SISKIYOU COUNTY LIBRARY

D0976119

ROTATION

Dunsmuir
8 28 14

McCloud
2 23 15

Montague

Mt. Shasta
5 10 15

Dunsmuir
9 19 15

Europ

OFFICIALLY
DISCARDED

Slovenia
p609

France
p183

Croatia
p119

Bosnia & Hercegovin
p75

Montenegro
p535

Portugal
p563

Spain
p649

Italy
p413

Albania
p42

Greece
p323

Turkey
p763

THIS EDITION WRITTEN AND RESEARCHED BY
Duncan Garwood

Alexis Averbuck, James Bainbridge, Mark Baker, Peter Dragicevich,
Mark Elliott, Anthony Ham, Tom Masters, Virginia Maxwell, Craig
McLachlan, Anja Mutić, Regis St Louis, Nicola Williams

PLAN YOUR TRIP

Welcome to Mediterranean Europe....6

Mediterranean Europe Map..............8

20 Top Experiences 10

Need to Know 20

If You Like 22

Month by Month....... 25

Itineraries 30

Countries at a Glance .. 35

ON THE ROAD

ALBANIA 42
Tirana................ 45
Northern Albania 52
Shkodra 52
Theth & Valbonë........ 54
Central Albania....... 54
Kruja.................. 55
Durrës 56
Apollonia 57
Berat.................. 57
Southern Coast....... 60
Vlora.................. 60
Drymades 61
Dhërmi 61
Himara 61
Vuno & Jal 62
Saranda 62
Eastern Albania....... 64
Gjirokastra............ 65
Understand Albania 66
Survival Guide......... 70

BOSNIA & HERCEGOVINA..... 75
Sarajevo.............. 78
Jahorina............... 90
Bjelašnica 91
Hercegovina 91
Mostar 92
Stolac................. 101
Eastern Bosnia & Hercegovina....... 102
Trebinje 102
Višegrad.............. 103
Central & Western Bosnia....... 104
Visoko................ 104
Travnik 105
Jajce................. 106
Banja Luka............ 107
Bihać 109
Understand Bosnia & Hercegovina......... 111

Survival Guide........ .115

CROATIA .... .119
Zagreb .... .121
Istria................ 136
Pula.................. 136
Rovinj 139
Poreč 142
Kvarner Region 144
Rijeka 144
Opatija 147
Krk Island 148
Dalmatia............. 149
Zadar 150
Split 152
Trogir 159
Hvar Island 160
Korčula Island......... 163
Mljet Island 164
Dubrovnik 166
Understand Croatia ...172
Survival Guide........177

FRANCE.......... 183
Paris................. 185
Disneyland Resort Paris ...217
Versailles 217
Chartres.............. 218
Lille, Flanders & the Somme 219
Lille.................. 219
Calais................ 222
Amiens............... 223
Normandy 224
Rouen................ 224
Bayeux 226
D-Day Beaches 227
Mont St-Michel........ 229
Brittany 229
Quimper.............. 230
St-Malo. 231
Champagne 234
Reims................ 234

BACKGAMMON PLAYERS, İSTANBUL (P765)

IZZET KERIBAR / GETTY IMAGES ©

TAPAS, MADRID (P651)

WALTER BIBIKOW / GETTY IMAGES ©

Contents

Épernay 236
Alsace & Lorraine. 237
Strasbourg 237
Nancy. 240
Metz 241
The Loire Valley 243
Blois 243
Tours. 245
Amboise. 247
**Burgundy &
the Rhône Valley. 248**
Dijon 248
Beaune. 250
Lyon 252
The French Alps 258
Chamonix 258
Annecy. 261
Grenoble 263
The Jura 265
Besançon. 265
The Dordogne 266
Sarlat-La-Canéda. 266
Les Eyzies-de-Tayac-
Sireuil. 268
The Atlantic Coast 268
Nantes 268
Poitiers. 270
Bordeaux 271
Lourdes 273
Biarritz. 274
**Languedoc-
Roussillon 275**
Nîmes 275
Toulouse. 277
Provence 280
Marseille 280
Aix-en-Provence 285
Avignon 287
**The French Riviera
& Monaco. 291**
Nice. 291
Cannes. 296
St-Tropez 298

Monaco 300
Corsica 303
Bastia 303
Calvi 305
Ajaccio 306
Bonifacio 307
Understand France. . . . 308
Survival Guide. 314
GREECE 323
Athens 325
Piraeus. 341
The Peloponnese 343
Patra. 343
Corinth 344
Ancient Corinth &
Acrocorinth 345
Nafplio 345
Epidavros. 347
Mycenae. 347
Sparta. 347
Mystras 348
Monemvasia & Gefyra . . 348
Gythio. 348
The Mani 349
Olympia 350
Central Greece 350
Delphi. 350
Meteora 351
Northern Greece. 352
Thessaloniki 352
Alexandroupolis 355
Mt Olympus. 355
Ioannina. 356
Zagorohoria
& Vikos Gorge 357
Igoumenitsa 357
Saronic Gulf Islands . . 357
Aegina 358
Poros 358
Hydra 358
Spetses 359
Cyclades. 359

Mykonos 359
Paros 363
Naxos 364
Ios 367
Santorini (Thira). 368
Crete. 371
Iraklio 372
Phaestos & Other
Minoan Sites 374
Rethymno 375
Hania 375
Samaria Gorge 376
Paleohora. 377
Lasithi Plateau 378
Agios Nikolaos 379
Sitia 379
Dodecanese 379
Rhodes 380
Karpathos 382
Symi 383
Kos 383
Patmos 385
**Northeastern Aegean
Islands 386**
Samos 386
Chios 387
Lesvos (Mytilini). 389
Sporades 391
Skiathos 391
Skopelos 392
Alonnisos 393
Ionian Islands 393
Corfu 393
Lefkada 396
Kefallonia 397
Ithaki 398
Zakynthos 398
Understand Greece . . . 400
Survival Guide. 405

ITALY 413
Rome 416
Ostia Antica. 445

Tivoli 445
Northern Italy 446
Genoa 446
Cinque Terre 448
Turin 450
Milan 452
Verona 456
Padua 457
Venice 458
Bologna 470
Ravenna 472
Tuscany 473
Florence 474
Pisa 485
Siena 487
Lucca 489
Umbria 491
Perugia 491
Assisi 493
Southern Italy 494
Naples 494
Capri 501
Sorrento 503
Amalfi Coast 504
Matera 506
Bari 507
Lecce 508
Sicily 509
Palermo 510
Aeolian Islands 514
Taormina 516
Mt Etna 517
Syracuse 517
Agrigento 519
Sardinia 520
Cagliari 520
Alghero 522
Understand Italy 524
Survival Guide 528

MONTENEGRO 535
Bay of Kotor 538
Herceg Novi 538

Perast 540
Kotor 540
Tivat 543
Adriatic Coast 544
Budva 544
Pržno & Sveti Stefan 545
Petrovac 546
Bar 546
Ulcinj 547
Central Montenegro . . .548
Lovćen National Park . . .548
Cetinje 548
Lake Skadar National
Park 549
Podgorica 551
Ostrog Monastery 553
Northern Mountains . . 554
Morača Canyon 554
Kolašin 554
Biogradska Gora
National Park 555
Durmitor
National Park 555
**Understand
Montenegro 557**
Survival Guide 560

PORTUGAL 563
Lisbon 566
Sintra 581

Cascais 583
The Algarve 583
Faro 585
Tavira 585
Lagos 586
Monchique 587
Silves 587
Sagres 588
Central Portugal 588
Évora 588
Monsaraz 590
Estremoz 590
Peniche 591
Óbidos 591
Nazaré 592
Tomar 592
Coimbra 593
Luso & the Buçaco Forest . .594
Serra da Estrela 595
The North 595
Porto 595
Along the Douro 601
Viana do Castelo 601
Braga 602
Parque Nacional
da Peneda-Gerês 603
Understand Portugal . . 604
Survival Guide 605

COLOSSEUM (P416). ROME

WIBOWO RUSLI / GETTY IMAGES ©

Contents

SLOVENIA **609**
Ljubljana **611**
Julian Alps **623**
Lake Bled 624
Lake Bohinj 628
Kranjska Gora 630
Soča Valley 631
Karst & Coast **633**
Postojna 633
Škocjan Caves 634
Koper 635
Piran 636
Portorož 640
Eastern Slovenia **640**
Maribor 641
Ptuj 641
Understand Slovenia . . **642**
Survival Guide **644**

SPAIN **649**
Madrid **651**
Castilla y León **674**
Ávila 674
Salamanca 675
Segovia 677
León 678
Castilla-La Mancha . . . **680**
Toledo 681
Catalonia **683**
Barcelona 683
Monestir de Montserrat . . 700
Girona 700
The Costa Brava 701
Tarragona 702
**Aragón, Basque
Country & Navarra** **703**
Aragón 703
Basque Country 705
Navarra 709
**Cantabria, Asturias
& Galicia** **711**
Cantabria 711
Asturias 711
Galicia 712

Valencia & Murcia **715**
Valencia 715
Alicante 719
Costa Blanca 720
Balearic Islands **720**
Mallorca 720
Ibiza 724
Menorca 726
Andalucía **727**
Seville 727
Córdoba 733
Granada 736
Costa de Almería 739
Málaga 740
Ronda 742
Algeciras 743
Cádiz 744
Tarifa 745
Gibraltar **746**
Extremadura **747**
Trujillo 747
Cáceres 748
Mérida 749
Understand Spain **750**
Survival Guide **755**

TURKEY **763**
İstanbul **765**
Edirne 781
Bursa 782
The Aegean Coast **784**
Gallipoli (Gelibolu)
Peninsula 784
Eceabat (Maydos) 784
Çanakkale 786
Behramkale & Assos 787
Ayvalık 788
Bergama (Pergamum) . . . 789
İzmir 790
Çeşme Peninsula 792
Selçuk 793
Ephesus (Efes) 794
Kuşadası 796
Bodrum 797

Marmaris 801
**The Mediterranean
Coast** **802**
Fethiye 802
Ölüdeniz 804
Patara 805
Kalkan 805
Kaş 806
Olympos & Çirali 809
Antalya 811
Side 814
Alanya 815
Anamur 816
Kızkalesi 816
Adana 817
Antakya (Hatay) 817
Central Anatolia **818**
Ankara 818
Konya 820
Cappadocia (Kapadokya) . . **821**
Göreme 823
Uçhisar 825
Zelve Valley 825
Ürgüp 825
Mustafapaşa 826
Kayseri 826
Eastern Turkey **827**
Mt Nemrut
National Park 828
Mardin 829
Van 830
Understand Turkey **831**
Survival Guide **837**

SURVIVAL GUIDE

Directory A–Z **848**
Transport **865**
Language **877**
Index **890**
Map Legend **909**

welcome to Mediterranean Europe

Cultural Calling

The cradle of Western civilisation, Mediterranean Europe boasts an unparalleled cultural legacy. Prehistoric paintings reveal the preoccupations of France's primeval cave dwellers; Greek and Roman monuments testify to the power and ambition of the ancient superpowers; Islamic art tells of Moorish sophistication; Gothic cathedrals, Renaissance palaces and baroque facades record the great artistic movements of history. The region's celebrated galleries and museums are pretty special, too, housing a considerable chunk of the Western world's combined art collection.

Food, Glorious Food

The region's passion for the finer things in life extends to the kitchen. Eating well is part and parcel of everyday life on the Med, as well as one of its great pleasures, and it doesn't have to cost a bomb. Picnicking on a loaf of freshly baked bread with cheese and olives and a bottle of wine bought from the local market could well turn out to be a holiday highlight. For dedicated foodies, France and Italy are the obvious destinations, but each country has its own culinary specialities – think tapas in Spain, kebaps in Turkey and souvlaki in Greece. And for wine buffs, the Mediterranean cellar is really quite something, with

Ancient ruins, awe-inspiring art, legendary cities and sun-kissed beaches – Mediterranean Europe is a visual and sensual feast. Visit once and you'll be hooked for life.

(left) Sveti Stefan beach (p545), Montenegro
(below) Carnevale revellers, Venice (p458), Italy

everything from world-famous vintages to thousands of cheerful local labels.

Natural Wonders

For many holidaymakers the Mediterranean's main appeal is the promise of summer sun and long, lazy days on the beach. Each year about 200 million visitors pour into the region, making it the world's top tourist destination. While not all head straight for the beach, many do – and with good reason. The Mediterranean's beaches are superb, ranging from big, sporty sands on Portugal's western seaboard to idyllic Sardinian hideaways and rocky platforms on Croatia's craggy Dalmatian coast. But there's more to the Med than the beach, and away from the coast the region's ancient landscape offers some truly spectacular natural sights: snow-clad Alpine peaks, bizarre rock formations, swaths of unspoiled forest and even a stunning fjord in Montenegro.

No Problem

Capping everything is the fact that Mediterranean Europe is an easy region in which to travel. Sure, services might not always be what you're used to, and some areas can be expensive, particularly in summer, but English is widely spoken, public transport more or less works, and with so many accommodation and eating options to choose from, you're sure to find somewhere to suit your style.

❯ Mediterranean Europe

Eiffel Tower, Paris, France
Towering monument
to French flair (p185)

Mt Triglav & Vršič Pass, Slovenia
Spectacular mountain
scenery (p629)

Venice, Italy
Romance, beauty
and canals (p458)

Alfama, Lisbon, Portugal
Atmospheric warren of
labyrinthine lanes (p566)

Alhambra, Granada, Spain
A palatial masterpiece of
Islamic art (p736)

Provence, France
Bright colours and coastal
splendour (p280)

Ancient Rome, Italy
Legends, ruins and
haunting views (p416)

La Sagrada Família, Barcelona, Spain
A unique work of
architectural genius (p690)

0   800 km
0   500 miles

NORWAY
Oslo

ATLANTIC
OCEAN

SCOTLAND
Edinburgh

North
Sea

DENMARK
Copenhagen

NORTHERN
IRELAND

Belfast
Dublin
Irish
Sea
IRELAND

WALES
Cardiff

ENGLAND
London

NETHERLANDS
Amsterdam

Berlin

GERMANY

St George's
Channel

English Channel

Brussels
BELGIUM

Rhine

Elb

LUXEMBOURG
Luxembourg
City

Seine
Paris

Loire

Danube

LIECHTENSTEIN
Vaduz

FRANCE   Bern
SWITZERLAND
Mt Blanc ▲
(4807m)   ALPS

Mt Trigl
(2864

ITALY
Venice

Bay of
Biscay
San Sebastián

PYRENEES
Andorra
la Vella   ANDORRA
Barcelona

Golfe
du Lion

Po
Provence   Monaco
Ligurian
Sea

Floren

San
Marin

Rom

Corsica
(France)

Douro

Ebro

PORTUGAL
Madrid
SPAIN

Lisbon

Balearic Islands
(Spain)

Sardinia
(Italy)

Tyrrhenia
Sea

Mediterranean Sea

Granada

Strait of
Gibraltar

Rabat

MOROCCO

Marrakesh

ATLAS MOUNTAINS

TUNISIA

WESTERN
SAHARA

ALGERIA

30°W   20°W   60°N   10°W   0° (Greenwich)   50°N   40°N   40°N   10°E   30°N

Mostar, Bosnia & Hercegovina
Visit Mostar's celebrated bridge (p92)

Bay of Kotor, Montenegro
A thrilling natural landscape (p538)

Meteora, Greece
Rock spires capped by monasteries (p351)

İstanbul, Turkey
Where East meets West (p765)

Berat, Albania
The 'town of a thousand windows' (p57)

Dubrovnik, Croatia
A marble gem of a city (p166)

Ephesus (Efes), Turkey
A stunningly preserved Roman city (p794)

20
TOP
EXPERIENCES

Ancient Rome, Italy

1 Rome's famous seven hills – in fact, there are nine – offer some superb vantage points. A favourite is the Palatine Hill (p417), a gorgeous green expanse of evocative ruins, towering umbrella pines and unforgettable views over the Roman Forum. This is where it all began, where Romulus supposedly founded the city and where the ancient Roman emperors lived in unimaginable luxury. Nowadays, it's a truly haunting spot, and as you walk the dusty paths you can almost sense the ghosts in the air. Roman Forum (p417)

La Sagrada Família, Barcelona, Spain

2 The Modernista brainchild of Antoni Gaudí remains a work in progress more than 80 years after his death. Fanciful and profound, inspired by nature and barely restrained by a Gothic style, Barcelona's quirky temple (p690) soars skyward with an almost playful majesty. The improbable angles and departures from architectural convention will have you shaking your head in disbelief, but the detail of the decorative flourishes on the Passion and Nativity facades are worth studying for hours.

SYLVAIN SONNET / GETTY IMAGES ©

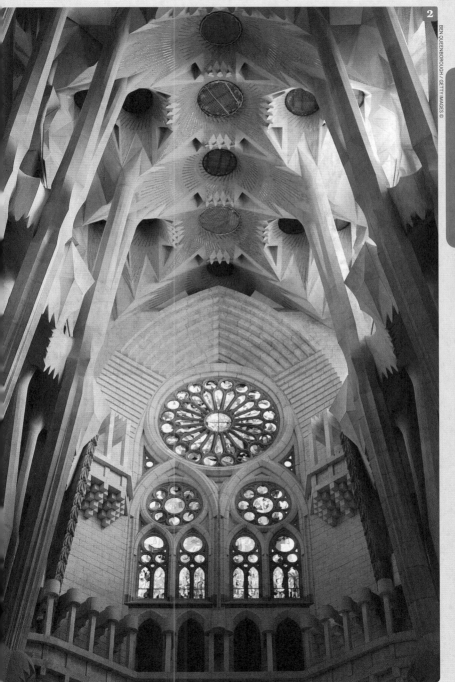

BEN QUEENBOROUGH / GETTY IMAGES ©

RUTH EASTHAM & MAX PAOLI / GETTY IMAGES ©

Venice, Italy

3 There's something special about Venice (p458) on a sunny winter's day. With far fewer tourists around and the light sharp and clear, it's the perfect time to lap up the city's unique and magical atmosphere. Ditch your map and wander Dorsoduro's shadowy back lanes while imagining secret assignations and whispered conspiracies at every turn. Then visit two of Venice's top galleries, the Galleria dell'Accademia and the Collezione Peggy Guggenheim, the latter housing works by many of the giants of 20th-century art.

Eiffel Tower, Paris, France

4 Seven million people visit the Eiffel Tower (p185) annually, but few disagree that each visit is unique. From an evening ascent amid twinkling lights to lunch in the company of a staggering city panorama, there are 101 ways to 'do' it. Pedal beneath it, skip the lift and hike up, buy a crêpe from a stand or a key ring from the street, snap yourself in front of it, visit at night or – our favourite – experience the odd special occasion when all 324m of it glows a different colour.

İstanbul, Turkey

5 Straddling Europe and Asia, the curriculum vitae of İstanbul (p765) includes stints as capital of the Byzantine and Ottoman Empires. It's quite simply one of the world's greatest cities. The historical highlights – the Aya Sofya, Blue Mosque, Topkapı Palace and Grand Bazaar – cluster in Sultanahmet. After marvelling at their ancient domes and glittering interiors, it's time to experience this 13-million-strong metropolis's vibrant contemporary life. Cross the Galata Bridge, passing ferries and fish-kebap stands, to Beyoğlu, a nightlife hot spot full of chic rooftop bars and rowdy taverns. Blue Mosque (p765)

5

CAROL POLICH PHOTO WORKSHOPS / GETTY IMAGES ©

Bay of Kotor, Montenegro

6 There's a sense of secrecy and mystery to the Bay of Kotor (p538). Grey mountain walls rise steeply from steely blue waters, getting higher and higher as you progress through their folds to the hidden reaches of the inner bay. Here, ancient stone settlements hug the shoreline, with Kotor's alleyways concealed in its innermost reaches behind hefty stone walls. Talk about drama! But you wouldn't expect anything else of the Balkans, where life is exuberantly Mediterranean and lived full of passion on these ancient streets.

6

KEITA SAWAKI / GETTY IMAGES ©

TONY WHEELER / GETTY IMAGES ©

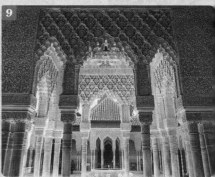

Berat, Albania

7 This wine-producing region's town (p57) reigns supreme in terms of Ottoman-style wonder and magic. The white, multi-windowed, Unesco-listed houses look down at the river below. Wander up the cobblestone paths to see them up close and meander through the living, breathing castle area (Kalasa) complete with a museum filled with stunning iconography by Onufri. Stay in Berat's Ottoman-style hostel or one of two traditional-homes-turned-hotels, and partake in the evening walk along the promenade for a truly enlivening experience. Kalasa (p58)

Alfama, Lisbon, Portugal

8 Alfama (p566), with its labyrinthine alleyways, hidden courtyards and curving, shadow-filled lanes, is a magical place to lose all sense of direction and delve into the soul of Lisbon. On the journey you'll pass breadbox-sized grocers; brilliantly tiled buildings; and cosy taverns filled with easy-going chatter, the scent of chargrilled sardines and the mournful rhythms of fado drifting in the breeze. Then you round a bend and catch sight of steeply pitched rooftops leading down to the glittering Tejo river and you know you're hooked.

Alhambra, Granada, Spain

9 The palace complex of the Alhambra (p736) is one of the most refined examples of Islamic art anywhere in the world and an enduring symbol of 800 years of Moorish rule of Al-Andalus. From afar, the Alhambra's red fortress towers dominate the Granada skyline, set against a backdrop of the Sierra Nevada's snow-capped peaks. Up close, the Alhambra's perfectly proportioned Generalife gardens complement the exquisite detail of the Palacio Nazaríes. Put simply, this is Spain's most beautiful monument.

Ephesus (Efes), Turkey

10 The eastern Mediterranean's best-preserved classical city (p794) is unique among historical sights: the tourists surging down the Curetes Way actually enhance the experience, evoking life in this busy Roman city. The capital of the Roman province of Asia, Ephesus had 250,000-plus inhabitants, many of them worshippers of the goddess Artemis. After 150 years of excavations, it is the place to get a feel for Graeco-Roman times. Near the jaw-dropping Library of Celsus, with its two storeys of pillars, are the Terraced Houses, the luxurious pads of the Roman elite.

Island-Hopping in the Adriatic, Croatia

11 From short jaunts between nearby islands to overnight rides along the length of the Croatian coast, travel by sea is a great and inexpensive way to see the Croatian side of the Adriatic. Take in the scenery of this stunning coastline as you whiz past some of Croatia's 1244 islands. If you have cash to splash, take it up a couple of notches and charter a sailboat to see the islands in style, propelled by winds and sea currents. Korčula Island (p163)

10

IZZET KERIBAR / GETTY IMAGES ©

11

M. GEBICKI / GETTY IMAGES ©

JEAN-BERNARD CARILLET / GETTY IMAGES ©

Provence, France

12 Captured on canvas by Van Gogh and Cézanne, Provence (p280) is a picture of bold primary colours and bucolic landscapes. Travel the area and you'll pass scented lavender fields, chestnut forests and silvery olive groves as you make for beautiful medieval cities and hilltop villages. But it's not all rural chic and perfect panoramas. On the southern coast, Marseille, the region's tough, compelling capital, exudes a gruff and edgy charm. One of the Mediterranean's great ports, this is the ideal place to try bouillabaisse, Provence's legendary fish dish.

Ancient Landmarks, Greece

13 From the magnificence of Athens' Acropolis (p329) to the skeletal remains of Knossos (p374), Greece's landscape is littered with ancient ruins. Top temples include the Parthenon, a stirring symbol of ancient glory; oracular Delphi (p350), perched above the Gulf of Corinth; and Olympia (p350), home to the first Olympic Games. The acoustically perfect theatre of Epidavros (p347) sits alongside the Sanctuary of Asclepius, an ancient healing centre, while offshore on Delos, the Sanctuary of Apollo (p362) marks the birthplace of the mythical god. Delphi (p350)

City Walls, Dubrovnik, Croatia

14 Get up close and personal with Dubrovnik by walking its spectacular city walls (p166), where history is unfurled from the battlements. No visit is complete without a leisurely walk along these ramparts, the finest in the world and Dubrovnik's main claim to fame. Built between the 13th and 16th centuries, they are still remarkably intact today and the vistas over the terracotta rooftops and the Adriatic Sea are sublime, especially at dusk when the sundown turns the hues dramatic and the panoramas unforgettable.

Mostar, Bosnia & Hercegovina

15 If the 1993 bombardment of Mostar's iconic 16th-century stone bridge underlined the pointlessness of Yugoslavia's civil war, its painstaking reconstruction has proved symbolic of a peaceful new era. Although parts of Mostar (p92) are still dotted with bombed-out buildings, the town continues to dust itself off. Its Ottoman quarter has been especially convincingly rebuilt and is once again a delightful patchwork of stone mosques, souvenir peddlers and cafes, and today it's tourists rather than militias who besiege the place.

Mt Triglav & Vršič Pass, Slovenia

16 They say you're not really Slovene until you've climbed Mt Triglav (p629). There's no rule about which particular route you take – there are about 20 ways up – but if you're a novice, ascend with a guide from the Pokljuka Plateau north of Bohinj. For a less strenuous yet no less thrilling journey, drive the Vršič Pass (p630), a spectacular mountain road that leads from alpine Gorenjska, past Mt Triglav itself and down to sunny Primorska and the bluer-than-blue Soča River in one hair-raising, spine-tingling hour.

RICHARD I'ANSON / GETTY IMAGES ©

JAN GREUNE / GETTY IMAGES ©

OLIVIER CIRENDINI / GETTY IMAGES ©

Florence & Tuscany, Italy

17 Florence (p474) has been seducing visitors for centuries and still today it casts a powerful spell. Its artistic treasures include celebrated masterpieces such as Michelangelo's figure-perfect *David* and Botticelli's revered Renaissance canvas *The Birth of Venus*. Florence's historic centre, overshadowed by Brunelleschi's landmark dome, sets the perfect scene for alfresco dining and relaxed wine drinking. If it all starts to get a bit much, head out to the country for a taste of the slow life amid Tuscany's picturesque vineyards and classic landscapes.

Meteora, Greece

18 The towering rock spires of Meteora (p351) are a stunning natural sight. But what makes them even more incredible are the elaborate 14th-century monasteries built on top of them. There were originally 24 monasteries (one for each pinnacle) but only six remain, accessible by stairs cut into the rock. Make the ascent and you're rewarded with breathtaking views of the surrounding landscape and, on quiet days, a sense of almost otherworldly serenity. For a completely different experience, Meteora's vertical peaks provide superb rock climbing. *Agias Varvaras Rousanou (p351)*

Touring the Loire Valley, France

19 With its extravagant chateaux, landscaped gardens and historic towns, the Loire Valley (p243) is made for touring. Pick up a car, or even better a bike, and castle-hop through the valley's wine-rich countryside. The chateaux, originally the country retreats of France's Renaissance royals and luxury-loving aristocrats, reveal spectacular architecture, from the fairy-tale chic of Château de Chenonceau to the classic proportions of Château de Cheverny and the Renaissance splendour of Château de Chambord. *Château de Chenonceau (p246)*

LATITUDESTOCK / GETTY IMAGES ©

Snacking in San Sebastián, Spain

20 Boasting more Michelin stars per capita than Paris, the Basque city of San Sebastián (p706) is one of Spain's top foodie destinations. To get into the swing of things, spend an evening bar-crawling around the Parte Vieya (Old Quarter), filling up on *pintxos* (Basque-style tapas). These bar snacks, traditionally accompanied by a cloudy white wine called *txakoli,* range from the classic (fresh fish cakes, marinated anchovies, wild mushrooms) to more innovative fusion fare prepared by the city's top chefs.

ALEX SEGRE / ALAMY ©

need to know

Buses
» Extensive network across the region; bus travel is often preferable in mountainous Eastern Europe.

Trains
» High-speed links across Western Europe; coverage patchy and services slow in Balkan countries.

When to Go

desert, dry climate
warm summer, mild winter
mild year round
mild summer, cold winter
cold climate

Paris GO Apr–Jun

Dubrovnik GO May–Sep

İstanbul GO Apr–May

Barcelona GO May–Jun & Sep

Rome GO Apr–Jun & Sep

Athens GO May–Jun

Your Daily Budget

Budget less than
€70
» Dorm beds: €10–40

» Pension double room: average €45 but can reach €110

» Markets and supermarkets for self-caterers

Midrange
€70–170
» Midrange hotel double room: €40–120 (up to €200 in some Western Europe capitals)

» B&Bs often offer good value for money

» Restaurant meals: from about €15

Top end over
€170
» Top-end hotel double room: from €100 (from €200 in some cities)

» Top restaurants often have cheaper fixed-price lunch menus

» Car hire: from €45 per day

High Season (Jun–Aug)
» Hot, sunny days and packed beaches.

» Peak rates in coastal areas; inland cities may have discounts in August.

» High season also during ski season (December to late March), Christmas, New Year and Easter.

Shoulder (Apr–May & Sep–Oct)
» Sunny spring days in April and May; September is still hot enough for the beach.

» Crowds and high prices in many cities; more space and lower prices on the coast.

Low Season (Nov–Mar)
» The coldest and wettest time of the year, with snow in mountainous areas.

» Prices are at their lowest.

» Many coastal resorts shut up for the winter.

Driving

» Car hire readily available across the region; tolls apply on many motorways. Road conditions not always great in Albania.

Ferries

» Good, safe network in the Mediterranean; book ahead for popular routes in peak season.

Bicycles

» Bike hire is widely available; can take bikes on trains and ferries for a small extra fee.

Planes

» National airlines and more than 30 low-cost carriers fly within Europe, ensuring a comprehensive network and competitive fares.

Websites

» **Lonely Planet** (www.lonelyplanet. com) Destination info, hotel bookings and traveller forum.

» **AFerry.com** (www. aferry.com) Research and book ferry tickets.

» **Seat 61** (www.seat61. com) Comprehensive A to Z of train travel.

» **Visit Europe** (www. visiteurope.com) Has practical advice and useful links.

» **Michelin** (www. michelin.com) Good for road directions and online maps.

» **Euroflights** (www. euroflights.info) Lists budget airlines and routes.

Money

The euro is used in France, Greece, Italy, Montenegro, Portugal, Slovenia and Spain.

» **Albania** Lekë, euro

» **Bosnia and Hercegovina (BiH)** Convertible mark, euro

» **Croatia** Kuna, euro

» **Turkey** Turkish lira, euro or US dollars

Visas

» No visas are required for most people for stays of up to 90 days in Schengen countries, plus Albania, BiH, Croatia and Montenegro.

» Citizens of Australia, the US, Canada and New Zealand need a visa for stays of longer than 90 days in the Schengen area.

» Australian, Canadian, UK and US citizens need a visa for Turkey – buy it on arrival.

Arriving

» **Roissy Charles de Gaulle Airport, Paris** Buses half-hourly from 5.45am to midnight, hourly from 12.30am

» **Leonardo da Vinci Airport, Rome** Trains every 30 minutes from 6.30am to 11.40pm; buses: 8.30am to 12.30am, plus four between 1.15am and 5am

» **Atatürk International Airport, İstanbul** Buses half-hourly from 4am to 1am; metro and trams: frequent from 5.40am to 1.40am

» **Barajas Airport, Madrid** Buses every 15 to 30 minutes; metro frequent from 6.05am to 2am

What to Take

» Travel insurance – make sure it covers any activities you might be doing.

» Driving licence and, if necessary, International Driving Permit.

» Photocopies of all important documents – so you're covered in case of theft.

» Plug adaptor, power transformer and mobile-phone recharger – so you can stay connected.

» Smart set of clothes – for that 'oh so chic' French restaurant.

» Sandals or thongs – for showers and pebbly beaches.

» Hat and shades – lifesavers when it's 35°C in the shade.

» Rain gear – it does rain in the Med, quite a lot in some months.

» Insect repellent – don't let the mosquitoes get to you.

» Bottle opener – picnics are much better when you can open the wine.

if you like...

Food & Drink

There's no finer place to indulge your appetites than the Mediterranean. With so many local specialities and traditional tipples to try, lovers of fine food and drink will be in seventh heaven.

Port Get to grips with Portugal's national drink in Porto, gateway to the port-producing Douro valley. (p595)

French Wine French wines have been setting the gold standard for centuries. Treat yourself to a taste by touring Burgundy's Côte d'Or vineyards. (p251)

Pizza Italy's culinary classic is best when prepared in a wood-fired oven and served with an ice-cold beer in a Neapolitan pizzeria. (p499)

Kebap This mainstay of Turkish cuisine comes in various forms, from the classic *döner* to the more sophisticated *İskender*. (p836)

Tapas Bar-hopping in Madrid becomes a culinary experience when eating tapas, Spain's legendary bar snacks. (p666)

Greek Salad A taverna staple ideal for a light summer lunch by the sea. (p404)

Museums & Galleries

Home to some of the world's most celebrated art, the region's museums and galleries boast works by French Impressionists, Spanish surrealists and the maestros of the Italian Renaissance, as well as many other revered artists.

Musée du Louvre One of the world's most famous museums, with an enormous collection – yet most eyes are drawn to Leonardo da Vinci's *Mona Lisa*. (p196)

Vatican Museums Michelangelo's Sistine Chapel frescoes are the highlight of the Vatican's mammoth museum complex. (p425)

Galleria degli Uffizi There's nowhere better to feast on Italian art than Florence, where the Renaissance kicked off in the late 15th century. (p475)

Museo del Prado Madrid's top art gallery features works by Spanish giants Goya, Velázquez, El Greco and many more. (p651)

National Archaeological Museum Finds from archaeological sites across Greece exhibited in Athens' most prestigious museum. (p330)

Ancient Ruins

Mediterranean Europe is littered with reminders of its ancient past. Ruined (and not-so-ruined) temples, amphitheatres, even entire towns, stand testament to the enduring skill of the region's pioneering engineers.

Parthenon Dating to the 5th century BC, Athens' staggering Doric temple encapsulates the glory of the once-powerful Greek empire. (p329)

Pompeii Almost 2000 years after it was destroyed by Mt Vesuvius, Italy's perfectly preserved ancient town is a thrilling sight. (p502)

Colosseum Rome's great gladiatorial arena is one of Italy's iconic monuments. (p416)

Ephesus Centred on a remarkable 25,000-seat theatre, the compelling ruins of Ephesus are Turkey's top ancient site. (p794)

Diocletian's Palace Built for a Croatian-born Roman emperor, this vast palace covers much of Split's historic centre. (p152)

Les Arènes Nîmes' stirring Roman amphitheatre once staged gory gladiatorial games; nowadays it's bullfights and historical recreations. (p276)

» Tapas (p755), Spain

Architecture

Mediterranean Europe is a dream destination for architecture buffs. Ancient temples stand alongside hulking Gothic churches, majestic mosques, baroque piazzas and avant-garde museums.

Pantheon Rome's epic temple is a staggering achievement and the high point of ancient Roman engineering. (p425)

Cathédrale de Notre Dame de Paris Paris' most famous and most visited cathedral is a towering masterpiece of early Gothic architecture. (p193)

Blue Mosque Islamic style finds perfect form in the Blue Mosque, one of İstanbul's most recognisable buildings. (p765)

St Peter's Square The Vatican's magnificent central piazza is a dazzling work of baroque urban design. (p424)

La Sagrada Família Barcelona's work-in-progress church was designed by Antoni Gaudí, famous exponent of 20th-century Catalan modernism. (p690)

Museo Guggenheim Since it was opened in Bilbao in 1997, Frank Gehry's striking museum has become a modern icon. (p708)

Medieval Towns

Against a backdrop of almost constant conflict, art and architecture flourished in the Middle Ages, giving rise to some wonderful towns and cities.

Siena Boasting a fine medieval cityscape, Siena radiates out from Piazza del Campo, setting of the city's famous Palio horse race. (p487)

Dubrovnik Dubrovnik's majestic medieval walls date to its heyday as an independent republic and rival to the powerful Venetians. (p166)

Santiago de Compostela Lording over Santiago's medieval centre is the city's landmark cathedral, a triumphant mix of architectural styles. (p712)

Rhodes Town Rhodes' Unesco-protected Old Town is a gem, lined with impressive buildings and surrounded by huge 12m-thick walls. (p381)

Kotor Situated at the head of a stunning fjord, walled Kotor is dramatically wedged between the sea and the steeply rising mountainside. (p540)

Carcassonne This walled city in southern France is protected by 52 stone towers and Europe's largest city fortifications. (p278)

Coastal Beauty

When it comes to spectacular scenery and shimmering seascapes, few areas can rival the Mediterranean. Its coastline is a magical mix of silky beaches, dreamy coves and precipitous cliffs, all lapped by lukewarm waters in a thousand shades of blue.

Amalfi Coast Italy's coastal pin-up is pure Mediterranean bliss, with cliffs plunging into sparkling azure waters and villages hanging onto vertiginous slopes. (p504)

Côte d'Azur Join the European jet set on the French Riviera as it snakes along the lavender-scented coast from one celebrity hot spot to the next. (p291)

Turquoise Coast A boat cruise is a popular way of exploring the clear blue waters, hidden coves and ancient ruins of Turkey's western Mediterranean coast. (p802)

Dalmatia Hundreds of verdant, unspoilt islands clutter the clear waters off Croatia's Adriatic coast. (p149)

Galicia Lighthouses and remote fishing villages pepper the wild cliffs of Galicia's Atlantic seaboard. (p715)

» Hvar Island (p160), Croatia

Islands

Ever since Odysseus stumbled across the Aegean on his return from Troy, island-hopping has been a popular Mediterranean pastime. The Greek islands are a favourite destination, but there are plenty of others littered across the seascape.

Santorini The result of a 3600-year-old volcanic eruption, Santorini is a classic island beauty with sheer, lava-clad cliffs, black beaches and sun-bleached villages. (p368)

Hvar Island Croatia's sunniest spot, Hvar is the most popular of the many islands floating off the Dalmatian coast. (p160)

Corsica Napoleon's birthplace is a weather-beaten old sea dog of an island with beautiful beaches and a wild, mountainous interior. (p303)

Sicily The Med's largest island boasts Europe's most volatile volcano (Mt Etna), ancient Greek ruins, fabulous food and glitzy resorts. (p509)

Menorca One of Spain's Balearic Islands, Menorca is a mecca for sun seekers with its pristine beaches and sandy bays. (p726)

Outdoor Activities

With its warm seas, snowy mountains and favourable climate, the Med is a sports lover's paradise. Whether you're after perfect snow powder or roaring surf, you'll find plenty of opportunities to feed your adrenalin habit.

Skiing Most of the region's top resorts are in the French and Italian Alps, but there's great-value skiing in Slovenia and Bosnia and Hercegovina. (p852)

Hiking There's excellent hiking across much of the region, particularly in mountainous areas such as the Italian Dolomites. (p852)

Diving Warm, shallow waters and the calcified wreck of a 3rd-century Roman ship make for fabulous diving off Croatia's Mljet Island. (p165)

Surfing Surfers head to the western edge of the continent for the thundering waves that crash in on central Portugal's Atlantic beaches. (p591)

Rafting One of the most popular outdoor pursuits in Montenegro is rafting along the Tara River in the Durmitor National Park. (p556)

Partying

Ever since ancient Greek philosophers raised the pursuit of pleasure to a philosophy, the Med has been a party hot spot. Modern-day hedonists are spoilt for choice, with everything from cutting-edge clubs to seafront bars and bacchanalian beach parties.

Ios & Mykonos Summer revellers flock to the bars and clubs on Ios and gay-friendly Mykonos, two of Greece's premier party destinations. (p359)

Ibiza Long a clubbing mecca, the Spanish island boasts some of the world's top clubs and regularly hosts big-name DJs. (p725)

Hvar Town The main town on Hvar Island rocks in summer, serving up the best nightlife on the Dalmatian coast. (p160)

Bodrum Up-for-it partygoers swell the clubs and bars of this ever popular resort on Turkey's Aegean coast. (p797)

Paris Catch a cabaret, dance till dawn or swoon over jazz in a shadowy basement bar – Paris by night offers limitless possibilities. (p212)

month by month

Top Events

1 **Carnival,** February

2 **Las Fallas de San José,** March

3 **Easter,** Late March or April

4 **Cannes Film Festival,** May

5 **Il Palio,** July

January

As the New Year celebrations die down, the winter cold digs in. This is a fine time to hit the ski slopes with good, fresh snow in the Alps and the Pyrenees.

🏃 Skiing, Region-Wide

Fresh snowfalls mean excellent conditions for skiing and snowboarding. The region's most famous resorts are in the French and Italian Alps but there's also excellent – and cheaper – skiing in the Pyrenees and Balkan countries. Slovenia and Bosnia and Hercegovina both offer exciting pistes.

February

The cold weather continues to provide ideal skiing conditions, while the winter quiet is shattered by high-spirited Carnival celebrations. Book accommodation if you're heading to a big Carnival destination.

⭐ Carnival, Region-Wide

In the run-up to Lent, Carnival is celebrated with wild processions, costumed parties and much eating and drinking. Events are held all over, but festivities are particularly exuberant in Cádiz (Spain), Rijeka (Croatia), Nice (France) and Venice (Italy).

March

The onset of spring brings blooming flowers, rising temperatures and unpredictable rainfall. Unless Easter falls in late March, it is still fairly quiet, even in the mountains where the ski season is starting to tail off.

⭐ Las Fallas de San José, Spain

Valencia is the place to be in the week leading up to 19 March. The city's annual party marathon (p719), held to celebrate St Joseph, is an explosive event of revelry, pageants and fireworks, culminating in the torching of hundreds of giant effigies.

April

Weather-wise April is glorious – sunshine and pleasant temperatures – but it can be busy, depending on when Easter falls. If travelling over Easter, expect crowds, memorable celebrations and high-season prices.

⭐ Feria de Abril, Spain

April is a festive time in Seville (p728). The week before Easter, Semana Santa is marked by sinister processions, while the Feria de Abril is a week-long fiesta of folklore, flamenco, tapas and sherry.

⭐ Easter, Region-Wide

Across the region, Easter week is marked by parades, solemn processions and passion plays. In Rome, the Pope leads a Good Friday procession around the Colosseum and, on Easter Sunday, he gives his traditional blessing in St Peter's Square.

⭐ Music Biennale Zagreb, Croatia

Held every odd-numbered year, Zagreb's headline event is one of Europe's top contemporary music festivals. Since it was established in 1961, it has grown in reputation and now attracts world-class performers from a range of musical backgrounds. See www.mbz.hr.

May

Beautiful sunny weather makes this a wonderful time to visit the region. Life on the coast is slowly starting up as hotels begin to open for the season and the festival calendar moves into top gear.

★★ May Day, Region-Wide

A public holiday across much of the region, May Day traditions differ from country to country: the French give each other *muguets* (lilies of the valley), the Greeks gather wildflowers, and the Italians descend on Rome for a vast open-air rock concert.

★★ Maggio Musicale Fiorentino, Italy

The curtain goes up on Italy's oldest arts festival, a month-long spectacle of opera, theatre, classical music, jazz and dance held at Florence's Teatro del Maggio Musicale Fiorentino.

★★ Queima das Fitas, Portugal

In the week following the first Thursday in May, students and townsfolk in Coimbra raucously celebrate the end of the academic year. Events kick off with a traditional fado serenade and climax with a parade of extravagantly decorated floats.

★★ Cannes Film Festival, France

Mid-month, the world's most influential and glamorous film festival rolls out the red carpet for the Hollywood A-list. Onlookers crowd La Croisette to catch a glimpse of their celluloid heroes and debate potential Palme d'Or winners.

★★ Fiesta de San Isidro, Spain

From the Friday preceding 15 May until the following Sunday, Madrid celebrates its patron saint with typical abandon. Roll up for costumed processions, concerts, bullfights and plenty of late-night revelry.

★★ Druga Godba, Slovenia

Ljubljana's flamboyant festival of alternative and world music features everything from new jazz to contemporary folk music. Alongside a rich concert program, there are also film screenings, workshops, debates and seminars. See www.drugagodba.si.

June

Summer has arrived and with it hot, sunny weather and a full festival schedule. This is a great time for sunning yourself on the beach before the holiday hordes descend and prices skyrocket.

★★ Palio delle Quattro Antiche Repubbliche Marinare, Italy

Historic rivalries are rekindled in the form of boat races between Italy's four ancient maritime republics: Pisa, Genoa, Amalfi and Venice. Before the races, representatives from each city don medieval garb and parade through the host city.

★★ International İstanbul Music Festival, Turkey

Catch a classical concert in a sultan's palace or a jazz jam in a 4th-century church during İstanbul's month-long music fest. In 2012 some 750 performers participated, including top orchestras from Berlin and Vienna. See http://muzik. iksv.org/en.

★★ Estate Romana, Italy

Between June and September, Rome's ruins, piazzas and parks stage events organised as part of this sweeping annual festival. The program is eclectic, featuring everything from film screenings to children's concerts, book readings and theatrical performances.

★★ INmusic Festival, Croatia

One of the Balkans' top music festivals, this two-day event near Lake Jarun in Zagreb features a strong international line-up – in recent years Franz Ferdinand, Gorillaz Sound System, Massive Attack and Lily Allen have all played. Get details at www.inmusic festival.com/en.

★★ Festa de Santo António, Portugal

On 12 and 13 June, Lisbon commemorates St Anthony with parades, street parties and unfeasible quantities of grilled sardines. The festival is part of the wide-ranging cultural event called Festas de Lisboa.

Hellenic Festival, Greece
The ancient theatre at Epidavros and the Odeon of Herodes Atticus are the headline venues of Athens' annual cultural shindig. The festival, which runs from mid-June to August, features music, dance, theatre, and much more besides. See www.greekfestival.gr.

Festa de São João, Portugal
One of Portugal's top festivals, the Festival of St John sees Porto's streets taken over by crowds of revellers wielding plastic hammers. Celebrations continue through the night of 23 June with fireworks, bonfires and beach parties.

Tarihi Kırkpınar Yağlı Güreş Festivali, Turkey
Huge crowds gather in Edirne in late June/early July to cheer greased-up wrestlers as they slap each other around during the Kırkpınar wrestling festival (p782). Dating back to the 14th century, this is the world's oldest wrestling event. Get details at www.kirkpinar.com.

July
Temperatures start to peak as schools break up for the long summer vacation. The coastal resorts are pretty busy by now and there are any number of festivals to check out.

Festival d'Avignon, France
Avignon's renowned arts festival is the oldest of its type in France and one of Europe's most famous. A month-long feast of drama, music, dance and poetry, it runs alongside the alternative fringe festival, Festival Off (www.avignonleoff.com). Check out www.festival-avignon.com.

Baščaršijske Noći, Bosnia & Hercegovina
Dance, music and theatre take to the streets of Sarajevo for the month-long Baščaršija Nights festival. All tastes are catered to, with everything from ballet and opera to film screenings, book readings and kids' events.

Zagreb Summer Evenings, Croatia
Zagreb's Upper Town buzzes to the sound of music and drama for much of July. The city's traditional summer festival showcases a range of musical forms, from classical to blues, jazz and world music.

Ljubljana Festival, Slovenia
Thousands flock to Slovenia's capital, Ljubljana, for the country's most important arts festival. Held throughout July and August, it has something for everyone, with world-class concerts, dance performances, lectures, children's workshops and exhibitions. Check out the website, www.ljubljanafestival.si.

Il Palio, Italy
Siena's legendary horse race, Il Palio, is held twice annually, on 2 July and 16 August. Accompanied by great pomp and medieval festivities, it's a ferocious affair, contested by jockeys riding bareback around the city's central square. For more information, see www.ilpalio.org.

Sanfermines, Spain
The Fiesta de San Fermín (Sanfermines; p710) is the week-long nonstop festival and party in Pamplona with the daily *encierro* (running of the bulls) as its centrepiece. Anything can happen, but it rarely ends well for the bull. The anti-bullfighting event, the Running of the Nudes, takes place two days earlier.

Bastille Day, France
Fireworks, balls, processions and a military parade in Paris mark France's national day on 14 July. Celebrated across the country, it excites much patriotic fervour and plenty of festive feasting.

Dubrovnik Summer Festival, Croatia
Dubrovnik's beautiful streets set the scintillating stage for Croatia's biggest summer arts festival. Local and international musicians, actors and artists perform at venues across the city throughout July and August. Get details at www.dubrovnik-festival.hr.

Split Summer Festival, Croatia
Music, drama and dance enjoy top billing at Split's

annual culture fest, held from mid-July to mid-August. Shows cover the full range, from classical music concerts and opera to experimental theatre performances and puppet shows.

 ### Festa del Redentore, Italy

On the third weekend in July, gondola regattas serve as the build up to a spectacular fireworks display in Venice. The much beloved festival was inaugurated in the 16th century to give thanks for the end of a plague epidemic.

 ### Mostar Bridge Diving Competition, Bosnia & Hercegovina

Crowds throng the rocky banks of the Neretva River to watch daredevil divers leap off Mostar's iconic bridge, Stari Most, and plunge into the green waters 21m below.

Umbria Jazz, Italy

Music aficionados flock to the medieval town of Perugia mid-month for Italy's premier jazz festival. A winter edition is also staged in the last days of December in the cliff-top town of Orvieto. Check www.umbriajazz.com for details.

 ### Nice Jazz Festival, France

International jazz greats lead this week-long party on the French Riviera. Louis Armstrong, Dizzy Gillespie and BB King have all headlined here, and the festival is a key date on the European jazz calendar. See www.nicejazzfestival.fr.

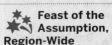

August

The height of summer. Much of the region is on holiday – most people in France and Italy take their annual vacation this month – making for packed resorts, quiet cities and traffic jams on coast-bound roads.

Feast of the Assumption, Region-Wide

Celebrated on 15 August, the Feast of the Assumption is the busiest holiday day of the year. Across the region, beaches are jam packed, cities slow to a standstill, and everyone basks in the summer sun.

Sarajevo Film Festival, Bosnia & Hercegovina

Since it was inaugurated in 1995, the Sarajevo Film Festival has become one of the largest film events in Europe and a major showcase for southeastern European movies. Commercial and art-house flicks are screened, almost all with English subtitles. For details see www.sff.ba.

Mostra del Cinema di Venezia, Italy

At the end of the month, movie big shots alight at Venice for the world's oldest film festival. The focus of attention is the Palazzo del Cinema on the Lido, a small slither of an island in Venice's lagoon.

September

September is a lovely month to be on the Med. The August crowds have gone home but it's still hot enough for sunbathing and swimming and there's great hiking in the region's many national parks.

Bienal de Flamenco, Spain

Give yourself up to the passion of Spain's largest flamenco festival, held in Seville every even-numbered year. The world's top flamenco stars strut their stuff before enthusiastic fans in venues across the city.

Festes de la Mercè, Spain

Barcelona's great annual bash is a bombastic affair, held over four days around 24 September. Highlights include eight-storey human towers and a procession of dragons that parades through the streets accompanied by deafening fireworks and bangers. See www.bcn.cat/merce.

Hiking, Region-Wide

Autumn, along with spring, is the ideal period for hiking. At higher altitudes, peaks are usually free of snow between June and September, making for great trekking in the Italian Dolomites (p474), Slovenia's Julian Alps (p623) and the Spanish Pyrenees (p705).

Adventure Race Montenegro

Montenegro's gruelling Adventure Race (p538) is not the only way to enjoy the Bay of Kotor's dramatic beauty, but it's certainly the toughest. Held in late September/early October, it involves an entire day of kayaking, mountain biking, trekking and orienteering. Check out www.adventure racemontenegro.com.

October

As coastal resorts wind down for the season, the focus returns inland. Warm weather and autumnal colours make for pleasant sightseeing, particularly in southerly areas, and accommodation rates start to drop.

✷✷ Romaeuropa, Italy

Established international performers join emerging stars at Rome's autumn festival of theatre, opera and dance. Events, staged between late September and October, range from full-on raves and avant-garde dance performances to installations, multimedia shows, recitals and readings. Get details at http://romaeuropa.net.

November

The wettest month of the year, November is a quiet time with not a whole lot going on. On the plus side, accommodation is cheap and there are few tourists around.

✷✷ International Jazz Festival, Bosnia & Hercegovina

One of the few events in November, Sarajevo's week-long jazz fest has a strong international reputation. Well-known musicians from around the world perform to enthusiastic crowds across the Bosnian capital. Get program details at www.jazzfest.ba.

Tirana Film Festival, Albania

Held in late November/early December, Albania's main film festival showcases features, shorts and works by local directors with prizes for best short fiction, animation, documentary and experimental. Get details at www.tiranafilmfest.com.

December

The build up to Christmas is a jolly time as crowds brave cold temperatures to shop at markets and enjoy the festive lights that adorn many towns and cities. Up in the mountains, the ski season kicks off mid-month.

✷✷ Fête des Lumières, France

A public holiday in many countries, 8 December is an important religious date, the Feast of the Immaculate Conception. In Lyon it coincides with the Festival of Lights, a spectacular sound and light show in the city's historic centre.

✷✷ Christmas, Region-Wide

Christmas is accompanied by the usual gift-giving traditions and family get-togethers. Highlights of the Christmas period include Strasbourg's famous Christmas market, the Marché de Noël, and Naples' elaborate *presepi* (nativity scenes).

itineraries

Whether you've got six days or 60, these itineraries provide a starting point for the trip of a lifetime. Want more inspiration? Head online to lonelyplanet.com/thorntree to chat with other travellers.

Two Weeks
City Highlights

> With only two weeks to travel, the challenge is to see as much as possible while doing justice to each place you visit. This whirlwind tour concentrates on four of the region's most seductive cities.
>
> Start with three days in the French capital, **Paris**. Check out the big sights – the Eiffel Tower, Notre Dame, the Louvre – and lap up the lifestyle in buzzing Montmartre and the Marais. Armed with your newly acquired savoir-faire, head south to **Madrid**, Spain's passionate capital. Admire the vast art collection at the Museo del Prado and pop into the king's royal palace, before an evening bar-hopping from one tapas joint to the next. After a couple of days, fly over to **Venice**, Italy's haunting and impossibly beautiful canal city. Here you'll have fun losing yourself in the atmospheric lanes and postcard-perfect piazzas, perhaps taking a gondola down the Grand Canal. From Venice, push on to the Eternal City. They say a lifetime's not enough for **Rome**, but three days should give you just enough time for the big sights – the Colosseum, the Roman Forum, the Vatican and the Sistine Chapel.

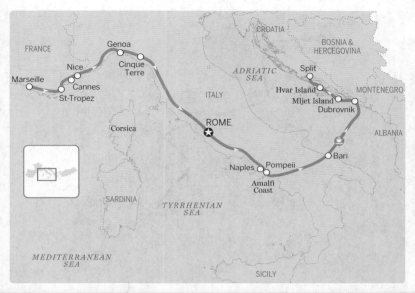

One Month
A Coastal Jaunt

Passing through the French Riviera, several Unesco-listed national parks and a number of full-blooded Mediterranean ports, this three-country route takes in some of the region's finest coastal scenery.

Start in **Marseille**, France's edgy, multi-ethnic Mediterranean port. A far cry from the postcard-pretty landscape that characterises much of the surrounding Provence region, it's a gritty, atmospheric city with some great sights and wonderful restaurants where you can sample a bowl of bouillabaisse. From Marseille, follow the coast eastwards along the fabled French Riviera. Top up your tan at **St-Tropez** and catch a film at **Cannes** as you wend your way along the coast to **Nice**, the Côte d'Azur's busy, cosmopolitan capital. From Nice, take a train to **Genoa**, where you can wander the same salty streets that once inspired local boy Christopher Columbus and eyeball sharks at Europe's second-largest aquarium. For more sea thrills take a day or two to explore the **Cinque Terre**, one of Italy's most spectacular stretches of coastline.

The road now leads to **Rome**, as all eventually do. Take in the big headline sights before continuing south to manic, in-your-face **Naples**. This sprawling city is not to everyone's taste but amid the chaos it harbours some truly amazing works of art, many taken from the nearby ruins of **Pompeii**. Continuing on, you'll come to the **Amalfi Coast**, a dreamy stretch of shimmering seascapes and plunging cliffs. From the Mediterranean coast, cross over to the Adriatic port of **Bari**, where you can catch a ferry for Croatia. While you wait to set sail, pass the time by investigating the lanes and Norman churches in Bari's labyrinthine Old Town. Over in Croatia, the first stop is **Dubrovnik**, the undisputed star of the Dalmatian coast. Once you've marvelled at the city's marble streets and baroque buildings, jump on a boat for some island hopping. Nearby, peaceful **Mljet Island** is a seductive mix of forests, vineyards and small villages, while further north **Hvar Island** boasts sunshine, beaches and a vibrant nightlife. From Hvar, it's a short ferry ride to **Split**, Croatia's second-largest city and home to the Unesco-listed Diocletian's Palace, one of Eastern Europe's greatest Roman monuments.

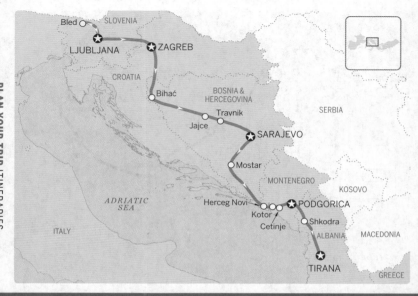

One Month
A Balkan Odyssey

Mountainous and covered in great swaths of forest, Slovenia and the Balkan countries present the tougher, more rugged side of the Mediterranean. This 1045km Eastern European odyssey leads through stunning mountain landscapes and beautiful towns as it snakes southwards from Slovenia to Albania.

To get you in the mood start with a few days in **Ljubljana**, Slovenia's cultured capital, enjoying the cafe life and exploring the city's landmark castle. Once done, head northwest to the lakeside town of **Bled**. A gorgeous spot in its own right, Bled makes a great base for hiking in the surrounding Julian Alps. From Bled double back to Ljubljana to pick up a bus to the Croatian capital, **Zagreb**. Hang around for a coffee or two in the Upper Town before pushing on to Bosnia and Hercegovina (BiH) and **Bihać**, a pretty staging post on the road to Sarajevo. Before reaching the Bosnian capital, take time to stop off at **Jajce**, famous for its catacombs, citadel and waterfall, and **Travnik**, home to some impressive castle ruins. After a few days enjoying **Sarajevo's** charming Turkish quarter and hip East–West vibe, continue south to **Mostar** and its scene-stealing bridge. Known as the Stari Most, this is one of BiH's most iconic sights, along with the divers who hurl themselves from it during the July diving competition.

From Mostar it's a straightforward bus journey to **Herceg Novi**, whose attractive walled town sits on Montenegro's coast at the mouth of the Bay of Kotor. A spectacular road winds its way along the bay to the magnificent medieval town of **Kotor**, wedged between dark mountains at the head of southern Europe's deepest fjord. The route here turns inland, through the thrilling Lovćen National Park, and on to Montenegro's former capital **Cetinje**. Continuing eastwards brings you to **Podgorica**, the nation's low-key modern capital. About 65km from Podgorica on the southeastern tip of Lake Shkodra, ancient **Shkodra** provides a good introduction to Albania as well as a convenient base for exploring the remote mountains around Theth. The last stretch of the tour leads south to the capital **Tirana**, once a model of drab Soviet-style urban blandness, now a crazy, colourful, buzzing city.

Three Weeks
Greek Island Hopping

With their beautiful beaches, ancient ruins and endless pleasures, the Greek Islands have been seducing travellers for millennia. Ferry services are reduced in winter, so this is a trip best undertaken in summer.

The obvious starting point is **Athens**, home to some of Europe's most iconic monuments. From nearby **Piraeus**, jump on a ferry for **Mykonos**, one of Greece's top island destinations. A hedonistic hot spot, it boasts action-packed beaches and a pretty whitewashed town. Before leaving, take time for a day trip to **Delos**, mythical birthplace of the god Apollo. From Mykonos, sail to **Naxos**, the largest and greenest of the Cyclades islands. Much more than a beach stop, its enticing main town and striking interior make it well worth exploring. From Naxos it's a quick ferry ride to laid-back **Paros** and the popular beaches of **Antiparos**. **Santorini** is one of the Aegean's most impressive islands, its volcanic cliffs sheering up from the blue sea. Greece's most southerly island, **Crete** makes a fitting finale. Just southwest of the main city **Iraklio** is **Knossos**, the ancient capital of Minoan Crete where the mythical Minotaur supposedly lived.

Two Weeks
Turkish Delights

Bridging the gap between East and West, Turkey is a compelling cauldron of culture and style.

The place to start is **İstanbul**, one of the world's great cities, whose highlights include the Topkapı Palace, Aya Sofya and Blue Mosque. Further round the Aegean coast, **Çanakkale** is a popular base for visiting **Gallipoli**, scene of vicious WWI fighting, and the legendary town of **Troy**. Following the coast, you arrive at **Bergama**, celebrated for the ruins of ancient Pergamum, once a powerful Middle Eastern kingdom. More classical treasures await at **Ephesus** (Efes), Turkey's answer to Pompeii, near **Selçuk**, home to the scarce remains of the Temple of Artemis, one of the Seven Wonders of the Ancient World. From Selçuk, push on to **Patara** and its magnificent 20km-long beach. Spend a day or two hanging out in a tree house in **Olympos** before heading on to **Antalya**, with its historic Ottoman district and ancient Roman harbour. At this point head inland to **Konya**, the birthplace of the whirling dervishes, which boasts some fine Seljuk architecture. Further northeast, the eerie, rocky landscape around **Göreme** is one of Turkey's most incredible sights.

PLAN YOUR TRIP ITINERARIES

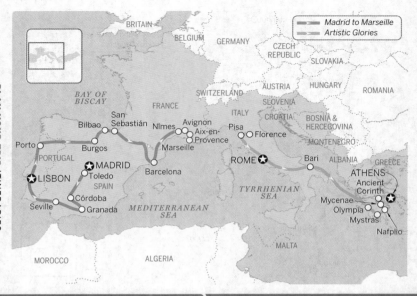

Five Weeks
Madrid to Marseille

> Taking in Spain, Portugal and France, this Franco-Iberian tour works either as a stand-alone itinerary or as half of a longer pan-Mediterranean trip.

Get off to a thumping start in Spain's capital **Madrid** before a day trip to **Toledo**, home of one of Spain's greatest Gothic cathedrals. Train down to Andalucía, stopping by **Córdoba** and **Granada** to admire stunning Islamic architecture, and **Seville** for its famous, full-blooded lifestyle. Head over to Portugal for stopovers in capital **Lisbon** and in **Porto**, where you can try the local tipple, port. Next, bus over to the cathedral city of **Burgos** en route to **Bilbao**, home of the extraordinary Museo Guggenheim. East of Bilbao, the seafront city of **San Sebastián** is considered Spain's culinary capital. Suitably sated, continue on to **Barcelona** for a look at the city's unique Modernista architecture. Continue northwards to **Nîmes**, a vibrant French city that houses some fine Roman ruins. To the east, **Avignon** provides an elegant introduction to Provence, France's showcase region renowned for its beautiful landscapes. As you head to the gripping Mediterranean port of **Marseille**, take a day to enjoy the bohemian chic of **Aix-en-Provence**, birthplace of artist Paul Cézanne.

Three Weeks
Artistic Glories

> Depending on how much time you have, this whistle-stop tour of Italy and Greece can either be undertaken as a trip in its own right or as a continuation of the Madrid to Marseille itinerary.

Kick off in **Florence**, the birthplace of the Renaissance and one of Italy's great art cities. After a few days ogling priceless treasures, drag yourself away for a quick stopover at **Pisa**, home to the world-famous Leaning Tower, en route to **Rome**, where you can marvel at headline sights such as the Colosseum, Pantheon and Michelangelo-frescoed Sistine Chapel. From Rome, pick up a train to the Adriatic port of **Bari** and a ferry for Patra. Once docked, head straight for **Olympia**, venue of the first Olympic Games in 776 BC. Continue to **Mystras**, famed for its Byzantine palaces and monasteries, before heading to **Nafplio**, a charming seaside town with Venetian-style houses and a striking hilltop fortress. Next, push on to mythical **Mycenae** and the ruins of **Ancient Corinth**. Across the water, **Athens** is a chaotic mix of the ancient and the modern. Not to be missed, the Parthenon dominates the cityscape from its position over the Acropolis, and the National Archaeological Museum houses the country's most important ancient artefacts.

countries at a glance

Stretching 4500km from Portugal's Atlantic coast to Turkey's eastern reaches, Mediterranean Europe encompasses a huge variety of people, places and beliefs. The region defies easy definition, but there are some things that all Med countries share – a handsome and ancient landscape, a turbulent history, a proud cultural legacy and a deeply ingrained respect for tradition. The vast majority of visitors head to the big holiday hot spots – France, Spain, Italy, Greece and Turkey – for the classic cocktail of sun, sea, culture, great food and timeless scenery. But venture off the beaten track and you'll encounter heartfelt hospitality and stunning natural beauty in the eastern Adriatic countries of Slovenia, Croatia, Bosnia and Hercegovina, Montenegro and Albania.

Albania

Scenery ✓✓✓
Beaches ✓✓✓
Culture ✓✓

Scenery

Albania's mountainous terrain, picturesque lakes and silent forests ensure swaths of stunning scenery. In the north, the Lake Koman Ferry provides spectacular passage up to the craggy Albanian Alps, while down south, the Llogaraja Pass National Park boasts dramatic mountainscapes.

Beaches

With everything from unspoiled bays to brash party strips, once-isolated Albania has beaches to rival those found anywhere on the Med. On the southern Ionian coast, popular destinations such as Drymades, Dhërmi and Himara attract the crowds while deserted coves lie waiting to be discovered.

Culture

More than museums and galleries, Albania specialises in castles, steeply stacked towns and the occasional ancient ruin. Highlights include Unesco-listed Berat and atmospheric ruins at Gjirokastra and Butrint.

p42

Bosnia & Hercegovina

Adventure Travel ✓✓✓
Scenery ✓✓
History ✓✓

Adventure Travel

Adrenalin junkies are spoiled for choice in Bosnia and Hercegovina (BiH). There's white-water rafting, kayaking and canyoning around Bihać, Banja Luka and Foča, skiing on world-class slopes near Sarajevo, and excellent hiking in the country's national parks.

Scenery

BiH's landscape is typical of the rugged Balkans: great, craggy peaks; deep, grey canyons; forested valleys; and fast-flowing rivers. For spectacular views make for the forested slopes of the Sutjeska National Park.

History

With its mixed Muslim and Christian heritage, BiH is a fascinating blend of historic cultures. Many of the country's top sights, including Sarajevo's old Turkish quarter and Mostar's Stari Most, testify to the country's past as an Ottoman province.

p75

Croatia

Scenery ✓✓✓
Islands ✓✓✓
Architecture ✓✓

Scenery

Croatia provides plenty of tasty eye candy. You can feast your eyes on virgin beaches and wildflowers at Rt Kamenjak, discover lakes, waterfalls and cascades in the Plitvice Lakes National Park, and explore pine-clad coves on Mljet Island.

Islands

Swimming in the crystalline waters off Croatia's 1778km Adriatic coast are some 1244 islands. The largest, busiest and most developed is Krk Island in the north, but sun seekers should head south to seductive Mljet and Hvar Island, said to be the country's sunniest spot.

Architecture

Croatia's historic towns and cities offer rich pickings for architecture buffs. You can admire ancient relics at Solin and Split, a Venetian fort in Hvar Town, and medieval city walls in Dubrovnik.

p119

France

Food & Wine ✓✓✓
Cities ✓✓✓
Landscapes ✓✓✓

Food & Wine

Oysters and foie gras, baguettes, smelly cheese and Bordeaux wine – France's foodie treasures are the stuff of gastronomic legend, and there's nowhere better to taste them than the country that gifted the world 'haute cuisine'.

Cities

France's great cities are at once exciting, fashionable, gritty and historic. Romance goes hand in hand with culture, couture and urban cool in Paris, while Lyon tops the culinary charts, Marseille bursts with colourful life, and Monaco woos the world's high-rollers.

Landscapes

France's landscape is as rich as it is varied, ranging from snow-capped Alpine peaks to the patchwork of primary colours that is Provence and the fairy-tale chateaux of the Loire Valley.

p183

Greece

Ancient Ruins ✓✓✓
Islands ✓✓✓
Food & Drink ✓✓

Ancient Ruins
Few countries do ruins like Greece and it's a thrilling experience to walk in the footsteps of the immortals at sites such as Athens' Acropolis; ancient Olympia, host of the first Olympic games; and Delphi, where pilgrims once queued to consult a verse-spouting oracle.

Islands
Island-hopping around the Greek Islands is a quintessential Mediterranean experience. Favourite destinations include party hot-spot Mykonos; Santorini, famous for its lava-clad cliffs and black volcanic beaches; and Rhodes, the largest of the Dodecanese islands.

Food & Drink
Generations of travellers have filled up on classic cheap eats such as gyros pitta (a Greek-style kebab), souvlaki (skewered meat) and Greek salads, all washed down with the local firewater, aniseed-flavoured ouzo.

p323

Italy

History ✓✓✓
Culture ✓✓✓
Food ✓✓✓

History
History, myth and legend come to life at Italy's historic sites. Ancient ruins resonate with epics of lost glories, Renaissance palaces harbour dark secrets, and baroque basilicas tell of papal plots and political intrigue.

Culture
Italy's many museums boast priceless artworks by the lorry load, with everything from ancient sculptures to modern design classics, while the nation's dedication to style, fashion and music makes for a rich and varied cultural landscape.

Food
Italian cuisine is imitated the world over but still nothing can compare to a pizza served straight from a wood-fired oven in a neighbourhood pizzeria or a humble bowl of pasta dished up in a family-run trattoria. Italian gelato (ice cream) is a national treasure not to be missed.

p413

Montenegro

Scenery ✓✓✓
Outdoor Pursuits ✓✓✓
Historic Sites ✓✓

Scenery
Montenegro crams an awful lot of stunning scenery into a very small space – jagged mountains; sheer-walled river canyons; long, sandy beaches; and the spectacular Bay of Kotor, Europe's most southerly fjord.

Outdoor Pursuits
Sports fans can get their fix on Montenegro's mountains, and in its rivers and lakes. Durmitor National Park provides the dramatic setting for skiing, hiking and rafting, while kayaking is a great way to explore Lake Skadar.

Historic Sites
Many of Montenegro's towns harbour handsome historic centres, including Kotor, Budva, and Perast, famous for its Venetian-style architecture. For a spiritual side trip head to Ostrog Monastery, dramatically sited on a steep cliff-face.

p535

Portugal

Towns & Cities ✓✓✓
Beaches ✓✓✓
Culture ✓✓

Towns & Cities
One of Europe's under-the-radar capitals, Lisbon is a low-key charmer oozing character. Other notable towns and cities include Porto, with its Unesco-listed historic centre, the university town of Coimbra, and the hilltop stunner Sintra.

Beaches
Beach aficionados will enjoy Portugal. There are excellent beaches all over but for the best head south to The Algarve, where you'll find everything from long sandy strips pounded by Atlantic surf to small secluded bays lapped by limpid, azure waters.

Culture
Music is a Portuguese passion and central to the country's cultural life. Soulful fado provides the soundtrack for Lisbon's atmospheric Alfama district while more modern tunes drive the city's thumping clubs. Bacchanalian street festivals provide a further excuse for red-blooded merrymaking.

p563

Slovenia

Scenery ✓✓✓
Outdoor Pursuits ✓✓✓
Towns & Cities ✓✓

Scenery
Even serial visitors to Slovenia regularly stop and stare, mesmerised by the sheer beauty of this tiny country. Pack your camera for staggering Alpine landscapes around Mt Triglav and picturesque Lake Bled.

Outdoor Pursuits
A wonderful, natural playground, Slovenia offers all sorts of sport. Bled and Bovec are popular centres offering canyoning, caving, kayaking and rafting, as well as hiking and mountain biking. Ski resorts pepper the mountains and you can go underground at the World Heritage–listed Škocjan Caves.

Towns & Cities
With its relaxed cafe culture, hilltop castle and smattering of museums and galleries, Ljubljana offers a fine introduction to Slovenia. Elsewhere, Bled is pure postcard material and Piran boasts ravishing Venetian architecture.

p609

Spain

Cities ✓✓✓
Food ✓✓✓
Beaches ✓✓✓

Cities
Unique Modernista architecture in Barcelona, awe-inspiring Moorish buildings in Córdoba and Granada, flamenco in Seville, art and clubbing in Madrid – Spain's great cities cater to all styles and tastes.

Food
For the food-loving traveller, Spain is a goldmine waiting to be tapped. Local specialities abound but the nation's greatest contribution to the culinary world is tapas. These tempting bar snacks are served across the country but are spectacularly good in San Sebastián, Spain's top foodie city.

Beaches
Sun seekers are spoiled for choice in Spain with a full gamut of beaches, from the wild, rocky coves of northern Galicia to the dreamy Mediterranean beaches of the Balearic Islands. For pure beach bliss, head to Menorca.

p649

Turkey

History ✓✓✓
Ancient Ruins ✓✓✓
Beaches ✓✓✓

History

From the ruins of Troy and the battlefields of Gallipoli to the domes, minarets and teeming markets of İstanbul, the former capital of the Byzantine and Ottoman Empires, history is writ large on Turkey's vast and varied landscape.

Ancient Ruins

Once a Roman provincial capital, Ephesus has survived in remarkable shape and its ruins are one of Turkey's headline sights. Elsewhere you can trawl ancient ruins at Troy and Pergamum, an important medical centre in ancient times.

Beaches

Turkey's Mediterranean seaboard, known as the Turquoise Coast, boasts some superb beaches and heavenly azure waters. Popular spots include Patara; the beautiful Butterfly Valley; Olympos, famed for its ancient ruins and tree houses; and Çıralı.

p763

Every listing is recommended by our authors, and their
favourite places are listed first

Look out for these icons:

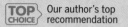 Our author's top
recommendation

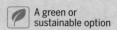 A green or
sustainable option

 No payment
required

ALBANIA 42
Tirana .45
Around Tirana 52
Northern Albania 52
Central Albania 54
Southern Coast 60
Eastern Albania 64
Understand Albania 66
Survival Guide 70

BOSNIA &
HERCEGOVINA 75
Sarajevo 78
Around Sarajevo 90
Hercegovina 91
Eastern Bosnia
& Hercegovina 102
Central &
Western Bosnia 104
Understand Bosnia
& Hercegovina 111
Survival Guide 115

CROATIA 119
Zagreb 121
Istria 136
Kvarner Region 144
Dalmatia 149
Understand Croatia 172
Survival Guide 177

FRANCE 183
Paris 185
Around Paris 217
Lille, Flanders &
the Somme 219

See the Index for a full list of destinations covered in this book.

On the Road

Normandy 224
Brittany 229
Champagne 234
Alsace & Lorraine 237
The Loire Valley 243
Burgundy &
the Rhône Valley 248
The French Alps 258
The Jura 265
The Dordogne 266
The Atlantic Coast 268
Languedoc-Roussillon 275
Provence 280
The French Riviera
& Monaco 291
Corsica 303
Understand France 308
Survival Guide 314

GREECE 323
Athens 325
Around Athens 341
The Peloponnese 343
Central Greece 350
Northern Greece 352
Saronic Gulf Islands 357
Cyclades 359
Crete 371
Dodecanese 379
Northeastern
Aegean Islands 386
Sporades 391
Ionian Islands 393
Understand Greece 400
Survival Guide 405

ITALY 413
Rome 416
Around Rome 445
Northern Italy 446
Tuscany 473
Umbria 491
Southern Italy 494
Sicily 509
Sardinia 520
Understand Italy 524
Survival Guide 528

MONTENEGRO 535
Bay of Kotor 538
Adriatic Coast 544
Central Montenegro 548
Northern Mountains 554
Understand Montenegro . . 557
Survival Guide 560

PORTUGAL 563
Lisbon 566
Around Lisbon 581
The Algarve 583
Central Portugal 588
The North 595
Understand Portugal 604
Survival Guide 605

SLOVENIA 609
Ljubljana 611
Julian Alps 623
Karst & Coast 633
Eastern Slovenia 640

Understand Slovenia 642
Survival Guide 644

SPAIN 649
Madrid 651
Around Madrid 673
Castilla y León 674
Castilla-La Mancha 680
Catalonia 683
Aragón, Basque
Country & Navarra 703
Cantabria, Asturias
& Galicia 711
Valencia & Murcia 715
Balearic Islands 720
Andalucía 727
Gibraltar 746
Extremadura 747
Understand Spain 750
Survival Guide 755

TURKEY 763
İstanbul 765
Around İstanbul 781
The Aegean Coast 784
The Mediterranean
Coast 802
Central Anatolia 818
Cappadocia
(Kapadokya) 821
Eastern Turkey 827
Understand Turkey 831
Survival Guide 837

Albania

Includes »

Tirana 45
Shkodra 52
Theth & Valbonë 54
Kruja 55
Durrës 56
Apollonia 57
Berat 57
Vlora 60
Drymades 61
Dhërmi 61
Himara 61
Vuno & Jal 62
Saranda 62
Gjirokastra 65
Understand Albania 66
Survival Guide 70

Why Go?

Albania has natural beauty in such abundance that you might wonder why it's taken 20 years for the country to take off as a tourist destination since the end of a particularly brutal strain of communism in 1991. So backward was Albania when it emerged blinking into the bright light of freedom that it needed two decades just to catch up with the rest of Eastern Europe. Now that it arguably has done so, Albania offers a remarkable array of unique attractions, not least due to this very isolation: ancient mountain codes of behaviour, forgotten archaeological sites and villages where time seems to have stood still are all on the menu. With its stunning mountain scenery, a thriving capital in Tirana and beaches to rival any elsewhere in the Mediterranean, Albania has become the sleeper hit of the Balkans. But hurry here, as word is well and truly out.

Best Places to Eat

» Kujtimi (p66)
» Era (p49)
» Tradita G&T (p53)
» Oda (p49)

Best Places to Stay

» Tradita G&T (p53)
» Hotel Rilindja (p54)
» Hotel Mangalemi (p59)
» Hotel Kalemi (p65)

When to Go
Tirana

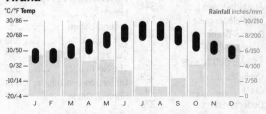

Jun Enjoy the perfect Mediterranean climate and deserted beaches.

Aug Albania's beaches may be packed, but this is a great time to explore the mountains.

Dec See features and shorts at the Tirana Film Festival, while the intrepid can snowshoe to Theth.

Connections

Albania has excellent connections in all directions: daily buses go to Kosovo, Montenegro, Macedonia and Greece. The southern seaport of Saranda is a short ferry trip from Greece's Corfu, while in summer ferries also connect Himara and Vlora to Corfu. Durrës has regular ferries to Italy. Travellers heading south from Croatia can pass through Montenegro to Shkodra (via Ulcinj), and loop through Albania before heading into Macedonia via Pogradec or Kosovo via the Lake Koman Ferry or new super-fast Albania–Kosovo highway. There are, however, no international train routes from Albania.

ITINERARIES

One Week

Spend a day in busy Tirana, checking out the various museums as well as the Blloku bars and nightclubs. On day two, head up the Dajti Express cable car and then make the two-hour trip to the Ottoman-era town of Berat. Spend a few nights in Berat, before continuing down the coast for a couple of days on the beach in Himara or Drymades. Loop around for one last night in charming Gjirokastra before returning to Tirana.

Two Weeks

Follow the first week itinerary and then head north into Albania's incredible 'Accursed Mountains'. Start in Shkodra, from where you can get transport to Koman for the stunning morning ferry ride to Fierzë. Continue the same day to the charming mountain village of Valbonë for a couple of nights, before trekking to Theth and spending your last couple of nights in the beautiful Theth National Park.

Essential Food & Drink

» **Byrek** Pastry with cheese or meat.
» **Fergesë** Baked peppers, egg and cheese, and occasionally meat.
» **Midhje** Wild or farmed mussels, often served fried.
» **Paçë koke** Sheep's head soup, usually served for breakfast.
» **Qofta** Flat or cylindrical minced-meat rissoles.
» **Sufllaqë** Doner kebab.
» **Tavë** Meat baked with cheese and egg.
» **Konjak** Local brandy.
» **Raki** Popular spirit made from grapes.
» **Raki mani** Spirit made from mulberries.

AT A GLANCE

» **Currency** lekë
» **Language** Albanian
» **Money** ATMs in most towns
» **Visas** Most visitors don't need one – a 90-day stamp is issued at the border

Fast Facts

» **Area** 28,748 sq km
» **Capital** Tirana
» **Country code** ☏355
» **Emergency** Ambulance ☏127, fire ☏128, police ☏129

Exchange Rates

Australia	A$1	114.59 lekë
Canada	C$1	107.95 lekë
Euro Zone	€1	140.19 lekë
Japan	¥100	116.24 lekë
New Zealand	NZ$1	91.85 lekë
UK	UK£1	165.99 lekë
USA	US$1	109.70 lekë

Set Your Budget

» **Budget hotel** €10–15 per person
» **Two-course meal** €8
» **Museum entrance** €1–3
» **Beer** €1.50
» **City transport ticket** 30 lekë

Resources

» **Albania-Hotel** (www.albania-hotel.com)
» **Balkanology** (www.balkanology.com/albania)
» **Journey to Valbona** (www.journeytovalbona.com)

Albania Highlights

1 Catch the **Lake Koman Ferry** (p55) through stunning mountain scenery, then continue to **Valbonë** and trek the 'Accursed Mountains'.

2 Explore the Unesco World Heritage–listed museum towns of dramatic **Berat** (p57), the so-called 'city of a thousand windows'.

3 Catch some sun at **Drymades** (p61), just one of the many beaches on the south's dramatic Ionian Coast.

4 Travel back in time to the ruins of **Butrint** (p64), hidden in the depths of a forest in a serene lakeside setting.

5 Feast your eyes on the wild colour schemes and experience the hip Blloku cafe culture in **Tirana** (p45).

6 Take a trip into the traditional Southern Albanian mountain town of **Gjirokastra** (p65), with is spectacular Ottoman-era mansions and impressive hilltop fortress.

TIRANA

🗐 04 / POP 764,000

Lively, colourful Tirana is the beating heart of Albania, where this tiny nation's hopes and dreams coalesce into a vibrant whirl of traffic, brash consumerism and unfettered fun. Having undergone a transformation of extraordinary proportions since it awoke from its communist slumber in the early 1990s, Tirana is now unrecognisable, with its buildings painted in horizontal primary colours, and public squares and pedestrianised streets a pleasure to wander.

Trendy Blloku buzzes with well-dressed *nouvelle bourgeoisie* hanging out in bars or zipping between boutiques, while the city's grand boulevards are lined with fascinating relics of its Ottoman, Italian and communist past – from delicate minarets to loud socialist murals. Tirana's traffic does daily battle with both itself and pedestrians in a constant scene of unmitigated chaos. Loud, crazy, colourful and dusty – Tirana is never dull.

◉ Sights

The centre of Tirana is Skanderbeg Sq, a large traffic island with an equestrian statue of the Albanian national hero at its centre. Running through the square is Tirana's main avenue, Blvd Zogu I, which becomes Blvd Dëshmorët e Kombit (Martyrs of the Nation Blvd) south of the square. At the street's northern end is Tirana's train station; head to the other end and you're at the small Tirana University building.

NORTH OF THE RIVER

Sheshi Skënderbej   SQUARE
(Skanderbeg Sq) Skanderbeg Sq is the best place to start witnessing Tirana's daily goings-on. Until it was pulled down by an angry mob in 1991, a 10m-high bronze statue of Enver Hoxha stood here, watching over a mainly car-free square. Now only the **equestrian statue of Skanderbeg** remains, deaf to the cacophony of screeching horns as cars four lanes deep try to shove their way through the battlefield below.

TOP CHOICE **National History Museum**   MUSEUM
(Muzeu Historik Kombëtar; Sheshi Skënderbej; adult/student 200/60 lekë; ◷10am-5pm Tue-Sat, to 2pm Sun) The largest museum in Albania holds most of the country's archaeological treasures and a replica of Skanderbeg's massive sword (how he held it, rode his horse

and fought at the same time is a mystery). The mosaic mural entitled *Albania* adorning the museum's facade shows Albanians victorious and proud from Illyrian times through to WWII. The collection is almost entirely signed in English and takes you chronologically from ancient Illyria to the postcommunist era. The highlight of the museum is a terrific exhibition of icons by Onufri, a renowned 16th-century Albanian master of colour. A disturbing and very important gallery devoted to those who suffered persecution under the communist regime is the most recent addition to the collection, though frustratingly almost none of this display is in English.

National Art Gallery   GALLERY
(Galeria Kombëtare e Arteve; www.gka.al; Blvd Dëshmorët e Kombit; admission 200 lekë; ◷10am-6pm Mon-Sat) Tracing the relatively brief history of Albanian painting from the early 19th century to the present day, this beautiful space also has temporary exhibits that are worth a look. Downstairs there's a small but interesting collection of 19th-century paintings depicting scenes from daily Albanian life, while upstairs the art takes on a political dimension with some truly fabulous examples of Albanian socialist realism.

Et'hem Bey Mosque   MOSQUE
(Sheshi Skënderbej; ◷8am-11am) To one side of Skanderbeg Sq, the 1789–1823 Et'hem

---

BUNKER LOVE

On the hillsides, beaches and generally most surfaces in Albania, you will notice small concrete domes (often in groups of three) with rectangular slits. Meet the bunkers: Enver Hoxha's concrete legacy, built from 1950 to 1985. Weighing in at 5 tonnes of concrete and iron, these little mushrooms are almost impossible to destroy. They were built to repel an invasion and can resist full tank assault – a fact proved by their chief engineer, who vouched for his creation's strength by standing inside one while it was bombarded by a tank. The shell-shocked engineer emerged unscathed, and tens of thousands were built. Today, some are creatively painted, one houses a tattoo artist, and some even house makeshift hostels.

Tirana

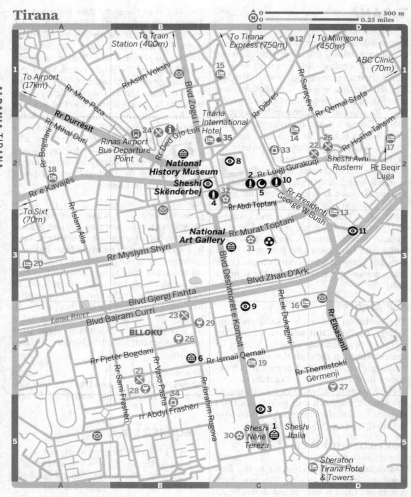

Bey Mosque was spared destruction during the atheism campaign of the late 1960s because of its status as a cultural monument. Small and elegant, it's one of the oldest buildings left in the city. Take your shoes off to look inside at the beautifully painted dome.

Clock Tower   TOWER
(Kulla e Sahatit; Rr Luigj Gurakuqi; admission 100 lekë; ⊙9am-1pm Mon, 9am-1pm & 4-6pm Thu; 🛜)
Behind the mosque is the tall clock tower, which you can climb for impressive views of the square. Further on up the street, look for

the socialist realist **statue of the Unknown Partisan**.

Palace of Culture   NOTABLE BUILDING
(Pallate Kulturës; Sheshi Skënderbej) To the east of Sheshi Skënderbej is the white stone Palace of Culture, which has a theatre, shops and art galleries. Construction of the palace began as a gift from the Soviet people in 1960 and was completed in 1966, years after the 1961 Soviet–Albanian split.

Fortress of Justinian   RUINS
(Rr Murat Toptani) If you turn up Rr Murat Toptani, behind the National Art Gallery,

Tirana

⊚ **Top Sights**
National Art Gallery C3
National History Museum B2
Sheshi Skënderbej B2

⊚ **Sights**
1 Archaeological Museum C5
2 Clock Tower C2
3 Congress Building C5
4 Equestrian Statue of Skanderbeg C2
5 Et'hem Bey Mosque C2
6 Former Residence of Enver
   Hoxha B4
7 Fortress of Justinian C3
8 Palace of Culture C2
9 Pyramid C4
10 Statue of the Unknown Partisan C2
11 Tanners' Bridge D3

⊕ **Activities, Courses & Tours**
12 Outdoor Albania C1

⊟ **Sleeping**
13 Brilant Antik D3
14 Capital Tirana Hotel C2
15 Freddy's Hostel C1
16 Green House C4
17 Hostel Albania D2
18 Hotel Serenity A2
19 Rogner Hotel Europapark Tirana C4

20 Tirana Backpacker Hostel A3

⊗ **Eating**
21 Era B4
   Green House .... (see 16)
22 Oda D2
23 Patisserie Française B4
24 Piazza B2
25 Stephen Centre D2

⊝ **Drinking**
26 Charl's B4
27 Kaon Beer Garden D4
28 Radio B4
29 Sky Club Bar B4

⊛ **Entertainment**
30 Academy of Arts C5
   Folie .... (see 31)
31 Kinema Millennium 2 .... C3
32 Theatre of Opera & Ballet C2

⊟ **Shopping**
   Adrion International Bookshop ..... (see 8)
33 Market C2
34 Natyral & Organik B5

⊙ **Transport**
   Avis .... (see 19)
35 Hertz C2

ALBANIA TIRANA

you'll pass the 6m-high walls of the Fortress of Justinian, the last remnants of a Byzantine-era castle. These days half a cinema/nightclub overflows over the top. East from here, on the corner of Rr Presidenti George W Bush and the Lana River, is **Tanners' Bridge**, a small 19th-century slippery-when-wet stone bridge.

SOUTH OF THE RIVER

Pyramid   NOTABLE BUILDING
(Blvd Dëshmorët e Kombit) Designed by Enver Hoxha's daughter and son-in-law and completed in 1988, this monstrously unattractive building was formerly the Enver Hoxha Museum, and more recently a convention centre and nightclub. Today, covered in graffiti and surrounded by the encampments of Tirana's homeless, its once white marble walls are now crumbling but no decision on whether to demolish or restore it appears to have yet been reached.

Congress Building   NOTABLE BUILDING
(Blvd Dëshmorët e Kombit) Another creation of the former dictator's daughter and son-in-law is the square Congress Building, just a little down the boulevard from the Pyramid. Follow Rr Ismail Qemali two streets north of the Congress Building and enter the once totally forbidden but now totally trendy Blloku area. This former Communist Party elite hang-out was opened to the general public for the first time in 1991. Security still guards the **former residence of Enver Hoxha** (cnr Rr Dëshmorët e 4 Shkurtit & Rr Ismail Qemali).

Archaeological Museum   MUSEUM
(Muzeu Arkeologik; Sheshi Nënë Tereza; admission 100 lekë; ⊙10.30am-2.30pm Mon-Fri) The collection here is comprehensive and impressive in parts, but there's no labelling in any language, nor tours in English offered, so unless this is your field, you may find yourself a little at a loss to get much out of the

museum. A total renovation is on the cards, but as one staff member pointed out to us, they've been waiting for this since 1985, so don't hold your breath.

Martyrs' Cemetery
CEMETERY

At the top of Rr Elbasanit is the Martyrs' Cemetery, where some 900 partisans who died in WWII are buried. The views over the city and surrounding mountains (including Mt Dajti to the east) are excellent, as is the sight of the immense, beautiful and strangely androgynous Mother Albania statue (1972). Hoxha was buried here in 1985 but in 1992 he was exhumed and interred in an ordinary graveyard elsewhere. Catch a municipal bus heading up Rr Elbasanit; the grand driveway is on your left.

👉 Tours

Get off the beaten track or discover Albania's tourist attractions with a Tirana-based tour company.

Albanian Experience
TOURS

(☑2272 055; www.albania-experience.al; Sheshi Italia, Sheraton Tirana Hotel) Organises tours of Albania with knowledgeable guides.

Outdoor Albania
TOURS

(☑2227 121; www.outdooralbania.com; Rr Sami Frasheri, Pallati Metropol) Excellent trail-blazing adventure tour agency offering hiking, rafting, snowshoeing, sea and white-water kayaking and, in summer, hikes through the Alps.

🎉 Festivals & Events

Tirana International Film Festival
CINEMA

(www.tiranafilmfest.com) This festival is held each late November/early December and features both short and feature films from its international competition winners, as well as new cinematic work from Albanian filmmakers.

🛏 Sleeping

🏆 TOP CHOICE Brilant Antik
HOTEL €€

(☑2251 166; www.hotelbrilant.com; Rr Jeronim de Rada 79; s/d €50/60; ❄🛜) This charming house-cum-hotel has plenty of character, a central location and welcoming English-speaking staff to ease you into Tirana life. Rooms are spacious, decently furnished with the odd antique, and breakfast downstairs is a veritable feast each morning.

Rogner Hotel Europapark Tirana
HOTEL €€€

(☑2235 035; www.hotel-europapark.com; Blvd Dëshmorët e Kombit; s €150-180, d €170-210, ste €240-290; ❄@🛜🏊) With an unbeatable location in the heart of the city, the Rogner is a peaceful oasis with a huge garden, tennis court and facilities such as banks, travel and car-rental agencies. The rooms are spacious, extremely comfortable and come with flat-screen TVs.

Green House
BOUTIQUE HOTEL €€€

(☑068 2072 262, 4521 015; www.greenhouse.al; Rr Jul Variboba 6; s/d €80/90; ❄🛜) In a cool spot in Tirana sits this modern 10-room hotel with downlit, stylish rooms that might be the city's coolest. Its sprawling downstairs terrace restaurant is a friendly expat hang-out with a varied menu and a long wine list. It looks up at one of Tirana's quirkiest buildings.

🏆 TOP CHOICE Tirana Backpacker Hostel
HOSTEL €

(☑068 3133 451, 068 4682 353; www.tiranahostel. com; Rr Myslym Shyri, Vila 7, behind Alpet petrol station; dm €13, d €40, without bathroom €28; ❄🛜) Albania's first ever hostel now boasts very smart new premises in the centre of town, and looks more like a fancy restaurant than a hostel at first glance. There are three six-bed dorms, all with their own facilities, and several comfortable doubles, including one with a great balcony. All rooms are equipped with air-con, but you'll need to pay €3 extra per room per night to turn it on. The place is very social, with a busy bar-restaurant downstairs and plenty of atmosphere.

Capital Tirana Hotel
HOTEL €€

(☑2258 575, 069 2080 931; www.capitaltiranahotel. com; Rr Qemal Stafa; s/d €40/65; P❄🛜) Opened in 2012, this thoroughly modern 29-room hotel just a stone's throw from Skanderbeg Sq is a welcome addition to Tirana's accommodation scene. It may be a little sterile and businesslike, but the rooms are of good quality with flat-screen TVs and minibars, staff are very helpful and the location on a busy shopping street is great.

Hostel Albania
HOSTEL €

(☑067 2783 798; www.hostel-albania.com; Rr Beqir Luga 56; dm €11-12, d €30; @🛜) This hostel has small four- and six-person dorms, though the basement's 14-bed dorm (€11) is the coolest spot in summer and dividers hide the fact that there are so many bunks down there. Zen space is in the outdoor shoes-off oriental lounge, and a filling breakfast with filter coffee is included. The artist owners provide great information about the local art scene, and the location is central.

Freddy's Hostel
HOTEL €

(☎2266 077, 068 2035 261; www.freddyshostel.com; Rr Bardhok Biba 75; dm €12, r €32-56; ❀☜) Freddy's is run by a friendly family whose knowledge of the city is second to none. The clean, basic bunk-free rooms have lockers and come in different configurations. Breakfast isn't included with the cheapest dorm places, but the central location is hard to beat. The owners can also arrange long-term apartment rentals.

Hotel Serenity
HOTEL €€

(☎2267 152; Rr Bogdani 4; s/d €25/40; ❀@☜) This villa-style hotel in a side street in central Tirana has a semi-boutique feel with stylish rooms and contemporary fittings. Despite the busy main road nearby, this is a quiet location. Rooms have tiled floors, minibars and TVs, and offer excellent value. Breakfast is not included.

Milingona
HOSTEL €

(☎069 2070 076, 069 2049 836; www.milingona-hostel.com; Rr Risa Cerova 197/2, off Rr Dibres; tent €7, dm €11-12, d €30; @☜) Now in a new location a 15-minute walk from Skanderbeg Sq, 'the Ant' takes up a large house in a residential district and is cared for by multilingual sisters Zhujeta and Rozana. There are large dorms (sleeping six and eight people), each of which shares facilities with another dorm on the same floor. There's a large shared kitchen, a living room, a roof terrace and a garden. To get here from the centre, walk up Rr Dibres, and when it splits, bear right after the Medresa, and Rr Risa Cerova is the first street on the right.

✖ Eating

Most of Tirana's best eating is in and around Blloku, a square of some 10 blocks of shops, restaurants, cafes and hotels situated one block west of Dëshmorët and along the Lana River in south Tirana.

TOP CHOICE Era
ALBANIAN, ITALIAN €€

(☎2266 662; www.era.al; Rr Ismail Qemali; mains 300-700 lekë; ☉11am-midnight; ✐) This local institution serves traditional Albanian and Italian fare in the heart of Blloku. The inventive menu includes oven-baked veal and

eggs, stuffed eggplant, pizza, and pilau with chicken and pine nuts. Be warned: it's sometimes quite hard to get a seat as it's fearsomely popular, so you may have to wait. Delivery and takeaway are both available.

TOP CHOICE Oda
ALBANIAN €€

(Rr Luigj Gurakuqi; mains 350-550 lekë; ☉noon-11pm) Bright flashing lights will guide you to this endearing little restaurant down a lane where you can choose from two brightly lit dining rooms or an atmospheric terrace. The place is stuffed full of traditional Albanian arts and crafts, and while its popularity with travellers means you won't feel like you've discovered a truly authentic slice of the country, the delicious menu and pleasant atmosphere make it well worth a visit.

Piazza
ITALIAN €€

(Rr Ded Gjo Luli; mains 400-700 lekë; ☉noon-11pm) Behind the national museum, this restaurant consistently gets rave reviews from visitors who enjoy the formal service, the stylish interior and the fine Italian cuisine. The fish is the speciality here, and it's cooked to perfection, while the wine list has some excellent local vintages.

Green House
ITALIAN €€

(Rr Jul Variboba 6; mains 400-800 lekë) Downstairs from the small eponymous hotel, the Green House boasts an enviable terrace that hums with the buzz of the local Blloku crowds day and night. The menu is strongly Italian leaning, but there are Albanian and other international dishes too.

Patisserie Française
BAKERY €

(Rr Dëshmorët e 4 Shkurtit 1; pastries from 150 lekë; ☉8am-10pm; ☜) This popular Blloku cafe has has an array of sweet pastries, macaroons and sandwiches plus good coffee to boot. It's a good breakfast option.

Stephen Centre
CAFE €€

(Rr Hoxha Tahsim 1; mains 400-700 lekë; ☉8am-8pm Mon-Sat; ☜) If you like your fries thin, your wi-fi free and the spirit Christian, here's the cafe for you. A veritable institution in Tirana, the Stephen Centre also offers accommodation upstairs in single-bed configurations (single/double €35/50).

☕ Drinking

Most of Tirana's nightspots are concentrated in the Blloku neighbourhood, and most will have you partying on to the wee hours.

Radio
BAR

(Rr Ismail Qemali 29/1) Set back from the street is this very cool yet understated and friendly bar. Check out the owner's collection of antique Albania-made radios while sipping cocktails with groovy locals.

Charl's
BAR

(Rr Pjetër Bogdani 36) Charl's is a consistently popular bar with Tirana's students because of its ever-varying live music on the weekends, and disco/dance crowd-pleasers the rest of the time. The relaxed vibe is enhanced by the bar's open-air garden.

Kaon Beer Garden
BEER HALL

(Rr Asim Zeneli; ⊙noon-1am) For those who hate the hassle of ordering beer after beer, here's Kaon. Its popular 'keg-on-the-table' approach means it can be hard to get a table in the evening (queuing is normal), but once you get in, it's a pleasant outdoor bar and restaurant in the fancy villa-filled part of town. You won't go hungry; Albanian meals start from 200 lekë. Locally brewed beer comes in standard glasses, or tabletop 2- and 3-litre 'roxys'.

Sky Club Bar
BAR

(Rr Dëshmorët e 4 Shkurtit, Sky Tower) Start your night here for spectacular city views from the revolving bar on top of one of the highest buildings in town.

☆ Entertainment

There is a good choice of entertainment options in Tirana, in the form of bars, clubs, cinema, performances, exhibitions and even 10-pin bowling. For the low-down on events and exhibitions, check posters around town. For alternative events, ask at Milingona hostel and Hostel Albania.

TOP CHOICE Tirana Express
GALLERY, MUSIC

(www.tiranaekspres.wordpress.com; Rr Karl Gega) This fantastic nonprofit arts project has converted a warehouse behind Tirana's semi-derelict train station into an arts space that hosts revolving temporary exhibits, concerts, installations and other events that appeal to Tirana's arty, alternative crowd. Go along and see what's on during your visit. Opening hours vary depending on what's on.

Folie
CLUB

(Rr Murat Toptani) This is where the big-name DJs come to play, and though the crowd can be a little more concerned with being seen than actually enjoying themselves, it's a great outdoor venue for a loud night out.

Kinema Millennium 2
CINEMA

(Rr Murat Toptani; tickets 300-500 lekë) Current-release movies that are cheaper the earlier in the day you go. At night it's a nightclub.

Theatre of Opera & Ballet
THEATRE

(⌨2224 753; www.tkob.al; Sheshi Skënderbej; tickets from 350 lekë; ⊙performances from 7pm, from 6pm winter) Check the listings and posters outside the theatre for performances.

Academy of Arts
THEATRE

(⌨2257 237; www.artacademy.al; Sheshi Nënë Tereza) Classical music and other performances take place throughout the year in either the large indoor theatre or the small open-air faux-classical amphitheatre; both are part of the university. Prices vary according to the program.

🛍 Shopping

Souvenir shops on Rr Durrësit and Blvd Zogu I sell red Albanian flags, red T-shirts, red lighters, bunker ashtrays and lively traditional textiles.

🌿Natyral & Organik
FOOD & DRINK

(Rr Vaso Pasha) This tiny store in Blloku not only supports small village producers by stocking their organic olive oil, honey, herbs, tea, eggs, spices, raki and cognac (these make great gifts, but be aware of customs regulations in the countries you're travelling through), it's also a centre for environmental activism.

Market
FOOD & DRINK

(Sheshi Avni Rustemi) Buy fruit, vegetables and deli produce here; nearby Rr Qemal Stafa has secondhand stalls selling everything from bicycles to bedheads.

Adrion International Bookshop
BOOKS

(Sheshi Skënderbej, Palace of Culture; ⊙9am-9pm Mon-Sat) The place to head for maps, guides and English-language books.

ℹ Information

Tirana has plenty of ATMs linked to international networks.

ABC Clinic (⌨2234 105; www.abchealth.org; Rr Qemal Stafa 260; ⊙9am-1pm Mon, Wed & Fri, to 5pm Tue & Thu) Has English-speaking Christian doctors and a range of services, including brief (600 lekë) and normal (1200 lekë) consultations.

Hygeia Hospital Tirana (☎2390 000; www.hygeia.al; Tirana-Durrës Hwy) This new Greek-owned private hospital has a 24-hour emergency department.

Post Office (Rr Çameria; ☼8am-8pm) A shiny and clean oasis in a street jutting west from Sheshi Skënderbej. Smaller offices operate around the city.

Tirana in Your Pocket (www.inyourpocket.com) Has a local team of writers providing up-to-date coverage of Tirana. It can be downloaded free or bought at bookshops, hotels and some of the larger kiosks for 500 lekë.

Tirana Tourist Information Centre (☎2223 313; www.tirana.gov.al; Rr Ded Gjo Luli; ☼9am-5pm Mon-Fri, to 2pm Sat) Friendly staff make getting information easy at this government-run initiative just off Skanderbeg Sq.

ℹ Getting There & Around

There's now a good network of city buses running around Tirana costing 30 lekë per journey (payable to the conductor), although most of the sights can be covered easily on foot.

Air

The modern **Nënë Tereza International Airport** (Mother Teresa Airport; ☎2381 800; www.tirana-airport.com.al) is at Rinas, 17km northwest of Tirana. The Rinas Express airport bus operates an hourly (8am to 7pm) service from Rr Mine Peza on the western side of the National History Museum for 250 lekë one way. The going taxi rate is 2000 to 2500 lekë. The airport is about 20 minutes' drive away, but plan for possible traffic jams.

Bicycle

This was the main form of transport for Albanians until the early 1990s, and it's having a

comeback (cyclists seem to make more headway in Tirana's regular traffic snarls). Bike hire is available from several hostels.

Bus

You have the option of buses or *furgons* (minibuses). There is no official bus station in Tirana, though there's a makeshift bus station beside the train station where some buses drop passengers off and depart from. Confusingly, other buses and *furgons* depart from ever-changing places in and around the city, so check locally for the latest departure points. You can almost guarantee that taxi drivers will be in the know; however, you may have to dissuade them from taking you the whole way.

Furgons are usually slightly more expensive than buses and leave when full. Buses for Pristina in Kosovo (€20, five hours, three daily) leave from beside the museum on Blvd Zogu 1. To Macedonia, there are buses via Struga (€15, five hours) to Tetovo (€20, seven to eight hours) and Skopje (€20, eight hours) from the same spot. Buses to Ulcinj (€20) and Budva (€30) in Montenegro depart from 6am in front of the tourist information centre. If you're heading to Athens (€35, 15 hours), buses leave at around either 8am or 7pm from outside the travel agencies on Blvd Zogu 1. Most bus services are fairly casual; you turn up and pay the driver.

Car

Lumani Enterprise (☎04-2235 021; www.lumani-enterprise.com) is a local car-hire company. International companies in Tirana include the following (each also has an outlet at the airport):

Avis (☎2235 011; www.avis.al; Blvd Dëshmorët e Kombit, Rogner Hotel Europapark)

DOMESTIC BUSES FROM TIRANA

DESTINATION	PRICE (LEKË)	DURATION	DISTANCE (KM)
Berat	400	2½hr	122
Durrës	150	1hr	38
Elbasan	300	1½hr	54
Fier	400	2hr	113
Gjirokastra	800	7hr	232
Korça	600	4hr	181
Kruja	150	30min	32
Pogradec	500	3½hr	150
Saranda	1200	7hr	284
Shkodra	300	2hr	116
Vlora	500	4hr	147

Europcar (2227 888; www.europcar.com; Rr Durrësit 61)

Hertz (2262 511; www.hertzalbania.com; Sheshi Skënderbej, Tirana Hotel International)

Sixt (068 2068 500, 2259 020; Rr e Kavajës 116)

Taxi

Taxi stands dot the city, and taxis charge 300 to 400 lekë for a ride inside Tirana and 600 lekë at night and to destinations outside the city centre. Reach agreement on price with the driver before setting off. **Radio Taxi** (224 4444), with 24-hour service, is particularly reliable.

Train

The rundown train station is at the northern end of Blvd Zogu I. Albania's trains range from sort of OK to very decrepit, and as a result Albanians only tend to travel by train if they can't afford the bus. Seven trains daily go to Durrës (70 lekë, one hour). Trains also depart for Elbasan (190 lekë, four hours, 2.10pm), Pogradec (2km out of town; 295 lekë, eight hours, 5.30am), Shkodra (145 lekë, 3½ hours, 1.15pm) and Vlora (250 lekë, 5¾ hours, 4.25pm). Check timetables at the station the day before travelling. Purchase tickets before hopping on the train.

AROUND TIRANA

Just 25km east of Tirana is **Mt Dajti National Park** (1611m). It is the most accessible mountain in the country, and many Tiranans go there to escape the city rush and have a spit-roast lamb lunch. A sky-high, Austrian-made cable car, **Dajti Express** (www.dajtiekspres.com; return 700 lekë; 9am-9pm Tue-Sun), takes 15 minutes to rise to (almost) the top. It's a scenic trip over bunkers, forest, farms and hilltops. Once there, you can avoid all the touts and their minibuses and take the opportunity to stroll through lovely, shady beech and pine forests. There are grassy picnic spots along the road to the right, but if you didn't pack a picnic, try the lamb roast and spectacular views from the wide terrace of the **Panorama Restaurant** (mains 500 lekë).

To get to the Dajti Express departure point, take the public bus from outside Tirana's clock tower to 'Porcelain' (30 lekë). From here, it's a 1.5km walk uphill, or you can wait for the free bus transfer. Taxis seem to charge what they want to the Dajti Express drop-off point, but the trip from Tirana should only cost 600 lekë. It's also possible to drive or cycle to the top.

NORTHERN ALBANIA

Northern Albania is a scenic wonderland where the incredible landscape of the 'Accursed Mountains' dominates and the rich and independent mountain culture strongly flavours all journeys. The north also boasts rich wildlife around beautiful Lake Shkodra, not to mention the ancient city of the same name. This may be the Albania of blood feuds, but anyone visiting northern Albania will be amazed by how friendly and welcoming locals are.

Shkodra

022 / POP 95,000

Shkodra (Shkodër), the traditional centre of the Gheg cultural region, is one of the oldest cities in Europe. The ancient Rozafa Fortress has stunning views over the nearby lake, while a concerted effort to renovate the buildings in the Old Town has made wandering through Shkodra a treat for the eyes. Many travellers pass through here between Tirana and Montenegro, or en route to the Lake Koman Ferry and the villages of Theth and Valbonë, but it's worth spending a night to soak up this pleasant and welcoming place.

As the Ottoman Empire declined in the late 18th century, Shkodra became the centre of a semi-independent *pashalik* (region governed by a pasha, an Ottoman high official), which led to a blossoming of commerce and crafts. In 1913 Montenegro attempted to annex Shkodra (it succeeded in taking Ulcinj), a move not approved of by the international community, and the town changed hands often during WWI. Badly damaged by an earthquake in 1979, Shkodra was subsequently repaired and is Albania's fifth-largest town. The communist-era Hotel Rozafa in the town centre does little to welcome guests, but it makes a good landmark: restaurants, the information centre and most of the town's sights are close by.

Sights

Rozafa Fortress CASTLE
(admission 200 lekë; 8am-10pm) Three kilometres southwest of Shkodra, near the southern end of Lake Shkodra, the Rozafa Fortress was founded by the Illyrians in antiquity and rebuilt much later by the Venetians and then the Turks. The fortress derives its name from a woman named

Rozafa, who was allegedly walled into the ramparts as an offering to the gods so that the construction would stand. The story goes that Rozafa asked that two holes be left in the stonework so that she could continue to breastfeed her baby. There's a spectacular wall sculpture of her near the entrance of the castle's **museum** (admission 150 lekë; ⊙8am-7pm). Some nursing women come to the fortress to smear their breasts with the milky water that seeps from the wall during some months of the year. Municipal buses (30 lekë) stop near the turnoff to the castle, and it's a short walk up from there.

Marubi Permanent Photo Exhibition
GALLERY

(Rr Muhamet Gjollesha; admission 100 lekë; ⊙8am-4pm Mon-Fri) Hidden behind a block of shops and flats, the Marubi Permanent Photo Exhibition has fantastic photography by the Marubi 'dynasty', Albania's first and foremost photographers. The first-ever photograph taken in Albania is here, taken by Pjetër Marubi in 1858. The exhibition shows fascinating portraits, places and events. Not only is this a rare insight into what things looked like in old Albania, it is also a small collection of mighty fine photographs. To get here, go northeast of the clock tower to Rr Çlirimi; Rr Muhamet Gjollesha darts off to the right. The exhibition is on the left in an unmarked building, but locals will help you find it if you ask.

🛏 Sleeping & Eating

TOP CHOICE **Tradita G&T**   BOUTIQUE HOTEL €€

(☑2240 537, 068 2086 056; www.traditagt.com; Rr Edith Durham; s/d/tr €35/50/55; P🅿🛜) By far the best choice in town, this innovative, well-managed guesthouse is a delight. Housed in a painstakingly restored 17th-century mansion that once belonged to a famous Shkodran writer, the Tradita heaves with Albanian arts and crafts and has traditional yet very comfortable rooms with terracotta-roofed bathrooms and locally woven bed linen. A homemade, homegrown breakfast awaits guests in the morning and the restaurant serves excellent fish dishes in an ethnographic museum atmosphere. If you're heading Lake Koman way, the owner can arrange for the bus to pick you up from the hotel, and very happily shares a great deal of local knowledge with guests.

Hotel Kaduku
HOTEL €€

(HK; ☑069 2551 230, 42 216; www.hotel-kaduku.com; Sheshi 5 Heronjtë; s/d/tr/ste €23/32/48/50; ✳🛜) This popular, modern hotel is behind Raiffeisen Bank on the roundabout near Hotel Rozafa. Its two wings have been renovated, but rooms are a little on the small side, and the bathrooms even more so. It's clean and friendly though, and the staff are able to provide information about getting to and from Theth.

Çoçja
ITALIAN €€

(Rr Hazan Riza; mains 300-800 lekë; ⊙10am-11pm) This classy place on a pleasant piazza a block north of the pedestrianised Rr Kolë Idromeno is all gleaming white tablecloths, timber floors and a refreshing lack of kitsch in the design choices. The menu encompasses great pizza as well as more exciting fare such as veal ribs and chicken fillet with mushrooms and cream. There's also a great little courtyard garden that's perfect for summer drinks.

Piazza Park
PIZZA €€

(Bul Skënderberg; mains 300-900 lekë) Where the locals return to, night after night, day after day for people-watching and overloud music. The pizza is good though, and you've the choice of eating indoors in a smart dining room, or outside on the busy summer terrace. It's right next to the Mother Teresa monument on the main drag.

❶ Information

The information office (a stand-alone booth) at the intersection of Bul Skënderberg and Rr Kolë Idromeno is open daily, and until 9pm in summer.

❶ Getting There & Away

BUS There are hourly *furgons* and buses to and from Tirana (300 lekë, two hours, 6am to 4pm). From Shkodra, *furgons* depart from outside Radio Shkodra near Hotel Rozafa. *Furgons* to Ulcinj in Montenegro leave at 9am and 4pm (600 lekë, two hours) from the other side of the park abutting Grand Hotel Europa. They fill quickly. From Ulcinj, buses leave for Shkodra at 6am and 12.30pm. Catch the 7am bus to Lake Koman (800 lekë, two hours) in time for the wonderful ferry trip along the lake to Fierzë near Kosovo. *Furgons* depart for Theth daily at 7am (700 lekë).

TAXI It costs between €40 and €45 for the trip from Shkodra to Uncinj in Montenegro, depending on your haggling skills.

TRAIN Trains depart Tirana daily at 1.15pm (145 lekë), and arrive in Shkodra at 4.50pm, but you'll need to be up early to catch the 5.40am train back. *Furgons* meet arriving trains.

Theth & Valbonë

These small villages deep in the 'Accursed Mountains' are all but deserted in winter (Theth locals head south to live in Shkodra), but come summer they're a magnet for those seeking beauty, isolation, mystery and adventure. From Theth, three circular hikes are very clearly marked out with red and white markers. It's possible to hike in the region without a guide, but they're helpful and charge between 3000 and 4000 lekë per day. Official guides charge €50.

The main hike is from Theth to Valbonë (or vice versa) and takes roughly six to seven hours. It takes around three hours to trek from Theth's centre (742m) to Valbonë pass (1812m), then a further two hours to the houses of Rragam and 1½ hours along a riverbed to near Bajram Curri. It's a spectacular hike and many visitors' highlight of Albania. If possible, combine it with the Koman Ferry for the ultimate Albanian mountain experience, though you're far better doing the circuit anticlockwise (ie going from Valbonë to Theth) if you choose to include the ferry.

◉ Sights

Kulla HISTORIC BUILDING
(Theth; admission €1) Visit this fascinating 'lock-in tower' in central Theth where men waited, protected, during a blood feud.

⨇ Sleeping & Eating

Many of Theth's traditional homes have become B&Bs (complete with Western-style bathrooms with hot showers), while in less developed Valbonë, hotels tend to be new builds specifically designed for the needs of travellers. Due to the absence of restaurants in both villages, hotels often include breakfast, lunch and dinner in the deal.

TOP CHOICE Hotel Rilindja GUESTHOUSE €€
(Valbonë; ☑067 3014 638; www.journeytovalbona. com; per tent €6, r €30-34) Pioneering tourism in Valbonë since 2005, the Albanian-American run Rilindja is a real treat and garners rave reviews from travellers who love the comfortable accommodation and excellent food. A new 12-room building was due to open in 2013 1km up the road from the original building, which is located at the entrance to Valbonë. The five rooms in the old

building share a bathroom, except for one that has private facilities. With fluent English spoken, the helpful owners can organise hikes, picnics and transport.

Çarku Guesthouse GUESTHOUSE €€
(Theth; ☑069 3164 211; www.guesthouse-thethi-carku.com; per person €25; ☉Apr-Oct) Book in advance for a bed in this charming family home with thick stone walls, timber floors, a garden and farm. Food is all grown locally and meals are delicious. It's well signposted as you enter the village.

Guesthouse Tërthorja GUESTHOUSE €€
(Theth; ☑069 3840 990; www.terthorja-guest-house-tethi.com; per person incl full board €25) This renovated guesthouse has whitewashed walls, a sports field, sports equipment and a resident cow. Accommodation is in rooms sleeping up to five people and there are stunning views of the mountains all around.

Hotel & Camping Tradita CHALET €€
(Valbonë; ☑067 301 4567, 067 383 800 14; s/d €25/50) This collection of five newly built chalets has a fantastic location in the middle of the village with extraordinary views in all directions. The pine cabins each come with hot water and private facilities, and the owner, Isa, also offers six further rooms in his adjacent stone house. There's a good restaurant on-site too.

❶ Getting There & Around

BUS Though Theth is only 70km from Shkodra, expect the occasionally hair-raising *furgon* trip to take four hours. The *furgon* leaves from Shkodra at 7am, and most hotels in town will be able to call ahead the night before and book you a seat on the bus, and sometimes, to have the bus pick you up from the hotel.
FERRY A popular route is to take the 7am *furgon* from Shkodra to the Koman Ferry, travel by ferry (two hours) then jump on a *furgon* from the ferry to Valbonë. If you're heading into Kosovo, it takes roughly 50 minutes to the border by car from the ferry terminal, but check that the car ferry is still running.
TAXI To get to Theth from Shkodra by taxi, expect to pay €100.

CENTRAL ALBANIA

Central Albania crams it all in. Travel an hour or two from Tirana and you can be Ottoman house-hopping in brilliant Berat, musing over ancient ruins in deserted Apol-

KRUJA EN FERENG SKANDERBERG'S TOWN

DON'T MISS

THE LAKE KOMAN FERRY

One of Albania's undisputed highlights is this superb three-hour ferry ride through the vast Lake Koman, connecting the towns of Koman and Fierzë. Lake Koman was created in 1978 when the River Drin was dammed, with the result that you can cruise through spectacular mountain scenery where many incredibly hardy peasants still live as they have for centuries, tucked away in tiny mountain villages.

The ferry is not set up for tourism, which makes the entire trip feel like a great adventure. The best way to experience the ride is to make a loop beginning and ending in Shkodra, and taking in Koman, Fierzë, Valbonë and Theth. Normally there are two ferries daily in the summer months – a passenger ferry that leaves Koman at 9am and a car ferry that leaves Koman at 10am. However, the car ferry didn't run in 2012 due to declining demand, and so it's likely that in future only the passenger ferry will run. Check www.journeytovalbona.com for the latest information.

The passenger ferry (500 lekë per person) arrives in Fierzë at around 1pm and is met by *furgons* that will take you to either Bajram Curri (200 lekë) or to Valbonë (400 lekë). There's no real reason to stay in Bajram Curri though, unless you plan to head to Kosovo. Hikers will want to head straight for Valbonë, where you can stay for a night or two before doing the stunning day hike to Theth, where you can stay for another night or two before taking a *furgon* back to Shkodra.

Ionia or haggling for antiques in an Ottoman bazaar in Kruja.

Kruja

📞 0511 / POP 20,000

Kruja is Skanderbeg's town. Yes, Albania's hero was born here, and although it was over 500 years ago, there's still a great deal of pride in the fact that he and his forces defended Kruja from the Ottomans until his death. As soon as you get off the *furgon,* you're face to knee with a statue of Skanderbeg wielding his mighty sword with one hand, and it just gets more Skanderdelic after that.

From the road below, Kruja's houses appear to sit in the lap of a mountain. An ancient castle juts out to one side, and the massive Skanderbeg Museum juts out of the castle itself. The local plaster industry is going strong so expect visibility-reducing plumes of smoke to cloud views of the Adriatic Sea. Kruja's sights can be covered in a few hours, making this an ideal town to visit en route to Tirana's airport.

👁 Sights

Castle   CASTLE
(⊙24hr) Inside Kruja's sprawling castle grounds are Albania flag sellers, pizza restaurants and an array of mildly interesting sights, though few actually castle-related.

National Ethnographic Museum   MUSEUM
(admission 300 lekë; ⊙9am-1pm & 4-7pm Tue-Sun)
This traditional home in the castle complex below the Skanderbeg Museum is one of the best in the country. Set in an original 19th-century Ottoman house that belonged to the affluent Toptani family, this museum shows the level of luxury and self-sufficiency the household maintained by producing its own food, drink, leather and weapons. They even had their very own mini *hammam* (Turkish bath) and watermill. The walls are lined with original frescos from 1764. The English-speaking guide's detailed explanations are excellent; offer a tip if you can.

Skanderbeg Museum   MUSEUM
(admission 200 lekë; ⊙9am-1pm & 4-7pm Tue-Sun) Designed by Enver Hoxha's daughter and son-in-law, this museum opened in 1982, and its spacious seven-level interior displays replicas of armour and paintings depicting Skanderbeg's struggle against the Ottomans. The museum is something of a secular shrine, and takes itself very seriously indeed, with giant statues and dramatic battle murals.

Teqe   MOSQUE
A short scramble down the cobblestone lane are the remains of a small *hammam* as well as a functioning *teqe* – a small place of worship for those practising the Bektashi branch of Islam. This beautifully decorated *teqe* has been maintained by

KRUJA: ENTERING SKANDERBEG'S TOWN

At a young age, Gjergj Kastrioti, the son of an Albanian prince, was handed over as a hostage to the Turks, who converted him to Islam and gave him a military education at Edirne in Turkey. There he became known as Iskander (after Alexander the Great) and Sultan Murat II promoted him to the rank of bey (governor), thus the name Skanderbeg.

In 1443 the Turks suffered a defeat at the hands of the Hungarians at Niš in present-day Serbia, and nationally minded Skanderbeg took the opportunity to abandon the Ottoman army and Islam and rally his fellow Albanians against the Turks. Skanderbeg made Kruja his seat of government between 1443 and 1468. Among the 13 Turkish invasions he subsequently repulsed was that led by his former commander, Murat II. Pope Calixtus III named Skanderbeg the 'captain general of the Holy See' and Venice formed an alliance with him. The Turks besieged Kruja four times. Though beaten back in 1450, 1466 and 1467, they finally took control of Kruja in 1478 (after Skanderbeg's death).

successive generations of the Dollma family since 1789. Skanderbeg himself reputedly planted the knotted olive tree at the front.

Bazaar   MARKET
This Ottoman-style bazaar is the country's best place for souvenir shopping and has WWII medical kits, antique gems and quality traditional ware, including beautifully embroidered tablecloths, copper coffee pots and plates. You can watch women using looms to make *kilims* (rugs) and purchase the results.

ℹ Getting There & Away

Kruja is 32km from Tirana. Make sure your *furgon* from Tirana (150 lekë, 30 minutes) is going to Kruja, not just Fush Kruja, the modern town below. It is very easy to reach the airport (150 lekë, 15 minutes) by *furgon* or taxi from here, and it's en route to Shkodra, though you'll need to pull over a bus on the busy Tirana–Shkodra highway as they don't drive up the mountain into the town itself.

Durrës
☑ 052

Durrës was once – albeit briefly – Albania's capital. It's now virtually an extension of Tirana, joined to the capital by a ceaseless urban corridor full of hypermarkets and car dealerships. Blessed with a decent 10km stretch of beach, Durrës is sadly a lesson in unplanned development; hundreds of hotels stand side by side, and it's terribly crowded in the summer months. Despite this, there's an interesting amphitheatre

to see, although the famous archaeological museum on the seafront has been demolished and a new one is currently being built on the same site.

◉ Sights

Amphitheatre of Durrës   RUINS
(Rr e Kalasë; admission 300 lekë; ⊙9am-7pm) The Amphitheatre of Durrës was built on the hillside inside the city walls in the early 2nd century AD. In its prime it had the capacity to seat 15,000 to 20,000 spectators, but these days a few inhabited houses occupy the stage, a reminder of its recent rediscovery (in 1966) and excavation. The Byzantine chapel in the amphitheatre has several beautiful mosaics. There are knowledgable English-speaking guides on site daily until 3pm; they work on a tipping basis.

⌂ Sleeping

Hotel Ani   HOTEL €€
(☑224 228; anihoteldurres@yahoo.it; 1 Shëtitorja Taulantia; r from €60; P※@🛜) This very smart property faces the site of the new archaeological museum and backs onto the seafront. The smart and classy lobby gives way to spacious and comfortable rooms, and service is friendly and efficient.

Nais Hotel   HOTEL €€
(☑230 375, 052 224 940; hotelnais@hotmail.com; Rr Lagja 1, off Bul Epidamni; r €25-40; ※🛜) Just a short wander from the amphitheatre in the centre of town, this friendly family-run place is a comfortable midrange option. Rooms are clean and modern, with a good breakfast served downstairs and the beachfront just moments away.

✕ Eating & Drinking

Palma   ITALIAN €€
(Rr Taulantia; mains 400-1000 lekë) One of the
better bets on the busy and commercial seafront, this smart place has a large menu of
pizza, grills and fish dishes, and is a great
spot to soak up the passing crowds.

Bar Torra   BAR
(Sheshi Mujo Ulqinaku) This Venetian tower
was opened by a team of local artists and
was one of the first private cafes in Albania. There are art displays (and cosy nooks)
downstairs, and in summer you can gaze
around Durrës from the top of the tower.

❶ Getting There & Away

BOAT Agencies around the train station sell tickets for the many ferry lines plying the Durrës–Bari
route (single deck €40, eight hours). **Venezia
Lines** (✆052 383 83; www.venezialines.com) has
the fastest boat to Bari (€60, 3½ hours). Ferries
also depart Durrës for Ancona most days in summer (€65, 17 hours) and at least three days a week
throughout the year.

BUS & FURGON *Furgons* (200 lekë, one hour)
and buses (150 lekë, one hour) to Tirana leave
from beside the train station when they're
full. Buses leave for Shkodra at 7.30am and
1.30pm (400 lekë, three hours). In summer,
long-distance buses and *furgons* going to and
from Saranda, Gjirokastra, Fier and Berat (400
lekë, 1½ hours) bypass this station, picking
up and dropping off passengers at the end of
Plazhi i Durrësi, east of the harbour, which can
be reached by the 'Plepa' orange municipal bus
(30 lekë, 10 minutes). In July and August many
buses connect Durrës with Pristina in Kosovo
(€15, five hours).

TRAIN Seven trains a day head to Tirana (70
lekë, one hour, 6.15am, 8.45am, 9.20am,
1.05pm, 3.12pm, 4.45pm and 8.05pm). Trains
also depart for Shkodra (1.05pm), Pogradec
(6.45am), Elbasan (6.45am, 3.25pm) and Vlore
(5.35pm). Check at the station for changes in
departure times.

Apollonia

The ruined city of ancient **Apollonia** (admission 700 lekë; ⊙9am-5pm) is 12km west of
Fier, which is 90km south of Durrës. Set
on rolling hills among olive groves, with
impressive views all around, Apollonia
(named after the god Apollo) was founded
by Greeks from Corinth and Corfu in 588
BC and quickly grew into an important city-
state, which minted its own currency and
benefited from a robust slave trade. Under
the Romans (from 229 BC), the city became
a great cultural centre with a famous school
of philosophy.

Julius Caesar rewarded Apollonia with
the title 'free city' for supporting him against
Gnaeus Pompeius Magnus (Pompey the
Great) during the civil war in the 1st century BC, and sent his nephew Octavius, the
future Emperor Augustus, to complete his
studies here.

After a series of military and natural disasters (including an earthquake in the 3rd
century AD that turned the river into a malarial swamp), the population moved south-
ward into present-day Vlora, and by the 5th
century only a small village with its own
bishop remained at Apollonia.

There is far less to see at Apollonia than
there is at Butrint, but there are some picturesque ruins within the 4km of city walls,
including a small original theatre and the
elegant pillars on the restored facade of the
city's 2nd-century-AD administrative centre. You may be able to see the 3rd-century-
BC **House of Mosaics** from a distance,
though they're often covered up with sand
for protection from the elements. Inside the
Museum of Apollonia complex is the Byzantine monastery and Church of St Mary,
which has gargoyles on the outside pillars.
Much of the site remains to be excavated,
but recent discoveries include a necropolis
outside the castle walls with graves from the
Bronze and Iron ages.

❶ Getting There & Away

Apollonia is best visited on a day trip from Tirana, Durrës, Vlora or Berat.

Furgons depart for the site (50 lekë) from
Fier's '24th August Bar' (ask locals for directions). From Fier, *furgons* head to Durrës (200
lekë, 1½ hours), Tirana (400 lekë, two hours),
Berat (300 lekë, one hour) and Vlora (200 lekë,
45 minutes).

If you'd prefer not to wait for the *furgon*, a taxi
will charge approximately 500 lekë one way
from Fier.

Berat

📞032 / POP 71,000
A highlight of any trip to Albania is a visit
to beautiful Berat. Its most striking feature
is the collection of white Ottoman houses
climbing up the hill to its castle, earning it
the title of 'town of a thousand windows'
and helping it join Gjirokastra on the list

of Unesco World Heritage sites in 2008. Its rugged mountain setting is particularly evocative when the clouds swirl around the tops of the minarets, or break up to show the icy top of Mt Tomorri.

The old quarters are lovely ensembles of whitewashed walls, tiled roofs and cobblestone roads. Surrounding the town, olive and cherry trees decorate the gentler slopes, while pine woods stand on the steeper inclines. The modern town is dominated by the huge dome of the brand-new Berat University, while elsewhere the bridges over the Osumi River to the charmingly unchanged Gorics side include a 1780 seven-arched stone footbridge.

In the 3rd century BC an Illyrian fortress called Antipatrea was built here on the site of an earlier settlement. The Byzantines strengthened the hilltop fortifications in the 5th and 6th centuries, as did the Bulgarians 400 years later. The Serbs, who occupied the citadel in 1345, renamed it Beligrad, or 'White City'. In 1450 the Ottoman Turks took the town. After a period of decline, in the 18th and 19th centuries the town began to thrive as a crafts centre specialising in woodcarving. Berat today is now a big centre for tourism in Albania, though it has managed to retain its easygoing charm and friendly atmosphere.

◉ Sights

TOP
CHOICE **Kalasa**   CASTLE
(admission 100 lekë, audio guide 500 lekë; ⊙24hr) The neighbourhood inside the castle's walls still lives and breathes; if you walk around this busy, ancient neighbourhood for long enough you'll invariably stumble into someone's courtyard thinking it's a church or ruin (no one seems to mind, though). In spring and summer the fragrance of chamomile is in the air (and underfoot), and wildflowers burst from every gap between the stones. The highest point is occupied by the Inner Fortress, where ruined stairs lead to a Tolkienesque water reservoir. Views are spectacular in all directions.

TOP
CHOICE **Onufri Museum**   GALLERY
(admission 200 lekë; ⊙9am-1pm & 4-7pm May-Sep, 9am-4pm Oct-Apr, closed Mon) Kala was traditionally a Christian neighbourhood, but fewer than a dozen of the 20 churches remain. The quarter's biggest church, **Church of the Dormition of St Mary** (Kisha Fjetja e Shën Mërisë), is the site of the

Onufri Museum. The church itself dates from 1797 and was built on the foundations of a 10th-century church. Onufri's spectacular 16th-century artworks are displayed on the ground level along with a beautifully gilded iconostasis.

Churches & Chapels   CHURCHES
Ask at the Onufri Museum if you can see the other churches and tiny chapels in Kala, including **St Theodore** (Shën Todher), close to the citadel gates; the substantial and picturesque **Church of the Holy Trinity** (Kisha Shën Triades), below the upper fortress; and the little chapels of **St Mary Blachernae** (Shën Mëri Vllaherna) and **St Nicholas** (Shënkolli). Some of the churches date back to the 13th century. Also keep an eye out for the **Red Mosque**, by the southern Kala walls, which was the first in Berat and dates back to the 15th century.

Chapel of St Michael   CHURCH
Perched on a cliff ledge below the citadel is the artfully positioned little chapel of St Michael (Shën Mihell), best viewed from the Gorica quarter.

Ethnographic Museum   MUSEUM
(admission 200 lekë; ⊙9am-1pm & 4-7pm May-Sep, 9am-4pm Oct-Apr, closed Mon) Down from the castle, this museum is in an 18th-century Ottoman house that's as interesting as the exhibits. The ground floor has displays of traditional clothes and the tools used by silversmiths and weavers, while the upper storey has kitchens, bedrooms and guest rooms decked out in traditional style. Check out the *mafil*, a kind of mezzanine looking into the lounge where the women of the house could keep an eye on male guests (and see when their cups needed to be filled). There are information sheets in Italian, French and English.

Mangalem Quarter   NEIGHBOURHOOD
Down in the traditionally Muslim Mangalem quarter, there are three grand mosques. The 16th-century **Sultan's Mosque** (Xhamia e Mbretit) is one of the oldest in Albania. The **Helveti teqe** behind the mosque has a beautiful carved ceiling and was specially designed with acoustic holes to improve the quality of sound during meetings. The Helveti, like the Bektashi, are a dervish order, or brotherhood, of Muslim mystics. The big mosque on the town square is the 16th-century **Lead Mosque** (Xhamia e Plumbit), so named because of the lead coating its

sphere-shaped domes. The 19th-century **Bachelors' Mosque** (Xhamia e Beqarëvet) is down by the Osumi River; look for the enchanting paintings on its external walls. This mosque was built for unmarried shop assistants and junior craftsmen, and is perched between some fine Ottoman-era shopfronts along the river.

🏃 Activities

Bogove Waterfall
HIKING

Catch the 8am or 9am *furgon* to Bogove via Skrappar, or a later bus to Polican then transfer to a *furgon* to Bogove. Lunch at Taverna Dafinat above the bus stop, then follow the path along the river (starting on the Berat side) to this icy waterfall.

Çobo Winery
WINE TASTING

(☏122 088; www.cobowineryonline.com; 🌐) The Çobo family winery is the best known in Albania, and it's worth checking out. Try its Shesh i Bardhe, Trebiano, Shesh i Izi and Kashmer wines, and, of course, its Raki me Arra. Any bus/*furgon* heading to Tirana can drop you off at the winery for 100 lekë.

Albania Rafting Group
TOURS

(☏2006 621; www.albrafting.com) This pioneering group runs rafting tours for all levels to some stunning gorges around Berat and Permet. Everyone from children to pensioners is welcome, and the various tours start at around €20 to €65 per person per day.

🛏 Sleeping & Eating

TOP CHOICE Hotel Mangalemi
HOTEL €€

(☏068 2323 238, 232 093; www.mangalemihotel. com; Rr Mihail Komneno; r from €35; P🐾) This hotel is housed in two sprawling Ottoman houses where all the rooms are beautifully furnished in traditional Berati style and balconies give superb views. Its terrace restaurant has great Albanian food with bonus views of Mt Tomorri. It's on the left side of the cobblestone road leading to the castle, just a short wander from the town centre.

TOP CHOICE Berat Backpackers
HOSTEL €

(☏069 474 8060, 069 3064 429; www.berat-backpackers.com; Gorica; tent/dm/r €7/12/28; 🕐Apr-Nov; @🐾) Albania's best hostel is the brainchild of Englishman Scott; he's transformed a traditional house in the Gorica quarter (across the river from Mangalem)

into a vine-clad hostel with a basement bar, alfresco drinking area and a cheery, relaxed atmosphere that money can't buy. There's a shaded camping area on the terrace, cheap laundry available, two airy dorms with original ceilings, and one excellent-value double room that shares the bathroom facilities with the dorms.

Hotel Muzaka
HOTEL €€

(☏231 999; www.hotelmuzaka.com; Gorica; s/d from €40/50; P🐾🐾🐾) This superb new addition to Berat's hotel scene is a careful restoration of an old stone mansion on the riverfront in Gorica, just over the footbridge from the centre of town. Wooden floorboards, gorgeous bathrooms and beautifully chosen pieces of furniture in the 10 spacious rooms make this a good option for those looking for some style as well as tradition in their accommodation.

White House
ITALIAN €€

(Rr Santa Lucia; mains 200-1000 lekë; 🕐8am-11pm) On the main road that runs north of the river, this smart place has a superb roof terrace with sweeping views over Berat, and serves up a mean pizza to boot. There's also a classier dining room downstairs with air-conditioning, perfect for a blowout meal.

Antigoni
ALBANIAN €€

(mains 600 lekë) This bustling restaurant may have an unusual style of service (some call it ignoring), but the Mangalem and Osumi River views from its upper levels are outstanding, and the food and local wine are both good.

ℹ️ Information

The town's **information centre** (www.bashkia-berat.com) is located in the council building, parallel to the Osumi River in new Berat.

ℹ️ Getting There & Away

Buses and *furgons* run between Tirana and Berat (400/500 lekë, 2½ hours) half-hourly until 3pm. From Tirana, buses leave from the 'Kombinati' station (catch the municipal bus from Sheshi Skënderbej to Kombinati for 30 lekë). In Berat, buses depart from and arrive in Sheshi Teodor Muzaka next to the Lead Mosque in the centre of town. There are buses to Vlora (350 lekë, 2½ hours, hourly until 2pm), Durrës (300 lekë, 1½ hours, five per day) and Saranda (1200 lekë, six hours, two daily at 8am and 2pm) via Gjirokastra (1000 lekë, four hours).

SOUTHERN COAST

With rough mountains falling head-first into bright blue seas, this area is wild and ready for exploration. The coastal drive between Vlora and Saranda is easily one of the most spectacular in Eastern Europe and shouldn't missed by any visitor to Albania. While beaches can be jam-packed in August, there's plenty of space, peace and happy-to-see-you faces in the low season. Sadly, the poorly planned development in the past decade has rather blighted many of the once-charming coastal villages, but there's still plenty of untouched beauty to be found here.

Vlora

☑033 / POP 184,000

It's here in sunny Vlora (the ancient Aulon) that the Adriatic Sea meets the Ionian, but the beaches are muddy and grubby, and the port town has really outgrown itself and is now a morass of overdevelopment. History buffs will still enjoy the museums and historic buildings, while beach lovers should hold out for the villages of Dhërmi, Drymades or Jal, all further south.

⦿ Sights

Sheshi i Flamurit   SQUARE
At Sheshi i Flamurit (Flag Sq), near the top of Sadik Zotaj, a magnificent socialist-realist **Independence Monument** stands proud against the sky with the flag bearer hoisting the double-headed eagle into the blue. Near the base of the monument lies the grave of local Ismail Qemali, the country's first prime minister.

Ethnographic Museum   MUSEUM
(Sheshi i Flamurit; admission 100 lekë; ⦿9am-noon Mon-Sat) This ethnographic museum is jam-

packed with relics of Albanian life. It's hidden behind an inconspicuous metal fence.

Muzeu Historik   MUSEUM
(Rr Ismail Qemali; ⦿8am-2pm daily, 5-8pm Tue-Thu in summer.) This antiquities museum opposite the ethnographic museum and just off Vlora's main square, Sheshi i Flamurit, has been renovated and has a good collection of ancient artefacts including Bronze Age relics and items from the Roman era. Labelling is spotty, however.

Muradi Mosque   MOSQUE
The 16th-century Muradi Mosque is a small elegant structure made of red and white stone, with a modest minaret; its exquisite design is attributed to one of the greatest Ottoman architects, Albanian-born Sinan Pasha.

**National Museum of
Independence**   MUSEUM
(admission 100 lekë; ⦿9am-1pm & 5-8pm Tue-Sun) Down by the harbour, the National Museum of Independence is housed in the villa that became the headquarters of Albania's first government in 1912. The preserved offices, historic photographs and famous balcony make it an interesting place to learn about Albania's short-lived, but long-remembered, 1912 independence.

❶ Getting There & Away

BUS & FURGON Buses (500 lekë, four hours) and *furgons* (600 lekë, three hours) to Tirana and Durrës (500 lekë, 2½ hours) whiz back and forth from 4am until 7pm. Buses to Saranda (900 lekë, six hours) and on to Gjirokastra (1000 lekë, seven hours) leave at 7am and 12.30pm. There are nine buses a day to Berat (300 lekë, two hours). Buses leave from Rr Rakip Malilaj; departures to Athens (€25) and cities in Italy (from €70) depart from Muradi Mosque.

FERRY Vlora to Brindisi in Italy takes around six hours. From Monday to Saturday there are

---

LLOGARAJA PASS NATIONAL PARK

Reaching the pine-tree-clad Llogaraja Pass National Park (1025m) is a highlight of travels in Albania. If you've been soaking up the sun on the southern coast's beaches, it seems impossible that after a steep hairpin-bend climb you'll be up in the mountains tucking into spit-roasted lamb and homemade wine. There's great scenery up here, including the *pisha flamur* (flag pine) – a tree resembling the eagle design on the Albanian flag. Watch clouds descending onto the mountain, shepherds on the plains guiding their herds, and thick forests where deer, wild boar and wolves roam. Check out the resident deer at the Tourist Village before heading across the road to the cute family-run cabins at **Hotel Andoni** (☑068 240 0929; cabins 4000 lekë). The family does a wonderful lamb roast lunch (800 lekë) here.

departures from Brindisi at 11pm and Vlora at noon (deck €35). There are also ferries to Corfu during the summer months with Finikas Lines.

TRAIN The daily train departs Tirana for Vlora at 4.30pm and Vlora for Tirana at 4.30am (250 lekë, five hours).

Drymades

As you zigzag down the mountain from the Llogaraja Pass National Park, the white crescent-shape beaches and azure waters lure you from below. The first beach before the alluvial fan is Palasa, and it's one of the last bar/restaurant/hotel-free beaches around.

The next beach along is Drymades beach. Turn right just after the beginning of the walk down to Dhërmi beach and you'll be on the sealed road that twists through olive groves. After a 20-minute walk you'll be on its rocky white beach.

🛏 Sleeping & Eating

TOP CHOICE Sea Turtle CAMPGROUND €
(☑069 4016 057; per person incl half-board from 1000 lekë; ☺Jun-Sep) This great little set-up is run by two brothers. Each summer they turn the family orange orchard into a vibrant tent city, and the price includes the tent (with mattresses, sheets and pillows), breakfast and a family-cooked dinner (served up in true camp style). Hot showers are under the shade of old fig trees.

Drymades Inn Resort CABINS €€
(☑069 2074 004, 069 2074 000; www.drymades-inn.al; s/d €40/60; ▣❋❄❋) This attractive constellation of blue-painted timber cabins under the shade of pine trees is just a step away from the blue sea and the glorious beach. There's a bar, restaurant and shaded playground, plus a classic beach bar with a straw roof. Prices halve off-peak, which is by far the best time to come, as in high summer it's rammed.

Dhërmi

Dhërmi beach is well and truly under the tourist trance in summer: expect booked-out accommodation and an almost unbearable rubbish problem. Despite this, there is fun to be had, and, if techno isn't your style, there's peace and quiet to be had, too. It's made up of lovely rocky outcrops, Mediterranean-blue water and tiny coves.

The beach is 1.5km below the Vlora–Saranda road, so ask the driver to stop at the turn-off on the Llogaraja side of the village. From here it's an easy 10-minute walk downhill.

🛏 Sleeping & Eating

Blu Blu CABINS €€
(☑068 6090 485; r from €80; ☺May-Oct; ❋❄) Hello? Whose stroke of genius is this? Turn left at the bottom of the road to Dhërmi, and follow the road almost to its end. Here you'll find one of the best 'no disco' beachside spots in Albania. Little white cabins with sea views sit among banana trees, and the bar/restaurant serves great food. Rooms start at €30 in May.

Hotel Greccia HOTEL €€
(☑069 6848 858, 069 5302 850; joanna_nino@hotmail.com; r from €60; ▣❋❄) This smart five-floor place is on the hillside just above the village on the road down from the coastal highway. It's well set up for a comfortable stay, with balconies giving great views over the sea or back towards the mountains, and sleekly minimalist rooms that are kept spotlessly clean.

Hotel Luciano RESTAURANT €€
(mains 400-700 lekë) Sure, the mosaic on the wall of this waterfront pizza and pasta joint says 'no', but it's a resounding 'yes' to its wood-fired pizzas. It's the first place you'll find after walking down the hill from the main road.

Himara

☎0393 / POP 4500
This sleepy town has fine beaches, a couple of pleasant Greek seafood tavernas, some smart modern hotels and an interesting Old Town high on the hill. Most of the ethnic Greek population left in the 1990s, but many have returned – Greek remains the mother tongue of its people. The lower town comprises three easily accessible rocky beaches and the town's hotels and restaurants. The main Vlora–Saranda road passes the entrance to the hilltop castle, which, like Berat's, still houses many people. A taxi to the castle from Himara costs 300 lekë.

🛏 Sleeping

Rapo's Resort LUXURY HOTEL €€€
(☑22 856; www.raposresorthotel.com; s & d €120-130; ❋❄❋) This top-end resort has smart

interior design, sparkling bathrooms and great service. It's near the beach, and also houses a massive swimming pool. For €9 anyone can relax by the pool for the day. Annoyingly at these high prices, wireless is limited to the lobby.

Kamping Himare CAMPGROUND €
(☑068 5298 940; www.himaracamping.com; tent per person 800 lekë; ☺Jun-Sep) Midnight movies in an open-air cinema add to the appeal of this camping ground across the road from the beach in an olive and orange grove. Tent rate includes mattresses, sheets and pillows. Try the restaurant's sublime pancakes (100 lekë) for breakfast.

Manolo BOUTIQUE HOTEL €€
(☑22 375; d €50) Right by the main beach in the centre of the village, Manolo is a cool bar downstairs with four contemporary and comfortable rooms that show good attention to detail and have sea views.

ℹ️ Getting There & Away

Buses to Saranda and Vlora pass through Himara in the early morning; check with locals exactly when, as schedules change all the time.

Vuno & Jal

Less than 10 minutes' drive from Himara is Vuno, a tiny hillside village above a picturesque beach (Jal, pronounced Yal). Outdoor Albania renovated Vuno's primary school, and each summer its classrooms are filled with blow-up beds and it becomes **Shkolla Hostel** (☑068 4682 353, 068 3133 451; www.tiranahostel.com; tent/dm €4/7; ☺late Jun-Aug). What it lacks in infrastructure and privacy it makes up for with its goat-bell soundtrack and evening campfire. From Vuno, walk over the bridge and follow the rocky path to your right past the cemetery.

It's a challenging 40-minute signed walk through olive groves to picturesque Jal, or a 5km walk along the main beach road. Jal was a victim of the permit police a few years ago, and since then new structures have taken on a temporary tone. Jal has two beaches; one has free camping while the other has a **camping ground** (including tent 2000 lekë) set back from the sea. Fresh seafood is bountiful in Jal and there are plenty of beachside restaurants in summer.

Saranda

☑0852 / POP 37,700

Saranda has grown rapidly in the past decade; skeletal high-rises crowd around its horseshoe shape and hundreds more are being built in the outlying region. Saranda is bustling in summer – buses are crowded with people carrying swimming paraphernalia and the weather means it's almost obligatory to go for a swim. A daily stream of Corfu holidaymakers take the 45-minute ferry trip to Albania, add the Albanian stamp to their passports and hit Butrint or the Blue Eye Spring before heading back.

The town's name comes from Ayii Saranda, an early monastery dedicated to 40 saints; its bombed remains (including some preserved frescos) are still high on the hill above the town. The town was called Porto Edda for a period in the 1940s, after Mussolini's daughter.

Saranda's stony beaches are quite decent and there are plenty of sights in and around town, including the mesmerising ancient archaeological site of Butrint and the hypnotic Blue Eye Spring. Between Saranda and Butrint, the lovely beaches and islands of Ksamil are perfect for a dip after a day of exploring.

Four main streets arc around Saranda's bay, including the waterfront promenade that becomes prime *xhiro* (evening walk) territory in the evening.

⊙ Sights

Synagogue RUINS
(Rr Skënderbeu; ☺24hr) This 5th-century synagogue is centrally located and is evidence of one of the earliest Balkan-Jewish communities.

Museum of Archaeology MUSEUM
(Rr Flamurit; ☺9am-2pm & 4-9pm) This office-like building houses a well-preserved 6th-century mosaic floor in its basement and has an interesting display about nearby Butrint. It's one block behind the harbour.

Castle of Lëkurësit CASTLE
This former castle is now a restaurant with superb views over Saranda and Butrint lagoon, especially at sunset. A taxi there costs about 1000 lekë return; arrange a time for the driver to pick you up, or it's a 15-minute walk up from the Saranda–Tirana road.

🛏 Sleeping

Hotel Porto Eda
HOTEL €€

(www.portoeda.com; Rr Jonianët; r €50; P❄✱🐕) Referencing the temporary name given to Saranda during the fascist occupation, this hotel is nevertheless a charming place and about as central as you can get, overlooking the harbour. The 24 rooms are comfortably and stylishly laid out, most with balconies, and the welcome is warm.

SR Backpackers
HOSTEL €

(☎069 4345 426; www.backpackerssr.hostel.com; Rr Mitat Hoxha 10; dm €11; @🐕) The hostel with the most central location in Saranda, this is also the cheapest option. Housed in an apartment and hosted by the gregarious English-speaking Tomi, the 14 beds here are spread over three dorms, each with its own balcony. There's one shared bathroom, a communal kitchen and a friendly atmosphere.

Hairy Lemon
HOSTEL €

(☎069 3559 317; www.hairylemonhostel.com; cnr Mitat Hoxha & E Arberit; dm €12; 🐕) With a prime 8th-floor location, a clean beach at its base and a friendly atmosphere, this Irish-run backpacker hostel is a good place to chill out. There's an open-plan kitchen and lounge, and two dorm rooms with fans and sea breezes. Follow the port road for around 10 minutes and continue when it becomes dirt; it's the orange-and-yellow apartment block on your right.

Hotel Palma
HOTEL €€

(☎22 929; Rr Mitat Hoxha; r from €30; ✱🐕) Right next to the port, this hotel is good value and an easy walk into the town. Some rooms have great views with large balconies and all are super-clean. If you're up for it, guests get free entry into the on-site summer disco.

🍴 Eating

Veliani
ALBANIAN €€

(Bul Hasan Tahsini; mains 450-1100 lekë) Right in the heart of town, this upmarket place right on the waterfront isn't cheap, but does an excellent selection of Albanian dishes, including its signature octopus in red wine – a true local speciality.

Pizza Limani
PIZZA €

(Bul Hasan Tahsini; pizza 400-800 lekë) The best pizza in town can be found on the seafront at this reliable and buzzing place with a giant terrace with superb harbour view and an excellent variety of tasty toppings on wood-fired oven-cooked dough.

Tani
SEAFOOD €

(mains 250-550 lekë) This portside seafood restaurant is run by chef Tani, who prides himself on serving dishes he's invented himself. The oven-baked filled mussels are a cheesy delight, and it's in a cool vine-draped location.

Dropulli
TRADITIONAL €

(cnr Rr Skënderbeu & Rr Mitro Dhmertika; mains 350 lekë) A local restaurant that has Albanian holidaymakers returning to it day after day has to be good, and vegetarians will love the melt-in-your-mouth stuffed peppers with tasty rice; ask for it to be served with potatoes.

ℹ Information

Banks with ATMs line the sea road (Rr 1 Maji) and the next street inland (Rr Skënderbeu).

Saranda's ZIT information centre (Rr Skënderbeu; ⊗8am-4pm Mon-Fri, 9am-2pm & 4-9pm Sat & Sun Oct-Jun, 8.30am-2pm & 4-10pm Jul-Sep) is the most established in Albania and provides information about transport and local sights. The newer, bigger tourist information centre on the promenade sells travel guides, souvenirs, Ismail Kadare novels and maps.

ℹ Getting There & Away

The ZIT information centre opposite the synagogue ruins has up-to-date bus timetables.

BUS The main bus station is uphill from the ruins on Rr Vangjel Pando. Municipal buses go to Butrint via Ksamil on the hour from 7am to 5pm (100 lekë, 30 minutes), leaving from the roundabout near the port and opposite ZIT. Buses to Tirana (1300 lekë, eight hours) via Gjirokastra (350 lekë) leave at 5am, 6.30am, 8.30am, 9.30am, 10.30am, 2pm and 10pm. The 5.30am and 9pm Tirana bus takes the coastal route (1300 lekë, eight hours) via Vlora (900 lekë). There are two buses and *furgons* an hour to Gjirokastra's new town (350 lekë, 1½ hours) – they all pass the turn-off to the Blue Eye Spring. Buses to Himara (400 lekë, two hours) leave around four times a day. Buses to the Greek border near Konispoli leave Saranda at 8am and 11am (200 lekë); otherwise you can reach the Greek border via Gjirokastra.

FERRY Finikas (☎067 2022 004, 260 57; www.finikas-lines.com; Rr Mithat Hoxha) at the port sells ferry tickets for Corfu with a daily departure at 10.30am (€19, 45 minutes). A slower boat departs daily at 4.30pm (€19, 90 minutes) and in summer a third ferry departs

Saranda at 4.30pm Thursdays, Saturdays and Sundays. From Corfu there are three ferries: one daily at 9am, one daily at 6.30pm and one at 9.15am Thursdays, Saturdays and Sundays. Note that Greek time is one hour ahead of Albanian time.

TAXI Taxis wait for customers at the bus stop and opposite Central Park on Rr Skënderbeu. A taxi to the Greek border at Kakavija costs 4000 lekë.

Around Saranda

BUTRINT

The ancient ruins of Butrint (www.butrint.org; admission 700 lekë; ⏱8am-dusk), 18km south of Saranda, are renowned for their size, beauty and tranquillity. They're in a fantastic natural setting and are part of a 29-sq-km national park. Set aside at least two hours to explore this fascinating place.

Although the site had been inhabited long before, Greeks from Corfu settled on the hill in Butrint (Buthrotum) in the 6th century BC. Within a century Butrint had become a fortified trading city with an acropolis. The lower town began to develop in the 3rd century BC, and many large stone buildings had already been built by the time the Romans took over in 167 BC. Butrint's prosperity continued throughout the Roman period, and the Byzantines made it an ecclesiastical centre. The city then went into a long decline and was abandoned until 1927, when Italian archaeologists arrived. These days Lord Rothschild's UK-based Butrint Foundation helps maintain the site.

As you enter the site the path leads to the right, to Butrint's 3rd-century-BC Greek theatre, secluded in the forest below the acropolis. Also in use during the Roman period, the theatre could seat about 2500 people. Close by are the small public baths, where geometric mosaics are buried under a layer of mesh and sand to protect them from the elements.

Deeper in the forest is a wall covered with crisp Greek inscriptions, and the 6th-century palaeo-Christian baptistry decorated with colourful mosaics of animals and birds, again under the sand. Beyond are the impressive arches of the 6th-century basilica, built over many years. A massive Cyclopean wall dating back to the 4th century BC is further on. Over one gate is a relief of a lion killing a bull, symbolic of a protective force vanquishing assailants.

The top of the hill is where the acropolis once was. There's now a castle here, housing an informative museum (⏱8am-4pm). The views from the museum's courtyard give you a good idea of the city's layout, and you can see the Vivari Channel connecting Lake Butrint to the Straits of Corfu. There are community-run stalls inside the gates where you can buy locally produced souvenirs.

❶ Getting There & Away

The municipal bus from Saranda to Butrint costs 100 lekë and leaves hourly from 7am to 5pm. It passes through Ksamil.

KSAMIL

Ksamil, 17km south of Saranda, has three small, dreamy islands within swimming distance and dozens of beachside bars and restaurants that open in the summer. The public Saranda–Butrint bus stops twice in the town (100 lekë; leaves hourly 1am to 5pm); either stop will get you to the pristine waters, though if you look closely you'll realise that the sand is trucked in.

Twenty-two kilometres east of Saranda, the Blue Eye Spring (Syri i Kaltër; per person/car 50/200 lekë) is a hypnotic pool of deep blue water surrounded by electric-blue edges like the iris of an eye. Bring your swimming gear and a towel, as it's a great spot for a dive into the cold water on a summer's day. It feeds the Bistrica River and its depth is unknown. It's a pleasant spot; blue dragonflies dash around the water, and the surrounding shady oak trees make a pleasant picnic spot, though it's often crowded in the summer months. There's a restaurant and cabins nearby. If you don't mind a 2km walk, any bus travelling between Saranda and Gjirokastra can drop you off at the spring's turn-off.

Hotel Joni (☎069 2091 554; s/d €20/25; ☎) is a clean hotel near the roundabout. There are plenty of 'rooms to rent' (averaging €20 per night) in private homes closer to the water, and seafood restaurants perch along the beachfront in summer.

EASTERN ALBANIA

Close to the Greek border and accessible from the Tirana–Saranda bus route is the Unesco World Heritage–listed town of Gjirokastra, surely one of Albania's most magical places and birthplace to two of its most famous sons. Expect bunker-covered mountains, winter-time snowfields and plenty of roads leading to Greece.

Gjirokastra

♪084 / POP 43,000

Defined by its castle, roads paved with chunky limestone and shale, imposing slate-roofed houses and views out to the Drina Valley, Gjirokastra is an intriguing hillside town described beautifully by Albania's most famous literary export and local-born author, Ismail Kadare (b 1936), in *Chronicles of Stone*. Archaeological evidence suggests there's been a settlement here for 2500 years, though these days it's the 600 'monumental' houses in town that attract visitors. Some of these magnificent houses, a blend of Ottoman and local architectural influence, have caved in on themselves, and Unesco funding is being spent to maintain them. Gjirokastra-born former dictator Enver Hoxha made sure his hometown was listed as a museum city, but after the fall of the communist regime the houses fell into disrepair.

◉ Sights

Gjirokastra Castle   CASTLE
(admission 200 lekë; ⊘8am-8pm) The town's moody castle hosts an eerie collection of armoury and is the setting for Gjirokastra's folk festival (held every four or five years). There's been a fortress here since the 12th century, although much of what can be seen today dates to the early 19th century. It's definitely worth the steep walk up from the Old Town, as well as an extra 200 lekë to visit its interior Museum Kombetar and see prison cells and more armoury. One of the more quirky sights on display is that of a recovered US Air Force jet that was shot down during the communist era.

TOP **Zekate House**   HISTORIC BUILDING
CHOICE
(admission 200 lekë; ⊘9am-6pm) This incredible three-storey house dates from 1811 and has twin towers and a double-arched facade. It's fascinating to nose around the almost totally unchanged interiors of an Ottoman-era home, especially the upstairs galleries, which are the most impressive. The owners live next door and collect the payments; to get here, follow the signs past the Hotel Kalemi and keep zigzagging up the hill.

Skenduli House   HISTORIC BUILDING
(Rr Ismail Kadare; admission 200 lekë; ⊘9am-7pm) The latest Ottoman-era mansion to receive a (partial) renovation, the Skenduli House

is well worth a visit and desperately needs contributions to pay for the remaining restoration work. You'll most likely be shown around by Mr Skenduli himself, who speaks Italian and some basic French, but no English. The house dates from 1700 and has many fascinating features.

Ethnographic Museum   MUSEUM
(admission 200 lekë; ⊘9am-6pm) This museum houses local homewares and was built on the site of Enver Hoxha's former house. Its collection is interesting if you're a fan of local arts and crafts, but don't come expecting anything about Hoxha himself.

Bazaar   HISTORIC SITE
The 'Neck of the Bazaar' makes up the centre of the Old Town and contains artisan shops that support masters of the local stone- and wood-carving industries.

🛏 Sleeping

Definitely stay in the scenic Old Town, though there are accommodation options in the new town if you can't find a room.

TOP **Hotel Kalemi**   HOTEL €€
CHOICE
(☎068 2234 373, 263 724; draguak@yahoo.com; Lagjia Palorto Gjirokastra; r €35; ℗❊@✿) This delightful, large Ottoman-style hotel has spacious rooms adorned with carved ceilings, antique furnishings and large communal areas, including a broad verandah with Drina Valley views. Some rooms even have fireplaces, though bathrooms can be on the cramped side. Breakfast (juice, tea, a boiled egg and bread with delicious fig jam) is an all-local affair.

Kotoni B&B   B&B €
(☎263 526, 069 2366 846; www.kotonihouse.com; Rr Bashkim Kokona 8; s/d from €20/25; ℗❊✿) Hosts Haxhi and Vita look after you in true Albanian style here: they love Gjirokastra and are happy to pass on information, as well as pack picnics for guests' day trips. The fact that these rooms are 220 years old makes up for their small size, while the astonishing views and friendly cats further sweeten the deal. Laundry is available, and fishing trips and hikes can be arranged.

Hotel Çajupi   HOTEL €€
(☎269 010; www.cajupi.com; Sheshi Çerçiz Topulli; s/d/tr €30/40/55; ❊) Aside from its relatively gargantuan size, it's hard to tell

that this breezy and friendly place was once the default communist-era hotel for foreigners. Rooms are spacious, clean and pleasant. The hotel is located on the main square of the Old Town, perfectly situated for exploration. Breakfast is a fairly lame affair, but the rooftop restaurant affords great views.

Hotel Sopoti HOSTEL €
(☏069 399 8922; Sheshi Çerçiz Topulli; per person 1000 lekë) The shared bathrooms here are extremely basic, but if you can get past that, this budget place is a steal. It boasts a great location in the heart of the Old Town, as well as clean rooms, many of which have gorgeous traditional floor tiles and balconies with superb valley views. If there's nobody at reception, go into the next-door cafe, where the owner works. Breakfast isn't included.

✕ Eating

TOP
CHOICE **Kujtimi** ALBANIAN €
(mains 200-600 lekë; ⊘11am-11pm) On the left-hand side of the path to Fantazia Restaurant is this wonderfully laid-back outdoor restaurant, run by the Dumi family. Try the delicious *trofte* (fried trout; 400 lekë), the *midhje* (fried mussels; 350 lekë) and *qifqi* (rice balls fried in herbs and egg, a local speciality). The terrace here is the perfect place to absorb the charms of the Old Town, and while it's popular with travellers, on a typical night it's still bustling with locals too.

Fantasia Restaurant ALBANIAN €€
(mains 200-750 lekë; ⊘noon-11pm) This modern place doesn't exactly overflow with local colour or traditional charm, but it has a large menu ranging from pizza to Albanian dishes, pastas and meat grills that keeps tour groups happy. It's located by a viewpoint with great views across the valley.

ℹ Information

The new town (no slate roofs here) is on the main Saranda–Tirana road, and a taxi up to or back from the Old Town is 300 lekë.
Information Centre (⊘8am-4pm Mon-Fri, 9am-2pm & 4-9pm Sat & Sun Oct-Jun, 8.30am-2pm & 4-10pm Jul-Sep) Opposite Çajupi Hotel behind the statue of the partisans.

ℹ Getting There & Away

Buses pass through the new town on their way to Tirana and Saranda, and *furgons* also go to Saranda (300 lekë, one hour). It takes about an hour to get to the Blue Eye Spring from Gjirokastra; buses to and from Saranda pass by its entrance, which is 2km from the spring itself. Buses to Tirana (1200 lekë, seven hours) leave on the hour from 5am – the last one passes through after 11pm. There are also irregular *furgons* to Berat (1000 lekë, four hours). From the bottom of the hill leading from the Old Town, turn left and walk 800m to find the ad hoc bus station just after the Eida petrol station.

UNDERSTAND ALBANIA

Albania Today

Albania managed to manoeuvre itself around the crippling economic crisis that gripped other European countries in 2008, and economic growth has continued. Despite this, infrastructure deficiencies still plague the country. Albania joined NATO in 2009 and may well become an official EU membership candidate in 2013, if elections to be held then are deemed fair.

History

Albanians call their country Shqipëria, and trace their roots to the ancient Illyrian tribes. Their language is descended from Illyrian, making it a rare survivor of the Roman and Slavic influxes and a European linguistic oddity on a par with Basque. The Illyrians occupied the western Balkans during the 2nd millennium BC. They built substantial fortified cities, mastered silver and copper mining, and became adept at sailing the Mediterranean. The Greeks arrived in the 7th century BC to establish self-governing colonies at Epidamnos (now Durrës), Apollonia and Butrint. They traded peacefully with the Illyrians, who formed tribal states in the 4th century BC.

Roman, Byzantine & Ottoman Rule

Inevitably the expanding Illyrian kingdom of the Ardiaei, based at Shkodra, came into conflict with Rome, which sent a fleet of 200 vessels against Queen Teuta in 229 BC. A long war resulted in the extension of Roman control over the entire Balkan area by 167 BC.

Under the Romans, Illyria enjoyed peace and prosperity, though large agricultural estates were worked by slaves. The Illyrians preserved their own language and traditions despite Roman rule. Over time the populace slowly replaced their old gods with the new Christian faith championed by Emperor Constantine. The main trade route between Rome and Constantinople, the Via Egnatia, ran from the port at Durrës.

When the Roman Empire was divided in AD 395, Illyria fell within the Eastern Empire, later known as the Byzantine Empire. Three early Byzantine emperors (Anastasius I, Justin I and Justinian I) were of Illyrian origin. Invasions by migrating peoples (Visigoths, Huns, Ostrogoths and Slavs) continued through the 5th and 6th centuries.

In 1344 Albania was annexed by Serbia, but after the defeat of Serbia by the Turks in 1389 the whole region was open to Ottoman attack. The Venetians occupied some coastal towns, and from 1443 to 1468 the national hero Skanderbeg (Gjergj Kastrioti) led Albanian resistance to the Turks from his castle at Kruja. Skanderbeg won all 25 battles he fought against the Turks, and even Sultan Mehmet-Fatih, the conqueror of Constantinople, could not take Kruja. After Skanderbeg's death the Ottomans overwhelmed Albanian resistance, taking control of the country in 1479, 26 years after Constantinople fell.

Ottoman rule lasted 400 years. Muslim citizens were favoured and were exempted from the janissary system, whereby Christian households had to give up one of their sons to convert to Islam and serve in the army. Consequently, many Albanians embraced the new faith.

Independent Albania

In 1878 the Albanian League at Prizren (in present-day Kosovo) began a struggle for autonomy that the Turkish army put down in 1881. Further uprisings between 1910 and 1912 culminated in a proclamation of independence and the formation of a provisional government led by Ismail Qemali at Vlora in 1912. These achievements were severely compromised when Kosovo, roughly one-third of Albania, was ceded to Serbia in 1913. The Great Powers tried to install a young German prince, Wilhelm of Wied, as ruler, but he wasn't accepted and returned home after six months. With the outbreak of WWI, Albania was occupied in succession by the armies of Greece, Serbia, France, Italy and Austria-Hungary.

In 1920 the capital city was moved from Durrës to less vulnerable Tirana. A republican government under the Orthodox priest Fan Noli helped to stabilise the country, but in 1924 it was overthrown by the interior minister, Ahmed Bey Zogu. A northern warlord, he declared himself King Zogu I in 1928, but his close collaboration with Italy backfired in April 1939 when Mussolini ordered an invasion of Albania. Zogu fled to Britain with his young wife, Geraldine, and newborn son, Leka, and used gold looted from the Albanian treasury to rent a floor at London's Ritz Hotel.

On 8 November 1941 the Albanian Communist Party was founded with Enver Hoxha as first secretary, a position he held until his death in April 1985. The communists led

ALBANIA HISTORY

FAMILY FEUD WITH BLOOD AS THE PRIZE

The *Kanun* (Code) was formalised in the 15th century by powerful northern chieftain Lekë Dukagjin. It consists of 1262 articles covering every aspect of daily life: work, marriage, family, property, hospitality, economy and so on. Though the *Kanun* was suppressed by the communists, there has been a revival of its strict precepts in northern Albania.

According to the *Kanun,* the most important things in life are honour and hospitality. If a member of a family (or one of their guests) is murdered, it becomes the duty of the male members of that clan to claim their blood debt by murdering a male member of the murderer's clan. This sparks an endless cycle of killing that doesn't end until either all the male members of one of the families are dead, or reconciliation is brokered through respected village elders.

Hospitality is so important in these parts of Albania that the guest takes on a godlike status. There are 38 articles giving instructions on how to treat a guest – an abundance of food, drink and comfort is at his or her disposal, and it is also the host's duty to avenge the murder of his guest, should this happen during their visit. It's worth reading *Broken April*, by Ismail Kadare, a brilliant exploration of people living under the *Kanun*.

the resistance against the Italians and, after 1943, against the Germans.

Communist Albania

In January 1946 the People's Republic of Albania was proclaimed, with Hoxha as president and 'Supreme Comrade'.

In September 1948 Albania broke off relations with Yugoslavia, which had hoped to incorporate the country into the Yugoslav Federation. Instead, it allied itself with Stalin's USSR and put into effect a series of Soviet-style economic plans – raising the ire of the USA and Britain, which made an ill-fated attempt to overthrow the government.

Albania collaborated closely with the USSR until 1960, despite Krushchev's denunciation of Stalin in his 1954 'secret speech'. However, when a heavy-handed Khrushchev demanded that a submarine base be set up at Vlora in 1961, Albania broke off diplomatic relations with the USSR and reoriented itself towards Maoist China.

From 1966 to 1967 Albania experienced a Chinese-style cultural revolution. Administrative workers were suddenly transferred to remote areas and younger cadres were placed in leading positions. The collectivisation of agriculture was completed and organised religion was completely banned.

Following the Soviet invasion of Czechoslovakia in 1968, Albania left the Warsaw Pact and embarked on a self-reliant defence policy. Some 60,000 igloo-shaped concrete bunkers were built at this time, the crumbling remains of which can still be seen all over the country today. Under the communists, some malarial swamps were drained, hydroelectric schemes and railway lines were built, and the literacy level was raised. Albania's people, however, lived in fear of the Sigurimi (secret police) and were not permitted to leave the country. Many were tortured, jailed or murdered for misdemeanours such as listening to foreign radio stations.

With the death of Mao Zedong in 1976 and the changes that followed in China after 1978, Albania's unique relationship with China also came to an end, and the country was left totally isolated and without allies. The economy was devastated and food shortages became more common.

Post-Hoxha

Hoxha died in April 1985 and his associate Ramiz Alia took over the leadership. Res-

trictions loosened (Albania was opened up to tourists in organised groups) but people no longer bothered to work on the collective farms, leading to food shortages in the cities. Industries began to fail and Tirana's population tripled as people took advantage of being able to freely move to the city.

In June 1990, inspired by the changes that were occurring elsewhere in Eastern Europe, around 4500 Albanians took refuge in Western embassies in Tirana. After a brief confrontation with the police and the Sigurimi, these people were allowed to board ships for Brindisi in Italy, where they were granted political asylum.

Following student demonstrations in December 1990, the government agreed to allow opposition parties, and the Democratic Party, led by heart surgeon Sali Berisha, was formed.

The March 1992 elections ended 47 years of communist rule, with parliament electing Sali Berisha president. Former president Alia was later placed under house arrest for writing articles critical of the Democratic government, and the leader of the Socialist Party, Fatos Nano, was also arrested on corruption charges.

During this time Albania switched from a tightly controlled communist regime to a rambunctious free-market free-for-all. A huge smuggling racket sprang up in which stolen Mercedes-Benz cars were brought into the country, and the port of Vlora became a major crossing point for illegal immigrants from Asia and the Middle East into Italy.

In 1996, 70% of Albanians lost their savings when private pyramid-investment schemes, believed to have been supported by the government, collapsed. Riots ensued, elections were called, and the victorious Socialist Party under Nano – who had been freed from prison by a rampaging mob – was able to restore some degree of security and investor confidence.

In 1999 a different type of crisis struck when 465,000 Kosovars fled to Albania as a result of a Serbian ethnic-cleansing campaign. The influx had a positive effect on Albania's economy, and strengthened the relationship between Albania and Kosovo.

For the past decade Albania has found itself in a kind of mini-boom, with a lot of money being poured into construction projects and infrastructure renewal. The general election of 2005 saw a return of Berisha's Democratic Party to government, and in 2009 they narrowly won again, forming a coalition with the Socialist Movement for Intergration (LSI).

People

Albania's population is made up of approximately 95% Albanians, 3% Greeks and 2% 'other' – comprising Vlachs, Roma, Serbs, Macedonians and Bulgarians. The majority of young people speak some English, but speaking a few words of Albanian (or Italian, and, on the south coast, Greek) will be useful. Like most Balkan people, Albanians shake their heads sideways to say yes *(po)* and usually nod and 'tsk' to say no *(jo* – pronounced 'yo'*)*. Albanians familiar with foreigners often take on the nod-for-yes way, which increases confusion.

The Ghegs in the north and the Tosks in the south have different dialects, music, dress and the usual jokes about each other's weaknesses.

Albanians are nominally 70% Muslim, 20% Christian Orthodox and 10% Catholic, but more realistic statistics estimate that up to 75% of Albanians are nonreligious. Religion was ruthlessly stamped out by the 1967 cultural revolution, when all mosques and churches were taken over by the state. By 1990 only about 5% of Albania's religious buildings were left intact. The rest had been turned into cinemas or army stores, or were destroyed. Albania remains a very secular society.

The Muslim faith has a branch called Bektashism, similar to Sufism, and its world headquarters were in Albania from 1925 to 1945. Bektashi followers go to *teqe* (temple-like buildings without a minaret), which are found on hilltops in towns where those of the faith fled persecution. Most Bektashis live in the southern half of the country.

Arts

Literature

One Albanian writer who is widely read outside Albania is Ismail Kadare (b 1936). In 2005 he won the inaugural Man Booker International Prize for his body of work. His books are a great source of information on Albanian traditions, history and social events, and exquisitely capture the atmosphere of the country's towns, as in the lyrical descriptions of Kadare's birthplace, Gjirokastra, in *Chronicle in Stone* (1971). *Broken April* (1990), set in the northern highlands before the 1939 Italian invasion, describes the life of a village boy who is next in line in a desperate cycle of blood vendettas.

Cinema

During Albania's isolationist years the only Western actor approved by Hoxha was UK actor Sir Norman Wisdom (he became quite a cult hero). However, with so few international movies to choose from, the local film industry had a captive audience. While much of its output was propagandist, by the 1980s this little country was turning out an extraordinary 14 films a year. Despite a general lack of funds, two movies have gone on to win awards at international film festivals. Gjergj Xhuvani's comedy *Slogans* (2001) is a warm and touching account of life during communist times. This was followed in 2002 by *Tirana Year Zero,* Fatmir Koci's bleak look at the pressures on the young to emigrate. *Lorna's Silence* (2008), a film about Albanians living in Belgium, was awarded in the 2008 Cannes Film Festival.

Music

Blaring from cars, bars, restaurants and mobile phones – music is something you get plenty of in Albania. Most modern Albanian music has clarinet threaded through it and a goat-skin drum beat behind it. Polyphony, the blending of several independent vocal or instrumental parts, dates from ancient Illyrian times, and can still be heard, particularly in the south.

Visual Arts

One of the first signs of the Albanian arts scene are the multicoloured buildings of Tirana, a project organised by the capital's former mayor, Edi Rama, himself an artist. The building's residents don't get a say in the colour or design, and come home to find their homes daubed in spots, paintings of trees, or even paintings of laundry drying under their windowsills.

One of the most delicious Albanian art treats is to be found in Berat's Onufri Museum. Onufri was the most outstanding Albanian icon painter of the 16th and 17th centuries, and his work is noted for its unique intensity of colour, derived from natural dyes that are as fresh now as the day he painted with them.

Environment

Albania consists of 30% vast interior plains, 362km of coast and a mountainous spine that runs its length. Mt Korab, at 2764m, is Albania's highest peak.

The country's large and beautiful lakes include the Balkans' biggest, Lake Shkodra, which borders Montenegro in the north, and the ancient Lake Ohrid in the east (one-third Albanian, two-thirds Macedonian). Albania's longest river is the Drin (280km), which originates in Kosovo and is fed by melting snow from mountains in Albania's north and east. Hydroelectricity has changed Albania's landscape: Lake Koman was once a river, and the blue water from the Blue Eye Spring near Saranda travels to the coast in open concrete channels via a hydroelectricity plant. Agriculture makes up a small percentage of land use, and citrus and olive trees spice up the coastal plains. Most rural householders grow their own food.

National Parks & Wildlife

The number of national parks in Albania has risen from six to 15 since 1966 and include Dajti, Llogara, Tomorri, Butrint, Valbonë and Theth. Most are protected only by their remoteness, and tree-felling and hunting still take place. Hiking maps of the national parks are available, though they can be hard to find (try *Wanderkarte Nord-albanien* for Theth).

Albania's Alps have become a 'must-do' for hikers, and they're home to brown bear, wolf, otter, marten, wild cat, wild boar and deer. Falcons and grouse are also Alpine favourites, and birdwatchers can also flock to wetlands at Lake Butrint, Karavasta Lagoon and Lake Shkodra (though the wetlands aren't pristine).

Lake Ohrid's trout is endangered (but still eaten), and endangered loggerhead turtles nest on the Ionian coast and on the Karaburun Peninsula, where there have also been sightings of critically endangered Mediterranean monk seals.

Environmental Issues

During communism, there were around 2000 cars in the country. Now it seems everyone has one, with many of Albania's older cars being diesel Mercedes-Benzes stolen from Western Europe. As a consequence of the explosion, air-pollution levels in Tirana are five to 10 times higher than in Western European countries.

Illegal logging and fishing reached epidemic proportions during the 1990s, and there are signs of it today; fishing for the endangered *koran* trout in Lake Ohrid continues, as does fishing with dynamite along the coast.

Albania was practically litter-free until the early 1990s, as everything was reused or recycled, but today there's literally rubbish everywhere. Walk around the perimeter of a hotel in a picturesque location and you'll come across its very unpicturesque dumping ground. Some Albanians are doing their bit to improve these conditions, and a 'raising awareness' campaign against litter was started by well-known Albanians in 2010.

Food & Drink

In coastal areas the calamari, mussels and fish will knock your socks off, while high-altitude areas such as Llogaraja have roast lamb worth climbing a mountain for.

Offal is popular; *fërgesë Tiranë* is a traditional Tirana dish of offal, eggs and tomatoes cooked in an earthenware pot.

Italian influences mean vegetarians will probably become vegitalians, and many restaurants serve pizza, pasta or grilled and stuffed vegetables.

Local Drinks

Raki is very popular. The two main types are grape raki (the most common) and *mani* (mulberry) raki. Ask for homemade if possible *(raki ë bërë në shtëpi)*. If wine is more your cup of tea, seek out the Çobo winery near Berat and its Shesh i Bardhe white. Local beers include Tirana, Norga (from Vlora) and Korça. Coffee remains the standard drink of choice at any time of day.

SURVIVAL GUIDE

Directory A–Z

Accommodation

With almost every house, bar and petrol station doubling as a hotel, you might think you'll never have trouble finding a bed in Albania, and you're right, though seaside towns are often booked out in August.

Homestays abound in Theth, while the number of camping grounds is increasing; you'll find them at Himare, Livadhi, Dhërmi and Drymades (from €4 per person). Most have hot showers, on-site restaurants and entertainment.

All but the most basic places have free wireless internet for guests.

The following price categories for the cost of a double room in high season are used in the listings in this chapter.

€ less than €30

€€ €30 to €80

€€€ more than €80

Activities

Hiking and adventure sports are gaining popularity in Albania, and **Outdoor Albania** (✆2227 121; www.outdooralbania.com; Rr Sami Frasheri, Pallati Metropol) is an excellent organisation at the forefront of the industry. Smaller operatives are starting up: **Albania Rafting** (✆2006 621; www.albrafting.com) runs rafting tours of the Osumi River and canyons in Berat. Hiking in the Alps, particularly around Theth and Valbonë, is popular (with and without guides), as is mountain biking around the country.

Business Hours

Banks 9am to 3.30pm Monday to Friday

Cafes & Bars 8am to midnight

Offices 8am to 5pm Monday to Friday

Restaurants 8am to midnight

Shops 8am to 7pm; siesta time can be any time between noon and 4pm

Embassies & Consulates

There is no Australian, Canadian, New Zealand or Irish embassy in Albania. The following embassies and consulates are in Tirana:

French Embassy (✆04-238 9700; www.ambafrance-al.org; Rr Skënderbej 14)

German Embassy (✆04-2274 505; www.tirana.diplo.de; Rr Skënderbej 8)

Netherlands Embassy (✆04-2240 828; www.albanie.nlambassade.org; Rr Asim Zeneli 10)

UK Embassy (✆04-2234 973; www.ukinalbania.fco.gov.uk; Rr Skënderbej 12)

US Embassy (✆04-2247 285; http://tirana.usembassy.gov; Rr Elbasanit 103)

Food

The following price categories for the cost of a main course are used in the listings in this chapter.

€ less than 200 lekë

€€ 200 lekë to 500 lekë

€€€ more than 500 lekë

Gay & Lesbian Travellers

Extensive antidiscrimination legislation became law in 2010, but did not extend to legalising same-sex marriage. Gay and lesbian life in Albania is alive and well but is not yet organised into clubs or organisations. Gaydar will serve gay and lesbian visitors well here: you'll have to ask on the street or online where the parties are. The alternative music and party scene in Tirana is queer-friendly.

Internet Access

If you've brought your own smartphone or laptop you can access free wi-fi in most hotels and many restaurants around the country. Internet cafes (increasingly rare) cost around 100 lekë per hour.

Money

The lekë is the official currency, though the euro is widely accepted; you'll get a better rate in general if you use lekë. Accommodation is generally quoted in euros but can be paid in either currency. ATMs (found in most of Albania's towns, bar remote villages) usually offer to dispense cash in either currency.

Albanian banknotes come in denominations of 100, 200, 500, 1000, 2000 and 5000 lekë. There are five, 10, 20, 50 and 100 lekë coins.

Albanian lekë can't be exchanged outside the country, so exchange them or spend them before you leave.

Credit cards are accepted only in the larger hotels, shops and travel agencies, and few of these are outside Tirana.

It's polite to leave your change as a tip.

Post

The postal system is fairly rudimentary – there are no postcodes, for example – and it certainly does not enjoy a reputation for efficiency.

Public Holidays

New Year's Day 1 January

Summer Day 16 March

Nevruz 23 March

Catholic Easter March or April

Orthodox Easter March or April

May Day 1 May

Mother Teresa Day 19 October

Independence Day 28 November

Liberation Day 29 November

Christmas Day 25 December

Telephone

Albania's country phone code is ☑355 (dial ☑+ or ☑00 first from a mobile phone).

Three established mobile-phone providers are Vodafone, AMC and Eagle, and a fourth licence has been promised. Don't expect isolated areas to have coverage (though most do, including Theth). Prepaid SIM cards cost around 1000 lekë and include credit. Mobile numbers begin with ☑06. To call an Albanian mobile number from abroad, dial ☑+355 then either ☑67, ☑68 or ☑69 (ie drop the 0).

Tourist Information

Tourist information offices with some English-speaking staff operate in Tirana, Shkodra, Saranda, Gjirokastra (www.gjirokastra.org) and Berat (www.bashkia-berat.net).

Travellers with Disabilities

High footpaths and unannounced potholes make life difficult for mobility-impaired travellers. Tirana's top hotels do cater to people with disabilities, and some smaller hotels are making an effort to be more accessible. The roads and castle entrances in Gjirokastra, Berat and Kruja are cobblestone, although taxis can get reasonably close.

Visas

Visas are not required for citizens of EU countries or nationals of Australia, Canada, New Zealand, Japan, South Korea, Norway, South Africa or the USA. Travellers from other countries should check www.mfa.gov.al. Passports are stamped for a 90-day stay.

A €10 entry and exit fee was abolished some years ago; do not be conned into paying this by taxi drivers at border crossings.

Women Travellers

Albania is a safe country for women travellers, but outside Tirana it is mainly men who go out and sit in bars and cafes in the evenings. You may tire of being asked why you're travelling alone.

Getting There & Away

Air

Nënë Tereza International Airport is 17km northwest of Tirana and is a modern, well-run terminal. There are no domestic flights within Albania. The following airlines fly to and from Albania:

Adria Airways (☑04-2272 666; www.adria.si) Flies to Ljubljana.

Air One (☑04-2230 023; www.flyairone.it) Flies to Milan, Pisa and Venice.

Alitalia (☑04-2230 023; www.alitalia.com) Flies to Rome, Verona, Turin, Naples, Florence, Genoa, Milan, Catania and Venice.

Austrian Airlines (☑04-2235 029; www.austrian.com) Flies to Vienna.

BelleAir (☑04-2240 175; www.belleair.it) Flies to Pristina, Ancona, Rimini, Forli, Bari, Pescara, Naples, Trieste, Perugia, Milan, Treviso, Turin, Palma, Bologna, Pisa, Florence, Rome, Geneva, London, Prague, Brussels and Vienna.

British Airways (☑04-2381 991; www.britishairways.com) Flies to London.

Lufthansa (☑04-2258 010; www.lufthansa.com) Flies to Vienna and Munich.

Olympic Air (☑04-2228 960; www.olympicair.com) Flies to Athens.

Turkish Airlines (☑04-2258 459; www.turkishairlines.com) Flies to İstanbul.

Land

BORDER CROSSINGS

There are no passenger trains into Albania, so your border-crossing options are buses, *furgons,* taxis or walking to a border and picking up transport on the other side.

Montenegro The main crossings link Shkodra to Ulcinj (Muriqan) and to Podgorica (Hani i Hotit).

Kosovo The closest border crossing to the Koman Ferry terminal is Morina, and further south is Qafë Prush. Near Kukës use Morinë for the highway to Tirana.

Macedonia Use Blato to get to Debar, quiet Qafë e Thanës to the north of Lake Ohrid, or Sveti Naum, near Pogradec, to its south. There's also a crossing at Stenje.

Greece The main border crossing to and from Greece is Kakavija on the road from Athens to Tirana. It's about half an hour from Gjirokastra and 250km west of Tirana, and can take up to three hours to pass through during summer. Kapshtica (near Korça) also gets long lines in summer. Konispoli is near Butrint in Albania's south.

BUS

From Tirana, regular buses head to Pristina, Kosovo; to Struga, Tetovo and Skopje in Macedonia; to Budva and Ulcinj in Montenegro; and to Athens and Thessaloniki in Greece. *Furgons* and buses leave Shkodra for Montenegro, and buses head to Kosovo from Durrës. Buses travel to Greece from Albanian towns on the southern coast and buses to Italy leave from Vlora.

CAR & MOTORCYCLE

To enter, you'll need a Green Card (proof of third-party insurance, issued by your insurer); check that your insurance covers Albania.

TAXI

Heading to Macedonia, taxis from Pogradec will drop you off just before the border at Tushëmisht/Sveti Naum. Alternatively, it's an easy 4km walk to the border from Pogradec. It's possible to organise a taxi (or, more usually, a person with a car) from where the Koman Ferry stops in Fierzë to Gjakove in Kosovo. Taxis commonly charge €40 from Shkodra to Ulcinj in Montenegro.

Sea

Two or three ferries per day ply the route between Saranda and Corfu, in Greece, and there are plenty of ferry companies making the journey to Italy from Vlora and Durrës, as well as additional ferries from Vlora to Corfu.

Getting Around

Bicycle

Cycling in Albania is tough but certainly feasible. Expect lousy road conditions including open drains, some abysmal driving from fellow road users and roads that barely qualify for the title. Organised groups head north for mountain biking, and cyclists are even spotted cycling the long and tough Korça–Gjirokastra road. Shkodra, Durrës and Tirana are towns where you'll see locals embracing the bike, and Tirana even has bike lanes.

Bus

The first bus/*furgon* departure is often at 5am and things slow down around lunchtime. There are many buses catering for the crowds along the coast in July and August. Fares are low, and you either pay the conductor on board or when you hop off.

Municipal buses operate in Tirana, Durrës, Shkodra and Vlora, and trips cost 30 lekë.

Car & Motorcycle

Albania's drivers are not the best in the world, mostly due to the communist era, when car ownership required a permit from the government, and only two were issued to nonparty members. As a result, the government didn't invest in new roads, and most Albanians were inexperienced motorists. Nowadays the road infrastructure is improving; there's an excellent highway from Tirana to Kosovo, and the coastal route from the Montenegro border to Butrint, near Saranda, is in good condition.

Tourists are driving cars, motorbikes and mobile homes into the country in greater numbers, and, apart from bad roads and bad drivers, it's generally hassle-free.

Off the main routes a 4WD is a good idea. Driving at night is particularly hazardous; follow another car on the road as there's rarely any road markings or street lighting.

DRIVING LICENCE

Foreign driving licences are all that's required to drive a car in Albania.

CAR HIRE

There are lots of car-hire companies operating out of Tirana, including all the major international agencies. Hiring a small car costs from €35 per day.

ROAD RULES

Drinking and driving is forbidden, and there is zero tolerance for blood-alcohol readings. Both motorcyclists and passengers must wear helmets. Speed limits are as low as 30km/h in built-up areas and 35km/h on the edges, and there are plenty of speed cameras monitoring the roads. Keep your car's papers with you, as police are active checkers.

Hitching

Though never entirely safe, hitchhiking is quite a common way for travellers to get around – though it's rare to see locals doing it.

Train

Albanians prefer bus and *furgon* travel, and when you see the speed and the state of the (barely) existing trains, you'll know why. However, the trains are dirt cheap and travelling on them is an adventure. Daily passenger trains leave Tirana for Durrës, Shkodra, Fier, Vlora, Elbasan and a few kilometres out of Pogradec. Check timetables at the station in person, and buy your ticket 10 minutes before departure. Albania is not connected to neighbouring countries by train.

Bosnia & Hercegovina

Includes »

Sarajevo...........................78
Jahorina 90
Bjelašnica......................91
Mostar 92
Stolac 101
Trebinje.........................102
Višegrad 103
Visoko...........................104
Travnik 105
Jajce 106
Banja Luka.....................107
Bihać.............................109
Understand Bosnia &
Hercegovina 111
Survival Guide...............115

Why Go?

This craggily beautiful land retains some lingering scars from the heartbreaking civil war in the 1990s. But today visitors will more likely remember Bosnia and Hercegovina (BiH) for its deep, unassuming human warmth and for the intriguing East-meets-West atmosphere born of fascinatingly blended Ottoman and Austro-Hungarian histories.

Major drawcards are the reincarnated antique centres of Sarajevo and Mostar, where rebuilt historical buildings counterpoint fashionable bars and wi-fi–equipped cafes. Elsewhere Socialist-era architectural monstrosities are surprisingly rare blots on predominantly rural landscapes. Many Bosnian towns are lovably small, wrapped around medieval castles and surrounded by mountain ridges or cascading river canyons. Few places in Europe offer better rafting or such accessible, inexpensive skiing.

Best Places to Eat

» Mala Kuhinja (p85)

» Bridge-view restaurants, Mostar (p98)

» Riverside restaurants on the Una (p111)

» Vinoteka Vukuje (p102)

Best Places to Stay

» Muslibegović House (p96)

» Hotel Platani (p102)

» Želenkovac (p110)

» Kostelski Buk (p111)

When to Go

Sarajevo

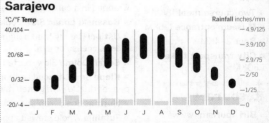

°C/°F Temp
40/104 —
20/68 —
0/32 —
-20/-4 —
J F M A M J J A S O N D

Rainfall inches/mm
— 4.9/125
— 3.9/100
— 2.9/75
— 2/50
— 1/25
— 0

Apr–Jun Beat the heat in Hercegovina; blooming flowers in Bosnia; peak-flowing rivers.

Jul Accommodation fills up in Mostar and Sarajevo but for beginners the rafting is best now.

Mid-Jan–mid-Mar Skiing gets cheaper after the New Year holidays.

AT A GLANCE

» **Currency** Convertible mark (KM, BAM)

» **Language** Bosnian, Croatian, Serbian

» **Money** ATMs widely available in towns

» **Visas** Not required for most visitors

Fast Facts

» **Area** 51,129 sq km

» **Capital** Sarajevo

» **Country code** ☑387

» **Emergency** Ambulance ☑124, fire ☑123, police ☑122

Exchange Rates

Australia	A$1	1.59KM
Canada	C$1	1.51KM
Euro Zone	€1	1.96KM
Japan	¥100	1.62KM
New Zealand	NZ$1	1.28KM
UK	UK£1	2.32KM
USA	US$1	1.53KM

Set Your Budget

» **Budget hotel room** 70KM

» **Two-course meal** 18KM

» **Museum entrance** 1–5KM

» **Beer** 2–4KM

» **City transport ticket** 1.80KM

Resources

» **BiH Tourism** (www.bhtourism.ba)

» **Bosnian Institute** (www.bosnia.org.uk)

» **Office of the High Representative** (www.ohr.int)

Connections

Regular buses link the Croatian coast to Mostar and Sarajevo plus there's a little-publicised Trebinje–Dubrovnik service. Trains link Sarajevo to Zagreb, Belgrade and Budapest-Keleti, the only direct overland link to Hungary. There are numerous bus connections to Serbia and Montenegro from Sarajevo, Višegrad and Trebinje.

ITINERARIES

Six Days

Arriving from Dubrovnik (coastal Croatia), roam Mostar's Old Town and join a day tour visiting Počitelj, Blagaj and the Kravice waterfalls. After two days in Sarajevo head for Jajce then bus down to Split (Croatia). Or visit Višegrad en route to Mokra Gora and Belgrade (Serbia).

Two Weeks

Add Trebinje and (if driving) historic Stolac between Dubrovnik and Mostar. Ski or go cycling around Bjelašnica, visit the controversial Visoko pyramid and old-town Travnik en route to Jajce, and consider adding in some high-adrenaline rafting from Banja Luka, Bihać or Foča.

Essential Food & Drink

» **Ćevapi (Ćevapčići)** Minced meat formed into cylindrical pellets and served in fresh bread with melting *kajmak* (thick semi-soured cream).

» **Pljeskavica** Patty-shaped Ćevapi.

» **Burek** Bosnian *burek* are cylindrical lengths of filo-pastry filled with minced meat, often wound into spirals. *Buredici* is the same served with *kajmak* and garlic, *sirnica* is filled instead with cheese, *krompiruša* with potato and *zeljanica* with spinach. Collectively these pies are called *pita*.

» **Sarma** Small *dolma*-parcels of rice and minced meat wrapped in a cabbage or other green leaf.

» **Bosanski Lonac** Slow-cooked meat-and-veg hotpot.

» **Uštipci** Bready fried dough-balls often eaten with sour cream, cheese or jam.

» **Sogan Dolma** Slow roasted onions filled with minced meat.

» **Klepe** Small ravioli-like triangles served in a butter-pepper drizzle with grated raw garlic.

» **Hurmastica** Syrup-soaked sponge fingers.

» **Tufahija** Whole stewed apple with walnut-filling and topped with whipped cream.

» **Ražnjići** Shish kebab (ie meat barbequed on skewers).

» **Pastrmka** Trout.

» **Rakija** Fruit brandy or grappa.

» **Ligne** Squid.

Bosnia & Hercegovina Highlights

1 Nose about Mostar's atmospheric Old Town and admire the magnificently rebuilt **Stari Most** (p92).

2 Raft down one of BiH's fast-flowing rivers – whether from **Foča** (p103) **Bihać** (p111) or **Banja Luka** (p107).

3 Ski the 1984 Olympic pistes at **Jahorina** (p90) or

Bjelašnica (p91) or explore the wild uplands behind them.

4 Potter around the timeless pedestrian lanes of **Sarajevo** (p78), and sample its fashionable cafes and eclectic nightlife.

5 Gaze through willow fronds at the Unesco-listed 16th-century bridge in

Višegrad (p103) that inspired a Nobel Prize–winning novel.

6 Wine and dine in historic little **Trebinje** (p102) and wander the low-key, stone-flagged Old Town.

7 Tune in to the mystical energy of **Visoko** (p104), asking yourself if you're really climbing the world's biggest pyramid.

SARAJEVO

☑ 033 / 436,000

In the 1990s Sarajevo was on the edge of annihilation. Today it's a vibrant yet very human city, notable for its attractive contours and East-meets-West ambience.

Beyond the stone-flagged alleys of central Baščaršija, 'Turkish Town', steep valley sides are fuzzed with red-roofed Bosnian houses and prickled with uncountable minarets, climbing towards green-topped mountain ridges. Westward, Sarajevo sprawls for over 10km through Novo Sarajevo and dreary Dobrinja past dismal ranks of bullet-scarred apartment blocks. At the westernmost end of the tramway spine, affluent Ilidža gives the city a final parkland flourish. In winter, Bjelašnica and Jahorina offer some of Europe's best-value skiing, barely 30km away.

History

Romans had bathed at Ilidža's sulphur springs a millennium earlier, but Sarajevo was officially 'founded' by 15th-century Turks. It rapidly grew wealthy as a silk-importing entrepôt and developed considerably during the 1530s when Ottoman governor Gazi-Husrevbey lavished the city with mosques and covered bazaars. In 1697 the city was burnt by Eugene of Savoy's Austrian army. When rebuilt, Sarajevo cautiously enclosed its upper flank in a large, fortified citadel, the remnants of which still dominate the Vratnik area.

The Austro-Hungarians were back more permanently in 1878 and erected many imposing central-European-style buildings. However, their rule was put on notice by Gavrilo Princip's fatal 1914 pistol shot that

killed Archduke Franz Ferdinand, plunging the world into WWI.

Less than a decade after hosting the 1984 Winter Olympics, Sarajevo endured an infamous siege that horrified the world. Between 1992 and 1995, Sarajevo's heritage of six centuries was pounded into rubble and its only access to the outside world was via a metre-wide, 800m-long tunnel under the airport. Bosnian Serb shelling and sniper fire killed over 10,500 Sarajevans and wounded 50,000 more. Uncountable white-stoned graves on Kovači and up near Koševo Stadium are a moving testimony to those terrible years.

⊙ Sights & Activities

The best way to really 'feel' the city is to stroll Old Sarajevo's pedestrian lanes and grand avenues and climb the gently picturesque slopes of Bjelave and Vratnik for sweeping views. Seeking out key museums is likely to take you into much more modern, businesslike Novo Sarajevo and on to park-filled Ilidža at the distant western end of the tram network.

OLD SARAJEVO

Baščaršija, the bustling old Turkish quarter is a warren of marble-flagged pedestrian courtyards and lanes full of mosques, copper workshops, jewellery shops and inviting restaurants. The riverbanks and avenues Ferhadija and Maršala Tita are well endowed with Austro-Hungarian architecture. And attesting to Sarajevo's traditional religious tolerance, you'll find within a couple of blocks several mosques, a synagogue, the artfully floodlit 1872 **Orthodox Cathedral** (Saborna Crkva Presvete Bogordice; Map p82; Trg Oslobođenja) and the **Catholic Cathedral** (Katedrala Srca Isusova; Map p82; Trg Fra Grge Martića 2; ⊙9am-4pm) where Pope John Paul II served mass in 1997. The area's charms are best discovered by wandering between the many street cafes.

Pigeon Square   NEIGHBOURHOOD
(Map p82) Nicknamed Pigeon Sq for all the birds, Baščaršija's central open space centres on the **Sebilj**, an ornate 1891 drinking fountain. It leads past the lively (if tourist-centric) coppersmith alley, **Kazandžiluk**, leading down to the garden-wrapped 16th-century **Baščaršija Džamija** (Baščaršija mosque; Map p82; Baščaršija 37).

Bursa Bezistan   MUSEUM
(Map p82; www.muzejsarajeva.ba; Abadžiluk 10; admission 3KM; ⊙10am-6pm Mon-Fri, 10am-3pm Sat) The six-domed 1551 Bursa Bezistan was

SARAJEVO IN TWO DAYS

Plunge into the pedestrianised 'Turkish' lanes of **Baščaršija** and the street cafes of **Ferhadija**. From the spot where a 1914 assassination kicked off WWI, cross the cute **Latin Bridge** for a beer at **Pivnica HS** or dinner overlooking the city rooftops at **Biban**.

Next day ponder the horrors of the 1990s siege era at the moving **History Museum** and unique **Tunnel Museum**. Recover with a drink at eccentrically Gothic **Zlatna Ribica** and a feisty gig at **Underground**.

originally a silk-trading bazaar. Today it's a small museum with bite-sized overviews of the city's history and a compelling model of Sarajevo as it looked in 1878.

Gazi-Husrevbey Mosque
MOSQUE

(Map p82; www.vakuf-gazi.ba; Saraći 18; admission 2KM; ⊘9am-noon, 2.30-3.30pm & 5-6.15pm May-Sep, closed Ramadan) Ottoman governor Gazi-Husrevbey funded a series of splendid 16th-century buildings of which this mosque forms the greatest centrepiece. Its cylindrical minaret contrasts photogenically with the elegant stone clock tower off Mudželeti Veliki alley. The associated **madrassa** (Religious School; Saraći 33-49) across Saraći is used for occasional exhibitions and book sales, its time-worn stonework contrasting conspicuously with the brand new library next door.

Vijećnica
ARCHITECTURE

(Map p82) With its storybook neo-Moorish facades, the 1892 Vijećnica is Sarajevo's most beautiful Austro-Hungarian era building. Originally the City Hall, Franz Ferdinand was on the way back from here when shot by Princip in 1914. It later became the Bosnian National Library. However, during the 1990s siege it was deliberately hit by a Serb incendiary shell. Around 90% of its irreplaceable collection of manuscripts and Bosnian books was destroyed and for nearly two decades the building remained a sorry skeleton. Reconstruction is finally advancing and due for completion in April 2014.

Sarajevo 1878–1918
HISTORICAL MUSEUM

(Map p82; Zelenih Beretki 2; admission 2KM; ⊘10am-6pm Mon-Fri, 10am-3pm Sat) This one-room exhibition examines the city's Austro-Hungarian–era history and the infamous 1914 assassination of Franz Ferdinand that happened right outside, ultimately triggering WWI.

Jewish Museum
MEDIEVAL SYNAGOGUE

(Muzej Jevreja BiH; Map p82; Mula Mustafe Bašeskije 40; admission 2KM; ⊘10am-6pm Mon-Fri, 10am-1pm Sun) More religiously open-minded than most of Western Europe in its day, the 15th-century Ottoman Empire offered refuge to the Sephardic Jews who had been evicted en masse from Spain in 1492. While conditions varied, Bosnian Jews mostly prospered, until WWII that is, when most of the 14,000-strong community fled or were murdered by Nazis. The community's story is well told in this 1581 Sephardic synagogue that still sees active worship during Rosh Hashana (Jewish New Year).

Academy of Arts
ARCHITECTURE

(Likovna Akademija; Map p82; www.alu.unsa.ba; Obala Maka Dizdara 3) Originally built in 1899 as an evangelical church, the Gothic Revival–style Academy of Arts looks like a mini version of Budapest's magnificent national parliament building. Since August 2012 it has been fronted by Festina Lente ('Hurry Slowly'), an Escheresque new footbridge that 'loops-the-loop'.

BJELAVE & VRATNIK

⌖TOP CHOICE Svrzo House
HOUSE MUSEUM

(Svrzina Kuća; Map p82; ☎535264; Glođina 8; admission 3KM; ⊘10am-6pm Mon-Fri, 10am-3pm Sat) An oasis of white-washed walls, cobbled courtyards and partly vine-draped dark timbers, this 18th-century house museum is brilliantly restored and appropriately furnished, helping visitors imagine Sarajevo life in eras past. Notice the *čekme dolaf* (food hatch), designed to prevent inter-sex fratenization.

Izetbegović Museum
MUSEUM

(Map p80; www.muzejalijaizetbegovica.ba; Ploča bb; admission 2KM; ⊘10am-6pm Mon-Fri, 10am-3pm Sat) Above the Kovači cemetery where he's buried, there's a small but fascinating museum to Alija Izetbegović. Even if you're not interested in BiH's first president, the setting (in the historic Kula Ploče Tower) is interesting and the visit lets you walk along a last surviving section of city wall emerging at the Kula Širokac Tower.

Vratnik
NEIGHBOURHOOD

The once-vast Vratnik Citadel was built in the 1720s and reinforced in 1816. Not much remains but there are superb views from the grassy-topped **Yellow Bastion** (Žuta Tabija; Map p80; Jekovac bb). Minibus 55 gets you reasonably close.

NOVO SARAJEVO

During the 1992–95 siege, the wide road from the airport (Zmaja od Bosne) was dubbed 'sniper alley' because Serb gunmen in surrounding hills could pick off civilians as they tried to cross it. The distinctive, pudding-and-custard coloured **Holiday Inn** (Map p80; www.holidaysarajevo.com; Zmaja Od Bosne 4) famously housed most of the embattled journalists covering that conflict.

Greater Sarajevo

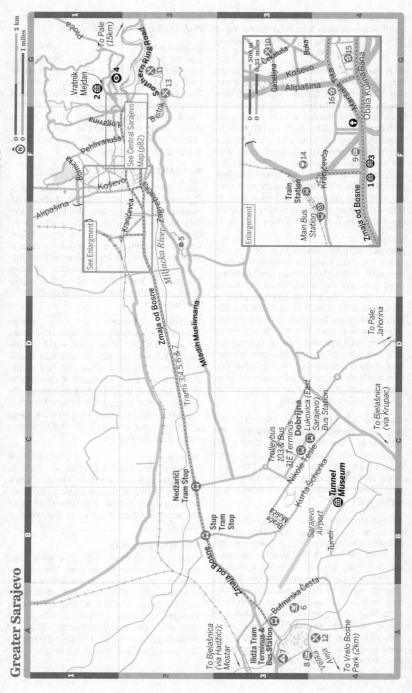

N

2 km
1 miles

To Pale (15km)

Ploča

Southern Ring Road

Vratnik Mejdan

Pehlivanuša

Bistrik

Logavina

Bolnia

Koševo

Alipašina

See Central Sarajevo Map (p82)

See Enlargement

Miljacka River
Zagrebačka

Kranjčeva

Zmaja od Bosne

Mlladih Muslimana

Trams 3,4,5,6 & 7

To Pale;
Jahorina

Dobrinja

Trolleybus
103 & Bus
31E Terminus

Nikole Tesle

Lukovica (East
Sarajevo)
Bus Station

Kurta Schorka

Tunnel
Museum

Nedžarići Tram Stop

Stup Tram Stop

To Bjelašnica
(via Krupac)

Brače
Mulića

Sarajevo Airport

Dobrinja

Zmaja od Bosne

Butmirska Cesta

Ilidža Tram
Terminus & Bus Station

To Bjelašnica
(via Hadžići);
Mostar

Velika
Aleja

To Vrelo Bosne
Park (2km)

Tuneli

Enlargement

500 m
0.25 miles

Cekaluša

Koševo

Buka

Gabelijna

Alipašina

Tita

Maršala Tita

Koševo

Obala Kulina Bana

Train
Station

Kranjčeva

Zmaja od Bosne

Main Bus
Station

Greater Sarajevo

◎ **Top Sights**
Tunnel Museum.. B4

◎ **Sights**
1 History Museum F4
2 Izetbegović Museum G1
3 National Museum F4
4 Yellow Bastion G1

◉ **Activities, Courses & Tours**
5 Green Visions E2
6 Termalna Rivijera A3

◍ **Sleeping**
7 AutoKamp Oaza A3

8 Casa Grande A3
9 Holiday Inn F4

◈ **Eating**
10 Avlija G3
11 Biban G2
12 Ildžis 1968 .... A4
13 Park Prinčeva G2

◉ **Drinking**
14 Caffe 35 .... F3

◈ **Entertainment**
15 FIS Kultura G4
16 Rooms Club & Restaurant G4

National Museum   MUSEUM
(Zemaljski Muzej Bosne-i-Hercegovine; Map
p80; www.zemaljskimuzej.ba; Zmaja od Bosne 3;
⊙temporarily closed) Bosnia's biggest and
best endowed museum closed in October
2012 due to persistent funding problems.
Ironically it had been a rare institution to
have remained at least partly functioning
throughout the siege era, and its impressive 1913 quadrangle of neo-classical 1913
buildings survived reasonably intact. As-
suming it reopens, the greatest highlights
are its Illyrian and Roman carvings and
especially the world-famous **Sarajevo
Haggadah**, a 14th-century Jewish codex
said to be worth a billion US dollars. Geraldine Brooks' 2007 historical novel *People
of the Book* is a part-fictionalised account
of how the Nazis failed to grab it during
WWII.

Outside at the front are some exceptional
medieval *stećci* (carved grave slabs).

History Museum   MUSEUM
(Map p80; Zmaja od Bosne 5; admission 4KM;
⊙9am-7pm Mon-Fri, 10am-2pm Sat-Sun) More
than half of the small but engrossing History Museum 'non-ideologically' charts the
course of the 1990s conflict. Affecting personal exhibits include examples of food aid,
DIY guns, stacks of Monopoly-style 1990s dinars and a makeshift siege-time 'home'. The
effect is emphasised by the building's miser-
able and still partly war-damaged 1970s architecture. Directly behind, the amusingly
tongue-in-cheek **Tito Cafe** (www.caffetito.
ba; ⊙24hr) has stormtrooper-helmet lampshades and garden seating surrounded by
WWII artillery pieces.

ILIDŽA & BUTMIR

TOP CHOICE **Tunnel Museum**   WAR MUSEUM
(Tunel Spasa; Map p80; www.tunelspasa.ba; Tuneli bb
1; admission 5KM; ⊙9.15am-5pm, last entry 4.30pm)
For much of the 1990s war, Sarajevo was
virtually surrounded by hostile Serb forces.
Butmir was the last Bosniak-held part of the
city still linked to the outside world. However,
between Butmir and Sarajevo lies the airport
runway. Although it was supposedly neutral
and under tenuous UN control, crossing it
would have been suicidal during the conflict.
The solution was a hand-dug 800m tunnel
beneath the runway. That was just enough to
keep Sarajevo supplied with arms and food
during the three-year siege. Most of the tunnel
has since collapsed, but this museum retains
a 20m section and gives visitors a glimpse of
its hopes and horrors. Photos are displayed
around the shell-pounded house that hides
the tunnel entrance and there's a 20-minute
video showing footage of the city bombardment and the wartime tunnel experience.

Joining a city tour that includes a visit
here can often prove cheaper than coming
by taxi and your guide can add a lot of useful
insight. Alternatively take tram 3 to Ilidža
(35 minutes, 11km from Baščaršija), then
switch to Kotorac-bound bus 32 (10 minutes,
twice hourly, 3km). Get off at the last stop,
walk across the bridge, then turn immediately left down Tuneli for 500m.

Vrelo Bosne Park   PARK
The focus of this extensive park is a patchwork of lush mini-islands at the cliff-mouth
source of the Bosna River. While it's not
worth a special trip from central Sarajevo,
if you're staying in Ilidža the park makes

Central Sarajevo

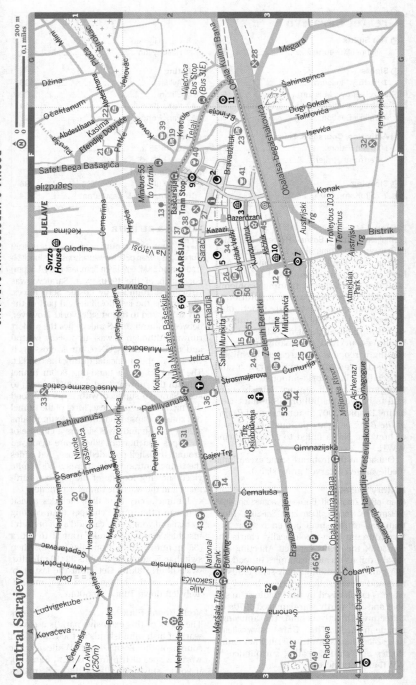

Central Sarajevo

◎ **Top Sights**
Svrzo House E1

◎ **Sights**
1 Academy of Arts A4
2 Baščaršija Džamija F2
3 Bursa Bezistan E3
4 Catholic Cathedral D2
5 Gazi-Husrevbey Mosque E3
6 Jewish Museum D2
7 Latin Bridge E3
8 Orthodox Cathedral C3
9 Pigeon Square F2
10 Sarajevo 1878–1918 .... E3
11 Vijećnica G3

◎ **Activities, Courses & Tours**
12 Insider E3
13 Sarajevo Funky Tours E2

◎ **Sleeping**
14 City Boutique Hotel C3
15 HCC Sarajevo Hostel D3
16 Hostel Old City D3
17 Hotel Art D3
18 Hotel Central D3
19 Hotel Kovači F2
20 Hotel Michele B1
21 Hotel Safir F1
22 Hotel Telal F1
23 Pansion Divan F3
24 Residence Rooms D3
25 Travellers Home D3
26 Villa Wien E3

◎ **Eating**
27 Dveri E2

28 Inat Kuća G3
29 Karuzo C2
30 Mala Kuhinja D2
31 Markale C2
32 Pivnica HS F4
33 Sushi San C1
34 To Be or Not to Be E3
35 Vegehana D2

◎ **Drinking**
36 Alfonso C2
37 Barhana E2
38 Caffe Divan E2
39 Čajdžinica Džirlo F2
40 Dibek F2
41 Kuća Sevdaha F3
42 Pravda A3
43 Zlatna Ribica B2

◎ **Entertainment**
44 Club Jež C3
45 Hacienda E3
46 National Theatre B4
47 Sloga A2
48 Underground B3

◎ **Shopping**
49 BuyBook A4
50 Dugi Bezistan E3
51 Šahinpašić D3

◎ **Transport**
52 BH Airlines A3
53 Gir C3

a pleasant outing accessible by horse-cart or on foot along Velika Aleja, an elegantly tree-lined pedestrian avenue stretching 3km from Ilidža's main hotel area.

Termalna Rivijera　SWIMMING
(Map p80; www.terme-ilidza.ba/en; Butmirska Cesta 18; adult/child Mon-Fri 13/10KM, Sat & Sun 15/12KM; ⊙9am-10pm Sun-Fri, 9am-2am Sat) A complex of indoor and outdoor swimming pools 600m east of Ilidža tram terminus.

☞ Tours

Insider　TOUR
(Map p82; ☎061-190591; www.sarajevoinsider.com; Zelenih Beretki 30; ⊙9am-6pm Mon-Fri, 9.30am-2pm Sat-Sun) Wide range of tours in and be-

yond Sarajevo. Popular daily offerings include the two-hour Tunnel Tour (€15, 2pm) and excellent three-hour 'Times of Misfortune' (€27, 11am), visiting sites related to the 1990s conflict. Tour customers get free entrance to Insider's two-room Siege 'museum' (otherwise 3KM), 17 photo-text panels explaining the Yugoslav conflict from Tito's death to Dayton.

Sarajevo Funky Tours　TOUR
(Map p82; ☎062-910546; www.sarajevofunkytours. com; Besarina Čikma 5) A similar range of tours to Insider.

Sarajevo Free Tour　TOUR
Impressive 90-minute city walking tour starting 3pm from the tourist office or

4.30pm from Insider. Runs most days in summer. Pay through tips.

Green Visions
TOUR

(Map p80; ☑717290; www.greenvisions.ba; opposite Radnićka 66; ◷9am-5pm Mon-Fri) Ecotourism specialist Green Visions offers a wide range of weekend and tailor-made hiking trips into the Bosnian mountains and villages with some fixed-day departures.

✯✯ Festivals & Events

Baščaršijske Noći
ARTS

(Baščaršija Nights; www.bascarsijskenoci.ba) Wide-ranging arts fest lasting all July.

Jazz Festival
MUSIC

(www.jazzfest.ba) Local and international jazz in early November.

Sarajevo Film Festival
FILM

(www.sff.ba) Globally acclaimed with commercial and art-house movies, most with English subtitles. Held in August or late July.

🛏 Sleeping

If you arrive without anywhere booked and everything seems full, there's still a chance of finding a bed through one of the three agencies on the north side of Mula Mustafe Bašeskije at Baščaršija tram stop.

CITY CENTRE

Hotel Michele
BOUTIQUE HOTEL €€€

(Map p82; ☑560310; www.hotelmichele.ba; Ivana Cankara 27; r €75-105, apt €120-150; ❋🛜) Behind the exterior of an oversized contemporary townhouse, this offbeat guesthouse welcomes you into a lobby-lounge full of portraits, pinned butterflies and elegant fittings. Age-effect elements are in evidence in the 12 new standard rooms but what draws celebrity guests including Morgan Freeman and Kevin Spacey are the vast, indulgently furnished apartments with antique (if sometimes mismatching) furniture.

🏆 TOP CHOICE Villa Wien
GUESTHOUSE €€

(Map p82; Ćurčiluk Veliki 3; s/d 143/186KM; ❋🛜) Six well-equipped rooms decorated in opulent pseudo–belle époque style are hidden away above the Wiener Café. They are relatively good value perhaps because there's no reception – you have to check in a few blocks away at the less impressive yet more expensive **Hotel Art** (Map p82; ☑232855; www.hotelart.ba; Ferhadija 30a; s/d/ste 183/236/306KM; P❋@🛜).

Hotel Central
HOTEL €€€

(Map p82; ☑033-561800; www.hotelcentral.ba; Cumurija 8; s/d/ste 200/240/300KM; ❋🛜🏊) Behind a grand Austro-Hungarian facade, most of this newly renovated 'hotel' is in fact an amazing three-floor gym complex with professional-standard weight rooms, saunas and big indoor pool manned by qualified sports training staff. The 15 huge, fashionably appointed guest rooms lead off corridors painted lugubriously deep purple.

🏆 TOP CHOICE Hostel Old City
HOSTEL €

(Map p82; ☑555355; www.hosteloldcity.ba; Sime Milutinovića 1; dm €15; ❋@🛜) One floor of a regal 1908 townhouse has been given a very impressive makeover in keeping with its heritage. Features include big lockers, well-constructed beds and a lounge with Latin Bridge balcony views.

Hotel Kovači
HOTEL €€

(Map p82; ☑573700; www.hotelkovaci.com; Kovači 12; s/d/tr/apt €50/70/90/100; ❋🛜) This wonderfully central family hotel blends a chic, understated modernism with a traditional design that incorporates overhanging ('doksat') windows. Its fresh white rooms are softened with photos of 19th-century Sarajevo on protruding panels.

City Boutique Hotel
BOUTIQUE HOTEL €€

(Map p82; ☑566850; www.cityhotel.ba; Mula Mustafe Bašekije 2; r Fri-Sat €76-91, Sun-Thu €94-114; ❋🛜) Contemporary, designer rooms in rectilinear modernist style feature striking colours and backlit ceiling panels. There's a 6th-floor self-serve lounge-cafe and rooftop terrace with limited views. Reception 24 hours.

Residence Rooms
HOSTEL €

(Map p82; ☑200157; www.residencerooms.ba; 1st fl, Saliha Muvekita 1; dm/s/d/tr €15/25/40/45; @🛜) High ceilings, ample common areas and widely spaced beds in the dorms all make for a convivial hostel experience. The lively bars directly outside can be a blessing or curse depending on your party plans.

HCC Sarajevo Hostel
HOSTEL €

(Map p82; ☑062-993330; www.hcc.ba; 3rd fl, Saliha Muvekita 2; dm €12-16, s €20-25, d €28-35; ❋@🛜) This sociable hostel has big lockers (padlock rental €1), a stylishly decorated kitchen/dining area and a bright lounge/lobby with DVDs to watch and a guitar to strum.

Pansion Divan
PENSION €

(Map p82; ☑061420254; www.facebook.com/pansion.divansarajevo; Brandžiluk 38; s €20-30, tw €30-35; 🛜) Above an Ali Baba's cave of a restaurant, these 10 neat, unfussy rooms with private bathrooms don't have reception or common room but at such bargain prices one can't complain. Wi-fi in five rooms.

Hotel Safir
HOTEL €€

(Map p82; ☑475040; www.hotelsafir.ba; Jagodića 3; s/d €50/72; ❋🛜) Off stairways featuring vibrantly colour-suffused flower photos, rooms come with little mirror 'windows', conical basins and beam-me-up-Scotty shower booths. Six out of eight have a kitchenette.

Travellers Home
HOSTEL €

(Map p82; ☑70 242 400; www.myhostel.ba; Ćumurija 4, 1st fl; dm 25-38KM; d 62-92KM; ⊗24hr; 🛜) One of Sarajevo's many high-ceilinged house-hostels, Travellers Home has outstandingly helpful, informative staff and a central yet peaceful locaton. Lockers are backpack-sized and power-points are accessible from each bunk.

Hotel Telal
HOTEL €

(Map p82; ☑525125; www.hotel-telal.ba; Abdesthana 4; s/d/tr/apt €30/40/45/60; ❋) Reception feels a little claustrophobic and the walls are thin but the en suite rooms are comparatively smart and well tended for the rock-bottom price.

ILIDŽA & AIRPORT AREA
Several indulgent yet well-priced hotels lie in green, pleasant Ilidža. Parking is easier here than downtown but it's a 35-minute tram ride from Sarajevo's old centre.

TOP CHOICE Casa Grande
HOTEL €€

(Map p80; ☑639280; www.casagrande-bih.com; Velika Aleja 2; s/d/tr/q 68/113/138/165KM; 🅿❋🛜) Designed like an aristocratic 1920s villa, the Casa Grande sits amid the plane trees right at the start of Ilidža's classic avenue, Velika Aleja. Rooms range from spacious to huge and are remarkably luxurious for the price. Expect satellite TV, leather-padded doors, 30-nozzle full-body shower pods and framed imitations of 'classic' art.

AutoKamp Oaza
CAMPING GROUND €

(Map p80; ☑636140; oaza@hoteliilidza.ba; per person 10KM, plus per tent/car/campervan 7/10/15KM, bungalows 60-105KM) Tree-shaded camping and caravan hook-ups (electricity 3KM extra)

tucked behind the Hotel Imzit, 1.5km west of Ilidža tram terminus.

✗ Eating
For inexpensive snack meals look along Bradžiluk or Kundurdžiluk: Bosna is a good place for cheap, fresh *burek*. Locals argue whether Hadžić, Mrkva or Željo is the best *ćevabdžinica* ('ćevapi servery').

CITY CENTRE

Mala Kuhinja
FUSION €€

(Map p82; ☑061 144741; www.malakuhinja.ba; Josipa Štadlera 6; meals 20-25KM; ⊗noon-4pm Mon-Sat) There's no menu at this tiny, fusion-food gem where the chefs simply ask you what you do/don't like and then set about making culinary magic. Sit at the three-seat 'bar' to watch the show in all its glory. Reservations advisable.

Dveri
EUROPEAN €€

(Map p82; ☑537020; www.dveri.co.ba; Prote Bakovića 12; meals 11-18KM; ⊗8am-11pm; 🛜📶) This tourist-friendly 'country cottage' eatery is densely hung with loops of garlic, corn cobs and gingham-curtained 'windows'. Classic European meat-based dishes are supplemented by inky risottos, vegie-stuffed eggplant and garlic-wine squid. There's a well-chosen wine list including some excellent Hercegovinian Blatinas.

To Be ~~or Not~~ to Be
INTERNATIONAL €€

(Map p82; ☑233265; Čizmedžiluk 5; meals 10-22KM; ⊗11am-11pm; 📶) Arched metal shutters creak open to reveal a tiny two-table room lovably decorated in traditional Bosnian style. Try the daring, tongue-tickling steak in chilli chocolate (22KM). The restaurant's name, with 'or Not' crossed out as a message of positivity, was originally a poster slogan for the 1994 Sarajevo Winter Festival, held against all odds during the siege.

Sushi San
SUSHI €

(Map p82; ☑833034; www.sarajevosushi.com; Muse Ćazima Ćatića 33 ; 2-piece sushi 5-6KM; ⊗11am-8pm Mon-Sat; 📶) The sushi master at this tiny six-stool box restaurant learned his trade in San Fransisco and manages to produce salmon nigiri that will impress even salmon-haters. Caters to various embassies.

Pivnica HS
INTERNATIONAL €€

(Map p82; sarajevska-pivara.ba/restaurant; Franjevačka 15; pasta 8-10KM; mains 13-25KM; ⊗10am-1am; 📶) If Willy Wonka built a beer hall it might look like this – a giant festival of Las

BOSNIA & HERCEGOVINA SARAJEVO

Vegas vaudeville. Meals are well presented and satisfying and this is the only place you can be sure of finding Sarajevskaya full range of tap beers (brewed next door).

Karuzo
SEAFOOD €€

(Map p82; ☑444647; www.karuzorestaurant.com; Dženetića Čikma 2; pasta 13-18KM, mains 15-35KM; ◷noon-3pm Mon-Fri, 6-11pm Mon-Sat; ☑◻) This friendly little meat-free restaurant is styled vaguely like a yacht's interior. Along with fish dishes and sushi there are some imaginative vegetarian options including chard pockets with smoked tofu and basil sauce. The owner is both waiter and chef so don't be in a hurry.

Inat Kuća
BOSNIAN €€

(Spite House; Map p82; ☑447867; www.inatkuca. ba; Velika Alifakovac 1; mains 12-20KM, snacks 10KM; ◷10am-10pm; ◻) This Sarajevo institution occupies a classic Ottoman-era house that's a veritable museum piece with central fire-flue, antique decor and a great little riverside terrace. The menu tells the story of its odd name but some of the typical Bosnian fare (stews, *dolme*) can be slightly lacklustre.

Vegehana
VEGETARIAN €

(Map p82; www.vegehana.ba/; Ferhadija 39; mains 5-10KM; ◷10am-9pm Mon-Fri, noon-9pm Sat; ☑◻) The first fully vegetarian, organic eatery in Sarajevo uses plenty of Tahina, quinoa, tofu and seitan meat-substitute.

Markale
MARKET

(Map p82; Mula Mustafe Bašeskije; ◷7am-5pm Mon-Sat, 7am-2pm Sun) Markale is an unassuming huddle of vegetable stalls. The massacre of marketgoers here in a 1995 Serb mortar attack proved a 'last straw', triggering NATO air strikes against the forces besieging Sarajevo.

GREATER SARAJEVO

Biban
BOSNIAN €€

(Map p80; ☑033-232026; Hošin Brijeg 95a; mains 7-16KM; ◷10am-10pm Mon-Fri, 10am-9pm Sun; ◻) Encompassing the whole Sarajevo Valley, Biban's panoramic city views trump even those of better-known Park Prinčeva, but the food is cheaper (and simpler) including typical meat dishes, squid and trout. The 10KM plates of *uštipci* (fist-size fried doughballs served with sour cream) are big enough to feed three people. Walk 600m uphill from Park Prinčeva, turning left after Nalina 15a.

Park Prinčeva
BALKAN, EUROPEAN €€€

(Map p80; ☑222708; www.parkprinceva.ba; Iza Hidra 7; meals 16-32KM; ◷9am-11pm; ◻) Like

Bono and Bill Clinton before you, gaze down across the city, the old city hall beautifully framed between rooftops, mosques and twinkling lights. Minibus 56 from Latin Bridge passes outside. Try the chicken in cherry sauce.

Avlija
BISTRO €€

(Map p80; ☑444 483; Sumbula Avde 2, opposite 53 Čekaluša; 9-20KM; ◷8am-11pm; ◻) Locals and in-the-know expats cosy up at painted wooden benches in this unpretentious covered yard, dangling with trailing potplants, strings of peppers and little witches. Generous portions of Central European pub food wash down merrily with local draft beers.

Ildžis 1968
ITALIAN €

(Map p80; Velika Aleja 3; mains 6-10KM, beer 2.50KM) Staying in Ilidža? Then consider drinking or dining at this rustic-effect wooden house filled with guitars, spinning wheels and giant model ships. At night it's very moodily lit and the woodland location is just as romantic by day. Pastas are copious, beautifully presented and served with oodles of Parmesan. It is two-minute stroll north of Casa Grande along tree-lined Velika Aleja.

🍷 Drinking

As chilly April melts into sunny May, terraces blossom and central Sarajevo becomes one giant street cafe.

Bars

TOP CHOICE / Zlatna Ribica
BAR

(Map p82; Kaptol 5; ◷10am-2am) This inspiring little cafe-bar is loaded with eccentricities, including drink menus hidden away in old books that dangle from lampshades. Music swerves unpredictably between jazz, Parisian croons, opera, reggae and The Muppets. Wine might arrive with a free scallop-shell of grapes. And the uniquely stocked toilet will have you laughing out loud.

Pravda
COCKTAIL BAR

(Map p82; www.pravda.ba; Radićeva 4c; ◷8am-midnight) Choose from marigold-patterned chill-out sofas or white-enamel perch-stools, then strike your pose amid Sarajevo's gilded youth. Oh no, don't say they've all gone next door to Cafe Nivea?! Or decamped to Dekanter?

Caffe 35
BAR

(Map p80; Avaz Twist Tower, 35th fl; coffee/cake/beer 2/3/4KM, sandwiches 3-5KM; ◷9am-11pm) If you're waiting for a train, what better place to do so than admiring a full city panorama from the 35th floor of 'The Balkans' Tallest Tower'. Upstairs for 1KM you can see the same views in the open air with bars instead of windows. The glass elevator coming back down feels like it's freefalling.

Barhana
BAR

(Map p82; Đugalina 8; beer/rakija 2/3KM, mains 6-20KM; ☺10am-midnight) Sample a selection of flavoured local shots in a hidden courtyard behind the equally enticing Babylon bar. A wide range of fair value meals is served.

Cafes

Kuća Sevdaha
CAFE

(Map p82; www.artkucasevdaha.ba/en/; Halači 5; ☺9am-11pm) Sip Bosnian coffee, juniper sherbet or rose water while nibbling local sweets and listening to the lilting wails of *sevdah*, traditional Bosnian music. The ancient building that surrounds the cafe's glassed-in fountain courtyard is now used as a museum celebrating great 20th-century *sevdah* performers (admission 3KM, open 10am to 6pm Tuesday to Sunday).

Caffe Divan
CARAVANSERAI

(Map p82; Morića Han, Saraći 77; ☺8am-midnight) Relax in wicker chairs beneath the wooden beams of a gorgeous, historic caravanserai courtyard whose stables now contain an alluring Iranian carpet shop. The restaurant section (kitchen till 10pm) serves good *klepe* (a kind of garlic ravioli).

Čajdžinica Džirlo
TEAHOUSE

(Map p82; www.facebook.com/CajdzinicaDzirlo; Kovači 16; ☺8am-10pm) Miniscule but brimming with character, Džirlo offers 45 types of tea (per pot 4KM), many of them made from distinctive Bosnian herbs. Good coffee and local sherbets are also available. It's on a steeply sloping stretch of Kovači amid old workshops including metal beaters and a coffee roaster.

Dibek
BAR

(Map p82; Laledžina 3; ☺8am-11pm) Smoking a hookah (*nargile* or water pipe; 5KM) is back in fashion as you'll see in this DJ-led bar that spreads colourful low stools beneath a central tree on a tiny Old Town square. Excellent coffee too.

Alfonso
CAFE

(Map p82; Trg Fra Grge Martica 4; ☺8am-11pm) Great espressos served at open-air pavement seating that sprawls around the Catholic cathedral, or inside where a hip interior includes a catwalk between cushioned sunken seat spaces.

☆ Entertainment
Nightclubs & Live Music

Within the old city, there are two small but ever-lively areas of late night music bars: around the Hacienda, and beneath HCC Sarajevo Hostel. Other clubs tend to be further west.

Underground
LIVE MUSIC

(Map p82; www.underground.ba; Maršala Tita 56; ☺7pm-5am) Especially on Friday and Saturday nights, talented bands give classic rock songs a romping rework in this medium-sized basement venue. Free entry, tap beers 2.50KM.

FIS Kultura
LIVE MUSIC

(Bock; Map p80; Musala bb; ☺6pm-2am) There's no sign so just follow the bass-beat to locate this tiny basement venue. Musical styles range wildly from grunge to punk to 'urban' party. Some nights private parties take over. It's on Musala, a north–south lane two blocks west of Radićeva.

Rooms Club & Restaurant
DJS, LIVE MUSIC

(Map p80; www.facebook.com/roomsclubsarajevo; Maršala Tita 7; ☺9.30pm-4am Wed, Fri & Sat) This subterranean trio of stone cavern rooms includes a restaurant that serves till 3am, a sofa-dotted lounge and a contrastingly boistrous bar-performance area with live gigs that pull in crowds after midnight, especially on Wednesdays. The 5KM cover includes one drink.

Club Jež
CLUB

(Map p82; http://jez.nash.ba/v2; Zelenih Beretki 14b; ☺9pm-late) This intimate stone-vaulted cavern club heaves with young local revellers overdosing on turbofolk. Cover charges (around 5KM) include one drink.

Sloga
CLUB

(Map p82; www.cinemas.ba; Seljo, Mehmeda Spahe 20; ☺8pm-3am) This cavernous, blood-red club-disco-dance hall caters to an excitable, predominantly student crowd but dancing is oddly impeded by rows of tables. Cover charge 5KM at weekends. Occasional concerts.

Hacienda
DJ

(Map p82; Bazerdzani 3; ☺10am-very late) The not-quite-Mexican food could be spicier. Not so the ambience, which by 2am has often morphed this cane-ceilinged cantina into one of the Old Town's most happening night spots. If it's quiet, try nearby alternatives **Pirates Pub** and **Caffe Red**.

Performing Arts

National Theatre PERFORMING ARTS
(Narodno Pozorište; Map p82; ☑221682; www.nps. ba; Obala Kulina Bana 9; tickets from 10KM; ☺box office 9am-noon & 4-7.30pm) Classically adorned with fiddly gilt mouldings, this proscenium-arched theatre hosts a ballet, opera, play or philharmonic concert virtually every night from mid-September to mid-June.

Shopping

Baščaršija's pedestrian lanes are full of jewellery stalls and wooden-shuttered souvenir shops flogging slippers, Bosnian flags, carpets, archetypal copperware and wooden spoons, though if you're heading to Mostar, you might find prices better there.

Some Sarajevo bookshops still stock the darkly humorous *Sarajevo Survival Guide*, originally published during the 1992–93 siege, as well as guidebooks, magazines and English-language books on ex-Yugoslavia.

Dugi Bezistan COVERED BAZAAR
(Map p82; www.vakuf-gazi.ba; ☺8am-8pm Mon-Fri, 9am-2pm Sat) Another of Gazi-Husrevbey's 16th-century architectural legacies, the stone-vaulted covered bazaar is little more than 100m long, but squint and you could be in Istanbul. Many of its 52 shops sell inexpensive souvenirs, cheap handbags and sunglasses (from 5KM).

BuyBook BOOKSHOP
(Map p82; ☑716450; www.buybook.ba; Radićeva 4; ☺9am-8pm Mon-Fri, 10am-6pm Sat)

Šahinpašić BOOKSHOP
(Map p82; ☑667210; www.btcsahinpasic.com; Vladislava Skarića 8; ☺9am-9pm Mon-Sat)

ℹ Information

ATMs are outside the bus station, inside the airport and sprinkled all over the city.

For currency exchanges, there's an airport **post-counter** (☺9am-5pm Mon-Fri), **Postbank** (☺8am-4pm Mon-Fri) branch hidden around the west side of the train station building and many banks along Ferhadija. At weekends try the Hotel Europe.

City.Ba (www.city.ba/en) Reviews of clubs, pubs, restaurants and more
Internet Caffe Baščaršija (Aščiluk bb; per hr 2KM; ☺8am-midnight)

Klinički Centar Univerziteta Sarajevo (☑445522; www.kcus.ba; 1st fl, DIP Bldg, Stepana Tomića bb/Bolnička 25 ; ☺8am-2pm Mon-Fri) English-speaking 'VIP Clinic' within the vast Koševo Hospital complex. Take bus 14 from Dom Armije to Hotel Belvedere and then walk 300m northwest.

Lonely Planet (www.lonelyplanet.com/bosnia-and-hercegovina/sarajevo)

Sarajevo Navigator Useful free maps and monthly guide pamphlets. Widely available.

Sonar (www.sonar.ba) Listings and information.

Tourist Office (Map p82; www.sarajevo-tourism.com; Sarači 58; ☺9am-8pm Mon-Fri, 10am-6pm Sat-Sun)

ℹ Getting There & Away

Air

An hour is ample for check-in at Sarajevo's modern but very compact international **airport** (☑234841; www.sarajevo-airport.ba; Kurta Schorka 36; ☺5am-11pm), about 12km southwest of Baščaršija.

Bus

Sarajevo's **main bus station** (Map p80; ☑213100; Put Života 8) primarily serves locations in the Federation, Croatia and Western Europe. Most services to the Republik Srpska (RS) and Serbia leave from **Lukovica (East Sarajevo) Bus Station** (Map p80; ☑057-317377; Nikole Tesle bb). The latter lies way out in the suburb of Dobrinja, 400m beyond the western terminus stop of trolleybus 103 and bus 31E. To some destinations, buses leave from both stations. For Jajce, take Banja Luka buses.

Train

From the **train station** (☑655330; Put Života 2) useful services include the following:
Belgrade (51.20KM, eight hours) Departs 11.49am.
Budapest (1st/2nd class 122.40KM, 11¼ hours) Departs 6.55am, routed via Osijek (Croatia, 55.40KM). Returns from Budapest-Keleti at 9.56am.
Mostar (9.90KM, 2¼ hours) Departs 7.05am, 8.05am and 6.18pm.
Zagreb (74.30KM, 9¼ hours) Trains depart 10.54am and 9.27pm. No couchette service.

ℹ Getting Around

To/From the Airport

Trolleybus 103 and bus 31E both run to the centre, picking up around 700m from the terminal. To find the stop turn right out of the airport following black-backed 'Hotel' signs. Take the first left, shimmy right-left-right past Hotel Octagon, then turn third right at the Panda car wash (Brače

BUSES FROM SARAJEVO

DESTINATION	DEPARTURE POINT	PRICE (KM)	DURATION	FREQUENCY
Banja Luka	Main bus station	32.90	5hr	5am, 7.45am, 9.15am, 2.30pm, 3.30pm, 4.30pm, 6.30pm
Banja Luka	East Sarajevo bus station	31	5hr	9.30am, 11.30am
Bihać	Main bus station	42	6½hr	7.30am, 1.30pm, 10pm
Belgrade (Serbia)	Main bus station	47	7½hr	6am
Belgrade (Serbia)	East Sarajevo bus station	40-55	8-11hr	8am, 9.45am, 12.30pm, 3pm, 10pm
Dubrovnik (Croatia)	Main bus station	47	7hr	7.15am, 10am, plus 2.30pm, 10.15pm summer
Foča	East Sarajevo bus station	9	1½hr	11.15am, 6.15pm, plus Trebinje, Podgorica & Herceg Novi services
Herceg Novi	East Sarajevo bus station	46	7½	9am plus summer specials
Jajce	Main bus station, East Sarajevo bus station	23.50	3½hr	Take Banja Luka buses
Ljubljana (Slovenia)	Main bus station	92	8½hr	8.40pm Tue, Fri, Sun
Mostar	Main bus station	18	2½hr	15 daily, 6.50am-7.55pm
Munich (Germany)	Main bus station	140	19hr	8am
Niš	East Sarajevo bus station	46	11hr	8.40am, 6pm
Novi Pazar	Main bus station	32	7-8hr	3pm, 9pm, 10pm
Pale	East Sarajevo bus station	3.50	40min	14 daily Mon-Fri, 6 on Sat & Sun
Pale	Main bus station	5.70	25min	7am, 10am, 2pm
Podgorica (Montenegro)	East Sarajevo bus station	36	6hr	8.15am, 2pm, 8pm, 10.30pm
Split (Croatia), via Mostar	Main bus station	53.50	7½hr	10am, 9pm, plus 7am in summer
Split (Croatia), via Livno	Main bus station	53.50	7¼hr	6am
Travnik	Main bus station	17	2hr	9 daily
Trebinje via Sutjeska National Park	East Sarajevo bus station	26	5hr	7.45am, 1pm, 4.05pm
Tuzla	Main bus station	21	3¼hr	9 daily
Visoko	Main bus station	6.30	50min	at least hourly by Kakanj bus
Vienna (Austria)	Main bus station	100	14½hr	11.15am
Zagreb (Croatia)	Main bus station	54	9½hr	6.30am, 12.30pm, 10pm
Zagreb (Croatia) via Bosanski Brod	Main bus station	54	8½hr	9.30am

Mulića 17). Before the Mercator Hypermarket (Mimar Sinana 1) cross the road and take the bus-trolleybus going back the way you've just come.

Metered taxis charge around 7KM to Ilidža, 16KM to Baščaršija. The airport closes 11pm to 5am.

Bicycle Rental

Gir (Map p82; ☑350 523; www.gir.ba; Zelenih Berekti 14a; city bike per hr/day/5-days 3/15/25KM, mountain bike 4/20/35KM; ☉10am-6pm) This cycle shop is 'hidden' within the commercial passageway that leads to Club Jež.

Car

Central Sarajevo isn't driver-friendly and hotel parking is very limited but a car makes it much easier to reach the surrounding mountain areas.

Public Transport

You can find timetables on www.gras.co.ba/hodnik.htm. Click 'Redove Voznje' then select mode of transport.

Single-ride tickets are 1.60/1.80KM from kiosks/drivers and must be stamped once aboard. Day tickets (5.60KM) are only sold from kiosks. They cover all trams and trolleybuses plus most buses (but not 31E).

Useful routes include the following. All service frequency reduces on Sunday.

Tram 3 (every four to seven minutes) From Ilidža passes the Holiday Inn then loops one way (anticlockwise) around Baščaršija. Last tram back to Ilidža departs Baščaršija at 12.10am.

Tram 1 (every 12 to 25 minutes) Starts at the train station then does the same loop as Tram 3. From the train station you could alternatively walk to the nearest Tram 3 stop in about seven minutes.

Trolleybus 103 (every six minutes till 11pm) Runs along the southern side of the city from Austrijski Trg passing near Green Visions en route to Dobrijna (35 minutes). Handy for Lukovica (East Sarajevo) bus station and the airport.

Bus 31E (three per hour, 6.30am to 10pm) Vijećnica to Dobrijna (for Lukovica bus station).

Taxi

Taxis from the central ranks (Latin Bridge, Hotel Kovači, etc) often want to fix a set fee. For reliable on-the-metre fares (2KM plus about 1KM per kilometre) call **Paja Taxis** (☑412555) .

AROUND SARAJEVO

Mountains rise directly behind the city, offering convenient access to winter skiing or summer rambles. Landmine dangers remain in some areas so stick to well-used paths especially in forests.

Jahorina
☑057

Of BiH's Olympic ski resorts, multi-piste **Jahorina** (www.oc-jahorina.com; ski pass per day/week 33/160KM, ski-set rentals per day 25-40KM) has by far the widest range of hotels, each within 300m of one of Jahorina's seven main ski lifts. In summer, Termag Hotel (p90) rents mountain bikes (per half-/full day 7/10KM) and quads (per hour for one/two people 50/70KM). There's an (over)heated indoor pool at **Hotel Board** (www.hotelboard-jahorina. com; guests/non-guests free/20KM; ☉10am-10pm year-round).

🛏 Sleeping & Eating

Hotels are strung out for 2.5km, starting from a small seasonal shopping 'village' where you'll find the cheaper *pansions* – all close out of season except Hotel Kristal. The Termag Hotel is 300m above, the Board is a little further then the road divides, passing the aging **Bistrica** one way, Dva Javora the other. Past the still-ruined Hotel Jahorina, the road tunnels beneath Rajska Vrata before dead-ending at the top of the Skočine Lift. Quoted ski-season rates are for mid-January to March with half-board; summer rates include breakfast only.

Termag Hotel HOTEL €€€
(☑270422; www.termaghotel.com; s/d/ste 115/152/200KM, new block 55-100KM, ski season d/ste from 240/300KM, new block 65-110KM; 🅿🖥🏊) Within an oversized mansion built in Scooby Doo Gothic style, the Termag is a beautifully designed fashion statement where traditional ideas and open fireplaces are given a stylish, modernist twist. Note that guests booking the new, less exclusive rooms in a 2013 humbacked extension will not enjoy free access to the sauna, pool and underground parking.

Rajska Vrata LODGE €€
(☑065 142244; www.jahorina-rajskavrata.com; d/tr €50/75; 🖥) Beside the longest piste in town, this perfect alpine ski-in cafe-restaurant has rustic sheepskin benches around a centrally flued real fire. The cosy pine-walled bedrooms are only available March to November.

Hotel Dva Javora HOTEL €€
(☑270481; www.hoteldvajavora.com; per person B&B 40KM, ski season 65-90KM; 🖥) Upstairs above a row of seasonal sports shops, the

modern lobby bar has an attractive, open feel. Rooms are fairly plain but with new pine beds and clean checkerboard bathrooms. Wi-fi in the bar.

Pansion Sport LODGE €€
(☑270333; www.pansion-sport.com; d Sun-Fri 54-80KM, Sat 84-124KM; ⊙mid-Dec–early Apr) Pleasant Swiss chalet–style guesthouse in the resort's 'village area'. There's a spacious glass-fronted bar full of big wicker chairs.

❶ Getting There & Away

Jahorina is 6.5km off the newly improved road leading between Istochno Sarajevo (27km) and Pale (13km). Buses run in ski season only, departing from Pale (3KM, 25 minutes) at 7am, 3pm and 11.30pm, returning from Hotel Bistrica.

Bjelašnica

☑033
BiH's second Olympic ski field rises above the two-hotel resort of Bjelašnica (www.bjelasnica.ba; ski pass per day/night/week 27/15/180KM), around 30km south of Sarajevo. An attraction here is the floodlit night skiing (6pm to 9pm) and, in summer, the possibilities of exploring the magical mountain villages (p91) behind. You can rent bicycles (per hour/day 5/30KM) and quads (per hour 60KM to 100KM) from the excellent new Hotel Han (☑584150; www.hotelhan.ba; s/d summer 56.50/95KM, d mid-Dec–Mar 155-185KM; ☎), a stylish yet reasonably priced

construction directly facing the main piste. Fronted by what looks like a giant Plexiglas pencil, the friendly but older Hotel Maršal (☑584129, 584100; www.hotel-marsal.ba; s/d summer 71.50/96KM, Christmas-early Mar d 116-136KM; ☎) rents skis, boots and poles (guests/non-guests per day 15/20KM) in season and has a nightclub.

Aimed at cross-country enthusiasts (it's away 5km from the downhill pistes), the great-value Hostel Feri (☑775555; www.feri.ba; Veliko Polje; per person summer/winter/New Year 74.20/94.20/114.20KM, s 54.60-84.60KM; ☎) charges the same per person whether you're in a double or six-bedded room. It's luxurious for a 'hostel', with flat-screen TVs, gym and ski-season-only sauna included.

On weekends in season bus 44 runs from Sarajevo's National Museum at 9am, returning at 3.30pm from Hotel Maršal. In summer you'll need wheels.

HERCEGOVINA

Hercegovina is the part of BiH that no one in the West ever mentions, if only because they can't pronounce it. The arid, Mediterranean landscape has a distinctive beauty punctuated with barren mountain ridges and photogenic river valleys. Famed for its fine wines and sun-packed fruits, Hercegovina is sparsely populated, but it has some intriguing historic towns and the Adriatic coast is just a skip away.

BJELAŠNICA'S MOUNTAIN VILLAGES

If you're driving, don't miss exploring the web of rural lanes tucked away in the uplands above Bjelašnica. Most famous is timeless Lukomir, 19km by a manageable unpaved road starting to the right of Aurora 97 snack-shack near Bjelašnica's Hotel Maršal. From a knoll that's less than five minutes' obvious climb beyond the road end in Lukomir village, a 360-degree panorama is one of the best in Bosnia encompassing the layered stone hamlet, sloping stony sheep pastures behind and a plunging gorge backed by a far horizon of rocky-knobbed peaks. There's a seasonal house-cafe in Lukomir but for a little more 'civilisation' head for Umoljani. Tucked into a partly wooded cwm, 16km from Bjelašnica, Umoljani has three little restaurant-cafes and two *pansions*. The Restoran Studeno Vrelo (☑061 709540; coffee/snack 1.50/5KM), the only one to open year-round, charges just 20KM per person to sleep in the cute three-bedroom log house behind. Koliba seasonal cafe displays excellent hiking maps on its exterior wall. Pansion Umoljani (☑061 228142) has a big-view terrace. The asphalted approach road to Umoljani is beautiful and there are *stećci* just above the road around 2.5km before the village. There's a hiking trail from Lukomir down to Umoljani but by road you need to backtrack 8km then descend via Milišići (which has its own appeal and some further great views) and turn right at the sharp junction 1.2km from Šabići. Green Visions (p84) and other agencies organise a range of summer activities to get you to and around this lovely area.

Mostar

♪036 / POP 111,600

At dusk the lights of numerous millhouse restaurants twinkle across gushing streamlets. Narrow Kujundžiluk 'gold alley' bustles joyously with trinket sellers. And in between, the Balkans' most celebrated bridge forms a majestic stone arc between reincarnated medieval towers. It's an enchanting scene. Do stay into the evening to see it without the summer hoards of day trippers. Indeed stay longer to enjoy memorable attractions in the surrounding area as well as pondering the city's darker side – still vivid scars of the 1990s conflict that remain visible beyond the cobbled lanes of the attractively restored Ottoman quarter. Be aware that between November and April most tourist facilities will be in wholescale hibernation.

History

Mostar means 'bridge-keeper', and the crossing of the Neretva River here has always been its raison d'être. In the mid-16th century, Mostar boomed as a key transport gateway within the powerful, expanding Ottoman Empire. Some 30 *esnafi* (craft guilds) included tanners (for whom the Tabhana was built), and goldsmiths (hence Kujundžiluk, 'gold alley'). In 1557, Suleyman the Magnificent ordered a swooping stone arch to replace the suspension bridge whose wobbling had previously terrified tradesmen as they gingerly crossed the fast-flowing Neretva River. The beautiful Stari Most (Old Bridge) that resulted was finished in 1566 and came to be appreciated as one of the era's engineering marvels. It survived the Italian occupation of WWII, but after standing for 427 years the bridge was destroyed in November 1993 by Bosnian Croat artillery in one of the most poignant and depressingly pointless moments of the whole Yugoslav civil war.

Ironically Muslims and Croats had initially fought together against Serb and Montenegrin forces that had started bombarding Mostar in April 1992. However, on 9 May 1993, a bitter conflict erupted between the former allies. A de facto frontline emerged north–south along the Bulvar and Aleksi Šantiće street with Croats to the west, Bosniaks to the east. For two years both sides swapped artillery fire and by 1995 Mostar resembled Dresden after WWII, with all its bridges destroyed and all but one of its 27

Ottoman-era mosques utterly ruined. Vast international assistance efforts rebuilt almost all of the Unesco-listed old city core, including the classic bridge, painstakingly reconstructed using 16th-century-style building techniques and stone from the original quarry. However, nearly two decades after the conflict, significant numbers of shattered buildings remain as ghostlike reminders. The psychological scars will take generations to heal and the city remains oddly schizophrenic, with two bus stations and two postal systems – one Bosniak and the other Croat.

◎ Sights

Stari Most
BRIDGE

The world-famous Stari Most (Old Bridge) is the indisputable visual focus that gives Mostar its special magic. The medieval bridge's pale stone magnificently throws back the golden glow of sunset or the tasteful night-time floodlighting. Numerous well-positioned cafes and restaurants, notably behind the **Tabhana** (an Ottoman-era enclosed courtyard), tempt you to sit and savour the scene. If you wait long enough you are likely to see someone jump 21m off the parapet into the icy Neretva below. This is not an attempt at suicide but an age-old tradition maintained by an elite group of young men. There's even an annual bridge-diving competition (July). At other times, however, divers will only generally jump once their hustlers have collected enough photo money from onlookers. If you want to jump yourself (from €25), ask at the **Bridge-Divers' Clubhouse** beside the bridge's western end. They can organise a wetsuit, basic training and two divers who await beside the river below in case of emergencies.

At the bridge's eastern side, the **Old Bridge Museum** (adult/student 5/3KM; ◎10am-6pm summer, 11am-2pm winter, closed Mon) has two parts, both offering relatively sparse exhibits. First you climb up a five-storey stone defence tower for partial views and interesting but limited displays about Stari Most's context and construction. Climb back down to walk through the bridge's archaeological bowels, and you'll emerge on Kujundžiluk.

Crooked Bridge
BRIDGE

(Kriva Ćuprija) Resembling Stari Most but in miniature, the pint-sized Crooked Bridge crosses the tiny Rabobolja creek amid a layered series of millhouse restaurants. The original bridge, weakened by wartime as-

IMAGES OF MOSTAR

At least four compelling videos of Mostar's demise and rebirth are on show around town. Each is subtly different but all include tragic footage of the moment the old bridge was blown apart. A decent free choice is within the **Old Hamam** (beside Tabhana; ☺10am-4pm May-Oct) where an exhibition looks building-by-building at Mostar's destruction and reconstruction. Bookshop **Galerija Old Bridge** (Stari Most; ☺9am-10pm), a former mosque right on the bridge's southwest parapet, plays and sells a similar DVD (€10). A 10-minute version concentrating more on bridge-diving is screened in a comfy cinema-style room at the Museum of Hercegovina. And there's a slow-moving 15-minute video shown at the Old Bridge Museum.

An **exhibition** (Helebija Kula, Stari Most; 6KM; ☺9am-8.30pm Apr-Nov) of around 50 black-and-white still photos depicting city life during wartime is shown within the semicircular Helebija Kula, a former gunpowder tower directly behind the Bridge Divers' Clubhouse. They're powerful images but there's no video and entry fees seem steep.

saults, was washed away by floods of 2000, but rebuilt a year later.

Koski Mehmed Paša Mosque
MOSQUE

(Mala Tepa 16; mosque/mosque & minaret 4/8KM; ☺8am-8pm Apr-Sep, 9am-5pm Oct, closed Nov-Mar) Entered from a gated courtyard, the rebuilt 1618 Koski Mehmed Paša Mosque lacks a certain finess in its interior but climbing the claustrophobic minaret allows you to enjoy sweeping town views. The most attractive part of the mosque complex is the small courtyard outside with its fountain taps and garden area (access free).

Bišćevića Ćošak
HOUSE

(Turkish House; Bišćevića 13; admission 4KM; ☺8.30am-6.30pm mid-Apr-Oct, closed winter except by tour) Bišćevića Ćošak is a slightly ramshackle 350-year-old Ottoman-Bosnian home with a colourfully furnished interior sporting a selection of traditional metalwork and carved wooden furniture. For interesting comparisons also visit the grander **Muslibegović House** (admission 4KM; ☺10am-6pm mid-Apr–mid-Oct), which now doubles as a boutique hotel (p96).

Former Front Line
HISTORIC AREA

Nearly two decades after the conflict, many buildings remain as bullet-pocked skeletal wrecks, especially along Mostar's former 'front line'. Every year more are restored but you'll still see several tragic ruins around Spanski Trg, including the triangular nine-storey tower that was once **Ljubljanska Banka** (Kralja Zvonimira bb). Meanwhile Trg Musala, once the heart of Austro-Hungarian Mostar, is still scarred by the stumpy war-ruined shell of the once splendid **Hotel Neretva** (Trg Musala).

Museum of Hercegovina
MUSEUM

(http://muzejhercegovine.com; Bajatova 4; admission 5KM; ☺8am-4pm Mon-Fri, 8am-1pm Sat) This small museum with archaeological and ethnographic sections, occupies the former house of Džemal Bijedić, former head of the Yugoslav government who died in mysterious circumstances in 1978. The unexplained plane wheels recall Mostar's Yugo-era aero-industry. Anton Zimlo's pre-WWI photos include a view of the Old Bridge carpet-decked for Austrian Emperor Franz Josef's 1910 visit.

Karađozbeg Mosque
MOSQUE

(Braće Fejića bb; mosque/mosque & minaret 4/8KM; ☺times vary, closed during prayers) Mostar's most important mosque, built in 1557 but heavily damaged during the war, is now completely renovated with distinctive lead-roofed wooden verandah and four-domed madrassa annexe now used as a clinic.

Roznamedži Ibrahimefendi Mosque
MOSQUE

(Braće Fejića bb) This early-17th-century mosque was the only one to survive the 1993–35 shelling relatively unscathed. Its associated **madrassa**, demolished in 1960, has now also been rebuilt, the reincarnation hosting shops and a cafe.

☞ Tours

Some homestays and hostels, including Majdas, Nina and **Miran's** (☏062 115333; www.hostelmiran-mostar.com; Pere Lažetića 13), offer walking tours around town and/or great-value full-day trips visiting Blagaj, Međugorje, Počitelj and the Kravice waterfalls for around 70KM. **Almira Travel** (☏551873; www.almira-travel.ba; Mala Tepa 9) offers alternative regional

Mostar

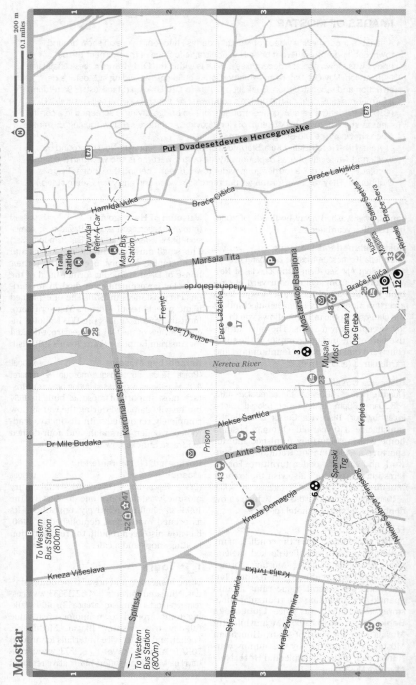

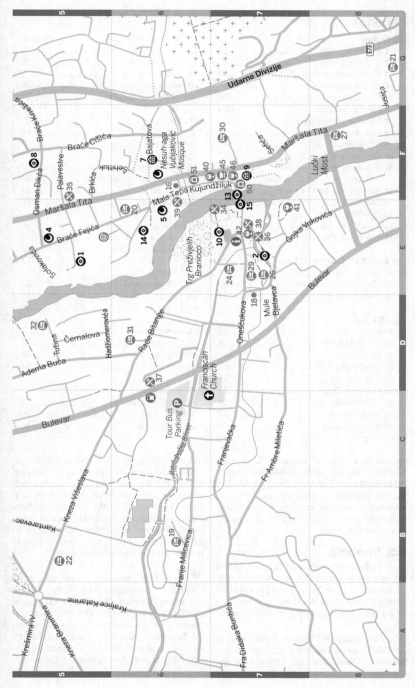

Mostar

◉ Sights
1 Biščevića Ćošak E5
2 Crooked Bridge E7
3 Hotel Neretva ruins D3
4 Karađozbeg Mosque E5
5 Koski Mehmed Paša Mosque E6
6 Ljubljanska Banka B4
7 Museum of Hercegovina F6
8 Muslibegović House F5
9 Old Bridge Museum F7
10 Old Hamam E7
11 Roznamedži Ibrahimefendi
   Madrassa E4
12 Roznamedži Ibrahimefendi
   Mosque E4
13 Stari Most F7
14 Tepa Vegetable Market E6
15 War Photo Exhibition E7

⊕ Activities, Courses & Tours
16 Almira Travel F6
17 Miran's Hostel & Tours D3
18 Tourist Info BH D7

🛏 Sleeping
19 Hostel Majdas B6
20 Hostel Miturno E6
21 Hostel Nina G8
22 Hostel Nina Annex B5
23 Hotel Bristol D4
24 Hotel Old Town E7
25 Hotel Pellegrino E4
26 Kriva Ćuprija E7
27 Kriva Ćuprija 2 .... F8

Muslibegović House .... (see 8)
28 Pansion Aldi D1
29 Pansion Oscar E7
30 Shangri-La F7
31 Villa Fortuna D6
32 Villa Mike D5

⊗ Eating
33 ABC E4
34 Babilon E7
35 Eko-Eli F5
36 Hindin Han E7
37 Konoba Boncampo D6
38 Šadrvan E7
39 Urban Grill E6

◎ Drinking
40 Ali Baba F6
41 Blasting Lounge E7
42 Caffe Marshall E7
43 Club Calamus C3
44 OKC Abrašević C3
45 Terasa F7
46 Wine & More F7

⊕ Entertainment
47 Cinestar B2
48 Club Oxygen D4
49 Romana Inn A4

⊜ Shopping
50 Galerija Old Bridge F7
51 Ismet Kurt F6
52 Mepas Mall B2

options in a range of European languages. **Tourist Info BH** (☎061 564146 561127; www. tourist-infobh.com; Oneščukova 39; ⊗8am-10.30pm May-Sep, 10am-8pm Oct-Apr) is pioneering an interesting series of rural experience tours including sunrise hill walking, farm-stays and cooking courses.

🛏 Sleeping

Most budget options are in people's homes without reception or full-time staff, so calling ahead can prove wise. Some are dormant during November to April but in others you might get a whole room for the dorm price.

TOP CHOICE **Muslibegović House** HISTORIC HOTEL €€ (☎551379; www.muslibegovichouse.com; Osman Đikća 41; s/d/ste €60/90/105; ❄🛜) In summer,

tourists pay to visit this restored late-17th-century Ottoman courtyard house, extended in 1871. But it's simultaneously an extremely charming boutique hotel. Room sizes and styles vary significantly, mixing excellent modern bathrooms with elements of traditional Bosnian, Turkish or even Moroccan design, notably in rooms 2 and 3. Double rooms cost €75 during low season.

🛏 **Hotel Old Town** BOUTIQUE HOTEL €€ (☎558877; www.oldtown.ba; Rade Bitange 9a; d/tr/q standard 180/250/300KM, deluxe 210/290/400KM; 🅿❄🛜) This super-central 10-room hotel is designed to look like a typical Bosnian house and sports handmade, specially designed wooden furniture. Meanwhile its state-of-the-art ecofriendly energy-saving systems include waste-burning furnaces for water heating and air circulation to save on air-con wastage. Standard rooms are tucked into sloping roof eaves.

Kriva Ćuprija
MILLHOUSE €€

(☑550953; www.motel-mostar.ba; r 70-130KM, apt 100-180KM; ❄️📶) Set above the famous little Crooked Bridge, this delightful central getaway enjoys the soothing sounds of gushing streams and charming mill-styled stone architecture. Idyllic views from the suites' semi-private terraces cram together old rooftops, minarets and a mountain-ridge backdrop. Rooms are impeccably clean if not necessarily large. Co-owned **Kriva Ćuprija 2** (Maršala Tita 186) is more stylishly appointed and has two hot-tubs on a rear deck but lacks the quaint location of the original.

Shangri-La
B&B €€

(☑551819; www.shangrila.com.ba; Kalhanska 10; d €49-59; P❄️📶) Quiet yet central, a pseudo-19th-century facade hides rooms that are contemporary and better appointed than those of many Mostar hotels. The rooftop views are hard to beat and the English-speaking hosts are faultlessly welcoming without being intrusive.

Hostel Majdas
HOSTEL €

(☑062 265324, 061 382940; www.hostelmajdas.com; 1st fl, Franje Milicevica 39; dm/d without bathroom €12/27; ⊙closed Oct-Mar; ❄️@📶) By sheer force of personality, and a very human awareness of traveller needs, the host family has transformed this once dreary tower-block apartment into Mostar's cult hostel. Space is tight in the colour-coordinated bunk dorms and little communal areas, but it's a great place to meet fellow travellers; there are lockers, FAQ and cultural-tip sheets, inexpensive laundry, a book exchange and a taxi sign-up sheet. Sharp-witted Bata runs popular full-day regional tours several times weekly.

Hotel Pellegrino
HOTEL €€

(☑062 969000; www.hotel-pellegrino.ba; Faladžića 1c; s €50-80, d €80-120; ❄️📶) The big pluses here are the oversized, elegantly appointed studio rooms (many with kitchenette) and excellent anti-allergenic bedding. But there is no reception, just a door-bell, and despite the five floors there are neither views nor a lift.

Hotel Bristol
BUSINESS HOTEL €€

(☑500100; www.bristol.ba; Mostarskog Bataljona; s/d from €50.50/81.50; ❄️📶) Classier than you'd guess from the rectilinear concrete exterior, there's an expansive piano bar, riverside terrace and a lift accessing the typical business-style rooms. There are desks even in the poky little singles.

Villa Fortuna
B&B €€

(☑551888; www.villafortuna.ba; Rade Bitange 34; s/d/tr/apt €30/40/60/80, incl breakfast €35/50/70/100; P❄️📶) Behind the bland travel-agency facade, fresh if compact air-con rooms lead off a hallway with a museum-like collection of local tools and metalwork. Behind is a sweet little private courtyard area in mock farmhouse style.

Villa Mike
HOMESTAY €€

(☑062 661535, 580929; www.villamike-mostar.com; Tutina 15; s/d without bathroom €30/50; ❄️📶🏊) Villa Mike is a private house offering four sparklingly clean, brand new homestay rooms sharing two bathrooms. The obliging owner speaks good English, but most remarkably there's an excellent private swimming pool in the walled backyard.

Hostel Nina
HOSTEL €

(☑061 382743; www.hostelnina.ba; Čelebica 18; dm/d without bathroom €11/22; ❄️@) Popular homestay-hostel run by an obliging English-speaking lady whose husband, a war survivor and former bridge jumper, runs regional tours that often end up over bargain beers at his bar in the Tabhana. Sometimes when the main hostel has been full, guests have been relocated to an **annex** that lacks much charm and is far less central.

Pansion Aldi
HOSTEL €

(☑061 273457, 552185; www.pansion-aldi.com; Laćina 69a; dm €10; P❄️@📶) Handy for the bus station, 17 beds in five large, simple rooms share a kitchenette and three small toilet-shower cubicles. It's slightly austere but there's a river-facing terrace garden.

Pansion Oscar
PENSION €

(☑580237, 061 823649; Oneščukova 33; s/d €30/40/45, s/d/tr/q without bathroom €20/30/50/60; ❄️📶) Oskar is essentially a pair of family homes above a summer-only cocktail/shisha garden-bar slap bang in the historic centre. Standards vary somewhat between the nine rooms, with the best in the eaves of the newer back house. They're not bookable through hostel websites so this is a good punt if you're arriving without reservations.

Hostel Miturno
HOSTEL €

(☑552408; www.hostel-miturno.ba; Braće Felića 67; dm/d €10/20; ⊙closed Jan & Feb; ❄️📶) Run by a youthful, music-loving crew, this central mini-hostel has a handful of rooms and small dorms above a main-street shop. The TV room-lobby is cramped but social and has a colourful graffiti-chic. Free coffee.

Eating

Cafes and restaurants with divine views of the river cluster along the riverbank near Stari Most. Although unapologetically tourist-oriented, their meal prices are only a *maraka* or two more than any ordinary dive. Along Mala Tepa and Braće Fejića you'll find a morning **vegetable market** (⊙6.30am-2pm), supermarkets and several inexpensive places for *ćevapi* and other Bosnian snacks.

Babilon
BALKAN €€

(Tabhana; mains 8-20KM; 🖂) Along with restaurants Bella Vista, Mlinica and Teatr next door, the Babilon has stupendous terrace views across the river to the Old Town and Stari Most. The food might be less impressive than the views, but some of the set 'tourist menus' are excellent value. Unlike several of its fellows, Babilon remains open in winter.

Hindin Han
BALKAN €€

(Jusovina bb; mains 7-20KM; ⊙11am-11pm; 🛜🖂) Hindin Han is a rebuilt historic building with several layers of summer terrace perched pleasantly above a side stream. Locals rate its food as better than most other equivalent tourist restaurants, and the stuffed squid certainly passes muster. The highly quaffable house wine costs 3.75KM per glass.

Šadrvan
BALKAN €€

(Jusovina 11; mains 7-23KM; ⊙closed Jan; 🖂) On a vine- and tree-shaded corner where the pedestrian lane from Stari Most divides, this tourist favourite has tables set around a trickling fountain made of old Turkish-style metalwork. The menu covers all bases and takes a stab at some vegetarian options. Meat-free *đuveć* (KM7) tastes like ratatouille on rice.

ABC
ITALIAN €

(📞061 194656; Braće Fejića 45; pizza & pasta 6-10KM, mains 13-17KM; ⊙9am-10.30pm Mon-Fri, noon-10.30pm Sat & Sun; 🖂) Above a popular cakeshop-cafe, this relaxed pastel-toned Italian restaurant is decorated with photos of old Mostar and dotted with aspidistras. Pizzas are bready but the pastas come with an extra bucketful of parmesan. Try plate-lickingly creamy Aurora tortellini (9KM).

Urban Grill
BOSNIAN €

(Mala Tepa 26; mains 5-17KM; ⊙8am-11pm Mon-Sat, 9am-11pm Sun) No longer limiting itself to *ćevapi*, this brightly modern take on Bosnian-rustic now serves a wider variety of local specialities but the secret trump card remains its little lower terrace with an unexpectedly excellent Old Bridge view.

Konoba Boncampo
BOSNIAN €€

(Husne Rebca 15 Bulevar; mains 8-18KM; ⊙8am-10.30pm) You'll wonder why on earth we've sent you to this hard-to-find, visually ordinary locals' eatery at the base of a residential tower block. But try their *mučkalica* ('everything' dish) and shots of Bosnia's best *slivovice* (plum brandy from Goražde) and you might understand.

Eko-Eli
BOSNIAN €

(Maršala Tita 115; mains 2.50-3.50KM; ⊙7am-11pm) Escape the tourists and watch typical Bosnian *pita* snacks (including *krompirača*, *sirnica*, *burek* and *zeljanica*) being baked over hot coals. Take away, eat at the communal table, or dine in the almost comically uninspired bar next door.

🍷 Drinking

Ali Baba
BAR

(Kujundžiluk; ⊙24hr Jun-Sep, 7am-7pm Oct, closed winter) Take a gaping cavern in the raw rock, add colourful low lighting, fat beats and Fashion TV and hey presto, you've got this one-off party bar. A dripping tunnel leads out to a second entrance on Maršala Tita.

OKC Abrašević
BAR

(📞561107; www.okcabrasevic.org; Alekse Šantića 25) This understatedly intellectual smoky box of a bar offers Mostar's most vibrantly alternative scene and has an attached venue for offbeat gigs. It's hidden away in an unsigned courtyard on the former front line. Draft beer from 2KM. Hours vary.

Terasa
CAFE

(Maršala Tita bb; ⊙weather dependent) This spectacular open-air perch-terrace surveys Stari Most and the old city towers from altogether new angles. Enter through the little roof-garden of art studio Atelje Novalić.

Club Calamus
COCKTAIL BAR

(Integra Bldg, 5th fl, Dr Ante Starčevića bb; ⊙10am-2am) DJs spin trancy beats after 10pm in this top-floor cocktail bar whose summer rooftop section affords fascinating if poignant views over some of Mostar's worst war ruins.

Caffe Marshall BAR
(Oneščukova bb; ☺8am-1am) This minuscule box bar has a ceiling draped with musical instruments and is often the latest to be active in the Old Bridge area.

Wine & More WINE BAR
(Mala Tepa; ☺9am-11pm; 🛜) Play Bacchus, sampling Trebinje's famous Tvrdoš Monastery wines (per glass 5KM) at barrel tables on the Old Town's time-polished stone stairways.

Blasting Lounge BAR
(Riverside; cocktails 5-10KM; ☺10am-late, closed mid-Nov–mid-May) Sip cocktails and fresh juice (no coffee machine) on a parasol-shaded bank of outdoor bag-cushions while gazing back at Stari Most.

☆ Entertainment

OKC Abrašević (p98) hosts occasional concerts and Ali Baba (p98) fills its summer cave with contemporary dance sounds, particularly on weekend party nights. There are several DJ cafes and nightclubs around the Rondo. Website www.bhclubbing.com gives upcoming listings.

Romana Inn DISCO
(www.romanainn.com; ☺10.30pm-5am Thu-Sat) Large, somewhat generic weekend disco.

Club Oxygen NIGHTCLUB
(www.biosphere.ba/biosfere-stranice-oxigen-en.html; Braće Fejića bb; ☺variable) Oxygen has DJ-parties and occasional live gigs.

Dom Herceg Stjepan Kosača CULTURAL CENTRE
(http://kosaca-mostar.com/; Rondo; 🛜) Diverse shows and concerts include occasional touring operas, ballets and theatre from Croatia.

Cinestar CINEMA
(www.blitz-cinestar-bh.ba) Multiplex in the big new **Mepas Mall** (www.mepas-mall.com; Kardinala Stepinca bb).

Shopping

The stone-roofed shop-houses of Kujundžiluk throw open metal shutters to sell colourfully inexpensive Turkish and Indian souvenirs including glittery velveteen slippers, pashmina-style wraps, fezzes, *boncuk* (evil-eye) pendants and Russian-style nested dolls. You can still find pens fashioned from old bullets and shell casings hammered into works of art. However, as supplies of war debris are finally being exhausted, artisans such as coppersmith **Ismet Kurt** (Kujundžiluk 5; ☺9am-8pm) are increasingly using old cutlery and trays instead as starting materials.

❶ Information

While no longer technically legal, in fact most businesses readily accept euros and Croatian

BUSES FROM MOSTAR (MAIN BUS STATION)

DESTINATION	PRICE (KM)	DURATION	FREQUENCY
Banja Luka via Jajce	25	6hr	1.30pm
Belgrade (Serbia)	58	11 hr	7.30pm, 9pm
Čapljina	6	40min	11.15am, 1pm, 3.25pm
Dubrovnik (Croatia)	32	3-4hr	7am, 10am, 12.30pm
Herceg Novi via Kotor	71	4½hr	7am (plus 2.30pm Fridays)
Sarajevo	20	2½hr	6am, 6.30am, 7am, 9am, 10am, 11am, 3pm, 4pm, 5pm, 6.15pm
Split (Croatia)	33	4½hr	6.15am, 7am, 11.15am, 12.50pm
Stolac	6	1hr	roughly hourly
Trebinje via Nevesinje	21	3hr	6.15am Mon-Sat, 3.30pm, 5.30pm
Vienna (Austria) via Maribor	110	12hr	8.30am
Zagreb (Croatia)	43-52	9½hr	7am, 9am, 8.15pm

kuna as well as marakas. Braće Fejića, the main commercial street, has banks, ATMs, a pharmacy, supermarkets and an internet cafe. Mostar websites include **Grad Mostar** (www.turizam. mostar.ba), the **Hercegovina Tourist Board** (www.hercegovina.ba) and **Visit Mostar** (www. visitmostar.org).

Bosniak Post Office (Braće Fejića bb; ⊙8am-8pm Mon-Fri, 8am-6pm Sat)

Croat Post Office (Dr Ante Starčevića bb; ⊙7am-7pm Mon-Sat, 9am-noon Sun)

Tourist Information Centre (☑397350; Trg Preživjelih Branioco; ⊙9am-9pm Jun-Sep, closed Oct-May) See also Tourist Info BH (p96).

⊙ Getting There & Around

AIR Mostar airport (OMO; ☑350992; www. mostar-airport.ba), 6km south of town off the Čapljina road, has no scheduled flights.

BICYCLE The souvenir stall beside the tourist info centre rents bicycles (per half-/full day €10/15) during the tourist season.

BUS Most long-distance buses use the **main bus station** (☑552025; Trg Ivana Krndelja) beside the train station. However, Renner buses to Stolac, a 4.30pm bus to Split (25KM) and seven weekday services to Međugorje (4KM, 45 minutes) start from the inconveniently located **western bus station** (☑348680; Autobusni Kolodvor; Vukovarska bb). It's around 800m from Mepas Mall, following Splitska west then the turning right at the third major junction. Yellow **Mostar Bus** (☑552250; www.mostarbus. ba/linije.asp) services to Blagaj start from opposite the train station and pick up passengers at Lučki Most stop.

CAR Hyundai Rent-A-Car (☑552404; www. hyundai.ba; main bus station; per day/week from 75/390KM; ⊙8am-11am & noon-4pm Mon-Fri, 9am-3pm Sat) offers good-value car hire including full insurance without deductible. Add 17% tax.

TRAIN Trains to Sarajevo (9.90KM, 2¼ hours) depart at 8.02am, 2.10pm and 6.43pm daily.

Around Mostar

By joining a tour or hiring a car you could visit Blagaj, Počitelj, Međugorje and the Kravice waterfalls all in one busy day.

BLAGAJ
☑036 / POP 4000

The signature sight in pretty Blagaj village is the half-timbered **Tekija** (Dervish House; www.fidantours.ba/tekke; ⊙8am-10pm summer, 8am-7pm winter) standing beside the surreally blue-green Buna River where it gushes out

of a cliff cave. Upstairs the Tekija's wobbly wooden interior entombs two 15th-century Tajik dervishes and attracts pious pilgrims. The best views are from across the river on a footpath leading behind the attractive riverside **Vrelo Restaurant** (☑572556; mains 8-27KM; ⊙9am-10pm).

Walking to the Tekija takes 10 minutes from the seasonal **tourist information booth** (⊙variable, closed Oct-Mar). En route you'll pass the **Ottoman Villa** (☑061 273459; www.velagomed.ba; Velagicevina bb; admission 2KM; ⊙10am-7pm, closed mid-Oct–Apr), an 18th-century Ottoman homestead with a unique set of island mill-meadow gardens. Out of hours the house's traditionally furnished little lounge transforms into the 'Oriental Nights' homestay room (€20 per person), by far the best of four guest rooms that share a single bathroom. There's a 'hanging garden' eating area outside and the French-speaking owner plans 'fair trade' tours. Alternatively, for accommodation try the friendly **Kayan Pansion** (☑061 241136, 572299; nevresakajan@yahoo.com; per person €10; ❋), offering 11 beds in seven interconnected rooms above an ultra-friendly family home with sizeable gym. It's unmarked, set back across a side road from the octagonal 1892 **Sultan Sulejman Mosque**.

Mostar Bus (www.mostarbus.ba/linije.asp) routes 10, 11 and 12 from Mostar all run to (or very near) Blagaj (2.10KM, 30 minutes), with 16 services on weekdays but only a handful at weekends (last return 8pm).

MEĐUGORJE
☑036 / POP 4300

On 24 June 1981 a vision appeared to six local teenagers in Međugorje (www.medjugorje.hr). What they believe they saw was a manifestation of the Holy Virgin. As a result, this formerly poor wine-making backwater has been utterly transformed into a bustling Catholic pilgrimage centre and continues to grow even though Rome has not officially acknowledged the visions' legitimacy. Today Međugorje has a blend of honest faith and cash-in tackiness that is reminiscent of Lourdes (France) or Fatima (Portugal) but there's little of beauty here and nonpilgrims generally find a one-hour visit ample to get the idea. The town's focus is double-towered 1969 **St James' Church** (Župna Crkva). In a garden 200m behind that, the mesmerising **Resurrected Saviour** (Uskrsli Spasitej) is a masterpiece of contemporary sculpture showing a 5m-tall metallic

Christ standing crucified yet cross-less, his manhood wrapped in scripture. At times the statue's right knee 'miraculously' weeps a colourless liquid that pilgrims queue to dab onto specially inscribed pads.

A 3km (5KM) taxi ride away at **Podbrdo** village, streams of the faithful climb **Brdo Ukazanja** (Apparition Hill) on red-earth paths studded with sharp stones. They're headed for a white statue of the Virgin Mary marking the site of the original 1981 visions. If you're fit you could nip up and back in 20 minutes but pilgrims spend an hour or more contemplating and praying at way stations, a few walking barefoot in deliberately painful acts of penitence.

For satelite mapped points of interest see www.medjugorjemap.com

POČITELJ
[📖]036 / POP 350

The stepped Ottoman-era fortress village of Počitelj is one of the most picture-perfect architectural ensembles in BiH. Cupped in a steep rocky amphitheatre, it's a warren of stairways climbing between ramshackle stone-roofed houses and pomegranate bushes. The large 1563 **Hadži Alijna Mosque** has been fully restored since the 1990s' destructions while the 16m **clock tower** (Sahat Kula) remains bell-less as it has been since 1917. The most iconic building is the climbable octagonal **Gavrakapetan Tower** in the still part-ruined **Utvrda** (Fort). But for even better panoramas climb to the uppermost rampart bastions. Breathtaking!

Accommodation is limited. Two new pine-walled **apartments** (d/tr €40/60; ❄) need to be pre-booked through English-speaking **Mediha Oruč** ([☎]062 481844), generally summer only. Year-round, simple **homestay rooms** ([☎]062 230023, 826468; per person €10) are rented by Razira Kajtaz who is often to be found hawking souvenirs at the gate-tower at the entrace to the Old Town. Three cafe-restaurants serve drinks and limited grill-meals.

Počitelj is right beside the main Split–Mostar road, 4km north of Čapljina. Mostar–Split, Mostar–Čapljina and some Mostar–Stolac buses pass by. By car, try to arrive an hour before sunset for perfect light and fewer Croatian tour groups.

KRAVICE WATERFALLS

In spring this stunning mini-Niagara of 25m **cascades** pounds itself into a dramatic, steamy fury. In summer the falls themselves are less impressive but surrounding pools become shallow enough for swimming. The site is 15 minutes' walk from a car park that's 4km down a dead-end road turning off the M6 (Čapljina–Ljubuški road). Turn at km42.5. There's no public transport.

Stolac
[📖]036 / POP 12,000

The attractive castle town of Stolac was the site of Roman Diluntum (3rd century AD) and became a prominent citadel from the 15th century. Stolac suffered serious conflict in 1993. The displaced population has long since returned and the town's greatest historical buildings have been painstakingly reconstructed. However, Stolac still hasn't fully recovered, war damage remains painfully evident and the only hotel has closed.

At the central junction, the large, mural-fronted 1519 **Čaršija Mosque** has been splendidly rebuilt. Following the Brevaga River upstream for 900m from here you'll pass the cute cubic **Ćuprija Mosque**, little stone-arched **Inat Ćuprija** (bridge) and three picturesque, if derelict, 17th-century stone **mill-races** before reaching unpretentious **Nota** (Kukovac bb; coffee/beer 1/2KM, pizza 4-7KM; ⏲8am-11pm) cafe-pizzeria. It's unmarked but obvious with a terrace on stilts above the lip of a clogged horseshoe of waterfall.

Downstream from Čaršija Mosque, the tree-lined main street (Hrvatske-Brante, aka Ada) passes a diagonal switchback track that leads up to the hefty **castle ruins**. Around 300m further along Hrvatske-Brante is another group of historic buildings, some rebuilt. Across the bridges, views of the castle

WINE DIVINE

Hercegovina's home-grown wines are a revelation. Local *živalka* grapes yield dry yet fruit-filled whites while suitably aged *blatina* and *vranac* reds can be velvety and complex. In restaurants, ordering *domaći* ('house') wine by the carafe (ie 'open') costs from just 15KM per litre. That's far less than by the bottle and ensures that you're drinking a really local drop. It's possible to visit a selection of rural wineries (see www.wineroute.ba) but it often pays to phone ahead.

site are most memorable from near the Auro petrol station, 50m south of the graffiti-covered bus station.

Beside the Mostar road 3km west of Stolac is **Radimlja Necropolis** (admission free). At first glimpse it looks like a quarryman's yard. But on closer inspection the group of around 110 blocks prove to include some of Bosnia's most important *stećci* (carved grave-markers). Entry is free if you ignore the book-bearing beggar.

Buses run Mostar–Stolac (6KM) approximately hourly. There's no Stolac–Trebinje bus whatsoever but you might persuade locals to act as taxi and take you to Ljubinje (20km, 40KM), from where a 4.15pm minibus runs daily to Trebinje (8KM, one hour). The Stolac–Ljubinje road crosses a former wartime no-man's-land passing the still bombed-out hilltop hamlet of Žegulja at km33.2.

EASTERN BOSNIA & HERCEGOVINA

To get quickly yet relatively easily off the main tourist trail, try linking Sarajevo or Mostar to Dubrovnik via Trebinje, or head to Belgrade via Višegrad. Both journeys take you through the semi-autonomous Republika Srpska.

Trebinje

📞059 / POP 36,000

It's just 28km from Dubrovnik (28km), but in tourist terms a whole world away. Trebinje's small, walled **Old Town** (Stari Grad) is attractive but very much 'lived in', its unpretentious cafes offering a fascinating opportunity to meet friendly local residents and hear Serb viewpoints on divisive recent history. The Old Town ramparts back onto the riverside near a 19th-century former Austro-Hungarian barracks which now houses the **Hercegovina Museum** (www.muzejhercegovine.org; Stari Grad 59; admission 2KM; ☺8am-2pm Mon-Fri, 10am-2pm Sat).

Trebinje's 1574 **Arslanagić Bridge** (Perovića Most), 700m northeast of Hotel Leotar, is a unique double-backed structure but it's sadly let down by the unexotic suburban location to which it was moved in the 1970s.

For phenomenal views, take the 2km winding lane leading east behind the hospital to hilltop Hercegovacka Gracanica. The compact but eye-catching **Presvete Bogorodice Church** (Hercegovačka Gračanica) was erected here in 2000 to re-house the bones of local hero Jovan Dučić. Its design is based on the 1321 Gračanica monastery in Kosovo, a building that's symbolically sacred to many Serbs. The brand new **Arhangel Mihailo Church** on a second hilltop across town provides a certain sense of urban symmetry.

Siniša Kunić (📞065 645224; www.walkwith-me.ba) offers small-group forest, hiking and pilgrimage trips.

🛏 Sleeping & Eating

Trebinje has half a dozen hotels including three motels across the river near the hospital. Within the Old Town, pizza windows sell slices for 1.50KM and there are many local-oriented cafe-bars including two at the river bank hidden behind the museum.

TOP CHOICE **Hotel Platani**   BOUTIQUE HOTEL €€
(http://hotel-platani-trebinje.com; Trg Svobode; s/d/tr Platani-1 63/85/100KM, Platani-2 72/104/128KM; ❇🛜) The Platani's two stone buildings both have distinctly Gallic-looking glass/wrought-iron overhangs and overlook the prettiest central square, shaded with chestnut and plane trees. Platini-1 is perfectly adequate but choose Platini-2 for its stylish contemporary rooms with virginal white sheets and Klimt-esque art. Some back rooms suffer road noise but it's fabulous value for money. So too is the excellent terrace restaurant where you can sip generous glasses of velvety Tvrdoš Vranac red wine for just 4KM.

TOP CHOICE **Vinoteka Vukoje 1982** WINE & CUISINE €€
(📞270370; www.podrum-vukoje.com; Mirna 28; mains 8-20KM; 🅿) Come for the free wine tasting (including Vukuje's irresistible Vranac Reserve) then stay for their imaginative cuisine employing a range of local herbs and meats. The two stylishly appointed new dining rooms have pale decor and sepia photos of the vineyards. From Hotel Platani it's 1.2km towards Bileća, 200m beyond the Niščić turn.

ℹ Information

Tourist Office (📞273410; www.trebinjeturizam.com; Jovan Dučića bb; ☺8am-8pm Mon-Fri, 8am-3pm Sat May-Oct, 8am-4pm Mon-Fri, 9am-2pm Sat Nov-Apr) Diagonally opposite Hotel Platani-1 near the Old Town's western gate.

ℹ Getting There & Away

The **bus station** (Autobusko Stajalište; Vojvode Stepe Stepanovića) is simply a shelter within a parking area, 200m west of the old town.

BUSES FROM TREBINJE

There are no buses to Stolac.

DESTINATION	PRICE (KM)	DURATION	FREQUENCY
Belgrade (Serbia) via Višegrad	52	11 hr	8am, 9.45pm
Dubrovnik (Croatia)	10	45min	10am Mon-Sat (returns at 1.30pm)
Foča	16	2½hr	take Belgrade, Novi Sad, Pale or Sarajevo buses
Ljubinje	8	1hr	3.05pm Mon-Fri, 7pm daily
Mostar via Nevesinje	24	3hr	6.15am, 10am, 2.30pm
Novi Sad	53	12hr	5.30pm
Pale	28.50	4½hr	5am
Podgorica via Nikšić	33	3½hr	8.30am, 3pm, 4.30pm
Sarajevo	26	4hr	5am, 7.30am, 11am

Trebinje To Višegrad

Trebinje–Belgrade and Trebinje–Sarajevo buses pass through the glorious **Sutjeska National Park** (www.npsutjeska.srbinje.net). Magnificent tree-dappled grey rock crags flank the Sutjeska canyon like scenes from classical Chinese paintings. A few kilometres further north the canyon opens out near an impressively vast concrete **Partizans' Memorial** commemorating the classic WWII battle of Tjentište. Mountaineers and hikers can explore more of the national park's scenic wonders with extreme-sports outfit **Encijan** (☑058-211150, 058-211220; www.pkencijan.com; Kraljapetra-I 1; ◷9am-5pm Mon-Sat), based in Foča (25km further north). Encijan also organises world-class rafting on the Tara River that cascades out of Europe's deepest canyon (across the Montenegrin border) then thunders over 21 rapids (class III to class IV in summer, class IV to class V in April).

Višegrad

☑058 / POP 20,000

A convenient stop between Sarajevo and Belgrade, Višegrad's main attraction is its 10-arch **Mehmet Paša Sokolović Bridge**. Built in 1571 it was immortalised in Ivo Andrić's Nobel Prize–winning classic *Bridge on the Drina*. To build on the connection, Višegrad is constructing **Andrićgrad** (www.andricgrad.com), a stone-walled mini 'old'

town that's due to open in 2014 as a historical fantasy cum cultural museum. Višegrad is otherwise architecturally unexciting but it's set between a series of impressive river canyons. On summer weekends there are usually **boat trips** (Sonja; ☑065-142742; per person incl lunch from 30KM) to explore them. Check booking details with the helpful **tourist office** (☑620950; www.visegradturizam.com; ul Kozachka; ◷8am-4pm Mon-Fri, 8am-3pm Sat) near the southern end of the old bridge. Their website has a town map.

A recently reconstructed narrow-gauge railway runs from Višegrad's decrepit station to Mokra Gora (Serbia), linking up with the popular Šargan 8 tourist train. In 2012 the service departed Višegrad weekends only at 3pm (adult/child 800/400 Serbian Dinars) but frequency should increase. The train makes a sightseeing stop at the historic, if almost totally reconstructed, **Dobrun Monastery** (km11.5, Višegrad–Belgrade road), a resonant site for Serbs as Karađorđe hid here immediately before launching the 1804 Serb uprising.

🛏 Sleeping & Eating

Hotel Višegrad   HOTEL **€€**
(☑620710; www.hotel.visegrad24.info; Trg Palih Boraca; s/d/tr 49/83/123KM; ◷7am-11pm; ☏) The facade is sickly yellow concrete, showers are feeble and decor's hardly stylish but friendly receptionists manage some English and the location is perfect, right at the riverside at the end of the historic bridge. The blandly

BUSES FROM VIŠEGRAD

DESTINATION	DEPARTURE POINT	PRICE (KM)	DURATION	FREQUENCY
Banja Luka	Hotel Višegrad	46	9hr	8am via Sarajevo
Belgrade (Serbia)	Hotel Višegrad	27	5½hr	5.15am
Belgrade (Serbia)	North side	27	5½hr	3.15am, 9.50am, 1.30pm
Foča	Hotel Višegrad	10	80min	7.15am, 9.30am
Mostar	North side	32	6hr	3.10am
Niš	North side	30	7hr	11.15am & alternate days 9.10pm
Sarajevo Lukavic	North side	19	3hr	12.45pm
Trebinje	North side	29	5hr	Overnight at 11.15pm
Užice	Hotel Višegrad	10	90min	11.30am, 6pm via Dobrun & Mokra Gora

boxlike restaurant (mains 6KM to 14KM) pumps out loud Europop, but its terrace frames bridge views between willow, pine and plane trees. And the inexpensive local fare is surprisingly well cooked. Wi-fi in restaurant only.

❶ Getting There & Away

Buses depart from outside the Hotel Višegrad as well as the north side of the old bridge and/or at Motel Okuka (1km northeast of the centre).

CENTRAL & WESTERN BOSNIA

West of Sarajevo lies a series of mildly interesting historic towns, green wooded hills, river canyons and rocky crags. The area offers ample opportunities for exploration and adrenaline-rush activities.

Visoko

📱 032 / POP 17,000

Once the capital of medieval Bosnia and the spiritual centre of the controversial Bosnian Church, this unremarkable leather-tanning town had been largely forgotten during the 20th century. Then Bosnian archaeologist Semir Osmanagic hatched a bold theory that Visoko's 250m-high Visočica Hill is in fact the **World's Greatest Pyramid** (Piramida Sunca; www.piramidasunca.ba), built approximately 12,000 years ago by a long-disappeared superculture.

The mainly forested 'Sun Pyramid' does indeed have a seemingly perfect pyramidal shape when viewed from some angles (despite a long ridge at the back) and plates of bafflingly hard ancient 'concrete' found here are cited as having once covered the hill, creating an artificially smoothed surface. Visits to the archaeological excavations (without/with guide 3/5KM) start with a stiff 20-minute climb from a car park and info point-ticket booth near Bistro Vidikovac. To get there from Visoko bus station takes around 15 minutes' walk starting by crossing the river towards the Motel Piramida-Sunca. However, imediately across the bridge turn left down Visoko's patchily attractive main street, Alije Izetbegovića, at the start of which is an **information office** (Alije Izetbegovića 53; ⊘8am-4pm Mon-Fri). Renamed Čaršijska, the street then curves to point directly towards the pyramid summit. After the bazaar veer left into Tvrtka/Mule Hodžić then turn right up the narrow asphalt lane directly beyond the church to find Bistro Vidikovac.

Other nearby hills are mooted to be lesser pyramids and archaeologists are busily investigating prehistoric subterranean labyrinths, notably the **Tunnel Ravne** (📱062 730299; admission 5KM; ⊘call ahead), of which more is excavated every year. Guided hardhat tours leave fairly regularly from an information booth outside (open 9am to 7pm) but you might have to wait a while. To find the site head 2km towards Kakanj from the Motel Piramida-Sunce. Turn left after the

Bingo Hypermarket and climb 500m up a tiny asphalt lane.

Young people come from across Europe to volunteer with the pyramids project and to soak up what many of them consider to be a potently spiritual earth energy that the valley exudes.

ⓘ Getting There & Away

Visoko is a stop for buses between Sarajevo (6.30KM, 50 minutes) and Kakanj (5KM, 35 minutes) running 18 times daily (seven times Sundays), last return to Sarajevo at 9.20pm. For Travnik and Jajce, direct buses depart Visoko at 8.10am, 9.50am, 2.10pm and 4.10pm or change in Zenica (14 buses on weekdays).

Travnik

☑030 / POP 27,500

Once the seat of Bosnia's Turkish viziers (Ottoman governors), Travnik is now best known for its sheep cheese – and as the birthplace of Nobel prize–winning author Ivo Andrić, who set his classic *Bosnian Chronicle* here. It's a pleasant place to spend a couple of hours when travelling between Sarajevo and Jajce.

For a basic walking tour exit the bus station to the south (down steps), cross a partly tree-shaded car park and turn left along Bosanska, Travnik's patchily interesting main street. You'll pass the distinctive **Sahat Kula** stone clocktower and 19th-century **Haji Alibey Mosque** before reaching the dreary Yugoslav-area **Hotel Lipa** (☑511604; Lažajeva 116/Bosanska 91; s/d/tr 52/84/111KM) in front of which the **Viziers' Turbe** is a pair of dome-sheltered collectons of Ottoman-era tombstones. At Bosanska's eastern end is Travnik's celebrated **Many Coloured Mosque** (Šasend Džamija; Bosanska 203) first built in 1757. Its fa-

mous murals have faded but it retains a little *bezistan* (mini-bazaar) built into the arches beneath its main prayer house.

Behind the mosque, take the pedestrian underpass beneath the M5 highway and follow Varoš steeply uphill to **Stari Grad** (☑518140; adult/student 2/1.50KM; ⊙8am-8pm Apr-Oct, by appointment Nov-Mar), Travnik's medieval grey-stone castle. Behind its extensively restored ramparts the multi-sided keep houses a modest museum of local history and costumes. Returning from the fortress, turn left on Musala beside the R&M store (Varoš 42) and immediately left again down the Hendek stairway. You'll emerge on Šumeća near Motel Aba. Turn left here to find Plava Voda (p106), a gaggle of restaurants flanking a merrily gurgling stream, criss-crossed by small bridges. Tucked behind here is the Moorish-styled **Elči-Ibrahimpaša Madrassa**.

🍴 Sleeping & Eating

Central hotels suffer from road rumble as do half a dozen other motels strung 10km along the eastbound M5. Travnik's better (but mostly winter-only) hotels are 27km northwest in the three-lift ski-resort of **Vlašić** (www.babanovac.net) above Babanovac village.

Motel Aba HOTEL €
(☑511462; www.aba.ba; Šumeća 166a; s 35-40KM, d/tr/q 50/70/80KM; �) Handily near to Plava Voda, Aba provides highly acceptable, unfussy en suite rooms at unbelievably reasonable prices. The stairs and road noise are minor niggles, wi-fi works well and there's limited free parking. Breakfast costs 10KM extra.

Blanca RESORT & SPA €€€
(☑519900; www.blancaresort.com; s €52-165, d €74-242, tr €132-273; ❉) If you don't mind driving

---

ANDRIĆ'S TRAVNIK

Readers who enjoyed *Bosnian Chronicle* can add several Andrić-related sites to their Travnik explorations. All are on or near Bosanska. An alien-eyed bust of the author sits in the churchyard of the **Sv Ivana Krstitelja Church** (Bosanska 93). The vine-covered old building now containing the banal **Caffe Consul** (Bosanska 135; coffee 1KM; ⊙8am-11pm) was indeed the *Chronicle*'s setting for the consul's house. Between Bosanska 171 and 169 head a short block north to find a traditionally styled Bosnian house designed to look like Andrić's birthplace and now containing a two-room **Andrić Museum** (☑518140; Zenjak 13; adult/student 2/1.50KM; ⊙9.30am-5pm Apr-Oct, 8am-4pm Mon-Fri, 10am-2pm Sat & Sun Nov-Mar). And across the stream from the Konoba Plava Voda (p106), is a moorish-styled cafe now called **Lutvina Kahva** (Plava Voda; ćevapi 2.50-9KM, mains 9-11KM; ⊙7am-10pm) that also featured in the book.

BUSES FROM TRAVNIK

DESTINATION	PRICE (KM)	DURATION	FREQUENCY
Babanovac	4	45min	10am, 3.10pm
Bihać	35.20	6hr	9.30am, 3.30pm, 4.20pm, 11.30pm
Jajce	8-12.70	1½hr	7.45am, 9.30am, 3pm, 4.20pm, 5.10pm, 5.30pm, 11.30pm
Sarajevo	15.50-17	2hr	6.50am, 8.05am, 9am, 10.40am, 12.15pm 3.40pm, 6.30pm, 7.30pm
Split (Croatia) via Bugojno	23-31	4½hr	6.50am, 8.20am, 11.10am, noon, 5.50pm
Zenica	5-7	1hr	25 daily

to Vlašić, the 2010 Blanca is a luxurious mountain getaway. Right at the base of the ski-jump, this complex uses wooden chalet elements to soften an overall sense of poised designer cool. Guests get free use of four different saunas, the indoor swimming pool has recliner chairs at view windows and unlike virtually every other Vlašić hotel it's open year-round. 'Classic' rooms have no view whatsoever while 'superior' rooms are huge. 'Premium' rooms strike the best balance.

Konoba Plava Voda   BOSNIAN €€
(Šumeće bb; meals 4.50-20KM; ☉7am-10pm; 🔊) This attractive warren of rooms is decked out like an ethnographic museum and has a tempting summer terrace in the attractive Plava Voda springs area. The menu is in English, portions generous and the kitchen stays open relatively late even off season.

Travnički Sir   CHEESE SHOP
(Bosanska 157; ☉8am-6pm Mon-Sat, 8am-3pm Sun) This small shop, overflowing with wooden churns, specialises in Travnik's trademark white cheese.

❶ Getting There & Away

Travnik's **bus station** (📞792761) is off Sehida (the M5 highway) around 500m west of centre. Its ticket office has keys for a left-luggage room (garderob).

Jajce

📞030 / POP 30,000
Above an impressive urban waterfall, Jajce's fortified Old Town climbs a steep rocky knoll to the powerful, ruined castle where Bosnia's medieval kings were once crowned.

The surrounding array of mountains, lakes and canyons make Jajce a potentially useful exploration base.

❖ Sights

Individually, none of old Jajce's attractions are major drawcards but together they make for an interesting two-hour exploration. Add in the surrounding lakes and canyons and you might want to stay for days.

For a quick visit, exit the bus station and walk anticlockwise around the bluff for views of the classic **waterfalls**. Before crossing the footbridge into town, you can visit the **AVNOJ Museum** (admission 2KM; ☉9am-5pm) for five minutes to contemplate a gilded polystyrene statue of Tito in the hall where Yugoslavia's postwar socialist constitution was formulated in 1943. Across the river, past several cafes burrowed into the rock-face and through the city wall via the **Travnik Gate** (Sadije Softića 1; ☉7am-11pm), you'll find Jajce's main shopping street. From the likeable Hotel Stari Grad you can escape the banal 20th-century architecture by climbing Svetog Luke past the new, if limited, **Ethno Museum** (Zavičajna Etno Zbinca; Svetog Luke bb; 1KM; ☉8am-4pm Mon-Fri, 9am-4pm Sat & Sun) and a 15th-century **campanile tower**. Peep into the **Catacombs** (Svetog Luke bb; admission 1KM; ☉9am-7pm May-Oct, 9am-5pm Nov-Apr), a small but imaginatively lit 15th-century crypt whose rough-carved sun-moon-cross centrepiece is a rare surviving memorial to the once independent Bosnian church. Up a stairway-street past the tiny, boxlike **Dizdar Džamija** (Women's Mosque) is the sturdy main **fortress** (adult/child 1/0.50KM; ☉8am-7pm). Inside is mostly bald grass but there are sweeping views from the ramparts.

To return, backtrack to the Dizdar Džamija, turn left along Stari Grad and descend a section of the citadel wall to the **Midway Tower** (Mala Tabija) before retrieving the lane to the Hotel Stari Grad.

Just outside the old city, one block north then west of the conspicuous hypermarket and boxy **Hotel Turist** (✆658151; www.hotel-turist98.com; Kraljice Katerine bb; s/d/tr/q 58/86/109/138KM; ✳) you'll find the **Mithraeum** (Mitrasova 12), a unique 4th-century sculpture featuring a bullfighting Mithras (the pre-Zoroastrian Persian sun god 'rediscovered' by mystical Romans). It's in a glass-sided enclosure at the end of Mitrasova.

The road on the south side of Hotel Turist, just before the bridge, leads west passing the good value Jajce Youth Hostel after 400m. Here guests can rent bicycles (per hour/day 4/10KM) and continue another 4km to the lovely **Pliva Lakes** (Plivsko Jezero) where wooded mountains reflect idyllically in calm, clear waters. Between the two main lakes, a collection of 17 **miniature watermills** form one of Bosnia's most photographed scenes. And 800m beyond, passing the well-organised **Autokamp** (✆647210; campsite per person 8KM; bungalow from s/d 38/56KM; ☉Apr–mid-Oct), you'll find two lakeside hotels including the bargain-priced Plaža Motel at the jetty where pleasure boats are rented in summer.

🛏 Sleeping & Eating

Hotel Stari Grad CENTRAL HOTEL €€
(✆654006; www.jajcetours.com; Svetog Luke 3; s/d 57/84KM, apt 82-154KM; ✳🐾) Although it's not actually old, beams, wood panelling and a heraldic fireplace give this comfortable little hotel a look of suavely modernised antiquity. Beneath the part-glass floor of the appealing lobby-restaurant (mains 10KM to 14KM) are the excavations of an Ottoman-era *hammam* (Turkish bath).

Jajce Youth Hostel HOSTEL €
(✆063 262168; www.jajce-youth-hostel.com; S Tomaševića 11; dm/d/tr 8/20/24KM; P@🐾) Offering some of the cheapest formal accommodation in rural Bosnia, rooms are neater than you'd guess from the slightly unkempt public spaces and all have en suite bathrooms.

Plaža Motel LAKESIDE MOTEL €
(✆647200; www.motel-plaza.com; M5 (Bihać hwy) km91; s/d/tr/q 40/70/99/120KM, pizza 7-11KM, mains 9-14KM) Simple, inexpensive rooms above a large lakeside restaurant whose summer dining terrace serves trout, pizza or *ćevapi* right at the waterfront. Jezero-bound buses pass by.

Banja Luka
✆051 / POP 232,000

Since 1998 Banja Luka has been what's probably Europe's least-known 'capital' (of the Republika Srpska). The city is lively

BUSES FROM JAJCE

DESTINATION	PRICE (KM)	DURATION	FREQUENCY
Banja Luka	8.50-12.80	1½hr	7.30am, 9.30am, 12.50pm, 4.20pm, 5.30pm, 6.50pm
Bihać	19-27.20	3½hr	7.30am, 11.30am, 12.30pm, 5.30pm
Jezero	2	15min	7.30am, 9.15am, 11.30am, 12.30pm, 4.40pm, 6.50pm
Mostar	18-18.50	5hr	1.25pm, 2.20pm
Sarajevo	23.50-27	3½hr	7.10am, 8.50am, 9.10am, 10.25am, 5.25pm, 12.30am
Split (Croatia)	31	4½hr	6am (from Split departs at 12.30pm)
Travnik	8-12.70	1¼hr	Take Zenica or Sarajevo buses
Zagreb (Croatia)	31-38	6½hr	7.30am, 8am, 10am, 11.15am, 12.30pm, 4pm, 6pm, 12.30am
Zenica	13.50-15	2¼hr	8.15am, 8.50am, 1.40pm, 3.15pm

more than lovely but it's a useful transport hub if you're planning rafting, canyoning or other adventure sports in the surrounding countryside. To organise any of the above contact **Guideline** (📞466411; www.guidelinebl.com; Kralja Petra 7; ☉8am-8pm Mon-Fri, 9am-2pm Sat, cafe 8am-10pm daily) whose brand new information centre doubles as a traveller cafe with free internet (not just wi-fi). Alternatively discuss things with the enthusiastic **tourist office** (📞490308; www.banjaluka-tourism.com; Kralja Petra 87; ☉8am-6pm Mon-Fri, 9am-2pm Sat). Both are conveniently found along the city's lengthy main drag, Kralja Petra.

Historic Banja Luka was ravaged by a 1969 earthquake then, late in the civil war, was flooded by Serb refugees from Croatia who dynamited over a dozen historic mosques. The most famous of these, the **Ferhadija Džamija** (Kralja Petra 42), is now being painstakingly reconstructed using traditional masonry techniques. On the riverside directly southeast, enclosing an area parkland, are the two-storey, 16th-century fortress walls of **Kastel Banja Luka**. Summer festivities held here include the famous **Demofest** (www.demofest.org; ☉late July), a play-off competition between up-and-coming raw garage bands.

Otherwise, only two central city blocks offer much architectural appeal. These surround the memorable **Orthodox Cathedral of Christ Saviour** (Saborni Hram Hrista Spasitelja; www.hhsbl.org; Trg Srpskih Vladara 3), rebuilt between 2004 and 2009 using alternate layers of crab-pink and mustard-yellow stone. Its domes are eye-catchingly gilded and its brick belltower looks like a Moroccan minaret on Viagra.

The Republic Srpska's sizeable 'national' **museum** (www.muzejrs.com; Đure Daničića 1; admission 1KM; ☉8am-7pm Mon-Fri, 10am-2pm Sat & Sun) has a scattering of stuffed birds but mainly walks visitors through the region's history from archaeological digs to horse worship to the horrors of the Ustashi concentration camps of WWII – which is a major culminating focus. Much is in English. The museum is entered from the east side of the large library/theatre building, a block east of the distinctive **1933 Hotel Palas** (Kralja Petra 60).

🛏 Sleeping & Eating

Running parallel to Kralja Petra, there are cheap snack bars in courtyards off Veselina Maslaše and many street cafes on its northern extension, Bana Milosavlevica. Close to the canoe club on Save Kovačevića, some 800m east of Ho(s)tel Hertz, are several characterful yet relatively inexpensive bars with tree-shaded riverside frontage: try **Monnet** (Save Kovačevića 42), **Deda Luka** (Save Kovačevića 32; beer/pizza from 1.20/3KM; ☉7am-midnight) or **Castra** (Save Kovačevića 46).

Vila Vrbas   BOUTIQUE HOTEL **€€**
(📞433840; Brace Potkonjaka 1; s/d/ste 80/110/130KM; P❄?) Polished, excellent-value guest rooms are available above this relatively upmarket restaurant with a spacious terrace shaded by plane trees. From here there are glimpses of the castle ramparts across the river.

Hotel Talija   BOUTIQUE HOTEL **€€**
(📞327460; www.hoteltalija.com; Srpska 9; s/d/apt standard 123.50/157/147KM, superior 143.50/177/247KM; ❄?) Above a classy pizzeria-cafe, the standard rooms are nothing exceptional but the brand new superior rooms are a whole level above with very elegant coffee-and-

BUSES FROM BANJA LUKA

DESTINATION	PRICE (KM)	DURATION (HR)	FREQUENCY
Belgrade (Serbia)	41.5	5¾-7½	many 5am-5pm plus 9pm & 11.30pm
Bihać	20	3	5.30am, 7.30am, 1pm, 2pm
Jajce	11.50	1½	6.40am, 7.45am, 1pm, 2pm, 4pm
Sarajevo	31	5	6.30am, 7.45am, 2.30pm, 4pm, 5pm, 12.30pm
Zagreb (Croatia)	31	7	3.15am, 6.30am, 8.45am, 9.10am, 11.30am, 4pm, 5.30pm

cream decor. Apartments give it all they've got with lashings of gilt and bold cubist-style artworks. It's 150m east of the cathedral on the road that passes MacTire (www.facebook.com/MacTire.Pub) Irish pub-restaurant.

Hotel Atina BUSINESS HOTEL €€
(☎334800; www.atinahotel.com; Slobodana Kokanovica 5; 92/124/144KM; P❋☎) Smart without undue extravagance; the main features are stylish rectilinear fittings and a helpfully central yet quiet location just east of the castle.

City Smile Hostel HOSTEL €
(☎214187; www.citysmilehostel.com; Skendera Kulenovića 16; dm/d 22/54KM; ☎) A large house turned into a friendly family-style hostel with a kitchen and small sitting area. Though officially on Skendera Kulenovića (the southwestern extension of Kralja Petra), the entrance is on Duška Koščige.

Ho(s)tel Herz HOSTEL €
(☎066 617627; www.hostelherz.com; Milana Rakića 22; dm/d/tr 22/70/100KM) One of several new hostels, this bright, tailor-made place has tight-packed dorms but their four private rooms are hotelstandard en suite affairs. Triples add a fold-out sofa. Breakfast 5KM. It's 300m east of Hotel Atina.

❶ Getting There & Away

AIR The **airport** (☎535210; www.banjaluka-airport.com) is 22km north. The only commercial flight is a stop-off on BH Airlines' thrice-weekly Sarajevo–Zürich run.

BICYCLE Mountain bikes can be rented from **Cycling Shop** (www.cyclingshop-banjaluka.com; Gundulićeva 104; per hr/day 2/15KM), 1.3km northeast of central Banja Luka.

BUS The **main bus** and **train stations** (☎922000; Prote N Kostića 38) are together, 3km north. Access by buses 6, 8 or 10 from near Hotel Palas (opposite the tourist office).

TRAIN Destinations include Zagreb (27KM, 4¼ hours) at 3.49pm and 2.10am and Sarajevo (25KM, five hours) at 1.17pm and 1.49am.

Around Banja Luka

VRBAS CANYONS

Between Jajce and Banja Luka the Vrbas River descends through a series of lakes and gorges that together form one of BiH's foremost adventure-sport playgrounds. At Karanovac, 11km from Banja Luka by bus 8A, **Rafting Centar Kanjon** (☎065 882085;

WORTH A TRIP

CASTLE CAPERS

Dotted between the faceless post-industrial towns of utterly untouristed northeastern Bosnia are several very photogenic medieval castle ruins.

Srebrenik Truly dramatic crag-top setting 6km east of Srebrenik town.

Tešanj Powerful ruins rise above a loveable Old Town square.

Vranduk Small ruins set in BiH's most idyllic castle village, around 10km north of Zenica.

Gradačac Gradačac town centre is dominated by a partly reconstructed castle with a restaurant on top.

Doboj The city is a drab railway junction but the castle hosts costumed festivals and there's a great little cafe-tower.

www.guidelinebl.com; Karanovac; ☉Apr-Oct) is a reliable, well-organised extreme-sports outfit offering guided canyoning (€25 including lunch), quad biking, hiking and especially top-class rafting. Rafting requires groups of at least four people but joining others is usually easy enough at short notice in summer. Some weekends there's a rare opportunity for floodlit night-rafting (with a week's advance reservation). Kanjon is building budget cottage accommodation and with its hypnotic river views, their splendid **Pastir Restaurant** (mains 7.50-15KM, uštipci 5KM) is one of the region's better dining spots.

Another decent stopping point if you're driving by is **Krupa na Vrbasu** (25km from Banja Luka). Set 700m off the main road here is a dainty set of cascades tumbling down between little wooden mill-huts. The tiny car park is overlooked by house-cafe **Krupski Slapovi** (coffee 1KM; ☉8am-10pm).

The Jajce road winds steeply on past two dams. The higher one is overlooked by the stubby rock ruins of what was once **Bočac Citadel**.

Bihać

☎037 / POP 80,000

In central Bihać, a closely clumped **church tower**, **turbe** (tomb) and 16th-century stone **tower-museum** (☎223214; admission 2KM;

WORTH A TRIP

ŽELENKOVAC

Lost in relatively remote forests, the eccentric 'eco-village' of **Želenkovac** (☑030-278649; www.zelenkovac.org; John Lenon Sq; bed per person 10-25KM) is an inspirationally alternative retreat based around a ramshackle former watermill transformed into a gallery-bar-cafe. Half a dozen Tolkeinesque wooden cottages offer rustic accommodation, some with open fireplaces and indoor bathrooms. International voluntary camps meet here, and there's a July artist colony week. Hiking possibilities abound though many visitors simply hang out and strum guitars with like-minded locals. To find Želenkovac turn off the Jajce–Bihać road at Podbrdo's Eco petrol station, head 7km south towards Baraći, then 500m (left) into the forest.

☑call ahead) look very photogenic viewed through the trees across gushing rapids. But that's about all there is to see here apart from nearby **Fethija Mosque**, converted from a rose-windowed medieval church in 1595. Bihać could make a staging post for reaching Croatia's marvellous **Plitvice Lakes** (www.np-plitvicka-jezera.hr) just 30km away (p136). Otherwise visit the **Una National Park information office** (www.nationalpark-una.ba; Bosanska 1; ☻8am-4.30pm Mon-Fri, 11am-3pm Sat, 11am-1pm Sun, closed weekends Nov-Apr) then head for the lovely Una Valley, preferably on a raft!

🛏 Sleeping & Eating

Opal Exclusive　　　RIVERSIDE HOTEL €€
(☑228586, 224182; www.hotelopalexclusive.net; Krupska bb; s/d/apt 89/138/196KM; P❄🕸) Hidden away but only 300m north of the centre, the Opal's spacious rooms vary considerably in attractiveness but the best are appealing with paintings in gilt frames and lovely views over the river rapids. Similar views are shared by the tree-shaded terrace restaurant (mains 7KM to 25KM) and the top-floor fitness room.

Villa Una　　　GUEST HOUSE €€
(☑311393; villa.una@bih.net.ha; Bihaćkih Branilaca 20; s/d/tr 52/74/96KM, superior s/d 62/84KM; ☻7-11am & 6-10pm; P❄🕸) In this very friendly *pansion*, homey standard rooms suffer some road noise but are every bit as comfortable as the rear 'superior' versions. It's very handy for the bus station with a frontage painted to look half-timbered.

❶ Getting There & Away

Disguised as a mini-casino, Bihać's **bus station** (☑311939) is 1km west of the centre, just off Bihaćkih Branilaća towards Sarajevo. Destinations include the following:

Banja Luka (22KM, three hours) Departs 5.30am, 7.30am, 1pm and 3pm via Bosanska Krupa and Otoka Bosanska.

Ostražac (4.50KM, 25 minutes) via **Kostela** (2.50KM, 10 minutes) Use Cazin-bound buses, 10 times daily on weekdays, 8.50am, 11.30am and 3.30pm Saturday, 3.30pm only Sunday.

Plitvice Jezero The 4.45pm Zagreb bus passes Plitvice (8KM). Otherwise change at Grabovac (11KM, 45 minutes).

Sarajevo (46KM, six to seven hours) Departs 12.45am, 7.30am, 2.30pm and 10pm, via Travnik.

Zagreb (25KM, three hours) Departs 4.45am, 10.20am, 2pm and 4.45pm.

Around Bihać

UNA RIVER VALLEY

The adorable Una River goes through varying moods. In the lush green gorges northwest of Bihać, some sections are as calm as mirrored opal while others gush over widely fanned rapids. There are lovely **watermill restaurants** at Bosanska Krupa and near Otoka Bosanska. And up 4km of hairpins above the valley, spookily Gothic **Ostrožac Fortress** (☑061 236641; www.ostrozac.com) is the most inspiring of several castle ruins.

Southwest of Bihać there's a complex of cascades at **Martin Brod** while the river's single most dramatic falls are at glorious **Štrbački Buk** (5KM; ☻8am-7pm May-Oct), which forms the centrepiece of the new **Una National Park** (www.nationalpark-una.ba). The easiest access is 8km along a good, largely flat unpaved lane from Orašac on the Kulen Vakuf road via National Park Gate 3. In dry conditions you can alternatively start from Gate 1 (Gorevac, 200m off the Bihać–Sarajevo road, 16km from Bihać) but that route uses 14km of woodland lanes that are rolling, very narrow and somewhat rocky (keep right then left at the only two turns en route).

The festive **Una Regatta** in late July sees hundreds of kayaks and rafts following a three-day course from Kulen-Vakuf to Bosanska Krupa via Bihać.

🏃 Activities

Various companies offer rafting (€25 to €55, six-person minimum), kayaking and a range of adventure sports. Each has its own campsite and provides transfers from Bihać since all are rurally based. Choices include the following:

Una Kiro Rafting RAFTING
(☎037-361110; www.una-kiro-rafting.com) A big multisport outfit with extensive if over-manicured facilities at the southeast edge of greater Bihać.

Bjeli Una Rafting RAFTING
(☎061 138853, 037-380222; www.una-rafting.ba; Klokot) At Klokot west of Bihać.

Una-Aqua RAFTING
(☎061 604313; www.una-aqua.com; Račić) Across the river from Neron at Račić.

🛏 Sleeping & Eating

TOP CHOICE **Kostelski Buk** RIVERSIDE HOTEL €€
(☎037-302340; www.kostelski-buk.com; M14, Kostela; s/d €40/59, superior €44/70.50; P❄🐾) The Louis XVI chairs and leather-padded doors might be a little glitzy for some tastes but rooms are superbly equipped, amply sized and come with luxurious mattresses worthy of a five-star hotel. Superior rooms have river views surveying a set of waterfall rapids. The view is shared by the terrace seating of the very reliable lower restaurant (mains 8KM to 30KM) whose excellent seafood platters (40KM for two people) wash down well with the Hercegovinian Riesling (per litre 20KM). It's 9km from Bihać towards Banja Luka.

Neron Touristički Centar RIVERSIDE ROOMS €
(☎061 142585; www.neronraft.com; Lohovo; per person without/with private bathroom 25/30KM; ☺May-Sep) Perched by the river at Lohovo where the Una's most testing rafting route ends (13km from Bihać, 5km southeast of Ripac), this museum-like cottage-restaurant (mains 7KM to 18KM)) and hotel is one of the most characterful dining/sleeping options on the Una. The three best rooms sleep three and come with kitchenette and views of the rapids.

Motel Estrada FAMILY HOTEL €
(☎070-218933; Ostrožac; per person 20KM) Homestay-style en suite rooms in the fifth unmarked house on the left up the Pročići road; 300m southwest of Ostrožac castle.

UNDERSTAND BOSNIA & HERCEGOVINA

Bosnia & Hercegovina Today

Under EU and American pressure BiH has centralised considerably over the last decade in a movement away from the original Dayton 'separate powers' concept. BiH now has a unified army, common passports and a single currency though there remain three separate postal systems. Many, but by no means all, refugees have returned and rebuilt their prewar homes. Politicians running the RS are less radically nationalist these days though during the October 2012 elections the spectre of eventual RS independence was publically raised. Meanwhile in the Federation, the relative complexity of the canton system has proved unwieldy leading to funding log-jams, most notably for the National Gallery and National Museum. While deep post-conflict scars remain, today economics, job security and corruption are the greatest concern for most Bosnians. Non-payment of wages is a growing worry for those working in the 'grey' private economy while getting certain decent government jobs is rumoured to cost applicants a hefty bribe. When reports suggested that political parties were paying 50KM for votes in the 2012 election, one harried working mother told us 'I wish they'd asked me! I'd have taken 40KM'.

History

Be aware that much of BiH's history remains highly controversial and is seen very differently according to one's ethno-religious viewpoint.

In AD 9 ancient Illyrian Bosnia was conquered by the Romans. Slavs arrived from the late 6th century and were dominant by 1180, when Bosnia first emerged as an independent entity under former Byzantine governor Ban Kulina. BiH had a patchy golden age between 1180 and 1463, peaking in the

Entities of BiH

Republika Srpska (Serbs)

Federation of Bosnia & Hercegovina (Muslims & Croats)

late 1370s when Bosnia's King Tvtko gained Hum (future Hercegovina) and controlled much of Dalmatia.

Blurring the borderline between Europe's Catholic west and Orthodox east, medieval Bosnia had its own independent church. This remains the source of many historical myths, but the long-popular idea that it was 'infected' by the Bulgarian Bogomil heresy is now largely discounted.

Turkish Ascendancy

Turkish raids whittled away at the country throughout the 15th century and by the 1460s most of Bosnia was under Ottoman control. Within a few generations, easy-going Sufi-inspired Islam became dominant among townspeople and landowners, many Bosnians converting as much to gain civil privileges as for spiritual enlightenment. However, a sizeable proportion of the serfs *(rayah)* remained Christian. Bosnians also became particularly prized soldiers in the Ottoman army, many rising eventually to high rank within the imperial court. The early Ottoman era also produced great advances in infrastructure, with fine mosques and bridges built by charitable bequests. Later, however, the Ottomans failed to follow the West's industrial revolution. By the 19th century the empire's economy was archaic, and all attempts to modernise the feudal system in BiH were strenuously resisted by the entrenched Bosnian-Muslim elite. In 1873 İstanbul's banking system collapsed under the weight of the high-living sultan's debts. To pay these debts the sultan demanded added taxes. But in 1874 BiH's harvests failed, so paying those taxes would have meant starving. With nothing left to lose the mostly Christian Bosnian peasants revolted, leading eventually to a messy tangle of pan-Balkan wars.

Austro-Hungarian Rule

These wars ended with the farcical 1878 Congress of Berlin, at which the Western powers carved up the western Ottoman lands. Austria-Hungary was 'invited' to occupy BiH, which was treated like a colony even though it theoretically remained under Ottoman sovereignty. An unprecedented period of development followed. Roads, railways and bridges were built. Coal mining and forestry became booming industries. Education encouraged a new generation of Bosnians to look towards Vienna. But new nationalist feelings were simmering: Bosnian Catholics increasingly identified with neighbouring Croatia (itself within Austria-Hungary) while Orthodox Bosnians sympathised with recently independent Serbia's dreams of a greater Serbian homeland. In between lay Bosnia's Muslims (40%), who belatedly started to develop a distinct Bosniak consciousness.

While Turkey was busy with the 1908 Young Turk revolution Austria-Hungary annexed BiH, undermining the aspirations of those who had dreamed of a pan-Slavic or greater Serbian future. The resultant scramble for the last remainders of Ottoman Europe kicked off the Balkan Wars of 1912 and 1913. No sooner had these been (unsatisfactorily) resolved than the heir to the Austrian throne was shot dead while visiting Sarajevo. One month later Austria declared war on Serbia and WWI swiftly followed.

BiH in Yugoslavia

WWI killed an astonishing 15% of the Bosnian population. It also brought down both the Turkish and Austro-Hungarian empires, leaving BiH to be absorbed into proto-Yugoslavia.

During WWII, BiH was occupied partly by Italy and partly by Germany, then absorbed into the newly created fascist state of Croatia. Croatia's Ustaše decimated Bosnia's Jewish population, and they also persecuted Serbs and Muslims. Meanwhile a pro-Nazi group of Bosnian Muslims committed their own atrocities against Bosnian Serbs while Serb Četniks and Tito's Communist Partizans put up some stalwart resistance to the Germans (as well as fighting each other). The BiH mountains proved ideal territory for Tito's flexible guerrilla army, whose greatest victories are still locally commemorated with vast memorials. In 1943, Tito's antifascist council meeting at Jajce famously formulated a constitution for an inclusive postwar, socialist Yugoslavia. BiH was granted republic status within that Yugoslavia but up until 1971 (when *Muslim* was defined as a Yugoslav 'ethnic group'), Bosniaks were not considered a distinct community and in censuses had to register as Croat, Serb or 'Other/Yugoslav'. Despite considerable mining in the northeast and the boost of the 1984 Sarajevo Winter Olympics, BiH's economy remained relatively underdeveloped.

The 1990s Conflict

In the post-Tito era, as Yugoslavia imploded, religio-linguistic (often dubbed 'ethnic') tensions were ratcheted up by the ultranationalist Serb leader Slobodan Milošević and equally radical Croatian leader Franjo Tuđman. Although these two were at war by spring 1991, they reputedly came up with a de facto agreement in which they planned to divide BiH between breakaway Croatia and rump Yugoslavia.

Under president Alija Izetbegović, BiH declared independence from Yugoslavia on 15 October 1991. Bosnian Serb parliamentarians wanted none of this and withdrew to set up their own government at Pale, 20km east of Sarajevo. BiH was recognised internationally as an independent state on 6 April 1992 but Sarajevo was already under siege both by Serb paramilitaries and by parts of the Yugoslav army (JNA).

Over the next three years a brutal and extraordinarily complex civil war raged. Best known is the campaign of 'ethnic' cleansing in northern and eastern BiH creating 300km 'pure'-Serb Republika Srpska (RS). But locals of each religion will readily admit that 'there were terrible criminals on our side too'. In western Hercegovina the Croat population armed itself with the help of neighbouring Croatia, eventually ejecting Serbs from their villages in a less reported but similarly brutal war.

Perhaps unaware of the secret Tuđman–Milošević understanding, Izetbegović had signed a formal military alliance with Croatia in June 1992. But by early 1993 fighting had broken out between Muslims and Croats, creating another war front. Croats attacked Muslims in Stolac and Mostar, bombarding their historic monuments and blasting Mostar's famous medieval bridge into the river. Muslim troops, including a small foreign *mujahedin* force, desecrated churches and attacked Croat villages, notably around Travnik.

UN Involvement

With atrocities on all sides, the West's reaction was confused and erratic. In August 1992, pictures of concentration-camp and rape-camp victims (mostly Muslim) found in northern Bosnia spurred the UN to create Unprofor, a protection force of 7500 peacekeeping troops. Unprofor secured the neutrality of Sarajevo airport well enough to allow the delivery of humanitarian aid, but overall proved notoriously impotent.

Ethnic cleansing of Muslims from Foča and Višegrad led the UN to declare 'safe zones' around the Muslim-majority towns of Srebrenica, Župa and Goražde. But rarely has the term 'safe' been so misused. When NATO belatedly authorised air strikes to protect these areas, the Serbs responded by capturing 300 Unprofor peacekeepers and chaining them to potential targets to keep the planes away.

WHAT'S IN A NAME?

Geographically Bosnia and Hercegovina (BiH) comprises Bosnia (in the north) and Hercegovina (Her-tse-GO-vina in the south), although the term 'Bosnian' refers to anyone from BiH, not just from Bosnia proper. Politically, BiH is divided into two entirely different entities. Southwest and central BiH falls mostly within the Federation of Bosnia and Hercegovina, usually shortened to 'the Federation'. Meanwhile most areas bordering Serbia, Montenegro and the northern arm of Croatia are within the Serb-dominated Republika Srpska (abbreviated RS). A few minor practicalities (stamps, phonecards) appear in different versions and the Cyrillic alphabet is more prominent in the RS, but these days casual visitors are unlikely to notice much immediately visible difference between the entities.

In July 1995 Dutch peacekeepers watched as the starving, supposedly 'safe' area of Srebrenica fell to a Bosnian Serb force led by the infamous Ratko Mladić. An estimated 8000 Muslim men were slaughtered in Europe's worst mass killings since WWII. Battered Goražde held out thanks to sporadically available UN food supplies. By this stage, Croatia had renewed its own internal offensive, expelling Serbs from the Krajina region of Croatia in August 1995. At least 150,000 of these dispossessed people then moved to the Serb-held areas of northern Bosnia.

Finally, another murderous Serb mortar attack on Sarajevo's main market (Markale) kick-started a shift in UN and NATO politics. An ultimatum to end the Serbs' siege of Sarajevo was made more persuasive through two weeks of NATO air strikes in September 1995. US president Bill Clinton's proposal for a peace conference in Dayton, Ohio, was accepted soon after.

The Dayton Agreement

While maintaining BiH's prewar external boundaries, Dayton divided the country into today's pair of roughly equally sized 'entities', each with limited autonomy. Finalising the border required considerable political and cartographic creativity and was only completed in 1999 when the last sticking point, Brčko, was belatedly given a self-governing status all of its own. Meanwhile BiH's curious rotating tripartite presidency has been kept in check by the EU's powerful High Representative (www.ohr.int).

For refugees (1.2 million abroad, and a million displaced within BiH), the Dayton Agreement emphasised the right to return to (or to sell) their prewar homes. International agencies donated very considerable funding to restore BiH's infrastructure, housing stock and historical monuments.

BOOKS

Bosnia: A Short History by Noel Malcolm is a very readable introduction to the complexities of Bosnian history. In *Not My Turn To Die,* by Savo Heleta, the memoirs of a besieged family at Goražde give insights into the strange mixture of terror, boredom and resignation of the 1990s conflict.

BuyBook (www.buybook.ba) produces several regional guidebooks.

People

Bosniaks (Bosnian Muslims, 48% of the population), Bosnian Serbs (Orthodox Christians, 37%) and Bosnian Croats (Catholics, 14%) differ by religion but are all Southern Slavs. Physically they are indistinguishable so the term 'ethnic cleansing', applied so often during the war, should more accurately have been called 'religio-linguistic forced expulsions'. The prewar population was mixed, with intermarriage common in the cities. Stronger divisions have inevitably appeared since the civil war of the 1990s which resulted in massive population shifts, changing the size and linguistic balance of many cities. Bosniaks now predominate in Sarajevo and central BiH, Bosnian Croats in western and southern Hercegovina, and Bosnian Serbs in the RS, which includes Istochno (East) Sarajevo and Banja Luka. Today social contact between members of the three groups remains somewhat limited. Religion is taken seriously as a badge of 'ethnicity' but spiritually most people are fairly secular.

Arts

Crafts

BiH crafts from *kilims* (woollen flat-weaves) to copperware and decoratively repurposed bullet casings are widely sold in Mostar's Kujundžiluk and Sarajevo's Baščaršija.

Stećci (singular *stećak*) are archetypal Bosnian forms of oversized medieval gravestones, best known at Radimlja near Stolac.

Literature

Bosnia's best-known writer, Ivo Andrić (1892–1975), won the 1961 Nobel Prize for Literature. With extraordinary psychological agility, his epic novel, the classic *Bridge on the Drina,* retells 350 years of Bosnian history as seen through the eyes of unsophisticated townsfolk in Višegrad. His *Travnik Chronicles* (aka *Bosnian Chronicle*) is also rich with human insight, portraying Bosnia through the eyes of jaded 19th-century foreign consuls in Travnik.

Many thought-provoking essays, short stories and poems explore the prickly subject of the 1990s conflict, often contrasting horrors against the victims' enduring humanity. Quality varies greatly but recommended collections include Miljenko

and alpine valleys, most famously in the magnificent Sutjeska National Park. In the far northeast the peaks subside into rolling bucolic hills flattening out altogether in the far north.

SURVIVAL GUIDE

Directory A–Z

Accommodation

Except in hostels, quoted room prices assume a private bathroom and breakfast unless otherwise indicated.

High season means June to September generally but late December to early March in ski resorts. In Mostar and Sarajevo summer prices rise 20% to 50% and touts appear at the bus stations. Our price ranges for a double room:

€ less than 80KM/€40

€€ 80KM/€40 to 190KM/€100

€€€ more than 190KM/€100

ACCOMMODATION TYPES

Hostels Usually bunk rooms in a semi-converted private home. Few have reception desks. Essentially Mostar, Sarajevo and Banja Luka only.

Hotels Anything from re-vamped Tito-era concrete monsters to elegantly restored Austro-Hungarian gems via modernist boxes and over-sized *pansions*.

Motels Generally new and suburban and ideal for those with cars. However, occasionally the term simply implies a lower midrange hotel so don't automatically assume there's much parking.

Pansions Anything from a glorified home-stay to a little boutique hotel.

Ski hotels From Christmas to mid-January availability is stretched and prices rise up to 50%. Most close during April to November.

Activities

Skiing Inexpensive yet high quality at Jahorina, Bjelašnica or Vlašić.

Rafting Reaches terrifyingly difficult class V in April/May but is more suitable for beginners in summer. Top spots are around Foča, Bihać and Banja Luka.

LANGUAGE

The people of BiH speak essentially the same language but it's referred to as 'Bosnian' (*bosanski*) in Muslim parts, 'Croatian' (*hrvatski*) in Croat-controlled areas and 'Serbian' (српски) in the RS. The Federation uses the Latin alphabet. The RS uses Cyrillic (ћирилица) but Latin (*latinica*) has wide parallel usage. Brčko uses both alphabets equally.

Key Bosnian phrases: *zdravo* (hello); *hvala* (thanks); *molim* (please), *koliko to košta?* (how much does it cost?).

Jergović's *Sarajevo Marlboro* and Semezdin Mehmedinović's *Sarajevo Blues*.

Movies

The relationship between two soldiers, one Muslim and one Serb, caught alone in the same trench during the Sarajevo siege was the theme for Danis Tanović's Oscar-winning 2002 film *No Man's Land*. The movie *Go West* takes on the deep taboo of homosexuality as a wartime Serb-Bosniak gay couple become a latter-day Romeo and Juliet. *Gori Vatra* (aka *Fuse*) is an irony-packed dark comedy set in the Bosnian castle town of Tešanj just after the war, parodying efforts to hide corruption and create a facade of ethnic reintegration for the sake of a proposed visit by US president Bill Clinton.

Music

Sevdah (traditional Bosnian music) typically uses heart-wrenching vocals to recount tales of unhappy amours, though singing it was once used as a subtle courting technique. Sarajevo has an annual **Jazz festival** (November) and a new October **Punkfest**. The post-industrial salt-mining city of Tuzla has vibrant rap and metal scenes.

Environment

BiH is predominantly mountainous. The mostly arid south (Hercegovina) dips one tiny toe of land into the Adriatic Sea at Neum then rises swiftly into bare limestone uplands carved with deep grey canyons. The central mountain core has some 30 peaks rising between 1700m and 2386m. Further north and east the landscape becomes increasingly forested with waterfalls

Hiking and mountain biking Many upland areas and national parks have mine-safe, marked trails.

Business Hours

Office hours 8am to 4pm Monday to Friday.

Banks 8am to 6pm Monday to Friday, 8.30am to 1.30pm Saturday.

Shops 8am to 6pm daily.

Restaurants 11.30am to 10.30pm, often later in summer. Restaurant closing time depends on customer demand more than fixed schedules.

Embassies & Consulates

You can find a list of foreign embassies and consulates in Sarajevo on http://www.bosnia. org.uk/bosnia/viewtype.cfm?typeID=229.

Food

Average costs for restaurant main courses:

€ less than 10KM

€€ 10KM to 25KM

€€€ more than 25KM

Gay & Lesbian Travellers

Although homosexuality was decriminalised per se in 1998 (2000 in the RS), attitudes remain very conservative. **Association Q** (www.queer.ba) nonetheless attempts to empower the self-reliance of the gay community in BiH. **Gay Romeo** (www.gayromeo.com) chat site reportedly has several hundred Sarajevo members.

Internet Access

Most hotels and some cafes offer free wi-fi.

Money

» ATMs accepting Visa and MasterCard are ubiquitous.

» Bosnia's convertible mark (KM or BAM) is pronounced *kai-em* or *maraka* and divided into 100 fenig. It's tied to the euro at approximately €1=1.96KM. Though no longer officially sanctioned, many businesses still unblinkingly accept euros, for minor purchases using a slightly cutomer-favourable 1:2 rate. Exchanging euros is markedly better than changing other currencies as there's no rate-split.

» Exchanging travellers cheques usually requires the original purchase receipt.

Post

BiH fascinates philatelists by having three parallel postal organisations, each issuing their own stamps: **BH Pošta** (www.posta.ba; Federation), **Pošte Srpske** (www.postesrpske. com; RS) and **HP Post** (www.post.ba; Croat areas, western Mostar).

Public Holidays

NATIONWIDE HOLIDAYS

New Year's Day 1 January

Independence Day 1 March

May Day 1 May

National Statehood Day 25 November

ADDITIONAL HOLIDAYS IN THE FEDERATION

Kurban Bajram (Islamic Feast of Sacrifice)

Ramazanski Bajram (end of Ramadan)

Gregorian Easter March/April

Gregorian Christmas 25 December

ADDITIONAL HOLIDAYS IN THE RS

Orthodox Easter April/May

Orthodox Christmas 6 January

Safe Travel

Landmines and unexploded ordnance still affect 2.8% of BiH's area. There were six mine-deaths in 2010. BHMAC (www.bhmac. org) clears more every year but total clearance isn't envisaged before 2019. Stick to asphalt/concrete surfaces or well-worn paths in affected areas, avoiding war-damaged buildings.

Telephone

Mobile-phone companies BH Mobile (☎061- and ☎062-), HT/EroNet (☎063-) and M-Tel (☎065-) all have virtually nationwide coverage.

Country code ☎+387

International operator ☎1201

Local directory information ☎1188

Travellers with Disabilities

Bosnia's steep townscapes are full of stairways and rough streets that can prove very awkward if you're disabled. A few places have wheelchair ramps in response to all the war wounded, but smaller hotels won't have lifts and disabled toilets remain extremely rare.

Visas

Stays of under 90 days require no visa for citizens of most Europeans countries and Australia, Brunei, Canada, Japan, Malaysia, New Zealand, Singapore, South Korea, Turkey and the USA. Other nationals should see www.mfa.ba for visa details and where to apply: several of those nationalities can get a visa on arrival at Sarajevo airport. You might require a letter of invitation or a tourist-agency voucher. Visitors without 150KM per day's intended stay could technically be refused entry, though checks are very rare.

Getting There & Away

Air

All flights use Sarajevo airport, though BH Airlines Zurich flights stop at Banja Luka. Alternatively consider flying to Dubrovnik, Split or Zagreb (Croatia) and connecting to BiH by bus or train.

The following airlines fly to Bosnia & Hercegovina:

Adria (www.adria.si) Via Ljubljana

Austrian (www.austrian.com) Via Vienna.

BH Airlines (Map p82; ☎768335, 033-550125; www.bhairlines.ba; Branilaca Sarajeva 15; ☺9am-5pm Mon-Fri, 9am-2pm Sat) Pronounced 'Bay-Ha', the national carrier flies a few time weekly from Sarajevo to Copenhagen, İstanbul and Zürich via Banja Luka.

Croatia Airlines (www.croatiaairlines.com) Via Zagreb.

Germanwings (www.germanwings.com) Köln-Bonn.

JAT (www.jat.com) Belgrade.

Lufthansa (www.lufthansa.com) Via Munich.

Norwegian (www.norwegian.no) Twice weekly to Stockholm and Oslo.

Turkish Airlines (www.thy.com) Via İstanbul.

Land
BUS

Buses to Zagreb and/or Split (Croatia) run at least daily from most towns in the Federation and to Serbia and/or Montenegro from many RS towns. Buses to Vienna and Germany run several times weekly from bigger BiH cities.

CAR & MOTORCYCLE

Drivers need Green Card insurance and an EU or International Driving Permit. Transiting Neum in a Croatian hire car is usually hassle-free.

TRAIN

The modest international network links Sarajevo to Belgrade, Zagreb (via Banja Luka), Budapest (via Osijek, Croatia) and to Ploče (coastal Croatia via Mostar).

Getting Around
Bicycle

Cyclists who can handle the hills will find BiH's secondary routes helpfully calm. There are off-road trails for mountain bikers but beware of straying from them in areas where landmines remain a danger.

Bus

Bus stations pre-sell tickets. Between towns it's normally easy enough to wave down any bus en route. Advance reservations are sometimes necessary for overnight routes or at peak holiday times. The biggest company, Centrotrans, has online timetables (click 'Red Vožnje').

Frequency drops drastically at weekends. Some shorter-hop routes stop altogether on Sundays.

Fares are around 7KM per hour travelled. Return tickets are often cheaper than two singles but are limited to one specific company. Expect to pay 2KM extra per stowed bag. Some bus-station ticket offices have a *garderob* for left luggage (from 2KM).

Car & Motorcycle

There's minimal public transport to BiH's most spectacular remote areas so having wheels can really transform your trip. Bosnia's winding roads are lightly trafficked and a delight for driving if you aren't in a hurry. **BIHAMK** (☎033 222210; www.bihamk.ba; Skenderija 23; annual membership 25KM; ☺8am-4.30pm Mon-Fri, 9am-noon Sat) offers road assistance and towing services (call ☎1282 or ☎1288).

HIRE

International chains are represented while smaller local outfits are often based at hotels. Most companies add 17% VAT. A good deal is Hyundai.ba; its standard rates include full insurance, theft protection and CDW. Pick-up/drop-off is possible at Mostar train station, Novo Sarajevo or Sarajevo airport without extra charge for open-jaws. Prices drop October to April.

ROAD RULES

Drive on the right. First-aid kit, warning triangle, reflective vest and spare bulb kits are compulsory.

» The blood-alcohol limit is 0.03%.
» Headlights must be kept on day and night.
» LPG availability is very limited.
» Parking is awkward in Mostar, central Trebinje and Sarajevo, but contrastingly easy elsewhere. In town centres expect to pay 1KM per hour (attendant or meter) when marked *parking naplatu*.
» Petrol is typically around 2% cheaper in RS than Federation.

» Seat belts are compulsory.
» Snow chains are compulsory on some mountain roads (November to April) and wherever snow is over 5cm deep.
» Speed limits vary: 130km/h (Kakanj–Sarajevo motorway), 100km/h (other dual carriageways), 80km/h (rural), 60km/h or less (in town). Absurdly slow limits are often posted with no obvious logic but police spot-checks are common.
» Winter tyres are compulsory mid-November to mid-April.

Train

Trains are slower and less frequent than buses but generally around 30% cheaper. **RS Railways** (www.zrs-rs.com/red_voznje.php) has full, up-to-date rail timetables.

Croatia

Includes »

Zagreb 121
Pula 136
Rovinj 139
Poreč 142
Rijeka 144
Opatija 147
Krk Island 148
Zadar 150
Split 152
Hvar Island 160
Korčula Island 163
Mljet Island 164
Dubrovnik 166
Understand Croatia 172
Survival Guide 177

Why Go?

Croatia has been touted as the 'new this' and the 'new that' for years since its re-emergence on the tourism scene, but it's now clear that it's a unique destination that holds its own and then some: this is a country with a glorious 1778km-long coast and a staggering 1244 islands. The Adriatic coast is a knockout: its sapphire waters draw visitors to remote islands, hidden coves and traditional fishing villages, all while touting the glitzy beach and yacht scene. Istria captivates with its gastronomic delights and wines, and the bars, clubs and festivals of Zagreb, Zadar and Split remain little-explored gems. Eight national parks showcase primeval beauty with their forests, mountains, rivers, lakes and waterfalls. and you can finish up in dazzling Dubrovnik in the south – just the right finale. Best of all, Croatia hasn't given in to mass tourism: there are pockets of unique culture and plenty to discover off the grid.

Best Places to Eat

- » Vinodol (p130)
- » Konoba Batelina (p138)
- » Foša (p151)
- » Bajamonti (p157)

Best Places to Stay

- » Studio Kairos (p129)
- » Goli + Bosi (p156)
- » Art Hotel Kalelarga (p151)
- » Lešić Dimitri Palace (p163)

When to Go
Zagreb

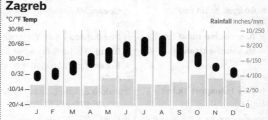

May & Sep Good weather, few tourists, full local events calendar, great for hiking

Jun Best time to visit: good weather, fewer people, lower prices and lots of festivals.

Jul–Aug Lots of sunshine, warm sea and summer festivals; many tourists and highest prices.

CROATIA

AT A GLANCE

» **Currency** Kuna (KN)

» **Language** Croatian

» **Money** ATMs available; credit cards accepted in most hotels and many restaurants

» **Visas** None for up to 90 days; South Africans and some other nationalities need them

Fast Facts

» **Area** 56,538 sq km

» **Capital** Zagreb

» **Country code** ☏385

» **Emergency** Ambulance ☏194, fire ☏193, police ☏192

Exchange Rates

Australia	A$1	6.21KN
Canada	C$1	5.85KN
Euro Zone	€1	7.60KN
Japan	¥100	6.30KN
New Zealand	NZ$1	4.97KN
UK	UK£1	8.99KN
USA	US$1	5.94KN

Set Your Budget

» **Budget hotel room** 450KN

» **Two-course meal** 150KN

» **Museum entrance** 10–40KN

» **Beer** 15KN

» **City transport ticket** 10KN

Resources

» **Adriatica.net** (www.adriatica.net)

» **Croatian National Tourist Board** (www.croatia.hr)

Connections

Croatia is a convenient transport hub for southeastern Europe and the Adriatic. Zagreb is connected by train and/or bus to Venice, Budapest, Belgrade, Ljubljana and Sarajevo in Bosnia and Hercegovina (BiH). Down south there are easy bus connections from Dubrovnik to Mostar and Sarajevo, and to Kotor (Montenegro). There are a number of ferries linking Croatia with Italy, including routes from Dubrovnik to Bari, and Split to Ancona.

ITINERARIES

One Week

After a day in dynamic Zagreb, delving into its simmering nightlife, fine restaurants and choice museums, head down to Split for a day and night at Diocletian's Palace, a living part of this exuberant seafront city. Then hop over to chic Hvar for a spot of partying and swimming off Pakleni Otoci. Next take it easy down the winding coastal road to magnificent Dubrovnik and take a day trip to Mljet for the final two days.

Two Weeks

After two days in Zagreb, head to Istria for a three-day stay, with Rovinj as the base, and day trips to Pula and Poreč. Go southeast next to the World Heritage–listed Plitvice Lakes National Park, a verdant maze of turquoise lakes and cascading waterfalls. After a quick visit, move on to Zadar, a real find of a city: historic, modern, active and packed with attractions. Then go on south to Split for a day or two. From here, take ferries to Hvar and then Korčula, spending a day or more on each island before ending with three days in Dubrovnik and an outing to Mljet.

Essential Food & Drink

» **Ćevapčići** Small spicy sausages of minced beef, lamb or pork.

» **Pljeskavica** An ex-Yugo version of a hamburger.

» **Ražnjići** Small chunks of pork grilled on a skewer.

» **Burek** Pastry stuffed with ground meat, spinach or cheese.

» **Rakija** Strong Croatian brandy comes in different flavours, from plum to honey.

» **Beer** Two top types of Croatian *pivo* (beer) are Zagreb's Ožujsko and Karlovačko from Karlovac.

ZAGREB

☑01 / POP 792,900

Everyone knows about Croatia's coast and islands, but a mention of the country's capital still draws the confused question: 'Is it worth visiting?' Here is the answer: Zagreb is a great destination, with lots of culture, arts, music, architecture, gastronomy and all the other things that make a quality capital.

Visually, Zagreb is a mixture of straight-laced Austro-Hungarian architecture and rough-around-the-edges socialist structures, its character a sometimes uneasy combination of these two elements. This mini metropolis is made for strolling the streets, drinking coffee in the permanently full cafes, popping into museums and galleries, and enjoying the theatres, concerts and cinema. It's a year-round outdoor city: in spring and summer everyone scurries to Jarun Lake in the southwest to swim, boat or dance the night away at lakeside discos, while in autumn and winter Zagrebians go skiing at Mt Medvednica, only a tram ride away, or hiking in nearby Samobor.

History

Zagreb's known history begins in medieval times with two hill settlements: Kaptol, now the site of Zagreb's cathedral, and Gradec. When the two merged in 1850, Zagreb was officially born.

The space now known as Trg Josipa Jelačića became the site of Zagreb's lucrative trade fairs, spurring construction around its edges. In the 19th century the economy expanded and cultural life blossomed with the development of a prosperous clothing trade and a rail link connecting Zagreb with Vienna and Budapest.

Between the two world wars, working-class neighbourhoods emerged in Zagreb between the railway and the Sava River, and new residential quarters were built on the southern slopes of Mt Medvednica. In April 1941, the Germans invaded Yugoslavia and entered Zagreb without resistance. Ante Pavelić and the Ustaše moved quickly to proclaim the establishment of the Independent State of Croatia (Nezavisna Država Hrvatska), with Zagreb as its capital.

In postwar Yugoslavia, Zagreb (to its chagrin) took second place to Belgrade but continued to expand. Zagreb was made the capital of Croatia in 1991, the same year that the country became independent.

◉ Sights

As the oldest part of Zagreb, the Upper Town (Gornji Grad) offers landmark buildings and churches from the earlier centuries of Zagreb's history. The Lower Town (Donji Grad) has the city's most interesting art museums and fine examples of 19th- and 20th-century architecture.

UPPER TOWN

Museum of Broken Relationships   MUSEUM
(http://brokenships.com; Ćirilometodska 2; adult/concession 25/20KN; ⊙9am-10.30pm Jun–mid-Oct, 9am-9pm mid-Oct–May) Explore mementos that remain after a relationship ends at Zagreb's quirkiest museum. On display are donations from around the globe, in a string of all-white rooms with vaulted ceilings. Exhibits hit on a range of emotions, from a can of love incense from Indiana that 'doesn't work' to an iron from Norway once used to straighten a wedding suit. Check out the adjacent store and the cosy cafe with sidewalk tables.

Dolac Market   MARKET
(⊙7am-3pm Mon-Fri, to 2pm Sat, to 1pm Sun) Zagreb's colourful Dolac is just north of Trg Josipa Jelačića. This buzzing centre of Zagreb's daily activity since the 1930s draws in traders from all over Croatia who flog their products here. The main part of the market is on an elevated square; the street level has indoor stalls selling meat and dairy products and, towards the square, flower stands.

**Cathedral of the Assumption
of the Blessed Virgin Mary**   CATHEDRAL
(Katedrala Marijina Uznešenja; Kaptol; ⊙10am-5pm Mon-Sat, 1-5pm Sun) Kaptol Sq is dominated by the twin neo-Gothic spires of this 1899 cathedral, formerly known as St Stephen's. Elements of an earlier medieval cathedral, destroyed by an earthquake in 1880, can be seen inside, including 13th-century frescoes, Renaissance pews, marble altars and a baroque pulpit. Note that you might be turned away if you're not dressed appropriately: no bare legs or shoulders.

Lotrščak Tower   HISTORICAL BUILDING
(Kula Lotrščak; Strossmayerovo Šetalište 9; adult/concession 10/5KN; ⊙9am-9pm) From Radićeva 5, off Trg Jelačića, a pedestrian walkway called Zakmardijeve Stube leads to this medieval tower, which can be climbed for a sweeping 360-degree view of the city.

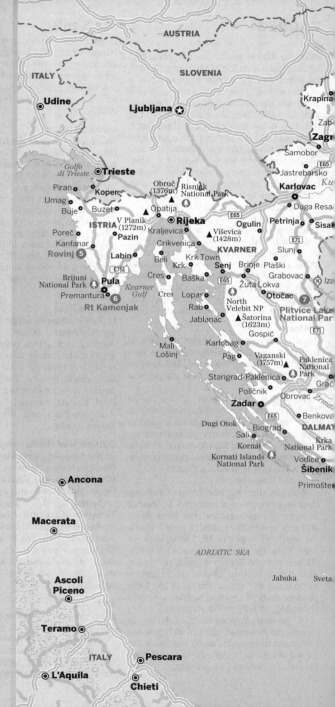

Croatia Highlights

1 Gape at the Old Town wall of **Dubrovnik** (p166), which surrounds luminous marble streets and finely ornamented buildings.

2 Admire the Venetian architecture and vibrant nightlife of **Hvar Town** (p160).

3 Indulge in the lively and historic delights of **Diocletian's Palace** (p152) in Split.

4 Explore the lakes, coves and island monastery of **Mljet** (p164).

5 Stroll the cobbled streets and unspoiled fishing port of **Rovinj** (p139).

6 Take in the wild landscapes of **Rt Kamenjak** (p137) cape near Pula.

7 Marvel at the turquoise lakes and waterfalls in **Plitvice Lakes National Park** (p136).

CROATIA ZAGREB

Zagreb

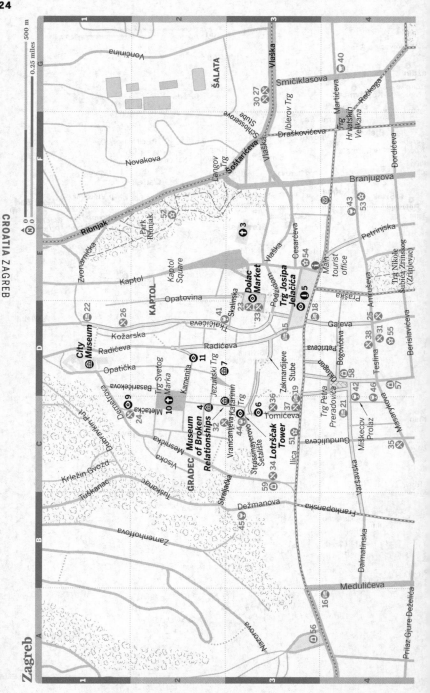

N
0   500 m
0   0.25 miles

Zvonarnička
Novakova
ŠALATA
Vončinina

Ribnjak
Park Ribnjak
52
Kaptol
Kaptol Square
KAPTOL
Opatovina
Skalinska
3
Vlaška
Langov Trg
Šoštarićeva
Schlosserove Stube
Smičiklasova
30 27
Iblerov Trg
Draškovićeva
Vlaška
Trg Martićeva
Trg Hrvatskih Velikana
Rackoga
40
Đorđićeva
Branjugova
Petrinjska
43 53
Cesarčeva
54
Main tourist office
City Museum
22
26
Kožarska
Radićeva
Opatička
Bošaričekova
Demetrova
6
Mletačka
10
24
GRADEC
Museum of Broken Relationships 4
32
Vranicanijeva
Visoka
Mesnička
Trg Svetog Marka
Kamenita
Jezuitski Trg
11
7
Katarinin Trg
44
Dolac Market
41
Trg Josipa Jelačića
23
33
15
18
Podgračka
5
Gajeva
Preradovićeva
Petrićeva
Bogovićeva
38 31
Teslina
25
Amruševa
Praška
Trg Nikole Šubića Zrinskog (Zrinjevac)
55
Benislavićeva
57
58
Ilica
Lotrščak Tower
6
36
37
Tomićeva
Zakmardijeve Stube
19
42
46
35
Dugoson
Trg Petra Preradovića
21
Miškecov Prolaz
Gundulićeva
Masarykova
Strossmayerovo Šetalište
34
Streljačka
59
Ilica
51
Frankopanska
Varšavska
Dežmanova
45
Dalmatinska
Zamenhofova
Tuškanac
Krležin Gvozd
Dubravkin Put
Meduliceva
16
56
Nazorova
Priliz Gjure Deželića
Priljaz Gjure Deželića

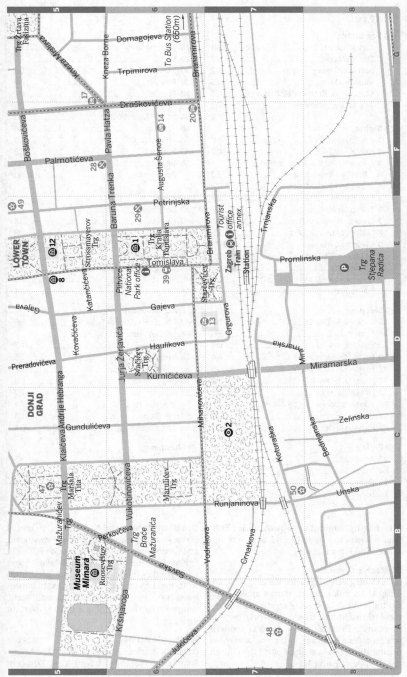

Trg Žrtava Fašizma

Trg Nikole

Kneza Borne

Domagojeva

Trpimirova

To Bus Station (650m)

Branimirova

Draškovićeva

17

Boškovićeva

Pavla Hatza

20

14

Palmotićeva

28

Baruna Trenka

Augusta Šenoe

LOWER TOWN

Strossmayerov Trg

Petrinjska

29

49

12

1

Trg Kralja Tomislava

Branimirova

Tourist office annex

Zagreb Tourist office

Train Station

8

Katančićeva

Plitvice National Park office

Tomislava

39

Promlinska

Gajeva

Gajeva

Starčevićev Trg

Grgurova

Trnjanska

P

Trg Stjepana Radića

Kovačićeva

Haulikova

13

Preradovićeva

Jurja Žerjavića

Svačićev Trg

Kumičićeva

Miramarska

Mitn

Zelinska

DONJI GRAD

Andrije Hebranga

Klaićeva

Gundulićeva

Mihanovićeva

2

Smarska

Koturaška

Bednjanska

47

Trg Maršala Tita

Vukotinovićeva

Marulićev Trg

Runjaninova

50

Unska

Mažuranićev Trg

Perkovčeva

Trg Braće Mažuranića

Vodnikova

Crnatkova

Museum Mimara

Roosevltov Trg

Baušce

Kršnjavoga

Jukićeva

48

Zagreb

◉ Top Sights

City Museum D1
Dolac Market E3
Lotrščak Tower C3
Museum Mimara B5
Museum of Broken Relationships C2
Trg Josipa Jelačića D3

◉ Sights

1 Art Pavilion E6
2 Botanical Garden C7
3 Cathedral of the Assumption of the
    Blessed Virgin Mary E3
4 Croatian Museum of Naïve Art C2
5 Equestrian Statue E3
6 Funicular Railway C3
7 Galerija Klovićevi Dvori D2
8 Gallery of Modern Art E5
9 Meštrović Atelier C1
10 St Mark's Church C2
11 Stone Gate D2
12 Strossmayer Gallery of Old
    Masters E5

◉ Sleeping

13 Esplanade Zagreb Hotel D6
14 Evistas F6
15 Fulir Hostel D3
16 Hobo Bear Hostel A4
17 Hostel Day and Night G5
18 Hotel Dubrovnik D3
19 Hotel Jägerhorn C3
20 Palmers Lodge Hostel Zagreb F6
21 Shappy Hostel C4
22 Taban Hostel D1

◉ Eating

23 Amfora D3
24 Didov San C1
25 Dinara D4
26 Ivica i Marica D1

27 Karijola G3
28 Konoba Čiho F5
29 Lari & Penati E6
30 Mali Bar G3
31 Pingvin D4
32 Prasac C2
33 Rubelj D3
34 Stari Fijaker 900 .... C3
35 Tip Top C4
36 Vallis Aurea C3
37 Vincek C3
38 Vinodol D4
    Zinfandel's .... (see 13)

◉ Drinking

39 Bacchus E6
40 Booksa G4
41 Cica D2
42 Kino Europa D4
43 Kolaž E4
44 Stross C3
45 Velvet B3
46 Vimpi C4

◉ Entertainment

47 Croatian National Theatre B5
48 Dražen Petrović Basketball
    Centre A7
49 Hotpot E5
50 KSET B7
51 Pepermint C3
52 Purgeraj E2
53 Rush Club F4
54 VIP Club E3
55 Zagrebačko Kazalište Mladih D4

◉ Shopping

56 Antiques Market A3
57 Natura Croatica D4
58 Profil Megastore D4
59 Prostor C3

The nearby **funicular railway** (ticket 5KN) was constructed in 1888 and connects the Lower and Upper Towns.

St Mark's Church   CHURCH
(Crkva Svetog Marka; Trg Svetog Marka 5; ☺7.30am-6.30pm) Its colourful tiled roof makes this Gothic church one of Zagreb's most emblematic buildings. Inside are works by Ivan Meštrović, Croatia's most famous modern sculptor. You can only enter the anteroom during the listed opening hours; the church itself is open during Mass.

Croatian Museum of Naïve Art   MUSEUM
(Hrvatski Muzej Naivne Umjetnosti; www.hmnu. org; Ćirilometodska 3; adult/concession 20/10KN; ☺10am-6pm Tue-Fri, to 1pm Sat & Sun) If you like Croatia's naïve art or want a good intro to it, head to this small museum. It houses over 1000 paintings, drawings and some sculpture by the discipline's most important artists.

Meštrović Atelier   ARTS CENTRE
(Mletačka 8; adult/concession 30/15KN; ☺10am-6pm Tue-Fri, to 1pm Sat & Sun) This 17th-cen-

tury building, the former home of Croatia's most recognised artist, Ivan Meštrović, now houses an excellent collection of some 100 sculptures, drawings, lithographs and pieces of furniture created by the artist.

City Museum
MUSEUM

(Muzej Grada Zagreba; www.mgz.hr; Opatička 20; adult/concession 30/20KN; ⊘10am-6pm Tue-Fri, 11am-7pm Sat, 10am-2pm Sun; 🖼) Check out the scale model of old Gradec, atmospheric background music and interactive exhibits that fascinate kids. There are summaries in English in each room of the museum, which is in the former Convent of St Claire (1650).

Galerija Klovićevi Dvori
ART GALLERY

(www.galerijaklovic.hr; Jezuitski trg 4; adult/concession 30/20KN; ⊘11am-7pm Tue-Sun) Housed in a former Jesuit monastery, this is the city's most prestigious space for exhibiting modern Croatian and international art. Note that the gallery closes in summer months.

Stone Gate
LANDMARK

Make sure you take a peek at this eastern gate to medieval Gradec Town, now a shrine. According to legend, a great fire in 1731 destroyed every part of the wooden gate except for the painting of the *Virgin and Child* by an unknown 17th-century artist.

LOWER TOWN

Trg Josipa Jelačića
SQUARE

Zagreb's main orientation point and the geographic heart of the city is Trg Josipa Jelačića. It has an **equestrian statue** of Jelačić, the 19th-century *ban* (viceroy or governor) who led Croatian troops into an unsuccessful battle with Hungary in the hope of winning more autonomy for his peo-

ple. The square is Zagreb's principal meeting point; sit in one of the cafes for quality people-watching.

Museum Mimara
MUSEUM

(Muzej Mimara; www.mimara.hr; Rooseveltov trg 5; adult/concession 40/30KN; ⊘10am-7pm Tue-Fri, to 5pm Sat, to 2pm Sun Jul-Sep, 10am-5pm Tue-Wed & Fri-Sat, to 7pm Thu, to 2pm Sun Oct-Jun) Ante Topić Mimara donated his diverse collection to Croatia. Housed in a neo-Renaissance palace, it includes icons, glassware, sculpture, Oriental art and works by renowned painters such as Rembrandt, Velázquez, Raphael and Degas.

Strossmayer Gallery of Old Masters
MUSEUM

(Strossmayerova Galerija Starih Majstora; Trg Nikole Šubića Zrinskog 11; adult/concession 30/10KN; ⊘10am-7pm Tue, to 4pm Wed-Fri, to 1pm Sat & Sun) Inside the neo-Renaissance Croatian Academy of Arts and Sciences, this gallery showcases the impressive fine-art collection donated to Zagreb by Bishop Strossmayer in 1884. The interior courtyard has the **Baška Slab** (1102) from Krk Island, one of the oldest inscriptions in the Croatian language.

Art Pavilion
ART GALLERY

(Umjetnički Pavilion; www.umjetnicki-pavilon.hr; Trg Kralja Tomislava 22; adult/concession 30/15KN; ⊘11am-7pm Tue-Sat, 10am-1pm Sun Sep–mid-Jul) The yellow Art Pavilion in a stunning 1897 art nouveau building presents changing exhibitions of contemporary art.

Gallery of Modern Art
ART GALLERY

(Moderna Galerija; www.moderna-galerija.hr; Andrije Hebranga 1; adult/concession 40/20KN; ⊘11am-6pm Tue-Fri, to 1pm Sat & Sun) With a glorious

---

ZAGREB IN TWO DAYS

Start your day with a stroll through Strossmayerov trg, Zagreb's oasis of greenery. Take a look at the **Strossmayer Gallery of Old Masters** and then walk to **Trg Josipa Jelačića**, the city's centre.

Head up to Kaptol Square for a look at the **Cathedral**, the centre of Zagreb's religious life. While in the Upper Town, pick up some fruit at **Dolac market** or have lunch at **Amfora**. Then get to know the work of Croatia's best sculptor at **Meštrović Atelier** and see his naïve-art legacy at the **Croatian Museum of Naïve Art**, followed by a visit to the quirky **Museum of Broken Relationships**. See the lay of the city from the top of **Lotrščak Tower**, then spend the evening bar-crawling along Tkalčićeva.

On the second day, tour the Lower Town museums, reserving an hour for the **Museum Mimara** and as long for the **Museum of Contemporary Art**. Lunch at **Vinodol** and digest in the **Botanical Garden**. Early evening is best at Preradovićev trg before dining and sampling some of Zagreb's nightlife.

display of Croatian artists of the last 200 years, this gallery offers an excellent overview of Croatia's vibrant arts scene.

Botanical Garden
GARDENS

(Botanički Vrt; Mihanovićeva bb; ⊘9am-2.30pm Mon & Tue, 9am-7pm Wed-Sun Apr-Oct) Laid out in 1890, the garden has 10,000 plant species, including 1800 tropical flora specimens. The landscaping has created restful corners and paths that seem a world away from bustling Zagreb.

OUTSIDE THE CENTRE

Museum of Contemporary Art
MUSEUM

(Muzej Suvremene Umjetnosti; www.msu.hr; Avenija Dubrovnik 17; adult/concession 30/15KN, 1st Wed of month free; ⊘11am-6pm Tue-Fri & Sun, to 8pm Sat) Housed in a dazzling new city icon designed by local starchitect Igor Franić, this swanky museum in Novi Zagreb, across the Sava River, puts on solo and thematic group shows by Croatian and international artists. The year-round schedule is packed with film, theatre, concerts and performance art.

Mirogoj
CEMETERY

(⊘6am-8pm Apr-Sep, 7am-6pm Oct-Mar) A 10-minute ride north of the city centre on bus 106 from the cathedral (or a half-hour walk through leafy streets) takes you to one of Europe's most beautiful cemeteries, a verdant resting place designed in 1876. The sculpted and artfully designed tombs lie beyond a majestic arcade topped by a string of cupolas.

FREE THRILLS

Though you'll have to pay to get into most of Zagreb's galleries and museums, there are some gorgeous parks and markets to be enjoyed for nowt – and there's always window shopping!

» Taste bits of food for free at Dolac (p121) – but don't be too cheeky!

» Smell the herbs at the Botanical Garden (p128).

» Enjoy the long walks around Maksimir Park (p128).

» See the magnificent Mirogoj cemetery (p128).

» Pop inside the ever-renovated cathedral (p121).

Maksimir Park
PARK

(www.park-maksimir.hr; Maksimirska bb; ⊘park 9am-dusk, info centre 10am-4pm Tue-Fri, to 6pm Sat & Sun mid-Apr–mid-Oct, 10am-4pm Tue-Fri, 8am-4pm Sat & Sun mid-Oct–mid-Apr) Another green delight is Maksimir Park, a peaceful wooded enclave covering 18 hectares; it is easily accessible by trams 11 and 12 from Trg Josipa Jelačića. Opened to the public in 1794, it was the first public promenade in southeastern Europe. There's also a modest zoo (www.zoo.hr; adult/children 30/20KN; ⊘9am-8pm) here.

Dražen Petrović Memorial Museum
MUSEUM

(☎48 43 146; Savska 30; tickets 10-20KN) Pay homage to Cibona's most famous player at this museum located south along Savska, on a small square just to the west.

Tours

ZET
BUS TOUR

(www.zet.hr) Zagreb's public transportation network operates open-deck tour buses (70KN) departing from Kaptol on a hop-on, hop-off basis from April through September.

Funky Zagreb
GUIDED TOUR

(www.funky-zagreb.com) Personalised tours that range in theme from wine tasting (200KN for three hours) to hiking in Zagreb's surroundings (from 635KN per person).

Blue Bike Tours
CYCLING

(www.zagrebbybike.com) Has two-hour tours (170KN) departing daily. Reserve ahead.

Zagreb Talks
WALKING TOUR

(www.zagrebtalks.com) Tours include Do You Speak Croatian? on Saturday mornings, which teaches you basic language skills (95KN; 75KN for students). From May through September only; otherwise by appointment.

Festivals & Events

For a complete listing of Zagreb events, see www.zagreb-touristinfo.hr.

Music Biennale Zagreb
MUSIC

(www.mbz.hr) Croatia's most important contemporary music event is held in April during odd-numbered years.

Subversive Festival
CULTURAL

(www.subversivefestival.com) Europe's activists and philosophers descend on Zagreb in droves for film screenings and lectures over two weeks in May.

INmusic Festival — MUSIC
(www.inmusicfestival.com) A three-day extravaganza every June, this is Zagreb's highest-profile music festival, with multiple stages by the Jarun Lake.

World Festival of Animated Film — FILM
(www.animafest.hr) This prestigious festival has been held in Zagreb annually in June since 1972.

Cest is D'Best — CULTURAL
(www.cestisdbest.com) In early June, it features five stages around the city centre, around 200 international performers and acts that include music, dance, theatre, art and sports.

Ljeto na Strossu — CULTURAL
(www.ljetonastrosu.com) From late May through late September, leafy Strossmayer Šetalište comes alive with free outdoor film screenings, concerts, art workshops and best-in-show mongrel dog competitions.

Eurokaz — THEATRE
(www.eurokaz.hr) Showcasing innovative theatre troupes and cutting-edge performances from all over the world in late June/early July.

Zagreb Summer Evenings — MUSIC
A cycle of concerts in the Upper Town each July, with the atrium of Galerija Klovićevi Dvori and the Gradec stage used for the performances of classical music, jazz, blues and world tunes.

World Theatre Festival — THEATRE
(www.zagrebtheatrefestival.hr) High-quality, contemporary theatre comes to Zagreb for a couple of weeks each September, often extending into early October.

🛏 Sleeping

Zagreb's accommodation scene has been undergoing a noticeable change, with many more budget options. Prices usually stay the same in all seasons, but be prepared for a 20% surcharge if you arrive during a festival or major event, in particular the autumn fair.

If you intend to stay in a private house or apartment – a good option if you want more privacy and a homey feel – try not to arrive on Sunday because most of the agencies will be closed, unless you've made prior arrangements. Prices for doubles run from about 300KN and studio apartments start at 400KN per night. There's usually a surcharge for staying only one night. Recommended agencies include **Evistas** (☑48 39 554; www.evistas.hr; Augusta Šenoe 28; s/d/apt from 240/290/340KN) and **InZagreb** (☑65 23 201; www.inzagreb.com; Remetinečka 13; apt 490-665KN).

TOP CHOICE Studio Kairos — B&B €€
(☑46 40 680; www.studio-kairos.com; Vlaška 92; s 380-440KN, d 560-660KN; ❄🖥) This adorable B&B has four well-appointed rooms in a street-level apartment. Rooms are decked out by theme and there's a cosy common space where breakfast is served. The main square (Trg Josipa Jelačića) is a 15-minute stroll away, a five-minute tram ride (take 11 or 12) or a five-minute bike ride (bikes are available for rent).

Esplanade Zagreb Hotel — HISTORIC HOTEL €€€
(☑45 66 666; www.esplanade.hr; Mihanovićeva 1; s/d 1385/1500KN; 🅿❄@🖥) Drenched in history, this six-storey hotel was built next to the train station in 1924 to welcome the *Orient Express* crowd in grand style. The art-deco masterpiece is replete with walls of swirling marble, immense staircases and wood-panelled lifts. Take a peek at the magnificent Emerald Ballroom and have a meal at superb **Zinfandel's restaurant** (Mihanovićeva 1; mains from 170KN).

Hotel Dubrovnik — HOTEL €€
(☑48 63 555; www.hotel-dubrovnik.hr; Gajeva 1; s/d from 740/885KN; 🅿❄🖥) Smack on the main square, this glass city landmark has 245 elegant units with old-school classic style and, from some, great views of the square. Check out the great specials and packages.

Hobo Bear Hostel — HOSTEL €
(☑48 46 636; www.hobobearhostel.com; Medulićeva 4; dm 135-175KN, d from 400KN; ❄@🖥) Inside a duplex apartment, this sparkling five-dorm hostel has exposed brick walls, hardwood floors, free lockers, a kitchen with free tea and coffee, a common room and book exchange. Take tram 1, 6 or 11 from Jelačića. The three doubles are across the street.

Hotel Jägerhorn — HOTEL €€
(☑48 33 877; www.jaegerhorn.hr; Ilica 14; s/d/apt 598/749/1052KN; 🅿❄@🖥) A charming little hotel that sits right underneath Lotršćak Tower (p121), the 'Hunter's Horn' has friend-

ly service and 18 spacious, classic rooms with good views (gaze over leafy Gradec from the top-floor attic rooms).

Funk Lounge Hostel HOSTEL €
(☑55 52 707; www.funkhostel.hr; Rendićeva 28b; dm 135-165KN, d 420KN; @🛜) Located steps from Maksimir Park, this new outpost of the original Funk Hostel (southwest of the centre) has friendly staff, neat rooms and a range of freebies, including breakfast and a shot of *rakija* in the on-site restaurant and bar.

The budget end of the market has picked up greatly and various hostel options now abound. The following hostels are worth checking out: **Shappy Hostel** (☑48 30 179; www.hostel-shappy.com; Varšavska 8; dm 128-170, d from 420KN; P✳@🛜), **Palmers Lodge Hostel Zagreb** (☑88 92 686; www.palmerslodge. com.hr; Branimirova 25; dm 120-150KN; @🛜), **Chillout Hostel Zagreb Downtown** (☑48 49 605; www.chillout-hostel-zagreb.com; Kačićeva 3b; dm 135-180KN; ✳@🛜), **Fulir Hostel** (☑48 30 882; www.fulir-hostel.com; Radićeva 3a; ✳@🛜), **Hostel Day and Night** (www.hosteldayand-night.com; Kneza Mislava 1), **Buzz Hostel** (☑23 20 267; www.buzzbackpackers.com; Babukićeva 1b; ✳@🛜) and **Taban Hostel** (www.tabanzagreb. com; Tkalčićeva 82).

✖ Eating

You'll have to love Croatian and Italian food to enjoy Zagreb's restaurants, but new places are branching out to include Japanese and other world cuisines. The biggest move is towards elegantly presented haute cuisine at haute prices.

You can pick up excellent fresh produce at Dolac market. The city centre's main streets, including Ilica, Teslina, Gajeva and Preradovićeva, are lined with fast-food joints and inexpensive snack bars.

Note that many restaurants close in August for their summer holiday, which typically lasts anywhere from two weeks to a month.

Vinodol CROATIAN €€
(Teslina 10; mains from 57KN) Well-prepared Central European fare much loved by local and overseas patrons. On warm days, eat on the covered patio entered through an ivy-clad passageway off Teslina. Highlights include the succulent lamb or veal and potatoes under *peka* (baked in a coal oven), as well as local mushrooms called *bukovače*.

Lari & Penati MODERN CROATIAN €
(Petrinjska 42a; mains from 40KN; ☺lunch & dinner Mon-Fri, lunch Sat) Small stylish bistro that serves up innovative lunch and dinner specials that change daily according to what's market fresh. The food is fab, the music cool and the few sidewalk tables lovely in warm weather. Closed for two weeks in August.

Tip Top SEAFOOD €
(Gundulićeva 18; mains from 55KN; ☺Mon-Sat) The excellent Dalmatian food is served by waitstaff sporting old socialist uniforms. Every day has its own set menu of mainstays.

Mali Bar TAPAS €€
(☑55 31 014; Vlaška 63; mains from 60KN; ☺closed Sun) This new spot by star chef Ana Ugarković shares the terraced space with Karijola (p130), hidden away in a *veža* (Zagreb alleyway). The cosy interior is earth-tone colourful and the food is focused on globally inspired tapas-style dishes. Book ahead.

Didov San DALMATIAN €€
(☑48 51 154; Mletačka 11; mains from 60KN) This Upper Town tavern features a rustic wooden interior with ceiling beams and tables on the streetside deck. Traditional fare hails from the Neretva River delta in Dalmatia's hinterland; try grilled frogs wrapped in proscuitto. Reserve ahead.

Karijola PIZZERIA €
(Vlaška 63; pizzas from 42KN; ☺Mon-Sat) Locals swear by the crispy thin-crust pizza churned out of a clay oven at this new location of Zagreb's best pizza joint. Expect high-quality toppings, such as smoked ham, olive oil, rich mozzarella, rocket and shiitake mushrooms.

Amfora SEAFOOD €
(Dolac 2; mains from 40KN; ☺lunch) This locals' lunch favourite serves super-fresh seafood straight from the market next door, paired with off-the-stalls veggies. This hole-in-the-wall has a few tables outside and an upstairs gallery with a nice market view.

Prasac MEDITERRANEAN €€
(☑48 51 411; Vranicanijeva 6; mains from 87KN; ☺Mon-Sat; 🛒) Creative Mediterranean fare is conjured up by the Croatian-Sicilian chef at this intimate place with wooden beamed ceilings and a few alfresco tables. The market-fresh food is superb, but the service is slow and the portions small. Reserve ahead.

Stari Fijaker 900
TRADITIONAL CROATIAN €

(Mesnička 6; mains from 50KN) Tradition reigns in the kitchen of this restaurant–beer hall with a decor of banquettes and white linen, so try the homemade sausages, bean stews and *štrukli* (dumplings filled with cottage cheese), or one of the cheaper daily dishes.

Ivica i Marica
TRADITIONAL CROATIAN €€

(Tkalčićeva 70; mains from 70KN) Based on the Brothers Grimm story *Hansel and Gretel*, this restaurant–cake shop is made to look like the gingerbread house from the tale, with waiters clad in traditional costumes. It has veggie and fish dishes plus meatier fare. The cakes and *štrukli* are great.

Konoba Čiho
SEAFOOD €€

(Pavla Hatza 15; mains from 80KN) An old-school Dalmatian *konoba* (simple family-run establishment), where, downstairs, you can get fish (by the kilo) and seafood grilled or stewed. Try the wide range of *rakija* and house wines.

Vallis Aurea
TRADITIONAL CROATIAN €

(Tomićeva 4; mains from 37KN; ⊘Mon-Sat) This true local eatery has some of the best home cooking you'll find in town, so it's no wonder that it's chock-a-block at lunchtime for its *gableci* (traditional lunches). Right by the lower end of the funicular.

Pingvin
SANDWICH SHOP €

(Teslina 7; ⊘9am-4am Mon-Sat, 6pm-2am Sun) This quick-bite institution, around since 1987, offers tasty designer sandwiches and salads which locals savour perched on a couple of bar stools.

Rubelj
FAST FOOD €

(Dolac 2; mains from 25KN) One of the many Rubeljs across town, this Dolac branch is a great place for a quick portion of *ćevapčići* (small spicy sausage of minced beef, lamb or pork).

Vincek
PASTRIES, CAKES €

(Ilica 18) This institution of a *slastičarna* (pastry shop) serves some of Zagreb's creamiest cakes. They recently got some serious competition, however, with **Torte i To** (Nova Ves 11, 2nd fl, Kaptol Centar).

Dinara
BAKERY €

(Gajeva 8) The best bakery in town churns out an impressive variety of baked goodies. Try the *bučnica* (filo pie with pumpkin). It also has branches at **Ilica** (Ilica 71) and **Preradovićeva** (Preradovićeva 1).

🍷 Drinking

In the Upper Town, chic Tkalčićeva is throbbing with bars and cafes. In the Lower Town, there's bar-lined Bogovićeva and Trg Petra Preradovića (known locally as Cvjetni trg), the most popular spot in the Lower Town for street performers and occasional bands.

One of the nicest ways to see Zagreb is to join in on the *špica* – Saturday-morning pre-lunch coffee drinking on the terraces along Bogovićeva, Preradovićeva and Tkalčićeva.

TOP CHOICE Cica
BAR

(Tkalčićeva 18) This tiny storefront bar is as underground as it gets on Tkalčićeva. Sample one or – if you dare – all of the 25 kinds of *rakija* that the place is famous for.

Booksa
CAFE

(www.booksa.hr; Martićeva 14d; ⊘11am-8pm Tue-Sun; 🛜) Bookworms, poets and oddballs all come to chat and drink coffee, browse the library, surf with free wireless and hear readings at this book-themed cafe. There are English-language readings here, too. It's a 10-minute stroll east of the main square. It's closed for three weeks from late July.

Stross
OUTDOOR BAR

(Strossmayerovo Šetalište; ⊘Jun-Sep) From June to September, a makeshift bar is set up at the Strossmayer promenade in the Upper Town, with cheap drinks and live music most nights. Come for the mixed-bag crowd, great city views and leafy ambience.

Bacchus
BAR

(Trg Kralja Tomislava 16; ⊘closed Sun) You'll be lucky if you score a table at Zagreb's funkiest courtyard garden – lush and hidden in a passageway. After 10pm the action moves inside the artsy subterranean space, which hosts poetry readings and oldies' nights.

Kino Europa
CAFE-BAR

(www.kinoeuropa.hr; Varšavska 3; ⊘Mon-Sat; 🛜♿) Zagreb's oldest cinema, from the 1920s, now houses a glass-enclosed cafe, wine bar and *grapperia*, with an outdoor terrace and free wireless. The cinema hosts daily film screenings and occasional dance parties.

Velvet
CAFE-BAR

(Dežmanova 9; ⊘8am-10pm Mon-Fri, to 3pm Sat, to 2pm Sun) Stylish spot for a good, but pricey, cup of java and a quick bite amid the minimalist-chic interior decked out by owner Saša Šekoranja, Zagreb's hippest florist.

GAY & LESBIAN ZAGREB

The gay and lesbian scene in Zagreb is finally becoming more open than it has previously been, although free-wheeling it isn't.

For more information, browse www.zagrebgayguide.com.

Kolaž (Amruševa 11) This basement speakeasy-style bar behind an un-marked door caters to a primarily gay crowd.

Rush Club (Amruševa 10) A younger gay and lesbian crowd mixes at this fun club in the city centre, with themed nights such as karaoke.

Hotpot (Petrinjska 31) This new club in town has quickly become one of the favourites.

Vimpi (Miškecov Prolaz 3) Gathering spot for Zagreb's lady-loving ladies.

Velvet Gallery next door, known as 'Black Velvet', stays open till 11pm (except Sunday).

☆ Entertainment

Zagreb doesn't register high on the night-life Richter scale, but it does have an ever-developing art and music scene. Its theatres and concert halls present a variety of programs throughout the year. Many are listed in the monthly brochure *Zagreb Events & Performances,* which is available from the main tourist office

Clubs

Club entry ranges from 20KN to 100KN. Clubs open around 10pm but most people show up around midnight. Most clubs open only from Thursday to Saturday.

VIP Club   CLUB
(www.vip-club.hr; Trg Josipa Jelačića 9; ⊙closed summer) This newcomer on the nightlife scene quickly became a favourite. A swank basement place on the main square, it offers a varied programme, from jazz to Balkan beats.

Tvornica   LIVE MUSIC
(www.tvornicakulture.com; Šubićeva 2) Excellent multimedia venue 20 minutes to the east of Trg Josipa Jelačića, showcasing live music performances, from Bosnian *sevdah* (Bos-

nian blues) to alternative punk rock. Check out the website to see what's on.

Aquarius   CLUB
(www.aquarius.hr; Jarun Lake) Past its heyday but still a fun lakeside club with a series of rooms that opens onto a huge terrace. House and techno are the standard fare but there are also hip-hop and R&B nights. During summer, Aquarius sets up shop at Zrće on Pag (p144).

Pepermint   CLUB
(www.pepermint-zagreb.com; Ilica 24) Small and chic city-centre club clad in white wood, with two levels and a well-to-do older crowd. Programs change weekly but the vintage rockabilly, twist and swing night on Wednesday is a definite hit.

Močvara   CLUB
(www.mochvara.hr; Trnjanski Nasip bb) In a former factory on the banks of the Sava River, 'Swamp' is one of Zagreb's best venues for the cream of alternative music and attractively dingy charm. Live acts range from dub and dancehall to world music and heavy metal.

KSET   CLUB
(www.kset.org; Unska 3) Zagreb's top music venue, with anyone who's anyone performing here – from ethno to hip-hop sounds. Saturday nights are dedicated to DJ music, when youngsters dance till late. You'll find gigs and events to suit most tastes.

Jabuka   CLUB
(Jabukovac 28) 'Apple' is an old-time fave, with 1980s hits played to a 30-something crowd that reminisces about the good old days when they were young and alternative. It's a taxi ride or a walk through the woods, set away in a posh area.

Medika   CLUB
(www.pierottijeva11.org; Pierottijeva 11) This artsy venue in an old pharmaceutical factory calls itself an 'autonomous cultural centre'. It's the city's first legalised squat with a program of concerts, art exhibits and parties fuelled by cheap beer and *rakija.*

Purgeraj   CLUB
(www.purgeraj.hr; Park Ribnjak 1) Live rock, blues and avant-garde jazz are on the music menu at this funky space that attracts a pretty young crowd. The brand-new Park just

merged with Purgeraj at the time of writing and started drawing in big-name bands.

Sport

Basketball is popular in Zagreb, home to the Cibona basketball team. There's a museum (p128) dedicated to Cibona star Dražen Petrović. Games take place frequently at the **Dražen Petrović Basketball Centre** (📞48 43 333; Savska 30; tickets from HRK35); tickets can be purchased at the door or online at www.cibona.com.

Performing Arts

Make the rounds of the theatres in person to check their programs. Tickets are usually available for even the best shows.

Zagrebačko Kazalište Mladih   THEATRE
(📞48 72 554; www.zekaem.hr; Teslina 7) Zagreb Youth Theatre, better known as ZKM, is considered the cradle of Croatia's contemporary theatre. It hosts several festivals.

Croatian National Theatre   THEATRE
(📞48 88 418; www.hnk.hr; Trg Maršala Tita 15) This neo-baroque theatre, established in 1895, stages opera and ballet performances.

Shopping

Ilica is Zagreb's main shopping street.

Prostor   FASHION
(www.multiracionalnakompanija.com; Mesnička 5; ⊙noon-8pm Mon-Fri, 10am-3pm Sat) A fantastic little art gallery and clothes shop, featuring some of the city's best independent artists and young designers. In a courtyard off Mesnička.

Natura Croatica   FOOD
(www.naturacroatica.com; Preradovićeva 8) Over 300 Croatian products and souvenirs are sold at this shop – from *rakija,* wines

and chocolates to jams, spices and truffle spreads. A perfect pitstop for gifts.

Profil Megastore   BOOKSTORE
(Bogovićeva 7) Inside an entryway, this most atmospheric of Zagreb bookstores has a great selection of books (many in English) and a nice cafe on the gallery.

Information

Discount Cards

Zagreb Card (www.zagrebcard.fivestars.hr; 24/72hr 60/90KN) Provides free travel on all public transport, a 50% discount on museum and gallery entries, plus discounts in some bars and restaurants, and on car rental. The card is sold at the main tourist office and many hostels, hotels, bars and shops.

Emergency

Police Station (📞45 63 311; Petrinjska 30)

Internet Access

Several cafes around town offer free wi-fi, including Booksa.

Sublink (📞48 19 993; www.sublink.hr; Teslina 12; per hr 15KN; ⊙9am-10pm Mon-Sat, 3-10pm Sun) The city's first cybercafe, still going strong.

Medical Services

Dental Emergency (📞48 28 488; Perkovčeva 3; ⊙10pm-6am)

KBC Rebro (📞23 88 888; Kišpatićeva 12; ⊙24hr) East of the city, provides emergency aid.

Pharmacy (📞48 16 198; Trg Josipa Jelačića 3; ⊙24hr)

Money

There are ATMs at the bus and train stations, the airport, and at numerous locations around town. Some banks in the train and bus stations accept travellers cheques. Exchange offices can be found in many locations around town.

MARKET DAYS

The Sunday **antiques market** (Britanski Trg; ⊙9am-2pm Sun) is one of central Zagreb's joys, but to see a flea market that's unmatched in the whole of Croatia, you have to head to **Hrelić** (⊙7am-3pm Wed & Sun). This huge open space is packed with anything – from car parts, cars and antique furniture to clothes, records, kitchenware, you name it. Shopping aside, it's also a great place to experience the truly Balkan part and chaotic fun of Zagreb – Roma music, bartering, grilled-meat smoke and general gusto. If you're going in the summer months, take a hat and slap on sunscreen – there's no shade.

By tram, take number 6 in the direction of Sopot, get off near the bridge and walk 15 minutes along the Sava to get to Hrelić; or take tram 14, get off at the last stop in Zapruđe and do the 15-minute walk from there.

Post

Post Office (☎66 26 453; Jurišićeva 13; ☺7am-8pm Mon-Fri, to 1pm Sat) Has a telephone centre.

Tourist Information

Main Tourist Office (☎info line 800 53 53, office 48 14 051; www.zagreb-touristinfo.hr; Trg Josipa Jelačića 11; ☺8.30am-9pm Mon-Fri, 9am-6pm Sat & Sun) Distributes free city maps and leaflets, and sells the Zagreb Card (p133).

Plitvice National Park Office (☎46 13 586; Trg Kralja Tomislava 19; ☺8am-4pm Mon-Fri) Has details and brochures mainly on Plitvice and Velebit but also on Croatia's other national parks.

Tourist Office Airport (☎62 65 091; ☺8.30am-9pm Mon-Fri, 9am-6pm Sat & Sun Jun-Sep) Handy for airport arrivals.

Tourist Office Annex (train station; ☺8.30am-9pm Mon-Fri, 9am-6pm Sat & Sun Jun-Sep, 8.30am-8pm Mon-Fri, 12.30-6.30pm Sat & Sun Oct-May) Same services as the main tourist office.

Travel Agencies

Atlas Travel Agency (☎48 07 300; www.atlas-croatia.com; Zrinjevac 17) Tours around Croatia.

Croatia Express (☎49 22 237; Trg Kralja Tomislava 17) Train reservations, car rental, air and ferry tickets, hotell bookings and a daily trip to the beach from June to September.

Zdenac Života (☎48 16 200; www.zdenac-zivota.hr; 2nd fl, Vlaška 40) Thematic sightseeing tours of Zagreb plus active day trips from the capital and multiday adventures around Croatia.

Websites

Lonely Planet (www.lonelyplanet.com/croatia/zagreb)

🛈 Getting There & Away

AIR Zagreb Airport (☎45 62 222; www.zagreb-airport.hr) Located 17km southeast of Zagreb, this is Croatia's major airport, offering a range of international and domestic services.

BUS Zagreb's bus station (☎060 313 333; www.akz.hr; Avenija M Držića 4) is 1km east of the train station. Trams 2, 3 and 6 run from the bus station to the train station. Tram 6 goes to Trg Josipa Jelačića. There's a **garderoba** (left-luggage office; 1st 4hr 20KN, then per hr 2.50KN; ☺24hr) at the bus station.

Before buying your ticket, ask about the arrival time – some of the buses take local roads and stop in every town en route. Note that listed schedules are somewhat reduced outside high season.

TRAIN The train station (☎060 333 444; www.hznet.hr; Trg Kralja Tomislava 12) is in the southern part of the city. As you come out of it, you'll see a series of parks and pavilions directly in front of you, which lead into the town centre. It's advisable to book train tickets in advance because of limited seating. There's a **garderoba** (Train station; lockers per 24hr 15KN; ☺24hr) left-luggage office at the station.

🛈 Getting Around

Zagreb is a fairly easy city to navigate. Traffic is bearable and the efficient tram system should be a model for other polluted, traffic-clogged European capitals.

To/From the Airport

The Croatia Airlines bus to the airport (30KN) leaves from the bus station every half-hour or hour from about 5am to 8pm, and returns from the airport on the same schedule. Taxis cost between 110KN and 300KN.

Car

Zagreb is a fairly easy city to navigate by car (boulevards are wide and parking in the city centre, although scarce, costs 10KN per hour). Watch out for trams buzzing around.

Motorists can call **Hrvatski Autoklub** (HAK, Croatian Auto Club; ☎46 40 800; www.hak.hr; Avenija Dubrovnik 44) at ☎1987 for help on the road.

International car-hire companies include **Budget Rent-a-Car** (☎46 73 603; www.budget.hr; Oreškovićeva 27) and **Hertz** (☎48 46 777; www.hertz.hr; Vukotinovićeva 4). Local companies usually have lower rates; try **Oryx** (☎61 15 800; www.oryx-rent.hr; Grada Vukovara 74), which has a desk at the airport.

Public Transport

Public transport is based on an efficient network of trams, although the city centre is compact enough to make them unnecessary. Buy tickets at newspaper kiosks for 12KN. Tickets can be used for transfers within 90 minutes, but only in one direction.

A *dnevna karta* (day ticket), valid on all public transport until 4am the next morning, is available for 40KN at most newspaper kiosks.

Make sure you validate your ticket when you get on the tram by inserting it in the yellow box.

Taxi

Until recently, Zagreb had only one taxi company which charged astronomical fees for even the shortest ride. That changed when other companies joined the fray; all have meters now and competitive rates. **Radio Taxi** (☎060 800 800, 1777) charges 10KN for a start and 5KN per kilometre; waiting time is 40KN per hour.

TRANSPORT FROM ZAGREB

Domestic Bus

DESTINATION	PRICE (KN)	DURATION (HR)	FREQUENCY (DAILY)
Dubrovnik	205-250	9½-11	9-12
Korčula	264	11	1
Krk	113-219	3-4½	8-10
Mali Lošinj	287-312	5-6	3
Plitvice	92-106	2-3	11-15
Poreč	156-232	4-4½	11
Pula	105-196	3½-5½	17-20
Rijeka	91-155	2½-4	20-25
Rovinj	150-195	4-6	9-11
Split	115-205	5-8½	32-34
Zadar	105-139	3½-5	31

International Bus

DESTINATION	PRICE (KN)	DURATION (HR)	FREQUENCY (DAILY)
Belgrade (Serbia)	220	6	5
Munich (Germany)	375	9½	2
Sarajevo (Bosnia & Hercegovina)	160-210	7-8	4-5
Vienna (Austria)	250	5-6	3

Domestic Train

DESTINATION	PRICE (KN)	DURATION (HR)	FREQUENCY (DAILY)
Rijeka	97	4-6	6
Split	189	5-7	3

International Train

DESTINATION	PRICE (KN)	DURATION (HR)	FREQUENCY (DAILY)
Banja Luka (Bosnia & Hercegovina)	105	4½-5	2
Belgrade (Serbia)	169	6½	4
Budapest (Hungary)	230	6-7	2
Ljubljana (Slovenia)	130	2½	6
Mostar (Bosnia & Hercegovina)	292	11½	1
Munich (Germany)	674	8½-9	3
Ploče (Italy)	320	13½	1
Sarajevo (Bosnia & Hercegovina)	231	8-9½	2
Venice (Italy)	450	11½	2
Vienna (Austria)	465	6-7	2

PLITVICE LAKES NATIONAL PARK

Between Zagreb and Zadar, **Plitvice Lakes National Park** (☑751 015; www.np-plitvicka-jezera.hr; adult/concession Apr-Oct 110/80KN, Nov-Mar 80/60KN; ⊙7am-8pm) comprises 19.5 hectares of wooded hills and 16 lakes, all connected by a series of waterfalls and cascades. The mineral-rich waters carve new paths through the rock, depositing tufa (new porous rock) in continually changing formations. Wooden footbridges follow the lakes and streams over, under and across the rumbling water for an exhilaratingly damp 18km. Swimming is not allowed. Your park admission also includes the boats and bus-trains you need to use to see the lakes. There is hotel accommodation onsite, and private accommodation just outside the park. Check the options with the Plitvice National Park Office (p134) in Zagreb.

Not all Zagreb–Zadar buses stop here as the quicker ones use the motorway, so check before boarding. You can check the schedules at www.akz.hr. The journey takes three hours from Zadar (95KN to 108KN) and 2½ hours from Zagreb (93KN to 106KN); there are 10 daily services.

Luggage can be left at the tourist information centre at the park's main entrance.

You'll have no trouble finding idle taxis, usually at blue-marked taxi signs; note that these are Radio Taxi stands.

For short city rides, **Taxi Cammeo** (☑060 71 00, 1212) is typically the cheapest, as the 15KN start fare includes the first two kilometres (it's 6KN for every subsequent kilometre).

ISTRIA

☑052

Continental Croatia meets the Adriatic in Istria (Istra to Croats), the heart-shaped 3600-sq-km peninsula just south of Trieste in Italy. While the bucolic interior of rolling hills and fertile plains attracts artsy visitors to its hilltop villages, rural hotels and farmhouse restaurants, the verdant indented coastline is enormously popular with the sun 'n sea set. Vast hotel complexes line much of the coast and its rocky beaches are not Croatia's best, but the facilities are wide-ranging, the sea is clean and secluded spots are still plentiful.

The coast, or 'Blue Istria', as the tourist board calls it, gets flooded with tourists in summer, but you can still feel alone in 'Green Istria' (the interior), even in mid-August. Add acclaimed gastronomy (starring fresh seafood, prime white truffles, wild asparagus, top-rated olive oils and award-winning wines), sprinkle it with historical charm and you have a little slice of heaven.

Pula

POP 57,800

The wealth of Roman architecture makes the otherwise workaday Pula (ancient Polensium) a standout among Croatia's larger cities. The star of the Roman show is the remarkably well-preserved Roman amphitheatre, which dominates the streetscape and doubles as a venue for summer concerts and festivals.

Historical attractions aside, Pula is a busy commercial city on the sea that has managed to retain a friendly small-town appeal. Just a short bus ride away, a series of beaches awaits at the resorts that occupy the Verudela Peninsula to the south. Although marred by residential and holiday developments, the coast is dotted with fragrant pine groves, seaside cafes and a clutch of fantastic restaurants. Further south along the indented shoreline, the Premantura Peninsula hides a spectacular nature park, the protected cape of Kamenjak.

⊙ Sights

THE CITY

The oldest part of the city follows the ancient Roman plan of streets circling the central citadel. Most shops, agencies and businesses are clustered in and around the Old Town as well as on Giardini, Carrarina, Istarska and Riva, which runs along the harbour. The new Riva is currently being renovated, which makes the harbourfront one big construction site; the work is expected to finish in late 2013.

Roman Amphitheatre HISTORIC BUILDING
(Arena; Flavijevska bb; adult/concession 40/20KN; ⊙8am-midnight Jul & Aug, around 8am-7pm Sep-Jun) Pula's most famous and imposing sight is this 1st-century amphitheatre, overlooking the harbour northeast of the Old Town. Built entirely from local limestone, the am-

phitheatre, known locally as the Arena, was designed to host gladiatorial contests, with seating for up to 20,000 spectators. In the chambers downstairs is a small **museum** with a display of ancient olive-oil equipment. **Pula Film Festival** (www.pulafilmfestival.hr) is held here every summer, as are pop and classical concerts.

Temple of Augustus   HISTORIC BUILDING
(Forum; adult/concession 20/10KN; ⊙9am-8pm Mon-Fri, to 3pm Sat & Sun Apr-Oct) This is the only visible remnant from the Roman era on the Forum, Pula's central meeting place from antiquity through the Middle Ages. This temple, erected from 2 BC to AD 14, now houses a small historical **museum** with captions in English.

Archaeological Museum   MUSEUM
(Arheološki Muzej; Carrarina 3; adult/concession 20/10KN; ⊙8am-8pm Mon-Fri, 9am-3pm Sat & Sun May-Sep, 9am-2pm Mon-Fri Oct-Apr) This museum presents archaeological finds from all over Istria. Even if you don't enter the museum, be sure to visit the large **sculpture garden** around it, and the **Roman theatre** behind. The garden, entered through 2nd-century twin gates, is the site of concerts in summer.

Zerostrasse   HISTORICAL SITE
(adult/concession 15/5KN; ⊙10am-10pm Jun–mid-Sep) This underground system of tunnels was built before and during WWI to shelter the city's population and serve as storage for ammunition. Now you can walk through several of its sections, which all lead to the middle, where a photo exhibit shows early aviation in Pula. There are three entrances – inquire at the tourism office.

Triumphal Arch of Sergius   RUINS
Along Carrarina are Roman walls, which mark the eastern boundary of old Pula. Follow these walls south and continue down Giardini to this majestic arch erected in 27 BC to commemorate three members of the Sergius family who achieved distinction in Pula.

THE COAST
Pula is surrounded by a half-circle of rocky beaches, each one with its own fan club. The most tourist-packed are undoubtedly those surrounding the hotel complex on the **Verudela Peninsula**, although some locals will dare to be seen at the small turquoise-coloured **Hawaii Beach** near the Hotel Park.

Rt Kamenjak   NATURE PARK
(www.kamenjak.hr; pedestrians & cyclists free, per car/scooter 25/20KN; ⊙7am-10pm) For seclusion, head out to the wild Rt Kamenjak on the Premantura Peninsula, 10km south of town. Istria's southernmost point, this gorgeous, entirely uninhabited cape has wildflowers (including 30 species of orchid), 30km of virgin beaches and coves, and a delightful beach bar, **Safari** (snacks 25-50KN; ⊙Apr-Sep), half-hidden in the bushes near the beach, about 3.5km from the entrance to the park. For the wildest and least-discovered stretch of the cape, head to Gornji Kamenjak, which lies between the village of Volme and Premantura. Watch out for strong currents if swimming off the southern cape. **Windsurf Bar** (⊘091 512 3646; www.windsurfing.hr; windsurfing equipment/courses per hr from 70/200KN) in Premantura rents bikes and windsurfing equipment and offers kayaking excursions. Take city bus 26 from Pula to Premantura (15KN), then rent a bike to get inside the park.

🏃 Activities
At the **Orca Diving Center** (⊘098 409 850; www.orcadiving.hr; Hotel Histria) on the Verudela Peninsula, you can arrange boat and wreck dives. In addition to windsurfing, Windsurf Bar (p137) in Premantura offers cycling (250KN) and kayaking (300KN) excursions.

An easy 41km **cycling trail** from Pula to Medulin follows the path of Roman gladiators. Check out **Istria Bike** (www.istria-bike.com), a tourist board–run website outlining trails, packages and agencies that offer cycling trips.

🛏 Sleeping
Pula's peak tourist season runs from the second week of July to late August. During this period it's wise to make advance reservations. The tip of the Verudela Peninsula, 4km southwest of the city centre, has been turned into a vast tourist complex replete with hotels and apartments.

Any travel agency can give you information and book you into one of the hotels, or you can contact **Arenaturist** (⊘529 400; www.arenaturist.hr; Splitska 1a).

The travel agencies in Pula can find you private accommodation, but there is little available in the town centre. Count on paying from 250KN to 490KN for a double room and from 300KN to 535KN for a two-person apartment. You can also browse the list of private accommodation at www.pulainfo.hr.

Hotel Amfiteatar
HOTEL €€

(☑375 600; www.hotelamfiteatar.com; Amfiteatarska 6; s/d 475/658KN; [P][✳][@][☎]) The swankiest spot in town, right by the amphitheatre, is a new hotel with contemporary rooms with upscale trimmings such as flat-screen TVs. The restaurant is one of Pula's best. There's a surcharge for stays of less than two nights.

Hostel Pipištrelo
HOSTEL €

(☑393 568; www.hostel-pipistrelo.com; Flaciusova 6; dm/s/d 124/148/296KN; [✳][@][☎]) With its colourful facade, this recent addition to Pula's hostel scene sits right across the harbour. Its quirky thematic rooms were done up by young Pula designers. It is cash-only and closed Sundays, so call ahead.

Hotel Scaletta
HOTEL €€

(☑541 025; www.hotel-scaletta.com; Flavijevska 26; s/d 505/732KN; [P][✳][☎]) There's a friendly family vibe at this cosy hotel. The rooms have tasteful decor and a bagful of trimmings (such as minibars). Plus it's just a hop and a skip from town, and a short walk from the Arena and the waterfront.

Riviera Guest House
HOTEL €€

(☑525 400; www.arenaturist.hr; Splitska 1; s/d 360/590KN; [☎]) This once-grand property in a Neo-Baroque 19th-century building is in dire need of a thorough overhaul. The saving grace: it's in the centre and the front rooms have water views.

Camping Stoja
CAMPING GROUND €

(☑387 144; www.arenacamps.com; Stoja 37; campsites per person/tent 58/37KN; ⊘Apr-Oct) The closest camping ground to Pula, 3km southwest of the centre, has lots of space on the shady promontory, with a restaurant and a diving centre. Take bus 1 to Stoja.

✕ Eating

The centre of Pula is full of tourist traps, so for the best food and good value you'll have to head out of town. For cheap bites, browse around the central market, where you'll find excellent sandwiches at **Garfield** (Narodni Trg 9; sandwiches from 25KN; ⊘9am-3pm Mon-Fri, to 2pm Sat) on the 1st floor. For a reliably good meal, head to the alfresco restaurant of Hotel Amfiteatar.

Vodnjanka
ISTRIAN €

(Vitezića 4; mains from 40KN; ⊘closed Sat dinner & Sun winter) Locals swear by the real-deal home cooking at this no-frills spot. It's cheap, casual, cash-only and has a small menu that concentrates on simple Istrian dishes. To get here, walk south on Radićeva to Vitezića.

TOP CHOICE Konoba Batelina
SEAFOOD €€

(☑573 767; Čimulje 25, Banjole; mains from 85KN; ⊘dinner) The superb food that awaits at this family-run tavern is worth a trek to Banjole village 3km east of Pula. The owner, fisherman and chef David Skoko, dishes out seafood that's some of the best and most creative you'll find in Istria. Reserve ahead.

Milan
MEDITERRANEAN €€

(www.milanpula.com; Stoja 4; mains from 85KN) An exclusive vibe, seasonal specialties, four sommeliers and an olive-oil expert on staff all create one of the city's best dining experiences. The five-course fish menu is well worth it.

Kantina
INTERNATIONAL €€

(Flanatička 16; mains from 70KN; ⊘Mon-Sat; [▣]) The beamed stone cellar of this Habsburg building has been redone in a modern style. The ownership and culinary helm changed recently so the food quality is hit and miss.

🍷 Drinking & Entertainment

Try to catch a concert in the spectacular amphitheatre (p136); the tourist office has schedules. Although most of the nightlife is out of the town centre, in mild weather the cafes on the Forum and along the pedestrian streets Kandlerova, Flanatička and Sergijevaca are lively people-watching spots. For beach-bar action, head to Verudela or Medulin.

TOP CHOICE Cabahia
BAR

(Širolina 4) This artsy hideaway in Veruda has a cosy wood-beamed interior, eclectic decor of old objects, dim lighting, South American flair and a great garden terrace out the back. It hosts concerts and gets packed on weekends. If it's too full, try the more laid-back **Bass** (Širolina 3), just across the street.

Cvajner
CAFE

(Forum 2) Snag a prime alfresco table at this artsy cafe right on the buzzing Forum and check out rotating exhibits in the funky interior, which showcases works by up-and-coming local artists.

Rojc
CULTURAL CENTRE

(www.rojcnet.pula.org; Gajeva 3) For an arty underground experience, check the program at Rojc, a converted army barracks that houses a multimedia art centre and studios with occasional concerts, exhibitions and other events.

DOMESTIC BUSES FROM PULA

DESTINATION	PRICE (KN)	DURATION (HR)	FREQUENCY (DAILY)
Dubrovnik	580	15	1
Poreč	72	1	5
Rovinj	38	¾	12
Split	392	10	2
Zadar	255	7	3
Zagreb	190	4	12

Zeppelin   BEACH BAR
(Saccorgiana Bay) Après-beach fun is on the menu at this new beach bar in Saccorgiana bay on Verudela, but it also does night parties ranging in theme from vodka to reggae and karaoke to martini.

ⓘ Information

Active Travel Istra (☑215 497; www.activa-istra.com; Scalierova 1) Excursions around Istria, adventure trips and concert tickets.

Hospital (☑376 548; Zagrebačka 34)

IstrAction (☑383 369; www.istraction.com; Prilaz Monte Cappelletta 3) Offers fun half-day tours to Kamenjak and around Pula's fortifications, as well as medieval-themed full-day excursions around Istria.

Main post office (Danteov trg 4; ⊙7am-8pm Mon-Fri, to 1pm Sat) You can make long-distance calls here. Check out the cool staircase inside.

MMC Luka (Istarska 30; per hr 25KN; ⊙8am-midnight Mon-Fri, to 3pm Sat) Internet access. There's also free wi-fi all around town; inquire at the tourism office about specific locations.

Tourist Ambulance (Flanatička 27; ⊙8am-9.30pm Mon-Fri Jul & Aug) Medical clinic.

Tourist Information Centre (☑212 987; www.pulainfo.hr; Forum 3; ⊙8am-9pm Mon-Fri, 9am-9pm Sat & Sun summer, around 8am-7pm rest of yr) Knowledgeable and friendly staff provide maps, brochures and schedules of events in Pula and around Istria. Pick up two useful booklets: *Domus Bonus*, which lists the best-quality private accommodation in Istria, and *Istra Gourmet*, with a list of all restaurants.

ⓘ Getting There & Away

BOAT Pula's harbour is located west of the bus station. **Jadroagent** (☑210 431; www.jadroagent.hr; Riva 14; ⊙7am-3pm Mon-Fri) has schedules and tickets for boats connecting Istria with the islands and south of Croatia.

Commodore Cruises (☑211 631; www.commodore-travel.hr; Riva 14) sells tickets for a catamaran between Pula and Zadar (100KN, five hours), which runs five times weekly from July through early September and twice weekly in June and the rest of September. There's a Wednesday boat service to Venice (430KN, 3½ hours) between June and September.

BUS From the Pula **bus station** (☑060 304 091; Šijanska 4), located 500m northeast of the town centre, there are buses heading to Rijeka (97KN, 1½hr) almost hourly. In summer, reserve a seat a day in advance. There's also a **garderoba** (left-luggage office; per hr 2.50KN; ⊙24hr) here.

There are weekly buses to Frankfurt and twice-weekly buses to Munich.

TRAIN Less than 1km north of town, the train station is near the sea along Kolodvorska. There is one direct train daily to Ljubljana (144KN, 4½ hours) and three to Zagreb (140KN, nine hours), but you must board a bus for part of the trip, from Lupoglav to Rijeka.

ⓘ Getting Around

The city buses of use to visitors are 1, which runs to Camping Stoja, and 2A and 3A to Verudela. The frequency varies from every 15 minutes to every half hour (from 5am to 11.30pm). Tickets are sold at *tisak* (news stands) for 6KN, or from the driver for 11KN.

Rovinj

POP 14,400

Rovinj (Rovigno in Italian) is coastal Istria's star attraction. It can get overrun with tourists in the summer months and residents are developing a sharp eye for maximising their profits (by upgrading hotels and restaurants to four-star status), but it remains one of the last true Mediterranean fishing ports. Fishermen haul their catch into the harbour in the early morning, followed by a horde of squawking gulls, and mend their nets before lunch.

The massive Church of St Euphemia, with its 60m-high tower, punctuates the peninsula.

Wooded hills and low-rise hotels surround the Old Town, which is webbed by steep, cobbled streets and piazzas. The 13 green, offshore islands of the Rovinj archipelago make for a pleasant afternoon away.

Sights

The Old Town of Rovinj is contained within an egg-shaped peninsula. There are two harbours – the northern open harbour and the small, protected harbour to the south. About 1.5km south is the Punta Corrente Forest Park and the wooded cape of **Zlatni Rt** (Golden Cape).

Church of St Euphemia   CHURCH
(Sveta Eufemija; Petra Stankovića; ☺10am-6pm Jun-Sep, 10am-4pm May, 10am-2pm Apr, by appointment Oct-Mar) The town's showcase is this imposing church, which dominates the Old Town from its hilltop location in the middle of the peninsula. Built in 1736, it's the largest baroque building in Istria, reflecting the period during the 18th century when Rovinj was its most populous town, an important fishing centre and the bulwark of the Venetian fleet.

Inside the church behind the right-hand altar, look for the marble **tomb of St Euphemia**, Rovinj's patron saint martyred in AD 304, whose body appeared in Rovinj one dark stormy night according to legend. The mighty 60m **bell tower** is topped by a copper statue of St Euphemia, which shows the direction of the wind by turning on a spindle. You can climb the tower (to the left of the altar) for 15KN.

Batana House   MUSEUM
(Pina Budicina 2; adult/child 10/5KN, with guide 15KN; ☺10am-2pm & 7-11pm Jun-Sep, 10am-2pm & 4-6pm Tue-Sun Oct-Jan & Mar-May) On the harbour, Batana House is a museum dedicated to the *batana*, a flat-bottomed fishing boat that stands as a symbol of Rovinj's seafaring and fishing traditions.

Grisia   STREET
(🏠) Lined with galleries where local artists sell their work, this cobbled street leads uphill from behind the elaborate 1679 **Balbi Arch** to St Euphemia. The winding narrow backstreets that spread around Grisia are an attraction in themselves. Windows, balconies, portals and squares are a pleasant confusion of styles – Gothic, Renaissance, baroque and neoclassical. On the second Sunday in August each year, Grisia becomes

an open-air **art exhibition**, with anyone from children to professional painters displaying their work.

Punta Corrente Forest Park   PARK
Follow the waterfront on foot or by bike past Hotel Park to this verdant area, locally known as Zlatni Rat, about 1.5km south. It's covered in oak and pine groves and boasts 10 species of cypress. You can swim off the rocks or just sit and admire the offshore islands.

Activities

Most people hop aboard a boat for swimming, snorkelling and sunbathing. A trip to Crveni Otok or Sveta Katarina is easily arranged. In summer, there are hourly boats from 5.30am till midnight to the islands of **Sveta Katarina** (return 30KN, 10 minutes) and **Crveni Otok** (return 40KN, 15 minutes). They leave from just opposite Hotel Adriatic and also from the Delfin ferry dock near Hotel Park.

Nadi Scuba Diving Centar (✆813 290; www.scuba.hr) and **Petra** (✆812 880; www.divingpetra.hr) offer daily boat dives. The main attraction is the Baron Gautsch wreck, an Austrian passenger steamer sunk in 1914 by a sea mine in 40m of water.

Cycling around Rovinj and the Punta Corrente Forest Park is a superb way to spend an afternoon. You can rent bicycles at many agencies around town, for around 20KN per hour or 70KN per day.

There are other exciting options, such as kayaking; book a trip through **Adistra** (✆095 838 3797; Carera 69). Nine-kilometre jaunts around the Rovinj archipelago cost 270KN; a 14km outing to the Limska Draga Fjord is 290KN.

Tours

Most travel agencies in Rovinj sell day trips to Venice (390KN to 520KN), Plitvice (500KN to 600KN) and Brijuni (380KN to 470KN). There are also fish picnics (250KN), panoramic cruises (100KN) and boat outings to Limska Draga Fjord (150KN). These can be slightly cheaper if booked through one of the independent operators that line the waterfront; **Delfin** (✆848 265) is reliable.

Sleeping

Rovinj has become Istria's destination of choice for hordes of summertime tourists, so reserving in advance is strongly recommended. Prices have been rising steadily and probably will continue to do so, as the city gears up to reach elite status.

If you want to stay in private accommodation, there is little available in the Old Town, where there's also no free parking and accommodation costs are higher. Double rooms start at 220KN in the high season, with a small discount for single occupancy; two-person apartments start at 330KN. Out of season, prices go down considerably.

The surcharge for a stay of less than three nights is up to 50%, and guests who stay only one night are sometimes punished with a 100% surcharge. Outside summer months, you should be able to bargain the surcharge away. You can book through one of the travel agencies.

Except for a few private options, most hotels and camping grounds in the area are managed by **Maistra** (www.maistra.com).

TOP CHOICE Hotel Lone DESIGN HOTEL €€€
(📞632 000; www.lonehotel.com; Luje Adamovića 31; s/d 1478/1847KN; P✳@🛜) Croatia's first design hotel, this 248-room powerhouse of style is a creation of Croatia's starchitects 3LHD. Rising over Lone bay, a 10-minute stroll from the Old Town, it has light-flooded rooms with private terraces, a restaurant and an extensive spa. Guests can use the pools at the next-door Monte Mulini.

Villa Valdibora HOTEL €€€
(📞845 040; www.valdibora.com; Silvano Chiurco 8; s/d 1080/1440KN; ✳🛜) The 11 rooms, suites and apartments in this historic building come with cool stone floors and upscale trimmings such as hydromassage showers. There's a fitness room, massages and bikes for rent.

Villa Baron Gautsch GUESTHOUSE €€
(📞840 538; www.baron-gautsch.com; IM Ronjgova 7; s/d 293/586KN; ✳🛜) This German-owned *pansion* (guesthouse), up the leafy street leading from Hotel Park, has 17 spick-and-span rooms, some with terraces and lovely views of the sea and the Old Town. It's cash (kuna) only.

Hotel Adriatic HOTEL €€€
(📞800 250; www.maistra.com; Pina Budicina bb; s/d 747/933KN; P✳🛜) The location of this hotel, right on the harbour, is excellent and the rooms are well-equipped, albeit in need of renovation and on the kitschy side. The pricier sea-view rooms have more space and newer fittings.

Porton Biondi CAMPING GROUND €
(📞813 557; www.portonbiondi.hr; Aleja Porton Biondi 1; campsites per person/tent 42/26KN; ⊙mid-Mar–Oct; 🐕) This beachside camping ground, which sleeps 1200, is about 700m from the Old Town.

✗ Eating

Picnickers can get supplies at the supermarket next to the bus station or at one of the Konzum stores around town.

Most of the restaurants that line the harbour offer the standard fish and meat mainstays at similar prices. For a more gourmet experience, you'll need to bypass the water vistas. Note that many restaurants shut their doors between lunch and dinner.

TOP CHOICE Male Madlene TAPAS €
(Križa 28; snacks from 30KN; ⊙11am-2pm & 7-11pm May-Sep) Adorable spot in the owner's tiny living room hanging over the sea, where she serves up creative tapas with market-fresh ingredients, based on old Italian recipes, plus great Istrian wines by the glass.

Monte MEDITERRANEAN €€€
(📞830 203; Montalbano 75; mains from 190KN) Rovinj's top restaurant, right below St Euphemia Church, is worth the hefty cost for the pure enjoyment of its beautifully presented dishes served on the elegant glassed-in terrace. Reserve ahead in high season.

Da Sergio PIZZERIA €
(Grisia 11; pizzas 28-71KN) It's worth waiting in line to get a table at this old-fashioned two-floor pizzeria that dishes out Rovinj's best thin-crust pizza. The best is Gogo, with fresh tomato and arugula (rocket) and prosciutto.

Kantinon SEAFOOD €
(Alda Rismonda 18; mains from 30KN) A fishing theme runs through this high-ceilinged canteen, which specialises in fresh seafood at low prices. The Batana fish plate for two is great value, as are the set menus.

Ulika MEDITERRANEAN €€
(Porečka 6; mains from 100KN; 🍴) Tucked away in an alleyway, this small, pretty tavern with streetside seating excludes the staples of Adriatic food kitsch (pizza, calamari) and instead features well-prepared, if pricey, Mediterranean fare.

Veli Jože FISH €
(Križa 3; mains from 50KN) Graze on good Istrian standards, either in the eclectic interior

BUSES FROM ROVINJ

DESTINATION	PRICE (KN)	DURATION	FREQUENCY (DAILY)
Dubrovnik	628	16hr	1
Labin	80	2hr	2
Poreč	35-50	50min	15
Pula	35-45	50min	20
Rijeka	93-127	1½-3hr	5
Split	444	11hr	1
Trieste (Italy)	100-120	1½hr	2
Zagreb	150-200	4-6hr	10

crammed with knick-knacks or at the clutch of outdoor tables with water views.

Drinking

Limbo CAFE-BAR
(Casale 22b; 🛜) Cosy cafe-bar with small candlelit tables and cushions laid out on the stairs leading to the Old Town's hilltop. It serves tasty snacks and good Prosecco.

Piassa Granda WINE BAR
(Veli trg 1) This stylish little wine bar with red walls and wood-beamed ceilings has 150 wine labels, mainly Istrian, 20 *rakija* varieties and delicious snacks.

Valentino COCKTAIL BAR
(Križa 28) Premium cocktail prices at this high-end spot include fantastic sunset views from cushions scattered on the water's edge.

Havana COCKTAIL BAR
(Aldo Negri bb) Tropical cocktails, Cuban cigars, straw parasols and the shade of tall pine trees make this open-air bar a popular spot.

ⓘ Information

There are ATMs and banks all around town. Most travel agencies will change money.
Globtour (📞814 130; www.globtour-turizam. hr; Alda Rismonda 2) Excursions and private accommodation.
Medical Centre (📞813 004; Istarska bb)
Planet (📞840 494; www.planetrovinj.com; Križa 1) Good bargains on private accommodation. Doubles as an internet cafe (6KN per 10 minutes) and has a printer.
Main post office (Matteo Benussi 4; ⊙8am-9pm Mon-Sat summer, 8am-7pm Mon-Fri, to 1pm Sat winter) You can make phone calls here.
Tourist office (📞811 566; www.tzgrovinj.hr; Pina Budicina 12; ⊙8am-10pm Jun-Sep, 8am-

3pm Mon-Fri, to 1pm Sat Oct-May) Has plenty of brochures and maps. Just off Trg Maršala Tita.

ⓘ Getting There & Around

The bus station is just to the southeast of the Old Town. There's a **garderoba** (left-luggage office; per day 10KN; ⊙6.30am-8pm).

Poreč

POP 20,600

Poreč (Parenzo in Italian) sits on a low, narrow peninsula halfway down the western coast of Istria. The ancient Roman town is the centrepiece of a vast system of resorts that stretch north and south, entirely devoted to summer tourism. While this is not the place for a quiet getaway (unless you come out of season), there is a World Heritage–listed basilica, a medley of Gothic, Romanesque and baroque buildings, well-developed tourist infrastructure and the pristine Istrian interior within easy reach.

⊙ Sights

The compact Old Town, called Parentium by the Romans, is based on a rectangular street plan. The ancient Decumanus with its polished stones is the main street running through the peninsula's middle, lined with shops and restaurants. Hotels, travel agencies and excursion boats are on the quayside Obala Maršala Tita, which runs from the small-boat harbour to the tip of the peninsula.

Euphrasian Basilica BASILICA
(Eufrazijeva bb; adult/concession 30/15KN; ⊙9am-6pm Mon-Sat, 2-6pm Sun Apr-Sep) The main reason to visit Poreč is to see the 6th-century Euphrasian Basilica, a World Heritage Site

and one of Europe's finest intact examples of Byzantine art. Built on the site of a 4th-century oratory, the sacral complex includes a church, an atrium and a baptistery. What packs in the crowds are the glittering wall mosaics in the apse, 6th-century masterpieces featuring biblical scenes, archangels and Istrian martyrs. The belfry affords an invigorating view of the Old Town.

Make sure to pop into the adjacent **Bishop's Palace**, which contains a display of ancient stone sculptures, religious paintings and 4th-century mosaics from the original oratory.

Sveti Nikola ISLAND

There are pebble and concrete beaches to choose from here, as well as rocky breakwaters, shady pine forests and great views of the town across the way. From May to October there are passenger boats every 30 minutes (from 6.45am to 1am) from the wharf on Obala Maršala Tita.

🏃 Activities

Many recreational activities are to be found outside the town in either Plava Laguna or Zelena Laguna. For details, pick up the yearly *Poreč Info & Events* booklet from the tourist office.

From April to October, a **tourist train** operates regularly from Šetalište Antona Štifanića by the marina to Plava Laguna (20KN) and Zelena Laguna (20KN). There's a **passenger boat** (15KN) that makes the same run from the ferry landing every hour from 9am till just before midnight.

The gentle rolling hills of the interior and the well-marked paths make **cycling** and **hiking** prime ways to explore the region. The tourist office issues a free map of roads and trails. You can rent a bike at many agencies around town for 80KN per day.

There is good diving in and around shoals and sandbanks in the area, as well as at the nearby Coriolanus, a British Royal Navy warship that sank in 1945. At **Diving Centre Poreč** (☑433 606; www.divingcenter-porec.com), boat dives start at 135KN (more for caves or wrecks) it's 355KN with full equipment rental.

🛏 Sleeping

Accommodation in Poreč is plentiful but gets booked ahead of time, so advance reservations are essential if you come in July or August.

Many travel agencies can help you find private accommodation. Expect to pay between 200KN and 250KN for a double room with private bathroom in the high season, plus a 30% surcharge for stays shorter than three nights. There is a limited number of rooms available in the Old Town, which has no parking. Look for the *Domus Bonus* certificate of quality in private accommodation.

Valamar Riviera Hotel HOTEL €€€
(☑400 800; www.valamar.com; Maršala Tita 15; s/d 1230/1455KN; P✳@�🛜) Rather swanky four-star incarnation right on the harbourfront, with a private beach on Sveti Nikola. Look out for online specials and packages.

Hotel Poreč HOTEL €€
(☑451 811; www.hotelporec.com; Rade Končara 1; s/d 496/760KN; P✳🛜) While the rooms inside this concrete box have uninspiring views over the bus station and the construction site for the shopping centre opposite, they're acceptable. They have balconies and it's an easy walk from the Old Town.

Camping Zelena Laguna CAMPING GROUND €
(☑410 102; www.lagunaporec.com; Zelena Laguna; campsite per adult/site 62/117KN; ⊙mid-Apr–Sep; ✳@🛜🏊) Well-equipped for sports, this camping ground 5km from the Old Town can house up to 2700 people. It has access to many beaches, including a naturist one.

🍴 Eating

Gourmet ITALIAN €€
(Eufrazijeva 26; mains from 60KN) Comforting Italian concoctions come in all shapes and forms here – penne, tagliatelle, fusilli, gnocchi and so on. There are also pizzas from a wood-fired oven as well as meat and seafood dishes. Tables spill out on the square.

⬛TOP CHOICE Konoba Daniela ISTRIAN €€
(☑460 519; Veleniki; mains from 65KN) In the sweet little village of Veleniki, 4.5km northeast of town, this rustic family-run tavern in an 1880s house is known for its steak tartare and seasonal Istrian mainstays. Taxis charge 80KN to 100KN one way.

Buffet Horizont FAST FOOD €
(Eufrazijeva 8; mains from 30KN) For cheap and tasty seafood snacks such as sardines, shrimp and calamari, look out for this yellow house with wooden benches outside.

Drinking & Entertainment

In the last couple of years, Poreč has turned into Istria's party capital, with nightlife hawks coming from all parts of Europe to let loose in its late-night clubs.

Rakijarnica   BAR

(Trg Marafor 10) Funky bar that specialises in *rakija*, serving up no less than 50 varieties. The vibe is boho and there are occasional live bands and DJs.

Torre Rotonda   CAFE-BAR

(Narodni trg 3a) Take the steep stairs to the top of the historic Round Tower and grab a table at the open-air cafe to watch the action on the quays.

Byblos   CLUB

(www.byblos.hr; Zelena Laguna 1) On weekends, celeb guest DJs such as David Morales crank out electro house tunes at this humongous open-air club, one of Croatia's hottest places to party.

ℹ Information

You can change money at any of the many travel agencies or banks. There are ATMs all around town. There's free wi-fi on Trg Slobode and along the seafront.

Cold Fusion (K Huguesa 2; per hr 30KN; ☉9am-10pm) A computer centre at the bus station.

Main post office (Trg Slobode 14; ☉8am-8pm Mon-Sat) Has a telephone centre.

Poreč Medical Centre (☎426 400; Maura Gioseffija 2)

Sunny Way (☎452 021; sunnyway@pu.t-com. hr; Negrija 1) Specialises in boat tickets and excursions to Italy and around Croatia.

Tourist office (☎451 293; www.to-porec.com; Zagrebačka 9; ☉8am-9pm Mon-Sat, 9am-1pm & 5-9pm Sun May-Sep, 8am-4pm Mon-Fri, 9am-1pm Sat Oct-Apr) Gives out lots of brochures and useful info.

ℹ Getting There & Away

The **bus station** (☎060 333 111; K Huguesa 2) is just outside the Old Town, behind Rade Končara, with a **garderoba** (left luggage; per hr 10KN; ☉6am-9pm). There are buses to Rovinj (42KN, 45 minutes, five daily), Zagreb (226KN, 4½ hours, five daily), Rijeka (89KN, 1½ hours, seven daily) and Pula (63KN, one to 1½ hours, five daily).

Ustica Line (www.usticalines.it) runs catamarans to Trieste every Saturday during the season (210KN, 1½ hours). There are four fast catamarans to Venice daily in high season (one way 250KN to 440KN, return 390KN to 880KN,

two hours), operated by **Venezia Lines** (www.venezialines.com) and **Commodore Cruises** (www.commodore-cruises.hr).

KVARNER REGION

 051

The Kvarner Gulf (Quarnero in Italian) covers 3300 sq km between Rijeka and Pag Island in the south, protected by the Velebit Range in the southeast, the Gorski Kotar in the east and the Učka massif in the northwest. Covered with luxuriant forests, lined with beaches and dotted with islands, the region has a mild gentle climate and a wealth of vegetation.

From the gateway city of Rijeka, Croatia's third-largest, you can easily connect to the foodie enclave of Volosko and the hiking trails inside the nature parks of Učka. The islands of Krk, Rab, Lošinj and Cres all have highly atmospheric old ports, and stretches of pristine coastline dotted with remote coves for superb swimming.

Rijeka

POP 128,700

Rijeka, Croatia's third-largest city, is an intriguing blend of gritty port and Hapsburg grandeur. Most people rush through en route to the islands or Dalmatia, but those who pause will discover charm and culture. Blend in with the coffee-sipping locals on the bustling Korzo pedestrian strip, take in the city museums and visit the imposing hilltop fortress of Trsat. Rijeka also boasts a good nightlife, intriguing festivals and Croatia's most colourful carnival.

Despite some regrettable architectural ventures in the outskirts, much of the centre is replete with ornate Austro-Hungarian–style buildings. It's a surprisingly verdant city once you've left its concrete core, which contains Croatia's largest port, with ships, cargo and cranes lining the waterfront.

Rijeka is a vital transport hub, but as there's no real beach in the city (and hotel options are few) most people base themselves in nearby Opatija.

◉ Sights

Trsat Castle   CASTLE

(adult/concession 15/5KN; ☉9am-8pm May-Oct, to 5pm Nov-Apr) High on a hill above the city is this semi-ruined, 13th-century fortress that houses two galleries and has great vistas from the open-air cafe.

Church of Our Lady of Trsat
CHURCH

(Crkva Gospe Trsatske; Frankopanski Trg; ⏰8am-5pm) Along with Trsat Castle, the other hill highlight is the Church of Our Lady of Trsat, a centuries-old magnet for believers that showcases an apparently miraculous icon of Virgin Mary.

City Monuments
MONUMENTS

(Trg Ivana Koblera) One of the few buildings to have survived the earthquake, the distinctive yellow **City Tower** (Gradski Toranj; Korzo) was originally a gate from the seafront to the city. The still-functioning clock was mounted in 1873.

Pass under the City Tower to the **Roman Gate** (Stara Vrata), which marks the former entrance to Praetorium, an ancient military complex; you can see the remains in a small excavation area.

Maritime & History Museum
MUSEUM

(Pomorski i Povijesni Muzej Hrvatskog Primorja; www.ppmhp.hr; Muzejski trg 1; adult/concession 10/5KN; ⏰9am-4pm Tue-Fri, to 1pm Sat) Housed in the Governor's Palace, this museum gives a vivid picture of life among seafarers, with model ships, sea charts, navigation instruments and portraits of captains.

Astronomical Centre
OBSERVATORY

(Astronomski Centar; www.rijekasport.hr; Sveti Križ 33; ⏰8am-11pm Tue-Sat) High on a hill in the east of the city, Croatia's first astronomical centre is a striking modern complex encompassing an observatory, planetarium and study centre. To get here, catch bus 7A from the centre.

✵ Festivals & Events

Rijeka Carnival
CARNIVAL

(www.ri-karneval.com.hr) This is the largest carnival in Croatia, with two weeks of pageants, street dances, concerts, masked balls, exhibitions and parades. It occurs between late January and early March, depending on when Easter falls.

Hartera
MUSIC

(www.hartera.com) Hartera is an annual electronic music festival with DJs and artists from across Europe. It's held in a former paper factory on the banks of the Rječina River over three days in mid-June.

⌂ Sleeping

Prices in Rijeka hotels generally stay the same year-round, except at popular carnival time, when you can expect to pay a surcharge. There are few private rooms in Rijeka itself; the tourist office (p146) lists these on its website. Nearby Opatija has a lot more accommodation.

Grand Hotel Bonavia
HOTEL €€€

(☏357 100; www.bonavia.hr; Dolac 4; s/d from 800/977KN; P❄@⊛) Right in the heart of town, this striking glass-fronted modernist building is Rijeka's top hotel. The rooms are well-equipped and comfort levels are high. There's a well-regarded restaurant, a spa and a stylish pavement cafe.

Best Western Hotel Jadran
HOTEL €€€

(☏216 600; www.jadran-hoteli.hr; Šetalište XIII Divizije 46; s/d from 706/833KN; P❄@⊛) Located 2km east of the centre, this attractive four-star hotel has seaview rooms where you can revel in the tremendous Adriatic vistas from your balcony right above the water. There's a tiny beach below.

Hotel Neboder
HOTEL €€

(☏373 538; www.jadran-hoteli.hr; Strossmayerova 1; s/d from 462/578KN; P❄@) An iconic design, this modernist tower block offers small, neat and modish rooms, most with balconies and amazing views; however, only the superior rooms have air-conditioning.

Youth Hostel
HOSTEL €

(☏406 420; www.hfhs.hr; Šetalište XIII Divizije 23; dm/s/d 130/236/314KN; @⊛) In the leafy residential area of Pečine, 2km east of the centre, this renovated 19th-century villa has clean, spacious (if plain) rooms and a communal TV area. Reserve ahead.

✗ Eating

There's very little choice on Sundays, when most places are closed. Many cafes on Korzo serve light meals.

Foodies should consider heading to nearby Volosko, 2km east of Opatija, where there's a strip of really high-quality restaurants.

TOP CHOICE Na Kantunu
SEAFOOD €€

(Demetrova 2; mains from 45KN) If you're lucky enough to grab a table at this tiny lunchtime spot on an industrial stretch of the port, you'll be treated to the superlative daily catch.

Kukuriku
CROATIAN €€€

(☏691 519; www.kukuriku.hr; Trg Matka Laginje 1a, Kastav; 6-course meals 380-550KN; ⏰closed Mon Nov-Easter) This opulent yet modern hotel-restaurant is owned by slow-food pioneer

Nenad Kukurin, who has a reputation for his innovative take on traditional Croatian recipes. Located in historic Kastav, Rijeka's hilltop suburb, it's worth the splurge. Take bus 18 from Rijeka (33 and 37 from Opatija).

Restaurant Spagho
ITALIAN €

(Ivana Zajca 24a; mains from 40KN) A stylish, modern Italian place with exposed brickwork, art and hip seating that offers delicious and filling portions of pasta, pizza, salads, and meat and fish dishes.

Zlatna Školjka
SEAFOOD €€

(Kružna 12; mains from 65KN) Savour the superbly prepared seafood and choice Croatian wines at this formal maritime-themed restaurant. The adjacent **Bracera** (Kružna 12; mains from 60KN), by the same owners, serves crusty pizza, even on a Sunday.

Mlinar
BAKERY €

(Frana Supila; items from 13KN; ⊙6am-8pm Mon-Fri, 6.30am-3pm Sat, 7am-1pm Sun) The best bakery in town, with delicious filled baguettes, wholemeal bread, croissants and *burek*.

🍷 Drinking

The main drags of Riva and Korzo are the best bet for a drink, with everything from lounge bars to no-nonsense pubs.

⌈TOP⌋ Gradena
⌊CHOICE⌋
CAFE

(www.bascinskiglasi.hr; Trsat; ☎) Set in the grounds of Trsat Castle, this happening cafebar with chillout music and friendly service would rate anywhere.

Filodrammatica Bookshop Cafe
CAFE

(☑498 141; www.vbz.hr; Korzo 28) A cafe and bar with luxurious decor and a VBZ (Croatia's biggest publisher) bookshop at the back, Filodrammatica also prides itself on specialist coffees and fresh, single-source beans.

Caffe Jazz Tunel
BAR

(☑327 116; www.jazztunel.com; Školjić 12; ⊙9am-2am Mon-Fri, 5pm-2am Sat) One of the city's most popular bars, it's crowded all week long, but full to bursting on Friday and Saturday nights when you can find live music or DJs rocking the night.

❶ Information

There are ATMs and exchange offices along Korzo and at the train station.

Hospital (☑658 111; Krešimirova 42)

Main post office (Korzo 13; ⊙7am-8pm Mon-Fri, to 2pm Sat) Has a telephone centre and an exchange office.

Tourist Information Centre (☑335 882; www.tz-rijeka.hr; Korzo 33a; ⊙8am-8pm Mon-Sat Apr-Sep, 8am-8pm Mon-Fri, to 2pm Sat Oct-Mar) Has good colour city maps, lots of brochures and private accommodation lists, though the staff can be aloof.

❶ Getting There & Away

BOAT Jadroagent (☑211 626; www.jadroagent.hr; Trg Ivana Koblera 2) Has information on all boats around Croatia.

Jadrolinija (☑211 444; www.jadrolinija.hr; Riječki Lukobran bb; ⊙8am-8pm Mon-Fri, 9am-5pm Sat & Sun) Sells tickets for the large coastal ferries that run all year between Rijeka and Dubrovnik on their way to Bari in Italy, via Split, Hvar, Korčula and Mljet. Check Jadrolinija's website for up-to-date schedules and prices. All ferries depart from the new ferry terminal.

BUS The **intercity bus station** (Trg Žabica) is west of the centre, at the western edge of Riva. The bus-station **garderoba** (left-luggage office; per day 15KN; ⊙5.30am-10.30pm) is at the cafe next door to the ticket office.

If you fly into Zagreb, there is a Croatia Airlines van that goes directly from Zagreb airport to Rijeka daily (160KN, two hours, 3.30pm). It goes back to Zagreb from Rijeka at 5am. There are three daily buses to Trieste (60KN, 2½ hours)

DOMESTIC BUSES FROM RIJEKA

DESTINATION	PRICE (KN)	DURATION (HR)	FREQUENCY (DAILY)
Dubrovnik	362-503	12-13	3-4
Krk	59	1-2	14
Pula	97	2¼	8
Rovinj	90	1-2	4
Split	253-330	8	6-7
Zadar	161-210	4-5	6-7
Zagreb	137-160	2¼-3	13-15

and one daily bus to Ljubljana (175KN, five hours). To get to Plitvice (142KN, four hours), you have to change in Otočac.

CAR AMC (☑338 800; www.amcrentacar.hr; Lukobran 4) Based in the new ferry terminal building, has cars starting from 250KN per day.

TRAIN The **train station** (☑213 333; Krešimirova 5) is a 10-minute walk east of the city centre; ther's a **garderoba** (left-luggage office; per day 15KN; ⏰4.30am-10.30pm). Seven daily trains run to Zagreb (100KN, four to five hours). There's one daily connection to Split (170KN, eight hours), though it involves a change at Ogulin. Two direct daily services head to Ljubljana (98KN, three hours) and one daily train goes to Vienna (319KN to 525KN, nine hours).

ℹ Getting Around

Taxis are very reasonable in Rijeka (if you use the right firm). **Cammeo** (☑313 313) cabs are modern, inexpensive, have meters and are highly recommended; a ride in the central area costs 20KN.

Opatija

POP 7870

Opatija stretches along the coast, just 15km west of Rijeka, its forested hills sloping down to the sparkling sea. It was this breathtaking location and the agreeable all-year climate that made Opatija the most fashionable seaside resort for the Viennese elite during the days of the Austro-Hungarian empire. The grand residences of the wealthy have since been revamped and turned into upscale hotels, with a particular accent on spa and health holidays. Foodies have been flocking from afar too, for the clutch of terrific restaurants in the nearby fishing village of Volosko.

Opatija sits on a narrow strip of land sandwiched between the sea and the foothills of Mt Učka. Ulica Maršala Tita is the main road that runs through town; it's lined with travel agencies, ATMs, restaurants, shops and hotels.

◉ Sights & Activities

Lungomare PROMENADE
The pretty Lungomare is the region's showcase. Lined with plush villas and ample gardens, this shady promenade winds along the sea for 12km from Volosko to Lovran. Along the way are innumerable rocky outcrops – a better option than Opatija's concrete beach.

Villa Angiolina HISTORICAL BUILDING
(Park Angiolina 1; ⏰9am-1pm & 4.30-9.30pm Tue-Sun summer, shorter hours rest of year) The re-stored Villa Angiolina houses the **Croatian Museum of Tourism**, a grand title for a modest collection of old photographs, postcards, brochures and posters tracing the history of travel. Don't miss a stroll around the verdant gardens that surround the villa, replete with gingko trees, sequoias, holm oaks and Japanese camellia (Opatija's symbol).

Učka Nature Park NATURE RESERVE
Opatija and the surrounding region offer some wonderful opportunities for hiking and biking around the Učka mountain range; the **tourist office** (☑293 753; www.pp-ucka.hr; Liganj 42; ⏰8am-4.30pm Mon-Fri) has maps and information.

⬛ Sleeping & Eating

There are no real budget hotels in Opatija, but there's plenty of value in the midrange and top end. Private rooms are abundant but a little more expensive than in other areas; expect to pay around 170KN to 240KN per person.

Maršala Tita is lined with serviceable restaurants that offer pizza, grilled meat and fish, but don't expect anything outstanding. Head to nearby Volosko for fine dining and regional specialties.

Villa Ariston HISTORIC HOTEL €€
(☑271 379; www.villa-ariston.com; Ulica Maršala Tita 179; s/d 600/800KN; P✳@☎) With a gorgeous location beside a rocky cove, this historic hotel has period charm and celeb cachet in spades (Coco Chanel and the Kennedys are former guests).

Hotel Opatija HOTEL €€
(☑271 388; www.hotel-opatija.hr; Trg Vladimira Gortana 2/1; r from 486KN; P✳@☎) The setting in a Habsburg-era mansion is the forte of this large hilltop three-star hotel with comfortable rooms, an amazing terrace, a small indoor seawater pool and lovely gardens.

Medveja CAMPING GROUND €
(☑291 191; medveja@liburnia.hr; campsites per adult/tent 44/32KN; ⏰Easter–mid-Oct) On a pretty pebble cove 10km south of Opatija, this camping ground has apartments and mobile homes for rent too.

Istranka ISTRIAN €
(Bože Milanovića 2; mains from 55KN) Graze on flavourful Istrian mainstays like *manestra* (vegetable and bean soup) at this rustic-themed tavern in a small street just up from Maršala Tita.

WORTH A TRIP

VOLOSKO

Volosko is one of the prettiest places on this coastline, a fishing village that has also become something of a restaurant mecca in recent years. This is not a tourist resort, and whether you're passing through for a drink or having a gourmet meal you'll enjoy the local ambience and wonderful setting.

Rijeka and Volosko are connected by bus, or you can walk along the coastal promenade from Opatija, a 30-minute stroll past bay trees, palms, figs and oaks and magnificent villas.

Tramerka (Andrije Mohorovičića 15; mains from 65KN; ⊘Tue-Sun) It doesn't have sea views but this wonderful place scores on every other level. Chef-patron Andrej Barbieri will expertly guide you through the short menu, chosen from the freshest available seafood (the *gregada* fish stew is just stupendous) and locally sourced meats.

Skalinada (www.skalinada.org; Put Uz Dol 17; meals from 80KN) An intimate, highly atmospheric little bistro-style place with sensitive lighting, exposed stone walls and a creative menu of Croatian food (small dishes or mains) using seasonal and local ingredients.

Drinking & Entertainment

Opatija is a pretty sedate place. Its Viennese-style coffee houses and hotel terraces are popular with the mature clientele, though there are a few stylish bars. Check out the slightly bohemian **Tantra** (Lido), which juts out into the Kvarner Gulf, and **Hemingway** (Zert 2), the original venue of what is now a nationwide chain of sleek cocktail bars.

❶ Information

Da Riva (☏272 990; www.da-riva.hr; Ulica Maršala Tita 170) A good source for private accommodation, and runs excursions around Croatia.

Linea Verde (☏701 107; www.lineaverde-croatia.com; Andrije Štangera 42, Volosko) Specialist agency with trips to Risnjak and Učka Nature Park and gourmet tours around Istria.

Tourist office (☏271 310; www.opatija-tourism.hr; Ulica Maršala Tita 128; ⊘8am-10pm Mon-Sat, 5-9pm Sun Jul & Aug, shorter hours rest of year) This office has knowledgeable staff and lots of maps, leaflets and brochures.

❶ Getting There & Away

Bus 32 runs through the centre of Rijeka along Adamićeva to the Opatija Riviera (20KN, 15km) as far as Lovran, every 20 minutes daily until late in the evening.

Krk Island

POP 16,400

Croatia's largest island, 409-sq-km Krk (Veglia in Italian) is also one of the busiest in the summer. It may not be the most beautiful or

lush island in Croatia – in fact, it's overdeveloped – but its decades of experience in tourism make it an easy place to visit, with good transport connections and well-organised infrastructure.

❶ Getting There & Around

The Krk toll bridge links the northern part of the island with the mainland, and a regular car ferry links Valbiska with Merag on Cres (passenger/car 18KN/115KN, 30 minutes) in summer.

Krk is also home to **Rijeka airport** (www.rijeka-airport.hr), the main hub for flights to the Kvarner region, which consist mostly of low-cost and charter flights during summer.

Rijeka and Krk Town are connected by nine to 13 daily bus services (56KN, one to two hours). Services are reduced on weekends.

Six daily buses run from Zagreb to Krk Town (179KN to 194KN, three to four hours). Note that some bus lines are more direct than others, which will stop in every village en route. **Autotrans** (www.autotrans.hr) has two quick daily buses.

KRK TOWN
POP 3370

The picturesque Krk Town makes a good base for exploring the island. It encompasses a medieval walled centre and, spreading out into the surrounding coves and hills, a modern development that includes a port, beaches, camping grounds and hotels.

◉ Sights

Highlights include the Romanesque **Cathedral of the Assumption** (Katedrala Uznešenja; Trg Svetog Kvirina; ⊘morning & evening Mass) and the fortified **Kaštel** (Trg Kamplin) facing the seafront on the northern edge of the Old

Town. The narrow cobbled streets that make up the pretty old quarter are worth a wander, although they're typically packed.

🛏 Sleeping & Eating

The Old Town only has one hotel; all the others are located in a large complex east of the centre and are very family orientated. Consult travel agencies for private accommodation. Note that the only hostel in town is pretty rundown.

⎯TOP⎯ Hotel Marina CHOICE BOUTIQUE HOTEL €€€

(📞221 357; www.hotelikrk.hr; Obala Hrvatske Mornarice 6; d 1460KN; 🅿❋@🛜) The only hotel in the Old Town enjoys a prime waterfront location and has 10 deluxe contemporary units.

Bor HOTEL €€

(📞220 200; www.hotelbor.hr; Šetalište Dražica 5; s/d from 480/960KN; ☉Apr-Oct; 🅿🛜) The 22 rooms are modest and without trimmings at this low-key hotel, but the seafront location amid mature pines makes it a worthwhile place to stay.

Autocamp Ježevac CAMPING GROUND €

(📞221 081; camping@valamar.com; Plavnička bb; campsite per adult/site 50/62KN; ☉mid-Apr–mid-Oct) Beachfront camping ground with shady pitches located on old farming terraces, with good swimming sites. It's a 10-minute walk southwest of town.

Konoba Nono CROATIAN €

(Krčkih Iseljenika 8; mains from 40KN) Savour local specialties like *šurlice sa junećim* (pasta topped with goulash), just a hop and a skip from the Old Town.

Galija PIZZERIA €

(www.galija-krk.com; Frankopanska 38; mains from 45KN) Munch your *margarita* or *vagabondo* pizza, grilled meat or fresh fish under beamed ceilings of this convivial part-*konoba*, part-pizzeria.

ℹ Information

The **main tourist office** (📞220 226; Vela Placa 1; ☉8am-3pm Mon-Fri) and **seasonal tourist office** (📞220 226; www.tz-krk.hr; Obala Hrvatske Mornarice bb; ☉8am-8pm Mon-Sat, 8am-2pm Sun Jun-Oct & Easter-May) distribute brochures and materials, including a map of hiking paths, and advice in many languages.

You can change money at any travel agency and there are numerous ATMs around town.

The bus from Rijeka stops at the station (no left-luggage office) by the harbour, a few minutes' walk from the Old Town.

DALMATIA

Roman ruins, spectacular beaches, old fishing ports, medieval architecture and unspoilt offshore islands make a trip to Dalmatia (Dalmacija) unforgettable. Occupying the central 375km of Croatia's Adriatic

---

LOŠINJ & CRES ISLANDS

Separated by an 11m-wide canal (with a bridge), these two highly scenic islands in the Kvarner archipelago are often treated as a single entity. On Lošinj, the more populated of the two, the pretty ports of Mali Lošinj and Veli Lošinj, ringed by pine forests and lush vegetation, attract plenty of summertime tourists. Consequently, there are varied sleeping and eating options. The waters around Lošinj are the first protected marine area for dolphins in the entire Mediterranean, watched over by the Mali Lošinj–based **Blue World** (www.blue-world.org) NGO.

Wilder, more barren Cres has a natural allure that's intoxicating and inspiring. Sparsely populated, it's covered in dense primeval forests and lined with a craggy coastline of soaring cliffs, hidden coves and ancient hilltop towns. The northern half of Cres, known as Tramuntana, is prime cruising terrain for the protected griffon vulture; see these giant birds at **Eco-Centre Caput Insulae** (📞840 525; www.supovi.hr; Beli 4; adult/concession 50/25KN; ☉9am-8pm, closed Nov-Mar), an excellent visitor centre in Beli on the eastern coast. The main seaside settlements lie on the western shore of Cres, while the highlands showcase the astounding medieval town of Lubenice.

The main maritime port of entry for the islands is Mali Lošinj, which is connected to Rijeka, Pula, Zadar and Venice in the summer. A variety of car ferries and catamaran boats are run by **Jadrolinija** (www.jadrolinija.hr), **Split Tours** (www.splittours.hr) and **Venezia Lines** (www.venezialines.com).

coast, Dalmatia offers a matchless combination of hedonism and historical discovery. The jagged coast is speckled with lush offshore islands and dotted with historic cities.

Split is the largest city in the region and a hub for bus and boat connections along the Adriatic, as well as home to the late-Roman Diocletian's Palace. Nearby are the early Roman ruins in Solin (Salona). Zadar has yet more Roman ruins and a wealth of churches. The architecture of Hvar and Korčula recalls the days when these islands were outposts of the Venetian empire. None can rival majestic Dubrovnik, a cultural and aesthetic jewel, while magical Mljet features isolated island beauty.

Zadar

023 / POP 73,400

Boasting a historic Old Town of Roman ruins and medieval churches, cosmopolitan cafes and quality museums, Zadar is an excellent city. It's not too crowded, it's not overrun with tourists and its two unique attractions – the sound-and-light spectacles of the Sea Organ and the Sun Salutation – need to be seen and heard to be believed.

It's not a picture-postcard kind of place, but the mix of beautiful Roman architecture, Hapsburg elegance, a wonderful seafront and some unsightly ordinary office blocks is what gives Zadar so much character – it's no Dubrovnik, but it's not a museum town either; this is a living, vibrant city, enjoyed by its residents and visitors alike.

The centre of town is not well blessed with hotels, though a few new places are springing up each year. Most visitors stay in the leafy resort area of Borik nearby. Zadar is a key transport hub with superb ferry connections to Croatia's Adriatic islands, Kvarner, southern Dalmatia and Italy.

◎ Sights

Sea Organ   MONUMENT

Zadar's incredible Sea Organ, designed by architect Nikola Bašić, has a hypnotic effect. Set within the perforated stone stairs that descend into the sea is a system of pipes and whistles that exudes wistful sighs when the movement of the sea pushes air through it.

Sun Salutation   MONUMENT

(🏃) Right next to the Sea Organ is the Sun Salutation, another wacky and wonderful Bašić creation. It's a 22m circle cut into the pavement, filled with 300 multilayered glass plates that collect the sun's energy during the day, and, together with the wave energy that makes the Sea Organ's sound, produce a trippy light show from sunset to sunrise that's meant to simulate the solar system.

Church of St Donat   CHURCH

(Crkva Svetog Donata; Šimuna Kožičića Benje; admission 15KN; ⊙9am-9pm May-Sep, to 4pm Oct-Apr) This circular 9th-century Byzantine structure was built over the Roman forum. A few architectural fragments are preserved inside. Notice the Latin inscriptions on the remains of the Roman sacrificial altars. Outside the church on the northwestern side is a pillar from the Roman era that served in the Middle Ages as a shame post, where wrongdoers were chained and publicly humiliated.

Museum of Ancient Glass   MUSEUM

(www.mas-zadar.hr; Poljana Zemaljskog Odbora 1; adult/concession 30/10KN; ⊙9am-9pm May-Sep, to 7pm Mon-Sat Oct-Apr) This is an impressive museum: its layout is superb, with giant lightboxes and ethereal music to make the experience special. The history and invention of glass is explained, through thousands of pieces on display: goblets, jars and vials; jewellery, rings and amulets.

Beaches   BEACHES

You can swim from the steps off the promenade and listen to the sound of the Sea Organ. There's a swimming area with diving boards, a small park and a cafe on the coastal promenade off Zvonimira. Bordered by pine trees and parks, the promenade takes you to a beach in front of Hotel Kolovare and then winds on for about a kilometre up the coast.

☞ Tours

Travel agencies offer boat cruises to Telašćica Bay and the beautiful Kornati Islands, which include lunch and a swim in the sea or a salt lake. Aquarius Travel Agency (p152) charges 250–300KN per person for a full-day trip, or ask around on Liburnska Obala (where the excursion boats are moored).

Organised trips to the national parks of Paklenica, Krka and Plitvice Lakes are also popular.

✺ Festivals & Events

Between July and September, the Zadar region showcases some of the globe's most celebrated electronic artists, bands and DJs. The ringmaster for these festivals is the Zadar-based Garden (p151) bar, but the festivals are held in a gorgeous new location, in the small village of Tisno, 45km south of Zadar. The original event, the **Garden Festival** (www.thegardenfestival.eu), has been running every July since 2006. By 2010, four other festivals (Soundwave, Suncebeat, Electric Elephant and Stop Making Sense) had joined the party between July and September.

🛏 Sleeping

Most visitors stay in the 'tourist settlement' of Borik, which isn't as bad as it sounds as it has good swimming, a nice promenade and lots of greenery. Most hotels in Borik date from Yugo days (or before) and there's also a hostel, camping ground and *sobe* (rooms) here too. Many hotels are managed by the Austria-based **Falkensteiner** (www.falkensteiner.com) group.

Contact travel agencies for private accommodation; very little is available in the Old Town, though.

ZADAR

TOP
CHOICE **Art Hotel Kalelarga** BOUTIQUE HOTEL €€€
(☑233 000; www.arthotel-kalelarga.com; Široka 23; s/d/ste 1225/1450/2300KN; P ❄ 🛜) Right in the heart of Zadar's Old Town, this 10-room boutique hotel is an understated beauty with a stylish cafe and spacious rooms in hues of sand and stone, with grand beds, elaborate lighting and cool lines. There is also a restaurant, which has tables on the main square.

Villa Hrešć HOTEL €€
(☑337 570; www.villa-hresc.hr; Obala Kneza Trpimira 28; s/d 670/850KN; P ❄ 🛜 🏊 👪) This condo-style villa is about a 20-minute walk from Zadar's historic sights. There's a coastal garden with an Old Town vista, and good-value rooms and apartments benefit from subtle colours and attractive decor. Some have massive terraces.

Hotel Venera GUESTHOUSE €€
(☑214 098; www.hotel-venera-zd.hr; Šime Ljubića 4a; d 460KN) A modest guesthouse that has two things going for it: a good location on a quiet street in the Old Town and the friendly family owners. Breakfast not included.

Student Hostel HOSTEL €
(☑224 840; Obala Kneza Branimira bb; dm 153KN; ☉Jul & Aug) This student dormitory turns into a hostel in July and August. It's centrally located – right across the footbridge – and has no-frills three-bed rooms.

BORIK

Autocamp Borik CAMPING GROUND €
(☑332 074; per adult 56KN, per campsite 94-146KN; ☉May-Oct) A good option for those who want easy access to Zadar, this camping ground is steps away from the shore at Borik. Pitches are shaded by tall pines.

🍴 Eating

Dining options in Zadar are eclectic and generally good value. You'll find elegant restaurants specialising in Dalmatian cuisine and no-nonsense canteen-style places offering filling grub.

Zadar's **market** (☉6am-3pm), off Jurja Barakovica, is one of Croatia's best.

TOP
CHOICE **Foša** MEDITERRANEAN €€
(www.fosa.hr; Kralja Dmitra Zvonimira 2; mains from 85KN) A classy place with a sleek interior and a gorgeous terrace that juts out into the harbour. Start by tasting the olive oils, and move on to a grilled Adriatic fish of your choice, though red-meat eaters won't be disappointed either.

Na po ure DALMATIAN €
(Špire Brusine 8; mains from 40KN) This unpretentious family-run *konoba* is the place to sate that appetite, with from-the-heart Dalmatian cooking: grilled lamb, calf's liver and fresh fish served with potatoes and vegetables.

Zalogajnica Ljepotica DALMATIAN €
(Obala Kneza Branimira 4b; mains from 35KN) The cheapest place in town prepares three to four dishes a day (think risotto, pasta and grilled meat) at knockout prices in a no-frills setting.

🍷 Drinking

Zadar has pavement cafes, lounge bars, boho bars and everything in between. Head to the district of Varoš on the southwest side of the Old Town for interesting little dive bars popular with students and arty types.

TOP
CHOICE **Garden** BAR, RESTAURANT
(www.thegardenzadar.com; Bedemi Zadarskih Pobuna; ☉late May-Oct) If anywhere can claim to have put Zadar on the map it's this remarkable bar-club-garden-restaurant perched on top of the old city walls with jaw-dropping harbour views. It's very Ibiza-esque, with cushion mattresses, secluded alcoves, vast sail-like sunshades, purple-and-white decor and contemporary electronic music.

Arsenal
BAR, RESTAURANT

(www.arsenalzadar.com; Trg Tri Bunara 1) A huge renovated shipping warehouse that now contains a lounge bar, a restaurant, a gallery and a cultural centre and has a cool, cultured vibe. There are musical events, good food and even a tourist-info desk (which may or may not be staffed).

Caffe Bar Lovre
CAFE

(Narodni trg 1) With a huge terrace on Narodni Trg, gorgeous Lovre has plenty of atmosphere and a heart-of-the-city vibe.

ⓘ Information

Aquarius Travel Agency (☑212 919; www.juresko.hr; Nova Vrata bb) Books accommodation and excursions.

Geris.net (Federica Grisogona 81; per hr 25KN) The city's best cybercafe.

Hospital (☑315 677; Bože Peričića 5)

Miatours (☑/fax 212 788; www.miatours.hr; Vrata Svetog Krševana) Arranges excursions and accommodation.

Post office (Poljana Pape Aleksandra III; ◷7.30am-9pm Mon-Sat, to 2pm Sun) You can make phone calls here and it has an ATM.

Tourist office (☑316 166; www.tzzadar.hr; Mihe Klaića 5; ◷8am-10pm Mon-Fri, to 9pm Sat & Sun Jun-Sep, to 8pm daily Oct-May) Publishes a good colour map and the free *Zadar City Guide*.

ⓘ Getting There & Away

AIR Zadar's airport, 12km east of the city, is served by **Croatia Airlines** (☑250 101; www.croatiaairlines.hr; Poljana Natka Nodila 7) and **Ryanair** (www.ryanair.com). A Croatia Airlines bus meets all flights and costs 23KN. For a taxi, call the very efficient and cheap **Lulić** (☑494 494).

BOAT On the harbour, **Jadrolinija** (☑254 800; www.jadrolinija.hr; Liburnska Obala 7) has tickets for all local ferries. Buy international tickets from **Jadroagent** (☑211 447; jadroagent-zadar@zd.t-com.hr; Poljana Natka Nodila 4), just inside the city walls.

BUS The **bus station** (☑211 035; www.liburnija-zadar.hr) is about 2km east of the Old Town and has daily buses to Zagreb (97KN to 147KN, 3½ to seven hours, every 30 minutes). Buses marked 'Poluotok' run from the bus station to the harbour and those marked 'Puntamika' (5 and 8) run to Borik every 20 minutes (hourly on Sunday). Tickets cost 10KN (15KN for two from a *tisak*).

TRAIN The **train station** (☑212 555; www.hznet.hr; Ante Starčevića 3) is adjacent to the bus station. There are six daily trains to Zagreb, but the journey time is very slow indeed; the fastest take over eight hours.

Split
☑021 / POP 178,200

The second-largest city in Croatia, Split (Spalato in Italian) is a great place to see Dalmatian life as it's really lived. Always buzzing, this exuberant city has just the right balance of tradition and modernity. Step inside Diocletian's Palace (a Unesco World Heritage site and one of the world's most impressive Roman monuments) and you'll see dozens of bars, restaurants and shops thriving amid the atmospheric old walls where Split life has been going on for thousands of years. To top it off, Split has a unique setting. Its dramatic coastal mountains act as the perfect backdrop to the turquoise waters of the Adriatic. You'll get a chance to appreciate this gorgeous cityscape when making a ferry journey to or from the city.

The Old Town is a vast open-air museum and the new information signs at the important sights explain a great deal of Split's history. The seafront promenade, Obala Hrvatskog Narodnog Preporoda, better known as Riva, is the best central reference point.

History

Split achieved fame when Roman emperor Diocletian (AD 245–313) had his retirement palace built here from 295 to 305. After his death the great stone palace continued to be used as a retreat by Roman rulers. When the neighbouring colony of Salona was abandoned in the 7th century, many of the Romanised inhabitants fled to Split and barricaded themselves behind the palace walls, where their descendants continue to live to this day.

⊙ Sights
DIOCLETIAN'S PALACE

Facing the harbour, **Diocletian's Palace** is one of the most imposing Roman ruins in existence. Don't expect a palace though, nor a museum – this is the living heart of the city, its labyrinthine streets packed with people, bars, shops and restaurants.

It was built as a military fortress, imperial residence and fortified town, with walls reinforced by square corner towers.

Each wall has a gate named after a metal: at the northern end is the **Golden Gate** (Zlatna Vrata), while the southern end has the **Bronze Gate**; the eastern gate is the **Silver Gate** and to the west is the **Iron Gate**. Between the eastern and western gates there's a straight road (Krešimirova; also known as Decumanus), which separates the imperial residence on the southern side. The Bronze Gate, in the southern wall, led from the living quarters to the sea.

There are 220 buildings within the palace boundaries, home to about 3000 people.

Town Museum   MUSEUM
(Muzej Grada Splita; www.mgst.net; Papalićeva 1; adult/concession 10/5KN; ⊘9am-9pm Tue-Fri, to 4pm Sat-Mon Jun-Sep, 10am-5pm Tue-Fri, to 1pm Sat-Mon Oct-May) Built for one of the many noblemen who lived within the palace in the Middle Ages, the Papalić Palace that houses the museum is considered a fine example of late-Gothic style. Its three floors showcase a collection of drawings, coats of arms, 17th-century weaponry and fine furniture. Captions are in Croatian.

FREE **Cathedral of St Domnius**   CATHEDRAL
(Katedrala Svetog Duje; Svetog Duje 5; cathedral/treasury/belfry 15/15/10KN; ⊘8am-7pm Mon-Sat, 12.30-6.30pm Sun Jun-Sep, sporadic hours Oct-May) On the eastern side of the Peristil, Split's cathedral was built as Diocletian's mausoleum. The oldest remnants inside are the remarkable 13th-century scenes from the life of Christ carved on the wooden entrance doors. The choir is furnished with 13th-century Romanesque seats that are the oldest in Dalma-

tia. The treasury is rich in reliquaries, icons, church robes and illuminated manuscripts. You can climb the Romanesque belfry.

Note that admission to the cathedral also gets you free access to the Temple of Jupiter and its crypt. For 35KN, you can get a ticket that includes access to the cathedral, treasury and belfry.

Temple of Jupiter   TEMPLE
(temple/crypt 5/5KN; ⊘8am-7pm Mon-Sat, 12.30-6.30pm Sun May-Sep) The headless sphinx in black granite guarding the entrance to the temple was imported from Egypt at the time of the temple's construction in the 5th century. Take a look at the barrel-vaulted ceiling and a decorative frieze on the walls. You can also pop into the crypt.

Ethnographic Museum   MUSEUM
(Etnografski Muzej; www.etnografski-muzej-split.hr; Severova 1; adult/concession 10/5KN; ⊘9am-7pm Mon-Fri, to 1pm Sat Jun-Sep, 9am-4pm Mon-Fri, to 1pm Sat Oct-May) This mildly interesting museum has a collection of photos of old Split, traditional costumes and memorabilia of important citizens. For great Old Town views, make sure you climb the staircase that leads to the Renaissance terrace on the southern edge of the vestibule. These views are reason enough to visit.

WORTH A TRIP

SOLIN (SALONA)

The ruin of the ancient city of Solin (known as Salona by the Romans), among the vineyards at the foot of mountains just northeast of Split, is the most interesting archaeological site in Croatia. Salona was the capital of the Roman province of Dalmatia from the time Julius Caesar elevated it to the status of colony. It held out against the barbarians and was only evacuated in AD 614 when the inhabitants fled to Split and neighbouring islands in the face of Avar and Slav attacks.

Begin your visit at the main entrance near Caffe Bar Salona, where you'll see an info-map of the complex. **Tusculum Museum** (admission 20KN; ⊘7am-7pm Mon-Fri, 8am-7pm Sat, 9am-1pm Sun Apr-Sep, shorter hours rest of year) is where you pay admission for the entire archaeological reserve (you'll get a brochure with a map) as well as for the small museum with interesting sculpture embedded in the walls and in the garden. Some of the highlights inside the complex include **Manastirine**, the fenced area behind the car park, a burial place for early Christian martyrs prior to the legalisation of Christianity; the excavated remains of **Kapljuč Basilica** – one of the early Christian cemeteries in Salona – and the 5th-century **Kapjinc Basilica** that sits inside it. Also look out for the **covered aqueduct** from the 1st century AD; the 5th-century **cathedral** with an octagonal baptistery; and the huge 2nd-century **amphitheatre**.

The ruins are easily accessible on Split city bus 1 (13KN), which goes all the way to the parking lot for Salona every half-hour from Trg Gaje Bulata. From Solin you can continue on to Trogir by catching westbound bus 37 (17KN) from the Širine crossroad. Take city bus 1 back to Širine and then walk for five minutes on the same road to get to the stop for bus 37 on the adjacent highway.

Central Split

CROATIA SPLIT

Map labels:

Plinarska

Ujevičeva
Poljana
30

Svačićeva

Porinova

Teutina

Trg
Gaje
Bulata

24

Croatian
Youth Hostel
Association

14

21

Tončićeva   Nigerova

Kralja Tomislava

Pistura

Matošića

Trogirska

17

Križeva

Domaldova

16

26

27

Ban Mladenova

Bana Josipa Jelačića

19

Kraj Sv Marije

Kružićeva

Obrov

Narodni
Trg

Bosanska

18

Trg
Republike

Marmontova

Zadarska

Šubićeva

6

12

Trg Franje Tuđmana

10

Morpurgova
poljana

Dobrić

25

Marulićeva

20

23

11

Tourist
Office

Trg
Brače
Radića

31   28

Obala Hrvatskog Narodnog Preporoda (Riva)

Trumbićeva Obala

Dosud

To Meštrović
Gallery (1.6km);
Kaštelet (2km)

Split Harbour

Obala
Lazareta

Peristil   SQUARE
This picturesque colonnaded square, with
a neo-Romanesque cathedral tower rising
above, is a great place for a break in the sun.
The **vestibule**, an open dome above the
ground-floor passageway at the southern
end of the Peristil, is overpoweringly grand
and cavernous.

Basement Halls   HISTORIC SITE
(adult/concession 35/15KN; ⊙9am-9pm daily Jun-
Sep, 9am-8pm Mon-Sat, to 6pm Sun Apr, May &

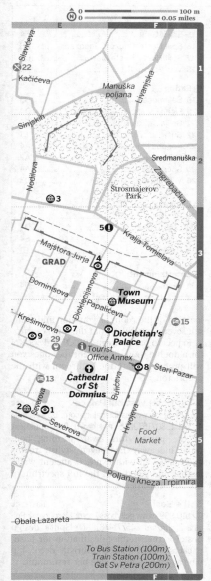

OUTSIDE THE PALACE WALLS

Gregorius of Nin
MONUMENT

(Grgur Ninski) This 10th-century statue is of the Croatian bishop who fought for the right to use old Croatian in liturgical services. Notice that his left big toe has been polished to a shine – it's said that rubbing the toe brings good luck.

Gallery of Fine Arts
GALLERY

(Galerija Umjetnina Split; www.galum.hr; Kralja Tomislava 15; adult/concession 20/10KN; ⊙11am-4pm Mon, to 7pm Tue-Fri, to 3pm Sat May-Sep, 9am-2pm Mon, to 5pm Tue-Fri, to 1pm Sat Oct-Apr) This gallery housed in a former hospital exhibits nearly 400 works of art spanning almost 700 years. Upstairs is the permanent collection; temporary exhibits downstairs change every few months. The pleasant cafe has a terrace overlooking the palace.

OUTSIDE CENTRAL SPLIT

Meštrović Gallery
GALLERY

(Galerija Meštrović; Šetalište Ivana Meštrovića 46; adult/concession 30/15KN; ⊙9am-7pm Tue-Sun May-Sep, shorter hours rest of year) At this stellar art museum, below Marjan to the west of the city centre, you'll see a comprehensive, nicely arranged collection of works by Ivan Meštrović, Croatia's premier modern sculptor. Don't miss the nearby **Kaštelet** (Šetalište Ivana Meštrovića 39; admission by Meštrović Gallery ticket; ⊙9am-7pm Tue-Sat, 10am-7pm Sun May-Sep, shorter hours rest of year), a fortress that Meštrović bought and restored to house his powerful Life of Christ wood reliefs.

Bačvice
BEACH

The most popular city beach is on the eponymous inlet. This biggish pebbly beach has good swimming, a lively ambience, a great cafe-bar and plenty of water games. There are showers and changing rooms at both ends of the beach.

🏃 Activities

Marjan
WALKING TRAIL

For an afternoon away from the city buzz, Marjan (178m) is the perfect destination. Considered the lungs of the city, this hilly nature reserve offers **trails** through fragrant pine forests, scenic **lookouts** and ancient **chapels**. There are different ways of reaching Marjan. Start from the stairway (Marjanske Skale) in Varoš, right behind the Church of Sveti Frane. It's a mild incline along old stone stairs and a scenic 10-minute trek to get to Vidilica (p158) cafe

Oct, shorter hours rest of year) Although mostly empty, save an exhibit or two, the rooms and corridors underneath the Diocletian's Palace exude a haunting timelessness that is well worth the price of a ticket.

Central Split

◎ Top Sights
Cathedral of St Domnius	E4
Diocletian's Palace	F4
Town Museum	F4

◎ Sights
1	Basement Halls	E5
	Bronze Gate	(see 1)
2	Ethnographic Museum	E5
3	Gallery of Fine Arts	E2
4	Golden Gate	E3
5	Gregorius of Nin	F3
6	Iron Gate	D4
7	Peristil	E4
8	Silver Gate	F4
9	Temple of Jupiter	E4

ⓘ Sleeping
10	Goli + Bosi	C4
11	Hotel Adriana	C4
12	Hotel Bellevue	B3
13	Hotel Vestibul Palace	E4
14	Silver Central Hostel	C2
15	Silver Gate	F4
16	Split Hostel Booze & Snooze	D3
17	Split Hostel Fiesta Siesta	D3
18	Villa Varoš	A3

✖ Eating
19	Bajamonti	B3
20	Figa	D4
21	Galija	B2
22	Gušt	E1
23	Konoba Matejuška	A4
24	Makrovega	A2
25	Šperun	A4
26	Villa Spiza	D3

🍷 Drinking
27	Bifora	D3
28	Ghetto Club	D4
29	Luxor	E4
30	Paradox	B1

✪ Entertainment
31	Fluid	D4

at the top. From here, right by the old Jewish cemetery, you can follow the marked trail, stopping en route to see the chapels, all the way to **Kašjuni cove**, a quieter beach option than the buzzing Bačvice.

✦ Festivals & Events

Carnival CULTURAL
This traditional February event sees locals dressing up and dancing in the streets for two very fun days.

Feast of St Duje RELIGIOUS
Otherwise known as Split Day, this 7 May feast involves much singing and dancing all around the city.

Split Summer Festival ARTS
(www.splitsko-ljeto.hr) From mid-July to mid-August, it features opera, drama, ballet and concerts on open-air stages.

🛏 Sleeping

Good budget accommodation has become more available in Split in the last couple of years but it's mostly comprised of hostels. Private accommodation is a great option and in summer you may be deluged at the bus station by women offering *sobe* (rooms available). You can also contact travel agencies. Make sure you are clear about the exact location of the room or you may find yourself several bus rides from the town centre.

Expect to pay between 300KN and 500KN for a double room; in the cheaper ones you will probably share the bathroom with the proprietor.

Hotel Vestibul Palace HOTEL €€€
(☎329 329; www.vestibulpalace.com; Iza Vestibula 4; s/d 1380/1670KN; P❄@☎) The poshest in the palace, this award-winning boutique hideaway has seven stylish rooms and suites, all with exposed ancient walls, leather and wood, and the full spectrum of upscale amenities.

Goli + Bosi HOSTEL €€
(☎510 999; www.gollybossy.com; Morpurgova Poljana 2; dm/s/d 245/714/818KN) Split's design hostel is the premier destination for flashpackers, with its sleek futuristic decor, hip vibe and a cool lobby cafe-bar-restaurant.

Hotel Bellevue HOTEL €€
(☎345 644; www.hotel-bellevue-split.hr; Bana Josipa Jelačića 2; s/d 620/865KN; P@) This atmospheric old classic has sure seen better days but it remains one of the more dreamy hotels in town, with regal-patterned wallpaper, art-deco elements, gauzy curtains and faded but well-kept rooms.

Villa Varoš GUESTHOUSE €€

(☑483 469; www.villavaros.hr; Miljenka Smoje 1; d/ste 600/900KN; ❋ 🛜) Owned by a New Yorker Croat, Villa Varoš is central, the rooms are simple, bright and airy, and the apartment has a Jacuzzi and a small terrace.

Hotel Adriana HOTEL €€€

(☑340 000; www.hotel-adriana.com; Hrvatskog Narodnog Preporoda 8; s/d 750/1100KN; ❋ 🛜) Good value, excellent location smack in the middle of the Riva. The rooms are not massively exciting, with navy curtains and beige furniture, but some have sea views.

CroParadise Split Hostels HOSTEL €

(☑091 444 4194; www.croparadise.com; Čulića Dvori 29; dm 180KN, d 400-500KN, apt from 500KN; ❋ @ 🛜) A great collection of three hostels – Blue, Green and Pink – inside converted apartments in the neighbourhood of Manuš. Five apartments are also available.

Silver Central Hostel HOSTEL €

(☑490 805; www.silvercentralhostel.com; Kralja Tomislava 1; dm 167-190KN; ❋ @ 🛜) In an upstairs apartment, this light-yellow-coloured boutique hostel has four dorm rooms and a pleasant lounge. It has a two-person apartment nearby and another hostel, **Silver Gate** (☑322 857; www.silvergatehostel.com; Hrvojeva 6; dm per person 167KN), near the food market.

Split Hostel Booze & Snooze HOSTEL €

(☑342 787; www.splithostel.com; Narodni trg 8; dm 200-215KN; ❋ @ 🛜) Run by a pair of Aussie Croat women, this party place at the heart of town has four dorms, a terrace, a book swap and boat trips. Its newer outpost, **Split Hostel Fiesta Siesta** (Kružićeva 5; dm 200-215KN, d 560KN; ❋ @ 🛜) has five sparkling dorms and one double above the popular Charlie's Backpacker Bar.

✖ Eating

Šperun SEAFOOD €

(Šperun 3; mains from 65KN; 🗐) A sweet little restaurant decked out with rustic details and exposed stone walls, this favourite among the foreigners churns out decent Dalmatian classics. **Šperun Deva**, a corner bistro across the street with a few tables outside, offers breakfasts, lighter summer fare and a great daily menu.

TOP
CHOICE **Figa** INTERNATIONAL €

(Buvinina 1; mains from 50KN) Split's coolest little restaurant and bar, with a funky interior

and tables on the stairs outside, Figa serves nice breakfasts, innovative dishes and a wide range of salads. There's live music some nights and the kitchen stays open late.

Konoba Matejuška DALMATIAN €

(Tomića Stine 3; mains from 50KN) Cosy, rustic tavern in an alleyway minutes from the seafront, it specialises in well-prepared seafood that also happens to be well priced.

Bajamonti INTERNATIONAL €€

(Trg Republike 1; mains from 75KN) Sleek restaurant and cafe on Trg Republike (Prokurative square), right off the Riva, with classic decor and excellent international fare. Grab a table on the square or on the mezzanine level inside.

TOP
CHOICE **Villa Spiza** DALMATIAN €

(Kružićeva 3; mains from 40KN; ⊙Mon-Sat) A locals' favourite within the palace walls, this low-key joint offers Dalmatian mainstays that change daily – think calamari, risotto, stuffed peppers – at low prices, served at the bar inside or at a couple of benches outside.

Makrovega VEGETARIAN €

(Leština 2; mains from 50KN; ⊙9am-8pm Mon-Fri, to 5pm Sat) A meat-free haven with a stylish, spacious interio, a delicious buffet and à la carte food that alternates between macrobiotic and vegetarian.

Galija PIZZERIA €

(Tončićeva 12; pizzas from 38KN) The go-to place for pizza for several decades now, Galija is the sort of joint where locals take you for a good, simple meal. Die-hard pizza fans have recently turned to the new favorite in town, **Gušt** (Slavićeva 1; pizzas from 32KN).

🍷 Drinking & Entertainment

Split is great for nightlife, especially in the spring and summer months. The palace walls are generally throbbing with loud music on Friday and Saturday nights.

Žbirac CAFE

(Bačvice bb) This beachfront cafe is like the locals' open-air living room, a cult hang-out with great sea views, swimming day and night and occasional concerts.

Bifora CAFE-BAR

(Bernardinova 5) A quirky crowd of locals frequents this artsy spot on a lovely little square, much loved for its intimate low-key vibe.

Ghetto Club   BAR

(Dosud 10) Split's most bohemian bar, in an intimate courtyard amid flowerbeds and a trickling fountain,with great music and a friendly atmosphere.

Luxor   CAFE-BAR

(Sveti Ivana 11) Touristy, yes, but it's great to have coffee and their delicious cake in the courtyard of the cathedral: cushions are laid out on the steps so you can watch the locals go about their business.

Vidilica   CAFE-BAR

(Nazorov Prilaz 1) Worth the climb up the stone stairs through the ancient Varoš quarter for a sunset drink at this hilltop cafe with amazing city and harbour views.

Paradox   WINE BAR

(Poljana Tina Ujevića 2) Stylish new wine bar with cool wine-glass chandeliers inside, alfresco tables and a great selection of well-priced Croatian wines and local cheeses.

Fluid   CLUB

(Dosud 1) This chic little spot is a jazzy party venue, pretty low-key and cool. Great for people-watching.

❶ Information

Internet Access

Several cafes around town, including Luxor offer free wi-fi access.

Backpackers Cafe (☑338 548; Kneza Domagoja bb; internet 30N; ⏰7am-9pm) Also sells used books, offers luggage storage and provides information for backpackers. There's happy hour for internet use between 3pm and 5pm, when it's 50% off.

Medical Services

KBC Firule (☑556 111; Spinčićeva 1) Hospital.

Money

You can change money at travel agencies or the post office. There are ATMs around the bus and train stations and throughout the city.

Post

Main post office (Kralja Tomislava 9; ⏰7.30am-7pm Mon-Fri, to 2.30pm Sat)

Tourist Information

Croatian Youth Hostel Association (☑396 031; www.hfhs.hr; Domilijina 8; ⏰8am-4pm Mon-Fri) Sells HI cards and has information about youth hostels all over Croatia.

Tourist Office (☑360 066; www.visitsplit.com; Hrvatskog Narodnog Preporoda 9; ⏰8am-9pm Mon-Sat, to 1pm Sun Apr–mid-Oct, 8am-8pm

Mon-Fri, to 1pm Sat mid-Oct–Mar) Has Split info and sells the Split Card (35KN), which offers free and reduced prices to attractions and discounts on car rental, restaurants, shops and hotels.

Tourist Office Annex (☑345 606; www.visitsplit.com; Peristil bb; ⏰9am-4pm Mon-Sat, 8am-1pm Sun Apr–mid-Oct, shorter hours rest of year) This tourist office annex on Peristil has shorter hours.

Travel Agencies

Daluma Travel (☑338 424; www.dalumatravel.hr; Kneza Domagoja 1) Arranges private accommodation, excursions and car rental.

Maestral (☑470 944; www.maestral.hr; Boškovića 13/15) Monastery stays, horseriding excursions, lighthouse holidays, trekking, sea kayaking and more.

Turist Biro (☑347 100; www.turistbiro-split.hr; Hrvatskog Narodnog Preporoda 12) Its forte is private accommodation and excursions.

❶ Getting There & Away

Air

Split airport (www.split-airport.hr) is 20km west of town, just 6km before Trogir. **Croatia Airlines** (☑362 997; www.croatiaairlines.hr; Hrvatskog Narodnog Preporoda 9; ⏰8am-4pm Mon-Fri) operates one-hour flights to Zagreb several times a day and a weekly flight to Dubrovnik (during summer only).

A couple of low-cost airlines fly to Split, including **Easyjet** (www.easyjet.com), **germanwings** (www.germanwings.com) and **Norwegian** (www.norwegian.com).

Boat

Jadrolinija (☑338 333; www.jadrolinija.hr; Gat Sv Duje bb) handles most of the coastal ferry lines and catamarans that operate between Split and the islands. There is also a twice-weekly ferry service between Rijeka and Split (147KN, 7.30pm Thursday and Sunday, arriving at 6am). Three times weekly a car ferry goes from Split to Ancona in Italy (435KN, nine to 11 hours).

In addition to Jadrolinija's boats, there is a fast passenger boat, the **Krilo** (www.krilo.hr), that goes to Hvar Town (45KN, one hour) daily and on to Korčula (65KN, 2¾ hours).

SNAV (☑322 252; www.snav.it) has daily ferries to Ancona (Italy) from June through mid-September (660KN; five hours) and to Pescara (Italy) from late July through August (6½ hours). Also departing to Ancona from Split are **BlueLine** (www.blueline-ferries.com) car ferries (from 480KN per person, 540KN per car, 10 to 12 hours), on some days via Hvar Town and Vis.

Car ferries and passenger lines depart from separate docks; the passenger lines leave from Obala Lazareta and car ferries from Gat Sv Duje. You can buy tickets from either the main Jadro-

BUSES FROM SPLIT

DESTINATION	PRICE (KN)	DURATION (HR)	FREQUENCY
Dubrovnik	115-145	4½	25 daily
Ljubljana (Slovenia)	320	10	1 daily
Međugorje (Bosnia & Hercegovina)	100	3-4	4 daily
Mostar (Bosnia & Hercegovina)	105-128	3½-4½	9 daily
Pula	423	10-11	3 daily
Rijeka	330	8-8½	11 daily
Sarajevo (Bosnia & Hercegovina)	220	6½-8	4 daily
Triesta (Italy)	284	10½	2 daily
Vienna (Austria)	57	11½	2 weekly
Zadar	99-128	3-4	27 daily
Zagreb	114-204	5-8	40 daily

linija office in the large ferry terminal opposite the bus station, or at one of the two stalls near the docks. In summer it's necessary to reserve at least a day in advance for a car ferry and you are asked to appear several hours before departure.

Bus

Advance bus tickets with seat reservations are recommended. Most buses leave from the main **bus station** (☑060 327 777; www.ak-split.hr) beside the harbour, where there's a **garderoba** (left-luggage office; 1st hr 5KN, then 1.50KN per hr; ☺6am-10pm).

Bus 37 goes to Split airport and Trogir (21KN, every 20 minutes), also stopping at Solin; it leaves from a local bus station on Domovinskog Rata, 1km northeast of the city centre, but it's faster and more convenient to take an intercity bus heading north to Zadar or Rijeka.

Note that Split–Dubrovnik buses pass briefly through Bosnian territory, so keep your passport handy for border-crossing points.

Train

There are five daily trains between Split **train station** (☑338 525; www.hznet.hr; Kneza Domagoja 9) and Zagreb (189KN, six to eight hours), two of which are overnight. There are also two trains a day from Split to Zadar (111KN, five hours) via Knin. The station is just behind the bus station and there's a **garderoba** (left-luggage office; per day 15KN; ☺6am-10pm).

ⓘ Getting Around

Buses by **Pleso Prijevoz** (www.plesoprijevoz. hr) and **Promet Žele** (www.split-airport.com.hr) depart to Split airport (30KN) from Obala Laza-reta several times daily. You can also take bus 37 from the local bus station on Domovinskog Rata (21KN, 50 minutes).

Buses run about every 15 minutes from 5.30am to 11.30pm. A one-zone ticket costs 11KN for one trip in central Split; it's 21KN to the surrounding districts.

Trogir

☑021 / POP 13,000

Gorgeous and tiny Trogir (formerly Trau) is beautifully set within medieval walls, its streets knotted and maze-like. It's fronted by a wide seaside promenade lined with bars and cafes and luxurious yachts docking in the summer. Trogir is unique among Dalmatian towns for its profuse collection of Romanesque and Renaissance architecture (which flourished under Venetian rule), and this, along with its magnificent cathedral, earned it World Heritage status in 1997.

Trogir is an easy day trip from Split and a relaxing place to spend a few days, taking a trip or two to nearby islands.

⊙ Sights

The heart of the Old Town, which occupies a tiny island in the narrow channel between Čiovo Island and the mainland, is a few minutes' walk from the bus station. After crossing the small bridge near the station, go through the north gate. Most sights can be seen on a 15-minute walk around this island.

Cathedral of St Lovro　　　CATHEDRAL
(Katedrala Svetog Lovre; Trg Ivana Pavla II; admission 25KN; ☺8am-8pm Mon-Sat, 2-6pm Sun Jun-Sep, shorter hours rest of year) The showcase of Trogir is this three-naved Venetian cathedral built from the 13th to 15th centuries. Its glory is

the **Romanesque portal** (1240) by Master Radovan, the earliest example of the nude in Dalmatian sculpture. Enter the building through an obscure back door to see the richly decorated Renaissance **Chapel of St Ivan**, choir stalls, pulpit and **treasury**, which contains an ivory triptych. You can even climb the 47m cathedral **tower** for a delightful view.

Kamerlengo Fortress
FORTRESS

(Tvrđava Kamerlengo; admission 20KN; ⊘9am-11pm May-Oct) Once connected to the city walls, the fortress was built around the 15th century. Today it hosts concerts during the **Trogir Summer** festival, which typically begins in mid-June and lasts through to late August.

Town Museum
MUSEUM

(Gradski Muzej; Gradska Vrata 4; admission 15KN; ⊘10am-5pm Jun-Sep, 9am-2pm Mon-Fri, to noon Sat Oct-May) Housed in the former Garagnin-Fanfogna palace, the museum has five rooms that exhibit books, documents, drawings and period costumes from Trogir's long history.

❶ Information

Atlas Trogir (☑881 374; www.atlas-trogir.hr; Kralja Zvonimira 10) This travel agency arranges private accommodation and runs excursions.

Portal Trogir (☑885 016; www.portal-trogir. com; Bana Berislavića 3) Private accommodation; bike, scooter and kayak rental; excursions, including quad safaris, rafting and canyoning; and internet. The agency runs a 90-minute walking tour of the Old Town twice a day from May to October, departing from outside the agency. It also rents out two-person kayaks for 250KN per day, which you can use to kayak around the island and to Pantan beach.

❶ Getting There & Away

Southbound intercity buses from Zadar (130km) and northbound buses from Split (28km) will drop you off in Trogir. Getting buses from Trogir to Zadar can be more difficult, as they often arrive full from Split.

City bus 37 from Split leaves every 20 minutes throughout the day, with a stop at Split airport en route to Trogir. You can buy the four-zone ticket (21KN) from the driver in either direction.

There are boats to and from Split four times daily (24KN) from Čiovo (150m to the left of the bridge).

Hvar Island

☑021 / POP 10,948

Hvar Island is the number-one carrier of Croatia's superlatives: it's the most luxurious island, the sunniest place in the country and, along with Dubrovnik, the most popular tourist destination. Hvar is also famed for its verdancy and its lavender fields, as well as other aromatic herbs such as rosemary.

The island's hub and busiest destination is Hvar Town. Visitors wander along the main square, explore the sights on the winding stone streets, swim on the numerous beaches or pop off to get into their birthday suits on the Pakleni Islands, but most of all they party at night. There are several good restaurants and a number of top hotels, as well as a couple of hostels.

Stari Grad (Old Town), on the island's north coast, is a more quiet, cultured and altogether sober affair than its stylish and stunning sister. If you're not after pulsating nightlife and thousands of people crushing each other along the streets in the high season, head for Stari Grad and enjoy Hvar at a more leisurely pace.

The interior of the island hides abandoned ancient hamlets, towering peaks and verdant, largely uncharted landscapes. It's worth exploring on a day trip, as is the southern end of the island, which has some of Hvar's most beautiful and isolated coves.

◉ Sights

St Stephen's Square
SQUARE

(Trg Svetog Stjepana) The centre of town is this rectangular square, which was formed by filling in an inlet that once stretched out from the bay. Notice the 1520 **well** at the square's northern end, which has a wrought-iron grill dating from 1780.

Franciscan Monastery & Museum
MONASTERY

(admission 25KN; ⊘9am-1pm & 5-7pm Mon-Sat) At the southeastern end of Hvar Town you'll find this 15th-century Renaissance monastery, with a wonderful collection of Venetian paintings in the adjoining church and a cloister garden with a cypress tree said to be more than 300 years old.

Fortica
FORTRESS

(admission 25KN; ⊘8am-10pm Jun-Sep) On the hill high above Hvar Town, this Venetian fortress (1551) is worth the climb up to appreciate the sweeping panoramic views. The fort was built to defend Hvar from the Turks, who sacked it in 1539 and 1571. There's a lovely cafe at the top.

Arsenal
HISTORIC BUILDING

(Trg Svetog Stjepana; arsenal & theatre 20KN; ⏱9am-9pm) Smack in the middle of Hvar Town is the imposing Gothic arsenal, and upstairs is Hvar's prize, the **Renaissance theatre** (Trg Svetog Stjepana; admission 10KN; ⏱9am-9pm) built in 1612 – reported to be the first theatre in Europe open to plebs and aristocrats alike.

Tours

Secret Hvar
GUIDED TOURS

(📞717 615; www.secrethvar.com; Trg Svetog Stjepana 4a) Don't miss the great off-road tours, which take in hidden beauties of the island's interior. It's worth every lipa of 600KN, which includes lunch in a traditional tavern and a stop on the beach.

Sleeping

As Hvar is one of the Adriatic's most popular destinations, don't expect many bargains. Most Hvar hotels are managed by **Sunčani Hvar Hotels** (www.suncanihvar.com). Accommodation in Hvar is extremely tight in July and August; try the travel agencies for help. Expect to pay anywhere from 150KN to 300KN per person for a room with a private bathroom in the town centre.

Family-run, private-apartment options are so many in Hvar that the choice can be overwhelming. Here are a few reliable, good-value apartments: **Apartments Ukić** (www.hvar-apartments-center.com), **Apartments Komazin** (www.croatia-hvar-apartments.com) and **Apartments Bracanović** (www.hvar-jagoda.com).

Hotel Riva
HOTEL €€€

(📞750 100; www.suncanihvar.com; Riva bb; s/d 1390/2617KN; ✳@) The luxury veteran on Hvar's hotel scene, this 100-year-old hotel has 54 smallish contemporary rooms and a great location right on the harbourfront, perfect for watching the yachts glide up and away.

TOP CHOICE Hotel Croatia
HOTEL €€€

(📞742 400; www.hotelcroatia.net; Majerovica bb; s/d 832/1110KN; P✳@🛜) Only a few steps from the sea, this medium-sized, rambling 1930s building sits among gorgeous, peaceful gardens. The rooms are simple and old-fashioned, many with balconies overlooking the gardens and the sea.

Hostel Marinero
HOSTEL €

(📞091 174 1601; Put Sv Marka 7; dm 200-240KN; ✳🛜) The location is the highlight at this six-dorm hostel right off the seafront. Dorms are basic but clean, and the restaurant downstairs is a good place to hang out. Be ready for some noise, as Kiva Bar is right next door.

Hvar Out Hostel
HOSTEL €

(📞717 375; hvarouthostel@gmail.com; Burak 23; dm 200-250KN; ✳@🛜) By the same owners as Split Hostel Booze & Snooze, this party place, steps from the harbour in the maze of the Old Town, has seven well-equipped dorms, a small shared kitchen and a terrace on the top floor.

Camping Vira
CAMPING GROUND €

(📞741 803; www.campingvira.com; campsite per adult/site 60/97KN; ⏱May–mid-Oct; P@🛜) This four-star camping ground on a beautiful wooded bay 4km from town is one of the best in Dalmatia. There's a gorgeous beach, a cafe and restaurant, and a volleyball pitch.

Eating

Hvar's eating scene is good and relatively varied, though, as with the hotels, restaurants often target affluent diners. Note that many restaurants close between lunch and dinner.

CROATIA HVAR ISLAND

WORTH A TRIP

PAKLENI ISLANDS

Most visitors to Hvar Town head to the Pakleni Islands (Pakleni Otoci), which got their name – 'Hell's Islands' in Croatian – from *paklina*, the resin that once coated boats and ships. This gorgeous chain of 21 wooded isles has crystal-clear seas, hidden beaches and deserted lagoons. Taxi boats leave regularly during the high season from in front of the Arsenal to the islands of **Jerolim** and **Stipanska** (35KN, 10 to 15 minutes), which are popular naturist islands (although nudity is not mandatory). They continue on to **Ždrilca** and **Mlini** (40KN) and, further out, **Palmižana** (60KN), which has a pebble beach and the **Meneghello Place** (www.palmizana.hr), a beautiful boutique complex of villas and bungalows scattered among lush tropical gardens. Run by the artsy Meneghello family, the estate holds music recitals, and features two excellent restaurants and an art gallery. Also on Palmižana are two top restaurant-cum-hang-out spots, Toto and Laganini.

Self-caterers can head to the supermarket next to the bus station, or pick up fresh supplies at the vegetable market next door.

Konoba Menego   DALMATIAN €€
(www.menego.hr; Groda bb; mains from 60KN) At this rustic old house, everything is decked out in Hvar antiques and the staff wear traditional outfits. Try the marinated meats, cheeses and vegetables, prepared the old-fashioned Dalmatian way.

Divino   MEDITERRANEAN €€€
(☎717 541; www.divino.com.hr; Put Križa 1 ; mains from 130KN; ☺dinner only) The fabulous location and the island's best wine list are reason enough to splurge at this swank restaurant. Add innovative food and dazzling views of the Pakleni Islands and there's a winning formula for a special night out.

Konoba Luviji   DALMATIAN €€
(☎091 519 8444; Jurja Novaka 6; mains from 50KN; ☺dinner) Food brought out of the wood oven at this tavern is simple, unfussy and tasty. Downstairs is the *konoba* where Dalmatian-style tapas are served; the upstairs restaurant has Old Town views.

Nonica   PASTRIES, CAKES €
(Burak 23; ☺8am-2pm & 5-11pm Mon-Sat, 8am-2pm Sun) Savour the best cakes in town, at this tiny storefront cafe right behind the Arsenal. Try the old-fashioned local biscuits such as *rafioli* and *forski koloc*.

Zlatna Školjka   MEDITERRANEAN €€€
(☎098 16 88 797; Petra Hektorovića 8; mains from 100KN; ☺dinner Sat & Sun) This slow-food, family-tun hideaway stands out for its creative fare conjured up by a local celebrity chef. Try the unbeatable *gregada* (fish stew) with lobster and sea snails; order in advance.

Drinking & Entertainment

Hvar has some of the best nightlife on the Adriatic coast.

Falko   BEACH BAR
(☺8am-10pm mid-May–mid-Sep) A 20-minute walk west from the town centre, past Hula-Hula and Hotel Amfora, brings you to this adorable hideaway in a pine forest just above the beach. Think low-key artsy vibe, homemade *rakija*, hammocks and a local crowd.

Carpe Diem   LOUNGE BAR
(www.carpe-diem-hvar.com; Riva) This swanky harbourfront spot is the mother of Croatia's coastal clubs, with house music spun nightly

by resident DJs. The **Carpe Diem Beach** (www.carpe-diem-beach.com) on the island of Stipanska is the hottest place to party (from June to September), with daytime beach fun and all-night parties.

Hula-Hula   BEACH BAR
(www.hulahulahvar.com) *The* spot to catch the sunset to the sound of techno and house music, Hula-Hula is known for its après-beach party (4pm to 9pm), where all of young trendy Hvar seems to descend for cocktails. To find it, head west along the seafront.

Kiva Bar   BAR
(www.kivabarhvar.com; Fabrika bb) This happening alleyway spot is packed to the rafters most nights, with a DJ spinning old dance, pop and rock classics that really get the crowd going.

Veneranda   CLUB
(admission 100-150KN; ☺10pm-4am) A former fortress on the slope above the seafront, Veneranda is Hvar's only real club, with a great sound system and late-night parties fulled by famous DJs.

ⓘ Information

Atlas Hvar (☎741 911; www.atlas-croatia.com) On the western side of the harbour, this travel agency finds private accommodation, rents bikes and boats, and books excursions to Vis, Bol and Dubrovnik.

Clinic (☎717 099; Biskupa Jurja Dubokovića 3) Medical clinic about 700m from the town centre, best for emergencies.

Del Primi (☎091 583 7864; www.delprimi-hvar.com; Burak 23) Travel agency specialising in private accommodation. Also rents jet skis.

Francesco (Burak bb; per hr 30KN; ☺8.30am-midnight) Internet cafe and call centre right behind the post office. Left luggage for 35KN per day and laundry service for 50KN per load.

Hvar Adventure (☎717 813; www.hvar-adventure.com; Obala bb) Adventure activities such as sailing, sea kayaking, cycling, hiking and rock climbing.

Pelegrini Tours (☎742 743; www.pelegrini-hvar.hr; Riva bb) Private accommodation, boat tickets to Italy with Blue Line, excursions (its daily trips to Pakleni Otoci are popular) and bike, scooter and boat rental.

Tourist office (☎741 059; www.tzhvar.hr; ☺8am-2pm & 3-9pm Jul & Aug, shorter hours rest of year) Right on Trg Svetog Stjepana.

ⓘ Getting There & Away

The local Jadrolinija (p158) car ferry from Split calls at Stari Grad (47KN, two hours) six times a day in summer. Jadrolinija also has three to five catamarans daily to Hvar Town (47KN, one hour). Krilo (p158), the fast passenger boat, travels once a day between Split and Hvar Town (45KN, one hour) in summer; it also goes on to Korčula (50KN, 1½ hours). You can buy tickets at Pelegrini Tours.

Connections to Italy are available in the summer season. Two Jadrolinija ferries a week (on Saturday and Sunday night) go from Stari Grad to Ancona in Italy. Blue Line (p180) also runs regular boats to Ancona from Hvar Town. Pelegrini Tours sells these tickets.

❶ Getting Around

Buses meet most ferries that dock at Stari Grad and go to Hvar Town (27KN, 20 minutes). There are 10 buses a day between Stari Grad and Hvar Town in summer, but services are reduced on Sunday and in the low season.

A taxi costs from 300KN to 350KN. **Radio Taxi Tihi** (☏ 098 338 824) is cheaper if there are a number of passengers to fill up the minivan.

Korčula Island

☏ 020 / POP 16,438

Rich in vineyards and olive trees, the island of Korčula was named Korkyra Melaina (Black Korčula) by the original Greek settlers because of its dense woods and plant life. As the largest island in an archipelago of 48, it provides plenty of opportunities for scenic drives, particularly along the southern coast.

Swimming opportunities abound in the many quiet coves and secluded beaches, while the interior produces some of Croatia's finest wine, especially dessert wines made from the *grk* grape cultivated around Lumbarda. Local olive oil is another product worth seeking out.

On a hilly peninsula jutting into the Adriatic sits Korčula Town, a striking walled town of round defensive towers and red-roofed houses. Resembling a miniature Dubrovnik, the gated, walled Old Town is crisscrossed by narrow stone streets designed to protect its inhabitants from the winds swirling around the peninsula.

◉ Sights

Other than the circuit of the city walls or walking along the shore, sightseeing in Korčula centres on Trg Sv Marka (St Mark's Sq).

St Mark's Cathedral   CATHEDRAL
(Katedrala Svetog Marka; Statuta 1214; ⊙9am-9pm Jul & Aug, Mass only Sep-Jun) Dominating Trg Svetog Marka, the 15th-century Gothic-Renaissance cathedral features works by Tintoretto (*Three Saints* and *The Annunciation*). Check out the modern sculptures in the baptistery too, including a *pietà* by Ivan Meštrović.

Town Museum   MUSEUM
(Gradski Muze; Statuta 1214; admission 25KN; ⊙9am-9pm daily Jun-Aug, 9am-1pm Mon-Sat Sep-May) The 16th-century Gabriellis Palace opposite the cathedral houses the museum, with a stone-carving collection, prehistoric objects, and Korčulan traditional, and art, furniture, textiles and portraits.

Marco Polo Museum   MUSEUM
(De Polo; admission 20KN; ⊙9am-7pm Jun-Sep, 10am-4pm May & Oct) It's said that Marco Polo was born in Korčula in 1254; you can visit what is believed to be his birthplace and climb the very steep steps for an eagle's-eye vista over the Korčula Peninsula and Adriatic.

☞ Tours

Travel agencies, like Atlas Travel Agency and Kantun Tours (p164), can set you up on an island tour or a day trip to Mljet and offer mountain biking, and sea-kayaking and snorkelling trips. In the summer season water taxis offer trips to **Badija Island**, which features a 15th-century Franciscan monastery and a naturist beach, and the nearby village of **Lumbarda**, both of which have sandy beaches.

🛏 Sleeping & Eating

Korčula's hotel scene is on the bulky and resort side. If you don't fancy staying in any of the big hotels, a more personal option is a guesthouse. Atlas Travel Agency (p164) and **Marko Polo Tours** (☏715 400; www.korcula. com; Biline 5; ⊙9am-9pm Mon-Fri, to 6pm Sat & Sun) arrange private rooms (from 250KN in high season).

TOP CHOICE **Lešić Dimitri Palace**   APARTMENTS €€€
(☏715 560; www.lesic-dimitri.com; Don Pavla Poše 1-6; apt 3363-9752KN; ❋☎) Exceptional in every way (including its rates). Spread over several town mansions, the six 'residences' have been finished to an impeccable standard, while keeping original details. The restaurant is the best in town, too.

Villa DePolo   APARTMENT, RENTAL ROOMS €
(☏711 621; tereza.depolo@du.t-com.hr; Svetog Nikole bb; d 350KN; ❋☎) These small, simple but attractive modern rooms (and apartment) come

WORTH A TRIP

OREBIĆ

Orebić, on the southern coast of the Pelješac Peninsula, has the best beaches in southern Dalmatia – sandy coves bordered by groves of tamarisk and pine. Only 2.5km across the water from Korčula Town, it makes a perfect day trip or an alternative base. After lazing on the beach, you can take advantage of some excellent hiking up and around Mt Ilija (961m) or poke around a couple of churches and museums. The best beach in Orebić is Trstenica cove, a 15-minute walk east along the shore from the port.

In Orebić the ferry terminal and the bus station are adjacent to each other. Korčula buses to Dubrovnik, Zagreb and Sarajevo stop at Orebić (on the harbourfront by the ferry port).

with comfortable beds; one has a terrace with amazing views. The location is excellent, a short walk from the Old Town.

Hotel Bon Repos　　　　　　　RESORT €€
(☑726 800; www.korcula-hotels.com; d 596KN; P@☎♨) On the road to Lumbarda, this huge hotel has manicured grounds, a large pool overlooking a small beach and a water-taxi service to Korčula Town.

TOP CHOICE **LD**　　　　MODERN MEDITERRANEAN €€
(☑715 560; www.lesic-dimitri.com; Don Pavla Poše 1-6; mains from 75KN) Korčula's finest restaurant, with tables right above the water, offers delectable combinations of Med ingredients and many wonderful Croatian choices.

TOP CHOICE **Konoba Komin**　　　　DALMATIAN €
(☑716 508; Don Iva Matijace; mains from 45KN) This family-run *konoba* looks almost medieval, with its *komin* (roaring fire), roasting meat, ancient stone walls and solid wooden tables. The menu is simple and delicious and the space tight, so book ahead.

☆ Entertainment

Between June and September there's Moreška sword dancing (tickets 100KN; 9pm Monday and Thursday) by the Old Town gate. The clash of swords and the graceful movements of the dancers/fighters make an exciting show. Travel agencies sell tickets.

❶ Information

There are several ATMs around town, including one at HVB Splitska Banka. You can also change money at the post office or at any of the travel agencies.

Atlas Travel Agency (☑711 231; atlas-korcula@du.htnet.hr; Plokata 19 Travnja bb) Represents American Express, runs excursions and finds private accommodation.

Hospital (☑711 137; Kalac bb) About 1km past Hotel Marko Polo.

Kantun Tours (☑715 622; www.kantun-tours.com; Plokata 19 Travnja bb) Private accommodation, lots of excursions, car hire and boat tickets, plus internet access (25KN per hour) and luggage storage.

Tourist office (☑715 701; www.korcula.net; Obala Franje Tuđmana 4; ◷8am-3pm & 5-8pm Mon-Sat, 9am-1pm Sun Jul & Aug, 8am-2pm Mon-Sat Sep-Jun) On the west harbour; an excellent source of information.

❶ Getting There & Around

There are buses to Dubrovnik (95KN, three hours, one to three daily) and one to Zagreb (245KN, 11 hours). Book ahead in summer.

The island has two major entry ports – Korčula Town and Vela Luka. All the **Jadrolinija** (☑715 410) ferries between Split and Dubrovnik stop in Korčula Town. If you're travelling between Split and Korčula you have several options.

There's a daily fast boat, the **Krilo** (www.krilo.hr), which runs from Split to Korčula (65KN, 2¾ hours) all year round, stopping at Hvar en route. Jadrolinija runs a passenger catamaran daily from June to September from Split to Vela Luka (70KN, two hours), stopping at Hvar and continuing on to Lastavo. There's also a regular afternoon car ferry between Split and Vela Luka (60KN, three hours) that stops at Hvar most days (although cars may not disembark at Hvar).

From the Pelješac Peninsula you'll find very regular boats link Orebić and Korčula. Passenger launches (20KN, 10 minutes, 13 daily June to September, at least five daily the rest of year) sail to the heart of Korčula Town. Car ferries (22KN, 15 minutes, at least 14 daily all year round) also run this route, but use the deeper port of Dominče, 3km from Korčula Town.

Scooters (320KN for 24 hours) and boats (610KN per day) are available from **Rent a Đir** (☑711 908; www.korcula-rent.net; Biline 5).

Mljet Island

☑020 / POP 1232

Of all the Adriatic islands, Mljet (Meleda in Italian) may be the most seductive. Much of the island is covered by forests and the rest is dotted with fields, vineyards and villages. The northwestern half of the island forms **Mljet National Park** (www.mljet.hr; adult/concession 100/50KN), where lush vegetation, pine forests and two saltwater lakes offer a scenic hideaway. It's an unspoiled oasis of tranquility that, according to legend, captivated Odysseus for seven years.

The island is 37km long, and has an average width of about 3km. The main points of entry are Pomena and Polače, two tiny towns about 5km apart.

Most people visit the island on excursions from Korčula or Dubrovnik (around 390KN and 245KN respectively), but it is possible to take a passenger boat from Dubrovnik or come on the regular ferry from Dubrovnik and stay a few days for hiking, cycling and boating.

◉ Sights & Activities

The highlights of the island are **Malo Jezero** and **Veliko Jezero**, the two lakes on the island's western end connected by a channel. In the middle of Veliko Jezero is an islet with a 12th-century **Benedictine monastery**, which contains a pricey but atmospheric restaurant.

There's a boat from Mali Most (about 1.5km from Pomena) on Malo Jezero that leaves for the island monastery every hour at 10 minutes past the hour. It's not possible to walk right around the larger lake as there's no bridge over the channel connecting the lakes to the sea. If you decide to swim it, keep in mind that the current can be strong.

Renting a **bicycle** (25/110KN per hour/day) is an excellent way to explore the national park. Several places including **Hotel Odisej** (744 022; www.hotelodisej.hr) in Pomena have bikes. Be aware that Pomena and Polače are separated by a steep hill. The bike path along the lake is an easier and very scenic pedal, but it doesn't link the two towns. You can rent a paddleboat and row over to the monastery but you'll need stamina.

The island offers some unusual opportunities for **diving**. There's a 3rd-century Roman wreck in relatively shallow water. The remains of the ship, including amphorae, have calcified over the centuries and this has protected them from pillaging. There's also a German torpedo boat from WWII and several walls to dive. Contact **Kronmar Diving** (744 022; Hotel Odisej).

🛏 Sleeping & Eating

The Polače tourist office arranges private accommodation (from around 250KN per double), but it's essential to make arrangements before peak season. You'll find more *sobe* signs around Pomena than Polače, and practically none at all in Sobra. Restaurants rent out rooms too.

TOP CHOICE Stermasi   APARTMENTS €€
(098 93 90 362; www.stermasi.hr; Saplunara; apt 368-625KN; ※) On the 'other' side of Mljet, these apartments are ideal if you want to enjoy the simple life and natural beauty of the island. Well-presented and bright, the nine modern units have terraces or private balconies. Sandy beaches are on your doorstep and guests get a 20% discount on meals at the amazing restaurant.

Soline 6   HOTEL €€
(744 024; www.soline6.com; Soline; d 598KN) This very green place is the only accommodation within the national park, with everything built from recycled products. Organic waste is composted, toilets are waterless and there's no electricity. The four studios are modern and equipped with private bathrooms, balconies and kitchens.

Camping Mungos   CAMPING GROUND €
(745 300; Babino Polje; campsite per person 54KN; ☺May-Sep) Close to the beach and the lovely grotto of Odysseus, this camping ground has a restaurant, currency exchange and a minimart.

Melita   CROATIAN €€
(www.mljet-restoranmelita.com; St Mary's Island, Veliko Jezero; mains from 60KN) A more romantic spot can't be found on the island – this is the restaurant attached to the church on the little island in the middle of the big lake.

CROATIA MLJET ISLAND

ℹ MLJET: INS & OUTS

Sightseeing boats from Korčula and the Dubrovnik catamarans arrive at Polače wharf in high season; Jadrolinija ferries use the Sobra port close to the centre of the island. The entry point for Mljet National Park is between Pomena and Polače. Your ticket includes bus and boat transfer to the Benedictine monastery. If you stay overnight on the island you only pay the park admission once.

ℹ Information

The **tourist office** (☑744 186; www.mljet.hr; ☺8am-1pm & 5-7pm Mon-Sat, 9am-noon Sun Jun-Sep, 8am-1pm Mon-Fri Oct-May) is in Polače and there's an ATM next door (and another at Hotel Odisej in Pomena). There are free brochures and a good walking map for sale. There's another ATM at the Hotel Odisej in Pomena.

Babino Polje, 18km east of Polače, is the island capital. It's home to another **tourist office** (☑745 125; www.mljet.hr; ☺9am-5pm Mon-Fri) and a post office.

ℹ Getting There & Away

Jadrolinija (p180) ferries stop only at Sobra (30KN, two hours) but the **G&V Line** (☑313 119; www.gv-line.hr) catamaran goes to Sobra (40KN, one hour) and Polače (54KN, 1½ hours) in the summer months, leaving Dubrovnik's Gruž harbour twice daily (9.15am and 7.10pm) and returning daily from Polače at 4.55pm, and twice daily from Sobra (6.15am and 5.35pm). You cannot reserve tickets in advance for this service; get to the harbour ticket office well in advance in high season to secure a seat (bicycles are not usually permitted either). In winter there's one daily catamaran. Tour boats from Korčula also run to Polače harbour in high season. Infrequent buses connect Sobra and Polače.

Dubrovnik

☑020 / POP 29,995

No matter whether you are visiting Dubrovnik for the first time or if you're returning again and again to this marvellous city, the sense of awe and beauty when you set eyes on the Stradun (the Old Town's main street) never fades. It's hard to imagine anyone, even the city's inhabitants, becoming jaded by its marble streets and baroque buildings, or failing to be inspired by a walk along the ancient city walls that protected a civilised, sophisticated republic for five centuries and that now look out onto the endless shimmer of the peaceful Adriatic.

History

Founded 1300 years ago by refugees from Epidaurus in Greece, medieval Dubrovnik (Ragusa until 1918) shook off Venetian control in the 14th century, becoming an independent republic and one of Venice's more important maritime rivals, trading with Egypt, Syria, Sicily, Spain, France and later Turkey. The double blow of an earthquake in 1667 and the opening of new trade routes to the east sent Ragusa into a slow decline, ending with Napoleon's conquest of the town in 1808.

The deliberate shelling of Dubrovnik by the Yugoslav army in 1991 sent shockwaves through the international community but, when the smoke cleared in 1992, traumatised residents cleared the rubble and set about repairing the damage. Reconstruction has been extraordinarily skilful. All of the damaged buildings have now been restored.

After a steep postwar decline in tourism, Dubrovnik has bounced back. Today it is the most prosperous, elegant and expensive city in Croatia and a real tourism magnet.

◉ Sights

All the sights are in the Old Town, which is entirely closed to cars. Looming above the city is Mt Srđ, which is connected by cable car to Dubrovnik. Pile Gate is the main entrance to the Old Town; the main street is Placa (better known as Stradun).

OLD TOWN

TOP CHOICE City Walls & Forts CITY WALLS

(Gradske Zidine; adult/concession 70/30KN; ☺9am-6.30pm Apr-Oct, 10am-3pm Nov-Mar) No visit to Dubrovnik would be complete without a walk around the city walls, the finest in the world and Dubrovnik's main claim to fame. Built between the 13th and 16th centuries, they enclose the entire city in a protective veil more than 2km long and up to 25m high, with two round and 14 square towers, two corner fortifications and a large fortress. The views over the town and sea are great – this walk could be the highlight of your visit. The main entrance and ticket office to the walls is by the 1537 **Pile Gate**. You can also enter at the **Ploče Gate** in the east (wise at really busy times). The walls can only be walked clockwise.

TOP CHOICE War Photo Limited PHOTOGRAPHIC GALLERY

(☑326 166; www.warphotoltd.com; Antuninska 6; admission 30KN; ☺9am-9pm daily Jun-Sep, to 3pm Tue-Sat & to 1pm Sun May & Oct) A powerful experience, this state-of-the-art photographic gallery has beautifully displayed and reproduced exhibitions curated by the gallery owner and former photojournalist Wade Goddard, who worked in the Balkans in the 1990s. In addition to temporary shows, there's a permanent exhibition devoted to the war in Yugoslavia. It closes from November to April.

Franciscan Monastery & Museum MONASTERY

(Muzej Franjevačkog Samostana; Placa 2; adult/concession 30/15KN; ☺9am-6pm) Inside this monastery complex is a mid-14th-century **cloister**, one of the most beautiful late-Romanesque structures in Dalmatia. Further inside you'll find the third-oldest functioning **pharmacy** in Europe, in business since 1391. The small monastery **museum** has a collection of relics, liturgical objects including chalices, paintings and gold jewellery and pharmacy items.

Dominican Monastery & Museum
MONASTERY

(Muzej Dominikanskog Samostana; off Ulica Svetog Dominika 4; adult/concession 20/10KN; ⊙9am-6pm May-Oct, to 5pm Nov-Apr) This imposing 14th-century structure in the northeastern corner of the city is a real architectural highlight, with a forbidding fortress-like exterior that shelters a rich trove of paintings from Dubrovnik's finest 15th- and 16th-century artists.

Rector's Palace
PALACE

(Pred Dvorom 3; adult/concession 35/15KN; audioguide 30KN; ⊙9am-6pm May-Oct, to 4pm Nov-Apr) This Gothic-Renaissance Rector's Palace built in the late 15th century houses a museum with artfully restored rooms, portraits, coats-of-arms and coins, evoking the glorious history of Dubrovnik. Today the atrium is often used for concerts during the Summer Festival (p169).

Cathedral of the Assumption of the Virgin
CATHEDRAL

(Stolna Crkva Velike Gospe; Poljana M Držića; ⊙morning & late-afternoon Mass) Completed in 1713 in a baroque style, the cathedral is notable for its fine altars. The cathedral **treasury** (Riznica; adult/concession 10/5KN; ⊙8am-5.30pm Mon-Sat, 11am-5.30pm Sun May-Oct, 10am-noon & 3-5pm Nov-Apr) contains relics of St Blaise as well as 138 gold and silver reliquaries largely made in the workshops of Dubrovnik's goldsmiths between the 11th and 17th centuries.

Sponza Palace
PALACE

(Placa) The 16th-century Sponza Palace was originally a customs house, then a minting house, a state treasury and a bank. Now it houses the **State Archives** (Državni Arhiv u Dubrovniku; admission 20KN; ⊙8am-3pm Mon-Fri, to 1pm Sat) and the **Memorial Room of the Defenders of Dubrovnik** (⊙10am-10pm Mon-Fri, 8am-1pm Sat), a heartbreaking collection of portraits of young people who perished between 1991 and 1995.

Onofrio Fountain
FOUNTAIN

One of Dubrovnik's most famous landmarks, Onofrio Fountain was built in 1438 as part of a water-supply system that involved bringing water from a well 12km away.

Serbian Orthodox Church & Museum
CHURCH, MUSEUM

(Muzej Pravoslavne Crkve; Od Puča 8; adult/concession 10/5KN; ⊙9am-2pm Mon-Sat) This 1877 Orthodox church has a fascinating collection of icons dating from the 15th to 19th centuries.

Synagogue
SYNAGOGUE

(Sinagoga; Žudioska 5; admission 20KN; ⊙10am-8pm Mon-Fri May-Oct, to 3pm Nov-Apr) The oldest Sephardic and second-oldest synagogue in the Balkans, dating back to the 15th century, has a small museum inside.

Orlando Column
MONUMENT

(Luža Sq) This popular meeting place used to be the spot where edicts, festivities and public verdicts were announced.

EAST OF THE OLD TOWN

TOP CHOICE Cable Car
CABLE CAR

(www.dubrovnikcablecar.com; Petra Krešimira IV; adult/concession 87/50KN; ⊙9am-10pm Tue-Sun May-Oct, shorter hours rest of year) Dubrovnik's cable car whisks you from just north of the city walls up to Mt Srđ in under four minutes, for a stupendous perspective of the city from a lofty 405m, down to the terracotta-tiled rooftops of the Old Town and the island of Lokrum, with the Adriatic and distant Elafiti Islands filling the horizon.

Homeland War Museum
MUSEUM

(www.tzdubrovnik.hr; admission 20KN; ⊙8am-6pm Apr-Oct, 9am-4pm Nov-Mar) Dedicated to the 'Homeland War' – as the 1990s war is dubbed in Croatia – this place inside a Napoleonic Fort, just above where the cable car drops you off, is interesting for those who want to learn more about Dubrovnik's wartime history.

THE COAST

The nicest beach that's walkable from the Old Town is below **Hotel Bellevue** (Petra Čingrije 7). In the Old Town, you can also swim below the two Buža bars.

Banje Beach
BEACH

(Outside Ploče Gate) Banje Beach is the most popular city beach, though it's even more crowded now that a section has been roped off for the exclusive EastWest Club (p171). Just southeast of here is **Sveti Jakov**, a good local beach that doesn't get rowdy and has showers, a bar and a restaurant. Buses 5 and 8 will get you there.

Dubrovnik

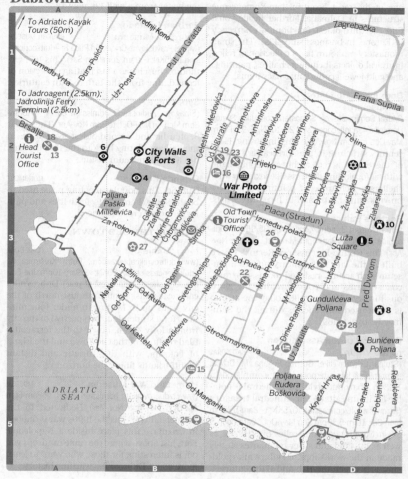

Lapad Bay   BEACH
Lapad Bay is brimming with hotel beaches that you can use without a problem; try the bay by Hotel Kompas. A little further on is the good shallow **Copacabana Beach** on Babin Kuk Peninsula. If you're a naturist, head down to **Cava**, signposted near Copacabana Beach. In the Old Town, you can also swim below the two Buža bars.

Lokrum Island   ISLAND
A better option than the mainland beaches is to take the **ferry** (return 40KN; ⊙last return boat 6pm) that shuttles roughly hourly in summer to lush Lokrum Island, a national park with a

rocky nudist beach (marked FKK), a botanical garden, the ruins of a medieval Benedictine monastery and an attractive cafe-restaurant.

🏃 Activities

Navis Underwater Explorers   DIVING
(☑099 35 02 773; www.navisdubrovnik.com; Copacabana Beach; ⦿) Recreational dives (including the wreck of the *Taranto*) and courses.

**Adriatic Kayak
Tours**   KAYAKING, WHITE-WATER RAFTING
(☑091 72 20 413; www.adriatickayaktours.com; Zrinsko Frankopanska 6) Kayak excursions (from a half-day paddle to a week-long trip);

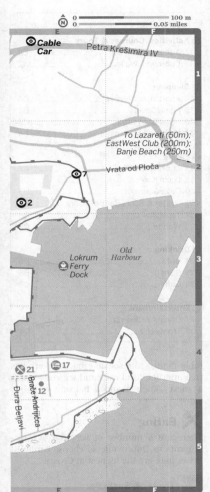

360KN) are very popular. Excursions to Korčula and Pelješac (390KN) are offered, too.

✹ Festivals & Events

The **Feast of St Blaise** is held on 3 February, and **Carnival** is also held in February.

Dubrovnik Summer Festival CULTURAL
(☎326 100; www.dubrovnik-festival.hr; tickets 50-300KN) A major cultural event over five weeks in July and August, with theatre, music and dance performances at different venues in the Old Town.

🛏 Sleeping

Private accommodation is generally the best option in Dubrovnik, which is the most expensive destination in Croatia. Beware the scramble of private owners at the bus station and ferry terminal: some provide what they say they offer while others are scamming. Expect to pay from 300KN for a double room, and from 500KN for an apartment in high season.

OLD TOWN

TOP CHOICE **Karmen Apartments** APARTMENTS €€
(☎098 619 282, 323 433; www.karmendu.com; Bandureva 1; apt 450-1200KN; ❄️🞀) Run by an Englishman who has lived in Dubrovnik for decades, these four inviting apartments with plenty of character enjoy a great location a stone's throw from Ploče harbour. Book well ahead.

TOP CHOICE **Fresh Sheets** HOSTEL €
(☎091 79 92 086; www.igotfresh.com; Sv Šimuna 15; dm/d 210/554KN; @🞀) The only hostel in the Old Town is a warm place right by the city walls, with clean and simple dorms and a double with a sea view. It's run by a hospitable crew who organise imaginative outings, international dinners and other fun stuff.

Apartments Amoret APARTMENTS €€
(☎091 53 04 910; www.dubrovnik-amoret.com; Dinke Ranjine 5; apt 755-1423KN; ❄️🞀) Spread over three historic buildings in the heart of the Old Town, Amoret offers 11 high-quality renovated studio apartments, all with bathrooms, a dash of art and parquetry flooring, and kitchenette-style cooking facilities.

Hotel Stari Grad BOUTIQUE HOTEL €€€
(☎322 244; www.hotelstarigrad.com; Od Sigurate 4; s/d 1350/1800KN; ❄️🞀) This Old Town hotel is all about location – it's very close to the Pile Gate and just off the Stradun. Its eight

it also offers white-water rafting on the Tara River in Montenegro.

👣 Tours

Dubrovnik Walks WALKING
(☎095 80 64 526; www.dubrovnikwalks.com) Excellent guided walks in English. One-hour Old Town tours (90KN) run twice daily. The meeting place is the Fuego club just west of the Pile Gate. No reservation is necessary.

Adriatic Explore BUS, BOAT
(☎323 400; www.adriatic-explore.com; Bandureva 4) Day trips to Mostar and Montenegro (both

Dubrovnik

◉ Top Sights
Cable Car E1
City Walls & Forts B2
War Photo Limited................................ C2

◉ Sights
1 Cathedral of the Assumption of
   the Virgin... D4
Cathedral of the Assumption of
   the Virgin Treasury .... (see 1)
2 Dominican Monastery &
   Museum...E2
3 Franciscan Monastery &
   Museum B2
Memorial Room of the
   Defenders of Dubrovnik............(see 10)
4 Onofrio Fountain................................. B2
5 Orlando Column...................................... D3
6 Pile Gate...A2
7 Ploče Gate..E2
8 Rector's Palace D4
9 Serbian Orthodox Church &
   Museum C3
10 Sponza Palace.. D3
State Archives..............................(see 10)
11 Synagogue.. D2

◉ Activities, Courses & Tours
12 Adriatic Explore E4
13 Dubrovnik Walks.............................A2

◉ Sleeping
14 Apartments Amoret................................C4
15 Fresh Sheets B4
16 Hotel Stari Grad......................................C2
17 Karmen Apartments E4

◉ Eating
18 Dubravka 1836 .... A2
19 Lucin Kantun C2
20 Oliva Gourmet.................................... D3
21 Oyster & Sushi Bar Bota Šare E4
22 Taj Mahal C3
23 Wanda C2

◉ Drinking
24 Buža D5
25 Buža II B5
26 Gaffe C3

◉ Entertainment
27 Open-Air Cinema...................................B3
28 Troubadur D4

rooms are smallish but neat and attractive. Staff are sweet and views from the rooftop terrace dramatic.

OUTSIDE THE OLD TOWN

Begović Boarding House   PRIVATE ACCOMMODATION €
(☎435 191; www.begovic-boarding-house.com; Primorska 17; dm/r/apt 150/320/385KN; P@) A steep walk uphill from Lapad harbourfront, this welcoming family-run place has smallish but clean pine-trimmed rooms, some opening out onto a communal garden with amazing views. There's free pick-up from the bus or ferry, free internet, a kitchen and excursions.

Hotel Ivka   HOTEL €€
(☎362 600; www.hotel-ivka.com; Put Sv Mihajla 21; s/d 593/785KN; P✿@☎) Modern three-star hotel with pleasant, spacious rooms that have wooden floors (and most have a balcony). Comfort levels are high given the prices. It's closer to Lapad and the ferry terminal than the Old Town, but on a regular bus route.

Dubrovnik Backpackers Club   HOSTEL €
(☎435 375; www.dubackpackers.com; Mostarska 2d; dm 120-170KN; @☎) Run by a very hospi-

table family, this sociable backpackers has free internet, local calls and tea/coffee, plus a guests' kitchen and a balcony with bay views.

🍴 Eating

There are a number of very average restaurants in Dubrovnik, so choose carefully. Prices here are the highest in Croatia.

TOP CHOICE Oyster & Sushi Bar Bota Šare   SUSHI €€
(☎324 034; www.bota-sare.hr; Od Pustijerne bb; oysters/sushi per piece from 12/15KN) Fresh Ston oysters and the best sushi this side of Dalmatia, plus an absolutely divine setting, with views of the cathedral from its terrace tables.

Lucin Kantun   CROATIAN €€
(☎321 003; Od Sigurate bb; mains from 80KN) A modest-looking place with shabby-chic decor, a few pavement tables and some of the most creative food in Dubrovnik. Virtually everything on the short meze-style menu is freshly cooked from an open kitchen so you may have to wait a while at busy times.

Taj Mahal   BOSNIAN, INTERNATIONAL €
(www.tajmahaldubrovnik.com; Nikole Gučetićeva 2; mains from 40KN) It's like an Aladdin's cave, with an interior loaded with Ottoman decorations and subdued lighting, and great Bosnian food. There are also three pavement tables.

Oliva Gourmet   MEDITERRANEAN €€
(☏324 076; www.pizza-oliva.com; Cvijete Zuzorić 2 ; mains from 100KN; ⊕) A lovely little place with a terrace on a tiny street and a cute interior with vintage pieces, dishing out simple and local food. The **Oliva Pizzeria**, next door, has good pizza.

Wanda   ITALIAN €€
(☏098 94 49 317; www.wandarestaurant.com; Prijeko 8; mains from 70KN) This is a very classy Italian, with good Croatian wines and dishes such as osso buco with saffron risotto and beautifully crafted pastas.

Dubravka 1836   INTERNATIONAL €
(www.dubravka1836.hr; Brsalje 1; mains from 49KN) This place has arguably Dubrovnik's best dining terrace, with stunning wall and sea views. Though it draws quite a touristy clientele, locals still rate the fresh fish, risotto and salads, pizza and pasta.

🍷 Drinking

TOP CHOICE **Buža**   BAR
(Ilije Sarake) Finding this isolated bar-on-a-cliff feels like a real discovery as you duck and dive around the city walls and finally see the entrance tunnel. It showcases tasteful music and a mellow crowd soaking up the vibes, views and sunshine.

Buža II   BAR
(Crijevićeva 9) Just a notch more upmarket than the original, this one is lower on the rocks and has a shaded terrace where you can snack on crisps, peanuts or sandwiches.

EastWest Club   COCKTAIL BAR
(www.ew-dubrovnik.com; Frana Supila bb) By day this upmarket outfit on Banje Beach rents out sun loungers and umbrellas and serves drinks to the bathers. When the rays lengthen, the cocktail bar opens.

Gaffe   IRISH PUB
(Miha Pracata bb) The busiest place in town, this huge pub has a homely interior and a long, covered side terrace.

☆ Entertainment

TOP CHOICE **Lazareti**   CULTURAL CENTRE
(☏324 633; www.lazareti.com; Frana Supila 8) Dubrovnik's best cultural centre, Lazareti hosts cinema nights, club nights, live music, gigs and pretty much all the best things in town.

Troubadur   LIVE MUSIC
(☏412 154; Bunićeva Poljana 2) Come to this corner bar, a legendary Dubrovnik venue, for live jazz concerts in the summer.

Open-Air Cinema   CINEMA
(Kumičića, Lapad) In two locations, it's open nightly in July and August with screenings starting after sundown. Also in the **Old Town** (Za Rokom).

ℹ Information

There are numerous ATMs in town, in Lapad and at the ferry terminal and bus station. Travel agencies and post offices will also exchange cash.

Atlas Travel Agency (www.atlas-croatia.com) With offices in Gruž Harbour (☏418 001; Obala Papa Ivana Pavla II 1, Gruž Harbour) and Pile Gate (☏442 574; Sv Đurđa 1, Pile Gate), this outfit organises excursions within Croatia and to Mostar and Montenegro. It also finds private accommodation.

Hospital (☏431 777; Dr Roka Mišetića) A kilometre south of Lapad Bay.

Lonely Planet (www.lonelyplanet.com/croatia/dubrovnik)

Main Post Office (cnr Široka & Od Puča)

Netcafé (www.netcafe.hr; Prijeko 21; per hr 30KN) A place to chill even if you're not surfing; has fast connections, CD burning, good drinks and coffee.

Tourist Office (www.tzdubrovnik.hr; ⊙8am-8pm daily Jun-Sep, 8am-3pm Mon-Fri & 9am-2pm Sat Oct-May) Maps, information and the indispensable *Dubrovnik Riviera* guide. The smart new head office (☏020 312 011; Brsalje 5) that's under construction just west of the Pile Gate should open by the time you read this. There are also offices at Gruž Harbour (☏417 983; Obala Stjepana Radića 27), the bus station (☏417 581; Obala Pape Ivana Pavla II 44a), Lapad (☏437 460; Šetalište Kralja Zvonimira 25) and at Široka (☏323 587; www.tzdubrovnik.hr; Široka 1; ⊙8am-8pm daily Jun-Sep, 8am-3pm Mon-Fri, 9am-2pm Sat Oct-May) in the Old Town.

ℹ Getting There & Away

Air

Daily flights to/from Zagreb are operated by **Croatia Airlines** (☏01 66 76 555; www.croatiaairlines.hr). Fares vary between 270KN

BUSES FROM DUBROVNIK

DESTINATION	PRICE (KN)	DURATION (HR)	FREQUENCY (DAILY)
Korčula	105	3	2
Kotor	130	2½	2-3
Mostar	130	3	3
Orebić	95	2½	2
Plitvice	350	10	1
Rijeka	370-510	13	4-5
Sarajevo	230	5	2
Split	140	4½	19
Zadar	190-230	8	8
Zagreb	270	11	7-8

for promo fares and around 760KN for flexi fares. The trip takes about an hour. Croatia Airlines also operate nonstop flights to Frankfurt and seasonal routes to cities such as Rome, Paris and Amsterdam.

Dubrovnik airport is served by over 20 other airlines from across Europe.

Boat

The **Jadrolinija ferry terminal** (✆418 000; www.jadrolinija.hr; Gruž Harbour) and the bus station are next to each other at Gruž, several kilometres northwest of the Old Town.

A twice-weekly Jadrolinija coastal ferry heads north to Korčula, Hvar, Split, Zadar and Rijeka. There's a local ferry that leaves Dubrovnik for Sobra and Polače on Mljet (60KN, 2½ hours) twice a week throughout the year; in summer there are also catamarans, which have a daily service to both Sobra and Polače (150KN, 1½ hours). Several daily ferries run year-round to the outlying Elafiti Islands of Koločep, Lopud and Šipan.

Ferries also go from Dubrovnik to Bari, in southern Italy; there are six a week in the summer season (300KN to 450KN, nine hours) and two in the winter months.

Jadroagent (✆419 000; Obala Stjepana Radića 32) books ferry tickets and has info.

Bus

Buses out of Dubrovnik **bus station** (✆060 305 070; Obala Pape Ivana Pavla II 44a) can be crowded, so book tickets ahead in summer. There's a **garderoba** (left-luggage office; 1st hr 7KN, then per hr 2KN; ☺4.30am-10pm) at the station.

Split–Dubrovnik buses pass briefly through Bosnian territory, so keep your passport handy for border-crossing points.

All bus schedules are detailed at www.libertas dubrovnik.hr.

❶ Getting Around

Čilipi international airport (www.airport-dubrovnik.hr) is 24km southeast of Dubrovnik. Atlas buses (35KN) leave from the main bus station irregularly, supposedly two hours before Croatia Airlines domestic flights, but it's best to check the latest schedule at the Atlas Travel Agency (p171) by the Pile Gate. These airport buses stop in Dubrovnik at Zagrebačka cesta, just north of the old town, en route out of the city (but not at the Pile Gate). Buses leave the airport for Dubrovnik bus station (via the Pile Gate in this direction) several times a day and are timed to coincide with arrivals; if your flight is late there's usually still one waiting.

Dubrovnik's buses run frequently and generally on time. The key tourist routes run until after 2am in summer, so if you're staying in Lapad there's no need to rush home. The fare is 15KN if you buy from the driver but only 12KN if you buy it at a kiosk.

UNDERSTAND CROATIA

Croatia Today

Croatia harbours a love-hate relationship with its own politicians, its political arena fuelled by constant drama. The pinnacle occurred in 2009, with the surprise resignation of then prime minister Ivo Sanader. In 2010 Sanader was arrested in Austria, in 2011 he was extradited to Croatia and later that year he was put on trial in Zagreb. The Sanader scandal remains the talk of the town; a fifth indictment on corruption charges was filed in September 2012.

Kukuriku Coalition

Croatian politics took a major turn in the 2011 parliamentary election, when the SDP joined three other centre-left parties to create the so-named Kukuriku coalition, an opposition bloc headed up by Zoran Milanović. Kukuriku won with an absolute majority, ousting Hrvatska Demokratska Zajednica (HDZ, Croatian Democratic Union), which had been in government for 16 of the 20 years since Croatia became independent in 1991.

Milanović took office as Croatia's prime minister in December 2011. But the slightly uplifted spirits quickly descended back into general discontent with politics, mainly due to the European debt crisis and the unpopular austerity measures that ensued.

EU Accession

In January 2012, about 44% of Croats turned up to vote in the referendum on European Union (EU) accession and supported the joining by a margin of two to one. But attitudes towards EU accession remain divided, in no small part due to the crisis. The divide aside, Croatia is slated to become the EU's 28th member state, which – on paper at least – will catapult it out of the Balkans and place it firmly in Central Europe. But the accession is no big bang; Croatia's inner strife remains.

Economic Woes

Croatia's economy has been in a shambles for several years, and the global downturn plus the EU crisis aren't helping. Unemployment is high, people's salaries are often months overdue, longstanding national companies are going bankrupt, pensions are ridiculously low and unemployment compensation isn't much better. Needless to say, from the point of view of the average Croat, life is tough and the global financial crisis has made itself clearly known. *Kriza* (crisis) is among the most uttered words in Croatia today; you'll hear it everywhere, all the time, like a mantra. Despite the double-dip recession, Croatia stands as a promising emerging market. It is compensating for the drastic drop in foreign investments by rapid growth in tourism revenue. It has, in fact, become the fastest-growing tourism market in the entire Mediterranean.

History

Since time immemorial, people have come and gone, invading, trading and settling. For long periods, the Croats have been ruled by and have fought off others – Venetians, Ottomans, Hungarians, Habsburgs, the French and the Germans. The creation of Yugoslavia after WWII brought some semblance of unity to the south Slavic nations. Yet it didn't last long. After the death of Yugoslav leader Tito in 1980, Yugoslavia slowly disintegrated, and a brutal civil war ensued.

Controversial Constituition

With political changes sweeping Eastern Europe, many Croats felt the time had come to separate from Yugoslavia, and the elections of April 1990 saw the victory of Franjo Tuđman's HDZ. On 22 December 1990, a new Croatian constitution changed the status of Serbs in Croatia from that of a 'constituent nation' to a national minority.

The constitution's failure to guarantee minority rights and mass dismissals of Serbs from the public service stimulated the 600,000-strong ethnic Serb community within Croatia to demand autonomy. In early 1991 Serb extremists within Croatia staged provocations designed to force federal military intervention. A May 1991 referendum (boycotted by the Serbs) produced a 93% vote in favour of independence, but when Croatia declared independence on 25 June 1991, the Serbian enclave of Krajina proclaimed its independence from Croatia.

War

Under pressure from the EC (now the EU), Croatia declared a three-month moratorium on its independence, but heavy fighting broke out in Krajina, Baranja (the area north of the Drava River opposite Osijek) and Slavonia. This initiated what Croats refer to as the Homeland War. The Serb-dominated Yugoslav People's Army intervened in support of Serbian irregulars, under the pretext of halting ethnic violence.

When the Croatian government ordered a shutdown of 32 federal military installations in the republic, the Yugoslav navy blockaded the Adriatic coast and laid siege to the strategic town of Vukovar on the Danube. During the summer of 1991, a quarter of Croatia fell to Serbian militias and the Yugoslav People's Army.

In late 1991, the federal army and the Montenegrin militia moved against Dubrovnik, and the presidential palace in Zagreb was hit by rockets from Yugoslav jets in an apparent assassination attempt on President Tuđman. When the three-month moratorium ended, Croatia declared full independence. Soon after, Vukovar finally fell when the Yugoslav army moved in, in one of the more bloodthirsty acts in all of the Yugoslav wars. During six months of fighting in Croatia, 10,000 people died, hundreds of thousands fled and tens of thousands of homes were destroyed.

Dayton Accord

Beginning on 3 January 1992, a UN-brokered ceasefire generally held. At the same time, the EU, succumbing to pressure from Germany, recognised Croatia. This was followed by US recognition, and in May 1992 Croatia was admitted to the UN.

The fighting continued until the Dayton Accord, signed in Paris in December 1995, recognised Croatia's traditional borders and provided for the return of eastern Slavonia. It was effected in January 1998. The transition proceeded relatively smoothly, but the two populations still regard each other with suspicion.

Postwar Politics

Franjo Tuđman's combination of authoritarianism and media control, and tendency to be influenced by the far right, no longer appealed to the postwar Croatian populace. By 1999 opposition parties united to work against Tuđman and the HDZ. Tuđman was hospitalised and died suddenly in late 1999, and planned elections were postponed until January 2000. Still, voters turned out in favour of a centre-left coalition, ousting the HDZ and voting in the centrist Stipe Mesić, who held the presidential throne for 10 years.

People

According to the 2011 census, Croatia has a population of roughly 4.3 million people, a decline from the prewar population of nearly five million. A discouraging economic outlook is largely responsible for a steady decline in Croatia's population, as educated young people leave in search of greater opportunities abroad. Then there was the still-recent war of the 1990s, during which about 50% of the Serbian population departed; less than half have returned. The post-independence economic crunch that followed sparked a mass exodus of Croats; some 120,000 emigrated. That was balanced out by the roughly equal number of ethnic Croat refugees who arrived from BiH and some 30,000 who came from the Vojvodina region of Serbia. These days, the recession-powered brain drain continues. It's not surprising: Croatia is right behind Spain and Greece when it comes to unemployment rates of young educated under-30s.

Religion

According to the most recent census, 87.8% of the population identifies as Catholic, 4.4% Orthodox, 1.3% Muslim, 0.3% Protestant and 6.2% other and unknown. Croats are overwhelmingly Roman Catholic, while Serbs belong to the Eastern Orthodox Church, a division that has its roots in the fall of the Roman Empire.

It would be difficult to overstate the extent to which Catholicism shapes the Croatian national identity. The Church is the most trusted institution in Croatia, rivalled only by the military. Religious holidays are celebrated with fervour and Sunday Mass is strongly attended.

Arts

Literature

Croatia's towering literary figure is 20th-century novelist and playwright Miroslav Krleža (1893–1981). His most popular novel is *The Return of Philip Latinovicz* (1932), which has been translated into English.

BOOKS

Lonely Planet's *Croatia* is a comprehensive guide to the country.

Interesting reads about Croatia include Rebecca West's *Black Lamb and Grey Falcon,* a classic travel book which recounts the writer's journeys through Croatia, Serbia, Bosnia, Macedonia and Montenegro in 1941. British writer Tony White retraced West's journey in *Another Fool in the Balkans* (2006), juxtaposing modern life in Serbia and Croatia with the region's political history. *Croatia: Travels in Undiscovered Country* (2003), by Tony Fabijančić, recounts the life of rural folks in a new Croatia. *Plum Brandy: Croatian Journeys* by Josip Novakovich is a sensitive exploration of his family's Croatian background.

Some contemporary writers worth reading include expat writer Dubravka Ugrešić, best known for her novels *The Culture of Lies* and *The Ministry of Pain*. Slavenka Drakulić's *Café Europa – Life After Communism* is an excellent read, while Miljenko Jergović's *Sarajevo Marlboro* and *Mama Leone* powerfully conjure up the atmosphere of life in pre-war Yugoslavia.

Music

Although Croatia has produced many fine classical musicians and composers, its most original musical contribution lies in its rich tradition of folk music. The instrument most often used in Croatian folk music is the *tamburica*, a three- or five-string mandolin that is plucked or strummed. Translated as 'group of people', *klapa* is an outgrowth of church-choir singing. The form is most popular in rural Dalmatia and can involve up to 10 voices singing in harmony.

There's a wealth of homegrown talent on Croatia's pop and rock music scene. Some of the most prominent pop, fusion and hip-hop bands are Hladno Pivo (Cold Beer), Pips Chips & Videoclips, TBF, Edo Maajka, Vještice (The Witches), Gustafi and the deliciously insane Let 3.

Visual Arts

Vlaho Bukovac (1855–1922) was the most notable Croatian painter in the late 19th century. Important early-20th-century painters include Miroslav Kraljević (1885–1913) and Josip Račić (1885–1908). Post-WWII artists experimented with abstract expressionism but this period is best remembered for the naive art that was typified by Ivan Generalić (1914–92). Recent trends have included minimalism, conceptual art and pop art. Contemporary Croatian artists worth checking out include Lovro Artuković, Sanja Iveković, Dalibor Martinis, Andreja Kulunčić, Sandra Sterle and Renata Poljak.

Environment

Croatia is shaped like a boomerang: from the Pannonian plains of Slavonia between the Sava, Drava and Danube Rivers, across hilly central Croatia to the Istrian peninsula, then south through Dalmatia along the rugged Adriatic coast.

The narrow Croatian coastal belt at the foot of the Dinaric Alps is only about 600km long as the crow flies, but it's so indented that the actual length is 1778km. If the 4012km of coastline around the offshore islands is added to the total, the length becomes 5790km. Most of the 'beaches' along this jagged coast consist of slabs of rock sprinkled with naturists. Don't come expecting to find sand, but the waters are sparkling clean, even around large towns.

Croatia's offshore islands are every bit as beautiful as those off the coast of Greece. There are 1244 islands and islets along the tectonically submerged Adriatic coastline, 50 of them inhabited. The largest are Cres, Krk, Mali Lošinj, Pag and Rab in the north; Dugi Otok in the middle; and Brač, Hvar, Korčula, Mljet and Vis in the south.

Wildlife

Deer are plentiful in the dense forests of Risnjak National Park, as are brown bears, wild cats and *ris* (lynx), from which the park gets its name. Occasionally a wolf or wild boar may appear but only rarely. Plitvice Lakes National Park, however, is an important refuge for wolves. The rare sea otter is also protected in Plitvice, as well as in Krka National Park. Two venomous snakes are endemic in Paklenica – the nose-horned viper and the European adder.

The griffon vulture, with a wingspan of 2.6m, has a permanent colony on Cres, and Paklenica National Park is rich in peregrine falcons, goshawks, sparrow hawks, buzzards and owls. Krka National Park is an important migration route and winter habitat for marsh birds as well as rare golden eagles and short-toed eagles. Kopački Rit Nature Park, near Osijek in eastern Croatia, is an extremely important bird refuge.

National Parks

When the Yugoslav federation collapsed, eight of its finest national parks ended up in Croatia. These have a total area of 96,135 sq km, of which 74,260 sq km is land and 21,875 sq km is water. Around 8% of Croatia is given over to its protected areas.

The dramatically formed karstic gorges and cliffs make Paklenica National Park along the coast a rock-climbing favourite. More rugged is the mountainous Northern Velebit National Park, a stunning patchwork of forests, peaks, ravines and ridges that backs northern Dalmatia and the Šibenik-Knin region. The abundant plant and animal life, including bears, wolves and deer, in the Plitvice Lakes National Park between Zagreb and Zadar has warranted its inclusion on Unesco's list of World Natural Heritage sites. Both Plitvice Lakes and Krka National Parks (near Šibenik) feature a dramatic series of cascades and incredible turquoise lakes.

The Kornati Islands consist of 140 sparsely inhabited and vegetated islands, islets and reefs scattered over 300 sq km – an Adriatic showpiece easily accessible on an organised tour from Zadar. The northwestern half of the island of Mljet has been named a national park due to its two highly indented saltwater lakes surrounded by lush vegetation. The Brijuni Islands near Pula are the most cultivated national park since they were developed as a tourist resort in the late 19th century and were the getaway paradise for Tito.

Environmental Issues

The lack of heavy industry in Croatia has had the happy effect of leaving its forests, coasts, rivers and air generally fresh and unpolluted, but, as ever, an increase in investment and development brings forth problems and threats to the environment.

With the tourist boom, the demand for fresh fish and shellfish has risen exponentially. The production of farmed sea bass, sea bream and tuna (for export) is rising substantially, resulting in environmental pressure along the coast. Croatian tuna farms capture the young fish for fattening before they have a chance to reproduce and replenish the wild-fish population.

Coastal and island forests face particular problems. The dry summers and brisk *maestrals* (strong, steady westerly winds) also pose substantial fire hazards along the coast. In the last 20 years, fires have destroyed 7% of Croatia's forests.

Food & Drink

Croatian food is a savoury smorgasbord of taste, echoing the varied cultures that have influenced the country over the course of its history. You'll find a sharp divide between the Italian-style cuisine along the coast and the flavours of Hungary, Austria and Turkey in the continental parts.

Staples & Specialities

Zagreb and northwestern Croatia favour the kind of hearty meat dishes you might find in Vienna. Juicy spit-roasted and baked meat features *janjetina* (lamb), *svinjetina* (pork) and *patka* (duck), often accompanied by *mlinci* (baked noodles) or *pečeni krumpir* (roast potatoes).

Coastal cuisine is typically Mediterranean, using a lot of olive oil, garlic, fresh fish and shellfish, and herbs. Along the coast, look for lightly breaded and fried *lignje* (squid) as a main course. For a special appetiser, try *paški sir*, a pungent, hard cheese from the island of Pag. Dalmatian *brodet* (stewed mixed fish served with polenta) is another regional treat.

Istrian cuisine has been attracting international foodies for its long gastronomic tradition, fresh foodstuffs and unique specialities. Typical dishes include *maneštra*, a thick vegetable-and-bean soup, *fuži*, hand-rolled pasta often served with truffles or game meat, and *fritaja* (omelette often served with seasonal veggies). Istrian wines and olive oil are highly rated.

Drinks

It's customary to have a small glass of brandy before a meal and to accompany the food with one of Croatia's many wines. Today winemaking is undergoing a renaissance in the hands of a new generation of winemakers with a focus on preserving indigenous varieties and revitalizing ancestral estates. Quality is rising, exports are increasing and the wines are garnering global awards and winning the affections of worldly wine lovers thirsty for authentic stories and unique terroirs. Croatians often mix their wine with water, calling it *bevanda*. *Rakija* (brandy) comes in different flavours. The most commonly drunk are *loza* (grape brandy), *šljivovica* (plum brandy) and *travarica* (herbal brandy).

The two top types of Croatian *pivo* (beer) are Zagreb's Ožujsko and Karlovačko from Karlovac. The small-distribution Velebitsko has a loyal following among in-the-know beer drinkers. You'll probably want to practise saying *živjeli!* (cheers!).

Where to Eat & Drink

Most restaurants cluster in the middle of the price spectrum – few are unbelievably cheap and few are exorbitantly expensive. A restaurant *(restoran)* is at the top of the food chain, generally presenting a more formal dining experience. A *gostionica* or *konoba* is usually a traditional family-run tavern. A *pivnica* is more like a pub, with a wide choice of beer. A *kavana* is a cafe. Self-service cafeterias are quick, easy and inexpensive, though the quality of the food tends to vary.

Restaurants are open long hours, often noon to 11pm (some midnight), but many close on Sunday out of peak season.

Vegetarians & Vegans

Outside of major cities like Zagreb, Rijeka, Split and Dubrovnik, vegetarian restaurants are few but Croatia's vegetables are usually locally grown and quite tasty. *Blitva* (swiss chard) is a nutritious side dish often served with potatoes. The hearty *štrukli* (baked cheese dumplings) are a good alternative too.

SURVIVAL GUIDE

Directory A–Z

Accommodation

Private accommodation is a lot more affordable in Croatia; it's very often great value if you don't mind foregoing hotel facilities.

Note that many establishments add a 30% charge for less than three-night stays and include 'residence tax', which is around 7KN per person per day. Prices quoted in this chapter do not include the residence tax.

The following price categories for the cost of double room with bathroom are used in the listings in this chapter.

€ less than 500KM

€€ 500KN to 900KN

€€€ more than 900KN

Breakfast is included in the prices for all hotels.

CAMPING

Nearly 100 camping grounds are scattered along the Croatian coast. Most operate from mid-April to mid-September, give or take a few weeks. The exact times change from year to year, so it's wise to call in advance if you're arriving at either end of the season.

Nudist camping grounds (marked FKK) are among the best, as their secluded locations ensure peace and quiet. Bear in mind that freelance camping is officially prohibited. A good site for camping information is www.camping.hr.

HOSTELS

The **Croatian YHA** (☐01-48 29 291; www.hfhs. hr; Savska 5/1, Zagreb) operates youth hostels in Rijeka, Dubrovnik, Zadar, Zagreb and Pula. Nonmembers pay an additional 10KN per person per day for a stamp on a welcome card; six stamps entitle you to membership. The Croatian YHA can also provide information about private youth hostels in Zadar, Dubrovnik and Zagreb.

HOTELS

Hotels are ranked from one to five stars with most in the two- and three-star range. In August, some hotels may demand a surcharge for stays of less than three or four nights, but this is usually waived during the rest of the year, when prices drop steeply. In Zagreb prices are the same all year.

PRIVATE ROOMS

The best value for money in Croatia is a private room or apartment, often within or attached to a local home – the equivalent of small private guesthouses in other countries. Book private accommodation through travel agencies, by dealing directly with proprietors who meet you at the local bus or ferry station, or by knocking on the doors of houses with *sobe* or *zimmer* (rooms available) signs.

Whether you deal with the owner directly or book through an agency, you'll pay a 30% surcharge for stays of less than four or three nights and sometimes 50% or even 100% more for a one-night stay, although you may be able to get them to waive the surcharge if you arrive in the low season. Some will even insist on a seven-night minimum stay in the high season.

If you land in a room or apartment without a blue *sobe* or *apartmani* sign outside, the proprietor is renting to you illegally (ie not paying residence tax). They will probably be reluctant to provide their full name or phone number and you'll have absolutely no recourse in case of a problem.

Activities

There are numerous outdoorsy activities in Croatia.

Cycling Croatia has become a popular destination for cycle enthusiasts. See www. bicikl.hr and www.pedala.com.hr.

Diving Most coastal and island resorts have dive shops. For more info see the **Croatian Association of Diving Tourism** (www.croprodive.info), **Croatian Diving Federation** (www.diving-hrs.hr) and **Pro Diving Croatia** (www.diving.hr).

Hiking For information about hiking in Croatia, see the **Croatian Mountaineering Association** (www.plsavez.hr).

Kayaking and rafting Zagreb-based **Huck Finn** (www.huck-finn.hr) is a good contact for sea and river kayaking packages as well as rafting.

Rock climbing and caving For details, contact the Croatian Mountaineering Association or check its speleological department website at www.speleologija.hr.

Windsurfing For info about windsurfing in Croatia, see the **Croatian Windsurfing Association** (www.hukjd.hr) or www.windsurfing.hr.

Yachting A good source of information is the **Association of Nautical Tourism** (Udruženje Nautičkog Turizma; ☎051 209 147; www.croatiacharter.com; Bulevar Oslobođenja 23, Rijeka), which represents all Croatian marinas, and **Adriatic Croatia International Club** (www.aci-club.hr).

Business Hours

Hours can vary across the year.

Banks 9am to 7pm Monday to Friday, 8am to 1pm or 9am to 2pm Saturday

Bars and cafes 8am to midnight

Offices 8am to 4pm or 9am to 5pm Monday to Friday, 8am to 1pm or 9am to 2pm Saturday

Restaurants noon to 11pm or midnight, closed Sunday out of peak season

Shops 8am to 8pm Monday to Friday, to 2pm or 3pm Saturday

Embassies & Consulates

The following are all in Zagreb.

Albanian Embassy (☎01-48 10 679; Jurišićeva 2a)

Australian Embassy (☎01-48 91 200; Nova Ves 11, Kaptol Centar)

Bosnia & Hercegovina Embassy (☎01-45 01 070; Torbarova 9)

Bulgarian Embassy (☎01-46 46 609; Nike Grškovića 31)

Canadian Embassy (☎01-48 81 200; Prilaz Gjure Deželića 4)

Czech Embassy (☎01-61 77 246; Radnička Cesta 47/6)

French Embassy (☎01-48 93 600; Andrije Hebranga 2)

German Embassy (☎01-61 58 100; Ulica Grada Vukovara 64)

Hungarian Embassy (☎01-48 90 900; Pantovčak 257)

Irish Embassy (☎01-63 10 025; Miramarska 23)

Netherlands Embassy (☎01-46 42 200; Medvešćak 56)

New Zealand Embassy (☎01-46 12 060; Vlaška 50a)

Polish Embassy (☎01-48 99 444; Krležin Gvozd 3)

Romanian Embassy (☎01-46 77 550; Mlinarska 43)

Serbian Embassy (☎01-45 79 067; Pantovčak 245)

Slovakian Embassy (☎01-48 77 070; Prilaz Gjure Deželića 10)

Slovenian Embassy (☎01-63 11 000; Savska cesta 41/annex)

UK Embassy (☎01-60 09 100; I Lučića 4)

US Embassy (☎01-66 12 200; Thomas Jefferson 2)

Food

Prices in this chapter are based on a main course.

€ less than 80KN

€€ 80KN to 150KN

€€€ more than 150KN

Gay & Lesbian Travellers

Homosexuality has been legal in Croatia since 1977 and is tolerated, but not welcomed with open arms. Public displays of affection between same-sex couples may be met with hostility, especially beyond the major cities.

Exclusively gay clubs are a rarity outside Zagreb, but many of the large discos attract a mixed crowd. On the coast, gay men gravitate to Rovinj, Hvar, Split and Dubrovnik, and tend to frequent naturist beaches.

In Zagreb, the last Saturday in June is Gay Pride Zagreb day.

Most Croatian websites devoted to the gay scene are in Croatian only, but a good starting point is www.travel.gay.hr.

Money

CREDIT CARDS

Amex, MasterCard, Visa and Diners Club cards are widely accepted in large hotels, stores and many restaurants, but don't count on cards to pay for private accommodation or meals in small restaurants. You'll find ATMs accepting MasterCard, Maestro, Cirrus, Plus and Visa in most bus and train stations, airports, all major cities and most small towns.

CURRENCY

Croatia uses the kuna (KN). Commonly circulated banknotes come in denominations of 500, 200, 100, 50, 20, 10 and five kuna. Each kuna is divided into 100 lipa. You'll find silver-coloured 50- and 20-lipa coins, and bronze-coloured 10-lipa coins.

TAX

Travellers who spend more than 740KN in one shop are entitled to a refund of the value-added tax (VAT), which is equivalent to 22% of the purchase price. In order to claim the refund, the merchant must fill out the Tax Cheque (required form), which you must present to the customs office upon leaving the country. Mail a stamped copy to the shop within six months, which will then credit your credit card with the appropriate sum.

TIPPING

If you're served well at a restaurant, you should round up the bill, but a service charge is always included. Bar bills and taxi fares can also be rounded up. Tour guides on day excursions expect to be tipped.

Public Holidays

New Year's Day 1 January

Epiphany 6 January

Easter Monday March/April

Labour Day 1 May

Corpus Christi 10 June

Day of Antifascist Resistance 22 June; marks the outbreak of resistance in 1941

Statehood Day 25 June

Homeland Thanksgiving Day 5 August

Feast of the Assumption 15 August

Independence Day 8 October

All Saints' Day 1 November

Christmas 25 and 26 December

Telephone

MOBILE PHONES

If you have an unlocked 3G phone, you can buy a SIM card for about 50KN. You can choose from four network providers: **VIP** (www.vip.hr), **T-Mobile** (www.t-mobile.hr), **Tomato** (www.tomato.com.hr) and **Tele2** (www.tele2.hr).

PHONE CODES

To call Croatia from abroad, dial your international access code, then ☎385 (the country code for Croatia), then the area code (without the initial ☎0) and the local number.

To call from region to region within Croatia, start with the area code (with the initial ☎0); drop it when dialling within the same code.

Phone numbers with the prefix ☎060 are either free or charged at a premium rate, so watch the small print. Phone numbers that begin with ☎09 are mobile phone numbers.

PHONECARDS

To make a phone call from Croatia, go to the town's main post office. You'll need a phone card to use public telephones. Phonecards are sold according to *impulsi* (units), and you can buy cards of 25 (15KN), 50 (30KN), 100 (50KN) and 200 (100KN) units. These can be purchased at any post office and most tobacco shops and newspaper kiosks.

Tourist Information

The **Croatian National Tourist Board** (www.croatia.hr) is a good source of info. There are regional tourist offices that supervise tourist development, and municipal tourist offices that have free brochures and information.

Travellers with Disabilities

Due to the number of wounded war veterans, more attention is being paid to the needs of disabled travellers in Croatia. Public toilets at bus stations, train stations, airports and large public venues are usually wheelchair accessible. Large hotels are wheelchair accessible, but very little private accommodation is. Bus and train stations in Zagreb, Zadar, Rijeka, Split and Dubrovnik are wheelchair accessible, but the local Jadrolinija ferries are not. For further information, get in touch with **Hrvatski Savez Udruga Tjelesnih Invalida** (☎01-48 12 004; www.hsuti.hr; Šoštarićeva 8, Zagreb), the Croatian union of associations for physically disabled persons.

Visas

Citizens of the EU, USA, Canada, Australia, New Zealand, Israel, Ireland, Singapore and the UK do not need a visa for stays of up to

90 days. South Africans must apply for a 90-day visa in Pretoria. Contact any Croatian embassy, consulate or travel agency abroad for information.

Getting There & Away

Getting to Croatia is becoming ever easier, especially if you're arriving in summer. Low-cost carriers are finally establishing routes to Croatia, and a plethora of bus and ferry routes shepherd holidaymakers to the coast.

Air

There are direct flights to Croatia from a number of European cities; however, there are no nonstop flights from North America to Croatia.

There are several major airports in Croatia.

Dubrovnik Airport (www.airport-dubrovnik. hr) Nonstop flights from Brussels, Cologne, Frankfurt, Hanover, London (Gatwick and Stansted), Manchester, Munich and Stuttgart.

Pula Airport (www.airport-pula.com) Nonstop flights from London (Gatwick) and Manchester.

Rijeka (www.rijeka-airport.hr) Nonstop flights from Cologne and Stuttgart.

Split Airport (www.split-airport.hr) Nonstop flights from Cologne, Frankfurt, London, Munich, Prague and Rome.

Zadar (www.zadar-airport.hr) Nonstop flights from Bari, Brussels, Dublin, London, Munich and more.

Zagreb Airport (www.zagreb-airport.hr) Direct flights from all European capitals, plus Cologne, Hamburg and Stuttgart.

Land

Croatia has border crossings with Hungary, Slovenia, BiH, Serbia and Montenegro.

Buses run to destinations throughout Europe.

From Austria, **Eurolines** (www.eurolines. com) operates buses from Vienna to several destinations in Croatia.

Bus services between Germany and Croatia are good, and fares are cheaper than the train. All buses are handled by **Deutsche Touring GmbH** (www.deutsche-touring. de); there are no Deutsche Touring offices in Croatia, but numerous travel agencies and bus stations sell its tickets.

Sea

Regular boats from the following companies connect Croatia with Italy:

Blue Line (www.blueline-ferries.com)

Commodore Cruises (www.commodore-cruises.hr)

Emilia Romagna Lines (www.emiliaromagnalines.it)

Jadrolinija (www.jadrolinija.hr)

Split Tours (www.splittours.hr)

SNAV (www.snav.com)

Termoli Jet (www.termolijet.it)

Ustica Lines (www.usticalines.it)

Venezia Lines (www.venezialines.com)

Getting Around

Air

Croatia Airlines (☏01-66 76 555; www.croatiaairlines.hr) Croatia Airlines is the only carrier for flights within Croatia. There are daily flights between Zagreb and Dubrovnik, Pula, Split and Zadar.

Bicycle

Cycling can be a great way to explore the islands. Relatively flat islands such as Pag and Mali Lošinj offer the most relaxed biking, but the winding, hilly roads on other islands offer spectacular views. Bicycles are easy to rent along the coast and on the islands. Some tourist offices, especially in the Kvarner and Istria regions, have maps of routes and can refer you to local bike-rental agencies. Even though it's not fully translated into English yet, www.pedala.hr is a great reference for cycling routes around Croatia.

Boat

JADROLINIJA FERRIES

Jadrolinija (www.jadrolinija.hr) operates an extensive network of car ferries and catamarans along the Adriatic coast. Ferries are a lot more comfortable than buses, though somewhat more expensive.

Services operate year-round, though they are less frequent in winter. Cabins should be booked a week ahead. Deck space is usually available on all sailings. You must buy tickets in advance at an agency or a Jadrolinija office. Tickets are not sold on board. In summer months, you need to check in two hours in advance if you bring a car.

Somewhat mediocre fixed-price menus in onboard restaurants cost about 100KN; the cafeteria only offers ham-and-cheese sandwiches for 30KN. Do as the Croats do: bring some food and drink with you.

LOCAL FERRIES

Local ferries connect the bigger offshore islands with each other and with the mainland, but you'll find many more ferries going from the mainland to the islands than from island to island.

On most lines, service is less frequent between October and April. Extra passenger boats are added in the summer; these are usually faster, more comfortable and more expensive. On some shorter routes, ferries run nonstop in summer and advance reservation is unnecessary.

Buy tickets at a Jadrolinija office or at a stall near the ferry (usually open 30 minutes prior to departure). There are no ticket sales on board. In summer, arrive one to two hours prior to departure, even if you've already bought your ticket.

Cars incur a charge; calculated according to the size of car and often very pricey. Reserve as far in advance as possible. Check in several hours in advance. Bicycles incur a small charge.

There is no meal service; you can buy drinks and snacks on board. Most locals bring their own food.

Bus

Bus services are excellent and relatively inexpensive. There are often a number of different companies handling each route so prices can vary substantially. Luggage stowed in the baggage compartment under the bus costs extra (7KN a piece, including insurance).

BUS COMPANIES

The companies listed here are among the largest.

Autotrans (☑060 30 20 10; www.autotrans. hr) Based in Rijeka. Connections to Istria, Zagreb, Varaždin and Kvarner.

Brioni Pula (☑052-535 155; www.brioni. hr) Based in Pula. Connections to Istria, Padua, Split, Trieste and Zagreb.

Contus (☑023-317 062) Based in Zadar. Connections to Split and Zagreb.

Croatiabus (☑01-61 13 073; www.croatiabus.hr) Connecting Zagreb with towns in Zagorje and Istria.

Samoborček (☑01-48 19 180; www. samoborcek.hr) Connecting Zagreb with towns in Dalmatia.

TICKETS & SCHEDULES

At large stations, bus tickets must be purchased at the office, not from drivers. Try to book ahead to be sure of a seat, especially in the summer.

Departure lists above the various windows at bus stations tell you which window sells tickets for your bus. On Croatian bus schedules, *vozi svaki dan* means 'every day' and *ne vozi nedjeljom i blagdanom* means 'no service Sunday and holidays'.

Some buses travel overnight, saving you a night's accommodation. Don't expect to get much sleep, though, as the inside lights will be on and music will be blasting the whole night. Take care not to be left behind at meal or rest stops, which usually occur about every two hours.

Car & Motorcycle

Croatia's motorway connecting Zagreb with Split is only a few years old and makes some routes much faster. Zagreb and Rijeka are now connected by motorway, and an Istrian motorway has shortened the travel time to Italy considerably.

Although the new roads are in excellent condition, there are stretches where service stations and facilities are few and far between. You can reach roadside assistance on ☑1987.

CAR HIRE

In order to rent a car you must be 21 or over, with a valid driving licence and a valid credit card.

Independent local companies are often much cheaper than the international chains, but the big companies offer one-way rentals. Sometimes you can get a lower car-rental rate by booking the car from abroad, or by booking a fly-drive package.

CAR INSURANCE

Third-party public liability insurance is included by law with car rentals, but make sure your quoted price includes full collision insurance, known as a collision damage waiver (CDW). Otherwise, your responsibility for damage done to the vehicle is usually determined as a percentage of the car's value, beginning at around 2000KN.

If you rent a car in Italy, many insurance companies will not insure you for a trip into Croatia. Border officials know this and may refuse you entry unless permission to drive into Croatia is clearly marked on the insurance documents.

Most car-rental companies in Trieste and Venice are familiar with this requirement and will furnish you with the correct stamp. Otherwise, you must make specific inquiries.

DRIVING LICENCE

Any valid driving licence is sufficient to drive legally and rent a car; an international driving licence is not necessary.

The **Hrvatski Autoklub** (HAK, Croatian Auto Club; ☏46 40 800; www.hak.hr; Avenija Dubrovnik 44) offers help and advice. For help on the road, you can contact the nationwide **HAK road assistance** (Vučna Služba; ☏987).

ON THE ROAD

Petrol stations are generally open from 7am to 7pm and often until 10pm in summer. Petrol is Eurosuper 95, Super 98, normal or diesel. See www.ina.hr for up-to-date fuel prices.

You have to pay tolls on all motorways, to use the Učka tunnel between Rijeka and Istria, to use the bridge to Krk Island, and on the road from Rijeka to Delnice.

For general news on Croatia's motorways and tolls, see www.hak.hr. The radio station HR2 broadcasts traffic reports in English every hour on the hour from July to early September.

ROAD RULES

In Croatia you drive on the right, and the use of seatbelts is mandatory. Unless otherwise posted, the speed limits for cars and motorcycles are 50km/h in built-up areas, 100km/h on main highways and 130km/h on motorways.

On two-lane highways, it's illegal to pass long military convoys or a line of cars caught behind a slow-moving truck.

It's illegal to drive with a blood alcohol content higher than 0.5%.

You are required to drive with your headlights on even during the day.

Local Transport

The main form of local transport is bus (although Zagreb and Osijek also have well-developed tram systems).

Buses in major cities such as Dubrovnik, Rijeka, Split and Zadar run about once every 20 minutes, less on Sunday. A ride is usually around 10KN, with a small discount if you buy tickets at a *tisak* (news stand).

Small medieval towns along the coast are generally closed to traffic and have infrequent links to outlying suburbs.

Bus transport within the islands is infrequent since most people have their own cars.

Train

Trains are less frequent than buses but more comfortable. For information about schedules, prices and services, contact **Croatian Railways** (Hrvatske Željeznice; ☏060 333 444; www.hznet.hr).

Zagreb is the hub for Croatia's less-than-extensive train system. No trains run along the coast and only a few coastal cities are connected with Zagreb. For travellers, the main lines of interest are the following:

Zagreb–Rijeka–Pula Via Lupoglava, where passengers switch to a bus.

Zagreb–Osijek

Zagreb–Split

Domestic trains are either 'express' or 'passenger' (local). Express trains have 1st- and 2nd-class cars, plus smoking and nonsmoking areas. A reservation is advisable for express trains.

Express trains are more expensive than passenger trains; any prices quoted in this chapter are for unreserved 2nd-class seating.

There are no couchettes on domestic services. There are sleeping cars on overnight trains between Zagreb and Split.

Baggage is free on trains; most stations have left-luggage services charging around 15KN a piece per day.

EU residents who hold an InterRail pass can use it in Croatia for free travel, but you're unlikely to take enough trains to justify the cost.

France

Includes »

Paris	185
Lille, Flanders & the Somme	219
Normandy	224
Brittany	229
Champagne	234
Alsace & Lorraine	237
The Loire Valley	243
Burgundy & the Rhône Valley	248
The French Alps	258
The Atlantic Coast	268
Bordeaux	271
Provence	280
The French Riviera & Monaco	291
Corsica	303

Best Places to Eat

» Beef Club (p204)
» Frenchie (p204)
» Septime (p205)
» La Table de Ventabren (p286)
» Les Vieilles Luges (p261)

Best Places to Stay

» Hôtel Amour (p204)
» Hôtel Crayon (p201)
» L'Épicerie (p286)
» Hôtel 7e Art (p297)
» Nice Pebbles (p294)

Why Go?

Few countries provoke such passion as La Belle France. Love it or loathe it, everyone has their own opinion about this Gallic Goliath. Snooty, sexy, superior, chic, infuriating, arrogant, officious and inspired in equal measures, the French have long lived according to their own idiosyncratic rules, and if the rest of the world doesn't always see eye-to-eye with them, well, *tant pis* (too bad) – it's the price you pay for being a culinary trendsetter, artistic pioneer and cultural icon.

If ever there was a country of contradictions, this is it. France is a deeply traditional place: castles, chateaux and ancient churches litter the landscape, while centuries-old principles of rich food, fine wine and joie de vivre underpin everyday life. Yet it is also a country that has one of Western Europe's most multicultural make-ups, not to mention a well-deserved reputation for artistic experimentation and architectural invention. Enjoy!

When to Go
Paris

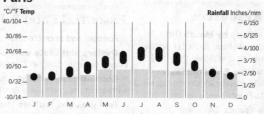

Dec–Mar Hit the French Alps, Jura or Pyrenees for some serious ski action. Eat truffles.

Apr–Jun France at its springtime best, *sans* crowds; June's Fête de la Musique gets you jigging.

Sep Cooling temperatures, abundant produce and the grape harvest; perfect for cycling through Provence.

FRANCE

AT A GLANCE

» **Currency** euro (€)

» **Language** French

» **Money** ATMs everywhere

» **Visas** Schengen rules apply

Fast Facts

» **Area** 551,000 sq km

» **Capital** Paris

» **Country code** 📞33

» **Emergency** 📞112

Exchange Rates

Australia	A$1	€0.82
Canada	C$1	€0.77
Japan	¥100	€0.83
New Zealand	NZ$1	€0.65
UK	UK£1	€1.18
USA	US$1	€0.78

Set Your Budget

» **Budget hotel room** €60–80

» **Two-course meal** €15–50

» **Museum entrance** €4–10

» **Glass of wine** €2–5

» **Paris metro ticket** €1.70

Resources

» **Paris by Mouth** (http://parisbymouth.com) Capital dining and drinking.

» **Wine Travel Guides** (www.winetravelguides.com) Guides to France's wine regions.

» **France 24** (www.france24.com/en/france) French news in English.

» **Lost in Cheeseland** (www.lostincheeseland.com) French life seen through the eyes of an American expat.

Connections

High-speed TGV trains link Paris' Gare du Nord with London's St Pancras (via the Channel Tunnel/Eurostar rail service) in just over two hours; Gare du Nord is also the point of departure for speedy trains to Brussels, Amsterdam and Cologne; and Gare de l'Est for Frankfurt. TGV Lyria trains whisk travellers from Paris' Gare de Lyon to Zurich in four hours. Many more trains make travelling between the French capital and pretty much any city in every neighbouring country a real pleasure. Ferry links from Cherbourg, St-Malo, Calais and other north-coast ports travel to England and Ireland; ferries from Marseille and Nice provide regular links with seaside towns in Corsica, Italy and North Africa.

Regular bus and rail links cross the French–Spanish border via the Pyrenees, and the French–Italian border via the Alps and the southern Mediterranean coast.

ITINERARIES

One Week

Start with a few days exploring Paris, taking in the Louvre, Eiffel Tower, Musée d'Orsay, Notre Dame, Montmartre and a boat trip along the Seine. Then head out to Normandy, Monet's garden at Giverny, and Versailles; or throw yourself into the Renaissance high life at chateaux in the Loire Valley.

Two Weeks

With Paris and surrounds having taken up much of the first week, concentrate on exploring one or two regions rather than trying to do too much in a whistlestop dash. High-speed TGV trains zip from Paris to every province: for prehistoric and gastronomic interest, head to the Dordogne; for architectural splendour, you can't top the Loire Valley; for typical French atmosphere, try the hill-top villages of Provence; and for sunshine and seafood, head to the French Riviera on the sparkling Med.

Essential Food & Drink

» **Fondue and raclette** Warming cheese dishes in the Alps.

» **Oysters and white wine** Everywhere on the Atlantic coast, but especially in Cancale and Bordeaux.

» **Bouillabaisse** Marseille's signature hearty fish stew, eaten with croutons and *rouille* (garlic-and-chilli mayonnaise).

» **Foie gras and truffles** The Dordogne features goose and 'black diamonds' from December to March. Provence is also good for indulging in the aphrodisiac-like fungi.

» **Piggy-part cuisine** Lyon is famous for its juicy *andouillette* (pig-intestine sausage); try it with a local Côtes du Rhône red.

» **Champagne** Tasting in century-old cellars is an essential part of Champagne's bubbly experience.

PARIS

POP 2.2 MILLION

What can be said about the sexy, sophisticated City of Lights that hasn't already been said a thousand times before? Quite simply, this is one of the world's great metropolises – a trendsetter, market leader and cultural capital for over a thousand years and still going strong. This is the place that gave the world the can-can and the cinematograph, a city that reinvented itself during the Renaissance, bopped to the beat of the jazz age, and positively glittered during the belle époque (literally, 'beautiful era').

As you might expect, Paris is strewn with historic architecture, glorious galleries and cultural treasures galore. But the modern-day city is much more than just a museum piece: it's a heady hodgepodge of cultures and ideas – a place to stroll the boulevards, shop till you drop, flop riverside, or simply do as the Parisians do and watch the world buzz by from a streetside cafe. Savour every moment.

History

The Parisii, a tribe of Celtic Gauls, settled the Île de la Cité in the 3rd century BC. Paris prospered during the Middle Ages and flourished during the Renaissance, when many of the city's most famous buildings were erected.

The excesses of Louis XVI and his queen, Marie Antoinette, led to an uprising of Parisians on 14 July 1789, and the storming of the Bastille prison – kick-starting the French Revolution.

In 1851 Emperor Napoléon III oversaw the construction of a more modern Paris, complete with wide boulevards, sculptured parks and a sewer system. Following the disastrous Franco-Prussian War and the establishment of the Third Republic, Paris entered its most resplendent period, the belle époque, famed for its art nouveau architecture and artistic and scientific advances. By the beginning of the 1930s, Paris had become a centre for the artistic avant-garde, and it remained so until the Nazi occupation of 1940–44.

After WWII, Paris regained its position as a creative centre and nurtured a revitalised liberalism that climaxed in student-led uprisings in 1968.

During the 1980s President François Mitterrand initiated several *grands projets,* building projects that garnered widespread approval even when the results were popular failures. In 2001 Bertrand Delanoë, a socialist with support from the Green Party, became Paris' – and a European capital's – first openly gay mayor. He returned to power for another term in the 2008 elections.

◉ Sights

LEFT BANK

Eiffel Tower   LANDMARK

(Map p188; ☎01 44 11 23 23; www.tour-eiffel.fr; lift to 3rd fl adult/12-24yr/4-12yr €14/12.50/9.50, lift to 2nd fl €8.50/7/4, stairs to 2nd fl €5/3.50/3; ⊙lifts & stairs 9am-midnight mid-Jun–Aug, lifts 9.30am-11pm, stairs 9.30am-6pm Sep–mid-Jun; Ⓜ Bir Hakeim or RER Champ de Mars-Tour Eiffel) Named after its designer, Gustave Eiffel, this Paris icon was built for the 1889 Exposition Universelle (World Fair), marking the centenary of the French Revolution. At the time it faced massive opposition

---

PARIS IN...

Two Days

Join a morning tour then focus on those Parisian icons: **Notre Dame**, the **Eiffel Tower** and the **Arc de Triomphe**. Late afternoon have a coffee or glass of wine on the **av des Champs-Élysées**, then mooch to Montmartre for dinner. On the second day enjoy the **Musée d'Orsay**, **Ste-Chapelle** and the **Musée Rodin**. Dine and revel in a night of mirth and gaiety in the dine-well, nightlife-buzzy Marais.

Four Days

With another two days, consider a cruise along the **Seine** or **Canal St-Martin** bookended by visits to the **Cimetière du Père Lachaise** and **Parc de la Villette**. By night take in a concert, opera or ballet at the **Palais Garnier** or **Opéra Bastille**, followed by a bar-club crawl along Ménilmontant's rue Oberkampf or through the Bastille area.

One Week

Seven days allows you to see a good many of the major sights and day-trip it out of Paris proper to surrounding areas such as **Versailles**.

France Highlights

1 Gorge on the iconic sights and sophistication of Europe's most hopelessly romantic city, **Paris** (p185)

2 Relive the French Renaissance with extraordinary chateaux built by kings and queens in the **Loire Valley** (p243)

3 Do a Bond and swoosh down slopes in the shadow of Mont Blanc in **Chamonix** (p258)

4 Dodge tides, stroll moonlit sand and immerse yourself in legend at island abbey **Mont St-Michel** (p229)

5 Savour ancient ruins, modern art, markets, lavender and hilltop villages in slow-paced **Provence** (p280)

6 Taste bubbly in ancient *caves* (cellars) in **Reims** (p234) and **Épernay** (p236), the heart of Champagne

7 Tuck into **Lyon's** piggy-driven cuisine in a traditional *bouchon* (p256)

8 Soak up the mystery of the world's best megaliths from the back of a Breton bicycle around **Carnac** (p229)

Greater Paris

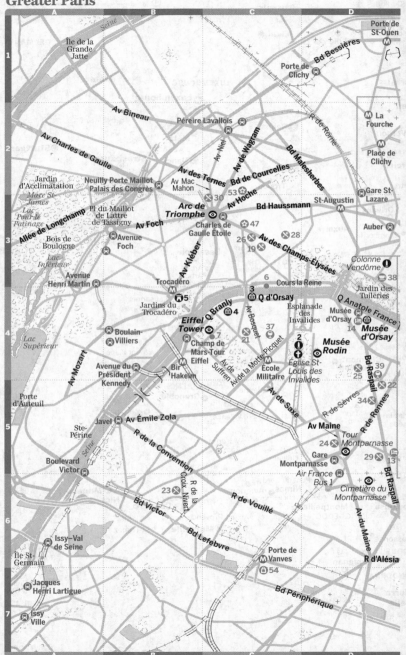

FRANCE PARIS

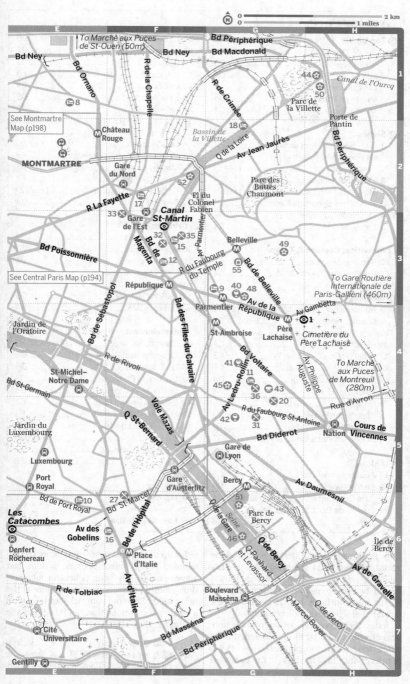

Greater Paris

◉ **Top Sights**
Arc de Triomphe....................................C3
Canal St-Martin F3
Eiffel Tower C4
Les Catacombes....................................E6
Musée d'Orsay D4
Musée Rodin D4

◉ **Sights**
1 Cimetière du Père Lachaise.................H4
Cité de l'Architecture et du
Patrimoine....................................(see 5)
2 Hôtel des Invalides C4
Musée de l'Armée ....(see 2)
3 Musée des Égouts de Paris..................C4
4 Musée du Quai Branly C4
5 Palais de Chaillot B4

➕ **Activities, Courses & Tours**
6 Bateaux-Mouches C3
7 Fat Tire Bike Tours C4

🛏 **Sleeping**
8 Au Sourire de Montmartre.....................E1
9 Cosmos Hôtel G3
10 Five Hotel E6
11 Hi Matic G4
12 Hôtel du Nord – Le Pari Vélo F3
13 L'Apostrophe D5
14 Le Bellechasse D4
15 Le Citizen Hotel....................................F3
16 Oops F6
République Hôtel ....(see 12)
17 St Christopher's Inn F2
18 St Christopher's Inn G2

🍽 **Eating**
19 Aubrac Corner C3
20 Bistrot Paul Bert G5
21 Café Constant.....................................C4
22 Cuisine de Bar D5
23 Jadis..B6

24 La Cabane à Huîtres............................D5
25 La Pâtisserie des Rêves D4
26 Ladurée C3
27 L'Agrume F6
28 Le Boudoir C3
29 Le Dôme..D5
30 Le Hide C3
31 Le Siffleur de Ballons G5
32 Le Verre Volé F3
Les Cocottes.................................(see 21)
33 Marché Couvert St-Quentin F3
34 Marché Raspail....................................D5
35 Pink Flamingo F3
Poilâne ....(see 22)
36 Septime...G4

🍷 **Drinking**
37 Alain Milliart C4
38 Angelina D3
39 Au Sauvignon D4
40 Café Charbon G3
41 La Fée Verte..G4
42 Le Baron Rouge G5
43 Le Pure Café G4

🎭 **Entertainment**
44 Cabaret Sauvage.................................H1
45 La Scène Bastille G4
46 Le Batofar G6
47 Le Lido de Paris C3
48 Le Nouveau Casino G3
49 Le Vieux Belleville...............................G3
50 Le Zénith H1
51 Palais Omnisports de Paris-
Bercy G6
52 Point Éphémère F2
53 Salle Pleyel...C2

🛍 **Shopping**
54 Marché aux Puces de la Porte
de Vanves C7
55 Marché Belleville G3

from Paris' artistic and literary elite, and the 'metal asparagus', as some Parisians snidely called it, was almost torn down in 1909 – spared because it proved an ideal platform for the transmitting antennas needed for the newfangled science of radiotelegraphy.

Today, the three levels are open to the public (entrance to the 1st level is included in all admission tickets), though the top level closes in heavy wind. Take the lifts (in the east, west and north pillars) or the stairs in the south pillar up to the 2nd platform. Highly recommended is the online booking system that allows you to buy your tickets in advance, thus avoiding the monumental queues at the ticket office. Print out your ticket or have it on a smart-phone screen that can be read by the scanner at the entrance.

Musée du Quai Branly   MUSEUM
(Map p188; www.quaibranly.fr; 37 quai Branly, 7e; adult/child €8.50/free; ⊙11am-7pm Tue, Wed & Sun,

11am-9pm Thu-Sat; MAlma-Marceau or RER Pont de l'Alma) No other museum in Paris provides such inspiration to those who appreciate the beauty of traditional craftsmanship. A tribute to the incredible diversity of human culture, it presents an overview of indigenous and folk art from around the world. Divided into four main sections, the museum showcases an impressive array of masks, carvings, weapons, jewellery and more, all displayed in a refreshingly unique interior without rooms or high walls. Don't miss the views from the 5th-floor restaurant Les Ombres.

Musée d'Orsay   MUSEUM
(Map p188; www.musee-orsay.fr; 62 rue de Lille, 7e; adult/18-25yr/under 18yr €9/6.50/free; ⊙9.30am-6pm Tue, Wed & Fri-Sun, to 9.45pm Thu; MAssemblée Nationale or RER Musée d'Orsay) The home of France's national collection from the impressionist, postimpressionist and art nouveau movements spanning from the 1840s and 1914 is the glorious former Gare d'Orsay railway station – itself an art nouveau showpiece. Highlights include Manet's *On The Beach* and *Woman With Fans*; Monet's gardens at Giverny; Cézanne's card players and still lifes; Renoir's *Ball at the Moulin de la Galette* and *Girls at the Piano*; Degas' ballerinas; Toulouse-Lautrec's cabaret dancers; and Van Gogh's self-portraits, *Bedroom in Arles* and *Starry Night*. There are also some magnificent decorative arts, graphic arts and sculptures.

Save time by prepurchasing tickets online or at Kiosque du Musée d'Orsay (⊙9am-5pm Tue-Fri school holidays, Tue only rest of year), in front of the museum, and head to entrance C. Admission drops to €6.50 after 4.30pm (after 6pm on Thursday).

Jardin du Luxembourg   PARK
(Map p194; numerous entrances; ⊙hrs vary; MSt-Sulpice, Rennes or Notre Dame des Champs, or RER Luxembourg) The voyeur's spot to peek on Parisians, this 23-hectare park is where Parisians of all ages flock to jog, practise t'ai chi, gossip with friends, read, romance, play tennis, stroll through terraced gardens and orchards heavy with apples, or chase 1920s sailboats around the octagonal Grand Bassin.

Palais du Luxembourg, at the northen end of the garden, was built in the 1620s for Marie de Médici, Henri IV's consort, to assuage her longing for the Pitti Palace in Florence, where she had spent her childhood. Since 1958 the palace has housed the Sénat (Senate; Map p194; ☎01 44 54 19 49; www.senat.fr; rue de Vaugirard; adult/18-25yr €8/6), occasion-

WANT MORE?

For in-depth information, reviews and recommendations at your fingertips, head to the Apple App Store to purchase Lonely Planet's *Paris City Guide* iPhone app.

Alternatively, head to **Lonely Planet** (www.lonelyplanet.com/france/paris) for planning advice, author recommendations, traveller reviews and insider tips.

ally visitable by guided tour. Top spot for sun-soaking – there are always loads of the garden's signature sage-green chairs here – is the southern side of the palace's 19th-century Orangery, where lemon and orange trees, palms, grenadiers and oleanders shelter from the cold.

Musée Rodin   GARDEN, MUSEUM
(Map p188; www.musee-rodin.fr; 79 rue de Varenne, 7e; adult/under 25yr permanent exhibition €7/5, garden €1/free; ⊙10am-5.45pm Tue-Sun; MVarenne) One of the most relaxing spots in the city, with a garden bespeckled with sculptures, this lovely art museum inside 18th-century Hôtel Biron displays vital bronze and marble sculptures by sculptor, painter, sketcher, engraver and collector Auguste Rodin. Highlights include that perennial crowd-pleaser *The Thinker*, and the sublime, the incomparable, that romance-hewn-in-marble called *The Kiss*. Buy tickets online to avoid queuing.

Les Catacombes   CEMETERY
(Map p188; www.catacombes.paris.fr; 1 av Colonel Henri Roi-Tanguy, 14e; adult/13-26yr/under 13yr €8/4/free; ⊙10am-5pm Tue-Sun; MDenfert Rochereau) Paris' most gruesome and macabre sight is this series of underground tunnels lined with skulls and bones exhumed from the city's overflowing cemeteries.

Created in 1810, the Catacombes takes visitors along 2km of subterranean passages with a mind-boggling amount of bones and skulls of millions of Parisians neatly packed along each and every wall. During WWII these tunnels were used as a headquarters by the Resistance; thrill-seeking *cataphiles* are often caught (and fined) roaming the tunnels at night.

Renting an audioguide greatly enhances the impossibly spooky experience.

FRANCE PARIS

MUSEUM TIPS

» If you're visiting more than two or three museums and monuments, buy a **Paris Museum Pass** (www.parismuseumpass.fr; 2/4/6 days €39/54/69), valid for entry to some 38 venues including the Louvre, Centre Pompidou, Musée d'Orsay, Musée Rodin and Château de Versailles. Pass-holders also get to bypass *looong* ticket queues at major attractions. Buy it online, at participating museums, tourist desks at airports, Fnac outlets and major metro stations.

» Most Paris museums are closed on Mondays, but some, including the Louvre and Centre Pompidou, are closed on Tuesdays instead.

» Paris' national museums are something of a bargain: admission is reduced for those aged over 60 years, and between 18 and 25; and completely free for EU residents under 26 years of age, anyone under 18 years, and everyone on the first Sunday of each month. These include: the Louvre, Musée National d'Art Moderne in the Pompidou, Musée du Quai Branly, Musée d'Orsay, Musée Rodin and Cité de l'Architecture et du Patrimoine.

» The following are free the first Sunday of the month from November to March: Arc de Triomphe, Conciergerie, Panthéon, Ste-Chapelle and the Tours de Notre Dame.

Musée des Égouts de Paris MUSEUM
(Map p188; place de la Résistance, 7e; adult/child €4.20/3.40; ⊙11am-5pm Sat-Wed May-Sep, 11am-4pm Sat-Wed Oct-Dec & Feb-Apr; MAlma Marceau or RER Pont de l'Alma) Raw sewage flows beneath your feet as you walk through 480m of odoriferous tunnels in this working sewer museum. Exhibitions cover the development of Paris' waste-water disposal system. Enter via a rectangular maintenance hole topped with a kiosk across the street from 93 quai d'Orsay, 7e.

Panthéon MAUSOLEUM
(Map p194; www.monum.fr; place du Panthéon; adult/under 18yr €8.50/free; ⊙10am-6.30pm Apr-Sep, to 6pm Oct-Mar; MMaubert-Mutualité, Cardinal Lemoine or RER Luxembourg) A superb example of 18th-century neoclassicism, this domed landmark was commissioned by Louis XV around 1750 as an abbey but due to financial and structural problems it wasn't completed until 1789. Two years later, the Constituent Assembly turned it into a secular mausoleum – now the eternal home of some of France's greatest thinkers including Voltaire, Jean-Jacques Rousseau, Louis Braille, Émile Zola and Jean Moulin. The first woman to be interred in the Panthéon was the two-time Nobel Prize–winner Marie Curie (1867-1934).

Hôtel des Invalides MONUMENT, MUSEUM
(Map p188; www.invalides.org; 129 rue de Grenelle, 7e; adult/child €9/free; ⊙10am-6pm Mon & Wed-Sun, 10am-9pm Tue, to 5pm Oct-Mar, closed 1st Mon of month; MInvalides) Hôtel des Invalides was built in the 1670s by Louis XIV to provide housing for 4000 *invalides* (disabled war

veterans). On 14 July 1789, a mob forced its way into the building and, after fierce fighting, seized 32,000 rifles before heading on to the prison at Bastille and the start of the French Revolution.

North of the main courtyard is the **Musée de l'Armée** (Army Museum; Map p188; www.invalides.org; 129 rue de Grenelle, 7e; ⊙10am-6pm Mon & Wed-Sat, to 9pm Tue), home to the nation's largest collection on French military history.

South are the **Église St-Louis des Invalides** and **Église du Dôme**, the latter of which contains the tomb of Napoléon I, comprising six coffins fitting into one another like a Russian *matryoshka* doll.

Palais de Chaillot PALACE
(Map p188; 17 place du Trocadéro et du 11 Novembre, 16e; MTrocadéro) The two curved, colonnaded wings of this palace and the terrace in between them afford an exceptional panorama of the **Jardins du Trocadéro**, the Seine and the Eiffel Tower. The palace's eastern wing houses the standout **Cité de l'Architecture et du Patrimoine** (Map p188; www.cite chaillot.fr; 1 place du Trocadéro et du 11 Novembre, 16e; adult/18-25yr/under 18yr €8/5/free; ⊙11am-7pm Wed-Mon, to 9pm Thu; MTrocadéro), devoted to French architecture and heritage.

Jardin des Plantes BOTANIC GARDEN
(Map p194; www.jardindesplantes.net; 57 rue Cuvier, 5e; adult/child €6/4; ⊙7.30am-7.45pm Apr–mid-Oct, 8.30am-5.30pm mid-Oct–Mar; MGare d'Austerlitz, Censier Daubenton or Jussieu) Paris' 24-hectare botanical gardens were created in 1626 as a medicinal herb garden for Louis XIII. On

its southern fringe is the Musée National d'Histoire Naturelle, France's natural-history museum.

Église St-Germain des Prés   CHURCH

(Map p194; www.eglise-sgp.org; 3 place St-Germain des Prés, 6e; ⊘8am-7pm Mon-Sat, 9am-8pm Sun; MSt-Germain des Prés) Paris' oldest standing church, the Romanesque St Germanus of the Fields, was built in the 11th century on the site of a 6th-century abbey and was the dominant place of worship in Paris until the arrival of Notre Dame.

Église St-Sulpice   CHURCH

(Map p194; www.paroisse-saint-sulpice-paris.org; place St-Sulpice, 6e; ⊘7.30am-7.30pm; MSt-Sulpice) Lined inside with 21 side chapels, this striking twin-towered church took six architects 150 years to build. What draws most people is not its Italianate facade with two rows of superimposed columns, its Counter-Reformation-influenced neoclassical decor or even the frescoes by Delacroix, but its setting for a murderous scene in Dan Brown's *Da Vinci Code*.

THE ISLANDS

Paris' twin set of islands could not be more different. Île de la Cité is bigger, full of sights and very touristy (few people live here). The site of the first settlement in Paris, around the 3rd century BC, and later the Roman town of Lutèce (Lutetia), Île de la Cité remained the centre of royal and ecclesiastical power throughout the Middle Ages. The seven decorated arches of Paris' oldest bridge, Pont Neuf, have linked Île de la Cité with both banks of the River Seine since 1607.

Smaller Île St-Louis is residential and quieter, with just enough boutiques and restaurants – and a legendary ice-cream maker – to attract visitors. The area around Pont St-Louis, the bridge across to the Île de la Cité, and Pont Louis Philippe, the bridge to the Marais, is one of the most romantic spots in Paris.

Cathédrale de
Notre Dame de Paris   CATHEDRAL

(Map p194; www.cathedraledeparis.com; 6 place du Parvis Notre Dame, 4e; admission free; ⊘7.45am-7pm; MCité) This is the heart of Paris: distances from Paris to every part of metropolitan France are measured from place du Parvis Notre Dame, the square in front of this French Gothic masterpiece. The most visited unticketed site in Paris, with upwards of 14 million visitors a year, No-

tre Dame is famed for its three spectacular rose windows and forest of ornate flying buttresses, best viewed from square Jean XXIII, the little park behind the cathedral. Built on a site occupied by earlier churches, it was begun in 1163 according to the design of Bishop Maurice de Sully, and largely completed by the early 14th century. Eugène Emmanuel Viollet-le-Duc carried out extensive renovations between 1845 and 1864.

The entrance to its famous towers, the Tours de Notre Dame (Notre Dame Towers; rue du Cloître Notre Dame, 4e; adult/18-25yr/under 18yr €8.50/5.50/free; ⊘10am-6.30pm daily Apr-Jun & Sep, 10am-6.30pm Mon-Fri, 10am-11pm Sat & Sun Jul & Aug, 10.30am-5.30pm daily Oct-Mar), is from the North Tower. Climb 422 spiralling steps and find yourself face-to-face with the cathedral's most frightening gargoyles, the 13-tonne bell Emmanuel (all of the cathedral's bells are named) and, last but not least, a spectacular view of Paris.

Ste-Chapelle   CHAPEL

(Map p194; 4 bd du Palais, 1er; adult/under 18yr €8.50/free; ⊘9.30am-5pm Nov-Feb, to 6pm Mar-Oct; MCité) Built in just under three years (compared with nearly 200 for Notre Dame), this gemlike Holy Chapel – the most exquisite of Paris' Gothic monuments – was consecrated in 1248 within the walls of the city's Palais de Justice (Law Courts). It was conceived by Louis IX to house his personal collection of holy relics (including the Holy Crown now kept in the treasury at Notre Dame), but is better known today for its dazzling, finely detailed stained glass.

A combined adult ticket with the Conciergerie costs €12.50.

Conciergerie   MONUMENT

(Map p194; www.monuments-nationaux.fr; 2 bd du Palais, Île de la Cité, 1er; adult/under 18yr €8.50/free, 1st Sun of month Nov-Mar free; ⊘9.30am-6pm; MCité) Built as a royal palace in the 14th century, this was the main prison during the Reign of Terror (1793–94), used to incarcerate alleged enemies of the Revolution before they were brought before the Revolutionary Tribunal, next door in the Palais de Justice. Queen Marie Antoinette was among the almost 2800 prisoners held here before being sent in tumbrels to the guillotine. The 14th-century Salle des Gens d'Armes (Cavalrymen's Hall), a fine example of Rayonnant Gothic style, is Europe's largest surviving medieval hall.

A joint ticket with Ste-Chapelle costs €12.50.

Central Paris

FRANCE PARIS

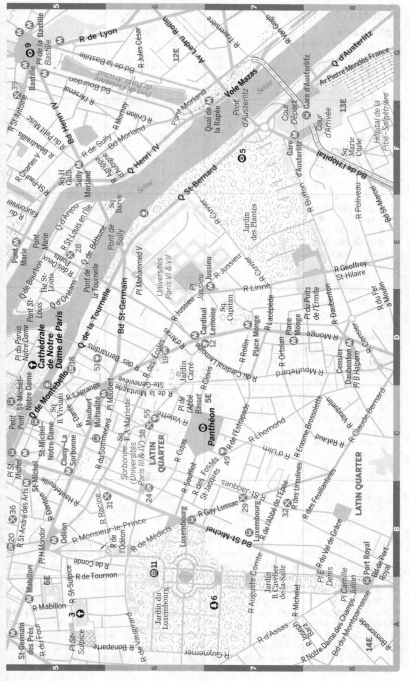

Central Paris

◉ Top Sights

Cathédrale de Notre Dame de
  Paris...D5
Centre Pompidou.................................D3
Musée du Louvre.................................B3
Musée Picasso......................................F3
Panthéon..C6
Ste-Chapelle...C4

◎ Sights

1 Conciergerie.......................................C4
2 Église St-Germain des Prés................A4
3 Église St-Sulpice................................A5
4 Forum des Halles................................C2
5 Jardin des Plantes.............................F7
6 Jardin du Luxembourg.......................A7
7 Maison de Victor Hugo......................F4
8 Musée Carnavalet..............................F4
9 Place de la Bastille............................G5
10 Place des Vosges..............................F4
11 Sénat...B6

✛ Activities, Courses & Tours

12 Gepetto et Vélos................................D7
13 Paris à Vélo, C'est Sympa!..................G3

🛏 Sleeping

14 BVJ Paris-Louvre..............................B2
15 Hôtel Crayon......................................B2
16 Hôtel du Petit Moulin........................F3
17 Hôtel Jeanne d'Arc............................F4
18 Hôtel les Degrés de Notre Dame..........D5
19 Hôtel Minerve....................................D6
20 Hôtel St-André des Arts....................B5
21 Hôtel Tiquetonne...............................D2
22 Le Pavillon de la Reine.....................F4
23 Maison Internationale de la
   Jeunesse et des Étudiants................E4
24 Select Hôtel.......................................B6

✗ Eating

25 Au Passage..G2

26 Au Pied de Fouet...............................A4
27 Beef Club...C2
28 Berthillon...E5
29 Bistrot Les Papilles...........................B7
30 Blend..C1
31 Bouillon Racine.................................B6
32 Boulangerie Bruno Solques................B7
33 Chez Marianne...................................E4
34 Cosi..A4
35 Frenchie...C1
36 KGB..B5
37 Kunitoraya...A1
38 Le Coupe-Chou..................................C6
39 Le Nôtre...G5
40 Marché aux Enfants Rouges.............F2
41 Nanashi...F2
42 Pink Flamingo...................................F3
43 Saveurs Végét'Halles........................C3
44 Spring..B3
45 Spring Épicerie.................................B3
46 Verjus...B1
47 Yam'Tcha...B2

☕ Drinking

48 3w Kafé..E4
49 Café de la Nouvelle Mairie...................C7
50 Café La Palette..................................A4
51 Curio Parlor Cocktail Club...................D5
52 Experimental Cocktail Club................C1
53 Kong...C3
54 Le Barav...F2
55 Le Pub St-Hilaire...............................C6
56 Le Tango..E2
57 Les Deux Magots...............................A4
58 Open Café..E3
59 Scream Club......................................G1

✪ Entertainment

60 Le Baiser Salé....................................C3

🛍 Shopping

61 Marché Bastille..................................G4

RIGHT BANK

Musée du Louvre   MUSEUM
(Map p194; ☎01 40 20 53 17; www.louvre.fr; rue de
Rivoli & quai des Tuileries, 1er; permanent/temporary
collection €11/12, both €15, under 18yr free; ⊙9am-
6pm Mon, Thu, Sat & Sun, to 9.45pm Wed & Fri;
Ⓜ Palais Royal–Musée du Louvre) The vast Palais
du Louvre was constructed as a fortress by
Philippe Auguste in the early 13th century
and rebuilt in the mid-16th century as a royal residence. The Revolutionary Convention
turned it into a national museum in 1793. Its
raison d'être: to present Western art from the
Middle Ages to about 1848 (at which point
the Musée d'Orsay takes over), as well as
works from ancient civilisations that formed
the starting point for Western art. Late 2012
saw the opening of the new Islamic art galleries in the restored **Cour Visconti**, topped
with an elegant, shimmering gold 'flying
carpet' roof designed by Italian architects
Mario Bellini and Rudy Ricciotti.

With some 35,000 paintings and objets d'art on display today, the sheer size and richness of the Louvre can be overwhelming; the south side facing the Seine is 700m long and it's said it would take nine months just to glance at every work. For many, the star attraction is Leonardo da Vinci's *La Joconde*, better known as the Mona Lisa (Room 6, 1st floor, Denon Wing). The most famous works from antiquity include the *Seated Scribe* (Room 22, 1st floor, Sully Wing), the *Code of Hammurabi* (Room 3, ground floor, Richelieu Wing), and that armless duo, the *Venus de Milo* (Room 16, ground floor, Sully Wing) and the *Winged Victory of Samothrace* (top of Daru staircase, 1st floor, Denon Wing). From the Renaissance, don't miss Michelangelo's *The Dying Slave* (Room 4, ground floor, Denon Wing) and works by Raphael, Botticelli and Titian (1st floor, Denon Wing). French masterpieces of the 19th century include Ingres' *The Turkish Bath* (off Room 60, 2nd floor, Sully Wing), Géricault's *The Raft of the Medusa* (Room 77, 1st floor, Denon Wing) and works by Corot, Delacroix and Fragonard (2nd floor, Sully Wing).

Arc de Triomphe   LANDMARK

(Map p188; www.monuments-nationaux.fr; place Charles de Gaulle; adult/18-25yr €9.50/6; ⊙10am-10.30pm, to 11pm Apr-Sep; MCharles de Gaulle–Étoile) If anything rivals the Eiffel Tower as the symbol of Paris, it's this magnificent 1836 monument to Napoléon's 1805 victory at Austerlitz. The intricately sculpted triumphal arch stands sentinel in the centre of place de l'Étoile. From the viewing platform on top of the arch (50m up via 284 steps; it's well worth the climb) you can see the dozen avenues that radiate from the arch.

Beneath the arch at ground level lies the **Tomb of the Unknown Soldier**, honouring the 1.3 million French soldiers who lost their lives in WWI; an eternal flame is rekindled daily at 6.30pm.

Centre Pompidou   MUSEUM

(Map p194; ☎01 44 78 12 33; www.centrepompidou.fr; place Georges Pompidou, 1er; museum, exhibitions & panorama adult/child €13/free; ⊙11am-9pm Wed-Mon; MRambuteau) Paris' premier cultural centre – designed inside out with utilitarian features such as plumbing, pipes, air vents and electrical cables forming part of the external facade to free up the interior space for exhibitions and events – has amazed visitors since it was inaugurated in 1977. Temporary exhibitions fill the ground floor **Forum du Centre Pompidou** and 6th-floor galleries, while the 4th and 5th floors host the **Musée National d'Art Moderne**, France's national collection of art dating from 1905 onwards, which includes works by the surrealists and cubists, as well as pop art and contemporary works.

Sweeping views of Paris thrill diners over lunch at the chic, hyperindustrial restaurant, Georges, on the 6th floor, and also from the rooftop terrace; admission is included in museum and exhibition tickets or buy a panorama ticket just for the roof.

West of the centre, **Place Georges Pompidou** and the nearby pedestrian streets attract buskers, musicians, jugglers and mime artists. South of the centre on **place Igor Stravinsky** are fanciful mechanical fountains of skeletons, hearts, treble clefs and a big pair of ruby-red lips, created by Jean Tinguely and Niki de Saint Phalle.

Basilique du Sacré-Cœur   BASILICA

(Map p198; www.sacre-coeur-montmartre.com; place du Parvis du Sacré-Cœur; Basilica dome admission €5, cash only; ⊙6am-10.30pm, dome 9am-7pm Apr-Sep, to 5.30pm Oct-Mar; MAnvers) Crowning the **Butte de Montmartre** (Montmartre Hill), Sacred Heart Basilica was begun in 1876 but not consecrated until 1919. Some 234 spiralling

THE LOUVRE: TICKETS & TOURS

To best navigate the collection, opt for a self-guided **thematic trail** (1½ to three hours; download trail brochures in advance from the website) or a self-paced **multimedia guide** (€5). More formal, English-language **guided tours** depart from the Hall Napoléon, which also has free English-language maps.

The main entrance and ticket windows are covered by the 21m-high **Grande Pyramide**, a glass pyramid designed by the Chinese-born American architect IM Pei. Avoid the queues outside the pyramid or at the Porte des Lions entrance by entering the Louvre complex via the underground shopping centre **Carrousel du Louvre**, at 99 rue de Rivoli. Buy your tickets in advance – and enter the museum with little or no queue – from the ticket machines inside the latter, by phoning 08 92 68 46 94 or 01 41 57 32 28, or from *billeteries* (ticket offices) inside Fnac or Virgin Megastores.

Montmartre

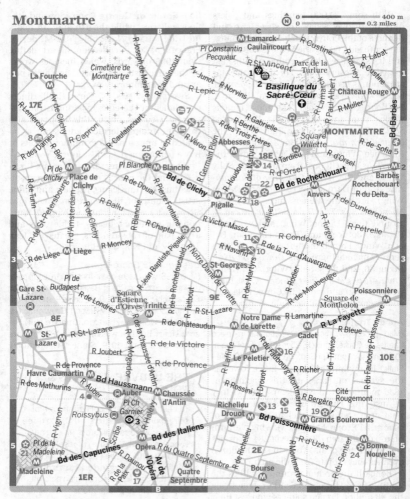

steps lead to its dome, which affords one of Paris' most spectacular panoramas – up to 30km on a clear day. The chapel-lined crypt, visited in conjunction with the dome, is huge.

Palais Garnier   OPERA HOUSE
(Map p198; ☎08 25 05 44 05; www.operadeparis. fr; cnr rues Scribe & Auber; visit adult/10-25yr/under 10yr €9/6/free, guided tour adult/10-25yr/under 10yr €13.50/9.50/6.50; ⊙10am-4.30pm; M Opéra) From Degas' ballerinas to Gaston Leroux's phantom and Chagall's ceiling, the layers of myth painted on gradually over the decades have bestowed a particular air of mystery and

drama to the Palais Garnier's ornate interior. Designed in 1860 by Charles Garnier – then an unknown 35-year-old architect – the opera house was part of Baron Haussmann's massive urban renovation project.

The opera is open for visits during the day; highlights include the opulent **Grand Staircase**, the **library-museum** (1st fl), where you'll find old show posters, costumes and original music scores, and the horseshoe-shaped **auditorium** (2nd fl), with its extravagant gilded interior and red velvet seats. Or reserve a spot on an English-language guided tour. Note that the

Montmartre

◎ Top Sights
Basilique du Sacré-Cœur......................C1

◎ Sights
1 Clos Montmartre C1
2 Musée de Montmartre C1
3 Palais Garnier... B5

✪ Activities, Courses & Tours
4 L'Open Tour A4
5 Vélib' D2

🛏 Sleeping
6 Hôtel Amour...C3
7 Hôtel des Arts.......................................B1
8 Hôtel Eldorado A2
9 Plug-Inn Hostel B2

✖ Eating
10 Arnaud Delmontel C3

11 Cul de Poule...C3
12 La Mascotte...B2
13 Le J'Go C5
14 Le Miroir...C2
15 Le Zinc des Cavistes C5
16 Les Pâtes Vivantes................................C4

◎ Drinking
17 Harry's New York Bar B5
18 La Fourmi..C2

✪ Entertainment
19 Au Limonaire D5
20 Bus Palladium...B3
21 Kiosque Théâtre Madeleine A5
22 La Cigale..C2
23 Le Divan du Monde C2
24 Le Rex Club...D5
25 Moulin Rouge..B2

auditorium cannot be visited when daytime rehearsals or matinees are scheduled; try to arrive before 1pm or check the website for the exact schedule.

Interestingly, a prop man at the opera house set up beehives on the roof a couple of decades ago – the honey, when available, is now sold at the gift shop.

Musée Picasso MUSEUM
(Map p194; ☎01 42 71 25 21; www.musee-picasso.fr; 5 rue de Thorigny; Ⓜ St-Paul or Chemin Vert) One of Paris' most beloved art collections opened its doors again after massive renovation works in summer 2013. Housed in the stunning, mid-17th-century Hôtel Salé, the Musée Picasso woos art lovers with more than 3500 drawings, engravings, paintings, ceramic works and sculptures by the *grand maître* (great master) Pablo Picasso (1881–1973). The extraordinary collection was donated to the French government by the artist's heirs in lieu of paying inheritance tax.

FREE **Musée Carnavalet** MUSEUM
(Map p194; www.carnavalet.paris.fr; 23 rue de Sévigné, 3e; ◷10am-6pm Tue-Sun; Ⓜ St-Paul, Chemin Vert or Rambuteau) One of the city's best free sights, this enormous 100-room ode to the history of Paris is housed in two elegant *hôtels particuliers* (historic mansions) in the Marais. Displays chart the history of Paris from Gallo-Roman to modern times: some of the nation's most important documents, paintings and objects from the French Revolution are here, as is Marcel Proust's cork-lined bedroom from his apartment on bd Haussmann where he wrote most of *À la Recherche du Temps Perdu* (In Search of Lost Time).

Place des Vosges SQUARE
(Map p194; place des Vosges, 4e; Ⓜ St-Paul or Bastille) Paris' oldest square, place des Vosges is a strikingly elegant ensemble of 36 symmetrical houses with ground-floor arcades, steep slate roofs and large dormer windows arranged around a large and leafy square. The square was named in 1800 to honour the Vosges *département* for being the first in France to pay its taxes.

Between 1832 and 1848 writer Victor Hugo lived in an apartment on the 3rd floor of the square's **Hôtel de Rohan-Guéménée**, now the museum **Maison de Victor Hugo** (Map p194; www.musee-hugo.paris.fr; admission free; ◷10am-6pm Tue-Sun; Ⓜ St-Paul or Bastille), devoted to his life and times.

Place de la Bastille SQUARE
(Map p194; Ⓜ Bastille) The Bastille, a 14th-century fortress built to protect the city gates, is the most famous Parisian monument that no longer exists. Transformed into a dreaded state prison under Cardinal Richelieu, it was demolished shortly after a mob stormed it on 14 July 1789. First impressions

DON'T MISS

CANAL ST-MARTIN

The shaded towpaths of the tranquil, 4.5km-long **Canal St-Martin** (Map p188; MRépublique, Jaurès, Jacques Bonsergent) are a wonderful place for a romantic stroll or a bike ride past nine locks, metal bridges and ordinary Parisian neighbourhoods. The canal's banks have undergone a real urban renaissance, and the southern stretch in particular is an ideal spot for cafe lounging, quayside summer picnics and late-night drinks. Hip new bistros have moved into the area (most are closed Sunday and often Monday) and if you're in Paris to tempt your taste buds, you'll wind up in these eastern suburbs sooner rather than later.

Linking the 10e arrondissement with **Parc de la Villette** in the 19e, the canal makes its famous dogleg turn in the 10e arrondissement. Parts of the waterway – which was built between 1806 and 1825 in order to link the Seine with the 108km-long **Canal de l'Ourcq** – are actually higher than the surrounding land. Take a **canal boat** cruise to savour the real flavour.

of today's busy traffic circle can be underwhelming. The bronze column topped with the gilded Spirit of Liberty commemorates victims of later revolutions in 1830 and 1848.

Cimetière du Père Lachaise　CEMETERY
(Map p188; ☎01 43 70 70 33; www.pere-lachaise.com; 16 rue du Repos & bd de Ménilmontant, 20e; admission free; ☺8am-6pm Mon-Fri, from 8.30am Sat, from 9am Sun; MPère Lachaise or Philippe Auguste) The world's most visited cemetery opened its one-way doors in 1804. Among the 800,000 people buried here are the composer Chopin; the playwright Molière; the poet Apollinaire; writers Balzac, Proust, Gertrude Stein and Colette; the actors Simone Signoret, Sarah Bernhardt and Yves Montand; the painters Pissarro, Seurat, Modigliani and Delacroix; the *chanteuse* Édith Piaf; the dancer Isadora Duncan; and even those immortal 12th-century lovers, Abélard and Héloïse, whose remains were disinterred and reburied here together in 1817 beneath a neo-Gothic tombstone. Particularly visited graves are those of Oscar Wilde (division 89) and 1960s rock star Jim Morrison (division 6).

🏃 Activities

Cycling

Paris is set to expand its 370km of cycling lanes to 700km by 2014. Many sections of road are shut to motorised traffic on Sundays and holidays. Pick up wheels with Vélib' (p216), join an organised bike tour or rent your own wheels and DIY with one of these outfits:

Gepetto et Vélos　CYCLING
(Map p194; www.gepetto-et-velos.com; 59 rue du Cardinal Lemoine, 5e; bicycles per day €15; ☺9am-1pm & 2-7.30pm Tue-Sat; MCardinal Lemoine)

Paris à Vélo, C'est Sympa!　CYCLING
(Map p194; www.parisvelosympa.com; 22 rue Alphonse Baudin, 11e; bicycles per day €20; ☺9.30am-1pm & 2-6pm Mon-Fri, 9am-1pm & 2-7pm Sat & Sun; MSt-Sébastien–Froissart)

👉 Tours

Fat Tire Bike Tours　CYCLING
(Map p188; ☎01 56 58 10 54; www.fattirebiketours.com) City bike tours, day and night, plus trips further afield to Versailles, Monet's garden in Giverny and the Normandy beaches. Tours generally meet opposite the Eiffel Tower's southern pillar at the start of the Champ de Mars; look for the yellow signs. Reserve in advance.

Bateaux-Mouches　BOAT TOUR
(Map p188; ☎01 42 25 96 10; www.bateauxmouches.com; Port de la Conférence, 8e; adult/4-12yr €11/5.50; ☺Apr-Dec; MAlma Marceau) River cruises (70 minutes) with commentary in French and English; set sail from the Right Bank, just east of Pont de l'Alma.

L'Open Tour　BUS TOUR
(Map p198; www.pariscityrama.com; 2-day passes adult/child €32/15) Hop-on, hop-off bus tours aboard an open-deck bus.

Paris Walks　WALKING TOUR
(www.paris-walks.com; adult/child €12/8) Highly rated by Lonely Planet readers, this long-established company runs thematic tours (fashion, chocolate, the French Revolution).

🎭 Festivals & Events

Fashion Week　FASHION
(www.pretparis.com; MPorte de Versailles) Prêt-à-Porter, the ready-to-wear fashion salon that

is held twice a year in late January and again in September, is a must for fashion buffs; it's held at the Parc des Expositions at Porte de Versailles, 15e.

Paris Plages
BEACH

(www.paris.fr) 'Paris Beaches' sees three waterfront areas transformed into sand-and-pebble 'beaches', complete with sun beds, beach umbrellas, atomisers, lounge chairs and palm trees; mid-July to mid-August.

Nuit Blanche
ART

(www.paris.fr) Museums, bars, clubs and so on don't sleep during Paris' 'White Night' all-nighter; first Saturday and Sunday of October.

Fête des Vendanges de Montmartre
HARVEST

(www.fetedesvendangesdemontmartre.com) This five-day festival during the second weekend in October celebrates Montmartre's grape harvest with costumes, speeches and a parade.

🛏 Sleeping

The Paris Convention & Visitors Bureau can find you a place to stay (no booking fee, but you need a credit card), though queues can be long in high season; it also has information on bed-and-breakfast accommodation.

LOUVRE & LES HALLES

The upside of this right-bank neighbourhood is its epicentral location, excellent transport links and proximity to many major sights and shops. However, the immediate area around the **Forum des Halles** (Map p194; www.forumdeshalles.com; 1 rue Pierre Lescot, 1er; ⊙shops 10am-8pm Mon-Sat; Ⓜ Les Halles or RER Châtelet–Les Halles) may be noisy/inconvenient during construction works (not due for completion until 2016).

Hôtel Tiquetonne
HOTEL €

(Map p194; ☑01 42 36 94 58; www.hoteltiquetonne. 6 rue Tiquetonne, 2e; d €65, with shared shower €45; 🛜; Ⓜ Étienne Marcel) What heart-warmingly good value this 45-room vintage cheapie is. This serious, well-tended address in the heart of party land has been in the hotel biz since the 1900s and is much-loved by a loyal clientele of all ages. Rooms straddle seven floors and sport an inoffensive mix of vintage decor – roughly 1930s to 1980s – with brand new bathrooms and parquet flooring in recently renovated rooms. Shared shower *jeton* (tokens) cost €5; ask at reception.

🔝 CHOICE Hôtel Crayon
BOUTIQUE HOTEL €€

(Map p194; ☑01 42 36 54 19; www.hotelcrayon. com; 25 rue du Bouloi, 1er; s €129-249, d €149-299; ✳🛜; Ⓜ Les Halles or Sentier) Line drawings by French artist Julie Gauthron bedeck walls and doors at this creative boutique hotel. The pencil (*le crayon*) is the theme, with rooms sporting a different shade of each floor's chosen colour – we love the coloured-glass shower doors and the books on the bedside table guests can swap and take home.

BVJ Paris-Louvre
HOSTEL €

(Map p194; ☑01 53 00 90 90; www.bvjhotel.com; 20 rue Jean-Jacques Rousseau, 1er; dm/d incl breakfast €30/70; @🛜; Ⓜ Louvre Rivoli) This modern, 200-bed hostel has doubles and bunks in a single-sex room for four to 10 people with showers down the corridor. Guests must be aged 18 to 35. Rooms are accessible from 2.30pm on the day you arrive. No kitchen facilities.

MARAIS & BASTILLE

Buzzing nightlife, hip shopping and an inexhaustible range of eating options ensure the popularity of this trendy, right-bank neighbourhood. Nearby Bastille has fewer

FRANCE PARIS

BOHEMIAN SOULS IN MONTMARTRE

No address better captures the *quartier*'s rebellious, bohemian and artsy past than **Musée de Montmartre** (Map p198; www.museedemontmartre.fr; 12 rue Cortot, 18e; adult/18-25yr/10-17yr €8/6/4; ⊙10am-6pm; Ⓜ Lamarck–Caulaincourt), one-time home to painters Renoir, Utrillo and Raoul Dufy. The 17th-century manor house-museum displays paintings, lithographs and documents; hosts art exhibitions by contemporary artists currently living in Montmartre; and its excellent bookshop sells bottles of the wine produced from grapes grown in the *quartier*'s very own vineyard, **Clos Montmartre** (Map p198; 18 rue des Saules, 18e).

Later, pay your respects to bohemian souls – writers Émile Zola, Alexandre Dumas and Stendhal, composer Jacques Offenbach, artist Edgar Degas, film director François Truffaut and dancer Vaslav Nijinsky among others – laid to rest in the Cimetière de Montmartre. Around since 1798, the cemetery is Paris' most famous after Père Lachaise.

RENTING AN APARTMENT

Be it a night, a week or longer, apartment rental is increasingly the modish way to stay in Paris. **Haven in Paris** (www.haveninparis.com) is recommended – it has luxury apartments from €575 per week.

Paris Attitude (www.parisattitude. com) Thousands of apartment rentals, professional service, reasonable fees.

Guest Apartment Services (www. guestapartment.com) Romantic apartment rentals on and around Paris' islands.

Room Sélection (www.room-selection. com) Select apartment rentals centred on the Marais.

tourists, allowing you to better glimpse the daily grind of the 'real' Paris.

TOP CHOICE / Hôtel Jeanne d'Arc HOTEL €€
(Map p194; ☎01 48 87 62 11; www.hoteljeannedarc. com; 3 rue de Jarente, 4e; s €65, d €81-96, tr €149, q €164; ☎; MSt-Paul) Book well in advance at this gorgeous address to snag one of its cosy, excellent-value rooms. Games to play, a painted rocking chair for tots in the bijou lounge, knick knacks everywhere, and the most extraordinary mirror in the breakfast room create a real 'family home' air to this 35-room house.

Le Pavillon de la Reine HISTORIC HOTEL €€€
(Map p194; ☎01 44 59 80 40; www.pavillonde lareine.com; 28 place des Vosges, 3e; d from €330; MChemin Vert) Dreamily set on Paris' most beautiful and elegant square, place des Vosges, this sumptuous address loaded with history doesn't come cheap. But who cares when you can sleep like a queen (indeed the hotel is named after Anne of Austria, queen to Louis XIII from 1615, who stayed here).

Cosmos Hôtel HOTEL €
(Map p188; ☎01 43 57 25 88; www.cosmos-hotel-paris.com; 35 rue Jean-Pierre Timbaud, 11e; s/d/tr €55/62/78; ☎; MRépublique) Cheap, brilliant value and just footsteps from the fun and happening bars, cafes and music clubs of increasingly trendy rue JPT, Cosmos is a shiny star with retro style on the budget-hotel scene. It has been around for 30-odd years but, unlike most other hotels in the same price bracket, Cosmos has been treated to a thoroughly modern makeover this century. Enjoy.

Hôtel du Petit Moulin BOUTIQUE HOTEL €€€
(Map p194; ☎01 42 74 10 10; www.hoteldupetit moulin.com; 29-31 rue du Poitou, 3e; d €190-350; MFilles du Calvaire) This 17-room hotel, a bakery at the time of Henri IV, was designed by Christian Lacroix. Pick from medieval and rococo Marais (rooms sporting exposed beams and dressed in toile de Jouy wallpaper), to more modern surrounds with contemporary murals and heart-shaped mirrors just this side of kitsch.

Hi Matic HOTEL €€
(Map p188; ☎01 43 67 56 56; www.hi-matic.net; 71 rue de Charonne, 11e; r €110-160; ✳@☎; MBastille) This odd place has staked its claim as the 'urban hotel of the future'. The plus side is eco-friendly features (LED energy-saving lights, natural pigments instead of paint) and a colourful, imaginative space-saving design (mattresses are rolled out onto tatamis at night) that some will find fun. The downside is that service is kept to a minimum – check-in is via computer, and the organic breakfast comes out of a vending machine.

Maison Internationale de la Jeunesse et des Étudiants HOSTEL €
(MIJE; Map p194; ☎01 42 74 23 45; www.mije.com; 6 rue de Fourcy, 4e; dm incl breakfast €31, annual membership €2.50; MSt-Paul) Sweep through the elegant front door and congratulate yourself on finding such magnificent digs. The MIJE runs three hostels in attractively renovated 17th- and 18th-century *hôtels particuliers* in the Marais. Rooms are closed from noon to 3pm, and curfew is 1am to 7am.

LATIN QUARTER
Midrange hotels in this good-value Left Bank neighbourhood are particularly popular with visiting academics, making rooms hardest to find during conferences (March to June and October).

Five Hotel DESIGN HOTEL €€€
(Map p188; ☎01 43 31 74 21; www.thefivehotel-paris. com; 3 rue Flatters, 5e; d €202-342; ✳☎; MLes Go-belins) Choose from one of five perfumes to fragrance your room at this contemporary romantic sanctum. Its private apartment, One by The Five, has a phenomenal 'suspended' bed.

Hôtel Minerve HOTEL €€
(Map p194; ☎01 43 26 26 04; www.parishotel minerve.com; 13 rue des Écoles, 5e; s €99, d €129-

165, tr €165; ❉@🛜; MCardinal Lemoine) Oriental carpets, antique books, frescoes of French monuments and reproduction 18th-century wallpaper make this family-run hotel a charming place to stay. Some rooms have small balconies with views of Notre Dame; two have tiny romantic courtyards.

Select Hôtel
BOUTIQUE HOTEL €€€

(Map p194; 🖉01 46 34 14 80; www.selecthotel.fr; 1 place de la Sorbonne, 5e; s €165, d €215-299, tr €309-320; ❉@🛜; MCluny–La Sorbonne) In the heart of the studenty Sorbonne area, the Select is a very Parisian art deco minipalace, with an atrium and cactus-strewn winter garden, an 18th-century vaulted breakfast room and 67 small but stylish bedrooms. The 1920s-style cocktail bar with 'library' is a delight.

Hôtel les Degrés de Notre Dame
HOTEL €€

(Map p194; 🖉01 55 42 88 88; www.lesdegreshotel. com; 10 rue des Grands Degrés, 5e; d incl breakfast €115-170; 🛜; MMaubert-Mutualité) Wonderfully old-school, with a winding timber staircase (no lift), and charming staff, the value is unbeatable at this hotel, a block from the Seine.

Oops
HOSTEL €

(Map p188; 🖉01 47 07 47 00; www.oops-paris. com; 50 av des Gobelins, 13e; dm/d €30/70; @🛜; MGobelins) A lurid candyfloss-pink lift scales the six floors of Paris' first 'design hostel', each painted a different colour. Well-sized doubles and modern but locker-less four- to six-bed dorms all have ensuites and some have Eiffel Tower views. No kitchen. No credit cards and no alcohol allowed.

ST-GERMAIN, ODÉON & LUXEMBOURG
Staying in chic St-Germain des Prés (6e) is a delight. But beware – budget places just don't exist in this part of the Left Bank.

TOP CHOICE L'Apostrophe
DESIGN HOTEL €€€

(Map p188; 🖉01 56 54 31 31; www.apostrophe-hotel. com; 3 rue de Chevreuse, 6e; d €150-350; ❉@🛜; MVavin) A street work-of-art with stencilled facade, this hotel's 16 rooms pay homage to the written word. Graffiti tags cover one wall of room U (for 'urbain') which has a ceiling shaped like a skateboard ramp. Room P (for 'Paris parody') sits in clouds overlooking Paris' rooftops.

Le Bellechasse
DESIGN HOTEL €€

(Map p188; 🖉01 45 50 22 31; www.lebellechasse. com; 8 rue de Bellechasse, 7e; d from €161; ❉🛜; MSolférino) Fashion designer Christian Lac-

roix's entrancing room themes make you feel like you've stepped into a larger-than-life oil painting. Mod cons include iPod docks and 200 TV channels.

Hôtel St-André des Arts
HOTEL €€

(Map p194; 🖉01 43 26 96 16; 66 rue St-André des Arts, 6e; s/d/tr/q incl breakfast €75/95/119/132; 🛜; MOdéon) Snug on a lively, restaurant-lined thoroughfare, this 31-room hotel is a veritable bargain in the centre of the action. Rooms are basic, but public areas are evocative of *vieux Paris* (old Paris) with beamed ceilings and stone walls.

GARE DU NORD, GARE DE L'EST & RÉPUBLIQUE
The areas around the Gare du Nord and Gare de l'Est are far from the prettiest parts of Paris, but decent-value hotels are a dime a dozen.

TOP CHOICE Le Citizen Hotel
BOUTIQUE HOTEL €€€

(Map p188; 🖉01 83 62 55 50; www.lecitizenhotel. com; 96 quai de Jemmapes, 10e; d €177-275, q €450; 🛜; MGare de l'Est, Jacques Bonsergent) A team of forward-thinking creative types put their heads together for this one, and the result is 12 alluring rooms equipped with iPads, filtered water and warm minimalist design.

Hôtel du Nord – Le Pari Vélo
HOTEL €€

(Map p188; 🖉01 42 01 66 00; www.hoteldunord-leparivelo.com; 47 rue Albert Thomas, 10e; s/d/q €71/85/110; 🛜; MRépublique) Beyond the bric-a-brac charm (and the ever popular dog, Pluto), Hôtel du Nord's other winning attribute is its prized location near place République. Bikes are on loan for guests.

République Hôtel
HOTEL €€

(Map p188; 🖉01 42 39 19 03; www.republiquehotel. com; 31 rue Albert Thomas, 10e; s €82, d €95-120, tr €120, q €169; 🛜; MRépublique) This hip spot is heavy on pop art – local street artists did some of the paintings here. Regardless of the garden gnomes in the breakfast room, you won't be able to fault the inexpensive rates and fantastic location off place République.

St Christopher's Inn
HOSTEL €

(Map p188; 🖉01 40 34 34 40; www.st-christophers. co.uk/paris-hostels; 68-74 quai de la Seine, 19e; dm €22-40, d from €70; @🛜; MRiquet or Jaurès) This is one of Paris' best, biggest and most up-to-date hostels with a modern design, four types of dorms (six- to 12-bed) and doubles with or without bathrooms. Other perks include a canal-side cafe, bar and a female-only floor. A new **branch** (Map p188; rue de Dunkerque) will open across from Gare du Nord.

MONTMARTRE & PIGALLE

What a charmer Montmartre is, with its varied accommodation scene embracing everything from boutique to bohemian, hostel to *hôtel particulier*.

TOP CHOICE Hôtel Amour
BOUTIQUE HOTEL **€€**

(Map p198; ☑01 48 78 31 80; www.hotelamourparis. fr; 8 rue Navarin, 9e; s €105, d €155-215; 📶; MSt-Georges or Pigalle) The inimitable black-clad Amour (formerly a love hotel by the hour) features original design and artwork – you won't find a more original place to lay your head in Paris at these prices.

Au Sourire de Montmartre
B&B **€€**

(Map p188; ☑06 64 64 72 86; www.sourire-de -montmartre.com; rue du Mont Cenis, 18e; r €125-170, apt per week €600; MJules Joffrin) This charming B&B on the backside of Montmartre has four rooms and a studio, each decorated with French antiques or Moroccan motifs. The surrounding neighbourhood is delightful, though slightly out of the way.

Hôtel Eldorado
HOTEL **€**

(Map p198; ☑01 45 22 35 21; www.eldoradohotel.fr; 18 rue des Dames, 17e; s €39-65, d €58-85, tr €75-93; 📶; MPlace de Clichy) This bohemian place is one of Paris' greatest finds: a welcoming, reasonably well-run place with 23 colourful rooms and a private back garden. Cheaper-category singles have washbasin only.

Hôtel des Arts
HOTEL **€€**

(Map p198; ☑01 46 06 30 52; www.arts-hotel-paris.com; 5 rue Tholozé, 18e; s €105, d €140-165; 📶; MAbbesses or Blanche) This attractive 50-room hotel, convenient to both place Pigalle and Montmartre, sports excellent-value midrange rooms; consider spending an extra €25 for the superior rooms, which have nicer views.

Plug-Inn Hostel
HOSTEL **€**

(Map p198; ☑01 42 58 42 58; www.plug-inn.fr; 7 rue Aristide Bruant, 18e; dm/d/tr incl breakfast €25/60/90; @📶; MAbbesses or Blanche) This hostel is much-loved for its central Montmartre location, four to five-person rooms each with shower, the kitchen, free breakfast and no curfew at night.

Eating

LOUVRE & LES HALLES

Trendy restaurants are on the rise in this epicentral area.

TOP CHOICE Beef Club
STEAK **€€**

(Map p194; ☑09 54 37 13 65; www.eccbeefclub. com; 58 rue Jean-Jacques Rousseau, 1er; mains €20-45; ⊘dinner; MLes Halles) No steak house is more chic or hip than this. Packed out ever since it threw its first T-bone on the grill in 2012, this beefy address is all about steak, prepared to sweet perfection by legendary Paris butcher Yves-Marie Le Bourdonnec. The vibe is hip New York and the downstairs cellar bar, Ballroom du Beef Club, shakes a mean cocktail (€12 to €15) courtesy of the Experimental Cocktail Club.

TOP CHOICE Frenchie
BISTRO **€€**

(Map p194; ☑01 40 39 96 19; www.frenchie -restaurant.com; 5-6 rue du Nil, 2e; menus €34, €38 & €45; ⊘dinner Mon-Fri; MSentier) This bijou bistro with wooden tables and old stone walls is always packed and for good reason: excellent-value dishes are modern, market-driven (the menu changes daily with a choice of two dishes by course) and prepared with just the right dose of unpretentious creative flair by French chef Gregory Marchand.

Reserve for one of two sittings (7pm or 9.30pm) two months in advance, arrive at 7pm and pray for a cancellation, or – failing that – share tapas-style small plates with friends across the street at no-reservations **Frenchie Bar à Vin**.

Verjus
INTERNATIONAL **€€€**

(Map p194; ☑01 42 97 54 40; www.verjusparis.com; 52 rue de Richelieu, 1er; 4-/6-course tasting menus €55/70, with wine pairings €85/110; ⊘dinner Mon-Fri; MBourse or Palais Royal–Musée du Louvre) Cuisine is contemporary and international at this hidden but hyped restaurant near Palais Royal that you really need to know about to find. Reservations are essential Thursday and Friday, but walk-ins Monday to Wednesday often end up with a table. And for diners who don't strike gold, there's the wine bar in the restaurant cellar famed in Parisian foodie circles for the best fried buttermilk chicken (€10) in town.

Yam'Tcha
FUSION **€€€**

(Map p194; ☑01 40 26 08 07; www.yamtcha.com; 4 rue Sauval, 1er; lunch/dinner menus from €50/85; ⊘lunch Wed-Sun, dinner Wed-Sat; MLouvre-Rivoli)

FRANCE PARIS

TOP FIVE PATISSERIES

Ladurée (Map p188; www.laduree.fr; 75 av des Champs-Élysées, 8e; pastries from €1.50; ⊙7.30am-11pm; MGeorge V) Paris' most historic and decadent; inventor of the *macaron*.

Le Nôtre (Map p194; www.lenotre.fr; 10 rue St-Antoine, 4e; MBastille) Delectable pastries and chocolate; 10-odd outlets around town.

La Pâtisserie des Rêves (Map p188; www.lapatisseriedesreves.com; 93 rue du Bac, 7e; ⊙10am-8.30pm Tue-Sat, 8.30am-2pm Sun; MRue du Bac) Extraordinary cakes and tarts showcased beneath glass at the chic 'art' gallery of big-name *pâtissier* Philippe Conticini.

Boulangerie Bruno Solques (Map p194; 243 rue St-Jacques, 5e; ⊙6.30am-8pm Mon-Fri; ♿; MPlace Monge or RER Luxembourg) Paris' most inventive *pâtissier*, Bruno Solques, excels at oddly shaped flat tarts and fruit-filled brioches.

Arnaud Delmontel (Map p198; 39 rue des Martyrs, 9e; ⊙7am-8.30pm Wed-Mon; MPigalle) Award-winning baguettes, gorgeous cakes, pastries to die for.

Adeline Grattard's ingeniously fused French and Chinese flavours has earned her a Michelin star. Pair dishes on the frequently changing menu with wine or exotic teas.

Spring MODERN FRENCH €€
(Map p194; ☎01 45 96 05 72; www.springparis.fr; 6 rue Bailleul, 1er; lunch/dinner menus €44/76; ⊙lunch & dinner Wed-Fri, dinner Tue & Sat; MPalais Royal–Musée du Louvre) One of the Right Bank's 'talk-of-the-town' addresses, with an American in the kitchen and stunning food. It has no printed menu, meaning hungry gourmets put their appetites in the hands of the chef and allow multilingual waiting staff to reveal what's cooking as each course is served. Advance reservations essential.

At lunchtime, nip to the **Spring Épicerie** (Map p194; www.springparis.fr; 52 rue de l'Arbre Sec, 1er; soup €12; ⊙noon-8pm Tue-Sat), a tiny wine shop which serves steaming bowls of chicken soup (€12) eaten at a bar stool or on the trot.

Kunitoraya JAPANESE €
(Map p194; www.kunitoraya.com; 39 rue Ste-Anne, 1er; mains €12-14; ⊙11.30am-10pm; MPyramides) Grab a stool at the kitchen bar and watch hip young Japanese chefs strut their stuff over steaming bowls of soup, *grands bols de riz* (big bowls of rice) and some of the best udon (handmade Japanese noodles) in town. No credit cards and no reservations.

Blend BURGERS €
(Map p194; www.blendhamburger.com; 44 rue d'Argout, 2e; burgers €10, lunch menus €15 & €17; ⊙lunch & dinner Mon-Sat; MSentier) A burger cannot simply be a burger in gourmet Paris,

where burger buffs dissolve into raptures of ecstacy at Blend. Think home-made brioche buns and ketchup, hand-cut meat and the most inventive of toppings that transform the humble burger into something really rather special.

Saveurs Végét'Halles VEGETARIAN €
(Map p194; ☎01 40 41 93 95; www.saveursvegethalles.fr; 41 rue des Bourdonnais, 1er; salads €11.90; ⊙lunch & dinner Mon-Sat; ♿; MChâtelet) This vegan eatery offers quite a few mock-meat dishes like *poulet végétal aux champignons* ('chicken' with mushrooms). No alcohol.

MARAIS & BASTILLE
The Marais is one of Paris' premier dining neighbourhoods; book ahead for weekend dining. Traditional bistros and neobistros vie for supremacy in neighbouring Bastille.

TOP CHOICE Septime MODERN FRENCH €€€
(Map p188; ☎01 43 67 38 29; 80 rue de Charonne, 11e; lunch/5-course menus €26/55; ⊙lunch Tue-Fri, dinner Mon-Fri; MCharonne) Reading the menu won't get you far given it more resembles a shopping list. But have no fear: alchemists in the kitchen produce truly beautiful creations, and the blue-smocked waitstaff go out of their way to ensure the culinary surprises are all pleasant ones.

Le Siffleur de Ballons WINE BAR €
(Map p188; www.lesiffleurdeballons.com; 34 rue de Citeaux, 12e; lunch menus €14, mains €7-15; ⊙10.30am-3pm & 5.30-10pm Tue-Sat; MFaidherbe Chaligny) With Tom Waits on the stereo and a few cactuses atop the register, this contemporary wine bar clearly has a dash of

TOP FIVE FOOD MARKETS

Marché Bastille (Map p194; bd Richard Lenoir; ⊙7am-2.30pm Thu & Sun; MBastille or Richard Lenoir) Paris' best outdoor food market.

Marché aux Enfants Rouges (Map p194; 39 rue de Bretagne, 3e; ⊙8.30am-1pm & 4-7.30pm Tue-Fri, 4-8pm Sat, 8.30am-2pm Sun; MFilles du Calvaire) The city's oldest food market, in the Marais, with food stalls and communal tables to lunch at.

Marché Belleville (Map p188; bd de Belleville, btwn rue Jean-Pierre Timbaud & rue du Faubourg du Temple, 11e & 20e; ⊙7am-2.30pm Tue & Fri; MBelleville or Couronnes) Fascinating entry into the large, vibrant communities of the eastern neighbourhoods, home to artists, students and immigrants from Africa, Asia and the Middle East.

Marché Couvert St-Quentin (Map p188; 85bis bd de Magenta, 10e) Iron-and-glass covered market built in 1866; lots of gourmet and upmarket food stalls.

Marché Raspail (Map p188; bd Raspail btwn rue de Rennes & rue du Cherche Midi, 6e; ⊙regular market 7am-2.30pm Tue & Fri, organic market 9am-3pm Sun; MRennes) Much-loved by foodies, particularly on Sunday for its organic produce.

California in its soul. The wines are French, natural, and paired to perfection with simple but delicious offerings: tartines, soups, lentil salad with truffle oil, cheeses and Iberian charcuterie plates. Look out for the weekly tastings with winemakers.

Bistrot Paul Bert
BISTRO €€

(Map p188; ☑01 43 72 24 01; 18 rue Paul Bert, 11e; 3-course lunch/dinner menus €18/36; ⊙lunch & dinner Tue-Sat; MFaidherbe-Chaligny) An address that stars on every 'best Paris bistro' list, Paul Bert serves perfectly executed classic dishes in a timeless setting.

Au Passage
BISTRO €€

(Map p194; ☑01 43 55 07 52; www.facebook.com/aupassage; 1bis passage de St-Sébastien, 11e; 2-/3-course lunch menus €13.50/19.50, dinners €20-35; ⊙lunch & dinner Mon-Fri, dinner Sat; MSt-Sébastien–Froissart) Have faith in talented Australian chef James Henry at this raved-about *petit bar de quartier* (neighbourhood bar) with vegetable crates piled scruffily in the window and a fridge filling one corner of the old-fashioned dining room.

The lunch menu – a good-value, uncomplicated choice of two starters and two mains – is chalked on the blackboard, while dinner sees waiting staff in jeans twirl in and out of the pocket-sized kitchen with tapas-style starters to share, followed by a feisty shoulder of lamb, side of beef or other meaty cut for the entire table.

Chez Marianne
JEWISH €€

(Map p194; 2 rue des Hospitalières St-Gervais, 4e; mains €19-24; ⊙noon-midnight; MSt-Paul) Absolutely heaving at lunchtime, Chez Marianne translates as elbow-to-elbow eating beneath age-old beams on copious portions of falafel, hummus, purées of aubergine and chickpeas, and 25-odd other *zakouski* (hors d'œuvres; plate of 4/5/6 for €12/14/16). Fare is Sephardic and a hole-in-the-wall window sells falafel in pita (€6) to munch on the move.

Nanashi
FUSION €

(Map p194; ☑09 60 00 25 59; www.nanashi.fr; 57 rue Charlot, 3e; bento €14-16; ⊙noon-midnight Mon-Fri, to 6pm Sat & Sun; MFilles du Calvaire) A fabulous lunch and after-dark address wedged between boutiques in the Haut Marais, this hip industrial space is uber-cool, ultra-healthy and great value. Pick from creative salads, soups and bento boxes, and don't miss the freshly squeezed fruit and veg cocktails. Weekend brunch €17.

LATIN QUARTER

From cheap student haunts to chandelier-lit palaces loaded with history, the 5e has something to suit every budget and culinary taste. Rue Mouffetard is famed for its food market and food shops; while its side streets, especially pedestrianised rue du Pot au Fer, cook up fine budget dining.

L'Agrume
NEOBISTRO €€

(Map p188; ☑01 43 31 86 48; 15 rue des Fossés St-Marcel, 5e; 2-/3-course lunch menus €19/24, mains €26-39; ⊙lunch & dinner Tue-Sat; MCensier Daubenton) Snagging a table at 'Citrus Fruit' is tough, but the reward is watching chefs work with seasonal produce in the open kitchen while you dine. You have a choice of table, bar stool or *comptoir* (counter). Lunching is magnificent value, while dinner is a no-choice *dégustation* (tasting) melody.

Bistrot Les Papilles
BISTRO €€

(Map p194; ☎01 43 25 20 79; www.lespapillesparis. com; 30 rue Gay Lussac, 5e; lunch/dinner menus from €22/31; ◐10.30am–midnight Mon-Sat; Ⓜ Raspail or RER Luxembourg) This hybrid bistro, wine cellar and *épicerie* (grocery) serves market-driven fare at simply dressed tables wedged beneath bottle-lined walls. Each weekday cooks up a different *marmite du marché* (market casserole). But what really sets it apart is its exceptional wine list.

Le Coupe-Chou
FRENCH €€

(Map p194; ☎01 46 33 68 69; www.lecoupechou. com; 9 & 11 rue de Lanneau, 5e; 2-/3-course lunch menus €27, mains €18-25; ◐Mon-Sat; Ⓜ Maubert-Mutualité) This maze of candlelit rooms inside a vine-clad 17th-century townhouse is overwhelmingly romantic. Ceilings are beamed, furnishings are antique, and background classical music mingles with the intimate chatter of diners. As in the days when Marlene Dietrich et al dined here, advance reservations are essential.

Le Coupe-Chou, incidentally, has nothing to do with cabbage *(chou);* rather it's named after the barber's razor once wielded with a deft hand in one of its seven rooms.

ST-GERMAIN, ODÉON & LUXEMBOURG

There's far more to this fabled pocket of Paris than the literary cafes of Sartre or the picnicking turf of Jardin de Luxembourg. Rue St-André des Arts (Ⓜ St-Michel or Odéon) is lined with places to dine lightly or lavishly, as is the stretch between Église St-Sulpice and Église St-Germain des Prés (especially rue des Canettes, rue Princesse and rue Guisarde).

TOP CHOICE Bouillon Racine
BRASSERIE €€

(Map p194; ☎01 44 32 15 60; www.bouillonracine. com; 3 rue Racine, 6e; lunch menu €14.50, menus €30-41; ◐noon–11pm; Ⓜ Cluny–La Sorbonne) This heritage-listed 1906 art nouveau 'soup kitchen', with mirrored walls, floral motifs and ceramic tiling, was built in 1906 to feed market workers. Superbly executed dishes inspired by age-old recipes include stuffed, spit-roasted suckling pig, pork shank in Rodenbach red beer, and scallops and shrimp with lobster coulis. Finish off your foray into gastronomic history with an old-fashioned sherbet.

Café Constant
NEOBISTRO €€

(Map p188; www.cafeconstant.com; 139 rue Ste-Dominique, 7e; 2-/3-course menus €16/23; ◐lunch & dinner Tue-Sun; Ⓜ École Militaire or RER Port de l'Alma) Take a former Michelin-star chef and a simple corner cafe and what do you get? This jam-packed address with original mosaic floor, wooden tables and huge queues every meal time. The pride and joy of Christian and Catherine Constant, it cooks up creative bistro cuisine, mixing old-fashioned grandma staples like *purée de mon enfance* (mashed potato from my childhood) with Sunday treats like foie-gras-stuffed quail and herb-roasted chicken. **Les Cocottes** (Map p188; www.leviolon dingres.com; 135 rue Ste-Dominique, 7e; 2-/3-course lunch menus €9/15, mains €14-28; ◐lunch & dinner Mon-Sat; Ⓜ École Militaire or RER Port de l'Alma), a couple of doors down, is another Constant hit.

KGB
FUSION €€

(Map p194; ☎01 46 33 00 85; http://zekitchengalerie. fr; 25 rue des Grands Augustins, 6e; 2-/3-course lunch menus €27/34, mains €27-32; ◐lunch & dinner Tue-Sat; Ⓜ St-Michel) Overtly art gallery in feel, KGB draws a hip crowd for its casual platters of

---

CANAL ST-MARTIN: A PARISIAN-PERFECT PICNIC

Not just another pizza place! *Mais non, chérie!* Once the weather warms up, the **Pink Flamingo** (Map p188; ☎01 42 02 31 70; www.pinkflamingopizza.com; 67 rue Bichat, 10e; pizzas €10.50-16; ◐lunch Tue-Sun, dinner daily; Ⓜ Jacques Bonsergent) unveils its secret weapon – pink helium balloons that the delivery guy uses to locate you and your perfect canalside picnic spot. Nip into the canalside pizzeria to order Paris' most inventive pizza (duck, apple and chèvre perhaps, or what about gorgonzola, figs and cured ham?), grab a balloon, and stroll off along the canal to your perfect picnic spot. There's also a **Marais branch** (Map p194; ☎01 42 71 28 20; 105 rue Vieille du Temple, 3e; pizzas €10.50-16; ◐noon-3pm & 7-11.30pm; Ⓜ St-Sébastien–Froissart).

To make your picnic Parisian perfect, buy a bottle of wine from nearby **Le Verre Volé** (Map p188; ☎01 48 03 17 34; 67 rue de Lancry, 10e; mains €13-16; ◐lunch & dinner; Ⓜ Jacques Bonsergent), a wine shop with a few tables, excellent wines (€5 to €60 per bottle, €4.50 per glass) and expert advice.

LOCAL KNOWLEDGE

PATRICIA WELLS, CULINARY SHOPPING SPREE

Cookery teacher and author of *The Food Lover's Guide to Paris*, American Patricia Wells (www.patriciawells.com) has lived, cooked and shopped in Paris since 1980, and is considered to have truly captured the soul of French cuisine.

What is it that makes Paris so wonderful for culinary shopping? The tradition, the quality, the quantity, the atmosphere and physical beauty!

Where do you shop? All over: the Sunday organic market at Rennes (Marché Raspail) – I love the dried fruits and nuts; Poilâne for bread; Quatrehomme for cheese; and Poissonnerie du Bac for fish. I shop regularly at Le Bon Marché's La Grande Épicerie de Paris; for special meals I order in advance and go from shop to shop – La Maison du Chocolat and Pierre Hermé for chocolate and cakes, and La Dernière Goutte for wine. That is the fun of Paris, and of France.

Your top food shopping tip? If you live in Paris, become a *client fidèle* so they reach in the back and give you the best stuff. If you only go once in a while, just smile and be friendly.

A perfect culinary souvenir from Paris? Fragonard, the perfume maker, has a great shop on bd St-Germain. They have a changing litany of *great* things for the home. Nothing is very expensive and the offerings change every few months. The gift wrapping alone is worth it!

Asian-influenced *hors d'œuvres*, creative pastas, and mains spanning roast pigeon with ginger and cranberry condiment, suckling lamb, and grilled seabass with lemongrass and mandarin dressing.

Cuisine de Bar SANDWICHES €
(Map p188; 8 rue du Cherche Midi, 6e; dishes €7.50-13; ☺8.30am-7pm Tue-Sat; Ⓜ Sèvres-Babylone) This is not any old sandwich bar, rather an ultrachic spot to lunch between designer boutiques on open sandwiches cut from celebrated **Poilâne** (Map p188; www.poilane. fr; 8 rue du Cherche Midi, 6e; ☺7.15am-8.15pm Mon-Sat; Ⓜ Sèvres-Babylone) bread and fabulously topped with gourmet goodies such as foie gras, smoked duck, gooey St-Marcellin cheese and Bayonne ham.

Au Pied de Fouet BISTRO €
(Map p194; ☎ 01 43 54 87 83; www.aupieddefouet. com; 50 rue St-Benoît, 6e; mains €9-12.50; ☺Mon-Sat; Ⓜ St-Germain des Prés) Wholly classic bistro dishes such as *entrecôte* (steak), *confit de canard* (duck cooked slowly its own fat) and *foie de volailles sauté* (pan-fried chicken livers) at this busy bistro are astonishingly good value. Round off your meal with a *tarte tatin*, wine-soaked prunes or a bowl of *fromage blanc* (a cross between yoghurt, sour cream and cream cheese).

Cosi SANDWICHES €
(Map p194; 54 rue de Seine, 6e; sandwich menus €10-15; ☺noon-11pm; ✸; Ⓜ Odéon) This might

just be Paris' most imaginative sandwich maker, with sandwich names like Stonker, Tom Dooley and Naked Willi chalked on the blackboard. Classical music plays in the background and homemade focaccia bread is still warm from the oven.

MONTPARNASSE

In the 1920s Montparnasse was one of Paris' premier avenues for cafe life and it still enjoys a clutch of worth-trying addresses.

Jadis NEOBISTRO €€
(Map p188; ☎ 01 45 57 73 20; www.bistrot-jadis.com; 202 rue de la Croix Nivert, 15e; lunch/dinner menus from €29/36; ☺lunch & dinner Mon-Fri; Ⓜ Boucicaut) This upmarket neobistro on the corner of a very unassuming street packs a modern punch thanks to the daring of rising-star chef, Guillaume Delage, who braises pork cheeks in beer and uses black rice instead of white. The chocolate soufflé – order it at the start of your meal – is divine.

TOP CHOICE La Cabane à Huîtres SEAFOOD €
(Map p188; ☎ 01 45 49 47 27; 4 rue Antoine Bourdelle, 14e; dozen oysters €14.50, menus €19.50; ☺lunch & dinner Wed-Sat; Ⓜ Montparnasse Bienvenüe) Wonderfully rustic, this wooden-styled *cabane* (cabin) with just nine tables is the pride and joy of fifth-generation oyster farmer Françis Dubourg, who splits his week between the capital and his oyster farm in Arcachon on the Atlantic Coast. The fixed menu includes a dozen oysters, foie gras, *magret de canard*

fumé (smoked duck breast) or smoked salmon and scrumptious desserts.

Le Dôme
BRASSERIE €€

(Map p188; ☎01 43 35 25 81; 108 bd du Montparnasse, 14e; mains €37-49, seafood platters €54; ⊙lunch & dinner; MVavin) A 1930s art deco extravaganza, Le Dôme is a monumental place for a meal service of the formal white-tablecloth and bow-tied-waiter variety. It's one of the swishest places around for shellfish platters piled high with fresh oysters, king prawns, crab claws and so on.

ÉTOILE & CHAMPS-ÉLYSÉES
The 8e arrondissement around the Champs-Élysées is known for its big-name chefs (Alain Ducasse, Pierre Gagnaire, Guy Savoy) and culinary icons (Taillevent), but there are all sorts of under-the-radar restaurants scattered in the backstreets where Parisians who live and work in the area dine. Gourmet food shops, some with attached eateries, garland **place Madeleine.**

Le Boudoir
FRENCH €€

(Map p188; ☎01 43 59 25 29; www.boudoirparis.fr; 25 rue du Colisée, 8e; lunch menus €25, mains €25-29; ⊙lunch Mon-Fri, dinner Tue-Sat; MSt-Philippe du Roule or Franklin D Roosevelt) Spread across two floors, the quirky salons here are works of art. Expect classy bistro fare prepared by chef Arnaud Nicolas, a recipient of France's top culinary honour.

Le Hide
FRENCH €€

(Map p188; ☎01 45 74 15 81; www.lehide.fr; 10 rue du Général Lanrezac, 17e; menus from €24; ⊙lunch Mon-Fri, dinner Mon-Sat; MCharles de Gaulle–Étoile) This tiny neighbourhood bistro serves scrumptious traditional French fare: snails, baked shoulder of lamb with pumpkin purée or monkfish in lemon butter. Unsurprisingly, this place fills up faster than you can scamper down the steps at the nearby Arc de Triomphe. Reserve well in advance.

Aubrac Corner
BURGERS €

(Map p188; www.aubrac-corner.com; 37 rue Marbeuf, 8e; sandwiches from €5, burgers from €9; ⊙7.30am-6.30pm Mon-Sat; MFranklin D Roosevelt) Burgers? On the Champs-Élysées? It might not sound all that French, but rest assured, this isn't fast food – it's actually the gourmet deli of a famous steakhouse. The burgers come with bowls of fries or *aligot* (mashed potatoes with melted cheese); take it all downstairs into the hidden wine cellar, a welcome refuge from the nonstop commotion outside.

OPÉRA & GRANDS BOULEVARDS
The neon-lit area around bd Montmartre forms one of the Right Bank's most animated cafe and dining districts.

Le J'Go
REGIONAL CUISINE €€

(Map p198; ☎01 40 22 09 09; www.lejgo.com; 4 rue Drouot, 9e; lunch/dinner menus €16/35; ⊙Mon-Sat; MRichelieu Drouot) This contemporary Toulouse-style bistro whisks you away to southwestern France. Its bright yellow walls are decorated with bull-fighting posters and the flavourful regional cooking is based around the rotisserie – not to mention other Gascogne standards like cassoulet and foie gras. Roasting takes a minimum of 20 minutes.

Les Pâtes Vivantes
CHINESE €

(Map p198; 46 rue du Faubourg Montmartre, 9e; noodles €9.50-12; ⊙Mon-Sat; MLe Peletier) Feast on *là miàn* (hand-pulled noodles) made to order in the age-old northern Chinese tradition. It packs in a crowd, so arrive early to stake out a table and watch as the nimble noodle maker works his magic.

Le Zinc des Cavistes
BAR, CAFE €

(Map p198; ☎01 47 70 88 64; 5 rue du Faubourg Montmartre, 9e; lunch menus €16, mains €11-19; ⊙8am-10.30pm; MGrands Boulevards) Don't tell the masses standing dutifully in the Chartier queue that there's a much better restaurant right next door – your formerly friendly waiter will probably run off screaming. A local favourite, Le Zinc des Cavistes is as good for a full-blown meal (duck confit, salads) as it is for sampling new vintages.

MONTMARTRE & PIGALLE
Neobistros, wine bars and world cuisine all feature in this area – pick and choose carefully to avoid tourist traps.

THE GOURMET GLACIER

Berthillon (Map p194; 31 rue St-Louis en l'Île, 4e; ice cream from €2; ⊙10am-8pm Wed-Sun; MPont Marie) on Île St-Louis is the place to head to for Paris' finest ice cream. There are 70 flavours to choose from, ranging from fruity cassis to chocolate, coffee, *marrons glacés* (candied chestnuts), *Agenaise* (Armagnac and prunes), *noisette* (hazelnut) and *nougat au miel* (honey nougat). One scoop just won't be enough...

TOP CHOICE Cul de Poule
MODERN FRENCH €€

(Map p198; ☑01 53 16 13 07; 53 rue des Martyrs, 9e; 2-/3-course menus lunch €15/18, dinner €23/28; ⊗closed Sun lunch; MPigalle) With plastic orange cafeteria seats outside, you probably wouldn't wander into the Cul de Poule by accident. But the light-hearted spirit (yes, there is a mounted chicken's *derrière* on the wall) is deceiving; this is one of the best and most affordable kitchens in the Pigalle neighbourhood, with excellent neobistro fare that emphasises quality ingredients from the French countryside.

Le Miroir
BISTRO €€

(Map p198; ☑01 46 06 50 73; 94 rue des Martyrs, 18e; lunch menus €18, dinner menus €25-40; ⊗lunch Tue-Sun, dinner Tue-Sat; MAbbesses) This unassuming modern bistro is smack in the middle of the Montmartre tourist trail, yet it remains a local favourite. There are lots of delightful pâtés and rillettes to start off with – guinea hen with dates, duck with mushrooms, haddock and lemon – followed by well-prepared standards like stuffed veal shoulder.

The lunch special includes a glass of wine, coffee and dessert; the Sunday brunch also gets the thumbs up. Afterwards, pop into its wine shop across the street.

La Mascotte
SEAFOOD, CAFE €€

(Map p198; ☑01 46 06 28 15; www.la-mascotte-montmartre.com; 52 rue des Abbesses, 18e; lunch/dinner menus €25/41; ⊗7am-midnight; MAbbesses) Founded in 1889, this unassuming bar is about as authentic as it gets in Montmartre. It specialises in quality seafood – oysters, lobster, scallops – and regional dishes (Auvergne sausage), but you can also pull up a seat at the bar for a simple glass of wine and a plate of charcuterie.

🍷 Drinking

The line between bars, cafes and bistros is blurred at best. Sitting at a table costs more than standing at the counter, more on a fancy square than a backstreet, more in the 8e than in the 18e. After 10pm many cafes charge a pricier *tarif de nuit* (night rate).

LOUVRE & LES HALLES

Angelina
TEAHOUSE

(Map p188; 226 rue de Rivoli, 1er; ⊗daily; MTuileries) This beautiful, high-ceilinged tearoom has exquisite furnishings, mirrored walls, fabulous fluffy cakes, and the best, most wonderfully sickening 'African' hot choco-

---

BAR-HOPPING STREETS

Prime Parisian drinking spots, perfect for evening meandering to soak up the scene:

Rue Vieille du Temple, 4e Marais cocktail of gay bars and chic cafes.

Rue Oberkampf & rue Jean-Pierre Timbaud, 11e Hip bars, bohemian hang-outs and atmospheric cafes.

Rue de Lappe, 11e Lively bars and clubs.

Rue Montmartre, 2e Atmospheric cafes.

Canal St-Martin, 10e Heady summer nights in casual canalside cafes.

Rue Princesse, 6e Student and sports bars.

---

late (€7.20), served with a pot of whipped cream and carafe of water.

Experimental Cocktail Club COCKTAIL BAR
(Map p194; www.experimentalcocktailclub.com; 37 rue St-Saveur, 2e; ⊗daily; MRéaumur-Sebastopol) Called ECC by trendies, this fabulous speakeasy with grey facade and old-beamed ceiling is effortlessly hip. Oozing spirit and soul, the cocktail bar – with retro-chic decor by American interior designer Cuoco Black and sister bars in London and New York – is a sophisticated flashback to those *années folles* (crazy years) of prohibition New York.

Cocktails (€12 to €15) are individual and fabulous, and DJs set the space partying until dawn at weekends. The same guys are behind the equally hip Ballroom cocktail bar in the cellar of the New Yorker–style Beef Club (p204).

Kong BAR
(Map p194; www.kong.fr; 1 rue du Pont Neuf, 1er; ⊗daily; MPont Neuf) Late nights at this Philippe Starck–designed riot of iridescent champagne-coloured vinyl booths, Japanese cartoon cut-outs and garden gnome stools see Paris' glam young set guzzling Dom Pérignon, nibbling on tapas-style platters (mains €20 to €40) and shaking their designer-clad booty on the tables.

If you can, try to snag a table *à l'étage* (upstairs) in the part-glass-roofed terrace-gallery, where light floods across the giant geisha swooning horizontally across the ceiling, and stunning river views (particularly at sunset) will make you swoon. Smokers will appreciate the *fumoir* (a tiny heated room with no windows or ceiling) accessible from here.

MARAIS & BASTILLE

TOP
CHOICE **Le Baron Rouge** WINE BAR

(Map p188; 1 rue Théophile Roussel, 12e; ⊘10am-2pm & 5-10pm Mon-Fri, 10am-10pm Sat, 10am-4pm Sun; MLedru-Rollin) Just about the ultimate Parisian wine-bar experience, this place has a dozen barrels of the stuff stacked up against the bottle-lined walls. As unpretentious as you'll find, it's a local meeting place where everyone is welcome and is especially busy on Sundays after the Marché d'Aligre wraps up. All the usual suspects – cheese, charcuterie and oysters – will keep your belly full.

For a small deposit, you can even fill up 1L bottles straight from the barrel for under €5.

Le Pure Café CAFE

(Map p188; 14 rue Jean Macé, 11e; ⊘daily; MCharonne) A classic Parisian haunt, this rustic, cherry-red corner cafe was featured in the art-house film *Before Sunset* but it's still a refreshingly unpretentious spot for a drink or well-crafted fare like veal with chestnut purée.

La Fée Verte BAR

(Map p188; 108 rue de la Roquette, 11e; dishes €10-16; ⊘daily; 🛜; MVoltaire) Yes, the 'Green Fairy' specialises in absinthe (served traditionally with spoons and sugar cubes), but this old-fashioned neighbourhood cafe and bar also serves terrific food, including Green Fairy cheeseburgers.

Le Barav WINE BAR

(Map p194; 📞01 48 04 57 59; www.lebarav.fr; 6 rue Charles-François Dupuis, 3e; ⊘Tue-Sat; MTemple) This hipster *bar à vin*, smart on one of the trendiest streets in the Haut Marais, oozes atmosphere – and one of the city's loveliest pavement terraces.

LATIN QUARTER

Café de la Nouvelle Mairie WINE BAR

(Map p194; 19 rue des Fossés St-Jacques, 5e; ⊘9am-8pm Mon-Fri; MCardinal-Lemoine) Shhhh... just around the corner from the Panthéon but hidden on a small, fountained square, this wine bar is a neighbourhood secret, serving blackboard-chalked wines by the glass or bottle. Tapas-style food is simple and delicious.

Curio Parlor Cocktail Club COCKTAIL BAR

(Map p194; www.curioparlor.com; 16 rue des Bernardins, 5e; ⊘7pm-2am Mon-Thu, to 4am Fri-Sun; MMaubert-Mutualité) Run by the same switched-on team as the Experimental Cocktail Club, this hybrid bar-club looks to the interwar *années folles* (crazy years) of 1920s Paris, London and New York for inspiration. Its racing-green facade with a simple brass plaque on the door is the height of discretion.

Le Pub St-Hilaire PUB

(Map p194; www.pubsainthilaire.com; 2 rue Valette, 5e; ⊘3pm-2am Mon-Thu, 3pm-4am Fri, 4pm-4am Sat, 4pm-midnight Sun; MMaubert-Mutualité) 'Buzzing' fails to do justice to the pulsating vibe inside this student-loved pub. Generous happy hours and a trio of pool tables, board games, music on two floors and hearty bar food pack out the place.

ST-GERMAIN, ODÉON & LUXEMBOURG

TOP
CHOICE **Les Deux Magots** CAFE

(Map p194; www.lesdeuxmagots.fr; 170 bd St-Germain, 6e; ⊘7.30am-1am; MSt-Germain des Prés) If ever there were a cafe that summed up St-Germain des Prés' early-20th-century literary scene, it's this former hangout of anyone who was anyone. You will spend *beaucoup* to sip a coffee in a wicker chair on the terrace shaded by dark-green awnings and geraniums spilling from window boxes, but it's an undeniable piece of Parisian history.

Au Sauvignon WINE BAR

(Map p188; 80 rue des Saints Pères, 7e; ⊘8.30am-10pm; MSèvres-Babylone) There's no more authentic *bar à vin* than this. Grab a table in the evening sun or head to the quintessential bistro interior, with an original zinc bar, tightly packed tables and hand-painted ceiling celebrating French viticultural tradition. Order a plate of *casse-croûtes au pain Poilâne* – toast with ham, pâté, terrine, smoked salmon, foie gras and so on.

Alain Milliart JUICE BAR

(Map p188; 📞01 45 55 63 86; www.alain-milliat.com; 159 rue de Grenelle, 7e; ⊘10am-10pm Tue-Sat; MLa Tour Maubourg) Alain Milliart's fruit juices, all 33 varieties bottled in the south of France, star at his Parisian juice bistro. His jams and compotes are equally lush. Rosé grape, green tomato juice or white peach nectar anyone?

Café La Palette CAFE
(Map p194; www.cafelapaletteparis.com; 43 rue de Seine, 6e; ⏰6.30am-2am Mon-Sat; ⓂMabillon) In the heart of gallery land, this *fin-de-siècle* cafe and erstwhile stomping ground of Paul Cézanne and Georges Braque attracts a grown-up set of fashion people and local art dealers. Its summer terrace is beautiful.

OPÉRA & GRANDS BOULEVARDS

Harry's New York Bar COCKTAIL BAR
(Map p198; www.harrysbar.fr; 5 rue Daunou, 2e; ⏰daily; ⓂOpéra) One of the most popular American-style bars in the prewar years, Harry's once welcomed writers like F Scott Fitzgerald and Ernest Hemingway, who no doubt sampled the bar's unique cocktail and creation: the Bloody Mary. The Cuban mahogany interior dates from the mid-19th century and was brought over from a Manhattan bar in 1911.

MONTMARTRE & PIGALLE

TOP CHOICE La Fourmi BAR, CAFE
(Map p198; 74 rue des Martyrs, 18e; ⏰8am-1am Mon-Thu, to 3am Fri & Sat, 10am-1am Sun; ⓂPigalle) A Pigalle institution, La Fourmi hits the mark with its high ceilings, long zinc bar and unpretentious vibe. Get up to speed on live music and club nights or sit down for a reasonably priced meal and drinks.

☆ Entertainment

From jazz cellars to comic theatre, garage beats to go-go dancers, world-class art galleries to avant-garde artist squats, Paris is *the* capital of *savoir-vivre*, with spectacular entertainment to suit every budget, every taste. To find out what's on, buy *Pariscope* (€0.40) or *Officiel des Spectacles* (www.offi.fr, in French) at Parisian news kiosks. *Billeteries* (ticket offices) in **Fnac** (www.fnac spectacles.com) and **Virgin Megastores** sell tickets.

If you go on the day of a performance, you can snag a half-price ticket (plus €3 commission) for ballet, theatre, opera and other performances at the discount-ticket outlet **Kiosque Théâtre Madeleine** (Map p198; opp 15 place de la Madeleine, 8e; ⏰12.30-8pm Tue-Sat, to 4pm Sun; ⓂMadeleine).

French-language websites www.billetteduc.com, www.ticketac.com and www.webguichet.com all sell discounted tickets.

Cabaret

Whirling lines of feather boa-clad, high-kicking dancers at grand-scale cabarets like the can-can creator, the Moulin Rouge, are a quintessential fixture on Paris' entertainment scene – for everyone but Parisians. Still, the dazzling sets, costumes and dancing guarantee an entertaining evening (or matinee).

Tickets to these spectacles start from around €90 (from €130 with lunch, from €150 with dinner), and usually include a half-bottle of champagne. Advance reservations are essential.

Moulin Rouge CABARET
(Map p198; ☏01 53 09 82 82; www.moulinrouge. fr; 82 bd de Clichy, 18e; ⓂBlanche) Immortalised in the posters of Toulouse-Lautrec, the Moulin Rouge twinkles beneath a 1925 replica of its original red windmill. Yes, it's rife with bus-tour crowds. But it's a whirl of fantastical costumes, sets, choreography and champagne.

FREE SHOWS

Paris' eclectic gaggle of clowns, mime artists, living statues, acrobats, rollerbladers, buskers and other street entertainers can be bags of fun and cost substantially less than a theatre ticket (a few coins in the hat is a sweet gesture). Some excellent musicians perform in the long echo-filled corridors of the metro, a privilege that artists have to audition for. Outside, you can be sure of a good show at:

Place Georges Pompidou, 4e In front of the Centre Pompidou.

Pont St-Louis, 4e Bridge linking Paris' two islands (best enjoyed with Berthillon ice cream in hand; see box text p209).

Pont au Double, 4e Pedestrian bridge linking Notre Dame with the Left Bank.

Place Jean du Bellay, 1er Musicians and fire-eaters near the Fontaine des Innocents.

Parc de la Villette, 19e African drummers at the weekend.

Place du Tertre, Montmartre, 18e Montmartre's original main square wins hands down as Paris' busiest street-artist stage.

GAY & LESBIAN PARIS

The Marais (4e), especially the areas around the intersection of rue Ste-Croix de la Bretonnerie and rue des Archives, and eastwards to rue Vieille du Temple, has been Paris' main centre of gay nightlife for some three decades. There are also a few bars and clubs within walking distance of bd de Sébastopol. Other venues are scattered city-wide. The lesbian scene is less public than its gregarious male counterpart, and centres around a few Marais cafes and bars, particularly along rues des Écouffes.

The single best source of info on gay and lesbian Paris is the **Centre Gai et Lesbien de Paris** (CGL; ☎01 43 57 21 47; www.centrelgbtparis.org; 61-63 rue Beaubourg, 3e; ⊙6-8pm Mon, 3.30-8pm Tue-Thu, 1-8pm Fri & Sat; Ⓜ Rambuteau or Arts et Métiers), with a large library and happening bar.

Our top choices include:

Open Café (Map p194; www.opencafe.fr; 17 rue des Archives, 4e; ⊙daily; Ⓜ Hôtel de Ville) This wide, white-seated pavement terrace in the Marais is prime talent-watching.

Scream Club (Map p194; www.scream-paris.com; 18 rue du Faubourg du Temple, 11e; ⊙daily; Ⓜ Belleville or Goncourt) Saturday night's the night at 'Paris' biggest gay party'

3w Kafé (Map p194; 8 rue des Écouffes, 4e; ⊙Tue-Sat; Ⓜ St-Paul) For women.

Le Tango (Map p194; www.boite-a-frissons.fr; 13 rue au Maire, 3e; ⊙Fri-Sun; Ⓜ Arts et Métiers) Historic 1930s dance hosting legendary gay tea dances.

Le Lido de Paris
CABARET

(Map p188; ☎01 40 76 56 10; www.lido.fr; 116bis av des Champs-Élysées, 8e; Ⓜ George V) Founded at the close of WWII, this gets top marks for its sets and the lavish costumes of its 70 artists, including the famed Bluebell Girls and now the Lido Boy Dancers.

Live Music

Palais Omnisports de Paris-Bercy (Map p188; www.bercy.fr; 8 bd de Bercy, 12e; Ⓜ Bercy); **Le Zénith** (Map p188; ☎01 55 80 09 38, 08 90 71 02 07; www.le-zenith.com; 211 av Jean Jaurès, 19e; Ⓜ Porte de Pantin) and **Stade de France** (☎08 92 39 01 00; www.stadefrance.com; rue Francis de Pressensé, ZAC du Cornillon Nord, St-Denis La Plaine; Ⓜ St-Denis-Porte de Paris) are Paris' big-name venues. But it's the smaller concert halls loaded with history and charm that most fans favour.

Salle Pleyel
CLASSICAL

(Map p188; ☎01 42 56 13 13; www.sallepleyel.fr; 252 rue du Faubourg St-Honoré, 8e; ⊙box office noon-7pm Mon-Sat, to 8pm on day of performance; Ⓜ Ternes) This highly regarded hall dating from the 1920s hosts many of Paris' finest classical-music recitals and concerts, including those by the celebrated **Orchestre de Paris** (www.orchestredeparis.com).

Point Éphémère
LIVE MUSIC

(Map p188; www.pointephemere.org; 200 quai de Valmy, 10e; ⊙noon-2am Mon-Sat, noon-10pm Sun;

☎; Ⓜ Louis Blanc) This arts and music venue by the Canal St-Martin attracts an underground crowd for drinks, meals, concerts, dance nights and even art exhibitions.

Le Nouveau Casino
LIVE MUSIC

(Map p188; www.nouveaucasino.net; 109 rue Oberkampf, 11e; ⊙Tue-Sun; Ⓜ Parmentier) This club-concert annexe of **Café Charbon** (Map p188; www.lecafecharbon.com; 109 rue Oberkampf, 11e; ⊙daily; ☎; Ⓜ Parmentier) has made a name for itself amid the bars of Oberkampf with its live music concerts and lively weekend club nights. Electro, pop, deep house, rock – the program is eclectic, underground and always up to the minute.

La Cigale
LIVE MUSIC

(Map p198; ☎01 49 25 81 75; www.lacigale.fr; 120 bd de Rochechouart, 18e; admission €25-60; Ⓜ Anvers or Pigalle) A historical monument, this music hall dates from 1887 but was redecorated 100 years later by Philippe Starck.

Le Vieux Belleville
LIVE MUSIC

(Map p188; www.le-vieux-belleville.com; 12 rue des Envierges, 20e; Ⓜ Pyrénées) This old-fashioned bistro and *musette* at the top of Parc de Belleville is an atmospheric venue for performances of *chansons* featuring accordions and an organ grinder.

Cabaret Sauvage
WORLD MUSIC

(Map p188; www.cabaretsauvage.com; 221 av Jean Jaurès, 19e; Ⓜ Porte de la Villette) This very cool space in the Parc de la Villette (it looks like a gigantic yurt) hosts African, reggae and raï concerts, and DJ nights that last till dawn. Occasional hip-hop and indie acts pass through.

Le Baiser Salé
LIVE MUSIC

(Map p194; www.lebaisersale.com; 58 rue des Lombards, 2e; ☺daily; Ⓜ Châtelet) One of several jazz clubs located on this street, this *salle de jazz* (jazz room) has concerts of jazz, Afro and Latin jazz and jazz fusion. Combining big names and unknown artists, it is known for its relaxed vibe and gift for discovering new talents. The Monday night *soirée bœuf* (jam session) is free.

Au Limonaire
LIVE MUSIC

(Map p198; ☏01 45 23 33 33; http://limonaire.free.fr; 18 cité Bergère, 9e; ☺7pm-midnight; Ⓜ Grands Boulevards) This little wine bar is one of the best places to listen to traditional French *chansons* and local singer-songwriters. Entry is free, the wine is good and dinner is served (plat du jour €7). Reserve if you plan to dine.

Clubbing

Paris' residential make-up means nightclubs aren't ubiquitous. Lacking a mainstream scene, clubbing tends to be underground and mobile, making blogs, forums and websites the savviest means of keeping apace with what's happening. The best DJs and their followings have short stints in a certain venue before moving on, and the scene's hippest *soirées clubbing* (clubbing events) float between venues – including the city's many dance-driven bars.

La Scène Bastille
NIGHTCLUB

(Map p188; www.scenebastille.com; 2bis rue des Taillandiers, 11e; ☺Thu-Sun; Ⓜ Bastille or Ledru-Rollin) The 'Bastille Scene' puts on a mixed bag of concerts but focuses on electro, funk and hip hop.

Le Batofar
NIGHTCLUB

(Map p188; www.batofar.org; opp 11 quai François Mauriac, 13e; ☺9pm-midnight Mon & Tue, to 4am or later Wed-Sun; Ⓜ Quai de la Gare or Bibliothèque) This much-loved, red-metal tugboat with rooftop bar and restaurant is known for its edgy, experimental music policy and live performances, mostly electro-oriented but also incorporating hiphop, new wave, rock, punk or jazz.

Le Divan du Monde
LIVE MUSIC

(Map p198; www.divandumonde.com; 75 rue des Martyrs, 18e; ☺Fri & Sat, open for events Mon-Fri; Ⓜ Pigalle) Inventive, open-minded, cross-cultural venue in Pigalle.

Le Rex Club
NIGHTCLUB

(Map p198; www.rexclub.com; 5 bd Poissonnière, 2e; ☺Wed-Sat; Ⓜ Bonne Nouvelle) Attached to the art deco Grand Rex cinema, this is Paris' premier house and techno venue where some of the world's hottest DJs strut their stuff on a 70-speaker, multidiffusion sound system.

Bus Palladium
NIGHTCLUB

(Map p198; www.lebuspalladium.com; 6 rue Pierre Fontaine, 9e; ☺11pm-5am Tue, Fri & Sat; Ⓜ Blanche) Once the place to be back in the 1960s, the Bus is now back in business 50 years later, with funky DJs and a mixed bag of performances by indie and pop groups.

🔒 Shopping

As in most capital cities, shops are spread across different neighbourhoods, inspiring very different styles of shopping. Annual, month-long *soldes* (sales) see prices slashed by as much as 50%; they start up in mid-January and again in mid-June.

Key areas to mooch with no particular purchase in mind are the maze of backstreet lanes in the Marais (3e and 4e), around St-Germain des Prés (6e), and parts of Montmartre and Pigalle (9e and 18e). Or perhaps you have something specific to buy?

Designer haute couture The world's most famous designers stylishly jostle for window space on av Montaigne, av Georges V and rue du Faubourg St-Honoré, 8e.

Chain-store fashion Find Gap, H&M, Zara and other major, super-sized chain stores on rue de Rivoli in the 1er, Les Halles in the 2e, and av des Champs-Élysées, 8e.

Department stores On and around bd Haussmann, 9e, including Paris' famous Galeries Lafayette at No 40 and Printemps at No 64.

Factory outlets Cut-price fashion for men, women and kids the length of rue d'Alésia, 14e.

Hip fashion & art Young designers crowd rue Charlot, 3e, and beyond in the northern Haut Marais.

Fine art & antiques Right Bank place des Vosges, 4e, and Left Bank Carré Rive Gauche, 6e.

Design Eames, eat your heart out! Boutique galleries specialising in modern furniture, art and design (1950s to present) stud rue Mazarine and rue de Seine, 6e.

Information

Dangers & Annoyances

Paris is generally safe. Metro stations best avoided late at night include: Châtelet-Les Halles and its corridors; Château Rouge in Montmartre; Gare du Nord; Strasbourg St-Denis; Réaumur Sébastopol; and Montparnasse Bienvenüe.

Pickpocketing and thefts from handbags and packs is a problem wherever there are crowds (especially of tourists).

Medical Services

American Hospital of Paris (☎01 46 41 25 25; www.american-hospital.org; 63 bd Victor Hugo, Neuilly-sur-Seine; MPont de Levallois) Private hospital offering emergency 24-hour medical and dental care.

Hertford British Hospital (☎01 47 59 59 59; www.ihfb.org; 3 rue Barbès, Levallois; MAnatole France) A less expensive, private, English-speaking option than the American Hospital.

Hôpital Hôtel Dieu (☎01 42 34 82 34; www.aphp.fr; 1 place du Parvis Notre Dame, 4e; MCité) One of the city's main government-run public hospitals; after 8pm use the emergency entrance on rue de la Cité.

Pharmacie Les Champs (☎01 45 62 02 41; Galerie des Champs, 84 av des Champs-Élysées, 8e; ⊙24hr; MGeorge V)

Tourist Information

Paris Convention & Visitors Bureau (Office de Tourisme et de Congrès de Paris; Map p188; ☎08 92 68 30 00; www.parisinfo.com; 25-27 rue des Pyramides, 1er; ⊙9am-7pm Jun-Oct, shorter hrs rest of year; MPyramides) Main tourist office with several branches around the city.

Getting There & Away

Air

Aéroport Roissy Charles de Gaulle (CDG; ☎01 70 36 39 50; www.aeroportsdeparis.fr) Three terminals, 30km northeast of Paris in the suburb of Roissy.

Aéroport d'Orly (ORY; ☎01 70 36 39 50; www.aeroportsdeparis.fr) Aéroport d'Orly is the older, smaller of Paris' two major airports, 19km south of the city.

Aéroport Beauvais (BVA; ☎08 92 68 20 66; www.aeroportbeauvais.com) Used by charter companies and budget airlines, 75km north of Paris.

TOP THREE FLEA MARKETS

Marché aux Puces de Montreuil (av du Professeur André Lemière, 20e; ⊙8am-7.30pm Sat-Mon; MPorte de Montreuil) Particularly known for its secondhand clothing, designer seconds, engravings, jewellery, linen, crockery and old furniture.

Marché aux Puces de St-Ouen (www.marcheauxpuces-saintouen.com; rue des Rosiers, av Michelet, rue Voltaire, rue Paul Bert & rue Jean-Henri Fabre; ⊙9am-6pm Sat, 10am-6pm Sun, 11am-5pm Mon; MPorte de Clignancourt) Around since the late 19th century, and said to be Europe's largest.

Marché aux Puces de la Porte de Vanves (Map p188; http://pucesdevanves.typepad.com; av Georges Lafenestre & av Marc Sangnier, 14e; ⊙from 7am Sat & Sun; MPorte de Vanves) The smallest and, some say, friendliest of the trio.

Bus

Eurolines (☎01 43 54 11 99; www.eurolines.fr; 55 rue St-Jacques, 5e; ⊙9.30am-6.30pm Mon-Fri, 10am-1pm & 2-5pm Sat; MCluny–La Sorbonne)

Gare Routiére Internationale de Paris-Galliéni (☎08 92 89 90 91; 28 av du Général de Gaulle; MGalliéni)

Train

Paris has six major train stations. For mainline train information contact **SNCF** (☎08 91 36 20 20, timetables 08 91 67 68 69; www.sncf.fr).

Gare d'Austerlitz (bd de l'Hôpital, 13e; MGare d'Austerlitz) Trains to/from Spain and Portugal, the Loire Valley and southwestern France.

Gare de l'Est (bd de Strasbourg, 10e; MGare de l'Est) Trains to/from Luxembourg, parts of Switzerland (Basel, Lucerne, Zurich), southern Germany (Frankfurt, Munich) and points further east; regular services to eastern France (Champagne, Alsace and Lorraine).

Gare de Lyon (bd Diderot, 12e; MGare de Lyon) Trains to/from parts of Switzerland (Bern, Geneva, Lausanne), Italy and points beyond; domestic services to areas southeast of Paris, including Dijon, Lyon, Provence, the Côte d'Azur and the Alps.

Gare Montparnasse (av du Maine & bd de Vaugirard, 15e; MMontparnasse Bienvenüe) Trains to/from Brittany and places en route from Paris (eg Chartres, Angers, Nantes);

also to Tours, Nantes, Bordeaux and other destinations in southwestern France.

Gare du Nord (rue de Dunkerque, 10e; MGare du Nord) Terminus of high-speed Thalys trains to/from Amsterdam, Brussels, Cologne and Geneva, and Eurostar to London; domestic services to Paris' northern suburbs and northern France.

Gare St-Lazare (rue St-Lazare & rue d'Amsterdam, 8e; MSt-Lazare) Trains to Normandy.

❶ Getting Around

To/From the Airports

Getting into town is straightforward and inexpensive thanks to a fleet of public-transport options. Bus drivers sell tickets. Children aged four to 11 years pay half-price on most services.

AÉROPORT ROISSY CHARLES DE GAULLE

RER B (☑32 46; www.ratp.fr; adult €9.10; ⊙5am-11pm) Departs every 10 to 15 minutes, serving Gare du Nord, Châtelet-Les Halles and St-Michel–Notre Dame stations in the city centre. Journey time approximately 35 minutes.

Air France Bus 2 (☑08 92 35 08 20; http://videocdn.airfrance.com/cars-airfrance; adult €15; ⊙6am-11pm) To/from the Arc de Triomphe and Porte Maillot metro station (35 to 50 minutes).

Air France Bus 4 (☑08 92 35 08 20; http://videocdn.airfrance.com/cars-airfrance; adult €16.50; ⊙6am-10pm from Roissy Charles de Gaulle, 6am-9.30pm from Paris) Shuttles every 30 minutes to/from Gare de Lyon and Gare Montparnasse (50 to 55 minutes).

Noctilien Buses 140 & 143 (☑32 46; www.noctilien.fr; adult €7.60; ⊙12.30am-5.30am) Hourly night buses to/from Gare de l'Est (140 & 143) and Gare de Nord (143).

RATP Bus 350 (☑32 46; www.ratp.fr; adult €5.10 or 3 metro tickets; ⊙5.30am-11pm) Every 30 minutes to/from Gare de l'Est and Gare du Nord (both one hour).

Roissybus (☑32 46; www.ratp.fr; adult €10; ⊙5.30am-11pm) Every 30 minutes to/from Opéra, 9e (45 minutes).

AÉROPORT D'ORLY

Air France Bus 1 (☑08 92 35 08 20; http://videocdn.airfrance.com/cars-airfrance; adult €11.50; ⊙5am-10.20pm from Orly, 6am-11.20pm from Invalides) Shuttle bus to/from Gare Montparnasse (35 minutes), Invalides in the 7e, and the Arc de Triomphe.

Orlybus (☑32 46; www.ratp.fr; adult €6.90; ⊙6am-11.20pm from Orly, 5.35am-11.05pm from Paris) RATP bus every 15 to 20 minutes to/from metro Denfert Rochereau (30 minutes) in the 14e.

Orlyval (☑32 46; www.ratp.fr; adult €10.75; ⊙6am-11pm) Orlyval automatic metro from

Orly to Antony station, then RER B to Gare du Nord, Châtelet-Les Halles and St-Michel–Notre Dame RER stations in the city centre.

BETWEEN ORLY & CHARLES DE GAULLE

Air France Shuttle Bus 3 (www.cars-airfrance.com; adult €20; ⊙6am-10.30pm) Every 30 minutes; journey time 30 to 45 minutes.

AÉROPORT PARIS-BEAUVAIS

Navette Officielle (Official Shuttle Bus; ☑08 92 68 20 64; airport 08 92 68 20 66; adult €15) Links Beauvais airport with metro station Porte de Maillot; journey time 1¼ hours.

Bicycle

Vélib' (www.velib.paris.fr; day/week subscription €1/5, bike hire per 1st/2nd/additional 30min free/€2/4) With this self-service bike scheme pick up a bike from one roadside Vélib' station and drop it off at another. To get a bike, first purchase a 1-/7-day subscription (€1.70/8) online or at any bike terminal (by credit card with a microchip).

Boat

Batobus (www.batobus.com; 1-/2-/5-day pass €15/18/21; ⊙10am-9.30pm Apr-Aug, to 7pm rest of year) Fleet of glassed-in trimarans dock at eight piers along the Seine; buy tickets at each stop or tourist offices and jump on and off as you like.

Public Transport

Paris' public transit system is operated by the **RATP** (www.ratp.fr). The same RATP tickets are valid on the metro, RER, buses, trams and Montmartre funicular. A single ticket is €1.70 while a *carnet* of 10 costs 12.70.

One ticket covers travel between any two metro stations (no return journeys) for 1½ hours; you can transfer between buses and between buses and trams, but not from metro to bus or vice versa.

Keep your ticket until you exit the station; ticket inspectors can fine you if you can't produce a valid ticket.

BUS Buses run from 5.30am to 8.30pm Monday to Saturday, with certain evening lines continuing until midnight or 12.30am, when hourly **Noctilien** (www.noctilien.fr) night buses kick in.

Short bus rides (ie rides in one or two bus zones) cost one metro/bus ticket (€1.70 or €1.90 direct from the driver); longer rides require two. Remember to punch single-journey tickets in the *composteur* (ticket machine) next to the driver.

METRO & RER Paris' underground network consists of the 14-line metro and the RER, a network of suburban train lines. Each metro train is known by the name of its terminus. The last metro train on each line begins sometime between 12.35am and 1.15am (2.15am Friday and Saturday), before starting up again around 5.30am.

TOURIST PASSES The **Mobilis Card** allows unlimited travel for one day in two to five zones (€6.40 to €14.20) on the metro, the RER, buses, trams and the Montmartre funicular; while the **Paris Visite** pass allows unlimited travel (including to/from airports) plus discounted entry to museums and activities and costs €9.75/15.85/21.60/31.15 for one to three zones for one/two/three/five days.

TRAVEL PASSES Navigo (www.navigo.fr), like London's Oyster or Hong Kong's Octopus cards, consists of a weekly, monthly or yearly unlimited pass that can be recharged at Navigo machines in most metro stations; swipe the card across the electronic panel to go through turnstiles. Standard Navigo passes, available to anyone with an address in Île de France, are free but take up to three weeks to be issued. Otherwise, pay €5 for a **Nagivo Découverte** (Navigo Discovery) card, issued on the spot. Both require a passport photo and can be recharged for periods of one week or more.

Otherwise, weekly tickets (*coupon hebdomadaire*) cost €19.15 for zones 1 and 2, valid Monday to Sunday.

Taxi

The flagfall is €2.40, plus €0.96 per km within the city limits from 10am and 5pm Monday to Saturday (Tarif A; white light on meter), and €1.21 per kilometre from 5pm to 10am, all day Sunday, and public holidays (Tarif B; orange light on meter).

Alpha Taxis (☎01 45 85 85 85; www.alpha taxis.com)

Taxis Bleus (☎01 49 36 10 10; www.taxis -bleus.com)

Taxis G7 (☎01 41 27 66 99; www.taxisg7.fr)

AROUND PARIS

Bordered by five rivers – the Epte, Aisne, Eure, Yonne and Marne – the area around Paris looks rather like a giant island, and indeed is known as Île de France. Centuries ago this was where French kings retreated to extravagant chateaux in Versailles and Fontainebleau. These days such royal castles have been joined by a kingdom of an altogether different kind.

Disneyland Resort Paris

In 1992, Mickey Mouse, Snow White and chums set up shop on reclaimed sugar-beet fields 32km east of Paris at a cost of €4.6 billion. Though not quite as over-the-top as its American cousin, France's Disneyland packs in the crowds nonetheless.

The main **Disneyland Park** (☺10am-8pm Mon-Fri, 9am-8pm Sat & Sun Sep-May, 9am-11pm Jun-Aug, hours can vary) comprises five *pays* (lands), including the 1900s idealised **Main St USA**, a recreation of the American Wild West in **Frontierland** with the legendary Big Thunder Mountain ride, futuristic **Discoveryland**, and the exotic-themed **Adventureland**, where you'll find the Pirates of the Caribbean and the spiralling 360-degrees roller coaster, Indiana Jones and the Temple of Peril. Pinocchio, Snow White and other fairy-tale characters come to life in the candy-coated heart of the park, **Fantasyland**.

Adjacent **Walt Disney Studios Park** (☺9am-7pm late Jun-early Sep, 10am-7pm Mon-Fri & 9am-7pm Sat & Sun early Sep-late Jun) has a sound stage, backlot and animation studios illustrating how films, TV programs and cartoons are produced.

Standard admission fees at **Disneyland Resort Paris** (☎hotel booking 01 60 30 60 30, restaurant reservations 01 60 30 40 50; www.disneylandparis.com; one-day admission adult/child €59/53; ☺hours vary; Ⓜ Marne-la-Vallée/Chessy) include admission to either Disneyland Park or Walt Disney, but there's always a multitude of different passes, special offers and accommodation/transport packages on offer.

Marne-la-Vallée/Chessy, Disneyland's RER station, is served by line A4; trains run every 15 minutes or so from central Paris (€7.10, 35 to 40 minutes).

Versailles
POP 88,930

Louis XIV transformed his father's hunting lodge into the monumental Château de Versailles in the mid-17th century, and it remains France's most famous, grandest palace. Situated in the prosperous, leafy and bourgeois suburb of Versailles, 28km southwest of Paris, the baroque palace was the kingdom's political capital and the seat of the royal court from 1682 up until 1789, when revolutionaries massacred the palace guard and dragged Louis XVI and Marie Antoinette back to Paris to be guillotined.

◉ Sights

Château de Versailles   PALACE
(☎01 30 83 78 00; www.chateauversailles.fr; admission passport (estate-wide access) €18, with

ⓘ **VERSAILLES TOP TIPS**

» Don't go on Monday (closed); avoid Tuesday and Sunday (busiest days).

» Queues for tickets and entering the chateau spiral out of control by noon: arrive early morning.

» Pre-purchase tickets on the chateau's website and head straight to Entrance A.

» Access areas otherwise off limits with a **guided tour** (📞01 30 83 77 88; tours €16; ⊙English-language tours 9.30am & 2pm Tue-Sun) of the Private Apartments of Louis XV and Louis XVI and the Opera House or Royal Chapel. Tour tickets include access to the most famous parts of the palace, such as the Hall of Mirrors and the King's and Queen's State Apartments; prebook online.

» The estate is vast: rent an **electric car** (📞01 39 66 97 66; per hr €30), **bike** (📞01 39 66 97 66; per hr €6.50) or **boat** (📞01 39 66 97 66; per hr €15).

» Be dazzled by 17th-century **Bassin de Neptune** (Neptune's Fountain) dancing during the **Grandes Eaux Musicales** (adult/child €7.50/6.50; ⊙11am-noon & 3.30-5pm Tue, Sat & Sun Apr-Sep) and after-dark **Grandes Eaux Nocturnes** (adult/child €23/19; ⊙9-11.20pm Sat mid-Jun–Aug), magical, summertime water displays set to classical music.

musical events €25, palace €15; ⊙8am-6pm Tue-Sat, 9am-6pm Sun Apr-Oct, 8.30am-5.30pm Tue-Sat, 9am-5.30pm Sun Nov-Mar) Built in the mid-17th century to project the absolute power of the French monarchy, Versailles reflects Louis XIV's taste for profligate luxury and his boundless appetite for grandstanding. In 1661 under the guidance of architect Louis Le Vau, painter and interior designer Charles Le Brun, and landscape artist André Le Nôtre, workers flattened hills, drained marshes and relocated forests to create the seemingly endless gardens, ponds and fountains. Inside, every moulding, cornice, ceiling and door was decorated with the most luxurious, ostentatious of appointments, peaking in opulence with the **Galerie des Glaces** (Hall of Mirrors), a 75m-long ballroom with 17 huge mirrors on one side and, on the other, an equal number of windows looking out over the gardens and the setting sun.

Until the current €400 million restoration program is completed in 2020 at least a part of the palace is likely to be clad in scaffolding when you visit.

✗ **Eating**

Eateries within the estate include tearoom **Angelina** (www.angelina-versailles.fr; mains €10-24; ⊙10am-6pm Tue-Sat Apr-Oct, to 5pm Tue-Sat Nov-Mar), famed for its decadent hot chocolate. In addition to the branch by the Petit Trianon, there's another inside the palace.

In the Louis XIV–created town of Versailles, rue de Satory is lined with restaurants serving cuisine from all over the globe.

For an enjoyable culinary experience, check out **La Cuisine de Bertrand** (www.lacuisinedebertrand.com), where you can learn traditional French cooking in Bertrand's Versailles home, followed by a meal with his family. Produce is from the chateau's Potager du Roi (royal veg patch).

À la Ferme REGIONAL CUISINE €€
(📞01 39 53 10 81; www.alaferme-versailles.com; 3 rue du Maréchal Joffre; lunch menus €13.80-23.90, dinner menus €19.50-23.90; ⊙Wed-Sun) Cowhide seats and rustic garlands strung from old wood beams add a country air to 'At the Farm', a temple to grilled meats and cuisine from southwest France.

ⓘ **Getting There & Away**

The easiest way to get to/from Versailles is aboard RER line C5 (€4.20, 45 minutes, every 15 minutes) from Paris' Left Bank RER stations to Versailles-Rive Gauche, 700m southeast of the chateau.

Chartres

POP 45,600

The magnificent 13th-century cathedral of Chartres, crowned by two very different spires – one Gothic, the other Romanesque – rises from rich farmland 88km southwest of Paris and dominates the medieval town. With its astonishing blue stained glass and other treasures, France's best-preserved medieval basilica is a must-see.

◉ Sights

Cathédrale Notre Dame   CATHEDRAL
(www.diocese-chartres.com; place de la Cathédrale;
⏰8.30am-7.30pm, to 10pm Tue, Fri & Sun Jun-Aug)
One of the crowning architectural achievements of Western civilisation, this 130m-
long Gothic cathedral was built during the
first quarter of the 13th century to replace a
Romanesque cathedral that had been devastated by fire – along with much of the town –
in 1194. It is France's best-preserved medieval
cathedral, having been spared postmedieval
modifications, the ravages of war and the
Reign of Terror.

The cathedral's west, north and south
entrances have superbly ornamented triple
portals, but the west entrance, known as the
Portail Royal, is the only one that predates
the fire. Carved from 1145 to 1155, its superb
statues represent the glory of Christ in the
centre, and the Nativity and the Ascension
to the right and left, respectively. The structure's other main Romanesque feature is the
105m-high **Clocher Vieux** (Old Bell Tower;
also called the Tour Sud or 'South Tower') -
the tallest Romanesque steeple still standing.
Superb views of three-tiered flying buttresses
and the 19th-century copper roof, turned
green by verdigris, reward the 350-step hike
up the 112m-high **Clocher Neuf** (New Bell
Tower, also known as North Tower).

Inside, 172 extraordinary **stained-glass
windows**, mainly from the 13th century,
form one of the most important ensembles
of medieval stained glass in the world. The
three most exquisite – renowned for the
depth and intensity of their tones, famously
known as 'Chartres blue' – are above the
west entrance and below the rose window.

To study the extraordinary detail of the
cathedral close up, rent binoculars (€2)
from Chartres **tourist office** (☎02 37 18 26
26; www.chartres-tourisme.com; place de la Cathédrale; ⏰9am-6pm Mon-Sat, 9.30am-5pm Sun),
across the square from the cathedral's main
entrance.

✕ Eating

TOP
CHOICE **Le Saint-Hilaire**   REGIONAL CUISINE €€
(☎02 37 30 97 57; www.restaurant-saint-hilaire.fr; 11
rue du Pont Saint-Hilaire; 2-/3-course menus from
€27/42; ⏰lunch & dinner Tue-Sat) Local products are transformed into to-die-for dishes –
think stuffed mushrooms with lentils, snails
in puff pastry with leek fondue, seasonal

lobster, aromatic cheese platters – at this
pistachio-painted, wood-beamed charmer.

La Chocolaterie   PATISSERIE, TEAHOUSE €
(14 place du Cygne; ⏰8am-7.30pm Tue-Sat, 10am-
7.30pm Sun & Mon) Revel in local life at the
open-air flower market are on place du
Cygne. Its hot chocolate and macarons, flavoured with orange, apricot, peanut, pineapple, and so on are sublime, as are its crêpes
and miniature madeleine sponge cakes.

❶ Getting There & Away

Frequent SNCF trains link Paris' Gare Montparnasse (€14.40, 55 to 70 minutes) with Chartres
via Versailles-Chantiers (€12.10, 45 minutes to
one hour).

LILLE, FLANDERS &
THE SOMME

When it comes to culture, cuisine, beer,
shopping and dramatic views of land
and sea, the friendly Ch'tis (residents of
France's northern tip) and their region
compete with the best France has to offer.
Highlights include Flemish-style Lille, the
cross-Channel shopping centre of Calais,
and the moving battlefields and cemeteries
of WWI.

Lille
POP 232,210
Lille (Rijsel in Flemish) may be the country's most underrated major city. In recent
decades this once-grimy industrial metropolis has transformed itself – with generous
government help – into a glittering and
self-confident cultural and commercial hub.
Highlights of the city include an attractive
Old Town with a strong Flemish accent, three
renowned art museums, stylish shopping and
a cutting-edge, student-driven nightlife.

◉ Sights

Vieux Lille   OLD TOWN
Lille's Old Town, which begins just north
of place du Général de Gaulle, is justly
proud of its restored 17th- and 18th-century
houses. Those along **rue de la Monnaie**
house the city's chicest boutiques and the
Musée de l'Hospice Comtesse (www.
mairie-lille.fr; 32 rue de la Monnaie; adult/student/
child €3.50/2.50/free; ⏰10am-12.30pm & 2-6pm,

closed Mon morning & Tue), featuring mainly religious art.

Palais des Beaux Arts   MUSEUM

(Fine Arts Museum; www.pba-lille.fr; place de la République; adult/student/child €6.50/4/free; ⊙2-6pm Mon, 10am-6pm Wed-Sun; MRépublique-Beaux Arts) Lille's world-renowned Fine Arts Museum displays a truly first-rate collection of 15th- to 20th-century paintings, including works by Rubens, Van Dyck and Manet.

Musée d'Art Moderne Lille-Métropole   MUSEUM

(☑03 20 19 68 68; www.musee-lam.fr; 1 allée du Musée; adult/student/child €7/5/free; ⊙10am-6pm Tue-Sun) Colourful, playful and just plain weird works of modern and contemporary art by masters such as Braque, Calder, Léger, Miró, Modigliani and Picasso are the big draw at this renowned, newly renovated museum and sculpture park in the Lille suburb of Villeneuve-d'Ascq, 9km east of Gare Lille-Europe. Take metro line 1 to Pont de Bois, then bus 41 (10 minutes) to Parc Urbain-Musée.

La Piscine Musée d'Art et d'Industrie   MUSEUM

(www.roubaix-lapiscine.com; 23 rue de l'Espérance, Roubaix; adult/child €4.50/free; ⊙11am-6pm Tue-Thu, 11am-8pm Fri, 1-6pm Sat & Sun; MGare Jean Lebas) Housed in an art deco municipal swimming pool (built 1927–32), this gallery, 12km northeast of Gare Lille-Europe, showcases fine arts, applied arts and sculpture in a delightfully watery environment.

🛏 Sleeping

TOP CHOICE L'Hermitage Gantois   DESIGN HOTEL €€€

(☑03 20 85 30 30; www.hotelhermitagegantois.com; 224 rue de Paris; d €219-455; @🛜; MMairie de Lille) This five-star hotel creates enchanting, harmonious spaces by complementing its rich architectural heritage – such as a Flemish-Gothic facade – with refined ultramodernism. The 67 rooms are huge and sumptuous, with Starck accessories next to Louis XV–style chairs and bathrooms that sparkle with Carrara marble. One of the four courtyards is home to a 220-year-old wisteria that's been declared a historic monument. The still-consecrated chapel was built in 1637.

Hotel Kanaï   HOTEL €

(☑03 20 57 14 78; www.hotelkanai.com; 10 rue de Bethune; s €47-98, d €65-115; ❋@🛜; MRihour) In the heart of Lille's pedestrian zone, this newer hotel offers reasonably priced rooms with a clean modern design, ranging from a cozy single tucked away on the top floor to spacious doubles with queen beds and couches; all come with coffee makers, attractive tiled bathrooms and cable internet connections. Wi-fi only reaches the lounge and breakfast area.

Hôtel Brueghel   HOTEL €€

(☑03 20 06 06 69; www.hotel-brueghel-lille.com; 5 parvis St-Maurice; s €79-95, d €89-105; 🛜; MGare Lille-Flandres) At this dependable midrange hotel halfway between Gare Lille-Flandres and the Grande Place, the 65 rooms mix vaguely antique furnishings with modern styling (though none of them offers as much Flemish charm as the lobby). Some south-facing rooms have sunny views of the adjacent church.

Auberge de Jeunesse   HOSTEL €

(☑03 20 57 08 94; www.fuaj.org; 12 rue Malpart; dm incl breakfast €21, d €42; ⊙Feb–mid-Dec; P@🛜; MMairie de Lille, République-Beaux Arts) This central former maternity hospital has 163 beds in rooms for two to eight, kitchen facilities and free parking. A few doubles have en-suite showers. Lockout 11am to 3pm (4pm Friday to Sunday).

Eating

Keep an eye out for *estaminets* (traditional eateries) serving Flemish specialities such as *carbonnade* (beef braised with Flemish beer, spice bread and brown sugar).

TOP CHOICE Chez la Vieille   FLEMISH €

(☑03 28 36 40 06; 60 rue de Gand; mains €10-14; ⊙dinner Mon, lunch & dinner Tue-Sat) Old-time prints, antiques and fresh hops hanging from the rafters create the cozy ambience of a Flemish village c 1900 at this beloved *estaminet*. Its sister restaurant Au Vieux de la Vieille (www.

OLD TOWN EAT STREETS

Rue de Gand Small, moderately priced French and Flemish restaurants.

Rue de la Monnaie Quirky restaurants here and on neighbouring side streets.

Rue Royale Ethnic cuisine (couscous, Japanese etc).

Rue Solférino & rue Masséna Lively, student-dominated cheap eats near the Palais des Beaux Arts.

estaminetlille.fr; 2-4 rue des Vieux Murs; mains €10-14; ☺lunch & dinner) serves an identical menu, with outdoor seating on picturesque cobblestoned Place de l'Oignon. The vibe at both is informal, but it's best to call ahead.

À l'Huîtrière SEAFOOD €€€
(☏03 20 55 43 41; www.huitriere.fr; 3 rue des Chats Bossus; lunch menus €45, dinner menu €110, oyster bar items from €15; ☺lunch & dinner Mon-Sat, lunch Sun Sep-Jul) On the 'Street of the Hunchback Cats', this sophisticated restaurant is well known for its fabulous seafood and wine cellar. For a lighter meal with a lower price tag, sit at the oyster bar up front, where stunning art deco trappings – including sea-themed mosaics and stained glass – create a colorful, more relaxed atmosphere.

Crêperie Beaurepaire CREPERIE €
(www.creperiebeaurepaire.com; 1 rue St-Étienne; crêpes €5-9; ☺lunch & dinner Mon-Sat; Ⓜ️Rihour) With its sunny beamed dining room, stone-walled cellar and sweet little outdoor courtyard, this hideaway just steps from place Charles de Gaulle is a lovely spot to enjoy crispy buckwheat galettes, salads and flaming dessert crêpes, accompanied by ceramic bowls full of cider.

La Source ORGANIC, VEGETARIAN €
(☏03 20 57 53 07; www.denislasource.com; 13 rue du Plat; menus €9.50-16; ☺11.30am-2pm Mon-Sat, 7-9pm Fri; ✍; Ⓜ️République Beaux Arts) This Lille institution serves delicious vegetarian, fowl and fish plats du jour, each accompanied by five hot veggie side dishes. The light, airy ambience and the diners exude health, well-being and cheer.

Marché de Wazemmes MARKET €
(place de la Nouvelle Aventure; ☺8am-2pm Tue-Thu, 8am-8pm Fri & Sat, 8am-3pm Sun & holidays; Ⓜ️Gambetta) Beloved foodie space, 1.7km southwest of the tourist office in Lille's working-class quarter of Wazemmes.

Drinking

Think two key nightlife zones: Vieux Lille's small, chic bars, and the student-oriented bars around rue Masséna and rue Solférino. In summer, pavement cafe terraces render place de la Théâtre in front of the opera prime beer-sipping terrain.

Meert TEAHOUSE
(www.meert.fr; 27 rue Esquermoise; waffles €3; ☺9.30am-7.30pm Tue-Sat, 9am-1pm & 3-7pm Sun;

NORTHERN BREWS

French Flanders brews some truly excellent *bière blonde* (lager) and *bière ambrée* (amber beer) with an alcohol content of up to 8.5%. Brands that give the Belgian brewers a run for their money include 3 Monts, Amadeus, Ambre des Flandres, Brasserie des 2 Caps, Ch'ti, Enfants de Gayant, Grain d'Orge, Hellemus, Jenlain, L'Angellus, La Wambrechies, Moulins d'Ascq, Raoul, Septante 5, St-Landelin, Triple Secret des Moines and Vieux Lille.

Ⓜ️Rihour) A delightful spot for morning coffee or mid-afternoon tea, this elegant tearoom dating to 1761 is beloved for its retro decor and its *gaufres* (waffles) filled with sweet Madagascan vanilla paste.

L'Illustration Café BAR, CAFE
(www.bar-lillustration.com; 18 rue Royale; ☺12.30pm-3am Mon-Sat, 3pm-3am Sun) Adorned with art nouveau woodwork and changing exhibits by local painters, this laid-back bar attracts artists, musicians, budding intellectuals and teachers in the mood to read, exchange weighty ideas – or just shoot the breeze. The mellow soundtrack mixes Western classical with jazz, French *chansons* and African beats.

ℹ️ Information

Tourist Office (☏from abroad +33 359 57 94 00, in France 08 91 56 20 04; www.lilletourism.com; place Rihour; ☺9am-6pm Mon-Sat, 10am-noon & 2-5pm Sun & holidays; Ⓜ️Rihour)

ℹ️ Getting There & Away

Lille has two train stations: Gare Lille-Flandres for regional services and trains to Paris' Gare du Nord (€42 to €58, one hour, 14 to 18 daily), and ultramodern Gare Lille-Europe for all other trains, including the Eurostar to London and TGV/Eurostar to Brussels-Nord (€18 to €25, 35 minutes, 12 daily).

Eurolines (☏08 92 89 90 91; www.eurolines.com; 23 parvis St-Maurice; Ⓜ️Gare Lille-Flandres) Serves cities such as Brussels (€18, 1½ hours), Amsterdam (€43, five hours) and London (€36, 5½ hours; by day via the Channel Tunnel, at night by ferry). Buses depart from blvd de Leeds near Gare Lille-Europe.

CÔTE D'OPALE

For a dramatic and beautiful intro to France, head to the 40km of majestic cliffs, sand dunes and beaches between Calais and Boulogne-sur-Mer. Known as the Côte d'Opale (Opal Coast) because of the ever-changing interplay of greys and blues in the sky and sea, it is a kaleidoscope of wind-buffeted coastal peaks, wide beaches and rolling farmland. The remains of Nazi Germany's Atlantic Wall, a chain of fortifications and gun emplacements built to prevent the Allied invasion that in the end took place in Normandy, stud the shore, which has been much loved by British beach-goers since Victorian times.

Protected by the **Parc Naturel Régional des Caps et Marais d'Opale** (www.parc-opale.fr), the area is criss-crossed by hiking paths, including the **GR120 Littoral trail** (with red-and-white trail markings) that snakes along the coast – except where the cliffs are in danger of collapse. Some trails are open to mountain bikers and horseriders. Each village along the Côte d'Opale has at least one camping ground, and most have places to eat.

By car, the D940 offers some truly spectacular vistas – or hop aboard Inglard's bus 44, which links the string of villages between Calais and Boulogne.

🛈 Getting Around

Lille's two metro lines, tramways and bus lines are run by **Transpole** (www.transpole.fr). Tickets (€1.40) are sold on buses but must be purchased *before* boarding a metro or tram. A *Pass Journée* (all-day pass) costs €4.10.

Calais

POP 75,240

As Churchill might have put it, 'Never in the field of human tourism have so many travellers passed through a place and so few stopped to visit'. Over 15 million people pass through Calais en route to the cross-Channel ferries, but few explore the town itself – it's worth it, if only to see Rodin's famous sculpture, *Les Bourgeois de Calais* (The Burghers of Calais).

👁 Sights

Beffroi de Calais   BELL TOWER
(Town Hall Belfry; place du Soldat Inconnu; adult/ child €5/3; ⏱10am-noon & 2-5.30pm, closed Mon Oct-Apr) An elevator whisks you to the top of Calais' town hall belfry, a Unesco World Heritage site, from where you can admire 360-degree views.

Burghers of Calais   SCULPTURE
(place du Soldat Inconnu) In front of Calais' Flemish Renaissance–style **Hôtel de Ville** (town hall) is Rodin's famous statue *Les Bourgeois de Calais* (The Burghers of Calais; 1895), honouring six local citizens who, in 1347, held off the besieging English forces for more than eight months. Edward III

was so impressed he ultimately spared the Calaisiens and their six leaders.

TOP CHOICE **Cité Internationale de la Dentelle et de la Mode**   MUSEUM
(International Centre of Lace & Fashion; ☎03 21 00 42 30; www.cite-dentelle.fr; 135 quai du Commerce; adult/child €5/2.50; ⏱10am-6pm Wed-Mon) Enter the intricate world of lace-making, the industry that once made Calais a textile powerhouse, at this informative, cutting-edge exhibition on the history of lace. Situated 500m southeast of the *hôtel de ville*.

🛏 Sleeping

Hôtel Meurice   HOTEL €€
(☎03 21 34 57 03; www.hotel-meurice.fr; 5-7 rue Edmond Roche; d €92-162; @🖥) This veteran downtown hotel with 39 rooms offers plenty of atmosphere, thanks to its grand lobby staircase, antique furnishings and breakfast room with garden views.

Auberge de Jeunesse   HOSTEL €
(☎03 21 34 70 20; www.auberge-jeunesse-calais. com; av Maréchal de Lattre de Tassigny; dm/s/tw incl breakfast €21/28/42; 🖥; 🚌3, 5, 9) Modern, well equipped and 200m from the beach.

🍴 Eating

Restaurants ring place d'Armes and are plentiful just south of there along rue Royale.

TOP CHOICE **Histoire Ancienne**   BISTRO €€
(☎03 21 34 11 20; www.histoire-ancienne.com; 20 rue Royale; lunch menus €15, dinner menus €19-28; ⏱lunch & dinner Tue-Sat, lunch Mon) Specialising

in French and regional dishes, some grilled over an open wood fire, this 1930s Paris-style bistro offers excellent value lunch and dinner menus in a classy dining room at the heart of town.

ℹ Information

Tourist office (☏03 21 96 62 40; www.calais-cotedopale.com; 12 bd Georges Clemenceau; ☉10am-6pm Mon-Sat, to 5pm Sun) Just across the bridge (north) from the train station.

ℹ Getting There & Around

Boat

Each day, over three dozen car ferries from Dover dock at Calais' bustling **car-ferry terminal**, 1.5km northeast of place d'Armes.

P&O Ferries (www.poferries.com; 41 place d'Armes) and **DFDS Seaways** (☏03 28 59 01 01; www.dfdsseaways.co.uk; ferry terminal) operate regular trans-Channel services. P&O accepts foot passengers; DFDS passengers with vehicles.

Shuttle buses (€2, roughly hourly from 11am to 6pm) link Gare Calais-Ville (train station) and place d'Armes (stop in front of Café de la Tour) with the car-ferry terminal. Departure times are posted at stops.

Bus

Ligne BCD (☏08 00 62 00 59; www.ligne-bcd.com) links Calais' train station (hours posted) with Dunkirk (€8.20, 50 minutes, six daily Monday to Friday, three Saturday).

Car & Motorcycle

To reach the Channel Tunnel's vehicle-loading area at Coquelles, 6km southwest of the town centre, follow the road signs on the A16 to 'Tunnel Sous La Manche' (exit 42).

Train

Calais has two train stations, linked by trains and a *navette* (shuttle bus; €2, free with train ticket).

Gare Calais-Ville (city centre) serves Amiens (€25.30, 2½ to 3½ hours, six daily), Boulogne (€7.70, 30 minutes, up to 19 daily), Dunkirk (€8.60, 50 minutes, two to six Monday to Saturday) and Lille-Flandres (€17.30, 1¼ hours, eight to 19 daily).

Gare Calais-Fréthun (TGV station 10km southwest of town near Channel Tunnel entrance) serves Paris' Gare du Nord (€44 to €61, 1¾ hours, three to six daily) and Eurostar to London's St Pancras (from €96, one hour, three daily).

Amiens

POP 137,030

One of France's most awe-inspiring Gothic cathedrals is reason enough to spend time in the former capital of Picardy, where Jules Verne spent the last two decades of his life. The mostly pedestrianised city centre, rebuilt after the war, is complemented by lovely green spaces along the Somme River. Some 25,000 students give the town a youthful feel.

◉ Sights

TOP CHOICE **Cathédrale Notre Dame** CATHEDRAL
(place Notre Dame; audioguide 1st/2nd person €4/3, north tower adult/child €5.50/free; ☉cathedral 8.30am-6.15pm daily, north tower afternoon only Wed-Mon) France's largest Gothic cathedral and a Unesco World Heritage Site, this magnificent structure was begun in 1220 to house the **skull of St John the Baptist**, framed in gold and jewels in the northern

FRANCE AMIENS

WORTH A TRIP

KILLING FIELDS

The **Battle of the Somme**, a WWI Allied offensive waged northeast of Amiens, was planned with the goal of relieving the pressure on the beleaguered French troops at Verdun. On 1 July 1916, two-dozen divisions of British, Commonwealth and French troops went 'over the top' in a massive assault along a 34km front. But German positions proved virtually unbreachable, and on the first day alone 21,392 Allied troops were killed and another 35,492 were wounded.

By the time the offensive was called off in mid-November, some 1.2 million lives had been lost: the British had advanced just 12km, the French 8km. The Battle of the Somme has since become a symbol of the meaningless slaughter of war and its killing fields and cemeteries have since become a site of pilgrimage (see www.somme-battlefields.com). Amiens tourist office supplies maps, guides and minibus tours.

outer wall of the ambulatory. Connoisseurs rave about the soaring Gothic arches (42.3m high over the transept), unity of style and immense interior.

Weather permitting, it's possible to climb the **north tower**; tickets are sold in the boutique to the left as you approach the west facade.

A free 45-minute **light show** bathes the cathedral's facade in vivid medieval colours nightly from mid-June to mid-September and for the month of December.

🛏️ Sleeping & Eating

Hôtel Victor Hugo   HOTEL €
(📞03 22 91 57 91; www.hotel-a-amiens.com; 2 rue de l'Oratoire; r €46-70; 🛜) Just a block from the cathedral, this friendly, family-run two-star hotel has 10 simple but comfortable rooms. Best value, if you don't mind a long stair climb, are the welcoming top-floor units (rooms 7 and 8) with rooftop views and lots of natural light.

Le T'chiot Zinc   BISTRO €
(📞03 22 91 43 79; 18 rue de Noyon; menus €13-27; ⊗closed Sun, also closed Mon Jul & Aug) Inviting, bistro-style decor reminiscent of the belle époque provides a fine backdrop for the tasty French and Picard cuisine, including fish dishes and *caghuse* (pork in a cream, wine vinegar and onion sauce). The proper Picard pronunciation of the restaurant's name is 'shtyoh-zang'.

ℹ️ Getting There & Away

Amiens is an important rail hub.
Calais-Ville €25.30, two to 2½ hours, six or seven daily.

DON'T MISS

THE CIDER ROAD

Normandy's signposted 40km **Route du Cidre**, about 20km east of Caen, wends its way through the **Pays d'Auge**, a rural area of orchards, pastures, hedgerows, half-timbered farmhouses and stud farms, through picturesque villages such as Cambremer and Beuvron-en-Auge. Along the way, signs reading 'Cru de Cambremer' indicate the way to about 20 small-scale, traditional producers who are happy to show you their facilities and sell you their home-grown cider (€3 a bottle) and Calvados (apple brandy).

Lille-Flandres €20.20, 1½ hours, six to 12 daily.
Paris' Gare du Nord €20.70, 1¼ to 1¾ hours, 14 to 30 daily.
Rouen €19.40, 1¼ hours, five daily.

NORMANDY

Famous for cows, cider and Camembert, this largely rural region (www.normandie-tourisme.fr) is one of France's most traditional – and most visited thanks to world-renowned sights such as the Bayeux Tapestry, historic D-Day beaches, Monet's garden at Giverny and spectacular Mont St-Michel.

Rouen

POP 119,927

With its elegant spires, beautifully restored medieval quarter and soaring Gothic cathedral, the ancient city of Rouen is a Normandy highlight. Devastated several times during the Middle Ages by fire and plague, the city was later badly damaged by WWII bombing raids, but has been meticulously rebuilt over the last six decades. The city makes an ideal base for exploring the northern Normandy coast.

◉ Sights

Église Jeanne d'Arc   CHURCH
(place du Vieux Marché; ⊗10am-noon & 2-6pm Apr-Oct) The old city's main thoroughfare, rue du Gros Horloge, runs from the cathedral west to **place du Vieux Marché**. Dedicated in 1979, the thrillingly bizarre Église Jeanne d'Arc, with its fish-scale exterior, marks the spot where 19-year-old Joan of Arc was burned at the stake in 1431.

Cathédrale Notre Dame   CATHEDRAL
(place de la Cathédrale; ⊗2-6pm Mon, 7.30am-7pm Tue-Sat, 8am-6pm Sun) Rouen's stunning Gothic cathedral, with its polished, brilliant-white facade, is the famous subject of a series of paintings by Monet. Its 75m-tall **Tour de Beurre** (Butter Tower) was financed by locals who donated to the cathedral in return for being allowed to eat butter during Lent – or so the story goes.

Musée des Beaux-Arts   MUSEUM
(📞02 35 71 28 40; www.rouen-musees.com; esplanade Marcel Duchamp; adult/child €5/free; ⊗10am-6pm Wed-Mon) Housed in a grand structure erected in 1870, Rouen's fine-arts museum features canvases by Caravaggio, Rubens,

LOUVRE-LENS

After years of anticipation, Europe's most ballyhooed new art museum has opened its doors. The innovative **Louvre-Lens** (www.louvrelens.fr; 6 rue Charles Lecocq, Lens; Galerie du Temps & Pavillon de Verre free through 2013; ⊙10am-6pm Wed-Mon) showcases hundreds of treasures from Paris' venerable Musée du Louvre in a purpose-built, state-of-the-art new exhibition space in the former coal mining town of Lens. The futuristic ensemble of buildings and surrounding parkland was designed to look like five river boats drifting haphazardly together on the grassed-over site of a former coal mine.

Intended to give museumgoers a completely different experience than its Parisian cousin, the Louvre-Lens is all about making art accessible to everyone, while showing off the Louvre's remarkable holdings in exciting new ways. Visitors are invited behind the scenes to view the museum's storerooms and watch art restoration personnel at work. There is no permanent collection; rather, the central 120m-long exhibition space, **Galerie du Temps**, displays a limited but significant, ever-rotating collection of 200+ pieces from the original Louvre. The museum's grand opening featured European masterpieces such as Delacroix's *Liberty Leading the People* and Raphael's *Portrait of Baldassare Castiglione* alongside works as diverse as ancient Mesopotamian tablets, Persian glazed tiles, Greek statues, Pompeiian frescoes, Roman bronzes, Islamic art from Spain to Syria, and 11th-century Italian mosaics.

A second building, the glass-walled **Pavillon de Verre**, displays annually changing themed exhibits (such as the Renaissance in 2013).

To celebrate Louvre-Lens' grand opening, the main collections are free of charge during 2013 (temporary exhibits cost €9). Lens, 18km north of Arras and 40km southwest of Lille, is accessible by TGV trains from Paris' Gare du Nord (€28 to €46, 65 to 70 minutes) and regional trains from Lille (€7.60, 40 minutes) and Arras (€4.20, 15 minutes).

Modigliani, Pissarro, Renoir, Sisley (lots) and (of course) several works by Monet.

🛏 Sleeping

TOP CHOICE Hôtel de Bourgtheroulde HOTEL €€€
(☑02 35 14 50 50; www.hotelsparouen.com; 15 place de la Pucelle; r €240-380; P❄🤚🛜🏊) This stunning conversion of an old private mansion brings a dash of glamour and luxury to Rouen's hotel scene. Rooms are large, gorgeously designed and feature beautiful bathrooms.

La Boulangerie B&B €€
(☑06 12 94 53 15; www.laboulangerie.fr; 59 rue St-Nicaise; d €77-92, q €150; P🛜) Tucked into a quiet side street slightly off the historic quarter, this adorable B&B occupying a former bakery offers three pleasingly decorated rooms. The largest 'Levain' room can sleep up to four people. Your charming hosts, Franck and Aminata, are a mine of local information.

Hôtel de la Cathédrale HOTEL €€
(☑02 35 71 57 95; www.hotel-de-la-cathedrale.fr; 12 rue St-Romain; s €66-86, d €76-104, q €143; @🛜) Hiding behind a 17th-century half-timbered facade, this atmospheric hotel has 27 stylishly refitted rooms, mostly overlooking a quiet plant-filled courtyard.

Auberge de Jeunesse Robec HOSTEL €
(☑02 35 08 18 50; www.fuaj.org; 3 rue de la Tour; dm/s/d incl breakfast €22/33/56; 🛜) The two- to eight-bed rooms at this modern hostel are comfortable and functional. Sadly, it's some way from the centre of town, off route de Darnétal – take bus T2 or T3 from Rouen's city centre and get off at the 'Auberge de Jeunesse' stop. Check in is from 5pm to 10pm only.

🍴 Eating

Little eateries crowd the north side of rue Martainville. For ethnic cuisine head two blocks south to rue des Augustins. More restaurants can be found along rue de Fontenelle (a block west of Église Jeanne d'Arc), and a few blocks east along rue Ecuyère.

TOP CHOICE Les Nymphéas FRENCH €€
(☑02 35 89 26 69; www.lesnympheas-rouen.com; 7-9 rue de la Pie; mains €29-37, menus €34-52; ⊙lunch & dinner Tue-Sat) Its formal table settings arrayed under 16th-century beams, this fine restaurant serves cuisine based on fresh ingredients.

DON'T MISS

MAISON DE CLAUDE MONET

Monet's home for the last 43 years of his life is now the delightful **Maison et Jardins de Claude Monet** (☑02 32 51 28 21; www.fondation-monet.com; adult/child €9/5; ☺9.30am-5.30pm Apr-Oct), where you can view the Impressionist's pastel-pink house and famous gardens with lily pond, Japanese bridge draped in purple wisteria, and so on. Early to late spring, daffodils, tulips, rhododendrons, wisteria and irises bloom in the flowery gardens, followed by poppies and lilies. By June, nasturtiums, roses and sweet peas are in flower, while September is the month to see dahlias, sunflowers and hollyhocks.

The gardens are in Giverny, 66km southeast of Rouen. Several trains (€10.80, 40 minutes) leave Rouen before noon, with hourly return trains between 5pm and 8pm. From Paris' Gare St-Lazare up to 15 daily trains run to Vernon (€13.30, 50 minutes), 7km west of Giverny, from where shuttle buses (€6.50 return, three to six daily April to October) shunt passengers to Giverny.

Let chef Patrick Kukurudz and his team seduce you with meat and fish dishes accompanied with divinely inspired sauces. Even the cheaper lunch menu (€34) is exquisite.

Minute et Mijoté BISTRO €€
(58 rue de Fontenelle; mains €20, menus €13-30; ☺lunch & dinner Mon-Sat) This smart bistro is one of our favourite finds in Rouen. The trademark here is freshness and great value for money, hence its fast-growing reputation. There's outdoor seating in summer.

L'Espiguette BISTRO €
(☑02 35 71 66 27; 25 place St-Amand; mains €13-19, lunch menu €11; ☺lunch & dinner Tue-Sat) A growing number of local connoisseurs are enthusiastic about this place, which overlooks a picturesque square. No culinary acrobatics here, just pared-down classics such as *joue de bœuf* (ox cheek), beef sirloin and salads. Its fixed-priced menu, with loads of good choices, is a great deal.

❶ Information

Tourist office (☑02 32 08 32 40; www.rouentourisme.com; 25 place de la Cathédrale; ☺9am-7pm Mon-Sat, 9.30am-12.30pm & 2-6pm Sun & holidays)

❶ Getting There & Away

TRAIN Direct services from Rouen train station, just north of the city centre.
Amiens from €19.40, 1¼ hours, four or five daily
Caen from €24.90, 1½ hours, eight to 10 daily
Dieppe from €11.10, 45 minutes, 14 to 16 daily Monday to Saturday, six Sunday
Le Havre €14.60, 50 minutes, 20 daily Monday to Saturday, 10 Sunday
Paris St-Lazare €21.90, 1¼ hours, at least hourly

Bayeux

POP 14,350

Bayeux has become famous throughout the English-speaking world thanks to a 68m-long piece of painstakingly embroidered cloth: the 11th-century Bayeux Tapestry, whose 58 scenes vividly tell the story of the Norman invasion of England in 1066. The town is also one of the few in Normandy to have survived WWII practically unscathed, with a centre crammed with 13th- to 18th-century buildings, wooden-framed Norman-style houses, and a spectacular Norman Gothic cathedral.

◉ Sights

TOP CHOICE **Bayeux Tapestry** TAPESTRY
(☑02 31 51 25 50; www.tapisserie-bayeux.fr; rue de Nesmond; adult/child incl audioguide €7.80/3.80; ☺9am-6.30pm mid-Mar–mid-Nov, to 7pm May-Aug, 9.30am-12.30pm & 2-6pm mid-Nov–mid-Mar) The world's most celebrated embroidery recounts the conquest of England from an unashamedly Norman perspective. Fifty-eight scenes fill the central canvas, and religious allegories and illustrations of everyday 11th-century life fill the borders. The final showdown at the Battle of Hastings is depicted in graphic fashion, complete with severed limbs and decapitated heads (along the bottom of scene 52); Halley's Comet, which blazed across the sky in 1066, appears in scene 32. Scholars believe the 68.3m-long tapestry was commissioned by Bishop Odo of Bayeux, William the Conqueror's half-brother, for the opening of Bayeux' cathedral in 1077.

Musée Mémorial de la Bataille de Normandie
MUSEUM

(Battle of Normandy Memorial Museum; bd Fabien Ware; adult/child €7/3.80; ⊙9.30am-6.30pm May-Sep, 10am-12.30pm & 2-6pm Oct-Apr) Using well-chosen photos, personal accounts, dioramas and wartime objects, this first-rate museum offers an excellent introduction to WWII in Normandy.

🛏 Sleeping

TOP CHOICE Les Logis du Rempart
B&B €

(✆02 31 92 50 40; www.lecornu.fr; 4 rue Bourbes-neur; d €60-80, q €130; 🐾) This *maison de famille* shelters three rooms oozing old-fashioned cosiness. The hosts run a tasting shop downstairs – the perfect place to stock up on top-quality, homemade Calvados and cider. Breakfast (€6) features organic apple juice and apple jelly.

Villa Lara
BOUTIQUE HOTEL €€€

(✆02 31 92 00 55; www.hotel-villalara.com; 6 place de Québec; d €180-280, ste €290-450; P❊🐾) Luxury and sophistication are the hallmarks of this 28-room boutique hotel, which opened in 2012. Clean lines, trendy colour schemes, top-quality fabrics and minimalist motifs distinguish the rooms, while other facilities include a bistro and a gym.

Hôtel Reine Mathilde
HOTEL €€

(✆02 31 92 08 13; www.hotel-bayeux-reinemathilde.fr; 23 rue Larcher; d €70-105; 🐾) Above a bustling local cafe of the same name, this family-run hotel is an excellent bet, right in the centre of town, with smallish but comfortable rooms. The annexe sports six sleek, spacious and sparkling rooms in a converted barn by the river.

✕ Eating

Local specialities to keep an eye out for include *cochon de Bayeux* (Bayeux-style pork). Rue St-Jean and rue St-Martin are home to a variety of cheap eateries and food shops.

La Rapière
REGIONAL CUISINE €€

(✆02 31 21 05 45; 53 rue St-Jean; menus €15-33.50; ⊙lunch & dinner Fri-Tue) Housed in a late-1400s mansion composed of stone walls and big wooden beams, this atmospheric restaurant specialises in Normandy staples such as terrines, duck and veal with Camembert. Four fixed-price menus assure a splendid meal on any budget.

La Reine Mathilde
CAKE SHOP €

(47 rue St-Martin; cakes from €2.50; ⊙8.30am-7.30pm Tue-Sun) A sumptuous, c 1900-style patisserie and *salon de thé* (tearoom) that's ideal if you've got a hankering for something sweet. There's seating here, making it prime breakfast and afternoon-tea terrain.

ⓘ Information

Tourist office (✆02 31 51 28 28; www.bessin-normandie.com; pont St-Jean; ⊙9.30am-12.30pm & 2-6pm)

ⓘ Getting There & Away

Trains link Bayeux with Caen (€6.20, 20 minutes, hourly), from where there are connections to Paris' Gare St-Lazare (€33.30, two hours) and Rouen (€24.90, 1½ hours).

D-Day Beaches

The D-Day landings, code-named 'Operation Overlord', were the largest military operation in history. Early on 6 June 1944,

---

WORTH A TRIP

RENOIR IN NORMANDY

Following the Seine valley west of Rouen, the D982 road winds through little towns, occasionally following the banks of the Seine as it climbs and descends. About 27km west of Rouen, in Jumièges, the **Abbaye de Jumièges** (✆02 35 37 24 02; Jumièges; adult/child €5/free; ⊙9.30am-6.30pm Jul-Aug, 9.30am-1pm & 2.30-5.30pm Sep-Jun) is an absolute must-see, even if you're not a history buff. With its ghostly white stone set off by a backdrop of trees, it's one of the most evocative ruins in Normandy. The church was begun in 1020, and William the Conqueror attended its consecration in 1067. It declined during the Hundred Years War and then enjoyed a renaissance under Charles VII. It continued to flourish until the 18th-century revolutionaries booted out the monks and allowed the buildings to be mined for building materials. Should you be tempted to overnight in Jumièges, consider staying at **Le Clos Fleuri** (✆06 16 72 29 53, 02 35 81 49 00; www.closfleuri76.fr; 2196 rte du Mesnil; s/d €42/48), an economical B&B just 1km away from the abbey.

DON'T MISS

CAEN MÉMORIAL

Caen's hi-tech, hugely impressive **Mémorial – Un Musée pour la Paix** (Memorial – A Museum for Peace; 02 31 06 06 45; www.memorial-caen.fr; esplanade Général Eisenhower, Caen; adult/child €18.80/16.30; ⏱9am-6.30pm, closed Jan & Mon mid-Nov–mid-Dec) uses sound, lighting, film, animation and lots of exhibits to graphically explore and evoke the events of WWII, D-Day landings and the ensuing Cold War. Tickets remain valid for 24 hours. The museum also runs D-Day beach tours.

Allied troops stormed ashore along 80km of beaches north of Bayeux, code-named (from west to east) Utah, Omaha, Gold, Juno and Sword. The landings on D-Day – called 'Jour J' in French – were followed by the Battle of Normandy, which ultimately led to the liberation of Europe from Nazi occupation. Memorial museums in Caen and Bayeux provide a comprehensive overview, and there are many small D-Day museums dotted along the coast. For context, see www.normandiememoire.com and www.6juin1944.com.

The most brutal fighting on D-Day took place 15km northwest of Bayeux along the stretch of coastline now known as **Omaha Beach**, today a glorious stretch of fine golden sand partly lined with sand dunes and summer homes. **Circuit de la Plage d'Omaha**, trail-marked with a yellow stripe, is a self-guided tour along the beach, surveyed from a bluff above by the huge **Normandy American Cemetery & Memorial** (www.abmc.gov; Colleville-sur-Mer; ⏱9am-5pm). Featured in the opening scenes of Steven Spielberg's *Saving Private Ryan*, this is the largest American cemetery in Europe.

☞ Tours

An organised minibus tour is an excellent way to get a sense of the D-Day beaches and their place in history. Bayeux tourist office (p227) handles reservations.

Mémorial MINIBUS TOURS
(www.memorial-caen.fr; adult/child €77/61) Excellent year-round minibus tours (four to five hours). Rates include entry to Mémorial. Book online.

Normandy Sightseeing Tours D-DAY TOUR
(02 31 51 70 52; www.normandywebguide.com) From May to October (and on request the rest of the year), this experienced outfit offers morning (adult/child €45/25) tours of various beaches and cemeteries. These can be combined into an all-day excursion (€90/50).

❶ Getting There & Away

Bus Verts (www.busverts.fr) bus 70 (two or three daily Monday to Saturday, more in summer) goes northwest from Bayeux to Colleville-sur-Mer and Omaha Beach (€2.30, 35 minutes).

CAMEMBERT COUNTRY

Some of the most enduring names in the pungent world of French *fromage* come from Normandy, including Pont L'Évêque, Livarot and, most famous of all, Camembert, all named after towns south of Honfleur, on or near the D579.

It's thought that monks first began experimenting with cheesemaking in the Pays d'Auge sometime in the 11th century, but the present-day varieties didn't emerge until around the 17th century. The invention of Camembert is generally credited to Marie Harel, who was supposedly given the secret of soft cheesemaking by an abbot from Brie on the run from Revolutionary mobs in 1790. Whatever truth there is in the legend, the cheese was a huge success at the local market in Vimoutiers, and production of Camembert quickly grew from a cottage industry into an international operation. The distinctive round wooden boxes, in which Camembert is wrapped, have been around since 1890; they were designed by a local engineer to protect the soft disc during long-distance travel.

If you're interested in seeing how the cheese is made, you can take a guided tour of the **Président Farm** (☏02 33 36 06 60; www.fermepresident.com; adult/child €3/2; ⏱10am-6pm Jun-Aug, 10am-6pm Apr & Sep-Oct, 10am-5pm Mar, closed Nov-Feb), an early-19th-century farm restored by Président, one of the region's largest Camembert producers in the centre of the town of **Camembert**, 60km south of Honfleur.

THE MORBIHAN MEGALITHS

Pre-dating Stonehenge by about a hundred years, **Carnac** comprises the world's greatest concentration of megalithic sites. There are more than 3000 of these upright stones scattered across the countryside between **Carnac-Ville** and **Locmariaquer** village, most of which were erected between 5000 BC and 3500 BC. No one's quite sure what purpose these sites served, although theories abound. A sacred site? Phallic fertility cult? Or maybe a celestial calendar? Even more mysterious is the question of their construction – no one really has the foggiest idea how the builders hacked and hauled these vast granite blocks several millennia before the wheel arrived in Brittany, let alone mechanical diggers.

Because of severe erosion, the sites are usually fenced off to allow vegetation to re-grow. **Guided tours** (€6) run in French year-round and in English from early July to late August. Sign up at the **Maison des Mégalithes** (☑02 97 52 29 81; rte des Alignements; tour adult/child €6/free; ⊙10am-8pm Jul & Aug, to 5.15pm Sep-Apr, to 7pm May & Jun). Opposite, the largest menhir field – with no fewer than 1099 stones – is the **Alignements du Ménec**, 1km north of Carnac-Ville. From here, the D196 heads northeast for about 1.5km to the **Alignements de Kermario**. Climb the stone observation tower midway along the site to see the alignment from above. Another 500m further on are the **Alignements de Kerlescan**, while the **Tumulus St-Michel**, 400m northeast of the Carnac-Ville tourist office, dates back to at least 5000 BC.

For background, Carnac's **Musée de Préhistoire** (☑02 97 52 22 04; www.museedecarnac.fr; 10 place de la Chapelle, Carnac-Ville; adult/child €5/2.50; ⊙10am-6pm) chronicles life in and around Carnac from the Palaeolithic and neolithic eras to the Middle Ages.

Mont St-Michel

On a rocky island opposite the coastal town of Pontorson, connected to the mainland by a narrow causeway, the sky-scraping turrets of the abbey of Mont St-Michel (☑02 33 89 80 00; www.monuments-nationaux.fr; adult/child incl guided tour €9/free; ⊙9am-7pm, last entry 1hr before closing) provide one of France's iconic sights. The surrounding bay is notorious for its fast-rising tides: at low tide the Mont is surrounded by bare sand for miles around; at high tide, just six hours later, the bay, causeway and nearby car parks can be submerged.

From the **tourist office** (☑02 33 60 14 30; www.ot-montsaintmichel.com; ⊙9am-12.30pm & 2-6.30pm Mon-Sat, 9am-noon & 2-6pm Sun), at the base of the mount, a cobbled street winds up to the **Église Abbatiale** (Abbey Church), incorporating elements of both Norman and Gothic architecture. Other notable sights include the arched **cloître** (cloister), the barrel-roofed **réfectoire** (dining hall), and the Gothic **Salle des Hôtes** (Guest Hall), dating from 1213. A one-hour tour is included with admission; English tours run hourly in summer, twice daily (11am and 3pm) in winter. In July and August, Monday to Saturday, there are illuminated *nocturnes* (night-time visits) with music from 9pm to 10pm.

Check the *horaire des marées* (tide table) at the tourist office. When the tide is out, you can walk all the way around Mont St-Michel, a distance of about 1km. Stray too far from the Mont and you risk getting stuck in wet sand – from which Norman soldiers are depicted being rescued in one scene of the Bayeux Tapestry – or being overtaken by the incoming tide, providing your next of kin with a great cocktail-party story.

Bus 6 (☑08 00 15 00 50; www.mobi50.com) links Mont St-Michel with Pontorson (€2.20, 13 minutes), from where there are two to three daily trains to/from Bayeux (€22.30, 1¾ hr) and Cherbourg (€28.10, three hours).

BRITTANY

Brittany is for explorers. Its wild, dramatic coastline, medieval towns, thick forests and the eeriest stone circles this side of Stonehenge make a trip here well worth the detour from the beaten track. This is a land of prehistoric mysticism, proud tradition and culinary wealth, where locals still remain fiercely independent, where Breton culture (and cider) is celebrated and where Paris feels a very long way away indeed.

BRETON MUSIC

Celtic culture is synonymous with music and Brittany is no exception. A wealth of indoor and outdoor festivals and concerts feature traditional instruments through to electronica, and everything in between, with some big-name international acts. Keep your finger on the pulse by picking up the free monthly 'zine *Ty Zicos* (www.tyzicos.com) in cafes and bars. In addition to an array of festivals and events, tune in to the region's top trio of music festivals each year.

Les Vieilles Charrues de Carhaix (www.vieillescharrues.asso.fr) Old-school crooners, electronic beats and more attract crowds of 300,000-plus to Carhaix in mid-July.

Astropolis (www.astropolis.org) Brest's electronic music fest in early August, with the main event atmospherically set in a castle.

Les Transmusicales de Rennes (www.lestrans.com) Groundbreaking indie bands in Rennes, in early December.

Quimper

POP 66,911

Small enough to feel like a village – with its slanted half-timbered houses and narrow cobbled streets – and large enough to buzz as the troubadour of Breton culture, Quimper (pronounced *kam-pair*) is the thriving capital of Finistère (meaning 'land's end'; in Breton *Penn ar Bed*, it means 'head of the world').

👁 Sights

Most of Quimper's historic architecture is concentrated in a tight triangle formed by place Médard, rue Kéréon, rue des Gentilhommes and its continuation, rue du Sallé, to place au Beurre.

Cathédrale St-Corentin CHURCH
(place Saint-Corentin; ⊙8.30am-noon & 1.30-6.30pm Mon-Sat, 8.30am-noon & 2-6.30 Sun) At the centre of the city is the cathedral with its distinctive kink, said to symbolise Christ's inclined head as he was dying on the cross. Construction began in 1239 but the cathedral's dramatic twin spires weren't added until the 19th century.

Musée Départemental Breton MUSEUM
(☑02 98 95 21 60; 1 rue du Roi Gradlon; adult/child €4/free; ⊙9am-6pm) Beside the cathedral, recessed behind a magnificent stone courtyard, this superb museum showcases Breton history, furniture, costumes, crafts and archaeology in a former bishop's palace.

🛏 Sleeping

Hôtel Manoir des Indes HOTEL €€
(☑02 98 55 48 40; www.manoir-hoteldesindes.com; 1 allée de Prad ar C'hras; s/d from €105/133; P 🕾 ✉) This stunning hotel conversion, located in an old manor house just a short drive from the centre of Quimper, has been restored with the original world-traveller owner in mind. Decor is minimalist and modern with Asian objets d'art, lots of exposed wood and a couple of elephants outside.

Camping Municipal CAMPGROUND €
(☑02 98 55 61 09; av des Oiseaux; sites €0.79, person €3.70, car €1.85; ⊙Jun-Oct; 🖵1) This wooded park is 1km west of the old city and 3km from the train station. From quai de l'Odet, follow rue Pont l'Abbé northwestwards and continue straight ahead where it veers left. Alternatively, take bus 1 from the train station to the Chaptal stop.

🍴 Eating

Crêperie du Quartier CREPERIE €
(☑02 98 64 29 30; 16 rue du Sallé; menus from €6, galettes €5-7.10) In a town where the humble crêpe is king, this cosy stone-lined place is one of the best. Its wide-ranging menu includes a *galette* of the week and, to follow up, you can go for the full monty: a crêpe stuffed with apple, caramel, ice cream, almonds and Chantilly. Wash it all down with a tipple from the range of local ciders.

L'Ambroisie GASTRONOMIC €€€
(☑02 98 95 00 02; www.ambroisie-quimper.com; 49 rue Elie Fréron; menus €25-62; ⊙lunch & dinner Tue-Sat, lunch Sun) Quimper's most celebrated gastronomic restaurant is sumptuously decorated with contemporary art and features elegant china on snow-white tablecloths. Regional produce provided by chef Gilbert Guyon's friends is used in the creation of house specials such as turbot with eschalots

as well as lots of those Breton favourites, scallops. Cooking classes on request.

Le Cosy Restaurant REGIONAL CUISINE €
(☑02 98 95 23 65; 2 rue du Sallé; mains €10-14.50; ⊙closed Sun, lunch Mon & dinner Tue) Make your way through the *épicerie* crammed with locally canned sardines, ciders and other Breton specialities to this eclectic dining room where you can tuck into top-quality gratins and *tartines*.

❶ Information

Tourist office (☑02 98 53 04 05; www.quimper-tourisme.com; place de la Résistance; ⊙9am-7pm Mon-Sat, 10am-12.45pm & 3-5.45pm Sun Jul-Aug, 9.30am-12.30pm & 1.30-6.30pm Mon-Sat, 10am-12.45pm Sun Jun & Sep)

❶ Getting There & Away

CAT/Viaoo (www.viaoo29.fr) Bus destinations include Brest (€6, 1¼ hours).

Frequent trains serve Brest (€16.50, 1¼ hours), Rennes (€28 to €34, 2½ hours) and Paris' Gare Montparnasse (€70 to €86, 4¾ hours).

St-Malo

POP 48,800

The mast-filled port of fortified St-Malo is inextricably tied up with the deep briny blue: the town became a key harbour during the 17th and 18th centuries, functioning as a base for merchant ships and government-sanctioned privateers, and these days it's a busy cross-Channel ferry port and summertime getaway.

◉ Sights

Walking on top of the city's sturdy 17th-century ramparts (1.8km) affords fine views of the old walled city known as **Intra-Muros** ('within the walls') or Ville Close – access the ramparts from any of the city gates.

Cathédrale St-Vincent CATHEDRAL
(place Jean de Châtillon; ⊙9.30am-6pm) The city's centrepiece was constructed between the 12th and 18th centuries. The battle to liberate St-Malo destroyed around 80% of the old city during August 1944, and damage to the cathedral was particularly severe.

Fort National RUIN
(www.fortnational.com; adult/child €5/3; ⊙Easter, school holidays & Jun–mid-Sep) From the city ramparts, spot the remains of St-Malo's former prison and the rocky islet of **Île du Grand Bé**, where the great St-Malo-born 18th-century writer Chateaubriand is buried. Walk at low tide, but check the tide times with the tourist office.

Musée du Château MUSEUM
(☑02 99 40 71 57; adult/child €6/3; ⊙10am-noon & 2-6pm Apr-Sep, Tue-Sun Oct-Mar) Within **Château de St-Malo**, built by the dukes of Brittany in the 15th and 16th centuries, this museum looks at the life and history of the city.

Grand Aquarium AQUARIUM
(☑02 99 21 19 00; www.aquarium-st-malo.com; av Général Patton; adult/child €16/11.50; ⊙9.30am-8pm; ⬆; ☐C1) Kids will adore the submarine ride and exhibits on local marine life at this excellent aquarium, about 4km south of the city centre. Bus C1 from the train station passes by every half-hour.

FRANCE ST-MALO

WORTH A TRIP

CULINARY CANCALE

No day trip from St-Malo is tastier than one to **Cancale** (www.cancale-tourisme.fr), an idyllic Breton fishing port 14km east, that's famed for its offshore *parcs à huîtres* (oyster beds).

Learn all about oyster farming at the **Ferme Marine** (☑02 99 89 69 99; www.ferme-marine.com; corniche de l'Aurore; adult/child €7/3.70; ⊙guided tours in French 11am, 3pm & 5pm Jul-Aug, in English 2pm, in German 4pm) and shop for oysters fresh from their beds at the **Marché aux Huîtres** (12 oysters from €3.50, lunch platters €20; ⊙9am-6pm), the local oyster market atmospherically clustered around the Pointe des Crolles lighthouse.

Le Coquillage (☑02 99 89 64 76; www.maisons-de-bricourt.com; 1 rue Duguesclin; menus €27-135; ⊙Mar-Dec), the sumptuous, Michelin-starred kitchen of superchef Olivier Roellinger, is housed in the gobsmackingly impressive Château Richeux, 4km south of Cancale. Crown the culinary experience with lunch or dinner here.

Keolis Emeraude (www.keolis-emeraude.com) runs buses from St-Malo (€2, 30 minutes) that stop in Cancale at Port de la Houle, next to the pungent fish market.

St-Malo

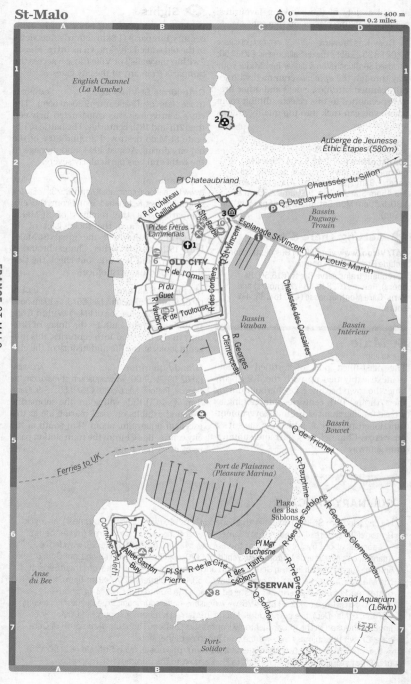

N 0 ———————— 400 m
0 ———————— 0.2 miles

*English Channel
(La Manche)*

2

Auberge de Jeunesse
Éthic Étapes (580m)

Chaussée du Sillon

Pl Chateaubriand

Q Duguay Trouin

R du Château
Gaillard

R Ste Barbe

3 🏛

P

Bassin
Duguay-
Trouin

Pl des Frères
Lammenais

1

Esplanade St-Vincent

6

OLD CITY

R de l'Orme

Av Louis Martin

R des Cordiers

Pl du
Guet

R Vauborel

5

R de Toulouse

Bassin
Vauban

Chaussée des Corsaires

Bassin
Intérieur

R Georges Clémenceau

Bassin
Bouvet

Q de Trichet

Ferries to UK

Port de Plaisance
(Pleasure Marina)

R Dauphine

R des Bas Sablons

R Georges Clémenceau

*Anse
du Bec*

Corniche d'Aleth

Allée Gaston
Buy

4

Pl St-
Pierre

R de la Cité

Plage
des Bas
Sablons

Pl Mgr
Duchesne

R des Hauts
Sablons

R Pré Brécel

ST-SERVAN

8

Q Solidor

*Grand Aquarium
(1.6km)*

*Port-
Solidor*

St-Malo

⊙ Sights
1 Cathédrale St-Vincent	B3
2 Fort National	C2
3 Musée du Château	C3

🛏 Sleeping
4 Camping Aleth	B6
5 Hôtel Quic en Groigne	B4
6 Hôtel San Pedro	B3

⊗ Eating
7 Le Bistro de Jean	B3
8 Le Bulot	C7
9 Le Chalut	B3

⊙ Drinking
10 La Cafe du Coin d'en Bas de la Rue du Bout de la Ville d'en Face du Port... La Java	C3

🛏 Sleeping

TOP CHOICE Hôtel Quic en Groigne BOUTIQUE HOTEL €€
(☎02 99 20 22 20; www.quic-en-groigne.com; 8 rue d'Estrées; s €64-72, d €79-102; ⊗closed mid-Nov–Feb; P🅿🛜) This exceptional hotel has 15 rooms that are the epitome of clean, simple style, and many a hotel twice the price should be envious of this place. If straight-out good value for money weren't enough then consider the staff who could hardly be more accommodating, an ideal location on a quiet old town street just a few metres from a (low-tide only) beach and secure lock-up parking.

Hôtel San Pedro HOTEL €€
(☎02 99 40 88 57; www.sanpedro-hotel.com; 1 rue Ste-Anne; s €58-60, d €69-79; P🛜) Tucked at the back of the old city, the San Pedro has cool, crisp, neutral-toned decor with subtle splashes of colour, friendly service and superb sea views.

Camping Aleth CAMPGROUND €
(☎06 78 96 10 62; www.camping-aleth.com; allée Gaston Buy, St-Servan; per 2-person tent €14.40; 🛜) Perched on a peninsula, Camping Aleth has panoramic 360-degree views and is close to beaches and some lively bars.

Auberge de Jeunesse Éthic Étapes HOSTEL €
(☎02 99 40 29 80; www.centrevarangot.com; 37 av du Père Umbricht; dm incl breakfast €21; @; 🛜3) This efficient place has a self-catering kitchen and free sports facilities. Take bus 3 from the train station.

🍴 Eating

TOP CHOICE Le Bistro de Jean BISTRO €
(☎02 99 40 98 68; 6 rue de la Corne-de-Cerf; mains €15-19, menus from €12; ⊗closed Wed & Sat lunch, all day Sun) Want to know where the locals choose to eat inside the walls? Peer through the windows of this lively and authentic bistro and you'll get your answer.

Le Chalut SEAFOOD €€
(☎02 99 56 71 58; 8 rue de la Corne-du-Cerf; menus €26-70; ⊗Wed-Sun) This unremarkable-looking establishment is, in fact, St-Malo's most celebrated restaurant. Its kitchen overflows with the best the Breton coastline has to offer – buttered turbot, line-caught sea bass and scallops in champagne sauce.

Le Bulot BISTRO €
(☎02 99 81 07 11; www.lebulot.com; 13 quai Sébastopol; menus €10-15, mains €8-14; ⊗closed dinner Sun Oct-May) A laidback neighbourhood bistro with a modern feel and views over the Port-Solidor (best appreciated on sunny days from the restaurant's raised wooden

FRANCE ST-MALO

FANCY UN CAFÉ?

The word 'eccentric' must have been coined to describe the extraordinary and insanely named **La Cafe du Coin d'en Bas de la Rue du Bout de la Ville d'en Face du Port... La Java** (☎02 99 56 41 90; www.lajavacafe.com; 3 rue Sante-Barbe). Think part-museum, part-toyshop and the work of art of an ever-so-slightly-twisted mind. Traditional French accordion music plays in the background and the beady eyes of hundreds of dolls and puppets keep watch from shelves and alcoves in the walls. Customers sit on swings, not chairs, and fake elephant tusks reach down out of the lamp shades. Even the opening times are odd: it opens at 8.31am on the dot during the week and 8.33am on weekends. And the drinks? Ah, well they're actually quite sane – a hundred different kinds of coffee and a quality beer range.

terrace). There's a short menu of delicious fusion dishes at bargain prices and they'll even serve you lunch after 2pm (a rare occurrence in anything other than tourist-class restaurants).

ℹ Information

Tourist office (📞€0.15 per min 08 25 13 52 00; www.saint-malo-tourisme.com; esplanade St-Vincent; ⊙9am-7.30pm Mon-Sat, 10am-6pm Sun) Just outside the walls.

ℹ Getting There & Away

Brittany Ferries (www.brittany-ferries.com) sails between St-Malo and Portsmouth, UK; **Condor Ferries** (www.condorferries.co.uk) runs to/from Poole via Jersey or Guernsey.

TGV train services include to/from Rennes (€13.60, one hour) and Paris' Gare Montparnasse (€52 to €64, three hours, up to 10 daily).

CHAMPAGNE

Known in Roman times as Campania, meaning 'plain', the agricultural region of Champagne is synonymous these days with its world-famous bubbly. This multimillion-dollar industry is strictly protected under French law, ensuring that only grapes grown in designated Champagne vineyards can truly lay claim to the hallowed title. The town of Épernay, 30km south of the regional capital of Reims, is the best place to head for *dégustation* (tasting), and a self-drive **Champagne Route** wends its way through the region's most celebrated vineyards.

Reims

POP 184,984

Over the course of a millennium (816 to 1825), some 34 sovereigns – among them two dozen kings – began their reigns in Reims' famed cathedral. Meticulously reconstructed after WWI and again following WWII, the city – whose name is pronounced something like 'rance' and is often anglicised as Rheims – is endowed with handsome pedestrian zones, well-tended parks, lively nightlife and a state-of-the-art tramway.

◉ Sights

TOP CHOICE Cathédrale Notre Dame CATHEDRAL
(www.cathedrale-reims.culture.fr; place du Cardinal Luçon; tower adult/child €7.50/free, incl Palais du Tau €11/free; ⊙7.30am-7.30pm, tower tours hourly 10am-5pm Tue-Sat, 2-5pm Sun Apr-Sep) The single most famous event to take place at this Gothic edifice, begun in 1211 and completed 100 years later, was the coronation of Charles VII, with Joan of Arc at his side, on 17 July 1429.

To get the most impressive first view of this Unesco World Heritage Site, approach the cathedral from the west, along rue Libergier. The finest stained-glass windows are the western facade's 12-petalled **great rose window**, its cobalt-blue neighbour below, and the **rose window** in the north transept (to the left as you walk from the entrance to the high altar), above the Flamboyant Gothic **organ case** (15th and 18th centuries). There are **windows by Chagall** (1974; a sign explains each panel) in the central axial chapel (directly behind the high altar) and, two chapels to the left, you'll find a **statue of Joan of Arc** in full body armour (1901).

End by climbing 250 steps up the **cathedral tower** on a one-hour tour. Book at Palais du Tau.

Palais du Tau MUSEUM
(http://palais-tau.monuments-nationaux.fr; 2 place du Cardinal Luçon; adult/child €7.50/free, incl cathedral tower €11/free; ⊙9.30am-6.30pm Tue-Sun) A Unesco World Heritage Site, this former archbishop's residence, constructed in 1690, was where French princes stayed before their coronations – and where they hosted sumptuous banquets afterwards. Now a museum, it displays truly exceptional statuary, liturgical objects and tapestries from the cathedral, some in the impressive Gothic-style **Salle de Tau** (Great Hall).

Basilique St-Rémi BASILICA
(place du Chanoine Ladame; ⊙8am-nightfall, to 7pm summer) This 121m-long former Benedictine abbey church, a Unesco World Heritage Site, mixes Romanesque elements from the mid-11th century (worn but stunning nave and transept) with early Gothic features from the latter half of the 12th century (choir). It is named in honour of Bishop Remigius, who baptised Clovis and 3000 Frankish warriors in 498. The 12th-century-style chandelier has 96 candles, one for each year of the life of St Rémi, whose tomb (in the choir) is marked by a mausoleum from the mid-1600s. The basilica is situated about 1.5km south-southeast of the tourist office; take the Citadine 1 or 2 or bus A or F to the St-Rémi stop.

☞ Tours

The bottle-filled cellars (10°C to 12°C – bring a sweater!) of eight Reims-area champagne houses can be visited by guided tour which ends, *naturellement,* with a tasting session.

The **Reims City Card** (€16), available at the tourist office, entitles you to the champagne-house visit (including tasting) and two audioguide tours of your choice.

Mumm CHAMPAGNE HOUSE
(☑03 26 49 59 70; www.mumm.com; 34 rue du Champ de Mars; tours €11; ☺tours begin 9am-11am & 2-5pm daily, closed Sun Nov-Feb) The only *maison* in central Reims was founded in 1827 and is now the world's third-largest producer (almost eight million bottles a year). Engaging and edifying one-hour tours take you through cellars filled with 25 million bottles of fine bubbly. Phone ahead if possible.

Taittinger CHAMPAGNE CELLAR
(☑03 26 85 84 33; www.taittinger.com; 9 place St-Niçaise; tours €16; ☺tours begin 9.30-11.50am & 2pm-4.20pm, closed Sat & Sun Dec–mid-Mar) Parts of the cellars here occupy 4th-century Roman stone quarries; other bits were excavated by 13th-century Benedictine monks. Situated 1.5km southeast of Reims centre; take the Citadine 1 or 2 bus to the St-Niçaise or Salines stops.

🛌 Sleeping

TOP CHOICE **Les Telliers** B&B €€
(☑09 53 79 80 74; http://telliers.fr; 18 rue des Telliers; s €76, d €87-110, tr €123, q €142; ☎) Enticingly positioned down a quiet alley near the cathedral, this bijou B&B extends one of Reims' warmest *bienvenues*. The high-ceilinged rooms are big on art-deco character, and are handsomely decorated with ornamental fireplaces, polished oak floors and the odd antique.

La Parenthèse B&B €€€
(☑03 26 40 39 57; www.laparenthese.fr; 83 rue Clovis; min 2-night stay d €170-220; ☎) Tucked away in the backstreets of old Reims, this little B&B has tasteful rooms with wood floors and bursts of pastel colour, all with kitchenettes.

Hôtel de la Paix HOTEL €€€
(☑03 26 40 04 08; www.bestwestern-lapaix-reims.com; 9 rue Buirette; d €170-220; ✱@☎☀) Outclassing most of Reims' midrange options, this contemporary, Best Western–affiliated hotel is the place to mellow in a pool, jacuzzi, hammam or Zen-like courtyard garden.

🍴 Eating

Place Drouet d'Erlon is lined with inexpensive restaurants and pub-cafes. More-discerning diners head to rue de Mars, adjacent to rue du Temple and place du Forum.

TOP CHOICE **Le Foch** GASTRONOMIC €€€
(☑03 26 47 48 22; www.lefoch.com; 37 bd Foch; lunch menus €31, dinner menus €48-80; ☺lunch Tue-Fri & Sun, dinner Tue-Sat) Michelin-starred Le Foch serves up cuisine as beautiful as it is delicious. Specialities like scallops with Jerusalem artichokes, pistachios and truffle emulsion are expertly paired with wines and presented with panache.

La Table Anna TRADITIONAL FRENCH €€
(☑03 26 89 12 12; 6 rue Gambetta; lunch menus €17, dinner menus €25-42; ☺lunch Tue-Sun, dinner Tue & Thu-Sun) So what if the decor is chintzy – there is a reason why this bistro is as busy as a beehive: friendly service and a menu packed with well-executed classics. The three-course, €17 lunch is a steal.

Brasserie Le Boulingrin BRASSERIE €€
(☑03 26 40 96 22; www.boulingrin.fr; 48 rue de Mars; menus €18.50-29; ☺lunch & dinner Mon-Sat) A genuine, old-time brasserie – the decor and zinc bar date back to 1925 – whose ambience and cuisine make it an enduring favourite. September to June, the culinary focus is *fruits de mer* (seafood).

🍷 Drinking

Café du Palais CAFE
(www.cafedupalais.fr; 14 place Myron-Herrick; ☺Tue-Sat) Run by the same family since 1930, this artdeco cafe is *the* place to sip a glass of champagne and see and be seen, at least if you're a *bon bourgeois* or a theatre type.

ℹ Information

Tourist office (☑08 92 70 13 51; www.reims-tourisme.com; 2 rue Guillaume de Machault; ☺9am-7pm Mon-Sat, 10am-6pm Sun & holidays)

ℹ Getting There & Away

Direct trains link Reims with Épernay (€6.50, 21 to 50 minutes, seven to 18 daily) and Paris' Gare de l'Est (€26 to €34, 12 to 17 daily), half of which are speedy TGVs (45 minutes).

FRANCE REIMS

Épernay

POP 25,000

Prosperous Épernay, 25km south of Reims, is the self-proclaimed *capitale du champagne* and home to many of the world's most celebrated champagne houses. Beneath the town's streets, some 200 million of bottles of champagne are slowly being aged, just waiting around to be popped open for some fizz-fuelled celebration.

◎ Sights & Activities

Many of Épernay's *maisons de champagne* (champagne houses) are based along the handsome and eminently strollable **av de Champagne**. Cellar tours end with a tasting and a visit to the factory-outlet bubbly shop.

Comtesse Lafond   CHAMPAGNE HOUSE
(🖉 03 86 39 18 33; www.deladoucette.net; 79 av de Champagne; 3-glass tasting €9, incl cellar tour €14; ◷10am-noon & 2-5.30pm daily) The whimsically turreted Comtesse Lafond is the most intimate and charming of the av de Champagne *maisons*. Tastings of three champagnes take place in the elegant salon or in manicured gardens overlooking vine-streaked hills.

Moët & Chandon   CHAMPAGNE HOUSE
(🖉 03 26 51 20 20; www.moet.com; 20 av de Champagne; adult incl 1/2 glasses €16.50/23, 10-18yr €9.50; ◷tours 9.30am-11.30am & 2-4.30pm, closed Sat & Sun mid-Nov–mid-Mar) Flying the Moët, French, European and Russian flags, this prestigious *maison* offers frequent one-hour tours that are among the region's most impressive. At the shop pick up a 15L bottle of Brut Impérial for €1500; a standard bottle costs €31.

Mercier   CHAMPAGNE HOUSE
(🖉 03 26 51 22 22; www.champagnemercier.fr; 68-70 av de Champagne; adult incl 1/2/3 glasses €11/16/19, 12-17yr €5.50; ◷tours 9.30-11.30am & 2-4.30pm, closed mid-Dec–mid-Feb) Everything here is flashy, including the 160,000L barrel that took two decades to build (for the Universal Exposition of 1889), the lift that transports you 30m underground, and the laser-guided touring train.

De Castellane   CHAMPAGNE HOUSE
(🖉 03 26 51 19 11; www.castellane.com; 64 av de Champagne; adult incl 1 glass €10, under 12yr free; ◷tours 10am-noon & 2-6pm, closed Christmas–mid-Mar) The 45-minute tours, in French and English, take in a museum dedicated to elucidating the *méthode champenoise* and its

diverse technologies. The reward for climbing the 237 steps up the 66m-high tower (built 1905) is a fine panoramic view.

🛏 Sleeping

TOP CHOICE Le Clos Raymi   HISTORIC HOTEL €€
(🖉 03 26 51 00 58; www.closraymi-hotel.com; 3 rue Joseph de Venoge; s €115, d €155-175; 🐾) Staying here is like being a personal guest of Monsieur Chandon of Champagne fame, who occupied this luxurious townhouse over a century ago. The seven romantic rooms have giant beds, high ceilings and parquet floors. In winter there's often a fire in the cosy art deco living room.

La Villa St-Pierre   HOTEL €
(🖉 03 26 54 40 80; www.villasaintpierre.fr; 14 av Paul Chandon; d €51-61; 🐾) In an early-20th-century mansion, this homey place, with 11 simple rooms, retains some of the charm of yesteryear.

✖ Eating & Drinking

La Grillade Gourmande   REGIONAL CUISINE €€
(🖉 03 26 55 44 22; www.lagrilladegourmande.com; 16 rue de Reims; menus €19-55; ◷lunch & dinner Tue-Sat) This chic, red-walled bistro is an inviting spot to try chargrilled meats and dishes rich in texture and flavour, such as crayfish pan-fried in champagne and lamb cooked in rosemary and honey until meltingly tender.

Chez Max   TRADITIONAL FRENCH €€
(🖉 03 26 55 23 59; www.chez-max.com; 13 av AA Thevenet, Magenta; menus €13.50-38.50; ◷lunch & dinner Tue-Sun, closed dinner Sun & Wed) No fuss, no frills, just good old-fashioned French cooking and a neighbourly vibe is what you'll get at Chez Max.

C. Comme   CHAMPAGNE BAR
(8 rue Gambetta; light meals €7.50-12, 6-glass champagne tasting €33; ◷10am-8.30pm Sun-Wed, 10am-11pm Thu, 10am-midnight Fri-Sat) The downstairs cellar has a stash of 300 different varieties of champagne; sample them (from €5.50 a glass) in the softly lit bar-bistro upstairs. Accompany your tipple with a tasting plate of regional cheese, charcuterie and *rillettes* (pork pâté).

❶ Information

Tourist Office (🖉 03 26 53 33 00; www.ot-epernay.fr; 7 av de Champagne; ◷9.30am-12.30pm & 1.30-7pm Mon-Sat, 11am-4pm Sun & holidays) Has excellent English brochures and maps on cellar visits, walking and cycling

FOODIE TRAILS

No matter whether you're planning to get behind the wheel for a morning, or pedal leisurely through the vineyards for a week, the picture-book **Route des Vins d'Alsace** (Alsace Wine Route) is a must. Swinging 170km from Marlenheim to Thann, the road is like a 'greatest hits' of Alsace, with its pastoral views, welcoming *caves* (cellars) and half-timbered villages. Go to www.alsace-route-des-vins.com to start planning.

Fancy cheese with your wine? Hit **Munster** to taste the pungent, creamy *fromage* first made by Benedictine monks. Munster tourist office (www.la-vallee-de-munster. com) arranges farmstays and dairy tours.

Having polished off the cheese and wine, it would be rude not to pass the chocolates, or gingerbread, or macarons, on the **Route du Chocolat et des Douceurs d'Alsace**. Pick up a map – 200km of sweet-toothed motoring – at Strasbourg tourist office.

options and car touring, and rents out a GPS unit (€7 per day) with self-guided vineyard driving tours in French, English and Dutch.

ⓘ Getting There & Away

Direct trains link Épernay to Reims (€6.20, 20 to 36 minutes, 11 to 18 daily) and Paris' Gare de l'Est (€21, 1¼ hours, five to 10 daily).

ALSACE & LORRAINE

Alsace is a one-off cultural hybrid. With its Germanic dialect and French sense of fashion, love of foie gras and *choucroute* (sauerkraut), fine wine *and* beer, this distinctive region often leaves you wondering quite where you are. Where are you? In the land of living fairy tales, where vineyards fade into watercolour distance, and hilltop castles mingle with the region's emblematic storks and half-timbered villages.

Lorraine has high culture and effortless grace thanks to its historic roll-call of dukes and art nouveau pioneers, who had an eye for grand designs and good living. Its blessedly underrated cities, cathedrals and art collections leave first-timers spellbound, while its WWI battlefields render visitors speechless.

Strasbourg

POP 276,136

Strasbourg is the perfect overture to all that is idiosyncratic about Alsace – walking a fine tightrope between France and Germany and between a medieval past and a progressive future, it pulls off its act in inimitable Alsatian style.

Tear your gaze away from that mesmerising Gothic cathedral for just a minute and you'll be roaming the old town's twisting alleys lined with crooked half-timbered houses à la Grimm; feasting in cosy *winstubs* (Alsatian taverns) by the canalside in Petite France; and marvelling at how a city that does Christmas markets and gingerbread so well can also be home to the glittering EU Quarter and France's second-largest student population.

⊙ Sights

Grande Île   HISTORIC QUARTER
(🚋Langstross) History seeps through the twisting lanes and cafe-rimmed plazas of Grande Île, Strasbourg's Unesco World Heritage–listed old town, made for aimless ambling. It cowers beneath the soaring magnificence of the cathedral and its sidekick, the gingerbready 15th-century **Maison Kammerzell**, with its ornate carvings and leaded windows. The lantern-lit alleys are most atmospheric at night, while the half-timbered houses and flowery canals of **Petite France** on the Grande Île's southwestern corner are fairytale pretty.

ⓘ STRASBOURG SAVER

The **Strasbourg Pass** (adult/child €14/7), a coupon book valid for three consecutive days, includes a visit to one museum, access to the cathedral platform, half a day's bicycle rental and a boat tour, plus hefty discounts on other tours.

Admission to all of Strasbourg's museums (www.musees-strasbourg.org), and to the cathedral's platform, is free on the first Sunday of the month.

Cathédrale Notre-Dame CATHEDRAL

(place de la Cathédrale; astronomical clock adult/child €2/1.50, platform adult/child €5/2.50; ☉7am-7pm, astronomical clock tickets sold from 11.45am, platform 9am-7.15pm; ⛴Langstross) At once immense and intricate, Strasbourg's centrepiece red-sandstone Gothic cathedral is a riot of filigree stonework and flying buttresses, leering gargoyles and lacy spires. The west facade was completed in 1284, but the 142m spire was not in place until 1439. The 30m-high Gothic-meets-Renaissance **astronomical clock** strikes solar noon at 12.30pm with a parade of carved wooden figures portraying the different stages of life and Jesus with his apostles.

A spiral staircase twists up to the 66m-high **platform** above the facade, from which the tower and its Gothic openwork spire soar another 76m.

Musée d'Art Moderne et Contemporain ART MUSEUM

(MAMCS; www.musees.strasbourg.eu; place Hans Jean Arp; adult/child €7/3.5; ☉10am-6pm Tue-Sun) This striking glass-and-steel cube showcases an outstanding collection of fine art, graphic art and photography. Kandinsky, Picasso, Magritte and Monet canvases hang out alongside curvaceous works by Strasbourg-born abstract artist Hans Jean Arp.

DON'T MISS

WHEN HELL WAS HELL

Hollywood gore seems tame compared with the tortures back when Hell really was hell. Sure to scare you into a life of chastity is *Les Amants Trépassés* (The Deceased Lovers), painted in 1470, showing a grotesque couple being punished for their illicit lust: both of their entrails are being devoured by dragon-headed snakes.

Track it down in Strasbourg's fabulous **Musée de l'Œuvre Notre Dame** (www.musees.strasbourg.org; 3 place du Château; adult/child €6/free; ☉10am-6pm Tue-Sun, to 8pm Thu; ⛴Langstross). Occupying a cluster of sublime 14th- and 16th-century buildings, the world-renowned ecclesiastical museum boasts one of Europe's premier collections of Romanesque, Gothic and Renaissance sculptures, 15th-century paintings, and stained glass.

Palais Rohan HISTORIC RESIDENCE

(2 place du Château; adult/child €6/free; ☉noon-6pm Mon & Wed-Fri, 10am-6pm Sat & Sun; ⛴Langstross) Hailed a 'Versailles in miniature', this opulent 18th-century residence was built for the city's princely bishops. The basement **Musée Archéologique** spans the Palaeolithic period to AD 800. The ground floor **Musée des Arts Décoratifs** evokes the lavish lifestyle of 18th-century nobility, and the 1st-floor **Musée des Beaux-Arts** showcases 14th- to 19th-century art.

☞ Tours

FREE **Cave des Hospices de Strasbourg** WINERY

(www.vins-des-hospices-de-strasbourg.fr; 1 place de l'Hôpital; ☉8.30am-noon & 1.30-5.30pm Mon-Fri, 9am-12.30pm Sat; ⛴Porte de l'Hôpital) Founded in 1395, this brick-vaulted wine cellar nestled deep in the bowels of Strasbourg's hospital has first-rate Alsatian wines.

Batorama BOAT TOUR

(www.batorama.fr; rue de Rohan; adult/child €9.20/4.80; ☉tours half-hourly 9.30am-7pm, hourly 8-10pm; ⛴Langstross) Scenic 70-minute boat trips along the storybook canals of Petite France.

Brasseries Kronenbourg BREWERY

(☏03 88 27 41 59; www.brasseries-kronenbourg.com; 68 rte d'Oberhausbergen; adult/child €6/4.50; ☉tours 1.30pm Tue-Sat; ⛴Ducs d'Alsace) Brewery tours in Cronenbourg, 2.5km northwest of Strasbourg's Grande Île; reserve in advance.

Festivals & Events

Vin chaud (mulled wine), spicy *bredele* and a Santa-loaded children's village feature in Strasbourg's festive **Marché de Noël** (Christmas Market; www.noel.strasbourg.eu), from the last Saturday in November to 24 December.

Raise a glass to Alsatian beer at October's **Mondial de la Bière** (www.mondialbierestrasbourg.com) or to wine at March's **Riesling du Monde** (www.portail-vins-du-monde.com).

🛏 Sleeping

Cour du Corbeau BOUTIQUE HOTEL €€€

(☏03 90 00 26 26; www.cour-corbeau.com; 6-8 rue des Couples; r €190-330; ❄@🤖; ⛴Porte de l'Hôpital) A 16th-century inn lovingly converted into a boutique hotel, Cour du Corbeau wins you over with its half-timbered charm and location steps from the river.

KATZENTHAL

Tiptoe off the tourist trail to Alsatian village **Katzenthal** (population 550), 9km west of Colmar and 80km south of Strasbourg. *Grand cru* vines ensnare the hillside, topped by the medieval ruins of Château du Wineck, from where walking trails into forest and vineyard begin.

Then there is the fabulous, family-run **Vignoble Klur** (☑03 89 80 94 29; www.klur.net; 105 rue des Trois Epis; apt €90-150, min 3-night stay), an organic winery and guest house that hosts wine tastings, Alsatian cookery classes and vineyard walks. Make yourself at home in a sunny apartment with kitchenette, read a book by an open fire in the salon, or unwind in the organic sauna. Oh, and don't miss Jean-Louis Frick's hilarious mural of hedonistic wine lovers above the entrance – it has raised a few local eyebrows, apparently.

Hôtel du Dragon   HOTEL €€
(☑03 88 35 79 80; www.dragon.fr; 12 rue du Dragon; s € 84-159, d €92-159; @⊛⊜; ⬚Porte de l'Hôpital) Step through a tree-shaded courtyard and into the blissful calm of this bijou hotel near Petite France.

Hôtel Régent Petite France DESIGN HOTEL €€€
(☑03 88 76 43 43; www.regent-hotels.com; 5 rue des Moulins; r €159-460; ❄@⊜; ⬚Alt Winmärik) Ice factory turned Strasbourg's hottest design hotel, this waterfront pile is quaint on the outside, ubercool inside. Work your relaxed look in the sauna, chic restaurant and champagne bar with dreamy River Ill views.

✗ Eating

Appetising restaurants abound on Grande Île: try canalside Petite France for Alsatian fare and half-timbered romance; Grand Rue for curbside kebabs and *tarte flambée;* and rue des Veaux or rue des Pucelles for hole-in-the-wall eateries serving the world on a plate.

Le Gavroche   MEDITERRANEAN €€
(☑03 88 36 82 89; www.restaurant-gavroche.com; 4 rue Klein; menu €38; ⊙Mon-Fri; ⬚; ⬚Porte de l'Hôpital) Bistro food is given a pinch of creativity and southern sunshine at intimate, softly lit Le Gavroche. Mains like veal in a mint crust with crispy polenta and coriander-infused artichoke tagine are followed by zingy desserts like lime tart with lemon-thyme sorbet.

Kobus   BISTRO €€
(☑03 88 32 59 71; www.restaurantkobus.com; 7 rue des Tonneliers; lunch/dinner menus €19.50/39.50; ⊙Tue-Sat; ⬚Langstross) Graphic artworks lend a contemporary feel to this stone-walled bistro with seasonal menu and a great €19.50 lunch deal.

Le Stras'   INTERNATIONAL €€
(☑03 88 35 34 46; 9 rue des Dentelles; mains €19-24; ⊙Tue-Sat; ⬚Langstross) The chef puts an innovative spin on seasonal ingredients at this beamed, gallery-style bistro in Petite France – a terrific choice for an intimate dinner.

🍫 Bistrot et Chocolat   CAFE €
(www.bistrotetchocolat.net; 8 rue de la Râpe; snacks €5-8, brunch €10-26; ⊙11am-7pm Tue-Fri, 10am-7pm Sat & Sun; ⬚⬚; ⬚Langstross) This boho-flavoured bistro is hailed for its solid and liquid organic chocolate (ginger is superb). The terrace is a local hangout for light bites; also good for weekend brunches and children's cooking classes.

❶ Information

Tourist office (☑03 88 52 28 28; www. otstrasbourg.fr; 17 place de la Cathédrale; ⊙9am-7pm) Runs an annexe in the southern wing of Strasbourg train station, 400m west of Grande Île.

❶ Getting There & Away

Air

Strasbourg's international **airport** (www.strasbourg.aeroport.fr) is 17km southwest of the city centre (towards Molsheim).

Ryanair links London Stansted with **Karlsruhe/Baden Baden airport** (www.badenairpark.de), 58km northeast of Strasbourg, across the Rhine in Germany.

Train

European cities with direct services include Basel SNCF (Bâle; €22, 1¼ hours, 25 daily), Brussels-Nord (€74, 5¼ hours, three daily), Karlsruhe (€25, 40 minutes, 16 daily) and Stuttgart (€47, 1¼ hours, four daily). Destinations within France include:

Paris Gare de l'Est €71, 2¼ hours, 19 daily

Lille €115, four hours, 17 daily

Lyon €71, 4½ hours, 14 daily

Marseille €161, 6¾ hours, 16 daily

Metz €24.50, two hours, 20 daily

Nancy €24, 1½ hours, 25 daily

Nancy

POP 108,597

Delightful Nancy has a refined air found nowhere else in Lorraine. With its resplendent central square, fine museums, medieval Old Town, formal gardens and shop windows sparkling with crystal, the former capital of the dukes of Lorraine catapults visitors back to the opulence of the 18th century (when much of the city centre was built).

◉ Sights

TOP CHOICE Place Stanislas   CITY SQUARE

Nancy's crowning glory is this neoclassical square, one of France's grandest public spaces and a Unesco World Heritage site. Your gaze will be drawn to an opulent ensemble of pale-stone buildings, gilded wrought-iron gateways and rococo fountains.

Musée de l'École de Nancy   ART MUSEUM

(School of Nancy Museum; www.ecole-de-nancy. com; 36-38 rue du Sergent Blandan; adult/child €6/4; ⊙10am-6pm Wed-Sun) This museum brings together art nouveau interiors, curvaceous glass and landscaped gardens, all in a 19th-century villa 2km southwest of the centre; take bus 122 or 123 to the Nancy Thermal or Paul-Painlevé stop.

Musée des Beaux-Arts   ART MUSEUM

(http://mban.nancy.fr; 3 place Stanislas; adult/child €6/free; ⊙10am-6pm Wed-Mon) Art nouveau glass creations by celebrated French glass maker Daum, and a rich selection of paintings from the 14th to 21st centuries, are among the star exhibits at this outstanding museum. Caravaggio, Rubens, Picasso and Monet masterpieces hang alongside works by Lorraine-born artists, such as Claude Lorrain's dreamlike baroque landscapes and the pared-down aesthetic of Nancy-born architect and designer Jean Prouvé (1901–1984)

🛏 Sleeping

TOP CHOICE Maison de Myon   B&B €€

(☑03 83 46 56 56; www.maisondemyon.com; 7 rue Mably; s/d €110/130, apt €150-200; 🖢) Slip behind the cathedral to reach this stately 17th-century house with wisteria-draped courtyard (is there a lovelier spot for breakfast?). Martine Quénot makes guests feel instantly at ease in her stylish home: wine tastings in the vaulted cellar, dinner alfresco, cookery classes – just say the word.

Hôtel des Prélats   HISTORIC HOTEL €€

(☑03 83 30 20 20; www.hoteldesprelats.com; 56 place Monseigneur Ruch; s €75-95, d €105-115; ❋🖢) Sleep in a former 17th-century bishop's palace right next to the cathedral. Service is as polished as the surrounds.

Hôtel de Guise   BOUTIQUE HOTEL €€

(☑03 83 32 24 68; www.hoteldeguise.com; 18 rue de Guise; s/d/tr/q €68/80/92/98; 🖢) Boutique chic meets 17th-century elegance at this hotel, with walled garden, down an old-town backstreet. Rooms are old-fashioned with antique furnishings, inlaid parquet and heavy drapes.

✗ Eating

Eats street rue des Maréchaux dishes up everything from French to Italian, tapas, seafood, Indian and Japanese. Then there's Grande Rue, peppered with sweet bistros.

La Primatiale   INTERNATIONAL €€

(☑03 83 30 44 03; www.la-primatiale.com; 14 rue de la Primatiale; menus €18-28; ⊙lunch Mon-Sat, dinner Mon & Wed-Sat) The food looks as good as it tastes at this upbeat, art-strewn bistro. Clean, bright flavours such as tartar of marinated salmon with dill and star anise and rack of lamb in a herb-olive crust reveal a definite Mediterranean slant.

Le V-Four   BISTRO €€

(☑03 83 32 49 48; 10 rue St-Michel; menus €19-50; ⊙lunch & dinner Tue-Sat, lunch Sun) With just a handful of tables, this petit bistro is all about intimacy and understated sophistication. Mulberry chairs and crisp white tablecloths set the scene for original creations like grilled scallops with wasabi cream and tomato confit. Book ahead.

Chez Tanésy – Le Gastrolâtre   BISTRO €€

(☑03 83 35 51 94; 23 Grande Rue; menus €27-45; ⊙Tue-Sat) A charmingly faded 16th-century townhouse is home to this cosy bistro with seasonal menu.

ℹ Information

Tourist office (☑03 83 35 22 41; www.ot-nancy.fr; place Stanislas; ⊙9am-7pm Mon-Sat, 10am-5pm Sun)

ℹ Getting There & Away

From the **train station** (place Thiers), 800m southwest of place Stanislas, destinations include:

Baccarat €10.50, 48 minutes, 15 daily

Metz €10, 38 minutes, 48 daily

DON'T MISS

CENTRE POMPIDOU-METZ

This architecturally innovative **museum** (www.centrepompidou-metz.fr; 1 parvis des Droits de l'Homme; adult/child €7/free; ⏱11am-6pm Mon, Wed & Sun, 11am-8pm Thu, Fri & Sat), dazzling white and sinuous, is the satellite branch of Paris' Centre Pompidou. Its gallery draws on Europe's largest collection of modern art to stage ambitious temporary exhibitions. The dynamic space also hosts top-drawer cultural events.

Paris Gare de l'Est €61, 1½ hours, 11 daily
Strasbourg €24, 1½ hours, 12 daily

Metz

POP 125,024

Straddling the confluence of the Moselle and Seille Rivers, Metz is Lorraine's graceful capital. Its Gothic marvel of a cathedral, Michelin star-studded dining scene, beautiful yellow-stone Old Town and regal Quartier Impérial (up for Unesco World Heritage status) are a joy to discover, but nothing can beat the city's show-stopping Centre Pompidou-Metz.

👁 Sights

FREE **Cathédrale St-Étienne**   CATHEDRAL
(place St-Étienne; audioguide €7, treasury & crypt adult/child €4/2; ⏱8am-6pm, treasury & crypt 9.30am-12.30pm & 1.30-5.30pm Mon-Sat, 1.30-5.30pm Sun) Exquisitely lit by kaleidoscopic curtains of 13th- to 20th-century stained glass, this cathedral is nicknamed 'God's lantern' and its sense of height and light is indeed spiritually uplifting. Flamboyant **Chagall windows** in startling jewel-coloured shades of ruby, gold, sapphire, topaz and amethyst adorn the ambulatory, which also harbours the **treasury**. The sculpture of the **Graoully** ('*grau*-lee'), a dragon said to have terrified pre-Christian Metz, lurks in the 15th-century **crypt**.

Quartier Impérial   HISTORIC QUARTER
The stately boulevards and bourgeois villas of the German Imperial Quarter, including rue Gambetta and av Foch, were the brainchild of Kaiser Wilhelm II. Built to trumpet the triumph of Metz' post-1871 status as part of the Second Reich, the architecture is a whimsical mix of art deco, neo-Romanesque and neo-Renaissance influences. Philippe Starck lamp posts juxtapose Teutonic sculptures, whose common theme is German imperial might, at the monumental Rhenish neo-Romanesque **train station**, completed in 1908.

🛏 Sleeping

TOP CHOICE **Hôtel de la Cathédrale**   HISTORIC HOTEL **€€**
(☑03 87 75 00 02; www.hotelcathedrale-metz.fr; 25 place de Chambre; d €75-110; 🛜) Expect a friendly welcome at this classy little hotel, occupying a 17th-century townhouse opposite the cathedral. Book well ahead for a cathedral view.

Péniche Alclair   HOUSEBOAT **€**
(☑06 37 67 16 18; www.chambrespenichemetz. com; allée St-Symphorien; r incl breakfast €70; 🛜) What a clever idea: this old barge has been revamped into a stylish blue houseboat, with two cheerful wood-floored rooms and watery views. Breakfast is served in your room or on the sundeck. It's a 15-minute stroll south of the centre along the river.

🍴 Eating

Metz has scores of appetising restaurants, many along and near the river. Place St-Jacques becomes one giant open-air cafe when the sun's out. Cobbled rue Taison and the arcades of place St-Louis shelter moderately priced bistros, pizzerias and cafes.

GO TO MARKET

If only every market were like Metz' grand **Marché Couvert** (Covered Market; place de la Cathédrale; ⏱8am-5.30pm Tue-Sat). Once a bishop's palace, now a temple to fresh local produce, this is the kind of place where you pop in for a baguette and struggle out an hour later with bags overflowing with charcuterie, ripe fruit and five different sorts of *fromage*.

Make a morning of it, stopping for an early, inexpensive lunch and a chat with the market's larger-than-life characters. **Chez Mauricette** (sandwiches €3-5, antipasti plate €5-7) tempts with Lorraine goodies from herby *saucisson* to local charcuterie and mirabelle pâté. Its neighbour, **Soupes á Soups** (soups €3.20), ladles out homemade soups, from mussel to creamy mushroom varieties.

FRANCE METZ

CHÂTEAUX TOURS

Hard-core indie travellers might balk at the idea of a tour, but don't dismiss them out of hand, especially if you don't have your own transport.

Shuttlebus & Minibus

April to August, Blois tourist office and TLC offer a twice-daily shuttle (€6) from Blois to the chateaux at Chambord, Cheverny and Beauregard.

Many private companies offer a choice of well-organised itineraries, taking in various combinations of Azay-le-Rideau, Villandry, Cheverny, Chambord and Chenonceau (plus wine-tasting tours). Half-day trips cost between €20 and €35; full-day trips range from €45 to €52. Entry to the chateaux isn't included, although you'll likely get a discount on tickets. Reserve via the tourist offices in Tours or Amboise, from where most tours depart.

Bicycle

The Loire Valley is mostly flat – it's excellent cycling country. **Loire à Vélo** (www.loire avelo.fr) maintains 800km of signposted routes. Pick up a guide from tourist offices, or download route maps, audioguides and bike-hire details online.

Détours de Loire (☑02 47 61 22 23; www.locationdevelos.com) has bike-rental shops in Tours and Blois and can deliver bikes; they also allow you to collect/return bikes along the route for a small surcharge. Classic bikes cost €14/59 per day/week; tandems €45 per day.

Les Châteaux à Vélo (☑in Blois 02 54 78 62 52; www.chateauxavelo.com; per day €12-14) has a bike-rental circuit between Blois, Chambord and Cheverny, 300km of marked trails and can shuttle you by minibus. Free route maps and MP3 guides online.

Something Different

Alain Caillemer (☑02 47 95 87 59; dcaillemer@rand.com; half-day tour per couple €75) Personalised vineyard and tasting tours with a bilingual (French-English) guide near his native Chinon.

Cheval et Châteaux (www.cheval-et-chateaux.com; multiday tour per person €1062-2124) Four- to seven-day horseback excursions combining visits to several of the Loire's best known chateaux with overnights in castle-based B&Bs. Rates include gourmet meals, wine, B&B accommodation, horses, gear and guide.

Art Montgolfières (☑02 54 32 08 11; www.art-montgolfieres.fr; solo/duo €205/390) The Loire Valley by hot-air balloon: one hour in the air, two hours preparing the balloon, dismantling it and drinking a celebratory glass of champagne.

Le Bistro des Sommeliers BISTRO €€
(☑03 87 63 40 20; 10 rue Pasteur; mains €16-20; ⊙closed Sat lunch, Sun) This no-nonsense bistro near the station prides itself on its warm ambiance and consistently good French cooking. *Entrecôtes* (rib-eye steaks) are succulent, *frites* (chips) crisp, salads well dressed and wines perfectly matched to mains. The three-course *prix fixe* menu is a bargain at €15.

Restaurant Thierry FUSION €€
(☑03 87 74 01 23; www.restaurant-thierry.fr; 5 rue des Piques; menus €19.50-36.50; ⊙closed Wed & Sun) Combining the historic backdrop of a 16th-century townhouse with the subtly spiced cuisine, lighting and bohemian flair of Morocco, this is one of Metz' most coveted tables.

ⓘ Information

Tourist office (☑03 87 55 53 76; http://tour isme.mairie-metz.fr; 2 place d'Armes; ⊙9am-7pm Mon-Sat, 10am-5pm Sun)

ⓘ Getting There & Away

Train it from Metz' ornate early-20th-century **train station** (pl du Général de Gaulle) to Paris' Gare de l'Est (€61, 80 minutes, 13 daily), Nancy (€10, 37 minutes, 48 daily) and Strasbourg (€24.50, 1¾ hours, 14 daily).

THE LOIRE VALLEY

One step removed from the French capital, the Loire was historically the place where princes, dukes and notable nobles established their country getaways, and the countryside is littered with some of the most extravagant architecture outside Versailles. From sky-topping turrets and glittering banquet halls to slate-crowned cupolas and crenellated towers, the hundreds of chateaux dotted along this valley, a Unesco World Heritage site, comprise 1000 years of astonishingly rich architectural and artistic treasures.

Blois

POP 40,057

Blois' historic chateau was the feudal seat of the powerful counts of Blois, and its grand halls, spiral staircases and sweeping court-yards provide a whistlestop tour through the key periods of French architecture. Sadly for chocoholics, the town's historic chocolate factory, Poulain, is off-limits to visitors.

◉ Sights

Blois' old city, heavily damaged by German attacks in 1940, retains its steep, twisting medieval streets.

Château Royal de Blois CHATEAU
(www.chateaudeblois.fr; place du Château; adult/child €9.50/4; ☉9am-6.30pm Apr-Sep, reduced hours rest of year) Blois' Royal Chateau makes an excellent introduction to the chateaux of the Loire Valley, with elements of Gothic (13th century), Flamboyant Gothic (1498–1503), early Renaissance (1515–24) and classical (1630s) architecture in its four grand wings.

Maison de la Magie MUSEUM
(www.maisondelamagie.fr; 1 place du Château; adult/child €8/5; ☉10am-12.30pm & 2-6.30pm Apr-Aug, 2-6.30pm Sep) Opposite Blois chateau is the former home of watchmaker, inventor and conjurer Jean Eugène Robert-Houdin (1805–71), after whom the great American magician Harry Houdini is named. Dragons emerge roaring from the windows on the hour, and the museum hosts magic shows and optical trickery.

🛏 Sleeping

TOP CHOICE **La Maison de Thomas** B&B €€
(☎02 54 46 12 10; www.lamaisondethomas.fr; 12 rue Beauvoir; s/d €75/85) Four spacious rooms and a friendly welcome await travelers at this homey bed and breakfast on a pedestrianised street. There's a wine cellar where you can sample local vintages.

Côté Loire HOTEL €
(☎02 54 78 07 86; www.coteloire.com; 2 place de la Grève; d €57-89; ☜) If it's charm and colours you want, head for the "Loire Coast". Its rooms come in cheery checks, bright pastels and the odd bit of exposed brick.

Hôtel Anne de Bretagne HOTEL €
(☎02 54 78 05 38; www.hotelannedebretagne.com; 31 av du Dr Jean Laigret; s €45-54, d €56-80; ☜) This creeper-covered hotel has friendly staff and a bar full of polished wood and vintage pictures. Modern rooms are finished in flowery wallpaper and stripy bedspreads.

✖ Eating

L'Orangerie GASTRONOMIC €€€
(☎02 54 78 05 36; www.orangerie-du-chateau.fr; 1 av du Dr Jean Laigret; menus €35-80; ☉lunch & dinner Tue-Sat) This acclaimed eatery is cloud nine for connoisseurs of haute cuisine. Plates are artfully stacked and the sparkling *salon* would make Louis XIV envious. On summer nights, dine in the courtyard.

Les Banquettes Rouges FRENCH €€
(☎02 54 78 74 92; www.lesbanquettesrouges.com; 16 rue des Trois Marchands; menus €17-32; ☉lunch & dinner Tue-Sat) Handwritten slate menus and wholesome food, think rabbit with marmalade, duck with lentils and salmon with apple vinaigrette, all done with a spicy twist, distinguish the 'Red Benches'.

Le Castelet FRENCH €€
(☎02 54 74 66 09; 40 rue St-Lubin; lunch menu incl wine €18, dinner menus €19-34; ☉lunch & dinner, closed Wed & Sun; ☒) This country restaurant emphasises seasonal ingredients and hearty traditional dishes such as *fondant de porc au cidre* (pork stewed in cider, accompanied by baked apples and potatoes au gratin).

ℹ Information

Tourist office (☎02 54 90 41 41; www.bloischambord.com; 23 place du Château; ☉9am-7pm)

ℹ Getting There & Away

BUS TLC operates buses from Blois' train station (€2) to Chambord (Line 3; 25 to 40 minutes, two Monday to Saturday) and Cheverny (Line 4; 45 minutes, six to eight Monday to Friday, two Saturday, one Sunday).

DON'T MISS

DOMAINE NATIONAL DE CHAMBORD

Chambord is not just about its chateau: **Domaine National de Chambord**, the vast hunting reserve ensnaring it, is a must-explore. While most of its 54 sq km is reserved strictly for high-ranking French government officials (hard to imagine the French president astride a galloping stallion), 10 sq km of its **walking, cycling** and **equestrian trails** are open to anyone.

A real highlight is **wildlife-spotting**, especially in September and October during the rutting season, when you can watch stags, boars and red deer woo and mate. Observation towers dot the park; set out at dawn or dusk to spot.

Or pedal around: hire bikes at the **rental kiosk** (☏02 54 33 37 54; per hr/half-/full day €7/11/15; ☉Apr-Oct) near the jetty on the Cosson River (where you can also rent boats). **Guided bike tours** (adult/child €10/6 plus bike hire) depart mid-August to September. Alternatively, join a **Land Rover Safari** (☏02 54 50 50 06; adult/child €20/12; ☉Apr-Sep).

TRAIN The train station is 600m uphill from the chateau, on av Jean Laigret.

Amboise €6.60, 20 minutes, 10 daily

Orléans €10.50, 45 minutes, hourly

Paris Gares d'Austerlitz and **Montparnasse** from €26.70, 1½ to two hours, 26 daily

Tours €10.20, 40 minutes, 13 daily

Around Blois

CHÂTEAU DE CHAMBORD

For full-blown chateau splendour, you can't top **Chambord** (☏02 54 50 40 00; www.chambord.org; adult/child €11/free, parking €4; ☉9am-6pm Apr–Sep, 10am-5pm Oct-Mar), constructed from 1519 by François I as a lavish base for hunting game in the Sologne forests, but eventually used for just 42 days during the king's 32-year reign (1515–47).

The chateau's most famous feature is its **double-helix staircase**, attributed by some to Leonardo da Vinci, who lived in Amboise (34km southwest) from 1516 until his death three years later. The Italianate **rooftop terrace**, surrounded by cupolas, domes, chimneys and slate roofs, was where the royal court assembled to watch military exercises and hunting parties returning at the end of the day.

Several times daily there are 1½-hour **guided tours** (€4) in English, and during school holidays **costumed tours** entertain kids.

Chambord is 16km east of Blois, 45km southwest of Orléans and 17km northeast of Cheverny.

CHÂTEAU DE CHEVERNY

Thought by many to be the most perfectly proportioned chateau of all, **Cheverny** (☏02 54 79 96 29; www.chateau-cheverny.fr; adult/child €8.70/5.70; ☉9.15am-6.45pm Jul & Aug, 9.15am-6.15pm Apr-Jun & Sep, 9.45am-5.30pm Oct, 9.45am-5pm Nov-Mar) represents the zenith of French classical architecture, the perfect blend of symmetry, geometry and aesthetic order. It has hardly been altered since its construction between 1625 and 1634. Inside is a formal dining room, bridal chamber and children's playroom (complete with Napoléon III–era toys), as well as a guards' room full of pikestaffs, claymores and suits of armour.

Near the chateau's gateway, the kennels house pedigreed French pointer/English foxhound hunting dogs still used by the owners of Cheverny; feeding time is the **Soupe des Chiens** (☉5pm Apr-Sep, 3pm Oct-Mar).

Behind the chateau is the 18th-century **Orangerie**, where many priceless art works (including the Mona Lisa) were stashed during WWII. Hérgé used the castle as a model for Moulinsart (Marlinspike) Hall, the ancestral home of Tintin's sidekick, Captain Haddock. **Les Secrets de Moulinsart** (combined ticket with chateau adult/child €13.20/9.10) explores the Tintin connections.

STAYING OVER

Just 2km south of Cheverny amid grassland, 19th-century farmhouse **La Levraudière** (☏02 54 79 81 99; www.lalevraudiere.fr; 1 chemin de la Levraudière; s €62, d €66-69, tr €85-90) is a perfect blend of tradition and modernity. Breakfast is around a slablike wooden table laden with fabulous homemade jams, while rooms are all about crisp linens and meticulous presentation.

Cheverny is 16km southeast of Blois and 17km southwest of Chambord. For buses to/from Blois see p243.

CHÂTEAU DE CHAUMONT

Set on a defensible bluff behind the Loire, **Chaumont-sur-Loire** (www.domaine-chaumont. fr; adult/child €10/6, with gardens €15.50/11; ⊙10am-6.30pm Apr-Sep, to 5 or 6pm Oct-Mar) presents a resolutely medieval face, with its cylindrical corner turrets and sturdy drawbridge. The castle became a short-lived residence for Catherine de Medici following the death of Henry II in 1560, and later passed into the hands of Diane de Poitiers (Henry II's mistress). A collection of vintage carriages is displayed inside the truly sumptuous **écuries** (stables), built in 1877.

Chaumont's gorgeous English-style gardens are finest during the annual **Festival International des Jardins** (International Garden Festival; adult/child €11/7.50; ⊙9.30am-sunset late Apr–mid-Oct). The chateau is 17km southwest of Blois and 20km northeast of Amboise. Onzain, a 2.5km walk from Chaumont across the Loire, has trains to Blois (€3.40, 10 minutes, 13 daily) and Tours (€8, 30 minutes, 10 daily).

Tours

POP 138,590

Hovering somewhere between the style of Paris and the conservative sturdiness of central France, Tours is a key staging post for exploring chateaux country. It's a smart, vivacious kind of town, filled with wide 18th-century boulevards, parks and imposing public buildings, as well as a busy university of some 25,000 students.

◉ Sights

Musée des Beaux-Arts　MUSEUM
(18 place François Sicard; adult/child €4/2; ⊙9am-12.45pm & 2-6pm Wed-Mon) Arranged around the courtyard of the archbishop's gorgeous palace, this fine-arts museum flaunts grand rooms with works spanning several centuries, including paintings by Delacroix, Degas and Monet, as well as a rare Rembrandt miniature and a Rubens *Madonna and Child*.

Cathédrale St-Gatien　CHURCH
(place de la Cathédrale; ⊙9am-7pm) With its twin towers, flying buttresses, stained glass and gargoyles, this cathedral is a showstopper. The interior dates from the 13th to

16th centuries, and the domed tops of the two 70m-high towers are Renaissance.

Musée du Compagnonnage　MUSEUM
(www.museecompagnonnage.fr; 8 rue Nationale; adult/child €5.30/3.50; ⊙9am-12.30pm & 2-6pm, closed Tue mid-Sep–mid-Jun) France has long prided itself on its *compagnonnages*, guild organisations of skilled labourers who have been responsible for everything from medieval cathedrals to the Statue of Liberty. Dozens of professions – from pastry chefs to locksmiths – are celebrated here through displays of their handiwork.

🛏 Sleeping

Hôtel Ronsard　BOUTIQUE HOTEL €
(☎02 47 05 25 36; www.hotel-ronsard.com; 2 rue Pimbert; s €58-72, d €66-78; ❄@🛜) This recently renovated hotel offers comfort and good value. Halls are lined with colourful photographs, while the sleek, modern and immaculate rooms incorporate muted tones of grey with sparkling white linens.

Hôtel Colbert　HOTEL €
(☎02 47 66 61 56; www.tours-hotel-colbert.fr; 78 rue Colbert; s €37-54, d €45-61; 🛜) In the heart of Tours' pedestrianised restaurant row, this newly remodeled, family-run hotel offers a welcoming haven amid the surrounding street life.

Hôtel Val de Loire　HOTEL €
(☎02 47 05 37 86; www.hotelvaldeloire.fr; 33 bd Heurteloup; s €45-58, d €55-78; 🛜) A prime location near the train station, friendly management and bright remodeled rooms make this an excellent midtown choice. Period features are nicely complemented by modern touches including new showers, double glazing and sound-dampening doors. The nicer back rooms downstairs have high ceilings and pleasant garden views, while the less expensive top-floor rooms are tucked under the eaves.

Auberge de Jeunesse du Vieux Tours　HOSTEL €
(☎02 47 37 81 58; www.fuaj.org/Tours; 5 rue Bretonneau; s/tw/tr incl breakfast €23/46/69; ⊙reception 8am-noon & 5-11pm; @🛜) This friendly, bustling HI hostel attracts a large foreign-student and young-worker contingent. Most rooms have only one to three beds; all share communal bathrooms, small kitchens and lounges. Bike rental.

WORTH A TRIP

TOP THREE CHATEAUX TRIPS

From Tours, a trio of drop-dead gorgeous castles beg to be devoured:

Château de Chenonceau (☎02 47 23 90 07; www.chenonceau.com; adult/child €11/8.50, with audioguide €15/12; ⊗9am-7pm Apr-Sep, reduced hours rest of year) This 16th-century castle is one of the Loire's most architecturally attractive. Framed by a glassy moat and sweeping gardens, and topped by turrets and towers, it's straight out of a fairy tale. Don't miss the yew-tree labyrinth and the 60m-long Grande Gallerie spanning the Cher River.

Château d'Azay-le-Rideau (☎02 47 45 42 04; azay-le-rideau.monuments-nationaux.fr/en; adult/child €8.50/free; ⊗9.30am-6pm Apr-Sep, to 7pm Jul & Aug, 10am-5.15pm Oct-Mar) Built in the 1500s on an island in the Indre River, this romantic, moat-ringed wonder flouts geometric windows, ordered turrets and decorative stonework. Don't miss: its loggia staircase and summertime **Promenade Nocturne** (adult/child €5/free).

Château de Villandry (☎02 47 50 02 09; www.chateauvillandry.com; château & gardens adult/child €9.50/5.50, gardens only €6.50/4; ⊗9am-6pm Apr-Oct, earlier rest of year, closed mid-Nov–Dec) One of the last major Renaissance chateaux to be built in the Loire, this one is famous for its gardens, which are nothing short of glorious. Don't miss the Jardin d'Ornement depicting fickle, passionate, tender and tragic love.

🍴 Eating

In the old city, place Plumereau, rue du Grand Marché and rue de la Rôtisserie are crammed with cheap eats (quality variable).

TOP CHOICE Cap Sud BISTRO €€
(☎02 47 05 24 81; capsudrestaurant.fr; 88 rue Colbert; lunch menus €15.50-19, dinner menus €24-36; ⊗lunch & dinner Tue-Sat) The hot-mod red interior combines nicely with genial service and refined culinary creations made from the freshest ingredients. Expect stylishly presented dishes such as warm St-Maure cheese with a pistachio-herb crumble and baby vegetables, or mullet fillet with sweet peppers, squid risotto and a ginger-tomato emulsion. Reserve in advance.

Tartines & Co BISTRO €
(6 rue des Fusillés; sandwiches €9-13; ⊗lunch Mon-Sat, dinner Wed-Fri) This snazzy little bistro reinvents the *croque* (toasted sandwich) amidst jazz and friendly chatter. Choose your topping (chicken, roasted veg, beef carpaccio, foie gras with artichokes and honey vinaigrette) and it's served up quick-as-a-flash on toasted artisanal bread.

L'Atelier Gourmand BISTRO €€
(☎02 47 38 59 87; www.lateliergourmand.fr; 37 rue Étienne Marcel; lunch/dinner menus €12/23; ⊗lunch Tue-Fri, dinner Mon-Sat) Another foodie address, but bring dark glasses: the puce-and-silver colour scheme is straight out of a Brett Easton Ellis novel. Everything's delivered with a modern spin, and many dishes feature intriguing blends of the sweet and savory.

Le Zinc FRENCH €€
(☎02 47 20 29 00; 27 place du Grand Marché; menus €19.50-24.50; ⊗lunch Tue & Thu-Sat, dinner Thu-Tue) More concerned with market-fresh staples sourced from the nearby Les Halles than with Michelin stars or haute cuisine cachet, this bistro impresses with authentic, attractive country classics.

ℹ Information

Tourist office (☎02 47 70 37 37; www. tours-tourisme.fr; 78-82 rue Bernard Palissy; ⊗8.30am-7pm Mon-Sat, 10am-12.30pm & 2.30-5pm Sun) Sells chateau tickets at a slight reduction.

ℹ Getting There & Away

AIR Tours-Val de Loire Airport (www.tours. aeroport.fr), 5km northeast, is linked to London's Stansted, Manchester, Dublin, Marseille; Porto by Ryanair; and Southampton by Flybe.

BUS Touraine Fil Vert (☎02 47 31 14 00; www. tourainefilvert.com; single ticket €1.80) line C links Tours bus station, next to the train station, with Amboise (40 minutes, 10 daily Monday to Saturday) and Chenonceaux (1¼ hours, one daily).

TRAIN Tours' central train station is linked to TGV station St-Pierre-des-Corps, 4km east, by frequent shuttle buses.

Amboise €5.20, 20 minutes, 13 daily
Blois €10.20, 40 minutes, 13 daily

Chenonceau €6.40, 25 minutes, eight daily

Paris Gare d'Austerlitz €32.90, two to 2¾ hours, five daily (slow trains)

Paris Gare Montparnasse €44 to €82, 1¼ hours, eight daily (high-speed TGVs)

Saumur €11.20, 45 minutes, hourly

Bordeaux €50, 2¾ hours, at least hourly

Nantes €29, 1½ hours, at least hourly

Amboise

POP 12,860

The childhood home of Charles VIII and final resting place of Leonardo da Vinci, elegant Amboise, 23km northeast of Tours, is pleasantly perched along the southern bank of the Loire and overlooked by its fortified chateau. With some seriously posh hotels and a wonderful weekend market, Amboise is a very popular base for exploring nearby chateaux; coach tours arrive en masse to visit da Vinci's Clos Lucé.

◉ Sights

Château Royal d'Amboise　　CASTLE
(www.chateau-amboise.com; place Michel Debré; adult/child €10.20/7, with audioguide €14.20/10; ☺9am-6pm Apr-Oct, earlier closing Nov-Mar) Sprawling across a rocky escarpment above town, this castle served as a weekend getaway from the official royal seat at nearby Blois. Charles VIII (r 1483–98), born and bred here, was responsible for the chateau's Italianate remodelling in 1492.

TOP CHOICE　**Le Clos Lucé**　　HISTORIC BUILDING
(www.vinci-closluce.com; 2 rue du Clos Lucé; adult/child €13.50/8.50; ☺9am-7pm Feb-Oct, 10am-6pm Nov-Jan; 🚸) Leonardo da Vinci took up residence at this grand manor house in 1516 on the invitation of François I, who was greatly enamoured of the Italian Renaissance. Already 64 by the time he arrived, da Vinci spent his time sketching, tinkering and dreaming up new contraptions, scale models of which are now abundantly displayed throughout the home and its expansive gardens.

Pagode de Chanteloup　　HISTORIC SITE
(www.pagode-chanteloup.com; adult/child €8.90/6.90; ☺10am-7pm May-Sep, reduced hours Oct-Apr) Two kilometres south of Amboise, this curiosity was built between 1775 and 1778 when the odd blend of classical French architecture and Chinese motifs were all the rage. Clamber to the top for glorious views. In summer, picnic hampers (€6.50 to €26)

are sold, you can rent rowing boats, and play free outdoor games.

🛏 Sleeping

Le Clos d'Amboise　　HISTORIC HOTEL €€€
(☏02 47 30 10 20; www.leclosamboise.com; 27 rue Rabelais; r €110-180, ste €210-310; ✳🛜🌊) Backed by a grassy lawn with 200-year-old trees and heated pool, this posh pad is country living in the heart of town.

Villa Mary　　B&B €€
(☏02 47 23 03 31; www.villa-mary.fr; 14 rue de la Concorde; d €90-120, apt per week €1180) Sandwiched between the river and chateau, this spacious 18th-century townhouse includes four lovingly restored, old-fashioned rooms plus a 200-square-metre top-floor apartment. The owner, a former economics professor and inveterate world traveller with a passion for history, lives onsite.

Centre Charles Péguy-Auberge de Jeunesse　　HOSTEL €
(☏02 47 30 60 90; www.mjcamboise.fr; Île d'Or; per person incl breakfast €19; @🛜) Efficient 72-bed boarding-school-style hostel on Île d'Or, an island in the middle of the Loire. Private rooms cost the same as dorms, making it an excellent budget option for solo travelers.

Hôtel Le Blason　　HOTEL €
(☏02 47 23 22 41; www.leblason.fr; 11 place Richelieu; s €50, d €53-63, q €83; ✳@🛜) Quirky, creaky budget hotel on a quiet square with 25 higgledy-piggledy rooms, wedged in around corridors: most are titchy, flowery

FRANCE AMBOISE

WORTH A TRIP

LUNCH IN THE COUNTRY

Renowned far and wide for its cosy atmosphere and superb food, country inn **Auberge de Launay** (☏02 47 30 16 82; www.aubergedelaunay.com; Le Haut Chantier, Limeray; menus €19.50-38; ☺lunch Tue-Fri, dinner Mon-Sat), 8km east of Amboise, merits the detour for anyone with their own wheels. Herbs and vegetables from the garden out back find their way into classic French meat, fish and poultry dishes, accompanied by a superb wine list and finished off with a divine artisanal cheese platter or desserts like wine-poached pears and homemade macarons.

and timber-beamed. Upstairs units under the eaves come with airconditioning.

Eating

La Fourchette FRENCH €€
(📞06 11 78 16 98; 9 rue Malebranche; lunch/dinner menus €15/24; ⊙lunch Tue-Sat, dinner Fri & Sat) Tucked into a back alley behind the tourist office, this is Amboise's favourite address for straightforward home cooking. Chef Christine makes you feel like you've been invited to her house with daily specials like *travers de porc* (spare ribs), *poulet rôti* (roast chicken) and *blanquette de veau* (veal stew).

Chez Bruno REGIONAL CUISINE €€
(📞02 47 57 73 49; place Michel Debré; menus from €15; ⊙lunch & dinner Tue-Sat) Uncork a host of local vintages in a coolly contemporary setting, accompanied by honest, inexpensive regional cooking. If you're after Loire Valley wine tips, this is the place.

Bigot PATISSERIE €
(www.bigot-amboise.com; place du Château; ⊙noon-7.30pm Mon, 9am-7.30pm Tue-Fri, 8.30am-7.30pm Sat & Sun) Since 1913 this cake and chocolate shop has been whipping up some of the Loire's creamiest cakes and gooiest treats.

❶ Information

Tourist office (📞02 47 57 09 28; www.amboise-valdeloire.com; ⊙9.30am-6pm Mon-Sat, 10am-1pm & 2-5pm Sun) In a riverside building opposite 7 quai du Général de Gaulle.

❶ Getting There & Around

From the **train station** (bd Gambetta), 1.5km north of the chateau on the opposite side of the Loire, local trains run at least hourly to **Tours** (€5.20, 20 minutes) and **Blois** (€6.60, 20 minutes). Four daily express trains also serve **Paris Gare d'Austerlitz** (€30.10, 1¾ hours).

BURGUNDY & THE RHÔNE VALLEY

If there's one place in France where you're really going to find out what makes the nation tick, it's Burgundy. Two of the country's enduring passions – food and wine – come together in this gorgeously rural region, and if you're a sucker for hearty food and the fruits of the vine, you'll be in seventh heaven.

WORTH A TRIP

MUSEOPARC ALÉSIA

Opened in 2012, the sensational **MuseoParc Alésia** (www.alesia.fr; 1 rte des Trois Ormeaux, Alise-Ste-Reine; ⊙9am-9pm Jul-Aug, 9am-6pm Apr-Jun & Sep, 10am-5pm Oct-Dec & Feb-Mar, closed Jan), near the village of Alise-Ste-Reine in the Pays d'Auxois, is well worth the drive from Dijon (67km). This was the site of what was once Alésia, the camp where Vercingétorix, the chief of the Gaulish coalitions, was defeated by Julius Caesar after a long siege. The defeat marked the end of the Gallic/Celtic heritage in France. You can visit the well-organised interpretative centre as well as the vestiges of the Gallo-Roman city that developed after the battle. Entertaining workshops for kids.

Dijon

POP 250,000

Dijon is one of France's most appealing cities. Filled with elegant medieval and Renaissance buildings, dashing Dijon is Burgundy's capital, and spiritual home of French mustard. Its lively Old Town is wonderful for strolling, especially if you like to leaven your cultural enrichment with excellent food, fine wine and shopping.

◎ Sights & Activities

Palais des Ducs et des États de Bourgogne PALACE
(Palace of the Dukes & States of Burgundy; place de la Libération) Once home to Burgundy's powerful dukes, this monumental palace with neoclassical facade overlooks **place de la Libération**, Old Dijon's magnificent central square dating from 1686. The palace's eastern wing houses the outstanding **Musée des Beaux-Arts**, whose entrance is next to the **Tour de Bar**, a squat 14th-century tower that once served as a prison.

Just off the **Cour d'Honneur**, the 46m-high, mid-15th-century **Tour Philippe le Bon** (adult/child €2.30/free; ⊙guided tours every 45min 9am-noon & 1.45-5.30pm late Nov–Easter, 1.30-3.30pm Wed, 9am-3.30pm Sat-Sun late Nov–Easter) affords fantastic views over the city. Spot Mont Blanc on a clear day.

Église Notre Dame
CHURCH

(place Notre-Dame) A block north of the Palais des Ducs, this church was built between 1220 and 1240. Its extraordinary facade's three tiers are lined with leering gargoyles separated by two rows of pencil-thin columns. Atop the church, the 14th-century **Horloge à Jacquemart**, transported from Flanders in 1383 by Philip the Bold who claimed it as a trophy of war, chimes every quarter-hour.

Around the north side of the church, **Rue de la Chouette** is named after the small stone *chouette* (owl) carved into the exterior corner of the chapel, diagonally across from No 24. Said to grant happiness and wisdom to those who stroke it, it has been worn smooth by generations of fortune-seekers.

Cathédrale St-Bénigne
CHURCH

(place St-Philbert) Built over the tomb of St Benignus (believed to have brought Christianity to Burgundy in the 2nd century), Dijon's Burgundian Gothic-style cathedral was built around 1300 as an abbey church.

FREE Musée de la Vie Bourguignonne
MUSEUM

(☑03 80 48 80 90; 17 rue Ste-Anne; ◎9am-noon & 2-6pm Wed-Mon) Housed in a 17th-century Cistercian convent, this museum explores village and town life in Burgundy in centuries past with evocative tableaux illustrating dress and traditional crafts. On the first floor, a whole street has been re-created.

🛏 Sleeping

Hôtel Le Jacquemart
HOTEL €

(☑03 80 60 09 60; www.hotel-lejacquemart.fr; 32 rue Verrerie; s €52-58, d €60-70; 🐾) In the heart of old Dijon, this two-star hotel is one of our favourite nests in town, with tidy, comfortable rooms and friendly staff. All the rooms are different; the best ones (Nos 5 and 6) are in a 17th-century annex just across the street; they're larger and better equipped than those within the hotel's original core, and combine vintage touches (stone walls, beamed ceiling) and modern conveniences.

Hôtel Le Sauvage
HOTEL €

(☑03 80 41 31 21; www.hotellesauvage.com; 64 rue Monge; s €48-59, d €53-64, tr €85; P🐾) Set in a 15th-century *relais de poste* (coaching inn) that ranges around a cobbled, vine-shaded courtyard, this little hotel is definitely good value. Rooms 10, 12, 14 and 17, with exposed beams, are the cosiest. It's in a lively area but the hotel is pleasingly quiet. Parking €5.

Hôtel Le Chambellan
HOTEL €

(☑03 80 67 12 67; www.hotel-chambellan.com; 92 rue Vannerie; s/d/tr/q €48/53/68/72, s/d with shared bathroom €35/38; 🐾) Built in 1730, this Old Town address has a vaguely medieval feel. Rooms come in cheerful tones of red, orange, pink and white; some have courtyard views.

Ethic Étapes Dijon
HOSTEL €

(Centre De Recontres et de Séjour Internationales, CRISD; ☑03 80 72 95 20; www.cri-dijon.com; 1 av Champollion; dm/s/d incl breakfast €21/40/52; P@🐾) This institutional but friendly, 219-bed hostel, 2.5km northeast of the centre, has modern, two- to six-bed rooms with private bathrooms. Take bus line 3 to the Dallas CRI stop.

A ROOM WITH A VINE VIEW

For those with their own wheels, two or four, beautiful stone-laced vintner villages around Dijon and Beaune hide some of Burgundy's most sought-after sleeping addresses:

Villa Louise Hôtel (☑03 80 26 46 70; www.hotel-villa-louise.fr; 9 rue Franche, Aloxe-Corton; d €100-195; P@🐾🏊) Who needs city life when you can stow away in vineyard-side luxury? This tranquil mansion on the Côte de Beaune houses dreamy rooms, an expansive garden, sauna, pool and wine cellar.

Domaine Corgette (☑03 80 21 68 08; www.domainecorgette.com; rue de la Perrière, St-Romain; d €85-110; P🐾) The sun-drenched terrace at this village winery faces dramatic cliffs. Rooms are light and airy with crisp linens, fireplaces and wooden floors.

Maison des Abeilles (☑03 80 62 95 42; www.chambres-beaune.fr; Magny-lès-Villers; d €63-68, q €112; 🐾) Sweet and jolly Jocelyne maintains this impeccably clean *chambre d'hôte* (B&B) with flowery garden in a village off the Route des Grands Crus. Breakfast is a homemade feast.

MAD ABOUT MUSTARD

If there is one pilgrimage to be made in Dijon it is to **Moutarde Maille** (☎03 80 30 41 02; www.maille.com; 32 rue de la Liberté; ☉10am-7pm Mon-Sat), the factory boutique of the company that makes Dijon's most famous mustard. The tangy odours of the sharp sauce assault your nostrils instantly upon entering and there are 36 different kinds to buy, including cassis-, truffle- or celery-flavoured; sample three on tap.

Or head to **Moutarderie Fallot** (Mustard Mill; www.fallot.com; 31 rue du Faubourg Bretonnière; adult/child €10/8; ☉tours 10am & 11.30am Mon-Sat, also afternoons summer, closed Nov-Mar 15) in neighbouring **Beaune** where Burgundy's last family-run, stone-ground mustard company offers tours of its facilities and mustard museum. Demonstrations include hand-milling mustard seeds – young kids love it! Reserve ahead at Beaune tourist office.

Eating

Eat streets loaded with restaurants include buzzy rue Berbisey, place Émile Zola, rue Amiral Roussin and around the perimeter of the covered market. Outdoor cafes fill place de la Libération.

DZ'Envies　　　　　　REGIONAL CUISINE €€
(☎03 80 50 09 26; www.dzenvies.com; 12 rue Odebert; mains €16-20, lunch menus €13-20, dinner menus €29-36; ☉Mon-Sat) This zinging restaurant with cheery decorative touches is a good choice if you're tired of heavy Burgundian classics. The menu always involves seasonal, fresh ingredients, and dishes are imaginatively prepared and beautifully presented. At €18, the lunchtime *I love Dijon* (yes) menu is a steal.

Chez Nous　　　　　　　　BISTRO €
(impasse Quentin; mains €7-8, lunch menus €10-13; ☉lunch noon-2pm Tue-Sat, bar 2pm-1am Mon, 11am-1am Tue-Sat) This quintessentially French *bar du coin* (neighbourhood bar), often crowded, hides down an alleyway near the covered market. At lunchtime join the flock and go for the fabulous-value *plat du jour* (daily special). Wash it all down with a glass of local wine (€2).

Chez Léon　　　　　　REGIONAL CUISINE €€
(☎03 80 50 01 07; www.restaurantchezleon.fr; 20 rue des Godrans; mains €11-29, lunch menus €15-21, dinner menus €22-27; ☉Tue-Sat) From bœuf bourguignon (beef marinated in young red wine) to *andouillettes* (chitterling sausages), this is the perfect primer course in hearty regional fare celebrated in a cosy and joyful atmosphere. The dining room is cluttered but there's outdoor seating in warm months.

ⓘ Information

Tourist office (☎08 92 70 05 58; www.visit dijon.com; 11 rue des Forges; ☉9am-6.30pm Mon-Sat, 10am-6pm Sun) Rents bicycles.

ⓘ Getting There & Away

BUS Transco (☎03 80 11 29 29; www.mobigo -bourgogne.com) Buses stop in front of the train station. Tickets sold on board (€1.50). Bus 44 goes to Nuits-St-Georges and Beaune. Bus 43 goes to Abbaye de Cîteaux.

TRAIN Trains leave the **train station** (www. voyages-sncf.com; rue du Dr Remy) for:

Lyon-Part Dieu from €22, 1½ hours, 25 daily

Marseille from €54, 3½ hours by TGV, six direct daily

Paris Gare de Lyon from €49, 1¾ hours by TGV, €42, three hours non-TGV, 25 daily

---

Beaune

POP 22,720

Beaune (pronounced 'bone'), 44km south of Dijon, is the unofficial capital of the Côte d'Or. This thriving town's raison d'être and the source of its joie de vivre is wine: making it, tasting it, selling it, but most of all, drinking it. Consequently, Beaune is one of the best places in all of France for wine tasting.

⊙ Sights & Activities

Beaune's amoeba-shaped old city is enclosed by **stone ramparts** sheltering wine cellars. Lined with overgrown gardens and ringed by a pathway, they make for a lovely stroll.

TOP CHOICE Hôtel-Dieu des Hospices de Beaune　　HISTORIC BUILDING

(www.hospices-de-beaune.com; rue de l'Hôtel-Dieu; adult/child €7/3; ☉9am-5.30pm) Built in 1443, this magnificent Gothic hospital (in operation until 1971) is famously topped by stunning turrets and pitched rooftops covered in multicoloured tiles. Interior highlights include the barrel-vaulted **Grande Salle** (look

A TRIP BETWEEN VINES

Burgundy's most renowned vintages come from the **Côte d'Or** (Golden Hillside), a range of hills made of limestone, flint and clay that runs south from Dijon for about 60km. The northern section, the **Côte de Nuits**, stretches from Marsannay-la-Côte south to Corgoloin and produces reds known for their robust, full-bodied character. The southern section, the **Côte de Beaune**, lies between Ladoix-Serrigny and Santenay and produces great reds and whites.

Tourist offices provide brochures: *The Burgundy Wine Road* is an excellent free booklet published by the Burgundy Tourist Board (www.bourgogne-tourisme.com) and *Roadmap to the Wines of Burgundy* is a useful map. There's also the **Route des Grands Crus** (www.road-of-the-fine-burgundy-wines.com), a signposted road route of some of the most celebrated Côte de Nuits vineyards. Mandatory tasting stops for oenophiles after nirvana include 16th-century **Château du Clos de Vougeot** (☑03 80 62 86 09; www.closdevougeot.fr; Vougeot; adult/child €4/3.10; ☺9am-5.30pm daily), with excellent guided tours, and **L'Imaginariim** (☑03 80 62 61 40; www.imaginarium-bourgogne. com; av du Jura, Nuits-St-Georges; adult/child €8/5; ☺2-7pm Mon, 10am-7pm Tue-Sun) with an entertaining wine museum, in Nuits-St-Georges.

Wine & Voyages (☑03 80 61 15 15; www.wineandvoyages.com; tours from €53) and **Alter & Go** (☑06 23 37 92 04; www.alterandgo.fr; tours from €70), with an emphasis on history and winemaking methods, run minibus tours in English; reserve online or at the Dijon tourist office.

for the dragons and peasant heads up on the roof beams); an 18th-century **pharmacy** lined with flasks once filled with elixirs and powders; and the multipanelled masterpiece **Polyptych of the Last Judgement** by 15th-century Flemish painter Rogier van der Weyden, depicting Judgment Day in glorious technicolour.

Cellar Visits   WINE TASTING

Millions of bottles of wine age to perfection in cool dark cellars beneath Beaune's buildings, streets and ramparts. Tasting opportunities abound and dozens of cellars can be visited by guided tour. Our favourites include the candlelit cellars of the former Église des Cordeliers, **Marché aux Vins** (www. marcheauxvins.com; 2 rue Nicolas Rolin; admission €10; ☺9.30-11.30am & 2-5.30pm, no midday closure Jul-Aug), where 15 wines can be sampled; and **Cellier de la Vieille Grange** (www.bourgogne-cellier.com; 27 bd Georges Clemenceau; ☺9am-noon & 2-7pm Wed-Sat, by appointment Sun-Tue), where locals flock to buy Burgundy wine *en vrac* (in bulk; bring your own jerrycan or buy a vinibag) for as little as €4.25 per litre for quality AOC wines. Tasting is done direct from barrels using a pipette. **Patriarche Père et Fils** (www.patriarche.com; 5 rue du Collège; audioguide tour €13; ☺9.30-11.30am & 2-5.30pm), lined with about five million bottles of wine, has Burgundy's largest cellars.

🛏 Sleeping

Hôtel des Remparts   HISTORIC HOTEL €€
(☑03 80 24 94 94; www.hotel-remparts-beaune. com; 48 rue Thiers; d €80-160; ℗❋🛜) Set around two delightful courtyards, this 17th-century townhouse has red-tiled or parquet floors and simple antique furniture. Some rooms come with exposed beams and a fireplace. Friendly staff rent bikes.

Abbaye de Maizières   HISTORIC HOTEL €€
(☑03 80 24 74 64; www.beaune-abbaye-maizieres. com; 19 rue Maizières; d €118-190; ❋@) This is a character-laden establishment inside a 12th-century abbey with modern rooms and contemporary furnishings. Rooms on the top floor offer views over Beaune's famed multicolour tile roofs.

Chez Marie   B&B €€
(☑06 64 63 48 20; www.chezmarieabeaune.com; 14 rue Poissonnerie; d €85-110; 🛜) Peace and calm five minutes from the centre of Beaune: Marie and her husband love having people to stay in their comfortable suburban house. Breakfast is served in a sweet garden. Bikes are available for rent.

🍴 Eating

Beaune harbours a host of excellent restaurants, many around place Carnot, place Félix Ziem and place Madeleine.

MONEY SAVER

If you'll be taking in a lot of sights and activities, including wine tasting, in the Beaune area, consider picking up the **Pass Pays Beaunois** at Beaune tourist offices. Ticket combos save 5% to 15% depending on the number of sights you plan to visit.

Loiseau des Vignes GASTRONOMIC €€€
(☑03 80 24 12 06; www.bernard-loiseau.com; 31 rue Maufoux; lunch menus €20-28, dinner menus €59-95; ⊘Tue-Sat) For that extra special meal, this culinary shrine is the place to go. Expect stunning concoctions ranging from caramelised pigeon to *quenelles de sandre* (dumplings made from pike fish), all exquisitely presented. And even the most budget-conscious can indulge – lunch menus are a bargain. In summer, the verdant garden is a plus.

Le Comptoir des Tontons REGIONAL CUISINE €€
(☑03 80 24 19 64; www.lecomptoirdestontons. com; 22 rue du Faubourg Madeleine; menus €25-36; ⊘Tue-Sat) Stylishly decorated in a hip bistro style, this local treasure entices with the passionate Burgundian cooking of chef Pepita. Most ingredients are organic and locally sourced.

Caves Madeleine FRENCH €€
(☑03 80 22 93 30; 8 rue du Faubourg Madeleine; mains €12-25, lunch menu €15; ⊘Mon-Wed & Sat, dinner Fri) This is a convivial restaurant where locals tuck into French classics such as *blanquette de veau* (veal stew) at long shared tables surrounded by wine racks.

ℹ Information

Tourist office (☑03 80 26 21 30; www. beaune-tourisme.fr; 6 bd Perpreuil; ⊘9am-7pm Mon-Sat, 9am-6pm Sun)

ℹ Getting There & Away

BUS Bus 44 links Beaune with Dijon (€1.50, 1½ hours, two to seven daily), stopping at Côte d'Or villages like Vougeot, Nuits-St-Georges and Aloxe-Corton.

Dijon €7.30, 25 minutes, 40 daily

Nuits-St-Georges from €4.50, 10 minutes, 40 daily

Paris Gare de Lyon from €41, 2¼ hours by TGV (non-TGV 3½ hours), 20 daily, two direct TGVs daily

Lyon-Part Dieu from €30, 1¾ hours, 16 daily

Lyon

POP 487,980

Gourmets, eat your heart out: Lyon is *the* gastronomic capital of France, with a lavish table of piggy-driven dishes and delicacies to savour. The city has been a commercial, industrial and banking powerhouse for the past 500 years, and is still France's second-largest conurbation, with outstanding art museums, a dynamic nightlife, green parks and a Unesco-listed Old Town.

◉ Sights

VIEUX LYON

Old Lyon, with its cobblestone streets and medieval and Renaissance houses below Fourvière hill, is divided into three quarters: St-Paul at the northern end, St-Jean in the middle and St-Georges in the south. Lovely old buildings languish on **rue du Bœuf, rue St-Jean** and **rue des Trois Maries**.

The partly Romanesque **Cathédrale St-Jean** (place St-Jean, 5e; ⊘8am-noon & 2-7pm; Ⓜ Vieux Lyon), seat of Lyon's 133rd bishop, was built from the late 11th to the early 16th centuries. Its **astronomical clock** chimes at noon, 2pm, 3pm and 4pm.

FOURVIÈRE

Over two millennia ago, the Romans built the city of Lugdunum on the slopes of Fourvière. Today, Lyon's 'hill of prayer' – topped by a basilica and the **Tour Métallique**, an Eiffel Tower–like structure built in 1893 and used as a TV transmitter – affords spectacular views of the city and its two rivers. Footpaths wind uphill, but the funicular is the least taxing way up.

Crowning Fourvière hill is the **Basilique Notre Dame de Fourvière** (www.fourviere. org; place de Fourvière, 5e; ⊘8am-7pm; funicular Fourvière funicular station), an iconic, 27m-high

WANT MORE?

For in-depth information, reviews and recommendations at your fingertips, head to the Apple App Store to purchase Lonely Planet's *Lyon City Guide* iPhone app.

Alternatively, head to **Lonely Planet** (www.lonelyplanet.com/france/burgundy-and-the-rhone/lyon) for planning advice, author recommendations, traveller reviews and insider tips.

basilica, a superb example of exaggerated 19th-century ecclesiastical architecture.

Around the corner, treasures from its interior enjoy pride of place in the **Musée d'Art Religieux** (8 place de Fourvière, 5e; adult/child €6/free; ☉10am-12.30pm & 2-5.30pm; funicular Fourvière funicular station).

PRESQU'ÎLE

The centrepiece of **place des Terreaux** is a 19th-century fountain sculpted by Frédéric-Auguste Bartholdi, creator of the Statue of Liberty. The **Musée des Beaux-Arts** (www.mba-lyon.fr; 20 place des Terreaux, 1er; adult/child incl audioguide €7/free; ☉10am-6pm Wed, Thu & Sat-Mon, 10.30am-6pm Fri; MHôtel de Ville) showcases France's finest collection of sculptures and paintings outside Paris.

Lyonnais silks are showcased at the **Musée des Tissus** (www.musee-des-tissus.com; 34 rue de la Charité, 2e; adult/child €10/7.50, after 4pm €8/5.50; ☉10am-5.30pm Tue-Sun; MAmpère). Next door, the **Musée des Arts Décoratifs** (34 Rue de la Charité, 2e; free with Musée des Tissus ticket; ☉10am-noon & 2-5.30pm Tue-Sun) displays 18th-century furniture, tapestries, wallpaper, ceramics and silver.

Laid out in the 17th century, **place Bellecour** – one of Europe's largest public squares – is pierced by an equestrian **statue of Louis XIV**. South of here, past **Gare de Perrache**, lies the once-downtrodden industrial area of **Lyon Confluence** (www.lyon-confluence.fr), where the Rhône and Saône meet. Trendy restaurants now line its quays, and the ambitious **Musée des Confluences** (www.museedesconfluences.fr; 28 Boulevard des Belges, 6e), a science-and-humanities museum inside a futuristic steel-and-glass transparent crystal, will open here in 2014.

North of place Bellecour, the charming hilltop quarter of **Croix Rousse** is famed for its lush outdoor food market and silk-weaving tradition, illustrated by the **Maison des Canuts** (www.maisondescanuts.com; 10-12 rue d'Ivry, 4e; adult/child €6.50/3.50; ☉10am-6pm Mon-Sat, guided tours 11am & 3.30pm; MCroix Rousse).

RIVE GAUCHE

Parc de la Tête d'Or　　　　　　　PARK
(www.loisirs-parcdelatetedor.com; bd des Belges, 6e; ☉6am-11pm Apr-Sep, to 9pm Oct-Mar; 🚌41, 47; MMasséna) France's largest urban park, landscaped in the 1860s, is graced by a lake (rent a rowing boat), botanic garden, rose garden, zoo, puppet theatre and tip-top **Musée d'Art Contemporain** (www.mac-lyon.com; 81 quai Charles de Gaulle, 6e; adult/child €8/free; ☉11am-

LYON CITY CARD

The **Lyon City Card** (www.lyon-france.com; 1/2/3 days adult €21/31/41, child €12.50/17.50/22.50) covers admission to every Lyon museum and the roof of Basilique Notre Dame de Fourvière, as well as guided city tours, a river excursion (April to October) and discounts on other selected attractions.

The card also includes unlimited travel on buses, trams, the funicular and metro. Buy it online (www.en.lyon-france.com/Lyon-City-Card), from the tourist office, or at some hotels.

6pm Wed-Fri, 10am-7pm Sat & Sun). Buses 41 and 47 link the park with metro Part-Dieu.

Musée Lumière　　　　　　　MUSEUM
(www.institut-lumiere.org; 25 rue du Premier Film, 8e; adult/child €6.50/5.50; ☉10am-6.30pm Tue-Sun; MMonplaisir-Lumière) Cinema's glorious beginnings are showcased at the art nouveau home of Antoine Lumière, who moved to Lyon with sons Auguste and Louis in 1870. The brothers shot the first reels of the world's first motion picture, *La Sortie des Usines Lumières* (Exit of the Lumières Factories) here in the grounds of one of their father's photographic factories on 19 March 1895. The former factory is the Hangar du Premier Film cinema today.

Centre d'Histoire de la Résistance et de la Déportation　　　　　MUSEUM
(www.chrd.lyon.fr; 14 av Berthelot, 7e; adult/child €4/free; ☉9am-5.30pm Wed-Sun; MPerrache or Jean Macé) The WWII headquarters of Gestapo commander Klaus Barbie evokes Lyon's role as the 'Capital of the Resistance' through moving multimedia exhibits. Re-opened after extensive remodeling in 2012, the museum's new sections include sound recordings of 30 deportees and Resistance fighters, plus a varied collection of everyday objects associated with the Resistance (including the parachute Jean Moulin used to re-enter France in 1942).

✺🎭 Festivals & Events

Fête des Lumières　　　　　WINTER FESTIVAL
(Festival of Lights; www.lumieres.lyon.fr) Over several days around the Feast of the Immaculate Conception (8 December), sound-and-light shows are projected onto key buildings, while locals illuminate window sills with candles.

FRANCE LYON

Lyon

200 m
0.1 miles

Q du Général Sarrail

5

To Les Halles
de Lyon (1.5km)

Pont
Morand

Q André Lassagne

Q André Lassagne

Pl Louis
Pradel

19

Cordeliers

Croix
Paquet

R du Griffon

3

R de la Bourse

Pl de la
Bourse

Montée St-Sébastien

R Romarin

Pl de la
Comédie

Hôtel de Ville

R de l'Arbre Sec

R Neuve

R Gentil

R de la
Poulaillerie

Pl François Régaud

R Imbert
Colomès

Le Village
des Créateurs

R René Leynaud

R des Capucins

Pl des
Terreaux

Musée des
Beaux-Arts

R du Bât d'Argent

R de la
Fromagerie

13

4

R Dubois

R des Tables Claudiennes

R Burdeau

R Ste-Catherine

1ER

R Paul Chenavard

6

R Mercière

Montée de la
Grande Côte

R Terme

R Aiguette

R Constantine

R Lanterne

15

2

R de la Platière

Q de la Pêcherie

Jardin des
Plantes

R de l'Annonciade

Pl
Sathonay

R Sergent Blandan

10

12

R du Jardin
des Plantes

R Pareille

8

7

Q de Bondy

Q Romain Rolland

17

Pl St-
Paul

R Octavio Mey

R François Vernay

R Lainerie

R de
Gadagne

R Juiverie

Gare
St-Paul

ST-PAUL

Q Pierre Scize

Q Pierre Scize

Saône

R Roger Radisson

5E

Fourvière
Hill

Tour
Métallique

1

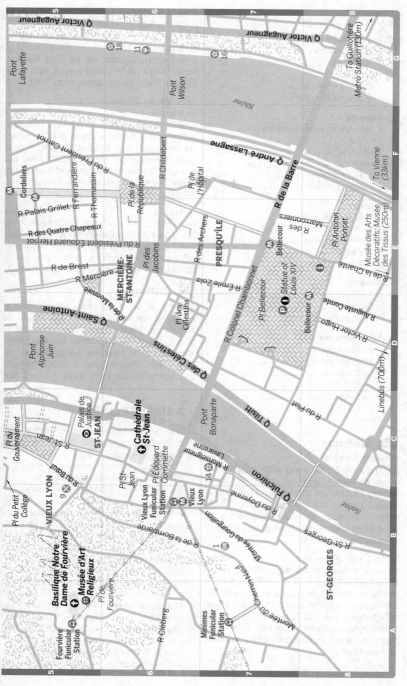

FRANCE LYON

Q Victor Augagneur

Q Victor Augagneur

Pont Lafayette

Pont Wilson

Rhône

To Guillotière
Metró Station (130m)

To Vienne (33km)

Cordeliers

R Palais Grillet

R Ferrandière

R Thomassin

R du Président Carnot

R Childebert

Pl de la République

Pl de l'Hôpital

Q André Lassagne

R de la Barre

R des Quatre Chapeaux

R du Président Édouard Herriot

Pl Jacobins

R des Archers

PRESQU'ÎLE

Pl d'Antonin Poncet

R des Marronniers

R de Brest

R Mercière

MERCIÈRE-ST-ANTOINE

R de la Monnaie

Pl des Jacobins

R des Cordeliers

R Émile Zola

Bellecour

Musée des Arts Décoratifs; Musée des Tissus (250m)

Q Saint-Antoine

Pl des Célestins

R Colonel Chambonnet

Pl Bellecour

Statue of Louis XIV

Bellecour

R Auguste Comte

R de la Charité

Pont Alphonse Juin

Q des Célestins

Pont Bonaparte

Q Tilsitt

R Victor Hugo

R du Plat

Linebus (700m)

Palais de Justice

R St-Jean

ST-JEAN

Cathédrale St-Jean

R Monseigneur Lavarenne

Q du Doyenné

Q Fulchiron

Saône

ST-GEORGES

R St-Georges

Pl du Gouvernement

R du Bœuf

VIEUX LYON

Pl du Petit Collège

Pl St-Jean

Pl Édouard Commette

Vieux Lyon Funicular Station

Vieux Lyon

Basilique Notre Dame de Fourvière

Musée d'Art Religieux

Fourvière Funicular Station

Pl de Fourvière

R Cléberg

R de la Bombarde

Montée du Gourguillon

Montée du Chemin Neuf

Minimes Funicular Station

Lyon

⊙ Top Sights

Basilique Notre Dame de
Fourvière A5
Cathédrale St-Jean C6
Musée d'Art Religieux A5
Musée des Beaux-Arts E3

🛏 Sleeping

1 Auberge de Jeunesse du Vieux
Lyon B7
2 Hôtel de Paris D3
3 Hôtel Iris F3
4 Hôtel Le Boulevardier E4
5 Péniche Barnum G3

✖ Eating

6 Café des Fédérations D3
7 Le Bistrot du Potager C2
8 Le Bouchon des Filles C2
9 Les Adrets B5
10 Magali et Martin D3

⊙ Drinking

11 La Passagère G6
12 Le Voxx D3
13 Le Wine Bar d'à Côté E4

⊕ Entertainment

14 (L'A)Kroche C7
15 Hot Club de Lyon D3
16 La Marquise G7
17 Le Club Théâtre B1
18 Le Sirius G6
19 Opéra de Lyon F2

🛏 Sleeping

Péniche Barnum   B&B €€

(☎06 63 64 37 39; www.peniche-barnum.com; 3 quai du Général Sarrail, 6e; d €120-150; ❄🐾; MFoch) Moored on the Rhône, Lyon's most unique B&B is this navy-and-timber barge with two smart en suite guestrooms, a book-filled lounge, and shaded deck terrace. Organic breakfasts €10.

Hôtel Le Boulevardier   HOTEL €

(☎04 78 28 48 22; www.leboulevardier.fr; 5 rue de la Fromagerie, 1er; s €47-56, d €49-59; 🐾; MHôtel de Ville, Cordeliers) Quirky touches like old skis and tennis racquets adorn the hallways at this bargain 11-room hotel. It's up a steep spiral staircase above a cool little bistro and jazz club of the same name, which doubles as reception.

Hôtel de Paris   HOTEL €€

(☎04 78 28 00 95; www.hoteldeparis-lyon.com; 16 rue de la Platière, 1er; s €52-92, d €64-135; ❄@🐾; MHôtel de Ville) This newly remodeled hotel in a 19th-century bourgeois building features bright decor and themed rooms with artsy designs. Some have a funky, retro '70s feel.

**Auberge de Jeunesse
du Vieux Lyon**   HOSTEL €

(☎04 78 15 05 50; www.fuaj.org/lyon; 41-45 montée du Chemin Neuf, 5e; dm incl breakfast €22; ⊙reception 7am-1pm, 2-8pm & 9pm-1am; @🐾; MVieux Lyon) Stunning city views unfold from the terrace of Lyon's only hostel, and from many of the (mostly six-bed) dorms. Bike parking, kitchen and laundry (wash-dry per load €4).

Hôtel Iris   HOTEL €

(☎04 78 39 93 80; www.hoteliris.fr; 36 rue de l'Arbre Sec, 1er; s €60-79, d €65-86; @; MHôtel de Ville) This basic but colourful dame in a centuries-old convent couldn't be better placed: its street brims with hip places to eat and drink.

✖ Eating

A flurry of big-name chefs preside over a sparkling restaurant line-up that embraces all genres: French, fusion, fast and international, as well as traditional Lyonnais *bouchons* (literally meaning 'bottle stopper' or 'traffic jam', but in Lyon a small, friendly bistro serving the city's local cuisine). See

---

A MARKET LUNCH

Shopping and munching lunch at the market is an unmissable part of the Lyon experience.

Pick up a round of impossibly runny St Marcellin from legendary cheesemonger **Mère Richard**, or a knobbly Jésus de Lyon from pork butcher **Collette Sibilia** at Lyon's famed indoor market **Les Halles de Lyon** (hallede lyon.free.fr; 102 cours Lafayette, 3e; ⊙8am-7pm Tue-Sat, to 1pm Sun; MPart-Dieu). Or simply sit down and enjoy a lunch of local produce, lip-smacking *coquillages* (shellfish) included, at one of its stalls.

Alternatively, meander up to the hilltop quarter of **Croix Rousse** and, December to April, indulge in oysters and a glass of white Côtes du Rhône on a cafe pavement terrace – before or after shopping at its huge and glorious morning food market on bd de la Croix Rousse.

www.lyonresto.com (in French) for reviews, videos and ratings.

Les Adrets
REGIONAL CUISINE €€

(☑04 78 38 24 30; 30 rue du Boeuf, 5e; lunch menu €15.50, dinner menus €23-45; ⊗lunch & dinner Mon-Fri; MVieux Lyon) This atmospheric spot serves some of Vieux Lyon's best food any time of day. The mix is half classic *bouchon* fare, half alternative choices like Parma ham and truffle risotto, or duck breast with roasted pears.

TOP CHOICE Le Bouchon des Filles
REGIONAL CUISINE €€

(☑04 78 30 40 44; 20 rue Sergent Blandan, 1er; menus €25; ⊗dinner daily, lunch Sun; MHôtel de Ville) This contemporary ode to Lyon's legendary culinary *mères* (mothers) is run by an enterprising crew of young women with deep roots in the local *bouchon* scene. The light and fluffy *quenelles* (Lyonnaise dumplings) are among the best you'll find in Lyon, and the rustic atmosphere is warm and welcoming.

Le Bistrot du Potager
TAPAS €

(☑04 78 29 61 59; www.lebistrotdupotager.com; 3 rue de la Martinière, 1er; tapas €5-12; ⊗lunch & dinner Tue-Sat; MHôtel de Ville) An offshoot of the renowned Potager des Halles restaurant next door, throngs of happy diners linger here over glasses of wine and Provençal duck carpaccio, grilled vegetables with pistou, stuffed artichokes, octopus salad, Tunisian-style chickpeas and platters of cheeses and charcuterie.

Magali et Martin
REGIONAL CUISINE €€

(☑04 72 00 88 01; www.magalietmartin.fr; 11 rue Augustins, 1er; lunch menus €19.50-23, dinner menus €29-35; ⊗lunch & dinner Mon-Fri; MHôtel de Ville) Watch chefs turn out traditional but lighter, more varied *bouchon*-influenced cuisine, at this sharp dining address.

Café des Fédérations
BOUCHON €€

(☑04 78 28 26 00; www.lesfedeslyon.com; 8-10 rue Major Martin, 1er; lunch/dinner menus from €19/25; ⊗lunch & dinner Mon-Sat; MHôtel de Ville) From the vast array of appetisers – lentils in mustardy sauce, slices of *rosette de Lyon* sausage, pickles, beets and more – clear through to a classic *baba au rhum* for dessert, this is *bouchon* dining at its finest.

🍷 Drinking & Entertainment

Cafe terraces on place des Terreaux buzz with all-hours drinkers, as do the British,

---

EAT STREETS

Rue St-Jean (MVieux Lyon) A surfeit of restaurants jam Vieux Lyon's pedestrian main street.

Cobbled rue Mercière, rue des Marronniers & place Antonin Poncet, 2e (MBellecour) Buzzing streets, chock-a-block with eating options (of widely varying quality) and pavement terraces overflowing in summer.

Rue du Garet & Rue Verdi, 1er (MHôtel de Ville) Twinset of parallel streets snug by Lyon's opera house on the Presqu'île.

Irish and other-styled pubs on nearby rue Ste-Catherine, 1er, and rue Lainerie and rue St-Jean, 5e, in Vieux Lyon.

Track new bars and nightclubs with *Le Petit Paumé* (www.petitpaume.com), a savvy city guide penned by local university students. Other what's on guides include **Lyon Poche** (www.lyonpoche.com) and **Le Petit Bulletin** (www.petit-bulletin.fr/lyon).

Tickets are sold at **Fnac Billetterie** (www. fnac.com/spectacles; 85 rue de la République, 2e; ⊗10am-7.30pm Mon-Sat; MBellecour).

Le Wine Bar d'à Côté
WINE BAR

(www.cave-vin-lyon.com; 7 rue Pleney, 1er; ⊗Mon-Sat; MCordeliers) Hidden in a tiny alleyway, this cultured wine bar feels like a rustic English gentlemen's club with leather sofa seating and a library.

Le Voxx
BAR

(1 rue d'Algérie, 1er; ⊗10am-3am daily; MHôtel de Ville) Minimalist but lively riverside bar packed with a mix of people, from students to city slickers.

Opéra de Lyon
OPERA HOUSE

(www.opera-lyon.com; place de la Comédie, 1er; MHôtel de Ville) Premier venue for opera, ballet and classical music.

(L'A)Kroche
LIVE MUSIC

(www.lakroche.fr; 8 rue Monseigneur Lavarenne, 5e; ⊗11am-1am Tue-Sat, 3-9pm Sun & Mon; MVieux Lyon) Hip concert cafe-bar with DJs spinning electro, soul, funk and disco; bands too.

Ninkasi Gerland
LIVE MUSIC

(www.ninkasi.fr; 267 rue Marcel Mérieux, 7e; ⊗10am-late; MStade de Gerland) Spilling over with a fun, frenetic crowd, this microbrewery dishes up DJs, bands and film projections amid a backdrop of fish-and-chips, build-your-own burgers and other un-French food.

Le Club Théâtre
PERFORMING ARTS

(www.thearte.fr; 4 impasse Flesselles, 1er; annual membership fee €2; MCroix Rousse) Hip and unique, this hybrid bar-nightclub-cultural centre sits inside Croix Rousse's old neighbourhood wash-house, with the central wash basin doubling as stage and dance floor.

Hot Club de Lyon
LIVE MUSIC

(www.hotclubjazz.com; 26 rue Lanterne, 1er; ⊘Tue-Sat; MHôtel de Ville) Lyon's leading jazz club, around since 1948.

Le Transbordeur
LIVE MUSIC

(www.transbordeur.fr; 3 bd de Stalingrad, Villeurbanne; trolleybus Cité Internationale/Transbordeur) In an old industrial building near the northeastern corner of the Parc de la Tête d'Or, Lyon's prime concert venue draws international acts on the European concert-tour circuit.

ℹ️ Information

Tourist office (☏04 72 77 69 69; www.lyon-france.com; place Bellecour, 2e; ⊘9am-6pm; MBellecour)

ℹ️ Getting There & Away

Air

Lyon-St-Exupéry Airport (www.lyon.aeroport.fr), 25km east of the city, serves 120 direct destinations across Europe and beyond, including many budget carriers.

DRINKS AFLOAT

Floating bars with DJs and live bands rock until around 3am aboard the string of *péniches* (river barges) moored along the Rhône's left bank. Scout out the section of quai Victor Augagneur between Pont Lafayette (MCordeliers or Guichard) and Pont de la Guillotière (MGuillotière).

Our favourites: laid-back **La Passagère** (21 quai Victor Augagneur, 3e; ⊘daily; MPlace Guichard - Bourse du Travail); party-hard **Le Sirius** (www.lesirius.com; 4 quai Victor Augagneur, 3e; ⊘daily; 🔊; MPlace Guichard - Bourse du Travail); and electro-oriented **La Marquise** (www.marquise.net; 20 quai Victor Augagneur, 3e; ⊘Tue-Sun; MPlace Guichard - Bourse du Travail).

Bus

In the Perrache complex, **Eurolines** (☏04 72 56 95 30; www.eurolines.fr; Gare de Perrache) and Spain-oriented **Linebús** (☏04 72 41 72 27; www.linebus.com; Gare de Perrache) have offices on the bus-station level of the Centre d'Échange (follow the 'Lignes Internationales' signs).

Train

Lyon has two main-line train stations: **Gare de la Part-Dieu** (MPart-Dieu), 1.5km east of the Rhône, and **Gare de Perrache** (MPerrache).

Destinations by direct TGV include:

Dijon from €29, two hours, at least seven daily

Lille-Europe from €90, three hours, at least 11 daily

Marseille from €45, 1¾ hours, every 30 to 60 minutes

Paris Gare de Lyon from €69, two hours, every 30 to 60 minutes

Paris Charles de Gaulle Airport from €69, two hours, at least 11 daily

Strasbourg €88, 3¾ hours, five daily

ℹ️ Getting Around

Tramway **Rhonexpress** (www.rhonexpress.net) links the airport with Part-Dieu train station in under 30 minutes. A single ticket costs €14.

Buses, trams, a four-line metro and two funiculars linking Vieux Lyon to Fourvière are run by **TCL** (www.tcl.fr). Public transport runs from around 5am to midnight. Tickets cost €1.60 while a *carnet* of 10 is €13.70; bring coins as machines don't accept notes (or some international credit cards). Time-stamp tickets on all forms of public transport or risk a fine.

Bikes are available from 200-odd bike stations thanks to **vélo'v** (www.velov.grandlyon.com; first 30min free, first/subsequent hr €1/2).

THE FRENCH ALPS

Whether it's paragliding among the peaks, hiking the trails or hurtling down a mountainside strapped to a pair of glorified toothpicks, the French Alps is the undisputed centre of adventure sports in France. Under Mont Blanc's 4810m of raw wilderness lies the country's most spectacular outdoor playground

---

Chamonix

POP 9378 / ELEV 1037M

With the pearly white peaks of the Mont Blanc massif as a sensational backdrop, being an icon comes naturally to Chamonix.

ERIC FAVRET: MOUNTAIN GUIDE

Eric Favret, guide with Compagnie des Guides de Chamonix, talked to Lonely Planet author Nicola Williams about his favourite local spots, views and thrills.

Aiguille du Midi The Aiguille du Midi, with one of the highest cable cars in the world, cannot be missed. Beyond the summit ridge is a world of snow and ice offering some of the greatest intermediate off-piste terrain in the Alps.

Off-Piste Thrills The Vallée Blanche has to be seen. But the Aiguille du Midi also has amazing off-piste runs, such as Envers du Plan, a slightly steeper and more advanced version of Vallée Blanche, offering dramatic views in the heart of the Mont Blanc range. There is also the less frequented run of the 'Virgin' or 'Black Needle' – a striking glacial run, it offers different views and a close-up look at the Giant's seracs.

Best-Ever Mont Blanc View No hesitation: the Traverse from Col des Montets to Lac Blanc. It's as popular as the Eiffel Tower for hikers in summer. I love swimming in mountain lakes, so I like to stop at Lac des Chéserys, just below, where it is quieter: what's better than a swim in pure mountain water, looking at Mont Blanc, the Grandes Jorasses and Aiguille Verte? This is what I call mountain landscape perfection!

First 'discovered' by Brits William Windham and Richard Pococke in 1741, this is the mecca of mountaineering. Its knife-edge peaks, plunging slopes and massive glaciers have enthralled generations of adventurers and thrill-seekers ever since. Its après-ski scene is equally pumping.

Sights

TOP CHOICE Aiguille du Midi VIEWPOINT

A jagged needle of rock rearing above glaciers, snowfields and rocky crags, 8km from the hump of Mont Blanc, the Aiguille du Midi (3842m) is one of Chamonix' most distinctive landmarks. If you can handle the height, the 360-degree views of the French, Swiss and Italian Alps from the summit are (quite literally) breathtaking.

Year-round, the vertiginous **Téléphérique de l'Aiguille de Midi** (place de l'Aiguille du Midi; adult/child return to Aiguille du Midi €46/39, Plan de l'Aiguille €26/22; ☺8.30am-4.30pm) cable car links Chamonix with the Aiguille du Midi. Halfway, Plan de l'Aiguille (2317m) is a terrific place to start hikes or paraglide. In summer you will need to obtain a boarding card (marked with the number of your departing *and* returning cable car) in addition to a ticket. Ensure that you bring warm clothes as even in summer the temperature rarely rises above -10°C at the top.

From the Aiguille du Midi, between late June and early September, you can continue for a further 30 minutes of mind-blowing scenery – think suspended glaciers and spurs, seracs and shimmering ice fields –

in the smaller bubbles of the **Télécabine Panoramic Mont Blanc** (adult/child return from Chamonix €70/59; ☺8.30am-3.30pm) to Pointe Helbronner (3466m) on the French–Italian border. From here another cable car descends to the Italian ski resort of Courmayeur.

Le Brévent VIEWPOINT

The highest peak on the western side of the valley, Le Brévent (2525m) has tremendous views of the Mont Blanc massif, myriad hiking trails, ledges to paraglide from and summit restaurant Le Panoramic. Reach it with the **Télécabine du Brévent** (29 rte Henriette d'Angeville; adult/child return €26/22; ☺8.50am-4.45pm).

Mer de Glace GLACIER

France's largest glacier, the glistening 200m-deep Mer de Glace (Sea of Ice) snakes 7km through mighty rock spires and turrets. The glacier moves up to 90m a year, and has become a popular attraction thanks to the rack-and-pinion railway line opened in 1908. The quaint red mountain train trundles up from **Gare du Montenvers** (35 place de la Mer de Glace; adult/child/family €26/22/79; ☺10am-4.30pm) in Chamonix to Montenvers (1913m), from where a cable car takes you down to the glacier and cave. Besides covering the 20-minute journey, the cable car and the ice cave, your ticket gets you entry into the crystal-laced **Galerie des Cristaux** and the new **Glaciorium**, spotlighting the birth, life and future of glaciers.

DON'T MISS

ADVENTURE KNOW-HOW

These guide companies have got it. So go on and create your own adventure:

Compagnie des Guides de Chamonix (☑04 50 53 00 88; www.chamonix-guides.com; 190 place de l'Église) The crème de la crème of mountain guides, founded in 1821. Guides for skiing, mountaineering, ice climbing, hiking, mountain biking and every other Alpine pastime.

Association Internationale des Guides du Mont Blanc (☑04 50 53 27 05; www. guides-du-montblanc.com; 85 rue des Moulins) Extreme skiing, mountaineering, glacier trekking, ice and rock climbing, and paragliding.

Aventure en Tête (☑04 50 54 05 11; www.aventureentete.com; 420 rte du Chapeau, Le Lavancher) Ski touring and ski-alpinism expeditions; free-ride and off-piste courses; mountaineering and climbing in summer.

Chamonix Experience (☑09 77 48 58 69; www.chamex.com; 49 place Edmond Desailloud) Courses in off-piste skiing, avalanche awareness, ice climbing and ski touring; in summer, rock and Alpine climbing.

Wrap up warm to experience the **Grotte de la Mer de Glace** (⊙late Dec-May & mid-Jun–Sep) ice cave, where frozen tunnels and ice sculptures change colour like mood rings.

The Mer de Glace can be reached on foot via the Grand Balcon Nord trail from Plan de l'Aiguille. The two-hour uphill trail from Chamonix starts near the summer luge track. Traversing the crevassed glacier requires proper equipment and an experienced guide.

🏃 Activities

Get the Mont Blanc lowdown on hiking, skiing and a zillion and one other adrenelin-pumping pursuits at the **Maison de la Montagne** (190 place de l'Église; ⊙8.30am-noon & 3-7pm), opposite the tourist office.

🛏 Sleeping

TOP CHOICE **Auberge du Manoir** HOTEL €€
(☑04 50 53 10 77; http://aubergedumanoir.com; 8 rte du Bouchet; s €109-122, d €126-176, q €178; ☎) This beautifully converted farmhouse ticks all the perfect alpine chalet boxes: pristine mountain views, pine-panelled rooms, outdoor hot tub, and a bar with open fire.

Hotel L'Oustalet HOTEL €€
(☑04 50 55 54 99; www.hotel-oustalet.com; 330 rue du Lyret; d/q €148/190; ☎⊠) You'll pray for snow at this alpine chalet near Aiguille du Midi cable car, just so you can curl up by the fire with a *chocolat chaud* (hot

chocolate) and unwind in the sauna and whirlpool. The rooms, including family ones, are snugly decorated in solid pine and open onto balconies with Mont Blanc views.

Hôtel Faucigny BOUTIQUE HOTEL €€
(☑04 50 53 01 17; www.hotelfaucigny-chamonix. com; 118 place de l'Église; s/d/q €90/120/170; ☎) This bijou hotel is a slice of minimalist alpine cool, with its charcoal-white rooms and slate-walled spa. Your hosts bend over backwards to please: free bike rental and afternoon tea, summer terrace with Mont Blanc views, open fire in winter, whirlpool and sauna.

Le Vert Hôtel HOTEL €€
(☑04 50 53 13 58; www.verthotel.com; 964 rte des Gaillands; s/d/tr/q € 80/103/129/151; ☎) Self-proclaimed 'Chamonix' house of sports and creativity', this party house 1km south of town has no-frills rooms, some with microscopically small bathrooms. But what people really come for is the all-happening, ultrahip bar, a regular venue for top DJs and live music. Minimum four-night stay.

Camping Mer de Glace CAMPGROUND €
(☑04 50 53 44 03; http://chamonix-camping. com; 200 chemin de la Bagna; sites €23.50; ⊙late Apr–Sep; ☎) Oh, what a beautiful morning! Draw back your tent flap and be dazzled by Mont Blanc and glaciated peaks at this campground, 2km northeast of Chamonix and an easy 20-minute stroll from the centre of town.

Eating

TOP CHOICE Les Vieilles Luges FRENCH €€
(☑06 84 42 37 00; www.lesvieillesluges.com;
Les Houches; menus €20-35; ☺lunch daily, dinner by reservation) This childhood dream
of a 250-year-old farmhouse can only be
reached by slipping on skis or taking a
scenic 20-minute hike from Maison Neuve
chairlift. Under low wood beams, Julie and
Claude spoil you with their home cooking
washed down with *vin chaud* (mulled wine)
warmed over a wood fire. Magic.

La Crèmerie du Glacier FRENCH €€
(☑04 50 54 07 52; www.lacremerieduglacier.fr; 766
chemin de la Glacière; menus €12-22; ☺lunch &
dinner Thu-Tue) Crazy as it sounds for a piste
restaurant, you might have to book to get a
chance to bite into La Crèmerie du Glacier's
world-famous *croûtes au fromage* (chunky
slices of toasted bread topped with melted
cheese). Ski to it on the red Pierre à Ric piste
in Les Grands Montets.

La Petite Kitchen INTERNATIONAL €€
(80 place du Poilu; 2-course lunch menus €12.50,
mains €18-28; ☺lunch & dinner Wed-Mon) The Little Kitchen is just that: a handful of tables
for the lucky few who get to indulge in its locally sourced feel-good food – filling English
breakfasts, steaks with homemade *frites* (hot
chips) and the stickiest of toffee puddings.

Le Bistrot GASTRONOMIC €€€
(☑04 50 53 57 64; www.lebistrotchamonix.com;
151 av de l'Aiguille du Midi; lunch menus €17-28,
dinner menus €50-85; ☺lunch & dinner daily; 🅿)
Michelin-starred chef Mickey experiments
with textures and seasonal flavours to
create taste sensations like pan-seared Arc-
tic char with chestnuts, and divine warm
chocolate macaroon with raspberry and red
pepper coulis.

Le GouThé TEAHOUSE €
(95 rue des Moulins; snacks €3-10; ☺9am-7pm
daily; 🅿) Welcome to the sweetest of tea
rooms: hot chocolates, macarons, *galettes*
(buckwheat crêpes) and crumbly homemade tarts.

Munchie FUSION €€
(☑04 50 53 45 41; www.munchie.eu; 87 rue des
Moulins; mains €19-24; ☺dinner daily) The style of
this trendy Swedish-run hangout is pan-Asian
fusion. Sittings go faster than musical chairs,
so it's worth a try even if you haven't booked.

🍷 Drinking & Entertainment

Nightlife rocks. In the centre, riverside rue
des Moulins boasts a line-up of après-ski
joints serving food as well as booze.

Chambre Neuf BAR
(272 av Michel Croz; 📶) Cover bands and raucous drinking make Room 9 one of Chamonix' liveliest party haunts. Conversations
about epic off-pistes and monster jumps
that are, like, totally mental, man, dominate
at every table.

MBC MICROBREWERY
(www.mbchx.com; 350 rte du Bouchet; ☺4pm-
2am) This trendy microbrewery run by four
Canadians is fab. Be it with their burgers,
cheesecake of the week, live music or amazing locally brewed and named beers (Blonde
de Chamonix, Stout des Drus, Blanche des
Guides etc), MBC delivers.

Elevation 1904 BAR
(259 av Michel Croz; ☺7am-11pm or later) Alpine
paraphernalia lines the walls of this merry
bet by the train station with an all-day snack
shack. The suntrap terrace is just right.

ℹ Information

Tourist office (☑04 50 53 00 24; www.
chamonix.com; 85 place du Triangle de l'Amitié;
☺8.30am-7pm)

ℹ Getting There & Away

BUS From **Chamonix bus station** (www.
sat-montblanc.com; place de la Gare), next to
the train station, five daily buses run to/from
Geneva airport (one way/return €33/55, 1½ to
two hours) and Courmayeur (one way/return
€13/20, 45 minutes). Advanced booking only.

TRAIN The Mont Blanc Express narrow-gauge
train trundles from St-Gervais-Le Fayet station,
23km west of Chamonix, to Martigny in Switzerland, stopping en route in Les Houches, Chamonix and Argentière. There are nine to 12 return
trips daily between Chamonix and St-Gervais
(€10, 45 minutes).

From St-Gervais-Le Fayet, there are trains to
most major French cities.

Annecy

POP 52,161 / ELEV 447M

Lac d'Annecy is one of the world's purest lakes,
receiving only rainwater, spring water and
mountain streams. Swimming in its sapphire
depths, surrounded by snowy mountains,

FREE WHEELER

Pick up a set of wheels to glide along the silky-smooth cycling path ensnaring Lake Annecy from **Vélonecy** (place de la Gare) at the train station for €15 per day (reduced to €5 with a valid train ticket). Or, in summer, simply head for the water and hire a bike lakeside from one of the many open-air stalls.

is a real Alpine highlight. Strolling the geranium-strewn streets of the historic Vieille Ville (Old Town) is not half bad either.

◉ Sights & Activities

Vieille Ville & Lakefront   HISTORIC QUARTER
It's a pleasure simply to wander aimlessly around Annecy's medieval old town, a photogenic jumble of narrow streets, turquoise canals and colonnaded passageways. Continue down to the tree-fringed lakefront and the flowery **Jardins de l'Europe**, linked to the popular picnic spot **Champ de Mars** by the poetic iron arch of the **Pont des Amours** (Lovers' Bridge).

🛏 Sleeping

Annecy Hostel   HOSTEL €
(☑09 53 12 02 90; www.annecyhostel.fr; 32 av de Loverchy; dm/d €22/55; ☎) Run by two well-travelled brothers, this newcomer makes backpackers' hearts sing with its bright and funky four-bed dorms, shared kitchen, chilled TV lounge, cheap bike rental and garden. It's a five-minute walk southwest of the old town.

Hôtel Alexandra   HOTEL €€
(☑04 50 52 84 33; www.hotelannecy-alexandra. fr; 19 rue Vaugelas; s/d/tr/q €55/75/95/110; ☎) Nice surprise: Annecy's most charming hotel is also one of its most affordable. The welcome is five-star, rooms are fresh and spotless – the best have balconies and canal views – and breakfast (€8) is a generous spread.

Splendid Hôtel   BOUTIQUE HOTEL €€
(☑04 50 45 20 00; www.hotel-annecy-lac.fr; 4 quai Eustache Chappuis; s/d €109/121; ✳☎) 'Splendid' sums up the lakefront position of this hotel, with breezy views from its boutique-chic, parquet-floor rooms.

Camping Les Rives du Lac   CAMPGROUND €
(☑04 50 52 40 14; www.lesrivesdulac-annecy.com; 331 chemin des Communaux; sites €23; ☒mid-Apr–Sep; ☒☎) Pitch your tent near the lakefront at this shady campground, 5km south of town in Sévrier. A cycling track runs into central Annecy from here.

✕ Eating

The old-town quays along Canal du Thiou are jam-packed with touristy cafes and pizzerias. Crêpes, kebabs, classic French cuisine – you'll find it all along pedestrianised rue Carnot, rue de l'Isle and rue Faubourg Ste-Claire.

 L'Esquisse   REGIONAL CUISINE €€
(☑04 50 44 80 59; www.esquisse-annecy.fr; 21 rue Royale; lunch menus €19-22, dinner menus €29-60; ☒lunch & dinner Mon-Tue & Thu-Sat) A talented husband-and-wife team run the show at this intimate bistro, with just six tables that fill predictably quickly. Carefully composed menus sing with natural, integral flavours, from wild mushrooms to spider crab.

La Ciboulette   GASTRONOMIC €€€
(☑04 50 45 74 57; www.laciboulette-annecy.com; 10 rue Vaugelas, cour du Pré Carré; menus €35-63; ☒lunch & dinner Tue-Sat) Such class! Crisp white linen and gold-kissed walls set the scene at this Michelin-starred place, where chef Georges Paccard cooks fresh seasonal specialities. Reservations are essential.

L'Étage   SAVOYARD €€
(☑04 50 51 03 28; 13 rue du Pâquier; menus €22-34; ☒lunch & dinner) Cheese, glorious cheese... *Fromage* is given pride of place in spot-on fondues and *raclette* (melting cheese, boiled potatoes, charcuterie and baby gherkins), with mellow music and cheerful staff as backdrop.

La Cuisine des Amis   BISTRO €€
(☑04 50 10 10 80; 9 rue du Pâquier; menus €15-31; ☒lunch & dinner; ☝) Opening onto a great people-watching terrace, this charcoal-walled bistro welcomes its clientele like *amis* (friends). Dine well on dishes like *marmite du pêcheur* (seafood stew) and Moroccan-style *pastilla* (crisp puff pastry pie filled with goat's cheese, figs and honey).

❶ Information

Tourist office (☑04 50 45 00 33; www.lac -annecy.com; Centre Bonlieu, 1 rue Jean Jaurès; ☒9am-6.30pm Mon-Sat, 10am-1pm Sun)

❶ Getting There & Away

BUS From the **bus station** (rue de l'Industrie), adjoining the train station, **Billetterie Crolard** (www.voyages-crolard.com) sells €1.50 tickets for roughly hourly buses to villages around the lake, local ski resorts and Lyon St-Exupéry airport (one-way/return €33/50, 2¼ hours). **Autocars Frossard** (www.frossard.eu) sells tickets for Geneva (€10.50, 1¾ hours, 16 daily).

TRAIN From Annecy's **train station** (place de la Gare), there are frequent trains to Lyon (€24.70, two hours) and Paris' Gare de Lyon (€76, four hours).

Grenoble

POP 158,221

With a dress-circle location overlooking the jagged mountains of the **Parc Naturel Régional de Chartreuse** and the **Parc Naturel Régional du Vercors**, Grenoble's backdrop is nothing short of extraordinary. At first glance the city iself is not quite so intoxicating, but taking a moment to linger rewards with fine museums, tasty dining and an effervescent nightlife buoyed by some 60,000 students.

◉ Sights

Fort de la Bastille   FORTRESS
(www.bastille-grenoble.com) Built high and mighty to withstand invasions by the dukes of Savoy, this 19th-century fort lures camera-toting crowds with its far-reaching views over Grenoble and the swiftly flowing River Isère to the peaks of the Vercors and, on cloud-free days, the snowy hump of Mont Blanc. Panels map out trails from gentle family walks to day hikes.

> ### MOUNTAIN ACTION!
>
> Get the scoop on mountain activities around Grenoble – skiing, snowboarding, ice climbing, walking, mountain biking, rock climbing and more – from knowledgeable staff at Grenoble's **Maison de la Montagne** (www.grenoble-montagne.com; 3 rue Raoul Blanchard; ⊙9.30am-12.30pm & 1-6pm Mon-Fri, 10am-1pm & 2-5pm Sat).
>
> If you're heading out for the day to one of the town's nearby ski resorts, jump lift-pass queues by buying your pass in advance from Grenoble's tourist office.

To reach the fort, hop aboard the riverside **Téléphérique Grenoble Bastille** (quai Stéphane Jay; adult/child one way €5/3, return €7/4.50; ⊙Feb-Dec). The ascent in glass bubbles, which climb 264m from the quay, is almost more fun than the fort itself.

TOP CHOICE **Musée de Grenoble**   MUSEUM
(www.museedegrenoble.fr; 5 place de Lavalette; adult/child €5/free; ⊙10am-6.30pm Wed-Mon) Also called the Musée des Beaux-Arts, Grenoble's boldest museum is renowned for its distinguished modern collection, including star pieces by Chagall, Matisse, Canaletto, Monet and Picasso.

Magasin Centre National d'Art Contemporain   MUSEUM
(www.magasin-cnac.org; 155 cours Berriat; adult/child €3.50/2; ⊙2-7pm Tue-Sun) Ensconced in a cavernous glass and steel warehouse built by Gustave Eiffel, this is one of Europe's leading centres of contemporary art. Take tram A to Berriat-Le Magasin stop, about 2km west of the town centre.

FREE **Musée Dauphinois**   MUSEUM
(www.musee-dauphinois.fr; 30 rue Maurice Gignoux; ⊙10am-6pm Wed-Mon) Atmospherically set in a 17th-century convent, this regional museum spells out alpine cultures, crafts and traditions, and the region's skiing history. Find it at the foot of the hill below Fort de la Bastille.

FREE **Musée de l'Ancien Évêché**   MUSEUM
(www.ancien-eveche-isere.fr; 2 rue Très Cloîtres; ⊙9am-6pm Mon, Tue, Thu & Fri, 1-6pm Wed, 11am-6pm Sat & Sun) On place Notre Dame, the Italianate **Cathédrale Notre Dame** and adjoining 13th-century **Bishops' Palace** – originally home to Grenoble's bishops – form this museum. The rich collection traces local history from prehistory to the 21st century, and takes visitors beneath the cathedral square to a crypt safeguarding old Roman walls and a baptistery dating from the 4th to 10th centuries.

FREE **Musée de la Résistance et de la Déportation de l'Isère**   MUSEUM
(www.resistance-en-isere.fr; 14 rue Hébert; ⊙9am-6pm Mon & Wed-Fri, 1.30-6pm Tue, 10am-6pm Sat & Sun) This emotive museum examines the deportation of Jews and other 'undesirables'

WORTH A TRIP

GREAT ESCAPES

Southwest of Grenoble, the gently rolling pastures and chiselled limestone peaks of the 1750-sq-km **Parc Natural Régional du Vercors** are the stuff of soft adventure. Quieter and cheaper than neighbouring Alpine resorts, the wildlife-rich park is a magnet for enthusiasts of fresh air, cross-country skiing, snowshoeing, caving and hiking. Its accommodation, moreover, is the stuff of Alpine dreams.

Les Allières (☑04 76 94 32 32; www.aubergedesallieres.com; Lans-en-Vercors; r with shared bathroom incl half board per person €47) This 1476m-high forest chalet offers no-frills digs (bunk beds, shared toilets) and wondrous mountain food (mains €18 to €30). The wood-fire *raclette* and *tarte aux myrtilles* (blueberry tart) are divine.

À la Crécia (☑04 76 95 46 98; www.gite-en-vercors.com; 436 Chemin des Cléments, Lans-en-Vercors; s/d/tr/q €58/63/78/93, dinner menus €19) Goats, pigs and poultry rule the roost at this 16th-century, solar-powered farm. Rooms are stylishly rustic with beams, earthy hues and mosaic bathrooms. Dinner is a farm-fresh feast.

Gîte La Verne (☑04 76 95 21 18; http://gite.laverne.free.fr; La Verne, Méaudre; apt per week for 4/8 people €500/750) Fitted with fully equipped kitchens, these beautiful apartments blend Alpine cosiness with mod cons. Whether you opt for self-catering or half-board, you'll luurv the *hammam* and outdoor Norwegian bath.

from Grenoble to Nazi camps during WWII in a cool-headed way. It also zooms in on the role of the Vercors region in the French Resistance.

🛏 Sleeping

Le Grand Hôtel   HOTEL €€
(☑04 76 51 22 59; www.grand-hotel-grenoble.fr; 5 rue de la République; r €118-245; ❄@🛜) Right in the thick of things, this newly revamped hotel raises the bar in Grenoble's style stakes with slick, monochromatic rooms, some with balconies looking out across the city to the Alps beyond.

Auberge de Jeunesse   HOSTEL €
(☑04 76 09 33 52; www.fuaj.org; 10 av du Grésivaudan; dm incl breakfast €21.50; 🛜) Grenoble's ultramodern, ecoconscious hostel is set in parkland, 5km from the centre. Take bus 1 to La Quinzaine stop, an easy two-minute walk from the hostel.

🍴 Eating & Drinking

Grenoble's most atmospheric bistros huddle on backstreets in the *quartier des Antiquaires* (Antiques Quarter). Don't miss local dish *gratin dauphinois* (finely sliced potatoes oven-baked in cream and a pinch of nutmeg).

La Petite Idée   FRENCH €€
(☑04 76 47 52 95; www.la-petite-idee.fr; 7 cours Jean Jaurès; menus €15.50-28; ☉lunch Sun-Fri,

dinner Tue-Sun; ♿) This sweet bistro had *la petite idée* (the little idea) to drum up business with market-fresh, seasonal dishes, as simple as rosemary-rubbed lamb with creamy *gratin dauphinois*. The setting is convivial and the €9.50 *plat du jour* is great value.

Ciao a Te   ITALIAN €€
(☑04 76 42 54 41; 2 rue de la Paix; mains €16.50-26; ☉lunch & dinner Tue-Sat, closed Aug) Stylish yet relaxed, Ciao dishes up authentic Italian cuisine. Book ahead.

Chez Mémé Paulette   CAFE €
(☑04 76 51 38 85; 2 rue St-Hugues; snacks €4-8; ☉lunch & dinner Tue-Sat) This old curiosity shop of a cafe is crammed with antique books, milk jugs, cuckoo clocks and other knick-knacks. It draws a young crowd with its wallet-friendly grub – from soups to *tartines* and homemade tarts.

Le 365   WINE BAR
(3 rue Bayard; ☉6pm-1am Tue-Sat) If Dionysus (god of wine) had a house, this is surely what it would look like: an irresistible clutter of bottles, oil paintings and candles that create an ultrarelaxed setting for quaffing one of the wines on offer.

ℹ Information

Tourist Office (☑04 76 42 41 41; www.grenoble-tourisme.com; 14 rue de la République; ☉9am-6.30pm Mon-Sat, 9am-2pm Sun)

ℹ️ Getting There & Away

Air

Several budget airlines fly to/from **Grenoble-Isère airport** (www.grenoble-airport.com), 45km northwest and linked by **shuttle bus** (www.grenoble-altitude.com; single/return €12.50/22, 45 minutes, twice daily Tue-Sat).

Bus

From the **bus station** (rue Émile Gueymard), next to the train station, **VFD** (www.vfd.fr) and **Transisère** (www.transisere.fr) run buses to/from various destinations including Geneva (€46.50, two hours) and Lyon St-Exupéry (€22, one hour) airports.

Train

From the **train station** (rue Émile Gueymard), frequent trains run to/from Paris' Gare de Lyon (from €80, 3½ hours) and Lyon (€20.50, 1½ hours).

THE JURA

The dark wooded hills, rolling dairy country and limestone plateaux of the Jura Mountains, stretching in an arc for 360km along the Franco-Swiss border from the Rhine to the Rhône, comprise one of the least explored pockets in France. Rural, deeply traditional and *un petit peu* eccentric, the Jura is the place if you're seeking serenity, authentic farmstays and a taste of mountain life.

The Jura – from a Gaulish word meaning 'forest' – is France's premier cross-country skiing area. The range is dotted with ski stations, and every year the region hosts the **Transjurassienne**, one of the world's toughest cross-country skiing events.

Besançon

POP 121,391

Home to a monumental Vauban citadel, France's first public museum, and the birthplace of Victor Hugo and the Lumière Brothers, Besançon has an extraordinary background and yet, remarkably, remains something of a secret. Straddling seven hills and hugging the banks of the River Doubs, the cultured capital of Franche-Comté remains refreshingly modest and untouristy, despite charms such as its graceful 18th-century old town, first-rate restaurants and happening bars pepped up by the city's students.

The opening of a new TGV station in the village of Auxon, 12km north, in late 2011, put Besançon firmly back on the map.

👁️ Sights

TOP CHOICE **Citadelle de Besançon** CITADEL

(www.citadelle.com; rue des Fusillés de la Résistance; adult/child €9/6; ☺9am-6pm) Besançon's crowning glory is this Unesco World Heritage–listed citadel designed by Vauban for Louis XIV in the late 17th century. It harbours three museums: the **Musée Comtois** covering local traditions, the **Musée d'Histoire Naturelle** on natural history, and the harrowing **Musée de la Résistance et de la Déportation** which look at the rise of Nazism and fascism, and the French Resistance movement. There's an **insectarium**, **aquarium**, pitch-black, ho-hum **noctarium** and an overly cramped **parc zoologique**.

TOP CHOICE **Musée des Beaux-Arts et d'Archéologie** MUSEUM

(www.musee-arts-besancon.org; 1 place de la Révolution; adult/child €5/free; ☺9.30am-noon & 2-6pm Wed-Mon) This museum was founded in 1694 (when the Louvre was but a twinkle in Paris' eye). The stellar collection spans Egyptian mummies, Neolithic tools and Gallo-Roman mosaics; a cavernous drawing cabinet with 5500 works, including Dürer, Delacroix and Rodin masterpieces; and 14th- to 20th-century painting with standouts by Titian, Rubens, Goya and Matisse.

☞ Tours

When the sun's out, a river cruise is a relaxed way to see Besançon. April to October, vessels dock beneath Pont de la République to take passengers on 1¼-hour cruises along the River Doubs, which include a glide

---

WORTH A TRIP

SALINE ROYALE

Envisaged by its designer, Claude-Nicolas Ledoux, as the 'ideal city', the 18th-century **Saline Royale** (Royal Saltworks; www.salineroyale.com; adult/child €7.50/3.50; ☺9am-noon & 2-6pm) in Arc-et-Senans, 35km southwest of Besançon, is a showpiece of early Industrial Age town planning. Although his urban dream was never fully realised, Ledoux's semicircular saltworks is now listed as a Unesco World Heritage site.

Regular trains link Besançon and Arc-et-Senans (€7, 30 minutes, 10 daily).

WORTH A TRIP

A WINE LOVER'S TRIP

Corkscrewing through some 80km of well-tended vines, pretty countryside and stone villages is the **Route des Vins de Jura** (Jura Wine Road; www.laroutedesvinsdujura. com). Linger in **Arbois**, Jura wine capital, where the history of its *vin jaune* is told in the **Musée de la Vigne et du Vin** (www.juramusees.fr; adult/child €3.50/3; ⊙10am-noon & 2-6pm Wed-Mon), inside the whimsical **Château Pécauld**. Next to the chateau, pick up the **Chemin des Vignes** (2.5km) walking trail or **Circuit des Vignes** (8km) mountain-bike route through vines.

Later, lunch on local organic produce at **La Balance Mets et Vins** (☑03 84 37 45 00; 47 rue de Courcelles, Arbois; menus €16.50-37; ⊙lunch & dinner Thu-Mon, lunch Tue & Wed; ☝). Its signature *coq au vin jaune et aux morilles* casserole, and crème brûlée doused in *vin jaune* are must-tastes, as are the wine *menus* with five glasses of Jurassienne wine (€17) or *vin jaune* (€25, including a vintage one). Kids can sniff, swirl and sip, too, with three kinds of organic grape juice (€7.80).

Above Arbois is **Pupillin**, a yellow-brick village famous for its wine production with several wine cellars to visit. Arbois' **tourist office** (☑03 84 66 55 50; www.arbois.com; 17 rue de l'Hôtel de Ville; ⊙9am-noon & 2-6pm Mon-Sat) has a list of many more. Trains links Arbois and Besançon (€9, 45 minutes, 10 daily).

along a 375m-long tunnel underneath the citadel.

Bateaux du Saut du Doubs   BOAT TOUR
(www.sautdudoubs.fr; adult/child €13/9; ⊙10am, 2.30pm & 4.30pm Jul & Aug)

🛏 Sleeping & Eating

TOP CHOICE **Charles Quint Hôtel**   HISTORIC HOTEL €€
(☑03 81 82 05 49; www.hotel-charlesquint.com; 3 rue du Chapître; d €89-145; ☝❄) This grand 18th-century townhouse is sublime, with a pool-clad garden slumbering in the shade of the citadel, behind the cathedral.

Hôtel Granvelle   HOTEL €
(☑03 81 81 33 92; www.hotel-granvelle.fr; 13 rue du Général Lecourbe; r €54-68; ❄@☝) You'll find 30 neat and tidy, if dated, rooms in this stone building below the citadel. 'Interactive' rooms have internet-linked computers and flatscreen TVs.

TOP CHOICE **Le Saint-Pierre**   MODERN FRENCH €€€
(☑03 81 81 20 99; www.restaurant-saintpierre.com; 104 rue Battant; menus €38-70; ⊙lunch Mon-Fri, dinner Mon-Sat) White tablecloths, exposed stone and subtle lighting are the perfect backdrop for the intense flavours of lobster fricassee with spinach and herb ravioli, expertly paired with regional wines. The three-course *menu marché* is excellent value at €38. The restaurant is 500m north of Grande Rue on the opposite side of the river.

ⓘ Getting There & Away

Besançon Gare Viotte is 800m uphill from the city centre. Useful routes:

Paris €60 to €85, 2¾ hours, 14 daily

Dijon €15, 70 minutes, 20 daily

Lyon €30 to €45, 2½ to three hours, 25 daily

Connections to major cities are quicker from the new **Gare de Besançon Franche-Comté TGV station**, 12km north of the centre and a 15-minute hop by train from Gare Viotte.

THE DORDOGNE

If it's French heart and soul you're after, look no further. Tucked in the country's southwestern corner, the Dordogne fuses history, culture and culinary sophistication in one unforgettably scenic package. The region is best known for its sturdy *bastides* (fortified towns), clifftop chateaux and spectacular prehistoric cave paintings, neighboured to the southwest by the Mediterranean-tinged region of **the Lot**, with its endless vintage vineyards.

Sarlat-La-Canéda
POP 9943

A gorgeous tangle of honey-coloured buildings, alleyways and secret squares make up this unmissable Dordogne village – a natural, if touristy, launchpad into the Vézère Valley.

Part of the fun of Sarlat is getting lost in its twisting alleyways and backstreets. **Rue Jean-Jacques Rousseau** or **rue Landry** are good starting points, but for the grandest buildings and *hôtels particuliers,* explore **rue des Consuls**. Whichever street you take, sooner or later you'll hit the **Cathédrale St-Sacerdos** (place du Peyrou), a real mix of architectural styles and periods: the belfry and western facade are the oldest parts.

Nearby, the former **Église Ste-Marie** (place de la Liberté) houses Sarlat's mouthwatering **Marché Couvert** (covered market) and a state-of-the-art **panoramic lift** (elevator), designed by French architect Jean Nouvel, in its bell tower.

🛏 Sleeping

Villa des Consuls　　　　B&B €€
(☏05 53 31 90 05; www.villaconsuls.fr; 3 rue Jean-Jacques Rousseau; d €82-103, apt €124-184; @🛜) Despite its Renaissance exterior, the enormous rooms here are modern through and through, with shiny wood floors, sofas and original roof trusses.

La Maison des Peyrat　　　HOTEL €€
(☏05 53 59 00 32; www.maisondespeyrat.com; Le Lac de la Plane; r €56-103) This beautiful 17th-century house with lovingly tended gardens sits on a hill about 1.5km from town. Its 11 generously sized rooms are fairly plain, but ooze country charisma.

Hôtel Les Récollets　　　HOTEL €
(☏05 53 31 36 00; www.hotel-recollets-sarlat.com; 4 rue Jean-Jacques Rousseau; d €49-89; ✲🛜) Budget rooms with an old town location, set around a pretty hidden courtyard.

🍴 Eating

 Le Grand Bleu　　　GASTRONOMIC €€€
(☏05 53 29 82 14; www.legrandbleu.eu; 43 av de la Gare; menus €36-65; ⊙lunch Thu-Sun, dinner Tue-Sat) For a proper supper, this Michelin-starred restaurant is the choice – think creative cuisine that makes maximum use of luxury produce: truffles, lobster, turbot and St-Jacques scallops. Cooking courses as well.

Le Bistrot　　　REGIONAL CUISINE €€
(☏05 53 28 28 40; place du Peyrou; menus €18.50-28.50; ⊙Mon-Sat) This dinky diner is the best of the bunch on cafe-clad place du Peyrou. Gingham cloths and tiny tables create a cosy bistro feel, and the menu's heavy on Sarlat classics – especially walnuts, *magret de canard* (duck breast) and *pommes sarladaises* (potatoes cooked in duck fat).

ℹ Information

Tourist Office (☏05 53 31 45 45; www.sarlat-tourisme.com; rue Tourny; ⊙9am-7pm Mon-Sat, 10am-1pm & 2-6pm Sun Jul & Aug, shorter hours Sep-Jun)

FRANCE SARLAT-LA-CANÉDA

TRUFFLE CAPITAL

For culinary connoisseurs there is just one reason to visit the Dordogne: black truffles *(truffes).* A subterranean fungi that thrives on the roots of oak trees, this mysterious little mushroom is notoriously capricious. The art of truffle-hunting is a closely guarded secret and vintage crops fetch as much as €1000 per kg. Truffles are sought after by top chefs for an infinite array of gourmet dishes, but black truffles are often best eaten quite simply in a plain egg omelette, shaved over buttered pasta or sliced on fresh crusty bread.

Truffles are hunted by dogs (and occasionally pigs) from December to March and sold at special truffle markets in the Dordogne, including in Périgueux, Sarlat and most notably, the 'world's truffle capital', **Sorges** (population 1234). This tiny village, 23km northeast of Périgueux on the N21, is the place to brush up on truffle culture; head to the **Ecomusée de la Truffe** (www.ecomusee-truffe-sorges.com; Le Bourg, Sorges; adult/child €5/2.50; ⊙9.30am-12.30pm & 2.30-6.30pm daily Jun-Sep, closed Mon Oct-May) and hook yourself up with a truffle hunt. **La Truffe Noire de Sorges** (☏06 08 45 09 48; www.truffe-sorges.com; tours €15-25; ⊙by reservation Dec-Feb & Jun-Sep) runs tours of *truffières* (the areas where truffles are cultivated), followed by a tasting.

Then there is **Auberge de la Truffe** (☏05 53 05 02 05; www.auberge-de-la-truffe.com; Sorges; r €55-81, f €110-145; ✲🏊) in the centre of Sorges, with its stylish and renowned **restaurant** (menus €23-57) serving sensational seasonal cuisine. For culinary connoisseurs there is just one fixed menu to order, the *menu truffe* (€100).

❶ Getting There & Away

The **train station** (ave de la Gare), 1.3km south of the old city, serves Périgueux (change at Le Buisson; €14.80, 1¾ hours, three daily) and Les Eyzies (change at Le Buisson; €9.80, 50 minutes to 2½ hours, three daily).

Les Eyzies-de-Tayac-Sireuil
POP 860

A hot base for touring the extraordinary cave collection of the **Vézère Valley**, this village is essentially a clutch of touristy shops strung along a central street. Its **Musée National de Préhistoire** (☎05 53 06 45 45; www.musee-prehistoire-eyzies.fr; 1 rue du Musée; adult/child €5/3, 1st Sun of month free; ☺9.30am-6pm Wed-Mon), rife with amazing prehistoric finds, makes a great introduction to the area.

About 250m north of the museum is the Cro-Magnon shelter of **Abri Pataud** (☎05 53 06 92 46; pataud@mnhn.fr; 20 rue du Moyen Âge; adult/child €5/3; ☺10am-noon & 2-6pm Sun-Thu), with an ibex carving dating from about 19,000 BC. Admission includes a guided tour (some in English).

Train services link Les Eyzies with Sarlat-la-Canéda.

THE ATLANTIC COAST

With quiet country roads winding through vine-striped hills and wild stretches of coastal sands interspersed with misty islands, the Atlantic coast is where France gets back to nature. Much more laid-back than the Med, this is the place to slow right down.

If you're a surf nut or a beach bum, then the sandy bays around Biarritz will be right up your alley, while oenophiles can sample the fruits of the vine in the high temple of French winemaking, Bordeaux. Towards the Pyrenees you'll find the Basque Country, which in many ways is closer to the culture of northern Spain than to the rest of France.

Nantes
POP 290,100

You can take Nantes out of Brittany (as happened when regional boundaries were redrawn during WWII), but you can't take Brittany out of its long-time capital, Nantes ('Naoned' in Breton). Spirited and innovative, this city has a long history of reinventing itself. Founded by Celts, the city later became France's foremost port, industrial cen-

---

DON'T MISS

PREHISTORIC PAINTINGS

Fantastic prehistoric **caves** with some of the world's finest **cave art** is what makes the Vézère Valley so very special. Most of the caves are closed in winter, and get very busy in summer. Visitor numbers are strictly limited, so you'll need to reserve well ahead.

Of the valley's 175 known sites, the most famous include **Grotte de Font de Gaume** (☎05 53 06 86 00; http://eyzies.monuments-nationaux.fr/; adult/child €7.50/free; ☺9.30am-5.30pm Sun-Fri mid-May–mid-Sep, 9.30am-12.30pm & 2-5.30pm Sun-Fri mid-Sep–mid-May), 1km northeast of Les Eyzies. About 14,000 years ago, prehistoric artists created the gallery of over 230 figures, including bison, reindeer, horses, mammoths, bears and wolves, of which 25 are on permanent display.

About 7km east of Les Eyzies, **Abri du Cap Blanc** (☎05 53 06 86 00; adult/child €7.50/free; ☺10am-6pm Sun-Fri mid-May–mid-Sep, 10am-noon & 2-6pm Sun-Fri mid-Sep–mid-May) showcases an unusual sculpture gallery of horses, bison and deer.

Then there is **Grotte de Rouffignac** (☎05 53 05 41 71; www.grotectderouffignac.fr; adult/child €6.50/4.20; ☺9-11.30am & 2-6pm Jul & Aug, 10-11.30am & 2-5pm Sep-Jun), sometimes known as the 'Cave of 100 Mammoths' because of its painted mammoths. Access to the caves, hidden in woodland 15km north of Les Eyzies, is aboard a trundling electric train.

Star of the show goes hands down to **Grotte de Lascaux** (Lascaux II; ☎05 53 51 95 03; www.semitour.com; adult/child €8.80/6; ☺9.30am-6pm), 2km southeast of Montignac, featuring an astonishing menagerie including oxen, deer, horses, reindeer and mammoth, as well as an amazing 5.5m bull, the largest cave drawing ever found. The original cave was closed to the public in 1963 to prevent damage to the paintings, but the most famous sections have been meticulously recreated in a second cave nearby – a massive undertaking that required some 20 artists and took 11 years.

NANTES CITY PASS

Sold at the tourist office, the **Pass Nantes** (one-/two-/three day pass €25/35/45) gets you unlimited travel on buses and trams, entry into museums and monuments, a guided tour, shopping discounts and various other handy extras.

tre and shipbuilding hub, and has recently reinvented itself again as a cultural centre and youthful metropolis – one in two Nantais is under 40!

Sights

TOP
CHOICE **Les Machines de l'Île de Nantes** THEME PARK
(www.lesmachines-nantes.fr; Parc des Chantiers, Blvd Léon Bureau; adult/child €7/5.50; ⏰10am-7pm Jul-Aug, hrs vary rest of year) Inside this fantasy world you can prance around on the back of a 45-tonne **mechanical elephant**, voyage on a boat through rough and dangerous oceans, or twirl through the sky aboard Le Carrousel des Mondes Marines; a 25m high funfair carousel like you've never seen before. Gallery tickets are good for the workshop, where you can watch these fantastical contraptions being built.

Château des Ducs de Bretagne CASTLE, MUSEUM
(www.chateau-nantes.fr; 4 place Marc Elder; adult/child €5/3; ⏰8am-7pm Apr-Oct, shorter hrs rest of year) Forget fusty furnishings – the stripped, light-filled interior of the restored Château des Ducs de Bretagne houses multimedia-rich exhibits detailing the city's history. Frequent temporary exhibitions (additional fee), too.

Musée Jules Verne MUSEUM
(www.julesverne.nantes.fr; 3 rue de l'Hermitage; adult/child €3/1.50; ⏰10am-7pm Tue-Sun) Overlooking the river, this is a magical museum with 1st-edition books, hand-edited manuscripts and cardboard theatre cut-outs. Child-friendly interactive displays introduce or reintroduce you to the work of Jules Verne, who was born in Nantes in 1828. The museum is a 2km walk down river from the town centre.

Musée des Beaux-Arts MUSEUM
(10 rue Georges Clemenceau; adult €3.50; ⏰10am-6pm Wed & Fri-Mon, to 8pm Thu) One of the finest collections of French paintings outside Paris hangs in the Musée des Beaux-Arts, with works by Georges de la Tour, Chagall, Monet,

Picasso and Kandinsky among others. Due to reopen after renovations in late 2013.

Sleeping

TOP
CHOICE **Hôtel Pommeraye** BOUTIQUE HOTEL €€
(☎02 40 48 78 79; www.hotel-pommeraye.com; 2 rue Boileau; s €54-139 d €59-144; ❄@🖥) Sleek and chic, this is more art gallery than hotel. Rooms have shimmering short-pile carpets and textured walls in shades of pale grey, gold, chocolate and violet.

Hôtel Amiral HOTEL €€
(☎02 40 69 20 21; www.hotel-nantes.fr; 26bis rue Scribe; s/d from €84/89; 🖥) The rooms at this excellent little hotel are fairly plain but the common areas are funky and the breakfast room a commotion of jungle plants. The family who run it are really helpful.

Hôtel Graslin HOTEL €€
(☎02 40 69 72 91; www.hotel-graslin.com; 1 rue Piron; r €59-109; 🖥) The unlikely (but very Nantes) marriage of art deco and the '70s at this refurbished hotel includes details like eggplant-and-orange wing chairs in the lounge.

Auberge de Jeunesse La Manu HOSTEL €
(☎02 40 29 29 20; www.fuaj.org/Nantes; 2 place de la Manu; dm incl breakfast €20.10; ⏰closed Christmas; 🖥) Housed in an old converted factory, this well-equipped 123-bed hostel is

FRANCE NANTES

DON'T MISS

INDUSTRIAL CHIC

Nantes has no shortage of edgy spots and there is no better place to start than the **Hangar à Bananes** (www.hangar-abananes.com; 21 quai des Antilles; ⏰daily till late), a rejuvenated banana-ripening warehouse on Île de Nantes with more than a dozen restaurants, bars and clubs (and combinations thereof), each hipper than the next. The front terraces of most face Daniel Buren's art installation **Anneaux de Buren** (quai des Antilles), illuminated at night.

Or try industrial-chic **Le Lieu Unique** (www.lelieuunique.com; 2 rue de la Biscuiterie), the one-time LU biscuit-factory-turned-performance-arts space where you can catch dance, theatre and contemporary art. Its restaurant, polished concrete bar buzzes and basement *hamman* (Turkish bath) buzzes.

WORTH A TRIP

GREEN VENICE

Floating along emerald waterways – tinted green in spring and summer by duckweed – in a kayak or rowing boat is a real Zen highlight. Dubbed *Venise Verte* (Green Venice), the **Parc Naturel Interrégional du Marais Poitevin** is a tranquil, bird-filled wetland covering some 800 sq km of wet and drained marshland, threaded with canals, cycling paths and the odd waterside village.

Boating and **cycling** are the only ways to explore and there is no shortage of bikes (per hour/half-day €6/13) and flat-bottomed boats (from €15/38) or kayaks (from €12/30) to rent from the Marais Poitevin's two main bases: tiny, honey-coloured **Coulon** and (our favourite, being a sucker for romance), the pretty village of **Arçais**. Try **Arçais Venise Verte** (www.veniseverteloisirs.fr), **Au Martin Pecheur** (www.aumartin pecheur.com) or **Bardet-Huttiers** (www.marais-arcais.com).

To ensure complete and utter head-over-the-heels love, stay overnight at the environmentally friendly **Maison Flore** (📞05 49 76 27 11; www.maisonflore.com; rue du Grand Port, Arçais; s/d €63/74; ⊘closed Christmas–mid-Feb; 🅿@🛜). Romantically set on Arçais' waterfront, the 10-room boutique hotel is painted the colours of local marsh plants such as the pale-green angelica and bright-purple iris. Books and board games in the lounge add a cosy touch and you can rent boats.

Getting to Green Venice is painful in anything other than your own car.

---

a 15-minute walk from the centre. Lock-out noon to 4pm. Take tram 1 to the Manufacture stop.

✖ Eating

Nantes' most cosmopolitan dining is in the medieval Bouffay quarter around rue de la Juiverie, rue des Petites Écuries and rue de la Bâclerie. Rue Jean Jacques Rousseau and rue Santeuil are other busy eat streets.

In March and November, buy sardines at street stalls all over town.

TOP CHOICE **Le Bistrot de l'Écrivain** MODERN FRENCH €€
(📞02 51 84 15 15; 15 rue Jean Jacques Rousseau; menus €14.50-18.50; ⊘Mon-Sat) Splashed in shades of red with wine bottles lining the walls, Le Bistrot de l'Écrivain is a relaxed place with all the Nantaise standards on the menu, plus dishes with an unexpected twist.

Les Pieds dans le Plat MODERN FRENCH €€
(📞02 40 69 25 15; 13 rue Jean-Jacques Rousseau; menus €13.50-25.50; ⊘11.30am-midnight) This modern French bistro has exposed stone walls, colourful paint work and is the real flavour of the month; advance reservations strongly advised.

Un Coin en Ville MODERN FRENCH €
(📞02 40 20 05 97; 2 place de la Bourse; menus from €14.95; ⊘lunch & dinner Mon-Fri, dinner only Sat) Expect flickering tea-light candles, soulful jazz and blues, and cooking that combines local produce with exotic styles, such as red curry with prawns and scallops.

ℹ Information

Tourist office (www.nantes-tourisme.com; 2 place St-Pierre & cours Olivier de Clisson; ⊘10am-6pm Mon-Sat, from 10.30am Thu)

ℹ Getting There & Away

AIR Aéroport International Nantes-Atlantique (www.nantes.aeroport.fr) is 12km southeast of town.

TRAIN Destinations from the **train station** (27 bd de Stalingrad) include Paris' Gare Montparnasse (from €58, two hours, 15 to 20 daily) and Bordeaux (€47, four hours, three or four daily).

Poitiers
POP 91,300

Inland from the coast, history-steeped Poitiers rose to prominence as the former capital of Poitou, the region governed by the Counts of Poitiers in the Middle Ages. Poitiers has one of the oldest universities in the country, first established in 1432 and today a lynchpin of this lively city.

◉ Sights

Église Notre Dame la Grande CHURCH
(place Charles de Gaulle) The earliest parts of this church date from the 11th century; three of the five choir chapels were added in the 15th century, with the six chapels along the

northern wall of the nave added in the 16th century. The only original frescoes are the faint 12th- or 13th-century works that adorn the U-shaped dome above the choir. Every evening from 21 June to the third weekend in September, spectacular colours are cinematically projected onto the west facade of this church.

Baptistère St-Jean   CHURCH
(rue Jean Jaurès; adult/child €2/1; ⊙10.30am-12.30pm & 3-6pm Wed-Mon Apr-Oct) Constructed in the 4th and 6th centuries on Roman foundations, Baptistère St-Jean, 100m south of Cathédrale St-Pierrel, was redecorated in the 10th century and used as a parish church. The octagonal hole under the frescos was used for total-immersion baptisms, practised until the 7th century. In July and August it's open daily.

Futuroscope   THEME PARK
(www.futuroscope.com; adult/child €35/26; ⊙10am-11.15pm Jul-Aug, shorter hrs Sep-Dec & Feb-Jun) This cinematic theme park, 10km north of Poitiers in Jaunay-Clan, takes you whizzing through space, diving into the deep blue ocean depths and on a close encounter with futuristic creatures. To keep things cutting edge, one-third of the attractions change annually. Many are motion-seat setups requiring a minimum height of 120cm. From Poitiers' train station take bus 1 or E (€1.30, 30 minutes).

🍴 Sleeping & Eating

Hôtel de l'Europe   HISTORIC HOTEL €
(☑05 49 88 12 00; www.hotel-europe-poitiers.com; 39 rue Carnot; s/d €59/65; ⊛) The main building of this elegant, very un-two-star-like hotel dates from 1710, with a sweeping staircase, oversized rooms and refined furnishings. The annexe has modern rooms.

Hôtel Central   HOTEL €
(☑05 49 01 79 79; www.hotel-central-poitiers.com; 35 place du Maréchal Leclerc; r from €52; ⊛) At the southern edge of a charming pedestrian district of half-timbered houses, this two-star place is a terrific little bargain. Rooms are (very!) snug but sunlit.

La Serrurerie   FRENCH €
(☑05 49 41 05 14; 28 rue des Grandes Écoles; menu €12.50, mains €10-17.50; ⊙8am-2am) Hecticly busy, this mosaic-and-steel bistro-bar is Poitiers' communal lounge-dining room. A chalked blackboard menu lists specialities

like *tournedos* (thick slices) of salmon, pastas and a crème brûlée you'll be dreaming about until your next visit.

ℹ Information
Tourist office (☑05 49 41 21 24; www.ot-poitiers.fr; 45 place Charles de Gaulle; ⊙10am-11pm)

ℹ Getting There & Away
The **train station** (☑36 35; bd du Grand Cerf) has direct links to Bordeaux (€24, 1¾ hours), Nantes (from €30, 3¼ hours) and Paris' Gare Montparnasse (from €47, 1½ hours, 12 daily).

Bordeaux
POP 240,500

The new millennium was a turning point for the city long nicknamed La Belle au Bois Dormant (Sleeping Beauty), when the mayor, ex-Prime Minister Alain Juppé, roused Bordeaux, pedestrianising its boulevards, restoring its neoclassical architecture, and implementing a hi-tech public-transport system. Today the city is a Unesco World Heritage site and, with its merry student population and 2.5 million-odd annual tourists, scarcely sleeps at all.

◎ Sights
Cathédrale St-André   CATHEDRAL
This Unesco World Heritage site is almost overshadowed by the gargoyled, 50m-high Gothic belfry, **Tour Pey-Berland** (adult/child €5.50/free; ⊙10am-1.15pm & 2-6pm Jun-Sep, shorter hrs rest of year). Erected between 1440 and 1466, its spire was topped off in 1863 with the statue of Notre Dame de l'Aquitaine (Our Lady of Aquitaine). Scaling the tower's 231 narrow steps rewards you with a spectacular panorama of Bordeaux city.

Museums and Galleries   MUSEUMS
Gallo-Roman statues and relics dating back 25,000 years are among the highlights at the impressive **Musée d'Aquitaine** (20 cours Pasteur), while an 1824 warehouse for French colonial produce (coffee, cocoa, peanuts, vanilla and the like) is the dramatic backdrop for cutting-edge modern art at the **CAPC Musée d'Art Contemporain** (rue Ferrére, Entrepôt 7; ⊙11am-6pm Tue & Thu-Sun, to 8pm Wed).

The evolution of Occidental art from the Renaissance to the mid-20th century fills the **Musée des Beaux-Arts** (20 cours d'Albret;

ON THE WINE TRAIL

Thirsty? The 1000-sq-km wine-growing area around the city of Bordeaux is, along with Burgundy, France's most important producer of top-quality wines. Whet your palate with Bordeaux tourist office's introduction wine-and-cheese courses (€24).

Serious students of the grape can enrol in a two-hour (€25) or two- to three-day course (€335 to €600) at the **École du Vin** (Wine School; ☑ 05 56 00 22 66; www. bordeaux.com) inside the **Maison du Vin de Bordeaux** (3 cours du 30 Juillet).

Bordeaux has over 5000 estates where grapes are grown, picked and turned into wine. Smaller chateaux often accept walk-in visitors, but at many places, especially better-known ones, you have to reserve in advance. If you have your own wheels, one of the easiest to visit is **Château Lanessan** (☑ 05 56 58 94 80; www.lanessan.com; Cussac-Fort-Medoc).

Favourite vine-framed villages brimming with charm and tasting/buying opportunities include medieval **St-Émilion** (www.saint-emilion-tourisme.com), port town **Pauillac** (www.pauillac-medoc.com) and **Listrac-Médoc**. In **Arsac-en-Médoc**, Philippe Raoux's vast glass-and-steel wine centre, **La Winery** (☑ 05 56 39 04 90; www.lawinery.fr; Rond-point des Vendangeurs, D1), stuns with concerts and contemporary art exhibitions alongside tastings to determine your *signe œnologique* ('wine sign'; booking required).

Many chateaux close during October's *vendange* (grape harvest).

⊙ 11am-6pm, closed Tue) inside the 1770s-built Hôtel de Ville.

Faience pottery, porcelain, gold, iron, glasswork and furniture are displayed at the **Musée des Arts Décoratifs** (39 rue Bouffard; ⊙ 2-6pm Wed-Mon).

Jardin Public   GARDEN
(cours de Verdun) Landscaping is artistic as well as informative at the Jardin Public, established in 1755 and laid out in the English style a century later.

🛏 Sleeping

TOP
CHOICE **Ecolodge des Chartrons**   B&B €€
(☑ 05 56 81 49 13; www.ecolodgedeschartrons.com; 23 rue Raze; s €96-118, d €98-134; 🔊) Hidden in a side street in Bordeaux' Chartrons wine merchant district, this *chambre d'hôte* is blazing a trail for ecofriendly sleeping with its solar-powered hot-water system, energy-efficient gas heating and hemp-based soundproofing. Each of the five rooms has a bathroom built from natural materials such as basalt. Organic breakfasts are served at a long timber table.

**Les Chambres au Coeur
de Bordeaux**   B&B €€
(☑ 05 56 52 43 58; www.aucoeurdebordeaux.fr; 28 rue Boulan; s/d from €85/95; 🔊) This swish B&B has five charming rooms that are a very Bordeaux-appropriate mix of old and new; free *apéro* each evening at 7pm.

La Maison Bord'eaux   BOUTIQUE HOTEL €€
(☑ 05 56 44 00 45; www.lamaisonbord-eaux.com; 113 rue du Docteur Albert Barraud; s/d from €145/165; P✳🔊) You'd expect to find a sumptuous 18th-century chateau with conifer-flanked courtyard and stable in the countryside, but this stunning *maison d'hôte* is right in the middle of the city. *Table d'hôte* available by arrangement (€35 to €150 including wine).

Auberge de Jeunesse   HOSTEL €
(☑ 05 56 33 00 70; www.auberge-jeunesse-bordeaux.com; 22 cours Barbey; dm incl sheets & breakfast €22.50; ⊙ reception closed 11am-2pm; 🔊) This ultra-modern building with kitchen reopened after renovation in 2013. From the train station, follow cours de la Marne northwest for 300m and turn left opposite the park; the hostel's about 250m ahead on your left.

🍴 Eating

Place du Parlement, rue du Pas St-Georges, rue des Faussets and place de la Victoire are loaded with dining addresses, as is the old waterfront warehouse district around quai des Marques – great for a sunset meal or drink.

TOP
CHOICE **Le Cheverus Café**   BISTRO €
(☑ 05 56 48 29 73; 81-83 rue du Loup; menus from €11.40; ⊙ Mon-Sat) This neighbourhood bistro is friendly, cosy and chaotically busy (be prepared to wait for a table at lunchtime). The food dares to veer slightly away from the

bistro standards of steak and chips; lunch *menus,* which include wine, are an all-out bargain. Come evening it morphs into something of a tapas bar.

TOP CHOICE **La Tupina** REGIONAL CUISINE €€
(☑05 56 91 56 37; www.latupina.com; 6 rue Porte de la Monnaie; menus €18-65, mains €27-45) Filled with the aroma of soup simmering inside an old *tupina* ('kettle' in Basque) over an open fire, this white-tableclothed place is feted far and wide for its seasonal southwestern French specialities. Find it a 10-minute walk upriver from the city centre, on a small side street. Any local can point you in the right direction.

La Boîte à Huîtres OYSTERS €€
(☑05 56 81 64 97; 36 cours du Chapeau Rouge; lunch menu €19, 6 oysters from €10) This rickety, wood-panelled place is the best place in Bordeaux to munch fresh Arcachon oysters. Traditionally they're served with sausage but you can have them in a number of different forms, including with foie gras.

Michels Bistrot BISTRO €
(15 rue du Pas-Saint-Georges; lunch menu €12) In Bordeaux's most bohemian quarter, this buzzing bistro is packed with students and those who wish they were still students. It's renowned for the quality of its beef – whether that be in hamburger form or a more classic steak. It's also a popular early evening *apéro* hangout.

ℹ Information

Main tourist office (☑05 56 00 66 00; www.bordeaux-tourisme.com; 12 cours du 30 Juillet; ☺9am-7.30pm Mon-Sat, 9.30am-6.30pm Sun)

ℹ Getting There & Away

AIR Bordeaux airport (p318) is in Mérignac, 10km west of the city centre, with domestic and some international services.

BUS Citram Aquitaine (www.citram.fr) runs most buses to destinations in the Gironde.

International bus operator **Eurolines** (☑05 56 92 50 42; 32 rue Charles Domercq) faces the train station.

TRAIN From Gare St-Jean, 3km from the centre:
Paris Gare Montparnasse €73, three hours, at least 16 daily
Nantes €47.70, four hours
Poitiers €38, 1¾ hours
Toulouse from €35.30, 2¼ hours

DON'T MISS

SATURDAY-MORNING OYSTERS

A classic Bordeaux experience is a Saturday morning spent slurping oysters and white wine from one of the seafood stands to be found at **Marché des Capucins** (six oysters & glass of wine €6; ☺7am-noon). Afterwards you can peruse the stalls while shopping for the freshest ingredients for a picnic in one of the city's parks. To get there, head south down cours Pasteur and once at place de la Victoire turn left onto rue Élie Gintrec.

Lourdes

In the heart of the Pyrenees, **Lourdes** has been one of the world's most important pilgrimage sites since 1858, when 14-year-old Bernadette Soubirous (1844–79) saw the Virgin Mary in a series of 18 visions that came to her in a grotto. The town now feels dangerously close to a religious theme park, with a roll-call of over six million miracle-seeking visitors and endless souvenir shops selling statues and Virgin Mary–shaped plastic bottles (just add holy water at the shrine). But the commercialism doesn't extend to the *sanctuaires* (sanctuaries) themselves, as they are mercifully souvenir-free.

Grotte de Massabielle (Massabielle Cave) is the most revered site in the area. The Esplanade des Processions, which is lined with enormous flickering candles left by previous pilgrims, leads along a river to the grotto's entrance, where people queue up to enter the cave or to dip in one of the baths. It's not for wallflowers: once you're behind the curtain, you're expected to strip off before being swaddled in a sheet and plunged backwards into the icy water.

The main 19th-century section of the sanctuaries is divided between the neo-Byzantine **Basilique du Rosaire**, the **crypt** and spire-topped **Basilique Supérieure** (Upper Basilica). From Palm Sunday to mid-October, nightly torchlight processions start from the Massabielle Grotto at 9pm, while at 5pm there's the **Procession Eucharistique** (Blessed Sacrament Procession) along Esplanade des Processions.

When the crowds of pilgrims get too much for you, seek refuge on the rocky 94m-high

DON'T MISS

DUNE DU PILAT

This colossal sand dune (sometimes referred to as the Dune de Pyla because of its location in the resort town of Pyla-sur-Mer), 65km west of Bordeaux, stretches from the mouth of the Bassin d'Arcachon southwards for almost 3km. Already the largest in Europe, it's spreading eastwards at 4.5m a year – it has swallowed trees, a road junction and even a hotel.

The view from the top – approximately 114m above sea level – is magnificent. To the west you can see the sandy shoals at the mouth of the **Bassin d'Arcachon**, including the **Banc d'Arguin bird reserve** and **Cap Ferret**. Dense dark-green pine forests stretch from the base of the dune eastwards almost as far as the eye can see.

Take care swimming in this area: powerful currents swirl out to sea from the deceptively tranquil *baïnes* (little bays).

Although an easy day trip from Bordeaux, the area around the dune is an enjoyable place to kick back for a while. Most people choose to camp in one of the swag of seasonal campgrounds. Lists and information on all of these (and more bricks-and-mortar-based accommodation) can be found at www.bassin-arcachon.com.

pinnacle of **Pic du Jer** – the panorama of Lourdes and the Pyrenees is inspiring. Walk three hours along a marked trail or ride six minutes in a century-old funicular. The summit is a superb picnic spot.

Lourdes is well connected by train; destinations include Bayonne (€22.40, 1¾ hours, up to four daily) and Paris' Gare Montparnasse (€75 to €107, 6½ hours, four daily).

Biarritz

POP 26,067

Edge your way south along the coast towards Spain and you arrive in stylish Biarritz, just as ritzy as its name suggests. The resort took off in the mid-19th century (Napoléon III had a rather soft spot for the place) and it still shimmers with architectural treasures from the belle époque and art deco eras. Big waves – some of Europe's best – and a beachy lifestyle are a magnet for Europe's hip surfing set.

◉ Sights & Activities

Biarritz' raison d'être is its fashionable beaches, particularly central **Grande Plage** and **Plage Miramar**, lined end to end with sunbathing bodies on hot summer days. Stripy 1920s-style beach tents can be hired for €9.50 per day. North of Pointe St-Martin, the adrenaline-pumping surfing beaches of **Anglet** (the final 't' is pronounced) continue northwards for more than 4km. Take bus 10 or 13 from the bottom of av Verdun (just near av Édouard VII).

TOP CHOICE Cité de l'Océan   MUSEUM

(☑05 59 22 75 40; www.citedelocean.com; 1 av de la Plage; adult/child €10.50/7; ☉10am-10pm) Inside an eye-catching, wave-shaped building south of town, this museum will teach you everything about the ocean and, in between, get you to ride to the depths of the ocean in a submarine and watch giant squid and sperm whales do battle. A combined ticket with the Musée de la Mer costs €17.50/13 per adult/child.

Musée de la Mer   MUSEUM

(☑05 59 22 75 40; www.museedelamer.com; Esplanade du Rocher de la Vierge; adult/child €13/9.50; ☉9.30am-midnight Jul-Aug, shorter hrs rest of year) Housed in a wonderful art deco building, Biarritz' Sea Museum is seething with underwater life from the Bay of Biscay and beyond. Its tanks house sharks and tropical reef fish, but it's the seals that steal the show (feeding times 10.30am and 5pm).

🛏 Sleeping

TOP CHOICE Hôtel Mirano   BOUTIQUE HOTEL €€

(☑05 59 23 11 63; www.hotelmirano.fr; 11 av Pasteur; d €68-130; P🐾) Squiggly purple, orange and black wallpaper and oversize orange perspex light fittings are some of the rad '70s touches at this retro boutique hotel, a 10-minute stroll from the town centre.

Hôtel de Silhouette   DESIGNER HOTEL €€€

(☑05 59 24 93 82; www.hotel-silhouette-biarritz.com; 30 rue Gambetta; d from €220; ❄🐾) This fabulous new addition to the Biarritz hotel scene has designer rooms with big-city attitude that would feel quite at home in an upmarket Manhattan apartment. In order to remind you that the countryside is close at hand there are a couple of 'sheep' in the garden and frequently changing outdoor art and sculpture exhibitions.

Hôtel Edouard VII   HISTORIC HOTEL €€
(✐05 59 22 39 80; www.hotel-edouardvii.com; 21 av Carnot; d €132-165; ❀⏚) From the ornate dining room full of gently tick-tocking clocks to the pots of lavender carefully colour coordinated to match the floral wallpaper, everything here screams 1920s Biarritz chic.

Auberge de Jeunesse de Biarritz   HOSTEL €
(✐05 59 41 76 00; www.hihostels.com; 8 rue Chiquito de Cambo; dm incl sheets & breakfast €24.20; ⏰reception 8.30-11.30am & 6-9pm, to noon & 10pm May-Sep, closed mid-Dec–early Jan; @⏚) This popular place offers outdoor activities including surfing. From the train station, follow the railway westwards for 800m.

✖ Eating

The area around covered market **Les Halles** (rue des Halles, rue du Centre, rue du Vieux Port) is the Biarritz hot spot for character-infused tapas bars loaded with tasty treats.

TOP
CHOICE **Casa Juan Pedro**   SEAFOOD €
(✐05 59 24 00 86; Port des Pêcheurs; mains €7-10) Down by the old port, this cute fishing-shack cooks up tuna, sardines and squid with plenty of friendly banter.

Le Crabe-Tambour   SEAFOOD €€
(✐05 59 23 24 53; 49 rue d'Espagne; menus €13-18) Named after the famous 1977 film of the same name (the owner was the cook for the film set), this local hangout serves great seafood for a price that is hard to fault.

Bistrot des Halles   BASQUE €€
(✐05 59 24 21 22; 1 rue du Centre; mains €15-17) One of a cluster of restaurants along rue du Centre that shop for their produce at the nearby covered market, this bustling place is known for its excellent fish and fresh modern French market fare.

♟ Drinking

Great bars stud rue du Port Vieux, place Clemenceau and the central food-market area.

Ventilo Caffé   BAR
(rue du Port Vieux; ⏰closed Tue Oct-Easter) Dressed up like a boudoir, this fun and funky place continues its domination of the Biarritz bar scene.

Arena Café Bar   BAR
(Plage du Port Vieux; ⏰9am-2am Apr-Sep, 10am-2am Wed-Sun Oct-Mar) Tucked into a tiny cove, this beachfront hang-out combines a style-conscious restaurant with a fashionista bar with DJs and sunset views.

ⓘ Information

Tourist office (✐05 59 22 37 10; www.biarritz. fr; square d'Ixelles; ⏰9am-7pm)

ⓘ Getting There & Away

AIR Biarritz-Anglet-Bayonne Airport (www. biarritz.aeroport.fr), 3km southeast of Biarritz, is served by several low-cost carriers.

BUS ATCRB buses (www.transdev-atcrb.com) runs services down the coast to the Spanish border.

TRAIN Biarritz-La Négresse train station, 3km south of town, is linked to the centre by bus A1.

LANGUEDOC-ROUSSILLON

Languedoc-Roussillon comes in three distinct flavours: Bas-Languedoc (Lower Languedoc), land of bullfighting, rugby and robust red wines, where the region's major sights are found; sunbaked Nîmes with its fine Roman amphitheatre; and fairy-tale Carcassonne, crowned with a ring of witch-hat turrets.

Inland, Haut Languedoc (Upper Languedoc) is a mountainous, sparsely populated terrain made for lovers of the great outdoors; while to the south sits Roussillon, snug against the rugged Pyrenees and frontier to Spanish Catalonia. Meanwhile, Languedoc's traditional centre, Toulouse, was shaved off when regional boundaries were redrawn almost half a century ago, but we've chosen to include it in this section.

Nîmes

POP 146,500

This buzzy city boasts some of France's best-preserved classical buildings, including a famous Roman amphitheatre, although the city is most famous for its sartorial export, *serge de Nîmes* – better known to cowboys, clubbers and couturiers as denim.

FESTIVE NÎMES

Nîmes becomes more Spanish than French during its two *férias* (bullfighting festivals): the five-day **Féria de Pentecôte** (Whitsuntide Festival) in June, and the three-day **Féria des Vendanges** celebrating the grape harvest on the third weekend in September. Each is marked by daily *corridas* (bullfights). Buy tickets in situ or online at the **Billeterie des Arènes** (www.arenesdenimes.com; 2 rue de la Violette).

⊙ Sights

A **Pass Nîmes Romaine** (adult/child €10/7.70), valid for three days, covers all three sights; buy one at the first place you visit.

Les Arènes   ROMAN SITES
(www.arenes-nimes.com; place des Arènes; adult/child €7.90/6; ⊙9am-8pm Jul-Aug, earlier closing at other times) Nîmes' twin-tiered amphitheatre, the best preserved in the Roman Empire, was built around AD 100 to stage gladiatorial contests and public executions – watched by an audience of 24,000 spectators. Public events of a less gory nature are held here today (although bullfights are still a regular fixture).

Maison Carrée   ROMAN SITES
(place de la Maison Carrée; adult/child €4.60/3.80; ⊙10am-8pm Jul-Aug, earlier closing at other times) This gleaming limestone temple built around AD 5 to honour Emperor Augustus' two adopted sons is not actually square, despite its name, which means 'Square House' – to the Romans, 'square' simply meant a building with right angles.

Carré d'Art   MUSEUM
(www.carreartmusee.com; place de la Maison Carrée; permanent collection free, exhibitions adult/child €5/3.70; ⊙10am-6pm Tue-Sun) The striking glass-and-steel art mseum facing the Maison Carrée was designed by British architect Sir Norman Foster. The rooftop restaurant makes a lovely lunch spot.

🛏 Sleeping

TOP CHOICE **Le Cheval Blanc**   HOTEL €€
(☑04 66 76 05 22; www.lechevalblanc-nimes.com; 1 place des Arènes; d €115, f €180-210; 🅟) A prime position overlooking Les Arènes and a spare, stripped-back style make this the swishest place to stay in central Nîmes. Bare wood, plaster and stone define the design, and there are several split-level apartments with galley kitchens. The building itself began life as a textile factory, but it feels deliciously modern now.

Hôtel Amphithéâtre   HOTEL €€
(☑04 66 67 28 51; www.hoteldelamphitheatre. com; 4 rue des Arènes; s/d €65/85) Tucked away along a narrow backstreet, this tall townhouse hotel run by an ex-pat Cornishman and his wife has chic and stylish rooms; some have balconies overlooking place du Marché.

Auberge de Jeunesse   HOSTEL €
(☑04 66 68 03 20; www.hinimes.com; 257 chemin de l'Auberge de Jeunesse, La Cigale; dm/d €15.55/36; ⊙reception 7.30am-1am) It's out in the sticks, 4km from the station, but there's lots in its favour: spacious dorms, family rooms, sweet garden with camping pitches, and a choice of self-catering kitchen or cafe. Take bus 1, direction Alès or Villeverte, to the Stade stop.

✗ Eating

Look out for *cassoulet* (pork, sausage and white bean stew, sometimes served with duck), aïoli and *rouille* (a spicy chilli mayonnaise).

L'Imprévu   MODERN FRENCH €€
(☑04 66 38 99 59; www.l-imprevu.com; 6 place d'Assas; mains €19.50-27.50; ⊙lunch & dinner) The simple, amber-stoned facade of this fine-dining French bistro looks homey, but the interior is light and contemporary, with swirly modern art, an open-plan kitchen and interior courtyard. There's a posh mix of *terre-et-mer* (surf-and-turf) dishes, mainly served à la carte.

Le Marché sur la Table   MODERN FRENCH €€
(☑04 66 67 22 50; 10 rue Littré; mains €18-22; ⊙Wed-Sun) Husband-and-wife team Éric and Caroline Vidal focus on organic ingredients picked up from the market. The interior feels homespun and there's a quiet courtyard for alfresco dining.

Carré d'Art   GASTRONOMIC €€
(☑04 66 67 52 40; www.restaurant-lecarredart.fr; 2 rue Gaston Boissier; 2-/3-course menu €24/29; ⊙Mon-Sat) Nîmes' top address for gourmet gastronomic dining.

DON'T MISS

PONT DU GARD

Southern France has some fine Roman sites, but for audacious engineering, nothing can top Unesco World Heritage site **Pont du Gard** ([phone]04 66 37 50 99; www.pontdugard.fr; car & up to 5 passengers €18, after 8pm €10, cyclists & walkers free; [clock]visitors centre & museum 9am-7pm Jun-Sep, 9am-6pm Mar-May & Sep, 9am-5pm Oct-Feb, car parks 9am-1am), 21km northeast of Nîmes. This three-tiered aqueduct was once part of a 50km-long system of water channels, built around 19 BC to transport water from Uzès to Nîmes. The scale is huge: 50m high, 275m long and graced with 35 precision-built arches, the bridge was sturdy enough to carry up to 20,000 cu metres of water per day. Each block was carved by hand and transported here from nearby quarries – no mean feat, considering the largest blocks weight over 5 tonnes.

The **Musée de la Romanité** provides background on the bridge's construction, while kids can try out educational activities in the **Ludo** play area. Nearby, the 1.4km **Mémoires de Garrigue** walking trail winds upstream through typically Mediterranean scrubland, and offers some of the best bridge views.

There are large car parks on both banks of the river, about 400m walk from the bridge. Parking costs a flat-rate €5.

Crowds can be a real problem in high summer; early evening is usually a great time to visit, especially since parking is free after 7pm and the bridge is stunningly lit after dark.

ℹ️ Information

Tourist office ([phone]04 66 58 38 00; www.ot-nimes.fr; 6 rue Auguste; [clock]8.30am-8pm Mon-Fri, 9am-7pm Sat, 10am-6pm Sun Jul & Aug, shorter hrs rest of year)

ℹ️ Getting There & Away

AIR Ryanair is the only airline to use Nîmes' **airport** ([phone]04 66 70 49 49; www.nimes-aeroport.fr), 10km southeast of the city on the A54.

BUS The **bus station** ([phone]04 66 38 59 43; rue Ste-Félicité) is next to the train station. Destinations include:

Pont du Gard 30 minutes, five to seven daily in summer

Uzès bus E52; 45 minutes, four to eight daily

TRAIN More than 12 TGVs daily run to/from Paris Gare de Lyon (€52 to €99.70, three hours). Local destinations include:

Arles €8 to €14, 30 minutes

Avignon €9, 30 minutes

Montpellier €9.20, 30 minutes

Toulouse

POP 446,200

Elegantly set at the confluence of the Canal du Midi and the River Garonne, this vibrant southern city – nicknamed *la ville rose* (the pink city) after the distinctive hot-pink stone used in many buildings – is one of France's liveliest metropolises. Busy, buzzy and bustling with students, this riverside dame has a history stretching back over 2000 years

and has been a hub for the aerospace industry since the 1930s. With a thriving cafe and cultural scene, a wealth of impressive *hôtels particuliers* and an enormously atmospheric old quarter, France's fourth-largest city is one place you'll love to linger.

👁 Sights

Place du Capitole   PUBLIC SQUARE
(place du Capitole) Toulouse's magnificent main square is the city's literal and metaphorical heart, where Toulousiens turn out en masse on sunny evenings to sip a coffee or an early aperitif at a pavement cafe. On the eastern side is the 128m-long facade of the **Capitole**, the city hall, built in the 1750s. To the south is the city's **Vieux Quartier** (Old Quarter), a tangle of lanes and leafy squares brimming with cafes, shops and eateries.

Basilique St-Sernin   CHURCH
(place St-Sernin; [clock]8.30am-noon & 2-6pm Mon-Sat, 8.30am-12.30pm & 2-7.30pm Sun) This red-brick basilica is one of France's best-preserved Romanesque structures. Inside, the soaring nave and delicate pillars harbour the tomb of St-Sernin, a Toulouse bishop martyred in 250 AD.

Musée des Augustins   MUSEUM
(www.augustins.org; 21 rue de Metz; adult/child €3/free; [clock]10am-6pm, to 9pm Wed) Toulouse's fabulous fine arts museum spans the centuries from the Roman era right through to the early 20th century. It's in a former

DON'T MISS

CARCASSONNE

Perched on a rocky hilltop and bristling with zig-zag battlements, stout walls and spiky turrets, the fortified city of Carcassonne looks like something out of a children's storybook from afar. It's most people's perfect idea of a medieval castle, and it's undoubtedly an impressive spectacle – not to mention one of the Languedoc's biggest tourist draws.

Unfortunately, the medieval magic's more than a tad tarnished by an annual influx of over four million visitors and it can be a tourist hell in high summer.

The old city, **La Cité**, is dramatically illuminated at night and enclosed by two rampart walls punctuated by 52 stone towers, Europe's largest city fortifications. Successive generations of Gauls, Romans, Visigoths, Moors, Franks and Cathars reinforced the walls, but only the lower sections are original; the rest, including the turrets, were stuck on by the 19th-century architect Viollet-le-Duc.

A drawbridge leads to the old gate of **Porte Narbonnaise** and rue Cros Mayrevieille en route to place Château and the 12th-century **Château Comtal** (adult/child €8.50/ free; ⊙10am-6.30pm Apr-Sep). South is **Basilique St-Nazaire** (⊙9-11.45am & 1.45-5 or 5.30pm), illuminated by delicate medieval rose windows.

Carcassonne is on the main rail line to/from Toulouse (€14, 50 minutes).

Augustinian monastery, and its two 14th-century cloister gardens are postcard-pretty.

Les Abattoirs MUSEUM
(www.lesabattoirs.org; 76 allées Charles de Fitte; adult/student & child €7/free; ⊙11am-7pm Wed-Sun) As its name suggests, this red-brick structure was once the city's main abattoir; now it's a cutting-edge art gallery.

☞ Tours

Toulouse is a river city, and you couldn't possibly leave without venturing out onto the water. March to November, several operators run scenic hour-long boat trips (adult/child €8/5) along the Garonne from quai de la Daurade; in summer, trips also pass through the St-Pierre lock onto the Canal du Midi and Canal de Brienne. Buy tickets on the boat, up to 10 minutes before departure, from **Les Bateaux Toulousains** (www.bateaux-toulousains.com), **Toulouses Croisières** (www.toulouse-croisieres.com) or **L'Occitania** (www.loccitania.fr).

Airbus Factory Tours AEROPLANES
(☎05 34 39 42 00; www.taxiway.fr) Dedicated plane-spotters can arrange a guided tour of Toulouse's massive J.L. Lagardère Airbus factory, 10km west in Colomiers. There are three options: the main tour of the A380 production line (adult/child €14.50/11.50), a 'Heritage Tour' of the factory's vintage planes (including Concorde, adult/child €11.50/10), and a 'Panoramic Tour' of the 700-hectare site by minibus (adult/child €10/8.50). Book in advance online or by phone; bring photo ID.

🛏 Sleeping

Les Loges de St-Sernin B&B €€
(☎05 61 24 44 44; www.leslogesdesaintsernin.com; 12 rue St-Bernard; r €125-150; ☎) Hidden behind an elegant rosy facade, Sylviane Tatin's lovely *chambre d'hôte* is a home away from home. The four rooms are huge, dolled up in shades of pink, lime and butter-yellow.

Hôtel St-Sernin BOUTIQUE HOTEL €€
(☎05 61 21 73 08; www.hotelstsernin.com; 2 rue St-Bernard; d from €130; ☎) This swish number opposite the Basilique St-Sernin has been stylishly renovated by a Parisian couple; the best rooms have floor-to-ceiling windows overlooking the basilica.

Hôtel La Chartreuse HOTEL €
(☎05 61 62 93 39; www.chartreusehotel.com; 4bis bd de Bonrepos; s/d/tr €45/51/63) Toulouse's station hotels are definitely on the scruffy side, but this family-run establishment is a welcome surprise: clean, friendly and quiet, with a lovely breakfast room and back garden patio.

🍴 Eating

Bd de Strasbourg, place St-Georges and place du Capitole are perfect spots for summer dining alfresco. Rue Pargaminières is the street for kebabs, burgers and other latenight student grub.

TOP CHOICE Chez Navarre REGIONAL CUISINE €€
(☎05 62 26 43 06; 49 Grande Rue Nazareth; menus €13-20; ⊙lunch & dinner Mon-Fri) Fancy rubbing shoulders with the locals? This *table d'hôte*

is the place, with honest Gascon cuisine served up beneath a creaky beamed ceiling at communal candlelit tables.

L'Air de Famille
MODERN FRENCH €€

(☎05 61 29 85 89; www.lairdefamille-restaurant. com; 20 place Victor Hugo; mains from €13; ⊙lunch Tue & Wed, lunch & dinner Thu-Sat) Expect the freshest of ingredients at this intimate bistro where chef Georges turns out a small but perfectly formed menu concentrating on classic *saveurs Toulousiens* (flavours of Toulouse). It's tiny, so book.

Les Halles Victor Hugo
BISTROS €

(place Victor Hugo; menus €10-20; ⊙lunch Tue-Sun) For a quintessentially Toulousien experience, join the punters at the string of tiny restaurants on the 1st floor of the Victor Hugo food market. They're lunchtime only, and the food is simple and unfussy, but they're full of character and the menus are brilliant value.

🍷 Drinking

Almost every square in the Vieux Quartier has at least one cafe-bar, busy day and night. After-dark streets include rue Castellane, rue Gabriel Péri and near the river around place St-Pierre.

Toulouse has a cracking live music and clubbing scene; see what's on at www. toulouse.sortir.eu.

Au Père Louis
HISTORIC BAR

(45 rue des Tourneurs; ⊙8.30am-3pm & 5-10.30pm Mon-Sat) This antique bar has been quenching the city's thirst since 1889, and it's crammed with interesting nooks and crannies, not to mention its fair share of colourful characters. There's a huge selection of wines and beers, and it feels very cosy.

Connexion Café
BAR, LIVE MUSIC

(www.connexion-cafe.com; 8 rue Gabriel Péri; ⊙from 5pm Mon-Sat) Housed in a converted carpark with old oil drums for tables, this lively bar hosts an eclectic line-up of events, from big-screen sports to live weekend gigs. When the weather's warm, they open up the plastic tarps and the action spills out onto the street.

La Maison
BAR

(9 rue Gabriel Péri; ⊙5pm-2am Sun-Fri, to 5am Sat) 'The House' is a hip, shabby-chic hang-out for students and trendy types, with plenty of scruffy sofas and secondhand chairs dotted around the lounge-style bar.

ℹ️ Information

Tourist office (☎05 61 11 02 22; www. toulouse-tourisme.com; Square Charles de Gaulle; ⊙9am-7pm daily)

ℹ️ Getting There & Away

AIR Toulouse-Blagnac Airport (www.toulouse. aeroport.fr/en), 8km northwest of the centre, has frequent flights to Paris and other large French and European cities. A **Navette Aéroport Flybus** (Airport Shuttle; ☎05 61 41 70 70; www. tisseo.fr) links it with town.

TRAIN Gare Matabiau (blvd Pierre Sémard), 1km northeast of the centre, is served by frequent TGVs to Bordeaux (€38, two hours) and east to Carcassonne (€15, 45 minutes to one hour).

DON'T MISS

CITÉ DE L'ESPACE

This fantastic **space museum** (☎08 20 37 72 33; www.cite-espace.com/en; av Jean Gonord; adult €19.50-23, child €14-15; ⊙9.30am-5pm or 6pm, to 7pm mid-Jul–Aug, closed Jan) on the city's eastern outskirts explores Toulouse's illustrious aeronautical history.

The city's high-flying credentials stretch all the way back to WWI, when it was a hub for pioneering mail flights to Africa and South America. Since WWII, Toulouse has been the centre of France's aerospace industry, developing many important aircraft (including Concorde and the 555-seat Airbus A380) as well as components for many international space programs.

The museum brings this interstellar industry vividly to life through hands-on exhibits including a shuttle simulator, planetarium, 3D cinema and simulated observatory. There are even full-scale replicas of iconic spacecraft including the Mir Space Station and a 53m-high Ariane 5 space rocket. Multilingual audioguides allow you to explore at your own pace, but you'll need a full day to do it justice.

To get there, catch Bus 15 from allée Jean Jaurès to the last stop, from where it's a 500m walk. Dodge queues by buying your tickets online or at the tourist office.

PROVENCE

Provence conjures up images of rolling lavender fields, blue skies, gorgeous villages, wonderful food and superb wine. It certainly delivers on all those fronts, but it's not just worth visiting for its good looks – dig a little deeper and you'll also discover the multicultural metropolis of Marseille, the artistic haven of Aix-en-Provence and the old Roman city of Arles.

Marseille

POP 858,902

There was a time when Marseille was the butt of French jokes. No more. The *cité phocéenne* has made an unprecedented comeback, undergoing a vast makeover. Marseillais will tell you that the city's rough-and-tumble edginess is part of its charm and that, for all its flaws, it is a very endearing place. They're right: Marseille grows on you with its unique history, souklike markets, millennia-old port and spectacular *corniches* (coastal roads) – all good reasons indeed why Marseille was chosen European Capital of Culture in 2013.

◉ Sights

Vieux Port   HISTORIC QUARTER
(MVieux Port) Ships have docked for more than 26 centuries at Marseile's colourful Old Port. The main commercial docks were transferred to the Joliette area north of here in the 1840s, but the old port stil over-

CENT SAVER

Buy a cent-saving **Marseille City Pass** (one-/two-day €22/29) at the tourist office. It covers admission to 15 museums, a city tour, unlimited public-transport travel, boat trips and so on.

flows with fishing boats, pleasure yachts and tourists.

Guarding the harbour are **Bas Fort St-Nicolas** and **Fort St-Jean**, founded in the 13th century by the Knights Hospitaller of St John of Jerusalem. The 40,000 sq metre state-of-the-art museum **Musée des Civilisations de l'Europe et de la Méditerranée** (MuCEM; Museum of European & Mediterranean Civilisations; ☑04 96 13 80 90; www.mucem.org; ⊙1pm-7pm Wed, Thu & Sat) will open inside in 2013.

Basilique Notre Dame de la Garde   CHURCH
(Montée de la Bonne Mère; ⊙7am-8pm Apr-Sep, to 7pm Oct-Mar) Everywhere you go in Marseille, you can see the opulent, domed 19th-century Romano-Byzantine basilica, privy to dazzling 360-degree panoramas of the city's sea of terracotta roofs below.

The church's bell tower is crowned by a 9.7m-tall gilded statue of the Virgin Mary on a 12m-high pedestal. Walk or take bus 60 from the Vieux Port.

Château d'If   ISLAND, CASTLE
(www.if.monuments-nationaux.fr; adult/child €5/free; ⊙9.30am-6.30pm May-Sep, to 4.45pm Tue-Sun Oct-

LES CALANQUES

Marseille abuts the wild and spectacular Les Calanques, a protected 20km stretch of high, rocky promontories rising from the bright turquoise sea. Sheer cliffs are occasionally interrupted by idyllic beach-fringed coves, many only possible to reach with kayak. They've been protected since 1975 and became a national park in 2012.

Calanque de Sormiou is the largest rocky inlet, with two seasonal restaurants cooking up fabulous views: **Le Château** (☑04 91 25 08 69; mains €18-24; ⊙Apr–mid-Oct) – the better food – and **Le Lunch** (☑04 91 25 05 39, 04 91 25 05 37; http://wp.resto.fr/lelunch; mains €16-28; ⊙Apr–mid-Oct) – nearer the water; both require advance reservation. By bus, take No 23 from the Rond Point du Prado metro stop to La Cayolle, from where it's a 3km walk (note diners with a table reservation can drive through; otherwise, the road is open to cars weekdays only September to June).

Marseille's tourist office leads guided hikes in Les Calanques and has information on walking trails (shut July and August due to forest-fire risk). For great views from out at sea hop aboard a boat trip to the wine-producing port of **Cassis**, 30km east along the coast, with **Croisières Marseille Calanques** (www.croisieres-marseille-calanques.com; 74 quai du Port).

Apr) Immortalised in Alexandre Dumas' 1844 novel *Le Comte de Monte Cristo* (The Count of Monte Cristo), this 16th-century fortress-turned-prison sits on an island 3.5km west of the Vieux Port. Political prisoners were incarcerated here, along with hundreds of Protestants, the Revolutionary hero Mirabeau, and the Communards of 1871.

Frioul If Express (www.frioul-if-express. com; 1 quai des Belges) boats leave for Château d'If from the Vieux Port. Over 15 daily departures in summer, fewer in winter (€10 return, 20 minutes).

TOP CHOICE Le Panier HISTORIC QUARTER
(MVieux Port) From the Vieux Port, hike north up to this fantastic history-woven quarter, dubbed Marseille's Montmartre as much for its sloping streets as its artsy ambience. In Greek Massilia it was the site of the *agora* (marketplace), hence its name, which means 'the basket'. During WWII the quarter was dynamited and afterwards rebuilt. Today it's a mishmash of lanes hiding artisan shops, *ateliers* (workshops) and terraced houses strung with drying washing.

Its centerpiece is the fascinating **Centre de la Vieille Charité** (2 rue de la Charité, 2e; both museums adult/student €5/2.50; MJoliette).

La Friche La Belle de Mai CULTURAL CENTRE
(04 95 04 95 04; www.lafriche.org; 41 rue Jobin; 49 to Jobin) This former sugar-refining plant and subsequent tobacco factory is now host to artists' workshops, cinema studios, radio stations, multimedia displays, alfresco installation art, skateboard camps and electro/world-music parties – enter the gregarious 'voice' of contemporary Marseille. Check its program online, view art in the **Galerie de la Friche Belle de Mai** (admission free; 3-7pm Tue-Sat) and dine in its stylishly industrial **Les Grandes Tables de la Friche** (04 95 04 95 85; www.lesgrande stables.com; 12 rue François Simon; mains €10; 8.30am-8pm Mon-Fri).

FREE Palais de Longchamp PALACE, PARK
(Longchamp Palace; bd Philippon; ; MCinq Avenues-Longchamp, Longchamp) This colonnaded 1860s palace houses Marseille's oldest museum, the **Musée des Beaux-Arts**, slated to reopen after renovations in 2013. The shaded park is one of central Marseille's few green spaces.

Sleeping

TOP CHOICE Casa Honoré B&B €€€
(04 96 11 01 62; www.casahonore.com; 123 rue Sainte; d incl breakfast €150-200; MVieux Port) Los Angeles meets Marseille at this four-room *maison d'hôte*, built around a central courtyard with lap pool shaded by banana trees. One complaint: some bathrooms are partitioned by curtains, not doors.

Hôtel Vertigo HOSTEL €
(04 91 91 07 11; www.hotelvertigo.fr; 42 rue des Petites Maries; dm/d €25/60; MGare St-Charles) This snappy boutique hostel kisses goodbye to dodgy bunks and hospital-like decor and says 'hello' to vintage posters, designer chrome kitchen and groovy communal spaces. No curfew (or lift, alas).

Le Ryad BOUTIQUE HOTEL €€
(04 91 47 74 54; www.leryad.fr; 16 rue Sénac de Meilhan; s €80-105, d €95-125, family €170; MNoailles, Canebière Garibaldi) Le Ryad draws sumptuous influence from Morocco. Beautiful bathrooms, garden-view rooms and great service make up for the sometimes-sketchy neighbourhood. Book the top-floor room (Mogador) for its rooftop terrace.

Mama Shelter DESIGN HOTEL €€
(01 43 48 48 48; www.mamashelter.com; 64 rue de la Loubière; d €99-139, q €159, ste €209; MNotre Dame du Monte–Cours Julien) The brainchild of Serge Trigano, son of Gilbert (Club Med creator), this affordable-chic new kid on the block sports design by Philippe Starck.

Eating

The Vieux Port overflows with restaurants, but choose carefully. Head to Cours Julien and its surrounding streets for world cuisine.

TOP CHOICE Le Café des Épices MODERN FRENCH €€
(04 91 91 22 69; www.cafedesepices.com; 4 rue du Lacydon; 3-course lunch/dinner menu €25/40; lunch Tue-Sat, dinner Thu-Fri; MVieux Port) One of Marseille's best young chefs, Arnaud de Grammont, infuses his cooking with a panoply of flavours...think squid ink spaghetti with sesame and perfectly cooked scallops, or tender roasted potatoes with hints of coriander and citrus, topped by the catch of the day.

FRANCE MARSEILLE

Marseille

FRANCE MARSEILLE

Mediterranean Sea

Joliette
LA JOLIETTE

Bassin de la Grande Joliette

Pl de la Joliette

Joliette

Gare Maritime

SNCM

République
Dames

R de Mazenod

Av Robert Schuman

1

R de l'Evêché

Pl des Moulins

Q de la Tourette

Av Vaudoyer

Pl de Lenche

R St-Laurent

Avant-Port de la Joliette

Fort St-Jean

3

Tunnel St-Laurent

Jardin du Pharo

Bas Fort St-Nicolas

Q de Rive

R des Catalans

Bd Charles Livon

Av Pasteur

R Sainte

5

Av de la Corse

Pl du 4 Septembre

R Cap Dessemond

Av de la Corse

R Sauveur

R Guidicelli

R Charras

Bd Tellene

Vallon des Auffes

R du Vallon

R des Auffes

Bd Marius Thomas

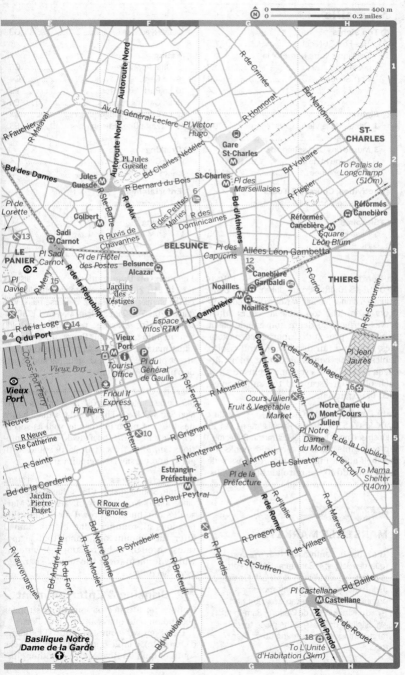

0 400 m
0 0.2 miles

FRANCE MARSEILLE

Marseille

◎ Top Sights
Bas Fort St-Nicolas C5
Basilique Notre Dame de la
Garde..E7
Fort St-Jean C4
Vieux Port...E4

◎ Sights
1 Centre de la Vieille Charité D3
2 Le Panier E3
3 Musée des Civilisations de
l'Europe et de la
Méditerranée C4

✪ Activities, Courses & Tours
4 Croisières Marseille Calanques.............E4

🛏 Sleeping
5 Casa Honoré D5
6 Hôtel Vertigo...F2

7 Le Ryad G3

✗ Eating
8 Café Populaire.......................................G6
9 La Cantinetta..G4
10 La Part des Anges F5
11 Le Café des Épices E4
12 Le Comptoir Dugommier......................G3
13 Pizzaria Chez Étienne E3

◎ Drinking
14 La Caravelle E4
15 Les Buvards E3

✪ Entertainment
16 L'Intermédiaire H4

⌂ Shopping
17 Fish Market..F4
18 Prado Market..H7

La Cantinetta   ITALIAN €

(☎04 91 48 10 48; 24 cours Julien; mains €9-19; ⊗lunch & dinner Tue-Sat; ⓜNotre Dame du Mont–Cours Julien) The top table at cours Julien serves perfectly al dente housemade pasta, paper-thin prosciutto, marinated vegetables, *bresaola* (air-dried beef) and risotto. Tables in the convivial dining room are cheek by jowl, and everyone seems to know each other. Or escape to the sun-dappled, tiled patio garden.

Café Populaire   BISTRO €

(☎04 91 02 53 96; 10 rue Paradis; mains €14-16; ⊗lunch & dinner Tue-Sat; ⓜEstrangin-Préfecture) Vintage tables and chairs, old books on the shelf and a fine collection of glass soda bottles all add to the retro air of this 1950s-styled jazz *comptoir* (counter).

DON'T MISS

MARSEILLE MARKETS

The small but enthralling **fish market** (quai des Belges; ⊗8am-1pm; ⓜVieux Port) is a daily fixture at the Vieux Port. **Cours Julien** hosts a Wednesday-morning organic fruit and vegetable market and **Prado Market** (av du Prado; ⊗8am-1pm; ⓜCastellane or Périer) is the place to go for anything and everything other than food.

Le Comptoir Dugommier   BISTRO €

(☎04 91 62 21 21; www.comptoirdugommier.fr; 14 bd Dugommier; mains €11-12, 3-course menu with drink €20; ⊗7.30am-3.30pm Mon-Wed, 7.30am-1am Thu & Fri; ⓜNoailles, ⏸Canebière Garibaldi) Tin molding, wooden floors and vintage signs make a homey escape from the busy street outside. The place gets packed for its downhome French fare.

Pizzaria Chez Étienne   REGIONAL CUISINE €

(43 rue de Lorette; mains €12-15; ⊗lunch & dinner Mon-Sat; ⓜColbert) This old Marseillais haunt has the best pizza in town as well as succulent *pavé de boeuf* (beef steak) and scrumptious *supions frits* (pan-fried squid with garlic and parsley). No credit cards.

La Part des Anges   BISTRO €

(33 rue Sainte; mains €15; ⊗lunch Mon-Sat, dinner daily) No address buzzes with Marseille's hip, buoyant crowd more than this fabulous all-rounder wine bistro, named after the amount of alcohol that evaporates through a barrel during wine or whisky fermentation: the angels' share *(la part des anges)*.

Drinking & Entertainment

Options for a coffee or something stronger abound on both quays at the Vieux Port.

Cafes crowd cours Honoré d'Estienne d'Orves (1e), a large open square two blocks south of quai de Rive Neuve. Another cluster overlooks place de la Préfecture, at the southern end of rue St-Ferréol (1er).

La Caravelle
BAR

(34 quai du Port; ⊙7am-2am; MVieux Port) Look up or miss this upstairs hideaway with tiny but treasured portside terrace. Fridays have live jazz 9pm to midnight.

Les Buvards
WINE BAR

(☑04 91 90 69 98; 34 Grand Rue; ⊙10am-1am; MVieux Port, ⓢSadi Carnot) Grand selection of natural wines and munchies.

L'Intermédiaire
NIGHTCLUB

(63 place Jean Jaurès; ⊙7pm-2am; MNotre Dame du Mont–Cours Julien) This grungy venue with graffitied walls is one of the best for live bands or DJs (usually techno or alternative).

❶ Information
Dangers & Annoyances

Petty crimes and muggings are common. Avoid the Belsunce area (southwest of the train station, bounded by La Canebière, cours Belsunce and rue d'Aix, rue Bernard du Bois and bd d'Athènes) at night. Walking La Canebiére is annoying, but generally not dangerous; expect to encounter kids peddling hash.

Tourist information

Tourist office (☑04 91 13 89 00; www.marseille -tourisme.com; 4 La Canebière; ⊙9am-7pm Mon-Sat, 10am-5pm Sun; MVieux Port)

❶ Getting There & Away
Air

Aéroport Marseille-Provence (p318), 25km northwest in Marignane, has numerous budget flights to various European destinations. **Shuttle buses** (☑Marseille 04 91 50 59 34, airport 04 42 14 31 27; www.lepilote.com) link it with Marseille Gare St-Charles (€8; 25 minutes, every 20 minutes).

Boat

The **passenger ferry terminal** (www.marseille -port.fr; MJoliette) is 250m south of Place de la Joliette (1er). **SNCM** (☑08 91 70 18 01; www. sncm.fr; 61 bd des Dames; MJoliette) boats sail to Corsica, Sardinia and North Africa.

Train

From Marseille's Gare St-Charles, trains including TGVs go all over France and Europe.
Avignon €24, 35 minutes
Lyon €50, 1¾ hours
Nice €35, 2½ hours
Paris Gare de Lyon €103, three hours

❶ Getting Around

Marseille has two metro lines, two tram lines and an extensive bus network, all run by **RTM** (☑04 91 91 92 10; www.rtm.fr; 6 rue des Fabres; ⊙8.30am-6pm Mon-Fri, 9am-12.30pm & 2-5.30pm Sat; MVieux Port), where you can obtain information and transport tickets (€1.50).

Pick up a bike from 100-plus stations across the city with **Le Vélo** (www.levelo-mpm.fr).

Aix-en-Provence
POP 141,895

Aix-en-Provence is to Provence what the Left Bank is to Paris: a pocket of bohemian chic crawling with students. It's hard to believe that 'Aix' (pronounced ex) is just 25km from chaotic, exotic Marseille. The city has been a cultural centre since the Middle Ages (two of the town's most famous sons are painter Paul Cézanne and novelist Émile Zola) but for all its polish, it's still a laid-back Provençal town at heart.

◉ Sights
Cours Mirabeau
HISTORIC QUARTER

No avenue better epitomises Provence's most graceful city than fountain-studded cours Mirabeau, sprinkled with elegant Renaissance *hôtels particuliers* and crowned with a summertime roof of leafy plane trees. Cézanne and Zola famously hung out at **Les Deux Garçons** (53 cours Mirabeau; ⊙7am-2am), a chic pavement cafe that buzzes with people-watchers despite its elevated prices and mediocre food.

Cézanne Sights
ART

To see where local lad Paul Cézanne (1839–1906) ate, drank and painted, follow the **Circuit de Cézanne** (Cézanne Trail), marked by footpath-embedded bronze plaques. The informative English-language guide to the plaques, *Cézanne's Footsteps*, is free at the tourist office. A mobile app, *City of Cézanne in Aix-en-Provence* (€2), is available online.

Cézanne's last studio, **Atelier Paul Cézanne** (www.atelier-cezanne.com; 9 av Paul Cézanne; adult/child €5.50/2; ⊙10am-noon & 2-6pm, closed Sun winter), 1.5km north of the tourist office, has been preserved and recreated (not all the tools and still-life models strewn around the single room were his) as it was at the time of his death. Take bus 1 or 20 to the Atelier Cézanne stop, or walk 1.5km from the centre. A 10-minute walk uphill from the

WORTH A TRIP

A CULINARY DETOUR

Hilltop village **Ventabren** (population 5000), 16km west of Aix, provides the perfect lazy-day detour. Meander sun-dappled cobbled lanes; peep inside a 17th-century church; and get drunk on dizzying views of Provence from old chateau ruins before a superb lunch or dinner at **La Table de Ventabren** (☎04 42 28 79 33; www.latabledeventabren.com; 1 rue Cézanne; menus €41-50; ⊙lunch Wed-Sun, dinner Tue-Sun). Chef Dan Bessoudo, honoured with a coveted Michelin star, creates inventive wholly modern French dishes and knockout desserts – served in summer on a romantic terrace facing distant mountains and starry skies. Reservations essential.

bus stop is the **Terrain des Peintres** (opp 62 av Paul Cézanne), a wonderful terraced garden perfect for a picnic, from where Cézanne, among others, painted the Montagne Ste-Victoire.

Visits to the both the Cézanne family country manor **Le Jas de Bouffan** (☎04 42 16 10 91; adult/child €5.50/2; ⊙guided tours 10.30am-5.30pm daily summer, less frequent other times; ☒6 to Corsy) and **Les Carrières de Bibemus** (Bibémus Quarries; ☎04 42 16 10 91; adult/child €6.60/3.10; ⊙tours 9.45am daily Jun-Sep, 10.30am & 5pm Mon, Wed, Fri & Sun Apr, May & Oct, 3pm Wed & Sat Jan-Mar), the cabin the artist rented in 1895 on the edge of town, must be reserved in advance at the tourist office.

Cathédrale St-Sauveur　　　CHURCH
(rue de la Roque; ⊙8am-noon & 2-6pm) A potpourri of styles, Aix cathedral was begun in the 12th century and enlarged over the next century. Acoustics make Gregorian chants (4.30pm Sunday) unforgettable.

Musée Granet　　　MUSEUM
(www.museegranet-aixenprovence.fr; place St-Jean de Malte; adult/child €4/free; ⊙11am-7pm Tue-Sun) Housed in a 17th-century priory, this exceptional museum covers 16th- to 20th-century Italian, Flemish and French works. Modern art reads like a who's-who: Picasso, Léger, Matisse, Monet, Klee, Van Gogh, Giacometti and, of course, Cézanne.

🛏 Sleeping

L'Épicerie　　　B&B €€
(☎06 08 85 38 68; www.unechambreenville.eu; 12 rue du Cancel; s incl breakfast €80-120, d incl breakfast €100-130; 🐑) This intimate B&B is the fabulous creation of born-and-bred Aixois lad, Luc. His breakfast room and *salon de thé* re-creates a 1950s grocery store, and the flowery garden out back is perfect for evening dining (book ahead).

Hôtel des Augustins　　　HOTEL €€
(☎04 42 27 28 59; www.hotel-augustins.com; 3 rue de la Masse; r €99-250; ✳🐑) A heartbeat from the hub of Aixois life, this former 15th-century convent has volumes of history: for example, Martin Luther stayed here after his excommunication from Rome.

Hôtel les Quatre Dauphins　　　BOUTIQUE HOTEL €
(☎04 42 38 16 39; www.lesquatredauphins.fr; 54 rue Roux Alphéran; s €55-60, d €70-85; ✳🐑) This sweet 13-room hotel is fresh and clean, with excellent new bathrooms. The tall terracotta-tiled staircase (no lift) leads to four attic rooms, with sloped beamed ceilings.

Hôtel Paul　　　HOTEL €
(☎04 42 23 23 89; http://www.aix-en-provence.com/hotelpaul; 10 av Pasteur; s/d/tr from €51/52/74; ℗🐑) On the edge of Vieil Aix, this bright, cheery bargain has a sweet garden and a TV lounge. There are fans in summer, free motorcycle and bike parking, and Wi-fi at €1.50 per 30 minutes. No credit cards.

🍴 Eating

Aix' sweetest treat is the marzipan-like local speciality, *calisson d'Aix,* a small, diamond-shaped, chewy delicacy made with ground almonds and fruit syrup. The daily **produce market** (place Richelme; ⊙mornings) sells olives, goat's cheese, garlic, lavender, honey, peaches, melons and other sun-kissed products.

TOP CHOICE **Restaurant Pierre Reboul**　　　GASTRONOMIC €€€
(☎04 42 20 58 26; www.restaurant-pierre-reboul.com; 11 Petite Rue St-Jean; 3-/7-/12-course menus €42/85/142; ⊙lunch Tue-Sat, dinner Wed-Sat, closed late Aug) Aix' newest culinary star invents playful, gorgeous creations in a relaxed dining room. The lunch special (€50), includes mineral water, coffee and a glass of perfectly paired wine.

Le Petit Verdot
FRENCH €€

(☑04 42 27 30 12; www.lepetitverdot.fr; 7 rue d'Entrecasteaux; mains €15-25; ☺dinner Mon-Sat, lunch Sat) Delicious menus are designed around what's in season and paired with excellent wines. Lively dining occurs around tabletops made of wine crates (expect to talk to your neighbour), and the gregarious owner speaks multiple languages.

Charlotte
BISTRO €€

(☑04 42 26 77 56; 32 rue des Bernardines; 2-/3-course menus €15.50/19; ☺lunch & dinner Tue-Sat; ⓓ) It's all very cosy at Charlotte, where everyone appears to know everyone. French classics like veal escalope and beef steak fill the handwritten menu, and there are always a couple of imaginative *plats du jour*. In summer everything moves into the garden.

La Mado
MODERN FRENCH €€

(Chez Madeleine; ☑04 42 38 28 02; www.lamado-aix.com; 4 place des Prêcheurs; lunch/dinner menus €18/32; ☺7am-2am) This smart daytime cafe and modern restaurant is an unbeatable spot for coffee and fashionable-people watching, or a delicious meal. It's been around for years, so the old guard dine while the hipsters shine.

❶ Information

Tourist office (☑04 42 16 11 61; www.aixen provencetourism.com; 37 av Giuseppi Verdi; ☺8.30am-7pm Mon-Sat, 10am-1pm & 2-6pm Sun Oct-Jun, to 8pm Jul-Sep)

❶ Getting There & Away

BUS From Aix' **bus station** (☑04 42 91 26 80, 08 91 02 40 25; av de l'Europe), a 10-minute walk southwest from La Rotonde, routes include Marseille (€5, 25 minutes), Arles (€9.20, 1½ hours) and Avignon (€17.40, 1¼ hours).

Half-hourly shuttle buses go to/from Aix TGV station and Aéroport Marseille-Provence.

TRAIN The only useful train from Aix' tiny **city centre train station** is to/from Marseille (€8, 45 minutes). **Aix TGV station**, 15km away, serves most of France; Marseille (€8, 20 daily) is a mere 12 minutes away.

Avignon

POP 92,454

Hooped by 4.3km of superbly preserved stone ramparts, this graceful city is the belle of Provence's ball. Famed for its annual performing arts festival and fabled bridge, Avignon is an ideal spot from which to step out into the sur-

CENT SAVER

The **Avignon Passion** discount card yields discounts of 10% to 50% on city museums, tours and monuments (pay full price at the first site, then discounts at each subsbequent site). The pass covers five people and is valid for 15 days. Available from the tourist office and tourist sites.

rounding region. Wrapping around the city, Avignon's defensive ramparts were built between 1359 and 1370, and are punctuated by a series of sturdy *portes* (gates).

◉ Sights

Palais des Papes
PALACE

(Papal Palace; www.palais-des-papes.com; place du Palais; adult/child €6/3; ☺9am-8pm Jul, 9am-9pm Aug, shorter hours Sep-Jun) This Unesco World Heritage site, the world's largest Gothic palace, was built when Pope Clement V abandoned Rome in 1309 to settle in Avignon, and it was the seat of papal power for 70-odd years. Today, it takes imagination to picture the former luxury of these vast, bare rooms, but PDA-style audio-video guides show 2- and 3D imagery of the once sumptuous furnishings.

Pont St-Bénézet
BRIDGE

(adult/child €4.50/3.50; ☺9am-8pm Jul, 9am-9pm Aug, shorter hours Sep-Jun) This fabled bridge, immortalised in the French nursery rhyme 'Sur le Pont d'Avignon', was completed in 1185 and rebuilt several times before all but four of its spans were washed away in the mid-1600s. See it free from the Rocher des Doms park, Pont Édouard Daladier or from across the river on Île de la Barhelasse's chemin des Berges.

Musée Calvet
GALLERY

(☑04 90 86 33 84; 65 rue Joseph Vernet; adult/ child €6/3; ☺10am-1pm & 2-6pm Wed-Mon) The elegant Hôtel de Villeneuve-Martignan (1741–54) provides a fitting backdrop for Avignon's fine-arts museum.

Musée du Petit Palais
MUSEUM

(www.petit-palais.org; place du Palais; adult/child €6/free; ☺10am-1pm & 2-6pm Wed-Mon) The bishops' palace houses outstanding collections of primitive, pre-Rennaissance, 13th-to 16th-century Italian religious paintings.

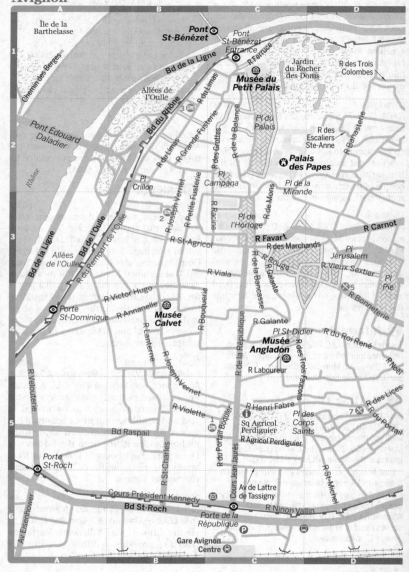

Musée Angladon　　　　　GALLERY
(www.angladon.com; 5 rue Laboureur; adult/child
€6/4; ☺1-6pm Tue-Sun Apr-Nov, 1-6pm Wed-Sun
Jan-Mar) This tiny museum harbours Impressionist treasures, including Van Gogh's
Railway Wagons – look closely and notice

the 'earth' isn't paint, but bare canvas. Also
displayed are a handful of early Picasso
sketches and artworks by Cézanne, Sisley,
Manet and Degas; upstairs are antiques
and 17th-century paintings.

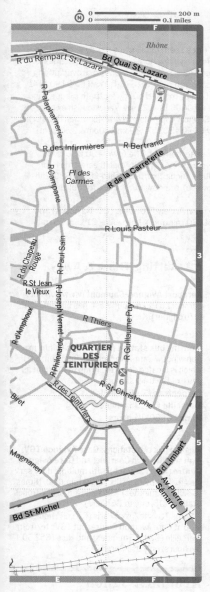

Avignon

◉ Top Sights

Musée Anglaldon	C4
Musée Calvet	B4
Musée du Petit Palais	C1
Palais des Papes	C2
Pont St-Bénézet	C1

🛏 Sleeping

1	Hôtel Boquier	C5
2	Hôtel Mignon	B3
3	Le Limas	B2
4	Lumani	F1

✴ Eating

5	Cuisine du Dimanche	D4
6	L'Atelier de Damien	F4
7	L'Epice and Love	D5

FRANCE AVIGNON

🛏 Sleeping

Le Limas B&B €€

(📞04 90 14 67 19; www.le-limas-avignon.com; 51 rue du Limas; d/tr incl breakfast from €120/200; ✳@) This chic B&B in an 18th-century townhouse is like something out of *Vogue Living*. Breakfast on the sun-drenched terrace is a treat, as is bubbly owner Marion.

Lumani B&B €€

(📞04 90 82 94 11; www.avignon-lumani.com; 37 rue du Rempart St-Lazare; d incl breakfast €100-170; ✳🛜) Art fills this fabulous *maison d'hôte,* a fount of inspiration for painters. Rooms include two suites and there's a fountained garden.

Hôtel Boquier HOTEL €

(📞04 90 82 34 43; www.hotel-boquier.com; 6 rue du Portail Boquier; d €50-70; ✳🛜) The owners' infectious enthusiasm informs this upbeat, colorful, small central hotel; try for themed rooms Morocco or Lavender. Excellent value.

Hôtel Mignon HOTEL €

(📞04 90 82 17 30; www.hotel-mignon.com; 12 rue Joseph Vernet; r incl breakfast €62-84; ✳@🛜) Cute and comfy, with 16 colorful rooms, this good-value hotel within the walled city is tops for no-frills budgeteers. Note: it has tiny baths and steep stairs.

✴ Festivals & Events

Hundreds of artists take to the stage and streets during the world-famous **Festival d'Avignon** (www.festival-avignon.com; ⊘Jul) and fringe **Festival Off** (www.avignonleoff.com; ⊘Jul), held early July to early August.

🍴 Eating

Place de l'Horloge's touristy cafes have so-so food. *Papaline d'Avignon* is a pink, chocolate ball filled with potent Mont Ventoux herbal liqueur.

VAN GOGH'S ARLES

If the winding streets and colourful houses of Arles seem familiar, it's hardly surprising – Vincent van Gogh lived here for much of his life in a yellow house on place Lamartine, and the town regularly featured in his canvases. His original house was destroyed during WWII, but you can still follow in Vincent's footsteps on the **Van Gogh Trail** (☑04 90 18 41 20; www.arlestourism.com; esplanade Charles de Gaulle), marked out by footpath plaques and a brochure handed out by the **tourist office** (☑04 90 18 41 20; www.arlestourisme.com; esplanade Charles de Gaulle; ⊗9am-6.45pm Apr-Sep, to 4.45pm Mon-Fri & 12.45pm Sun Oct-Mar); there is also a branch at the **train station** (☑04 90 43 33 57; ⊗9am-1.30pm & 2.30-5pm Mon-Fri Apr-Sep).

Two millennia ago, Arles was a major Roman settlement. The town's 20,000-seat amphitheatre and 12,000-seat theatre, known as the **Arénes** (Amphitheatre; rue Henri Vadon) and the **Théâtre Antique** (www.theatre-antique.com; adult/child €8.50/6.50, 2nd child free; ⊗9am-6pm Mar-Oct, 9am-4.30pm Nov-Feb), are nowadays used for cultural events and bullfights.

Telleschi (☑04 42 28 40 22) buses go to/from Aix-en-Provence (€9, 1½ hours) and there are regular trains to/from Nîmes (€7.50, 30 minutes), Marseille (€13.55, 55 minutes) and Avignon (€6.50, 20 minutes).

TOP CHOICE Cuisine du Dimanche PROVENÇAL €€
(☑04 90 82 99 10; www.lacuisinedudimanche.com; 31 rue Bonneterie; mains €15-25; ⊗daily Jun-Sep, Tue-Sat Oct-May) Spitfire chef Marie shops every morning at Les Halles to find the freshest ingredients for her earthy flavour-packed cooking. The menu changes daily, but specialities include scallops and simple roast chicken with pan gravy.

L'Atelier de Damien MODERN FRENCH €€
(☑04 90 82 57 35; 54 rue Guillaume Puy; lunch/dinner menus €13.50/26; ⊗lunch Mon-Sat, dinner Wed-Sat) Unframed paintings and worn tile floors lend a rough-around-the-edges look to this off-the-tourist-radar restaurant on Avignon's less-glamorous side. Chef Damien Demazure draws inspiration from market-fresh ingredients, combining French with Asian – ginger, lemongrass and coriander are his favorites. Expect excellent fish, foie gras, and caramel-candy cake.

L'Epice and Love FRENCH €
(☑04 90 82 45 96; 30 rue des Lices; mains €11-12; ⊗dinner Mon-Sat) Tables are cheek by jowl at this tiny bohemian restaurant with nothing fancy, just straightforward bistro fare, stews, roasts and other reliably good, home-style French dishes. Cash only.

❶ Information

Tourist Office (Main) (41 cours Jean Jaurès; ⊗ 9am-6pm Mon-Fri, 9am-5pm Sat, 10am-noon Sun Nov-Mar, 9am-6pm Mon-Sat, 10am-5pm Sun Apr-Oct)

❶ Getting There & Away

Air

Aéroport Avignon-Caumont (www.avignon.aeroport.fr), 8km southeast, has budget flights to/from the UK.

Bus

From the **bus station** (bd St-Roch; ⊗information window 8am-7pm Mon-Fri, 8am-1pm Sat), which is located down the ramp to the right as you exit the train station:

Carpentras €2, 45 minutes
Marseille €22, 35 minutes
Nîmes €1.50, 1¼ hours

Train

Avignon has two stations. **Gare Avignon TGV**, 4km southwest in Courtine; and **Gare Avignon Centre** (42 bd St-Roch), with multiple daily services to/from: Arles (€6.50, 20 minutes), Nîmes (€8.50, 30 minutes), Marseille airport (Vitrolles Station, €16, one to 1½ hours).

Some TGVs to/from Paris (€75, 3½ hours) stop at Gare Avignon Centre, but TGVs to/from Marseille (€29, 35 minutes) and Nice (€52.50, 3¼ hours) only use Gare TGV.

Around Avignon

LES BAUX DE PROVENCE

At the heart of the Alpilles, spectacularly perched above picture-perfect rolling hills of vineyards, olive groves and orchards, is the hilltop village of Les Baux de Provence. Van Gogh painted it and if you stroll around the deep dungeons, up crumbling towers and

DON'T MISS

CARPENTRAS MARKET

Don't miss **Carpentras**, 25km north-east of Avignon, on a Friday morning when its streets and squares spill over with hundreds of market stalls laden with breads, honeys, cheeses, olives, fruit and a rainbow of *berlingots* (the local striped, pillow-shaped hard-boiled sweet). Late November to March, pungent black-truffle stalls murmur with hushed-tones transactions.

around the maze-like ruins of **Château des Baux** (www.chateau-baux-provence.com; adult/child €7.60/5.70; ⊙9am-6pm Sep-Jun, 9am-8pm Jul & Aug) you'll see why. Lunch afterwards at legendary **L'Oustau de Baumanière** (☑04 90 54 33 07; www.oustaudebaumaniere.com; menus €95-150; ✐).

VAISON-LA-ROMAINE

This traditional market town 17km north of Avignon still has a thriving Tuesday-morning market, a delightful cobbled medieval quarter and a rich Roman legacy. It also makes a great base for hiking and cycling jaunts into the limestone ridge of the nearby **Dentelles de Montmirail** and also up the 'Giant of Provence', **Mont Ventoux** (1912m).

The **Gallo-Roman ruins** (adult/child €8/3.50; ⊙closed Jan-early Feb) of Vasio Vocontiorum, the city that flourished here between the 6th and 2nd centuries BC, fill two central Vaison sites. Two neighbourhoods of this once-opulent city, Puymin (with the still-functioning 6000-seat **Théâtre Antique**) and La Villasse, lie on either side of the tourist office and av du Général-de-Gaulle. To make sense of the remains (and gather your audioguide), head for the **archaeological museum**, which revives Vaison's Roman past with incredible swag – superb mosaics, carved masks, and statues that include a 3rd-century silver bust and marble renderings of Hadrian and wife Sabina.

From the bus station, 400m east of the town centre on av des Choralies, there are services to/from Avignon (€4, 1½ hours via Orange).

THE FRENCH RIVIERA & MONACO

With its glistening seas, idyllic beaches and fabulous weather, the French Riviera (Côte d'Azur in French) screams exclusivity, extravagance and excess. It has been a favourite getaway for the European jet set since Victorian times and there is nowhere more chichi or glam in France than St-Tropez, Cannes and super-rich, sovereign Monaco.

But it's not just a high-roller's playground. Culture vultures will revel in the region's thriving art scene: the Riviera has fine art museums and rich Roman ruins to explore, while millions descend on this southern stripo of coast purely to bronze their bodies, smell the lavender and soak up the hip Mediterranean vibe.

Nice

POP 344,460

Riviera queen Nice is what good living is all about – shimmering shores, the very best of Mediterranean food, a unique historical heritage, free museums, a charming Old Town, exceptional art and Alpine wilderness within an hour's drive. To get stuck-in straight away, make a beeline upon arrival for **Promenade des Anglais**, Nice's curvaceous palm-lined seafront that follows its busy pebble beach for 6km from the city centre to the airport.

◉ Sights

TOP CHOICE **Vieux Nice** HISTORIC QUARTER
(⊙food markets 6am-1.30pm Tue-Sun) Ditch the map and get lost in this mellow-hued rabbit warren of 18th-century passages, alleyways, historic churches and hidden squares. **Cours Saleya**, running parallel to

DON'T MISS

THE CORNICHES

Some of the Riviera's most spectacular scenery stretches east between Nice and Monaco. A trio of *corniches* (coastal roads) hugs the cliffs between the two seaside cities, each higher up the hill than the last. The middle *corniche* ends in Monaco; the upper and lower continue to Menton near the French-Italian border.

FRANCE NICE

Nice

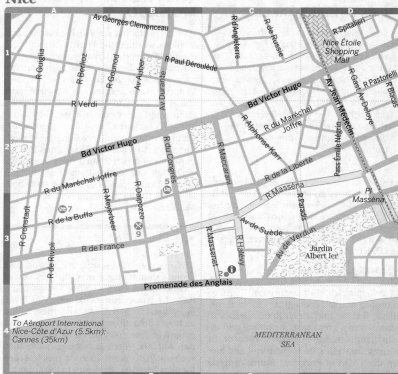

FRANCE NICE

Nice

◉ Top Sights
Cathédrale Ste-Réparate.......................F3
Chapelle de la Miséricorde F3
MAMAC G1
Parc du Château G4
Vieux Nice F3

✛ Activities, Courses & Tours
1 Centre du Patrimoine Walking
   Tours E3
2 Nice Guided Walking Tours C3
3 Trans Côte d'Azur...............................H3

🛏 Sleeping
4 Hôtel Wilson...E2
5 Nice Garden Hôtel B2

6 Nice Pebbles...F1
7 Villa Rivoli..A3

✖ Eating
8 Fenocchio F3
9 La Cave de l'Origine B3
10 La Merenda..E3
11 Le Bistrot d'Antoine F3
12 Le Comptoir du Marché.......................F3
13 Luna Rossa E2
14 Zucca Magica H2

🍷 Drinking
15 L'Abat-Jour...F3
16 Le Smarties F1
17 Les Distilleries Idéales F3

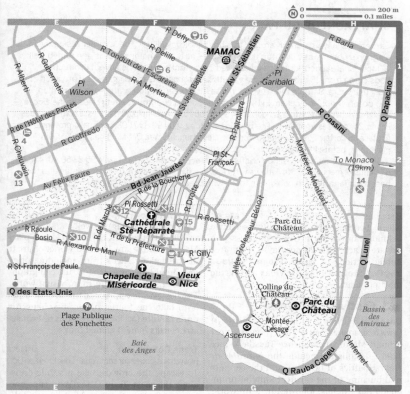

the seafront, remains a joyous, thriving market square with one of France's most vibrant food and flower markets. Rue de la Boucherie and rue Pairolièreare excellent for food shopping, a daily fish market fills place St François, and baroque aficionados will fall head over heels in love with architectural gems such as **Cathédrale Ste-Réparate** (place Rossetti) and the exuberant **Chapelle de la Miséricorde** (cours Saleya).

MAMAC
MUSEUM

(Musée d'Art Moderne et d'Art Contemporain; www.mamac-nice.org; promenade des Arts; ⊙10am-6pm Tue-Sun) This ode to contemporary art houses some fantastic avant-garde art from the 1960s to the present, including iconic pop art from Roy Lichtenstein and Andy Warhol's 1965 *Campbell's Soup Can*. An awesome panorama of Vieux Nice unfolds from its rooftop garden-gallery.

FREE Musée Matisse
GALLERY

(www.musee-matisse-nice.org; 164 av des Arènes de Cimiez; ⊙10am-6pm Wed-Mon) About 2km north in the leafy quarter of Cimiez, this museum houses a fascinating assortment of works by Matisse. Its permanent collection is displayed in a red-ochre 17th-century Genoese villa overlooking an olive-tree-studded park. Temporary exhibitions are hosted in the futuristic basement building. The artist is buried in the **Monastère de Cimiez** cemetery, across the park from the museum.

Musée National Marc Chagall
GALLERY

(www.musee-chagall.fr; 4 av Dr Ménard; adult/child €7.50/5.50; ⊙10am-5pm Wed-Mon Oct-Jun, to 6pm Jul-Sep) Discover the largest public collection of works by Belarusian painter Marc Chagall (1887–1985) in this small museum, a 20-minute walk from the centre (signposted from av de l'Olivetto).

WORTH A TRIP

CHÂTEAUNEUF-DU-PAPE

Carpets of vineyards unfurl around this tiny medieval village. The summer residence of Avignon's popes was built atop the wall here – all that remains today is one ruined wall.

Most Châteauneuf-du-Pape wine is red, and strict regulations govern production. Reds come from 13 different grape varieties – grenache is the biggie – and are aged at least five years. Sample them over a free tasting (*dégustation gratuite*) at more than two dozen shops and cellars in the village, or book a two-hour tasting class at the **École de Dégustation** (Tasting School; ☑04 90 83 56 15; www.oenologie-mouriesse.com; 2 rue des Papes; 2hr courses from €40). The **tourist office** (☑04 90 83 71 08; www.pays-provence.fr; place du Portail; ☺9.30am-6pm Mon-Sat, closed lunch & Wed Oct-May) has a list of wine-producing estates that do cellar visits, tastings and tours.

Perched beneath the ruined chateau, **Le Verger des Papes** (☑04 90 83 50 40; 4 rue du Château; menus €20-30; ☺hours vary) has a leafy terrace with knockout vistas and the best traditional French cooking in town, with bread made in a wood-fired oven.

Beaches
BEACHES

Nice's beaches are all pebbly; sensitive behinds can opt for a comfy mattress at a private beach (€15–20 per day). Of the free public sections of beach, **Plage Publique des Ponchettes**, opposite Vieux Nice, is the most popular.

🎊 Festivals & Events

Carnaval de Nice
CARNIVAL

(www.nicecarnaval.com) Held each year around Mardi Gras (Shrove Tuesday) since 1294 – highlights include the *batailles de fleurs* (battles of flowers), and the ceremonial burning of the carnival king on promenade des Anglais, followed by a fireworks display.

Nice Jazz Festival
MUSIC FESTIVAL

(www.nicejazzfestival.fr) France's original jazz festival has taken on a life of its own in its new promenade location, with fringe concerts popping up all around the venue, from Vieux Nice to Massena and the shopping streets around Rue de France.

👉 Tours

Nice Guided Walking Tours
WALKING TOUR

The best way to discover Nice's rich heritage is to take a guided walking tour. The **Centre du Patrimoine** (75 quai des Etats-Unis; ☺8.30am-1pm & 2-5pm Mon-Thu, to 3.45pm) runs a two-hour Vieux Nice Baroque tour (Tuesday afternoon), as well as themed tours, including art deco, neoclassical and belle époque Nice. The tourist office runs a 2½-hour Vieux Nice tour in English (adult/child €12/6) at 9.30am on Saturday.

Art With The Tram
TRAM TOUR

(www.tramway-nice.org) As well as Jaume Plensa's glow-in-the-dark *Conversation* on place Masséna, there are 13 more works of art to discover along Nice's tram, including original sound bites at each stop, the calligraphy of the tram's stops and more visual works. The best way to appreciate this artistic input is to take the tourist office's two-hour **Art dans la Ville** (adult/child €8/3, plus €2 for transport; ☺tours 7pm Fri) guided tour.

Trans Côte d'Azur
BOAT TOUR

(www.trans-cote-azur.com; quai Lunel; ☺Apr-Oct) To escape the crowds, take a scenic cruise along the coast. Trans Côte d'Azur runs one-hour trips along the Baie des Anges and the Rade de Villefranche (adult/child €16/10) from April to October. From mid-June to mid-September it also runs regular excursions to Île Ste-Marguerite (€35/25, crossing one hour), St-Tropez (€58/44, crossing 2½ hours) and Monaco (€34/ 25, crossing 45 minutes). Reservations are essential.

🛏 Sleeping

Nice Garden Hôtel
BOUTIQUE HOTEL €€

(☑04 93 87 35 63; www.nicegardenhotel.com; 11 rue du Congrès; s/d €75/100; ❄🕸) Heavy iron gates hide this gem. Nine rooms are a subtle blend of old and new, and overlook a delightful garden with orange tree. Amazingly, all this charm and peacefulness is just two blocks from the promenade.

TOP CHOICE Nice Pebbles
SELF-CONTAINED €€

(☑04 97 20 27 30; www.nicepebbles.com; 23 rue Gioffredo; 1-/3-bedroom apt from €105/320; 🕸🕸) The concept is simple: the quality of a four-star boutique hotel in holiday flats. Apartments (one to three bedrooms) are equipped with flat-screen TV, kitchen, linen bedding and, in some cases, wi-fi, swimming pool, and balcony, and come with a useful starter pack (no need to rush to the supermarket). Nightly rates are significantly cheaper during low season.

Villa Saint-Exupéry
HOSTEL €€
(☏04 93 84 42 83; www.villahostels.com; 22 av Gravier; dm/s/d incl breakfast €25-30/45/90; @ 🛜) Set in a lovely converted monastery in the north of Nice, this is a great place. Chill out in the 24-hour common room housed in the old stained-glass chapel, sip a €1 beer on the barbecue terrace and stock up on travel tips.

Villa staff will pick you up from the nearby Comte de Falicon tram stop or St-Maurice stop for bus 23 (direct from the airport) when you first arrive. Rates include breakfast.

Villa Rivoli
BOUTIQUE HOTEL €€
(☏04 93 88 80 25; www.villa-rivoli.com; 10 rue de Rivoli; s/d/q from 85/99/210; ❄🛜) Built in 1890, this stately villa feels like your own pied-à-terre in the heart of Nice. Take breakfast in the garden's sun-dappled shade, or in the grand belle époque *salon*.

Hôtel Wilson
BOUTIQUE HOTEL €
(☏04 93 85 47 79; www.hotel-wilson-nice.com; 39 rue de l'Hôtel des Postes; s/d €50/55; 🛜) Many years of travelling, an experimental nature and exquisite taste have turned Jean-Marie's rambling flat into a compelling place to stay. The 16 rooms have individual, carefully crafted decor, and share the eclectic dining room.

✖ Eating

Niçois nibbles include *socca* (a thin layer of chickpea flour and olive oil batter), *salade niçoise* and *farcis* (stuffed vegetables). Restaurants in Vieux Nice are a mixed bag, so choose carefully.

ᴛᴏᴘ Le Bistrot d'Antoine
MODERN FRENCH €€
(☏04 93 85 29 57; 27 rue de la Préfecture; mains €13-18; ◷lunch & dinner Tue-Sat) This brasserie is full every night (booking essential), yet the 'bistro chic' cuisine never wavers, the staff are cool as cucumbers, the atmosphere is reliably jovial and the prices incredibly good value.

Luna Rossa
ITALIAN €€
(☏04 93 85 55 66; www.lelunarossa.com; 3 rue Chauvain; mains €15-25; ◷Tue-Fri, dinner Sat)

Luna Rossa is like your dream Mediterranean dinner come true: fresh pasta, exquisitely cooked seafood, sun-kissed vegetables and divine meats.

Fenocchio
ICE CREAM €
(2 place Rossetti; ice cream from €2; ◷9am-midnight Feb-Oct) Dither too long over the 70-plus flavours of ice cream and sorbet at this unforgettable *glacier* (ice-cream shop) and you'll never make it to the front of the queue. Eschew predictable favourites and indulge in a new taste sensation: black olive, tomato-basil, avocado, rosemary or lavender.

La Cave de l'Origine
MODERN FRENCH €€
(☏04 83 50 09 60; 3 rue Dalpozzo; mains €15-22; ◷lunch & dinner Tue-Sat) This sleek new wine bar–restaurant has as much substance as style: great selection of wines by the glass, many local, and fantastic advice about what to pair with your food (well-executed, modern French fare with a touch of fusion).

Le Comptoir du Marché
MODERN FRENCH €
(☏04 93 13 45 01; 8 rue du Marché; mains €13-15; ◷lunch & dinner Tue-Sat) Vintage kitchen decor, recession-proof prices and a creative cuisine that gives a modern twist to French traditional recipes is the secret to the Counter's huge success.

La Merenda
NIÇOIS €
(4 rue Raoul Bosio; mains €12-15; ◷Mon-Fri) Simple, solid Niçois cuisine by former Michelin-starred chef Dominique Le Stanc draws the crowds to this pocket-sized bistro. No credit cards.

Zucca Magica
VEGETARIAN €€
(☏04 93 56 25 27; www.lazuccamagica.com; 4bis quai Papacino; menus €30; ◷Tue-Sat; ✈) The Magic Pumpkin serves a fixed five-course menu, dictated simply by the market and the chef's fancy. Seating is amid a fabulous collection of pumpkins and fairy lights.

🍷 Drinking & Entertainment

Vieux Nice's streets are stuffed with bars and cafes.

ᴛᴏᴘ Les Distilleries Idéales
CAFE
(24 rue de la Préfecture; ◷9am-12.30am) Whether you're after an espresso on your way to the cours Saleya market or an *apéritif* (complete with cheese and charcuterie platters, €5.20) before trying out one of Nice's

fabulous restaurants, Les Distilleries is one of the most atmospheric bars in town.

Le Smarties BAR
(http://nicesmarties.free.fr; 10 rue Défly; ⊙6pm-2am Tue-Sat) We love Smarties' sexy '70s swirly orange style, which draws a hot-looking straight-gay crowd. On weekends, the tiny dance floor fills when DJs spin deep house, electro, techno and occasionally disco; weekdays are mellower. Free tapas with happy hour (nightly 6pm to 9pm).

L'Abat-Jour BAR
(25 rue Benoît Bunico) With its vintage furniture, rotating art exhibitions and alternative music, l'Abat-Jour is all the rage with Nice's young and trendy crowd. The basement has live music or DJ sessions.

❶ Information

Tourist Office (📞08 92 70 74 07; www.nicetourisme.com; 5 promenade des Anglais; ⊙9am-6pm Mon-Sat) Also runs a branch at the train station.

❶ Getting There & Away

Air

Nice-Côte d'Azur airport is 6km west of Nice, by the sea. A taxi to Nice centre costs around €25.

» Buses 98 and 99 link the airport terminal with Nice Gare Routière and Nice train station (€4, 35 minutes, every 20 minutes).

» Bus 110 (€18, hourly) links the airport with Monaco (40 minutes).

Boat

Nice is the main port for ferries to Corsica. **SNCM** (www.sncm.fr; quai du Commerce, ferry terminal) and **Corsica Ferries** (www.corsicaferries.com; quai Lunel) are the two main companies.

Bus

There are excellent intercity services around Nice. All journeys cost €1. The bus station was demolished in 2011 so bus stops are now scattered around the *coulée verte*. Smartphone users can also download the very useful Ligne d'Azur app or visit the company's office.

Train

From **Gare Nice Ville** (av Thiers), 1.2km north of the beach, there are frequent services to Cannes (€6.40, 40 minutes) and Monaco (€3.60, 20 minutes).

WORTH A TRIP

THE PINE CONE TRAIN

Chugging between mountains and the sea, narrow-gauge railway **Train des Pignes** (Pine Cone Train; www.train provence.com) is one of France's most picturesque train rides. Rising to 1000m, with breathtaking views, the 151km-long track between Nice and Digne-les-Bains passes through the scarcely populated back country of little-known Haute Provence.

Day-trip suggestion: a picnic and meander around the historical centre and citadel of the beautiful medieval village of **Entrevaux** (€20 return, 1½ hours).

Cannes

POP 74,445

Most have heard of Cannes and its celebrity film festival. The latter only lasts for two weeks in May, but the buzz and glitz linger all year thanks to regular visits from celebrities who come here to indulge in designer shopping, beaches and the palace hotels of the Riviera's glammest seafront, bd de la Croisette.

Offshore lie the idyllic islands, Îles de Lérins, the unexpected key to 2000-plus years of history – from Ligurian fishing communities (200 BC) to one of Europe's oldest religious communities (5th century AD) and the enigmatic Man in the Iron Mask.

◉ Sights & Activities

La Croisette ARCHITECTURE
The multistarred hotels and couture shops that line the famous bd de la Croisette (aka La Croisette) may be the preserve of the rich and famous, but anyone can enjoy the palm-shaded promenade and take in the atmosphere. In fact, it's a favourite amongst Cannois (natives of Cannes), particularly at night when it's lit with bright colours.

There are great views of the bay and nearby Estérel mountains, and stunning art deco architecture among the seafront palaces, such as the **Martinez** or the legendary **Carlton InterContinental** – its twin cupolas were modelled on the breasts of the courtesan La Belle Otéro, infamous for her string of lovers.

Not so elegant but imposing nonetheless is the **Palais des Festivals** (Festival Palace; bd de la Croisette; guided tours adult/child €3/free; ⏱guided tours 2.30pm Jun-Apr), host to the world's most glamorous film festival. Climb the red carpet, walk down the auditorium, tread the stage and learn about cinema's most glamorous event and its numerous anecdotes on a **Palais des Festivals guided tour** (adult/child €3/free; ⏱1½ hr); tickets can only be booked in person at the tourist office.

Beaches
BEACHES

Cannes is blessed with sandy beaches although much of bd de la Croisette is taken up by private beaches (open to all). This arrangement leaves only a small strip of free sand near the Palais des Festivals for the bathing hoi polloi; the much bigger **Plage du Midi** (bd Jean Hibert) and **Plage de la Bocca**, west from Vieux Port, are also free.

Le Suquet
HISTORIC QUARTER

Cannes' historic quarter, pre-dating the glitz and glam of the town's festival days, retains a quaint village feel with its steep, meandering alleyways. There are wonderful views of the Baie de Cannes from the top of the hill.

Îles de Lérins
ISLANDS

Although just 20 minutes away by boat, these tranquil islands feel far from the madding crowd. **Île Ste-Marguerite**, where the mysterious Man in the Iron Mask was incarcerated during the late 17th century, is known for its bone-white beaches, eucalyptus groves and small marine museum. Tiny **Île St-Honorat** has been a monastery since the 5th century. Boats leave Cannes from quai des Îles on the western side of the harbour.

🛏 Sleeping

TOP CHOICE **Hôtel Le Canberra** BOUTIQUE HOTEL €€€
(☎04 97 06 95 00; www.hotel-cannes-canberra.com; 120 rue d'Antibes; d from €255; ✳@🛜🏊) This boutique stunner, just a couple of blocks back from La Croisette, is the epitome of Cannes glamour: designer grey rooms with splashes of candy pink, sexy black-marble bathrooms with coloured lighting, heated pool (April to October) in a bamboo-filled garden, intimate atmosphere (there are just 35 rooms) and impeccable service. Rooms overlooking rue d'Antibes are cheaper.

Le Romanesque BOUTIQUE HOTEL €€
(☎04 93 68 04 20; 10 rue du Batéguier; s/d/tr €89/109/149; ✳🛜) Every room is individually decorated at this eight-room boutique charmer in the heart of the Carré d'Or nightlife district (book a back room if you're a light sleeper). Favourite rooms include Charlotte, with its sun-drenched bath; and Elizabeth, the former maid's quarters, with low, sloping beamed ceilings. Gay-friendly. Great service.

Hôtel 7e Art BOUTIQUE HOTEL €
(☎04 93 68 66 66; www.7arthotel.com; 23 rue Maréchal Joffre; s €68, d €60-98; ✳🛜) Hôtel 7e Art has put boutique style within reach of budgeters. The snappy design of putty-coloured walls, padded headboards and pop art, and perks like iPod docks in every room, far exceed what you'd expect at this price.

FRANCE CANNES

WORTH A TRIP

THE SCENT OF THE CÔTE D'AZUR

Mosey some 20km northwest of Cannes to inhale the sweet smell of lavender, jasmine, mimosa and orange-blossom fields. In **Grasse**, one of France's leading perfume producers, dozens of perfumeries create essences to sell to factories (for aromatically enhanced foodstuffs and soaps) as well as to prestigious couture houses – the highly trained noses of local perfume-makers can identify 3000 scents in a single whiff.

Learn about three millennia of perfume-making at the **Musée International de la Parfumerie** (MIP; www.museesdegrasse.com; 2 bd du Jeu de Ballon; adult/child €3/free; ⏱11am-6pm Wed-Mon; 👪) and watch the process first-hand during a guided tour at **Fragonard** (www.fragonard.com; 20 bd Fragonard; ⏱9am-6pm Feb-Oct, 9am-12.30pm & 2-6pm Nov-Jan) perfumery, the easiest to reach by foot. The tourist office has information on other perfumeries and field trips to local flower farms, including the **Domaine de Manon** (☎06 12 18 02 69; www.le-domaine-de-manon.com; 36 chemin du Servan, Plascassier; admission €6). Roses are picked mid-May to mid-June, jasmine July to late October.

Hôtel Le Mistral
BOUTIQUE HOTEL €€

(☎04 93 39 91 46; www.mistral-hotel.com; 13 rue des Belges; d from €89; ✳🛜) This small boutique hotel wins the *palme d'or* for best value in town: rooms are decked out in flattering red and plum tones, bathrooms feature lovely designer fittings, there are seaviews from the top floor, and the hotel is a mere 50m from La Croisette.

 Eating

TOP CHOICE / Sea Sens
FUSION €€

(☎04 63 36 05 06; www.five-hotel-cannes.com; Five Hotel & Spa, 1 rue Notre Dame; 2-/3-course lunch menu €29/39, mains €26-55; 🛜🍴) Run by the brilliant Pourcel brothers, Cannes' latest food sensation serves divine food blending French gastronomy and Asian elegance, with panoramic views of Le Suquet and Cannes' rooftops on the side. Come here for lunch to make the best of the great-value menus.

Mantel
MODERN EUROPEAN €€

(☎04 93 39 13 10; www.restaurantmantel.com; 22 rue St-Antoine; menus €25-38; ⊙Fri-Mon, dinner Tue & Thu) Discover why Noël Mantel is the hotshot of the Cannois gastronomic scene at his refined old-town restaurant. Try the wonderfully tender glazed veal shank in balsamic vinegar or the original poached octopus *bourride*-style. Best of all though, you get not one but two desserts from pastry-chef wonder Christian Gonthier, who bakes the bread, and prepares the sweets served with coffee.

Aux Bons Enfants
FRENCH €€

(80 rue Meynadier; menus €23; ⊙Tue-Sat) A people's-choice place since 1935, this informal restaurant cooks up regional dishes such as aïoli *garni* (aïoli with vegetables), *daube* (beef stew), and *rascasse meunière* (pan-fried rockfish), all in a convivial atmosphere. No credit cards and no booking.

PhilCat
DELICATESSEN €

(La Pantiéro; sandwiches & salads €4-6.50; ⊙8.30am-5pm) Don't be put off by Phillipe and Catherine's unassuming prefab cabin on the Pantiéro: this is Cannes' best lunch house. Huge salads, made to order, are piled high with delicious fresh ingredients. Or if you're *really* hungry, try one of their phenomenal *pan bagna* (a moist sandwich bursting with Provençal flavours).

ⓘ Information

Tourist office (☎04 92 99 84 22; www. cannes.travel; Palais des Festivals, bd de la Croisette; ⊙9am-7pm)

ⓘ Getting There & Away

BUS From the **bus station** (place Cornut-Gentille), buses serve Nice (€1, 1½ hours) and Nice airport (€16, 50 minutes, half-hourly).

TRAIN From Cannes train station there are at least hourly services to/from:

Nice €6.40, 40 minutes

Antibes €2.70, 12 minutes

Monaco €8.70, one hour

Marseille €28.40, two hours

St-Tropez
POP 4986

In the soft autumn or winter light, it's hard to believe the pretty terracotta fishing village of St-Tropez is a stop on the Riviera celebrity circuit. It seems far removed from its glitzy siblings further up the coast, but come spring or summer, it's a different world: the population increases tenfold, prices triple and fun-seekers pile in to party till dawn, strut around the luxury-yacht-packed Vieux Port and enjoy the creature comforts of exclusive A-listers' beaches in the Baie de Pampelonne.

⊙ Sights & Activities

Musée de l'Annonciade
MUSEUM

(place Grammont; adult/child €6/4; ⊙10am-noon & 2-6pm Wed-Mon Oct & Dec-May, 10am-noon & 3-7pm Wed-Mon Jun-Sep) In a gracefully converted 16th-century chapel, this famous art museum showcases an impressive collection of modern

---

DON'T MISS

THE MARKET

One of southern France's busiest and best, St-Tropez's **place des Lices market** (⊙mornings Tue & Sat) is a highlight of local life, with colourful stalls groaning under the weight of plump fruit and veg, mounds of olives, local cheeses, chestnut purée and fragrant herbs. Afterwards meander to the port and duck beneath the stone arch to the bijou **fish market** (⊙mornings Tue-Sun, daily summer), hidden between stone walls on place aux Herbes.

TOP FIVE BEACH EATS

Book lunch (well ahead) at the following, open May to September and around €15 to €40 for a main.

Club 55 (www.leclub55.fr; 43 bd Patch, Pampelonne) St-Tropez's oldest-running beach club, this 1950s address was the crew canteen for the filming of *And God Created Woman* with Brigitte Bardot. The rich and famous flock here to be seen, although the food is nothing special.

Nikki Beach (www.nikkibeach.com/sttropez; rte de l'Epi, Epi Plage) Favoured by dance-on-the-bar celebs such as Paris Hilton and Pamela Anderson, the deafening scene ends at midnight.

Aqua Club (04 94 79 84 35; www.aqua-club-plage.fr; rte de l'Epi, Pampelonne; mains €22-29; Jan-Oct) Friendly mixed, gay-straight crowd, the most diverse by far.

Moorea Plage (04 94 97 18 17; www.moorea-plage-st-tropez.com; rte des Plages, Tahiti; mains €15-29) Ideal for conversation and backgammon (supplied); tops for steak.

Liberty Plage (04 94 79 80 62; www.plageleliberty.com; chemin des Tamaris, Pampelonne; mains €17-19; year-round) Clothing optional – eat naked.

art infused with that legendary Côte d'Azur light. Pointillist Paul Signac bought a house in St-Tropez in 1892 and introduced others to the area. The museum's collection includes his *St-Tropez, Le Quai* (1899) and *St-Tropez, Coucher de Soleil au Bois de Pins* (1896), which hangs juxtaposed with a window-view of contemporary St-Tropez.

Plage de Pampelonne   BEACH
The golden sands of **Plage de Tahiti**, 4km southeast of town, morph into the 5km-long, celebrity-studded **Plage de Pampelonne**, which sports a line-up of exclusive beach restaurants and clubs in summer. The bus to Ramatuelle stops at various points along a road, 1km inland from the beach.

Citadelle de St-Tropez   HISTORIC SITE
(admission €2.50; 10am-6.30pm) Built in 1602 to defend the coast against Spain, the citadel dominates the hillside overlooking St-Tropez to the east. The views (and peacocks!) are fantastic. Its dungeons shelter a **Musée Naval**, dedicated to the town's maritime history and the Allied landings in August 1944.

🛏 Sleeping

St-Tropez is no shoestring destination, but multistar camping grounds abound on the road to Plage de Pampelonne.

TOP CHOICE **Hôtel Lou Cagnard**   PENSION €€
(04 94 97 04 24; www.hotel-lou-cagnard.com; 18 av Paul Roussel; d €75-156; Jan-Oct;) Book well ahead for this great-value courtyard charmer, shaded by lemon and fig trees.

This pretty Provençal house with lavender shutters has its very own jasmine-scented garden, strung with fairy lights at night. The cheapest rooms have private washbasin and standup-bathtub but share a toilet; 15 of the 19 rooms have aircon.

Hôtel Le Colombier   HOTEL €€
(04 94 97 05 31; http://lecolombierhotel.free.fr; impasse des Conquettes; r €84-158, without bathroom €76;) An immaculately clean converted house, five minutes' walk from place des Lices, the Colombier's fresh, summery decor is feminine and uncluttered, with pale pink bedrooms and vintage furniture.

Pastis   HOTEL €€€
(04 98 12 56 50; www.pastis-st-tropez.com; 61 av du Général Leclerc; d from €200;) This stunning townhouse-turned-hotel is the brainchild of an English couple besotted with Provence and passionate about modern art. You'll die for the pop-art-inspired interior, and long for a swim in the emerald-green pool.

🍽 Eating

Quai Jean Jaurès at the Vieux Port is littered with restaurants and cafes.

 Auberge de l'Oumède   PROVENÇAL €€
(04 94 44 11 11; www.aubergedeloumede.com; Chemin de l'Oumède; mains €39-59; d from €225; dinner Tue-Sat May–mid-Sep, dinner daily Jul & Aug;) Epicureans come from far and wide to sample Jean-Pierre Frezia's Provençal cuisine served in a sea of vineyards. Dining at this isolated *bastide* down a

FRANCE ST-TROPEZ

ⓘ TRAFFIC-JAM DODGER

To skip the worst of July and August's high-season traffic, motorists get off the A8 at Le Muy (exit 35), take the D558 road through the Massif des Maures and via La Garde Freinet to **Port Grimaud**, park and hop aboard a **Les Bateaux Verts** (☎04 94 49 29 39; www.bateauxverts.com; quai Jean Jaurès) shuttle boat (15 minutes) to St-Tropez.

single-lane track is indeed a rare treat. It has seven rooms and a pool – handy should you really not want to leave.

Auberge des Maures   PROVENÇAL €€
(☎04 94 97 01 50; 4 rue du Docteur Boutin; mains €31-39; ☺dinner) The town's oldest restaurant remains the locals' choice for always-good, copious portions of earthy Provençal cooking, like *daube* (a Provençal beef stew) or tapenade-stuffed lamb shoulder. Book a table (essential) on the leafy courtyard.

Le Sporting   BRASSERIE €€
(☎04 94 97 00 65; place des Lices; mains €14-24; ☺8am-1am) There's a bit of everything on the menu at always-packed Le Sporting, but the speciality is a hamburger topped with *foie gras* and morel cream sauce. The Brittany-born owner also serves perfect buckwheat crêpes, honest lunch deals (€13), and a simple salad and *croque monsieur*.

ⓘ Information

Tourist office (☎04 94 97 45 21; www.ot-saint -tropez.com; quai Jean Jaurès; ☺9.30am-8pm Jul & Aug, 9.30am-12.30pm & 2-7pm Apr-Jun & Sep–mid-Oct, 9.30am-12.30pm & 2-6pm mid-Oct–Mar)

ⓘ Getting There & Away

From the **bus station** (☎04 94 56 25 74; av du Général de Gaulle) buses run by **VarLib** (www. varlib.fr) serve Ramatuelle (€2, 35 minutes) and St-Raphaël train station (€2, 1¼ hours) via Grimaud, Port Grimaud and Fréjus. There are four daily buses to Toulon-Hyères airport (€15, 1½ hours).

Monaco

☎377 / POP 32,350

Your first glimpse of this pocket-sized principality will probably make your heart sink: after all the gorgeous medieval hilltop vil-

lages, glittering beaches and secluded peninsulas of the surrounding area, Monaco's concrete high-rises and astronomic prices come as a shock.

But Monaco is beguiling. The world's second-smallest state (a smidgen bigger than the Vatican), it is as famous for its tax-haven status as for its glittering casino, sports scene (Formula One, world-famous circus festival and tennis open) and a royal family on a par with British royals for best gossip fodder. For visitors, it just means an exciting trip: from an evening at the stunning casino, to a visit of the excellent Musée Océanographique to a spot of celebrity/royalty spotting, Monaco is a fun day out on the Riviera.

In terms of practicalities, Monaco is a sovereign state but has no border control. It has its own flag (red and white), national holiday (19 November) and telephone country code (377), but the official language is French and the country uses the euro even though it is not part of the European Union.

Most visit Monaco as a day trip from Nice, a 20-minute train ride away.

⊙ Sights & Activities

Casino de Monte Carlo   CASINO
(www.casinomontecarlo.com; place du Casino; ☺European Rooms from noon Sat & Sun, from 2pm Mon-Fri) Living out your James Bond fantasies just doesn't get any better than at Monte Carlo's monumental, richly decorated showpiece, the 1910-built casino. The European Rooms have poker/slot machines, French roulette and *trente et quarante* (a card game), while the Private Rooms offer

Monaco

⊙ Top Sights

Casino de Monte Carlo	C3
Cathédrale de Monaco	B6
Le Rocher	B6
Musée Océanographique de Monaco	C6
Palais du Prince	A6

⊗ Eating

1	Café Llorca	D1
2	La Montgolfière	B6
3	Zelo's	D1

⊙ Drinking

4	Brasserie de Monaco	B5

Monaco

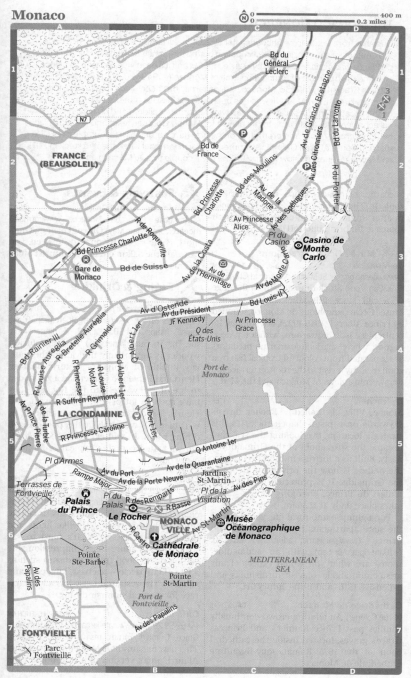

0 400 m
0 0.2 miles

FRANCE MONACO

Bd du Général Leclerc

Av de Grande Bretagne

Bd du Larvotto

R du Portier

Av des Citronniers

Bd de France

FRANCE (BEAUSOLEIL)

N7

Bd Princesse Charlotte

Bd des Moulins

Av de la Madone

Av des Spélugues

Av Princesse Alice

Pl du Casino

Casino de Monte Carlo

R de Roqueville

Bd Princesse Charlotte

Gare de Monaco

Bd de Suisse

Av de la Costa

Av de l'Hermitage

Av de

Av de Monte Carlo

Bd Louis II

Av d'Ostende

Av du Président JF Kennedy

Av Princesse Grace

Q des États-Unis

Bd Rainier III

Louise Aureglia

R Bretelle Aureglia

R Grimaldi

Bd Albert 1er

Q Albert 1er

Port de Monaco

R Princesse Notari

R Louise

Av Prince Pierre

R de la Turbie

R Suffren Reymond

LA CONDAMINE

R Princesse Caroline

Q Albert 1er

Q Antoine 1er

Pl d'Armes

Av de la Quarantaine

Rampe Major

Av du Port

Av de la Porte Neuve

Jardins St-Martin

Av des Pins

Terrasses de Fontvieille

Pl du Palais

R des Remparts

R Basse

Pl de la Visitation

Av St-Martin

Palais du Prince

Le Rocher

MONACO VILLE

Musée Océanographique de Monaco

R Castro

Cathédrale de Monaco

MEDITERRANEAN SEA

Pointe Ste-Barbe

Av des Papalins

Pointe St-Martin

Port de Fontvieille

FONTVIEILLE

Av des Papalins

Parc Fontvieille

THE MONACO MONARCHY

Originally from Genoa in neighbouring Italy, the Grimaldi family has ruled Monaco since 1297, except for the principality's occupation during the French Revolution. Monaco's independence was again recognised by France in 1860, and it's been independent ever since.

Since the marriage of Prince Rainier III of Monaco (r 1949–2005) to Hollywood actress Grace Kelly in 1956, Monaco's ruling family has been a nonstop feature in gossip magazines. Even Albert II, who has been prince since his father's death in 2005, hasn't escaped media scrutiny: he has two illegitimate children and no legal heirs, but his achievements as an athlete (he played for Monaco football team and is a judo black belt), his charity work and promotion of the arts have earned him favourable press. He married South African Olympic swimmer and former model Charlene Wittstock in 2011, and Monégasques are now waiting for the royal couple to give Monaco an heir.

baccarat, blackjack, craps and American roulette. The jacket-and-tie dress code kicks in after 8pm. Minimum entry age for both rooms is 18; bring photo ID.

TOP CHOICE Musée Océanographique de Monaco
AQUARIUM

(www.oceano.org; av St-Martin; adult/child €13/6.50; ⊗9.30am-7pm) Stuck dramatically to the edge of a cliff since 1910, the world-renowned Musée Océanographique de Monaco, founded by Prince Albert I (1848-1922), is a stunner. Its centrepiece is its **aquarium**, with a 6m-deep **lagoon** where sharks and marine predators are separated from colourful tropical fish by a coral reef. Pay a visit to the rooftop terrace too for sweeping views of Monaco and the Med.

Le Rocher
HISTORIC QUARTER

Monaco Ville, also called Le Rocher, thrusts skywards on a pistol-shaped rock. It's this strategic location, overlooking the sea, that became the stronghold of the Grimaldi dynasty. Built as a fortress in the 13th century, the **palace** is now the private residence of the Grimaldis. It is protected by the Carabiniers du Prince; **changing of the guard** takes place daily at 11.55am.

For a glimpse into royal life, you can tour the state apartments inside the **Palais du Prince** (www.palais.mc; adult/child €8/3.50; ⊗10am-6pm Apr-Sep) with an audioguide; rooms are what you would expect of any aristocratic abode - lavish furnishings and expensive 18th- and 19th-century art.

Cathédrale de Monaco
CATHEDRAL

(4 rue Colonel) An adoring crowd continually shuffles past Prince Rainier's and Princess Grace's graves, located inside the cathedral choir of the 1875 Romanesque-Byzantine Cathédrale de Monaco.

✯✯ Festivals & Events

Formula One Grand Prix
SPORTS

(Automobile Club de Monaco; www.formula1monaco.com; ⊗late May) One of Formula One's most iconic races. If you're dead keen, you can walk the 3.2km circuit; the tourist office has maps.

✖ Eating & Drinking

TOP CHOICE La Montgolfière
FUSION €€

(☑97 98 61 59; www.lamontgolfiere.mc; 16 rue Basse; mains €21-30; ⊗lunch & dinner Mon, Tue, Thu, Fri, Sun, dinner Sat) This tiny fusion wonder is an unlikely find amid the touristy jumble of Monaco's historic quarter. Henri and Fabienne Geraci had a great idea to breathe new life into the Rocher. They have spent a lot of time in Malaysia, and Henri's fusion cuisine is outstanding, as is Fabienne's welcome in the pocket-sized dining room. In winter, Henri cooks *bourride*, a salted cod stew typical of Monaco, every day.

Zelo's
FUSION €€

(☑99 99 25 50; 10 av Princesse Grace, Grimaldi Forum; mains €25-30; ⊗dinner) With enormous chandeliers, intensely blue walls, a ceiling fitted with hundreds of starlike lights and uninterrupted sea views, it's hard to say which makes more of an impression, the setting or the food (modern dishes such as a trio of Carpaccio – sea bass, king crab and salmon). The restaurant also has a huge terrace for magical summer dining.

Café Llorca
MODERN FRENCH €€

(☑99 99 29 29; www.cafellorca.mc; 10 av Princesse Grace, Grimaldi Forum; mains €15-26; ⊗lunch) This new restaurant is Michelin-starred-chef Alain Llorca's version of a traditional cafe:

the menu is classic French fare (pork loin with sautéed potatoes; *daube*, a local beef stew) but elevated to new heights in taste and presentation. In summer, tables are set out on the terrace overlooking the sea.

TOP CHOICE **Brasserie de Monaco** MICROBREWERY (www.brasseriedemonaco.com; 36 rte de la Piscine; ⊙11am-1pm Sun-Thu, 11am-3am Fri & Sat) Tourists and locals rub shoulders at Monaco's only microbrewery, which crafts rich organic ales and lager, and serves tasty (if pricey) antipasti plates. Happy hour is 5pm to 8pm.

❶ Information

Telephone
Calls between Monaco and France are international calls. Dial 00 followed by Monaco's country code (377) when calling Monaco from France or elsewhere abroad. To phone France from Monaco, dial 00 and France's country code (33).

Tourist information
Tourist office (www.visitmonaco.com; 2a bd des Moulins; ⊙9am-7pm Mon-Sat, 11am-1pm Sun) From mid-June to late September additional tourist-info kiosks mushroom around the harbour and train station.

❶ Getting There & Away
Monaco's **train station** (av Prince Pierre) has frequent trains to Nice (€3.60, 20 minutes), and east to Menton (€2, 10 minutes) and beyond into Italy.

One thing to note if planning a day trip to Monaco is that its sparkly, state-of-the-art train station has no lockers to stash your bags.

CORSICA

The rugged island of Corsica (Corse in French) is officially a part of France, but remains fiercely proud of its own culture, history and language. It's one of the Mediterranean's most dramatic islands, with a bevy of beautiful beaches, glitzy ports and a mountainous, maquis-covered interior to explore, as well as a wild, independent spirit all of its own.

The island has long had a love-hate relationship with the mother mainland – you'll see plenty of anti-French slogans and 'Corsicanised' road signs – but that doesn't seem to deter the millions of French tourists who descend on the island every summer. Prices skyrocket and accommodation is at a premium during the peak season between July and August, so you're much better off saving your visit for spring and autumn.

Bastia
POP 44,170

Filled with heart, soul and character, the bustling old port of Bastia is a good surprise. Sure, it might not measure up to Ajaccio's sexy style or the architectural appeal of Bonifacio, but it has an irresistible magnetism. Allow yourself at least a day to drink in the narrow old-town alleyways of Terra Vecchia, the seething Vieux Port (Old Port), dramatic 16th-century citadel perched up high, and the compelling history museum.

◉ Sights & Activities
Even by Corsican standards, Bastia is a pocket-sized city. The 19th-century central square of **place St-Nicholas** sprawls along the seafront between the ferry port and harbour. Named after the patron saint of sailors – a nod to Corsica's seagoing heritage – the square is lined with plane trees, busy cafes and a **statue of Napoléon Bonaparte**, Corsica's famous son.

A network of narrow lanes leads south towards the neighbourhood of **Terra Vecchia**, a muddle of crumbling apartments and balconied blocks. Further south, the Vieux Port is ringed by pastel-coloured tenements and buzzy brasseries, as well as the twin-towered **Église St-Jean Baptiste**. The best views of the harbour are from the **Jetée du Dragon** (Dragon Jetty) or from the hillside park of **Jardin Romieu**, reached via a twisting staircase from the waterfront. Behind the garden looms Bastia's sunbaked **citadel**, built from the 15th to 17th centuries as a stronghold for the city's Genoese masters. Inside the citadel, the **Palais des Gouverneurs** (Governers Palace) houses Bastia's top-notch local history museum, **Musée d'Histoire de Bastia** (📞04 95 31 09 12; www.musee-bastia.com; place

FRANCE BASTIA

MONEY MATTERS

Many restaurants and hotels in Corsica don't accept credit cards, and *chambres d'hôtes* (B&Bs) hardly ever: those that do quite frequently refuse card payments for amounts typically less than €15.

CORSICAN ICE

Wrapping your lips around a rich Corsican ice cream, flavoured with one of the island's distinctive edible products, is an essential part of the Bastia experience. And no address does it better than **Raugi** (2 rue du Chanoine Colombani; one/two/three scoops €1.30/2.60/3.90, cups €5-20), an ice-cream house dating to 1937, with its main cafe in town and a waterfront **takeaway parlour** (quai du 1er Bataillon de Choc) at the old port. Flavours range from bog-standard raspberry, lemon and so on to Corsican chestnut, mandarin, fig, aromatic *senteur de maquis* (scent of Corsican herbal scrubland) and sweet *myrte* (myrtle). Forget the chocolate flake; top it off with a *canistrelli* (local biscuit) stuck in the top.

du Donjon; admission €5; ⊘10am-7.30pm Tue-Sun Jul–mid-Sep, shorter hrs mid-Sep–Jun).

🛏 Sleeping

TOP CHOICE **Hôtel Central**　　　　　HOTEL €€
(☑04 95 31 71 12; www.centralhotel.fr; 3 rue Miot; s €77, d €90; 🛜) From the vintage, black-and-white-tiled floor in the entrance to the sweeping staircase and eclectic jumble of pot plants in the minscule interior courtyard, this family-run address oozes 1940s grace.

Hôtel Les Voyageurs　　　　HOTEL €€
(☑04 95 34 90 80; www.hotel-lesvoyageurs.com; 9 av Maréchal Sébastiani; s €60-85, d €75-100, q €110-150; P ❄ 🛜) In a city where parking can be tricky, the garage here is a big plus. Combine this with a gorgeous ginger facade, shabby-chic oyster-grey shutters and a modern three-star interior, and you'll be well pleased.

🍴 Eating

Tasty all-day options abound around the Vieux Port and along quai des Martyrs. Market stalls packed with local produce spill across **place de l'Hôtel de Ville** every Saturday and Sunday morning.

Le Lavezzi　　　　MODERN FRENCH €€
(☑04 95 31 05 73; 8 rue St-Jean; mains €20-35, lunch menus €19) A boutique address design-loving gourmets will love, Le Lavezzi is completely different. Its artsy interior is fabulous

and funky, and the real heart stealer is the twinset of 1st-floor balconies with prime old-port views.

Petite Marie　　　　REGIONAL CUISINE €€
(☑04 95 32 47 83; 2 rue des Zéphyrs; mains €16-19; ⊘dinner Mon-Sat) Everything is home baked at Petite Marie, a bolt-hole hidden away in an alley a couple of blocks from the Vieux Port. Do as locals do and kick-start your feast with *friture de rougets* (battered, fried red mullet) followed by grilled crayfish. No frozen *frites* (fries) – only hand cut, homemade – and no credit cards.

ℹ Information

Tourist office (☑04 95 54 20 40; www.bastia-tourisme.com; place St-Nicolas; ⊘8am-6pm Mon-Sat, 8am-noon Sun)

ℹ Getting There & Away

Air

Aéroport Bastia-Poretta (www.bastia.aeroport.fr), 24km south, is linked by bus (€9, 30 minutes, 10 daily) with the Préfecture building in town.

Boat

Bastia Port (www.bastia.port.fr) has two ferry terminals; ferry companies have information

ℹ TRAMWAY DE LA BALAGNE

You may well tremble as the *trinighellu* (trembler) – as the **Tramway de la Balagne** (☑04 95 60 00 50, 04 95 65 00 61) is affectionately called – trundles periously close to the shore along sand-covered tracks between Calvi and Île Rousse. The dinky little train is the easiest way to access the numerous hidden coves and beaches sprinkled along the coast: you'll avoid traffic jams and experience an unforgettable trip alongside getaway beaches. The train runs four to eight times daily April to September, calling at 15 stations en route, all by request only. Out of season, regular trains run by **Chemins de Fer de la Corse** (☑04 95 32 80 57; http://train-corse.com) cover the same route. Hop off at an intermediate rocky cove or, for fine golden sand, leave the train at Algajola or Plage de Bodri, the last stop before Île Rousse. It costs €5.40 one-way.

offices in the **Southern Ferry Terminal** (www.port-de-bastia.net), usually open for same-day ticket sales a couple of hours before sailings. Ferries sail to/from Marseille, Toulon and Nice (mainland France), and Livorno, Savona, Piombino and Genoa (Italy).

Corsica Ferries (☎08 25 09 50 95; www.corsica-ferries.fr; 5bis rue Chanoine Leschi)

La Méridionale (☎08 10 20 13 20; www.lameridionale.fr; Port de Commerce)

Moby Lines (☎04 95 34 84 94; www.mobylines.com; 4 rue du Commandant Luce de Casabianca)

SNCM (☎32 60; www.sncm.fr)

Bus & Train

The **bus station** (1 rue du Nouveau Port) is north of place St-Nicolas and bus stops are scattered around town. Many buses depart from in front of Bastia **train station** (av Maréchal Sébastiani), the departure point for daily trains to Ajaccio (€25, 3¾ hours, four daily) via Corte (1¾ hours), and Calvi (three hours, three or four daily) via Île Rousse.

Transports Santini (☎04 95 37 02 98) Seasonal buses to Île Rousse (€15, 1¾ hrs, six weekly) leave from the train station.

Eurocorse Voyages (☎04 95 31 73 76; www.eurocorse.com; 1 rue Nouveau Port) Buses to Ajaccio (€21, three hours) via Corte (€11.50, two hours) twice daily except on Sunday from Bastia bus station.

Les Rapides Bleus (☎04 95 31 03 79; www.rapides-bleus.com; 1 av Maréchal Sébastiani) Buses leave from in front of the post office to Porto-Vecchio (€22, three hours) twice daily except Sunday.

Calvi

POP 5486

Basking between the fiery orange bastions of its 15th-century citadel and the glittering waters of a moon-shaped bay, Calvi feels closer to the chichi sophistication of a French Riviera resort than a historic Corsican port. Palatial yachts dock along its harbourside, while above the quay the watchtowers of the town's Genoese stronghold stand guard, proffering sweeping views inland to Monte Cinto (2706m).

Calvi's 15th-century **citadel** – also known as the Haute Ville (Upper City) – sits on a rocky promontory above the Basse Ville (Lower Town). Down below, its stellar 4km-long sandy **beach** begins at the marina and runs east around the Golfe de Calvi. Rent kayaks and windsurfs on the sand, and hook up with local diving schools by the **tourist office** (☎04 95 65 16 67; www.balagne-corsica.com; Port de Plaisance; ⏰9am-noon & 2-6pm daily Jul & Aug, Mon-Sat May, Jun, Sep & Oct, Mon-Fri Nov-Apr) at the marina.

DON'T MISS

CHEZ TAO

You won't find cooler (or more amazing sea views with cocktail in hand) than **Chez Tao**, (☎04 95 65 00 73; rue St-Antoine; ⏰Jun-Sep) a super-slick piano bar of mythical standing up high within the citadel. Founded in 1935 by White Russian émigré Tao Kanbey de Kerekoff, the lavishly decorated vaulted room still lures hedonistic hipsters seven decades on.

Sleeping & Eating

Hôtel Le Magnolia HOTEL €€

(☎04 95 65 19 16; www.hotel-le-magnolia.com; rue Alsace-Lorraine; d €70-150; ⏰Apr-Nov; ❄@📶) An oasis from the harbourside fizz, this attractive mansion sits behind a beautiful high-walled courtyard garden pierced by a handsome magnolia tree. Pretty much every room has a lovely outlook – Calvi rooftops, garden or sea – and connecting doubles makes it an instant hit with families.

Camping La Pinède CAMPGROUND €

(☎04 95 65 17 80; www.camping-calvi.com; rte de la Pinède; tent, car & 2 adults €34; ⏰Apr-Oct; P🏊) Handy for town and beach; mobile homes and chalets too.

A Candella TRADITIONAL CORSICAN €€

(☎04 95 65 42 13; 9 rue St-Antoine; mains €15-25) One of a handful of addresses to eat within the citadel, A Candella stands out for its romantic, golden-hued terrace of stone strung with pretty flowers in pots and olive trees. The food is Corsican hearty, and the sea view is the most marvellous you could hope for.

Getting There & Away

BOAT From Calvi's **ferry terminal** (quai Landry) regular ferries sail to/from Nice (France) and Savona (Italy).

BUS Les Beaux Voyages (☎04 95 65 15 02; place de la Porteuse d'Eau) runs daily buses to Bastia (2½ hours) via Île Rousse (15 minutes).

TRAIN Calvi's train station connects with Ajaccio (five hours, two daily) and Bastia (three hours) via Ponte Leccia.

DON'T MISS

LES CALANQUES

No amount of hyperbole can capture the astounding beauty of **Les Calanques de Piana** (E Calanche in Corsican), sculpted cliffs teetering above the Golfe de Porto that rear up from the sea in staggering scarlet pillars, teetering columns, towers and irregularly shaped boulders of pink, ochre and ginger. Flaming red in the sunlight, this natural ensemble of gargantuan proportions is one of Corsica's most iconic, awe-inspiring sights. And as you sway around switchback after switchback along the rock-riddled 10km stretch of the D81 south of Porto towards the village of **Piana** (pop 500; www. otpiana.com), one mesmerising vista piggybacks another.

For the full technicolour experience, savour Les Calanques on foot. Trails start near **Pont de Mezzanu**, a road bridge on the D81 about 3km north of Piana. In the village itself, the **tourist office** (www.otpiana.com; place Mairie; ⊙9am-6pm Mon-Fri) stocks the leaflet *Piana: Sentiers de Randonnée*, detailing six walks. Afterwards, sand-flop on the idyllic beaches of **Ficajola** and **Arone**, 5km and 11km southwest respectively. Or splurge on lunch with a view at Corsica's original luxury hotel, **Les Roches Rouges** (☑04 95 27 81 81; www.lesrochesrouges.com; D81; s €102-123, d €114-136, tr €156-176, q €177-213; ⊙Apr-Oct; ☞), in business since 1912. Faded grandeur at its best, a meal in its superb gourmet restaurant (or, should you fancy staying over, a sea-view room) is worth every cent; at the very least partake in a drink on the romantic stone terrace to savour the truly extraordinary vista.

Ajaccio

POP 65,000

With its sweeping bay and buzzing centre replete with mellow-toned buildings, cafes and yacht-packed marina, Ajaccio, Corsica's main metropolis, is all class and seduction. Looming over this elegant port city is the spectre of Corsica's great general: Napoléon Bonaparte was born here in 1769 and the city is dotted with statues and museums relating to the diminutive dictator (starting with the main street in Ajaccio, cours Napoléon).

◉ Sights & Activities

Palais Fesch – Musée des Beaux-Arts
MUSEUM

(www.musee-fesch.com; 50-52 rue du Cardinal Fesch; adult/child €8/5; ⊙10.30am-6pm Mon, Wed & Sat, noon-6pm Thu, Fri & Sun year-round, to 8.30pm Fri Jul & Aug) This superb museum established by Napoléon's uncle has France's largest collection of Italian paintings outside the Louvre. Mostly the works of minor or anonymous 14th- to 19th-century artists, there are also canvases by Titian, Fra Bartolomeo, Veronese, Botticelli and Bellini.

Maison Bonaparte
MUSEUM

(☑04 95 21 43 89; www.musee-maisonbonaparte. fr; rue St-Charles; adult/child €7/5.50; ⊙10.30am-12.30am & 1.15-6pm Tue-Sun Apr-Sep, 10am-noon & 2-4.45pm Oct-Mar) Napoléon spent his first nine years in this house, host to various memorabilia of the emperor and his siblings, including a glass medallion containing a lock of his hair. It's closed Monday mornings.

Boat Trips
TOURS

Kiosks on the quayside opposite place du Maréchal Foch sell tickets for seasonal boat trips around the Golfe d'Ajaccio and Îles Sanguinaires (€27), and excursions to the **Réserve Naturelle de Scandola** (adult/child €50/35).

🛏 Sleeping

TOP CHOICE **Hôtel Kallisté**
HOTEL €€

(☑04 95 51 34 45; www.hotel-kalliste-ajaccio.com; 51 cours Napoléon; s/d/tr €77/95/123; P❄@☞) Exposed brick, neutral tones, terracotta tiles and a funky glass lift conjure a neo-boutique feel at the Kallisté, which occupies a typical 19th-century Ajaccio townhouse. Facilities are fab – wi-fi, satellite TV, a copious buffet breakfast for a mere €4 extra, and the convenience of a hotel car park in a city where parking can be downright hellish.

Hôtel Marengo
HOTEL €

(☑04 95 21 43 66; www.hotel-marengo.com; 2 rue Marengo; d €65-89, tr €95-115; ⊙Apr-Oct; ❄) For something nearer to the sand, try this charmingly eccentric small hotel near the beach. Rooms have a balcony, there's a quiet flower-filled courtyard and reception is an agreeable clutter of tasteful prints and personal objects. Find it down a cul de sac off bd Madame Mère.

✖ Eating

Le 20123 TRADITIONAL CORSICAN €€
(☎04 95 21 50 05; www.20123.fr; 2 rue du Roi de Rome; menus €34.50; ☺dinner Tue-Sun) This fabulous, one-of-a-kind place started life in the village of Pila Canale (postcode 20123 – get it?), and when the owner upped sticks to Ajaccio he decided to take the old village with him – water pump, washing line, life-sized dolls in traditional dress, central square et al. It all sounds a bit tacky, but you won't find many more character-filled places in Corsica. Needless to say, the food is 100% authentic, too - everyone feasts on the same four-course *menu,* presented orally, built solely from local produce and traditional recipes, and – amazingly – unchanged for 25 years.

L'Altru Versu GASTRONOMIC €€
(☎04 95 50 05 22; www.laltruversu.com; rte des Sanguinaires, Les Sept Chapelles; mains €20-30; ☺lunch & dinner daily Jun-Sep, lunch & dinner Tue-Sun Oct-May; ✯) Ajaccio's top-notch restaurant belongs to the Mezzacqui brothers who are passionate gastronomes and excellent singers – they hitch on their guitars and serenade guests each Friday and Saturday night.

Da Mama TRADITIONAL CORSICAN €
(☎04 95 21 39 44; 3 passage de la Ghinghetta; lunch menus €12, dinner menus €17-25; ☺dinner Mon, lunch & dinner Tue-Sat) Staunchly Corsican cuisine aside, the main draw of this unfussy eatery is its location in the shade of a magnificent rubber tree down a narrow alley.

ⓘ Information

Tourist office (www.ajaccio-tourisme.com; 3 bd du Roi Jérôme; ☺8am-7pm Mon-Sat, 9am-1pm Sun)

ⓘ Getting There & Away

AIR Bus 8 (€4.50, 20 minutes) links **Aéroport d'Ajaccio-Campo dell'Oro** (☎04 95 23 56 56; www.ajaccio.aeroport.fr), 8km east, with Ajaccio's train and bus stations.
BOAT Boats to/from Toulon, Nice and Marseille depart from Ajaccio's **Terminal Maritime et Routier** (☎04 95 51 21 80; www.2a.cci.fr; quai L'Herminier).

BUS Local bus companies have ticket kiosks inside the ferry terminal building, the arrival/departure point for buses.
TRAIN From the **train station** (place de la Gare), services include Bastia (four hours, three to four daily), Corte (two hours, three to four daily) and Calvi (five hours, two daily; change at Ponte Leccia).

Bonifacio

POP 2973

With its glittering harbour, dramatic perch atop creamy white cliffs, and stout citadel teetering above the cornflower-blue waters of the Bouches de Bonifacio, this dazzling port is an essential stop. Just a short hop from Sardinia, Bonifacio has a distinctly Italianate feel: sun-bleached townhouses, dangling washing lines and murky chapels cram the web of alleyways of the old citadel while, down below on the harbourside, brasseries and boat kiosks tout their wares to the droves of day trippers.

⊙ Sights & Activities

Citadel (Haute Ville) HISTORIC NEIGHBOURHOOD
Much of Bonifacio's charm comes from strolling the citadel's shady streets, several spanned by arched aqueducts designed to collect rainwater to fill the communal cistern opposite **Église Ste-Marie Majeure**. From the marina, the paved **steps of montée du Rastello** and **montée St-Roch** bring you up to the citadel's old gateway, complete with an original 16th-century drawbridge. Inside the gateway is the 13th-century **Bastion de l'Étendard** (adult/child €2.50/free; ☺9am-7pm Mon-Fri, 10am-6pm Sat & Sun Apr-Oct), home to a small history museum. Stroll the ramparts to **place du Marché** and **place de la Manichella** for jaw-dropping views over the Bouches de Bonifacio.

DON'T MISS

THE PERFECT PICTURE

If you're after that perfect snapshot, don't miss the fantastic, easy walk along the cliffs to the **Phare de Pertusato**, a lighthouse from where the seamless views of the cliffs, Îles Lavezzi, Bonifacio and Sardinia are memorable. Pick up the trail just to the left of the sharp bend on the hill up to Bonifacio's citadel. Count 1½ hours for the 5.6km round trip.

From the citadel, the **Escalier du Roi d'Aragon** (King of Aragon's stairway; adult/under 12yr €2.50/free; ⊙9am-7pm Mon-Fri, 10am-6pm Sat & Sun Apr-Oct) cuts down the southern cliffface. Legend says its 187 steep steps were carved in a single night by Aragonese troops during the siege of 1420, only for troops to be rebuffed by retaliating Bonifacio residents at the top. In reality, the steps served as an access path to an underground freshwater well.

Îles Lavezzi   ARCHIPELAGO

Paradise! This protected clutch of uninhabited islets were made for those who love nothing better than splashing in tranquil lapis-lazuli waters. The 65-hectare Île Lavezzi, which gives its name to the whole archipelago, is the most accessible of the islands. Savage beauty aside, the island's superb natural pools and scenic stretches of sand beg for long-and-lazy sunbathing and swimming sessions. In summer, various companies organise **boat trips** here; buy tickets at the booths located on Bonifacio's marina and bring your own picnic lunch.

🛏 Sleeping & Eating

TOP CHOICE **Domaine de Licetto**   HOTEL €€

(☑04 95 73 03 59; www.licetto.com; rte du Phare de Pertusato; s €55-85, d €70-105, q €115-175; ⊙Apr-Oct; 🅿) Tucked in the maquis just a couple of kilometres east of Bonifacio, this motel-style address is a lovely surprise. Its seven minimalist rooms sport stylishly modern bathrooms, well-chosen furnishings and each has a terrace with table and chairs made for lounging alfresco in the surrounding peace and quiet. The restaurant on the estate is a feast in traditional dining and, best of all, Bonifacio town is a short idyllic walk away along the clifftop coastal path.

TOP CHOICE **Kissing Pigs**   MODERN CORSICAN €

(☑04 95 73 56 09; quai Banda del Ferro; mains €9-15) Soothingly positioned by the harbour, this widely acclaimed restaurant and wine bar serves savoury fare in a seductively cosy interior, complete with wooden fixtures and swinging sausages. It's famed for its cheese and charcuterie platters; for the indecisive, the combination *moitié-moitié* (half-half) is perfect. The Corsican wine list is another hit.

ⓘ Information

Tourist office (www.bonifacio.fr; 2 rue Fred Scamaroni; ⊙9am-8pm Jul & Aug, to 7pm May, Jun & Sep, 9am-noon & 2-6pm Oct-Apr)

ⓘ Getting There & Away

AIR A taxi into town from **Aéroport de Figari** (www.figari.aeroport.fr), 21km north, costs about €40.

BOAT Saremar and Moby Lines sail between Bonifacio and Santa Teresa di Gallura (on the neighbouring island of Sardinia) in summer.

UNDERSTAND FRANCE

History

Prehistory

Neanderthals were the first to live in France (about 90,000 to 40,000 BC). Cro-Magnons followed 35,000 years ago and left behind cave paintings and engravings, especially around the Vézère Valley in the Dordogne. Neolithic people (about 7500 to 4000 years ago) created France's incredible menhirs (standing stones) and dolmens (megalithic tombs), especially in Brittany.

The Celtic Gauls arrived between 1500 and 500 BC, and were superseded by the Romans for around five centuries after Julius Caesar took control around 52 BC, until the Franks and Alemanii overran the country.

The Frankish Merovingian and Carolingian dynasties ruled from the 5th to the 10th century AD. In 732 Charles Martel defeated the Moors, preventing France from falling under Muslim rule. Martel's grandson, Charlemagne (742–814), extended the power and boundaries of the kingdom and was crowned Holy Roman Emperor in 800.

The Early French Kings

The tale of William the Conqueror's invasion of England in 1066 is recorded in the Bayeux Tapestry, sowing the seeds for a fierce rivalry between France and England that peaked with the Hundred Years War (1337–1453).

Following the occupation of Paris by the English-allied dukes of Burgundy, John Plantagenet was made regent of France on behalf of England's King Henry VI in 1422. Less than a decade later, he was crowned king at Paris' Notre Dame cathedral. Luckily for the French, a 17-year-old warrior called Jeanne d'Arc (Joan of Arc) came along in 1429. She persuaded Charles VII that she had a divine mission from God to expel the English from France. Following her capture by the Burgundians and subsequent sale to the English in 1430, Joan was convicted of witchcraft and heresy and burned at the stake in Rouen, on the site now marked by the city's cathedral.

Despite Charles' promised corination in July 1429, battles waged between the English and the French until 1453, when the English were driven out of France once and for all, marking the end of the war.

The arrival of Italian Renaissance culture during the reign of François I (r 1515–47) ushered in some of France's finest chateaux, especially in the Loire Valley.

The period from 1562 to 1598 was one of the bloodiest periods in French history. Ideological disagreement between the Huguenots (French Protestants) and the Catholic monarchy escalated into the French Wars of Religion.

The Sun King

Louis XIV, Le Roi Soleil (the Sun King), ascended the throne in 1643, and spent the next 60 years in a series of bloody wars. He also constructed the fabulous palace at Versailles.

Louis XV ascended to the throne in 1715 and shifted the royal court back to Paris. As the 18th century progressed, the ancient regime became increasingly out of step with the needs of the country. Antiestablishment and anticlerical ideas expressed by Voltaire, Rousseau and Montesquieu further threatened the royal reign.

Revolution to Republic

Social and economic crisis marked the 18th century. Discontent among the French populace turned violent when a Parisian mob stormed the prison at Bastille on the 14th of July 1789. France was declared a constitutional monarchy and Louis XVI was publicly guillotined in January 1793 on Paris' place de la Concorde.

The Reign of Terror between September 1793 and July 1794 saw religious freedoms revoked, churches closed, cathedrals turned into 'Temples of Reason' and thousands beheaded. In the chaos, a dashing young Corsican general named Napoléon Bonaparte (1769–1821) stepped from the shadows.

In 1799 Napoléon I assumed power and in 1804 he was crowned emperor of France at Notre Dame. Napoléon waged several wars in which France gained control over most of Europe. Two years later, Allied armies entered Paris, exiled Napoléon to Elba and restored the French throne at the Congress of Vienna (1814–15).

In 1815 Napoléon escaped, entering Paris on 20 May. His glorious 'Hundred Days' back in power ended with the Battle of Waterloo and his exile to the island of St Helena, where he died in 1821.

Second Republic to Second Empire

The subsequent years were marked by civil strife and political unrest, with monarchists and revolutionaries vying for power. Louis-Philippe (r 1830–48), a constitutional monarch, was chosen by parliament but ousted by the 1848 Revolution. The Second Republic was established and Napoléon's nephew, Louis Napoléon Bonaparte, was elected president. But in 1851 Louis Napoléon led a coup d'état and proclaimed himself Emperor Napoléon III of the Second Empire (1852–70).

France did enjoy significant economic growth during this period. Paris was transformed under urban planner Baron Haussmann (1809–91), who created the 12 huge boulevards radiating from the Arc de Triomphe. But Napoléon III embroiled France in various catastrophic conflicts, including the Crimean War (1853–56) and the Franco-Prussian War (1870–71), which ended with Prussia taking the emperor prisoner. Upon hearing the news, defiant Parisian masses took to the streets demanding a republic be declared – enter the Third Republic.

The World Wars

The 20th century was marked by two of the bloodiest conflicts in the nation's history, beginning with the Great War (WWI). The northeastern part of France bore the brunt of the devastating trench warfare between Allied and German forces: 1.3 million French soldiers were killed and almost one million injured, and the battlefields of the Somme have become powerful symbols of the unimaginable costs and ultimate futility of modern warfare.

After the war, the Treaty of Versailles imposed heavy reparations on the defeated nations, including the return of Alsace-Lorraine, which the French had lost to Germany in 1871. These punitive terms sowed the seeds for future unrest, when the fanatic leader Adolf Hitler rose to power and promised to restore the German nation's pride, power and territory. Despite constructing a lavish series of defences (the so-called Maginot Line) along its German border, France was rapidly overrun and surrendered in June 1940. The occupying Germans divided France into an Occupied Zone (in the north and west) and a puppet state in the south, centring on the spa town of Vichy.

The British Army was driven from France during the Battle of Dunkirk in 1940. Four years later, on 6 June 1944, Allied forces stormed the coastline of Normandy in the D-Day landings. The bloody Battle of Normandy followed and Paris was liberated on 25 August.

The Fourth Republic

In the first postwar election in 1945, the wartime leader of the Free French, Général Charles de Gaulle, was appointed head of the government,; he quickly sensed that the tide was turning against him and he resigned in 1946.

Progress rebuilding France's shattered economy and infrastructure was slow. By 1947 France was forced to turn to the USA for loans as part of the Marshall Plan to rebuild Europe. The economy gathered steam in the 1950s but the decade marked the end of French colonialism in Vietnam and in Algeria. The Algerian war of independence (1954–62) was particularly brutal, characterised by torture and massacre meted out to nationalist Algerians.

The Modern Era

De Gaulle assumed the presidency again in 1958, followed by his prime minister Georges Pompidou (in power 1969–74), Valéry Giscard d'Estaing (in power 1974–81), François Mitterrand (in power 1981–95), and the centre-right president Jacques Chirac, who (among other things) oversaw the country's adoption of the euro in 1999.

Presidential elections in 2007 ushered out Jacques Chirac (in his 70s with two terms under his belt) and brought in Nicolas Sarkozy. Dynamic, ambitious and media-savvy, the former interior minister and chairman of centre-right party UMP wooed voters with policies about job creation, lower taxes, crime crackdown and help for France's substantial immigrant population – issues that had particular pulling power coming from the son of a Hungarian immigrant father and Greek Jewish-French mother. Personal affairs dominated his first few months in office as he divorced his wife Cecilia and wed Italian multimillionaire singer Carla Bruni.

Unemployment soared during the 2008 global banking crisis that saw the French government inject €10.5 billion into France's six major banks. Sarkozy's party received a battering in the 2010 regional elections which saw the left scoop 54% of votes and take control of 21 out of 22 regions on mainland France and Corsica. Government popularity hit an all-time low.

France Today

Presidential elections in spring 2012 ushered in France's first socialist president since François Mitterand left office in 1995. The presidential campaign saw Sarkozy vie for a second term in office against left-wing candidate François Hollande (b 1954) of the Socialist party. Sarkozy promised to modernise the French economy, reduce the number of immigrants to France, and lower France's budget deficit; but with the electorate tired of the austerity policies of the Conservatives, it was Hollande's ambitious talk of reducing unemployment (at a 12-year high), clearing the country's debts (by 2017), upping tax on corporations and salaries over €1 million per annum, and increasing the minimum salary, that proved the more appealing platform. Parliamentary elections a month later sealed Hollande's grip on power with the Socialists winning a comfortable majority in France's 577-seat National Assembly, thus paving the way for Hollande to govern France during Europe's biggest economic crisis in decades.

Culturally, France is savouring a high. Art lovers are bursting with excitement over the reopening in Paris, after months of painstaking renovation, of both the Musée Picasso and the country's most prestigious theatre, the Comédie Française, where Molière trod the boards. At the 2012 Academy Awards, the French-made silent film *The Artist,* starring the quintessentially French Jean Dujardin, scooped five Oscars to effectively herald the renaissance of French cinema; while the grand opening of the striking new Louvre-Lens art museum in northern France promises to inject new creativity into the conventional French museum experience.

Arts

Literature

France has made huge contributions to European literature. The philosophical work of Voltaire (1694–1778) and Jean-Jacques Rousseau dominated the 18th century. A century later, the poems and novels of Victor Hugo – *Les Misérables* and *Notre Dame de Paris* (*The Hunchback of Notre Dame*)

MULTICULTURAL MUSINGS

No French writer better delves into the mind and politics of France's ethnic population than Faïza Guène (b 1985), writing in a notable 'urban slang' style, born and bred on a ghetto housing estate outside Paris. Her second semi-autobiographical novel, *Du Rêve pour les Oeufs* (2006), is published in English as *Dreams from the Endz* (2008). Another French writer to address ethnic issues so engagingly is JMG Le Clézio, born in Nice to a Niçois mother and Mauritian father. He grew up in Nigeria and won the 2008 Nobel Prize in Literature, confirming France's ranking as the country with the most literary Nobel Prize winners.

among them – became landmarks of French Romanticism.

In 1857 two literary landmarks were published: *Madame Bovary* by Gustave Flaubert (1821–80) and Charles Baudelaire's collection of poems, *Les Fleurs du Mal* (The Flowers of Evil). Émile Zola (1840–1902) meanwhile strove to convert novel-writing from an art to a science in his series *Les Rougon-Macquart*.

Symbolists Paul Verlaine (1844–96) and Stéphane Mallarmé (1842–98) aimed to express mental states through their poetry, while Verlaine's poems, along with those of Arthur Rimbaud (1854–91), are seen as French literature's first modern poems.

After WWII, the existentialist movement developed around the lively debates of Jean-Paul Sartre (1905–80), Simone de Beauvoir (1908–86) and Albert Camus (1913–60) over coffee and cigarettes in Paris' Left Bank cafes.

Contemporary authors include Françoise Sagan, Pascal Quignard, Anna Gavalda, Emmanuel Carrère and Yasmina Khadra (actually a man, a former colonel in the Algerian army, who adopted his wife's name as a nom de plume).

Marc Levy is France's best-selling writer, whose novels have been translated into 42 languages. *L'étrange voyage de Monsieur Daldry* (The Strange Journey of Mr Daldry; 2011) is his latest.

Cinema

Cinematographic pioneers the Lumière brothers shot the world's first-ever motion picture in March 1895 and French film flourished in the following decades. The post-WWII *nouvelle vague* (new wave) filmmakers, such as Claude Chabrol, Jean-Luc Godard and François Truffaut, pioneered the advent of modern cinema, using fractured narratives, documentary camerawork and highly personal subjects.

Big-name stars, slick production values and nostalgia were the dominant motifs in the 1980s, as filmmakers switched to costume dramas, comedies and 'heritage movies'. Claude Berri's depiction of prewar Provence in *Jean de Florette* (1986), Jean-Paul Rappeneau's *Cyrano de Bergerac* (1990) and *Bon Voyage* (2003), set in 1940s Paris – all starring France's best-known (and biggest-nosed) actor, Gérard Depardieu – found huge audiences in France and abroad.

Massive international box-office hit *Le Fabuleux Destin de Amélie Poulain* (*Amélie;* 2001) is a feel-good story about a Parisian do-gooder. *Bienvenue chez les Ch'tis* (2008) is another big film of recent years, which debunks grim stereotypes about the industrialised regions of the north of France with high jinks and hilarity.

'New French Extremity' is the tag given to the socially conscious, transgressive films of talented Paris-born, Africa-raised filmmaker Claire Denis. *Chocolat* (1988) and *Matériel Blanc* (*White Material;* 2009), scripted by Parisian novelist Marie NDiaye, both explore the legacy of French colonialism.

No French film has ever wooed the world at large quite like *The Artist* (2011), a silent B&W, romantic comedy set in 1920s Hollywood that scooped five Oscars heralding the renaissance of French film.

Music

French musical luminaries Charles Gounod (1818–93), César Franck (1822–90) and *Carmen* creator Georges Bizet (1838–75) among them were a dime a dozen in the 19th centu-

WORLD-CLASS WORLD MUSIC

No artist has cemented France's reputation in world music more than Paris-born, Franco-Congolese rapper, slam poet and three-time Victoire de la Musique-award winner, Abd al Malik. His albums, *Gibraltar* (2006), *Dante* (2008) and *Château Rouge* (2010) are classics.

ry. Claude Debussy (1862–1918) revolutionised classical music with *Prélude à l'Après-Midi d'un Faune* (Prelude to the Afternoon of a Faun); while Maurice Ravel (1875–1937) peppered his work, including *Boléro*, with sensuousness and tonal colour.

Jazz was the hot sound of 1920s Paris with the likes of Sidney Bechet, Kenny Clarke, Bud Powell and Dexter Gordon filling clubs in the capital.

The *chanson française*, a folkish tradition dating from medieval troubadours, was revived in the 1930s by Edith Piaf and Charles Trenet. In the 1950s, Paris' Left Bank cabarets nurtured *chansonniers* (cabaret singers) like Léo Ferré, Georges Brassens, Claude Nougaro, Jacques Brel and the much-loved crooner Serge Gainsbourg.

Frenc electronic music (think Daft Punk and Air) has a global following, while French rap never stops breaking new ground, pioneered in the 1990s by MC Solaar and continued by young French rappers such as Disiz La Peste, Monsieur R, the trio Malekal Morte, Marseille's home-grown IAM and five-piece band KDD from Toulouse. Cyprus-born Diam's (short for *'diamant'* meaning 'diamond'; www.diams-lesite.com), who arrived in Paris aged seven, is one of France's few female rappers, while Brittany's Manau trio engagingly fuses hip hop with traditional Celtic sounds.

French pop music has evolved massively since the 1960s *yéyé* (imitative rock) days of Johnny Hallyday. Particularly strong is world music, from Algerian raï and other North African music (artists include Natacha Atlas) to Senegalese *mbalax* (Youssou N'Dour) and West Indian zouk (Kassav, Zouk Machine). Musicians who combine many of these elements include Paris-born Manu Chao and Franco-Algerian Rachid Taja.

Architecture

Southern France is the place to find France's Gallo-Roman legacy, especially at the Pont du Gard (c 19 BC), and the amphitheatres in Nîmes and Arles (c 100 BC).

Several centuries later, architects adopted Gallo-Roman motifs in Romanesque masterpieces such as Poitier's Église Notre Dame la Grande, dating from the 11th to 16th centuries.

Impressive 12th-century Gothic structures include Avignon's pontifical palace, Chartres' cathedral and, of course, Notre Dame in Paris.

Art nouveau (1850–1910) combined iron, brick, glass and ceramics in new ways. See it for yourself at Paris' metro entrances and in the Musée d'Orsay.

Contemporary buildings to look out for include the once-reviled (now much-revered) Centre Pompidou and IM Pei's glass pyramid at the Louvre. In the provinces, notable buildings include Strasbourg's European Parliament, a 1920s art deco swimming pool-turned-art museum in Lille, the stunning new Centre Pompidou in Metz, and Louvre-Lens, in the former mining town of Lens.

Painting

An extraordinary flowering of artistic talent occurred in 19th- and 20th-century France. The Impressionists, who endeavoured to capture the ever-changing aspects of reflected light, included Edouard Manet, Claude Monet, Edgar Degas, Camille Pissarro, and Pierre-Auguste Renoir. They were followed by the likes of Paul Cézanne (who lived in Aix-en-Provence) and Paul Gauguin, as well as the fauvist Henri Matisse (a resident of Nice on the French Riviera) and Cubists including Spanish-born Pablo Picasso and Georges Braque.

Environment

The Land

Hexagon-shaped France is the largest country in Europe after Russia and Ukraine. The country's 3200km-long coastline ranges from chalk cliffs (Normandy) to fine sand (Atlantic coast) and pebbly beaches (Mediterranean coast).

Europe's highest peak, Mont Blanc (4810m), crowns the French Alps along France's eastern border, while the rugged Pyrenees define France's 450km-long border with Spain, peaking at 3404m. The country's major river systems include the Garonne, Rhône, Seine, and France's longest river, the Loire.

Wildlife

France has more mammals (around 110) than any other country in Europe. Couple this with 363 bird species, 30 types of amphibian, 36 varieties of reptile and 72 kinds of fish, and wildlife-watchers are in paradise. Several distinctive animals can still be found in the Alps and Pyrenees, including the marmot, *chamois* (mountain antelope), *bouquetin* (Alpine ibex) and *mouflon* (wild mountain sheep), introduced in the 1950s. The *loup* (wolf) disappeared from France in the 1930s, but was reintroduced to the Parc National du Mercantour in 1992. The *aigle royal* (golden eagle) is a rare but hugely rewarding sight in the French mountain parks.

National Parks

The proportion of protected land is low relative to the country's size: seven national parks (www.parcsnationaux-fr.com) fully protect around 0.8% of the country. Another 13% is protected by 45 regional parks (www.parcs-naturels-regionaux.tm.fr) and a further few percent by 320 smaller nature reserves (www.reserves-naturelles.org).

Environmental Issues

Summer forest fires are an annual hazard. Wetlands, essential for the survival of a great number of species, are shrinking. More than two million hectares – 3% of French territory – are considered important wetlands, but only 4% of this land is protected.

France generates around 80% of its electricity from nuclear power stations – the highest ratio in the world – with the rest coming from carbon-fuelled power stations and renewable resources (mainly wind farms and hydroelectric dams). Indeed, one of the last decisions Nicolas Sarkozy made as French president was to guarantee, in February 2012, the life of France's nuclear-power stations for another 40 years. Costing an extraordinary €6 billion, the country's most recent nuclear reactor, Flamanville 3, on Normandy's west coast near Cherbourg, is due for completion in 2016.

Europe's largest solar-powered electricity-generating farm sits 1000m-high on a south-facing slope near the tiny village of Curbans in Provence. Since its inauguration in 2011 the farm's 150-hectare array of photovoltaic cells – 145,000 panels in all – have removed 120,000 metric tonnes of carbon dioxide annually from the French energy bill.

Food & Drink

France means food. Every region has its distinctive cuisine, from the rich classic dishes of Burgundy, the Dordogne, Lyon and Normandy, to the sun-filled Mediterranean flavours of Provence, Languedoc and Corsica. Broadly speaking, the hot south tends to favour olive oil, garlic and tomatoes, while the cooler pastoral north favours cream and butter. Coastal areas overflow with mussels, oysters and saltwater fish.

A countrywide essential is *pain* (bread), typically eaten with every meal. Order in a restaurant and within minutes a basket should be on your table. Except in a handful of top-end gastronomic restaurants, butter (unsalted) is never an accompaniment. The long, thin *baguette* is the classic 'loaf', but there are countless others.

France *is* cheese land. There are nearly 500 varieties of *fromage* (cheese), ranging from world-known classics such as Brie, Camembert and Époisses de Bourgogne (France's smelliest cheese?) to local varieties available only in the regions where they're made. At meal times, cheese is always served after the main course and before dessert.

Charcuterie – hams, *saucissons* (salamis), sausages, black pudding and the fabulous *andouillette* (pig intestine sausage) – is the backbone of any self-respecting French picnic. Traditionally charcuterie is made only from pork, though other meats (beef, veal, chicken or goose) go into sausages, salamis, blood puddings and other cured and salted meats.

MONT ST-MICHEL

Environmental protection is rarely straightforward, as recent developments at the iconic, abbey-crowned mount of Mont St-Michel demonstrate. A €200 million project is designed to stop the mythical bay silting up by building a dam, ridding the mount of cars and motorised vehicles from its traffic-congested foot, and replacing the original tidal causeway trodden by pilgrims since 1879 with an ultralightweight bridge (by 2014). This would allow the 14m-high tidal waters for which this part of Normandy is famed to swirl without environmental consequence. Yet, just as the motorised vehicles go and the 2.5 million annual visitors embrace the final leg of one of France's top tourist pilgrimages on foot or by shuttle, Mont St-Michel risks losing its Unesco World Heritage status. The reason: the proposed construction of offshore turbine farms some 20km out to sea from the priceless mount.

The principal wine-producing regions are Alsace, Bordeaux, Burgundy, Champagne, Languedoc-Roussillon, the Loire region and the Rhône. Areas such as Burgundy comprise many well-known districts, including Chablis, Beaujolais and Mâcon, while Bordeaux encompasses Médoc, St-Émilion and Sauternes among many others. Northern France and Alsace produce excellent local beers; *bière à la pression* (draught beer) is served by the *demi* (about 33cL).

Coffee and mineral water are drunk by the gallon in France. In restaurants, save cents by asking for a jug of tap water *(une carafe d'eau)* rather than pricier bottled water. The most common coffee, simply called *un café* in French, is espresso – ordering anything other than this at the end of a meal is a real faux pas.

Where to Eat & Drink

Auberge Country inn serving traditional country fare, often attached to a rural B&B or small hotel.

Ferme auberge Working farm that cooks up meals built squarely from local farm products.

Bistro (also spelled *bistrot*) Anything from a pub or bar with snacks and light meals to a small, fully fledged restaurant.

Brasserie Like a cafe except it serves full meals, drinks and coffee from morning till 11pm or even later. Classic fare includes *choucroute* (sauerkraut) and *moules-frites* (mussels and fries).

Cafe Serves basic food as well as drinks, most commonly a chunk of baguette filled with Camembert or pâté and *cornichons* (mini gherkins), a *croque-monsieur* (grilled ham and toasted-cheese sandwich) or *croque-madame* (a toasted-cheese sandwich topped with a fried egg).

Creperie Casual address specialising in sweet crêpes and savoury galettes.

Restaurant Serves lunch and dinner five or six days; standard opening hours are noon-2.30 or 3pm, and 7-10 or 11pm.

Salon de thé Tearoom often serving light lunches (quiche, salads, pies and tarts) as well as cakes, pastries, tea and coffee.

SURVIVAL GUIDE

Directory A–Z
Accommodation

France has accommodation to suit every taste, budget and mood.

» Budget covers everything from barebones hostels to simple family-run places; midrange means a few extra creature comforts such as satellite TV, airconditioning and free wi-fi; while top-end places stretch from luxury five-star chains with the mod cons and swimming pools to boutique-chic chalets in the Alps.

» Accommodation costs vary wildly between regions: what will buy you a night in a romantic *chambre d'hôte* (B&B) in the countryside may only get you a dorm bed in major cities and ski resorts.

» Many tourist offices make room reservations, often for a fee of €5, but many only do so if you stop by in person. In the French Alps, ski-resort tourist offices operate a central reservation service.

PRICE RANGES

Our reviews refer to the cost of a double room with private bathroom, except in hostels or where otherwise specified. Quoted rates are for high season, which is July and August in southern France (Provence and the French Riviera, Languedoc-Roussilon, Corsica) and December to March in the French Alps. Prices exclude breakfast unless otherwise noted.

€€€ more than €180 (€200 in Paris)

€€ €80 to €180 (€110 to €200 in Paris)

€ below €80 (€110 in Paris)

THE MENU

In France a menu is not the card given to you in restaurants listing what's cooking (la carte in French). Rather, *un menu* is a preset, three-course meal at a fixed price – by far the best-value dining around and available in 99% of restaurants.

Lunch *menus* often include a glass of wine and/or coffee, and are a great way of dining at otherwise unaffordable gastronomic addresses.

All but top-end places often offer *une formule* too, a cheaper lunchtime option usually comprising the *plat du jour* (dish of the day) plus a starter or dessert.

B&BS

For charm, a heartfelt *bienvenue* (welcome) and home cooking, it's hard to beat a *chambre d'hôte* (B&B). Pick up lists at local tourist offices or online:

Bienvenue à la Ferme (www.bienvenue-a-la -ferme.com)

Chambres d'Hôtes France (www.chambres dhotesfrance.com)

Fleurs de Soleil (www.fleursdesoleil.fr) Selective collection of 550 stylish *maisons d'hôte,* mainly in rural France.

Gîtes de France (www.gites-de-france.com) France's primary umbrella organisation for B&Bs and *gîtes* (self-catering houses and apartments).

Samedi Midi Éditions (www.samedimidi. com) Choose your *chambre d'hôte* by location or theme (romance, golf, design, cooking courses).

CAMPING

Camping has never been more *en vogue.* **Gîtes de France** (www.gites-de-france.com) and **Bienvenue à la Ferme** (www.bienvenue-a -la-ferme.com) coordinate camping on farms.

» Most camping grounds open March or April to October.

» Euro-economisers should look for good-value but no-frills *campings municipaux* (municipal camping grounds).

» Camping in nondesignated spots (*camping sauvage*) is illegal in France. Easy-to-navigate websites with campsites searchable by location and facilities:

Camping en France (www.camping.fr)

Camping France (www.campingfrance.com)

Guide du Camping (www.guideducamping. com)

Cabanes de France (www.cabanes-de-france. com) Tree houses.

HOSTELS

Hostels range from funky to threadbare.

» A dorm bed in an *auberge de jeunesse* (youth hostel) costs about €25 in Paris, and anything from €10.50 to €28 in the provinces; sheets are always included and often breakfast too.

» To prevent outbreaks of bed bugs, sleeping bags are no longer permitted.

» All hostels are nonsmoking.

HOTELS

French hotels almost never include breakfast in their advertised nightly rates.

WHICH FLOOR?

In France, as elsewhere in Europe, 'ground floor' refers to the floor at street level; the 1st floor – what would be called the 2nd floor in the US – is the floor above that.

» Hotels in France are rated with one to five stars; ratings are based on objective criteria (eg size of entry hall), not service, decor or cleanliness.

» A double room has one double bed (or two singles pushed together); a room with twin beds is more expensive, as is a room with bathtub instead of shower.

Activities

From glaciers, rivers and canyons in the Alps to porcelain-smooth cycling trails in the Dordogne and Loire Valley – not to mention 3200km of coastline stretching from Italy to Spain and from the Basque country to the Straits of Dover – France's landscapes offer exhilarating outdoor escapes.

» The French countryside is criss-crossed by a staggering 120,000km of *sentiers balisés* (marked walking paths), which pass through every imaginable terrain in every region of the country. No permit is needed to hike.

» The best-known trails are the *sentiers de grande randonnée* (GR), long-distance paths marked by red-and-white-striped track indicators.

» For complete details on regional activities, courses, equipment rental, clubs, companies and organisations, contact local tourist offices.

Business Hours

» French business hours are regulated by a maze of government regulations, including the 35-hour working week.

» The midday break is uncommon in Paris but, in general, gets longer the further south you go.

» French law requires most businesses to close Sunday; exceptions include grocery stores, *boulangeries,* florists and businesses catering to the tourist trade.

» In many places shops close on Monday.

» Many service stations open 24 hours a day and stock basic groceries.

» Restaurants generally close one or two days of the week.

FRANCE DIRECTORY A–Z

STANDARD OPENING HOURS

We've only listed business hours where they differ from the following standards:

BUSINESS	OPENING HOURS
Bank	9am-noon & 2-5pm Mon-Fri or Tue-Sat
Bar	7pm-1am Mon-Sat
Cafe	7am or 8am-10pm or 11pm Mon-Sat
Nightclub	10pm-3am, 4am or 5am Thu-Sat
Post office	8.30am or 9am-5pm or 6pm Mon-Fri, 8am-noon Sat
Restaurant	lunch noon-2.30pm (or 3pm in Paris), dinner 7-11pm (until 10pm to midnight in Paris) six days a week
Shop	9am or 10am-7pm Mon-Sat (often with lunch break noon-1.30pm)
Supermarket	8.30am-7pm Mon-Sat, 8.30am-12.30pm Sun

» Most (but not all) national museums are closed on Tuesday, while most local museums are closed on Monday, though in summer some open daily. Some museums close for lunch.

Embassies & Consulates

All foreign embassies are in Paris.
» Many countries – including Canada, Japan, the UK, USA and most European countries – also have consulates in other major cities such as Bordeaux, Lyon, Nice, Marseille and Strasbourg.
» To find a consulate or an embassy not listed here, visit www.embassiesabroad.com or look up *'ambassade'* in the super user-friendly **Pages Jaunes** (Yellow Pages; www. pagesjaunes.fr).

Australia (☑01 40 59 33 00; www.france.emb assy.gov.au; 4 rue Jean Rey, 15e; Ⓜ Bir Hakeim)

Canada (☑01 44 43 29 00; www.amb-canada.fr; 35 av Montaigne, 8e; Ⓜ Franklin D Roosevelt)

Japan (☑01 48 88 62 00; www.amb-japon.fr; 7 av Hoche, 8e; Ⓜ Courcelles)

New Zealand (☑01 45 01 43 43; www.nz embassy.com; 7ter rue Léonard de Vinci, 16e; Ⓜ Victor Hugo)

UK (☑01 44 51 31 00; http://ukinfrance.fco.gov. uk; 35 rue du Faubourg St-Honoré, 8e; Ⓜ Concorde)

USA (☑01 43 12 22 22; http://france.usembassy. gov; 4 av Gabriel, 8e; Ⓜ Concorde)

Food

Price ranges refer to a two-course meal:
€€€ more than €50

€€ €15 to €50

€ below €15

Gay & Lesbian Travellers

Gay mayors (including Paris' very own Bertrand Delanoë), artists and film directors, camper-than-camp fashion designers...the rainbow flag flies high in France, one of Europe's most liberal countries when it comes to homosexuality.
» Major gay and lesbian organisations are based in Paris.
» Bordeaux, Lille, Lyon, Toulouse and many other towns have active communities.
» Attitudes towards homosexuality tend to be more conservative in the countryside and villages.
» Gay Pride marches are held in major French cities from mid-May to early July. Online try:

French Government Tourist Office (www. us.franceguide.com/special-interests/gay-friendly) Information about 'the gay-friendly destination par excellence'.

France Queer Resources Directory (www. france.qrd.org) Gay and lesbian directory.

Language Courses

» The website www.studyabroadlinks. com can help you find specific courses and summer programs, while www.edufrance.fr/ en has information about university study.
» All manner of French-language courses are available in Paris and provincial towns and cities; many arrange accommodation.
» Prices and courses vary greatly and the content can often be tailored to your specific needs (for a fee).
Some schools you might consider:

Centre de Linguistique Appliquée de Besançon (☑03 81 66 52 00; http://cla.univ

-fcomte.fr; 6 rue Gabriel Plançon, Besançon) One of France's largest language schools in a beautiful city.

Centre Méditerranéen d'Études Françaises (www.monte-carlo.mc/centremed; chemin des Oliviers, Cap d'Ail) Mythical French Riviera school around since 1952.

Eurocentres (www.eurocentres.com) Trio of small, affiliated schools in Amboise, La Rochelle and Paris.

Aix-Marseille Université (www.univ-provence.fr; 29 av Robert Schumann, Aix-en-Provence) A hot choice in Provence; semester-long courses as well as summer classes.

Legal Matters

French police have wide powers of stop-and-search and can demand proof of identity at any time. Foreigners must be able to prove their legal status in France (eg passport, visa, residency permit).

Money

Credit and debit cards are accepted almost everywhere in France.

» Some places (eg 24hr petrol stations and some *autoroute* toll machines) only take credit cards with chips and PINs.

» In Paris and major cities, *bureaux de change* (exchange bureaux) are fast, easy, open longer hours and offer competitive exchange rates.

For lost cards, call:

Amex (☑01 47 77 72 00)

Diners Club (☑08 10 31 41 59)

MasterCard (☑08 00 90 13 87)

Visa (Carte Bleue; ☑08 00 90 11 79)

Public Holidays

New Year's Day (Jour de l'An) 1 January

Easter Sunday & Monday (Pâques & lundi de Pâques) March or April

May Day (Fête du Travail) 1 May – traditional parades.

Victoire 1945 8 May – commemorates the Allied victory in Europe that ended WWII.

Ascension Thursday (Ascension) May – celebrated on the 40th day after Easter.

Pentecost/Whit Sunday & Whit Monday (Pentecôte & lundi de Pentecôte) Mid-May to mid-June – celebrated on the seventh Sunday after Easter.

Bastille Day/National Day (Fête Nationale) 14 July – *the* national holiday.

Assumption Day (Assomption) 15 August

All Saints' Day (Toussaint) 1 November

Remembrance Day (L'onze novembre) 11 November – marks the WWI armistice.

Christmas (Noël) 25 December

Telephone
MOBILE PHONES

French mobile phones numbers begin with 06 or 07.

» France uses GSM 900/1800, compatible with the rest of Europe and Australia but not with the North American GSM 1900 or the totally different system in Japan (though some North Americans have tri-band phones that work here).

» It's usually cheaper to buy your own French SIM card (€20 to €30) sold at ubiquitous outlets run by France's three mobile phone companies, **Bouygues** (www.bouyguestelecom.fr), France Telecom's **Orange** (www.orange.com) and **SFR** (www.sfr.com).

» Recharge cards are sold at *tabacs* (tobacconists) and newsagents; domestic prepaid calls cost about €0.50 per minute.

PHONE CODES

Calling France from abroad Dial your country's international access code, ☑33 (France's country code), and the 10-digit local number *without* the initial 0.

DRUGS & ALCOHOL

» French law does not distinguish between 'hard' and 'soft' drugs.

» The penalty for any personal use of *stupéfiants* (including cannabis, amphetamines, ecstasy and heroin) can be a one-year jail sentence and a €3750 fine but, depending on the circumstances, it might be anything from a stern word to a compulsory rehab program.

» Importing, possessing, selling or buying drugs can get you up to 10 years' prison and a fine of up to €500,000.

» *Ivresse* (drunkeness) in public is punishable by a monetary fine.

Calling internationally from France

Dial ☎00 (the international access code), the country code, area code (without the initial zero if there is one) and local number.

Directory inquiries For France Telecom's *service des renseignements* (directory inquiries), dial ☎11 87 12 or use the online service for free www.118712.fr.

International directory inquiries For numbers outside France, dial ☎11 87 00.

Emergency number ☎112, can be dialled from public phones without a phonecard.

Toilets

» Public toilets, signposted WC or *toilettes,* are not always plentiful in France.
» Love them (sci-fi geek) or loathe them (claustrophobe), France has its fair share of 24hr self-cleaning toilets, €0.50 in Paris and free elsewhere.
» Some older cafes and restaurants still have the hole-in-the-floor squat toilets.
» The French are blasé about unisex toilets; save your blushes when tiptoeing past the urinals to reach the loo.

Visas

For up-to-date details on visa requirements, visit the **French Foreign Affairs Ministry** (www.diplomatie.gouv.fr).

Visa requirements:
» EU nationals and citizens of Iceland, Norway and Switzerland need only a passport or national identity card to enter France and stay in the country, even for stays of over 90 days. Citizens of new EU member states may be subject to various limitations on living and working in France.
» Citizens of Australia, the USA, Canada Israel, Hong Kong, Japan, Malaysia, New Zealand, Singapore, South Korea and many Latin American countries do not need visas to visit France as tourists for up to 90 days. For longer stays of over 90 days, contact your nearest French embassy or consulate.
» Other people wishing to come to France as tourists have to apply for a Schengen Visa.
» Tourist visas cannot be changed into student visas after arrival. However, short-term visas are available for students sitting university-entrance exams in France.

Getting There & Away

Entering the Country

Entering France from other parts of the continental EU should be a breeze – no border checkpoints or customs thanks to the Schengen Agreement signed by all of France's neighbours except the UK, the Channel Islands and Andorra. For these three entities, old-fashioned document and customs checks remain the norm, at least when exiting France (when entering France in the case of Andorra).

INTERNATIONAL AIRPORTS

Paris Charles de Gaulle (CDG; www.aeroportsdeparis.fr)

Paris Orly (ORY; www.aeroportsdeparis.fr)

Aéroport de Bordeaux (www.bordeaux.aeroport.fr)

Aéroport de Lille (www.lille.aeroport.fr)

Aéroport International Strasbourg (www.strasbourg.aeroport.fr)

Aéroport Lyon-Saint Exupéry (www.lyonaeroports.com)

Aéroport Marseille-Provence (www.marseille.aeroport.fr)

Aéroport Nantes Atlantique (www.nantes.aeroport.fr)

Aéroport Nice-Côte d'Azur (http://societe.nice.aeroport.fr)

Aéroport Toulouse-Blagnac (www.toulouse.aeroport.fr)

EuroAirport (Basel-Mulhouse-Freiburg; www.euroairport.com)

Land

BUS

Eurolines (☎in France 08 92 89 90 91; www.euro lines.eu), a grouping of 32 long-haul coach operators (including the UK's National Express), links France with cities all across Europe and in Morocco and Russia. Discounts are available to people under 26 and over 60. Make advance reservations, especially in July and August.

The standard Paris–London fare is between €45 and €59, but the trip – including a Channel crossing by ferry or the Chunnel (Channel tunnel) – can cost as little as €13 if you book 45 days ahead.

CAR & MOTORCYCLE

A right-hand-drive vehicle brought to France from the UK or Ireland must have deflectors affixed to the headlights to avoid dazzling oncoming traffic.

Departing from the UK, **Eurotunnel Le Shuttle** (www.eurotunnel.com) trains whisk bicycles, motorcycles, cars and coaches in 35 minutes from Folkestone through the Channel Tunnel to Coquelles, 5km southwest of Calais. Shuttles run 24 hours a day, with up to three departures an hour during peak periods. The earlier you book, the less you pay. Fares for a car, including up to nine passengers, start at £30.

TRAIN
Rail services – including a dwindling number of overnight services to/from Spain, Italy and Germany – link France with virtually every country in Europe. Book tickets and get train information from **Rail Europe** (www.raileurope.com). In France ticketing is handled by **SNCF** (☑from abroad +33 8 92 35 35 35, in France 36 35; www.sncf.com); internet bookings are possible but they won't post tickets outside France.

High-speed train travel between France and the UK, Belgium, the Netherlands, Germany and Austria is covered by **Railteam** (www.railteam.co.uk) and **TGV-Europe** (www.tgv-europe.com).

Certain rail services between France and its continental neighbours are marketed under a number of unique brand names:

Elipsos (www.elipsos.com) Luxurious 'train-hotel' services to Spain.

TGV Lyria (www.tgv-lyria.fr) To Switzerland.

Thalys (www.thalys.com) Thalys trains pull into Paris' Gare du Nord from Brussels, Amsterdam and Cologne.

Eurostar (☑France 08 92 35 35 39, UK 08432 186 186; www.eurostar.com) Runs from London St Pancras station to Paris Gare du Nord in 2¼ hours, with onward connections to destinations all over France. Ski trains connecting England with the French Alps run weekends mid-December to mid-April.

Sample Train Fares

ROUTE	FULL FARE (€)	DURATION (HR)
Amsterdam–Paris	89	3¼
Madrid–Blois	153	12½
Berlin–Paris	189	8
Brussels–Paris	69	1½
Dijon–Milan	80	7
Paris–Venice	100	11¾
Geneva–Marseille	50	3½
Vienna-Strasbourg	153	9¾

SEA
Regular ferries travel to France from Italy, the UK, Channel Islands and Ireland. Several ferry companies ply the waters between Corsica and Italy.

INTERNATIONAL FERRY ROUTES

COMPANY	ROUTES	WEBSITE
Brittany Ferries	England–Normandy, England–Brittany, Ireland-Brittany	www.brittany-ferries.co.uk; www.brittanyferries.ie
Celtic Link Ferries	Ireland–Normandy	www.celticlinkferries.com
Condor Ferries	England–Normandy, England–Brittany, Channel Islands–Brittany	www.condorferries.com
CTN	Tunisia–France	www.ctn.com.tn
Irish Ferries	Ireland–Normandy, Ireland–Brittany	www.irishferries.ie; www.shamrock-irlande.com, in French
LD Lines	England–Channel Ports, England–Normandy	www.ldlines.co.uk
Manche Îles Express	Channel Islands–Normandy	www.manche-iles-express.com
Norfolk Line (DFDS Seaways)	England–Channel Ports	www.norfolkline.com
P&O Ferries	England–Channel Ports	www.poferries.com
SNCM	Algeria–France, Sardinia–France, Tunisia–France	www.sncm.fr
Transmanche Ferries	England–Normandy	www.transmancheferries.com

Getting Around

Air

France's vaunted high-speed train network has made rail travel between some cities (eg from Paris to Lyon and Marseille) faster and easier than flying.

Air France (www.airfrance.com) and its subsidiaries **Brit Air** (www.britair.fr) and **Régional** (☎36 54; www.regional.com) control the lion's share of France's long-protected domestic airline industry. Good deals can be had if you buy your ticket well in advance (at least 42 days ahead for the very best deals), stay over a Saturday night and don't mind tickets that can't be changed or reimbursed.

Budget carriers offering flights within France include **easyJet** (www.easyjet.com), **Airlinair** (www.airlinair.com), **Twin Jet** (www.twinjet.net) and **Air Corsica** (www.aircorsica.com).

Bus

You're nearly always better off travelling by train in France if possible, as the SNCF domestic railway system is heavily subsidised by the government and is much more reliable than local bus companies. Nevertheless, buses are widely used for short-distance travel within *départements*, especially in rural areas with relatively few train lines (eg Brittany and Normandy).

Bicycle

France is a great place to cycle. Not only is much of the countryside drop-dead gorgeous, but the country has an extensive network of secondary and tertiary roads with relatively light traffic, and a growing number of urban and rural *pistes cyclables* (bike paths and lanes); see **Voie Vertes** (www.voiesvertes.com). French train company SNCF does its best to make travelling with a bicycle easy; see www.velo.sncf.com for full details.

Most French cities and towns have at least one bike shop that rents out mountain bikes (VTT; around €15 a day), road bikes (VTCs) and cheaper city bikes. You have to leave ID and/or a deposit (often a credit-card slip) that you forfeit if the bike is damaged or stolen. A growing number of cities have automatic bike rental systems.

Car & Motorcycle

A car gives you exceptional freedom and allows you to visit more-remote parts of France.

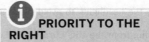

ⓘ PRIORITY TO THE RIGHT

Under the *priorité à droite* (priority to the right) rule, any car entering an intersection from a road on your right has the right of way, unless the intersection is marked 'vous n'avez pas la priorité' (you do not have right of way) or 'cédez le passage' (give way).

But it can be expensive and, in cities, parking and traffic are frequently a major headache. Motorcyclists will find France great for touring, with winding roads of good quality and lots of stunning scenery.

BRINGING YOUR OWN VEHICLE

All foreign motor vehicles entering France must display a sticker or licence plate identifying its country of registration. If you're bringing a right-hand-drive vehicle remember to fix deflectors on your headlights to avoid dazzling oncoming traffic.

DRIVING LICENCE & DOCUMENTS

All drivers must carry a national ID card or passport; a valid driving licence (*permis de conduire;* most foreign licences can be used in France for up to a year); car-ownership papers, known as a *carte grise* (grey card); and proof of third-party (liability) insurance.

FUEL & TOLLS

Essence (petrol), also known as *carburant* (fuel), costs around €1.45/L for 95 unleaded (Sans Plomb 95 or SP95, usually available from a green pump), and €1.30 for diesel (*diesel, gazole* or *gasoil*, usually available from a yellow pump). Filling up *(faire le plein)* is most expensive along *autoroutes* and cheapest at supermarkets on town outskirts.

Many French motorways (*autoroutes*) are fitted with toll *(péage)* stations that charge a fee based on the distance you've travelled; factor in these costs when driving.

HIRE

To hire a car you'll usually need to be over 21 and in possession of a valid driving licence and a credit card. Auto transmissions are *very* rare in France; you'll need to order one well in advance.

There are major car rental companies with offices across France and Europe.

INSURANCE

Unlimited third-party liability insurance is mandatory in France. Third-party liability insurance is provided by car-rental companies, but collision-damage waivers (CDW) vary between companies. When comparing rates check the *franchise* (excess). Your credit card may cover CDW if you use it to pay for the car rental.

ROAD RULES

Cars drive on the right in France. Speed limits on French roads are as follows:

» 50km/h in built-up areas
» 90km/h (80km/h if it's raining) on N and D highways
» 110km/h (100km/h if it's raining) on dual carriageways
» 130km/h (110km/h if it's raining) on *autoroutes*

Child-seat rules:

» Children under 10 are not permitted to ride in the front seat (unless the back is already occupied by other children under 10).
» A child under 13kg must travel in a backward-facing child seat (permitted in the front seat only for babies under 9kg and if the airbag is deactivated).
» Up to age 10 and/or a minimum height of 140cm, children must use a size-appropriate type of front-facing child seat or booster.

Other key rules of the road:

» Blood-alcohol limit is 0.05% (0.5g per litre of blood) – the equivalent of two glasses of wine for a 75kg adult. Police often conduct random breathalyser tests and penalties can be severe, including imprisonment.
» Mobile phones may be used only if they are equipped with a hands-free kit or speakerphone.
» All passengers must wear seatbelts.
» All vehicles must carry a reflective safety jacket (stored inside the car, not the trunk/boot), a reflective triangle, and a portable, single-use breathalyser kit. The fine for not carrying any of these items is €90.
» Riders of any type of two-wheeled vehicle with a motor (except motor-assisted bicycles) must wear a helmet.
» North American drivers, remember: turning right on a red light is illegal.

Train

France's superb rail network is operated by the state-owned **SNCF** (www.sncf.com); many rural towns not on the SNCF train network are served by SNCF buses.

The flagship trains on French railways are the superfast TGVs, which reach speeds in excess of 200mph and can whisk you from Paris to the Côte d'Azur in as little as three hours.

Many non-high-speed lines are also served by TGV trains; otherwise you'll find yourself aboard a non-TGV train, referred to as a *corail* or TER *(train express régional)*.

TGV lines and key stations:

TGV Nord, Thalys & Eurostar Link Paris Gare du Nord with Arras, Lille, Calais, Brussels (Bruxelles-Midi), Amsterdam, Cologne and, via the Channel Tunnel, Ashford, Ebbsfleet and London St Pancras.

TGV Est Européen Connects Paris Gare de l'Est with Reims, Nancy, Metz, Strasbourg, Zurich and Germany, including Frankfurt and Stuttgart. At present, the super-high-speed track stretches only as far east as Lorraine but it's supposed to reach Strasbourg in 2016.

TGV Sud-Est & TGV Midi-Méditerranée Link Paris Gare de Lyon with the southeast, including Dijon, Lyon, Geneva, the Alps, Avignon, Marseille, Nice and Montpellier.

TGV Atlantique Sud-Ouest & TGV Atlantique Ouest Link Paris Gare Montparnasse with western and southwestern France, including Brittany (Rennes, Brest, Quimper), Tours, Nantes, Poitiers, La Rochelle, Bordeaux, Biarritz and Toulouse.

TGV Rhin-Rhône France's most recent high-speed rail route – the first section of which opened in December 2011 – bypasses Paris altogether in its bid to better link the provinces. Six services a day speed between Strasbourg and Lyon, with most continuing south to Marseille or Montpellier on the Mediterranean.

VALIDATE YOURSELF

Before boarding any train, you must validate *(composter)* your ticket by time-stamping it in a *composter*, one of those yellow posts located on the way to the platform. If you forget (or don't have a ticket for some other reason), find a conductor on the train before they find you – or risk an unwelcome fine.

FRANCE GETTING AROUND

SNCF TRAIN FARES & DISCOUNTS

The Basics

» Full-fare return travel costs twice as much as a one-way fare.

» 1st-class travel, where available, costs 20% to 30% extra.

» Ticket prices for some trains, including most TGVs, are pricier during peak periods.

» The further in advance you reserve, the lower the fares.

» Children under four travel for free (€8.50 to any destination if they need a seat).

» Children aged four to 11 travel for half price.

Discount Tickets

Prem's The SNCF's most heavily discounted, use-or-lose tickets, sold online, by phone and at ticket windows/machines a maximum of 90 days and minimum 14 days before you travel.

Bons Plans A grab-bag of cheap options for different routes/dates, advertised online under the tab 'Dernière Minute' (Last Minute).

iDTGV Cheap tickets on advance-purchase TGV travel between about 30 cities; only sold at www.idtgv.com.

Discount Cards

Reductions of 25% to 60% are available with several discount cards (valid for one year):

Carte 12-25 (www.12-25-sncf.com; €50) For travellers aged 12 to 25 years.

Carte Enfant Plus (www.enfantplus-sncf.com; €71) For one to four adults travelling with a child aged four to 11 years.

Carte Escapades (www.escapades-sncf.com; €76) Discounts on return journeys of at least 200km that include a Saturday night away or only involve travel on a Saturday or Sunday; for 26- to 59-year-olds.

Carte Sénior (www.senior-sncf.com; €57) Travellers over 60 years.

TICKETS

Buying online at the various SNCF websites can reward with you some great reductions on fares, but be warned – these are generally intended for domestic travellers, and if you're buying abroad be aware of the pitfalls. Many tickets can't be posted outside France, and if you buy with a non-French credit card, you might not be able to use it in the automated ticket collection machines at many French stations. Buying from a ticket office may not secure you the cheapest fare, but at least you'll be sure of being able to pick up your ticket.

RAIL PASSES

The **InterRail One Country Pass** (www.interrailnet.com; 3/4/6/8 days €205/226/288/319, 12–25yr €139/149/190/211), valid in France, entitles residents of Europe who do not live in France to unlimited travel on SNCF trains for three to eight days over a month.

Greece Ελλάδα

Includes »

Athens 325
The Peloponnese 343
Thessaloniki 352
Saronic Gulf Islands 357
Mykonos 359
Paros 363
Naxos 364
Ios 367
Santorini (Thira) 368
Crete 371
Dodecanese 379
Rhodes 380
Sporades 391
Ionian Islands 393
Corfu 393

Why Go?

Don't let headline-grabbing financial woes put you off going to Greece. The alluring combination of history and hedonism, which has made Greece one of the most popular destinations on the planet, continues to beckon, and now is as good a time as ever to turn up for some fun in the sun. Within easy reach of magnificent archaeological sites are breathtaking beaches and relaxed tavernas serving everything from ouzo to octopus. Wanderers can island-hop to their heart's content, while party types can enjoy pulsating nightlife in Greece's vibrant modern cities and on islands such as Mykonos, Ios and Santorini. Add welcoming locals with an enticing culture to the mix and it's easy to see why most visitors head home vowing to come back. Travellers to Greece inevitably end up with a favourite site they long to return to – get out there and find yours.

Best Places to Eat

» Marco Polo Café (p382)
» Alaloum (p346)
» Café Avyssinia (p335)
» Spondi (p337)
» Taverna Lava (p370)

Best Places to Stay

» 1700 (p357)
» Amfitriti Pension (p345)
» Francesco's (p368)
» Pension Sofi (p366)
» Hotel Afendoulis (p384)

When to Go

Athens

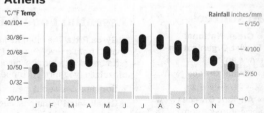

May & Jun Greece opens the shutters in time for Orthodox Easter; the best months to visit.

Jul & Aug Be prepared to battle summer crowds, high prices and soaring temperatures.

Sep & Oct The season winds down; a relaxing and pleasant time to head to Greece.

AT A GLANCE

» **Currency** euro (€)

» **Language** Greek

» **Money** ATMs all over; banks open Mon-Fri

» **Visas** Schengen rules apply

Fast Facts

» **Area** 131,944 sq km

» **Capital** Athens

» **Country code** ☑30

» **Emergency** ☑112

Exchange Rates

Australia	A$1	€0.82
Canada	C$1	€0.77
Japan	¥100	€0.83
New Zealand	NZ$1	€0.65
UK	UK£1	€1.18
USA	US$1	€0.78

Set Your Budget

» **Budget hotel room** €50

» **Two-course meal** €20

» **Museum entrance** €5

» **Beer** €2.50

» **Athens metro ticket** €1.40

Resources

» **Greek National Tourist Organisation** (www.gnto.gr)

» **Virtual Greece** (www.greecevirtual.gr)

» **Ancient Greece** (www.ancientgreece.com)

» **Greek Ferries** (www.openseas.gr)

Connections

For those visiting Greece as part of a trip around Europe, there are various exciting options for reaching onward destinations overland or by sea.

There are regular ferry connections between Greece and the Italian ports of Ancona, Bari, Brindisi and Venice. Similarly, there are ferries operating between the Greek islands of Rhodes, Kos, Samos, Chios and Lesvos and the Aegean coast of Turkey. Island-hopping doesn't have to take you back to Athens.

Overland, it's possible to reach Albania, Bulgaria, the Former Yugoslav Republic of Macedonia (FYROM) and Turkey from Greece. If you've got your own wheels, you can drive through border crossings with these four countries. There are train and bus connections with Greece's neighbours, but check ahead, as these have been affected by the financial crisis. At the time of writing, no international train services from Greece were running.

ITINERARIES

One Week

Explore Athens' museums and ancient sites on day one before spending a couple of days in the Peloponnese visiting Nafplio, Mycenae and Olympia; ferry to the Cyclades and enjoy Mykonos and spectacular Santorini.

One Month

Give yourself some more time in Athens and the Peloponnese, then visit the Ionian Islands for a few days. Explore the villages of Zagorohoria before travelling back to Athens via Meteora and Delphi. Take a ferry from Piraeus south to Mykonos, then island-hop via Santorini to Crete. After exploring Crete, take the ferry east to Rhodes, then north to Symi, Kos and Samos. Carry on north to Chios, then head to Lesvos. Take the ferry back to Piraeus when you're out of time or money.

Essential Food & Drink

» **Gyros Pitta** The ultimate in cheap eats. Pork or chicken shaved from a revolving stack of sizzling meat is wrapped in pitta bread with tomato, onion, fried potatoes and lashings of tzatziki (yoghurt, cucumber and garlic). Costs €2 to €3.

» **Souvlaki** Skewered meat, usually pork.

» **Greek salad** Tomatoes, cucumber, onion, feta and olives.

» **Grilled octopus** All the better with a glass of ouzo.

» **Ouzo** Sipped slowly, this legendary aniseed-flavoured tipple turns a cloudy white when ice and water are added.

» **Raki** Cretan fire water produced from grape skins.

» **Greek coffee** A legacy of Ottoman rule, Greek coffee should be tried at least once.

ATHENS   AΘHNA

POP 3.8 MILLION

Ancient and modern, with equal measures of grunge and grace, bustling Athens is a heady mix of history and edginess. Iconic monuments mingle with first-rate muse- ums, lively cafes and alfresco dining, and it's downright fun. With Greece's financial difficulties Athens has revealed its more restive aspect, but take the time to look beneath the surface and you'll discover a complex metropolis full of vibrant subcultures.

Greece Highlights

1 Island-hop (p410) at your own pace under the Aegean sun

2 In **Athens** (p325), trace the ancient to the modern from the Acropolis to booming nightclubs

3 Lose yourself within the medieval walls of **Rhodes Old Town** (p381)

4 Search for the oracle amidst the dazzling ruins of **Delphi** (p350)

5 Stare dumbfounded at the dramatic volcanic caldera of incomparable **Santorini** (p368)

6 Sip **ouzo** (p404) while munching on grilled octopus

7 Climb russet rock pinnacles to the exquisite monasteries of **Meteora** (p351)

8 Hike through Crete's stupendous **Samaria Gorge** (p376)

9 Let your cares float away from the pristine west-coast beaches of **Lefkada** (p396)

10 Use quaint **Nafplio** (p345) as a base for exploring the back roads and ruins of the Peloponnese

Central Athens

GREECE ATHENS

To Larisis Train Station (300m)

To Gagarin 205 Club (1.9km); Liossion Terminal B (2.3km); Kiffisos Terminal A (2.6km)

OMONIA

Metaxourghio

Agiou Konstantinou

Omonia

Plateia Omonias

Plateia Karaiskaki

Ahilleos

Leof Athinon

Plateia Eleotrivion

Plateia Ramnes

Naousis

Kastorias

Leof Konstantinoupoleos

Keramikos

GAZI

Pireos

Pireos (Tsaldari Panagi)

Plateia Kotzia

1 Sapfous

Plateia Eleftherias (Koumoundourou)

PSYRRI

37

11

31

47

42

40

35

15

Thisio Park

THISIO

Plateia Afea

Plateia Thisiou

Plateia Agion Asomaton

Thisio

MONASTIRAKI

Plateia Monastirakiou

Plateia Agia Irini

Ancient Agora

Roman Agora

ANAFIOTIKA

Acropolis

Hill of the Nymphs

24

Areopagus Hill

See Plaka & Monastiraki Map (p334)

14

To Venue (40m); Benaki Museum Pireos Annexe (200m)

Petralona

52

4

Filopappou Hill

Dionysiou Areopagitou

Rovertou Galli

To Marble House Pension (90m)

Syngrou-Fix

23

32

27

48

44

21

57

58

54

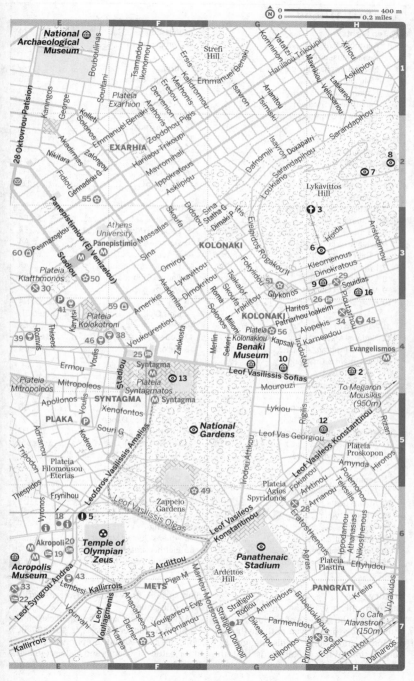

Map labels and features (as printed):

0 — 400 m
0 — 0.2 miles

National Archaeological Museum

Strefi Hill

Plateia Exarhion

EXARHIA

Athens University

Panepistimio (El Venizelou)

KOLONAKI

Lykavittos Hill

55

60

Stadiou

Plateia Klafthmonos

30

41

Plateia Kolokotroni

59

50

51

Glykonos

Kleomenous

Dinokratous

29

9

16

26

Haritos

Patriarhou Ioakeim

34

45

KOLONAKI

Plateia Kolonakiou

56

Alopekis

Karneadou

Benaki Museum

10

39

46

38

25

Syntagma

Plateia Syntagmatos

13

SYNTAGMA

Syntagma

Leof Vasilissis Sofias

Mourouzi

2

Evangelismos

To Megaron Mousikis (950m)

PLAKA

Plateia Mitropoleos

Xenofontos

Lykiou

12

National Gardens

Leof Vas Georgiou

Leof Vasileos Konstantinou

Plateia Proskopon

Plateia Filomousou Eterias

Frynihou

18

5

Zappeio Gardens

49

Plateia Agios Spyridonos

28

Akropoli

20

19

Temple of Olympian Zeus

Leof Vasileos Konstantinou

Ardittou

Panathenaic Stadium

Plateia Plastira

PANGRATI

Acropolis Museum

33

43

Kallirois

22

METS

Ardettos Hill

To Cafe Alavastron (150m)

53

17

36

Kallirrois

3

6

7

8

+ + +

Central Athens

◎ Top Sights

Acropolis Museum	E6
Benaki Museum	G4
National Archaeological Museum	E1
National Gardens	F5
Panathenaic Stadium	G6
Temple of Olympian Zeus	E6

◎ Sights

1	Andreas Melas & Helena Papadopoulos Gallery	C3
2	Byzantine & Christian Museum	H4
3	Chapel of Agios Giorgios	H3
4	Filopappou Hill	C7
5	Hadrian's Arch	E6
6	Lykavittos Funicular Railway	H3
7	Lykavittos Hill	H2
8	Lykavittos Theatre	H2
9	Medusa Art Gallery	H3
10	Museum of Cycladic Art	G4
11	Museum of Islamic Art	C3
12	National Museum of Contemporary Art	H5
13	Parliament & Changing of the Guard	F4
14	Stoa of Eumenes	D6
15	Technopolis	A4
16	Xippas Gallery	H3

✪ Activities, Courses & Tours

17	Athens Centre	G7
18	Athens Segway Tours	E6

▢ Sleeping

19	Athens Backpackers	E6
20	Athens Gate	E6
21	Athens Style	D4
22	Hera Hotel	E7
23	Hotel Cecil	D3
24	Hotel Erechthion	C5
25	Hotel Grande Bretagne	F4

26	Periscope	H4
27	Tempi Hotel	D4

✪ Eating

28	Cucina Povera	G6
29	Filippou	H3
30	Kalnterimi	E3
31	Kanella	A3
32	Mama Roux	D4
33	Mani Mani	E7
34	Oikeio	H4
35	Sardelles	A4
36	Spondi	H7
37	Varoulko	B3

◎ Drinking

38	42 Bar	F4
39	Baba Au Rum	E4
40	Gazarte	A4
41	Gin Joint	E4
42	Hoxton	A3
43	Lamda Club	E6
44	Magaze	D4
45	Mai Tai	H4
	Noiz Club	(see 31)
46	Seven Jokers	E4
47	Sodade	A3
48	Tailor Made	D4

✪ Entertainment

49	Aigli Cinema	F6
50	Astor	E3
51	Dexameni	G3
52	Dora Stratou Dance Theatre	B7
	Greek National Opera	(see 55)
53	Half Note Jazz Club	F7
54	National Theatre	D2
55	Olympia Theatre	E2
56	Rock'n'Roll	G4
57	Stoa Athanaton	D3

◎ Shopping

58	Athens Central Market	D3
59	Eleftheroudakis	F4
60	To Pantopoleion	E3

History

The early history of the city of Athens, named after the goddess of wisdom Athena, is inextricably interwoven with mythology, making it impossible to disentangle fact from fiction. What is known is that the hilltop site of the Acropolis, with two abundant springs, drew some of Greece's earliest Neolithic settlers.

Athens' golden age, the pinnacle of the classical era under Pericles (r 461–429 BC), came after the Persian Empire was repulsed at the battles of Salamis and Plataea (480–479 BC). The city has passed through many hands and cast off myriad invaders, from Sparta to Philip II of Macedon, the Roman and Byzantine Empires, and, most recently, the Ottoman Empire. In 1834 Athens superseded Nafplio as the capital of independent Greece.

⊙ Sights

TOP
CHOICE **Acropolis** HISTORIC SITE
(Map p334; ☑210 321 0219; http://odysseus.culture.gr; adult/child €12/6; ☉8am-8pm Mon-Fri, to 3pm Sat & Sun; ⓂAkropoli) Arguably the most important ancient monument in the Western world, the Acropolis attracts multitudes of visitors, so head there in the early morning or late afternoon.

The site was inhabited in Neolithic times and the first temples were built during the Mycenaean era in homage to the goddess Athena. People lived on the Acropolis until the late 6th century BC, but in 510 BC the Delphic oracle declared that the Acropolis should be the province of the gods. When all of the buildings were reduced to ashes by the Persians on the eve of the Battle of Salamis (480 BC), Pericles set about rebuilding a city purely of temples.

Enter near the **Beule Gate**, a Roman arch added in the 3rd century AD. Beyond this lies the **Propylaea**, the enormous columned gate that was the city's entrance in ancient times. Damaged in the 17th century when lightning set off a Turkish gunpowder cache, it's since been restored. South of the Propylaea, the small, beautiful **Temple of Athena Nike** has been recently restored.

It's the **Parthenon**, however, that epitomises the glory of ancient Greece. Completed in 438 BC, it's unsurpassed in grace and harmony. To achieve the appearance of perfect form, columns become narrower towards the top and the bases curve upward slightly towards the ends – effects that make them look straight. The remains of its metopes, pediments and frieze can be seen at the Acropolis Museum.

The Parthenon was built to house the great statue of Athena commissioned by Pericles, and to serve as the new treasury. In AD 426 the gold-plated 12m-high statue was taken to Constantinople, where it disappeared.

To the north, lies the **Erechtheion** and its much-photographed caryatids, the six maidens who support its southern portico. These are plaster casts – the originals are in the Acropolis Museum (and one is in London).

ATHENS IN TWO DAYS

Walk the deserted morning streets of the charming Plaka district to reach the **Acropolis** and **Ancient Agora**, beating the crowds. Dig in to *mezedhes* at **Tzitzikas & Mermingas** before spending the afternoon at the **Acropolis Museum** and the **National Archaeological Museum**. Enjoy Parthenon views over dinner at **Café Avyssinia** or sup on gyros at **Thanasis**.

On day two, watch the changing of the guard at **Plateia Syntagmatos** (Syntagma Sq) before crossing the **National Gardens** to the **Panathenaic Stadium** and the **Temple of Olympian Zeus**. Visit the wonderful **Benaki Museum**, **Byzantine & Christian Museum** or the **Museum of Cycladic Art**, then rest up for a night out in **Gazi**.

On the southern slope of the Acropolis, the importance of theatre in the everyday lives of ancient Athenians is made manifest in the enormous **Theatre of Dionysos** (☑210 322 4625; Dionysiou Areopagitou; admission €2, free with Acropolis Pass; ☉8am-8pm Mon-Fri, 8am-3pm Sat & Sun; underground rail Akropoli). Built between 340 and 330 BC on the site of an earlier theatre dating to the 6th century BC, it held 17,000 people. The **Stoa of Eumenes** (Map p326), built as a shelter and promenade for theatre audiences, runs west to the **Odeon of Herodes Atticus** (☑210 324 1807; www.hellenicfestival.gr; Dionysiou Areopagitou; underground rail Akropoli), built in Roman times (and open only for performances).

Acropolis Museum MUSEUM
(Map p326; ☑210 900 0901; www.theacropolismuseum.gr; Dionysiou Areopagitou 15, Makrygianni; admission €5; ☉8am-8pm Tue-Sun, to 10pm Fri; ⓂAkropoli) Don't miss this superb museum on the southern base of the hill, and magnificently reflecting the Parthenon on its glass facade; it houses the surviving treasures of the Acropolis.

Bathed in natural light, the 1st-floor **Archaic Gallery** is a forest of statues, including stunning examples of 6th-century *kore* (maidens). Finds from temples pre-dating the Parthenon include sculptures such as Heracles slaying the Lernaian Hydra, and a lioness devouring a bull.

ℹ UNCERTAIN TIMES

» Due to the financial difficulties in Greece, which became acute starting in 2010, opening hours, prices and even the existence of some establishments have fluctuated much more than usual.

» At the time of writing the government was running many archaeological sites on their shorter winter hours (closing around 3pm). This could change.

» If in doubt, call ahead.

The museum's crowning glory is the top-floor **Parthenon Gallery**, a glass hall built in alignment with the Parthenon, which is visible through the windows. It showcases the temple's metopes and 160m frieze shown in sequence for the first time in over 200 years. Interspersed between the golden-hued originals, white plaster replicates the controversial Parthenon Marbles removed by Lord Elgin in 1801 and later sold to the British Museum.

Other highlights include five **caryatids**, the maiden columns that held up the Erechtheion (the sixth is in the British Museum), a giant floral acroterion and a movie illustrating the history of the Acropolis.

The surprisingly good-value restaurant has superb views; there's also a fine museum shop.

Ancient Agora   HISTORIC SITE
(Map p334; ☎210 321 0185; http://odysseus.culture.gr; Adrianou; adult/child €4/2, free with Acropolis pass; ☉8am-3pm, museum closed 8-11am Mon; ⓜMonastiraki) The Ancient Agora was the marketplace of early Athens and the focal point of civic and social life; Socrates spent time here expounding his philosophy. The main monuments of the Agora are the well-preserved **Temple of Hephaestus** (Monastiraki), the 11th-century **Church of the Holy Apostles** (Monastiraki) and the reconstructed **Stoa of Attalos**, which houses the site's excellent **museum**.

Roman Agora   HISTORIC SITE
(Map p334; ☎210 324 5220; cnr Pelopida & Eolou, Monastiraki; adult/child €2/1, free with Acropolis pass; ☉8.30am-3pm; ⓜMonastiraki) The Romans built their agora just east of the ancient Athenian Agora. The wonderful **Tower of the Winds** was built in the 1st century

BC by Syrian astronomer Andronicus. Each side represents a point of the compass and has a relief carving depicting the associated wind.

TOP CHOICE National Archaeological Museum   MUSEUM
(Map p326; ☎210 821 7717; www.namuseum.gr; 28 Oktovriou-Patision 44, Exarhia; adult/child €7/free; ☉1-8pm Mon, 8am-3pm Tue-Sun; ⓜViktoria, 🚎2, 4, 5, 9 or 11 Polytechnio stop) One of the world's great museums, the National Archaeological Museum contains significant finds from major archaeological sites throughout Greece. The vast collections of Greek art masterpieces include exquisite **Mycenaean gold artefacts**, **Minoan frescos** from Santorini and stunning, enormous statues.

Temple of Olympian Zeus   RUIN
(Map p326; ☎210 922 6330; adult/child €2/free, free with Acropolis pass; ☉8am-3pm; ⓜSyntagma, Akropoli) Begun in the 6th century BC, Greece's largest temple is impressive for the sheer size of its Corinthian columns: 17m high with a base diameter of 1.7m. It took more than 700 years to build, with Emperor Hadrian overseeing its completion in AD 131, and sits behind **Hadrian's Arch** (Map p326; cnr Leoforos Vasilissis Olgas & Leoforos Vasilissis Amalias; ⓜSyntagma).

Panathenaic Stadium   HISTORIC SITE
(Map p326; Leoforos Vasileos Konstantinou, Pangrati; adult/child €3/1.50; ☉8am-7pm; ⓜAkropoli) The Panathenaic Stadium, built in the 4th century BC as a venue for the Panathenaic athletic contests, was restored (including seats of Pentelic marble for 70,000 spectators) and hosted the first modern Olympic Games in 1896, as well as some events of the 2004 Olympics.

Benaki Museum   MUSEUM
(Map p326; ☎210 367 1000; www.benaki.gr; Koumbari 1, cnr Leoforos Vasilissis Sofias, Kolonaki; adult/child €7/free, free Thu; ☉9am-5pm Wed, Fri & Sat, to midnight Thu, to 3pm Sun; ⓜSyntagma, Evangelismos) This superb museum houses an extravagant collection, including ancient sculpture, Persian, Byzantine and Coptic objects, Chinese ceramics, icons, El Greco paintings and fabulous traditional costumes. The museum's annexes around the city: **Museum of Islamic Art** (Map p326; ☎210 325 1311; Agion Asomaton 22 & Dipylou 12, Keramikos; adult/child €7/free; ☉9am-5pm Thu-Sun; ⓜThisio) and **Benaki**

Museum Pireos Annexe (📞210 345 3111; www.benaki.gr; Pireos 138, cnr Andronikou, Rouf; admission €5; ⊙10am-6pm Wed, Thu & Sun, to 10pm Fri & Sat, closed Aug; Ⓜ Keramikos).

Museum of Cycladic Art MUSEUM
(Map p326; 📞210 722 8321; www.cycladic.gr; Neofytou Douka 4, cnr Leoforos Vasilissis Sofias, Kolonaki; adult/child €7/free; ⊙10am-5pm Mon, Wed, Fri & Sat, 10am-8pm Thu, 11am-5pm Sun; Ⓜ Evangelismos) This wonderful private museum was custom-built to display its extraordinary collection of Cycladic art, with an emphasis on the early Bronze Age. It's easy to see how the graceful marble statues, some dating from 3000 BC to 2000 BC, influenced the art of Modigliani and Picasso.

TOP CHOICE **Byzantine & Christian Museum** MUSEUM
(Map p326; 📞210 721 1027; www.byzantinemuseum.gr; Leoforos Vasilissis Sofias 22, Kolonaki; adult/child €4/free; ⊙9am-4pm Tue-Sun; Ⓜ Evangelismos) This outstanding museum presents a priceless collection of Christian art, dating from the 3rd to 20th centuries, exceptionally presented in expansive multilevel galleries in a restored villa. Artefacts include icons, frescoes, sculptures, textiles, manuscripts, vestments and mosaics.

FREE **Parliament & Changing of the Guard** CEREMONY
(Map p326; Plateia Syntagmatos; Ⓜ Syntagma) In front of the parliament building on Plateia Syntagmatos, the traditionally costumed *evzones* (guards) of the **Tomb of the Unknown Soldier** change every hour on the hour. On Sunday at 11am, a whole platoon marches down Vasilissis Sofias to the tomb, accompanied by a band.

FREE **Filopappou Hill** LANDMARK, PARK
(Map p326; Ⓜ Akropoli) Also called the Hill of the Muses, Filopappou is identifiable southwest of the Acropolis by the **Monument of Filopappos** at its summit. Built between AD 114 and 116, it honours Julius Antiochus Filopappos, a prominent Roman consul. The hill's pine-clad slopes offer superb views, with some of the best vantage points for photographing the Acropolis. Small paths weave all over the hill, but the paved path to the top starts near the *periptero* (kiosk) on Dionysiou Areopagitou. After 250m, the path passes the **Church of Agios**

ⓘ **CHEAPER BY THE HALF-DOZEN**

The €12 ticket at the Acropolis (valid for four days) includes entry to the other significant ancient sites: Ancient Agora, Roman Agora, Keramikos, Temple of Olympian Zeus and the Theatre of Dionysos.

Enter the sites free on the first Sunday of the month (except for July, August and September) and on certain holidays. Anyone aged under 19 years or with an EU student card gets in free.

Dimitrios Loumbardiaris, which contains fine frescoes.

FREE **Lykavittos Hill** LANDMARK
(Map p326; Ⓜ Evangelismos) Pine-covered Lykavittos is the highest of the eight hills dotting Athens. Climb to the summit for stunning views of the city, the Attic basin and the islands of Salamis and Aegina (pollution permitting). Little **Chapel of Agios Giorgios** is floodlit at night and open-air **Lykavittos Theatre** hosts concerts in summer.

The main path up starts at the top of Loukianou, or take the **funicular railway** from the top of Ploutarhou.

FREE **National Gardens** GARDENS
(Map p326; entrance on Leoforos Vasilissis Sofias & Leoforos Vasilissis Amalias, Syntagma; ⊙7am-dusk; Ⓜ Syntagma) A delightful, shady refuge during summer, these gardens contain a large playground, a duck pond and a tranquil cafe.

☞ **Tours**

The usual city tours exist like open-bus **CitySightseeing Athens** (Map p334; 📞210 922 0604; www.city-sightseeing.com; Plateia Syntagmatos, Syntagma; adult/child €15/6.50; ⊙every 30min 9am-8pm; Ⓜ Syntagma), **Athens Segway Tours** (Map p326; 📞210 322 2500; www.athenssegwaytours.com; Eschinou 9, Plaka; 2hr tour €59; Ⓜ Akropoli) or the volunteer **This is My Athens** (www.thisisathens.org). Get out of town on the cheap with **Athens: Adventures** (📞210 922 4044; www.athensadventures.gr). Hike or kayak with **Trekking Hellas** (📞210 331 0323; www.trekking.gr; Saripolou 10, Exarhia; Ⓜ Viktoria).

CONTEMPORARY ART

Athens is not all about ancient art. For a taste of the contemporary, visit:

Taf (The Art Foundation; Map p334; www.theartfoundation.gr; Normanou 5, Monastiraki; ⊙1pm-midnight; MMonastiraki) Eclectic art and music gallery.

Onassis Cultural Centre (www.sgt.gr; Leoforos Syngrou 109, Neos Kosmos; MSyngrou-Fix) Multimillion-euro visual and performing arts centre.

National Museum of Contemporary Art (Map p326; www.emst.gr; Leoforos Vas Georgiou B 17-19, enter from Rigilis; adult/child €3/free; ⊙11am-7pm Tue, Wed & Fri-Sun, to 10pm Thu; MEvangelismos) Will be moving to the old Fix brewery on Leoforos Syngrou.

Xippas Gallery (Map p326; Patriarhou Ioakeim 53, Kolonaki; ⊙Tue-Sat; MEvangelismos)

Medusa Art Gallery (Map p326; www.medusaartgallery.com; Xenokratous 7, Kolonaki; MEvangelismos)

Andreas Melas & Helena Papadopoulos Gallery (Map p326; http://melaspapadopoulos.com; Epikourou 26, cnr Korinis, Psyrri; ⊙noon-6pm Tue-Fri, noon-4pm Sat; MOmonia)

Technopolis (Map p326; ☎210 346 7322; Pireos 100, Gazi; MKeramikos) Former gasworks turned cultural centre.

Festivals include:

Art-Athina (www.art-athina.gr) International art in May.

Athens Biennial (www.athensbiennial.org) Every two years from June to October.

ReMap (www.remap.org) Parallel event to the Biennial, exhibiting in abandoned buildings.

⚐ Festivals

Hellenic Festival PERFORMING ARTS
(www.greekfestival.gr; ⊙late May-Oct) Top lineup of local and international music, dance and theatre in venues across Athens and Epidavros' ancient theatre.

🛏 Sleeping

Discounts apply in low season, for longer stays and online. Book well ahead for July and August.

Plaka

Central Hotel BOUTIQUE HOTEL €€
(Map p334; ☎210 323 4357; www.centralhotel.gr; Apollonos 21, Plaka; s/d incl breakfast from €80/100; ❄@; MSyntagma) Pass through the sleek lobby and by the attentive staff to spacious white rooms hung with original art and decked out with all the mod cons. Some balconies have Acropolis views, as does the rooftop, where you can sunbake and relax in the Jacuzzi.

New BOUTIQUE HOTEL €€€
(Map p334; ☎210 628 4565; www.yeshotels.gr; Filellinon 16, Plaka; s/d incl breakfast from €170/185; P❄☈; MSyntagma) Smart New is the latest entry on the high-end Athens scene. Whether you dig the groovy, designer furniture or the pillow menu (tell 'em how you like it!), you'll find some sort of decadent treat to tickle your fancy.

Hotel Adonis HOTEL €
(Map p334; ☎210 324 9737; www.hotel-adonis.gr; 3 Kodrou St, Plaka; s/d/tr incl breakfast €45/55/75; ❄@☈; MSyntagma) Comfortable rooms, newly renovated bathrooms, conscientious staff and Acropolis views from the breakfast room/bar keep folks coming back.

Niki Hotel HOTEL €€
(Map p334; ☎210 322 0913; www.nikihotel.gr; Nikis 27, Syntagma; s/d/tr incl breakfast €55/65/118; ❄@☈; MSyntagma) This small hotel bordering Plaka with contemporary furnishings has well-appointed rooms and a two-level suite for families (€145), with Acropolis-view balconies.

Plaka Hotel HOTEL €€
(Map p334; ☎210 322 2096; www.plakahotel.gr; Kapnikareas 7, cnr Mitropoleos, Plaka; s/d/tr incl breakfast from €90/110/125; ❄☈; MMonastiraki) Folks come here not for the tidy, bland rooms but for the excellent Acropolis views from the rooftop garden and top-floor digs.

Hotel Acropolis House
PENSION €€

(Map p334; ☎210 322 2344; www.acropolishouse. gr; Kodrou 6-8, Plaka; s €65, d €65-82, tr from €113, q from €136, all incl breakfast; ❄🖳; MSyntagma) This well-situated hotel in a 19th-century house feels more pension than hotel, with a comfy sitting room and hospitable management. Guests chat amicably over breakfast.

Student & Travellers' Inn
HOSTEL €

(Map p334; ☎210 324 4808; www.studenttravellersinn.com; Kydathineon 16, Plaka; dm €20-22, s/d/tr €45/55/65, without bathroom €30/50/60; ❄@🖳; MSyntagma) The mixed-sex dorms may be spartan and housekeeping a bit lean, but extras (laundry, left luggage) make up for it.

Monastiraki

TOP CHOICE **Magna Grecia**
BOUTIQUE HOTEL €€

(Map p334; ☎210 324 0314; www.magnagreciahotel.com; Mitropoleos 54, Monastiraki; d incl breakfast €95-135; ❄🖳; MMonastiraki) Enjoy Acropolis views from the front rooms and rooftop terrace in a historic building opposite the cathedral. Imaginatve, luxe rooms sport comfortable mattresses.

Hotel Cecil
HOTEL €€

(Map p326; ☎210 321 7079; www.cecil.gr; Athinas 39, Monastiraki; s/d/tr incl breakfast from €55/70/85; ❄@🖳; MMonastiraki) Aromatic spices waft into the lobby from nearby Asian markets, but double-pane windows keep the high-ceilinged rooms in this classical building quiet.

Tempi Hotel
HOTEL €

(Map p326; ☎210 321 3175; www.tempihotel.gr; Eolou 29, Monastiraki; d/tr €57/67, s/d without bathroom €35/47; ❄🖳; MMonastiraki) No-frills rooms may be tiny, but some have balconies overlooking Plateia Agia Irini. A communal kitchen and nearby markets make it ideal for self-caterers.

Syntagma

Hotel Grande Bretagne
LUXURY HOTEL €€€

(Map p326; ☎210 333 0000; www.grandebretagne.gr; Vasileos Georgiou 1, Syntagma; r/ste from €275/960; P❄@🖳; MSyntagma) Dripping with elegance and old-world charm, *the* place to stay in Athens has always has been these deluxe digs. Built in 1862 to accommodate visiting heads of state, it ranks among the great hotels of the world. From the decadent, chandeliered lobby, to the exquisite guestrooms, divine spa and rooftop restaurant, this place is built for pampering.

Makrygianni & Koukaki

TOP CHOICE **Athens Backpackers**
HOSTEL, APARTMENT €

(Map p326; ☎210 922 4044; www.backpackers. gr; Makri 12, Makrygianni; dm incl breakfast €23-28, 2-/4-/6-person apt €90/120/150; ❄@🖳; MAkropoli) This excellent, popular hostel also has great apartments and boasts a rooftop party bar with Acropolis views, kitchen, daily movies, and the friendly Aussie management hosts (free!) barbecues. Breakfast and nonalcoholic drinks are included; long-term storage, laundry and airport pick-up available.

TOP CHOICE **Athens Gate**
BUSINESS HOTEL €€

(Map p326; ☎210 923 8302; www.athensgate.gr; Leoforos Syngrou Andrea 10, Makrygianni; s/d incl breakfast from €120/130; ❄@🖳; MAkropoli) With stunning views over the Temple of Olympian Zeus from the spacious front rooms, and a central (if busy) location, this totally refurbished hotel is a great find. Stylish, immaculate rooms have all the mod cons, staff are friendly and breakfast is served on the superb rooftop terrace with 360-degree Athens views.

Hera Hotel
BOUTIQUE HOTEL €€

(Map p326; ☎210 923 6682; www.herahotel.gr; Falirou 9, Makrygianni; s/d from €75/90, ste from €180; ❄@🖳; MAkropoli) The ornate interior complements the hotel's lovely neoclassical facade. The rooftop garden, restaurant and bar boast spectacular views and it is a short walk to the Acropolis and Plaka.

Marble House Pension
PENSION €

(☎210 923 4058; www.marblehouse.gr; Zini 35a, Koukaki; s/d/tr €35/45/55, d/tr/q without bathroom €40/50/65; ❄🖳; MSyngrou-Fix) This long-standing Athens favourite is on a quiet cul-de-sac 10 minutes' walk from Plaka. Step through the garden to quiet, spotless rooms. For air-con add €9.

Psyrri & Thisio

Athens Style
HOSTEL, APARTMENT €

(Map p326; ☎210 322 5010; www.athenstyle. com; Agias Theklas 10, Psyrri; dm €20-28, s/d/tr €51/80/96, apt from €90; ❄@; MMonastiraki) This bright, arty hostel, the newest in town, has dorm beds and well-equipped apartments. The cool basement lounge holds art exhibitions, a pool table and home cinema; the rooftop bar has Acropolis views.

GREECE ATHENS

Plaka & Monastiraki

200 m
0.1 miles

SYNTAGMA

Plateia
Syntagmatos

Stadiou

Karageorgi Servias

Othonos

Xenofontos

Bus X95 to Airport

Bus 040 to Piraeus

Filellinon

Zappeio
Gardens

Leof Vassilissis Amalias

Nikis

Nikis

Souri G

Voulis

Voulis

Skoufou

Voulis

Voulis

Pendelis

Axarlian

Diomias

Petraki

Patroou

Apollonos

Ipitou

Kodrou

Plateia
Sofiros
Kydaθhineon

Dedalou

Tsatsou K

Pittakou

Nikis

PLAKA

Patroou

Iperidou

Angelou Geronta

Aφroditis

Heфaistou

Lysikratous

Goura

Thalou

Periklous

Fokionos

Mitropoleos

 Spartias

Thoukididou

Navarhou Nikodimou

Nekropos

Adrianou

Farmaki

Shelley

Heфestou

Epimenidou

Evangelistrias

Ktena

Church of
Agios
Eleftherios

Apollonos

Flessa

Scholiou

Tripodon

Rangova

Shelley

Vyronos

Thespidos

Stratonos

ANAFIOTIKA

Plateia
Mitropoleos

Mnisikleous

Plateia
Kapnikareas

Kyrristou

Lysiou

Prytaniou

Old Acropolis
Museum

Ermou

Ermou

Plateia
Monastirakiou

Monastiraki

Pandrosou

Eolou

Kalogrioni

Plateia
Arhaia
Agoras Adrianou

Adrianou

Thrasyvoulou

Klepsydras

**Roman
Agora**

Panos

Tholou

Mitroou

Aretousas

Theorias

Dioskouron

Theorias

Acropolis

MONASTIRAKI

**Monastiraki
Flea Market**

Areos

Kladou

Dexippou

Pelopida

PeΚklis

Vrysakiou

Taxiarhon

**Ancient
Agora**

Theorias

Acropolis
Main
Entrance

Thisio

Astingos

Agiou Filippou

Adrianou

Apostolou Pavlou

Plaka & Monastiraki

◎ Top Sights

Acropolis	C4
Ancient Agora	B2
Monastiraki Flea Market	B1
Roman Agora	D2

◎ Sights

1 Beule Gate	C4
2 Church of the Holy Apostles	B2
3 Erechtheion	D3
4 Parthenon	D4
5 Propylaea	C4
6 Stoa of Attalos	B2
7 Taf	C1
8 Temple of Athena Nike	C4
9 Temple of Hephaestus	A1
10 Theatre of Dionysos	D4
11 Tower of the Winds	D2

◎ Activities, Courses & Tours

12 CitySightseeing Athens	G1

◎ Sleeping

13 Central Hotel	F2
14 Hotel Acropolis House	F3
15 Hotel Adonis	F3
16 Magna Grecia	E1
17 New	G3
18 Niki Hotel	F2
19 Plaka Hotel	D1
20 Student & Travellers' Inn	F3

◎ Eating

21 Avocado	F2
22 Café Avyssinia	B1
23 Filistron	A3
24 Palia Taverna Tou Psara	E3
25 Paradosiako	F2
26 Platanos	D2
27 Thanasis	C1
28 Tzitzikas & Mermingas	F1

◎ Drinking

29 Brettos	E4

◎ Entertainment

30 Cine Paris	F3
31 Odeon of Herodes Atticus	C4

◎ Shopping

32 Eleftheroudakis	F2
33 Ioanna Kourbela	E3
34 Public	G1

Hotel Erechthion
HOTEL **€**

(Map p326; ☑210 345 9606; www.hotelerechthion.gr; Flammarion 8, cnr Agias Marinas, Thisio; s/d/tr €40/60/70; ❀☞; Ⓜ Thisio) Simple, clean rooms with TVs, refrigerators, veneer furniture and basic bathrooms are not the highlights here. Much more impressive are the fantastic Acropolis views from the balconies, the low price and the homey neighbourhood.

Kolonaki

Periscope
BOUTIQUE HOTEL **€€**

(Map p326; ☑210 729 7200; www.periscope.gr; Haritos 22, Kolonaki; d incl breakfast from €145; ❀☞; Ⓜ Evangelismos) A hip hotel with a cool, edgy look, this place has comfortable minimalist rooms with all the mod cons and a quiet location.

✗ Eating

In addition to mainstay tavernas, Athens has upscale eateries (wear your most stylish togs at night). Eat streets include Mitropoleos, Adrianou and Navarchou Apostoli in Monastiraki, the area around Plateia Psyrri, and Gazi, near Keramikos metro.

The fruit and vegetable **market** (Varvakios Agora; Map p326; Athinas, btwn Sofokleous & Evripidou; ⊙7am-3pm Mon-Sat; Ⓜ Monastiraki, Panepistimio, Omonia) is opposite the meat market.

Syntagma & Monastiraki

Café Avyssinia
MEZEDHES **€**

(Map p334; ☑210 321 7047; www.avissinia.gr; Kynetou 7, Monastiraki; mains €10-16; ⊙11am-1am Tue-Sat, to 7pm Sun; Ⓜ Monastiraki) Hidden away on the edge of grungy Plateia Avyssinias in the middle of the flea market, this *mezedhopoleio* (*mezedhes* restaurant) gets top marks for atmosphere, and the food is not far behind. Often has live music on weekends.

Tzitzikas & Mermingas
MEZEDHES **€**

(Map p334; ☑210 324 7607; Mitropoleos 12-14, Syntagma; mezedhes €6-11; Ⓜ Syntagma) Greek merchandise lines the walls of this cheery, modern *mezedhopoleio*. The great range of delicious and creative *mezedhes* (appetisers) draws a bustling local crowd. Don't miss the decadent honey-coated fried cheese with ham...it's the kind of special dish that will haunt your future dreams.

Mama Roux
INTERNATIONAL €

(Map p326; ☑213 004 8382; Eoulou 48-50, Monastiraki; mains €5-10; ☺9am-midnight Tue-Sat, to 5pm Mon, noon-5pm Sun; ☎; ⓂMonastiraki) Downtown's hottest cheap-eats restaurant fills up with locals digging into a fresh, delicious mix of dishes: from real burritos and Cajun specials to whopping American-style burgers.

Kalnterimi
TAVERNA €

(Map p326; ☑210 331 0049; www.kalnterimi.gr; Plateia Agion Theodoron, cnr Skouleniou; mains €5-8; ☺lunch & dinner; ⓂPanepistimio) Find your way back behind the Church of Agii Theodori to this open-air taverna offering Greek food at its most authentic. Everything is fresh-cooked and delicious.

Thanasis
SOUVLAKI €

(Map p334; ☑210 324 4705; Mitropoleos 69, Monastiraki; gyros €2.50; ☺8.30am-2.30am; ⓂMonastiraki) In the heart of Athens' souvlaki hub, Thanasis is known for its kebabs on pitta with grilled tomato and onions. Live music, grill aromas and crowds give the area an almost permanently festive air.

Plaka & Makrygianni

TOP CHOICE Mani Mani
REGIONAL CUISINE €

(Map p326; ☑210 921 8180; www.manimani.com.gr; Falirou 10, Makrygianni; mains €10-16; ☺3pm-12.30am Tue-Thu, from 1pm Fri & Sat, 1-5.30pm Sun, closed Jul & Aug; ⓂAkropoli) Sample cuisine from Mani in the Peloponnese, such as tangy sausage with orange. Most dishes can be ordered as half-serves (at half-price), allowing you to try a wide range.

Paradosiako
TAVERNA €

(Map p334; ☑210 321 4121; Voulis 44a, Plaka; mains €5-11; ☎; ⓂSyntagma) For great traditional fare, you can't beat this inconspicuous, no-frills taverna on the periphery of Plaka. Choose from daily specials such as delicious shrimp *saganaki* (fried Greek cheese).

Avocado
VEGETARIAN €

(Map p334; ☑210 323 7878; www.avocadoathens.com; Nikis 30, Plaka; mains €6.50-9.50; ☺11am-10pm Mon-Sat, to 7pm Sun; ☎☑; ⓂSyntagma) A full array of vegan, gluten-free and organic treats (a rarity in Greece). Enjoy everything from fresh juices and sandwiches to quinoa with eggplant or mixed veg coconut curry.

Cucina Povera
MEDITERRANEAN €

(Map p326; ☑210 756 6008; www.cucinapovera.gr; Efforionos 13, Pangrati; mains €9-14; ☺dinner Tue-Sat, brunch Sun; ⓂEvangelismos) Dishes can be occasionally incandescent, like the salad with avocado, pear and goat cheese. The dining room embodies relaxed hipness, and the wine list rocks.

Platanos
TAVERNA €

(Map p334; ☑210 322 0666; Diogenous 4, Plaka; mains €7-9; ☺lunch & dinner; ⓂMonastiraki) Tasty, home-cooked-style Greek cuisine include delicious lamb dishes, and we love the leafy courtyard.

Palia Taverna Tou Psara
TAVERNA €€

(Map p334; ☑210 321 8734; www.psaras-taverna.gr; Erehtheos 16, Plaka; mains €12-24; ☺11am-12.30pm Wed-Mon; ⓂAkropoli) Situated on a path leading up towards the Acropolis, this gem of a taverna is one of Plaka's best, serving scrumptious *mezedhes* and excellent fish and meat classics on a tree-lined terrace.

Keramikos, Thisio & Gazi

Varoulko
SEAFOOD €€€

(Map p326; ☑210 522 8400; www.varoulko.gr; Pireos 80, Keramikos; mains €35-60; ☺from 8.30pm Mon-Sat; ⓂThisio, Keramikos) For a magical Greek dining experience, you can't beat the winning combination of Acropolis views and delicious seafood by celebrated Michelin-starred chef Lefteris Lazarou. Athenian celebrities feast in an airy, glass-fronted dining room.

Kanella
TAVERNA €

(Map p326; ☑210 347 6320; Leoforos Konstantinoupoleos 70, Gazi; dishes €7-10; ☺1.30pm-late; ⓂKeramikos) Home-made village-style bread, mismatched retro crockery and brown-paper tablecloths set the tone for this trendy, modern taverna serving regional Greek cuisine.

Filistron
MEZEDHES €€

(Map p334; ☑210 346 7554; Apostolou Pavlou 23, Thisio; mezedhes €8-14; ☺lunch & dinner Tue-Sun; ⓂThisio) Book a prized table on the rooftop terrace of this excellent *mezedhopoleio*, which enjoys breathtaking Acropolis- and Lykavittos-views.

Sardelles
SEAFOOD €€

(Map p326; ☑210 347 8050; Persefonis 15, Gazi; fish dishes €10-17; ⓂKeramikos) As the name suggests (Sardelles means 'sardines'), , this modern fish taverna facing the illuminated gasworks specialises in seafood *mezedhes*.

Kolonaki & Pangrati

TOP CHOICE Spondi
MEDITERRANEAN €€€

(Map p326; 210 752 0658; Pyrronos 5, Pangrati; mains €35-50; ⊗8pm-late) Dining in this superb restaurant's gorgeous vaulted cellar or in its bougainvillea-draped courtyard in summer is quite an understatedly elegant affair. Chef Arnaud Bignon has won two Michelin stars, creating extravagant seasonal menus adhering to French technique but embodying vibrant Greek flavours.

TOP CHOICE Oikeio
TAVERNA €

(Map p326; 210 725 9216; Ploutarhou 15, Kolonaki; mains €7-13; ⊗1pm-2.30am Mon-Sat; MEvangelismos) With excellent home-style cooking, this modern taverna lives up to its name ('Homey'). The intimate bistro atmosphere spills out to tables on the pavement for glitterati-watching without the usual high Kolonaki bill. Reservations recommended.

Filippou
TAVERNA €

(Map p326; 210 721 6390; Xenokratous 19, Kolonaki; mains €8-12; ⊗lunch & dinner, closed Sat night & Sun; MEvangelismos) Filippou has been dishing out yummy Greek dishes since 1923. Think soul cooking, with white linen, in the heart of chic Kolonaki.

Drinking

Athenians know how to party. Everyone has their favourite *steki* (hang-out), but expect people to show up after midnight. Head to Gazi (around Voutadon and the Keramikos metro station), Kolonaki (around Ploutarhou and Haritos, or Skoufa and Omirou) or Monastiraki (around Plateia Karytsi or Kolokotroni) and explore!

Omonia is best avoided late at night, and although Exarhia has a bohemian bar scene, the neighbourhood has been affected recently by street demonstrations.

Kolonaki has a mind-boggling array of cafes off Plateia Kolonakiou on Skoufa and Tsakalof. Another cafe-thick area is Adrianou, along the Ancient Agora.

Hoxton
BAR

(Map p326; Voutadon 42, Gazi; MKeramikos) Kick back on overstuffed leather couches under modern art in this industrial space that fills up late with bohemians, ruggers and the occasional pop star.

Mai Tai
BAR

(Map p326; Ploutarhou 18, Kolonaki; MEvangelismos) Jam-packed with well-heeled young

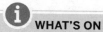

WHAT'S ON

For comprehensive events listings, with links to online ticket sales points, try: www.breathtakingathens.gr, www.el culture.gr, www.tickethour.com, www. tickethouse.gr, www.ticketservices.gr. The *Kathimerini* supplement inside the *International Herald Tribune* contains event listings and a cinema guide.

Athenians, this is just one in a group of happening spots in Kolonaki.

Seven Jokers
BAR

(Map p326; Voulis 7, Syntagma; MSyntagma) Lively and central Seven Jokers anchors the party block, also shared by spacious **42** (Kolokotroni 3, Syntagma) around the corner, for cocktails in wood-panelled splendour, with **Baba Au Rum** (Klitiou 6, Syntagma; MSyntagma) and **Gin Joint** (Lada 1, Syntagma; MSyntagma) nearby.

Gazarte
BAR

(Map p326; 210 346 0347; www.gazarte.gr; Voutadon 32-34, Gazi; MKeramikos) Trendy crowd takes in mainstream music and rooftop city views including the Acropolis.

Brettos
BAR

(Map p334; Kydathineon 41, Plaka; MAkropoli) This bar-distillery is back-lit by an eye-catching collection of coloured bottles.

Tailor Made
CAFE, BAR

(Map p326; 213 004 9645; www.tailormade.gr; Plateia Agia Irini 2, Monastiraki; MMonastiraki) Cheerful Athenians spill from the mod art-festooned micro-roastery to tables alongside the flower market. At night it turns into a happening cocktail and wine bar.

Entertainment
Nightclubs

Athenians go clubbing after midnight and dress up. In summer try beachfront venues.

Rock'n'Roll
CLUB, BAR

(Map p326; 210 721 7127; Plateia Kolonakiou, Kolonaki; MEvangelismos) Dependably fun, with a casual-cool Kolonaki crowd.

TOP CHOICE Venue
CLUB

(210 341 1410; www.venue-club.com; Pireos 130, Rouf; ⊗Sep-May; MKeramikos) Arguably the city's biggest dance club: three-stage dance floor and an energetic crowd.

GREECE ATHENS

WANT MORE?

For in-depth information, reviews and recommendations at your fingertips, head to the Apple App Store to purchase Lonely Planet's *Athens City Guide* iPhone app.

Alternatively, head to **Lonely Planet** (www.lonelyplanet.com/greece/athens) for planning advice, author recommendations, traveller reviews and insider tips.

Akrotiri CLUB
(☎210 985 9147; www.akrotirilounge.gr; Vasileos Georgiou B5, Agios Kosmas) Beach-side in summer with a capacity for 3000 people, bars and lounges cover multiple levels.

Gay & Lesbian Venues

Gay bars cluster in Gazi near the railway line on Leoforos Konstantinoupoleos and Megalou Alexandrou, as well as Makrygianni, Psyrri, Metaxourghio and Exarhia. Check out www.athensinfoguide.com, www.gay.gr or a copy of the *Greek Gay Guide* booklet at newspaper kiosks.

Sodade GAY
(Map p326; ☎210 346 8657; www.sodade.gr; Triptolemou 10, Gazi; Ⓜ Keramikos) Tiny, sleek and super-fun for dancing. It draws a great group.

Noiz Club LESBIAN
(Map p326; ☎210 342 4771; www.noizclub.gr; Evmolpidon 41, Gazi; Ⓜ Keramikos) In Gazi's gay triangle, for a female crowd.

Lamda Club GAY
(Map p326; ☎210 942 4202; Lembesi 15, cnr Leoforos Syngrou, Makrygianni; Ⓜ Akropoli) Busy, three levels and not for the faint of heart.

Magaze CAFE, BAR
(Map p326; ☎210 324 3740; Eolou 33, Monastiraki; Ⓜ Monastiraki) All-day hang-out with Acropolis views from pavement tables; lively bar after sunset.

Live Music

In summer, concerts rock plazas and parks; some clubs shut down. Most authentic *rembetika* venues close during summer, but you can see a popularised version at some tavernas in Psyrri.

TOP
CHOICE **Half Note Jazz Club** JAZZ
(Map p326; ☎210 921 3310; www.halfnote.gr; Trivonianou 17, Mets; Ⓜ Akropoli) Dark, smoky venue for serious jazz.

Cafe Alavastron LIVE MUSIC
(☎210 756 0102; www.cafealavastron.gr; Damareos 78, Pangrati) Eclectic mix of modern jazz, ethnic and Greek music in a casual, intimate venue.

TOP
CHOICE **Gagarin 205 Club** LIVE MUSIC
(www.gagarin205.gr; Liosion 205, Thymarakia; Ⓜ Agios Nikolaos) Interesting international and local rock acts.

TOP
CHOICE **Stoa Athanaton** REMBETIKA
(Map p326; ☎210 321 4362; Sofokleous 19, Central Market; ⊘3-6pm & midnight-6am Mon-Sat, closed Jun-Sep; Ⓜ Monastiraki, Panepistimio, Omonia) Located above the meat market, this is still *the* place to listen to *rembetika*, often referred to as Greek blues.

Classical Music, Theatre & Dance

In summer, the excellent Hellenic Festival (p10) swings into action.

Megaron Mousikis PERFORMING ARTS
(Athens Concert Hall; ☎210 728 2333; www.megaron.gr; Kokkali 1, cnr Leoforos Vasilissis Sofias, Ilissia; ⊘box office 10am-6pm Mon-Fri, to 2pm Sat; Ⓜ Megaro Mousikis) Superb concert venue hosting winter performances by local and international artists.

National Theatre THEATRE
(Map p326; ☎210 522 3243; www.n-t.gr; Agiou Konstantinou 22-24, Omonia; Ⓜ Omonia) Contemporary plays and ancient theatre on the main stage and other venues.

Olympia Theatre PERFORMING ARTS
(Map p326; ☎210 361 2461; Akadimias 59, Exarhia; Ⓜ Panepistimio) November to June: ballet, symphony and the **Greek National Opera** (Ethniki Lyriki Skini; Map p326; ☎210 360 0180; www.nationalopera.gr).

Dora Stratou
Dance Theatre TRADITIONAL DANCE
(Map p326; ☎210 921 4650; www.grdance.org; Filopappou Hill; adult/child €15/5; ⊘performances 9.30pm Wed-Fri, 8.15pm Sat & Sun Jun-Sep; Ⓜ Petralona) Traditional folk-dancing shows feature more than 75 musicians and dancers in an open-air amphitheatre.

Cinema

Most cinemas, like **Astor** (Map p326; 210 323 1297; Stadiou 28, Syntagma; MPanepistimio), show recent releases in their original language; tickets cost around €8. In summer, watch outdoors at **Aigli Cinema** (Map p326; ⏺210 336 9369; Zappeio Gardens, Syntagma; MSyntagma), **Dexameni** (Map p326; ⏺210 362 3942; Plateia Dexameni, Kolonaki; MEvangelismos) or **Cine Paris** (Map p334; ⏺210 322 0721; Kydathineon 22, Plaka; MSyntagma).

 ## Shopping

Shop for cool jewellery, clothes, shoes and souvenirs such as backgammon sets, hand-woven textiles, olive-oil beauty products, worry beads and ceramics. Find boutiques around Syntagma, from the Attica department store past Voukourestiou and on Ermou; designer brands and cool shops in Kolonaki; and souvenirs, folk art and leather in Plaka and Monastiraki.

Monastiraki Flea Market   MARKET
(Map p334; Adrianou, Monastiraki; ⏺daily; MMonastiraki) Enthralling; spreads daily from Plateia Monastirakiou.

To Pantopoleion   FOOD, DRINK
(Map p326; ⏺210 323 4612; Sofokleous 1, Omonia; MPanepistimio) Expansive store selling traditional food products from all over Greece.

Ioanna Kourbela   CLOTHING
(Map p334; ⏺210 322 4591; www.ioannakourbela.com; Adrianou 109, Plaka; MSytnatgma) Classic, cool fashion by a young Greek designer.

Eleftheroudakis   BOOKS
Syntagma (Map p326; ⏺210 331 4180; Panepistimiou 17, Syntagma; MSyntagma); **Plaka** (Map p334; ⏺210 322 9388; Nikis 20, Plaka; MSyntagma) English-language books.

Public   BOOKS, ELECTRONICS
(Map p334; ⏺210 324 6210; Plateia Syntagmatos, Syntagma; 🛜; MSyntagma) English-language books on 3rd floor.

ℹ Information

Emergency

Visitor Emergency Assistance (⏺112) Toll-free, 24 hours; in English.

Tourist Police (⏺210 920 0724, 24hr 171; Veïkou 43-45, Koukaki; ⏺8am-10pm; MSyngrou-Fix)

Police Station (⏺210 725 7000; Plateia Syntagmatos; MSyntagma) Phone ⏺100 for the police.

SOS Doctors (⏺1016, 210 821 1888; ⏺24hr) Pay service with English-speaking doctors.

Ambulance/First-aid Advice (⏺166)

Internet Access

There are free wi-fi hot spots at Plateia Syntagmatos, Thisio, Gazi, the port of Piraeus, many cafes and on the 3rd floor of Public (see above).

 ## DANGERS & ANNOYANCES

» Crime has heightened in Athens with the onset of the financial crisis. Though violent street crime remains relatively rare, travellers should be alert on the streets, especially at night, and beware the traps listed here.

» Streets surrounding Omonia have become markedly seedier, with an increase in prostitutes and junkies; avoid the area, especially at night.

» Watch for pickpockets on the metro and at the markets.

» When taking taxis, ask the driver to use the meter or negotiate a price in advance. Ignore stories that the hotel you've chosen is closed or full: they're angling for a commission from another hotel.

» Bar scams are commonplace, particularly in Plaka and Syntagma. They go something like this: friendly Greek approaches solo male traveller, discovers traveller is new to Athens, and reveals that he, too, is from out of town. However, friendly Greek knows a great bar where they order drinks and equally friendly owner offers another drink. Women appear and more drinks are served; at the end of the night the traveller is hit with an exorbitant bill.

» The recent financial reforms in Greece have caused strikes in Athens. If there is a strike while you are here (check http://livingingreece.gr/strikes), confirm that the sights you wish to see will be open and the transport you are planning to use will be running. Picketers tend to march in Plateia Syntagmatos.

Internet Resources

Official visitor site (www.breathtakingathens.gr)

Media

Kathimerini (www.ekathimerini.com) and **Athens News** (www.athensnews.gr) have English-language coverage.

Money

Banks suround Plateia Syntagmatos.

Eurochange (210 331 2462; Karageorgi Servias 2, Syntagma; 8am-9pm; Syntagma)

Telephone

Kiosks sell phonecards for public phones and prepaid SIM cards for mobiles.

Tourist Information

EOT (Greek National Tourist Organisation; 210 331 0716, 210 331 0347; www.visitgreece.gr; Dionysiou Areopagitou 18-20, Makrygianni; 8am-8pm Mon-Fri, 10am-4pm Sat & Sun May-Sep, 9am-7pm Mon-Fri Oct-Apr; Akropoli)

Athens Information Kiosk Acropolis (Acropolis; 9am-9pm Jun-Aug; Akropoli)

Athens Information Kiosk Airport (210 353 0390; www.breathtakingathens.com; Airport; 8am-8pm; Airport) Maps, transport information and all Athens info.

Getting There & Away

Air

Modern **Eleftherios Venizelos International Airport** (ATH; 210 353 0000; www.aia.gr), 27km east of Athens.

Boat

Most ferries, hydrofoils and high-speed catamarans leave from the massive port at Piraeus. Some depart from smaller ports at Rafina and Lavrio.

Bus

KTEL (14505; www.ktel.org) Athens has two main intercity bus stations, one 5km and one 7km to the north of Omonia. Tourist offices have timetables.

Mavromateon Terminal (210 822 5148, 210 880 8000; cnr Leoforos Alexandras & 28 Oktovriou-Patision, Pedion Areos; Viktoria) Buses for destinations in southern Attica leave from this terminal, about 250m north of the National Archaeological Museum.

Kifissos Terminal A (210 512 4910; Kifissou 100, Peristeri; Agios Antonios) Buses to the Peloponnese, Igoumenitsa, Ionian Islands, Florina, Ioannina, Kastoria, Edessa and Thessaloniki, among other destinations. Bus 051 goes to central Athens (junction of Zinonos and Menandrou, near Omonia) every 15 minutes from 5am to midnight. Taxis to Syntagma cost about €8.

Liossion Terminal B (210 831 7153; Liossion 260, Thymarakia; Agios Nikolaos) Buses to Trikala (for Meteora), Delphi, Larissa, Thiva, Volos and other destinations. To get here, take bus 024 from outside the main gate of the National Gardens on Amalias and ask to get off at Praktoria KTEL. Get off the bus at Liossion 260, turn right onto Gousiou and you'll see the terminal.

Car & Motorcycle

The airport has car rental, and Syngrou, just south of the Temple of Olympian Zeus, is dotted with car-hire firms, though driving in Athens is treacherous.

Avis (210 322 4951; Leoforos Vasilissis Amalias 48, Makrygianni; Akropoli)

Budget (210 922 4200; Leoforos Syngrou Andrea 23, Makrygianni; Akropoli)

Europcar (210 921 1444; Leoforos Syngrou Andrea 25, Makrygianni; Akropoli)

Train

Intercity trains to central and northern Greece depart from the central **Larisis train station**, about 1km northwest of Plateia Omonias. For the Peloponnese, take the suburban rail to Kiato and change for other OSE services, or check for available lines at the Larisis station. International trains have been discontinued.

OSE Office (210 529 7005, in English 1110; www.ose.gr; Karolou 1, Omonia; 8am-3pm Mon-Fri; Metaxourghio)

Getting Around

To/From the Airport

BUS Tickets cost €5. Twenty-four-hour services:

Plateia Syntagmatos (Bus X95, 60 to 90 minutes, every 15 minutes) The Syntagma stop is on Othonos.

Piraeus Port (Bus X96, 1½ hrs, every 20 minutes)

Terminal A (Kifissos) Bus Station (Bus X93, 35 minutes, every 30 minutes)

METRO Blue line 3 links the airport to the city centre in around 40 minutes; it operates from Monastiraki from 5.50am to midnight, and from the airport from 5.30am to 11.30pm. Tickets (€8) are valid for all public transport for 90 minutes. Fare for two or more passengers is €14 total.

TAXI Fares vary according to the time of day and level of traffic; expect at least €35 from the airport to the centre, and €50 to Piraeus. Both trips can take up to an hour, more in heavy traffic.

Public Transport

The metro, tram and bus system makes getting around central Athens and to Piraeus easy. Athens' road traffic can be horrendous. Get maps and timetables at the tourist offices or **Athens Urban Transport Organisation** (OASA; ☎185; www.oasa.gr; ☺6.30am-11.30pm Mon-Fri, 7.30am-10.30pm Sat & Sun).

BUS & TROLLEYBUS

Buses and electric trolleybuses operate every 15 minutes from 5am to midnight.

Piraeus From Syntagma and Filellinon to Akti Xaveriou catch Bus 040; from Omonia end of Athinas to Plateia Themistokleous, catch Bus 049.

METRO

Trains operate from 5am to midnight (Friday and Saturday to around 2am), every three to 10 minutes. Get timetables at www.ametro.gr.

TAXI

Flag fall is €1.16 with an additional surcharge of €1.05 from ports and train and bus stations, and €3.77 from the airport; then the day rate (tariff 1 on the meter) is €0.66 per kilometre. The night rate (tariff 2 on the meter, from midnight to 5am) is €1.16 per kilometre. Baggage costs €0.38 per item over 10kg. Minimum fare is €3.10. Booking a radio taxi costs €1.88 extra. Fixed rates are posted at the airport.

Taxibeat (https://taxibeat.gr) Mobile app for hailing available taxis by location and rating. Can book from abroad.

Athina 1 (☎210 921 2800)

Enotita (☎801 115 1000)

Ikaros (☎210 515 2800)

TRAIN

Fast **suburban rail** (☎1110; www.trainose.gr) links Athens with the airport, Piraeus, the outer regions and the northern Peloponnese. It connects to the metro at Larisis, Doukissis Plakentias and Nerantziotissa stations, and goes from the airport to Kiato.

AROUND ATHENS

Piraeus   Πειραιάς

TRANSPORT HUB
POP 179,500

The highlights of Greece's main port and ferry hub are the otherworldly rows of ferries, ships and hydrofoils filling its seemingly endless quays. It takes around 40 minutes to get here (10km) from Athens' centre by

TICKETS & PASSES

Tickets good for 90 minutes (€1.40), a 24-hour travel pass (€4) and a weekly ticket (€14) are valid for all forms of public transport except for airport services. Bus/trolleybus-only tickets (€1.20) cannot be used on the metro. Children under six travel free; people under 18 and over 65 pay half-fare. Buy tickets in metro stations, transport kiosks, or most *periptera* (street kiosks). Validate the ticket in the machine as you board your transport of choice.

metro, so there's no reason to stay in shabby Piraeus. The Mikrolimano (Small Harbour), with its cafes and fish restaurants, reveals the city's gentler side.

🛏 Sleeping

Piraeus Theoxenia   LUXURY HOTEL €€
(☎210 411 2550; www.theoxeniapalace.com; Karaoli Dimitriou 23; s/d/tr incl breakfast €99/110/150; ❄@🛜; MPiraeus) Piraeus' most upmarket, central hotel, with plump bathrobes and satellite TV; get the best deals online.

Hotel Triton   HOTEL €€
(☎210 417 3457; www.htriton.gr; Tsamadou 8; s/d/tr incl breakfast €45/70/80; ❄@; MPiraeus) Refurbished hotel with simple executive-style rooms; a treat compared with Piraeus' usual run-down joints.

🍴 Eating

If you're killing time, take trolleybus 20 to Mikrolimano for harbourfront seafood.

Rakadiko   TAVERNA €
(☎210 417 8470; Stoa Kouvelou, Karaoli Dimitriou 5; mains €12-20; ☺lunch & dinner Tue-Sat) Under grapevines, dine quietly on *mezedhes* from all over Greece. Live *rembetika* on weekends.

Mandragoras   DELI €
(☎210 417 2961; Gounari 14; ☺7.30am-4pm Mon, Wed & Sat, to 8pm Tue, Thu & Fri) Fantastic array of fresh Greek products.

General Market   MARKET €
(Dimosthenous; ☺6am-4pm Mon-Fri)

Piraikon   SUPERMARKET €
(Makras Stoas 1; ☺8am-8pm Mon-Fri, to 4pm Sat)

GREECE PIRAEUS

Piraeus

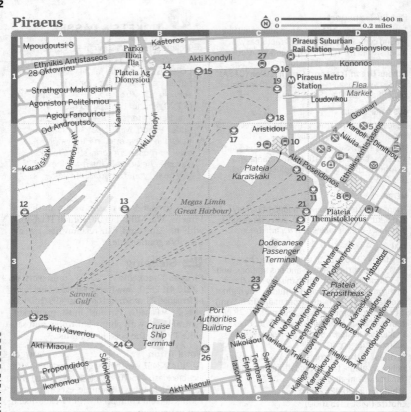

GREECE PIRAEUS

Piraeus

🛌 Sleeping

1 Hotel Triton	D2
2 Piraeus Theoxenia	D2

🍴 Eating

3 General Market	D2
4 Mandragoras	D2
5 Rakadiko	D2

🛍 Shopping

6 Piraikon	D2

ℹ Transport

7 Bus 040 to Syntagma	D2
8 Bus 049 to Omonia	D2
9 Bus Station	C2
10 Bus X96 to Airport	C2
11 Catamarans & Hydrofoils to the Peloponnese & Saronic Gulf	D2
12 Gate E1 (for the Dodecanese)	A2
13 Gate E2 (for Crete & Northeastern Aegean Islands)	B2
14 Gate E3	B1
15 Gate E4 (for Crete)	B1
16 Gate E5	C1
17 Gate E7	C2
18 Gate E7 (for the Cyclades)	C1
19 Gate E7 (for the Western & Central Cyclades)	C1
20 Gate E8 (for the Saronic Gulf Islands)	C2
21 Gate E9 (for the Cyclades)	C2
22 Gate E9 (for the Cyclades, Samos, Ikaria)	C3
23 Gate E10	C3
24 Gate E11	B4
25 Gate E12	A4
26 International Ferries	B4
27 Shuttle Bus to Gates E1 to E3	C1

ℹ Information

Internet Access Free wi-fi around the port.
Left Luggage At the metro station (€3 per 24 hours).

ℹ Getting There & Away

Boat

All ferry companies have online timetables and booths on the quays. EOT (p340) in Athens has a weekly schedule, or check www.openseas.gr. Schedules are reduced in April, May and October, and are radically cut in winter, especially to smaller islands. When buying tickets, confirm the departure point. For more details contact the **Piraeus Port Authority** (☎1441; www.olp.gr).

Hellenic Seaways (☎210 419 9000; www. hellenicseaways.gr; cnr Akti Kondyli & Elotikou) operates high-speed hydrofoils and catamarans to the Cyclades from early April to the end of October, and year-round services to the Saronic Gulf Islands. Other high-speed services include **Aegean Speedlines** (☎210 969 0950; www. aegeanspeedlines.gr).

Bus

The **X96** Piraeus–Athens Airport Express (€5) leaves from the southwestern corner of Plateia Karaïskaki. **Bus 040** goes to Syntagma in downtown Athens.

Metro

The fastest and most convenient link to Athens is the metro (€1.40, 40 minutes, every 10 minutes, 5am to midnight), near the ferries.

Train

Piraeus has a station for Athens' suburban rail.

ℹ Getting Around

Local bus 904 runs between the metro station and Zea Marina.

THE PELOPONNESE
ΠΕΛΟΠΟΝΝΗΣΟΣ

The Peloponnese encompasses a breathtaking array of landscapes, villages and ruins, where much of Greek history has played out. It's home to Olympia, birthplace of the Olympic Games; the ancient archaeological sites of magical Epidavros, Mycenae and Corinth; the fairy-tale Byzantine city of Mystras; and ancient Sparta.

Two of Greece's most memorable towns grace its shores: Venetian-style Nafplio and romantic Monemvasia. The isolated Mani Peninsula, best known for its wild landscape and people, bristles with fortified tower settlements and is blanketed with a colourful collection of spectacular wildflowers in spring.

Patra   Πάτρα
POP 168,900

Greece's third-largest city, Patra is the principal ferry port for the Ionian Islands and Italy. Despite its 3000-year history, ancient sites and vibrant social life, few travellers linger here longer than necessary to transfer to their ferries.

◉ Sights

FREE **Archaeological Museum of Patras**   MUSEUM
(☎261 042 0645; cnr Amerikis & Patras-Athens National Rd; ⊗8.30am-3pm Tue-Sun) The country's second-largest museum features objects from prehistoric to Roman times.

FREE **Kastro**   CASTLE
(⊗8.30am-3pm Tue-Sun) The Byzantine castle, originally Roman-built around AD 550, but rebuilt since, has excellent views to the Ionian Islands.

🎉 Festivals

Patras Carnival   MARDI GRAS
(www.carnivalpatras.gr) Wild weekend of costume parades and floats in spring.

🛏 Sleeping

Pension Nikos   HOTEL €
(☎261 062 3757; cnr Patreos 3 & Agiou Andreou 121; s/d/tr €30/40/55, s/d without bathroom €25/35; ❄) Marble stairs lead to spotlessly clean rooms smack in the city centre.

Olympic Star Hotel   BUSINESS HOTEL €€
(☎261 062 2939; www.olympicstar.gr; Agiou Nikolau 46; s/d/tr incl breakfast €55/70/90; ❄🐾) Business-style rooms feature hydro showers.

🍴 Eating & Drinking

Scores of stylish cafes and fast-food eateries lie between Kolokotroni and Ermou; drinking hot spots cluster on Agiou Nikolaou and near pedestrainised Riga Fereou. Pedestrianised Trion Navarhon is lined with tavernas.

Kouzina tis Kornilias   BISTRO €
(☎261 027 2987; Plateia Kapodistrio 4; mains €8-14; ⊗dinner, lunch Sat & Sun) Dig in to Turkish braised beef with aubergine puree (€14) and

other delicate specialities in this cool bistro tucked in the corner of a quiet square.

Mythos TAVERNA €
(☏261 032 9984; cnr Trion Navarhon 181 & Riga Fereou; mains €8-14; ☉dinner) Friendly waiters serve excellent home-cooked Greek classics in a chandelier-strewn town house.

Dia Discount Supermarket SUPERMARKET €
(Agiou Andreou 29; ☉Mon-Sat)

❶ Information

Tourist Office (☏261 046 1741; www.info centerpatras.gr; Agiou Andreou 12-14, btwn Zaimi & Aratou; ☉7.30am-9pm; ☏) Friendly multilingual staff with information on transport. A kiosk in central Plateia Trion Symahon operates from 7.30am to 9pm in summer.

Tourist Police (☏261 069 5191; Gounari 52; ☉7.30am-9pm)

❶ Getting There & Away
Boat

Schedules vary; the tourist office provides timetables. Ticket agencies line the waterfront.

Strintzis (☏261 024 0000; www.strintzis ferries.gr) sails to:
Ithaki (€18.60, four hours, one daily)
Kefallonia (€18.20, 2¾ hours, one to two daily)
Minoan Lines (☏261 042 6000; www.minoan. gr), **ANEK Lines** (☏261 022 6053; www.anek. gr) and others sail to:
Igoumenitsa (€25, seven hours, one daily)
Italy (from €65/70 to Venice/Ancona)

WORTH A TRIP

DIAKOFTO–KALAVRYTA RAILWAY
ΔΙΑΚΟΦΤΟ–ΚΑΛΑΒΡΥΤΑ

This spectacular rack-and-pinion **train** (☏26910 43206), built in the 1890s, crawls up the deep **Vouraïkos river gorge** from the small coastal town of Diakofto, one hour east of Patra, to the mountain resort of Kalavryta, 22km away. It's a thrilling one-hour journey, with dramatic scenery best viewed from any forward-facing seat. They book up, so buy tickets (€10, five daily) in advance at any train station or online at **Trainose** (www.trainose. gr). Visit www.odontotos.com for more information.

Bus

Services from **KTEL Achaia bus station** (☏261 062 3886; cnr Zaimi 2 & Othonos Amalias):
Athens (€20, three hours, half-hourly, via Corinth)
Ioannina (€24, 4½ hours, two daily)
Kalamata (€23, four hours, two daily)
Kalavryta (€7, two hours, two daily)
Pyrgos (for Olympia; €10, two hours, 10 daily)
Thessaloniki (€44, seven hours, four daily)

Buses to the Ionian Islands, via the port of Kyllini, leave from the **KTEL Lefkada & Zakynthos bus station** (☏261 022 0993; www.ktel -zakynthos.gr; Othonos Amalias 48) or nearby **KTEL Kefallonia bus station** (☏261 027 4938; Othonos Amalias 58).

Train

At the time of research, train lines from **Patra train station** (☏261 063 9108; Othonos Amalias 27) were under construction and may reopen in 2013. Replacement buses serve Athens' Kiato station (connects to suburban rail), Diakofto, Kalamata and Pyrgos (for Olympia).

Corinth Κόρινθος
POP 26,400

Drab, modern Corinth (ko-rin-thoss), 6km west of the Corinth Canal, is an uninspiring town; it's better to stay in the village near Ancient Corinth if visiting the ruins.

🛏 Sleeping

Hotel Ephira HOTEL €
(☏27410 22434; www.ephirahotel.gr; Ethnikis Andistasis 52; d €50; ❄☀☏) Corinth's smartest hotel is comfortably furnished, but hides a few blemishes. Suites are a notch more upmarket.

Blue Dolphin Camping CAMPGROUND €
(☏27410 25766; www.camping-blue-dolphin.gr; campsites per tent/adult €5/6.50; ☉Apr-Oct; ☀) Has a beach, decent facilities and offers tours. It's at Lecheon, about 4km west of Corinth, just after the ancient Corinth turnoff. Offers pick-up from train or bus stations.

❶ Getting There & Away

BUS Buses to Athens (€8, 1½ hours, halfhourly) and Ancient Corinth (€1.70, 20 minutes, hourly) leave from the **KTEL Korinthos bus station** (☏27410 75425; www.ktel-korinthias. gr; Dimocratias 4). Buses to the rest of the Peloponnese leave from the **Corinth Isthmus (Peloponnese) KTEL bus station** (☏27410 73987, 27410 83000) on the Peloponnese side of the Corinth Canal. All buses from Athens to the Peloponnese stop here. To get there from Corinth, catch one of the frequent local buses to Loutraki.

TRAIN At the time of research, train lines to Patra and Athens were closed for construction; they may reopen in 2013. The *proastiako* suburban train at nearby Kiato goes to Athens airport (€12, one hour, eight daily). Buses to/from the *proastiako* station go to/from Corinth's Plateia Kentriki (€1.50, 20 minutes).

Ancient Corinth & Acrocorinth
Αρχαία Κόρινθος & Ακροκόρινθος

Seven kilometres southwest of Corinth's modern city, the ruins of **Ancient Corinth** (☏27410 31207; site & museum €6; ☺8.30am-8pm Apr-Oct, to 3pm Nov-Mar) and its lovely museum lie at the edge of a small village in the midst of fields sweeping to the sea. It was one of ancient Greece's wealthiest cities, but earthquakes and invasions have left only one Greek monument remaining: the imposing **Temple of Apollo**; the rest of the ruins are Roman. **Acrocorinth** (☺8am-3pm), the remains of a citadel built on a massive outcrop of limestone, looms majestically over the site.

The great-value digs at **Tasos Taverna & Rooms** (☏27410 31225; s/d/tr €30/45/55; ✱), 200m from the museum, are spotlessly clean and above an excellent eatery serving Greek classics.

Nafplio
Ναύπλιο
POP 14,000

Elegant Venetian houses and neoclassical mansions dripping with crimson bougainvillea cascade down Nafplio's hillside to the azure sea. Vibrant cafes, shops and restaurants fill winding pedestrian streets. Crenulated Palamidi Fortress perches above it all. What's not to love?

◉ Sights

Palamidi Fortress FORTRESS
(☏27520 28036; admission €4; ☺8am-7.30pm May–mid-Oct, to 4.30pm mid-Oct–Apr) Enjoy spectacular views of the town and surrounding coast from the magnificent hilltop fortress built by the Venetians between 1711 and 1714.

WORTH A TRIP

THE WINE ROAD

The Nemea region, in the rolling hills southwest of Corinth, is one of Greece's premier wine-producing areas, famous for its full-bodied reds from the local *agiorgitiko* grape and a white from *roditis* grapes. Some wineries offer tastings:

Skouras (☏27510 23688; www.skouras wines.com) Northwest of Argos.

Ktima (☏27460 24190; www.palivos.gr; Ancient Nemea) Palivou

Lafkioti (☏27460 31000; www.lafkiotis. gr; Ancient Kleonai) Located 3km east of Ancient Nemea.

Gaia Wines (☏27460 22057; www.gaia -wines.gr; Koutsi) North of Nemea.

Archaeological Museum MUSEUM
(☏27520 27502; Plateia Syntagmatos; admission €3; ☺noon-4pm Mon, 9am-4pm Tue-Sun) Fine exhibits include fire middens from 32,000 BC and bronze armour from near Mycenae (12th to 13th centuries BC).

Peloponnese Folklore Foundation Museum MUSEUM
(☏27520 28379; www.pli.gr; Vas Alexandrou 1; admission €2; ☺9am-2.30pm) One of Greece's best small museums, with displays of vibrant regional costumes and rotating exhibitions.

🛏 Sleeping

Exquisite hotels abound in Nafplio. The Old Town is *the* place to stay, but it has few budget options. Friday to Sunday the town fills and prices rise; book ahead. Cheaper spots dot the road to Argos and Tolo.

Amfitriti Pension PENSION €€
(☏27520 96250; www.amfitriti-pension.gr; Kapodistriou 24; d incl breakfast from €60; ✱🐾) Quaint antiques fill these intimate rooms in a house in the Old Town. You can also enjoy stellar views at its nearby sister hotel, **Amfitriti Belvedere**, which is chock-full of brightly coloured tapestries and emits a feeling of cheery serenity.

Pension Marianna PENSION €€
(☏27520 24256; www.pensionmarianna.gr; Potamianou 9; s/d/tr incl breakfast €50/65/85;

P ✳ 🛜) Welcoming owners epitomise Greek *filoxenia* (hospitality) and serve delicious organic breakfasts. Up a steep set of stairs, and tucked under the fortress walls, a dizzying array of rooms intermix with sea-view terraces.

Adiandi BOUTIQUE HOTEL €€
(✆27520 22073; www.hotel-adiandi.com; Othonos 31; r incl breakfast €75-120; ✳🛜) Rooms in this fun and upmarket place are quirkily decorated with artistic bedheads fashioned from doors and contemporary decor. Fantastic farm-fresh breakfasts.

Hotel Byron PENSION €
(✆27520 22351; www.byronhotel.gr; Platonos 2; d incl breakfast from €45; ✳) Tucked into two fine Venetian buildings, iron bedsteads, rich carpets and period furniture fill immaculate rooms.

Hotel Grande Bretagne LUXURY HOTEL €€
(✆27520 96200; www.grandebretagne.com.gr; Plateia Filellinon; d incl breakfast from €115; ✳🛜) In the heart of Nafplio's cafe action and overlooking the sea, this splendidly restored hotel with high ceilings, antiques and chandeliers radiates plush opulence.

Kapodistrias PENSION €
(✆27520 29366; www.hotelkapodistrias.gr; Kokinou 20; d incl breakfast from €50; ☺Mar–mid-Oct; ✳🛜) Beautiful rooms, many with elegant canopy beds, come with sea or old-town views.

Pension Dimitris Bekas PENSION €
(✆27520 24594; Efthimiopoulou 26; s/d/tr €25/30/45) The only good, central budget option. Clean, homey rooms (some with shared bath) have a top-value location on the slopes of the Akronafplia, and the owner has a killer baseball cap collection.

✕ Eating

Nafplio's Old Town streets are loaded with standard tavernas; those on Staïkopoulou or overlooking the port on Bouboulinas get jam-packed on weekends. Vasilissis Olgas is better, with tavernas like **Aeolos** (✆27520 26828; Vasilissis Olgas 30; mains €5-13) and **To Omorfo Tavernaki** (✆27520 25944; Vasilissis Olgas 1; mains €7-14).

TOP CHOICE **Alaloum** GREEK €€
(✆27520 29883; Papanikolaou 10; mains €10-18) Heaping creative interpretations of traditional dishes like rooster, veal or homemade

pasta can be shared. Everything is made from scratch and salads are a meal in their own right.

TOP CHOICE **Antica Gelateria di Roma** ICE CREAM €
(✆27520 23520; cnr Farmakopoulou & Komninou) The best (yes, best) traditional gelati outside Italy.

To Kentrikon CAFE €
(✆27520 29933; Plateia Syntagmatos; mains €4-10) Relax under the shady trees on this pretty square during extensive breakfasts. Best coffees and teas.

Arapakos SEAFOOD €€
(✆27520 27675; www.arapakos.gr; Bouboulinas 81; mains €10-15) The best of the boardwalk catch for fresh seafood.

🛍 Shopping

Nafplio shopping is a delight, with jewellery workshops like **Metallagi** (✆27520 21267; Sofroni 3), boutiques and wonderful regional products, such as worry beads, honey, wine and handicrafts.

Odyssey BOOKS
(✆27520 23430; Plateia Syntagmatos) International papers, magazines and novels.

🍷 Drinking & Entertainment

Wander the Old Town to cafe- and bar-hop the lively scene. You could start at newcomer **O Mavros Gatos** (Sofroni 1), or creative stalwarts near Plateia Syntagmatos like **Cafe Rosso** (Komninou 5), where every table is different.

TOP CHOICE **Fougaro** CULTURAL CENTRE
(✆27520 96005; www.fougaro.gr; Asklipiou 98) Nafplio's marquee arts and cultural centre opened with fanfare in 2012 in an impeccably renovated factory that now houses an art shop, library, cafe and exhibition spaces, and holds performing arts programs.

ℹ Information

Emergency
Tourist Police (✆27520 28131; Kountouridou 16)

Tourist Information
Staikos Tours (✆27520 27950; Bouboulinas 50) Helpful; Avis rental cars; full travel services like occasional day-long boat trips (www.pegasus-cruises.gr) to Spetses, Hydra and Monemvasia.

GORGE YOURSELF

The picturesque prefecture of **Arkadia** occupies much of the central Peloponnese and is synonymous with grassy meadows, forested mountains and gurgling streams. West of Tripoli, a tangle of medieval villages and narrow winding roads weave into valleys of dense vegetation beneath the **Menalon Mountains**. These areas are best accessed by car.

Wonderful walks along the **Lousios Gorge** leave from **Dimitsana** (population 230), a delightful medieval village built amphitheatrically on two hills at the beginning of the gorge. It sits 11km north of **Stemnitsa** (population 412), another gorge gateway and a striking village of stone houses and Byzantine churches.

Trekking Hellas (☑697 445 9753, 27910 25978; www.trekkinghellas.gr) offers rafting (from €50) on the nearby Lousios and Alfios Rivers, gorge hikes (from €20) and multi-day tours (€275).

Leonidio (population 3224), 90km east of Sparta, is dramatically set at the mouth of the **Badron Gorge**. Some older residents still speak Tsakonika, a distinctive dialect from the time of ancient Sparta.

ⓘ Getting There & Away

KTEL Argolis Bus Station (☑27520 27323; www.ktel-argolidas.gr; Syngrou 8) has the following services:

Argos (for Peloponnese connections; €1.60, 30 minutes, half-hourly)

Athens (via Corinth; €13.10, 2½ hours, hourly)

Epidavros (€2.90, 45 minutes, two Mon-Sat)

Mycenae (€2.90, one hour, three daily)

Epidavros   Επίδαυρος

Spectacular World Heritage–listed **Epidavros** (☑27530 22009; admission €6; ☺8am-6pm Apr-Oct, to 5pm Nov-Mar) was the sanctuary of Asclepius, god of medicine. Amid pine-covered hills, the magnificent **theatre** is still a venue during the Hellenic Festival, but don't miss the peaceful **Sanctuary of Asclepius**, an ancient spa and healing centre.

Go as a day trip from Nafplio (€2.90, 45 minutes, two daily buses Monday to Saturday).

For an early-morning visit to the site, stay at the **Hotel Avaton** (☑27530 22178; s/d €40/50; P❋), 1km away, at the junction of the road to Kranidi.

Mycenae   Μυκήνες

Although settled as early as the 6th millennium BC, **Ancient Mycenae** (☑27510 76585; admission €8; ☺8am-7pm Mon-Sat, to 4pm Sun Jun-Sep, 8am-6pm Mon-Sat, to 4pm Sun Oct-May)

, pronounced mih-*kee*-nes, was at its most powerful from 1600 to 1200 BC. Mycenae's grand entrance, the **Lion Gate**, is Europe's oldest monumental sculpture. Homer accurately described Mycenae as being 'rich in gold': excavations of **Grave Circle A** by Heinrich Schliemann in the 1870s uncovered magnificent gold treasures, such as the Mask of Agamemnon, now on display at Athens' National Archaeological Museum.

Most people visit on day trips from Nafplio, but the bare-bones **Belle Helene Hotel** (☑27510 76225; Christou Tsounta; d without bathroom, incl breakfast €35) is where Schliemann lived during excavations.

Three buses go daily to Mycenae from Argos (€1.60, 30 minutes) and Nafplio (€2.90, one hour).

Sparta   Σπάρτη

POP 14,200

Cheerful, unpretentious modern Sparta (*spar*-tee) is at odds with its ancient Spartan image of discipline and deprivation. Although there's little to see, the town makes a convenient base from which to visit Mystras.

Modern **Hotel Lakonia** (☑27310 28951; www.lakoniahotel.gr; Palaeologou 89; s/d from €40/55; ❋☎) maintains comfy, welcoming rooms with spotless bathrooms. **Hotel Maniatis** (☑27310 22665; www.maniatishotel.gr; Paleologou 72-76; s/d incl breakfast €80/100; ❋☎) offers the sleekest digs in town.

The sweet smell of spices inundates **Restaurant Elysse** (☑27310 29896; Palaeologou 113; mains €6-12), which is run by a friendly

Greek-Canadian family. Locals chill out next door at **Café Ouzeri** (mains €4-6).

Sparta's **KTEL Lakonia bus station** (☑27310 26441; cnr Lykourgou & Thivronos), on the east edge of town, services Athens (€20, 3½ hours, eight daily) via Corinth, Gythio (€4.50, one hour, five daily), Monemvasia (€11, two hours, three daily) and Mystras (€2, 30 minutes, 11 daily).

Mystras · Μυστράς

Magical **Mystras** (☑27310 83377; adult/child €5/3; ⊙8.30am-5.30pm Mon-Sat, to 3pm Sun, sometimes longer in summer) was once the effective capital of the Byzantine Empire. Ruins of palaces, monasteries and churches, most of them dating from between 1271 and 1460, nestle at the base of the Taÿgetos Mountains, and are surrounded by verdant olive and orange groves.

Allow half a day to explore the site. While only 7km from Sparta, staying in the village nearby allows you to get there early before it heats up. Enjoy exquisite views and a beautiful swimming pool at **Hotel Byzantion** (☑27310 83309; www.byzantionhotel.gr; s/d/tr €50/70/80; P❄@☎). Have a decadent escape at **Hotel Pyrgos Mystra** (☑27310 20870; www.pyrgosmystra.com; Manousaki 3; d incl breakfast €200; ❄), with its lovingly appointed rooms in a restored mansion.

Camp at **Castle View** (☑27310 83303; www.castleview.gr; campsites per adult/tent/car €6/4/4, 2-person bungalow €30; ⊙Apr-Oct; ☎), about 1km before Mystras village and set in olive trees, or **Camping Paleologio Mystras** (☑27310 22724; campsites per adult/tent/car €7/4/4; ⊙year-round; ☎), 2km west of Sparta and approximately 4km from Mystras. Buses will stop outside either if you ask.

Several tavernas serve traditional Greek meals.

Monemvasia & Gefyra
Μονεμβάσια & Γέφυρα
POP 1320

Slip out along a narrow causeway, up around the edge of a towering rock rising dramatically from the sea and arrive at the exquisite walled village of Monemvasia. Enter the *kastro* (castle), which was separated from mainland Gefyra by an earthquake in AD 375, through a narrow tunnel on foot, and emerge into a stunning (carless) warren of cobblestone streets and stone houses. Beat the throngs of day trippers by staying over.

Signposted steps lead up to the ruins of a **fortress** built by the Venetians in the 16th century, and the Byzantine **Church of Agia Sophia**, perched precariously on the edge of the cliff. Views are spectacular, and wildflowers grow shoulder-high in spring.

🛏 Sleeping & Eating

Staying in a hotel in the *kastro* could be one of the most romantic things you ever do (ask for discounts in low season), but if you're on a tight budget stay in Gefyra.

Three traditional Greek tavernas sit cheek to cheek in Monemvasia's old town: **Matoula** (☑27320 61660; mains €8-13), **Marianthi** (☑27320 61371; mains €8-13) and **To Kanoni** (☑27320 61387; mains €8-13). You can't really go wrong with any of them.

TOP CHOICE **Hotel Malvasia**   HISTORIC HOTEL €€
(☑27320 61160; malvasia@otenet.gr; d/apt from €60/100; ❄) A variety of cosy, traditionally decorated rooms and apartments (most with sea views) are scattered around the Old Town. Another branch, known as the **Malvasia Hotel** (http://malvasia-hotel.gr), has higher-end rooms.

Hotel Aktaion   HOTEL €
(☑27320 61234; www.aktaion-monemvasia.gr; s/d €40/50) This clean, sunny hotel, on the Gefyra end of the causeway, has balconies with views of the sea and 'the rock'.

Taverna O Botsalo   TAVERNA €
(☑27320 61486; mains €4-9) Just down the wharf on the mainland; serves savoury meals.

❶ Getting There & Away

Buses stop in Gefyra at the friendly **Malvasia Travel** (☑27320 61752), where you can buy tickets. Four daily buses travel to Athens (€32, six hours) via Corinth and Sparta (€11, 2½ hours).

Gythio · Γύθειο
POP 4490

Gythio (*yee*-thih-o) was once the port of ancient Sparta. Now it's an earthy fishing town and gateway to the rugged, much more beautiful Mani Peninsula.

Peaceful **Marathonisi islet**, linked to the mainland by a causeway, is said to be ancient Cranae, where Paris (prince of Troy) and Helen (the wife of Menelaus of Sparta) consummated the love affair that sparked the Trojan War. You'll find the tiny **Museum of Mani History** (☑27330 24484; admission €2; ⊙8am-2.30pm) here in an 18th-century tower.

🛏 Sleeping & Eating

The waterfront is packed with fish taverna, like **I Gonia** (Vassilis Pavlou; mains €6-15), and cafes.

Hotel La Boheme   BOUTIQUE HOTEL €
(☑27330 21992; www.labohemehotel.gr; Tzani Tzanitaki; s/d incl breakfast €45/60; ₱❋@) Sea views, upmarket rooms and a zippy downstairs bar-restaurant draw crowds.

Camping Meltemi   CAMPGROUND €
(☑27330 23260; www.campingmeltemi.gr; campsites per tent/adult €5.50/6, bungalows €30-60; ⊙Apr-Oct; ❋≋) Birds chirp in these idyllic silver olive groves, 3km south of Gythio; private beach, swimming pool and summer beauty contests! The Areopoli bus stops here.

Xenia Karlaftis Rooms to Rent   PENSION €
(☑27330 22719; opp Marathonisi islet; s/d €25/40) Friendly owner Voula keeps clean (if worn) rooms and offers kitchen access. Several nearby places are of similar quality if you can't get in here.

❶ Getting There & Away

BUS The **KTEL Lakonia bus station** (☑27330 22228; http://ktel-lakonias.gr; cnr Vasileos Georgios & Evrikleos) is on the square near Hotel Aktion.

Areopoli (€2.80, 30 minutes, four daily)
Athens (€24, 4½ hours, six daily)
Geroliminas (€6, 1¼ hours, one daily)
Sparta (€4.50, one hour, four daily)

CAR & BOAT LANE Lines (www.lane.gr) has a weekly ferry to Crete (€23, seven hours) via Kythira (€11, 2½ hours) and Antikythira. Schedules change; check with **Rozakis Travel** (☑27330 22207; rosakigy@otenet.gr; Pavlou 5) which also rents cars.

The Mani   Η Μάνη

The exquisite Mani completely lives up to its reputation for rugged beauty, with abundant wildflowers in spring and dramatic juxtapositions of sea and the Taÿgetos Mountains (threaded with wonderful walking trails). The Mani occupies the central peninsula of the southern Peloponnese and is divided into two regions: the arid Lakonian (inner) Mani in the south and the verdant Messinian (outer) Mani in the northwest near Kalamata. Explore the winding roads by car.

LAKONIAN MANI

For centuries the Maniots were a law unto themselves, renowned for their fierce independence and their spectacularly murderous internal feuds. To this day, bizarre tower settlements built as refuges during clan wars dot the rocky slopes of Lakonian Mani.

Areopoli (population 775), 30km southwest of Gythio and named after Ares, the god of war, is a warren of cobblestone and ancient towers. Stay in a tastefully decorated 200-year-old tower house at **Londas Pension** (☑27330 51360; www.londas.com; near Church of Taxiarhes; s/d/tr incl breakfast €65/75/103, s/d without bathroom €56/65). For a cushy boutique hotel experience, book in at **Areos Polis** (☑27330 51028; www.areospolis.gr; s/d/tr incl breakfast from €40/65/80; ❋❄).

Step behind the counter to choose from the scrumptious specials at **Nicola's Corner Taverna** (☑27330 51366; Plateia Athanaton; mains €8-10), on the central square.

The **bus station** (☑27330 51229) services Athens (€28, four daily) via Gythio (€2.80, 30 minutes), Itilo (for the Messinian Mani, €2, 20 minutes, two daily Monday to Saturday), Gerolimenas (€3.40, 45 minutes, three daily) and the Diros Caves (€1.60, 15 minutes, one daily).

Eleven kilometres south, the extensive, though touristy **Diros Caves** (☑27330 52222; adult/child €12/7; ⊙8.30am-5.30pm Jun-Sep, to 3pm Oct-May) contain a subterranean river. In neighbouring **Pyrgos Dirou**, stay over at chic **Vlyhada** (☑27330 52469; www.vlyhada.gr; d incl breakfast €70; ₱❋).

Gerolimenas, a tranquil fishing village on a sheltered bay 20km further south, is home to the exceedingly popular boutique establishment **Kyrimai Hotel** (☑27330 54288; www.kyrimai.gr; d incl breakfast from €110; ₱❋≋). Groovy music and mood lighting fill this exquisitely renovated castle with a seaside swimming pool and top-notch restaurant.

MESSINIAN MANI

Stone hamlets dot aquamarine swimming coves. Silver olive groves climb the foothills to the snow-capped Taÿgetos Mountains. Explore the splendid meandering roads and hiking trails from Itilo to Kalamata.

GREECE THE MANI

The people of the enchanting seaside village of **Kardamyli**, 37km south of Kalamata, know how good they've got it. Sir Patrick Leigh Fermor famously wrote about his rambles here in *Mani: Travels in the Southern Peloponnese*. Trekkers come for the magnificent **Vyros Gorge**. Walks are well organised and colour-coded.

Kardamyli has a good choice of small hotels and private rooms for all budgets; book ahead for summer.

Notos Hotel (☑27210 73730; www.notos hotel.gr; studio €110, apt €135-160; P✳) is really a boutique hamlet of individual stone houses with fully equipped kitchens, verandas and views overlooking the village, the mountains and the sea.

Olympia Koumounakou Rooms (☑27210 73623; s/d €30/40) is basic but clean and popular with backpackers, who like the communal kitchen and courtyard.

Beautiful **Elies** (☑27210 73140; mains €6-12; ☺lunch), right by the beach 1km north of town, is worth a lunchtime stop.

Kardamyli is on the main bus route from Itilo to Kalamata (€4, one hour) and two to four buses stop daily at the central square.

Olympia Ολυμπία

POP 1000

Tucked alongside the Kladeos River, in fertile delta country, the modern town of Olympia supports the extensive ruins of the same name. The first Olympics were staged here in 776 BC, and every four years thereafter until AD 394, when Emperor Theodosius I banned them. During the competition the city-states were bound by a sacred truce to stop fighting and take part in athletic events and cultural exhibitions.

Ancient Olympia (☑26240 22517; adult/child €6/3, site & museum €9/5; ☺8am-8pm Apr-Oct, 8.30am-3pm Nov-Mar) is dominated by the immense ruined **Temple of Zeus**, to whom the games were dedicated. Don't miss the statue of **Hermes of Praxiteles**, at the exceptional **Archaeological Museum** (adult/child €6/3; ☺1.30-8pm Mon, 8am-8pm Tue-Sun Apr-Oct, to 3pm Nov-Mar).

Sparkling-clean **Pension Posidon** (☑26240 22567; www.pensionposidon.gr; Stefanopoulou 9; s/d/tr €35/40/50; ✳) and quiet, spacious **Hotel Pelops** (☑26240 22543; www.hotelpelops.gr; Varela 2; s/d/tr incl breakfast €40/50/70; ☺✳@☞) offer the best value in the centre. Family-run **Best Western Europa** (☑26240 22650; www.hoteleuropa.gr; Drouva 1; s/d €80/100; P✳@☞☀) perches on a hill above town and has gorgeous sweeping vistas from room balconies and the wonderful swimming pool.

Pitch your tent in the leafy grove at **Camping Diana** (☑26240 22314; www.camping-diana.gr; campsites per tent/adult €6/8; ☀), 250m west of town.

There are no outstanding favourites among Olympia's ho-hum restaurants. Take your pick, or head to outer villages. **O Thea** (☑26240 23264; mains €6-11; ☺dinner year-round, lunch May-Oct), 1.5km north in Floka, offers hearty taverna fare and terrace views. Call to ensure it's open outside high season.

Olympia Municipal Tourist Office (☑26240 22262; Praxitelous Kondyli; ☺9am-3pm Mon-Fri May-Sep) has transport schedules.

Catch buses at the stop on the north end of town. Northbound buses go via Pyrgos (€2, 30 minutes), where you connect to buses for Athens, Corinth and Patra. Two buses go east from Olympia to Tripoli (€12, 2½ hours) – you must reserve ahead at **KTEL Pyrgos** (☑26210 20600; www.ktelileias. gr). Local trains run daily to Pyrgos (€1, 30 minutes).

CENTRAL GREECE
ΚΕΝΤΡΙΚΗ ΕΛΛΑΔΑ

This dramatic landscape of deep gorges, rugged mountains and fertile valleys is home to the magical stone pinnacle-topping monasteries of Meteora and the iconic ruins of ancient Delphi, where Alexander the Great sought advice from the Delphic oracle. Established in 1938, **Parnassos National Park** (www.routes.gr), to the north of Delphi, attracts naturalists, hikers (it's part of the E4 European long-distance path) and skiers.

Delphi Δελφοί

POP 2800

Modern Delphi and its adjoining ruins hang stunningly on the slopes of Mt Parnassos overlooking the shimmering Gulf of Corinth.

According to mythology, Zeus released two eagles at opposite ends of the world and they met here, thus making Delphi the centre of the world. By the 6th century BC, **Ancient Delphi** (☑22650 82312; www.culture. gr; site or museum €6, combined adult/concession

€9/5; ⊙8am-3pm; sometimes varies) had become the Sanctuary of Apollo. Thousands of pilgrims flocked here to consult the middle-aged female oracle who sat at the mouth of a fume-emitting chasm. After sacrificing a sheep or goat, pilgrims would ask a question, and a priest would translate the oracle's response into verse. Wars, voyages and business transactions were undertaken on the strength of these prophecies. From the entrance, take the **Sacred Way** up to the **Temple of Apollo**, where the oracle sat. From here the path continues to the well-preserved **theatre** and **stadium**.

Opposite the main site and down the hill some 100m, don't miss the **Sanctuary of Athena** and the much-photographed **Tholos**, a 4th-century-BC columned rotunda of Pentelic marble.

In the town centre, the welcoming **Hotel Hermes** (☑22650 82318; www.hermeshotel.com.gr; Vasileon Pavlou & Friderikis 27; s/d incl breakfast €40/50; ❄) has spacious rooms sporting balconies with excellent valley views. **Hotel Appolonia** (☑22650 82919; www.hotelapollonia.gr; Ifeigenias 37-39; s/d/tr incl breakfast €60/80/100; ❄@🗢) is a bit more upmarket.

Apollon Camping (☑22650 82762; www.apolloncamping.gr; campsites per person/tent €8.50/4; P@🗢🏊), 2km west of town, has great facilities, including restaurant, pool and minimarket.

Specialities at **Taverna Vakhos** (☑22650 83186; Apollonos 31; mains €6-17) include stuffed zucchini flowers and rabbit stew. Locals pack **Taverna Gargadouas** (☑22650 82488; Vasileon Pavlou & Friderikis; mains €6-10) for grilled meats and slow-roasted lamb.

The **bus station** (☑22660 82317), post office and banks are all on modern Delphi's main street, Vasileon Pavlou. Six buses a day go to Athens (€15.50, three hours). Take a bus to Lamia (€9.20, two hours, two daily) or Trikala (€14, 4½ hours, two daily) to transfer for Meteora.

Meteora   Μετέωρα

Meteora (meh-*teh*-o-rah) should be a certified Wonder of the World with its magnificent late-14th-century monasteries perched dramatically atop enormous rocky pinnacles. Try not to miss it. The tranquil village of **Kastraki**, 2km from Kalambaka, is the best base for visiting.

While there were once monasteries on all 24 pinnacles, only six are still occupied:

WORTH A TRIP

PELION PENINSULA

The **Pelion Peninsula**, a dramatic mountain range whose highest peak is Pourianos Stavros (1624m), was inhabited, according to mythology, by half-man and half-horse *kentavri* (centaurs). Today it is a verdant destination for trekkers. The largely inaccessible eastern flank consists of high cliffs that plunge into the sea. The gentler western flank coils round the Pagasitikos Gulf.

Megalou Meteorou (Grand Meteoron; ☑24320 22278; ⊙9am-5pm Wed-Mon Apr-Oct, to 4pm Thu-Mon Nov-Mar), **Varlaam** (☑24320 22277; ⊙9am-4pm Sat-Thu Apr-Oct, to 3pm Sat-Wed Nov-Mar), **Agiou Stefanou** (☑24320 22279; ⊙9am-1.30pm & 3.30-5.30pm Tue-Sun Apr-Oct, 9.30am-1pm & 3-5pm Nov-Mar), **Agias Triados** (Holy Trinity; ☑24320 22220; ⊙9am-5pm Fri-Wed Apr-Oct, 10am-3pm Nov-Mar), **Agiou Nikolaou Anapafsa** (☑24320 22375; ⊙9am-3.30pm Sat-Thu) and **Agias Varvaras Rousanou** (⊙9am-6pm Thu-Tue Apr-Oct, to 4pm Nov-Mar). Admission is €2 for each monastery and strict dress codes apply (no bare shoulders or knees and women must wear skirts; borrow a long skirt at the door if you don't have one). Walk the footpaths between monasteries, drive the back asphalt road, or take the bus (€1.20, 20 minutes) that departs from Kalambaka and Kastraki at 9am, and returns at 1pm.

Meteora's stunning rocks are also a climbing paradise. Licensed mountain guide **Lazaros Botelis** (☑694 804 3655, 24320 79165; meteora.guide@gmail.gr; Kastraki) and mountaineering instructor **Kostas Liolos** (☑69725 67582; ksds_liolios@yahoo.com; Kalambaka) show the way.

🛏 Sleeping & Eating

CHOICE **Doupiani House**   PENSION €
(☑24320 75326; www.doupianihouse.com; s/d/tr incl breakfast €40/50/60; P❄@🗢) Gregarious hosts Thanassis and Toula Nakis offer this comfy home from which to explore or simply enjoy the panoramic views. Request a balcony room.

Vrachos Camping   CAMPGROUND €
(☑24320 22293; www.campingmeteora.gr; campsites per tent/adult €9/free; 🏊) Great views, excellent facilities and a good taverna; a short stroll from Kastraki.

GREECE METEORA

Taverna Paradisos TAVERNA €
(☏24320 22723; mains €6.50-9) Look for outstanding traditional meals with spectacular views.

Taverna Gardenia TAVERNA, PENSION €
(☏24320 22504; Kastrakiou St; mains €6-9; s/d/tr incl breakfast €35/45/55) Freshest Greek food served with aplomb and more splendid views. The owners also have good-value, spacious rooms.

❶ Getting There & Around

Local buses shuttle between Kalambaka and Kastraki (€1.90). Hourly buses go from Kalambaka's **KTEL bus station** (☏24320 22432; Ikonomou) to the transport hub of Trikala (€2, 30 minutes), from where buses go to Ioannina (€13.10, three hours, two daily) and Athens (€27, 4½ hours, seven daily).

From Kalambaka **train station** (☏24320 22451), trains run to Athens (regular/IC €15/25, 5½/4½ hours, both twice daily) and Thessaloniki (€13, four hours, three daily).

NORTHERN GREECE
ΒΟΡΕΙΑ ΕΛΛΑΔΑ

Northern Greece is graced with magnificent mountains, thick forests, tranquil lakes and archaeological sites. It's easy to get off the beaten track and experience aspects of Greece noticeably different to other mainland areas and the islands.

Thessaloniki
Θεσσαλονίκη

POP 342,200

Dodge cherry sellers in the street, smell spices in the air and enjoy waterfront breezes in Thessaloniki (thess-ah-lo-*nee*-kih), also known as Salonica. The second city of Byzantium and of modern Greece boasts countless Byzantine churches, a smattering of Roman ruins, engaging museums, shopping to rival Athens, fine restaurants and a lively cafe scene and nightlife.

◉ Sights & Activites

Check out the seafront **White Tower** (Lefkos Pyrgos; ☏231 026 7832; www.lpth.gr; ⊙8.30am-3pm Tue-Sun) and wander *hammams* (Turkish baths), Ottoman and Roman sites, and

churches such as the enormous, 5th-century **Church of Agios Dimitrios** (☏231 027 0008; Agiou Dimitriou 97; ⊙8am-10pm).

The award-winning **Museum of Byzantine Culture** (☏231 330 6400; www.mbp. gr; Leoforos Stratou 2; admission €4; ⊙9am-4pm) beautifully displays splendid sculptures, mosaics, icons and other intriguing artefacts. The **Archaeological Museum** (☏231 083 0538; www.amth.gr; Manoli Andronikou 6; admission €6; ⊙10am-6pm Mon, 9am-6pm Tue-Sat, 9am-4pm Sun) showcases prehistoric, ancient Macedonian and Hellenistic finds.

The compelling **Thessaloniki Centre of Contemporary Art** (☏231 059 3270; www. cact.gr; Warehouse B1; ⊙10am-6pm Tue-Sat, 11am-3pm Sun) and hip **Thessaloniki Museum of Photography** (☏231 056 6716; www.thmphoto. gr; Warehouse A, Thessaloniki Port; admission €2; ⊙11am-7pm Tue-Sun), beside the port, are worth an hour.

Wonderfully seen on foot, Thessaloniki can also be zigzagged by **bus tour** (ticket €3; ⊙hourly 8am-9pm Jun-Sep, 9am-4pm Oct-May) leaving from the White Tower. Get information at the tourist office.

🛏 Sleeping

Steep discounts abound during summer; prices rise during conventions (listed at www.helexpo.gr).

Electra Palace Hotel LUXURY HOTEL €€€
(☏231 029 4000; www.electrahotels.gr; Plateia Aristotelous 9; d from €150; ❈@⊛☀) Dive into five-star seafront pampering: impeccable service, plush rooms, a rooftop bar, indoor and outdoor swimming pools and a *hammam*.

Rent Rooms Thessaloniki HOSTEL €
(☏231 020 4080; www.rentrooms-thessaloniki. com; Konstantinou Melenikou 9, near Kamara; dm/s/d/tr/q incl breakfast €19/38/49/67/82; ❈☀) Cheery, clean and modern, with a back-garden cafe looking onto the Rotunda. Communal breakfast-cafe nook and cheap bike hire add to the appeal. Some dorms/rooms have minikitchens, and all have bathrooms. Book ahead.

Hotel Orestias Kastorias HOTEL €
(☏231 027 6517; www.okhotel.gr; Agnostou Stratiotou 14; s/d/tr €37/46/58; ❈@☀) A friendly favourite with cosy, clean rooms, renovated in 2011.

Thessaloniki

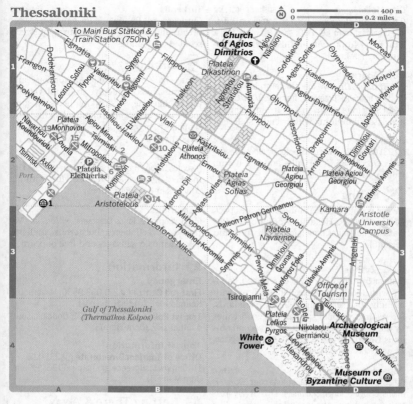

GREECE THESSALONIKI

Thessaloniki

◎ Top Sights
Archaeological Museum	D4
Church of Agios Dimitrios	C1
Museum of Byzantine Culture	D4
White Tower	C4

◎ Sights
1	Thessaloniki Centre of Contemporary Art	A2

⊟ Sleeping
2	City Hotel	B2
3	Electra Palace Hotel	B2
4	Hotel Orestias Kastorias	C1
5	Hotel Pella	B1
6	Hotel Tourist	B2
7	Rent Rooms Thessaloniki	D2

⊗ Eating
8	Dore Zythos	C4
9	Kitchen Bar	A2
10	Modiano Market	B2
11	Myrsini	C4
12	O Arhontis	B2
13	Paparouna	A2
14	Turkenlis	B2
15	Zythos	A2

⊝ Drinking
16	Gambrinus	B1
17	Spiti Mou	A1

City Hotel
BUSINESS HOTEL €€

(☑2310269421; www.cityhotel.gr; Komninon 11; d/tr incl breakfast from €90/110; ❄@☎) Ask for a light-filled front room in this excellently located stylish hotel.

Hotel Tourist
BUSINESS HOTEL €

(☑231 027 0501; www.touristhotel.gr; Mitropoleos 21; s/d/tr/q incl breakfast from €50/58/68/85; ❄@) Spacious rooms in a charming, central, neoclassical building with friendly staff.

Hotel Pella
HOTEL €

(☑231 052 4221; www.pella-hotel.gr; Ionos Dragoumi 63; s/d €30/36; ❄☎) Quiet and family-run, with spotless rooms.

Eating

Tavernas dot Plateia Athonos and cafes pack Leoforos Nikis. Head to **Modiano Market** (Vassiliou Irakliou or Ermo) for fresh fruit and vegetables.

TOP CHOICE Zythos
TAVERNA €

(Katouni 5; mains €8-12; ⏰lunch & dinner) Popular with locals, this excellent taverna with friendly staff serves up delicious standards, interesting regional specialities, good wines by the glass and beers on tap. Its second outlet is **Dore Zythos** (☑231 027 9010; Tsirogianni 7), near the White Tower.

Paparouna
GREEK €

(☑231 051 0852; www.paparouna.com; Doxis 7; mains €8-16; ⏰lunch & dinner) This lively restaurant whips up inventive cuisine like chicken with peppermint and honey.

Myrsini
CRETAN €

(☑231 022 8300; Tsopela 2; mains €8-12; ⏰Sep-Jun) Hearty portions of delicious Cretan dishes such as roast rabbit and *myzithropitakia* (flaky filo triangles with sweet sheep's-milk cheese).

Kitchen Bar
INTERNATIONAL €

(☑231 050 2241; www.kitchenbar.com.gr; Warehouse B, Thessaloniki Port; mains €8-13; ⏰lunch & dinner) This perennial favourite offers both drinks and artfully prepared eclectic food, in a sumptuously decorated, renovated warehouse with waterfront tables.

O Arhontis
STREET FOOD €

(Ermou 26; mains €5; ⏰11am-5pm) Eat delicious grilled sausages and potatoes off butcher's paper at this popular workers' eatery in Modiano Market.

Turkenlis
BAKERY €

(Aristotelous 4) Renowned for *tzoureki* (sweet bread) and a mind-boggling array of sweet-scented confections.

🍷 Drinking

Funky bars line Plateia Aristotelous and Leoforos Nikis, while Syngrou and Valaoritou Sts have newer drinking holes. In summer many city-centre nightclubs close and reopen in bigger spaces outdoors, on the airport road.

Spiti Mou
BAR

(Leontos Sofou 26, cnr Egnatia; ⏰1pm-late; ☎) Unmarked entrance and relaxed vibe, with big couches and eclectic tunes.

Gambrinus
BAR

(cnr Valaoritou & Ionos Dragoumi; ⏰Mon-Sat) Variety of Czech beers, boisterous students, eclectic music, sausages and free popcorn.

ℹ️ Information

Emergency
First-Aid Centre (☑231 053 0530; Navarhou Koundourioti 10) Near the port.
Tourist Police (☑231 055 4871; Dodekanisou 4, 5th fl; ⏰7.30am-11pm)

Tourist Information
Office of Tourism Directorate (☑231 022 1100; www.visitgreece.gr; Tsimiski 136; ⏰9am-3pm Mon-Fri)

ℹ️ Getting There & Away

Air

Makedonia Airport (SKG; ☑231 047 3212; www.thessalonikiairport.com) is 16km southeast of the centre and served by local bus 78 (www.oasth.gr; €0.80, one hour, from 5am to 10pm). Taxis cost €12 (20 minutes).

Olympic Air, Aegean Airlines and **Astra Airlines** (☑231 048 9392; www.astra-airlines.gr) fly throughout Greece.

Boat

Weekly ferries go to, among others, Limnos (€22, eight hours), Lesvos (€32, 14 hours) and Chios (€35, 19 hours). **Karaharisis Travel & Shipping Agency** (☑231 052 4544; Navarhou Koundourioti 8) handles tickets.

Bus

The **main bus station** (☑231 059 5408; www.ktel-thes.gr; Monastiriou 319) services Athens (€42, 6¼ hours, 10 daily), Ioannina (€30, 4¾ hours, six daily) and other destinations. Buses to

HALKIDIKI ΧΑΛΚΙΔΙΚΗ

Beautiful pine-covered Halkidiki is a three-pronged peninsula that extends into the Aegean Sea, southeast of Thessaloniki. Splendid, if built-up, sandy beaches rim its 500km of coastline. The middle **Sithonian Peninsula** is most spectacular. With camping and rooms to rent, it is more suited to independent travellers than overdeveloped **Kassandra Peninsula**, although Kassandra has the summertime **Sani Jazz Festival** (www.sanifestival.gr). You'll need your own wheels to explore Halkidiki properly.

Halkidiki's third prong is occupied by the all-male Monastic Republic of **Mt Athos** (known in Greek as Agion Oros, the Holy Mountain), where 20 monasteries full of priceless treasures stand amid an impressive landscape of gorges, mountains and sea. Only men may visit, a permit is required and the summer waiting-list is long. Start months in advance by contacting the Thessaloniki-based **Mt Athos Pilgrims' Bureau** (231 025 2578; pilgrimsbureau@c-lab.gr; Egnatia 109; 9am-1pm Mon-Fri, 10am-noon Sat).

the Halkidiki Peninsula leave from the **Halkidiki bus terminal** (231 031 6555; www.ktel-chalkidikis.gr; Karakasi 68).

At the time of writing, small bus companies, mostly across from the courthouse (Dikastirion), provided the only services to international destinations like Skopje, Sofia and Bucharest. Try **Simeonidis Tours** (231 054 0970; www.simeonidistours.gr; 26 Oktovriou 14). Train company OSE has run buses to Sofia and Tirana but service was in flux at the time of writing. Check at the office on the eastern side of the train station.

Train

The **train station** (231 059 9421; www.trainose.gr; Monastiriou) serves Athens (regular/IC €28/36, 6¾/5½ hours, seven/10 daily) but other lines like Alexandroupolis have been reduced, and all international trains were discontinued at the time of writing. Check schedules at the **train ticket office** (OSE; 231 059 8120; Aristotelous 18) or the station.

Alexandroupolis
Αλεξανδρούπολη

POP 59,900

Alexandroupolis (ah-lex-an-*dhroo*-po-lih) and nearby Komotini (ko-mo-tih-*nee*) enjoy lively student atmospheres that make for a satisfying stopover on the way to Turkey or Samothraki.

Waterfront **Hotel Bao Bab** (25510 34823; Alexandroupoli–Komotini Hwy; s/d/tr incl breakfast €40/50/60; P❄@), 1km west of town, has large, comfortable rooms and an excellent restaurant. Downtown, **Hotel Marianna** (25510 81456; Malgaron 11; s/d €40/50) has small, clean rooms.

Tuck into today's fresh catch at **Psarotaverna tis Kyra Dimitras** (25510 34434; cnr Kountourioti & Dikastirion; fish €6-11).

Alexandroupoli's cool nightspots change with the whims of its students. Leoforos Dimokratias has trendy bars; cafes line the waterfront.

The **municipal tourist office** (25510 64184; Leoforos Dimokratias 306; 7.30am-3pm) is helpful.

❶ Getting There & Away

AIR & BOAT Dimokritos Airport (25510 89300; www.alxd.gr), 7km east of town, is served by Olympic Air and Aegean Airlines.
Sever Travel (25510 22555; sever1@otenet.gr; Megalou Alexandrou 24) handles ferry (to Samothraki and Limnos) and airline tickets.
BUS The **bus station** (25510 26479; Eleftheriou Venizelou 36) has departures to the following:

Athens (€64, 10 hours, one daily)
Thessaloniki (€30, 3¾ hours, nine daily)
İstanbul (Turkey; OSE bus €15, six hours, one daily Tue-Sun)
TRAIN At the time of writing, international trains were cancelled. Other schedules change. Check ahead at the **train station** (25510 26395; www.trainose.gr).
Athens (€50, 14 hours, one daily)
Thessaloniki (€9, seven hours, four daily)

Mt Olympus
Όλυμπος Όρος

Just as it did for the ancients, Greece's highest mountain, the cloud-covered lair of the Greek pantheon, fires the visitor's imagination today. The highest of Olympus' eight peaks is **Mytikas** (2917m), popular with trekkers, who use **Litohoro** (305m), 5km inland from the Athens–Thessaloniki highway, as their base. The main route up takes two days, with a stay overnight at one of the **refuges** (☻May-Oct). Good protective clothing is essential, even in summer. **EOS** (Greek Alpine Club; ☎23520 84544; Plateia Kentriki, Litohoro; ☻Mon-Sat Jun-Sep) has information on treks.

From the **bus station** (☎23520 81271; Agiou Nikolaou, Litohoro) 13 buses daily go to Thessaloniki (€9, 1¼ hours) and three to Athens (€33, 5½ hours). Litohoro's **train station**, 9km away, gets 10 daily trains on the Athens–Volos–Thessaloniki line.

Xenonas Papanikolaou
GUESTHOUSE €
(☎23520 81236; www.xenonas-papanikolaou.gr; Nikolaou Episkopou Kitrous 1; s/d incl breakfast €45/55; P ☀@) This romantic guesthouse sits in a flowery garden up in the backstreets, a world away from tourist crowds.

Olympos Beach Camping
CAMPGROUND €
(☎23520 22111; www.olympos-beach.gr; campsites per adult/tent €7/6, bungalows €45; ☻Apr-Oct) Has a booming waterfront lounge and a pleasant beach.

TOP CHOICE Gastrodromio En Olympio
GREEK €
(☎23520 21300; Plateia Eleftherias; mains €7-13; ☻lunch & dinner) One of Greece's best country restaurants serves up specialities such as *soutzoukakia* (minced meat with cumin and mint) and delicious wild mushrooms with an impressive regional wine list and gorgeous Olympus views.

Ioannina Ιωάννινα

POP 64,500

Charming Ioannina (ih-o-*ah*-nih-nah) on the western shore of Lake Pamvotida at the foot of the Pindos Mountains, was a major intellectual centre during Ottoman rule. Today it's a thriving university town with a lively waterfront cafe scene.

☉ Sights

Kastro
NEIGHBOURHOOD
The narrow stone streets of the evocative old quarter sit on a small peninsula jutting into the lake. Within its impressive fortifications, **Its Kale**, an inner citadel with lovely grounds and lake views, is home to the splendid **Fetiye Cami** (Victory Mosque),

built in 1611, and the gemlike **Byzantine Museum** (☎26510 25989; admission €3; ☻8am-5pm Tue-Sun).

Lake Pamvotida
LAKE
The lake's serene *nisi* (island) shelters four **monasteries** among its trees. Frequent ferries (€2) leave from near Plateia Mavili.

🛏 Sleeping

TOP CHOICE Filyra
BOUTIQUE HOTEL €
(☎26510 83560; http://hotelfilyra.gr; alley off Andronikou Paleologou 18; s/d €45/55; P ☀) Five Old Town self-catering suites fill up fast. The affiliated **Traditional Hotel Dafni** (Ioustinianou 12; s/d/q €45/65/90) is built into the Kastro's outer walls.

Hotel Kastro
PENSION €€
(☎26510 22866; www.hotelkastro.gr; Andronikou Paleologou 57; s/d incl breakfast €50/65; P ☀) Ask for a high-ceilinged upstairs room at this quaint hotel, across from Its Kale.

Limnopoula Camping
CAMPGROUND €
(☎26510 25265; Kanari 10; campsites per tent/adult €4/8; ☻Apr-Oct) Tree-lined and splendidly set on the edge of the lake 2km northwest of town.

✗ Eating & Drinking

Scores of cafes and restaurants line the waterfront. Enjoy a cold beer on a sunny day in Its Kale, at its exquisitely situated **cafe** (mains €4-8).

Sirios
GREEK €
(☎26510 77070; www.seirioskouzina.gr; Patriarhou Evangelidi 1; mains €8-12; ☻noon-11pm) An imaginative menu of decidedly delicious dishes, ranging from braised rooster to pork cutlets.

Taverna To Manteio
TAVERNA €
(☎26510 25452; Plateia Georgiou 15; mains €7-8; ☻lunch & dinner Tue-Sun) Join local families along the flower-filled Its Kale wall for deliciously simple *mezedhes,* salads and grills.

Ananta
BAR
(cnr Anexartisias & Stoa Labei) Rock out in the shadows of the long bar.

❶ Information

EOT (Tourist Office; ☎26510 41142; Dodonis 39; ☻7.30am-2.30pm Mon-Fri)
EOS (Greek Alpine Club; ☎26510 22138; Despotatou Ipirou 2; ☻7-9pm Mon-Fri)

ⓘ Getting There & Away

AIR Aegean Airlines (☑26510 64444) and **Olympic Air** (☑26510 26518) fly to Athens. Slow buses ply the 2km road into town.

BUS The **station** (☑26510 26286; Georgiou Papandreou) is 300m north of Plateia Dimokratias.

Athens (€40, 6½ hours, nine daily)

Igoumenitsa (€9.80, 1¼ hours, eight daily)

Thessaloniki (€32, 4¾ hours, six daily)

Trikala (€15.50, 2¼ hours, two daily)

Zagorohoria & Vikos Gorge
Τα Ζαγοροχώρια & Χαράδρα του Βικού

Do not miss the spectacular Zagori region, with its deep gorges, abundant wildlife, dense forests and snowcapped mountains. Some 46 charming villages, famous for their grey-slate architecture, and known collectively as the Zagorohoria, are sprinkled across a large expanse of the Pindos Mountains north of Ioannina. These beautifully restored gems were once only connected by stone paths and arching footbridges, but paved roads now wind between them. Get information on walks from Ioannina's EOT and EOS offices. Book ahead during high season (Christmas, Greek Easter and August); prices plummet in low season.

Tiny, carless **Dilofo** makes for a peaceful sojourn, especially if you lodge at excellent **Gaia** (☑26530 22570; www.gaia-dilofo.gr; s/d/tr incl breakfast from €60/70/80; 🖥) or **Arhontiko Dilofo** (☑26530 22455; www.dilofo.com; d incl breakfast from €55; ℗) and sup on the square at **Sopotseli** (☑26530 22629; mains €5-7).

Delightful **Monodendri**, known for its special pitta bread, is a popular departure point for treks through dramatic 12km-long, 900m-deep **Vikos Gorge**, with its sheer limestone walls. Get cosy at quaint **Archontiko Zarkada** (☑26530 71305; www.monodendri.com; s/d incl breakfast €40/60; ℗), one of Greece's best-value small hotels.

Exquisite inns with attached tavernas abound in remote (but popular) twin villages **Megalo Papingo** and **Mikro Papingo**. Visit the **WWF Information Centre** (www.wwf.gr; Mikro Papingo; ◷11am-5.30pm Fri-Wed) to learn about the area.

In Megalo Papingo, simple **Lakis** (☑26530 41087; d incl breakfast €35) is a *domatia* (B&B), taverna and store. Spectacular views and family-friendly studios add to the charms of **Papaevangelou** (☑26530 41135; www.ho-

telpapaevangelou.gr; d/studio incl breakfast from €75/120). Stylish **Tsoumani** (☑26530 41893; www.tsoumanisnikos.gr; d incl breakfast from €70; 🖥) also serves some of the best food around. Two friendly brothers run charming **Xenonas tou Kouli** (☑26530 41115; d €60).

Hide away in Mikro Papingo's sweetly rustic **Xenonas Dias** (☑26530 41257; www.diaspapigo.gr; s/d incl breakfast €40/55) or fabulous, sumptuously minimalist **1700** (☑26530 41179; www.mikropapigo.gr; d from €80).

Infrequent buses run to Ioannina from Dilofo (€3.80, 40 minutes, three weekly), Monodendri (€3.60, one hour, three weekly) and the Papingos (€5.10, two hours, three weekly). It's best to explore by rental car from Ioannina; in a pinch take an (expensive) taxi.

Igoumenitsa
Ηγουμενίτσα

TRANSPORT HUB
POP 9160

Though tucked beneath verdant hills and lying on the sea, this characterless port is little more than a ferry hub: keep moving.

If you must stay over, look for *domatia* signs or opt for the most modern: **Angelika Pallas Hotel** (☑26650 26100; www.angelikapallas.gr; Agion Apostolon 145; s/d/tr incl breakfast from €60/70/90; ❄🖥) across from the Corfu ferry terminal. It also has a restaurant.

The **bus station** (☑26650 22309) services Ioannina (€9.80, 2½ hours, nine daily) and Athens (€45, eight hours, five daily).

Several companies operate 90-minute **ferries to Corfu** (☑26650 99460; person/car €10/40; ◷hourly) and hydrofoils in summer. International ferries go to the Italian ports of Ancona, Bari, Brindisi and Venice. Ticket agencies line the port. Book ahead for car tickets or sleeping cabins.

SARONIC GULF ISLANDS
ΝΗΣΙΑ ΤΟΥ ΣΑΡΩΝΙΚΟΥ

Scattered about the Saronic Gulf, these islands are within easy reach of Athens. The Saronics are named after the mythical King Saron of Argos, a keen hunter who drowned while chasing a deer that had swum into the gulf to escape.

You can either island-hop through the group then return to Piraeus, or carry on to the Peloponnese from any of the islands mentioned.

HELLENIC WILDLIFE HOSPITAL

While some Greeks may not appear too environmentally minded, others are making a sterling effort to face the country's ecological problems head-on. The **Hellenic Wildlife Hospital** (☑22970 28367; www.ekpaz.gr; ☉by appointment) on the Saronic Gulf island of Aegina is one such place. As the oldest and largest wildlife rehabilitation centre in southern Europe, it tackles damage caused to wild birds and animals from hunting and pollution, and runs projects such as the release of raptors into the wilds of Crete and Northern Greece. You can visit the centre for free, though donations are appreciated. Better yet, the centre welcomes volunteers and accommodation is supplied.

Aegina   Αίγινα

POP 14,500

Once a major player in the Hellenic world, thanks to its strategic position at the mouth of the gulf, Aegina (*eh*-yee-nah) now enjoys its position as Greece's premier producer of pistachios. Pick up a bag before you leave!

Bustling **Aegina Town**, on the west coast, is the island's capital and main port. There is no official tourist office, but information can be gleaned at www.aeginagreece.com.

The impressive **Temple of Aphaia** (adult/under 18yr €4/free; ☉8am-6.30pm) is a well-preserved Doric temple 12km east of Aegina Town. It's said to have served as a model for the construction of the Parthenon. Standing on a pine-clad hill with imposing views out over the gulf, it is well worth a visit. Buses from Aegina Town to the small resort of Agia Marina can drop you at the site.

In Aegina Town, **Hotel Rastoni** (☑22970 27039; www.rastoni.gr; d/tr incl breakfast €90/120; [P][✳][@][✿]), a boutique hotel with excellent service, gets a big thumbs up for its quiet location, spacious rooms and lovely garden. **Electra Pension** (☑22970 26715; www.aegina-electra.gr; s/d €45/50; [✳][✿]) is in a quiet corner of town with rooms that are impeccable and comfy.

A flotilla of ferries (€9.50, 70 minutes) and hydrofoils (€13.50, 40 minutes) ply the waters between Aegina and Piraeus with great regularity. You can head back to Pi-

raeus, carry on through the Saronic Gulf Islands or take a boat to Methana (€5.70, 40 minutes) on the Peloponnese. There is a good public bus service on the island.

Poros   Πόρος

POP 5250

Only a few hundred metres from the village of Galatas on the shores of the mountainous Peloponnese, Poros is an attractive island with a friendly feel that is worth the effort. **Poros Town**, on the island's southern coast, is a haven for yachties, and with boats from all over tied up along the waterfront, there is a happy mood in the air.

Seven Brothers Hotel (☑22980 23412; www.7brothers.gr; s/d/tr €55/65/75; [✳][✿]) is conveniently close to the hydrofoil dock. This modern hotel has bright, comfy rooms with balconies and impressive bathrooms.

There is no tourist office, but also no shortage of businesses hoping to sell you your onward ticket. Hit www.poros.gr for extensive information.

There are ferry (€12.80, 2½ hours) and hydrofoil (€22.20, one hour) services daily between Poros and Piraeus. The ferries go via Aegina (€8.30, 1¼ hours), while the hydrofoils go direct. Many of the outbound boats head on to Hydra and Spetses. Small boats shuttle back and forth between Poros and Galatas (€1, five minutes) on the Peloponnese.

Hydra   Ύδρα

POP 2900

The catwalk queen of the Saronics, Hydra (*ee*-drah) is a delight. On the northern side of this sparsely populated island, **Hydra Town** has a picturesque horseshoe-shaped harbour with gracious white and pastel stone mansions stacked up the rocky hillsides that surround it. The island is known as a retreat for artists, writers and celebrities, and wears its celebrity with panache.

A major attraction is Hydra's tranquillity. Forget noisy motorbikes keeping you awake half the night! There are no motorised vehicles – apart from sanitation trucks – and the main forms of transport are foot and donkey.

Pension Erofili (☑22980 54049; www.pensionerofili.gr; Tombazi; s/d/tr €45/55/65; [✳][✿]), tucked away in the inner town, has clean, comfortable rooms, an attractive courtyard and breakfast features homemade preserves and jams. The owners add a friendly sparkle. **Hotel Miranda** (☎22980 52230; www.mirandahotel.gr; Miaouli; s/d incl breakfast €120/140; ❋) is worth a splurge. Originally built in 1810 as the mansion of a wealthy Hydriot sea captain, this stylish place retains much of its historical character and is a National Heritage building.

There is no tourist office, but check out www.hydra.com.gr for detailed information.

High-speed boat services (€25.50, 1½ hours) connect Hydra with Piraeus seven times daily. There are also services to Ermioni and Porto Heli on the Peloponnese mainland, inbound boats to Poros and outbound boats to Spetses.

Spetses   Σπέτσες

POP 4400

Spetses is an appealing island that is packed with visitors in summer. Its attractiveness is largely thanks to Spetses-born philanthropist Sotirios Anargyrios, who made a fortune in the US after emigrating in 1848. Anargyrios returned in 1914, bought two-thirds of the then-barren island, planted Aleppo pines, financed the island's road system and commissioned many of the town's grandest buildings.

Spetses Town, the main port, sprawls along half the northeast coast of the island.

Opposite the small town beach to the east of the ferry quay, **Villa Marina** (☎22980 72646; www.villamarinaspetses.com; s/d €55/65; ❋) is a convenient, welcoming place with tidy rooms. Ask for a sea view.

There is no tourist office. See the website www.spetsesdirect.com for more information.

High-speed boats head regularly to Piraeus (€35, 2¼ hours). Another option is to carry on to the Peloponnese mainland on boats to Ermioni (€7.50, 30 minutes) or Porto Heli (€5.50, 15 minutes).

CYCLADES   ΚΥΚΛΑΔΕΣ

The Cyclades (kih-*klah*-dez) are Greek islands to dream about. Named after the rough *kyklos* (circle) they form around the island of Delos, they are rugged outcrops of rock in the azure Aegean, speckled with white cubist buildings and blue-domed Byzantine churches. Throw in sun-blasted golden beaches, more than a dash of hedon-

ism and a fascinating culture, and it's easy to see why many find the Cyclades irresistible.

Some of the islands, such as Mykonos, Ios and Santorini, have seized tourism with great enthusiasm. Prepare to battle the crowds if you turn up at the height of summer. Others are little more than clumps of rock, with a village, secluded coves and a few curious tourists. Ferry services rarely run in winter, while from July to September the Cyclades are vulnerable to the *meltemi*, a fierce northeasterly wind that can play havoc with ferry schedules.

History

Said to have been inhabited since at least 7000 BC, the Cyclades enjoyed a flourishing Bronze Age civilisation (3000–1100 BC), more or less concurrent with the Minoan civilisation. From the 4th century AD, the islands, like the rest of Greece, suffered a series of invasions and occupations. The Turks turned up in 1537 but neglected the Cyclades to the extent that they became backwaters prone to raids by pirates – hence the labyrinthine character of their towns, which was meant to confuse attackers. On some islands the whole population moved into the mountainous interior to escape the pirates, while on others they braved it out on the coast. Consequently, the *hora* (main town) is on the coast on some islands, while on others it is inland.

The Cyclades became part of independent Greece in 1827. During WWII they were occupied by the Italians. Before the revival of the islands' fortunes by the tourist boom that began in the 1970s, many islanders lived in poverty and many more headed for the mainland or emigrated to America or Australia in search of work.

Mykonos   Μύκονος

POP 8000

Sophisticated Mykonos glitters happily under the Aegean sun, shamelessly surviving on tourism. The island has something for everyone, with marvellous beaches, romantic sunsets, chic boutiques, excellent restaurants and bars, and its long-held reputation as a mecca for gay travellers. The maze of white-walled streets in Mykonos Town was designed to confuse pirates, and it certainly manages to captivate and confuse the crowds that consume the island's capital in summer.

Mykonos

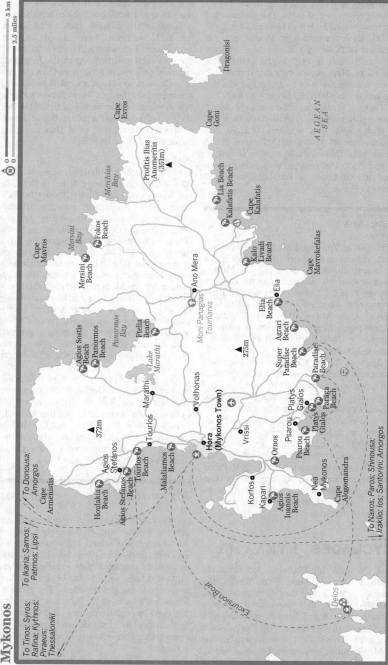

To Tinos; Syros;
Rafina; Kythnos;
Piraeus;
Thessaloniki

To Ikaria; Samos;
Patmos; Lipsi

To Donousa;
Amorgos

Cape
Armenistis

Houlakia
Beach

Agios Stefanos
Beach

Agios
Stefanos

Tourlos
Beach

Tourlos

372m

Malaliamos
Beach

Hora
(Mykonos Town)

Vrissi

Korfos

Kapari

Agios
Ioannis
Beach

Nea
Mykonos

Cape
Alogomandra

Ornos

Psarou
Beach

Psarou

Platys
Gialos

Platys
Gialos

Paraga
Beach

Paranga

To Naxos; Paros; Shinousa;
Iraklio; Ios; Santorini; Amorgos

Delos

Excursion Boat

Super
Paradise
Beach

Paradise
Beach

Agrari
Beach

Elia
Beach

Elia

Kalo
Livadi
Beach

Cape
Mavrokefalas

275m

Moni Panagias
Tourlianis

Ano Mera

Vothonas

Marathi

Lake
Marathi

Pelia
Beach

Panormos
Beach

Agios Sostis
Beach

Panormos
Bay

Mersini
Beach

Cape
Mavros

Mersini
Bay

Fokos
Beach

Merchias
Bay

Profitis Ilias
Anomeritis
(351m)

Cape
Evros

Cape
Goni

Lia Beach

Kalafatis Beach

Cape
Kalafatis

AEGEAN
SEA

Dragonisi

5 km

2.5 miles

Sights & Activities

Mykonos Town
NEIGHBOURHOOD

A stroll around Mykonos Town, shuffling through snaking streets with blinding white walls and balconies of flowers is a must for any visitor. This is the centre of the action on the island. **Little Venice**, where the sea laps up to the edge of the restaurants and bars, and Mykonos' famous hilltop row of **windmills** should be included in the spots-to-see list. You're bound to run into one of Mykonos' famous resident pelicans on your walk.

Beaches

The island's most popular beaches are on the southern coast. **Platys Gialos** has wall-to-wall sun lounges, while nudity is not uncommon at **Paradise Beach**, **Super Paradise**, **Agrari** and gay-friendly **Elia**.

Sleeping

Rooms in Mykonos Town fill up quickly in high season; book ahead. Prices mentioned are for the peak season – they plummet further than on most islands outside of July and August.

Mykonos has two camping areas, both on the south coast. Minibuses from both meet the ferries, and buses go regularly into town.

TOP CHOICE Carbonaki Hotel
BOUTIQUE HOTEL €€€

(www.carbonaki.gr; 23 Panahrantou; s/d/tr/q €140/168/210/240; ❄🛜) This family-run place on the edge of the old town has bright and comfortable rooms dotted around a sunny central courtyard. Throw in a Jacuzzi, sauna and delightful ambiance and this is a top place to stay.

Hotel Philippi
HOTEL €€

(☎22890 22294; www.philippihotel.com; 25 Kalogera, Mykonos Town; s €60-90, d €75-120; ❄🛜) In the heart of the *hora,* Philippi, one of Mykonos' few affordable options, has spacious and clean rooms that open onto a railed veranda overlooking a lush garden. An extremely peaceful, pleasant place to stay. Free wi-fi.

Hotel Lefteris
HOTEL €€

(☎22890 23128; www.lefterishotel.gr; 9 Apollonas, Mykonos Town; s/d €99/129, studios €239-279; ❄@) Tucked away just up from Plateia Taxi (Taxi Sq), Lefteris has bright, comfy rooms, and a relaxing sun terrace with superb views over town. A good international meeting place.

CYCLADIC CONNECTIONS

For planning purposes, it's worth noting that once the season kicks in, a batch of companies run daily catamarans and ferries up and down the Cyclades. You can start from Piraeus (for Athens), Iraklio on Crete, or just about anywhere in-between.

One boat heads south daily from Piraeus to Paros, Naxos, Ios and Santorini, returning along the same route. There's also a daily run from Piraeus to Syros, Tinos and Mykonos.

Heading north from Iraklio, another catamaran runs to Santorini, Ios, Paros, Mykonos and return.

If it all get a bits much to comprehend (the schedules are constantly changing!), check the online guide **Open Seas** (www.openseas.gr).

Island-hopping through the Cyclades from Piraeus to Crete (or vice-versa) is getting easier and easier – though ease of travel means there are more people out there doing it!

Paradise Beach Camping
CAMPGROUND €

(☎22890 22852; www.paradisemykonos.com; campsites per tent/person €5/10; @🛜) There are lots of options here on the south coast of the island, including camping, beach cabins and apartments, as well as bars, a swimming pool, games etc. It is skin-to-skin mayhem in summer with a real party atmosphere. The website has it all.

Eating

There is no shortage of places to eat and drink in Mykonos Town. Cheap eateries are found around Plateia Taxi and the southern bus station. Restaurants offering abundant seafood abound in Little Venice and towards the Delos excursion boats. Mykonos' top touts are its two resident pelicans, who wander the restaurants looking for handouts, often with visitors following them.

Fato a Mano
MEDITERRANEAN €

(Plateia Meletopoulou; mains €8-15) In the middle of the maze, this place is worth taking the effort to find. It serves up tasty Mediterranean and traditional Greek dishes with pride.

WORTH A TRIP

DELOS ΔΗΛΟΣ

Southwest of Mykonos, the island of **Delos** (sites & museum €5; ⏱8.30am-3pm Tue-Sun) is the Cyclades' archaeological jewel. The opportunity to clamber among the ruins shouldn't be missed.

According to mythology, Delos was the birthplace of Apollo – the god of light, poetry, music, healing and prophecy. The island flourished as an important religious and commercial centre from the 3rd millennium BC, reaching its apex of power in the 5th century BC.

Ruins include the **Sanctuary of Apollo**, containing temples dedicated to him, and the **Terrace of the Lions**. These proud beasts were carved in the early 6th century BC using marble from Naxos to guard the sacred area. The original lions are in the island's **museum**, with replicas on the original site. The **Sacred Lake** (dry since 1926) is where Leto supposedly gave birth to Apollo, while the **Theatre Quarter** is where private houses were built around the **Theatre of Delos**.

The climb up **Mt Kynthos** (113m), the island's highest point, is a highlight. The view of Delos and the surrounding islands is spectacular, and it's easy to see how the Cyclades got their name.

Take a sunhat, sunscreen and sturdy footwear. The island's cafeteria sells food and drinks. Staying overnight on Delos is forbidden.

Numerous boat companies offer trips from Mykonos to Delos (€18 return, 30 minutes) between 9am and 1pm. The return boats leave Delos between noon and 3pm. There is also a €5 per person entry fee on arrival at Delos.

Katerina's   GREEK €€

(Agion Anargyron; mains €11-25) Long a legendary bar in Little Venice with breath-taking views out over the water, Katerina's has added an excellent restaurant offering up Greek dishes. The seafood is superb.

 Drinking & Entertainment

The waterfront is perfect for sitting with a drink and watching an interesting array of passers-by, while Little Venice has bars with dreamy views and water lapping below your feet.

Long feted as a gay travel destination, there are many gay-centric clubs and hangouts. The waterfront area, between the Old Harbour and the Church of Paraportiani, is popular for late night gay interaction.

Cavo Paradiso   CLUB

(☑22890 27205; www.cavoparadiso.gr) For those who want to go the whole hog, this place 300m above Paradise Beach picks up around 2am and boasts a pool the shape of Mykonos. A bus transports clubbers from town in summer.

ⓘ **Information**

Mykonos Accommodation Centre (☑22890 23408; www.mykonos-accommodation.com; Enoplon Dynameon 10) This helpful place can do it all, from arranging hotels to tours.

Hoteliers Association of Mykonos (☑22890 24540; www.mha.gr; ⏱9.30am-4pm Apr-Oct) At the old port; can book accommodation. They also have a desk at the airport.

Island Mykonos Travel (☑22890 22232; www.discovergreece.org) On Plateia Taxi, where the port road meets the town; helpful for travel information, hotels, transfers and tickets.

ⓘ **Getting There & Around**

Mykonos Town has two ferry quays. The old quay, where the smaller ferries and catamarans dock, is 400m north of the town waterfront. The new quay, where the bigger boats dock, is 2.5km north of town. Buses meet arriving ferries. When leaving Mykonos, double-check which quay your boat leaves from.

Air

There are daily flights connecting Mykonos airport (JMK) to Athens, plus a growing number of international flights winging in directly from May to September. Don't just assume you'll have to fly through Athens to get to Mykonos. The airport is 3km southeast of the town centre; €1.60 by bus from the southern bus station.

Boat

Daily ferries (€32, five hours) and catamarans (€50, three hours) arrive from Piraeus. From Mykonos, there are daily ferries and hydrofoils to most major Cycladic islands, daily services to Crete, and less-frequent services to the northeastern Aegean Islands and the Dodecanese.

GREECE MYKONOS

Bus

The northern bus station is near the old port. It serves Agios Stefanos, Elia, Kalafatis and Ano Mera. The southern bus station, a 300m walk up from the windmills, serves the airport, Agios Ioannis, Psarou, Platys Gialos and Paradise Beach.

Local Boats

In summer, *caiques* (small fishing boats) from Mykonos Town and Platys Gialos putter to Paradise, Super Paradise, Agrari and Elia beaches.

Paros   Πάρος
POP 13,000

Paros is an attractive, laid-back island with an enticing main town, good swimming beaches and terraced hills that build up to Mt Profitis Ilias (770m). It has long been prosperous, thanks to an abundance of pure white marble (from which the *Venus de Milo* and Napoleon's tomb were sculpted).

Paros' main town and port is **Parikia**, on the west coast. Opposite the ferry terminal, on the far side of Windmill roundabout, is Plateia Mavrogenous, the main square. Agora, also known as Market St, the main commercial thoroughfare, runs southwest from the far end of the square.

◎ Sights

Panagia Ekatondapyliani   CHURCH
(Parikia; ⊙7.30am-9.30pm) Dating from AD 326 and known for its beautiful ornate interior, this is one of the most impressive churches in the Cyclades. Within the church compound, the **Byzantine Museum** (admission €1.50; ⊙9.30am-2pm & 6-9pm) has an interesting collection of icons and artefacts.

🏃 Activities

A great option on Paros is to rent a scooter or car at one of the many outlets in Parikia and cruise around the island. There are sealed

Paros & Antiparos

roads the whole way, and the opportunity to explore villages such as **Naoussa**, **Marpissa** and **Aliki**, and swim at beaches such as **Logaras**, **Punda** and **Golden Beach**. Naoussa is a cute little fishing village on the northeastern coast that is all geared up to welcome tourists.

Less than 2km from Paros, the small island of **Antiparos** has fantastic beaches, which have made it wildly popular. Another attraction is its **Cave of Antiparos** (admission €3.60; ⏲10.45am-3.45pm summer), considered to be one of Europe's best.

Sleeping

TOP CHOICE **Pension Sofia** PENSION €€
(☎22840 22085; www.sofiapension-paros.com; Parikia; d/tr €75/90; P❄@📶) If you don't mind a stroll to town, this place, with a beautifully tended garden and immaculate rooms, is a great option that won't be regretted. It's run with pride and passion.

Rooms Mike PENSION €
(☎22840 22856; www.roomsmike.com; Parikia; s/d/tr €25/40/60; ❄📶) A popular and friendly place, Mike's offers a good location and local advice. There are options of rooms with shared facilities through to fully self-contained units with kitchens. Mike's sign is easy to spot from the quay, away to the left.

Rooms Rena PENSION €
(☎22840 22220; www.cycladesnet.gr/rena; Parikia; s/d/tr €35/45/55; ❄📶) The quiet, well-kept rooms here are excellent value. Turn left from the pier then right at the ancient cemetery and follow the signs.

Koula Camping CAMPGROUND €
(☎22840 22801; www.campingkoula.gr; campsites per tent/person €4/8; ⏲Apr-Oct; P📶) A pleasant shaded spot behind the beach at the north end of the waterfront. They have free transfers to and from the port.

Eating & Drinking

Budget eating spots are easy to find near the Windmill roundabout in Parikia. Head along the waterfront to the west of the ferry quay to find a line-up of restaurants and drinking establishments that gaze out at the setting sun. It's hard to beat **Pebbles Jazz Bar** for ambience. There are also a number of good eating and drinking options along Market St, which more or less parallels the waterfront.

Happy Green Cows VEGETARIAN €€
(dishes €12-18; ⏲dinner; 🖉) Cheerful service goes with the quirky name of this little eatery, a vegetarian's delight at the back of the main square. It's a touch pricey, but worth it for the often saucily named dishes.

Levantis GREEK €€
(Kastro; dishes €11-19) A courtyard garden setting enhances the experience at this long-established restaurant at the heart of Kastro that serves excellent house wine.

Information

There is no tourist office. See www.parosweb.com for information.

Santorineos Travel (☎22840 24245; www.traveltoparos.gr) On the waterfront near the Windmill roundabout; good for ticketing, information and luggage storage.

Getting There & Around

Air

Paros' airport (PAS) has daily flight connections with Athens. The airport is 8km south of Parikia; €1.50 by bus.

Boat

Parikia is a major ferry hub with daily connections to Piraeus (€32.50, five hours) and frequent ferries and catamarans to Naxos, Ios, Santorini, Mykonos and Crete. The fast boats generally take half the time but are more expensive (eg a fast boat to Piraeus takes 2½ hours but costs €40). The Dodecanese and the northeastern Aegean Islands are also well serviced from here.

Bus

From Parikia there are frequent bus services to the entire island. A free green bus runs around Parikia at regular intervals from early morning to late at night.

Local Boats

In summer there are excursion boats to Antiparos from Parikia port, or you can catch a bus to Pounta and ferry across.

Naxos Νάξος

POP 12,000

The largest of the Cyclades islands, Naxos could probably survive without tourism – unlike many of its neighbouring islands. Green and fertile, Naxos produces olives, grapes, figs, citrus, corn and potatoes. The island is well worth taking the time to explore, with its fascinating main town, excel-

lent beaches, remote villages and striking interior.

Naxos Town, on the west coast, is the island's capital and port. The ferry quay is at the northern end of the waterfront, with the bus terminal out front. The island of Paros seems surprisingly close, directly to the west.

◉ Sights & Activities

Kastro   CASTLE
Behind the waterfront in Naxos Town, narrow alleyways scramble up to the spectacular hilltop 13th-century *kastro,* where the Venetian Catholics lived. The *kastro* looks out over the town, and has a well-stocked **archaeological museum** (admission €3; ☺8.30am-3pm Tue-Sun).

Temple of Apollo   ARCHAEOLOGICAL SITE
From the ferry quay it's a short stroll to the unfinished Temple of Apollo, Naxos' most fa-

mous landmark. Though there's not much to see other than two columns with a crowning lintel, people gather at sunset for views back to the whitewashed houses of town.

Beaches

The popular beach of **Agios Georgios** is just a 10-minute walk south from the main waterfront. Beyond it, wonderful sandy beaches stretch as far south as **Pyrgaki Beach**. **Agia Anna Beach**, 6km from town, and **Plaka Beach** are lined with accommodation and packed in summer.

Villages

A hire car or scooter will help reveal Naxos' dramatic and rugged landscape. The **Tragaea** region has tranquil villages, churches atop rocky crags and huge olive groves. **Filoti**, the largest inland settlement, perches on the slopes of **Mt Zeus** (1004m), the highest peak in the Cyclades. The historic village of

DON'T MISS

KITRON-TASTING IN HALKI

The historic village of Halki, which lies at the heart of the Tragaea region, is a top spot to try *kitron*, a liqueur unique to Naxos. Usually consumed cold after meals, *kitron* is made from the fruit of the citron (*Citrus medica*). The fruit may be barely edible in its raw state, but when it and its leaves are boiled with pure alcohol, the result is a tasty concoction that has been keeping Naxians happy since the 1870s. While the exact recipe is top secret, visitors can taste it and stock up on supplies at the **Vallindras Distillery** (☎22850 31220; ☺10am-11pm Jul-Aug, 10am-6pm May-Jun & Sep-Oct) in Halki's main square. There is a **Kitron Museum** (admission free), complimentary tastings, and a shop selling the distillery's products.

Halki, one-time centre of Naxian commerce, is well worth a visit.

Apollonas is a lovely spot near Naxos' northern tip. There's a **beach**, excellent taverna, and the mysterious 10.5m **kouros** (naked male statue), constructed in the 7th century BC, lying abandoned and unfinished in an ancient marble quarry.

🛏 Sleeping

TOP CHOICE **Pension Sofi** PENSION €

(☎22850 23077; www.pensionsofi.gr; r €30-90; ☺year-round; ❋🛜) Run by members of the Koufopoulos family, Pension Sofi is in Naxos Town, while their **Studios Panos** (☎22850 26078; www.studiospanos.com; Agios Georgios Beach; r €30-75; ❋🛜) is a 10-minute walk away near Agios Georgios Beach. Guests are met with family-made wine, and immaculate rooms come with bathroom and kitchen. Rates at both places halve out of the high season. Call ahead for pick-up at the port.

Hotel Grotta HOTEL €€

(☎22850 22215; www.hotelgrotta.gr; s/d incl breakfast €70/85; 🅿❋@🛜🏊) Overlooking Grotta Beach at the northern end of town, this modern hotel has comfortable and immaculate rooms, a Jacuzzi and minipool, and offers great sea views.

Camping Maragas CAMPGROUND €

(☎22850 42552; www.maragascamping.gr; campsites €9, d €45, studio €70) On Agia Anna Beach to the south of town, this place has all sorts of options, including camping, rooms and studios, and there is a restaurant and minimarket on-site.

🍴 Eating & Drinking

Naxos Town's waterfront is lined with eating and drinking establishments. Head into Market St in the Old Town, just down from the ferry quay, to find quality tavernas. South of the waterfront, but only a few minutes' walk away, Plateia Main is home to plenty of excellent eateries.

TOP CHOICE **Picasso** MEXICAN €

(www.picassoismexican.com; Agiou Arseniou; dishes €6-18; ☺all day Jun-Sep, dinner only Oct-May) Definitely the best Mexican fare in Greece (and possibly in Europe!). Just off Plateia Main, Picasso boasts that it serves 'extraordinary Mexican food' and it does. It also offers up exquisite frozen margaritas.

Metaximas TAVERNA €

(Market St; dishes €8-20) Tucked away in the little maze that is Market St, Metaximas serves Naxian seafood at its best. Try the grilled octopus.

ℹ Information

There's no official tourist information office. Try www.naxos-greece.net for more information.

Zas Travel (☎22850 23330; www.zastravel.com) Good for boat and air tickets, car rental, internet and luggage storage.

ℹ Getting There & Around

AIR **Naxos airport** (JNX) has daily flight connections with Athens. The airport is 3km south of town; no buses – a taxi costs €15.

BOAT There are daily ferries (€31, five hours) and catamarans (€48, 3¾ hours) from Naxos to Piraeus, and good ferry and hydrofoil connections to most Cycladic islands and Crete.

BUS Buses travel to most villages regularly from the bus terminal in front of the port.

CAR & MOTORCYCLE Having your own wheels is a good option on Naxos. Car and motorcycle rentals are readily available in Naxos Town.

Ios   Ιος

POP 1900

Ios has long held a reputation as 'Party Island'. There are wall-to-wall bars and nightclubs in 'the village' that thump all night, and fantastic fun facilities at Milopotas Beach that entertain all day. You won't leave disappointed if you're there to party.

But there's more to Ios than just hedonistic activities. British poet and novelist Lawrence Durrell thought highly of Ios as a place of poetry and beauty, and there is an enduring claim that Homer was buried here, with his alleged tomb in the north of the island.

Ios' three population centres are close together on the west coast. Ormos is the port, where ferries arrive. Two kilometres inland and up overlooking the port is 'the village', Hora, while 2km down from Hora to the southeast is Milopotas Beach.

◉ Sights & Activities

The village has an intrinsic charm with its labyrinth of white-walled streets, and it's very easy to get lost, even if you haven't had one too many. Milopotas has everything a resort beach could ask for and parties hard. A rental car or scooter is a good option for exploring Ios.

Skarkos   ARCHAEOLOGICAL SITE

('The Snail'; ⊗8.30am-3pm Tue-Sun) An award-winning archaeological triumph for Ios! This Bronze Age settlement crowns a low hill in the plain just to the north of Hora, and its excavations have been opened to the public. There are interpretation boards in Greek and English.

Manganari Beach   BEACH

This isolated beach on the south coast is reached by rental vehicle, or by excursion boat or bus in summer. It's a beautiful spot

Ios

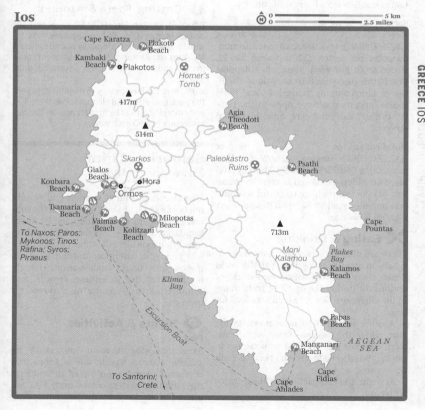

GREECE IOS

and the drive on Ios' newest sealed road is an experience in itself.

Homer's Tomb
TOMB

You'll need your own wheels to get here, 12km north of Hora.

Meltemi Water Sports
WATER SPORTS

(☎22860 91680; www.meltemiwatersports.com) This outfit at Milopotas Beach's far end has everything a beach could possibly provide, including rental windsurfers, sailboats and canoes.

🛏 Sleeping

TOP CHOICE Francesco's
HOSTEL €

(☎22860 91223; www.francescos.net; s €40-45, d €50-60 ; ❄@🛜🏊) A lively meeting place in the village with superlative views from its terrace bar, legendary Francesco's is convenient for party-going, and rates halve out of high season. The party spirit rules here. Long established and very well run.

Far Out Camping & Beach Club
CAMPGROUND €

(☎22860 91468; www.faroutclub.com; Milopotas; campsites per person €12, bungalows €15-22, studios €100; 🅿@🛜🏊) Right on Milopotas Beach, this place has tons of options. Facilities include camping, bungalows and hotel rooms, and its pools are open to the public. It also has rental cars, quad bikes and scooters.

Hotel Nissos Ios
HOTEL €€

(☎22860 91610; www.nissosios-hotel.com; Milopotas; s/d/tr €60/75/90; ❄@🛜) This cheerful place on Milopotas Beach is great for families. Rooms feature huge colourful wall murals, and the excellent Bamboo Restaurant & Pizzeria is on-site.

🍴 Eating & Drinking

There are numerous places in the village to get cheap eats like gyros. Down at Milopotas Beach, there's a great bakery and stacks of options for during the day. The restaurants in the village are of a very high standard for later.

Another option is to head down to the port, where the tavernas serve superb seafood. The port may be filled with visitors in the day, but it's the locals who head there in the evening.

At night, the compact little village erupts with bars.

Ali Baba's
THAI €

(Hora; dishes €7-12) This great Ios favourite is the place for tasty Thai dishes. The service is very upbeat and there's a garden courtyard. It's on the same street as the Emporiki bank.

Pithari
GREEK €

(Hora; mains from €10) Behind the cathedral at the entrance to the Hora, Pithari offers an excellent array of tasty dishes; the seafood spaghetti is especially good.

Blue Note
BAR

(Hora) A perennial village favourite, where happy hour continues all night long!

❶ Information

There's no tourist office. See www.iosgreece. com for more information.

Acteon Travel (☎22860 91343; www.acteon. gr) Has offices in Ormos, the village and Milopotas and is extremely helpful.

❶ Getting There & Around

BOAT Ios has daily ferry (€32.50, seven hours) and catamaran (€55, 3½ hours) connections with Piraeus. Being strategically placed between Mykonos and Santorini, there are frequent catamarans and ferries to the major Cycladic islands and Crete.

BUS There are buses every 15 minutes between the port, the village and Milopotas Beach until early morning. Buses head to Manganari Beach in summer (€3.50 each way).

Santorini (Thira)
Σαντορίνη (Θήρα)

POP 13,500

Stunning Santorini is unique and should not be missed. The startling sight of the submerged caldera almost encircled by sheer lava-layered cliffs – topped off by clifftop towns that look like a dusting of icing sugar – will grab your attention and not let it go. If you turn up in high season, though, be prepared for relentless crowds and commercialism – Santorini survives on tourism.

◉ Sights & Activities

Fira

Santorini's vibrant main town with its snaking narrow streets full of shops and restaurants perches on top of the caldera; the stunning caldera views from Fira are unparalleled.

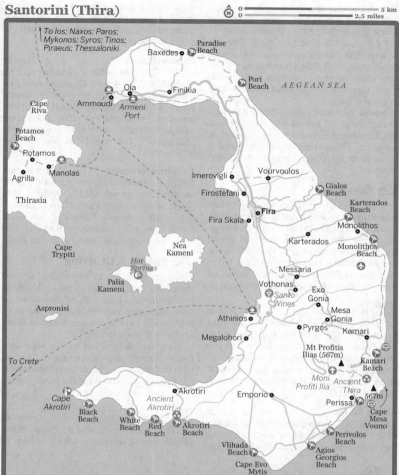

MUSEUMS

The exceptional **Museum of Prehistoric Thira** (admission €3; ☉8.30am-8pm Tue-Sun), which has wonderful displays of artefacts predominantly from ancient Akrotiri, is two blocks south of the main square. **Megaron Gyzi Museum** (admission €3.50; ☉10.30am-1.30pm & 5-8pm Mon-Sat, 10.30am-4.30pm Sun), behind the Catholic cathedral, houses local memorabilia, including photographs of Fira before and after the 1956 earthquake.

Around the Island

At the north of the island, the intriguing village of **Oia** (ee-ah), famed for its postcard

sunsets, is less hectic than Fira and a must-visit. Its caldera-facing tavernas are superb spots for brunch. There's a path from Fira to Oia along the top of the caldera that takes three to four hours to walk; otherwise take a taxi or bus.

Excavations in 1967 uncovered the remarkably well-preserved Minoan settlement of **Akrotiri** at the south of the island, with its remains of two- and three-storey buildings. Akrotiri has recently reopened to the public after a seven-year hiatus.

Santorini's black-sand **beaches** of **Perissa** and **Kamari** sizzle – beach mats are essential. Sitting on a mountain between the two are the atmospheric ruins of **Ancient Thira**, first settled in the 9th century BC.

Of the surrounding islets, only **Thirasia** is inhabited. Visitors can clamber around on volcanic lava on **Nea Kameni** then swim into warm springs in the sea at **Palia Kameni**; there are various excursions available to get you there.

Santo Wines (☎22860 22596; www.santo wines.gr; Pyrgos) is a great spot to try the delectable Assyrtico crisp dry white wine while savouring unbelievable views. Santorini is home to an increasing number of excellent wineries.

Sleeping

Few of Fira's sleeping options are cheap, especially anywhere with a caldera view. Ask about transfers when you make a booking; many places offer free port and airport transfers. If you are out of the high season and don't have a booking, a veritable scrum of accommodation owners will battle for your attention when you get off the boat.

TOP CHOICE Hotel Keti   HOTEL €€
(☎22860 22324; www.hotelketi.gr; Agiou Mina, Fira; d/tr €95/120; ❄🅢) Overlooking the caldera, with views to die for, Hotel Keti is a smaller place with traditional rooms carved into the cliffs. Some rooms have Jacuzzis. Head down next to Hotel Atlantis and follow the signs.

Aroma Suites   BOUTIQUE HOTEL €€
(☎22860 24112; www.aromasuites.gr; Agiou Mina; s €120, d €140-160; ❄🅢) At the southern end of Fira on the caldera edge, this delightful bou-

tique hotel has charming owners to match. Stylish modern facilities enhance traditional caldera interiors. Rates are substantially reduced in low season.

Pension Petros   PENSION €€
(☎22860 22573; www.hotelpetros-santorini.gr; Fira; s/d/tr €60/70/85; ❄🅢🅢) Three hundred metres east of the square, Petros offers decent rooms at good rates, free airport- and port-transfers, but no caldera views. It's a good affordable option, with rates halving outside high season. The friendly family also has other hotels.

Santorini Camping   CAMPGROUND €
(☎22860 22944; www.santorinicamping.gr; Fira; campsites per person €12.50; 🅿@🅢) This place, 500m east of Fira's main square, is the cheapest option. There are campsites, dormitories and rooms, as well as a restaurant, bar, minimarket and swimming pool.

✗ Eating & Drinking

Cheap eateries are in abundance around the square in Fira. Prices tend to double at restaurants and bars with caldera views, so don't glaze over too early. Many of the more popular bars and clubs are clustered along Erythrou Stavrou in Fira.

Many diners head out to Oia, legendary for its superb sunsets, timing their meal with the setting sun, while good-value tavernas line the waterfronts at the beach resorts of Kamari and Perissa.

TOP CHOICE Selene   GREEK €€
(☎22860 22249; www.selene.gr; Pyrgos; dishes €15-30) Out in the lovely hill-top village of

---

ℹ️ **SANTORINI ON A BUDGET**

Spectacular Santorini will take your breath away, and if you're on a tight budget, its prices might too. Expect to pay through the nose for caldera views at accommodation and eating establishments in and around Fira.

A budget alternative with the added bonus of a stunning black-sand beach is to head out to Perissa, on the southeast coast, and stay at **Stelios Place** (☎22860 81860; www.steliosplace.com; r €30-120; 🅿❄🅢🅢). Stelios is an excellent option one block back from the beach. There's a refreshing pool, very friendly service and free port- and airport-transfers. Rates halve out of high season.

All of your needs will be catered for in Perissa, which has bars and restaurants lining the waterfront. **Taverna Lava** (☎22860 81776), at the southern end of the waterfront, is an island-wide favourite that features a mouth-watering menu. Or just head back into the kitchen, see what Yiannis has conjured up for the day's meals and pick whatever looks good.

Public buses run regularly into Fira.

Pyrgos, Selene is in the heart of Santorinian farming and culinary culture, and specialises in creative cuisine based on Cycladic produce and unique local ingredients, such as small tomatoes and fava beans. The wine cellar houses some of Santorini's best.

Fanari   GREEK €

(☏22860 25107; www.fanari-restaurant.gr; Fira; dishes €7-20) On the street leading down to the old port, Fanari serves up both tasty traditional dishes and superlative views.

ℹ Information

There is no tourist office. Try www.santorini.net for more information.

Dakoutros Travel (☏22860 22958; www.dakoutrostravel.gr; ⊙8.30am-10pm) Just down from the square and opposite the taxi station in Fira; extremely helpful and good for ticketing.

ℹ Getting There & Around

The bus station and taxi station are just south of Fira's main square, Plateia Theotokopoulou. The new port of Athinios, where most ferries dock, is 10km south of Fira by road. The old port of Fira Skala, used by cruise ships and excursion boats, is directly below Fira and accessed by cable car (adult/child €4/2 one way), donkey (€5, up only) or by foot (588 steps).

Air

Santorini airport (JTR) has daily flight connections with Athens, plus a growing number of domestic destinations and direct international flights from all over Europe. The airport is 5km southeast of Fira; frequent buses (€1.50) and taxis (€12).

Boat

There are daily ferries (€33.50, nine hours) and fast boats (€60, 5¼ hours) to Piraeus; daily connections in summer to Mykonos, Ios, Naxos, Paros and Iraklio; and ferries to the smaller islands in the Cyclades. Large ferries use Athinios port, where they are met by buses and taxis.

Bus

Buses go frequently to Oia, Kamari, Perissa and Akrotiri from Fira. Port buses usually leave Fira, Kamari and Perissa one to 1½ hours before ferry departures.

Car & Motorcycle

A car or scooter is a great option on Santorini. There are plenty of places to rent them (from €30 per day).

CRETE   ΚΡΗΤΗ

POP 550,000

Crete is Greece's largest and most southerly island and its size and distance from the rest of Greece give it the feel of a different country. With its dramatic landscape and unique cultural identity, Crete is a delight to explore.

The island is split by a spectacular chain of mountains running east to west. Major towns are on the more hospitable northern coast, while most of the southern coast is too precipitous to support large settlements. The rugged mountainous interior, dotted with caves and sliced by dramatic gorges, offers rigorous hiking and climbing.

While Crete's proud, friendly and hospitable people have enthusiastically embraced tourism, they continue to fiercely protect their traditions and culture – and it is the people that remain a major part of the island's appeal.

For more detailed information, snap up a copy of Lonely Planet's *Crete*. Good websites on Crete include www.interkriti.org and www.explorecrete.com.

History

Crete was the birthplace of Minoan culture, Europe's first advanced civilisation, which flourished between 2800 and 1450 BC. Very little is known of Minoan civilisation, which came to an abrupt end, possibly destroyed by Santorini's volcanic eruption in around 1650 BC. Later, Crete passed from the warlike Dorians to the Romans, and then to the Genoese, who in turn sold it to the Venetians. Under the Venetians, Crete became a refuge for artists, writers and philosophers, who fled after it fell to the Turks. Their influence inspired the young Cretan painter Domenikos Theotokopoulos, who moved to Spain and there won immortality as the great El Greco.

The Turks conquered Crete in 1670. In 1898 Crete became a British protectorate after a series of insurrections and was united with independent Greece in 1913. There was fierce fighting during WWII when a German airborne invasion defeated Allied forces in the 10-day Battle of Crete. A fierce resistance movement drew heavy German reprisals, including the slaughter of whole villages.

Crete

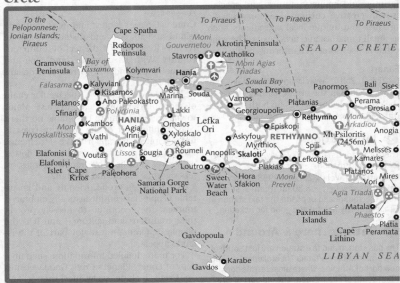

Iraklio   Ηράκλειο

POP 138,000

Iraklio (ee-*rah*-klee-oh; often spelt Heraklion), Crete's capital and economic hub, is a bustling modern city and the fifth-largest in Greece. It has a lively city centre, an excellent archaeological museum and is close to Knossos, Crete's major visitor attraction.

Iraklio's harbours face north into the Sea of Crete. The old harbour is instantly recognisable, as it is protected by the old Venetian fortress. The new harbour is 400m east. Plateia Venizelou, known for its Lion Fountain, is the heart of the city, 400m south of the old harbour up 25 Avgoustou.

⊙ Sights & Activities

Archaeological Museum   MUSEUM
(www.odysseus.culture.gr; Xanthoudidou 2; adult/student €4/2; ☺8.30am-3pm Nov-Mar) The outstanding Minoan collection here is second only to that of the national museum in Athens. The museum was under long-term reconstruction at the time of research, but its key exhibits are beautifully displayed in an annex.

Koules Venetian Fortress   FORTRESS
(admission €2; ☺8.30am-7pm Tue-Sun May-Oct, to 3pm Nov-Apr) Protecting the old harbour, this impressive fortress is also known as Rocca al Mare, which, like the city walls, was built by the Venetians in the 16th century. It stopped the Turks for 21 years and later became a Turkish prison for Cretan rebels.

City Walls   FORTRESS
Iraklio burst out of its city walls long ago, but these massive Venetian fortifications, with seven bastions and four gates, are still very conspicuous, dwarfing the concrete structures of the 20th century.

Morosini Fountain   FOUNTAIN
(Plateia Venizelou) Iraklio's much loved 'lion fountain', built in 1628 by the Venetians, spurts water from four lions into eight ornate U-shaped marble troughs.

⛏ Cretan Adventures   OUTDOORS
(☑28103   32772;   www.cretanadventures.gr; Evans 10, 3rd fl) Cretan Adventures is a well-regarded local company run by Fondas Spinthaikos that can organise hiking tours, mountain biking, and other specialist and extreme activities.

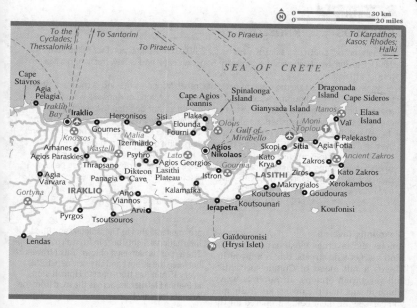

Sleeping

Lato Hotel TOP CHOICE BOUTIQUE HOTEL €€

(☎28102 28103; www.lato.gr; Epimenidou 15; d incl breakfast €90-120; P✹@☎) This stylish boutique hotel overlooking the waterfront is a top place to stay. Ask for a room with harbour views. The contemporary interior design extends to the bar, breakfast restaurant and **Brillant** (☎28102 28103; www.brillantrestaurant.gr; mains €10-25), the superb fine-dining restaurant on the ground floor. From May to October, the restaurant renames itself **Herb's Garden** and moves to the hotel rooftop for alfresco dining with harbour views.

Kronos Hotel HOTEL €

(☎28102 82240; www.kronoshotel.gr; Sofokli Venizelou 2; s/d €44/50; ✹@☎) After a thorough makeover, this waterfront hotel has polevaulted to the top of the budget hotel category. The comfortable rooms have double-glazed windows and balconies. Ask for one of the rooms with sea views.

Hotel Mirabello HOTEL €

(☎28102 85052; www.mirabello-hotel.gr; Theotokopoulou 20; s/d €42/48; ✹@☎) A pleasant, relaxed budget hotel on a quiet street in the centre of town, this place is run by an ex-sea captain who has travelled the world. A good-value option.

Eating & Drinking

There's a congregation of cheap eateries, bars and cafes in the Plateia Venizelou (Morosini Fountain) and El Greco Park area. The places around the park are packed at night. Head down towards the old harbour for plenty of seafood options.

DON'T MISS

MARKET ON 1866

Heading inland from Lion Fountain, cross the main street diagonally to the left and you'll be on Odos 1866 (1866 St). This bustling, colourful market street, perfect for people-watching, has everything on offer from fruit and vegetables to honey, herbs and succulent olives. Crete is known for its leather goods and this is a good spot to purchase them.

KNOSSOS ΚΝΩΣΣΟΣ

Five kilometres south of Iraklio, **Knossos** (☎28102 31940; admission €6; ⏱8am-7pm Jun-Oct, to 3pm Nov-May) was the capital of Minoan Crete, and is now the island's major tourist attraction.

Knossos (k-nos-os) is the most famous of Crete's Minoan sites and is the inspiration for the myth of the Minotaur. According to legend, King Minos of Knossos was given a magnificent white bull to sacrifice to the god Poseidon, but decided to keep it. This enraged Poseidon, who punished the king by causing his wife Pasiphae to fall in love with the animal. The result of this odd union was the Minotaur – half-man and half-bull – who lived in a labyrinth beneath the king's palace, munching on youths and maidens.

In 1900 Arthur Evans uncovered the ruins of Knossos. Although archaeologists tend to disparage Evans' reconstruction, the buildings – incorporating an immense palace, courtyards, private apartments, baths, lively frescos and more – give a fine idea of what a Minoan palace might have looked like.

Buses to Knossos (€1.50, 20 minutes, three per hour) leave from Bus Station A.

Giakoumis Taverna TAVERNA €

Among the tavernas clustered around the 1866 market side streets, this is a favourite. There's a full menu of Cretan specialities and vegetarian options. Turnover is heavy, which means that the dishes are fresh, and you can see the meat being prepared for the grill.

Ippokambos Ouzerie SEAFOOD €

Many locals come to this classic Iraklio haunt at the edge of the tourist-driven waterfront dining strip. Take a peek inside at the fresh trays and pots of *mayirefta* (ready-cooked meals) such as baked cuttlefish, and dine at one of the sidewalk tables or on the promenade across the road.

Veneto CAFE

(☎28102 23686; Epimenidou 9) This cafe has the best view of the harbour and fortress from its lovely terrace. It's in an historic building near Lato Hotel.

ℹ Information

Visit www.heraklion.gr for more information about the city.

Tourist Office (☎28102 46299; Xanthoudidou 1; ⏱8.30am-8.30pm Apr-Oct, to 3pm Nov-Mar)

Skoutelis Travel (☎28102 80808; www.skoutelis rentacar.gr; 25 Avgoustou 20) Between Lion Fountain and the old harbour, handles airline and ferry bookings, runs tours and rents cars.

ℹ Getting There & Around

Air

Flights depart daily from Iraklio's Nikos Kazantzakis airport (HER) for Athens and there are regular flights to Thessaloniki and Rhodes. International flights buzz in from all over Europe. The airport is 5km east of town. Bus 1 travels between the airport and city centre (€1.20) every 15 minutes from 6am to 11pm. It stops at Plateia Eleftherias, across the road from the Archaeological Museum.

Boat

Daily ferries service Piraeus (€37, seven hours), and catamarans head daily to Santorini and continue on to other Cycladic islands. Ferries sail east to Rhodes (€28, 12 hours) via Agios Nikolaos, Sitia, Kasos, Karpathos and Halki.

Bus

KTEL (Koino Tamio Eispraxeon Leoforion; http://www.bus-service-crete-ktel.com/) runs the buses on Crete and has useful tourist information inside Bus Station A.

Iraklio has two bus stations. The main **Bus Station A** is just inland from the new harbour and serves eastern Crete (Agios Nikolaos, Ierapetra, Sitia, Malia and the Lasithi Plateau), as well as Hania and Rethymno. **Bus Station B**, 50m beyond the Hania Gate, serves the southern route (Phaestos, Matala and Anogia).

Phaestos & Other Minoan Sites Φαιστός

Phaestos (☎29820 42315; admission €6; ⏱8am-7pm May-Oct, to 5pm Nov-Apr), 63km southwest of Iraklio, is Crete's second-most important Minoan site. While not as impressive as Knossos, Phaestos (fes-tos) is still worth a visit for its stunning views of the surrounding Mesara plain and Mt Psiloritis (2456m; also known as Mt Ida). The layout is similar to Knossos, with rooms arranged around a central courtyard. Eight buses a day head to Phaestos from Iraklio's Bus Station B (€6.30, 1½ hours).

Other important Minoan sites can be found at **Malia**, 34km east of Iraklio, where there's a palace complex and adjoining town, and **Zakros**, 40km southeast of Sitia, the last Minoan palace to have been discovered, in 1962.

Rethymno   Ρέθυμνο

POP 28,000

Rethymno (*reth*-im-no) is Crete's third-largest town. It's also one of the island's architectural treasures, due to its stunning fortress and mix of Venetian and Turkish houses in the old quarter. Most spots of interest are within a small area around the old Venetian harbour.

The old quarter is on a peninsula that juts out into the Sea of Crete; the fortress sits at its head, while the Venetian harbour, ferry quay and beach are on its eastern side. El Venizelou is the main strip along the waterfront and beach.

Rethymno's 16th-century **Venetian fortezza** (Fortress; Paleokastro Hill; admission €4; ⊘8am-8pm May-Oct) is the site of the city's ancient acropolis and affords great views across the town and mountains. The main gate is on the eastern side of the fortress, opposite the interesting **archaeological museum** (☑28310 54668; admission €3; ⊘8.30am-3pm Tue-Sun), which was once a prison.

Happy Walker (☑28310 52920; www.happy-walker.com; Tombazi 56) runs an excellent program of daily walks in the countryside and also longer walking tours.

Sea Front (☑28310 51981; www.rethymnoatcrete.com; Arkadiou 159; d €40-50; ✴🤝) has all sorts of sleeping options and is ideally positioned with beach views and spacious rooms. **Hotel Fortezza** (☑28310 55551; www.fortezza.gr; Melissinou 16; s/d incl breakfast €75/88; P✴🤝🏊) is more upmarket; with a refreshing pool, it's in a refurbished old building in the heart of the Old Town. **Rethymno Youth Hostel** (☑28310 22848; www.yhrethymno.com; Tombazi 41; dm €11; 🤝) is a well-run place with crowded dorms, free hot showers and no curfew.

The **municipal tourist office** (☑28310 29148; www.rethymno.gr; Eleftheriou Venizelou; ⊘9am-8.30pm), on the beach side of El Venizelou, is convenient and helpful. **Ellotia Tours** (☑28310 24533; www.rethymnoatcrete.com; Arkadiou 155) will answer all transport, accommodation and tour enquiries.

There are regular ferries between Piraeus and Rethymno (€30, nine hours), and a high-speed service in summer. Buses depart regularly to Iraklio (€7.60, 1½ hours) and Hania (€6.20, one hour).

Hania   Χανιά

POP 54,000

Crete's most romantic, evocative and alluring town, Hania (hahn-*yah*; often spelt Chania) is the former capital and the island's second-largest city. There is a rich mosaic of Venetian and Ottoman architecture, particularly in the area of the old harbour, which lures tourists in droves. Modern Hania retains the exoticism of a city caught between East and West, and is an excellent base for exploring nearby idyllic beaches and a spectacular mountainous interior.

◉ Sights & Activities

Old Harbour   HISTORIC SITE
From Plateia 1866 in the middle of town, the old harbour is a short walk down Halidon. A stroll around here is a must for any visitor to Hania. It is worth the 1.5km walk around the sea wall to get to the Venetian **lighthouse** at the entrance to the harbour.

Venetian Fortifications   FORTRESS
Part of a defensive system built by the Venetians from 1538, Hania's massive fortifications remain impressive. Best preserved is the western wall, running from the Firkas Fortress at the western entrance to the Old Harbour.

Archaeological Museum   MUSEUM
(Halidon 30; admission €2; ⊘8.30am-3pm Tue-Sun) The museum is housed in a 16th-century Venetian church that the Turks made into a mosque. The building, 200m up Halidon from the Old Harbour, became a movie theatre in 1913 and then was a munitions depot for the Germans during WWII.

Food Market   MARKET
Hania's covered food market, in a massive cross-shaped building 400m southeast of the Old Harbour, is definitely worth an inspection.

🛏 Sleeping

TOP CHOICE **Pension Lena**   PENSION €

(☏28210 86860; www.lenachania.gr; Ritsou 5; s/d €35/55; ❋❄) For some real character in where you stay, Lena's pension (in an old Turkish building near the mouth of the old harbour) is the place to go. Help yourself to one of the appealing rooms if proprietor Lena isn't there – pick from the available ones on the list on the blackboard.

Amphora Hotel   HOTEL €€

(☏28210 93224; www.amphora.gr; Parodos Theotokopoulou 20; s/d €95/120; ❋❄) Most easily found from the waterfront, this is Hania's most historically evocative hotel. Amphora is in an impressively restored Venetian mansion with elegantly decorated rooms around a courtyard. The hotel also runs the **waterfront restaurant**, which ranks as the best along that golden mile.

Vranas Studios   APARTMENT €

(☏28210 58618; www.vranas.gr; Agion Deka 10; studio €40-70; ❋❄) This place is on a lively pedestrian street and has spacious, immaculately maintained studios with kitchenettes. All rooms have polished wooden floors, balconies, TVs and telephones.

Camping Hania   CAMPGROUND €

(☏28210 31138; www.camping-chania.gr; Agii Apostoli; campsites per tent/person €4/7; P❄) Take the Kalamaki Beach bus from the east corner of Plateia 1866 (every 15 minutes) to get to this camping ground, which is 3km west of town on the beach. There is a restaurant, bar and minimarket.

🍴 Eating & Drinking

The entire waterfront of the old harbour is lined with restaurants and tavernas, many of which qualify as tourist traps. Watch out for touts trying to reel you in. There are a number of good options one street back.

TOP CHOICE **Michelas**   GREEK €

(☏28210 90026; mains €4-12; ☉10am-4pm Mon-Sat) Serving up authentic Cretan specialities at reasonable prices for 75 years, this family-run place in the Food Market uses only local ingredients and cooks up a great selection each day that you can peruse, then choose from.

Taverna Tamam   TAVERNA €€

(☏28210 58639; Zambeliou 49; mains €10-20; ☟) A taverna in an old converted *hammam* (Turkish bathhouse) one street back from the Old Harbour, Tamam has tables that spill out onto the street. This place has tasty soups and a superb selection of vegetarian specialities.

Café Kriti   BAR

(Kalergon 22; ☉8pm-late) Near the eastern end of the Venetian harbour, Kriti is known for its down-to-earth atmosphere and live traditional Cretan music.

ℹ Information

For more information visit the **Hania website** (www.chania.gr).

Tellus Travel (☏28210 91500; www.tellustravel.gr; Halidon 108; ☉8am-11pm) Has schedules and does ticketing, plus it rents out cars.

Tourist Information Office (☏28210 36155; Kydonias 29; ☉8am-2.30pm) Under the town hall; helpful and provides practical information and maps.

ℹ Getting There & Away

Air

There are several flights a day between Hania airport (CHQ) and Athens, plus a number of flights to Thessaloniki each week. An increasing number of international flights are winging directly into Hania from around Europe. The airport is 14km east of town on the Akrotiri Peninsula. Taxis to town cost €20; buses cost €2.30.

Boat

Daily ferries sail between Piraeus (€35, nine hours) and the port of Souda, 9km southeast of Hania. Frequent buses (€1.65) and taxis (€10) connect town and Souda.

Bus

Frequent buses run along Crete's northern coast to Iraklio (€13.80, 2¾ hours, half-hourly) and Rethymno (€6.20, one hour, half hourly); buses run less frequently to Paleohora (€7.60, one hour 50 minutes, four daily), Omalos (€6.90, one hour, three daily) and Hora Sfakion (€7.60, 1½ hours, three daily) from the main bus station.

Hania's bus station is on Kydonias, two blocks southwest of Plateia 1866, one of the city's main squares. Buses for the beaches west of Hania leave from the eastern side of Plateia 1866.

Samaria Gorge
Φαράγγι της Σαμαριάς

The **Samaria Gorge** (☏28250 67179; admission €5; ☉6am-3pm May–mid-Oct) is one of Europe's most spectacular gorges and a superb hike. Walkers should take rugged footwear,

ℹ BEAT THE CROWDS AT SAMARIA

The Samaria Gorge walk is extremely popular and can get quite crowded, especially in summer. Most walkers have given the gorge a day and are on a rushed trip from Hania or other northern-coast cities.

If you've got a bit of time on your hands, and decide to do things on your own, there are a couple of excellent options.

One is to take the afternoon bus from Hania and spend the night in the Cretan mountains at 1200m above sea level in **Omalos** (population 30) at the very pleasant **Neos Omalos Hotel** (☑28210 67269; www.neos-omalos.gr; s/d €25/35; ✳@). The hotel's restaurant serves excellent Cretan cuisine and local wine by the litre (€6); there's a shuttle to the start of the gorge track the next morning. Keen hikers may want to stay here a couple of nights and tackle Mt Gingilos (2080m; five hours return from Xyloskalo) before hiking the gorge.

Another option is to leave from Hania in the morning, but let the sprinters go and take your time hiking through this stupendous gorge. When you hit the coast at **Agia Roumeli** (population 125), down a cool beer and take a dip in the refreshing Libyan Sea. There are a number of restaurants and **Paralia Taverna & Rooms** (☑28250 91408; www.taverna-paralia.com; d €30; ✳📶), right on the waterfront, is a good spot to stay the night. The next day you can take a ferry either west to Sougia or Paleohora, or east to Loutro or Hora Sfakion.

food, drinks and sun protection for this strenuous five- to six-hour trek.

You can do the walk as part of an excursion tour, or independently by taking the Omalos bus from the main bus station in Hania (€6.90, one hour) to the head of the gorge at Xyloskalo (1230m). It's a 16.7km walk (all downhill) to Agia Roumeli on the coast, from where you take a boat to Hora Sfakion (€10, 1¼ hours) and then a bus back to Hania (€7.60, 1½ hours). You are not allowed to spend the night in the gorge, so you need to complete the walk in a day.

Paleohora Παλαιόχωρα

POP 2200

Paleohora (pal-ee-o-*hor*-a) has a sleepy end-of-the-line feel about it. Isolated and a bit hard to get to, the village is on a peninsula with a sandy beach to the west and a pebbly beach to the east. On summer evenings the main street is closed to traffic and the tavernas move onto the road. If you're after a relaxing few days, Paleohora is a great spot to chill out.

Heading south from the bus stop, you'll find the main street, which is called Eleftheriou Venizelou.

The ruins of the 13th-century **Venetian castle** are worth clambering over, although there's not much left after the fortress was destroyed by the Turks, the pirate Barbarossa in the 16th-century and then the Germans during WWII.

Homestay Anonymous (☑28230 41509; www.cityofpaleochora.gr/cp; s/d/tr €23/28/32; ✳) is a great option with its warm service and communal kitchen. Across the road from the sandy beach, the refurbished **Poseidon Hotel** (☑28230 41374; www.poseidon-paleohora.com; s/d/apt €35/40/50; ✳@) has a mix of tidy double rooms, studios and apartments. **Camping Paleohora** (☑28230 41120; campsites per tent/person €3/5) is 1.5km northeast of town, near the pebble beach. There's a taverna but no minimarket here.

There are plenty of eating options on the main street. Vegetarians rave about **Third Eye** (mains from €5; 🍴), just inland from the sandy beach.

There's a welcoming **tourist office** (☑28230 41507; ⏱10am-1pm & 6-9pm Wed-Mon May-Oct) on the pebble beach road near the harbour and ferry quay. The opening hours listed here are indicative only! Back on the main street, **Notos Rentals/Tsiskakis Travel** (☑28230 42110; www.notoscar.com; ⏱8am-10pm) handles almost everything, including tickets, rental cars/scooters and internet access.

There are four to six buses daily between Hania and Paleohora (€7.60, two hours). In summer, a bus for those hiking Samaria Gorge leaves for Omalos (€5.50, two hours) each morning at 6.15am. It also drops off hikers at the head of the Agia Irini Gorge.

WORTH A TRIP

SOUTHWEST COAST VILLAGES

Crete's southern coastline at its western end is dotted with remote, attractive little villages that are brilliant spots to take it easy for a few days.

Heading east from Paleohora are Sougia, Agia Roumeli, Loutro and Hora Sfakion. No road links the coastal resorts, but a daily boat from Paleohora to Sougia (€8.50, one hour), Agia Roumeli (€12.50, 1½ hours), Loutro (€14, 2½ hours) and Hora Sfakion (€16, three hours) connects the villages in summer. The ferry leaves Paleohora at 9.45am and returns along the same route from Hora Sfakion at 1pm. See www.sfakia-crete.com/sfakia-crete/ferries.html for up-to-date information.

If you're a keen hiker, keep in mind that it's also possible to walk right along this southern coast.

Sougia

At the mouth of the Agia Irini gorge, Sougia (soo-yah) is a laid-back and refreshingly undeveloped spot with a wide curve of sand-and-pebble beach. The 14.5km (six hours) walk from Paleohora is popular, as is the Agia Irini gorge walk which ends (or starts!) in Sougia. It's possible to get here by ferry, by car or on foot. Stay at **Santa Irene Hotel** (28230 51342; www.santa-irene.gr; d/tr €55/70; ❄️⚡), a smart beachside complex of apartments and studios that has its own cafe and bar.

Agia Roumeli

At the mouth of the Samaria Gorge, Agia Roumeli bristles with gorge-walkers from mid-afternoon until the ferry comes to take them away. Once they are gone, this pleasant little town goes into quiet mode until the first walkers turn up early afternoon the following day. Take your time to enjoy the village. Right on the waterfront, Paralia Taverna & Rooms (p377) offers everything you need; excellent views, tasty Cretan cuisine, cold beer and simple, clean rooms.

Loutro

This tiny village is a particularly picturesque spot, curled around the only natural harbour on the southern coast of Crete. With no vehicle access, the only way in is by boat or on foot. If you decide to walk, the track from Hora Sfakion comes via the stunning Sweetwater Beach. **Hotel Porto Loutro** (28250 91433; www.hotelportoloutro.com; s/d incl breakfast €50/60; ❄️@) has tasteful rooms with balconies overlooking the harbour. The village beach, excellent walks, rental kayaks and boat transfers to Sweetwater Beach will help to fill in a peaceful few days. Take a book and chill out.

Hora Sfakion

Renowned in Cretan history for its rebellious streak, Hora Sfakion is an amiable town. WWII history buffs know this as the place where thousands of Allied troops were evacuated by sea after the Battle of Crete. To the visitor with a bit of time, Hora Sfakion offers a row of seafront tavernas serving fresh seafood, some intriguing and eccentric locals, and an opportunity to see 'the real Crete'. **Hotel Stavris** (28250 91220; http://www.hotel-stavris-chora-sfakion.com; s/d/tr €31/36/41; ❄️⚡) has simple rooms and breakfast outside in its courtyard.

Start or finish your southwest coast villages sojourn in Hora Sfakion. There are four buses daily both to and from Hania (€7.60, two hours).

Lasithi Plateau
Οροπέδιο Λασιθίου

The mountain-fringed Lasithi Plateau in eastern Crete is laid out like an immense patchwork quilt. At 900m above sea level, it is a vast flat expanse of orchards and fields, once dotted with thousands of stone windmills with white canvas sails. There are still plenty of windmills, but most are now of the rusted metal variety and don't work.

There are 20 villages around the periphery of the plain, the largest being **Tzermiado** (population 750), **Agios Georgios** (population 550) and **Psyhro** (population 210).

The **Dikteon Cave** (☑28440 31316; admission €4; ☺8am-6pm Jun-Oct, to 2.30pm Nov-May) is where, according to mythology, Rhea hid the newborn Zeus from Cronos, his offspring-gobbling father. The cave, which covers 2200 sq metres and features numerous stalactites and stalagmites, is 1km from the village of Psyhro.

There are daily buses to the area from Iraklio and Agios Nikolaos, though having your own wheels would make life a lot easier.

Agios Nikolaos
Αγιος Νικόλαος

Agios Nikolaos (*ah-yee-os nih-ko-laos*) is an attractive former fishing village on Crete's northeast coast. The de facto town centre is around the picturesque **Voulismeni Lake**, which is ringed with cafes and tavernas, and is linked to the sea by a short canal. The ferry port is 150m past the canal.

The two nice little beaches in town, **Kytroplatia** and **Ammos**, get a bit crowded in summer. **Almyros Beach**, about 1km south, gets less so. Agios Nikolaos acts as a base for excursion tours to **Spinalonga Island**. The island's massive fortress was built by the Venetians in 1579 but taken by the Turks in 1715. It later became a leper colony. Nowadays it's a fascinating place to explore. Tours cost around €25.

Pergola Hotel (☑28410 28152; Sarolidi 20; s/d €35-40; ❋🛜) is a friendly family-run place out near the ferry port, with clean rooms, balconies and sea views. **Du Lac Hotel** (☑28410 22711; www.dulachotel.gr; Oktovriou 17; s/d €40/60; ❋🛜) is a refurbished hotel in a great location with views out over the lake.

Finding a place to eat will not be a problem; there are a lot of options around the lake. **Taverna Itanos** (☑28410 25340; Kyprou 1; mains €6-12), tucked away on a backstreet off the main square, is superb, has reasonable prices and offers the opportunity to wander into the kitchen and see what looks good.

The very helpful **municipal tourist office** (☑28410 22357; www.agiosnikolaos.gr; ☺8am-9pm Apr-Nov) is on the north side of the bridge over the canal and does a good job of finding sleeping options.

Buses to Iraklio run every 30 minutes (€7.10, 1½ hours).

Sitia   Σητεία
POP 9000

Sitia (si-*tee*-a) is a laid-back little town in the northeastern corner of Crete that has escaped much of the tourism frenzy along the north coast. It is on an attractive bay flanked by mountains, and is an easy place to unwind.

The main square, Plateia Iroon Plytehniou, is in the corner of the bay, and recognisable by its palm trees and statue of a dying soldier.

Porto Belis Travel (☑28430 22370; www.portobelis-crete.gr; Karamanli Aven 34), on the waterfront just before the start of the town beach, is a one-stop shop, handling ticketing, rental cars and scooters, and accommodation bookings in town. It also runs **Porto Belis House** (☑28430 22370; d/q €35/60; ❋🛜) above the travel agency. These rooms are immaculate, have kitchens and look straight out onto the beach.

Itanos Hotel (☑28430 22900; www.itanoshotel.com; Karamanli 4; s/d incl breakfast €50/68; ❋@) is an upmarket establishment next to the square with its own excellent **Itanos Taverna** on the waterfront outside the front door.

The waterfront is lined with tavernas. **Balcony** (☑28430 25084; www.balcony-restaurant.com; Foundalidou 19; mains €12-19), a couple of streets back, is the finest dining in Sitia. It's in a charmingly decorated neoclassical building.

The helpful **tourist office** (☑28430 28300; Karamanli; ☺9.30am-2.30pm & 5-8.30pm Mon-Fri, 9.30am-2pm Sat), on the waterfront, has town maps.

Sitia airport (JSH) has flights to Athens. There are buses daily to Iraklio (€14.70, 3½ hours) via Agios Nikolaos (€7.60, 1½ hours).

DODECANESE
ΔΩΔΕΚΑΝΗΣΑ

Strung out along the coast of western Turkey, the 12 main islands of the Dodecanese (*dodeca* means 12) have suffered a turbulent past of invasions and occupations that have endowed them with a fascinating diversity.

Conquered successively by the Romans, the Arabs, the Knights of St John, the Turks, the Italians, then liberated from the Germans by British and Greek commandos in

1944, the Dodecanese became part of Greece in 1947. These days, tourists rule.

The islands themselves range from the verdant and mountainous to the rocky and dry. While Rhodes and Kos host highly developed tourism, the more remote islands await those in search of traditional island life.

Rhodes   Ρόδος

POP 98,000

Rhodes (Rodos in Greek) is the largest island in the Dodecanese. According to mythology, the sun god Helios chose Rhodes as his bride and bestowed light, warmth and vegetation upon her. The blessing seems to have paid off, for Rhodes produces more flowers and sunny days than most Greek islands. Throw in an east coast of virtually uninterrupted sandy beaches and it's easy to understand why sun-starved northern Europeans flock here.

ⓘ Getting There & Away

Air

There are plenty of flights daily between Rhodes' **Diagoras airport** (RHO) and Athens, plus less-regular flights to Karpathos, Kastellorizo, Thessaloniki, Iraklio and Samos. Options are growing.

Rhodes

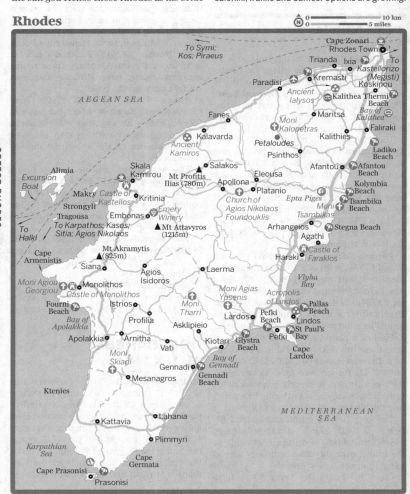

TALKING TURKEY

Turkey is so close that it looks like you could swim there from many of the Dodecanese and Northeastern Aegean islands. Here are the boat options:

Marmaris or Fethiye from Rhodes (p625)

Bodrum from Kos (p629)

Kuşadasi (near Ephesus) from Samos (p630)

Çeşme (near İzmir) from Chios (p633)

Dikili (near Ayvalık) from Lesvos (p633)

International charter flights swarm in summer, plus budget airlines fly in with scheduled flights. The airport is on the west coast, 16km southwest of Rhodes Town; 25 minutes and €2.20 by bus.

Boat

Rhodes is the main port of the Dodecanese and there is a complex array of departures. There are daily ferries from Rhodes to Piraeus (€59, 13 hours). Most sail via the Dodecanese north of Rhodes, but at least twice a week there is a service via Karpathos, Crete and the Cyclades.

In summer, catamaran services run up and down the Dodecanese daily from Rhodes to Symi, Kos, Kalymnos, Nisyros, Tilos, Patmos and Leros.

To Turkey

There are boats between Rhodes and Marmaris in Turkey (one-way/return including port taxes,

€50/75, 50 minutes). Check www.marmarisinfo.com for up-to-date details.

You can also travel between Rhodes and Fethi-ye, Turkey (one way/return including port taxes €50/75, 90 minutes). See www.alaturkaturkey.com.

RHODES TOWN

POP 56,000

Rhodes' capital is Rhodes Town, on the northern tip of the island. Its **Old Town**, the largest inhabited medieval town in Europe, is enclosed within massive walls and is a joy to explore. To the north is **New Town**, the commercial centre. The **town beach**, which looks out at Turkey runs around the peninsula at the northern end of New Town.

The main port, **Commercial Harbour**, is east of the Old Town, and is where the big interisland ferries dock. Northwest of here is **Mandraki Harbour**, lined with excursion boats and smaller ferries, hydrofoils and catamarans. It was the supposed site of the Colossus of Rhodes, a 32m-high bronze statue of Apollo built over 12 years (294–282 BC). The statue stood for a mere 65 years before being toppled by an earthquake.

🛏 Sleeping

TOP CHOICE / Marco
Polo Mansion   BOUTIQUE HOTEL €€

(22410 25562; www.marcopolomansion.gr; Agiou Fanouriou 40, Old Town; d incl breakfast from €90-180; ✳🅿🛜) In a 15th-century building in the Turkish quarter of the Old Town, this place is rich in Ottoman-era colours and features

GREECE RHODES

DON'T MISS

OLD TOWN

A wander around Rhodes' World Heritage–listed Old Town is a must. It is reputedly the world's finest surviving example of medieval fortification, with 12m-thick walls. Throngs of visitors pack its busier streets and eating, sleeping and shopping options abound.

The Knights of St John lived in the Knights' Quarter in the northern end of the Old Town. The cobbled **Odos Ippoton** (Ave of the Knights) is lined with magnificent medieval buildings, the most imposing of which is the **Palace of the Grand Masters** (22410 23359; admission €6; ⊗8.30am-3pm Tue-Sun), which was restored, but never used, as a holiday home for Mussolini.

The 15th-century Knight's Hospital now houses the **Archaeological Museum** (22410 27657; Plateia Mousiou; admission €3; ⊗8am-4pm Tue-Sun). The splendid building was restored by the Italians and has an impressive collection that includes the ethereal marble statue *Aphrodite of Rhodes*.

The pink-domed **Mosque of Süleyman**, at the top of Sokratous, was built in 1522 to commemorate the Ottoman victory against the knights, then rebuilt in 1808.

You can take a pleasant walk around the imposing walls of the Old Town via the wide and pedestrianised moat walk.

DON'T MISS

MARCO POLO CAFÉ

A top spot to eat in Rhodes. **Marco Polo Café** (📞22410 25562; www.marco polomansion.gr; Agiou Fanouriou 40, Old Town) is worth finding in the back-streets of the Old Town. Owner Efi is as tastefully colourful as her mansion and garden restaurant. This place serves its guests with a rare passion – and the desserts are exquisite!

in glossy European magazines. In the secluded garden is the highly recommended Marco Polo Café.

TOP CHOICE Mango Rooms PENSION €
(📞22410 24877; www.mango.gr; Plateia Dorieos 3, Old Town; s/d/tr €44/58/66; ❋@☎) A good-value, friendly one-stop shop near the back of the Old Town, Mango has an outdoor restaurant, bar and internet cafe down below, six well-kept rooms above, and a sunny terrace on top. Open year-round.

Hotel Andreas PENSION €€
(📞22410 34156; www.hotelandreas.com; Omirou 28d, Old Town; s/d/tr €45/70/85; ❋@☎) Tasteful Hotel Andreas has individually decorated rooms and terrific views from its terrace. Rates differ by room; check it all out online, and choose your room before you go.

Hotel International HOTEL €€
(📞22410 24595; www.international-hotel.gr; 12 Kazouli St, New Town; s/d/tr €45/60/75; ❋☎) In New Town, the International is a friendly family-run operation with immaculately clean and good-value rooms only a few minutes from Rhodes' main town beach. It's a 10-minute stroll to Old Town, and prices drop by a third out of high season.

✗ Eating & Drinking

There's food and drink everywhere you look in Rhodes. Outside the city walls are many cheap places in the New Market, at the southern end of Mandraki Harbour. Head further north into New Town for countless restaurants and bars.

Inside the walls, Old Town has it all in terms of touts and over-priced tavernas trying to separate less-savvy tourists from their euro. The back alleys tend to throw up better-quality eateries and prices. Delve into the maze and see what you can come up with.

To Meltemi TAVERNA €
(Kountourioti 8; mains €10-15) At the northern end of Mandraki Harbour, To Meltemi is one place worth heading to. Gaze out on Turkey from this beachside taverna where the seafood is superb. Try the grilled calamari stuffed with tomato and feta, and inspect the old photos of Rhodes.

❶ Information

For more information, visit the Rodos website (www.rodos.gr).

Tourist Information Office (EOT; 📞22410 35226; cnr Makariou & Papagou; ⏰8am-2.45pm Mon-Fri) Has brochures, maps and *Rodos News*, a free English-language newspaper.

Triton Holidays (📞22410 21690; www.triton dmc.gr; Plastira 9, Mandraki) In the New Town, this place is exceptionally helpful, handling accommodation bookings, ticketing and rental cars. The island-hopping experts, Triton can provide up-to-date advice in these times of constantly changing flight and boat schedules. Email ahead for advice.

❶ Getting Around

BUS Rhodes Town has two bus stations a block apart next to the New Market. The west-side bus station serves the airport, Kamiros (€4.60, 55 minutes) and the west coast. The east-side bus station serves the east coast, Lindos (€5, 1½ hours) and the inland southern villages.

AROUND THE ISLAND

The **Acropolis of Lindos** (admission €6; ⏰8.30am-6pm Tue-Sun Jun-Aug, to 2.30pm Sep-May), 47km south from Rhodes Town, is an ancient city spectacularly perched atop a 116m-high rocky outcrop. Below is the town of **Lindos**, a tangle of streets with elaborately decorated 17th-century houses.

The extensive ruins of **Kamiros**, an ancient Doric city on the west coast, are well preserved, with the remains of houses, baths, a cemetery and a temple, but the site should be visited as much for its lovely setting on a gentle hillside overlooking the sea.

Karpathos Κάρπαθος
POP 6000

The elongated, mountainous island of Karpathos (*kar*-pah-thos), midway between Crete and Rhodes, is a scenic, hype-free place with a cosy port, numerous beaches and unspoilt villages. It is a wealthy island, reputedly receiving more money from emigrants living abroad than any other Greek island.

The main port and capital is **Pigadia**, on the southeast coast. The northern village of **Olymbos** is like a living museum. Locals wear traditional outfits and the facades of houses are decorated with bright plaster reliefs.

A great option on Karpathos is to hire a car and tour this rugged island on its excellent roads. The 19km stretch from Spoa to Olymbos may finally be sealed by the time you read this. Check before you go though!

Elias Rooms (☏22450 22446; www.elias rooms.com; s/d €35/40; 🛜) is an excellent accommodation option. Owner Elias is a mine of information and his rooms have great views while being in a quiet part of town. Elias' website can tell you all you need to know about Karpathos and he is happy to provide information by email.

Possi Travel (☏22450 22235; www.possi -holidays.gr; ⏱8am-1pm & 5.30-8.30pm), on pedestrianised Apodimon Karpathion, can suggest local tours and handles air and ferry tickets.

In summer, **Karpathos airport** (AOK), 13km southwest of Pigadia, has daily flights to Rhodes and Athens. With a huge new terminal, international charter flights also wing their way in. There are two ferries a week to Rhodes (€23, four hours) and two to Piraeus (€41, 17 hours) via Crete and the Cyclades.

There are also excursions from Pigadia to Diafani, at the north of the island, that include a bus trip to Olymbos.

WORTH A TRIP

CRYSTAL CLEAR

If you like mind-bogglingly clear water when you go to the beach, head to Karpathos for some of the clearest turquoise wet stuff to be seen anywhere. **Apella** and **Ahata** beaches, both north of Pigadia, are stunning; **Ammoöpi**, 8km south of the capital, will make you drool. Karpathos' top beaches are best accessed with your own wheels.

southern end of the island. Its **museum** is impressive, but try to avoid the hordes of day trippers who arrive at around 10.30am on excursion boats from Rhodes.

Budget accommodation is scarce. **Rooms Katerina** (☏69451 30112, 22460 71813; www.symigreece.com/sg/villakaterina; d €30; ❄🛜) is excellent, but get in quick as there are only three rooms. There is a communal kitchen with breathtaking views down over the port, and helpful Katerina is happy to answer all your questions.

On the waterfront next to the clock tower, **Hotel Nireus** (☏22460 72400; www.nireus-hotel.gr; s/d incl breakfast €80/115; ❄🛜) is bright, friendly, has free wi-fi and the bonus of being able to swim right out front.

Kalodoukas Holidays (☏22460 71077; www.kalodoukas.gr) handles accommodation bookings, ticketing and has a book of walking trails on the island.

There are frequent boats between Rhodes and Kos that stop at Symi, as well as daily excursion boats from Rhodes. **Symi Tours** (www.symitours.com) runs excursions on Saturdays to Datça in Turkey for €40.

Small taxi boats visit inaccessible east-coast beaches daily in summer, including spectacular Agios Georgious, backed by a 150m sheer cliff.

Symi   Σύμη

POP 2600

Simply superb, Symi is an inviting island to the north of Rhodes that should be on all island-hopper itineraries. The port town of **Gialos** is a Greek treasure, with pastel-coloured mansions heaped up the hills surrounding the protective little harbour. Symi is swamped by day trippers from Rhodes, and it's worth staying over to enjoy the island in cruise control. The town is divided into Gialos, the port and the tranquil *horio* (village) above it, accessible by taxi, bus or 360 steps from the harbour.

There is no tourist office. The best source of information is the free monthly English-language **Symi Visitor** (www.symivisitor.com), which includes maps of the town.

The **Monastery of Panormitis** (⏱dawn-sunset) is a hugely popular complex at the

Kos   Κως

POP 17,900

Captivating Kos, only 5km from the Turkish peninsula of Bodrum, is popular with history buffs as the birthplace of Hippocrates (460–377 BC), the father of medicine. The island also attracts an entirely different crowd – sun-worshipping beach lovers from northern Europe who flock here during summer. Tourism rules the roost, and whether you are there to explore the Castle of the Knights or to party till you drop, Kos should keep you happy for at least a few days.

Kos Town is based around a circular harbour, protected by the imposing Castle of the Knights, at the eastern end of the island. The ferry quay is just to the north of the castle.

◉ Sights & Activities

Kos Town has recently developed a number of **bicycle paths** and renting a bike from one of the many places along the waterfront is a great option for getting around town and seeing the sights.

If the historical stuff is all too much, wander around and relax with the Scandinavians at the town beach past the northern end of the harbour.

Castle of the Knights   CASTLE
(☑22420 27927; admission €4; ⊙8am-2.30pm Tue-Sun) Built in the 14th century, this impressive castle protected the knights from the encroaching Ottomans, and was originally separated from town by a moat. That moat is now Finikon, a major street. Entrance to the castle is over the stone bridge behind the Hippocrates Plane Tree.

THE KNIGHTS OF ST JOHN

Do some island-hopping in the Dodecanese and you'll quickly realise that the Knights of St John left behind a whole lot of castles.

Originally formed as the Knights Hospitaller in Jerusalem in AD 1080 to provide care for poor and sick pilgrims, the knights relocated to Rhodes (via Cyprus) after the loss of Jerusalem in the First Crusade. They ousted the ruling Genoese in 1309, built a stack of castles in the Dodecanese to protect their new home, then set about irking the neighbours by committing acts of piracy against Ottoman shipping. Sultan Süleyman the Magnificent, not a man you'd want to irk, took offence and set about dislodging the knights from their strongholds. Rhodes finally capitulated in 1523 and the remaining knights relocated to Malta. They set up there as the Sovereign Military Hospitaller of Jerusalem, of Rhodes, and of Malta.

Asklipieion   ARCHAEOLOGICAL SITE
(☑22420 28763; adult/student €4/3; ⊙8am-7.30pm Tue-Sun) On a pine-clad hill 4km southwest of Kos Town stand the extensive ruins of the renowned healing centre where Hippocrates practised medicine. Groups of doctors come from all over the world to visit.

Ancient Agora   RUIN
The ancient agora, with the ruins of the **Shrine of Aphrodite** and **Temple of Hercules**, is just off Plateia Eleftherias. North of the agora is the **Hippocrates Plane Tree**, under which the man himself is said to have taught his pupils.

🛏 Sleeping

TOP CHOICE **Hotel Afendoulis**   HOTEL €
(☑22420 25321; www.afendoulishotel.com; Evripilou 1; s/d €30/50; ⊙Mar-Nov; ❄@🛰) In a pleasant, quiet area about 500m south of the ferry quay, this well-kept hotel won't disappoint. Run by the charismatic English-speaking Alexis, this is a great place to relax and enjoy Kos. Port- and bus-station transfers are complimentary, and you can get your laundry done here.

Hotel Sonia   HOTEL €
(☑22420 28798; www.hotelsonia.gr; Irodotou 9; s/d/tr €35/50/85; ❄🛰) Recently refurbished, Sonia's place has long been a popular spot to stay in Kos. It has large rooms and a relaxing veranda and garden. They'll pick you up at the port or bus station for free and there are laundry facilities on site. It's back behind the Dolphin roundabout.

✗ Eating & Drinking

Restaurants line the central waterfront of the old harbour, but you might want to hit the backstreets for value. There are plenty of cheap places to eat on the beach to the north of the harbour, and a dozen discos and clubs around the streets of Diakon and Nafklirou, just north of the agora.

Stadium Restaurant   SEAFOOD €
(☑22420 27880; mains €10-18) On the long waterfront 500m southeast of the castle, Stadium serves succulent seafood at good prices, along with excellent views of Turkey.

❶ Information

Visit www.kosinfo.gr for more information.
Exas Travel (☑22420 28545; www.exas.gr) Near the Archaeological Museum, in the heart

of town, to the southwest of the harbour; handles schedules, ticketing and excursions.

Municipal Tourist Office (22420 24460; www.kosinfo.gr; Vasileos Georgiou 1; ⊙8am-2.30pm & 3-10pm Mon-Fri, 9am-2pm Sat May-Oct) On the waterfront directly south of the port; provides maps and accommodation information.

Getting There & Around

Air
There are daily flights to Athens from Kos' Ippokratis airport (KGS), which is 28km southwest of Kos Town. International charters and scheduled flights wing in throughout the summer from around Europe. Get to/from the airport by bus (€4) or taxi (€30).

Boat
There are frequent ferries from Rhodes to Kos that continue on to Piraeus (€53, 10 hours), as well as ferries heading the opposite way. Daily fast-boat connections head north to Patmos and Samos, and south to Symi and Rhodes.

To Turkey
In summer boats depart daily for Bodrum in Turkey (€20 return, one hour). Wander the waterfront and take your pick.

Bus
There is a good public bus system on Kos, with the bus station on Kleopatras, near the ruins at the back of town.

Mini-Train
Next to the tourist office is a blue mini-train for Asklipion (€5 return, hourly, Tuesday to Sunday) and a green mini-train that does city tours (€4, 20 minutes).

Patmos   Πάτμος

POP 3050

Patmos has a sense of 'spirit of place', and with its great beaches and relaxed atmosphere, it's a superb place to unwind.

The main town and port of Skala is about halfway down the east coast of Patmos, with a protected harbour. Towering above Skala to the south is the *hora*, crowned by the immense Monastery of St John the Theologian.

◉ Sights & Activities

Beaches   BEACHES

Patmos' coastline provides secluded coves, mostly with pebble beaches. The best is **Psili Ammos**, in the south, reached by excursion boat from Skala port. **Lambi Beach**, on the

WORTH A TRIP

ST JOHN & THE APOCALYPSE

For the religiously motivated, Patmos is not to be missed. Orthodox and Western Christians have long made pilgrimages to Patmos, for it was here that John the Divine ensconced himself in a cave and wrote the Book of Revelation.

The **Cave of the Apocalypse** (admission free, treasury €6; ⊙8am-1.30pm daily & 4-6pm Tue, Thu & Sun) is halfway between the port and Hora. Take a bus from the port or hike up the Byzantine path, which starts from a signposted spot on the Skala–Hora road.

The **Monastery of St John the Theologian** (admission free; ⊙8am-1.30pm daily & 4-6pm Tue, Thu & Sun) looks more like a castle than a monastery and tops Patmos like a crown. It exhibits all kinds of monastic treasures, and attending a service here is unforgettable.

north coast, is a pebble-beach-lover's dream come true.

🛏 Sleeping

Pension Maria Pascalidis   PENSION €
(22470 32152; s/d without bathroom €20/30) Maria has cosy rooms in a fragrant citrus-tree garden on the road heading up to the Hora and Monastery. A travellers' favourite, guests share a communal bathroom and kitchen.

Blue Bay Hotel   BOUTIQUE HOTEL €€
(22470 31165; www.bluebaypatmos.gr; s/d/ tr incl breakfast €65/90/108; ※@☎) South of the harbour in Skala, this recommended waterfront hotel has superb rooms, internet access, and breakfast included in its rates (which tumble outside of high season).

❶ Information

See the websites www.patmosweb.gr, and www. patmos-island.com for more information.

Apollon Travel (22470 31324; apollontravel@stratas.gr) On the waterfront; handles schedules and ticketing.

Tourist Office (22470 31666; ⊙8am-6pm Mon-Fri Jun-Sep) In the white building opposite the port in Skala, along with the post office and police station.

GREECE PATMOS

ⓘ Getting There & Away

BOAT Patmos is well connected, with ferries to Piraeus (€37, seven hours) and south to Rhodes (€32, six hours). In summer, daily high-speed services head south to Kos and Rhodes, and north to Samos.

NORTHEASTERN AEGEAN ISLANDS
ΤΑ ΝΗΣΙΑ ΤΟΥ ΒΟΡΕΙΟ ΑΝΑΤΟΛΙΚΟ ΑΙΓΑΙΟΥ

One of Greece's best-kept secrets, these far-flung islands are strewn across the north-eastern corner of the Aegean Sea, closer to Turkey than mainland Greece. They harbour unspoilt scenery, welcoming locals, fascinating independent cultures and remain relatively calm even when other Greek islands are sagging with tourists at the height of summer.

Samos   Σάμος

POP 32,800

A lush mountainous island only 3km from Turkey, Samos has a glorious history as the legendary birthplace of Hera, wife and sister of god-of-all-gods Zeus. Samos was an important centre of Hellenic culture, and the mathematician Pythagoras and storyteller Aesop are among its sons. The island has beaches that bake in summer, and a hinterland that is superb for hiking. Spring brings with it pink flamingos, wildflowers and orchids that the island grows for export, while summer brings throngs of package tourists.

ⓘ Getting There & Around

Air

There are daily flights to Athens from **Samos airport** (SMI), 4km west of Pythagorio, plus less-regular flights to Iraklio, Rhodes, Chios and Thessaloniki. Charter flights wing in from Europe in summer.

Boat

Samos has two main ports: Vathy (Samos Town) in the northeast and Pythagorio on the southeast coast. Those coming from the south by boat generally arrive in Pythagorio. Big ferries use Vathy. Once you're on Samos and have onward tickets, double-check where your boat is leaving from. Buses between the two take 25 minutes.

A maritime hub, Samos offers daily ferries to Piraeus (€48, 10 hours), plus ferries heading north to Chios and west to the Cyclades. Once the season is up and going, fast speed services head south to Patmos and continue to Kos.

Bus

You can get to most of the island's villages and beaches by bus.

Car & Motorcycle

Rental cars and scooters are readily available around the island (cars/scooters from €60/30 per day).

To Turkey

There are daily ferries to Kuşadasi (for Ephesus) in Turkey (one-way/return €35/45, plus €10 port taxes). Day excursions are also available from April to October. Check with ITSA Travel in Vathy for up-to-date details.

VATHY (SAMOS TOWN)   ΒΑΘΥ ΣΑΜΟΣ

POP 2030

Busy Vathy is an attractive working port town. Most of the action is along Themis-

Samos

tokleous Sofouli, the main street that runs along the waterfront. The main square, Plateia Pythagorou, in the middle of the waterfront, is recognisable by its four palm trees and statue of a lion.

The **Archaeological Museum** (adult/student €3/2, free Sun; ☺8.30am-3pm Tue-Sun) by the municipal gardens, is first-rate and one of the best in the islands.

Pythagoras Hotel (☎22730 28601; www.pythagorashotel.com; Kallistratou 12; s/d/tr €20/35/45; ☺Feb-Nov; ✳@☎) is a friendly, great-value place with a convivial atmosphere, run by English-speaking Stelio. There is a restaurant serving tasty home-cooked meals, a bar, satellite TV and internet access. Facing inland, the hotel is 400m to the left of the quay. Call ahead for free pick-up on arrival.

Ino Village Hotel (☎22730 23241; www.inovillagehotel.com; Kalami; s/d/tr incl breakfast €65/80/100; P✳☎☀) is an impressive, elegant place in the hills north of the ferry quay. Its **Elea Restaurant** on the terrace serves up both invigorated Greek cuisine and views over town and the harbour.

ITSA Travel (☎22730 23605; www.itsatravelsamos.gr), opposite the quay, is helpful with travel enquiries, excursions, accommodation and luggage storage.

To get to Vathy's bus station, follow the waterfront south and turn left onto Lekati, 250m south of Plateia Pythagorou (just before the police station).

PYTHAGORIO ΠΥΘΑΓΟΡΕΙΟ
POP 1300

Pretty Pythagorio, 25 minutes south of Vathy by bus, is where you'll disembark if you've come by boat from Patmos. It is a small, enticing town with a yacht-lined harbour and a holiday atmosphere.

The 1034m-long **Evpalinos Tunnel** (adult/student €4/2; ☺8am-8pm Tue-Sun), built in the 6th century BC, was dug by political prisoners and used as an aqueduct to bring water from Mt Ampelos (1140m). In the Middle Ages, locals hid out in it during pirate raids. It's a 20-minute walk north of town.

Polyxeni Hotel (☎22730 61590; www.polyxenihotel.com; s/d/tr €40/45/55; ✳☎) is a fun place to stay in the heart of the waterfront action. **Pension Despina** (☎22730 61677; www.samosrooms.gr/despina; A Nikolaou; d €35; ✳☎), a block back from the water, offers simple studios and rooms, some with balconies and kitchenettes.

Tavernas and bars line the waterfront. **Poseidon Restaurant** (☎22730 62530; mains

THAT TRIANGLE MAN

You don't need much of an imagination to figure out where the cute little town of Pythagorio got its name! The impressive statue of Pythagoras and his triangle on the town's waterfront should have you recalling his theorem from your high school maths days. If right-angled triangles weren't your thing, buy a T-shirt with the theorem emblazoned on it to remind you.

from €7), on the small town beach, past the jetty with the Pythagoras statue on it, offers superb seafood.

The cordial **municipal tourist office** (☎22730 61389; deap5@otenet.gr; ☺8am-9.30pm) is two blocks from the waterfront on the main street, Lykourgou Logotheti. The bus stop is two blocks further inland on the same street.

Around Samos

Ireon (adult/student €4/2; ☺8.30am-8pm Tue-Sun), the legendary birthplace of the goddess Hera, is 8km west of Pythagorio. The temple at this World Heritage site was enormous – four times the Parthenon – though only one column remains.

The captivating villages of **Vourliotes** and **Manolates**, on the slopes of imposing Mt Ampelos, northwest of Vathy, are excellent walking territory and have many marked pathways.

Choice beaches include **Tsamadou** on the north coast, **Votsalakia** in the southwest and **Psili Ammos** to the east of Pythagorio. The latter is sandy and stares straight out at Turkey, barely a couple of kilometres away.

Chios Χίος
POP 54,000

Due to its thriving shipping and mastic industries (mastic produces the resin used in chewing gum), Chios (*hee*-os) has never really bothered much with tourism. If you are an off-the-beaten-track type of Greek Islands traveller, you'll find Chios all the more appealing.

Chios Town, on the island's eastern coast, is a working port and home to half the island's inhabitants. A main street runs in a semicircle

THE ORIGINAL CHEWING GUM

Chios is home to the world's only gum-producing mastic trees and the southern *masti-hohoria* (mastic villages) were wealthy for centuries. Not only were they wealthy, but the mastic trees are also said to have saved them when the Turks came and slaughtered the rest of the island's residents. The sultan's reputed fondness for mastic chewing gum – and the rumour that his harem girls used it for keeping their teeth clean and their breath fresh – meant that the *mastihohoria* were spared.

These days, **Masticulture Ecotourism Activities** (☎22710 76084; www.masticulture.com) in the southern village of Mesta, introduces visitors to the local history and culture, including mastic cultivation tours. In Chios Town, on the waterfront, **Mastihashop** (☎22710 81600; www.mastihashop.com; Leoforos Egeou 36) sells products such as mastic chewing gum, toothpaste and soaps, and **Mastic Spa** (☎22710 28643; www.masticspa.com; Leoforos Egeou 12) sells mastic-based cosmetics.

around the port, with most ferries docking at its northern end. The *kastro* (old Turkish quarter) is to the north of the ferry quay, and Plateia Vounakiou, the main square, is just south and inland from the quay.

◉ Sights & Activities

In Chios Town, **Philip Argenti Museum** (Korais; admission €1.50; ⊙8am-2pm Mon-Thu, to 2pm & 5-7.30pm Fri, 8am-12.30pm Sat) contains the treasures of the wealthy Argenti family.

World Heritage–listed **Nea Moni** (New Monastery; admission free; ⊙8am-1pm & 4-8pm) is 14km west of Chios Town and reveals some fine Byzantine art, with mosaics dating from the 11th century. The mosaics survived, but the resident monks were massacred by the Turks in 1822. You can see their dented skulls in the chapel at the monastery's entrance.

Those in the ghost village of **Anavatos**, 10km from Nea Moni and built on a precipitous cliff, preferred a different fate, hurling themselves off the cliff rather than being taken captive by the Turks.

Pyrgi, 24km southwest of Chios Town, is one of Greece's most unusual villages. The facades of the town's dwellings are decorated with intricate grey-and-white geometric patterns and motifs. The tiny medieval town of **Mesta**, 10km from Pyrgi and nestled within fortified walls, features cobbled streets, overhead arches and a labyrinth of streets designed to confuse pirates.

🛏 Sleeping

TOP
CHOICE **Chios Rooms**　　　　PENSION €
(☎22710 20198; www.chiosrooms.gr; Leoforos Egeou 110; s/d/tr €30/35/45; 🛜) A top location to stay, this place is upstairs in a restored neoclassical house on the waterfront at the southern

end of the harbour. It has bright, airy rooms, some with en suite bathrooms, and is being restored lovingly by its Kiwi owner, Don, who is a mine of information on Chios.

Hotel Kyma　　　　HOTEL €€
(☎22710 44500; kyma@chi.forthnet.gr; Evgenias Handris 1; s/d/tr incl breakfast €70/90/110; ❄🛜) Just past the southern end of the waterfront, this place occupies a charismatic century-old mansion and is run by the enthusiastic multilingual Theodoris. Ask for a room overlooking the sea.

🍴 Eating

The waterfront has ample options in the way of eateries and bars, though for cheap eats, head one street back onto El Venizelou, which is lined with shops. The Plateia Vounakiou area, inland from where the ferries dock, also has up some good options.

TOP
CHOICE **Hotzas Taverna**　　　　TAVERNA €
(☎22710 42787; Kondyli 3; mains from €6) Up the back of town, Hotzas is known by locals to provide the best Greek fare on the island. Get a local to mark it on a map, and enjoy the walk. It's worth the effort of finding.

ℹ Information

Check out the **Chios website** (www.chios.gr) for more information.
Agean Travel (☎22710 41277; www.aegeanspirit.gr; Leoforos Egeou 114)
Municipal Tourist Office (☎22710 44389; infochio@otenet.gr; Kanari 18; ⊙7am-3pm & 6.30-10pm Apr-Oct, to 3pm Nov-Mar) Information on accommodation, car rental, bus and boat schedules.

Getting There & Around

Air

There are daily flights from Chios airport (JKH) to Athens and some to Rhodes, Samos, Lesvos and Thessaloniki. The airport is 4km south of Chios Town; there's no bus, a taxi costs €8.

Boat

Ferries sail daily to Piraeus (€32.50, six hours) and Lesvos (€19.50, three hours). Boats also head out less regularly to Thessaloniki and Samos.

Bus

Chios Town has two bus stations. Blue buses go regularly to local villages and Karfas Beach, and leave from the local bus station at the main square. Buses to Pyrgi (€2.70) and Mesta (€3.90) and other distant points leave from the long-distance bus station on the waterfront near the ferry quay.

To Turkey

Boats to Turkey run all year from Chios, with daily sailings from July to September to Çeşme (one-way/return €25/30), near İzmir. For details, check out **Miniotis Lines** (22710 24670; www.miniotis.gr; Neorion 24).

Lesvos (Mytilini) Λέσβος (Μυτιλήνη)

POP 93,500

Lesvos, or Mytilini as it is often called, tends to do things in a big way. The third-largest of the Greek Islands after Crete and Evia, Lesvos produces half the world's ouzo and is home to over 11 million olive trees. Mountainous yet fertile, the island presents excellent hiking and birdwatching opportunities, but remains relatively untouched in terms of tourism development.

Lesvos has always been a centre of philosophy and artistic achievement, and to this day is a spawning ground for innovative ideas in the arts and politics. An excellent source of information on the island is www.greeknet.com.

The two main towns on the island are the capital, **Mytilini**, on the southeast coast, and attractive **Mithymna** on the north coast.

Getting There & Away

Air

Written up on flight schedules as Mytilene, Lesvos' Odysseas airport (MJT) has daily connections with Athens, plus flights to Thessaloniki,

Iraklio and a growing number of domestic destinations. The airport is 8km south of Mytilini town; a taxi costs €9 and a bus to town costs €1.50.

Boat

In summer there are daily fast/slow boats to Piraeus (€37/27, eight/13 hours) via Chios, and boats to Limnos, Thessaloniki and Samos.

To Turkey

There are regular ferries a week to Dikeli port (which serves Ayvalık) and to Fokias (which serves İzmir). Stop by Zoumboulis Tours in Mytilini for ticketing and schedules.

MYTILINI ΜΥΤΙΛΗΝΗ
POP 27,300

The capital and main port, Mytilini, is built between two harbours (north and south) with an imposing fortress on the promontory to the east. All ferries dock at the southern harbour, and most of the town's action is around this waterfront. With a large university campus, Mytilini is a lively place year-round.

Sights & Activities

Archaeological Museum MUSEUM
(8 Noemvriou; adult/child €3/2; 8.30am-3pm Tue-Sun) Mytilini's excellent neoclassical Archaeological Museum has a fascinating collection from Neolithic to Roman times.

SAPPHO, LESBIANS & LESVOS

Sappho, one of Greece's great ancient poets, was born on Lesvos during the 7th century BC. Most of her work was devoted to love and desire, and the objects of her affection were often female. Because of this, Sappho's name and birthplace have come to be associated with female homosexuality.

These days, Lesvos is visited by many lesbians paying homage to Sappho. The whole island is very gay-friendly, in particular the southwestern beach resort of Skala Eresou, which is built over ancient Eresos, where Sappho was born. The village is well set up to cater to lesbian needs and has a 'Women Together' festival held annually in September. Check out www.sapphotravel.com for details.

There is an excellent statue of Sappho in the main square on the waterfront in Mytilini.

Teriade Museum
MUSEUM
(☎22510 23372; admission €2; ☺8.30am-2pm & 5-8pm Tue-Sun) Take a local bus 4km south of Mytilini to the village of Varia, where an unexpected treasure awaits: the Teriade Museum, with its astonishing collection of paintings by world-renowned artists like Picasso, Chagall, Miro, Le Corbusier and Matisse.

Theophilos Museum
MUSEUM
(admission €2; ☺9am-1pm & 5-8pm Tue-Sun) This shrine to the prolific folk painter and Lesvos native Theophilos is located 4km south of Mytilini in Varia village, next to the Teriade Museum.

Fortress
FORTRESS
(adult/student €2/1; ☺8am-2.30pm Tue-Sun) Mytilini's impressive fortress was built in early Byzantine times and enlarged by the Turks. The pine forest surrounding it is a superb place for a stroll or to have a picnic.

🛏 Sleeping

Porto Lesvos 1 Hotel
HOTEL €€
(☎22510 41771; www.portolesvos.gr; Komninaki 21; s/d/tr incl breakfast €50/60/70; ❄🐾) This hotel has attractive rooms and service – right down to robes and slippers – in a restored building one block back from the waterfront.

Pension Thalia
PENSION €
(☎22510 24640; Kinikiou 1; s/d €25/30) This pension has clean, bright rooms in a large house. It is about a five-minute walk north of the main square, up Ermou, the road that links the south and north harbours. Follow the signs from the corner of Ermou and Adramytiou.

🍴 Eating & Drinking
Mytilini's top spots are a road or two back at the northern end of the harbour.

Stou Mihali
GREEK €
(☎22510 43311; Ikarias 7, Plateia Sapphou; mains €4-10; ☺9am-9pm) It's getting hard to find a free table at lunch at this tasty and inexpensive place. Everything is good; try the *soutzoukakia*, *imam baïldi* (roast eggplant) and Greek salad.

Mousiko Kafenio
CAFE
(cnr Mitropoleos & Vernardaki; ☺7.30am-2am) This relaxed, arty student cafe just in from the waterfront is full of colour, with eclectic paintings, mirrors and well-worn wooden fixtures.

ℹ Information
See www.lesvos.net for more information.

Tourist Office (EOT; ☎22510 42512; 6 Aristarhou; ☺9am-1pm Mon-Fri) Located 50m up Aristarhou inland from the quay; offers brochures and maps, but its opening hours are limited.

Zoumboulis Tours (☎22510 37755; Kountourioti 69) On the waterfront; handles flights, boat schedules, ticketing and excursions to Turkey.

ℹ Getting Around
Mytilini has two bus stations. For local buses, head along the waterfront to the main square. For long-distance buses, walk 600m from the ferry along the waterfront to El Venizelou and turn right until you reach Agia Irinis park, which is next to the station. There are regular services in summer to Mithymna and Skala Eresou.

MITHYMNA
ΜΗΘΥΜΝΑ
POP 1500

The gracious, preserved town of Mithymna (known by locals as Molyvos) is 62km north of Mytilini. Cobbled streets canopied by flowering vines wind up the hill below the impressive castle. The town is full of cosy tavernas and genteel stone cottages.

The noble **Genoese castle** (admission €2; ☺8.30am-7pm Tue-Sun) perches above the town like a crown and affords tremendous views out to Turkey. Pebbly **Mithymna Beach** sits below the town and is good for swimming. Don't forget to stroll down to the harbour.

Eftalou hot springs (public/private bath per person €4/5; ☺6am-9pm), 4km from town on the beach, is a superb bathhouse complex with a whitewashed dome and steaming, pebbled pool.

Nassos Guest House (☎22530 71432; www.nassosguesthouse.com; Arionis; d/tr without bathroom €20/35; 🐾) is an airy, friendly place with shared facilities and a communal kitchen, in an old Turkish house oozing character. With rapturous views, it's highly recommended. It's the only blue house below the castle.

Betty's Restaurant (☎22530 71421; Agora; mains €3-12) has superb home-style Greek food, views and atmosphere in a building that was once a notorious bordello. Betty also has a couple of **cottages** (☎22530 71022; www.bettyscottages.molivos.net; cottages €50) with kitchens in her garden.

From the bus station, walk straight ahead towards the town for 100m to the helpful **municipal tourist office** (www.mithymna.gr), which has good maps. Some 50m further on, the cobbled main thoroughfare of 17 Noemvriou heads up to the right. Go straight to get to the colourful fishing port.

Buses to Mithymna (€6.90) take 1¾ hours from Mytilini, though a rental car is a good option.

AROUND THE ISLAND

Southern Lesvos is dominated by **Mt Olympus** (968m) and the very pretty village of **Agiasos**, which has good artisan workshops making everything from handcrafted furniture to pottery.

Western Lesvos is known for its petrified forest, with petrified wood at least 500,000 years old, and for the gay-friendly town of **Skala Eresou**, the birthplace of Sappho, see boxed text p389.

SPORADES ΣΠΟΡΑΔΕΣ

Scattered to the southeast of the Pelion Peninsula, to which they were joined in prehistoric times, the 11 islands that make up the Sporades group have mountainous terrain, dense vegetation and are surrounded by scintillatingly clear seas.

The main ports for the Sporades are Volos and Agios Konstantinos on the mainland.

Skiathos   Σκιάθος

POP 6150

Lush and green, Skiathos has a beach resort feel about it. Charter flights bring loads of package tourists, but the island still oozes enjoyment. Skiathos Town and some excellent beaches are on the hospitable south coast, while the north coast is precipitous and less accessible.

Skiathos Town's main thoroughfare is Papadiamanti, named after the 19th-century novelist Alexandros Papadiamanti, who was born here. It runs inland opposite the quay.

● Sights & Activities

Beaches

Skiathos has superb beaches, particularly on the south coast. **Koukounaries** is popular with families. A stroll over the headland, **Big Banana Beach** is stunning, but if you want an all-over tan, head a tad further to **Little Banana Beach**, where bathing suits are a rarity.

MOVIES UNDER THE STARS

Greece has such great weather in summer that not only does it have a history of open-air theatre, there is also an open-air cinema culture. **Cinema Attikon** (24720 22352; ticket €7), on Skiathos Town's main street of Papadiamanti, is a great example. You can catch current English-language movies under the stars, sip a beer and practise speed-reading Greek subtitles at the same time! Films are usually shown in their original language in Greece (ie not dubbed).

A number of other islands have similar outdoor cinemas.

Boat Trips

At the Old Harbour in Skiathos Town, there are all sorts of offerings in terms of **boat excursions** – trips to nearby beaches (€10), trips around Skiathos Island (€25) and full-day trips that take in Skopelos, Alonnisos and the Marine Park (€35).

🛏 Sleeping

TOP CHOICE **Hotel Bourtzi**   BOUTIQUE HOTEL €€ (24270 21304; www.hotelbourtzi.gr; s/d/tr incl breakfast €80/115/140; P ✳ 🛜 🛝) On upper Papadiamanti, the swanky Bourtzi escapes much of the downtown noise and features lovely rooms, along with an inviting garden and pool.

Pension Pandora   PENSION € (694 413 7377, 24270 24357; www.skiathosinfo.com/accomm/pension-pandora; r €30-70; P ✳ 🛜) Run by the effervescent Georgina, this family-run place is 10 minutes' walk north of the quay and a great budget option. The spotless rooms have TV, kitchens and balconies. Georgina also has two exceptional apartments just off Papadiamanti.

Camping Koukounaries   CAMPGROUND € (24270 49250; campsites per tent/person €4/10; P) This place, 30 minutes from town by bus and at the southwestern end of the island, is at beautiful Koukounaries Beach. There are good facilities, a minimarket and a taverna.

ECOTOURISM ON THE RISE

In a country not noted for its ecological long-sightedness, locals (especially the fishermen) initially struggled with the idea of the **National Marine Park of Alonnisos** when it was established in 1992 to protect the highly endangered Mediterranean monk seal and to promote the recovery of fish stocks.

These days, though, the people of the Sporades have caught on to the advantages of having such a park on their doorstep. Ecotourism is on the rise, with daily excursions on licensed boats into the park from Skiathos, Skopelos and Alonnisos. Though your odds of seeing the shy monk seal aren't great – it's on the list of the 20 most endangered species worldwide – the chances of cruising among pods of dolphins (striped, bottlenose and common) are high.

✗ Eating & Drinking

Skiathos Town is brimming with eateries. There are seafood options around the Old Harbour, and some excellent places up the stairs from there behind the small church.

TOP CHOICE Piccolo   ITALIAN €
(☑24270 22780; www.firponet.com/piccolo; mains from €8) This Italian place behind the church up from the Old Harbour does exquisite pizzas and pastas in a lovely setting.

1901   GREEK €€
(☑69485 26701; www.skiathos1901.gr; mains from €15) A superb fine-dining restaurant with a glowing reputation, 1901 is up Grigoriou, above the church up from the Old Harbour.

Kentavros   BAR
(☑24270 22980) A popular drinking spot just off Plateia Papadiamanti. Expect a mellow ambience and mixture of rock, jazz and blues.

ⓘ Information

See the website www.skiathosinfo.com for more information.

Heliotropio Travel (☑24270 22430; www. heliotropio.gr) Opposite the ferry quay; handles ticketing and rents cars and scooters.

Tourist Information Booth (☑24270 23172) At the port, but it opens irregularly.

ⓘ Getting There & Around

AIR Along with numerous charter flights from northern Europe, in summer there is a daily flight from Athens and one from Thessaloniki. Skiathos airport (JSI) is 2km northeast of Skiathos Town.

BOAT There are frequent daily hydrofoils to/ from the mainland ports of Volos (€34, 1¼ hours) and Agios Konstantinos (€36, two hours), as well as cheaper ferries. The hydrofoils head to/from Skopelos (€12, 45 minutes) and Alonnisos (€18, one hour). In summer there is also a hydrofoil to Thessaloniki (€47, 4½ hours).

BUS Crowded buses ply the south-coast road between Skiathos Town and Koukounaries every 30 minutes between 7.30am and 11pm year-round, stopping at all the beaches along the way. The bus stop is at the eastern end of the harbour.

Skopelos   Σκόπελος
POP 4700

A mountainous island, Skopelos is covered in pine forests, vineyards, olive groves and fruit orchards. While the northwest coast is exposed with high cliffs, the southeast is sheltered and harbours pleasant pebbled beaches. The island's main port and capital of **Skopelos Town**, on the east coast, skirts a semicircular bay and clambers in tiers up a hillside, culminating in a ruined fortress.

The island was used in the filming of *Mamma Mia*. The crew took over Skopelos Town's accommodation for a month and filmed at Agnontas and Kastani beaches on the western coast.

Pension Sotos (☑24240 22549; www.sko-pelos.net/sotos; s/d €30/45; ❄️📶), in the middle of the waterfront, has big rooms in an enchanting old Skopelete building. Check out individual rooms and its different prices online before you go. **Hotel Regina** (☑24240 22138; www.skopelosweb.gr/regina; s/d incl breakfast €45/60; ❄️📶) has bright and cheery rooms with balconies. The hotel's rooftop signage is easily spotted from the waterfront.

Top spot in town to chill out is under the huge plane tree at **Platanos Jazz Bar** (☑24240 23661) on the waterfront. It's open all day, plays wicked jazz and blues, and is the ideal place to recover from, or prepare for, a hangover.

In Skopelos Town, there is no tourist office, but **Thalpos Holidays** (☑24240 29036; www.holidayislands.com), on the waterfront, is handy for accommodation and tours. The bus station is next to the port. Excursion boats along the waterfront offer trips into the marine park.

Hydrofoils dash daily to Skiathos (€12, 45 minutes), Alonnisos (€9, 20 minutes), Volos (€44, 2¼ hours) and Agios Konstantinos (€44, three hours). Most hydrofoils also call in at Loutraki, the port below Glossa on the northwest coast of the island. There is also a daily ferry along the same route that costs less but takes longer. There are frequent buses from Skopelos Town to Glossa (€4.80, one hour) stopping at all beaches along the way.

Alonnisos   Αλόννησος
POP 2700

Green, serene Alonnisos is at the end of the line and the least visited of the Sporades' main islands. The west coast is mostly precipitous cliffs, but the east coast is speckled with pebble-and-sand beaches. The island is well known as a walking destination.

The port village of Patitiri was slapped together in 1965 after an earthquake destroyed the hilltop capital of **Alonnisos Town**.

Pension Pleiades (☑24240 65235; www. pleiadeshotel.gr; s/d/tr from €25/35/50; ❋@) looks out over the harbour and is visible from the quay. The rooms are immaculate, balconied, bright and cheerful. There's also a good restaurant. **Liadromia Hotel** (☑24240 65521; www.liadromia.gr; d/tr/ste incl breakfast €50/70/95; P❋@☎) is an excellent-value place with tons of character, overlooking Patitiri's harbour. Follow the stairway opposite the National Bank. **Camping Rocks** (☑24240 65410; campsites per person €6) is a shady, basic camping ground. It is a steep hike about 1.5km from the port.

There is no tourist office, but on the waterfront, **Alonnisos Travel** (☑24240 66000; www.alonnisostravel.gr) handles boat scheduling and ticketing.

There are ferries with varying regularity connecting Alonnisos to Volos and Agios Konstantinos via Skopelos and Skiathos. Hydrofoils provide the most regular schedules between the islands. They travel several times a day to Skopelos Town (€9, 20 minutes), Skiathos (€16, 1½ hours), Volos (€44, three hours) and Agios Konstantinos (€44, four hours).

THE GREAT CHEESE PIE DEBATE

Tyropita (cheese pie), almost deified in its birthplace of the Sporades, is made with goat cheese rolled in delicate filo dough, coiled up, then fried quickly and served hot. The locals love it, but its origins are a source of hot debate.

Those from Alonnisos claim it evolved in the wood-fired oven kitchens of their island and was 'taken' to Skopelos in the 1950s, when farmers went to work on their neighbouring island. What smarts on Alonnisos is that the pie has become famous throughout Greece thanks to a popular TV host who credited Skopelos with its origin – and it is known as the 'Skopelos Cheese Pie'. Those on Alonnisos are cheesed off, to say the least!

IONIAN ISLANDS
ΤΑ ΕΠΤΑΝΗΣΑ

The idyllic cypress- and fir-covered Ionian Islands stretch down the western coast of Greece from Corfu in the north to Kythira, off the southern tip of the Peloponnese. Mountainous, with dramatic cliff-backed beaches, soft light and turquoise water, they're more Italian in feel, offering a contrasting experience to other Greek islands. Invest in a hire car to get to small villages tucked along quiet back roads. Prices drop in low season.

Corfu   Κέρκυρα
POP 122,700

Many consider Corfu, or Kerkyra (*ker*-kih-rah) in Greek, to be Greece's most beautiful island – the unfortunate consequence of which is that it's overbuilt and often overrun with crowds.

ⓘ Getting There & Away
Air

Ioannis Kapodistrias Airport (CFU; ☑26610 30180) is 3km from Corfu Town. **Olympic Air** (☑801 801 0101) and **Aegean Airlines** (☑26610 27100) fly daily to Athens and a few times a week to Thessaloniki.

Sky Express (www.skyexpress.gr) operates seasonal routes to Preveza, Kefallonia, Zakynthos, Kythira and Crete. Charter planes and

Corfu

easyJet fly internationally in summer. A taxi from the airport to the centre costs around €12. Buses 6 and 10 stop 800m from the airport.

Boat

Ferries go to Igoumenitsa (€10, 1½ hours, hourly). In summer, daily ferries and hydrofoils go to Paxi, and international ferries (Italy, Albania) also stop in Patra (€35, six hours).

Bus

Daily **buses** (26610 28898; www.ktelkerkyras. gr) to Athens (€50, 8½ hours) and Thessaloniki

(€45, eight hours) leave from Corfu's **long-distance bus station** (26610 28927; Ioannou Theotoki).

CORFU TOWN
POP 28,800

Built on a promontory and wedged between two fortresses, Corfu's Old Town is a tangle of narrow walking streets through gorgeous Venetian buildings. Explore the winding alleys and surprising plazas in the early morning or late afternoon to avoid the hordes of day trippers seeking souvenirs.

◉ Sights

TOP CHOICE Museum of Asian Art   MUSEUM

(☑26610 30443; adult/child €4/2; ⊙8.30am-8pm Tue-Sun Jun-Oct, 8.30am-2.30pm Tue-Sun Nov-May) Housed in the **Palace of St Michael & St George** this art collection is expertly curated with extensive English-language placards. Approximately 10,000 artefacts collected from China, Japan, India, Tibet and Thailand include priceless prehistoric bronzes, ceramics, jade figurines and coins.

TOP CHOICE Palaio Frourio   FORTRESS

(☑26610 48310; adult/concession €4/2; ⊙8am-8pm May-Oct, 8.30am-3pm Nov-Mar) Constructed by the Venetians in the 15th century on the remains of a Byzantine castle and further altered by the British, the Palaio Frourio stands on an eastern promontory; the Neo Frourio (New Fortress) lies to the northwest.

Antivouniotissa Museum   MUSEUM

(☑26610 38313; off Arseniou; admission €2; ⊙8am-2.30pm Tue-Sun) Exquisite basilica with an outstanding collection of Byzantine icons and artefacts dating from the 13th to the 17th centuries.

Mon Repos Estate   PARK

(Kanoni Peninsula; ⊙8am-7pm May-Oct, to 5pm Nov-Apr) Sprawling gardens boast two Doric temples.

Church of Agios Spiridon   CHURCH

(Agios Spiridonos) Richly decorated church displays the remains of St Spiridon.

Archaeological Museum   MUSEUM

(☑26610 30680; P Vraïla 5; admission €3; ⊙8.30am-3pm Tue-Sun) Houses a collection of finds from Mycenaean to classical times.

⌂ Sleeping

Accommodation prices fluctuate wildly depending on season; book ahead.

TOP CHOICE Bella Venezia   BOUTIQUE HOTEL €€

(☑26610 46500; www.bellaveneziahotel.com; N Zambeli 4; s/d incl breakfast from €100/120; ❋❋☎) Impeccable and understated; contemporary rooms are decked out in cream linens and marbles.

City Marina Hotel   HOTEL €€

(☑26610 39505; www.citymarina.gr; Donzelot 15, Old Port; s/d €75/80; ❋☎) Recently renovated and with some sea views, light-filled rooms are managed by friendly staff.

Hermes Hotel   HOTEL €

(☑26610 39268; www.hermes-hotel.gr; Markora 12; s/d/tr €50/60/75; ❋☎) Completely refurbished, pleasant, well-appointed rooms in the New Town.

✗ Eating & Drinking

Corfu has excellent restaurants. Cafes and bars line the arcaded Liston. Try Corfu Beer.

La Cucina   ITALIAN €€

(☑26610 45029; Guilford 17; mains €10-25) Every detail is cared for at this intimate bistro (and its annex down the street), from the hand-rolled tortelloni to the inventive pizzas and murals on the walls.

Rex   MEDITERRANEAN €€

(☑26610 39649; Kapodistriou 66; mains €8-21) Set back from the Liston, this elegant restaurant elevates Greek home cooking to fine dining.

Chrisomalis   TAVERNA €

(☑26610 30342; N Theotoki 6; mains €8-13) In the heart of the Old Town, this Ma and Pa operation dishes out the classics.

Rouvas   TAVERNA €

(☑26610 31182; S Desilla 13; mains €5-8; ⊙9am-5pm) A favourite lunch stop for locals.

To Dimarchio   ITALIAN, GREEK €€

(☑26610 39031; Plateia Dimarchio; mains €9-25) Relax in a luxuriant rose garden on a charming square.

ⓘ Information

Tourist Police (☑26610 30265; Samartzi 4, 3rd fl)

ⓘ Getting Around

Blue buses (€1.10 to €1.50) for villages near Corfu Town leave from Plateia San Rocco. Services to other destinations (around Corfu €1.60 to €4.40) leave from the long distance bus terminal.

AROUND THE ISLAND

To explore fully all regions of the island your own transport is best. Much of the coast just north of Corfu Town is overwhelmed with beach resorts, the south is quieter, and the west has beautiful, if popular, coastline. The **Corfu Trail** (www.thecorfutrail.com) traverses the island north to south.

In **Kassiopi**, **Manessis Apartments** (☑26610 34990; http://manessiskassiopi.com; 4-person apt €100; ❋☎) offers water-view apartments. In Sgombou, **Casa Lucia**

WORTH A TRIP

PAXI (ΠΑΞΟΙ)

Paxi lives up to its reputation as one of the Ionians' most idyllic and picturesque islands. At only 10km by 4km it's the smallest of the main holiday islands and makes a fine escape from Corfu's quicker-paced pleasures.

(☑26610 91419; www.casa-lucia-corfu.com; studios & cottages €70-120; Pᴁ) is a garden complex of lovely cottages with a strong alternative ethos. Don't miss a dinner at one of the island's best tavernas, **Klimataria** (Bellos; ☑26610 71201; mains €8-14; ☉dinner) in Benitses.

To gain an aerial view of the gorgeous cypress-backed bays around **Paleokastritsa**, the west coast's main resort, go to the quiet village of **Lakones**. Backpackers head to **Pelekas Beach** for low-key **Rolling Stone** (☑26610 94942; www.pelekasbeach.com; r/apt €35/98; @☎) or ramshackle **Sunrock** (☑26610 94637; www.sunrockcorfu.com; dm/r per person €18/24; @ᴁ), a full-board hostel. Further south, good beaches surround tiny **Agios Gordios**.

Lefkada   Λευκάδα

POP 22,500

Joined to the mainland by a narrow isthmus, fertile Lefkada with its mountainous interior and pine forests also boasts truly splendid beaches and one of the hottest windsurfing spots in Europe.

ⓘ Getting There & Around

AIR Sky Express flies to Preveza-Aktio airport (PVK), 20km to the north.

BOAT West Ferry (www.westferry.gr) has an ever-changing schedule from Vasiliki to Kefallonia.

Ionian Pelagos (☑26450 31520) occasionally goes from Vasiliki via Piso Aetos (Ithaki) to Sami (Kefallonia).

Book with **Samba Tours** (☑26450 31520; www.sambatours.gr; Vasiliki) or **Borsalino Travel** (☑26450 92528; Nydri).

BUS & CAR KTEL Bus Station Lefkada Town (☑26450 22364; Ant Tzeveleki)

Athens (€32, 5½ hours, four daily)
Igoumenitsa (€12, two hours, daily)
Patra (€15, three hours, three weekly)
Preveza (€2.90, 30 minutes, six daily)

Thessaloniki (€41.50, eight hours, two weekly)
Rent cars in Lefkada Town, Nydri or Vasiliki.

LEFKADA TOWN

Most travellers' first port of call, Lefkada Town remains laid-back except for August high season. The town's unique earthquake-resistant corrugated-steel architecture somehow blends with its attractive marina, waterfront cafes and vibrant pedestrian thoroughfares.

🛏 Sleeping & Eating

Restaurants and cafes line the main street, **Dorpfeld**, central **Plateia Agiou Spyridonos** and the waterfront.

Boschetto Hotel   BOUTIQUE HOTEL €€
(☑26450 24967; www.boschettohotel.com; Dorpfeld 1; d incl breakfast from €80; ᴁ@☎) Exquisite c 1900 building with four custom-designed rooms and one suite tricked out with all the chicest amenities.

Hotel Santa Maura   HOTEL €
(☑26450 21308; Dorpfeld; s/d/tr incl breakfast €50/60/70; ᴁ☎) Think tropical Bahamas with sky-blue and shell-pink interiors and breezy balconies; best rooms on the top floor.

Pension Pirofani   HOTEL €€
(☑26450 25844; Dorpfeld; r €60-80; ᴁᴁ☎) Modern rooms have balconies for prime people-watching.

Ey Zhn   INTERNATIONAL €
(☑69746 41160; Filarmonikis 8; mains €7-12; ☉dinner Jan-Oct) Roadhouse meets artist's loft at this ambience-rich restaurant with excellent, eclectic food.

AROUND THE ISLAND

With its lovely bay, **Nydri** is unfortunately blighted by tacky souvenir shops and touristy tavernas. Lefkada's true gifts are its west-coast beaches. Cliffs drop to broad sweeps of white sand and turquoise waters. Explore! Tiny, bohemian **Agios Nikitas** village draws travellers, but gets very crowded in summer. Nearby, in Athani, get simple clean studios at **Aloni Studios** (☑26450 33604; www.aloni studios-lefkada.com; r €40; Pᴁ).

Southernmost eucalyptus-scented **Vasiliki** is popular with windsurfers. Organise lessons through **Club Vass** (☑26450 31588; www.clubvass.com). Overlooking the port, **Pension Holidays** (☑26450 31426; s/d €45/50; ᴁᴁ☎) has great-value rooms with kitchens.

Kefalonia Κεφαλλονιά

POP 37,800

Tranquil cypress- and fir-covered Kefalonia, the largest Ionian island, is breathtakingly beautiful with rugged mountain ranges, rich vineyards, soaring coastal cliffs and golden beaches. It has not succumbed to package tourism to the extent that some of the other Ionian Islands have and remains low-key outside resort areas. Due to the widespread destruction of an earthquake in 1953, much of the island's historic architecture was levelled; Assos and Fiskardo are exceptions.

ⓘ Getting There & Around

Air

Olympic Air (☑26710 41511) flies to Athens, and **Sky Express** serves the Ionians and Crete, from **Kefallonia Airport** (☑26710 41511), 9km south of Argostoli.

Boat

Ionian Ferries (www.ionianferries.gr) connects Poros and Argostoli to Kyllini (Peloponnese).
Ionian Pelagos (☑26450 31520) links Sami with Astakos (Peloponnese; sometimes via Piso Aetos in Ithaki).
Strintzis Lines (www.strintzisferries.gr) connects Sami with Patra (Peloponnese) and Vathy or Piso Aetos (Ithaki).
West Ferry (www.westferry.gr) loops from Fiskardo, and sometimes Sami, to Frikes (Ithaki) and Vasiliki.

In high season some ferries connect Sami with Bari, Italy. **Nautilus Travel** (☑26740 41440; Fiskardo) has information and tickets.

Bus

Three daily buses connect **KTEL Bus Station Argostoli** (☑26710 22276; Antoni Tritsi 5) with Athens (€47, seven hours) via Patra (€26, four hours). Buses also go to Athens from Sami (two daily), Poros (one daily) and Lixouri (one daily). Local buses don't run on Sunday.

Car

A car is best for exploring. **Pama Travel** (☑26740 41033; www.pamatravel.com; Fiskardo) rents cars and boats. **Karavomilos** (☑26740 22779; Sami) delivers cars.

FISKARDO

Pretty Fiskardo, with its pastel-coloured Venetian buildings set around a picturesque bay, is popular with European yachties but it's still peaceful enough to appeal to independent travellers. Take lovely walks to sheltered coves for swimming.

🛏 Sleeping

Archontiko PENSION €€
(☑26740 41342; r from €70; ⧉) Overlooking the harbour, people-watch from the balconies of luxurious rooms in a restored stone mansion.

Regina's Rooms PENSION €
(☑26740 41125; d/tr €40/50; ⧉) Some of its colourful, breezy rooms have bay views or kitchenettes.

✕ Eating

Fiskardo has no shortage of excellent waterside restaurants.

TOP CHOICE Tassia MEDITERRANEAN €€
(☑26740 41205; mains €7-25) This unassuming but famous Fiskardo institution run by Tassia Dendrinou, celebrated chef and writer, serves up excellent seafood and Greek dishes.

Café Tselenti ITALIAN €€
(☑26740 41344; mains €10-23) Enjoy outstanding Italian classics served by friendly waiters; tucked back in a romantic plaza.

AROUND THE ISLAND

In **Argostoli**, the capital, stay over at **Vivian Villa** (☑26710 23396; www.kefalonia-vivianvilla.gr; Deladetsima 11; d/tr/apt €60/65/100; ⧉⧈) with its big, bright rooms and friendly owners. Sample inventive Mediterranean cooking at

GREECE KEFALLONIA

KEFALLONIA HIGH-SEASON FERRIES

FROM	TO	FARE (€)	DURATION (HR)
Argostoli	Kyllini (Peloponnese)	14	5
Pesada	Agios Nikolaos (Zakynthos)	8.50	1½
Poros	Kyllini	10	1½
Sami	Bari (Italy)	45	12
Sami	Patra (Peloponnese)	19	2¾
Sami	Piso Aetos & Vathy (Ithaki)	3/7	45min

Casa Grec (☑26710 24091; Metaxa 12; mains €12-22; ☺dinner nightly, closed Sun & Mon Nov-Apr) or top Kefallonian cuisine at **Arhontiko** (☑26710 27213; 5 Risospaston; mains €7-17; ☺breakfast, lunch & dinner).

Straddling a slender isthmus on the northwest coast, the petite pastel-coloured village of **Assos** watches over the ruins of a Venetian fortress perched upon a pine-covered peninsula. Eat at **Platanos** (☑69446 71804; mains €6-15; ☺breakfast, lunch & dinner Easter-Oct) for home-cooked food at its best. Splendid **Myrtos Beach**, 13km south of Assos, is spellbinding from above, with post-card views from the precarious roadway.

Near **Sami**, eat at **Paradise Beach** (Dendrinos; ☑26740 61392; Agia Evfymia; mains €6-13; ☺lunch & dinner mid-May–mid-Oct), a renowned Kefallonian taverna.

The interior **Omala Valley** is home to **Robola wines** (www.robola.gr). **Paliki Peninsula** is filled with under-explored beauty.

Ithaki   Ιθάκη

POP 1550

Odysseus' long-lost home in Homer's *Odyssey*, Ithaki (ancient Ithaca) remains a pristine island blessed with cypress-covered hills and beautiful turquoise coves.

ℹ Getting There & Away

Strintzis Lines (www.strintzisferries.gr) has two ferries daily connecting Vathy or Piso Aetos with Patra (Peloponnese) via Sami (Kefallonia).

Ionian Pelagos (☑26450 31520) goes daily in high season between Piso Aetos, Sami and Astakos (mainland).

West Ferry (www.westferry.gr) has an ever-changing schedule from Frikes to Vasiliki (Lefkada); sometimes it goes to Fiskardo, but at the time of research was considering cutting the Frikes stop.

Check routes and schedules at **Delas Tours** (☑26740 32104; www.ithaca.com.gr) or **Polyctor Tours** (☑26740 33120; www.ithakiholidays.com) in Vathy.

KIONI

Tucked in a tiny, tranquil bay, Kioni is a wonderful place to chill for a few days.

Individuals rent rooms and **Captain's Apartments** (☑26740 31481; www.captains-apartments.gr; 2-/4-person apt €60/70; ☀) has shipshape, spacious apartments with kitchens, satellite TV and balconies overlooking the valley and village. **Mythos** (mains €6-10) taverna on the harbour has excellent *pastit-*

ℹ **FERRY BETWEEN ZAKYNTHOS & KEFALLONIA**

From the northern port of Agios Nikolaos a ferry serves Pesada in southern Kefallonia twice daily from May to October (€8, 1½ hours). Get tickets at **Chionis Tours** (☑26950 23894; Lomvardou 8, Zakynthos Town). *BUT*, in high season, there are only two buses a week from Zakynthos Town to Agios Nikolaos and two buses daily from Pesada to Argostoli (Kefallonia), making crossing without your own transport difficult. An alternative is to cross to Kyllini and catch another ferry to Kefallonia.

sio (a thick noodle and ground beef casserole). Comfy **Cafe Spavento** (per hr €2) has internet.

AROUND THE ISLAND

The dusty port of **Frikes**, where some ferries dock, is a funkier alternative to Kioni and has rooms to rent.

Vathy, Ithaki's small, bustling capital, is the spot for hiring cars and getting cash (no banks in Kioni). Elegant mansions rise from around its bay and **Hotel Perantzada** (☑26740 33496; www.arthotel.gr/perantzada; Odyssea Androutsou; s/d incl breakfast from €120/150; ☺Easter–mid-Oct; ❉@☎☀) occupies two with sensational rooms. **Odyssey Apartments** (☑26740 33400; www.ithaki-odyssey.com; d €60-80, studio €100, 1-/2-bedroom apt €120/150; ℙ❉☀) overlooks town (500m up) and the sea with spotless studios and a pool.

Zakynthos   Ζάκυνθος

POP 41,000

The beautiful island of Zakynthos, or Zante, has stunning coves, dramatic cliffs and extensive beaches, but unfortunately is swamped by package-tour groups, so only a few special spots warrant your time.

ℹ Getting There & Around

AIR The **airport** (ZTH; ☑26950 28322) is 6km from Zakynthos Town. **Olympic Air** flies to Athens; **Sky Express** flies to Corfu via Kefallonia and Preveza, or to Crete; **easyJet** flies occasionally to Gatwick and Milan; **Air Berlin** flies to German cities.

BOAT Ionian Ferries (☑26950 22083/49500; www.ionianferries.gr; Lomvardou 40 & 72,

Zakynthos Town) travels from Zakynthos Town to Kyllini (Peloponnese; €8.50, one hour, four to seven daily).

Occasional ferries go to Brindisi, Italy (€75, 15½ hours), some via Igoumenitsa and Corfu (€32, 8¾hr, two weekly).

BUS The **KTEL bus station** (📞26950 22255; www.ktel-zakynthos.gr) is west of Zakynthos town. Budget an additional €8.50 for the ferry to Kyllini.

Athens (€26, six hours, four daily)
Patra (€8.50, 3½ hours, four daily)
Thessaloniki (€50, 10 hours, three weekly)

Local buses serve major resort towns.

CAR Europcar (📞26950 41541; Plateia Agiou Louka, Zakynthos Town) Delivers to the airport.

ZAKYNTHOS TOWN

The island's attractive Venetian capital and port were painstakingly reconstructed after the 1953 earthquake. The pine-tree-filled **Kastro** (📞26950 48099; admission €3; ⏰8.30am-2.30pm Tue-Sun), a ruined Venetian fortress high above town, makes for a peaceful outing. The **Byzantine Museum** (📞26950 42714; Plateia Solomou; admission €3; ⏰8.30am-3pm Tue-Sun) houses fabulous ecclesiastical art rescued from churches razed in the earthquake.

🍽 Sleeping & Eating

Restaurants abound but, as in most of the island, they tend to be overpriced and not overly inspiring. In Zakynthos Town, try **Mesathes** (📞26950 49315; Ethnikis Antistaseos; mains €9-11) for an elegant meal.

TOP CHOICE Hotel Strada Marina   HOTEL €€
(📞26950 42761; www.stradamarina.gr; Lombardou 14; s/d incl breakfast from €60/70; ✴🎄🏊) Well-situated, portside rooms have balconies with sea views.

Hotel Diana   HOTEL €€
(📞26950 28547; Plateia Agiou Markou; r incl breakfast from €60; ✴@🎄) This comfortable and well-appointed hotel in a good, central location has a two-bedroom family suite (€100).

Camping Zante   CAMPGROUND €
(📞26950 61710; www.zantecamping.gr; Ampula Beach; campsites per person/tent €6/5; @🏊) Decent beachside camping 5km north of Zakynthos Town.

TOP CHOICE Malanos   TAVERNA €
(📞26950 45936; www.malanos.gr; Agiou Athanasiou, Kiri area; mains €5-10; ⏰noon-4pm & 8pm-late) Serves up Zakynthos specialities like rooster, rabbit and wild boar. South, in the countryside; ask a local for directions.

AROUND THE ISLAND

Transport of your own is really necessary to unlock the charms of Zakynthos. The **Vasilikos Peninsula** is the pretty green region southeast of Zakynthos Town and fringing **Laganas Bay** with its long, lovely **Gerakas Beach**. The area has been declared **National Marine Park of Zakynthos** (NMPZ; www.nmp-zak.org) in order to protect the endangered loggerhead turtles that come ashore to lay their eggs in August, the peak of the tourist invasion. Inform yourself before exploring so as not to accidentally disrupt buried eggs.

Cape Keri, near the island's southernmost point, has spectacular views of sheer cliffs and beaches. **Villa Christina** (📞26950 49208; viganelichristina@hotmail.com; Limni Keriou; studio €50-55, apt €60-80, maisonette €150; ⏰May-Oct; 🅿✴@🏊) is tops for tidy apartments in lush gardens with a pool. **Tartaruga Camping** (📞26950 51967; www.tartaruga-camping.com; camp sites per adult/car/tent €5/3/3.60, r per person €15; ⏰Apr-Oct; 🅿✴@🎄), signed on the road from Laganas to Keri, sprawls through terraced olive groves and pines next to the sea.

Continue north and try to arrive early at remote **Limnionas** for swimming in crystal-clear turquoise coves, or explore lovely **Louha** tumbling down a central valley.

Many descend on famous **Shipwreck Beach**, magnificent photos of which grace every tourist brochure about Zakynthos. It is in Navagio Bay, at the northwest tip of the island. From above, a lookout platform gives

GREECE ZAKYNTHOS

WORTH A TRIP

KYTHIRA   ΚΥΘΗΡΑ

Kythira, despite its proximity to the Peloponnese, is considered a part of the Ionian Island group. Genuinely unspoilt, the population (3330) is spread among more than 40 villages with a white-cube Cycladic feel. Mythology suggests that Aphrodite was born in Kythira, but Cypriots claim otherwise. Tourism remains low-key except in July and August, when the island goes mad. Easiest way to get there: fly or get a ferry in Diakofti or Neapoli in the Peloponnese. **LANE Lines** (www.lane.gr) sometimes links Piraeus.

great views. For a (crowded in high season) sea-level look, take a boat from Cape Skinari near Agios Nikolaos, Porto Vromi or Alykes. Cape Skinari's **Windmill** (📞26950 31132; www.potamitisbros.gr; d €60; ❄) has quaint rooms, impressive views, cooking facilities and sea access.

UNDERSTAND GREECE

History

With its strategic position at the crossroads of Europe and Asia, Greece has endured a long and turbulent history. During the Bronze Age (3000–1200 BC in Greece), the advanced Cycladic, Minoan and Mycenaean civilisations flourished. The Mycenaeans were swept aside in the 12th century BC by the warrior-like Dorians, who introduced Greece to the Iron Age. The next 400 years are often referred to as the dark ages, a period about which little is known.

By 800 BC, when Homer's *Odyssey* and *Iliad* were first written down, Greece was undergoing a cultural and military revival with the evolution of the city states, the most powerful of which were Athens and Sparta. Greater Greece (Magna Graecia) was created, with southern Italy as an important component. The unified Greeks repelled the

ORIGINAL OLYMPICS

The Olympic tradition emerged around the 11th century BC as a paean to the Greek gods, in the form of contests of athletic feats that were attended initially by notable men and women, who assembled before the sanctuary priests and swore to uphold solemn oaths. By the 8th century BC, the attendance had grown to include a wide confederacy of city states, and the festival morphed into a male-only major event lasting five days at the site of Olympia. A ceremonial truce was enforced for the duration of the games. Crowds of spectators lined the tracks, where competitors vied for victory in athletics, chariot races, wrestling and boxing. Three millennia later, while the scale and scope of the games may have expanded considerably, the basic format has remained essentially unchanged.

Persians twice, at Marathon (490 BC) and Salamis (480 BC). Victory over Persia was followed by unparalleled growth and prosperity known as the classical (or golden) age.

The Golden Age

During this period, Pericles commissioned the Parthenon, Sophocles wrote *Oedipus the King* and Socrates taught young Athenians to think. The golden age ended with the Peloponnesian War (431–404 BC), when the militaristic Spartans defeated the Athenians. They failed to notice the expansion of Macedonia under King Philip II, who easily conquered the war-weary city states.

Philip's ambitions were surpassed by those of his son, Alexander the Great, who marched triumphantly into Asia Minor, Egypt, Persia and what are now parts of Afghanistan and India. In 323 BC he met an untimely death at the age of 33, and his generals divided his empire between themselves.

Roman Rule & the Byzantine Empire

Roman incursions into Greece began in 205 BC. By 146 BC Greece and Macedonia had become Roman provinces. After the subdivision of the Roman Empire into eastern and western empires in AD 395, Greece became part of the Eastern (Byzantine) Empire, based at Constantinople.

In the centuries that followed, Venetians, Franks, Normans, Slavs, Persians, Arabs and, finally, Turks, took turns chipping away at the Byzantine Empire.

The Ottoman Empire & Independence

After the end of the Byzantine Empire in 1453, when Constantinople fell to the Turks, most of Greece became part of the Ottoman Empire. Crete was not captured until 1670, leaving Corfu as the only island not occupied by the Turks. By the 19th century the Ottoman Empire was in decline. The Greeks, seeing nationalism sweep through Europe, fought the War of Independence (1821–22). Greek independence was proclaimed on 13 January 1822, only for arguments among the leaders who had been united against the Turks to escalate into civil war. The Turks, with the help of the Egyptians, tried to retake Greece, but the great powers – Britain, France and Russia – intervened in 1827, and Ioannis Kapodistrias was elected the first Greek president.

Kapodistrias was assassinated in 1831 and the European powers stepped in once again, declaring that Greece should become a monarchy. In January 1833 Otho of Bavaria was installed as king. His ambition, called the Great Idea, was to unite all the lands of the Greek people to the Greek motherland. In 1862 he was peacefully ousted and the Greeks chose George I, a Danish prince, as king.

During WWI Prime Minister Venizelos allied Greece with France and Britain. King Constantine (George's son), who was married to the kaiser's sister Sophia, disputed this and left the country.

Smyrna & WWII

After the war Venizelos resurrected the Great Idea. Underestimating the new-found power of Turkey under the leadership of Atatürk (Mustafa Kemal), he sent forces to occupy Smyrna (the present-day Turkish port of İzmir), with its large Greek population. The army was heavily defeated and this led to a brutal population exchange between the two countries in 1923.

In 1930 George II, Constantine's son, was reinstated as king; he appointed the dictator General Metaxas as prime minister. Metaxas' grandiose ambition was to combine aspects of Greece's ancient and Byzantine past to create a Third Greek Civilisation. However, his chief claim to fame is his celebrated *ohi* (no) to Mussolini's request to allow Italian troops into Greece in 1940.

Greece fell to Germany in 1941 and resistance movements, polarised into royalist and communist factions, staged a bloody civil war lasting until 1949. The civil war was the trigger for a mass exodus that saw almost one million Greeks head off to countries such as Australia, Canada and the USA. Entire villages were abandoned as people gambled on a new start in cities such as Melbourne, Toronto, Chicago and New York.

The Colonels' Coup

Continuing political instability led to the colonels' coup d'état in 1967. The colonels' junta distinguished itself with its appalling brutality, repression and political incompetence. In 1974 it attempted to assassinate Cyprus' leader, Archbishop Makarios, and when he escaped the junta replaced him with the extremist Nikos Samson, prompting Turkey to occupy North Cyprus. The continued Turkish occupation of Cyprus remains one of the most contentious issues in Greek politics. The junta had little choice but to hand back power to the people. In November 1974 a plebiscite voted against restoration of the monarchy. Greece became a republic with the right-wing New Democracy (ND) party taking power.

The 1980s & 1990s

In 1981 Greece entered the European Community (now the EU) as its 10th, smallest and poorest member. Andreas Papandreou's Panhellenic Socialist Movement (Pasok) won the next election, giving Greece its first socialist government. Pasok, which ruled for most of the next two decades, promised the removal of US air bases and withdrawal from NATO, but delivered only rising unemployment and spiralling debt.

Elections in 1990 brought the ND party back to power, but tough economic reforms made the government unpopular and in 1993, Greeks again turned to Pasok and the ailing Papandreou. He had little option but to continue with the austerity program and became equally unpopular until he stood down in 1996 due to ill health. Pasok then abandoned its leftist policies, elected economist and lawyer Costas Simitis as leader, and romped to victory later that year.

The New Millennium

Simitis' government focused strongly on further integration with Europe and in January 2001 admission to the euro club was approved; Greece duly adopted the currency in 2002 and prices have been on the rise ever since.

Greece tilted to the right and in March 2004 elected the ND party led by Costas Karamanlis. This new broom was fortuitous, as the Olympic preparations were running late and suffering budget problems. While the Olympics were successful, Greece is still counting the cost.

During the long hot summer of 2007, forest fires threatened Athens and caused untold damage in the western Peloponnese, Epiros and Evia. Later that year, Karamanlis' government was returned to power for a second term, but amid growing discontent that included massive general strikes and riots, was turfed out in elections in October 2009 in favour of Pasok and George Papandreou, son and grandson of former prime ministers.

RECOGNISE THAT TWANG?

Don't be surprised if your hotel receptionist or waiter speaks perfect English with an Australian twang. A growing stream of young second- and third-generation Greeks are repatriating from the USA, Australia, Canada and other reaches of the Greek diaspora. A huge number of Greeks emigrated during their country's tumultuous history and it is said that over five million people of Greek descent live in 140 countries around the world. Strong sentimental attractions endure and many expat Greeks are involved in the political and cultural life of their ancestral islands, and many retire in Greece.

Greece Today

Textbooks are being written on Greece's 2010 financial crisis. Simply put, Greece almost fell over from years of over-borrowing, over-spending and breaking eurozone rules on deficit management. Financially crippled and looking likely to drag other failing eurozone economies down with it, Greece was on the receiving end of a succession of bail-out packages to help right the ship. Needless to say, austerity measures to help balance the budget were not popular, with citizens angry about cuts in spending, pensions and salaries, along with higher taxes.

Strikes and riots made world news and in May 2012 elections, no party or coalition of parties was able to form a government. New elections were called for June and in what was seen worldwide as a vote that would determine if Greece remained in the eurozone, a coalition of three parties formed a government with New Democracy's Antonis Samaris as prime minister.

Samaris hopes to keep both Greece's creditors and its populace happy, but without doubt, tough times are ahead.

People

Greece's population has topped 11.2 million, with around one-third of the people living in the Greater Athens area and more than two-thirds living in cities – confirming that Greece is now a primarily urban society. Less than 15% live on the islands, the most populous being Crete, Evia and Corfu. Greece has an ageing population and declining birth rate, with big families a thing of the past. Population growth over the last couple of decades is due to a flood of migrants, both legal and illegal.

About 95% of the Greek population belongs to the Greek Orthodox Church. The remainder is split between the Roman Catholic, Protestant, Evangelist, Jewish and Muslim faiths. While older Greeks and those in rural areas tend to be deeply religious, most young people are decidedly more secular.

The Greek year is centred on the saints' days and festivals of the church calendar. Name days (celebrating your namesake saint) are celebrated more than birthdays. Most people are named after a saint, as are boats, suburbs and train stations.

Orthodox Easter is usually at a different time than Easter celebrated by Western churches, though generally in April/May.

Arts

The arts have been integral to Greek life since ancient times, with architecture having had the most profound influence. Greek temples, seen throughout history as symbolic of democracy, were the inspiration for architectural movements such as the Italian Renaissance. Today masses of cheap concrete apartment blocks built in the 20th century in Greece's major cities belie this architectural legacy.

Thankfully, the great works of Greek literature are not as easily besmirched. The first and greatest Ancient Greek writer was Homer, author of *Iliad* and *Odyssey,* telling the story of the Trojan War and the subsequent wanderings of Odysseus.

Pindar (c 518–438 BC) is regarded as the pre-eminent lyric poet of ancient Greece and was commissioned to recite his odes at the Olympic Games. The great writers of love poetry were Sappho (6th century BC) and Alcaeus (5th century BC), both of whom lived on Lesvos. Sappho's poetic descriptions of her affections for women gave rise to the term 'lesbian'.

The Alexandrian Constantine Cavafy (1863–1933) revolutionised Greek poetry by introducing a personal, conversational style. Later, poet George Seferis (1900–71) won the Nobel Prize for literature in 1963, as did Odysseus Elytis (1911–96) in 1979. Nikos Kazantzakis, author of *Zorba the Greek* and numerous novels, plays and poems, is the most famous of 20th-century Greek novelists.

Greece's most famous painter was a young Cretan called Domenikos Theotokopoulos, who moved to Spain in 1577 and became known as the great El Greco. Famous painters of the 20th century include Konstantinos Parthenis and, later, George Bouzianis, whose work can be viewed at the National Art Gallery in Athens.

Music has been a facet of Greek life since ancient times. When visiting Greece today, your trip will inevitably be accompanied by the plucked-string sound of the ubiquitous bouzouki. The bouzouki is one of the main instruments of *rembetika* music – which is in many ways the Greek equivalent of the American blues and has its roots in the sufferings of refugees from Asia Minor in the 1920s.

Dance is also an integral part of Greek life. Whether at a wedding, nightclub or village celebration, traditional dance is widely practised.

Drama continues to feature in domestic arts, particularly in Athens and Thessaloniki. In summer, Greek dramas are staged in the ancient theatres where they were originally performed.

Greek film has for many years been associated with the work of film-maker Theo Angelopoulos, who won Cannes' Palme d'Or in 1998 with *An Eternity and One Day*. Yorgos Lanthimos was nominated for an Academy Award for Best Foreign Language Film for *Dogtooth* (Kynodonta) in 2011. However, the most internationally acclaimed film remains to be the 1964 classic, *Zorba the Greek*.

Greek TV is dominated by chat shows, sport and foreign movies, only to be interrupted by localised versions of the latest American 'reality TV' hit.

Environment

The Land

Greece sits at the southern tip of the Balkan Peninsula. Of its 1400 islands, only 169 are inhabited. The land mass is 131,944 sq km and Greek territorial waters cover a further 400,000 sq km. Nowhere in Greece is much more than 100km from the sea.

Around 80% of the land is mountainous, with less than a quarter of the country suitable for agriculture.

Greece sits in one of the most seismically active regions in the world – the eastern Mediterranean lies at the meeting point of three continental plates: the Eurasian, African and Arabian. Consequently, Greece has had more than 20,000 earthquakes in the last 40 years, most of them very minor.

Wildlife

The variety of flora in Greece is unrivalled in Europe, with a dazzling array of spectacular wildflowers best seen in the mountains of Crete and the southern Peloponnese.

You won't encounter many animals in the wild, mainly due to hunting. Wild boar, still found in the north, is a favourite target. Squirrels, rabbits, hares, foxes and weasels are all fairly common on the mainland. Reptiles are well represented by snakes, including several poisonous viper species.

Lake Mikri Prespa in Macedonia has the richest colony of fish-eating birds in Europe, while the Dadia Forest Reserve in Thrace counts such majestic birds as the golden eagle and the giant black vulture among its residents.

The brown bear, Europe's largest land mammal, still survives in very small numbers in the mountains of northern Greece, as does the grey wolf.

Europe's rarest mammal, the monk seal, once very common in the Mediterranean Sea, is now on the brink of extinction in Europe. There are about 400 left in Europe, half of which live in Greece. About 40 frequent the Ionian Sea and the rest are found in the Aegean.

The waters around Zakynthos are home to Europe's last large sea turtle colony, that of the loggerhead turtle *(Careta careta)*. The **Sea Turtle Protection Society of Greece** (☎21052 31342; www.archelon.gr) runs monitoring programs and is always on the look-out for volunteers.

National Parks

While facilities in Greek national parks aren't on par with many other countries, all have refuges and some have marked hiking trails. The most visited parks are Mt Parnitha, north of Athens, and the Samaria Gorge on Crete. The others are Vikos-Aoös and Prespa National Parks in Epiros; Mt Olympus on the border of Thessaly and Macedonia; and Parnassos and Iti National Parks in central Greece. There is also a national marine park off the coast of Alonnisos, and another around the Bay of Laganas area off Zakynthos.

GREECE ENVIRONMENT

Environmental Issues

Greece is belatedly becoming environmentally conscious but, regrettably, it's too late for some regions. Deforestation and soil erosion are problems that go back thousands of years, with olive cultivation and goats being the main culprits. Forest fires are also a major problem, with an estimated 250 sq km destroyed every year.

General environmental awareness remains at a depressingly low level, especially where litter is concerned. The problem is particularly bad in rural areas, where roadsides are strewn with aluminium cans and plastic packaging hurled from passing cars. It is somewhat surprising that the waters of the Aegean are as clear as they are considering how many cigarette butts are tossed off ferries.

Food & Drink

Snacks

Greece has a great range of fast-food options. Foremost among them are gyros and souvlaki. The gyros is a giant skewer laden with seasoned meat that grills slowly as it rotates, the meat being steadily trimmed from the outside. Souvlaki are small cubes of meat cooked on a skewer. Both are served wrapped in pitta bread with salad and lashings of tzatziki (a yogurt, cucumber and garlic dip). Other snacks are pretzel rings, spanakopita (spinach and cheese pie) and *tyropita* (cheese pie).

Starters

Greece is famous for its appetisers, known as *mezedhes* (literally, 'tastes'; meze for short). Standards include tzatziki, *melitzanosalata* (aubergine dip), taramasalata (fish-roe dip), dolmadhes (stuffed vine leaves; dolmas for short), *fasolia* (beans) and *oktapodi* (octopus). A selection of three or four starters represents a good meal and makes an excellent vegetarian option.

Mains

You'll find moussaka (layers of aubergine and mince, topped with béchamel sauce and baked) on every menu, alongside a number of other taverna staples. They include *moschari* (oven-baked veal and potatoes), *keftedes* (meatballs), *stifado* (meat stew), *pastitsio* (baked dish of macaroni with minced meat and béchamel sauce) and *yemista* (either tomatoes or green peppers stuffed with minced meat and rice).

Kalamaria (fried squid) is the most popular (and cheapest) seafood, while *barbouni* (red mullet) and *sifias* (swordfish) tend to be more expensive than meat dishes.

Fortunately for vegetarians, salad is a mainstay of the Greek diet. The most popular is *horiatiki salata,* normally listed on English-language menus as Greek salad. It's a delicious mixed salad comprising cucumbers, peppers, onions, olives, tomatoes and feta cheese. For the full scoop on Greece's legendary feta cheese, check out www.feta.gr.

Desserts

Most Greek desserts are Turkish in origin and are variations on pastry soaked in honey, such as baklava (thin layers of pastry filled with honey and nuts). Delicious Greek yogurt also makes a great dessert, especially with honey.

Drinks

Bottled mineral water is cheap and available everywhere, as are soft drinks and packaged juices.

Mythos, in its distinctive green bottle, and Alfa, are popular Greek beers.

Greece is traditionally a wine-drinking society. An increasingly good range of wines

---

THE ART OF OUZO

Ouzo is Greece's most famous but misunderstood tipple. While it can be drunk as an aperitif, for most Greeks ouzo has come to embody a way of socialising – best enjoyed during a lazy, extended summer afternoon of seafood *mezedhes* (appetisers) by the beach. Ouzo is sipped slowly and ritually to clean the palate between tastes. It is served in small bottles or *karafakia* (carafes) with water and a bowl of ice cubes – and is commonly drunk on the rocks, diluted with water (it turns a cloudy white). Mixing it with cola is a foreign abomination!

Made from distilled grapes, ouzo is also distilled with residuals from fruit, grains and potatoes, and flavoured with spices, primarily aniseed, giving it that liquorice flavour. The best ouzo is produced on Lesvos and there are more than 360 brands.

NO MORE SMOKE

Legislation that brought in anti-smoking laws similar to those throughout Europe in 2009 was not exactly popular with Greeks, the EU's biggest smokers. Smoking is now officially banned inside public places, with the penalty fines placed on the business owners.

made from traditional grape varieties is available. Wine enthusiasts should take a look at www.allaboutgreekwine.com. Retsina, wine flavoured with pine-tree resin, is a tasty alternative – though an acquired taste for some. Most tavernas will offer locally made house wines by the carafe.

Metaxa, Greece's dominant brandy, is sweet, while if you are offered some raki, make sure to take a small sip first!

'Greek' coffee should be tried at least once, but don't drink the mudlike grounds at the bottom!

Where to Eat & Drink

The most common variety of restaurant in Greece is the taverna, traditionally an extension of the Greek home table. *Estiatorio* is Greek for restaurant and often has the same dishes as a taverna but with higher prices. A *psistaria* specialises in charcoal-grilled dishes, while a *psarotaverna* specialises in fish. *Ouzeria* (ouzo bars) often have such a range of *mezedhes* that they can be regarded as eateries. Many restaurants are open for lunch and dinner daily during high season.

Kafeneia are the smoke-filled cafes where men gather to drink 'Greek' coffee, play backgammon and cards, and engage in heated political discussion. Every Greek town you'll visit now has at least one cafe-bar where Greece's youth while away hours over a frappé (frothy ice coffee).

Buying and preparing your own food is easy in Greece – every town of consequence has a supermarket, as well as fruit and vegetable shops.

To have a go at producing your own Greek culinary masterpieces, check out www.gourmed.gr. You'll also find information on the healthy Greek diet at www.mediterraneandiet.gr, while www.oliveoil.gr can tell you all about one of Greece's best-known products.

SURVIVAL GUIDE

Directory A–Z
Accommodation

Campgrounds Generally open from April to October; standard facilities include hot showers, kitchens, restaurants and minimarkets – and often a swimming pool; **Panhellenic Camping Association** (21036 21560; www.panhellenic-camping-union.gr).

Domatia Greek equivalent of a B&B, minus the breakfast; don't worry about finding them – owners will find you as they greet ferries and buses shouting 'room!'.

Hotels Classified as deluxe, or A, B, C, D or E class; ratings seldom seem to have much bearing on the price, which is determined more by season and location.

Mountain refuges Listed in *Greece Mountain Refuges & Ski Centres,* available free of charge at EOT and EOS (Ellinikos Orivatikos Syndesmos, the Greek Alpine Club) offices.

Youth hostels In most major towns and on some islands; **Greek Youth Hostel Organisation** (21075 19530; www.athens-yhostel.com).

SEASONAL PRICES

'High season' is usually in July and August. If you turn up in the 'middle' or 'shoulder seasons' (May and June; September and October) expect to pay significantly less. During 'low season' (late October to late April) prices can be up to 50% cheaper, but a lot of places, especially on the islands, virtually close their shutters for winter. Websites will usually display these differences in price.

Greek accommodation is subject to strict price controls, and by law a notice must be displayed in every room stating the category of the room and the seasonal price. It's usually on the back of the door. If you think there's something amiss, contact the Tourist Police.

PRICE RANGES

Prices quoted in listings are for high season (usually July and August) and include a private bathroom.

€€€ more than €150

€€ €60 to €150

€ less than €60

Business Hours

Banks 8am to 2.30pm Monday to Thursday, 8am to 2pm Friday (in cities, also: 3.30p 6.30pm Monday to Friday, 8am to 1.30pm Saturday)

Cafes 10am to midnight

Post offices 7.30am to 2pm Monday Friday (in cities 7.30am to 8pm Monday Friday, 7.30am- to 2pm Saturday)

Restaurants 11am to 3pm & 7pm to 1am (varies greatly)

Supermarkets 8am to 8pm Monday to Friday, 8am to 3pm Saturday

Street kiosks (*Periptera*) early to late Monday to Sunday

Children

It's safe and easy to travel with children in Greece, as Greeks tends to be very family-oriented. See www.greece4kids.com.

» Be very careful crossing roads with kids!
» Travel on ferries, buses and trains is free to age four; half-fare to age 10 (ferries) or 12 (buses and trains).
» Kids' menus abound.

ⓘ HAPHAZARD OPENING HOURS

It's worth noting that with businesses associated with tourism, opening hours can be rather haphazard. In high season when there are plenty of visitors around, restaurants, cafes, nightclubs and souvenir shops are pretty much open whenever they think they can do good business. If there are few people around, some businesses will simply close early or won't bother opening at all. And in low season, some places, including some sleeping options, may close up for months at a time.

Customs Regulations

There are no longer duty-free restrictions within the EU.

It is strictly forbidden to export antiquities (anything over 100 years old) without an export permit.

Embassies & Consulates

Australian Embassy (☑210 870 4000; www.greece.embassy.gov.au; Ambelokipi, 6th fl, Thon Building, cnr Leoforos Alexandras & Leoforos Kifisias)

Canadian Embassy (☑210 727 3400; www.greece.gc.ca; Genadiou 4)

Japanese Embassy (☑210 670 9900; www.gr.emb-japan.go.jp; Ethnikís Antistáseos 46, Halandri)

New Zealand Embassy (☑210 687 4701; www.nzembassy.com; Kifisias 268, Halandri)

UK Embassy (☑210 723 6211; www.ukingreece. fco.gov.uk; Ploutarhou 1)

US Embassy (☑210 721 2951; http://athens. usembassy.gov; Leoforos Vasilissis Sofias 91)

Food

Price ranges for Eating are as follows:

€€€ more than €40

€€ €15 to €40

€ less than €15

Gay & Lesbian Travellers

The church plays a significant role in shaping society's views on issues such as sexuality, and homosexuality is generally frowned-upon.

It is wise to be discreet and to avoid open displays of togetherness. That said, Greece is a popular destination for gay travellers.

Athens has a busy gay scene that packs up and heads to the islands for summer, with Mykonos famous for its bars, beaches and hedonism, and Eresos on Lesvos something of a pilgrimage for lesbians.

Internet Access

Greece has embraced the internet big-time, but charges differ wildly (as does speed of access). Most midrange and top-end hotels will offer their guests some form of internet connection, and laptop-wielding visitors will often be able to connect to wi-fi at hotels and most internet cafes.

Language Courses

For intensive language courses check out the **Athens Centre** (Map p326; ☎210 701 2268; www.athenscentre.gr; Arhimidous 48, Mets; Ⓜ Akropoli).

Money

ATMs Everywhere except the smallest villages.

Bargaining While souvenir shops will generally bargain, prices in other shops are normally clearly marked and non-negotiable; accommodation is nearly always negotiable outside peak season, especially for longer stays.

Cash Currency is king at street kiosks and small shops, and especially in the countryside.

Changing currency Banks, post offices and currency exchange offices are all over the places; exchange all major currencies.

Credit cards Generally accepted, but may not be on smaller islands or in small villages.

Tipping The service charge is included on the bill in restaurants, but it is the custom to 'round up the bill'; same for taxis.

Post

Tahydromia (post offices) are easily identified by the yellow sign outside.

Regular postboxes are yellow; red postboxes are for express mail.

The postal rate for postcards and airmail letters within the EU is €0.60; to other destinations it's €0.80.

Public Holidays

New Year's Day 1 January

Epiphany 6 January

First Sunday in Lent February

Greek Independence Day 25 March

Good Friday/Easter Sunday March/April

May Day (Protomagia) 1 May

Feast of the Assumption 15 August

Ohi Day 28 October

Christmas Day 25 December

St Stephen's Day 26 December

Safe Travel

Crime is traditionally low in Greece, but on the rise. Watch out for bar scams and *bombes* (spiked drinks), and be wary of pickpockets on the Athens metro, around Omonia and at the flea market. Generally speaking, thefts from tourists are often committed by other tourists.

Telephone

Maintained by Organismos Tilepikoinonion Ellados, known as OTE (o-*teh*). Public phones are everywhere, take all phonecards and are easy to use; pressing the 'i' button brings up the operating instructions in English.

For directory inquiries within Greece, call ☎131 or ☎132; for international directory enquiries, it's ☎161 or ☎162.

MOBILE PHONES

Mobile phones are a must-have in Greece. If you have a compatible GSM phone from a country with a global roaming agreement with Greece, you'll be able to use your phone there.

There are several mobile service providers in Greece; **CosmOTE** (www.cosmote.gr) has the best coverage. You can purchase a Greek SIM card for around €20.

The use of a mobile phone while driving in Greece is prohibited.

PHONE CODES

Telephone codes are part of the 10-digit number within Greece.

The landline prefix is 2 and for mobiles it's 6.

PHONECARDS

All public phones use OTE phonecards; sold at OTE offices and street kiosks. Phonecards come in €3, €5 and €10 versions; local calls cost €0.30 for three minutes. Discount-card schemes are available, offering much better value for money.

Time

There's one time zone throughout Greece, which is two hours ahead of GMT/UTC and three hours ahead on daylight-savings time (from the last Sunday in March to the last Sunday in October).

Toilets

Public toilets are rare, except at airports and bus and train stations.

Most places have Western-style toilets, but some public toilets may be Asian-style squat toilets.

Greek plumbing can't handle toilet paper: anything larger than a postage stamp will cause a blockage. Put your used toilet paper, sanitary napkins and tampons in the small bin provided next to every toilet.

Tourist Information

There's an EOT office or local tourist office in almost every town of consequence and on many of the islands, plus **Tourist Police** in popular destinations; they can also provide information. Head here if you think you've been ripped off.

Greek National Tourist Organisation (GNTO; www.gnto.gr) Known as EOT within Greece.

Travellers with Disabilities

Most hotels, museums and ancient sites are not wheelchair accessible; the uneven terrain is an issue even for able-bodied people. Few facilities exist for the visually or hearing impaired. Check out www.greecetravel.com/handicapped.

Visas

Visitors from most countries don't need a visa for Greece. Countries whose nationals can stay in Greece for up to three months include Australia, Canada, all EU countries, Iceland, Israel, Japan, New Zealand and the USA.

Getting There & Away

Air

Most visitors arrive by air, mostly into Athens. There are 17 international airports in Greece; most handle only summer charter flights to the islands.

There's a growing number of direct scheduled services into Greece by European budget airlines – Olympic Air (www.olympicair.com) and Aegean Airlines (www.aegeanair.com) also fly internationally.

Land

BORDER CROSSINGS

You can drive or ride through the following border crossings.

From Albania:

Kakavia (60km northwest of Ioannina)

Sagiada (28km north of Igoumenitsa)

Mertziani (17km west of Konitsa)

Krystallopigi (14km west of Kotas)

From Bulgaria:

Promahonas (109km northeast of Thessaloniki)

Ormenio (41km from Serres)

Exohi (50km north of Drama)

INTERNATIONAL AIRPORTS

CITY	AIRPORT	DESIGNATION
Aktion (for Lefkada)	Aktion National Airport	PVK
Athens	Eleftherios Venizelos Airport	ATH
Corfu	Corfu Intl Airport	CFU
Hania (Crete)	Hania Intl Airport	CHQ
Iraklio	Nikos Kazantzakis Airport	HER
Kalamata	Kalamata Intl Airport	KLX
Karpathos	Karpathos National Airport	AOK
Kavala	Alexander the Great Airport	KVA
Kefallonia	Kefallonia Intl Airport	EFL
Kos	Hippocrates Intl Airport	KGS
Mykonos	Mykonos National Airport	JMK
Rhodes	Diagoras Airport	RHO
Samos	Samos Intl Airport	SMI
Santorini (Thira)	Santorini National Airport	JTR
Skiathos	Skiathos National Airport	JSI
Thessaloniki	Macedonia Airport	SKG
Zakynthos	Zakynthos Intl Airport	ZTH

LONDON TO ATHENS OVERLAND

For overland enthusiasts, a trip from London to Athens can be accomplished in two days, taking in some gorgeous scenery along the way. A sample itinerary from London would see you catching the Eurostar to Paris and then an overnight sleeper train to Bologna in Italy. From there, a coastal train takes you to Bari, where there's an overnight boat to Patra on the Peloponnese. From Patra, it's a 4½-hour train journey to Athens.

From Macedonia:

Evzoni (68km north of Thessaloniki)

Niki (16km north of Florina)

Doïrani (31km north of Kilkis)

From Turkey:

Kipi (43km east of Alexandroupolis)

Kastanies (139km northeast of Alexandroupolis)

BUS

The **Hellenic Railways Organisation** (OSE; www.ose.gr) has been operating the following routes, but international buses are somewhat in limbo due to Greece's financial problems. Check the current status well in advance.

Albania Athens–Tirana overnight bus (16 hours, daily) via Ioannina and Gjirokastra

Bulgaria Athens–Sofia bus (15 hours, six weekly); Thessaloniki–Sofia (7½ hours, four daily)

Turkey Athens–İstanbul (22 hours, six weekly); stops at Thessaloniki (seven hours) and Alexandroupolis (13 hours)

TRAIN

Both international and domestic train routes have been severely curtailed due to the financial problems. Be sure to check the current situation well in advance. The following routes may or may not be in operation.

Bulgaria Sofia–Athens (18 hours, daily) via Thessaloniki

Macedonia Thessaloniki–Skopje (five hours, twice daily)

Turkey İstanbul–Thessaloniki (12 hours, daily)

Russia Thessaloniki–Moscow (70 hours, weekly, summer only)

Sea

Check out ferry routes, schedules and services online at www.greekferries.gr.

If you are travelling on a rail pass, check to see if ferry travel between Italy and Greece is included. Some ferries are free, others give a discount. On some routes you will need to make reservations.

ALBANIA

Saranda Petrakis Lines (☑26610 38690; www.ionian-cruises.com) has daily hydrofoils to Corfu (25 minutes).

ITALY

Ancona Patra (20 hours, three daily, summer)

Bari Patra (14½ hours, daily) via Corfu (eight hours) and Keffalonia (14 hours); also to Igoumenitsa (11½ hours, daily)

Brindisi Patra (15 hours, Apr–early Oct) via Igoumenitsa

Venice Patra (30 hours, up to 12 weekly, summer) via Corfu (25 hours)

TURKEY

Boat services operate between Turkey's Aegean coast and the Greek Islands.

Marmaris and Fethiye Rhodes (daily in summer, twice weekly in winter)

Bodrum Kos (one hour, daily in summer)

Kuşadası Samos (one hour, daily in summer, weekly in winter)

Çeşme Chios (one hour, daily in summer)

Ayvalık Lesvos (one hour, four times weekly in summer)

GREECE GETTING THERE & AWAY

MOVING ON?

For tips, recommendations and reviews beyond Greece, head to www.shop.lonelyplanet.com, where you can purchase downloadable PDFs of the Albania and Turkey chapters from Lonely Planet's *Mediterranean Europe* guide, or the Macedonia and Bulgaria chapters from *Eastern Europe*.

Getting Around

Greece has a comprehensive transport system and is easy to get around.

Air

Domestic air travel has been very price competitive of late, and it's sometimes cheaper to fly than take the ferry, especially if you book ahead online. A plan to merge Olympic Air and Aegean Airlines was prohibited by the European Commission in January 2011 due to its potential effect on competition and prices.

DOMESTIC AIRLINES

Aegean Airlines (A3; www.aegeanair.com) The big competition for Olympic Air offers newer aircraft and similar prices on popular routes.

Astra Airlines (A2; www.astra-airlines.gr) Based in Thessaloniki; a newcomer flying limited routes.

Athens Airways (☑210 669 6600, 801 801 4000; www.athensairways.com) New kid on the block, but growing steadily.

Olympic Air (OA; www.olympicair.com) Recently privatised; has the most extensive network.

Sky Express (☑281 022 3500; www.sky express.gr) Based in Iraklio, Crete; mainly flies routes that the big two don't.

Bicycle

Greece has very hilly terrain and the summer heat can be stifling. In addition, many drivers totally disregard the road rules.

See www.cyclegreece.gr for bicycle tour ideas. Bicycles are carried for free on ferries.

Rental bicycles are available at most tourist centres, but are generally for pedalling around town rather than for serious riding. Prices generally range from €10 to €20 per day.

Boat

FERRY

Ferries come in all shapes and sizes, from state-of-the-art 'superferries' that run on the major routes, to ageing open ferries that operate local services to outlying islands.

Newer high-speed ferries are slashing travel times, but cost much more.

'Classes' on ferries are largely a thing of the past; you have the option of 'deck class', which is the cheapest ticket, or 'cabin class' with air-con cabins and a decent lounge and restaurant.

When buying tickets you will automatically be given deck class.

Tickets can be bought at the last minute at the dock, but in high season, some boats may be full – plan ahead.

The Greek Ships app for smartphones can be used for real-time tracking to see if your ferry is going to turn up on time – seach for 'Greek Ships' in your app store.

 ISLAND-HOPPING

For many, the idea of meandering from island to island by boat in the Greek Islands is the ultimate dream. It's still a lot of fun, but to some extent not what it used to be. Many of those slow, romantic old ferries you may have seen in the movies have disappeared, replaced by big modern people-movers. If you turn up in high season you might find it just as stressful as rush hour back home.

It's still possible to get away from it all, but it will require some thought – head to smaller islands off the beaten path before high season kicks in. Every island has a boat service of some sort!

Boat operations are highly seasonal and based on the tourist trade, so there's not a lot happening in winter. Services pick up from April, and during July and August Greece's seas are a mass of wake and wash.

Summer also brings the *meltemi*, a strong dry northerly wind that can blow for days and cause havoc to ferry schedules.

In any season, changes to schedules can take place at the last minute. Be prepared to be flexible. Boats seldom arrive early, but often arrive late! And some don't come at all. Think of it as part of the fun.

Check out www.openseas.gr for schedules, costs and links to individual boat company websites.

Main Ferry Routes

CATAMARAN

High-speed catamarans have become an important part of the island travel scene and are much less prone to cancellation in rough weather.

Catamaran fares are generally more expensive than ferries and about the same as hydrofoils.

HYDROFOIL

Hydrofoils are a faster alternative to ferries on some routes, take half the time, but cost twice as much. Most routes will operate only during the high season.

Tickets for hydrofoils must be bought in advance and they are often sold with seat allocation.

Bus

Long-distance buses are operated by **KTEL** (www.ktel.org). Fares are fixed by the government and service routes can be found on the company's website. Buses are comfortable, generally run on time, reasonably priced – eg Athens–Volos (€25, five hours) and Athens–Patra (€17, three hours) – and there are frequent services on all major routes. Tickets should be bought at least an hour in advance to ensure a seat. Buses don't have toilets and refreshments, but stop for a break every couple of hours.

Car & Motorcycle

Driving yourself is a great way to explore areas in Greece that are off the beaten track, but be careful – Greece has the highest road-fatality rate in Europe. The road network has improved dramatically in recent years, but freeway tolls are fairly hefty.

Almost all islands are served by car ferries, but they are expensive; costs vary by the size of the vehicle.

The Greek automobile club, **ELPA** (www. elpa.gr), generally offers reciprocal services to

ROAD RULES

» Drive on the right.

» Overtake on the left (not all Greeks do this!).

» Compulsory to wear seatbelts in the front seats, and in the back if they are fitted.

» Drink-driving laws are strict; a blood alcohol content of 0.05% incurs a fine of around €150 and over 0.08% is a criminal offence.

members of other national motoring associations. If your vehicle breaks down, dial ☑104.

EU-registered vehicles are allowed free entry into Greece for six months without road taxes being due; a green card (international third party insurance) is all that's required.

RENTAL CARS

Available just about anywhere in Greece, you'll get better rates with local rental-car companies than with the big multinational outfits. Check the insurance waivers closely; check how they can assist in case of a breakdown.

High-season weekly rates start at about €280 for the smallest models, dropping to €200 in winter – add tax and extras. Major companies will request a credit-card deposit.

Minimum driving age in Greece is 18, but most car-hire firms require a driver of 21 or over.

RENTAL MOPEDS & MOTORCYCLES

These are available for hire everywhere. Regulations stipulate that you need a valid motorcycle licence stating proficiency for the size of motorcycle you wish to rent – from 50cc upwards.

Mopeds and 50cc motorcycles range from €10 to €25 per day or from €25 per day for a 250cc motorcycle. Outside high season, rates drop considerably.

Ensure that the bike is in good working order and the brakes work well, and check that your travel insurance covers you for injury resulting from motorcycle accidents.

Public Transport

Bus All major towns have local bus systems.

Metro Athens is the only city with a metro system.

TAXI

Taxis are widely available and reasonably priced. Yellow city cabs are metered; rates double between midnight and 5am. Grey rural taxis do not have meters; settle on a price before you get in.

Athens taxi drivers are gifted in their ability to somehow make a little bit extra with every fare. If you have a complaint, note the cab number and contact the Tourist Police. Rural taxi drivers are generally honest, friendly and helpful.

Train

Greece's train services were in a precarious state at the time of research. Check the Greek Railways Organisation website (www.ose.gr) for the latest.

Greece has only two main lines: Athens north to Thessaloniki and Alexandroupolis, and Athens to the Peloponnese.

There are a number of branch lines, eg Pyrgos–Olympia line and the spectacular Diakofto–Kalavryta mountain railway.

InterRail and Eurail passes are valid; you still need to make a reservation.

In summer make reservations at least two days in advance.

Italy

Includes »

Rome	416
Turin	450
Milan	452
Venice	458
Bologna	470
Ravenna	472
Florence	474
Pisa	485
Siena	487
Lucca	489
Naples	494
Matera	506
Lecce	508
Sicily	509
Sardinia	520

Why Go?

Italians really do know how to live well. Ever since the Etruscans came, liked what they saw and decided to stay and party, the locals have embraced the finer things in life. Here, family, faith, friendship, food and wine reign supreme, contributing to the famous Italian *dolce vita* (sweet life).

Travellers have been falling under Italy's spell ever since the days of the 18th-century Grand Tour, enticed by its sun-kissed landscape, delectable cuisine and extraordinary art. This is the home of gently rolling Tuscan hills and postcard-perfect coastlines, and the place where simple dishes such as pizza and pasta regularly attain culinary perfection. It's where Michelangelo shocked the establishment with his assertively humanist sculptures and Caravaggio shocked everyone else with his criminal highjinks and darkly atmospheric paintings.

So make like Julius Caesar. Come and see – you're bound to be conquered.

Best Places to Eat

» Enoteca Provincia Romana (p437)
» L'Osteria di Giovanni (p482)
» Piccolo Napoli (p513)
» Osteria de' Poeti (p471)
» Cucina Casareccia (p509)

Best Places to Stay

» Academy Hostel (p481)
» Art Hotel Boston (p450)
» Belludi37 (p458)
» Novecento (p462)
» Hostel of the Sun (p498)

When to Go

Rome

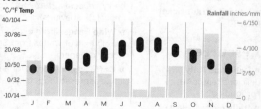

Apr & May Perfect spring temperatures and blooming wildflowers make hikers happy.

Jul Summer means beach weather and a packed festival calendar.

Oct Enjoy mild temperatures, autumn cuisine and the *vendemmia* (grape harvest).

AT A GLANCE

- » **Currency** euro (€)
- » **Language** Italian
- » **Money** ATMs widespread; credit cards widely accepted
- » **Visas** Schengen rules apply

Fast Facts

- » **Area** 301,230 sq km
- » **Capital** Rome
- » **Country code** ☏39
- » **Emergency** ☏112

Exchange Rates

Australia	A$1	€0.82
Canada	C$1	€0.77
Japan	¥100	€0.83
New Zealand	NZ$1	€0.65
UK	UK£1	€1.18
USA	US$1	€0.78

Set Your Budget

- » **Budget hotel room** €50–110
- » **Two-course meal** €20–40 (pizza €10–15)
- » **Museum entrance** €6.50–15
- » **Beer** €2.50–5
- » **Intercity train ticket** €12–80

Resources

- » **Delicious Italy** (www.deliciousitaly.com) For foodies.
- » **Italia** (www.italia.it) Official tourism site.
- » **Lonely Planet** (www.lonelyplanet.com/italy) Destination information, hotel bookings, travellers forum and more.

Connections

Milan and Venice are northern Italy's two main transport hubs. From Milan, trains run to cities across Western Europe, including Paris, Geneva and Zürich. Venice is better placed for Eastern Europe, with rail connections to Ljubljana, Zagreb, Belgrade and Vienna. You can also pick up ferries in Venice for Croatia. Down the east coast, there are ferries from Bari to various Greek ports, as well as to Bar and Dubrovnik. Ferries to Barcelona leave from Genoa, and ferries to Tunis from both Genoa and Palermo.

ITINERARIES

One Week

A one-week whistle-stop tour of Italy is enough to take in the country's three most famous cities. After a couple of days exploring Venice's unique canal-scape, head south to Florence, Italy's great Renaissance city. Two days will whet your appetite for the artistic and architectural treasures waiting to be discovered on your final days in Rome.

Two Weeks

After the first week, continue south for some sea and southern passion. Spend a day dodging traffic in Naples, a day investigating the ruins at Pompeii and a day or two admiring the Amalfi Coast. Then backtrack to Naples for a ferry to Palermo and the gastronomic delights of Sicily, or to Cagliari and Sardinia's magical beaches.

Essential Food & Drink

- » **Pizza** Two varieties: Roman, with a thin crispy base; and Neapolitan, with a higher, more doughy base. The best are always prepared in a *forno a legna* (wood-fired oven).
- » **Gelato** Popular ice-cream flavours include *fragola* (strawberry), *nocciola* (hazelnut) and *stracciatella* (milk with chocolate shavings).
- » **Wine** Ranges from big-name reds such as Piedmont's Barolo to light whites from Sardinia and sparkling *prosecco* from the Veneto.
- » **Caffè** Join the locals for a morning cappuccino or post-lunch espresso, both taken standing at a bar.

Italy Highlights

1 Face up to iconic monuments in Italy's mesmerising capital, **Rome** (p416)

2 Take to the water and cruise past palaces, churches and piazzas in **Venice** (p458)

3 Explore the Renaissance time capsule of **Florence** (p474)

4 Feast on foodie delights and medieval architecture in hedonistic **Bologna** (p470)

5 Explore ancient rock dwellings in **Matera** (p506)

6 Taste the world's best pizza in **Naples** (p494)

7 Admire glorious Gothic architecture and Renaissance art in **Siena** (p487)

8 Visit regal palaces, magnificent museums and historic cafes in **Turin** (p450)

9 Take in an open-air opera in **Verona** (p456), one of Italy's most romantic cities.

10 Enjoy a bike ride and picnic atop the medieval city walls in **Lucca** (p489).

ROME

ITALY ROME

POP 2.76 MILLION

Even in this country of exquisite cities, Rome is special. Pulsating, seductive and utterly disarming, the Italian capital is an epic, monumental metropolis that will steal your heart and haunt your soul. They say a lifetime's not enough *(Roma, non basta una vita)*, but even on a short visit you'll be swept off your feet by its artistic and architectural masterpieces, its operatic piazzas, romantic corners and cobbled lanes. Yet while history reverberates all around, modern life is lived to the full – priests in designer shades walk through the Vatican talking into smartphones, scooters scream through medieval alleyways, fashionable drinkers sip *aperitivi* on baroque piazzas. It's this intoxicating mix of past and present, of style and urban grit, that makes Rome such a rich and compelling place.

History

According to legend Rome was founded by Romulus and Remus in 753 BC. Historians debate this, but archaeological evidence has confirmed the existence of a settlement on the Palatine Hill in that period.

The city was originally ruled by a king, but in 509 BC the Roman Republic was founded. Over the next five centuries the Republic flourished, growing to become the dominant force in the Western world. The end came in the 1st century BC when internal rivalries led to the murder of Julius Caesar in 44 BC and the outbreak of civil war between Octavian and Mark Antony. Octavian emerged victorious and was made Rome's first emperor with the title Augustus.

By AD 100 Rome had a population of 1.5 million and was the *caput mundi* (Capital of the World), but by the 5th century decline had set in. In 476 Romulus Augustulus, the last emperor of the Western Roman Empire, was deposed.

By this time Rome's Christian roots had taken hold. Christianity had been spreading since the 1st century AD, and under Constantine it received official recognition. Pope Gregory I (590–604) did much to strengthen the Church's grip over the city, laying the foundations for its later role as capital of the Catholic Church.

Under the Renaissance popes of the 15th and 16th centuries, Rome was given an extensive facelift. But trouble was never far away and in 1527 the city was sacked by Spanish forces under Charles V.

ROMA PASS

The **Roma Pass** (www.romapass.it; 3 days €30) provides free admission to two museums or sites (choose from a list of 45), as well as reduced entry to extra sites, unlimited city transport and discounted entry to other exhibitions and events. Valid for three days, it's available online or from tourist information points and participating museums.

By the 17th century Rome needed rebuilding, and turned to baroque masters Bernini and Borromini. With their exuberant churches, fountains and *palazzi* (palaces), these two bitter rivals changed the face of the city. A building boom following the declaration of Rome as the capital of a newly-unified Italy also profoundly influenced the look of the city, as did Mussolini and post-WWII expansion.

◉ Sights

Most of Rome's sights are concentrated in the area between Stazione Termini and the Vatican. Halfway between the two, the Pantheon and Piazza Navona lie at the heart of the *centro storico* (historic centre), while to the southeast, the Colosseum lords it over the city's ancient core.

ANCIENT ROME

Colosseum AMPHITHEATRE
(Map p422; ☑06 399 67 700; www.coopculture.it; Piazza del Colosseo; adult/reduced/EU child incl Roman Forum & Palatino €12/7.50/free, audioguide €5.50 ☉8.30am-1hr before sunset; Ⓜ Colosseo) Rome's great gladiatorial arena is the most thrilling of its ancient sights. Originally known as the Flavian Amphitheatre, the 50,000-seat Colosseum was started by Emperor Vespasian in AD 72 and finished by his son Titus in AD 80. It was clad in travertine and covered by a huge canvas awning that was held aloft by 240 masts. Inside, tiered seating encircled the sand-covered arena, itself built over underground chambers (known as the hypogeum), where animals were caged and elaborate stage sets prepared. Games involved gladiators fighting wild animals or each other, but contrary to Hollywood folklore, bouts rarely ended in death.

The top tier and hypogeum can be visited on guided tours (€6 or €8 for both), which must be booked in advance, either at www. pierreci.it or by calling ☑06 399 67 700.

ROME IN...

Two Days

Get to grips with ancient Rome at the **Colosseum**, the **Roman Forum** and the **Palatino**. Spend the afternoon exploring the **Capitoline Museums** before an evening in **Trastevere**. On day two, hit the **Vatican**. Marvel at **St Peter's Basilica** and the **Sistine Chapel** in the **Vatican Museums**. Afterwards, ditch your guidebook and get happily lost in the animated streets around **Piazza Navona** and the **Pantheon**.

Four Days

With another couple of days, book a visit to the outstanding **Museo e Galleria Borghese** and check out **Piazza del Popolo**, the **Spanish Steps** and **Trevi Fountain**. Venture out to **Via Appia Antica** to explore the catacombs, and, if you can handle more art, take in the **Galleria Doria Pamphilj** and **Museo Nazionale Romano: Palazzo Massimo alle Terme**. In the evenings, sip in style in the bohemian **Monti** district or let your hair down with a concert at the **Auditorium Parco della Musica**.

West of the Colosseum, the **Arco di Costantino** (Map p422; Ⓜ Colosseo) was built to celebrate Constantine's victory over rival Maxentius at the battle of Milvian Bridge in AD 312.

Palatino   RUINS
(Palatine Hill; Map p422; ☑06 399 67 700; www.coopculture.it; Via di San Gregorio 30; adult/reduced/EU child incl Colosseum & Roman Forum €12/7.50/free, audioguide €5; ◷8.30am-1hr before sunset; Ⓜ Colosseo) Rising above the Roman Forum, the Palatine Hill is where Romulus supposedly killed his twin Remus and founded the city in 753 BC. Archaeological evidence can't prove the legend, but it has dated human habitation here to the 8th century BC. Later, the Palatine was Rome's most exclusive neighbourhood and the emperor Augustus lived here all his life. After Rome's fall, it fell into disrepair, and in the Middle Ages churches and castles were built over the ruins and wealthy Renaissance families established gardens here.

Most of the area is covered by the ruins of Emperor Domitian's vast complex, which served as the main imperial palace for 300 years. Divided into the **Domus Flavia** (Imperial Palace), **Domus Augustana** (Emperor's Residence) and a **stadio** (Stadium), it was built in the 1st century AD.

Among the best-preserved buildings on the Palatine Hill is the **Casa di Livia**, home of Augustus' wife Livia, and, in front, Augustus' separate residence, the frescoed **Casa di Augusto** (◷11am-3.30pm Mon, Wed, Sat & Sun).

For grandstand views over the Roman Forum, head to the **Orti Farnesiani** gardens in the north of the complex.

Roman Forum   RUINS
(Foro Romano; Map p422; ☑06 399 67 700; www.coopculture.it; Largo della Salara Vecchia; adult/reduced/EU child incl Colosseum & Palatino €12/7.50/free, audioguide €5; ◷8.30am-1hr before sunset) Now a collection of fascinating, if rather confusing, ruins, the Roman Forum was ancient Rome's showpiece centre, a grandiose district of temples, basilicas and vibrant public spaces. Originally an Etruscan burial ground, the area was first developed in the 7th century BC, and became the social, political and commercial heart of the Roman world. Its importance declined after the fall of the Roman Empire, until eventually the site was used as pasture land and plundered for marble.

As you enter from Largo della Salara Vecchia, ahead to your left is the **Tempio di Antonino e Faustina** (Map p422), built by the senate in AD 141 and transformed into a

COLOSSEUM TIPS

Follow these tips to beat the queues:

» Buy your ticket from the Palatine entrance (about 250m away at Via di San Gregorio 30) or the Roman Forum (Largo della Salara Vecchia).

» Get the Roma Pass, which is valid for three days and a whole host of sites.

» Book your ticket online at www.coopculture.it (plus booking fee of €1.50).

» Join an official English-language tour – €5 on top of the regular Colosseum ticket price.

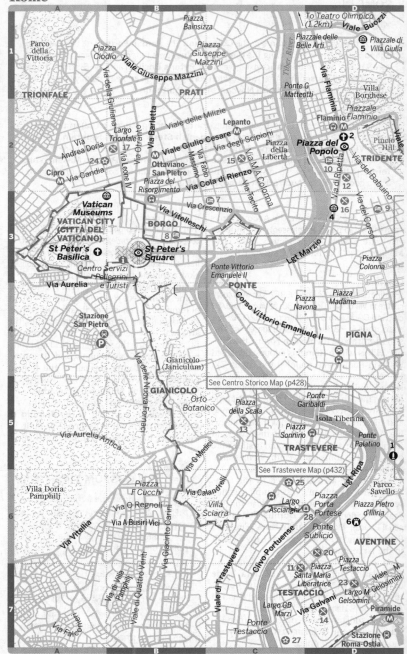

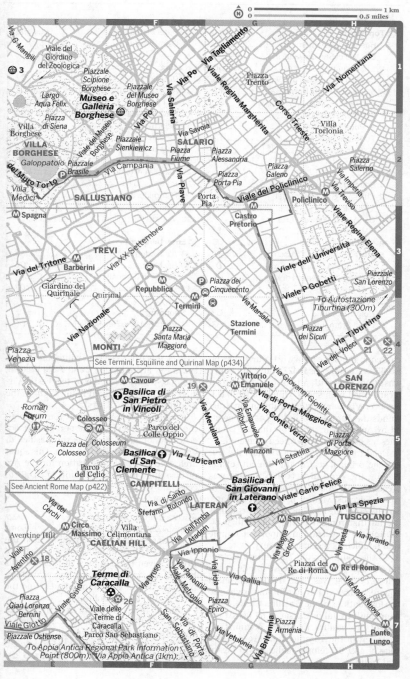

Rome

◉ Top Sights
Basilica di San Clemente F5
Basilica di San Giovanni in
Laterano G6
Basilica di San Pietro in Vincoli F5
Museo e Galleria Borghese....................F2
Piazza del Popolo D2
St Peter's Basilica..................................A3
St Peter's Square B3
Terme di Caracalla F7
Vatican Museums...................................A3

◎ Sights
1 Bocca della Verità..................................D5
2 Chiesa di Santa Maria del
Popolo...D2
3 Galleria Nazionale d'Arte
Moderna..E1
4 Museo dell'Ara Pacis D3
5 Museo Nazionale Etrusco di
Villa Giulia..D1
6 Priorato dei Cavalieri di Malta D6

🛌 Sleeping
7 Colors Hotel C3
8 Hotel Bramante B3

9 Hotel Panda D3
10 Okapi Rooms D2

✕ Eating
11 00100 Pizza...C7
12 Al Gran Sasso D2
13 Da Lucia C5
14 Flavio al Velavevodetto.........................D7
15 Gelarmony C2
16 'Gusto...D3
17 Hostaria Dino & Tony.............................B2
18 Il Gelato E6
19 Panella l'Arte del Pane F4
20 Pizzeria Da Remo D6
21 Pommidoro...H4
22 Tram Tram..H4
23 Volpetti Più D7

✪ Entertainment
24 Alexanderplatz A2
25 Big Mama..C6
26 Terme di Caracalla F7
27 Villaggio Globale....................................C7

🛍 Shopping
28 Porta Portese Flea Market D6

church in the 8th century. To your right, the **Basilica Aemilia** (Map p422), built in 179 BC, was 100m long with a two-storey porticoed facade lined with shops. Opposite the basilica, over **Via Sacra**, the Forum's main drag, stands the **Tempio di Giulio Cesare**, erected by Augustus in 29 BC on the site where Caesar's body had earlier been cremated.

Head right up Via Sacra to reach the **Curia**, the original seat of the Roman senate. Nearby, the **Arco di Settimio Severo** was erected in AD 203 to honour Emperor Septimus Severus' victory over the Parthians. Southwest of the arch, eight granite columns are all that remain of the 5th-century BC **Tempio di Saturno**, an important temple that doubled as the state treasury.

To the southeast, the 7th-century **Colonna di Foca** (Column of Phocus) stands at the centre of what was once the forum's main square, Piazza del Foro. To your right are the foundations of the **Basilica Giulia**, a law court built by Julius Caesar in 55 BC. At the end of the basilica rise three columns, all that's left of the **Tempio di Castore e Polluce**, a 489 BC temple dedicated to Castor and Pollux.

Back towards Via Sacra, white statues line the grassy atrium of the **Casa delle Vestali**, the once-luxurious home of the Vestal Virgins who kept the sacred flame alight in the adjoining **Tempio di Vesta**.

Continuing up Via Sacra, you come to the vast **Basilica di Massenzio** (Basilica di Costantino), also known as the Basilica di Costantino, and the **Arco di Tito**. This squat arch, said to be the inspiration for the Arc de Triomphe in Paris, was built in AD 81 to celebrate victories against Jewish rebels in Jerusalem.

Piazza del Campidoglio   PIAZZA
(Map p422; 🚇Piazza Venezia) This elegant Michelangelo-designed piazza sits atop the Capitoline Hill (Campidoglio), the lowest of Rome's seven hills. In ancient times, it was home to the city's two most important temples: one dedicated to Juno Moneta and the other to Jupiter Capitolinus.

You can reach the piazza from the Roman Forum but the most dramatic approach is via the graceful **Cordonata** staircase. At the top, the piazza is flanked by three *palazzi:* **Palazzo Nuovo** on the left, **Palazzo dei**

Conservatori on the right, and **Palazzo Senatorio**, seat of Rome's City Hall since 1143. In the centre, the bronze **statue of Marcus Aurelius** is a copy; the original is in the Capitoline Museums.

Capitoline Museums MUSEUM
(Musei Capitolini; Map p422; ☑06 06 08; www.musei capitolini.org; Piazza del Campidoglio 1; adult/reduced/child €9.50/7.50/free plus possible exhibition supplement, audioguide €5; ☺9am-8pm Tue-Sun, last admission 7pm; ☐Piazza Venezia) Housed in Palazzo dei Conservatori and Palazzo Nuovo on Piazza del Campidoglio, the Capitoline Museums are the world's oldest public museums, dating to 1471. Their collection of classical art is one of Italy's finest, including masterpieces such as the *Lupa Capitolina* (Capitoline Wolf), a sculpture of Romulus and Remus under a wolf, and the *Galata morente* (Dying Gaul), a moving depiction of a dying Gaul. The rich 2nd-floor **pinacoteca** (picture gallery) contains paintings by the likes of Titian, Tintoretto, Van Dyck, Rubens and Caravaggio.

Chiesa di Santa Maria in Aracoeli CHURCH
(Map p422; Piazza Santa Maria in Aracoeli; ☺9am-12.30pm & 2.30-5.30pm; ☐Piazza Venezia) Marking the highest point of the Campidoglio, this 6th-century church sits on the site of the Roman temple to Juno Moneta. According to legend it was here that the Tiburtine Sybil told Augustus of the coming birth of Christ, and the church still has a strong association with the nativity.

FREE **Il Vittoriano** MONUMENT
(Map p422; Piazza Venezia; ☺9.30am-5.30pm summer, to 4.30pm winter; ☐Piazza Venezia) Love it or loathe it as most locals do, you can't ignore Il Vittoriano (aka the *Altare della Patria;* Altar of the Fatherland), the massive mountain of marble that looms over Piazza Venezia. Begun in 1885 to honour Italy's first king, Vittorio Emanuele II, it incorporates the **Tomb of the Unknown Soldier** and the **Museo Centrale del Risorgimento** (Map p422; Via di San Pietro in Carcere; admission free; ☺9.30am-6.30pm; ☐Piazza Venezia), documenting Italian unification. At the back, a **panoramic lift** (Map p422; adult/reduced €7/3.50; ☺9.30am-6.30pm Mon-Thu, to 7.30pm Fri-Sun) whisks you up to the top for Rome's best 360-degree views.

Over the square, the 15th-century **Palazzo Venezia** (Map p434; Piazza Venezia; ☐Piazza Venezia) was the first of Rome's great Renaissance *palazzi*. Mussolini had his office here and there's now a museum of medieval and Renaissance art.

Mercati di Traiano Museo dei Fori Imperiali MUSEUM
(Map p434; ☑06 06 08; www.mercatiditraiano.it; Via IV Novembre 94; adult/reduced €9.50/7.50, plus possible exhibition supplement; ☺9am-7pm Tue-Sun, last admission 6pm; ☐Via IV Novembre) This striking museum brings to life the **Mercati di Traiano**, emperor Trajan's great 2nd-century market complex. From the main hallway, a lift whisks you up to the **Torre delle Milizie** (Militia Tower), a 13th-century red-brick tower, and the upper levels of the vast three-storey semi-circular construction that once housed hundreds of market traders.

Bocca della Verità MONUMENT
(Map p418; Piazza Bocca della Verità 18; donation €0.50; ☺9.30am-4.50pm winter, to 5.50pm summer; ☐Piazza Bocca della Verità) A mask-shaped round marble disc that was once part of an ancient fountain, or possibly an ancient manhole cover, the Mouth of Truth is one of Rome's great curiosities. According to legend, if you put your hand in the carved mouth and tell a lie, it will bite your hand off.

The mouth is in the portico of the **Chiesa di Santa Maria in Cosmedin**, one of Rome's most beautiful medieval churches.

THE VATICAN
The world's smallest sovereign state – it covers just 0.44 sq km – the Vatican is the modern vestige of the Papal States. This papal empire encompassed Rome and much of central Italy for more than a thousand years until it was forcibly incorporated into the Italian state during unification in 1861. Relations between Italy and the landless papacy remained strained until 1929 when Mussolini and Pope Pius XI signed the Lateran Treaty, formally establishing the Vatican State.

WANT MORE?

For in-depth information, reviews and recommendations at your fingertips, head to the Apple App Store to purchase Lonely Planet's *Rome City Guide* iPhone app.

Alternatively, head to **Lonely Planet** (www.lonelyplanet.com/italy/rome) for planning advice, author recommendations, traveller reviews and insider tips.

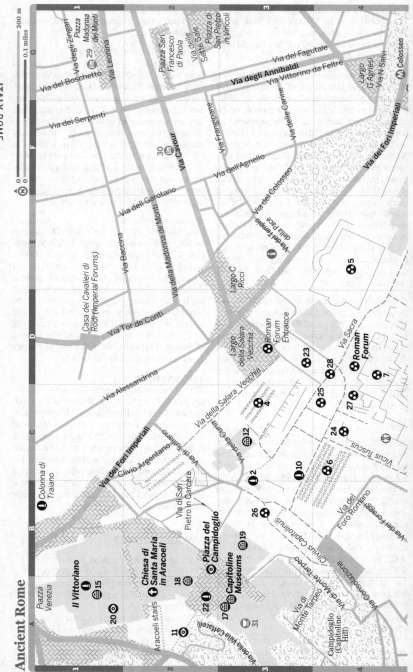

Ancient Rome

N

0 ————— 200 m
0 ————— 0.1 miles

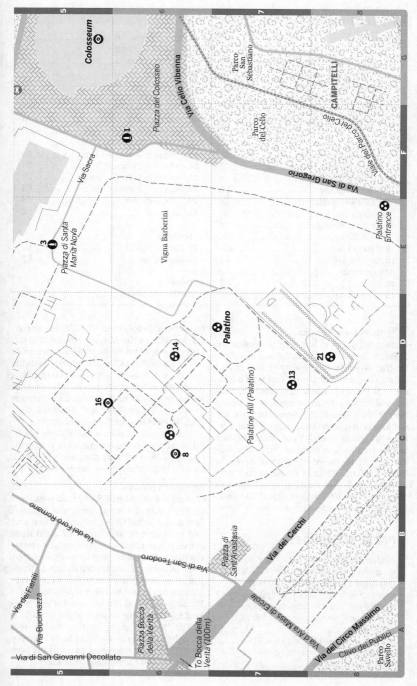

Ancient Rome

⊚ Top Sights

Capitoline Museums	A3
Chiesa di Santa Maria in Aracoeli	A2
Colosseum	G5
Il Vittoriano	A1
Palatino	D7
Piazza del Campidoglio	B2
Roman Forum	D4

⊚ Sights

1	Arco di Costantino	F6
2	Arco di Settimio Severo	C3
3	Arco di Tito	E5
4	Basilica Aemilia	C3
5	Basilica di Massenzio	E4
6	Basilica Giulia	C4
7	Casa delle Vestali	D4
8	Casa di Augusto	C6
9	Casa di Livia	C6
10	Colonna di Foca	C3
11	Cordonata	A2
12	Curia	C3
13	Domus Augustana	D7

14	Domus Flavia	D6
15	Museo Centrale del Risorgimento	A1
16	Orti Farnesiani	C5
17	Palazzo dei Conservatori	A3
18	Palazzo Nuovo	A2
19	Palazzo Senatorio	B3
20	Panoramic Lift	A1
21	Stadio	D8
22	Statue of Marcus Aurelius	A2
23	Tempio di Antonino e Faustina	D3
24	Tempio di Castore e Polluce	C4
25	Tempio di Giulio Cesare	C4
26	Tempio di Saturno	B3
27	Tempio di Vesta	C4
28	Via Sacra	D4

⊜ Sleeping

29	Duca d'Alba	G1
30	Nicolas Inn	F2

⊜ Drinking

31	Caffè Capitolino	A3

FREE **St Peter's Basilica** CHURCH
(Basilica di San Pietro; Map p418; www.vatican.va; St Peter's Square; ⊙7am-7pm Apr-Sep, to 6.30pm Oct-Mar; Ⓜ Ottaviano-San Pietro) In this city of outstanding churches, none can hold a candle to St Peter's Basilica, Italy's biggest, richest and most spectacular church. Standing over St Peter's tomb, the current basilica, the world's second largest, was built atop an earlier 4th-century church by an army of major league architects and artists, including Bramante, who produced the original design in 1506, Raphael, Antonio de Sangallo, Carlo Maderno and Michelangelo, who took over the project in 1507 and designed the soaring 120m-high dome. The entrance to climb

---

PAPAL AUDIENCES

At 11am on Wednesday, the Pope addresses his flock at the Vatican (in July and August in Castel Gandolfo near Rome). For details of how to apply for free tickets, see the Vatican website (www.vatican.va/various/prefettura/index_en.html).

He also blesses the crowd in St Peter's Square on Sunday at noon – no tickets are required.

---

the **dome** (with/without lift €7/5; ⊙8am-6pm Apr-Sep, 8am-5pm Oct-Mar) is to the right of the stairs that lead up to the basilica's atrium.

The cavernous 187m-long interior contains numerous treasures, including two of Italy's most celebrated masterpieces: Michelangelo's hauntingly beautiful *Pietà*, the only work to carry his signature; and Bernini's 29m-high **baldachin** over the main altar.

Note that the basilica is one of Rome's busiest attractions, so expect queues in peak periods. Also, dress rules are stringently enforced, so no shorts, miniskirts or sleeveless tops.

St Peter's Square PIAZZA
(Piazza San Pietro; Map p418; Ⓜ Ottaviano-San Pietro) The Vatican's central space was designed by baroque artist Gian Lorenzo Bernini and laid out between 1656 and 1667. Seen from above, it resembles a keyhole with two semicircular colonnades, each consisting of four rows of Doric columns, encircling a giant ellipse that straightens out to funnel believers into the basilica. The effect was deliberate – Bernini described the colonnades as representing 'the motherly arms of the church'.

The 25m obelisk in the centre was brought to Rome by Caligula from Heliopolis in Egypt and later used as a turning post for the chariot races in Nero's circus.

Vatican Museums MUSEUM
(Musei Vaticani; Map p418; ☎06 698 84 676; http://
mv.vatican.va; Viale Vaticano; adult/reduced/child
€16/8/free, admission free last Sun of month; ⊙9am-
6pm Mon-Sat, last admission 4pm, 9am-2pm last Sun
of month, last admission 12.30pm; ⓂOttaviano-San
Pietro) Boasting one of the world's great art
collections, the Vatican Museums are housed
in the Palazzo Apostolico Vaticano, a vast
5.5-hectare complex comprising two palaces
and three internal courtyards. You'll never
cover it all in one day – there are about 7km
of exhibits – so it pays to be selective.

For spectacular classical statuary, head
to the **Museo Pio-Clementino**, home to
the peerless *Apollo Belvedere* and the 1st-
century *Laocoön,* both in the Cortile Ottagono (Octagonal Courtyard). Further on, beyond the magnificent **Galleria delle Carte
Geografiche** (Map Gallery), are the **Stanze
di Raffaello** (Raphael Rooms). These were
once the private apartments of Pope Julius
II, and are adorned with frescos by Raphael
and his students, including Raphael's great
masterpiece *La Scuola di Atene* (The School
of Athens) in the Stanza della Segnatura.

From the Raphael Rooms, it's a short walk
on to the **Sistine Chapel** (Cappella Sistina),
the museums' grand finale. This soaring
15th-century chapel, where the papal con-
clave is locked to elect the pope, is home to
two of the world's most celebrated works of
art – Michelangelo's ceiling frescos and his
Giudizio Universale (Last Judgment). The
chapel was originally built in 1484 for Pope
Sixtus IV, after whom it was named, but it was
Julius II who commissioned Michelangelo to
decorate it in 1508. Over the next four years,
the artist painted the entire 800-sq-metre
ceiling with episodes from the book of Gen-
esis. Twenty-two years later he returned at the
behest of Pope Clement VII to paint the *Last
Judgment* on the 200-sq-metre west wall. The
other walls of the chapel feature frescos produced by a crack team of Renaissance artists
including Botticelli, Domenico Ghirlandaio,
Pinturicchio and Luca Signorelli.

CENTRO STORICO

FREE **Pantheon** CHURCH
(Map p428; Piazza della Rotonda; audioguide €5;
⊙8.30am-7.30pm Mon-Sat, 9am-6pm Sun; ⊡Lar-
go di Torre Argentina) A striking 2000-year-
old temple, now church, the Pantheon is
the best preserved of ancient Rome's great
monuments. In its current form it dates to
around AD 120 when the Emperor Hadrian

**ⓘ QUEUE JUMPING AT
THE VATICAN MUSEUMS**

To reduce waiting time:

» Book tickets at http://biglietteria
musei.vatican.va/musei/tickets (plus
booking fee of €4).

» Time your visit: Wednesday mornings are good as everyone is at the
Pope's weekly audience at St Peter's;
on other days, afternoon is better than
the morning; avoid Mondays, when
many other museums are shut.

built over Marcus Agrippa's original 27 BC
temple (Agrippa's name remains inscribed
on the pediment). The **dome**, considered
the Romans' greatest architectural achievement, was the largest in the world until
the 15th century and is still the largest un-
reinforced concrete dome ever built. It's a
mind-boggling structure whose harmonious
appearance is due to a precisely calibrated
symmetry – its diameter is exactly equal
to the Pantheon's interior height of 43.3m.
Light (and rain, which drains away through
22 holes in the floor) enters through the
oculus, an 8.7m opening that acts as a com-
pression ring, absorbing and redistributing
the dome's vast structural forces.

Inside, you'll find the tombs of Raphael and
kings Vittorio Emanuele II and Umberto I.

Piazza Navona PIAZZA
(Map p428; ⊡Corso del Rinascimento) With its
ornate fountains, baroque *palazzi,* pavement
cafes and colourful cast of street artists, hawk-
ers, tourists and pigeons, Piazza Navona is
Rome's most celebrated square. Built over the
ruins of the 1st-century Stadio di Domiziano
(Domitian's Stadium), it was paved in the
15th century and for almost 300 years hosted
the city's main market.

Of the piazza's three fountains, the grand
centrepiece is Gian Lorenzo Bernini's 1651
Fontana dei Quattro Fiumi (Fountain of the
Four Rivers), a monumental ensemble repre-
senting the rivers Nile, Ganges, Danube and
Plate.

Campo de' Fiori PIAZZA
(Map p428; ⊡Corso Vittorio Emanuele II) Noisy,
colourful 'Il Campo' is a major focus of Roman life: by day it hosts a much-loved market, while at night it morphs into a raucous
open-air pub. For centuries this was the site
of public executions, and it was here that

VATICAN MUSEUMS ITINERARY

Follow this three-hour itinerary for the museums' greatest hits.

Cortile della Pigna First stop is this impressive courtyard, named after the huge Augustan-era bronze pine cone in the monumental niche. Cross the courtyard into the long corridor that is the Museo Chiaramonti and head left up the stairs.

Museo Pio-Clementino This stunning museum showcases some of the Vatican's finest classical statuary. Follow the flow of people through the Cortile Ottagono and push onto the Sala Croce Greca (Greek Cross Room) from where stairs lead up to the 1st floor of the Belvedere Palace.

Galleria dei Candelabri The Gallery of the Candelabra is the first of three galleries that run the length of the palace. It gets very crowded up here as you're funnelled through the Galleria degli Arazzi (Tapestry Gallery) and onto the striking Galleria delle Carte Geografiche (Map Gallery). At the end of the corridor, carry on through the Sala Sobieski to the Sala di Costantino, the first of the four Raphael Rooms.

Stanze di Raffaello (Raphael Rooms) Anywhere else these magnificent frescoed chambers would be the star attraction but here they're the warm-up for the grand finale, the Sistine Chapel. To get there, follow the one-way system past the modern art section and through the chapel's small and surprisingly discreet visitors' entrance.

Sistine Chapel Once in the chapel, head to the far wall for the best views of the frescos.

Castel Sant'Angelo (Map p428; ☏06 681 91 11; Lungotevere Castello 50; adult/reduced/EU child €8.50/6/free, plus possible exhibition supplement; ⊗9am-7.30pm Tue-Sun, last admission 6.30pm; ☐Piazza Pia) An instantly recognisable landmark, this chunky round-keeped castle was built in the 2nd century AD as a mausoleum for the emperor Hadrian. It was converted into a papal fortress in the 6th century and now houses a museum with an assorted collection of sculptures, paintings, weapons and furniture. The terrace offers great views.

philosopher monk Giordano Bruno (the hooded figure in Ettore Ferrari's sinister statue) was burned at the stake for heresy in 1600.

Palazzo Farnese
PALACE

(Map p428; www.inventerrome.com; Piazza Farnese; admission €5; ⊗guided tours 3pm, 4pm, 5pm Mon, Wed & Fri, advance booking obligatory; ☐Corso Vittorio Emanuele II) One of Rome's most impressive Renaissance *palazzi,* now home to the French Embassy, this 16th-century palace was designed and built by a trio of top architects – Antonio da Sangallo the Younger, Michelangelo and Giacomo della Porta. Inside, the highlight is a series of frescos by Annibale Carracci, said by some to rival Michelangelo's in the Sistine Chapel. Visits are by guided tour only.

Galleria Doria Pamphilj
MUSEUM

(Map p428; ☏06 679 73 23; www.dopart.it; Via del Corso 305; adult/reduced €11/7.50; ⊗9am-7pm, last admission 6pm; ☐Piazza Venezia) Behind the grimy grey walls of Palazzo Doria Pamphilj is one of Rome's finest private art collections, with works by Raphael, Tintoretto, Brueghel, Titian, Caravaggio and Bernini.

The undisputed highlight is the Velázquez portrait of Pope Innocent X, who grumbled that the portrait was 'too real'.

Trevi Fountain
FOUNTAIN

(Fontana di Trevi; Map p434; Piazza di Trevi; Ⓜ Barberini) Immortalised by Anita Ekberg's sensual dip in Fellini's *La dolce vita,* the Trevi Fountain is Rome's largest and most famous fountain. The flamboyant ensemble was designed by Nicola Salvi in 1732 and depicts Neptune in a shell-shaped chariot being led by the Tritons and two sea horses representing the moods of the sea. The water comes from the *aqua virgo,* a 1st-century BC underground aqueduct, and the name 'Trevi' refers to the *tre vie* (three roads) that converge at the fountain.

The custom is to throw a coin into the fountain, thus ensuring your return to Rome. On average about €3000 is chucked away daily.

Galleria Nazionale d'Arte Antica: Palazzo Barberini
GALLERY

(Map p434; ☏06 3 28 10; www.gebart.it; Via delle Quattro Fontane 13; adult/reduced €7/3.50, with Palazzo Corsini €9/4.50; ⊗8.30am-7pm Tue-Sun; Ⓜ Barberini) A must for anyone who's into Renaissance and baroque art, this sumpt uous gallery is housed in Palazzo Barberini, one of Rome's most spectacular *palazzi*. Inside, you'll find works by Raphael, Caravaggio, Guido Reni, Bernini, Filippo Lippi and Holbein, as well as Pietro da Cortona's breathtaking *Trionfo della Divina Provvidenza* (Triumph of Divine Providence).

Spanish Steps
ARCHITECTURE

(Map p434; Piazza di Spagna; M Spagna) Rising above Piazza di Spagna, the Spanish Steps, aka the Scalinata della Trinità dei Monti, have been a magnet for foreigners since the 18th century. The piazza was named after the Spanish embassy to the Holy See, although the staircase, which was built with French money in 1725, leads to the French church, **Chiesa della Trinità dei Monti** (Map p434; Piazza Trinità dei Monti; ⊙6am-8pm Tue-Sun; M Spagna). At the foot of the steps, the fountain of a sinking boat, the **Barcaccia** (1627), is believed to be by Pietro Bernini, father of the more famous Gian Lorenzo. Opposite, Via dei Condotti is Rome's top shopping strip.

Piazza del Popolo
PIAZZA

(Map p418; M Flaminio) This elegant landmark square was laid out in 1538 at the point of convergence of three roads – Via di Ripetta, Via del Corso and Via del Babuino – at what was then Rome's northern entrance. Guarding its southern approach are the twin 17th-century churches of **Santa Maria dei Miracoli** and **Santa Maria in Montesanto**, while on the northern flank is the **Porta del Popolo**, created by Bernini in 1655. The 36m-high obelisk in the centre was brought by Augustus from Heliopolis in ancient Egypt.

Chiesa di Santa Maria del Popolo
CHURCH

(Map p418; Piazza del Popolo; ⊙7.30am-noon & 4-7pm; M Flaminio) On the northern side of Piazza del Popolo stands one of Rome's earliest and richest Renaissance churches. The first chapel was built in 1099 to exorcise the ghost of Nero, who was buried on this spot and whose ghost was said to haunt the area, but its current form dates to 1472. Inside, the star attraction is the pair of Caravaggio masterpieces: the *Conversione di San Paolo* (Conversion of St Paul) and the *Crocifissione di San Pietro* (Crucifixion of St Peter).

TOP CHOICE Museo dell'Ara Pacis
MUSEUM

(Map p418; ☑06 06 08; http://en.arapacis.it; Lungotevere in Augusta; adult/reduced €8.50/6.50; ⊙9am-7pm Tue-Sun, last admission 6pm; M Flaminio) The first modern construction in Rome's

FREE THRILLS

Surprisingly, some of Rome's most famous sights are free:

» Trevi Fountain
» Spanish Steps
» Pantheon
» Bocca della Verità
» All churches, including St Peter's Basilica
» Vatican Museums on the last Sunday of the month

historic centre since WWII, Richard Meier's white pavilion houses the **Ara Pacis Augustae** (Altar of Peace), one of the most important works of ancient Roman sculpture. The vast marble altar was completed in 13 BC as a monument to the peace that Augustus established both at home and abroad.

VILLA BORGHESE

Just north of the *centro storico*, Villa Borghese is Rome's best-known park. The grounds, which were created in the 17th century by Cardinal Scipione Borghese, are accessible from Piazzale Flaminio, Pincio Hill and the top of Via Vittorio Veneto. Bike hire is available at various points, typically costing €5 per hour.

TOP CHOICE Museo e Galleria Borghese
MUSEUM

(Map p418; ☑06 3 28 10; www.galleriaborghese.it; Piazzale del Museo Borghese 5; adult/reduced €9/4.50, plus €2 booking fee and possible exhibition supplement; ⊙9am-7pm Tue-Sun, pre-booking necessary; ☐ Via Pinciana) If you only have time, or inclination, for one art gallery in Rome, make it this one. Housing the 'queen of all private art collections', it boasts paintings by Caravaggio, Botticelli and Raphael, as well as some spectacular sculptures by Gian Lorenzo Bernini. There are highlights at every turn, but look out for Bernini's *Ratto di Proserpina* (Rape of Persephone) and *Apollo e Dafne;* Antonio Canova's *Venere vincitrice* (Conquering Venus); and the Caravaggios in room VIII.

Note that you'll need to pre-book your ticket and enter at an allotted time.

Museo Nazionale Etrusco di Villa Giulia
MUSEUM

(Map p418; ☑06 322 65 71; www.villagiulia.beni culturali.it; Piazzale di Villa Giulia; adult/reduced/child €8/4/free; ⊙Villa Giulia 8.30am-7.30pm

Centro Storico

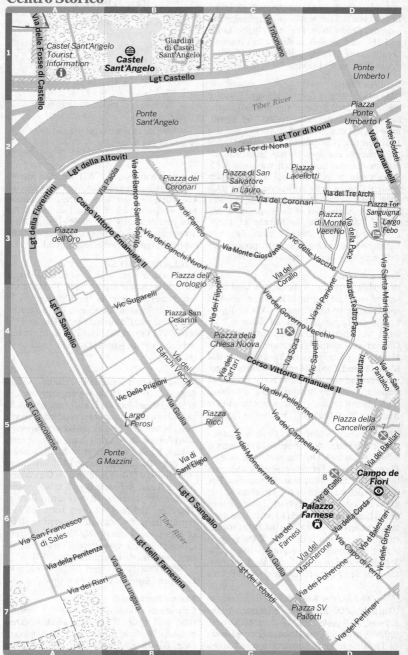

ITALY ROME

A | **B** | **C** | **D**

Via delle Fosse di Castello

Castel Sant'Angelo Tourist Information

Castel Sant'Angelo

Giardini di Castel Sant'Angelo

Via Triboniano

Lgt Castello

Ponte Umberto I

Tiber River

Ponte Sant'Angelo

Lgt Tor di Nona

Piazza Ponte Umberto I

Via dei Soldati

Via G Zanardelli

Lgt della Altoviti

Via di Tor di Nona

Via Paola

Via del Banco di Santo Spirito

Piazza del Coronari

Piazza di San Salvatore in Lauro

Piazza Lacellotti

Via dei Coronari

Via dei Tre Archi

Piazza Tor Sanguigna

Lgt della Fiorentini

Corso Vittorio Emanuele II

Via di Panico

Via dei Banchi Nuovi

Via Monte Giordana

Vic delle Vacche

Piazza di Monte Vecchio

Via della Pace

Largo Febo

Via Santa Maria dell'Anima

Piazza dell'Oro

Vic Sugarelli

Piazza dell' Orologio

Via dei Filippini

Via del Corallo

Via del Governo Vecchio

Via di Parione

Via del Teatro Pace

Piazza San Cesarini

Piazza della Chiesa Nuova

Via dei Cartari

Via di Sora

Vic Savelli

Corso Vittorio Emanuele II

Tratarina

Via di San Pantaleo

Lgt D Sangallo

Via dei Banchi Vecchi

Vic Delle Prigioni

Via Giulia

Largo L Perosi

Piazza Ricci

Via del Pellegrino

Via dei Cappellari

Piazza della Cancelleria

Via dei Baullari

Lgt Giancolense

Ponte G Mazzini

Via di Sant'Eligio

Via di Monserrato

Campo de Fiori

Vic di Gallo

Palazzo Farnese

Via della Corda

Via San Francesco di Sales

Via della Penitenza

Via dei Riari

Via della Lungara

Lgt della Farnesina

Lgt D Sangallo

Tiber River

Via dei Farnesi

Via Giulia

Via del Mascherone

Via Capo di Ferro

Via d Balestrari

Via dei Polverone

Lgt dei Tebaldi

Piazza SV Pallotti

Vic delle Grotte

Via dei Pettinari

A | **B** | **C** | **D**

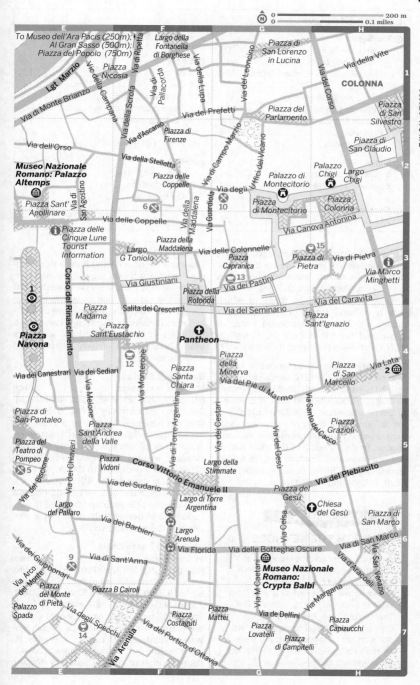

To Museo dell'Ara Pacis (250m);
Al Gran Sasso (500m);
Piazza del Popolo (750m)

Largo della
Fontanella
di Borghese

Piazza di
San Lorenzo
in Lucina

Via della Vite

Lgt Marzio

Piazza
Nicosia

Via di
Pallacorda

Via dei Prefetti

COLONNA

Via del Corso

Via di Monte Brianzo

Via della Campana

Via della Scrofa

Via di Ripetta

Via della Lupa

Via del Leoncino

Piazza del
Parlamento

Piazza
di San
Silvestro

Via dell'Orso

Via d'Ascanio

Piazza di
Firenze

Via di Campo Marzio

Piazza del
Parlamento

Piazza di
San Claudio

Via della Stelletta

Museo Nazionale
Romano: Palazzo
Altemps

Piazza delle
Coppelle

Via di Sant'Agostino

Uffici del Vicario

Palazzo di
Montecitorio

Palazzo
Chigi

Largo
Chigi

Piazza Sant'
Apollinare

6 ✕

Via degli
10 ✕

Via della Maddalena

Via Guardiola

Piazza
di Montecitorio

Piazza
Colonna

Piazza delle
Cinque Lune
Tourist
Information

Via delle Coppelle

Via Canova Antonina

Piazza della
Maddalena

Via delle Colonnelle

Piazza
Capranica

15 ✕

Piazza di
Pietra

Via di Pietra

Largo
G Toniolo

Via Giustiniani

13 ✕

Via dei Pastini

Via Marco
Minghetti

Corso del Rinascimento

1 ◉

Piazza della
Rotonda

Via del Seminario

Via del Caravita

2 ◉

Piazza
Navona

Piazza
Madama

Salita dei Crescenzi

Piazza
Sant'Ignazio

Piazza
Sant'Eustachio

Pantheon

Piazza
della
Minerva

Via dei Canestrari

Via dei Sediari

12 ✕

Piazza
Santa
Chiara

Via del Piè di Marmo

Piazza
di San
Marcello

Via Lata

2 ⌂

Via Monterone

Via di Torre Argentina

Via dei Cestari

Via Santo del Cacco

Piazza di
San Pantaleo

Via del Gesù

Piazza
Grazioli

Piazza del
Teatro di
Pompeo

5 ✕

Via dei Chiavari

Piazza
Sant'Andrea
della Valle

Piazza
Vidoni

Corso Vittorio Emanuele II

Largo della
Stimmate

Via del Plebiscito

Via dei Bresciani

Via del Sudario

Largo di Torre
Argentina

Piazza del
Gesù

Chiesa
del Gesù

Piazza di
San Marco

Largo
del Pallaro

Via dei Barbieri

Largo
Arenula

Via Celsa

Via di San Marco

Via d'Aracoeli

Via San Venanzio

Via Arco
del Monte

9 ✕

Via di Sant'Anna

Via Florida

Via delle Botteghe Oscure

Museo Nazionale
Romano:
Crypta Balbi

Piazza
del Monte
di Pietà

Piazza B Cairoli

Via M Caetani

Via Margana

Via dei Giubbonari

Palazzo
Spada

Via degli Specchi

14 ✕

Via Arenula

Via del Portico d'Ottavia

Piazza
Costaguti

Piazza
Mattei

Piazza
Lovatelli

Via de Delfini

Piazza
di Campitelli

Piazza
Capizucchi

Centro Storico

◎ **Top Sights**

Campo de' Fiori..D6
Castel Sant'Angelo..................................B1
Museo Nazionale Romano: Crypta
  Balbi...G6
Museo Nazionale Romano:
  Palazzo Altemps.................................E2
Palazzo Farnese.......................................D6
Pantheon..F4
Piazza Navona...E4

◎ **Sights**

1 Fontana dei Quattro Fiumi.....................E3
2 Galleria Doria Pamphilj.........................H4

🛏 **Sleeping**

3 Hotel Raphaël...D3

4 Relais Palazzo Taverna..........................C3

✖ **Eating**

5 Baffetto 2...E5
6 Casa Coppelle..F2
7 Ditirambo...D5
8 Forno di Campo de' Fiori.......................D6
9 Forno Roscioli...E6
10 Giolitti..G2
11 Pizzeria da Baffetto.............................C4

🍷 **Drinking**

12 Caffè Sant'Eustachio..........................F4
13 La Tazza d'Oro......................................G3
14 Open Baladin..E7
15 Salotto 42..H3

Tue-Sun, Villa Poniatowski 9am-1.45pm Tue-Sat; 🚇Via delle Belle Arti) Italy's finest collection of Etruscan treasures is beautifully housed in Villa Giulia, Pope Julius III's 16th-century pleasure palace. Exhibits, many of which came from burial tombs in northern Lazio, include a polychrome terracotta statue of *Apollo* and the 6th-century BC *Sarcofago degli Sposi* (Sarcophagus of the Betrothed).

Galleria Nazionale d'Arte Moderna GALLERY (Map p418; ☎06 3229 8221; www.gnam.benicul-turali.it; Viale delle Belle Arti 131, disabled entrance Via Gramsci 71; adult/reduced €8/4, plus possible exhibition supplement; ⏰8.30am-7.30pm Tue-Sun; 🚇Piazza Thorvaldsen) Set in a vast belle époque palace, this oft-overlooked museum displays works by some of the most important exponents of modern art, including Modigliani, De Chirico, Cezanne, Kandinsky, Klimt, Pollock and Henry Moore.

LOCAL KNOWLEDGE

THROUGH THE KEYHOLE

Head up to the Aventine Hill for one of Rome's best views. At the southern end of Via Santa Sabina stands the **Priorato dei Cavalieri di Malta** (Map p418), the Roman headquarters of the Cavalieri di Malta (Knights of Malta). The building is closed to the public, but look through its keyhole and you'll see the dome of St Peter's perfectly aligned at the end of a hedge-lined avenue.

TRASTEVERE

Trastevere is one of central Rome's most vivacious neighbourhoods, a tightly packed warren of ochre *palazzi,* ivy-clad facades and photogenic lanes. Taking its name from the Latin *trans Tiberium,* meaning over the Tiber, it was originally a working-class district, but has since been gentrified and is today a trendy hang-out full of bars, trattorias and restaurants.

**Basilica di Santa
Maria in Trastevere** CHURCH (Map p432; ☎06 581 94 43; Piazza Santa Maria in Trastevere; ⏰7.30am-9pm; 🚇Viale di Trastevere, 🚋Viale di Trastevere) Nestled in a quiet corner of **Piazza Santa Maria in Trastevere**, Trastevere's picturesque focal square, this exquisite basilica is believed to be Rome's oldest church dedicated to the Virgin Mary. It originally dates to the 4th century, but a 12th-century makeover saw the addition of a Romanesque bell tower and frescoed facade. Inside, the glittering 12th-century apse mosaics are the main drawcard.

**Basilica di Santa Cecilia
in Trastevere** CHURCH (Map p432; ☎06 589 92 89; Piazza di Santa Cecilia; basilica free, fresco & crypt each €2.50; ⏰basilica & crypt 9.30am-2.30pm & 4-7.30pm, fresco 10am-2.30pm Mon-Sat; 🚇Viale di Trastevere, 🚋Viale di Trastevere) The last resting place of St Cecilia, the patron saint of music, this church features a stunning 13th-century fresco by Pietro Cavallini and, below the altar, a breathtaking sculpture of St Cecilia by Stefano

Moderno. Beneath the basilica, you can visit excavations of several Roman houses.

TERMINI & ESQUILINE

The largest of Rome's seven hills, the Esquiline (Esquilino) extends from the Colosseum up to Stazione Termini, Rome's main transport hub.

Basilica di San Pietro in Vincoli CHURCH
(Map p418; ☑06 978 44 950; Piazza di San Pietro in Vincoli 4a; ⊗8am-12.30pm & 3-7pm Apr-Sep, to 6pm Oct-Mar; ⓂCavour) Pilgrims and art lovers flock to this church, just off Via Cavour, for two reasons: to see the chains worn by St Peter before his crucifixion (hence the church's name – St Peter in Chains), and to marvel at Michelangelo's *Moses,* the centrepiece of his unfinished tomb for Pope Julius II.

Basilica di Santa Maria Maggiore CHURCH
(Map p434; ☑06 698 86 800; Piazza Santa Maria Maggiore; basilica free, museum €3, loggia €2; ⊗7am-7pm, museum & loggia 9.30am-6.30pm; 🚇Piazza Santa Maria Maggiore) One of Rome's four patriarchal basilicas, this hulking church was built in AD 352 on the site of a miraculous snowfall. An architectural hybrid, it has a 14th-century Romanesque belfry (at 75m Rome's highest), an 18th-century baroque facade, a largely baroque interior and a series of glorious 5th-century mosaics.

SAN GIOVANNI & CAELIAN HILL

Basilica di San Giovanni in Laterano CATHEDRAL
(Map p418; Piazza di San Giovanni in Laterano 4; basilica free, cloister €3; ⊗7am-6.30pm, cloister 9am-6pm; ⓂSan Giovanni) For a thousand years this monumental cathedral was the most important church in Christendom. Founded by Constantine in AD 324, it was the first Christian basilica built in the city and, until the late 14th century, was the pope's main place of worship. It is still Rome's official cathedral and the pope's seat as bishop of Rome. It has been revamped several times, most notably by baroque maestro Borromini in the run-up to the 1650 Jubilee, and by Alessandro Galilei who added the monumental facade in the 18th century.

Basilica di San Clemente CHURCH
(Map p418; www.basilicasanclemente.com; Via di San Giovanni in Laterano; church/excavations free/€5; ⊗9am-12.30pm & 3-6pm Mon-Sat, noon-6pm Sun; ⓂColosseo) Nowhere better illustrates the various stages of Rome's turbulent history than this fascinating, multilayered church. The ground-level, 12th-century basilica sits atop a 4th-century church which, in turn, stands over a 2nd-century temple dedicated to the pagan god Mithras and a 1st-century Roman house. Beneath everything are foundations dating from the Roman Republic.

MUSEO NAZIONALE ROMANO

Spread over four sites, the Museo Nazionale Romano (National Roman Museum) houses one of the world's most important collections of classical art. A combined ticket including each of the sites costs adult/EU child €7/free (plus possible €3 exhibition supplement), and is valid for three days.

Palazzo Massimo alle Terme (Map p434; ☑06 399 67 700; www.coopculture.it; Largo di Villa Peretti 1; adult/reduced/EU child €7/3.50/free, audioguide €5; ⊗9am-7.45pm Tue-Sun; ⓂTermini) A fabulous museum with amazing frescos and wall paintings.

Terme di Diocleziano (Map p434; ☑06 399 67 700; www.coopculture.it; Viale Enrico de Nicola 78; adult/reduced/EU child €10/6.50/free 3-day integrated ticket includes Palazzo Massimo alle Terme & Aula Ottagona, audioguide €5; ⊗9am-7.30pm Tue-Sun; ⓂTermini) Ancient epigraphs and tomb artefacts in the Terme di Diocleziano (Diocletian's Baths), ancient Rome's largest baths complex.

Palazzo Altemps (Map p428; ☑06 399 67 700; http://archeoroma.beniculturali.it/en/museums/national-roman-museum-palazzo-altemps; Piazza Sant'Apollinare 44; adult/reduced/EU child €7/3.50/free plus possible €3 exhibition supplement; ⊗9am-7.45pm Tue-Sun; 🚇Corso del Rinascimento) Wonderful classical sculpture in an exquisite Renaissance *palazzo*.

Crypta Balbi (Map p428; ☑06 399 67 700; http://archeoroma.beniculturali.it/en/museums/national-roman-museum-crypta-balbi; Via delle Botteghe Oscure 31; adult/reduced/EU child €7/3.50/free plus possible €3 exhibition supplement; ⊗9am-7.45pm Tue-Sun ; 🚇Via delle Botteghe Oscure) Set atop an ancient Roman theatre, the Teatro di Balbus (13 BC).

Trastevere

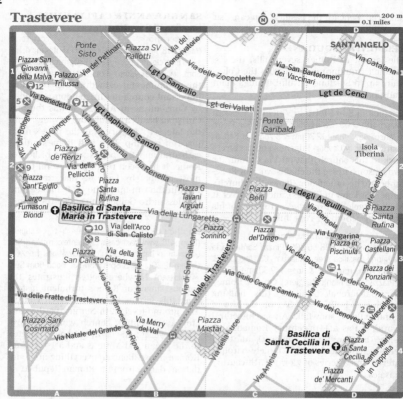

Terme di Caracalla

RUINS

(Map p418; ☏ 06 399 67 700; www.coopculture.it; Viale delle Terme di Caracalla 52; adult/reduced/EU child €7/4/free, audioguide €5; ⊙9am-1hr before sunset Tue-Sun, 9am-2pm Mon year-round; ☐Viale delle Terme di Caracalla) The vast ruins of the Terme di Caracalla are an awe-inspiring sight. Inaugurated in AD 217, the 10-hectare leisure complex could hold up to 1600 people and included richly decorated pools, gymnasiums, libraries, shops and gardens. The ruins are now used to stage summer opera.

✵✵ Festivals & Events

Rome's year-round festival calendar ranges from the religious to the ribald, with traditional religious and historical celebrations, performing-arts festivals and an international film festival.

Easter

RELIGIOUS

On Good Friday, the pope leads a candlelit procession around the Colosseum. At noon on Easter Sunday he blesses the crowds in St Peter's Square.

Settimana della Cultura

CULTURAL

(www.beniculturali.it) During Culture Week admission is free to state-run museums, monuments, galleries and otherwise closed sites. Dates change annually but it's usually in April.

Natale di Roma

CULTURAL

Rome celebrates its birthday on 21 April with music, historical recreations, fireworks and free entry to many museums.

Primo Maggio

MUSIC

Rome's free May Day rock concert attracts huge crowds and top Italian performers to Piazza di San Giovanni in Laterano.

Estate Romana

CULTURAL

(www.estateromana.comune.roma.it) From June to October Rome's big summer festival includes hundreds of cultural events and activities.

Trastevere

◎ **Top Sights**

Basilica di Santa Cecilia in
Trastevere...D4
Basilica di Santa Maria in
Trastevere...A2

🛏 **Sleeping**

1 Arco del Lauro.....................................D3
2 Maria-Rosa Guesthouse....................D4
3 Villa Della Fonte...............................A2

🍽 **Eating**

4 Da Enzo...D4
5 Dar Poeta..A1
6 Forno la Renella.................................A2
7 Hostaria dar Buttero.........................C3
8 Paris..A3
9 Trattoria degli Amici.........................A2

🍷 **Drinking**

10 Bar San Calisto..................................A3
11 Freni e Frizioni..................................A1
12 Ma Che Siete Venuti a Fà..................A1

Festa dei Santi Pietro e Paolo   RELIGIOUS
Rome celebrates its patron saints Peter and Paul on 29 June. Festivities are centred on St Peter's Basilica and Via Ostiense.

Festa de'Noantri   CULTURAL
Trastevere's annual party, held in the third week of July, involves plenty of food, wine, prayer and dancing.

RomaEuropa   CULTURAL
(http://romaeuropa.net) From late September to November, top international artists take to the stage for Rome's premier dance and drama festival.

**Festival Internazionale
del Film di Roma**   FILM
(www.romacinemafest.org) Held at the Auditorium Parco della Musica in late October or early November, Rome's film festival rolls out the red carpet for Hollywood hotshots and Italian celebs.

🛏 Sleeping

Rome has plenty of accommodation, but rates are universally high. The best, most atmospheric places to stay are the *centro storico*, the Prati area near the Vatican and Trastevere. If you're on a tight budget, most hostels and cheap *pensioni* (guesthouses) are in the Termini area. You'll find a full list of accommodation options (with prices) at www.060608.it.

Always try to book ahead, even if it's just for the first night. But if you arrive without a booking, there's a **hotel reservation service** (Map p434; ☎06 699 10 00; booking fee €3; ⊙7am-10pm) next to the tourist office at Stazione Termini.

ANCIENT ROME

Nicolas Inn   B&B €€
(Map p422; ☎06 9761 8483; www.nicolasinn.com; Via Cavour 295, 1st fl; s €95-160, d €100-180; ❄🅐; Ⓜ️Cavour) This sunny B&B offers a warm welcome and a convenient location, a stone's throw from the Roman Forum. Run by a friendly couple, it has four big guest rooms, each with homely furnishings, colourful pictures and large en suite bathrooms.

Duca d'Alba   HOTEL €€
(Map p422; ☎06 48 44 71; www.hotelducadalba.com; Via Leonina 14; r €70-200; ❄🅐; Ⓜ️Cavour) This refined four-star sits amid the boutiques and wine bars of the hip Monti district. It's a tight squeeze, but the individually decorated guest rooms are sleek and stylish with parquet floors and modern grey-white colour schemes.

THE VATICAN

Hotel Bramante   HOTEL €€€
(Map p418; ☎06 6880 6426; www.hotelbramante.com; Vicolo delle Palline 24-25; s €100-160, d €140-240, tr €170-250, q €175-260; ❄🅐; 🚌Piazza del Risorgimento) Tucked away in an alley under the Vatican walls, the Hotel Bramante exudes country-house charm with its quietly elegant rooms and cosy internal courtyard. It's housed in the 16th-century building where architect Domenico Fontana lived before Pope Sixtus V banished him from Rome.

Colors Hotel   HOTEL €
(Map p418; ☎06 687 40 30; www.colorshotel.com; Via Boezio 31; s €35-90, d €45-125; ❄🅐; 🚌Via Cola di Rienzo) Popular with young travellers, this is a bright budget hotel with smart, vibrantly coloured rooms spread over three floors (no lift, though). There are also cheaper rooms with shared bathrooms and, from June to August, dorms (€12 to €35 per person) for guests under 38 years of age.

CENTRO STORICO

TOP CHOICE **Daphne Inn**   BOUTIQUE HOTEL €€
(Map p434; ☎06 8745 0086; www.daphne-rome.com; Via di San Basilio 55; s €110-180, d €140-230, without bathroom s€70-130, d €90-160; ❄🅐;

Termini, Esquiline and Quirinal

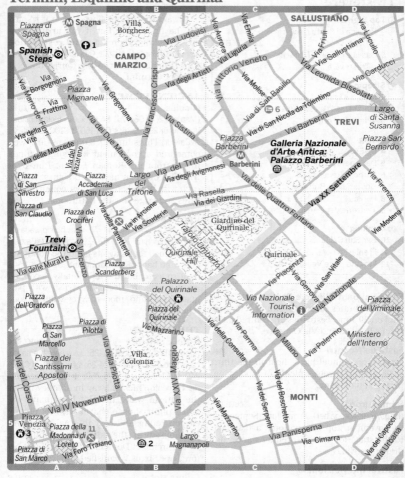

ITALY ROME

Ⓜ Barberini) Daphne is a gem. Spread over two sites (Daphne Veneto and Daphne Trevi) near Piazza Barberini, it offers value for money, exceptional service and chic modern rooms. The English-speaking staff go that extra mile, even lending guests a cell phone during their stay.

TOP CHOICE Hotel Panda
PENSION €

(Map p418; ☏06 678 0179; www.hotelpanda.it; Via della Croce 35; s €65-80, d €85-108, tr €120-140, q €180; ☏; Ⓜ Spagna) A great position near the Spanish Steps, small, simply furnished rooms, and honest rates ensure a year-round

stream of travellers to this budget stalwart. Cheaper rooms are also available with shared bathrooms. Breakfast, which is optional, costs €5 and is served in a nearby bar.

Okapi Rooms
HOTEL €

(Map p418; ☏06 3260 9815; www.okapirooms.it; Via della Penna 57; s €65-80, d €85-120, tr €110-140, q €120-180; ✳☏; Ⓜ Flaminio) Occupying a tall townhouse near Piazza del Popolo, the Okapi is a bargain low-midrange option. Rooms, spread over six floors, are small and simple with cream walls, terracotta-tiled floors and tiny en suite bathrooms. Several also have small terraces.

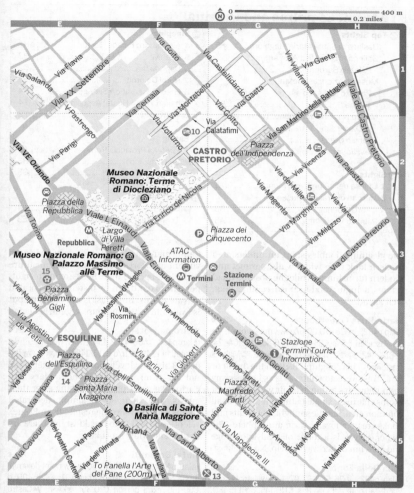

Relais Palazzo Taverna   BOUTIQUE HOTEL €€
(Map p428; ☑06 2039 8064; www.relaispalazzo
taverna.com; Via dei Gabrielli 92; s €80-140, d €80-
150, tr €120-240; ❋ @ 🛜; 🚇Corso del Rinascimento)
Housed in a 15th-century *palazzo,* this boutique hotel is superbly located in the heart
of the *centro storico.* Its six rooms cut a stylish dash with white wood-beamed ceilings,
funky wallpaper and dark parquet. Tea- and
coffee-making facilities add a homey touch.

Hotel Raphaël   HISTORIC HOTEL €€€
(Map p428; ☑06 68 28 31; www.raphaelhotel.com;
Largo Febo 2; d from €280; ❋ 🛜; 🚇Corso del Rinascimento) An ivy-clad landmark just off
Piazza Navona, the Raphaël boasts a serious art collection – Picasso ceramics and
lithographs by Miró – as well as minimalist
Richard Meier–designed rooms and a panoramic rooftop restaurant.

TRASTEVERE

[TOP CHOICE] Arco del Lauro   B&B €
(Map p432; ☑9am-2pm 06 9784 0350, mobile 346
2443212; www.arcodellauro.it; Via Arco de' Tolomei
27; s €75-125, d €95-145; ❋ @ 🛜; 🚇Viale di Trastevere, 🚋Viale di Trastevere) This friendly B&B is
in a medieval *palazzo* on a narrow cobbled
street in Trastevere's quieter eastern half. Its

Termini, Esquiline and Quirinal

⊙ Top Sights

Basilica di Santa Maria Maggiore	F5
Galleria Nazionale d'Arte Antica: Palazzo Barberini	C2
Museo Nazionale Romano: Palazzo Massimo alle Terme	F3
Museo Nazionale Romano: Terme di Diocleziano	F2
Spanish Steps	A1
Trevi Fountain	A3

⊙ Sights

1 Chiesa della Trinità dei Monti	A1
2 Mercati di Traiano Museo dei Fori Imperiali	B5
3 Palazzo Venezia	A5

🛏 Sleeping

4 Alessandro Palace Hostel	H2
5 Beehive	H2
6 Daphne Inn	C2
7 Hotel Dolomiti	H1
8 Hotel Reservation Service	G4
9 Italian Youth Hostel Association	F4
10 Welrome Hotel	F2

⊗ Eating

11 Enoteca Provincia Romana	A5
12 San Crispino	B3
13 Trattoria Monti	G5

✪ Entertainment

14 Orbis	E4
15 Teatro dell'Opera di Roma	E3

five gleaming doubles sport an understated modern look with white walls, parquet and modern furnishings, while the upstairs quad retains a high wood-beamed ceiling. Book well ahead.

Maria-Rosa Guesthouse B&B €
(Map p432; ☑338 770 00 67; www.maria-rosa.it; Via dei Vascellari 55; s €53-73, d €66-86, tr €104-124, q €122-142; @ �; 🚇Viale di Trastevere, 🚇Viale di Trastevere) This delightful B&B on the 3rd floor of a Trastevere townhouse is a home away from home. It's a simple affair with two guest rooms sharing a single bathroom and a small common area, but the sunlight, pot plants and books create a lovely, warm atmosphere. The owner, Sylvie, is a fount of local knowledge and goes out of her way to help. No breakfast.

Villa Della Fonte B&B €€
(Map p432; ☑06 580 37 97; www.villafonte.com; Via della Fonte dell'Olio 8; s €110-145, d €135-180; 🕸�; 🚇Viale di Trastevere, 🚇Viale di Trastevere) Near Piazza Santa Maria in Trastevere, this charming B&B occupies an ivy-clad, 17th-century *palazzo*.The five rooms are small but tastefully decorated and there's a sunny garden terrace for alfresco breakfasts.

TERMINI & ESQUILINE

TOP CHOICE **Beehive** HOSTEL €
(Map p434; ☑06 4470 4553; www.the-beehive. com; Via Marghera 8; dm €25-30, s €50-60, d €90-100, without bathroom s €40-50, d €80-90, tr €95-105; 🕸�; 🚇Termini) More boutique chic than backpacker crashpad, the Beehive is one of the best hostels in town. Run by a southern

Californian couple, it's an oasis of style with vibrant art works, funky modular furniture and a laid-back lounge. Beds are in an eight-person mixed dorm or tastefully decorated private rooms. Breakfast is not included but is available at the in-house vegetarian cafe.

Welrome Hotel HOTEL €
(Map p434; ☑06 4782 4343; www.welrome.it; Via Calatafimi 15-19; d/tr/q €110/148/187; 🕸�; 🚇Termini) This is a lovely, low-key budget hotel not far from Termini. Owners Mary and Carlo take great pride in looking after their guests, and their seven simply decorated rooms provide welcome respite from Rome's relentless streets. No breakfast but there are kettles and fridges available.

Hotel Dolomiti HOTEL €
(Map p434; ☑06 495 72 56; www.hotel-dolomiti. it; Via San Martino della Battaglia 11; s €45-100, d €60-160, extra person €20-35; 🕸@�; 🚇Castro Pretorio) A warm, family-run hotel, the Dolomiti is a reliable option. Rooms, which come with cream walls, cherry-wood furniture and prints of chubby-cheeked cherubs, are spread over three floors of a big apartment block not far from Termini.

Alessandro Palace Hostel HOSTEL €
(Map p434; ☑06 446 19 58; www.hostelsalessandro.com; Via Vicenza 42; dm €19-35, d €70-120, tr €95-120; 🕸@�; 🚇Castro Pretorio) A long-standing favourite in the Termini area, this slick hostel offers spick-and-span hotel-style rooms, as well as dorms sleeping from four to eight. It's managed by an efficient inter-

VIA APPIA ANTICA

Completed in 190 BC, ancient Rome's *regina viarum* (queen of roads) connected the capital with Brindisi on Italy's southern Adriatic coast. Nowadays, Via Appia Antica (The Appian Way) is one of Rome's most exclusive addresses, a beautiful cobbled thoroughfare flanked by grassy fields, ancient ruins and towering pine trees. But it has a dark history – it was here that Spartacus and 6000 of his slave rebels were crucified in 71 BC, and it was here that the early Christians buried their dead in underground catacombs.

The two main catacombs are the **Catacombe di San Sebastiano** (☑06 785 03 50; www.catacombe.org; Via Appia Antica 136; adult/reduced/child €8/5/free; ☺10am-5pm Mon-Sat, closed mid-Nov–mid-Dec; 🚌Via Appia Antica), which extends beneath the **Basilica di San Sebastiano**, and the **Catacombe di San Callisto** (☑06 513 01 51; www.cata-combe.roma.it; Via Appia Antica 110 & 126; adult/reduced €8/5; ☺9am-noon & 2-5pm, closed Wed mid-Jan–mid-Feb; 🚌Via Appia Antica), where the remains of thousands of Christians have been unearthed.

To get to Via Appia Antica, take bus 660 from Colli Albani metro station (line A) or bus 118 from Piramide (line B).

For information on the area, stop off at the **Appia Antica Regional Park Information Point** (☑06 513 53 16; www.parcoappiaantica.org; Via Appia Antica 58-60; ☺9.30am-1.30pm & 2-5.30pm Mon-Sat, to 4.30pm winter, 9.30am-6.30pm Sun).

national crew, has 24-hour reception, and serves cut-price beer in the hostel bar.

✖ Eating

Eating out is one of the great joys of visiting Rome and everywhere you go you'll find trattorias, pizzerias, *gelaterie* (ice-cream shops) and restaurants. Traditional Roman cooking holds sway but *cucina creativa* (creative cooking) has taken off in recent years and there are plenty of exciting, contemporary restaurants to try.

The best areas are the *centro storico* and Trastevere, but there are also excellent choices in San Lorenzo east of Termini and Testaccio. Watch out for overpriced tourist traps around Termini and the Vatican.

Roman specialities include *cacio e pepe* (pasta with pecorino cheese, black pepper and olive oil), *pasta all'amatriciana* (with tomato, pancetta and chilli), *fiori di zucca* (fried courgette flowers) and *carciofi alla romana* (artichokes with garlic, mint and parsley).

ANCIENT ROME

TOP CHOICE **Enoteca Provincia Romana** TRADITIONAL ITALIAN €€
(Map p434; ☑06 699 40 273; Via Foro Traiano 82-4; mains €17, aperitif from €5; ☺11am-11pm Mon-Sat; 🚌Via dei Fori Imperiali) Specialising in regional food and wine, this stylish wine bar-cum-restaurant offers a daily menu of pastas and mains, wine by the glass, finger foods and an evening aperitif. Service is friendly and with

an enviable location overlooking the Colonna di Traiano, it's a top choice. Lunchtimes are busy but it quietens in the evening.

THE VATICAN

Hostaria Dino & Tony TRATTORIA €€
(Map p418; ☑06 397 33 284; Via Leone IV 60; mains €12; ☺Mon-Sat, closed Aug; Ⓜ Ottaviano-San Pietro) An authentic trattoria in the Vatican area. Kick off with the monumental antipasto before plunging into its signature dish, *rigatoni all' amatriciana*. Finish up with a *granita di caffè* (a crushed ice coffee served with a full inch of whipped cream). No credit cards.

CENTRO STORICO

TOP CHOICE **Casa Coppelle** MEDITERRANEAN €€
(Map p428; ☑06 688 91 707; www.casacoppelle. it; Piazza delle Coppelle 49; meals €35; 🚌Corso del Rinascimento) Exposed brick walls, books, flowers and subdued lighting set the stage for wonderful French-inspired food at this intimate, romantic restaurant. There's a full range of starters and pastas but the real *tour de force* is the steak served with crisp, thinly sliced potato crisps. Book ahead.

Al Gran Sasso TRATTORIA €€
(Map p418; ☑06 321 48 83; www.trattoriaalgran sasso.com; Via di Ripetta 32; mains €13; ☺lunch & dinner Sun-Fri; Ⓜ Flaminio) The perfect lunchtime spot, this is a classic, dyed-in-the-wool trattoria. It's a relaxed place with a welcoming vibe, garish murals on the walls (strangely, often a good sign) and tasty country food.

HOW TO EAT & DRINK FOR LESS

» Lunch on *pizza al taglio* (pizza by the slice) and ice cream; dine on bar snacks over an *aperitivo* (aperitif).

» Take advantage of the fixed-price lunch menus that some restaurants offer.

» Fill up on the bread they bring you when you sit down – you'll pay for it whether you eat it or not.

» Drink standing at the bar rather than sitting at a table.

Forno di Campo de' Fiori
BAKERY €

(Map p428; Campo de' Fiori 22; pizza slices about €3; ⊗7.30am-2.30pm & 4.45-8pm Mon-Sat; ☐Corso Vittorio Emanuele II) This is one of Rome's best bakeries, serving bread, panini and delicious straight-from-the-oven *pizza al taglio* (by the slice). Aficionados swear by the *pizza bianca* (white pizza), but the panini and *pizza rossa* (with tomato) are just as good.

Pizzeria da Baffetto
PIZZERIA €

(Map p428; ☑06 686 16 17; www.pizzeriabaffetto.it; Via del Governo Vecchio 114; pizzas €6-9; ⊗6.30pm-1am; ☐Corso Vittorio Emanuele II) For the full-on Roman pizza experience, get down to this local institution. Meals are raucous, chaotic and fast, but the thin-crust pizzas are spot on and the vibe is fun. To partake, join the queue and wait to be squeezed in wherever there's room. There's also **Baffetto 2** (Map p428; Piazza del Teatro di Pompeo 18; ⊗6.30pm-12.30am Mon & Wed-Fri, 12.30-3.30pm & 6.30pm-12.30am Sat & Sun; ☐Corso Vittorio Emanuele II) near Campo de' Fiori.

Ditirambo
MODERN ITALIAN €€

(Map p428; ☑06 687 16 26; www.ristoranteditirambo.it; Piazza della Cancelleria 72; meals €40; ⊗closed lunch Mon; ☐Corso Vittorio Emanuele II) This popular new-wave trattoria dishes up a laid-back atmosphere and innovative, organic cooking. The menu changes regularly, but there's always a good choice of vegetarian dishes such as ricotta ravioli with cherry tomatoes and capers. Book ahead.

TOP CHOICE Forno Roscioli
PIZZA, BAKERY €

(Map p428; Via dei Chiavari 34; pizza slices from €2, snacks from €1.50; ⊗7.30am-8pm Mon-Fri, 7.30am-2.30pm Sat; ☐Via Arenula) Join the lunchtime crowds at this revered bakery for a slice of *pizza bianca* or a freshly baked pastry. There's also a counter serving hot pastas and vegetable side dishes.

'Gusto
RISTORANTE €

(Map p418; ☑06 322 62 73; Piazza Augusto Imperatore 9; pizzas €7-10; ☐Via del Corso) All exposed brickwork and industrial chic, this '90s-style warehouse operation is a lunchtime favourite with office workers, serving everything from thick-crust pizza to cheese platters, salads and overpriced fusion food. At lunch the buffet is a bargain.

TRASTEVERE

Trattoria degli Amici
TRATTORIA €€

(Map p432; ☑06 580 60 33; www.trattoriadegliamici.org; Piazza Sant'Egidio 6; mains €15; ☐Viale di Trastevere, ☐Viale di Trastevere) Boasting a prime piazza location, this cheerful trattoria is run by a local charity and staffed by volunteers and people with disabilities who welcome guests with a warmth not always apparent in this touristy neck of the woods. With its outside tables, it's a lovely place to dig into well-prepared Italian classics and enjoy the neighbourhood vibe.

Da Lucia
TRATTORIA €€

(Map p418; ☑06 580 36 01; Vicolo del Mattinato 2; mains €12.50; ⊗Tue-Sun; ☐Viale di Trastevere, ☐Viale di Trastevere) For a real Trastevere experience, search out this terrific neighbourhood trattoria on a hidden cobbled backstreet. It's popular with locals and tourists alike for its authentic Roman soul food, including a fine *spaghetti alla gricia* (with pancetta and cheese). Cash only.

Paris
RISTORANTE €€€

(Map p432; ☑06 581 53 78; www.ristoranteparis.it; Piazza San Calisto 7a; meals €55; ⊗Tue-Sat, lunch only Sun; ☐Viale di Trastevere, ☐Viale di Trastevere) An elegant, old-fashioned restaurant set in a 17th-century building, Paris is a great place to experience traditional Roman-Jewish cuisine. Signature dishes include *fritto misto con baccalà* (deep-fried vegetables with salt cod) and *carciofi alla giudia* (Jewish-style fried artichokes).

Dar Poeta
PIZZERIA €

(Map p432; ☑06 588 05 16; Vicolo del Bologna 46; pizzas from €6; ⊗lunch & dinner; ☐Piazza Trilussa) Loud and always busy, this much-loved pizzeria guarantees a bustling, cheery atmosphere and hearty wood-fired pizzas that fall somewhere between wafer-thin Roman pizzas and the softer, doughier Neapolitan version. Expect queues.

Forno la Renella
BAKERY €

(Map p432; ☎06 581 72 65; Via del Moro 15-16; pizza slices from €2.50; ☉7am-2am Tue-Sat, to 10pm Sun & Mon; ☐Piazza Trilussa) The wood-fired ovens at this historic Trastevere bakery have been firing for decades, producing a delicious daily batch of pizza, bread and biscuits.

Hostaria dar Buttero
TRATTORIA €€

(Map p432; ☎06 580 05 17; Via della Lungaretta; mains €13; ☉Mon-Sat; ☐Viale di Trastevere, ☐Viale di Trastevere) On Trastevere's quieter eastern side, this is a typical old-school trattoria, attracting a mixed crowd of tourists and Romans. The menu lists all the usual pastas, grilled meats and pizzas (evenings only), but the food is well cooked, the atmosphere is convivial and the prices are right for the area.

Da Enzo
TRATTORIA €€

(Map p432; ☎06 581 83 55; www.daenzoal29.com; Via dei Vascellari 29; meals €35; ☉Mon-Sat; ☐Viale di Trastevere, ☐Viale di Trastevere) This rough-around-the-edges Trastevere institution is as authentic as it gets. Don't expect silver service; just traditional Roman food dished up to crowds of hungry diners. Menu stalwarts include *cacio e pepe* and *polpette al sugo* (meat balls in tomato sauce).

TESTACCIO

TOP CHOICE Flavio al Velavevodetto
TRATTORIA €€

(Map p418; ☎06 574 41 94; www.flavioalvelavevodetto.it; Via di Monte Testaccio 97-99; meals €30-35; ☉closed Sat lunch & Sun summer; ☐Via Marmorata) This welcoming Testaccio eatery is the sort of place that gives Roman trattorias a good name. Housed in a rustic Pompeian-red villa, complete with intimate covered courtyard and an open-air terrace, it specialises in earthy, no-nonsense Italian food, prepared with skill and served in mountainous portions.

TOP CHOICE 00100 Pizza
PIZZA €

(Map p418; www.00100pizza.com; Via Branca 88; pizza slices from €3, trapizzini from €3.50; ☉noon-11pm; ☐Via Marmorata) A pocket-size pizza pusher, this is one of a select group of Roman takeaways with culinary ambitions. As well as pizzas topped with unusual combos – cream of chickpea; mozzarella, gorgonzola and port – the trademark here is the *trapizzini,* small cones of pizza base stuffed with fillers like *polpette al sugo.*

Pizzeria Da Remo
PIZZERIA €

(Map p418; ☎06 574 62 70; Piazza Santa Maria Liberatrice 44; pizzas from €5.50; ☉7pm-1am Mon-Sat; ☐Via Marmorata) Remo is one of Rome's most popular pizzerias, its spartan interior always full of noisy young Romans. Tick your order on a sheet of paper slapped down by an overstretched waiter and wait for your huge, sizzling, charred disc. Queues are the norm after 8.30pm.

Volpetti Più
CAFETERIA €

(Map p418; Via Volta 8; mains €8; ☉10.30am-3.30pm & 5.30-9.30pm Mon-Sat; ☐Via Marmorata) One of the few places in town where you can sit down and eat well for less than €20. Volpetti Più is a sumptuous *tavola calda* ('hot table') offering an opulent choice of pizza, pasta, soup, meat, vegetables and fried nibbles.

GELATO GALORE

To get the best out of Rome's *gelaterie* (ice-cream shops) look for the words *'produzione proprio'*, meaning 'own production'. As a rough guide, expect to pay from €1.50 for a *cono* (cone) or *coppa* (tub). Our choice of the city's finest:

San Crispino (Map p434; ☎06 679 39 24; Via della Panetteria 42; ice cream from €2.30; ☉noon-12.30am Mon, Wed, Thu & Sun, 11am-1.30am Fri & Sat; Ⓜ Barberini) Near the Trevi Fountain, it serves natural, seasonal flavours – think *fichi secci* (dried figs) and *miele* (honey) – in tubs only.

Gelarmony (Map p418; Via Marcantonio Colonna 34; ice cream from €1.50; ☉10am-late; Ⓜ Lepanto) A Sicilian *gelateria* serving 60 flavours and heavenly *cannoli* (pastry tubes filled with ricotta and candied fruit).

Il Gelato (Map p418; Viale Aventino 59; ☉11am-9pm Tue-Sun, to 10.30pm daily summer; Ⓜ Circo Massimo) Creative, preservative-free combos from Rome's *gelato* king Claudio Torcè.

Gelateria Giolitti (Map p428; ☎06 699 12 43; www.giolitti.it; Via degli Uffici del Vicario 40; ☉7am-1am; ☐Via del Corso) Rome's most famous *gelateria,* near the Pantheon.

TERMINI & ESQUILINE

Trattoria Monti
RISTORANTE €€

(Map p434; ☑06 446 65 73; Via di San Vito 13a; meals €45; ☺lunch & dinner Tue-Sat, lunch Sun, closed Aug; Ⓜ Vittorio Emanuele) Loved by locals and visitors alike, this intimate, arched restaurant – it's a trattoria in name only – serves top-notch regional cooking from Le Marche (a hilly region on Italy's Adriatic coast). Expect exemplary game stews and pungent truffles, as well as wonderful fried starters like *olive ascolane* (fried meat-stuffed olives). Book for dinner.

Panella l'Arte del Pane
BAKERY, CAFE €

(Map p418; ☑06 487 24 35; Via Merulana 54; pizza slices around €3; ☺noon-midnight Mon-Sat, 10am-4pm Sun Mar-Oct; Ⓜ Vittorio Emanuele) A devilishly tempting bakery-cum-cafe-cum-deli with a sumptuous array of *pizza al taglio*, *supplì* (fried rice balls), focaccia and fried croquettes. You can sit outside – perfect for a leisurely breakfast or chilled drink – or perch on a high stool and eye the shelves of gourmet delicacies.

Pommidoro
TRATTORIA €€

(Map p418; ☑06 445 26 92; Piazza dei Sanniti 44; meals €35; ☺Mon-Sat, closed Aug; ☐Via Tiburtina) Unchanged throughout San Lorenzo's metamorphosis from working-class district to bohemian enclave, century-old Pommidoro is a much-loved local institution. It was a favourite of film director Pier Paolo Pasolini, and contemporary celebs still stop by, but it's an unpretentious place with traditional food and magnificent grilled meats.

Tram Tram
OSTERIA €€

(Map p418; ☑06 49 04 16; www.tramtram.it; Via dei Reti 44; meals around €40; ☺12.30-3.30pm & 7.30-11.30pm Tue-Sun; ☐Via Tiburtina) This cosy San Lorenzo *osteria* (tavern) takes its name from the trams that rattle past outside. Very popular locally, it offers tasty traditional dishes and wonderful Sicilian-inspired seafood such as *alici frittodorate* (fried anchovies) and *involtini di pesce spada* (swordfish rolls). Book ahead.

🍷 Drinking

Rome has plenty of drinking venues, ranging from neighbourhood hang-outs to elegant streetside cafes, dressy lounge bars and Irish-theme pubs. During the day, bars are generally visited for a quick coffee while early evening sees the city's hipsters descend on the fashionable watering holes for *aperitivi* (aperitifs).

Much of the action is in the *centro storico* – Campo de' Fiori fills with young, rowdy drinkers, while the lanes around Piazza Navona host a more calm, dressier scene. Over the river, Trastevere is another popular spot with dozens of bars and pubs, while to the east of Termini, San Lorenzo and Pigneto attract students and bohemian uptowners.

TOP CHOICE Caffè Sant'Eustachio
CAFE

(Map p428; Piazza Sant'Eustachio 82; ☺8.30am-1am Sun-Thu, to 1.30am Fri, to 2am Sat; ☐Corso del Rinascimento) This small, unassuming cafe, generally three-deep at the bar, is famous for its *gran caffè*, said by many to be the best coffee in town. Created by beating the first drops of espresso and several teaspoons of sugar into a frothy paste, then adding the rest of the coffee, it's guaranteed to put some zing into your sightseeing.

Open Baladin
BAR

(Map p428; www.openbaladinroma.it; Via degli Specchi 6; ☺12pm-2am; ☐Via Arenula) This designer bar is a leading light on Rome's burgeoning beer scene. It's a slick, stylish place with more than 40 beers on tap and up to 100 bottled beers, many produced by Italian artisanal breweries.

La Tazza d'Oro
CAFE

(Map p428; Via degli Orfani 84-86; ☺7am-8pm Mon-Sat, 10.30am-7.30pm Sun; ☐Via del Corso) A busy, burnished cafe, this is one of Rome's best coffee houses. Its espresso hits the mark perfectly and there's a range of delicious coffee concoctions, including *a* refreshing *granita di caffè*.

Salotto 42
BAR

(Map p428; www.salotto42.it; Piazza di Pietra 42; ☺10am-2am Tue-Sat, to midnight Sun & Mon; ☐Via del Corso) On a picturesque piazza facing a 2nd-century Roman temple, this is a hip lounge bar, complete with vintage armchairs, suede sofas and heavy-as-houses designer tomes. Come for the daily lunch buffet or to hang out with the beautiful people over an aperitif.

Ma Che Siete Venuti a Fà
PUB

(Map p432; Via Benedetta 25; ☺11am-2am; ☐Piazza Trilussa) This pint-sized pub – whose name, a football chant, translates politely as 'What did you come here for?' – is a beer-buff's paradise, packing a huge number of artisanal beers into its tiny interior.

Freni e Frizioni
BAR

(Map p432; www.freniefrizioni.com; Via del Politeama 4-6; ☺6.30pm-2am; ☐Piazza Trilussa)

Housed in a former garage – hence its name meaning 'breaks' and 'clutches' – this designer-grunge bar draws a spritz-loving crowd that flocks here to slurp on mojitos and fill up at the popular 7pm *aperitivo*.

Caffè Capitolino
CAFE

(Map p422; Piazzale Caffarelli 4; ⊙9am-7.30pm Tue-Sun; ☐Piazza Venezia) The stylish rooftop cafe of the Musei Capitolini is a good place for a timeout over a coffee, cool drink or light snack. And you don't need a museum ticket to drink here – it's accessible via an independent entrance on Piazza Caffarelli.

Bar San Calisto
CAFE

(Map p432; Piazza San Calisto 3-5; ⊙6am-2am Mon-Sat; ☐Viale di Trastevere, ☐Viale di Trastevere) Down-at-heel 'Sanca' is a perennial Trastevere favourite. A motley crew of students, punks, alcoholics, affected bohemians and card-playing *nonni* (grandpas) congregate here for dirt-cheap drinks and the bar's legendary chocolate – drunk hot in winter, eaten as ice cream in summer.

☆ Entertainment

Rome has a thriving cultural scene, with a year-round calendar of concerts, performances and festivals. In summer, the Estate Romana (p432) festival sponsors hundreds of cultural events, many staged in atmospheric parks, piazzas and churches. Autumn is another good time, with festivals dedicated to dance, drama and jazz.

A useful listings guide is *Trova Roma*, a free insert which comes with *La Repubblica* newspaper every Thursday. Upcoming events are also listed on www.turismoroma. it, www.060608.it and www.auditorium.com.

For tickets, try **Orbis** (Map p434; ☑06 474 4776; Piazza dell'Esquilino 37), which accepts cash payment only, or the online agency **Hellò Ticket** (☑800 90 70 80; www.helloticket.it).

Classical Music & Opera

TOP
CHOICE **Auditorium**
Parco della Musica
CONCERT VENUE

(☑06 802 41 281; www.auditorium.com; Viale Pietro de Coubertin 30; ☐shuttle bus M from Stazione Termini, ☐Viale Tiziano) This Renzo Piano–designed modernist complex is Rome's cultural hub and premier concert venue. Its three concert halls and 3000-seat open-air arena stage everything from classical music concerts to tango exhibitions, book readings and film screenings. The auditorium is also

home to Rome's top orchestra, the world-class Orchestra dell'Accademia Nazionale di Santa Cecilia (www.santacecilia.it).

Teatro Olimpico
THEATRE

(☑06 326 59 91; www.teatroolimpico.it; Piazza Gentile da Fabriano 17; ☐Piazza Mancini, ☐Piazza Mancini) The Accademia Filarmonica Romana (www.filarmonicaromana.org), one of Rome's major classical music organisations, stages a varied program of classical and chamber music here as well as opera, ballet and contemporary multimedia events.

Teatro dell'Opera di Roma
OPERA

(Map p434; ☑06 4817 003; www.operaroma.it; Piazza Beniamino Gigli; ballet €12-80; opera €17-150; ⊙box office 9am-5pm Mon-Sat, 9am-1.30pm Sun; ⓂRepubblica) Rome's premier opera house also stages the city's ballet company. The opera season runs from December to June, with summer performances staged at the **Terme di Caracalla** (Map p418; Viale delle Terme di Caracalla 52; ☐Viale delle Terme di Caracalla).

Nightclubs & Live Music

Clubbing action caters to most tastes, with DJs spinning everything from lounge and jazz to house, dancehall and hip hop. The scene is centred on Testaccio and the Ostiense area, although you'll also find places in Trastevere and the *centro storico*. Out from the centre, San Lorenzo and Pigneto are happening areas.

You'll need to dress the part for the big clubs, which can be tricky to get into, especially for groups of men. Gigs are often listed for 10pm but don't kick off until around 11pm, while clubs rarely hot up much before midnight or 1am. Admission is often free but drinks are expensive, typically €10 to €16. Note also that many clubs shut between mid-June and mid-September.

TOP
CHOICE **Circolo degli Artisti**
CLUB

(www.circoloartisti.it; Via Casilina Vecchia 42; ⊙7pm-2am Tue-Thu, to 4.30am Fri-Sun; ☐Ponte Casilino) East of the Pigneto district, this kicking club offers one of Rome's best nights out with top live music from Italian and international bands, cracking DJ turns, and a large garden area for outdoor beer. Admission is either free or a bargain.

Alexanderplatz
JAZZ

(Map p418; www.alexanderplatz.it; Via Ostia 9; ⊙concerts 9.45pm Sun-Thu, 10.30pm Sat & Sun;

Ⓜ Ottaviano-San Pietro) Rome's top jazz joint attracts international performers – regulars include George Coleman and Lionel Hampton – and a passionate, knowledgeable crowd. In July and August the club goes alfresco at the under-the-stars Villa Celimontana Jazz Festival.

Big Mama   BLUES

(Map p418; www.bigmama.it; Vicolo di San Francesco a Ripa 18; ⊙9pm-1.30am, show 10.30pm Thu-Sat, closed Jun-Sep; ⛴Viale di Trastevere, ⛴Viale di Trastevere) To wallow in the Eternal City blues, there's only one place to go – this cramped Trastevere basement. There are weekly residences from well-known Italian musicians and regular blues, jazz, funk, soul and R&B concerts by international acts.

Goa   NIGHTCLUB

(www.goaclub.com; Via Libetta 13; ⊙11.30pm-4.30am Thu-Sat; Ⓜ Garbatella) Goa is Rome's serious super-club, with international names, a fashion-forward crowd, podium dancers and heavies on the door. Thursday is always a big night with top European DJs.

Villaggio Globale   CLUB, LIVE MUSIC

(Map p418; www.ecn.org/villaggioglobale/joomla; Via Monte del Cocci 22; ⛴Via Marmorata) For a warehouse-party vibe, head to Testaccio and Rome's best-known *centro sociale* (an ex-squat turned cultural centre) in the city's graffiti-sprayed former slaughterhouse. Entrance is cheap, the beer flows and the sound systems serve a steady supply of dancehall, reggae, dubstep and drum'n'bass.

🛍 Shopping

Rome boasts the usual cast of flagship chain stores and glitzy designer outlets, but what makes shopping here fun is its legion of small, independent shops – historic, family-owned delis, small-label fashion boutiques, artists' studios, neighbourhood markets. For designer clothes head to Via dei Condotti and the area around Piazza di Spagna, while for something more left-field check out the vintage shops and boutiques on Via del Governo Vecchio, around Campo de' Fiori, and in the Monti neighbourhood.

Rome's markets are great places for bargain hunting. The most famous, **Porta Portese** (Map p418; Piazza Porta Portese; ⊙7am-1pm Sun; ⛴Viale di Trastevere), is held every Sunday morning near Trastevere, and sells everything from antiques to clothes, bikes, bags and furniture.

For the best bargains, time your visit to coincide with the *saldi* (sales). Winter sales run from early January to mid-February and summer sales from July to early September.

❶ Information

Dangers & Annoyances

Rome is not a dangerous city but petty theft can be a problem. Watch out for pickpockets around the big tourist sites, at Stazione Termini and on crowded public transport – the 64 Vatican bus is notorious.

Emergency

Ambulance (☑118)

Fire (☑115)

Police (☑113, 112)

Main Police Station (Questura; ☑06 4 68 61; http://questure.poliziadistato.it; Via San Vitale 15; ⊙8.30am-11.30pm Mon-Fri, 3-5pm Tue & Thu)

Internet Access

Free wi-fi is widely available in hostels, B&Bs and hotels. Some places also provide laptops/computers for guests' use. Internet cafes are fairly thin on the ground, with costs usually between €4 and €6 per hour.

Medical Services

For problems that don't require hospital treatment call the **Guardia Medica Turistica** (☑06 7730 6650; Via Emilio Morosini 30). For emergency treatment, go to the *pronto soccorso* (casualty) section of an *ospedale* (hospital). Pharmacists will serve prescriptions and can provide basic medical advice.

Pharmacy (☑06 488 00 19; Piazza Cinquecento 51; ⊙7.30am-10pm daily) There's also a pharmacy in Stazione Termini, next to platform 1, open 7.30am to 10pm.

Ospedale Santo Spirito (☑06 6 83 51; Lungotevere in Sassia 1) Near the Vatican; multilingual staff.

Policlinico Umberto I (☑06 4 99 71; www.policlinicoumberto1.it; Viale del Policlinico 155) East of Stazione Termini.

Money

ATMs are liberally scattered around the city.

Most midrange and top-end hotels accept credit cards, as do most restaurants and large shops. Some cheaper *pensioni,* trattorias and pizzerias only accept cash. Don't rely on credit cards at museums or galleries.

There are money-exchange booths at Stazione Termini and Fiumicino and Ciampino airports.

Tourist Information

For phone enquiries, the Comune di Roma runs a multilingual **tourist information line** (📞060608; www.060608.it; ⏰9am-9pm).

There are tourist information points at **Fiumicino** (Terminal 3, International Arrivals; ⏰8am-7.30pm) and **Ciampino** (International Arrivals, baggage reclaim area; ⏰9am-6.30pm) airports. Also at the following locations across the city, open 9.30am to 7pm (except at Stazione Termini):

Castel Sant'Angelo Tourist Information (Map p428; Piazza Pia; ⏰9.30am-7pm)

Fori Imperiali Tourist Information (Map p422; Via dei Fori Imperiali; ⏰9.30am-7pm; 🚇Via dei Fori Imperiali)

Piazza delle Cinque Lune Tourist Information (Map p428; ⏰9.30am-7pm) Near Piazza Navona.

Stazione Termini Tourist Information (Map p434; ⏰8am-8.30pm) In the hall that runs parallel to platform 24.

Via Marco Minghetti Tourist Information (Map p428; ⏰9.30am-7pm) Near the Trevi Fountain.

Via Nazionale Tourist Information (Map p434; ⏰9.30am-7pm)

For information about the Vatican, contact the **Centro Servizi Pellegrini e Turisti** (Map p418; 📞06 6988 1662; St Peter's Square; ⏰8.30am-6pm Mon-Sat).

Websites

060608 (www.060608.it) Provides information on sites, shows, transport etc.

Coop Culture (www.coopculture.it) Information and ticketing for Rome's monuments, museums and galleries.

Turismo Roma (www.turismoroma.it) Rome's official tourist website.

Vatican (www.vatican.va) The Vatican's official website.

ⓘ Getting There & Away

Air

Rome's main international airport, Leonardo da Vinci (p531), better known as Fiumicino, is on the coast 30km west of the city. The much smaller Ciampino airport (p532), 15km southeast of the city centre, is the hub for low-cost carrier **Ryanair** (www.ryanair.com).

Boat

Rome's port is at Civitavecchia, about 80km north of Rome.

Ferry bookings can be made at the Termini-based **Agenzia 365** (📞06 474 09 23; www.agenzie365.it; ⏰8am-9pm), at travel agents or online at www.traghettionline.net. You can also buy directly at the port.

Half-hourly trains depart from Roma Termini to Civitavecchia (€5 to €14.50, 40 minutes to one hour). On arrival, it's about 700m to the port (to your right) as you exit the station.

The main ferry companies:

Grimaldi Lines (📞081 49 64 44; www.grimaldi-lines.com) To/from Trapani (Sicily), Porto Torres (Sardinia), Barcelona (Spain) and Tunis (Tunisia).

Tirrenia (📞89 21 23; www.tirrenia.it) To/from Arbatax, Cagliari and Olbia (all Sardinia).

Bus

Long-distance national and international buses use the Autostazione Tiburtina in front of Stazione Tiburtina. Take metro line B to Tiburtina.

You can get tickets from the offices next to the bus terminus or at travel agencies. Bus operators:

Interbus (📞091 34 25 25; www.interbus.it) To/from Sicily.

Marozzi (📞080 579 01 11; www.marozzivt.it) To/from Sorrento, Bari, Matera and Lecce.

SENA (📞0861 199 19 00; www.sena.it) To/from Siena, Bologna and Milan.

Sulga (📞800 09 96 61; www.sulga.it) To/from Perugia, Assisi and Ravenna.

Car & Motorcycle

Driving into central Rome is a challenge, involving traffic restrictions, one-way systems, a shortage of street parking and aggressive drivers.

The city is circled by the Grande Raccordo Anulare (GRA), to which all autostradas (motorways) connect, including the main A1 north–south artery (the Autostrada del Sole), and the A12, which runs to Civitavecchia and Fiumicino airport.

CAR HIRE

Rental cars are available at the airport and Stazione Termini. As well as international companies, try **Maggiore National** (www.maggiore.it)

Near Termini, **Bici & Baci** (📞06 482 84 43; www.bicibaci.com; Via del Viminale 5; ⏰8am-7pm) is one of many agencies renting out scooters. Bank on from €19 per day.

Train

Almost all trains arrive at and depart from Stazione Termini. There are regular connections to other European countries, all major Italian cities, and many smaller towns.

Train information is available from the customer service area on the main concourse to the left of the ticket desks. Alternatively, check www.trenitalia.com, or phone the **Trenitalia Call Centre** (📞89 20 21; ⏰24hr).

Left luggage (1st 5hr €5, 6-12hr per hr €0.70, 13hr & over per hr €0.30; ⏰6am-11pm) is on the lower ground floor under platform 24.

Rome's second train station is Stazione Tiburtina, a short ride away on metro line B.

❶ Getting Around

To/From the Airport

FIUMICINO

The easiest way to get to/from the airport is by train but there are also bus services. The set taxi fare to the city centre is €48 (valid for up to four people with luggage).

Cotral Bus (www.cotralspa.it; one-way €5, €7 if bought on bus) Runs to/from Stazione Tiburtina via Stazione Termini. Eight daily departures including night services from the airport at 1.15am, 2.15am, 3.30am and 5am, and from Tiburtina at 12.30am, 1.15am, 2.30am and 3.45am. Journey time is one hour.

FR1 Train (€8) Connects the airport to Trastevere, Ostiense and Tiburtina stations, but not Termini. Departures from the airport every 15 minutes (hourly on Sunday and public holidays) between 5.58am and 11.28pm; from Ostiense between 5.18am and 10.48pm.

Leonardo Express Train (adult/child €14/free) Runs to/from platform 24 at Stazione Termini. Departures from the airport every 30 minutes between 6.38am and 11.38pm, from Termini between 5.52am and 10.52pm. Journey time is 30 minutes.

SIT Bus (☎06 591 68 26; www.sitbusshuttle.it; Fiumicino one-way €6 or €5 online, €4/6 from/to Ciampino) From the airport regular departures between 8.30am and 12.30am to Via Marsala outside Stazione Termini; from Termini between 9.30am and 1.10am. Tickets are available on the bus. Journey time is one hour.

CIAMPINO

The best option is to take one of the regular bus services into the city centre. Alternatively, you can take a bus to Ciampino train station and then pick up a train to Stazione Termini. The set taxi fare is €30.

Cotral Bus (www.cotralspa.it; one-way €3.90) Runs 15 daily services to/from Via Giolitti near Stazione Termini. Also buses to/from Anagnina metro station (€1.20) and Ciampino train station (€1.20), where you can get a train to Stazione Termini (€1.30).

SIT Bus (www.sitbusshuttle.com; from airport €4, to airport €6) Regular departures from the airport to Via Marsala outside Stazione Termini between 7.45am and 11.15pm, and from Termini between 4.30am and 9.30pm. Get tickets on the bus. Journey time is 45 minutes.

Terravision Bus (www.terravision.eu; one-way €4) Twice hourly departures to/from Via Marsala outside Stazione Termini. From the airport, services are between 8.15am and 12.15am;

from Via Marsala between 4.30am and 9.20pm. Buy tickets at Terracafé in front of the Via Marsala bus stop. Journey time is 40 minutes.

Car & Motorcycle

Most of the *centro storico* is closed to normal traffic from 6.30am to 6pm Monday to Friday, from 2pm to 6pm Saturday, and from 11pm to 3am Friday to Sunday – see http://muovi.roma. it for details of the capital's limited traffic zones (*zone a traffico limitato;* ZTL).

PARKING

Blue lines denote pay-and-display parking spaces with tickets available from meters (coins only) and *tabacchi* (tobacconists). Expect to pay up to €1.20 per hour between 8am and 8pm (11pm in some places). After 8pm (or 11pm) parking is generally free until 8am the next morning. If your car gets towed away, check with the **traffic police** (☎06 676 92 303).

Car parks:

Piazzale dei Partigiani (per hr/day €0.77/5; ◷6am-11pm)

Stazione Termini (Piazza dei Cinquecento; per hr/day €2/18; ◷6am-1am)

Villa Borghese (Viale del Galoppatoio 33; per hr/day €2.20/20; ◷24hr)

Public Transport

Rome's public transport system includes buses, trams, metro and a suburban train network.

TICKETS

Tickets are valid for all forms of transport and come in various forms:

Single (BIT; €1.50) Valid for 100 minutes, during which time you can use as many buses or trams as you like but can only go once on the metro.

Daily (BIG; €6) Unlimited travel until midnight of the day of purchase.

Three-day (BTI; €16.50) Unlimited travel for three days.

Weekly (CIS; €24) Unlimited travel for seven days.

Buy tickets at *tabacchi,* newsstands and from vending machines at main bus stops and metro stations. They must be purchased before you start your journey and validated in the machines on buses, at the entrance gates to the metro or at train stations. Ticketless riders risk an on-the-spot €50 fine.

Children under 10 travel free.

BUS

Buses and trams are run by **ATAC** (☎06 5 70 03; www.atac.roma.it). The main bus station is in front of Stazione Termini on Piazza dei Cinquecento, where there's an **information booth** (Map p434; ◷7.30am-8pm). Other important hubs are at Largo di Torre Argentina and Piazza Venezia.

Buses generally run from about 5.30am until midnight, with limited services throughout the night.

METRO

Rome's two main metro lines, A (orange) and B (blue), cross at Termini, the only point at which you can change from one line to the other. There is a third line 'B1', which serves the northern suburbs, but you're unlikely to need it.

Take line A for the Trevi Fountain (Barberini), Spanish Steps (Spagna) and Vatican (Ottaviano-San Pietro); line B for the Colosseum (Colosseo).

Trains run between 5.30am and 11.30pm (to 1.30am on Friday and Saturday).

Taxi

Official licensed taxis are white with the symbol of Rome on the doors. Always go with the metered fare, never an arranged price (the set fares to and from the airports are exceptions). Official rates are posted in taxis.

You can hail a taxi, but it's often easier to wait at a rank or phone for one. There are major taxi ranks at the airports, **Stazione Termini**, **Largo di Torre Argentina**, **Piazza della Repubblica** and the **Colosseum**. You can book a taxi by phoning the Comune di Roma's automated **taxi line** (☑06 06 09) or calling a taxi company direct:

La Capitale (☑06 49 94)

Radio Taxi (☑06 35 70)

Samarcanda (☑06 55 51)

AROUND ROME

Ostia Antica

An easy day trip from Rome, the well-preserved ruins of Ostia Antica, ancient Rome's main seaport, form one of Italy's most compelling and under-appreciated archaeological sites. The city was founded in the 4th century BC at the mouth of the Tiber and developed into a major port with a population of around 100,000. Decline came in the 5th century when barbarian invasions and an outbreak of malaria led to its abandonment and slow burial in river silt, thanks to which it has survived so well.

The ruins, the **Scavi Archeologici di Ostia Antica** (☑06 563 52 830; www.ostiaantica.info; adult/reduced/EU child €6.50/3.25/free, plus possible exhibition supplement; ☉8.30am-6pm Tue-Sun Apr-Oct, to 5pm Mar, to 4pm Nov-Dec & Jan-Feb), are spread out and you'll need a few hours to do them justice.

The main thoroughfare, the **Decumanus Maximus** leads from the city's entrance, **Porta Romana**, to highlights such as the **Terme di Nettuno** (Baths of Neptune) and the steeply stacked **amphitheatre**. Behind the theatre, the **Piazzale delle Corporazioni** (Forum of the Corporations) housed Ostia's merchant guilds and is decorated with well-preserved mosaics. Further towards Porta Marina, the **Thermopolium** is an ancient cafe complete with a bar and fresco advertising the bill of fare.

To get to Ostia Antica take the Ostia Lido train (25 minutes, half-hourly) from Stazione Porta San Paolo next to Piramide metro station. The journey is covered by standard public-transport tickets. By car, take Via del Mare or Via Ostiense and follow signs for the *scavi*.

Tivoli

POP 56,530

An ancient resort town and playground for the Renaissance rich, hilltop Tivoli is home to two Unesco-listed sites: Villa Adriana, Emperor Hadrian's sprawling summer residence, and Villa d'Este, a Renaissance villa famous for its garden fountains. You can cover both in a day trip from Rome, but you'll have to start early.

🅾 Sights

TOP CHOICE ✓ **Villa Adriana**   ARCHAEOLOGICAL SITE
(☑06 399 67 900; www.villaadriana.beniculturali.it; adult/reduced/EU child €8/4/free, plus possible exhibition supplement, car park €3; ☉9am-1hr before sunset) Emperor Hadrian's sprawling 1st-century summer residence, 5km outside Tivoli proper, was one of the largest and most sumptuous villas in the Roman Empire. Hadrian personally designed much of it, taking inspiration from buildings he'd seen around the world. The **pecile**, a large porticoed pool, was a reproduction of a building in Athens, and the **canopo** is a copy of the sanctuary of Serapis near Alexandria. To the east of the *pecile* is Hadrian's private retreat, the **Teatro Marittimo**.

Allow several hours to explore the site.

Villa d'Este   GARDENS
(☑0774 331 20 70; www.villadestetivoli.info; Piazza Trento; adult/reduced/EU child €8.50/4/free, plus possible exhibition supplement; ☉8.30am-1hr before sunset Tue-Sun) In Tivoli's hilltop centre, the Renaissance Villa d'Este was originally a Benedictine convent before Lucrezia Bor-

gia's son, Cardinal Ippolito d'Este, transformed into a pleasure palace in 1550. Later, in the 19th century, the composer Franz Liszt lived and worked here.

More than the villa itself, it's the elaborate gardens and fountains that are the main attraction. Highlights include the **Fountain of the Organ**, an extravagant baroque ensemble that uses water pressure to play music through a concealed organ, and the 130m-long **Avenue of the Hundred Fountains**.

❶ Information

Information is available at the **tourist information point** (⌨0774 31 35 36; Piazzale delle Nazione Unite; ⊙9.30am-5.30pm Tue-Sun) near the bus stop in the *centro storico*.

❶ Getting There & Away

Tivoli is 30km east of Rome and accessible by Cotral bus (€1.30, 50 minutes, every 10 minutes) from Ponte Mammolo metro station. The fastest route by car is on the Rome–L'Aquila autostrada (A24).

To get to Villa Adriana from Tivoli town centre, take CAT bus 4 or 4X (€1, 10 minutes, half-hourly) from Largo Garibaldi.

NORTHERN ITALY

Italy's well-heeled north is a fascinating area of historical wealth and natural diversity. Bordered by the northern Alps and boasting some of the country's most spectacular coastline, it also encompasses Italy's largest lowland area, the fertile Po valley plain. Of the cities, it's Venice that hogs the limelight, but in their own way Turin, Genoa and Bologna offer plenty to the open-minded traveller. Verona is justifiably considered one of Italy's most beautiful cities, while Padua and Ravenna harbour celebrated artistic treasures.

Genoa

POP 607,900

One of the Mediterranean's great ports, Genoa (Genova) is an absorbing city of aristocratic *palazzi,* dark, malodorous alleyways, Gothic architecture and industrial sprawl. Its shadowy, sometimes seedy, *centro storico* teems with life while its grand palaces house artistic treasures amassed during its heyday as a powerful maritime republic known as La Superba. The city's main draw – apart from its cosmopolitan air and sense of history (Christopher Columbus was born here in 1451) – is its aquarium, Europe's second largest.

◉ Sights

Most sights are in the *centro storico* and Porto Antico (Old Port) between the city's two main train stations: Stazione Brignole and Stazione Principe.

For assiduous museum-goers, the **museum card** (24/48hr €12/16) gives free admission to 22 museums and discounted entry to the aquarium and other sights. Buy it at tourist offices or participating museums.

Piazza de Ferrari   PIAZZA

Genoa's main piazza is a good place to start exploring the city. Grandiose and impressive, it's centred on an exuberant fountain and ringed by imposing *palazzi* – **Palazzo della Borsa**, Italy's former stock exchange, **Teatro Carlo Felice**, the city's neoclassical opera house, and the huge **Palazzo Ducale** (www.palazzoducale.genova.it; Piazza Giacomo Matteotti 9; admission depends on exhibition; ⊙exhibitions 9am-9pm), once the seat of the city's rulers but now used to host major art exhibitions.

Musei di Strada Nuova   MUSEUM

(www.museidigenova.it; combined ticket adult/concession €8/6; ⊙9am-7pm Tue-Fri, 10am-7pm Sat & Sun) Genoa's main museums are in a series of *palazzi* on Via Garibaldi, where the city's richest families once lived. The three most important, known collectively as the Musei di Strada Nuova, are housed in **Palazzo Bianco** (Via Garibaldi 11), **Palazzo Rosso** (Via Garibaldi 18) and **Palazzo Doria-Tursi** (www.museidigenova.it; Via Garibaldi 9). The first two feature works by Flemish, Dutch, Spanish and Italian masters, while the third displays the personal effects of Genoa's legendary violinist Niccolò Paganini. Tickets, valid for all three museums, are available from the bookshop in Palazzo Doria-Tursi.

Cattedrale di San Lorenzo   CHURCH

(Piazza San Lorenzo; ⊙8am-noon & 3-7pm) Genoa's Gothic-Romanesque cathedral is notable for its striking black-and-white-striped facade. Fronted by twisting columns and crouching lions, it was first consecrated in 1118 but the two bell towers and cupola were added in the 16th century.

Acquario di Genova   AQUARIUM

(☎010 2 34 51; www.acquariodigenova.it; Ponte Spinola; adult/child €19/13; ⊙8.30am-10pm daily Jul & Aug, varied hrs rest of year) The main attraction in Genoa's **Porto Antico** is Europe's second-largest aquarium. Designed by Italian architect Renzo Piano, it houses 5000 animals in six million litres of water.

Renzo Piano was also responsible for two of the port's other landmarks: the **Biosfere** (Ponte Spinola; adult/child €5/3.50; ⊙10am-7pm mid-Mar–mid-Nov, 10am-5pm rest of year), a giant glass ball housing a tropical ecosystem, and the **Bigo** (Calata Cattaneo; adult/child €4/3; ⊙10am-11pm Jun-Aug, 2-6pm Mon, 10am-6pm Tue-Sun Mar-May, Sep & Oct, 10am-5pm Sat & Sun Nov-Feb), an eye-catching panoramic lift.

🛏 Sleeping

TOP CHOICE **Hotel Cairoli**   HOTEL €€

(☎010 246 14 54; www.hotelcairoligenova.com; Via Cairoli 14/4; r €60-160; ❋@☎) Colourful, friendly and central, the Cairoli makes quite an impression. Rooms are themed on works by celebrated modern artists and the public spaces, which include a communal library, chill-out area, internet room and fully equipped gym, create a bright, welcoming vibe.

Locanda di Palazzo Cicala   BOUTIQUE HOTEL €€

(☎010 251 88 24; www.palazzocicala.it; Piazza San Lorenzo 16; r €109-129, ste €159-219; ❋@☎) Housed in a grand 16th-century *palazzo* opposite the cathedral, this welcoming boutique hotel has huge high-ceilinged rooms replete with parquet and slick designer furniture. There are also several apartments available in nearby buildings.

Albergo Carola   PENSION €

(☎010 839 13 40; www.pensionecarola.com; 3rd fl, Via Groppallo 4; d €60-90, without bathroom s €23-50, d €40-90; ☎) This is a classic family-run *pensione* with nine simple, well-kept rooms on the 3rd floor of a lovely old building near Stazione Brignole. Rates don't include breakfast.

Ostello Genova   HOSTEL €

(☎010 242 24 57; www.ostellogenova.it; Via Costanzi 120; dm €17, s/d €28/50, without bathroom s/d €24/44; ⊙reception 9am-3.30pm & midnight-7am Feb–mid-Dec; P☎) A steep bus ride from the centre, Genoa's hillside hostel is a functional, institutional affair with basic facilities and sweeping city views. Hostelling International (HI) cards, which are available at check-in, are mandatory. Catch bus 40 from Stazione Brignole or Via Napoli.

🍴 Eating

Ligurian specialities include pesto (a sauce of basil, garlic, pine nuts and Parmesan cheese) served with *trofie* (pasta curls), and focaccia (flat bread made with olive oil).

Trattoria della Raibetta   TRATTORIA €€

(www.trattoriadellaraibetta.it; Vico Caprettari 10-12; mains €14; ⊙Tue-Sun) For a taste of authentic Genoese cooking, search out this inviting trattoria near the Porto Antico. It's a snug place with a low, brick-vaulted ceiling, pale yellow walls, and a thoughtful menu featuring minestrone and pesto alongside steaks and fresh seafood.

Regina Margherita   RISTORANTE €€

(☎010 595 57 53; Piazza della Vittoria 89-103; mains from €15, pizzas from €6) A bright, modern setup with a two-floor interior and a small outdoor terrace. It's not in a particularly enticing location – on Piazza della Vittoria – but it's very popular and the food is excellent. Speciality of the house is the wood-fired Neapolitan pizza.

La Cremeria delle Erbe   GELATERIA €

(Piazza delle Erbe 15-17; cones from €2; ⊙11am-1am Mon-Thu & Sun, to 2am Fri & Sat) On humming cafe-clad Piazza delle Erbe, this fab *gelateria* is perfectly placed for a quick ice-cream fix. The cream-based flavours are especially good, including a blissful *millefoglie*.

Osteria San Matteo   OSTERIA €€

(☎010 247 32 82; Piazza San Matteo 4r; mains €13) With its wood beams and exposed-brick walls, this is an inviting *osteria* in the heart of the *centro storico*. It serves a full menu but the reasonably priced seafood is the thing to go for.

🍷 Drinking & Entertainment

Action centres on the *centro storico,* with a number of good bars clustered around Piazza delle Erbe.

Mcafé   CAFE

(Piazza Giacomo Matteotti 5; ⊙8am-9.30pm Tue-Fri, 10am-9.30pm Sat & Sun) This swish cafe in the atrium of Palazzo Ducale is good anytime of the day – for a morning cappuccino, a quick lunchtime bite or an evening *aperitivo*. Upstairs, a restaurant serves set lunch menus (€12) on weekdays and brunch (€16) at weekends.

Storico Lounge Café CAFE
(Piazza de Ferrari 34/36r; ⊘6am-3am) The daily *aperitivo* (5pm to 10.30pm) draws a mixed crowd to this popular cafe overlooking Piazza de Ferrari. Grab a square-side table and join the locals over a cool, well-mixed cocktail and snacks from the abundant buffet.

Teatro Carlo Felice THEATRE
(☑010 538 12 24; www.carlofelice.it; Passo Eugenio Montale 4) Genoa's historic four-stage opera house stages a full program of opera, ballet and classical music. Tickets generally start at around €23 for ballet and €25 for opera.

❶ Information

There are tourist offices at: **Airport** (☑010 601 52 47; Airport; ⊘10am-1pm & 1.30-6.30pm); **De Ferrari** (☑010 860 61 22; www.visitgenoa. it; Largo Pertini 13; ⊘10am-1pm & 3-6pm Mon-Sat); **Via Garibaldi** (☑010 557 29 03; Via Garibaldi 12r; ⊘9am-6.30pm); **Antico Porto.** (010 557 42 00; Piazza Caricamento; ⊘9am-6.30pm summer, to 6pm winter)

❶ Getting There & Around

Air

Genoa's **Cristoforo Colombo airport** (☑010 6 01 51; www.airport.genova.it) is 6km west of the city. To get to/from it, the Volabus shuttle connects with Stazione Brignole and Stazione Principe (€6, 30 minutes, hourly 5.20am to 10.10pm to airport, 6am to 11.30pm from airport). Buy tickets on board or at tourist offices.

A taxi costs €7 per person (minimum three peole) from Stazione Principe and €8 from Brignole. For fewer than three people the minimum rate is €15.

Boat

Ferries sail to/from Spain, Sicily, Sardinia, Corsica and Tunisia from **Terminal Traghetti** (Ferry Terminal; www.porto.genova.it; Via Milano 51), west of the city centre. Ferry companies:

Grandi Navi Veloci (GNV; ☑010 209 45 91; www.gnv.it) To/from Sicily (Palermo from €58, 20½ hours), Barcelona (€95, 19½ hours) and Tunis (€99, 23½ hours).

Moby Lines (☑199 30 30 40; www.mobylines. it) To/from Sardinia (Olbia from €80.85, 11 hours).

Tirrenia (☑89 21 23; www.tirrenia.it) To/from Sardinia (Porto Torres €54, 10 hours), Olbia (€54, 9¾ hours) and Arbatax (€55, 14½ hours).

Bus

Buses to international and regional destinations depart from Piazza della Vittoria, south of Stazione Brignole. Book tickets at **Geotravels** (Piazza della Vittoria 57).

Local buses are run by **AMT** (www.amt.genova.it). Tickets cost €1.50 and are valid for 100 minutes. Bus 20 runs from Via Luigi Cadorna near Stazione Brignole up to Piazza de Ferrari and Via Andrea Doria, stopping near Stazione Principe.

AMT tickets are also valid on Genoa's small metro system.

Train

There are direct trains to Turin (€18, two hours, up to 15 daily), Milan (€18.50, 1½ hours, hourly), Pisa (€18, two to three hours, up to 14 daily) and Rome (€44 to €58.50, 4½ to 5½ hours, nine daily). Regional trains to La Spezia serve the Cinque Terre (€7.30, two hours, hourly).

It generally makes little difference whether you leave from Brignole or Principe.

Cinque Terre

Liguria's eastern Riviera boasts some of Italy's most dramatic coastline, the highlight of which is the Unesco-listed **Parco Nazionale delle Cinque Terre** (Cinque Terre National Park) just north of La Spezia. Running for 18km, this awesome stretch of plunging cliffs and vine-covered hills is named after its five tiny villages: Riomaggiore, Manarola, Corniglia, Vernazza and Monterosso.

The area's beauty masks its vulnerability; in autumn 2011 heavy rainfall caused severe flooding and mudslides, leaving four people dead. Further problems arose a year later when four Australian tourists were injured by rockfalls on the coast's most popular trail. The villages are now up and running again but several paths remain closed.

It gets very crowded in summer, so try to come in spring or autumn. You can either visit on a day trip from Genoa or La Spezia, or stay overnight in one of the five villages.

◉ Sights & Activities

The Cinque Terre villages are linked by the 9km **Sentiero Azzurro** (Blue Trail; admission with Cinque Terre Card), a magnificent, mildly challenging five-hour trail. The path, which is marked No 2 on maps, is in four stages, the easiest of which is the first from Riomaggiore to Manarola (Via dell'Amore; 20 minutes) and the second from Manarola to Corniglia (one hour). For the final two stages, you'll need to be fit and wearing proper walking shoes. The stretch from Corniglia to Vernazza takes approximately 1½ hours and from Vernazza to Monterosso it's two hours. Make sure you bring a hat, sunscreen and plenty of water if walking in hot weather. At the time of writing, the Sentiero was closed for reconstruction work after the floods in 2011 and rockfalls in 2012. For the latest information check www.parconazionale5terre.it.

The Sentiero Azzurro is just one of a network of footpaths and cycle trails that crisscross the park – details are available from the park offices. If water sports are more your thing, you can hire snorkelling gear (€10 per day) and kayaks (double €10 per hour) at the **Diving Center 5 Terre** (www.5terrediving.com; Via San Giacomo) in Riomaggiore. It also offers a snorkelling boat tour for €20.

🛏 Sleeping & Eating

L'Eremo sul Mare B&B €
(📞346 019 58 80; www.eremosulmare.com; d €80-110; ❄) On the Sentiero Azzurro, about a 15-minute steep walk from Vernazza, this charming B&B is set in an idyllic cliffside position. With only three rooms and stunning sea views, it's a wonderful spot for a romantic escape. Cash only.

Hotel Ca' d'Andrean HOTEL €
(📞0187 92 00 40; www.cadandrean.it; Via Doscovolo 101, Manarola; s €55-75, d €70-105; ❄📶) An excellent family-run hotel offering comfortable rooms and value-for-money in the upper part of Manarola. Rooms are big and cool with tiled floors and unobtrusive furniture; some also have private terraces. Breakfast (€6) is served in the garden. No credit cards.

Ostello 5 Terre HOSTEL €
(📞0187 92 00 39; www.hostel5terre.com; Via Riccobaldi 21, Manarola; dm €20-23, d €55-65, q €88-100; @📶) In Manarola, this is a decent private-run hostel with bright single-sex dorms and private rooms with en suite bathrooms. Extras include breakfast (€5) and dinner (€10), laundry facilities and a book exchange. Book at least a week ahead in summer.

Dau Cila MODERN ITALIAN €€
(📞0187 76 00 32; www.ristorantedaucila.com; Via San Giacomo 65, Riomaggiore; mains €18; ⊙8am-2am Mar-Oct) Perched within pebble-lobbing distance of Riomaggiore's snug harbour, Dau Cila is a smart restaurant-cum-*enoteca* (wine bar) specialising in excellent local wine and classy seafood such as *paccheri* (large pasta rings) with cuttlefish and red cabbage.

CINQUE TERRE CARD

To walk the Sentiero Azzurro or any other of the Cinque Terre paths, you'll need a Cinque Terre Card. This comes in two forms:

Cinque Terre Card (adult/child 1 day €5/2.50, 2 days €8/4, family card 1/2 days €12.50/20) Available at all park offices.

Cinque Terre Treno Card (adult/child 1 day €10/6, 2 days €19) As for the Cinque Terre Card plus unlimited train travel between La Spezia and the five villages.

Marina Piccola SEAFOOD €
(📞0187 76 20 65; www.hotelmarinapiccola.com; Via Lo Scalo 16, Manarola; mains €16, s/d €90/120, half-/full-board per person €90/105; ❄📶) Dine on fresh-off-the-boat seafood and house speciality *zuppa di datteri* (date soup) at this popular harbour-side restaurant in Manarola. If you want to stay, the adjoining hotel has small, comfortable rooms.

ℹ Information

The most convenient **information office** (📞0187 92 06 33; ⊙8am-7pm) is at Riomaggiore train station. There are also offices in the stations at Manarola, Corniglia, Vernazza, Monterosso and La Spezia (most open 8am to 7pm).

Online information is available at www.parconazionale5terre.it and www.cinqueterre.com.

ℹ Getting There & Away

Boat

Between July and September, **Golfo Paradiso** (📞0185 77 20 91; www.golfoparadiso.it) operates excursions from Genoa's Porto Antico to Vernazza and Monterosso. These cost €18 one-way, €33 return.

From late March to October, **Consorzio Marittimo Turistico 5 Terre** (📞0187 73 29 87; www.navigazionegolfodeipoeti.it) runs daily ferries between La Spezia and four of the villages (not Corniglia), costing €18 one-way. Return trips are covered by a daily ticket (weekdays/weekends €25/27).

Train

From Genoa Principe (€7.30) and Brignole (€6.60) direct trains run to Riomaggiore (1½ to two hours, 18 daily), stopping at each of the Cinque Terre villages.

Between 4.30am and 11.10pm, one to three trains an hour crawl up the coast from La Spezia to Levanto (€3.30, 30 minutes), stopping at all of the villages en route.

Turin

POP 907,600

First-time visitors are often surprised by Turin (Torino). Expecting a bleak, industrial sprawl dominated by Fiat factories, they are instead confronted with a dynamic and attractive city full of regal *palazzi*, historic cafes, baroque piazzas and world-class museums. The city was the seat of the royal Savoy family for centuries, and between 1861 and 1864 was Italy's first post-unification capital. More recently, it hosted the 2006 Winter Olympics and was European Capital of Design in 2008.

⊙ Sights

Serious sightseers should consider the **Torino & Piedmont Card** (2/3/5/7 days €25/29/34/37, junior 2 days €12), available at tourist offices, which gives free entry to 180 museums, monuments and castles, as well as discounts on tourist attractions and car rental.

Mole Antonelliana
MUSEUM

(Via Montebello 20) The symbol of Turin, this 167m tower with its distinctive aluminium spire appears on the Italian two-cent coin. It was originally intended as a synagogue but now houses the enjoyable **Museo Nazionale del Cinema** (www.museonazionaledelcinema.org; adult/reduced €9/7, incl panoramic lift €12/9; ⊙9am-8pm Tue-Fri & Sun, to 11pm Sat) and its comprehensive collection of film memorabilia. Don't miss the glass **panoramic lift** (Mole Antonelliana Tower; adult/reduced €6/4, incl museum €12/9; ⊙10am-8pm Tue-Fri & Sun, to 11pm Sat), which whisks you up 85m to the Mole's roof terrace in 59 seconds.

Museo Egizio
MUSEUM

(Egyptian Museum; www.museoegizio.org; Via Accademia delle Scienze 6; adult/reduced €8/6; ⊙8.30am-7.30pm Tue-Sun) Opened in 1824, this legendary museum houses the most important collection of Egyptian treasure outside of Cairo. Two of many highlights are a statue of Ramesses II (one of the world's most important pieces of Egyptian art) and over 500 items found in the tomb of Kha and Merit (from 1400 BC).

Piazza Castello
PIAZZA

Turin's grandest square is bordered by porticoed promenades and regal palaces. Dominating the piazza, the part-medieval, part-baroque **Palazzo Madama**, the original seat of the Italian parliament, is home to the **Museo Civico d'Arte Antica** (www.palaz-zomadamatorino.it; Piazza Castello; adult/reduced €10/8; ⊙10am-6pm Tue-Sat, to 7pm Sun), whose impressive collection includes Gothic and Renaissance paintings and some interesting majolica work. To the north, statues of Castor and Pollux guard the entrance to the **Palazzo Reale** (Piazza Castello; adult/reduced €10/5; ⊙8.30am-7.30pm Tue-Sun), built for Carlo Emanuele II around 1646. The palace's **Giardino Reale** (Royal Garden; admission free; ⊙9am-1hr before sunset) was designed by André le Nôtre, who also created the gardens at Versailles.

A short walk away, **Piazza San Carlo**, known as Turin's drawing room, is famous for its cafes and twin baroque churches **San Carlo** and **Santa Cristina**.

Cattedrale di San Giovanni Battista
CHURCH

(Piazza San Giovanni; ⊙8am-noon & 3-7pm) Turin's 15th-century cathedral houses the famous **Shroud of Turin** (*Sindone*), supposedly the cloth used to wrap the crucified Christ. A copy is on permanent display in front of the altar, while the real thing is kept in a vacuum-sealed box and rarely revealed.

Pinacoteca Giovanni e Marella Agnelli
GALLERY

(www.pinacoteca-agnelli.it; Via Nizza 230; adult/reduced €4/2.50; ⊙10:30am-7pm Tue-Sun) This Renzo Piano–designed modern art gallery displays masterpieces by Canaletto, Renoir, Manet, Matisse and Picasso in the Lingotto, Fiat's former car factory.

⊨ Sleeping

🆃🅾🅿 Art Hotel Boston
BOUTIQUE HOTEL €€€

(☎011 50 03 59; www.hotelbostontorino.it; Via Massena 70; s €80-120, d €110-400; ❋@🛜) The Boston's austere facade gives no inkling of the explosion of modern art inside. Public areas are filled with original works by Warhol, Lichtenstein and Aldo Mondino, while individually styled guest rooms are themed on subjects as diverse as Lavazza coffee, the Diabolik comic character, Ayrton Senna and Pablo Picasso.

Hotel Montevecchio
HOTEL €€

(☎011 562 00 23; www.hotelmontevecchio.com; Via Montevecchio 13; s €40-90, d €55-140; @🛜) In a quiet residential area 300m from Stazione Porta Nuova, this two-star offers a friendly welcome and bright, good-sized rooms. Useful extras include a laundry service and wi-fi (€1 for 30 minutes).

HISTORIC CAFES

Turin is home to an impressive array of historic cafes:

Baratti & Milano (☎011 561 30 60; Piazza Castello 27; mains about €10-15; ☺8am-9pm Tue-Sun) Serving coffee and confectionary since 1875.

Caffè San Carlo (Piazza San Carlo 156; ☺8am-midnight Tue-Fri, to 1am Sat, to 9pm Mon) Dates from 1822.

Caffè Torino (Piazza San Carlo 204; ☺7.30am-1am) A relative newcomer, this art nouveau gem opened in 1903.

Neuv Caval'd Brôns (Piazza San Carlo 155; ☺7.30am-1am) A 20th-century imposter named after the equestrian statue of Emanuele Filiberto on Piazza San Carlo.

San Tommaso 10 (Via San Tommaso 10; ☺8am-midnight Mon-Sat) This is where Lavazza started. It now serves an unorthodox array of flavoured coffees as well as all the classics.

L'Orso Poeta
B&B €€

(☎011 517 89 96; www.orsopoeta-bed-and-breakfast.it; Corso Vittorio Emanuele II 10; s/d €70/110; ❀☎) A welcoming B&B in a historic apartment building by the Po River. Its two small, pastel-shaded rooms have bathrooms and lots of character. Note that it's closed in August, December and January.

Alpi Resort Hotel
BUSINESS HOTEL €

(☎011 812 96 77; www.hotelalpiresort.it; Via A Bonafous 5; s €54-65, d €69-85; ❀☎) A businesslike three-star in an excellent location just off Piazza Vittorio Veneto. Its impeccably clean, carpeted rooms are quiet and comfortable, if rather characterless.

✖ Eating & Drinking

Turin has a reputation for magnificent gelato, which you can sample at outlets of **Grom** (www.grom.it; Piazza Pietro Paleocapa; ☺11am-midnight Sun-Thu, to 1am Fri & Sat) at Piazza Paleocapa 1d, Via Accademia delle Scienze 4 and Via Garibaldi 11, or the critically acclaimed newcomer **+ Di Un Gelato** (www.piudiungelato. it; Galleria Subalpina 32, entrance on Piazza Carlo Alberto; small cone or tub €2; ☺12.30am-8pm Mon-Fri, to 10pm Sat & Sun).

Early evening is the time to make for one of the city's cafes and enjoy an *aperitivo* (about €8) accompanied by a sumptuous buffet (included in the price). Popular *aperitivo* precincts include Piazza Emanuele Filiberto and environs, and Piazza Vittorio Veneto: try **I Tre Galli** (www.3galli.com; Via Sant'Agostino 25; ☺12.30am-2.30pm & 6.30pm-midnight Mon-Wed, to 2am Thu-Sat) or **La Drogheria** (www.la-drogheria.it; Piazza Vittorio Veneto 18; ☺10am-2am).

L'Hamburgheria di Eataly
BURGERS €

(Piazza Solferino 16a; burgers from €5.50; ☺11am-11pm Mon-Thu & Sun, to 1am Sat) Run by the Slow Food–backed Eataly chain, this cool burger bar takes fast food upmarket with a smart brick-and-steel interior and select menu. Choose your gourmet burger, made from locally sourced Piedmontese beef, and sit back with a bottle of artisanal beer as you wait.

Sfashion
PIZZERIA €

(☎011 516 00 85; Via Cesare Battisti 13; pizzas from €5.80, mains from €8.50) Overlooking Piazza Carlo Alberto, Sfashion is currently the hottest pizza ticket in town. The Neapolitan-style pizzas fly like hot bullets from the ovens of this kooky cafe-cum-pizzeria owned by local TV celebrity Piero Chiambretti.

Otto Etre Quarti
PIZZERIA, RISTORANTE €€

(☎011 517 63 67; Piazza Solferino 8c; pizzas from €5, mains from €15) Claim a table in one of 8¾'s high-ceilinged dining rooms or on the square-side terrace and feast on fab pizzas or tasty pastas such as *cavatelli con salsiccia e zafferano* (small fingers of pasta with sausage and saffron).

❶ Information

The city's efficient **tourist office** (☎010 53 51 81; www.turismotorino.org) has branches at **Porta Nuova station** (☺9am-6pm Mon-Sat, to 3pm Sun), **Piazza Castello** (☺9am-7pm) and **Via Giuseppe Verdi** (☺9am-7pm) near the Mole Antonelliana.

❶ Getting There & Around

In Caselle, 16km northwest of the city centre, **Turin airport** (www.turin-airport.com) serves flights to/from European and national destinations.

Sadem (www.sadem.it) runs an airport shuttle (€5.50 or €6 on board, 40 minutes, half-hourly) between the airport and Porta Nuova train station. A taxi costs approximately €35 to €40.

Direct trains connect with Milan (€11 to €30, one to two hours, up to 30 daily), Florence (€65, three hours, seven daily), Genoa (€18, two hours, up to 15 daily) and Rome (€90, 4¼ hours, nine daily).

Milan

POP 1.32 MILLION

Few Italian cities polarise opinion like Milan, Italy's financial and fashion capital. Some people love the cosmopolitan, can-do atmosphere, the vibrant cultural scene and the sophisticated shopping; others grumble that the city's dirty, ugly and expensive. Certainly, it lacks the picture-postcard beauty of many Italian towns, but in among the urban hustle are some truly great sights – Leonardo da Vinci's *Last Supper,* the immense Duomo and the world-famous La Scala opera house.

Originally founded by Celtic tribes in the 7th century BC, Milan was conquered by the Romans in 222 BC and developed into a major trading and transport centre. From the 13th century it flourished under the rule of two powerful families, the Visconti and Sforza.

◉ Sights

Milan's main attractions are concentrated in the area between Piazza del Duomo and Castello Sforzesco. To get to the piazza from Stazione Centrale, take the yellow MM3 underground line.

Duomo   CHURCH
(www.duomomilano.it; Piazza del Duomo; roof stairs/lift €7/12; ⊗7am-6.45pm, roof stairs 9am-6.30pm, lift 9am-8.30pm; ⓂDuomo) With a capacity of 40,000 people, this is the world's largest Gothic cathedral and the third-largest church in Europe. Commissioned in 1386 to a florid French-Gothic design and finished nearly 600 years later, it's a fairy-tale ensemble of 3200 statues, 135 spires and 146 stained-glass windows. Climb to the roof for memorable city views with tickets bought at the nearby **Duomo Information Point** (⎘02 720 23 375; www.duomomilano.it; Via dell'Arcivescovado 1; ⊗9am-8.30pm).

Galleria Vittorio Emanuele II ARCHITECTURE
(Piazza del Duomo; ⓂDuomo) Opening onto Piazza Duomo, the neoclassical Galleria Vittorio Emanuele is a soaring iron-and-glass shopping arcade known locally as *il salotto bueno,* the city's fine drawing room. Long-standing Milanese tradition claims you can ward off bad luck by grinding your heel into the testicles of the mosaic bull on the floor.

Teatro alla Scala   OPERA HOUSE
(La Scala; www.teatroallascala.org; Via Filodrammatici 2) Milan's legendary opera house hides its sumptuous six-tiered interior behind a surprisingly severe exterior. You can peek inside as part of a visit to the theatre's **Museo Teatrale alla Scala** (La Scala Museum; ⎘02 433 53 521; Largo Ghiringhelli 1; adult/child €6/4; ⊗9am-12.30pm & 1.30-5.30pm) providing there are no performances or rehearsals in progress.

The Last Supper   MURAL
(Il Cenacolo Vinciano; ⎘02 928 00 360; www.cenacolovinciano.net; Piazza Santa Maria delle Grazie 2; adult/reduced/EU child €6.50/3.25/free, plus booking fee €1.50; ⊗8.15am-6.45pm Tue-Sun; ⓂCadorna) Milan's most famous tourist attraction – Leonardo da Vinci's mural of *The Last Supper* – is in the Cenacolo Vinciano, the refectory of the **Chiesa di Santa Maria delle Grazie**, west of the city centre. To see it you need to book ahead or take a city tour.

Castello Sforzesco   CASTLE
(⎘02 884 63 700; www.milanocastello.it; Piazza Castello; ⊗7am-7pm summer, to 6pm winter; ⓂCairoli) Originally a Visconti fortress, this immense red-brick castle was later home to the Sforza dynasty that ruled Renaissance Milan. Today, it shelters the **Musei del Castello** (www.milanocastello.it; Piazza Castello 3; adult/EU child €3/free; ⊗9am-5.30pm Tue-Sun), a series of museums dedicated to art, sculpture, archaeology and music. Entry is free on Friday between 2pm and 5.30pm and on Tuesday, Wednesday, Thursday, Saturday and Sunday between 4.30pm and 5.30pm.

Pinacoteca di Brera   GALLERY
(⎘02 722 63 264; www.brera.beniculturali.it; Via Brera 28; adult/concession/EU child €6/3/free; ⊗8.30am-7.15pm Tue-Sun; ⓂLanza) Above the prestigious Brera Academy, this gallery houses Milan's most impressive collection of old masters, including works by Rembrandt, Goya, van Dyck, Titian, Tintoretto and Caravaggio. A highlight is Andrea Mantegna's brutal masterpiece *Cristo morto nel Sepolcro e tre Dolenti* (Lamentation over the Dead Christ).

Central Milan

Central Milan

◎ Top Sights
Castello Sforzesco	A1
Duomo	C3
Galleria Vittorio Emanuele II	C3
Teatro alla Scala	C2

◎ Sights
1 Musei del Castello	A1
2 Museo Teatrale alla Scala	C2
3 Pinacoteca di Brera	C1

✪ Activities, Courses & Tours
4 Autostradale	A2

🛌 Sleeping
5 Ariston Hotel	A4

✗ Eating
6 Peck Delicatessen	B3
7 Peck Italian Bar	B3

✪ Entertainment
8 Box Office	C3
9 Teatro alla Scala	C2

☞ Tours

Autostradale (☏02 720 01 304; www.auto stradale.it; Piazza Castello 1) runs walking tours (€20) and three-hour multilingual bus tours (€60) that take in the main sights and include entry to *The Last Supper*. Book tickets online or at the Autostradale office.

🛏 Sleeping

Milan is a business city, which means hotels are expensive and it can be hard to find a room, particularly when trade fairs are on (which is often). Booking is essential.

Antica Locanda Leonardo HOTEL €€€
(✆02 480 14 197; www.anticalocandaleonardo.com; Corso Magenta 78; s €120, d €170-265; ❄@🐾) A charming little hotel in a 19th-century *palazzo* near Leonardo's *Last Supper*. Rooms are individually styled but there's a homey feel about the place with period furniture, plush drapes, parquet and pot plants.

Hotel De Albertis HOTEL €€
(✆02 738 34 09; www.hoteldealbertis.it; Via De Albertis 7; s €50-100, d €50-160; @🐾) Out from the centre in a leafy residential street, this small hotel is a welcoming, family-run affair. There are few frills but rooms are clean and quiet, and breakfast is made with locally sourced organic produce. Take bus 92 from Stazione Centrale or 27 from the Duomo.

Zebra Hostel HOSTEL €
(✆02 367 05 185; www.zebrahostel.it; Viale Regina Margherita 9; dm €24-29; ❄@🐾) Good budget accommodation is thin on the ground in Milan, which makes this vibrant hostel all the more welcome. Winner of a 2012 Hostel World 'Hoscar', it's colourful and cheerfully decorated with excellent communal facilities, a fully equipped kitchen, and clean mixed and same-sex dorms.

Ariston Hotel HOTEL €€€
(✆02 720 00 556; www.aristonhotel.com; Largo Carrobbio 2; s €66-280, d €80-400; ❄@🐾) A business-style hotel offering decent three-star rooms about 10 minutes' walk from Piazza del Duomo. Check the website for low-season deals.

🍴 Eating & Drinking

Local specialities include *risotto alla milanese* (saffron-infused risotto cooked in bone-marrow stock) and *cotoletta alla milanese* (breaded veal cutlet).

There are hundreds of bars and restaurants in Milan but as a general rule, the area around the Duomo is full of smart business-oriented restaurants, Brera is a fashionable bar haunt and the lively Navigli canal district caters to all tastes.

Piccola Ischia PIZZERIA €
(✆02 204 76 13; Via Morgagni 7; pizzas €3-8; ⊗lunch & dinner Mon, Tue, Thu & Fri, dinner only Sat & Sun) This bustling, boisterous pizzeria brings a touch of Naples to Milan. Everything from the wood-fired pizza to the Campanian potato croquettes and exuberant decor screams of the sunny south. It's hugely popular so book or expect to queue. Also does takeaway.

El Brellin RISTORANTE €€€
(✆02 581 01 351; www.brellin.com; cnr Vicolo dei Lavandai 14 & Alzaia Naviglio Grande 14; mains €20; ⊗lunch & dinner daily, cafe from 6pm) Atmospheric El Brellin is housed in a 1700s laundry in the Navigli district. Its candlelit garden is a charming spot to linger over Milanese classics like *ossobuco* (oxtail) *con risotto alla milanese* while watching the canal-side parade. If you just just fancy a drink, *aperitivi* are served from 6pm.

Rinomata GELATERIA €
(Ripa di Porta Ticinese; ice creams from €2.50) If dining in Navigli, skip dessert and grab an ice cream from this historic hole-in-the-wall *gelateria*. Its fabulous interior features old-fashioned fridges and glass-fronted cabinets filled with cones – and the gelato is good, too.

Peck Italian Bar ITALIAN €€
(✆02 869 30 17; www.peck.it; Via Cesare Cantù 3; mains from €16.50; ⊗7.30am-8.30pm Mon-Fri, 9am-8.30pm Sat; ❄; Ⓜ Duomo) Round the corner from the legendary **Peck Delicatessen** (Via Spadari 9), this bar oozes Milanese chic. Black-jacketed waiters serve coffees, wine and a daily dose of pasta to a stylish, sharply dressed crowd.

BQ Navigli BAR
(Birra Artigianale di Qualità; Via Alzaia Naviglio Grande 44; ⊗6pm-2am) In recent years Italy has been rediscovering the joys of beer and this canal-front bar has a fine selection of local brews ranging from light lagers to dark, hardcore bitters. Panini and *piadine* (pitta bread-style rolls) provide the solids.

☆ Entertainment

Milan offers a rich and vibrant cultural scene, ranging from opera at La Scala to world-class football and cutting-edge club nights. September is a good time for classical-music fans, as the city co-hosts the **Torino Milano Festival Internazionale della Musica** (www.mitosettembremusica.it).

The opera season at **Teatro alla Scala** (✆02 8 87 91; www.teatroallascala.org; Piazza della Scala; Ⓜ Duomo) runs from November to July, but you can see theatre, ballet and concerts year-round, with the exception of August.

FOOTBALL IN MILAN

Milan is home to Italy's two most successful *calcio* (football) teams: the Berlusconi-owned AC Milan and Internazionale, aka Inter. During the season (September to May), the two clubs play on alternate Sundays at the **Stadio Giuseppe Meazza** (Via Piccolomini 5; Lotto), aka the San Siro. Match tickets (from €18) are available from branches of Banca Intesa (AC Milan) and Banca Popolare di Milano (Inter). To get to the stadium on match days, take the free shuttle bus from the Lotto (MM1) metro station.

Tickets are available online or from the **box office** (Galleria del Sagrato; noon-6pm) beneath Piazza del Duomo. Bank on €12 to €187 for opera and €10 to €115 for ballet performances.

For jazz, **Blue Note** (02 690 16 888; www. bluenotemilano.com; Via Borsieri 37; tickets €20-35; Tue-Sun Sep-Jul; Zara, Garibaldi) stages top international and Italian performers.

Shopping

For designer clobber head to the so-called Golden Quad, the area around Via della Spiga, Via Sant'Andrea, Via Monte Napoleone and Via Alessandro Manzoni. Street markets are held around the canals, notably on Viale Papiniano on Tuesday mornings and Saturdays.

Information

There are tourist offices at **Piazza Castello** (02 774 04 343; Piazza Castello 1; 9am-6pm Mon-Fri, 9am-1.30pm & 2-6pm Sat, to 5pm Sun) and **Stazione Centrale** (02 774 04 318; opposite platform 13, Stazione Centrale; 9am-6pm Mon-Fri, 9am-1.30pm & 2-6pm Sat, to 5pm Sun).

Useful websites include www.visitamilano.it and www.hellomilano.it.

Pharmacy (02 669 07 35; Stazione Centrale; 24hr)

Police Station (02 6 22 61; Via Fatebenefratelli 11)

Getting There & Away

Air

Most international flights fly into Malpensa Airport (p532), about 50km northwest of Milan. Domestic and some European flights use **Linate airport** (LIN; flight information 02 23 23 23;

www.milanolinate.eu/it), about 7km east of the city. Low-cost airlines often use **Orio al Serio airport** (BG; 035 32 63 23; www.sacbo.it), near Bergamo.

Train

Regular daily trains depart Stazione Centrale for Venice (€36, 2½ hours), Bologna (€40, one hour), Florence (€50, 1¾ hours), Rome (€86, three to 3½ hours) and other Italian and European cities. Note that these prices are for the fast Frecce services.

Most regional trains also stop at Stazione Nord in Piazzale Cadorna.

Getting Around
To/From the Airport

MALPENSA

Malpensa Shuttle (02 585 83 185; www. malpensashuttle.it; adult/child €10/5) Buses run to/from Piazza Luigi di Savoia next to Stazione Centrale every 20 minutes between 4.15am and 12.30pm. Buy tickets at Stazione Centrale or the airport. Journey time is 50 minutes.

Malpensa Bus Express (02 805 81 354; www.autostradale.it; adult/child €10/5) To/from Piazza Luigi di Savoia half-hourly between 4am and 12.40am. The trip takes 50 minutes.

Malpensa Express (800 50 00 05; www. malpensaexpress.it) Trains depart every 30 minutes to Terminal 1 from Stazione Centrale (adult/child €10/5, 45 minutes) and Stazione Nord (adult/child €11/5, 40 minutes).

LINATE

ATM (800 80 81 81; www.atm-mi.it) Local bus 73 runs from Piazza San Babila every 10 to 15 minutes between 5.30am and 12.30am. Use a regular bus ticket (€1.50).

Starfly (02 585 87 237; www.starfly.net; €5) Buses to/from Piazza Luigi di Savoia half-hourly between 5.30am and 10.45pm. Journey time is 30 minutes. Buy tickets at newsstands or on board.

ORIO AL SERIO

Autostradale (02 720 01 304; www. autostradale.it; €5) Half-hourly buses to/from Piazza Luigi di Savoia between 4am and 11.30pm. Journey time is one hour.

Orio Shuttle (035 33 07 06; www.orio shuttle.com; adult/child €8/3, one hour) Runs half-hourly to/from outside Stazione Centrale (one hour) between 3am and 12.15am.

Bus & Metro

Milan's excellent public transport system is run by ATM (p455). Tickets (€1.50) are valid for one underground ride or up to 90 minutes' travel on city buses and trams. A day ticket costs €4.50. Buy them at metro stations, *tabacchi* and newsstands.

Verona

POP 263,700

Wander Verona's atmospheric streets and you'll understand why Shakespeare set *Romeo and Juliet* here – this is one of Italy's most beautiful and romantic cities. Known as *piccola Roma* (little Rome) for its importance in imperial days, its heyday came in the 13th and 14th centuries when it was ruled by the Della Scala (aka Scaligeri) family, who built *palazzi* and bridges, sponsored Giotto, Dante and Petrarch, oppressed their subjects and feuded with everyone else.

◉ Sights

The **Verona Card** (www.veronacard.it; 2/5 days €15/20), available from tourist offices, sites and *tabacchi*, covers city transport and the city's main monuments and churches.

Arena di Verona   AMPHITHEATRE
(www.arena.it; Piazza Brà; adult/reduced/child €6/4.50/free; ⊙1.30am-7.30pm Mon plus 8.30am-7.30pm Tue-Sun, to 4.30pm on performance days) In the corner of Piazza Brà, the 1st-century pink marble Arena is the third-largest Roman amphitheatre in Italy. And although it can no longer seat 30,000, it still draws sizeable crowds to its summer opera performances.

Casa di Giulietta   MUSEUM
(Juliet's House; ☑045 803 43 03; Via Cappello 23; adult/reduced €6/4.50 or with VeronaCard; ⊙8.30am-7.30pm Tue-Sun, 1.30-7.30pm Mon) Juliet and her lover Romeo were entirely fictional characters but that doesn't stop visitors flocking to this 14th-century *palazzo* to act out their romantic fantasies and add their lovelorn words to the graffiti on the arched gateway.

Piazzas   PIAZZA
Set over the city's Roman forum, **Piazza delle Erbe** is lined with sumptuous *palazzi* and filled with touristy market stalls. Through the **Arco della Costa**, the quieter **Piazza dei Signori** is flanked by the early Renaissance **Loggia del Consiglio**, aka the Loggia Fra Gioconda, and the **Palazzo del Podestà**, the 14th-century residence of Cangrande I, the most celebrated of the Della Scala rulers. Nearby, the **Arche Scaligere** are the Della Scala family's elaborate Gothic tombs.

Basilica di San Zeno Maggiore   CHURCH
(www.chieseverona.it; Piazza San Zeno; adult/child €2.50/free, incl Verona church €6 or with VeronaCard; ⊙8.30am-6pm Tue-Sat, 12.30-6pm Sun Mar-Oct, 10am-1pm & 1.30-5pm Tue-Sat, 12.30-5pm Sun Nov-Feb) This masterpiece of Romanesque architecture honours the city's patron saint. Note Mantegna's 1457–59 altarpiece, *Maestà della Vergine* (Majesty of the Virgin), and the 12th-century bronze doors.

🛏 Sleeping

High-season prices apply during the opera season and it is absolutely essential to book for this period. If you arrive without a booking, the tourist office has a hotel reservation service.

Hotel Aurora   HOTEL €€€
(☑045 59 47 17; www.hotelaurora.biz; Piazza delle Erbe; s €100-160, d €110-240; ❄🖀🛇) Gleaming after a recent makeover, this friendly three-star is right in the heart of the action on central Piazza delle Erbe. Rooms, some of which have piazza views, are smart with laminated parquet, polished wood and modern mosaic-tiled bathrooms. Breakfast can be enjoyed on a lovely terrace overlooking the piazza.

Appartamenti L'Ospite   APARTMENT €€
(☑045 803 69 94; www.lospite.com; Via XX Settembre 3; apt 1 or 2 people €35-105, apt 2-4 people €40-180; ❄🖀🛇) Over the river from the *centro storico*, L'Ospite has six self-contained apartments for up to four people. Simple and bright with fully equipped kitchens, they come with wi-fi and are ideal for families.

Villa Francescatti   HOSTEL €
(☑045 59 03 60; www.ostelloverona.it; Salita Fontana del Ferro 15; dm €18-20; ⊙7am-midnight) This HI youth hostel is in a 16th-century villa a 20-minute walk from central Verona. Dinners cost €9 (reservations required); there are no cooking facilities. Rooms are off limits 9am to 5pm, but you can use the common rooms. Catch bus 73 (weekdays) or bus 90 (Sunday and holidays) from the train station. There's a strict 11.30pm curfew.

🍴 Eating

Boiled meats are a Veronese speciality, as is crisp Soave white wine.

Al Pompiere   TRATTORIA €€
(☑045 803 05 37; www.alpompiere.com; Vicolo Regina d'Ungheria 5; mains €16; ⊙Tue-Sat) Near the

Casa di Giulietta, this handsome trattoria – think low wooden ceiling, hanging sausages and framed photos – is famed for its vast cheese selection and house-cured *salumi*. Make a meal of the starters with wine by the glass, or fill up on robust meaty mains. Reservations recommended.

Trattoria Al Bersagliere TRATTORIA €€
(✆045 800 48 24; www.trattoriaalbersagliere.it; Via Dietro Pallone 1; mains €11-15; ☺Tue-Sat) With its wood-beamed ceilings and internal courtyard, this much-loved trattoria is a lovely place to dine on rustic Veronese cooking such as *pasta e fasoi* (Veneto-style bean soup) and *patissada de Caval con polenta* (stewed horse meat with polenta), a local speciality since the 15th century.

Café Noir CAFE €
(✆045 803 05 00; Via Pellicciai 12; mains €7; ☺7.30am-9pm Mon-Sat) This popular cafe is a favourite with local shoppers who stop by for fresh lunchtime salads, daily pastas and simple risottos. No dinner.

☆ Entertainment

Tickets for the opera season at the **Arena** (✆045 800 51 51; www.arena.it; Piazza Brà; tickets €23-200; ☺opera season mid-Jun–early Sep) are available online or at various places across town, including the tourist office; see the website for details.

❶ Information

Information, opera tickets and hotel reservations are available at the central **tourist office** (✆045 806 86 80; www.tourism.verona.it; Via degli Alpini 9; ☺9am-7pm Mon-Sat, 10am-4pm Sun) just off Piazza Brà. There's a second **office** (✆045 861 91 63; Verona-Villafranca airport; ☺10am-4pm Mon & Tue, to 5pm Wed-Sat) in the airport arrivals hall.

❶ Getting There & Around

The **Aeroporto di Verona** (Valerio Catullo airport; ✆045 809 56 66; www.aeroportodelgarda.it), 12km outside the city, is accessible by bus from the train station (€6, 20 minutes, every 20 minutes between 5.15am and 11.10pm).

From stand A outside the train station, buses 90, 92, 93, 98 and 510 run to Piazza Brà. Tickets cost €1.30 or €1.50 if bought on board.

Direct trains connect with Milan (€11.30 to €19, one hour 20 minutes to two hours, three hourly), Venice (€7.40 to €19, 50 minutes to 2¼ hours, half-hourly) and Bologna (€8.90 to €19, 50 minutes to 1½ hours, 20 daily).

Padua

POP 214,200

The elegant city of Padua (Padova) sees only a fraction of the visitors who pile into nearby Venice. Yet, it's a fascinating place, a handsome medieval city with a long and cultured past (Galileo taught astronomy at the city university), one of the world's oldest (Shakespeare set parts of *The Taming of the Shrew* here), and Giotto painted one of Italy's greatest works of art in the city's Cappella degli Scrovegni.

◉ Sights

The **PadovaCard** (www.padovacard.it; per 48/72hr €16/21) provides free parking, public transport and entry to many sights, including the Cappella degli Scrovegni (plus €1 booking fee). Get it at tourist offices or participating sites.

Cappella degli Scrovegni CHURCH
(✆049 201 00 20; www.cappelladegliscrovegni.it; Piazza Eremitani 8; adult/reduced €13/8; ☺9am-7pm Mon, to 10pm Tue-Sun Mar-Oct, 9am-7pm Nov-Dec, by reservation only) Giotto's frescos in the Scrovegni chapel – named after the banker Enrico Scrovegni who originally commissioned it – are among the defining works of early Renaissance art. Painted between 1303 and 1305, the 38 colourful panels cover the chapel from floor to ceiling, depicting events from the life of Christ and the Virgin Mary.

Visits, which must be booked online or by phone at least 24 hours beforehand, last only 15 minutes and are preceded by a mandatory, 15-minute video introduction.

The picture galleries in the nearby **Musei Civici agli Eremitani** (✆049 8204 5450; Piazza Eremitani 8; adult/reduced €10/8; ☺9am-7pm Tue-Sun) are home to an impressive collection of paintings and sculptures, including two Giottos.

FREE **Basilica di Sant'Antonio** CHURCH
(Il Santo; www.basilicadelsanto.org; Piazza del Santo; ☺6.20am-7.45pm Apr-Oct, to 7pm Nov-Mar) On the other side of the *centro storico* from the Cappella degli Scrovegni is this domed basilica, a major pilgrimage site. Thousands come to pay homage to the town's patron saint, St Anthony (1193–1231), whose gaudy tomb is covered with requests and thanks for miracle cures and the recovery of lost objects.

Outside, Donatello's 1453 equestrian statue, which commemorates a 15th-century

ITALY PADUA

Venetian mercenary called Gattamelata ('Honeyed Cat'), is considered the first great Italian Renaissance bronze.

🛌 Sleeping

TOP CHOICE Belludi37
BOUTIQUE HOTEL €€

(☑049 66 56 33; www.belludi37.it; Via Luca Belludi 37; s €97, d €120-145; ❋🐾) This sleek boutique hotel ticks all the boxes, providing excellent value for money, a central location near the Basilica di Sant'Antonio, a chic, contemporary look, and friendly, helpful staff. Parking is also available for €15 per night. Highly recommended.

Albergo Verdi
HOTEL €

(☑049 836 41 63; www.albergoverdipadova.it; Via Dondi dall'Orologio 7; s €70, d €100; ❋@🐾) A modern three star offering spruce, bright rooms and mod cons such as wi-fi (€2 per three hours) and satellite TV. The guest rooms are not the biggest but it's a friendly place and the central location near Piazza dei Signori is handy for the sights.

Ostello Città di Padova
HOSTEL €

(☑049 875 22 19; www.ostellopadova.it; Via Aleardi 30; dm €19-23, d €76; ⊙reception 7.15-9.30am & 3.30-11.30pm; 🐾) On a quiet side street in the *centro storico*, Padua's rather drab youth hostel has functional dorms with bunk beds for four to six people. Take bus 8 or 12 or the tram from the train station to Via Cavalletto, then follow on foot.

🍴 Eating & Drinking

TOP CHOICE Godenda
MODERN ITALIAN €€

(☑049 877 41 92; www.godenda.it; Via Squarcione 4/6; meals €25-40; ⊙10am-3pm & 6pm-2am Mon-Sat) Hidden under an ancient portico, this foodie favourite sets a fashionable, contemporary stage for creative modern dishes such as *crema di patate al curry con sauté di cozze* (curried mashed potato with sautéed mussels) as well as traditional cheese platters and tasty vegetable pastas. Reservations recommended.

L'Anfora
OSTERIA €€

(☑049 65 66 29; Via dei Soncin 13; meals €25-30; ⊙9am-11pm Mon-Sat) At this laid-back *osteria* with bare wooden tables and racked wine bottles, the menu changes daily, with the emphasis on regional, local dishes. It can get pretty busy, particularly on Saturday nights, so book ahead.

Antica Osteria dal Capo
OSTERIA €€

(☑049 66 31 05; www.osteriadalcapo.it; Via degli Obizzi 2; mains €10-16; ⊙Tue-Sat) A cosy *osteria* serving earthy Veneto cuisine. Seafood features strongly on the seasonal menu alongside hearty vegetable soups and old-school meat dishes like *fegato alla veneziana con polenta* (Venetian-style liver and onions with polenta). Reservations recommended.

ℹ️ Information

There are tourist offices: at the **train station** (☑049 875 20 77; www.turismopadova.it; ⊙9.15am-7pm Mon-Sat, 9am-noon Sun), **Galleria Pedrocchi** (☑049 876 79 27; www.turismo padova.it; Vicolo Pedrocchi; ⊙9am-1.30pm & 3-7pm Mon-Sat) and **Piazza del Santo** (☑049 875 30 87; www.turismopadova.it; ⊙10.30am-1.30pm & 3-6pm Tue-Sun).

ℹ️ Getting There & Away

Busitalia (☑049 820 68 44; www.fsbusitalia. it) buses leave from the bus station outside the train station for Venice's Marco Polo airport (€8 or €10 on board, one hour, hourly between 6.25am and 8.25pm), stopping off at Venice en route.

Regional trains serve Venice (€3.50, one hour, every 20 minutes), Verona (€5.95, 1½ hours, hourly) and Bologna (€9, 1½ hours, hourly).

Venice

POP 270,900

Venice (Venezia) is a hauntingly beautiful city. At every turn you're assailed by unforgettable images – tiny bridges crossing limpid canals, delivery barges jostling chintzy gondolas, excited tourists posing on Piazza San Marco. Its celebrated sights are legion and its labyrinthine backstreets exude a unique, almost eerie, atmosphere, redolent of dark passions and dangerous secrets. Parts of the Cannaregio, Dorsoduro and Castello *sestieri* (districts) rarely see many tourists, and you can lose yourself for hours in the lanes between the Accademia and train station.

Despite its romantic reputation, the reality of modern Venice is a city besieged by rising tides and up to 20 million visitors a year. This and the sky-high property prices mean that most locals live over the lagoon in Mestre.

History

Venice's origins date to the 5th and 6th centuries when barbarian invasions forced the

Greater Venice

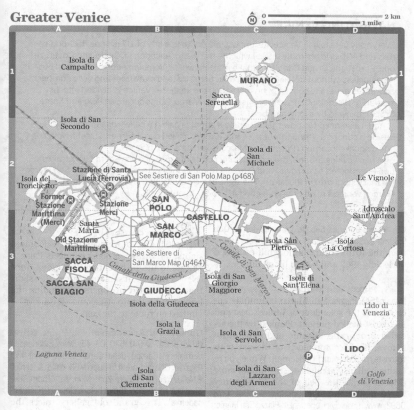

Veneto's inhabitants to seek refuge on the lagoon's islands. Initially the city was ruled by the Byzantines from Ravenna, but in 726 the Venetians went it alone and elected their first doge (duke). Over successive centuries, the Venetian Republic grew into a great merchant power, dominating half the Mediterranean and the trade routes to the Levant – it was from Venice that Marco Polo set out for China in 1271. Decline began in the 16th century and in 1797 the city authorities opened the gates to Napoleon, who, in turn, handed the city over to the Austrians. In 1866, Venice was incorporated into the Kingdom of Italy.

◉ Sights

Whet your sightseeing appetite by taking *vaporetto* (small passenger ferry) No 1 along the **Grand Canal** lined with rococo, Gothic, Moorish and Renaissance palaces. Alight at Piazza San Marco, Venice's main square.

Basilica di San Marco CHURCH
(St Mark's Basilica; Map p464; ☎041 270 83 11; www. basilicasanmarco.it; Piazza San Marco; ⊙9.45am-4.45pm Mon-Sat, 2-4pm Sun & holidays, baggage storage 9.30am-5.30pm; ⊠San Marco) With its spangled spires, Byzantine domes, luminous mosaics and lavish marble work, Venice's signature church is an unforgettable sight. It was first built to house the corpse of St Mark, but the original chapel was destroyed by fire in 932 and a new basilica was built over it in 1094. For the next 500 years it was a work in progress as successive doges added mosaics and embellishments looted from the East.

Inside, behind the main altar, check out the **Pala d'Oro** (admission €2; ⊙9.45am-5pm Mon-Sat, 2-4.30pm Sun, to 4pm winter), a stunning gold altarpiece decorated with priceless jewels.

Outside in the piazza, the basilica's 99m freestanding **campanile** (Bell Tower; www. basilicasanmarco.it; Piazza San Marco; admission

NAVIGATING VENICE

Everybody gets lost in Venice. It's impossible not to in a city of 117 islands, 150-odd canals and 400 bridges (only four of which – the Rialto, Accademia, Scalzi and Costituzione – cross the Grand Canal). To make matters worse, Venetian addresses are all but meaningless without detailed walking directions. Instead of a street and civic number, addresses generally consist of no more than the *sestiere* (Venice is divided into six *sestieri* or districts: Cannaregio, Castello, San Marco, Dorsoduro, San Polo and Santa Croce) followed by a long number.

You'll also need to know that in Venice a street is called a *calle, ruga* or *salizada;* beside a canal it's a *fondamenta*. A canal is a *rio,* a filled canal-turned-street a *rio terrà,* and a square a *campo* (Piazza San Marco is Venice's only piazza).

When walking around, the most helpful points of reference are Santa Lucia train station (signposted as *ferrovia*) and Piazzale Roma in the northwest, and Piazza San Marco (St Mark's Square) in the south. The signposted path from the station to Piazza San Marco (Venice's main drag) is a good 40- to 50-minute walk.

€8; ☉9am-9pm Jul-Sep, to 7pm Apr-Jun & Oct, 9.30am-3.45pm Nov-Mar; ⛴San Marco) dates from the 10th century, although it collapsed on 14 July 1902 and had to be rebuilt.

TOP CHOICE Piazza San Marco PIAZZA

(Map p464) Piazza San Marco beautifully encapsulates the splendour of Venice's past and its tourist-fuelled present. Flanked by the arcaded **Procuratie Vecchie** and **Procuratie Nuove**, it's filled for much of the day with tourists, pigeons and policemen. While you're taking it all in, you might see the bronze *mori* (Moors) strike the bell of the 15th-century **Torre dell'Orologio** (Clock Tower; ☏041 4273 0892; www.museicivicineziani.it; Piazza San Marco; adult/reduced with Museum Pass €12/7; ☉tours in English 10am & 11am Mon-Wed, 2pm & 3pm Thu-Sun, in Italian noon & 4pm daily, in French 2pm & 3pm Mon-Wed, 10am & 11am Thu-Sun; ⛴San Marco).

TOP CHOICE Palazzo Ducale MUSEUM

(Ducal Palace; Map p464; ☏848 08 20 00; www.palazzoducale.visitmuve.it; Piazzetta San Marco 52; adult/reduced/child incl Museo Correr €16/8/free or with Museum Pass; ☉8.30am-7pm Apr-Oct, to 5.30pm Nov-Mar; ⛴San Zaccaria) The official residence of the doges from the 9th century and the seat of the Republic's government, Palazzo Ducale also housed Venice's prisons. The doges' apartments on the 1st floor are suitably lavish, but it's the vast **Sala del Maggiore Consiglio** on the 2nd floor that will really take your breath away. Measuring 53m by 25m, this echoing hall is dominated by Tintoretto's *Paradiso* (Paradise), one of the world's largest oil paintings.

TOP CHOICE Ponte dei Sospiri BRIDGE

(Map p464) One of Venice's most celebrated sights, the Bridge of Sighs connects Palazzo Ducale to the 16th-century *Priggione Nove* (New Prisons). It's named after the sighs that condemned prisoners – including the legendary lothario Giacomo Casanova – emitted en route to the cells.

Gallerie dell'Accademia GALLERY

(Map p464; ☏041 520 03 45; www.gallerieaccademia.org; Campo della Carità 1050; ticket incl Palazzo Grimani adult/reduced/EU child & senior €14/11/free; ☉8.15am-2pm Mon, to 7.15pm Tue-Sun, last admission 45min before closing; P; ⛴Accademia) This grand old gallery traces the development of Venetian art from the 14th to the 18th century. You'll find works by Bellini, Titian, Carpaccio, Tintoretto, Giorgione and Veronese, whose controversial *Feast in the House of Levi* was condemned by the church Inquisition for its depiction of dogs, drunks and dwarfs cavorting with the apostles.

TOP CHOICE Collezione Peggy Guggenheim GALLERY

(Map p464; ☏041 240 54 11; www.guggenheim-venice.it; Dorsoduro 701, Palazzo Venier dei Leoni; adult/reduced/child €12/7/free; ☉10am-6pm Wed-Mon) The American heiress Peggy Guggenheim was one of the great art collectors of the 20th century. Her spellbinding collection, displayed here in her former home, runs the gamut of modern art with works by Picasso, Pollock, Braque, Kandinsky, Klee and many more. In the sculpture garden you'll find the graves of Peggy and her dogs.

Palazzo Grassi   MUSEUM
(Map p464; ✆box office 199 13 91 39, 041 523 16 80; www.palazzograssi.it; Campo San Samuele 3231; adult/reduced/child €15/10/free, 72hr ticket incl Punta della Dogana €20/15/free; ⊕10am-7pm Wed-Mon; ⛴San Samuele) One of the most impressive buildings on the Grand Canal, the 18th-century Palazzo Grassi provides the dramatic setting for exhibitions and installations by big-name contemporary artists like Jeff Koons and Richard Prince. In 2009, the museum opened a second exhibition space, the **Punta della Dogana** (Map p464; ✆041 271 90 39; www.palazzograssi.it; adult/reduced/child €15/10/free, incl Palazzo Grassi €20/15/free; ⊕10am-7pm Wed-Mon; ⛴Salute).

Churches   CHURCH
As in much of Italy, Venice's churches harbour innumerable treasures; unusually, though, you have to pay to get into many of them. The Chorus Pass (p462) gives admission to 16 of the city's most important churches, which otherwise charge adult/reduced €3/1.50.

Scene of the annual Festa del Redentore (Feast of the Redeemer), the **Chiesa del Santissimo Redentore** (Church of the Redeemer; Campo del SS Redentore 194; adult/reduced/child €3/1.50/free or with Chorus Pass; ⊕10am-5pm Mon-Sat; ⛴Redentore) was built by Palladio on the island of Giudecca to commemorate the end of the Great Plague in 1577.

At the entrance to the Grand Canal, the 17th-century **Chiesa di Santa Maria della Salute** (La Salute; Map p464; ✆041 241 10 18; www.seminariovenezia.it; Campo della Salute 1b; admission free, sacristy adult/reduced €3/1.50; ⊕9am-noon & 3-5.30pm; ⛴Salute) contains works by Tintoretto and Titian. Arguably the greatest of Venetian artists, Titian is buried in the **Basilica di Santa Maria Gloriosa dei Frari** (www.basilicadeifrari.it; Campo dei Frari, San Polo; adult/reduced/child €3/1.50/free or Chorus Pass; ⊕9am-6pm Mon-Sat, 1-6pm Sun), near his celebrated *Assunta* (Assumption; 1518).

The Lido   ISLAND
Unless you're on the Lido for the Venice Film Festival, the main reason to visit is to head to the beach. One of the best is **Alberoni**, in the south of the island.

The Lido is accessible by various *vaporetti*, including Nos 1 and 2 from San Zaccaria.

Islands   ISLAND
The island of **Murano** is the home of Venetian glass. Tour a factory for a behind-the-

scenes look at production or visit the **Museo del Vetro** (Glass Museum; ✆041 73 95 86; www. museovetro.visitmuve.it; Fondamenta Giustinian 8; adult/reduced €8/5.50; ⊕10am-6pm Apr-Oct, to 5pm Nov-Mar; ⛴Museo) near the Museo *vaporetto* stop. **Burano**, with its cheery pastel-coloured houses, is renowned for its lace. **Torcello**, the republic's original island settlement, was largely abandoned due to malaria and now counts no more than 80 residents. Its not-to-be-missed Byzantine cathedral, the **Basilica di Santa Maria Assunta** (Piazza Torcello; adult/reduced €5/4, incl museum €8/6; ⊕10.30am-6pm Mar-Oct, 10am-5pm Nov-Feb; ⛴Torcello), is Venice's oldest.

To get to Murano take *vaporetto* 4.1, 4.2 from San Zaccaria or Fondamente Nove. For Burano take No 12 from Fondamente Nove. Torcello is linked to Burano by *vaporetto* 9.

🏃 Activities

Be prepared to pay through the nose for that quintessential Venetian experience, a **gondola ride**. Official rates start at €80 or €100 from 7pm to 8am – these prices are per gondola (maximum six people). Additional time is charged in 20-minute increments (day/night €40/50). Haggling is unlikely to get you a reduction but you can save money by taking a gondola tour with the tourist office or a reliable tour operator.

☞ Tours

Between April and October, Venice's tourist offices offer a range of tours, including a 35-minute gondola ride (€28 per person), a 40-minute gondola serenade (€40), a 1½-hour city walking tour (€21) and a four-hour trip to Murano, Burano and Torcello (€20).

There are also private outfits running tours, including **TU.RI.VE** (✆041 241 34 22; www.turive.it), which organises itineraries exploring the city's Byzantine heritage (€36) and legends (€20).

TOILETS

Don't get caught short. You'll find public toilets at the train station, Piazzale Roma, Ponte dell'Accademia, Campo San Bartolomeo, and by the Giardini ex Reali near Piazza San Marco. To use them you'll need €1.50 in change.

ⓘ ADMISSION DISCOUNTS

Venice Card (☏041 24 24; www.venicecard.com; adult/junior €39.90/29.90; ☺call centre 8am-7.30pm), valid for seven days, gives free entry to Palazzo Ducale, 10 civic museums, the 16 churches covered by the Chorus Pass, as well as discounts on exhibitions, concerts and parking. Buy it at tourist offices and HelloVenezia booths.

Venice Card San Marco (☏041 24 24; www.venicecard.com; €24.90) provides free admission to Palazzo Ducale, three civic museums and three Chorus churches, plus discounts on exhibitions, concerts and parking. Available at tourist offices and HelloVenezia booths.

Rolling Venice Card (☏041 24 24; www.hellovenezia.com; 14-29yr €4) offers discounts on food, accommodation, shopping, transport and museums. Get it at tourist offices and HelloVenezia booths. You'll need ID.

Museum Pass (Musei Civici Pass; www.visitmuve.it; adult/reduced €20/14) is valid for single entry to 10 civic museums, or just the four museums around Piazza San Marco (adult/concession €16/8). Buy it at participating museums or online at www.visitmuve.it or www.veniceconnected.com.

Chorus Pass (☏041 275 04 62; www.chorusvenezia.org; adult/reduced/child €10/7/free) covers admission to 16 of Venice's major churches and is available online or at the churches.

✦✦ Festivals & Events

Carnevale   CARNIVAL
(www.carnevale.venezia.it) Venice's carnival celebrations take over town in the two-week run-up to Ash Wednesday. Costume parties are held in every *campo* (square) until a Grand Canal flotilla marks the end of festivities.

Palio delle Quattro
Antiche Repubbliche Marinare   BOAT RACE
(Regatta of the Four Ancient Maritime Republics) Venice, Amalfi, Genoa and Pisa take turns to host this historic regatta in early June. It will be in Venice in 2015.

Venice Biennale   ART
(www.labiennale.org) An important exhibition of international visual arts. It's held every odd-numbered year from June to November.

Festa del Redentore   RELIGIOUS
(Feast of the Redeemer; www.turismovenezia.it) Held on the third weekend in July; celebrations climax with a spectacular fireworks display.

Venice Architecture Biennale   ARCHITECTURE
(www.labiennale.org) This major architecture shindig is held every even-numbered year from late August to November.

Venice Film Festival   FILM
(Mostra del Cinema di Venezia; www.labiennale.org/en/cinema) Italy's top film fest comes to town in late August or early September at the Lido's Palazzo del Cinema.

Regata Storica   BOAT RACE
(www.comune.venezia.it) Costumed parades precede gondola races on the Grand Canal; held on the first Sunday in September.

🛏 Sleeping

Venice is Italy's most expensive city. It's always advisable to book ahead, especially at weekends, in May and September, and during Carnevale and other holidays.

SAN MARCO

TOP CHOICE Novecento   BOUTIQUE HOTEL €€
(Map p464; ☏041 241 37 65; www.novecento.biz; Calle del Dose 2683/84; d €140-300; ❄🗗; 🚇Santa Maria del Giglio) Sporting a bohemian-chic oriental look, the Novecento is a real charmer. Its nine individually decorated rooms feature Turkish kilim pillows, Fortuny draperies, carved bedsteads and immaculate designer bathrooms, while its garden is a gorgeous spot for a leisurely breakfast.

PalazzinaG   BOUTIQUE HOTEL €€€
(Map p464; ☏041 528 46 44; www.palazzinag.com; San Marco 3247; r from €288; ❄🗗) Luxury goes hand in hand with a fashionable Philippe Stark design at this Grand Canal boutique hotel. Common areas are lavishly decorated while the light-drenched rooms cleverly use mirrors and white furnishings to maximise space.

DORSODURO

Pensione La Calcina
HOTEL €€

(☑041 520 64 66; www.lacalcina.com; Fondamenta Zattere ai Gesuati 780, Dorsoduro 780; s €90-170, d €110-310; ❄️🌐) A historic landmark on the Giudecca canalfront, this centuries-old hotel exudes character. Author John Ruskin stayed here in 1877 (in room 2) and there's an air of quiet gentility about the sunny antique-clad rooms. Out front, the elegant bar/restaurant is a prime spot for a relaxed waterfront meal.

SAN POLO & SANTA CROCE

TOP CHOICE Oltre il Giardino
BOUTIQUE HOTEL €€

(Map p468; ☑041 275 00 15; www.oltreilgiardino -venezia.com; Fondamenta Contarini, San Polo 2542; d incl breakfast €180-250; ❄️@; 🚤San Tomà) Once home to Alma Mahler, the composer's widow, this gorgeous hotel is hidden behind a walled garden full of pomegranate, olive and magnolia trees. Inside, six sharply designed rooms combine mod cons and deftly chosen antiques to stylish effect.

Ca' Angeli
BOUTIQUE HOTEL €€

(☑041 523 24 80; www.caangeli.it; Calle del Traghetto de la Madonnetta 1434, San Polo; d incl breakfast €70-215; ❄️🌐; 🚤San Silvestro) An elegant choice overlooking the Grand Canal, Ca' Angeli offers tastefully decorated rooms and suites with canal views. Staff are friendly, the organic breakfast is excellent, and wi-fi is free if you book through the hotel's website.

Pensione Guerrato
INN €€

(Map p468; ☑041 528 59 27; www.pensioneguerra to.it; Calle Drio la Scimia 240a, San Polo; d/tr/q incl breakfast €145/165/185; ❄️🌐; 🚤Rialto Mercato) Housed in a 13th-century tower near the Rialto market, this hospitable *pensione* has comfortable, good-sized rooms on several floors (no lift) and friendly, helpful owners. Check the website for low-season offers.

Hotel Alex
PENSION €

(Map p468; ☑041 523 13 41; www.hotelalexinvenice. com; Rio Terà, San Polo 2606; d €60-124, tr €80-150, q €100-190, without bathroom s €35-60, d €40-94, tr €60-120, q €80-144; 🌐; 🚤San Tomà) In a quiet spot near Campo dei Frari, no-frills Alex offers 11 simple but decent-sized rooms, some of which come with a balcony overlooking two canals.

L'Imbarcadero
HOSTEL €

(☑392 584 06 00; www.hostelvenice.net; cnr Imbarcadero Riva de Biasio & Calle Zen, Santa Croce; dm from €27, r per person €32-40; 🌐) This is a popular hostel with decent mixed and female-only dorms and private rooms with shared bathrooms. It's not the easiest place to find, although only about five minutes' walk from the train station.

CANNAREGIO

Giardino dei Melograni
GUESTHOUSE €€

(☑041 822 61 31; www.pardesrimonim.net; Ghetto Nuovo, Cannaregio 2873/c; s €70-100, d €80-160, tr €110-190, q €140-220; ❄️🌐) Run by Venice's Jewish community, the 'Garden of Pomegranates' is a sparkling new kosher residence. It's wonderfully located on the tranquil Campo Ghetto Nuovo and offers 14 modern white-grey rooms and a courtyard restaurant serving Jewish and Venetian cuisine (€25 for a meal or €30 on Friday night and Saturday lunch).

Hotel Bernardi
HOTEL €

(Map p468; ☑041 522 72 57; www.hotelbernardi. com; SS Apostoli Calle dell'Oca 4366; s €48-72, d €57-90, f €75-130, without bathroom s €25-32, d €45-62; ❄️🌐) Just off Venice's main drag, this excellent budget option has rooms spread over two sites – this, the main hotel, and a nearby annexe. Rooms come in various shapes and sizes but the general look is classic Venetian with chandeliers, wooden beams, rugs and antiques.

CASTELLO

Foresteria Valdese
HOSTEL €

(Palazzo Cavagnis; ☑041 528 67 97; www.foresteri-avenezia.it; Castello 5170; dm €30-35, d €70-140, q €95-190; 🚤Ospedale, San Zaccaria) One of the cheapest sleeps in the *centro storico*, this hostel is run by the Waldensian church and housed in a rambling old palace with 18th-century frescos, canal views and a range of rooms. Adding to the deal are free music concerts, usually held at 6pm on Wednesdays.

Ca' Valeri
B&B €€

(☑041 241 15 30; www.locandacavaleri.com; Ramo Corazzieri 3845; r €69-280, ste €79-280; ❄️🌐) To escape the teeming hordes, search out this far-flung retreat whose classically decorated rooms provide a lovely base for exploring the nearby Arsenale.

Sestiere di San Marco

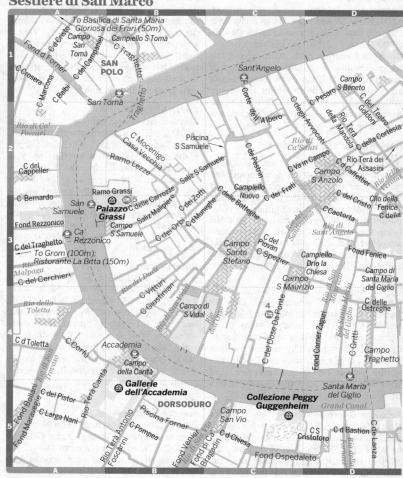

Sestiere di San Marco

◎ Top Sights

Basilica di San Marco	H2
Collezione Peggy Guggenheim	C5
Gallerie dell'Accademia	B5
Palazzo Ducale	H3
Palazzo Grassi	B3
Piazza San Marco	G3
Ponte dei Sospiri	H3
Punta della Dogana	F5

◎ Sights

1 Basilica di Santa Maria della Salute	E5

2 Campanile	G3
3 Torre dell'Orologio	G2

🛏 Sleeping

4 Novecento	C4
5 PalazzinaG	B3

🍷 Drinking

6 Caffè Florian	G3
7 Harry's Bar	F4

✦ Entertainment

8 Teatro La Fenice	E3

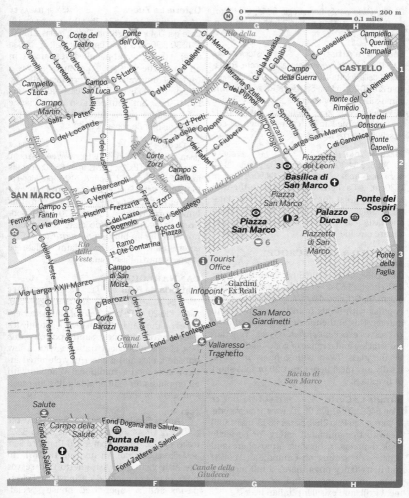

🍴 Eating

Venetian specialities include *risi e bisi* (pea soup thickened with rice) and *sarde in saor* (fried sardines marinated in vinegar and onions).

DORSODURO

Ristorante La Bitta
RISTORANTE €€

(📞041 523 05 31; Calle Lunga San Barnaba 2753a; meals €30-40; ⏰dinner Mon-Sat; 🚤Ca' Rezzonico) With its woody bottle-lined interior and attractive internal courtyard, this is a lovely place to enjoy rustic dishes such as *tagliolini con verdure e zenzero* (thin pasta ribbons with vegetables and ginger) and *galletto al peperone* (chicken with peppers). Cash only.

Grom
GELATERIA €

(📞041 099 17 51; www.grom.it; Campo San Barnaba 2461; gelati €2.50-4; ⏰11am-midnight Sun-Thu, to 1am Fri & Sat; ♿; 🚤Ca' Rezzonico) An ice cream from this Slow Food–rated *galeteria* is the perfect pick-me-up. Seasonal flavours are made with top ingredients from around the world – lemons and almonds from Sicily, chocolate from South America, cinnamon from Sri Lanka. There's a second

Grom (Map p468; Cannaregio 3844, Ca' d'Oro) on the main station to San Marco strip near Ca' d'Oro.

Enoteca Ai Artisti RISTORANTE €€€

(☎041 523 89 44; www.enotecaartisti.com; Fondamenta della Toletta 1169a; meals €40-50; ◷noon-4pm & 6.30-10pm Mon-Sat; ⛴Ca' Rezzonico) This canal-side wine bar serves a serious choice of wines by the glass, delicious cheese platters and refined main courses such as sea bass with herbs and salad.

Pizza Al Volo PIZZERIA €

(☎041 522 54 30; Campo Santa Margherita 2944; pizza slices from €2, small pizzas €4.50-7; ◷noon-11.30pm; ⛴Ca' Rezzonico) A hole-in-the-wall takeaway great for a quick lunch or late-night filler. Grab a slice – they're cheap and tasty – and munch away on the vibrant square outside.

SAN POLO & SANTA CROCE

All'Arco VENETIAN €

(Map p468; ☎041 520 56 66; Calle dell'Ochialer 436; cicheti €1.50-4; ◷8am-3.30pm Mon-Sat, plus 6-9pm Apr-Oct, closed Jul & Aug; ⛴Rialto Mercato) Popular with locals from the nearby Rialto market, this authentic neighbourhood *osteria* serves excellent *cicheti* (typical Venetian bar snacks) and a range of good-quality wine by the glass. Even with copious *prosecco*, hardly any meal here tops €20 or falls short of five stars.

Birraria La Corte PIZZERIA, RISTORANTE €€

(Map p468; ☎041 275 05 70; www.birrarialacorte. it; Campo San Polo 2168; pizzas €8-13, mains €15) Head to this animated eatery for perfectly cooked pizzas, a buzzing atmosphere and square-side seating on Campo San Polo. If you don't fancy pizza there's a full menu of pastas and mains, including a mammoth meat grill, and excellent Italian beers.

Vecio Fritolin VENETIAN €€€

(Map p468; ☎041 522 28 81; www.veciofritolin.it; Calle della Regina 2262, Santa Croce; mains €25, tasting menu €55; ◷noon-2.30pm & 7-10.30pm Wed-Sun, 7-10.30pm Tue; ⛴San Stae) Traditionally a *fritolin* was an eatery where diners sat at a communal table and tucked into fried fish. This is the modern equivalent, if considerably smarter and more sophisticated. The menu includes meat and vegetable dishes, but the headline act is the top-quality seafood, sourced daily from the nearby Rialto market.

Osteria La Zucca MODERN ITALIAN €€

(Map p468; ☎041 524 15 70; www.lazucca.it; Calle del Tintor 1762, Santa Croce; mains €10-20; ◷12.30-2.30pm & 7-10.30pm Mon-Sat; ⚲; ⛴San Stae) A snug wood-panelled restaurant in an out-of-the-way spot, La Zucca serves a range of innovative Mediterranean dishes. The emphasis is on fresh, seasonal vegetarian dishes, but you can also order classic meat dishes such as duck with green apple or English-style roast beef.

Ae Oche PIZZERIA €

(Map p468; ☎041 524 11 61; www.aeoche.com; Calle del Tentor 1552a; pizzas from €5.50, aperitifs from €2.50; ◷noon-2.30pm & 7-10.30pm Mon-Fri, to 11.30pm Sat & Sun; ⛴San Stae) Students and budget-minded foodies converge on this bubbly pizzeria for a choice of 70-plus wood-fired pizzas and well-priced ale. Keep things hot with the lip-buzzing *mangiafuoco* (fire-eater) made with spicy salami, Calabrese peppers and Tabasco sauce.

CANNAREGIO

Trattoria da Bepi VENETIAN €€

(Map p468; ☎041 528 50 31; Cannaregio 4550; mains €10-20; ◷Fri-Wed) One of the better eateries on the touristy main drag – actually it's a few metres off it near Santi Apostoli – this is a classic old-school trattoria with a few outside tables and a cheerfully cluttered interior. The food is traditional Venetian with an emphasis on seafood, including an excellent *sarde in saor*.

Anice Stellato VENETIAN €€€

(☎041 72 07 44; Fondamenta della Sensa 3272; mains €18-23; ◷noon-2pm & 7.30-11pm Wed-Sun; ⛴Madonna dell'Orto) An inviting trattoria in the little-visited Jewish ghetto that serves huge plates of seafood antipasti, delicious pastas and a super-sized house speciality of fried fish with polenta. Book a table outside by the boats or share a communal table inside.

Fiaschetteria Toscana RISTORANTE €€€

(Map p468; ☎041 528 52 81; Salizada San Giovanni Grisostomo 5719; mains €22-40, tasting menu €48; ◷lunch & dinner Thu-Mon, dinner Wed; ⛴Ca' d'Oro) This formal, old-fashioned restaurant specialises in classic local cuisine and fresh lagoon seafood, but varies the formula with a few Tuscan triumphs, including delectable Chianina-beef steaks. Tuscan wines also feature on the mighty 600-label wine list.

Da Marisa
TRATTORIA €€

(☑041 72 02 11; Fondamenta di San Giobbe 652b; lunch set price €15, dinner €35-40; ☺lunch daily, dinner Tue & Thu-Sat) Search out this modest family-run trattoria for a taste of authentic Venetian home cooking and sunset views over the lagoon. Expect brusque service and a fixed daily menu, which is mostly meat but sometimes seafood. Reservations recommended. Cash only.

Drinking

Al Mercà
WINE BAR

(Map p468; ☑393 992 47 81; Campo Cesare Battisti 213; ☺9.30am-2.30pm & 6-9pm Mon-Sat; ⛴Rialto-Mercato) This hole-in-the-wall bar draws daily crowds for its excellent snacks (meatballs and mini-panini from €1.50) and keenly priced drinks, including top-notch *prosecco* and DOC wines by the glass (from €2).

TOP CHOICE Cantina Do Spade
PUB

(Map p468; ☑041 521 05 83; www.cantinadospade. it; Calle delle Do Spade 860; ☺10am-3pm & 6-10pm) A warm, woody neighbourhood *osteria* great for a relaxed glass of local wine or a double-malt beer. Keep hunger at bay by snacking on *cicheti* (from €1) such as *sarde fritte* (fried sardines), anchovies and meatballs.

Muro Venezia
BAR

(Map p468; www.murovinoecucina.it; Campo Cesare Battisti, San Polo 222; ☺9am-3pm & 4pm-2am Mon-Sat, 4pm-2am Sun) The centre of a happening nightlife scene in the market squares of the Rialto, Muro is the watering hole of choice for young locals, who spill out into the square with their drinks. Come at Saturday lunch to enjoy a plate of fried fish and glass of Chardonnay for €8.

Il Caffè Rosso
CAFE, BAR

(☑041 528 79 98; Campo Santa Margherita 2963; ☺7am-1am Mon-Sat; ⛴Ca' Rezzonico) The most popular of the bars and cafes on vibrant Campo Santa Margherita. Its sunny piazza seating fills quickly with students drawn by the laid-back buzz and 6pm Spritz cocktails.

Harry's Bar
BAR

(Map p464; ☑041 528 57 77; Calle Vallaresso 1323; cocktails €12-22; ☺10.30am-11pm; ⛴San Marco) To try a Bellini (white peach pulp and *prosecco*) at the bar that invented them is to follow in prestigious footsteps – Ernest Hemingway, Charlie Chaplin and Orson Welles have all drunk here, and Woody Allen likes to pop in when in town.

Ancorà
WINE BAR

(Map p468; ☑041 520 70 66; www.ancoravenezia. it; San Polo 120, Fabbriche Vecchie; ☺10am-2am; ⛴Rialto) Jazz, Grand Canal views, *prosecco*, raw oysters and modern romance are house specialities at this chic cocktail bar tucked under the porticos of the Rialto's waterfront warehouses.

TOP CHOICE Caffè Florian
CAFE

(Map p464; ☑041 520 56 41; www.caffeflorian.com; Piazza San Marco 56/59; drinks €6.50-16; ☺10am-midnight Thu-Tue; ⛴San Marco) With its historic pedigree (it opened in 1720), house orchestra and eye-watering prices (a cappuccino costs €9), Venice's most celebrated cafe is everything you'd expect it be. Byron, Goethe and Rousseau are among the luminaries who have sipped here.

⭐ Entertainment

Upcoming events are listed in the free *Shows & Events* guide, available at tourist offices, and at www.veneziadavivere.com. Tickets for most events are sold at **HelloVenezia ticket outlets** (☑041 24 24; www.hellovenezia. it) in front of the train station, at Piazzale Roma and near key *vaporetto* stops.

Teatro La Fenice
OPERA

(Map p464; ☑041 78 65 11; www.teatrolafenice.it; Campo San Fantin 1965; adult/reduced €8.50/6, opera tickets from €40; ☺tours 9.30am-6pm) One of Italy's top opera houses, La Fenice hosts a year-round program of opera, ballet and classical music. You can also visit on a guided tour between 9.30am and 6pm most days – check www.festfenice.com for details.

ℹ️ Information

Emergency
Police Station (☑041 270 55 11; Castello 5053, Fondamenta di San Lorenzo)

Medical Services
Ospedale Civile (☑041 529 41 11; Campo SS Giovanni e Paolo 6777)

Tourist Information
Pick up the free *Shows & Events* guide at tourist offices. It contains comprehensive city listings and up-to-date details of exhibitions and events. The tourist offices also sell a handy map of the city (€2.50).

Tourist Office (Azienda di Promozione Turistica; ☑041 529 87 11; www.turismovenezia.it) Marco Polo (Marco Polo airport, arrivals hall; ☺9am-8pm); Piazzale Roma (Piazzale Roma, ground fl, multistorey car park; ☺9.30am-

Sestiere di San Polo

ITALY VENICE

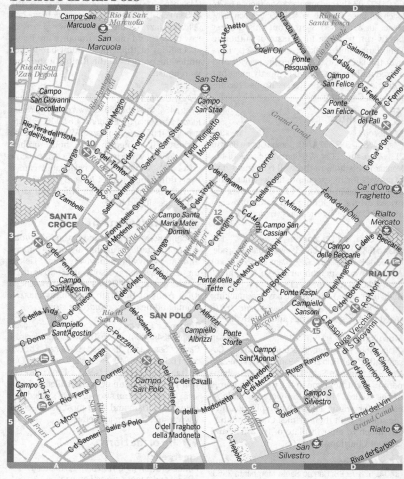

Sestiere di San Polo

Sleeping
1 Hotel Alex A5
2 Hotel Bernardi... E2
3 Oltre il Giardino A4
4 Pensione Guerrato D3

Eating
5 Ae Oche A3
6 All'Arco D4
7 Birraria La Corte B4
8 Fiaschetteria Toscana........................... F3

9 Grom D2
10 Osteria La Zucca A2
11 Trattoria da Bepi................................... F2
12 Vecio Fritolin.. C3

Drinking
13 Al Mercà E4
14 Ancorà E4
15 Cantina Do Spade................................. D4
16 Muro Venezia.. E3

ITALY VENICE

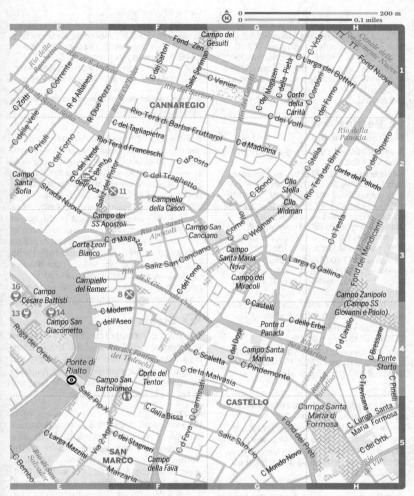

2.30pm; 🚉Santa Chiara); Piazza San Marco (Piazza San Marco 71f; ⊘9am-7pm; 🚉San Marco); Stazione di Santa Lucia (Stazione di Santa Lucia; ⊘9am-7pm Nov-Mar, 1.30-7pm Apr-Oct; 🚉Ferrovia Santa Lucia); Venice Pavilion (📞041 529 87 11; fax 041 523 03 99; Venice Pavilion, next to the Giardini Ex Reali, near St Mark's Square; ⊘9am-6pm)

ⓘ Getting There & Away

Air

Most flights land at **Marco Polo airport** (📞041 260 92 60; www.veniceairport.it), 12km outside Venice. Ryanair flies to **Treviso airport** (📞0422

31 51 11; www.trevisoairport.it; Via Noalese 63), about 30km away.

Boat

Venezia Lines (📞041 882 11 01; www.venezia-lines.com) operates high-speed boats to/from several ports in Croatia between mid-April and early October, including Pola (€69 to €74).

Bus

ACTV (Azienda del Consorzio Trasporti Veneziano; 📞041 24 24; www.actv.it) buses service surrounding areas, including Mestre, Padua and Treviso. Tickets and information are available at the bus station in Piazzale Roma.

Train

Venice's Stazione di Santa Lucia is directly linked by regional trains to Padua (€3.50, one hour, every 20 minutes) and Verona (€7.40 to €19, 50 minutes to 2¼ hours, half-hourly), and has fast services to/from Bologna, Milan, Rome and Florence. International trains run to/from points in France, Germany, Austria and Switzerland.

Getting Around

To/From the Airport

To get to/from Marco Polo airport there are several options.

Alilaguna (041 240 17 01; www.alilaguna.com; Marco Polo airport) operates three fast-ferry lines (€15/27 one-way/return, approximately half-hourly) – the *Arancio* (Orange) line goes to Piazza San Marco via Rialto and the Grand Canal; the *Blu* (Blue) line stops off at Murano, the Lido and San Marco; and the *Rosso* (Red) line runs to Murano and the Lido.

There is an **ATVO** (Azienda Trasporti Veneto Orientale; 0421 59 46 71; www.atvo.it) shuttle bus to/from Piazzale Roma (€6/11 one-way/return, 20 minutes, half-hourly).

By bus, take **ACTV** (www.actv.it) bus 5 (€6/11 one-way/return, 25 minutes, half-hourly).

Water taxis to/from the train station cost €100 for up to five passengers.

For Treviso airport, there's an ATVO shuttle bus (one-way/return €7/13, 70 minutes, six times daily) to/from Piazzale Roma.

Boat

The city's main mode of public transport is the *vaporetto*. Useful routes include:

1 From Piazzale Roma to the train station and down the Grand Canal to San Marco and the Lido.

2 From San Zaccaria (near San Marco) to the Lido via Giudecca, Piazzale Roma, the train station and Rialto.

4.1 To/from Murano via Fondamente Nove, the train station, Piazzale Roma, Giudecca and San Zaccaria.

9 From Burano to Torcello and vice versa.

Tickets, available from ACTV and HelloVenezia booths at the major *vaporetti* stops, are expensive: €7 for a single trip; €18 for 12 hours; €20 for 24 hours; €25 for 36 hours; €30 for two days; €35 for three days; €50 for seven days.

There are significant discounts for holders of the Rolling Venice Card and all tickets are cheaper if you purchase them online at www.veniceconnected.com.

The poor man's gondola, *traghetti* (€2 per crossing), are used to cross the Grand Canal where there's no nearby bridge.

Car & Motorcycle

Vehicles must be parked on Tronchetto or at Piazzale Roma (cars are allowed on the Lido – take ferry 17 from Tronchetto). The car parks cost €24 to €26 per day for a small car, €27 to €29 for a big car. It's generally cheaper to leave your wheels in Mestre and get a train over to Venice.

Bologna

POP 380,200

Boasting a boisterous bonhomie rare in Italy's reserved north, Bologna is one of Italy's great unsung destinations. Its medieval centre is an eye-catching ensemble of red-brick *palazzi*, Renaissance towers and 40km of arcaded porticos, and there are enough sights to excite without exhausting. A university town since 1088 (Europe's oldest), it is also one of Italy's foremost foodie destinations, home to the eponymous bolognese sauce *(ragù)* as well as *tortellini* (pasta pockets stuffed with meat), lasagne and *mortadella* (aka baloney or Bologna sausage). Trattorias and restaurants abound and the large student population ensures a high-spirited nightlife.

Sights

The city has recently introduced a **Bologna Welcome Card** (€20), available in tourist offices, which gives free entrance to city-run museums, public transport for 24 hours or two tickets for the airport shuttle bus, and discounts in shops and restaurants.

Piazza Maggiore PIAZZA

Pedestrianised Piazza Maggiore is Bologna's showpiece square. Overlooking it are several impressive Renaissance *palazzi* and the Gothic **Basilica di San Petronio** (Piazza Maggiore; 8am-1pm & 3-6pm), the world's fifth-largest church. Work began on the basilica, which is dedicated to Petronius, the city's patron saint, in 1390, but it was never finished and still today the facade is incomplete.

To the basilica's west, **Palazzo Comunale** (Bologna's Town Hall) is home to the city's art collection, the **Collezioni Comunali d'Arte** (051 20 36 29; Palazzo Comunale; adult/reduced/child €5/3/free; 9am-6.30pm Tue-Fri, 10am-6.30pm Sat & Sun), and the **Museo Morandi** (tel, info 051 20 36 29; www.mambo-bologna.org/museomorandi; Palazzo Comunale; adult/reduced €6/4; 11am-6pm Tue-Fri, 11am-8pm Sat & Sun) dedicated to the work of Giorgio Morandi. At the time of research the Museo Morandi was about to be temporarily transferred to the MAMbo to allow for repair work.

Adjacent to the square, Piazza del Nettuno is named after the 16th-century **Fontana del Nettuno** (Neptune's Fountain), featuring an impressively muscled Neptune.

Le Due Torri
TOWER

(Torre degli Asinelli admission €3; ⊙Torre degli Asinelli 9am-6pm, to 5pm Oct-May) Standing sentinel over Piazza di Porta Ravegnana are Bologna's two leaning towers. You can climb the taller of the two, the 97.6m-high **Torre degli Asinelli**, which was built between 1109 and 1119. The neighbouring 48m-high **Torre Garisenda** is sensibly out of bounds given its drunken 3.2m tilt.

Basilica di San Domenico
CHURCH

(Piazza San Domenico 13; ⊙9.30am-12.30pm & 3.30-6.30pm Mon-Fri, to 5.30pm Sat & Sun) This 13th-century church is noteworthy for the elaborate sarcophagus of San Domenico, founder of the Dominican order. The tomb stands in the **Cappella di San Domenico**, which was designed by Nicola Pisano and later added to by Michelangelo.

Museo Civico Archeologico
MUSEUM

(Via dell'Archiginnasio 2; adult/reduced/child €5/3/free; ⊙9am-3pm Tue-Fri, 10am-6.30pm Sat & Sun) Impressive in its breadth of historical coverage, this museum displays well-documented Egyptian and Roman artefacts along with one of Italy's best Etruscan collections.

MAMbo
MUSEUM

(Museo d'Arte Moderna di Bologna; www.mambo-bologna-org; Via Don Minzoni 14; adult/reduced/child €6/4/free; ⊙noon-6pm Tue, Wed & Fri, to 10pm Thu, to 8pm Sat & Sun) An excellent modern-art museum in a converted bakery.

🛏 Sleeping

Accommodation is largely geared to the business market so there are few budget options. Avoid the busy spring and autumn trade fairs when prices skyrocket and reservations are essential.

Il Convento dei Fiori di Seta
BOUTIQUE HOTEL €€€

(☑051 27 20 39; www.silkflowersnunnery.com; Via Orfeo 34; r €140-420, ste €250-520; ❄️@📶) This seductive boutique hotel is a model of sophisticated design. Housed in a 15th-century convent, it features contemporary furniture juxtaposed against exposed brick walls and religious frescos, Mapplethorpe-inspired flower motives and mosaic-tiled bathrooms.

Albergo delle Drapperie
HOTEL €

(☑051 22 39 55; www.albergodrapperie.com; Via delle Drapperie 5; s €60-70, d €75-85; ❄️📶) Bed down in the heart of the atmospheric Quadrilatero district at this welcoming three-star. Rooms, which all differ slightly, are attractive with wood-beamed ceilings, wrought-iron beds and the occasional brick arch. Breakfast costs €5 extra and wi-fi €2. At a second site, the **Residence delle Drapperie** (☑051 22 39 55; www.residencedrapperie.com; Via Galliera 48; apt from €55) has 10 mini-apartments for stays of two nights or more.

Hotel University Bologna
HOTEL €€

(☑051 22 97 13; www.hoteluniversitybologna.com; Via Mentana 7; d €70-250; ❄️@📶) A low-key three-star offering value for money and an excellent location in the orange-hued university district. There are few frills but the functionally furnished rooms are comfortable and it's great to be in such a lively neighbourhood.

Albergo Panorama
PENSION €

(☑051 22 18 02; www.hotelpanoramabologna.it; Via Livraghi 1, 4th fl; d €65-90, without bathroom s €40-60, d €55-70, tr €70-90, q €90-120; ❄️📶) A budget bolthole within easy walking distance of Piazza Maggiore, this is a cheerful old-school *pensione* with simple, spacious rooms, lovely rooftop views, and flowers in the hallway. Note that air-con is only in rooms overlooking the street. Cash only.

🍴 Eating

Foodie hot spots include the university district northeast of Via Rizzoli and the Quadrilatero district east of Piazza Maggiore.

Osteria de' Poeti
RISTORANTE €€

(www.osteriadepoeti.com; Via de' Poeti 1b; mains €12; ⊙closed dinner Mon & Sun) In the wine cellar of a 14th-century *palazzo*, this historic eatery is a bastion of old-style service and classic local cuisine. Take a table by the stone fireplace and enjoy warming regional staples such as *tortellini in brodo di carne* (in a meat broth). Evenings feature frequent live music.

Il Saraceno
RISTORANTE €€

(☑051 23 66 28; www.ristorantesaracenobologna.com; Via Calcavinazzi 2; pizzas from €5, mains €12-20) Popular with lunching locals, this is a good all-purpose eatery just off central Via Ugo Basso. Tables are on a small outdoor terrace or in a smart white-grey interior, and the menu covers all bases, from steak to seafood, pasta to pizza.

Trattoria del Rosso
TRATTORIA €

(☑051 23 67 30; www.trattoriadelrosso.com; Via A Righi 30; daily menu €10, mains €7.50-10) The oldest trattoria in town is the perfect place for a cheap lunchtime fill-up. Sit down to filling pastas and honest journeyman's fare, cooked simply and served fast.

La Sorbetteria Castiglione
GELATERIA €

(www.lasorbetteria.it; Via Castiglione 44; ☺8.30am-midnight Tue-Sat, 9am-11.30pm Sun) A walk out of the centre, this much-vaunted *gelateria* produces superb ice cream, as well as *granite* (crushed ice drinks), *frappè* (milk shakes) and smoothies.

Drinking & Entertainment

Bologna's nightlife is one of the most vibrant in the country, with a huge number of bars, cafes and clubs. Thirsty students congregate on and around Piazza Verdi, while the fashionable Quadrilatero district hosts a dressier, more upmarket scene.

Café de Paris
BAR

(Piazza del Francia 1c; ☺7.30am-3am Mon-Sat, 4pm-3am Sun) Modish bar with daily aperitifs between 7.30pm and 9.30pm.

La Scuderia
BAR, CAFE

(www.lascuderia.bo.it; Piazza Verdi 2; ☺8am-2.30am; ☺) A popular student hang-out housed in medieval stables. *Aperitivi* and regular live music.

Caffè degli Orefici
CAFE

(Via Orefici 6; ☺Mon-Sat) A modern cafe next to a historic coffee shop.

Cantina Bentivoglio
JAZZ

(www.cantinabentivoglio.it; Via Mascarella 4b; ☺8pm-2am) Bologna's top jazz joint is part wine bar (choose from over 500 labels), part restaurant (the set-price menu costs €30) and part concert venue (there's live music nightly).

Cassero
CLUB

(www.cassero.it; Via Don Minzoni 18) Saturday and Wednesday are the big nights at this legendary gay and lesbian (but not only) club, home of Italy's Arcigay organisation.

ℹ Information

HOSPITAL Ospedale Maggiore (☑051 647 81 11; Largo Nigrisoli 2)

TOURIST INFORMATION Bologna (www.bolognawelcome.com), Airport (☑051 647 21 13; ☺9am-7pm Mon-Sat, to 4pm Sun); Piazza Maggiore (☑051 23 96 60; Piazza Maggiore 1/e; ☺9am-7pm Mon-Sat, 10am-5pm Sun)

ℹ Getting There & Around

Air

European and domestic flights serve **Guglielmo Marconi airport** (☑051 647 96 15; www.bologna-airport.it), 6km northwest of the city. From the airport, an Aerobus shuttle (€6, 30 minutes, every 15 to 30 minutes) connects with the main train station; tickets can be bought on board.

Bus

National and international coaches depart from the bus station on Piazza XX Settembre. However, for most destinations the train is a better bet.

Bologna's efficient bus system is run by **ATC** (www.atc.bo.it). To get to the centre from the train station take bus A, 25 or 30 (€1.20).

Train

Bologna is a major rail hub. From the central train station on Piazza delle Medaglie d'Oro, fast trains run to Venice (€30, 1½ hours, hourly), Florence (€24 to €36, 40 minutes, half-hourly), Rome (€56 to €81, 2½ hours, half-hourly) and Milan (€32 to €40, one to two hours, hourly).

Ravenna
POP 158,700

Easily accessible from Bologna, and worth a day trip at the very least, the refined town of Ravenna is famous for its remarkable Early Christian mosaics. These Unesco-listed treasures, relics of the town's golden age as capital of the Western Roman and Byzantine Empires, have been impressing visitors ever since the 13th century when Dante described them in his *Divine Comedy* (much of which was written here).

Adding to the town's cultural credentials is the **Ravenna Festival** (www.ravennafestival.org), which sees classical music concerts staged across town in June and July.

⊙ Sights

Mosaics
MOSAICS

Ravenna's mosaics are spread over several sites in and around town. The five main ones – Basilica di San Vitale, Mausoleo di Galla Placida, Basilica di Sant'Appollinare Nuovo, Museo Arcivescovile and Battistero Neoniano – are covered by a single ticket (adult/reduced/child €9.50/8.50/free) which is available at any of the five locations.

On the northern edge of the *centro storico*, the sombre exterior of the 6th-century **Basilica di San Vitale** (Via Fiandrini, entrance on Via San Vitale; ☺9am-7pm Apr-Sep, to 5.30pm Mar & Oct, 9.30am-5pm Nov-Feb) hides a dazzling interior with mosaics depicting Old Testament scenes. In the same complex, the small **Mausoleo di Galla Placidia** (Via Fiandrini; ⊙9am-7pm Apr-Sep, to 5.30pm Mar & Oct, 9.30am-5pm Nov-Feb) contains the city's oldest mosaics, dating to around AD 430. Note that between March and mid-September there's a €2 booking fee for the Mausoleum.

Adjoining Ravenna's unremarkable cathedral, the **Museo Arcivescovile** (Piazza Arcivescovado; ⊙9am-7pm Apr-Sep, 9.30am-5.30pm Oct & Mar, 10am-5pm Nov-Feb) boasts an exquisite 6th-century ivory throne, while next door in the **Battistero Neoniano** (Piazza del Duomo; ⊙9am-7pm Apr-Sep, 9.30am-5.30pm Mar & Oct, 10am-5pm Nov-Feb) the baptism of Christ and the apostles is represented in the domed roof mosaics. To the east, the **Basilica di Sant'Apollinare Nuovo** (Via di Roma; ⊙9am-7pm Apr-Sep, 9.30am-5.30pm Mar & Oct, 10am-5pm Nov-Feb) boasts, among other things, a superb mosaic depicting a procession of martyrs headed towards Christ and his apostles.

Five kilometres southeast of town, the apse mosaic of the **Basilica di Sant'Apollinare in Classe** (Via Romea Sud; adult/reduced/child €5/2.50/free; ⊙8.30am-7.30pm Mon-Sat, 1-7.30pm Sun) is a must-see. Take bus 4 (€1.20) from Piazza Caduti per la Libertà.

FREE **Dante's Tomb** MAUSOLEUM

(Via Dante Alighieri 9; admission free; ⊙9.30am-6.30pm) Italy's greatest literary hero, Dante Alighieri (1265–1321), spent the last 20 years of his life in Ravenna after he was expelled from his hometown, Florence, in 1302. As a perpetual act of penance, Florence still supplies the oil for the lamp that burns continuously in his tomb.

🛏 Sleeping & Eating

Ostello Galletti Abbiosi HOSTEL €

(☑0544 3 13 13; www.galletti.ra.it; Via Roma 140; s €50, d €70-140; P🅿︎@🅰︎) More hotel than hostel, this excellent budget option occupies an aristocratic 18th-century *palazzo*. As a result, rooms are spacious and high-ceilinged, there's a monumental staircase, a handsome internal courtyard and even an on-site chapel.

Hotel Sant'Andrea HOTEL €€

(☑0544 21 55 64; www.santandreahotel.com; Via Cattaneo 33; s €50-100, d €80-180; 🅰︎@🅰︎) In the *centro storico*, this charming three-star provides elegant accommodation in a converted convent. A grand wooden staircase leads up to smart, carpeted rooms overlooking a lawned garden where breakfast is served in spring and summer.

La Gardela TRATTORIA €

(☑0544 21 71 47; Via Ponte Marino 3; mains €8-16, fixed-price menu €15/25; ⊙closed Thu) A cheerful, unpretentious place that gives you exactly what you want from an Italian trattoria – large helpings of hearty home-cooked food, a jovial, warm atmosphere and efficient service. Particularly good value is the €15 set menu, ideal for lunch.

Ca' de Vèn RISTORANTE €€

(☑0544 3 01 63; Via Corrado Ricci 24; mains €12-18; ⊙Tue-Sun) Yes, it's touristy, but this cavernous *enoteca*-cum-restaurant is still a memorable spot for a meal and glass of wine. Housed in a 15th-century *palazzo* with frescoed domes and vaulted brick ceilings, it offers a full menu of regional specialities, cheese and *piadine* (sandwiches made with a local flatbread), alongside an encyclopaedic wine list.

❶ Information

Information is available online at www.turismo.ravenna.it and at three tourist offices – the **main office** (☑0544 3 54 04; Via Salara 8; ⊙8.30am-7pm Mon-Sat, 10am-6pm Sun) and branches at **Teodorico** (☑0544 45 15 39; Via delle Industrie 14; ⊙9.30am-12.30pm & 3.30-6.30pm) and **Classe** (☑0544 47 36 61; Via Romea Sud 266, Classe; ⊙9.30am-12.30pm & 3.30-6.30pm).

❶ Getting There & Around

Regional trains run to/from Bologna (€6.80, 1½ hours, 14 daily) and destinations on the east coast.

In town, cycling is popular. The main tourist office runs a free bike-hire service to visitors aged 18 or over (take ID).

TUSCANY

Tuscany is one of those places that well and truly lives up to its hype. The fabled landscape of rolling, vine-covered hills dotted with cypress trees and stone villas has long been considered the embodiment of rural chic, and its historically intact cities are home to a significant portfolio of the world's medieval and Renaissance art. Some people never venture beyond Florence, but those who do are inevitably enchanted by their visits to hilltop towns, medieval monasteries, picturesque wine estates and some of Italy's best restaurants.

WORTH A TRIP

THE DOLOMITES

A Unesco Natural Heritage site since 2009, the Dolomites stretch across the northern regions of **Trentino-Alto Adige** and the **Veneto**. Their stabbing sawtooth peaks and vertiginous walls provide thrilling scenery and superb sport.

Ski resorts abound, offering downhill and cross-country skiing as well as snowboarding and other winter sports. Facilities are generally excellent and accommodation is widely available. Ski passes cover either single resorts or a combination of slopes – the most comprehensive is the **Dolomiti Superski pass** (www.dolomitisuperski.com; high season 3-/6-day pass €144/254) which accesses 1220km of runs in 12 valleys. Popular ski destinations include **Cortina d'Ampezzo**, one of Italy's most fashionable, expensive and well-equipped resorts; **Canazei** in the **Val di Fassa**; and **Ortisei**, **Santa Cristina** and **Selva Gardena** in the **Val Gardena**.

Hiking opportunities run the gamut from kid-friendly strolls to hard-core mountain treks. Trails are well marked with numbers on red-and-white bands or inside coloured triangles on the *Alte Vie* (High Routes). Recommended areas include the **Alpe di Siusi**, a vast plateau above the Val Gardena; the area around Cortina; and the **Pale di San Martino**, a highland plateau accessible by cable car from **San Martino di Castrozza**.

Tourist offices in individual resorts can provide local advice, but for area-wide information contact the offices in **Trento** (☏0461 21 60 00; www.apt.trento.it; Via Manci 2; ◷9am-7pm) and **Bolzano** (☏0471 30 70 00; www.bolzano-bozen.it; Piazza Walther 8; ◷9am-7pm Mon-Fri, 9.30am-6pm Sat). The best online resource is www.dolomiti.org.

Most places are accessible by bus, with services run by **Trentino Trasporti** (☏0461 82 10 00; www.ttesercizio.it) in Trento; **SAD** (☏0471 45 01 11; www.sad.it) in Alto Adige; and **Dolomiti Bus** (☏0437 21 71 11; www.dolomitibus.it) in the Veneto. During winter, most resorts also offer 'ski bus' services.

Florence

POP 371,300

Visitors have rhapsodised about the beauty of Florence (Firenze) for centuries, and once here you'll appreciate why. An essential stop on every Italian itinerary, this Renaissance time capsule is busy year-round, but even the enormous and inevitable crowds of tourists fail to diminish its lustre. A list of the city's famous sons reads like a Renaissance who's who – under 'M' alone you'll find Medici, Machiavelli and Michelangelo – and its treasure trove of galleries, museums and churches showcases a magnificent array of Renaissance artworks.

History

Many hold that Florentia was founded by Julius Caesar around 59 BC, but archaeological evidence suggests an earlier village, possibly founded by the Etruscans around 200 BC. Though it was a rich merchant city by the 12th century, Florence's golden age took a bit longer to arrive, and did so under the auspices of the Medici family. They ruled the city between the 14th and 17th centuries and their visionary patronage of writers, artists and thinkers culminated in the Renaissance.

The Medicis were succeeded in the 18th century by the French House of Lorraine, which ruled until 1860, when the city was incorporated into the kingdom of Italy. From 1865 to 1870, Florence was capital of the fledgling kingdom.

During WWII, parts of the city were destroyed by bombing and in 1966 a devastating flood destroyed or damaged many important works of art. Recent decades have been blessedly free of such events, and the city is undergoing a modern Renaissance spearheaded by the opening of cultural institutions such as the Palazzo Strozzi and the long-overdue restoration and expansion of the Uffizi Gallery.

◉ Sights

From the main train station, Stazione Santa Maria Novella, it's a 550m walk along Via de' Panzani and Via de' Cerretani to the Duomo. From Piazza di San Giovanni, next to the Duomo, Via Roma leads down to Piazza della Repubblica and continues as Via Calimala and Via Por Santa Maria to the Ponte Vecchio.

There are seven major neighbourhoods in Florence's *centro storico*: Duomo and

Piazza della Signoria, Santa Maria Novella, San Lorenzo, San Marco, Santa Croce, Oltrarno and Boboli/San Miniato al Monte. Most of these owe their names to the significant basilicas located within their borders, which make excellent navigational landmarks.

Piazza del Duomo & Around PIAZZA

Photographs don't do justice to the exterior of Florence's Gothic **Duomo** (Cattedrale di Santa Maria del Fiore, St Mary of the Flower; www.duomofirenze.it; dome admission €10, crypt admission €3, campanile adult/child €7/free; ☉10am-5pm Mon-Wed & Fri, to 3.30pm Thu, to 4.45pm Sat, to 3.30pm 1st Sat of month, 1.30-4.45pm Sun, Mass in English 5pm Sat, dome 8.30am-7pm Mon-Fri, to 5.40pm Sat, crypt 10am-5pm Mon-Wed & Fri, to 4.45pm Sat, campanile 8.30am-7.30pm). While they reproduce the startling colours of the tiered red, green and white marble facade and the beautiful symmetry of the dome, they fail to give any real sense of its monumental size and its importance as the city's major landmark. Officially known as the Cattedrale di Santa Maria del Fiore, the building's construction began in 1294 but the cathedral itself wasn't consecrated until 1436. Construction of its most famous feature, the enormous octagonal **Cupola** (admission €10), was overseen by Brunelleschi after his design won a public competition in 1420. There's a magnificent view from the top of the cupola, but the climb is steep (463 steps) and also extremely cramped in places, so it's best avoided if you are unfit or claustrophobic.

The cathedral's interior is decorated with frescos by Vasari and Zuccari, and the stained-glass windows are by Donatello, Paolo Uccello and Lorenzo Ghiberti. The facade is a 19th-century replacement of the unfinished original, pulled down in the 16th century.

The design of the 82m **Campanile** (bell tower; www.operaduomo.firenze.it; adult €7; ☉9am-6pm) was begun by Giotto in 1334 and completed after his death by Andrea Pisano and Francesco Talenti. The views from the top make the 414-step climb worthwhile.

The stunning Romanesque **Battistero** (Baptistry; Piazza di San Giovanni; admission €6; ☉11.15am-6.30pm Mon-Sat, 8.30am-2pm 1st Sat of every month, till 11pm Thu-Sat Jun-22 Sep, 8.30am-2pm Sun) is one of the oldest buildings in Florence. Built on the site of a Roman temple between the 5th and 11th centuries, it's famous for its gilded-bronze doors, particularly Lorenzo Ghiberti's *Gate of Paradise*.

Surprisingly overlooked by the crowds, the **Museo dell'Opera di Santa Maria del Fiore** (Cathedral Museum; www.operaduomo.firenze.it; Piazza del Duomo 9; admission €7; ☉9am-6pm Mon-Sat, 9am-1pm Sun) safeguards treasures that once adorned the Duomo, Battistero and Campanile and is one of the city's most impressive museums. Its collection includes Ghiberti's *Gate of Paradise* panels (those on the Baptistry doors are copies) and a Pietà by Michelangelo.

Three cumulative tickets are available: €13 for entrance to the Cupola and the Museo dell'Opera di Santa Maria del Fiore; €17 for the Campanile, Battistero and Museo; and €26.50 for every Duomo sight (valid four days). All can be purchased at the ticket desk at the Museo.

Galleria degli Uffizi MUSEUM

(Uffizi Gallery; www.uffizi.firenze.it; Piazzale degli Uffizi 6; adult/reduced €6.50/3.25, incl temporary exhibition €11/5.50; ☉8.15am-6.05pm Tue-Sun) This magnificent gallery safeguards the Medici family's private art collection, which was bequeathed to the city in 1743 on the condition that it never leaves Florence. It occupies the Palazzo degli Uffizi, a handsome structure built between 1560 and 1580 to house government offices.

A major refurbishment and redevelopment of the gallery was under way as this book went to print. The completion date was uncertain, although nine new exhibition rooms opened in mid-2012 and remaining works are progressing.

The gallery is home to the world's greatest collection of Italian Renaissance art. Highlights include Simone Martini's shimmering *Annunciation* (room 3); Piero della Francesca's famous profile portraits of the Duke and Duchess of Urbino (room 7); Botticelli's *Birth of Venus* and *Allegory of Spring* (Primavera; rooms 10 to 14); Leonardo da Vinci's *Annunciation* (room 15); and Michelangelo's *Holy Family* (room 25). Allow at least four hours for your visit.

For a break, head to the gallery's rooftop cafe. Members of the Medici family once congregated here to watch events in the Piazza della Signoria.

Piazza della Signoria PIAZZA

(cnr Via Calimaruzza & Via de' Calzaiuoli) The city's most splendid piazza was created in the 13th century and has been the hub of Florentine

Florence

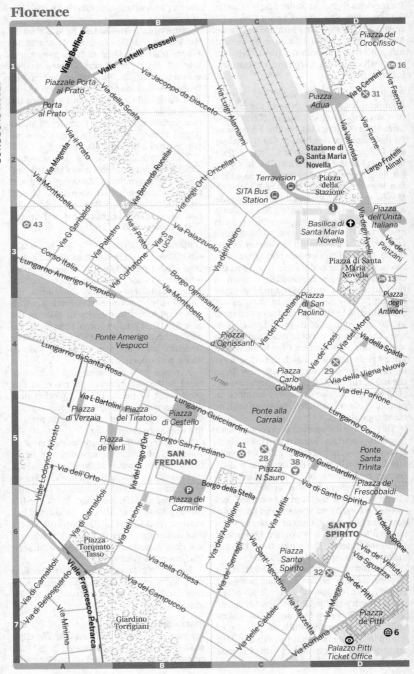

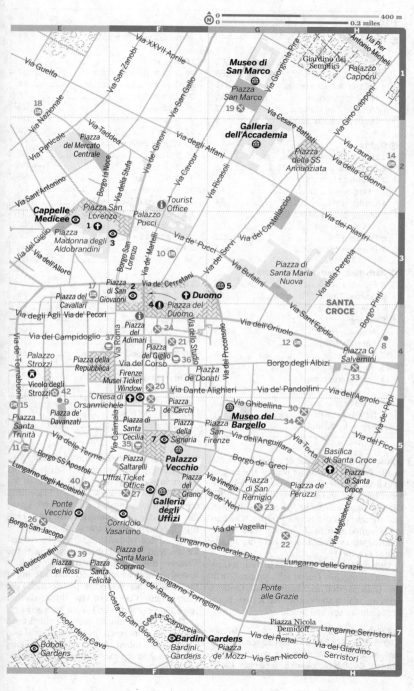

0 — 400 m
0 — 0.2 miles

Via Pier Antonio Micheli

Via Guelfa

Via XXVII Aprile

Museo di San Marco

Giardino dei Semplici

Palazzo Capponi

Via San Zanobi

Via Giorgio La Pira

Via Cesare Battisti

Via Gino Capponi

18

Via Nazionale

Via Taddea

Via San Gallo

Piazza San Marco

19

Galleria dell'Accademia

Via Panicale

Piazza del Mercato Centrale

Via de' Ginori

Via degli Alfani

Via Laura

Via della Colonna

14

Via Sant'Antonino

Borgo la Noce

Via della Stufa

Via Cavour

Via Ricasoli

Piazza della SS Annunziata

Via dei Pilastri

Cappelle Medicee

Piazza San Lorenzo

1

Palazzo Pucci

Tourist Office

Via del Giglio

Piazza Madonna degli Aldobrandini

3

Via de' Martelli

Via de' Pucci

Via dei Servi

Via del Castellaccio

Via del Giglio

Borgo San Lorenzo

10

Piazza di Santa Maria Nuova

Via della Pergola

Via dell'Alloro

17

Piazza di San Giovanni

2

Via de' Cerretani

Via Bufalini

SANTA CROCE

Borgo Pinti

Via degli Agli

Piazza del Cavallari

Via de' Pecori

4

Duomo

5

Piazza del Duomo

Via dell'Oriuolo

Via Sant'Egidio

Via de' Tornabuoni

Via del Campidoglio

Piazza del Adimari

24

Via dello Studio

12

Piazza G Salvemini

8

Palazzo Strozzi

Piazza della Repubblica

37

Via Roma

Piazza del Giglio

21

36

Via del Proconsolo

33

Vicolo degli Strozzi

42

Via del Corso

Piazza de' Donati

Borgo degli Albizi

Via de' Pandolfini

Via dell'Agnolo

15

9

Firenze Musei Ticket Window

20

Via Dante Alighieri

Via Ghibellina

30

Via de' Pepi

Piazza de' Davanzati

Chiesa di Orsanmichele

25

Piazza de' Cerchi

Museo del Bargello

34

Via del Fico

Piazza Santa Trinità

11

Via Calimala

Piazza di Santa Cecilia

Piazza della Signoria

Piazza San Firenze

Via Torta

Basilica di Santa Croce

Via delle Terme

35

7

Via dell'Anguillara

Piazza di Santa Croce

Borgo SS Apostoli

Piazza Saltarelli

Palazzo Vecchio

Borgo de' Greci

40

Uffizi Ticket Office

27

Piazza del Grano

Via Vinegia

Piazza di San Remigio

Piazza de' Peruzzi

Lungarno degli Acciaiuoli

Galleria degli Uffizi

Via de' Neri

23

Ponte Vecchio

Corridoio Vasariano

Via de' Vagellai

22

Via Maggliabecchi

Borgo San Jacopo

Lungarno Generale Diaz

Via Guicciardini

39

Piazza di Santa Maria Soprarno

Lungarno delle Grazie

Piazza dei Rossi

26

Piazza Santa Felicità

Via de' Bardi

Ponte alle Grazie

Costa di San Giorgio

Lungarno Torrigiani

Vicolo della Cava

Costa Scarpuccia

Bardini Gardens

Piazza Nicola Demidoff

Lungarno Serristori

Boboli Gardens

Bardini Gardens

Piazza de' Mozzi

Via dei Renai

Via San Niccolò

Via del Giardino Serristori

Florence

◎ **Top Sights**

Cappelle Medicee E3
Duomo...F3
Galleria degli Uffizi................................F6
Galleria dell'Accademia........................G2
Museo del Bargello...............................G5
Museo di San Marco..............................G1
Palazzo Vecchio.....................................F5

◎ **Sights**

1 Basilica di San Lorenzo.......................E3
2 Battistero F3
3 Biblioteca Laurenziana
   Medicea F3
4 Campanile F4
5 Museo dell'Opera di Santa
   Maria del Fiore G3
6 Palazzo Pitti D7
7 Piazza della Signoria F5

◎ **Activities, Courses & Tours**

8 Florence by Bike H4
9 Walking Tours of Florence E5

◎ **Sleeping**

10 Academy Hostel F3
11 Hotel Cestelli...E5
12 Hotel Dalí...G4
13 Hotel L'Orologio.....................................D3
14 Hotel Morandi alla
   Crocetta H2
15 Hotel Scoti..E5
16 Ostello Archi Rossi D1
17 Relais del Duomo...................................E3

18 Sette Angeli Rooms E1

◎ **Eating**

19 Accademia Ristorante G1
20 Cantinetta dei Verrazzano F4
21 Coquinarius F4
22 Del Fagioli G6
23 Gelateria dei Neri.................................. G6
24 Grom F4
25 I Due Fratellini.......................................F5
26 Il Ristoro...E6
   'Ino ....(see 13)
27 'Ino F6
28 La Carraia C5
29 L'Osteria di Giovanni............................D4
30 Osteria del Caffè Italiano G5
31 Trattoria I Due S....................................D1
32 Trattoria La Casalinga D6
33 Vestri H4
34 Vivoli G5

◎ **Drinking**

35 Caffè Rivoire F5
36 Chiaroscuro F4
37 Gilli..F4
38 Il Santino C5
39 Le Volpi e l'Uva E6
40 Sky Lounge Continentale E5

◎ **Entertainment**

41 La Cité...C5
42 Odeon Cinehall E4
43 Teatro del Maggio
   Musicale Fiorentino.............................A3

political and social life ever since. It is home to the Palazzo Vecchio as well as the Loggia dei Lanzi, an open-air showcase of sculpture from the 14th and 16th centuries – look for Giambologna's *Rape of the Sabine Women* and Agnolo Gaddi's *Seven Virtues*. The loggia is named after the *Lanzichenecchi* (Swiss Guards) who were stationed here during the rule of Cosimo I.

Other statues in the piazza include a copy of Michelangelo's *David* (the original is in the Galleria dell'Accademia) and Cellini's *Perseus,* which shows the Greek hero holding Medusa's severed head.

Palazzo Vecchio   MUSEUM
(☑055 276 82 24; www.palazzovecchio-family museum.it; Piazza della Signoria; museum adult/ reduced/ €6.50/4.50, tower €6.50, combined ticket €10; ⊙museum 9am-7pm Fri-Wed, to 2pm Thu; tower 10am-5pm Fri-Wed, to 2pm Thu, longer hrs in summer) Built between 1298 and 1340 for the Signoria, the highest level of Florentine republican government, this palace became the residence of Cosimo I in the 16th century. It remains the mayor's office today.

The series of lavish apartments created for the Medici is well worth seeing, as is the **Salone dei Cinquecento** (16th-Century Room), created within the original building in the 1490s to accommodate the Consiglio dei Cinquecento (Council of Five Hundred) that ruled Florence at the end of the 15th century.

The best way to visit is on a guided tour. These cost a mere €2 (or €1 per tour if two or more are taken on the same day). Book in advance at the ticket desk, by telephone or by email.

Museo del Bargello   MUSEUM

(☑055 294 883; www.polomuseale.firenze.it; Via del Proconsolo 4; adult/EU 18-25/EU child & senior €4/2/free, incl temporary exhibition €6/3/free; ☺8.15am-4.20pm Tue-Sun & 1st & 3rd Mon of month) Home to Italy's most comprehensive collection of Tuscan Renaissance sculpture, the Bargello features Donatello's two versions of *David* (one in marble and the other in bronze) plus a number of important early works by Michelangelo.

Palazzo Pitti   MUSEUM

(☑055 294 883; www.polomuseale.firenze.it; Piazza Pitti; ticket one adult/EU 18-25/EU child & senior €8.50/4.25/free, ticket two €7/3.50/free, ticket three €11.50/5.75/free; ☺8.15am-4.30pm Tue-Sun, longer hours high season, closed 1st & last Mon of month) Originally commissioned by the Pitti family, great rivals of the Medici, this vast 15th-century palace was acquired by Cosimo I and Eleonoradi Toledo in 1549 and became the Medici family residence. It remained the official residence of Florence's rulers until 1919, when the Savoys gave it to the state.

Today it houses four museums, of which the **Galleria Palatina** is the most important. Works by Raphael, Botticelli, Caravaggio, Filippo Lippi, Titian and Rubens adorn its lavishly decorated rooms, culminating in the **Appartamenti Reali** (Royal Apartments), which retain their late-19th-century decoration. Three other museums – the **Museo degli Argenti** (Medici Treasury), **Galleria d'Arte Moderna** (Gallery of Modern Art) and **Galleria del Costume** (Costume Gallery) – are located within the palace buildings.

Behind the palace are the **Boboli Gardens** (Giardino di Boboli) and the adjacent **Bardini Gardens** (Giardino di Bardini).

Ticketing can be confusing: ticket one gives entrance to the Galleria Palatina, Appartamenti Reali and Galleria d'Arte Moderna; ticket two gives entrance to the Museo degli Argenti and Galleria del Costume, plus the Boboli and Bardini Gardens; and ticket three gives entrance to all museums and gardens and is valid for three days.

Galleria dell'Accademia   MUSEUM

(☑055 29 48 83; Via Ricasoli 60; adult/EU 18-25/EU child & senior €6.50/3.25/free; ☺8.15am-6.20pm Tue-Sun) Expect a lengthy queue when visiting the home of Michelangelo's *David*. Fortunately, the most famous statue in the world is well worth the wait. Carved from a single block of marble, the nude warrior assumed his pedestal in the Piazza della Signoria in 1504, providing Florentines with a powerful emblem of power, liberty and civic pride. The statue was moved here in 1873.

Adjacent rooms contain paintings by Andrea Orcagna, Taddeo Gaddi, Domenico Ghirlandaio, Filippino Lippi and Sandro Botticelli.

Basilica di San Lorenzo   CHURCH

(Piazza San Lorenzo; adult/child €3.50/free; ☺10am-5pm Mon-Sat year-round, 1.30-5pm Sun Mar-Oct) One of the city's finest examples of Renaissance architecture, this basilica was designed by Brunelleschi in the 15th century and includes his austerely beautiful **Sagrestia Vecchia** (Old Sacristry), which features sculptural decoration by Donatello. Michelangelo was commissioned to design the building's facade in 1518 but his design in white Carrara marble was never executed, hence its rough, unfinished appearance. He also designed the attached **Biblioteca Medicea Laurenziana** (Medici Library; www.bml.firenze.sbn.it; Piazza San Lorenzo 9; admission €3, incl basilica €6; ☺9.30am-1.30pm Mon-Fri), with its sensuously curvaceous staircase.

Cappelle Medicee   MAUSOLEUM

(☑055 294 883; www.polomuseale.firenze.it; Piazza Madonna degli Aldobrandini; adult/EU 18-25/EU child & senior €6/3/free; ☺8.15am-1.20pm, till 4.20pm late Mar-early Nov, closed 2nd & 4th Sun & 1st, 3rd & 5th Mon of month) Principal burial place of the Medici rulers, this mausoleum is home to the stark but graceful **Sagrestia Nuova** (New Sacristy), Michelangelo's first architectural work and the showcase for three of his most haunting sculptures: *Dawn and Dusk, Night and Day* and *Madonna and Child.*

TOP CHOICE Museo di San Marco   MUSEUM

(☑055 294 883; www.polomuseale.firenze.it; Piazza San Marco 1; adult/EU 18-25/EU child & senior €4/2/free; ☺8.15am-1.20pm Mon-Fri, 8.15am-4.20pm Sat & Sun, closed 1st, 3rd & 5th Sun & 2nd & 4th Mon of month) Housed in a Dominican monastery, this spiritually uplifting museum is a showcase of the work of Fra Angelico, who decorated the cells with deeply devotional frescos to guide the meditation of his fellow friars. His most famous work, *Annunciation* (c 1450), is at the top of the stairs that lead to the cells.

CUTTING THE QUEUES

Sightseeing in Florence can entail hours spent in queues. Fortunately, there are two ways of saving time – one of which can also save you money.

For €4 extra per museum you can book tickets for the Uffizi and Galleria dell'Accademia (the museums with the longest queues) through **Firenze Musei** (Florence Museums; ☑055 29 48 83; www.firenzemusei.it; ☺telephone booking line 8.30am-6.30pm Mon-Fri, 8.30am-12.30pm Sat). Book online in advance, or purchase tickets in person before your visit from the ticket desks at the Palazzo Pitti, Museo di San Marco or at the rear of the Chiesa di Orsanmichele.

If you are planning to visit most of the major museums, consider purchasing a **Firenze Card** (www.firenzecard.it; €50). These are valid for 72 hours, allow the holder to bypass both advance booking and queues, and also give free entry to one accompanying child under 18 (EU citizens only). Cards can be purchased online, at the tourist information offices opposite Stazione Santa Maria Novella and in Via Cavour, and at the ticket desks at the Palazzo Pitti, Palazzi Vecchio and Galleria degli Uffizi (door 2).

☞ Tours

Cycling

A number of Florence-based companies offer cycling tours of Chianti, sometimes leaving by minibus and getting on bikes in Chianti and at other times doing the full tour by bike. Most include lunch and a wine-tasting, and are offered from March to October.

Florence by Bike   CYCLING
(☑055 48 89 92; www.florencebybike.it; Via San Zanobi 120r) This shop hires mountain, hybrid and race bikes (€22 to €37 per day) and provides self-guided itineraries and maps of tours through Chianti. It also offers a 32km-long day tour of northern Chianti (adult/under 26 €79/71).

I Bike Italy   CYCLING
(☑055 012 39 94; www.ibikeitaly.com) One-day guided tours in Chianti (€80) and a two-hour guided ride around Florence (including gelato; €25). 10% student discount.

I Bike Tuscany   CYCLING
(☑335 812 07 69; www.ibiketuscany.com) One-day rides in the Florentine Hills, in Chianti and from Chianti to Siena (with bus transfers from Florence), led by former bike racer Marco Vignoli, cost €95 to €145.

Walking

Freya's Florence   WALKING
(☑349 074 89 07; www.freyasflorence.com; per hr €70) A knowledgeable and enthusiastic Australian-born, Florence-based private tour guide; you'll pay admission fees on top of the guiding fee.

Walking Tours of Florence   WALKING
(☑055 264 50 33; www.italy.artviva.com; Via de' Sassetti 1; tours per person from €25) The Artviva outfit offers a range of city tours, all led by English-speaking guides.

☆☆ Festivals & Events

Scoppio del Carro   EASTER
A cart of fireworks is exploded in front of the cathedral at 11am on Easter Sunday – get there at least two hours early to grab a good position.

Maggio Musicale Fiorentino   ARTS
(www.maggiofiorentino.com) Italy's oldest arts festival is held in the Teatro del Maggio Musicale Fiorentino and stages performances of theatre, classical music, jazz and dance; April to June.

Festa di San Giovanni   MIDSUMMER
Florence celebrates its patron saint, John, with a *calcio storico* (historical football) match on Piazza di Santa Croce and fireworks over Piazzale Michelangelo; 24 June.

🛏 Sleeping

Although there are hundreds of hotels in Florence, it's still prudent to book ahead. Look out for low-season website deals – prices often drop by up to 50%.

DUOMO & PIAZZA DELLA SIGNORIA

Hotel Dalí   HOTEL €
(☑055 234 07 06; www.hoteldali.com; Via dell'Oriuolo 17; d/tr €85/110, apt from €95, with shared bathroom s/d €40/70; ℗@🛜) This overwhelmingly friendly hotel offers 10 light and airy rooms with double-glazed windows, tea- and coffee-making facilities and ceiling fans; the best

overlook the rear garden. Parking is included in the room cost, but breakfast isn't. The owners also offer three nearby self-catering apartments sleeping between two and six.

Relais del Duomo   B&B €

(☏055 21 01 47; www.relaisdelduomo.it; Piazza dell'Olio 2; s €40-90, d €70-130) The location is the prime selling point of this B&B on a quiet traffic-free street around the corner from the Duomo. The four pastel-coloured rooms are simple, but comfortable, and manager Elisabetta is extremely helpful.

Hotel Cestelli   PENSION €

(☏055 21 42 13; www.hotelcestelli.com; Borgo SS Apostoli 25; d €50-100, ste €80-115, without bathroom s €40-60, d €50-80; ⊙closed Jan-Feb, Aug) Run by Florentine photographer Alessio and his Japanese wife Asumi, this eight-room hotel on the 1st floor of a 12th-century *palazzo* is wonderfully located. Though dark, rooms are attractively furnished, clean, quiet and cool. No breakfast.

SANTA MARIA NOVELLA

TOP CHOICE Hotel L'Orologio   BOUTIQUE HOTEL €€€

(☏055 27 73 80; www.hotelorologioflorence.com; Piazza di Santa Maria Novella 24; r €160-550; P✳@☎) This design-driven hotel has four stars, five floors and 54 well-equipped and extremely comfortable rooms. The magnificent top-floor breakfast area commands views over Piazza Santa Maria Novella, and the elegant ground floor offers lounges and a popular wine bar.

Ostello Archi Rossi   HOSTEL €

(☏055 29 08 04; www.hostelarchirossi.com; Via Faenza 94r; dm €18-27, s €30-60, d €55-80; ⊙closed 2 weeks Dec; @☎) Guests' paintings and graffiti pattern the walls at this ever-busy hostel near Stazione di Santa Maria Novella. Rooms and dorms are simple but very clean, and there's a pleasant garden area. Bonuses include free breakfast, computers in some rooms, free guided walking tours and free pasta-and-salad meals six nights per week in the low season.

TOP CHOICE Hotel Scoti   PENSION €

(☏055 29 21 28; www.hotelscoti.com; Via de' Tornabuoni 7; s €29-75, d €45-125, tr €75-150; ☎) Wedged between Prada and McQueen, this *pensione* on Florence's most famous and glamorous shopping strip is a splendid mix of old-fashioned charm and value for money. Run with smiling aplomb by Australian Doreen and Italian Carmello, it offers 16 clean and comfortable rooms and a magnificent frescoed living room. Breakfast costs €5.

SAN LORENZO

TOP CHOICE Academy Hostel   HOSTEL €

(☏055 239 86 65; www.academyhostel.eu; Via Ricasoli 9; dm €32-34, d with shared bathroom €76, s/d €42/86; ✳@☎) The philosophy of this truly excellent small hostel close to the Duomo is that cheap accommodation shouldn't compromise comfort. Its immaculately maintained dorms sleep between four and six, and come with night lights, lockers and one shower and toilet for every four beds. Rates include breakfast.

Johlea & Johanna   B&B €€

(☏055 462 72 96, 055 463 32 92; www.johanna.it; d €60-165; ✳@☎) This highly regarded, professionally run operation has two elegant suite apartments and more than a dozen beautifully decorated and well-equipped ensuite B&B rooms housed in five historic residences in the quiet San Marco and San Lorenzo districts. One (Johanna 2) has parking, another (Antica Dimora Johlea) has a terrace with wonderful views and all offer a delicious breakfast and all-day tea, coffee (Nespresso) and cake. The pick of the bunch is Antica Dimora Johlea.

Sette Angeli Rooms   B&B €

(☏393 949 08 10; www.setteangelirooms.com; Via Nazionale 31; s €45-60, d €85-110, tr €95-135; ✳☎) Tucked behind the central market on a mainstream shopping street, Seven Angels is a tantalising mix of great value and recent renovation. Its rooms are perfectly comfortable and guests can pay an extra €10 to use the self-catering kitchen corner.

SAN MARCO

Hotel Morandi alla Crocetta   HOTEL €€

(☏055 234 47 47; www.hotelmorandi.it; Via Laura 50; s €70-140, d €93-220, tr €130-195, q €150-370; P✳☎) This medieval convent-turned-hotel away from the madding crowd is a stunner. Rooms have traditional furnishings and an old-fashioned ambience; a couple have handkerchief-sized gardens to laze in and one (No 29) is the frescoed former chapel.

SAN MINIATO AL MONTE

Campeggio Michelangelo   CAMPGROUND €

(☏055 681 19 77; www.ecvacanze.it; Viale Michelangelo 80; campsite adult €9.50-11.70, child 3-11 free-€6.90, car & tent €12.50-15.30; P@) Just off Piazzale Michelangelo, this large and comparatively leafy site has lovely city views.

Take bus 13 from Stazione di Santa Maria Novella or walk – steeply uphill!

Eating

Classic Tuscan dishes include *ribollita* (a heavy vegetable soup) and *bistecca alla fiorentina* (Florentine steak served rare). Chianti is the local tipple.

DUOMO & PIAZZA DELLA SIGNORIA

'Ino   SANDWICHES €
(Via dei Georgofili 3r-7r; panini €8, tasting platter €12; ☾11am-8pm Mon-Sat, noon-5pm Sun) Artisan ingredients are sourced locally and utilised creatively at this stylish address near the Uffizi. Create your own combination or pick a house special and scoff on the spot with a glass of wine. There's another **branch** in the Hotel l'Orologio on piazza Santa Maria Novella.

Cantinetta dei Verrazzano   BAKERY €
(Via dei Tavolini 18-20; focaccias €3-3.50; ☾noon-9pm Mon-Sat) Together, a *forno* (baker's oven) and *cantinetta* (small cellar) equal a match made in heaven. Head here for a foccacia straight from the oven and a glass of wine from the Verrazzano estate in Chianti.

I Due Fratellini   SANDWICHES €
(www.iduefratellini.com; Via dei Cimatori 38r; panini €3; ☾9am-8pm Mon-Sat, closed Fri & Sat 2nd half of Jun & all Aug) This hole-in-the-wall has been in business since 1875. Locals flock here to order panini filled to order and eaten standing in the street.

Coquinarius   WINE BAR
(www.coquinarius.com; Via delle Oche 11r; crostini & carpacci €4; ☾noon-10.30pm) Nestled within the shadow of the Duomo, this *enoteca* is extremely popular with tourists – try the justly famous ravioli with cheese and pear. Note: at the time of research, a move to a nearby location was on the cards; telephone ahead for an update.

SANTA MARIA NOVELLA

L'Osteria di Giovanni   TUSCAN €€€
(☎055 28 48 97; www.osteriadigiovanni.it; Via del Moro 22; mains €20-27; ☾dinner Mon-Fri, lunch & dinner Sat & Sun) The house antipasto is a great way to sample Tuscan specialities such as *crostini* (small toasts with toppings) and *lardo* (pork fat), and both the pasta dishes and the *bistecca alla fiorentina* are sensational. Everything a perfect neighbourhood eatery should be, and then some.

SAN LORENZO

Trattoria I Due G   TRATTORIA €€
(☎055 21 86 23; www.trattoriai2g.com; Via B Cennini 6r; mains €10-17; ☾lunch & dinner Mon-Sat) There isn't a tourist in sight at this old-fashioned trattoria near the train station (well, there wasn't before we published this review). Huge servings of tasty salads, pastas and mains tempt every palate, but the sentimental favourite is undoubtedly the delicious *pollo fritto* (fried chicken).

SAN MARCO

Accademia Ristorante   TRATTORIA €€
(☎055 21 73 43; www.ristoranteaccademia.it; Piazza San Marco 7r; mains €12-22, pizzas €6-18; ☾lunch & dinner) There aren't too many decent eateries in this area, which is one of the reasons why this family-run restaurant is perennially packed. Factors such as friendly staff, cheerful decor and consistently tasty food help, too.

SANTA CROCE

Trattoria Cibrèo   TRATTORIA €€
(Via dei Macci 122r; meals €30; ☾lunch & dinner Tue-Sat Sep-Jul) The small casual dining annexe of Florence's most famous (and considerably more expensive) restaurant is a gem. *Primi* include a justly famous fish soup and *secondi* comprise a small main dish matched with a side of seasonal vegetables; everything is exceptionally well priced considering its quality. No reservations and no credit cards.

Del Fagioli   TRATTORIA €
(☎055 24 42 85; Corso Tintori 47r; mains €8.50-10; ☾lunch & dinner Mon-Fri, closed Aug) This Slow Food favourite near the Basilica di Santa Croce is the archetypical Tuscan trattoria. It opened in 1966 and has been serving well-priced bean dishes, soups and roasted meats to throngs of appreciative local workers and residents ever since. No credit cards.

Osteria del Caffè Italiano   TUSCAN €€€
(☎055 28 90 20; www.caffeitaliano.it; Via dell'Isola delle Stinche 11-13r; meals €45; ☾lunch & dinner Tue-Sun) This old-fashioned *osteria* occupies the ground floor of a 14th-century *palazzo* and is an excellent spot to try the city's famous *bistecca alla fiorentina* (per kg €60). The adjoining **pizzeria** (pizzas €7 to €8) offers a choice of three pizza types – margherita, napoli and marinara – which are best enjoyed with an icy-cold beer (€6). No credit cards at the pizzeria.

TOP FIVE GELATERIE

There are plenty of places offering *gelato artiginale* (traditional, usually homemade, ice cream and sorbet). Flavours change according to what fruit is in season, and a small cone or tub can cost anywhere from €2 to €3.

La Carraia (Piazza Nazario Sauro 25r; tubs €1.50-6,cones €1.50-3; ⊙9am-11pm summer, to 10pm winter) Look for the ever-present queue next to the Ponte Carraia, and you will find this fantastic *gelateria*.

Gelateria dei Neri (Via de' Neri 22r; ⊙9am-midnight) Semifreddo-style gelato that is cheaper than its competitors; known for its Giotto (almond, hazelnut and coconut) flavour.

Gelateria Vivoli (Via dell'Isola delle Stinche 7; ⊙7.30am-midnight Tue-Sat, 9am-midnight Sun Apr-Oct, to 9pm Nov-Mar) Choose a flavour from the huge choice on offer (the chocolate with orange is a perennial favourite) and scoff it in the pretty piazza opposite; tubs only.

Grom (www.grom.it; cnr Via del Campanile & Via delle Oche; ⊙10.30am-midnight Apr-Sep, to 11pm Oct-Mar) Delectable flavours and often-organic ingredients.

Vestri (www.vestri.it; Borgo degli Albizi 11r; ⊙10.30am-8pm Mon-Sat) Specialises in chocolate; go for the decadent white chocolate with wild strawberries or the chocolate with pepper.

OLTRANO

La Casalinga
TRATTORIA €
(☏055 21 86 24; Via de' Michelozzi 9r; mains €10; ⊙lunch & dinner Mon-Sat) Family run and locally loved, this busy place is one of Florence's cheapest trattorias. You'll be relegated behind locals in the queue – it's a fact of life and not worth protesting – with the eventual reward being hearty peasant dishes such as *bollito misto con salsa verde* (mixed boiled meats with green sauce).

Il Ristoro
TUSCAN €
(☏055 264 55 69; Borgo San Jacopo 48r; mains €10; ⊙noon-4pm Mon, noon-10pm Tue-Sun) A disarmingly simple address not to be missed; this two-room restaurant with deli counter is a great budget choice. Pick from classics like *pappa al pomodoro* (tomato and bread soup) or a plate of cold cuts and swoon over views of the Arno swirling beneath your feet.

Drinking

TOP CHOICE Le Volpi e l'Uva
WINE BAR
(www.levolpieluva.com; Piazza dei Rossi 1; crostini €6.50, cheese and meat platter €8; ⊙11am-9pm Mon-Sat) This intimate *enoteca con degustazione* (wine bar with tasting) offers an impressive list of wines by the glass (€4 to €8). To attain true bliss indulge in *crostini* topped with honeyed speck or *lardo*, or a platter of boutique Tuscan cheese and meat.

Caffè Rivoire
CAFE
(Piazza della Signoria 4; ⊙Tue-Sun) Rivoire's terrace has the best view in the city. Settle in for a long *aperitivo* or coffee break – it's worth the high prices.

Gilli
CAFE, BAR
(www.gilli.it; Piazza della Repubblica 39r; ⊙Wed-Mon) The city's grandest cafe, Gilli has been serving excellent coffee and delicious cakes since 1733. Claiming a table on the piazza is *molto* expensive – we prefer standing at the spacious Liberty-style bar.

Chiaroscuro
CAFE, BAR
(www.chiaroscuro.it; Via del Corso 36r; ⊙7.30am-9pm Mon-Sat, noon-9pm Sun, closed 1 week mid-Aug) This casual cafe roasts its own beans and serves what may well be the best coffee in Florence. Its *aperitivo* buffet (6pm to 8pm) is justly popular.

Sky Lounge Continentale
BAR
(www.continentale.it; Vicolo dell'Oro 6r; ⊙2.30-11.30pm daily Apr-Sep) Accessible from the 5th floor of the Ferragamo-owned Hotel Continentale, this chic bar has amazing views over the Arno. Dress the part or feel out of place.

TOP CHOICE Il Santino
WINE BAR
(Via Santo Spirito 34; soup €5, antipasti €6-10, panini €5.50; ⊙daily) This pocket-sized wine bar is the much-loved sibling of Il Santo Bevitore, one of the city's most fashionable eateries. Go early to claim a stool, graze on antipasti and choose from a list of quality wines by the glass; later in the evening drinkers spill out onto the street.

☆ Entertainment

Florence's definitive monthly listings guide, *Firenze Spettacolo* (€2), is sold at newsstands and has a small English-language section on the final pages.

Concerts, opera and dance are performed year-round at the **Teatro Comunale** (📞055 28 72 22; www.maggiofiorentino.com; Corso Italia 16), also the venue for events organised by the Maggio Musicale Fiorentino.

English-language films are screened at the **Odeon Cinehall** (📞055 29 50 51; www.cinehall.it; Piazza Strozzi 2; ⊗Oct-Jun).

La Cité   LIVE MUSIC
(www.lacitelibreria.info; Borgo San Frediano 20r; ⊗3pm-1am Mon-Thu, 5pm-2am Fri & Sat; 📶) By day it'a a cafe-bookshop, but by night this intimate space morphs into a vibrant live-music space: think swing, fusion, jam-session jazz.

ℹ Information

Emergency

Police Station (Questura; 📞055 4 97 71; http://questure.poliziadistato.it; Via Zara 2; ⊗24hr)

Medical Services

Dr Stephen Kerr: Medical Service (📞335 836 16 82, 055 28 80 55; www.dr-kerr.com; Piazza Mercato Nuovo 1; ⊗3-5pm Mon-Fri, or by appointment) Resident British doctor.

Emergency Doctor (Guardia Medica; 📞north of the Arno 055 233 94 56, south of the Arno 055 21 56 16) For a doctor at night, weekends or on public holidays.

Tourist Information

Tourist Offices (www.firenzeturismo.it) Located at Via Cavour (📞055 29 08 33, 055 29 08 32; www.firenzeturismo.it; Via Cavour 1r; ⊗8:30am-6:30pm Mon-Sat); the airport (📞055 31 58 74; ⊗8.30am-6.30pm); Piazza della Stazione (📞055 21 22 45; www.commune.fi.it; Piazza della Stazione 4; ⊗8.30am-7pm Mon-Sat, to 2pm Sun) and the Bigallo (📞055 28 84 96; www.comune.fi.it; Loggia del Bigallo, Piazza San Giovanni 1; ⊗9am-7pm Mon-Sat, 9am-2pm Sun).

ℹ Getting There & Away

Air

The main airport serving Florence is Pisa international airport (p532). There's also the small, city **Florence airport** (www.aeroporto.firenze.it), 5km northwest of Florence.

Bus

The **SITA bus station** (www.sitabus.it; Via Santa Caterina da Siena 17r; ⊗information office 8.30am-12.30pm & 3-6pm Mon-Fri, 8.30am-12.30pm Sat) is just south of the train station. Buses leave for Siena (€7.80, 1¼ hours, every 30 to 60 minutes) and San Gimignano via Poggibonsi (€6.80, 1¼ hours, 14 daily).

Car & Motorcycle

Florence is connected by the A1 autostrada to Bologna and Milan in the north and Rome and Naples to the south. The A11 links Florence with Pisa and the coast, and a *superstrada* (expressway) joins the city to Siena.

Train

Florence is well connected by train. There are regular services to/from Pisa (Regionale €7.80, one hour, every 30 minutes), Rome (Freccia Rossa; €29, 90 minutes, hourly), Venice (Freccia Argento; €29 to €45, 2¼ hours, 12 daily) and Milan (Freccia Rossa; €39 to €49, 1¾ hours, hourly).

ℹ Getting Around

To/From the Airport

ATAF (📞800 42 45 00; www.ataf.net) runs a shuttle bus (€5, 25 minutes, half-hourly from 5.30am to 11pm) connecting Florence airport with the SITA bus station.

Taxis charge a fixed rate of €20 plus €1 per bag (€23.30 at night) for the trip between Florence airport and the *centro storico*.

Terravision (www.terravision.eu) runs a bus service between Pisa (Galileo Galilei) airport and the paved bus park in front of Stazione Santa Maria Novella (one-way/return €6/10, 70 minutes, 12 daily). In Florence, buy your tickets at the Terravision desk inside Deanna Café, opposite the station.

Autostradale also runs a bus service between Pisa airport (one-way/return €6/10) and Stazione Santa Maria Novella. In Florence, tickets are available from the newsstand at the tram stop next to the station.

A limited number of trains run from Pisa airport directly to Florence each day (€7.80, one hour); regular services run to Pisa Centrale from where you can change to a Florence train.

Bus

ATAF buses service the city centre and Fiesole, a picturesque small town in the hills 8km northeast of Florence. Take bus 7 from Piazza San Marco for Fiesole, and bus 12 or 13 from Stazione Santa Maria Novella for Piazzale Michelangelo. Tickets (90 minutes €1.20) are sold at *tabacchi* and newsstands – you can also buy a 90-minute ticket on board the bus (€2).

Car & Motorcycle

Note that there is a strict Limited Traffic Zone (ZTL) in the *centro storico* from 7.30am to 7.30pm Monday to Friday and 7.30am to 6pm on Saturday. Fines are hefty if you enter the centre during these times without a special permit having been organised by your hotel in advance. For information about the ZTL go to www.comune.fi.it.

The ZTL means that the best option is to leave your car in a car park and use public transport to access the centre. Porta al Prato is a good choice as it's only one tram stop away from Santa Maria Novella. It charges €1 for the first hour, €2 per hour for the second or subsequent hour, or €20 per 24 hours. Buy tickets for the tram (No 1 to/from Villa Costanza; €1.20) from the machines at the tram stop. Details of other car parks are available from **Firenze Parcheggi** (☑ 055 500 19 94; www.firenzeparcheggi.it).

Pisa

POP 88,300

Most people know Pisa as the home of an architectural project gone terribly wrong, but the Leaning Tower is just one of a number of noteworthy sights in this compact and compelling university city.

Pisa's golden age came in the 12th and 13th centuries when it was a maritime power rivalling Genoa and Venice. It was eventually defeated by the Genoese in 1284, and in 1406 it fell to Florence. Under the Medici, the arts and sciences flourished and Galileo Galilei (1564–1642) taught at the university.

◉ Sights & Activities

The Piazza dei Miracoli is a straightforward 1.5km walk from the bus and train stations – follow Viale F Crispi north, cross the Ponte Solferino over the Arno and continue straight up Via Roma to Campo dei Miracoli.

Piazza dei Miracoli   PIAZZA
(Campo dei Miracoli; www.opapisa.it; ⊙10am-5pm Jan-Feb & Nov-Dec, 9am-6pm Mar, 8am-8pm Apr-Sep, 9am-7pm Oct) Pisans claim that the Piazza dei Miracoli is among the most beautiful urban spaces in the world. Certainly, the immaculate walled lawns provide a gorgeous setting for the architecturally harmonious Romanesque architectural trio of cathedral, baptistry and tower.

The centrepiece is the **Duomo** (Piazza dei Miracoli; adult/reduced €2/1, admission free Nov-Feb; ⊙10am-8pm Apr-Sep, 10am-7pm Oct, 10am-12.45pm & 2-5pm Nov-Feb, 10am-6pm Mar), the construction of which began in 1064. It has a graceful tiered facade and a cavernous interior featuring a carved marble pulpit by Giovanni Pisano. The transept's bronze doors are by Bonanno Pisano.

Construction of the cupcake-like **Battistero** (Piazza dei Miracoli; ⊙8.30am-8pm Apr-Sep, 9am-7pm Oct, 10am-5pm Nov-Feb, 9am-6pm Mar) to the west of the Duomo started in 1153 and was completed under the supervision of Nicola and Giovanni Pisano in 1260. Inside, note Nicola Pisano's beautiful pulpit.

But it's to the campanile, better known as the **Leaning Tower** (Torre Pendente; €15 at ticket office, €17 when booked online; ⊙8.30am-8pm Apr-May & Sep, 8.30am-11pm Jun-Aug, 9am-7pm Oct, 9.30am-5.30pm Nov & Feb, 10am-4.30pm Dec-Jan, 9am-5.30pm Mar), that all eyes are drawn. Construction began in 1173 under the supervision of Bonanno Pisano, but his plans came a cropper almost immediately. Only three of the tower's seven tiers were completed before it started tilting – continuing at a rate of about 1mm per year. By 1990 the lean had reached 5.5 degrees – a tenth of a degree beyond the critical point established by computer models. Stability was finally ensured in 1998 when a combination of biased weighting and soil drilling forced the tower into a safer position. Today it's almost 4.1m off the perpendicular.

PIAZZA DEI MIRACOLI TICKETING

Ticket pricing for Piazza dei Miracoli sights is complicated. Tickets to the Leaning Tower and Duomo are sold individually, but for the remaining sights combined tickets are available. These cost €5/6/8/10 for one/two/four/five sights and cover the Duomo, Baptistry, Camposanto cemetery, Museo dell'Opera del Duomo and Museo delle Sinópie. Entry for children aged under 10 years is free for all sights except the Tower. Any ticket will also give access to the multimedia and information areas located in the Museo Dell'Opera del Duomo and Museo delle Sinópie.

Tickets are sold at two **ticket offices** (www.opapisa.it; Piazza dei Miracoli; ⊙8am-7.30pm Apr-Sep, 8.30am-7pm Oct, 9am-5pm Nov & Feb, 9.30am-4.30pm Dec-Jan, 8.30am-6pm Mar) on the piazza: the central ticket office is behind the tower and a second office is in the entrance foyer of the Museo delle Sinópie. To ensure your visit to the tower, book tickets via the website at least 15 days in advance.

Visits to the tower are limited to groups of 40, and children under eight years are not allowed entrance; entry times are staggered and queuing is inevitable. It is wise to book ahead.

Flanking the Campo, the beautiful **Camposanto cemetery** (Piazza dei Miracoli; ⊙8.30am-8pm Apr-Sep, 9am-7pm Oct, 10am-5pm Nov-Feb, 9am-6pm Mar) is said to contain soil shipped from Calvary during the crusades. Look out for the 14th-century fresco *The Triumph of Death* on the southern cloister wall.

A free audioguide to the sight is available in podcast format at www.opapisa.it. Guided tours of the piazza are conducted by **Pisa Guide** (☎333 614 49 24; www.pisaguide. com; adult/child 10-18yr/child under 10yr €8/6/free; ⊙11am-noon Fri-Sun Oct-May).

🛏 Sleeping

Many people visit Pisa on a day trip from Florence, but if you're keen to sample the lively bar scene at night there are a few decent overnight options.

Hostel Pisa Tower　　　　HOSTEL €
(☎329 701 73 87, 050 520 24 54; www.hostelpisatower.it; Via Piave 4; dm €18-22, apt €49-69; @�) This extremely friendly place near the Piazza dei Miracoli opened in 2011. Occupying a villa with a rear garden, it is cheerful, clean and comfortable but suffers from a lack of communal kitchen and bathroom facilities (only two showers and two toilets for 22 beds). The apartment sleeps two or three and has a small kitchen and private car park; wi-fi is free but internet access costs €4 per hour.

Hostel Pisa　　　　HOSTEL €
(☎050 520 18 41; www.hostelpisa.it; Via Corridoni 29; dm €15, d/t €40/56, d with shared bathroom €35; @�) Opened in 2011, this hostel is close to the train station (expect noise) and offers characterless, but cheap and clean, accommodation. There's a communal kitchen, a concrete courtyard with ping-pong table, and a lounge with TV and pool table. Breakfast costs €5.50 and bike rental (24 hour) costs €10. Rooms are hot in summer.

Royal Victoria Hotel　　　　HOTEL €€
(☎050 94 01 11; www.royalvictoria.it; Lungarno Pacinotti 12; d €65-150, ste €150-190, without bathroom r €30-80; ⌘�) This doyen of Pisan hotels has been run with pride by the Piegaja family since 1837. Rooms vary, but most are a perfect shabby-chic mix of antique ambience and modern-day comfort. The flowery 4th-floor terrace is a highlight.

🍴 Eating & Drinking

The best restaurants and bars are in the streets around Piazza Dante Alighieri, Piazza Vettovaglie and along the riverbank.

Il Montino　　　　PIZZERIA €
(Vicolo del Monte 1; pizza slices €1.50; ⊙10.30am-3pm & 5-10pm Mon-Sat) Students and sophisticates alike adore the *cecina* (chickpea pizza) and *spuma* (sweet, nonalcoholic drink) that are the specialities of this local institution. Order to go or claim one of the outdoor tables.

biOsteria 050　　　　ORGANIC €
(☎050 54 31 06; www.zerocinquanta.com; Via San Francesco 36; burgers €6.50-8.50, mains €9.50-13; ⊙lunch Mon-Sun, dinner Tue-Sun; �) The chef here uses produce that is strictly local and organic to create his tasty dishes. There are ample choices for vegetarians and coeliac sufferers, and excellent-value daily lunch specials are chalked on the board outside.

Bar Pasticceria Salza　　　CAFE, PASTICCERIA €
(Borgo Stretto 44; ⊙8am-8.30pm Apr-Oct, shorter hours Tue-Sun Nov-Mar) This old-fashioned cafe and cake shop has been tempting Pisans off Borgo Stretto and into sugar-induced indulgence since the 1920s.

Sottobosco　　　　CAFE
(www.sottoboscocafe.it; Piazza San Paolo all'Orto; ⊙10am-midnight Tue-Fri, noon-1am Sat, 7pm-midnight Sun) What a tourist-free breath of fresh air this bohemian cafe is! Enjoy coffee, herbal teas, pastries and light lunches during the day, or head here on Friday, Saturday and Sunday nights for live music (often jazz).

ℹ Information

For city information, check www.pisaunicaterra. it or pop into the tourist office at the airport or in the city centre.

ℹ Getting There & Around

Pisa international airport (p532) is linked to the city centre by train (€1.40, five minutes, 15 daily), or by the **CPT** (www.cpt.pisa.it) LAM Rossa bus (€1.10, 10 minutes, every 10 minutes). Buy bus tickets at the newsstand at the train station or any *tabacchi*.

A taxi between the airport and the city centre costs €15 (€20 at night).

Terravision buses depart from the airport to Florence (one-way/return €6/10, 70 minutes, 12 daily). **Train Spa** (www.trainspa.it) shuttle buses go to Siena via Poggibonsi (€14, one daily).

Regular trains run to Lucca (Regionale €3.30, 30 minutes, every 30 to 60 minutes), Florence (Regionale €7.80, 1¼ hours, every 30 minutes), Rome (Freccia Bianca €19 to €44.50, three hours, five daily) and Genoa (InterCity €9 to €18, 2½ hours, eight daily).

Siena

POP 54,600

Siena is one of Italy's most enchanting medieval towns. Its walled centre, a beautifully preserved warren of dark lanes punctuated with Gothic *palazzi,* has at its centre Piazza del Campo (known as Il Campo), the sloping square that is the venue for the city's famous annual horse race, Il Palio.

According to legend, Siena was founded by the sons of Remus (one of the founders of Rome). In the Middle Ages its dramatic rise caused political and cultural friction with nearby Florence and the two cities strove to outdo each other with their artistic and architectural achievements. Painters of the Sienese School (most notably in the 13th to 15th centuries) produced significant works of art, many of which are on show in the city's impressive museums and churches.

◉ Sights

From the train station take bus 8 or 9 (€1.10) to Piazza Gramsci, from where Piazza del Campo is a short, signposted walk away. Buy your ticket from the *tabacchi* at the station.

From the bus station it's a 10-minute walk up Via La Lizza and Via delle Terme. The centre's main streets – the Banchi di Sopra, Via di Città and Banchi di Sotto – curve around Il Campo.

Piazza del Campo   PIAZZA

Il Campo has been Siena's civic and social centre for nearly 600 years. Near the top of the slope is a copy of the **Fonte Gaia** (Happy Fountain), decorated in 1419 by Sienese sculptor Jacopo della Quercia. The recently restored originals are on show in the Complesso Museale Santa Maria della Scala. Down the slope from the fountain is the **Palazzo Comunale** (aka Palazzo Pubblico), a striking example of Sienese Gothic architecture that is home to the splendid Museo Civico.

ⓉⓄⓅ CHOICE Museo Civico   MUSEUM

(www.comune.siena.it; Palazzo Comunale; adult/EU reduced €8/4.50; ⏲10am-6.15pm mid-Mar–Oct, to 5.15pm Nov–mid-Mar) The collection here includes Simone Martini's famous *Maestà* (Virgin Mary in Majesty; 1315–16) and his oft-reproduced fresco (1328–30) of Guidoriccio da Fogliano, a captain of the Sienese army.

Also here is the most important secular painting of the Renaissance, Ambrogio Lorenzetti's fresco cycle known as the *Allegories of Good and Bad Government* (c 1337–40).

The museum is on the 1st floor of the *palazzo;* from the ground floor it is possible to access the **Torre del Mangia** (admission €8; ⏲10am-7pm Mar–mid-Oct, to 4pm mid-Oct–Feb), a 102m-high bell tower offering great views over the city. A combined ticket to the museum and tower costs €13.

Duomo   CHURCH

(www.operaduomo.siena.it; Piazza del Duomo; admission Mar-Oct €3, Nov-Feb free; ⏲10.30am-7pm Mon-Sat, 1.30-6pm Sun Mar-Oct, 10.30am-5.30pm Mon-Sat, 1.30-5.30pm Sun Nov-Feb) Siena's cathedral is one of Italy's greatest Gothic churches. Begun in 1196, it was opened in 1215, although work continued on features such as the apse and dome well into the 13th century. The magnificent facade of white, green and red polychrome marble was finished towards the end of the 14th century and the mosaics in the gables are 19th-century additions. Notable features include the carved pulpit by Giovanni and Nicola Pisano, Donatello's bronze of St John the Baptist and the inlaid marble floor, decorated with 56 panels depicting historical and biblical subjects. The most valuable panels are kept covered and are revealed only from 21 August through 27 October each year (admission is €7 during this period).

Through a door from the north aisle is the **Libreria Piccolomini** (Piccolomini Library; Piazza Jacopo della Quercia, Duomo Nuovo), which is decorated with vivid narrative frescos by Pinturicchio.

Battistero di San Giovanni   BAPTISTRY

(Piazza San Giovanni; admission €4; ⏲10.30am-7pm Mon-Sat & 1.30-6pm Sun Mar-Oct, 10.30am-5.30pm Mon-Sat & 1.30-5.30pm Sun Nov-Feb) While this baptistry's Gothic facade has remained unfinished, the interior is richly decorated with frescos. The centrepiece is a marble font by Jacopo della Quercia, decorated with bronze panels in relief and depicting the life of St John the Baptist. Artists include Lorenzo

Ghiberti (*Baptism of Christ* and *St John in Prison*) and Donatello (*Herod's Feast*).

Museo Opera del Duomo   MUSEUM

(Piazza del Duomo; admission €7; ⊙10.30am-7pm Mon-Sat & 1.30-6pm Sun Mar-Oct, 10.30am-5.30pm Mon-Sat & 1.30-5.30pm Sun Nov-Feb) This museum is home to a large collection of Sienese painting and sculpture, including an entire room dedicated to the work of Duccio di Buoninsegna, the most significant painter of the Sienese School. The ticket also includes access to a panoramic terrace.

Complesso Museale
Santa Maria della Scala   CULTURAL BUILDING

(www.santamariadellascala.com; Piazza del Duomo 1; adult/reduced/child under 11 €6/3.50/free; ⊙10.30am-4pm, till 6.30pm in high season) This former hospital, parts of which date to the 13th century, is directly opposite the Duomo and houses three museums – the Archaeological Museum, Art Museum for Children, and Center of Contemporary Art (SMS Contemporanea) – as well as a variety of historic halls, chapels and temporary exhibition spaces. Though the atmospheric **Archaeological Museum** housed in the basement tunnels is impressive, the complex's undoubted highlight is the upstairs **Pellegrinaio** (Pilgrim's Hall), with its vivid 15th-century frescos.

✦ Festivals & Events

Siena's great annual event is the **Palio** (⊙2 Jul & 16 Aug), a pageant culminating in a bareback horse race round Il Campo. The city is divided into 17 *contrade* (districts), of which 10 are chosen annually to compete for the *palio* (silk banner).

🛏 Sleeping

It's always advisable to book in advance, but for August and the Palio, it's essential.

TOP CHOICE **Campo Regio Relais**   BOUTIQUE HOTEL €€€

(☎0577 22 20 73; www.camporegio.com; Via della Sapienza 25; s €150-300, d €190-300, ste €250-600; ❋@🛜) Siena's most charming hotel occupies a 16th-century *palazzo* and has only six rooms, all of which are individually decorated and luxuriously equipped. Breakfast is served in the sumptuous lounge or on the terrace, which has a sensational view of the Duomo and Torre del Mangia.

TOP CHOICE **Hotel Alma Domus**   HOTEL €

(☎0577 4 41 77; www.hotelalmadomus.it; Via Camporegio 37; s €40-48, d €60-85, tr €80-110; ❋@🛜)

COMBINATION PASSES

There are a number of money-saving passes to Siena's churches and museums on offer:

Siena Itinerari d'Arte (SIA) Museo Civico, Complesso Museale Santa Maria della Scala, Museo Opera del Duomo and Battistero (€17 mid-March to October, €14 November to mid-March, valid seven days).

Musei Comunali Ticket Museo Civico and Complesso Museale Santa Maria della Scala (€11, valid two days).

OPA Si Pass Duomo, Libraria Piccolomini, Battistero, Museo Opera del Duomo and Panoramic Terrace (€12, valid three days).

All three passes can be purchased at the Duomo ticket office. The Siena Itinerari d'Arte and Musei Comunali Ticket are also available at the ticket offices at the Museo Civico and Complesso Museale Santa Maria della Scala.

Owned by the Catholic diocese and still home to six Dominican nuns who act as guardians at the Casa Santuario di Santa Caterina (in the same complex), this convent is now privately operated as a budget hotel. Many of the spotlessly clean rooms have views over the narrow green Fontebranda valley across to the Duomo. There's a 1am curfew.

Antica Residenza Cicogna   B&B €

(☎0577 28 56 13; www.anticaresidenzacicogna.it; Via dei Termini 67; s €70-90, d €85-110, ste €120-150; ❋@🛜) Charming host Elisa supervised the recent restoration of this 13th-century building and will happily recount its history (it's been owned by her family for generations). The seven rooms are clean and well maintained, with comfortable beds, painted ceilings and tiled floors.

🍴 Eating & Drinking

Traditional Sienese dishes include *panzanella* (summer salad of soaked bread, basil, onion and tomatoes), *pappardelle con la lepre* (ribbon pasta with hare) and panforte (a rich cake of almonds, honey and candied fruit).

TOP CHOICE **Enoteca I Terzi**   MODERN ITALIAN €€

(☎0577 4 43 29; www.enotecaiterzi.it; Via dei Termini 7; mains €18; ⊙11am-1am Mon-Sat) Close to the

Campo but off the well-beaten tourist trail, this classy, modern *enoteca* is a favourite with bankers from the nearby headquarters of the Monte dei Paschi di Siena bank, who love to linger over their working lunches of handmade pasta, flavoursome risotto and succulent grilled meats.

Morbidi DELI €
(Via Banchi di Sopra 75; ⊙9am-8pm Mon-Sat, lunch buffet 12.30-2.30pm) Local gastronomes shop here, as the range of cheese, cured meats and imported delicacies is the best in Siena. If you are self-catering you can join them, but make sure you also investigate the downstairs lunch buffet (€12), which offers fantastic value.

Kopa Kabana GELATERIA €
(www.gelateriakopakabana.it; Via dei Rossi 52-55; gelati €1.70-2.30; ⊙11am-midnight mid-Feb–mid-Nov) Come here for fresh gelato made by self-proclaimed ice-cream master, Fabio (we're pleased to concur).

Caffè Fiorella CAFE
(www.torrefazionefiorella.it; Via di Città 13; ⊙7am-8pm Mon-Sat) Squeeze into this tiny space behind the Campo to enjoy Siena's best coffee. In summer, the coffee granita with a dollop of cream is a wonderful indulgence.

ⓘ Information
Tourist Office (☐0577 28 05 51; www.terre siena.it; Piazza del Campo 56; ⊙9am-7pm)

ⓘ Getting There & Away
Siena is not on a main train line, so it's easier to arrive by bus. From the bus station on Piazza Gramsci, SITA/Siena Mobilità buses run to Florence (€7.80, 1½ hours, every 30 to 60 minutes) and San Gimignano (€6, 1¼ hours, hourly), either direct or via Poggibonsi. A Train SPA bus travels to Pisa airport (€14, two hours, one daily).

Sena (☐861 199 19 00; www.sena.it) operates services to/from Rome Tiburtina and Fiumicino Airport (€23, 3½/4 hours, 11 daily weekdays, fewer on weekends), Milan (€36, 4½ hours, five daily), Perugia (€12, 1½ hours, one daily) and Naples (€32, 6½ hours, one daily). Services to Naples depart from outside the railway station.

Both Train Siena Mobilità and Sena have ticket offices underneath the piazza.

There's a ZTL in the *centro storico*, although visitors can drop off luggage at their hotel, then leave (make sure the hotel reception reports your licence number or you will be fined). The paid car parks at San Francesco and Santa Caterina (aka Fontebranda) each charge €1.60

per hour and have a *scala mobile* (escalator) to take you into the centre. For details, check www. sienaparcheggi.com (in Italian).

Lucca
POP 85,000
Lucca is a love-at-first-sight type of place. Hidden behind monumental Renaissance walls, its *historic centre* is chock-full of handsome churches, excellent restaurants and tempting *pasticcerie*. Founded by the Etruscans, it became a city state in the 12th century and stayed that way for 600 years. Most of its streets and monuments date from this period.

From the train station walk across Piazza Ricasoli, cross Viale Regina Margherita, and then follow the path across the grass and through the wall to reach the centre.

⊙ Sights & Activities
A two-hour guided walking tour of the historical centre (adult/child under 15yr €10/free) leaves from the Città di Lucca tourist office at 2pm every day between April and September.

Opera buffs should visit in July and August, when the **Puccini Festival** (www. puccinifestival.it) is held in a purpose-built outdoor theatre in the nearby settlement of Torre del Lago. For other festivals and events, check www.luccaitinera.it.

City Walls FORTRESS
Lucca's massive *mura* (walls), built around the old city in the 16th and 17th centuries and defended by 126 cannons, remain in almost perfect condition. Twelve metres high and 4km in length, the ramparts are crowned with a tree-lined footpath that looks down on the old town and out towards the Apuane Alps – it's the perfect spot to stroll, cycle, run and get a feel for local Lucchesi life.

Cattedrale di San Martino CHURCH
(Piazza San Martino; sacristy adult/reduced €2/1.50; ⊙7am-6pm Apr-Sep, to 5pm Oct-Mar) Lucca's predominantly Romanesque cathedral dates to the start of the 11th century. Its exquisite façade was constructed in the prevailing Lucca-Pisan style and designed to accommodate the pre-existing campanile. Inside, there's a simply fashioned image of a dark-skinned, life-sized Christ on a wooden crucifix, known as the *Volto Santo*, and a magnificent *Last Supper* by Tintoretto. The **sacristy** features Domenico Ghirlandaio's 1479 *Madonna Enthroned with Saints* and a marble memorial carved by Jacopo della Quercia in 1407.

Chiesa e Battistero dei SS Giovanni e Reparata
ARCHAEOLOGICAL SITE

(☎0583 49 05 30; Piazza San Giovanni; adult/concession €2.50/1.50) The 12th-century interior of this deconsecrated church is a hauntingly atmospheric setting for one-hour opera recitals staged by **Puccini e la sua Lucca** (☎340 810 60 42; www.puccinielasualucca.com; adult/reduced €17/13; ⊗7pm daily mid-Mar–Oct, 7pm Fri-Wed Nov–mid-Mar) every evening from mid-March to November. Professional singers present a one-hour program of arias and duets dominated by the music of Puccini. Tickets are available from the church between 10am and 6pm.

Casa Natale Giacomo Puccini
MUSEUM

(☎0583 58 40 28; www.puccinimuseum.it; Corte San Lorenzo 9; adult/reduced €7/5; ⊗10am-6pm Wed-Mon Apr-Oct, 11am-5pm Wed-Mon Nov-Mar) The great composer was born in this modest house in 1858. It's now a somewhat dull showcase of everyday objects telling the tale of the composer's life. For afficionados only.

🛏 Sleeping

2italia
APARTMENT €€

(☎3355 20 82 51; www.2italia.com; Via della Anfiteatro 74; apt for 2 adults & up to 4 children €150-170; ☎) This clutch of family-friendly self-catering apartments overlooks Piazza Anfiteatro, one of the city's major landmarks. Available on a nightly basis (minimum two nights), they sleep up to six, have fully equipped kitchen and washing machine, and come with sheets and towels. The owners also organise cycling tours, cooking courses, wine tastings and olive pickings.

Ostello San Frediano
HOSTEL €

(☎0583 46 99 57; www.ostellolucca.it; Via della Cavallerizza 12; dm/s/d/tr €22/45/65/80, without bathroom dm €20; P@☎) Comfort and service levels are high at this HI-affiliated hostel set in a lovely garden. There are 149 beds in private rooms and segregated dorms, a courtyard and a grandiose dining room (breakfast €3 to €5, dinner €11). Wi-fi and parking are free; internet access costs €1 per hour.

Piccolo Hotel Puccini
HOTEL €

(☎0583 5 54 21; www.hotelpuccini.com; Via di Poggio 9; s €50-73, d €70-97; ✳☎) Close to the Casa Natale Giacomo Puccini, this well-run, small hotel has rooms with old-fashioned decor, satellite TV and small clean bathrooms. Breakfast costs €3.

🍴 Eating

La Pecora Nera
TRATTORIA €

(☎0583 46 97 38; www.lapecoraneralucca.it; Piazza San Francesco 4; pizzas €5-9, mains €8.50-13; ⊗lunch Sat, dinner Wed-Sun) The Black Sheep is the only Lucchesi restaurant recommended by the Slow Food Movement. It also scores extra brownie points for social responsibility (its profits fund workshops for young people with Down syndrome). The menu features pizzas (dinner only), Tuscan favourites and daily specials.

Taddeucci
PASTICCERIA €

(www.taddeucci.com; Piazza San Michele 34; 300/600/900g loaf €4.50/9/13.50; ⊗8.30am-7.45pm, closed Thu winter) This *pasticceria* is where the traditional Lucchesi treat of *buccellato* was created in 1881. These ring-shaped loaves made with flour, sultanas, sugar and aniseed seeds are the perfect accompaniment to a mid-morning or afternoon espresso.

Forno Giusti
BAKERY €

(Via Santa Lucia 20; pizzas & filled focaccias per kg €8-16; ⊗7am-1pm & 4-7.30pm Mon, Tue & Thu-Sat, 7am-1.30pm Wed, 4-7.30pm Sun) The best way to enjoy a Lucchese lunch is to picnic on the walls, particularly if you buy delectable provisions from this excellent bakery.

Da Felice
PIZZERIA €

(www.pizzeriadafelice.com; Via Buia 12; focaccias €1-3.50, pizza slices €1.30; ⊗10am-8.30pm Mon-Sat) This buzzing local favourite behind Piazza San Michele serves *cecina* and *castagnacci* (chestnut cakes).

ℹ Information

The **Città di Lucca tourist office** (☎0583 58 31 50; www.luccaitinera.it; Piazzale Verdi; ⊗9am-7pm Apr-Oct, to 5pm Nov-Mar) holds luggage (€7.50 per day), offers toilet facilities (€0.50), hires bicycles (€2.50 per hour), operates an internet point (€1 per 30 minutes), sells concert tickets, and supplies free maps and information. In the high season there's another tourist office near **Porta Elisa** (☎0583 355 51 00; www.luccatourist.it; Piazza Napoleone; ⊗10am-1pm & 2-6pm Mon-Sat).

ℹ Getting There & Around

The bus station is on Piazzale Giuseppe Verdi, near Porta Vittorio Emanuele Santa Anna. From the bus station **VaiBus** (www.vaibus.it; ⊗hourly Mon-Sat, every 2 hours Sun) buses run to/from Pisa airport (€3, one hour).

Lucca is on the Florence–Pisa–Viareggio train line. Regional trains run to/from Florence (€7,

SAN GIMIGNANO

This tiny hilltop town deep in the Tuscan countryside is a mecca for day-trippers from Florence and Siena. Its nickname is 'The Medieval Manhattan' courtesy of the 11th-century towers that soar above its pristine *centro storico*. Originally 72 were built as monuments to the town's wealth but only 14 remain.

The **tourist office** (📞0577 94 00 08; www.sangimignano.com; Piazza del Duomo 1; ⏰10am-1pm & 3-7pm Mar-Oct, 10am-1pm & 2-6pm Nov-Feb) is a short walk from Piazza dei Martiri di Montemaggio, the nearest San Gimignano has to a bus terminal. Next door, the **Palazzo Comunale** (Piazza del Duomo; gallery & tower admission adult/reduced €5/4; ⏰6.30am-7pm Apr-Sep, 11am-5.30pm Oct-Mar) houses San Gimignano's art gallery (the **Pinacoteca**) and tallest tower, the Torre Grossa.

Nearby, the Romanesque cathedral, known as the **Collegiata** (Piazza del Duomo; adult/child €3.50/1.50; ⏰10am-7.10pm Mon-Fri, to 5.10pm Sat, 12.30-7.10pm Sun Apr-Oct, shorter hours rest of year, closed 2nd half Nov & Jan), boasts an interior covered with 14th-century frescos by Bartolo di Fredi, Lippo Memmi and Tadeo di Bartolo. The small **Cappella di Santa Fina** off the south aisle features frescos by Domenico Ghirlandaio.

While in town, be sure to sample the local wine, Vernaccia, while marvelling at the spectacular view from the terrace of the **Museo del Vino** (Wine Museum; Parco della Rocca; admission free; ⏰11.30am-6.30pm mid-Mar–Oct), which is located next to the Rocca (fortress).

For lunch, head to **Dal Bertelli** (Via Capassi 30; panini €3-5, glasses of wine €1.50; ⏰1-7pm Mar-early Jan) for a panino made with local artisan ingredients, followed by an icy delight from the justly famous **Gelateria di Piazza** (www.gelateriadipiazza.com; Piazza della Cisterna 4; gelati €1.80- 2.50; ⏰8.30am-11pm Mar–mid-Nov).

Regular buses link San Gimignano with Florence (€6.80, 1¼ hours, 14 daily), travelling via Poggibonsi. There are also services to/from Siena (€6, 1¼ hours, hourly).

1½ hours, every 30 to 90 minutes) and Pisa (€3.30, 30 minutes, every 30 to 60 minutes).

There are plenty of car parks around the walls. Most charge €1.50 per hour between 8am and 6.30pm.

Cicli Bizzarri (📞0583 49 66 82; www.cicli bizzarri.net; Piazza Santa Maria 32; ⏰9am-7pm) and **Biciclette Poli** (📞0583 49 37 87; www.bici clettepoli.com; Piazza Santa Maria 42; ⏰9am-7pm) on Piazza Santa Maria rent bikes for €3 per hour (€8 for an electric bike).

UMBRIA

Dubbed the 'green heart of Italy', this predominantly rural region harbours some of Italy's best-preserved historic *borghi* (villages) and many important artistic, religious and architectural treasures. The regional capital, Perugia, provides a convenient base, with Assisi and Orvieto easy day trips away.

Perugia

POP 168,200

With its hilltop medieval centre and international student population, Perugia is Umbria's largest and most cosmopolitan city. There's not a lot to see here, but the presence of the University for Foreigners ensures a buzz that's not always apparent in the region's sleepy hinterland. In July, music fans inundate the city for the prestigious **Umbria Jazz Festival** (www.umbria jazz.com) and in the third week of October the **Eurochocolate** (📞075 502 58 80; www. eurochocolate.com) festival lures chocoholics from across the globe.

Perugia has a bloody and lively past. In the Middle Ages, the Baglioni and Oddi families fought for control of the city, while later, as a papal satellite, the city fought with its neighbours. All the while art and culture thrived: painter Perugino and Raphael, his student, both worked here.

The *centro storico* is on top of the hill, the train station is at the bottom and the regional bus station, Piazza dei Partigiani, is halfway between the two. From Piazza Partigiani there are *scale mobili* (escalators) going up to Piazza Italia, where local buses terminate. From Piazza Italia, pedestrianised Corso Vannucci runs up to Piazza IV Novembre, the city's focal point.

☉ Sights

The **Perugia Città Museo Card** (adult/student €10/6) gives one adult and one child aged under 18 years access to five city museums and is valid for 48 hours.

Piazza IV Novembre   PIAZZA

This meeting point for Etruscans and Romans and former medieval political centre is now a popular gathering place for students and tourists. The 14th-century **Cattedrale di San Lorenzo** (☑075 572 38 32; Piazza IV Novembre; ☺8am-noon & 4-6.30pm) forms an impressive backdrop and the 13th-century **Fontana Maggiore** (Great Fountain) carved by Nicola and Giovanni Pisano provides a stolid centrepoint.

Palazzo dei Priori   MUSEUM

Constructed between the 13th and 14th centuries and formerly the headquarters of the city's magistrature, this *palazzo* now houses some of the best museums in Perugia, including Umbria's foremost art gallery, the stunning **Galleria Nazionale dell'Umbria** (☑800 69 76 16; Corso Vannucci 19; adult/EU 18-25/EU under 18 & over 65 €6.50/3.25/free; ☺8.30am-6.30pm Tue-Sun). An art historian's dream, it showcases 30 rooms of works featuring everything from Byzantine art to the 16th-century creations of home town heroes Pinturicchio and Perugino.

The same building also holds what some consider the most beautiful bank in the world, the **Nobile Collegio del Cambio** (Exchange Hall; ☑075 572 85 99; Corso Vannucci 25; adult/reduced €4.50/2.60; ☺9am-12.30pm & 2.30-5.30pm Mon-Sat, 9am-1pm Sun, closed Mon afternoon Nov–mid-Mar). Its walls are adorned with frescos by Perugino – look for his self-portrait in the painted frame.

COURSES

The **Università per Stranieri** (☑075 5 74 61; www.unistrapg.it; Piazza Fortebraccio 4, Palazzo Gallenga) runs hundreds of courses in language, art, history, music and architecture.

🛏 Sleeping

Primavera Minihotel   PENSION €

(☑075 572 16 57; www.primaveraminihotel.it; Via Vincioli 8; s €45-65, d €70-100, tr €95-120; ❄@🛜) On the top floor of a 16th-century *palazzo*, this well-run two-star *pensione* has eight modern rooms that are as clean as they are comfortable (ask for the top-floor room with terrace). Only a few rooms have air-con; breakfast costs an extra €5 to €8.

Ostello di Perugia   HOSTEL €

(☑075 572 28 80; www.ostello.perugia.it; Via Bontempi 13; dm €16, sheet supplement €2; ☺mid-Jan–mid-Dec) If the 10am to 4pm lockout doesn't scare you off, you're sure to appreciate the sweeping countryside view and wafting sounds of church bells from the hostel's terrace, where guests often gather after making dinner. Enjoy the 16th-century frescoed ceilings and tidy four- to six-person rooms.

🍴 Eating

⬆TOP CHOICE Sandri   CAFE, PASTICCERIA €

(☑075 572 41 12; Corso Vannucci 32; ☺8am-8pm Tue-Sun) Sandri has been serving sweet temptations and the best coffee in town since 1860. Sit at a table on the *corso* or stand at the bar and eye off the decadent cakes, pastries and chocolates on offer.

Civico 25   UMBRIAN €€

(☑075 571 63 76; Via della Viola 25; mains €13.50-14; ☺dinner Mon-Sat) There's lots to like about this *enoteca* – great jazz on the sound system, friendly staff, delicious food and an excellent range of wine by the glass.

Pizzeria Mediterranea   PIZZERIA €

(☑075 572 13 22; Piazza Piccinino 11/12; pizzas €5-12; ☺lunch & dinner) Perugians know to come here for the best pizza in town. The wood-fired brick oven cooks margherita and other choices that can be topped with *mozzarella di bufala* (fresh buffalo-milk mozzarella) for a small surcharge.

ℹ Information

City maps and printed mini-guides are available at the **tourist office** (☑075 573 64 58; www.perugia.umbria2000.it; Piazza Matteotti 18; ☺8.30am-6.30pm). For information about what's on in town, buy a copy of *Viva Perugia* (€1) from a local newsstand.

ℹ Getting There & Away

From the intercity bus station on Piazza dei Partigiani, **Sulga** (☑800 09 96 61; www.sulga.it) buses depart for Florence (€10.10, two hours, twice weekly), Rome's Tiburtina bus station (€16, 2½ hours, five daily), Fiumicino airport (€23, 3¾ hours, three daily Monday to Saturday, two Sunday), Naples (€23, 4½ hours, two daily), Assisi (€3.20, 50 minutes, five daily) and Orvieto (€6.90, two hours, once daily). Sena buses go to Siena (€12, 1½ hours, once daily).

Regional trains connect with Rome (€11.20, 2¾ hours, six daily) and Florence (€12.35, two hours, seven daily).

❶ Getting Around

From the train station, take the *minimetrò* (€1.50) to the Pincetto stop just below Piazza Matteotti, or bus G to Piazza Italia, bus C to Piazza Cavallini behind the Cattedrale di San Lorenzo or bus R to Via XIV Settembre near Piazza Matteotti (tickets all €1.50, €2 if purchased on bus). From the intercity bus station on Piazza dei Partigiani, take the free *scala mobila*.

The centre is mostly closed to traffic, so it's best to park in the free car park at Pian di Massiano and take the *minimetrò* into the centre. Otherwise, the supervised car park at Piazza dei Partigiani charges €16 per 24 hours.

Assisi

POP 28,200

St Francis was born here in 1182, making this medieval town a major destination for millions of pilgrims. Its major sight is the Basilica di San Francesco, a treasure trove of Renaissance frescos.

◉ Sights

Dress rules are applied rigidly at the main religious sights, so no shorts, miniskirts, low-cut dresses or tops. To book guided tours (in English) of the Basilica di San Francesco, telephone or email its **information office** (☑075 819 00 84; www.sanfrancescoassisi.org; ⊙9.15am-noon & 2.15-5.30pm Mon-Sat).

Churches   CHURCH

The **Basilica di San Francesco** (☑075 81 90 01; Piazza di San Francesco; ⊙Reliquary Chapel 9am-6pm daily, 1-4.30pm holidays) comprises two churches. The **upper church** (⊙8.30am-6.45pm Easter-Oct, to 6pm Nov-Easter) was damaged during a severe earthquake in 1997, but has since been restored to its former glory. Built between 1230 and 1253 in the Italian Gothic style, it features a huge fresco cycle by Giottoi.

Downstairs in the dimly lit **lower church** (⊙6am-6.45pm Easter-Oct, to 6pm Nov-Easter), constructed between 1228 and 1230, you'll find a series of colourful frescos by Simone Martini, Cimabue and Pietro Lorenzetti. The **crypt** where St Francis lies buried is below the church.

The 13th-century **Basilica di Santa Chiara** (☑075 81 22 82; Piazza Santa Chiara; ⊙6.30am-noon & 2-7pm Apr-Oct, to 6pm Nov-Mar) contains the remains of St Clare, friend of St Francis and founder of the Order of Poor Clares.

🛏 Sleeping & Eating

You'll need to book ahead during peak times: Easter, August and September, and the Feast of St Francis (3 and 4 October). The tourist office can supply a list of convents and monasteries offering accommodation to pilgrims.

WORTH A TRIP

ORVIETO

Strategically located on the major train line and autostrada between Rome and Florence, this spectacularly sited hilltop town has one major drawcard: its simply extraordinary Gothic-style **Cattedrale** (☑0763 34 11 67; www.opsm.it; Piazza Duomo; admission €3; ⊙9.30am-7pm Mon-Sat Apr-Oct, to 6pm Sat Mar & Oct, 9.30am-1pm & 2.30-5pm Mon-Sat Nov-Feb, 1-6.30pm Sun Jun-Sep, to 5.30pm Sun Mar-May & Oct, 2.30-5.30pm Sun Nov-Feb). Construction of the cathedral commenced in 1290 and took three centuries to complete. Its facade is perhaps the most beautiful to grace any Italian church. The cathedral has a stark but ethereally beautiful interior and its two chapels are decorated with major works of art including Luca Signorelli's *The Last Judgment* fresco cycle.

The **tourist office** (☑0763 34 17 72; info@iat.orvieto.tr.it; Piazza Duomo 24; ⊙8.15am-1.50pm & 4-7pm Mon-Fri, 10am-1pm & 3-6pm Sat & Sun) is opposite the cathedral, and one of Umbria's best restaurants, **I Sette Consoli** (☑0763 34 39 11; www.isetteconsoli.it; Piazza Sant'Angelo 1/a; mains €19-20, 6-course degustation menu €42; ⊙lunch & dinner Thu-Tue), is nearby.

If you arrive by train, you'll need to take a **cable car** (€1 each way, €0.80 with train ticket; ⊙every 10min 7.05am-8.25pm Mon-Fri, every 15min 8.15am-8pm Sat & Sun) up to the town centre. Tickets are available from the *tabacchi* at the station.

Trains run to/from Florence (Intercity; €9 to €20, 1¾ hours, hourly) and Rome (Regionale €7.50, 80 minutes, hourly). To get here from Perugia (€7.10, 1¾ hours), you'll need to change trains at Terontola-Cortona.

Hotel Alexander
B&B €€

(☑075 81 61 90; http://hotelalexanderassisi.it; Piazza Chiesa Nuova 6; s €60-80, d €80-140; ☏) Smack-bang in the centre of town, this safe choice offers nine rooms that vary in size – try to get the one on the top floor, which is huge and has great countryside views. The decor is modern and breakfast in served in your room.

Ostello della Pace
HOSTEL €

(☑075 81 67 67; www.assisihostel.com; Via Valecchie 177; dm incl breakfast €17-19, r from €40; ☉1 Mar-8 Nov & 27 Dec-6 Jan; [P][@]) Student groups, couples appreciating the handful of private rooms, backpackers and pilgrims are all welcome at Assisi's HI hostel. Thrifty travellers will appreciate the dinners (€10.50), hikers will appreciate the boxed lunches (€7) and everyone will appreciate the idyllic setting. You'll find it just off the road coming in from Santa Maria degli Angeli.

Trattoria da Erminio
TRATTORIA €

(☑075 81 25 06; www.trattoriadaerminio.it; Via Montecavallo 19; mains €7-11, set menus €16; ☉lunch & dinner Fri-Wed, closed Feb & 1st half of Jul) Da Erminio is known for its grilled meats, which are prepared on a huge fireplace in the main dining area. In summer, tables on the pretty cobbled street are hot property. You'll find it in the upper town near Piazza Matteotti.

Trattoria Pallotta
TRATTORIA €€

(☑075 81 26 49; www.pallottaassisi.it; Vicolo della Volta Pinta; mains €12-18, set menus €18-27; ☉lunch & dinner Wed-Mon) Head through the Volta Pinta (Painted Vault) off Piazza del Comune into this old-fashioned eatery. They offer all the Umbrian classics here – rabbit, homemade *strangozzi* (pasta) and pigeon – as well as an excellent *antipasto della casa* (house antipasto; €9). Vegetarians are well catered for.

Mangiar di Vino
RISTORANTE €€

(☑0758 15 51 32; www.mangiardivino.it; Via Francalancia 2; mains €10-18, pizzas €7-8) This modern *enoteca* on the *passaggiata* (evening walk) route between Piazza del Comune and Piazza Santa Chiara serves pastas, simple mains and pizzas. It's a good choice for *aperitivo*, and the two-course *menu del giorno* (menu of the day) is excellent value at only €16.

❶ Information

Tourist Office (☑075 813 86 80; www.assisi. regioneumbria.eu; Piazza del Comune 22; ☉8am-2pm & 3-6pm Mon-Fri, 9.30am-5pm Sat & Sun, later in summer) Supplies maps, brochures and practical information.

❶ Getting There & Away

It is better to travel to Assisi by bus rather than train, as the train station is 4km from Assisi proper, in Santa Maria degli Angeli. Buses arrive at and depart from Piazza Matteotti, stopping at Piazza Unita d'Italia below the basilica en route.

Sulga buses connect Assisi with Perugia (€3.20, 50 minutes, five daily), Rome (€18, three hours, one daily) and Florence (€12.50, 2½ hours, twice weekly).

If you arrive by train, a bus (Linea C; €1, half-hourly) runs between Piazza Matteotti and the station. Regional trains run to Perugia (€2.40, 20 minutes, hourly).

SOUTHERN ITALY

Southern Italy is a robust contrast to the genteel north. Its beaches, baroque towns and classical ruins exist alongside ugly urban sprawl and scruffy coastal development (sometimes in the space of a few kilometres) and its residents are a raucous lot who are often wary of interlopers, be they from other countries or the regions north of Rome.

Yet for all its flaws – organised crime, corrupt officialdom, unchecked and outrageous property development – *il mezzogiorno* (the midday sun, as southern Italy is known) is an essential part of every Italian itinerary, offering cheeky charm, culinary masterpieces and architectural treasures galore.

Naples
POP 959,600

Naples (Napoli) is dirty, noisy, dishevelled and totally exhilarating. Founded by Greek colonists, it became a thriving Roman city and was later the Bourbon capital of the Kingdom of the Two Sicilies. In the 18th century it was one of Europe's great cities, something you'll readily believe as you marvel at its profusion of baroque *palazzi*.

The city fronts the waterfront and is divided into *quartieri* (districts). A convenient point of reference is Stazione Centrale, which forms the eastern flank of Piazza Garibaldi, Naples' ugly transport hub. From Piazza Garibaldi, Corso Umberto I skirts the *centro storico*, which is centred on two parallel roads: Via San Biagio dei Librai and its continuation Via Benedetto Croce (together known as Spaccanapoli); and Via dei Tribunali. West of the *centro storico*, Via Toledo, Naples' main shopping strip, leads down to Piazza del Plebiscito. South of here lies the seafront Santa Lucia district; to the west is Chiaia, an upmarket and extremely fashionable area. Above it all, Vomero is a natural balcony with grand views.

◉ Sights

TOP CHOICE **Museo Archeologico Nazionale** MUSEUM

(☑081 44 01 66; Piazza Museo Nazionale 19; admission €6.50; ☺9am-7.30pm Wed-Mon; Ⓜ Museo, Piazza Cavour) If you visit only one museum in southern Italy, make it this one. Boasting priceless classical sculptures as well as mosaics and frescos from Pompeii and Herculaneum, its collection is mind-bogglingly impressive.

Many of the exhibits once belonged to the Farnese family, including the mighty *Toro Farnese* (Farnese Bull) in Room XVI and the muscle-bound *Ercole* (Hercules) in Room XI. The mezzanine floor is home to an exquisite collection of Pompeian mosaics, including *La battaglia di Alessandro contro Dario* (The Battle of Alexander against Darius) in Room LXI and the amusing *Scene di commedia: musici ambulanti* (Comedy Scene: Street Musicians) in room LIX.

Beyond the mosaics, the **Gabinetto Segreto** (Secret Chamber) contains a small but much-studied collection of ancient erotica.

Cappella Sansevero CHAPEL

(☑081 551 84 70; www.museosansevero.it; Via Francesco de Sanctis 19; adult/EU student/child under 10 €7/5/free; ☺10am-5.40pm Mon & Wed-Sat, to 1.10pm Sun; Ⓜ Dante) This chapel sports a sumptuous baroque interior and is home to the *Cristo velato* (Veiled Christ), Giuseppe Sanmartino's incredibly lifelike sculpture of a recumbent dead Christ covered by a veil.

Basilica di Santa Chiara CHURCH

(☑081 195 75 915; www.monasterodisantachiara.eu; Via Benedetto Croce; cloisters adult/reduced €5/3.50; ☺basilica 7.30am-1pm & 4.30-8pm, cloisters 9.30am-5pm Mon-Sat, 10am-2pm Sun; Ⓜ Dante) This huge basilica is actually a 20th-century recreation of Gagliardo Primario's 14th-century original, which was severely damaged in World War II. The pièce de résistance, however, is the basilica's adjoining **Chiostro Maiolicato** (Nuns' Cloister), encrusted with colourful 17th-century majolica tiles and frescos.

Palazzo Reale MUSEUM

(Royal Palace; ☑081 40 04 54; Piazza del Plebiscito; adult/reduced/EU under 18 & over 65 €4/3/free; ☺9am-7pm Thu-Tue) This former residence of the Bourbon and Savoy kings now houses a

❶ DISCOUNT CARDS

Campania ArteCards (☑0639 96 76 50, 800 60 06 01; www.campaniaartecard. it) offer discounted admission to museums in Naples and Campania. Choose the version that suits you best; some include free public transport. The Tutti la Regione three-day card (adult/EU 18-25 €27/20) includes free Unicocampania public transport (including the Alibus from Napoli airport) and free entrance to your choice of two museums and sights, including Pompeii and the Museo Archeologico Nazionale di Napoli. The seven-day card (€30) includes free entrance to five museums or sights and a 50% discount to all others (no transport, though). The cards are available at participating museums, at Capodichino airport, at Stazione Centrale in Naples, online or through the call centre.

museum showcasing baroque and neoclassical furnishings, statues and paintings. Among the many highlights is the **Teatrino di Corte**, a lavish private theatre built in 1768 to celebrate the marriage of Ferdinand IV and Marie Caroline of Austria.

Certosa e Museo di San Martino MUSEUM

(☑848 80 02 88; Largo San Martino 5; adult/reduced €6/3; ☺8.30am-6.30pm Thu-Tue) Originally built by Charles of Anjou in 1325, this former Carthusian monastery houses a superb collection of Neapolitan art. Highlights include the main church and sacristy, the 16th-century Chiostro Grande (Great Cloister), the 'Images and Memories of Naples' exhibition in the Quarto del Priore (Priors Quarters) and the Sezione Presepiale, which houses a whimsical collection of rare Neapolitan *presepi* (nativity scenes) carved in the 18th and 19th centuries.

The easiest way to get up to Vomero is to take the Funiculore Centrale (€1.20) from Stazione Cumana di Montesanto, near Via Toledo.

Catacomba di San Gennaro ARCHAEOLOGICAL SITE

(☑081 744 37 14; www.catacombedinapoli.it; Via Tondo di Capodimonte 13; adult/reduced €8/5; ☺1hr tours every hour 10am-5pm Mon-Sat, to 1pm Sun) Naples' oldest catacomb became a Christian pilgrimage site when the body of the city's patron saint, Gennaro, was interred

Central Naples

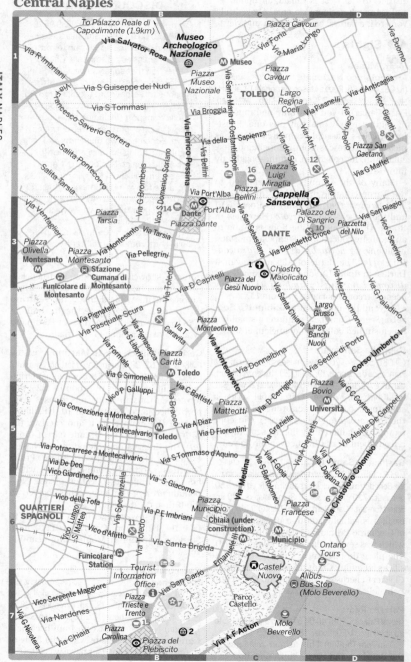

To Palazzo Reale di
Capodimonte (1.9km)

Via R Imbriani

Via Salvator Rosa

Museo Archeologico Nazionale

Piazza Cavour

Via Foria

Via Maria Longo

Via Duomo

Piazza Museo Nazionale

Museo

Via Santa Maria di Costantinopoli

Piazza Cavour

Via S Guiseppe dei Nudi

Via S Tommasi

Via Francesco Saverio Correra

TOLEDO

Largo Regina Coeli

Via d'Anticaglia

Vico Giganti

Via Broggia

Via della Sapienza

Via Pisanelli

Via San Paolo

8

Salita Pontecorvo

Via Enrico Pessina

Via Atri

Via del Sole

Piazza San Gaetano

Salita Tarsia

Via Bellini

5

16

Piazza Luigi Miraglia

12

Via Nilo

Via G Maffei

Via Ventaglieri

Via G Brombeis

Vico S Domenico Soriano

Via Port'Alba

Piazza Bellini

Port'Alba

Cappella Sansevero

Piazza Olivella

14

Dante

Piazza Dante

Via San Sebastiano

Palazzo dei Di Sangrio

Via San Biagio

Vico S Severino

Montesanto

Piazza Montesanto

Via Montesanto

Via Tarsia

Piazzetta del Nilo

Piazza Tarsia

Via Pellegrini

10

DANTE

Via Benedetto Croce

Via Mezzocannone

Via G Paladino

Stazione Cumana di Montesanto

Funicolare di Montesanto

Via Toledo

Via D Capitelli

Piazza del Gesù Nuovo

1

Chiostro Maiolicato

Largo Giusso

Via Pignatelli

Via Pasquale Scura

9

Via T Caravita

Piazza Monteoliveto

Via Santa Chiara

Largo Banchi Nuovi

Via Pignasecca

Via S Liborio

Via Formale

Piazza Carità

Via Monteoliveto

Via Donnalbina

Via Sedile di Porto

Corso Umberto I

Via G Simonelli

Toledo

Via C Battisti

Via D Cerriglio

Piazza Bovio

Via G C Cortese

Vico P Galluppi

Piazza Matteotti

Via A Diaz

Università

Via Concezione a Montecalvario

Via Bracco

Piazza Matteotti

Via D Fiorentini

Via Graziella

Via Alside De Gasperi

Via Montecalvario

Toledo

Via Potracarrese a Montecalvario

Via S Tommaso d'Aquino

Via F Gioia

Via A-Depretis

Via S Nicola alla Dogana

Via Cristoforo Colombo

QUARTIERI SPAGNOLI

Via De Deo
Vico Giardinetto

Via S Giacomo

Via Speranzella

Via Medina

Via S Bartolomeo

4

6

Vico della Tofa

Via P E Imbriani

Piazza Municipio

Via Lungo S Matteo

11

Via Toledo

Piazza Francese

Via A F Acton

Funicolare Station

Tourist Information Office

3

Via Santa Brigida

Chiaia (under construction)

Municipio

Ontano Tours

Vico Sergente Maggiore

17

Via San Carlo

Piazza Trieste e Trento

Emanuele III

Castel Nuovo

Alibus
Bus Stop
(Molo Beverello)

Via G Nicotera

Via Nardones

15

Piazza Carolina

Piazza del Plebiscito

2

Parco Castello

Molo Beverello

Via Chiaia

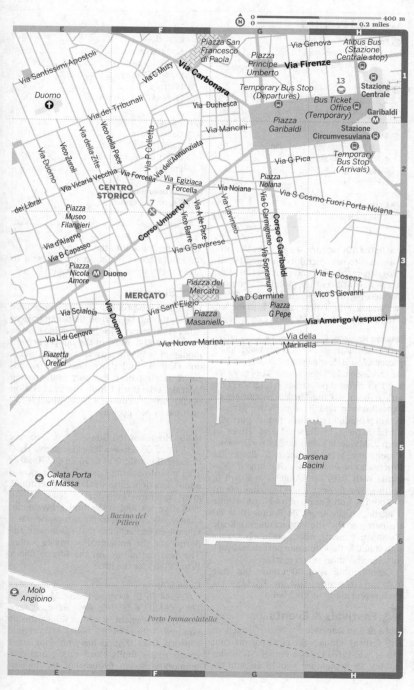

0 — 400 m
0 — 0.2 miles

Via Genova

Piazza San Francesco di Paola

Piazza Principe Umberto

Via Firenze

Alibus Bus (Stazione Centrale stop)

Via Santissimi Apostoli

Via C Muzy

Via Carbonara

Temporary Bus Stop (Departures)

13

Bus Ticket Office (Temporary)

Stazione Centrale

Duomo

Via dei Tribunali

Via Duchesca

Piazza Garibaldi

Garibaldi

Via della Pace

Vico della Zite

Vico Zuroli

Via P Colletta

Via dell'Annunziata

Via Mancini

Stazione Circumvesuviana

Via Duomo

Via Vicaria Vecchia

Via Forcella

Via Egiziaca a Forcella

Via G Pica

Temporary Bus Stop (Arrivals)

dei Librai

CENTRO STORICO

7

Piazza Nolana

Via Nolana

Via S Cosmo Fuori Porta Nolana

Piazza Museo Filangieri

Via d'Alagno

Via B Capasso

Corso Umberto I

Vico Barre

Via A de Pace

Via Lavinaio

Via C Carmignano

Corso G Garibaldi

Via G Savarese

Via Soppramuro

Piazza Nicola Amore

Duomo

MERCATO

Piazza del Mercato

Via D Carmine

Via E Cosenz

Vico S Giovanni

Via Scialoia

Via Duomo

Via Sant'Eligio

Piazza Masaniello

Piazza G Pepe

Via Amerigo Vespucci

Via L di Genova

Via Nuova Marina

Via della Marinella

Piazzetta Orefici

Calata Porta di Massa

Darsena Bacini

Bacino del Piliero

Molo Angioino

Porto Immacolatella

Central Naples

◎ **Top Sights**
Cappella Sansevero D3
Museo Archeologico Nazionale............ B1

◎ **Sights**
1 Basilica di Santa Chiara C3
2 Palazzo Reale B7

◎ **Sleeping**
3 Art Resort Galleria Umberto B6
4 Hostel of the Sun D6
5 Hotel Piazza Bellini C2
6 Romeo Hotel D6

◎ **Eating**
7 Da Michele F2

8 Di Matteo D2
9 Fantasia Gelati B4
La Stanza del Gusto .... (see 5)
10 Palazzo Petrucci D3
11 Pintauro B6
12 Pizzeria Gino Sorbillo D2

◎ **Drinking**
13 Caffè Mexico H1
14 Caffè Mexico B3
15 Gran Caffè Gambrinus B7
16 Intra Moenia C2

◎ **Entertainment**
17 Teatro San Carlo B7

here in the 5th century. It's an evocative other world of tombs, corridors and broad vestibules decorated with 2nd-century Christian frescos and 5th-century mosaics. Tours are operated by the Cooperativa Sociale Onlus 'La Paranza', whose ticket office is to the left of the Chiesa di Madre di Buon Consiglio.

Palazzo Reale di Capodimonte   PALACE
(✆081 749 91 11; Parco di Capodimonte; adult/reduced €7.50/3.75; ⊗museum 8.30am-6pm Thu-Tue, park 7.45am-1hr before sunset; ☐R4 to Via Miano) This colossal palace set in a 130-hectare park is home to the **Museo Nazionale di Capodimonte** and its superlative art collection. Highlights include family portraits of the Farnese by Raphael and Titian in room 2, Masaccio's celebrated *Crocifissione* (Crucifixion; 1426) in Room 3, Botticelli's *Madonna col Bambino e due angeli* (Madonna with Baby and Angels) in Room 6, Bellini's *Trasfigurazione* (Transfiguration) in Room 8, and Caravaggio's *Flagellazione* (Flagellation) in Room 78. Rooms 31 to 60 are occupied by the Appartamento Reale (Royal Apartment), which positively heaves with valuable Capodimonte porcelain, heavy curtains and shiny inlaid marble.

Capodimonte is a 30-minute bus ride from the city centre; take bus R4 from Via Medina and alight at Via Miano.

✫✫ Festivals & Events

Festa di San Gennaro   RELIGIOUS
This festival honours the city's patron saint and is held three times a year (first Sunday in May, 19 September and 16 December). Thousands pack into the Duomo to witness the saint's blood liquefy, a miracle said to save the city from potential disasters.

⌂ Sleeping

You'll have no problem finding somewhere to stay, though be warned that many places suffer from street noise, and double-glazing is not common. Most of the budget accommodation is in the ugly area around Stazione Centrale and down near the port; if you're staying near the port and arriving by train, take tram 1 from the train station (€1.20) rather than the R2 bus, which is frequented by pickpockets.

TOP CHOICE Hostel of the Sun   HOSTEL €
(✆081 420 63 93; www.hostelnapoli.com; Via G Melisurgo 15; dm €15-20, s €25-35, d €60-70; ❄ �🤶) This award-winning hostel has the lot – a handy location close to the ferry terminal, great facilities (including a bar), helpful staff, free tea and coffee and a breezy, inclusive vibe. Adding to the atmosphere is a vibrant colour scheme that extends to the dorms and the hotel-quality private rooms. The best dorms are on the higher floors. Bring €0.05 for the lift.

Casa D'Anna   GUESTHOUSE €€
(✆081 44 66 11; www.casadanna.it; Via Cristallini 138; s €67-102, d €95-145; ❄ � 🤶; Ⓜ Piazza Cavour, Museo) An elegant guesthouse lavishishly equipped with antiques, books and original artwork, Casa D'Anna has only four guest rooms that skilfully blend classic and contemporary design features of the highest

quality. Breakfast includes homemade baked treats and jams. Two-night minimum stay.

Hotel Piazza Bellini
BOUTIQUE HOTEL €€

(☏081 45 17 32; www.hotelpiazzabellini.com; Via Costantinopoli 101; s €70-140, d €80-165; ❋@🛜; MDante) Only steps away from buzzing nightspot Piazza Bellini, this sleek hotel inhabits a 16th-century *palazzo* and its cool white spaces are adorned with original majolica tiles and the work of emerging artists. Rooms offer pared-back chic, with comfortable beds and small bathrooms.

B&B Cappella Vecchia
B&B €

(☏081 240 51 17; www.cappellavecchia11.it; Vico Santa Maria a Cappella Vecchia 11; s €50-80, d €75-120; ❋@🛜; 🚌C24 to Piazza dei Martiri) Run by a super-helpful young couple, this B&B is a first-rate choice. There are six simple, comfy rooms and a spacious communal area for breakfast. Check the website for monthly packages.

UNA Napoli
BUSINESS HOTEL €€

(☏081 563 69 01; www.unahotels.it/en/una_hotel_napoli/napoli_hotels.htm; Piazza Garibaldi 10; r €84-151; ❋@🛜) A convenient location opposite the train station and excellent online specials mean that it's well worth considering this well-run business hotel. Rooms are blessedly quiet due to double-glazed windows and have every amenity you will need.

Art Resort Galleria Umberto
BOUTIQUE HOTEL €€

(☏081 497 62 81; www.artresortgalleriaumberto.it; Galleria Umberto I 83, 4th fl, Via Toledo, Quartieri Spagnoli; r €94-193; ❋@🛜) For a taste of Neapolitan glitz and grandeur, book into this boutique hotel secreted on an upper floor of the magnificent Galleria Umberto I. The price includes a delicious buffet breakfast and evening *aperitivo*. You'll need €0.10 for the lift.

Romeo Hotel
LUXURY HOTEL €€€

(☏081 017 50 01; www.romeohotel.it; Via Cristoforo Colombo 45; r €150-330, ste €240-400; ❋@🛜) A quick walk from the ferries takes you to this relatively new hotel and design buff's dream. Designed by Paul Tange (son of Japanese starchitect Kenzo Tange), it features luxe rooms, A-list art and furniture, a glam sushi bar, a rooftop restaurant and a truly jaw-dropping spa centre.

✖ Eating

Neapolitans are justifiably proud of their food. The pizza was created here – there are any number of toppings but locals favour margherita (tomato, mozzarella and basil) or marinara (tomato, garlic, oregano and olive oil), cooked in a wood-fired oven. Pizzerias serving the 'real thing' have a sign on their door – *la vera pizza napoletana* (the real Neapolitan pizza).

For something sweet try a *sfogliatella*, a flaky pastry filled with sweet orange-flavoured ricotta that is ideally served warm.

Pizza

TOP CHOICE▸ Pizzeria Gino Sorbillo
PIZZERIA €

(☏081 44 66 43; www.accademiadellapizza.it; Via dei Tribunali 32; pizzas from €2.50; ⊘Mon-Sat; MDante) The clamouring crowds say it all: Gino Sorbillo is the city's pizza king. Be sure to go to Gino – there are two other Sorbillo pizzerias on the same block, all from one family of 21 pizza-making siblings.

Da Michele
PIZZERIA €

(☏081 553 92 04; www.damichele.net; Via Cesare Sersale 1; small/medium/large pizzas €4/5/6; ⊘Mon-Sat) Da Michele has been serving since 1870, and its popularity shows no sign of waning. Things are plain and simple here: unadorned marble tabletops, brisk service and two types of pizza – margherita or marinara. Just show up, take a ticket and wait your turn.

Di Matteo
PIZZERIA €

(☏081 45 52 62; Via dei Tribunali 94; snacks €0.50, pizzas from €2.50; ⊘9am-midnight Mon-Sat; 🅿; 🚌C55 to Via Duomo) The little street stall at this no-frills pizzeria sells some of the city's best fried snacks, from golden *crocchè* (potato croquettes) to nourishing *arancini* (fried rice balls). Head inside for low lighting, surly waiters and lip-smacking pizzas.

Not Pizza

La Stanza del Gusto
OSTERIA €€

(☏081 40 15 78; www.lastanzadelgusto.com; Via Costantinopoli 100; soup €10, platters €13-20, filled panini €5-8; ⊘11am-midnight Tue-Sat, till 4pm Sun; MDante) There's a restaurant serving modern twists on local favourites upstairs, but we prefer the atmospheric *osteria* on the ground floor, where it's possible to enjoy a glass of wine accompanied by a cheese or *salumi* (cured meat) platter, panino (lunch only) or bowl of soup.

Palazzo Petrucci
MODERN ITALIAN €€€

(☏081 552 40 68; www.palazzopetrucci.it; Piazza San Domenico Maggiore 4; mains €16-25, degustation menu €55; ⊘lunch Tue-Sun, dinner Mon-Sat; MDante) Progressive Petrucci is a breath of fresh air, exciting palates with mostly successful new-school creations that balance technique and flavour well. The fine-dining air may be a bit stuffy for some.

TOP CHOICE Pintauro
PASTICCERIA €

(☏348 778 16 45; Via Toledo 275; sfogliatelle €2; ⊙8am-2pm & 2.30-8pm Mon-Sat, 9am-2pm Sun Sep-May) This cinnamon-scented local institution sells warm *sfogliatelle* dusted with icing sugar to shoppers on Via Toleda. Delicious!

Fantasia Gelati
GELATERIA €

(☏081 551 12 12; Via Toledo 381; gelato from €2; ⊙7.30am-midnight; Ⓜ Toledo) Head here for the city's finest gelato. The heavenly, made-on-site flavours include a dangerously dense chocolate *'cuore nero'* (dark heart). There's another branch in Vomero.

🍷 Drinking

Caffè Mexico
CAFE

(Piazza Dante 86; ⊙7am-8.30pm Mon-Sat) This retro gem makes the best coffee in the city. The espresso is served *zuccherato* (sweetened), so request it *amaro* if you drink it unadorned. In summer, the *caffè freddo con panna* (iced coffee with cream) is a treat. There's another branch at Piazza Garibaldi 70.

Gran Caffè Gambrinus
CAFE

(www.caffegambrinus.com; Via Chiaia 1-2; ⊙7am-2am) Naples' most venerable cafe features a showy art nouveau interior and a cast of self-conscious drinkers served by smart, waistcoated waiters. It's great value when you stand at the bar.

Intra Moenia
CAFE

(☏081 29 07 20; Piazza Bellini 70; ⊙10am-2am; 🛜; Ⓜ Dante) This arty cafe-bookshop-bar on Piazza Bellini attracts a bohemian crowd who adore its laid-back, literary ambience.

☆ Entertainment

Opera fans will enjoy an evening at Teatro San Carlo (☏081 797 23 31; www.teatrosancarlo.it; Via San Carlo 98; ⊙box office 10am-7pm Tue-Sat, 10am-3.30pm Sun), the oldest opera house in Italy. The opera season runs from December to May and performances of music and ballet are held at other times of the year.

In May, the **Maggio dei Monumenti** festival stages concerts and cultural activities in museums and monuments around town. Entry to most of these is free; check details with a tourist office.

ℹ Information

Dangers & Annoyances

Despite Naples' notoriety as a Mafia hot spot, the city is pretty safe. That said, travellers should be careful about walking alone late at night near Stazione Centrale and Piazza Dante. Petty crime is also widespread – be vigilant for pickpockets (especially on the city's public transport) and be on guard against moped bandits.

Emergency

Police Station (Questura; ☏081 794 11 11; Via Medina 75)

Medical Services

Ospedale Loreto-Mare (Hospital; ☏081 254 27 93; Via Amerigo Vespucci 26) On the waterfront, near the train station.

Tourist Information

There are several **tourist information points** (www.inaples.it) around town: Piazza del **Gesù Nuovo** (Piazza del Gesù Nuovo 7; ⊙9.30am-1.30pm & 2.30-6.30pm Mon-Sat, 9.30am-1.30pm Sun), Via **Santa Lucia** (☏081 240 09 14; Via Santa Lucia; ⊙9am-7pm daily) and Via **San Carlo** (☏081 40 23 94; Via San Carlo; ⊙9.30am-1.30pm & 2.30-6.30pm Mon-Sat, 9.30am-1.30pm Sun).

ℹ Getting There & Away

Air

Capodichino airport (p532), 7km northeast of the city centre, is southern Italy's main airport. Flights operate to most Italian cities and up to 30 European destinations, as well as New York.

Boat

A fleet of *traghetti* (ferries), *aliscafi* (hydrofoils) and *navi veloci* (fast ships) connect Naples with Sorrento, the bay islands, the Amalfi Coast, Salerno, Sicily and Sardinia. Most fast ferries and hydrofoils leave from Molo Beverello; a few services to Capri, Ischia and Procida also leave from Molo Mergellina. Ferries for Sicily and Sardinia sail from Molo Angioino, next to Molo Beverello, and also from the neighbouring Calata Porta di Massa.

Tickets for shorter journeys can be bought at Molo Beverello or Molo Mergellina. For longer journeys try **Ontano Tours** (☏081 551 71 64; www.ontanotour.it; Molo Angioino; ⊙8.30am-8pm Mon-Sat), in the car park in front of Molo Angioino. You can also purchase tickets online.

Note that ferry services are pared back in winter and adverse sea conditions may affect sailing schedules.

The major companies servicing Naples: **Alilauro** (☏081 497 22 38; www.alilauro.it) To/from Sorrento (€11, bags €2 each, 35 minutes, five daily).

Caremar (☎199 11 66 55; www.caremar.it) Runs services from Naples to Capri (ferry/hydrofoil €11.50/18.80, 80/50 minutes, frequent in summer).

Gescab (☎081 807 18 12; www.gescab.it) Runs hydrofoils to Sorrento (€11, 35 minutes, six daily).

Metrò del Mare (☎199 60 07 00; www.metro delmare.net) Usually runs services between Naples and Sorrento, Positano and Amalfi over the summer months, but had suspended services when this book went to print.

NLG (☎081 552 07 63; www.navlib.it) To/from Capri (€20.20, nine daily) and Sorrento (€12.10, nine daily).

Siremar (☎199 11 88 66; www.siremar.it) Operates boats to the Aeolian Islands and Milazzo (seat from €70.20, six times weekly in summer, twice weekly in the low season).

SNAV (☎091 428 55 55; www.snav.it) Runs hydrofoils to Capri (€19.80, seven daily) and Sorrento (€13.10, five daily) as well as ferries to Palermo (from €48, 10 hours, one daily). In summer there are daily services to the Aeolian Islands.

Tirrenia (☎081 720 11 11; www.tirrenia.it) Twice-weekly service to and from Cagliari (from €45, 11¼ hours) and a daily service to Palermo (from €34).

TTT Lines (☎081 580 27 44; www.tttlines.it) To/from Catania (from €38, 11 hours, one daily).

Bus

Most long-distance buses leave from the temporary bus stop in Piazza Garibaldi, opposite the Hotel Cavour. **Miccolis** (☎081 20 03 80; www.miccolis-spa.it) runs buses to Bari (€19, three hours, three daily) and Lecce (€32, three hours, three daily) via Brindisi (€29, five hours). **Marino** (☎080 311 23 35; www.marinobus.it) operates services to Matera (€19, 4¼ hours, two daily). Buy tickets and catch buses from the temporary ticket booth in front of Stazione Centrale.

Car & Motorcycle

The city is easily accessible from Rome on the A1 autostrada. The Naples–Pompeii–Salerno motorway (A3) connects with the coastal road to Sorrento and the Amalfi Coast. If you value your sanity, skip driving in Naples itself.

Train

Most trains stop at Stazione Centrale, which incorporates Stazione Garibaldi. There are up to 30 trains daily to Rome (Intercity €19, 2¼ hours) and a few to Palermo (Intercity €29, nine hours).

The **Circumvesuviana** (☎081 772 24 44; www.vesuviana.it), accessible through Stazione Centrale, operates a service to Sorrento (€4, 65 minutes) via Ercolano for Herculaneum (€2.10, 10 minutes), Pompeii (€2.10, 35 minutes) and

other towns along the coast. There are about 40 trains daily running between 5am and 10.40pm, with reduced services on Sunday.

ⓘ Getting Around

To/From the Airport

By public transport you can either take the regular **ANM** (☎800 63 95 25; www.unicocampania.it) bus 3S (€1.10, 20 minutes, half-hourly) from Piazza Garibaldi, or the Alibus airport shuttle (€3, 45 minutes) from Piazza del Municipio or Stazione Centrale. This operates every 30 minutes between 6am and midnight.

Taxi fares are set at €16 to/from the *centro storico* and €19 to/from the port.

Public Transport

You can travel around Naples by bus, metro and funicular. Journeys are covered by the **Unico Napoli ticket** (www.unicocampania.it), which comes in various forms: the standard ticket, valid for 90 minutes, costs €1.20; a daily pass is €3.60 and a weekend daily ticket is €3. Note that these tickets are not valid on the Circumvesuviana line.

Taxi

Taxi fares are set at €6 between the *centro storico* and Piazza Garibaldi and from the centre to the port. A trip from Piazza Garibaldi to the port costs €11. There's a €3 surcharge after 10pm (€5.50 on Sunday).

Be warned that there are a number of unlicensed taxi drivers operating from outside the train station; only use official white taxis.

Capri

POP 14,200

The most visited of the islands in the Bay of Naples, Capri deserves more than a quick day trip. Beyond the glamorous veneer of chichi cafes and designer boutiques is an island of rugged seascapes, desolate Roman ruins and a surprisingly unspoiled rural inland.

Emperor Augustus made Capri his private playground and Tiberius retired there in AD 27. Its modern incarnation as a tourist destination dates to the early 20th century when it was invaded by an army of European artists, writers and Russian revolutionaries, drawn as much by the beauty of the local boys as by the thrilling landscape.

The island is easily reached from Naples and Sorrento. Hydrofoils and ferries dock at Marina Grande, from where it's a short funicular ride up to Capri, the main town. A further bus ride takes you up to the island's second settlement, Anacapri.

ITALY CAPRI

POMPEII & HERCULANEUM

On 24 August AD 79 Mt Vesuvius erupted, submerging the town of Pompeii in lapilli (burning fragments of pumice stone) and the town of Herculaneum in mud. As a result, both towns were destroyed and over 2000 residents died. The Unesco-listed ruins of both provide remarkable models of working Roman cities, complete with streets, temples, houses, baths, forums, taverns, shops and even a brothel. Exploring both gives a fascinating glimpse into ancient Roman life.

Visitors can choose to visit one site, or can purchase a combination ticket that covers both and is valid for three days.

To visit **Herculaneum** (☏081 732 43 38; www.pompeiisites.org; Corso Resina 6, Ercolano; adult/EU 18-24/EU under 18 & over 65 €11/5.50, combined ticket incl Pompeii; ⊙8.30am-6pm Apr-Oct, to 3.30pm Nov-Mar; ☒Ercolano-Scavi), take the Circumvesuviana train from Naples (€2.10, 10 minutes), alight at the Ercolano stop and walk straight down the main street to reach the archaeological site. Highlights include the Sede degli Augustali, the Casa del Salone Nero and the Casa Sannitica.

For **Pompeii** (☏081 857 53 47; www.pompeiisites.org; entrances at Porta Marina & Piazza Anfiteatro; adult/EU 18-24/EU under 18 & over 65 €11/5.50/free, combined ticket incl Herculaneum €20/10; ⊙8.30am-6pm Apr-Oct, 8.30am-3.30pm Nov-Mar), take the Circumvesuviana to the Pompeii Scavi-Villa dei Misteri stop (€2.10, 35 minutes), located right next to the Porta Marina entrance to the ruins. There's a huge amount to see here, but be sure not to miss the Lupanare (Brothel), the Casa del Menandro, the *anfiteatro* (ampitheatre) and the Villa dei Misteri with its extraordinary frescos.

For the best views on the island, take the **seggiovia** (chairlift; one-way/return €7/10; ⊙9am-5pm Mar-Oct, 9am-3pm Nov-Feb) up from Piazza Vittoria to the summit of **Mt Solaro** (589m), Capri's highest point.

👁 Sights & Activities

Grotta Azzurra   CAVE
(Blue Grotto; admission €12.50; ⊙9am–3pm) This stunning sea cave illuminated by an otherworldly blue light is Capri's major attraction and is best visited in the morning. Boats leave from Marina Grande (return incl Grotto entrance €24.50); allow a good hour or so. Alternatively, take a bus from Viale Tommaso de Tommaso in Anacapri (€1.80, 15 minutes) or take a bus to Piazza Vittoria and then follow the pedestrian-only path down Via G Orlandi, Via Pagliaro and Via Grotta Azzurra (35 minutes). Note that the grotto is not visitable when seas are rough or tides are high.

Giardini di Augusto   GARDENS
(Gardens of Augustus; admission €1; ⊙9am-1hr before sunset) Once you've explored Capri Town's picture-perfect streets, head to this garden to enjoy breaktaking views. From here Via Krupp zigzags down to Marina Piccola.

Villa Jovis   RUIN
(Jupiter's Villa; ☏081 837 06 34; Via Amaiuri; adult/reduced €2/1; ⊙9am-1hr before sunset) This was the largest and most sumptuous of the island's 12 Roman villas and was Tiberius' main Capri residence. Although not in great shape today, it gives a good idea of the scale on which the emperor liked to live.

🛏 Sleeping

Capri has plenty of top-end hotels, but few genuinely budget options. Always book ahead, as hotel space is at a premium during summer and many places close between November and Easter.

Hotel Villa Eva   HOTEL €€
(☏081 837 15 49; www.villaeva.com; Via La Fabbrica 8, Anacapri; r €100-120; ⊙Mar-Oct; ▣@☰) Hidden among fruit and olive trees, Villa Eva has rooms with lashings of character, a swimming pool and treetop views down to the sea. To get here take a taxi (€30) or the Grotta Azzurra bus from Anacapri and ask the driver where to get off.

Hotel La Tosca   PENSION €€
(☏081 837 09 89; www.latoscahotel.com; Via Dalmazio Birago 5, Capri Town; s €50-100, d €75-160; ⊙Apr-Oct; ▣☎) This charming one-star *pensione* is hidden down a quiet back lane overlooking the mountains and away from the glitz of the centre. Plain but comfortable rooms have large bathrooms and several have private terraces.

Capri Palace
LUXURY HOTEL €€€

(☑081 978 01 11; www.capripalace.com; Via Capodimonte 2b, Anacapri; s/d/ste from €195/295/620; ☺Apr-Oct; ❋☎☂) This ultra-fashionable retreat has a stylish Mediterranean-style decor and is full of contemporary art. Guests rarely leave the hotel grounds, taking full advantage of the huge pool, on-site health spa and top-notch L'Olivo restaurant. There's a three-night minimum stay in high season.

✗ Eating & Drinking

Be warned that restaurants on Capri are overpriced and underwhelming. Many close between November and Easter.

La Taverna di Pulcinella
PIZZERIA €

(☑081 837 64 85; Via Tiberio 7; pizzas from €7; ☺Apr-Oct) If you can bear being served by waiters in Punchinello (Pulcinella) costumes, you'll be rewarded by what are generally acknowledged to be the best pizzas on Capri.

Salemeria da Aldo
DELI €

(Via Cristoforo Colombo 26; panini from €3.50) Ignore the restaurant touts and head straight to this honest portside deli, where bespectacled Aldo will make you his legendary *panino alla Caprese* (crusty bread stuffed with silky mozzarella and tomatoes from his own garden).

Lo Sfizietto
GELATERIA €

(☑081 837 00 91; Via Longano 6) Located just off La Piazzetta, this *gelateria* uses only organic ingredients with choices that include *cremolate* with 60% fresh fruit and the namesake choice *sfizietto* (caramel with pine nuts).

Pulalli
WINE BAR

(Piazza Umberto I 4; mains €25; ☺Wed-Mon) Climb the clock-tower steps to the right of Capri Town's tourist office and your reward is this laid-back local hang-out, where fabulous *vino* meets a discerning selection of cheeses, *salumi* and pastas.

❶ Information

Information is available online at www.capritourism.com or from one of the three tourist offices: **Marina Grande** (☑081 837 06 34; ☺8.30am-2.30pm Mon-Sat Nov-Mar, 9.15am-1.15pm & 3.15-6.15pm daily Apr-Jun & Sep-Oct, 9am-1pm & 3.30-6.45pm daily Jul & Aug), **Capri Town** (☑081 837 06 86; Piazza Umberto 1; ☺9.15am-1.15pm & 3-6.15pm Mon-Sat Nov-Mar, 8.30am-8.30pm Mon-Sat Apr-Oct) and **Anacapri** (☑081 837 15 24; Via G Orlando 59; ☺9am-3pm Mon-Sat Mar-Oct).

❶ Getting There & Around

There are year-round hydrofoils and ferries to Capri from Naples. Timetables and fare details are available online at www.capritourism.com; look under 'Shipping timetable'.

From Naples, ferries depart from Calata Porta di Massa and hydrofoils from Molo Beverello and Mergellina. Services are regular and tickets cost €19 to €21 (hydrofoil), €17.80 (fast ferry) and €11.50 (ferry).

There are services to/from Sorrento (hydrofoil €17 to €18, fast ferry €15 to €16.20, 20 minutes, 11 daily) and from Easter to November there are also services to Positano (€15.50, 45 minutes, four daily).

On the island, buses run from Capri Town to/from Marina Grande, Anacapri and Marina Piccola. There are also buses from Marina Grande to Anacapri. Single tickets cost €1.80 on all routes, as does the funicular (€1.80) that links Marina Grande with Capri Town in a four-minute trip.

Taxis between Marina Grande and Capri Town cost €15 (€20 to Anacapri) and can carry up to six people.

A private tour around the island by motorboat (stopping for a swim and at the Grotta Azzurra on the way) costs between €150 and €200 per group; a couple of companies based at Marina Grande offer one-hour public tours (€15).

Sorrento

POP 16,600

A stunning location overlooking the Bay of Naples and Mt Vesuvius makes Sorrento a popular package-holiday destination despite the fact that it has no decent beach. Its profusion of sweet-smelling citrus trees and laid-back local lifestyle are certainly attractive, and its relative proximity to the Amalfi Coast, Pompeii and Capri make it a good base for those who don't wish to deal with the chaos and cacophony of Naples.

The centre of town is Piazza Tasso, a short distance northwest of the train and bus station. From Marina Piccola, where ferries and hydrofoils dock, walk south along Via Marina Piccola then climb the steps or take the *ascensore* (lift; €1) to reach the piazza.

◉ Sights & Activities

You'll probably spend most of your time in the *centro storico*, which is full of narrow streets lined with shops, cafes, churches and restaurants. To the north, the **Villa Comunale Park** (☺8am-midnight) commands grand views over the sea to Mt Vesuvius.

The two main swimming spots are **Marina Piccola** and **Marina Grande**, although neither is especially appealing. Nicer by far is **Bagni Regina Giovanna**, a rocky beach set among the ruins of a Roman villa, 2km west of town.

🛏 Sleeping

Casa Astarita   B&B **€**
(☑081 877 49 06; www.casastarita.com; Corso Italia 67, Sorrento; s €50-100, d €70-120, tr €85-145; ❋@☎) Housed in a 16th-century building on the town's major *passaggiata* strip, this family-run place offers six quiet rooms combining rustic charm with modern comforts (iPod docks, Apple TV, kettle, fridge). The colourful decor is extremely attractive, and all rooms are freshly painted and immaculately maintained.

Ulisse Deluxe Hostel   HOSTEL **€**
(☑081 877 47 53; www.ulissedeluxe.com; Via del Mare 22; dm €18-28, s €45-75, d €50-100; P❋@☎) Resembling a three-star hotel, the Ulisse offers quiet modern rooms and single-sex dorms (all with bathroom). The decor is a bit sterile and the ambience impersonal, but the efficient staff, excellent amenities and clean, comfortable rooms certainly compensate. Breakfast costs an extra €7, use of the pool in the attached wellness centre €5 and parking €10. To find it, walk west along Via Corso and then down the stairway next to the hospital.

🍴 Eating & Drinking

Aurora Light   CAMPANIAN **€€**
(☑081 877 26 31; www.auroralight.it; Piazza Tasso 3-4; mains €15) Close examination of its seasonally driven menu shows that Aurora Light's enthusiastic young owner enjoys giving traditional Campanian dishes an innovative twist. There are plenty of vegetarian options on offer.

Garden   CAMPANIAN **€€**
(☑081 878 11 95; Corso Italia 50-52; mains €15; ⊘closed Jan-Mar) Enjoy local and Italian wines by the glass accompanied by slices of prosciutto and cheese in the sophisticated downstairs wine bar, or head to the upstairs terrace garden where the menu includes all the mainstay pasta dishes and plenty of seafood.

ℹ Information

The main **tourist office** (☑081 807 40 33; Via Luigi De Maio 35; ⊘8.30am-4.10pm Mon-Sat) is near Piazza San Antonino, but there are also information points at **Marina Piccola** (⊘8am-1pm) and on **Corso Italia** (⊘9am-1pm & 3-10pm)

near Piazza Tasso. Note that their opening hours can be erratic, especially in the low season.

ℹ Getting There & Away

Circumvesuviana trains run half-hourly between Sorrento and Naples (€4, 65 minutes) via Pompeii (€2.10, 30 minutes) and Ercolano (€2.10, 45 minutes). A daily ticket covering all stops on the route costs €12 (€6.30 on weekends) and a daily ticket covering stops at Ercolano, Pompeii and Sorrento costs €6.30 (€3.40 on weekends).

Curreri (☑081 801 54 20; www.curreriviaggi.it) buses travel between Naples' Capodichino airport and the front of Sorrento train station (€10, 90 minutes, six daily). Buy tickets on the bus.

Regular SITA buses leave from the train station for the Amalfi Coast, stopping in Positano (40 minutes) and then continuing to Amalfi (90 minutes). See the boxed text for ticket prices. When travelling from Sorrento to Amalfi, sit on the left-hand side of the bus for the best views; from Amalfi to Sorrento, sit on the right.

There are boat services to Capri (€17 to €18 hydrofoil, €15 to €16.20 fast ferry, 20 minutes, 11 daily) and Naples (return hydrofoil €22, 35 minutes, six daily).

Amalfi Coast

Stretching 50km along the southern side of the Sorrentine Peninsula, the Amalfi Coast (Costiera Amalfitana) is a postcard-perfect vision of shimmering blue water fringed by vertiginous cliffs to which whitewashed villages with terraced lemon groves cling. This Unesco-protected area is one of Italy's top tourist destinations, attracting hundreds of thousands of visitors each year (70% of them between June and September).

ℹ Getting There & Away

There are two main entry points to the Amalfi Coast: Sorrento and Salerno. Both can be accessed by train from Naples (Sorrento on the Circumvesuviana and Salerno on Treitalia).

Regular SITA buses run from Sorrento to Positano (40 minutes) and Amalfi (90 minutes), and from Salerno to Amalfi (75 minutes). All trips are covered by a 90-minute or greater Unico Costiera travel card.

Boat services are generally limited to the period between April and October. Gescab-**Alicost** (☑089 87 14 83; www.alicost.it) operates one daily ferry/hydrofoil from Salerno to Amalfi (€7/9), Positano (€11/13) and Capri (€18.50/20). It also runs daily ferries from Sorrento to Positano (€13) and Amalfi (€14). **TraVelMar** (☑089 87 29 50; www.travelmar.it) and

Mètro del Mare also run services over summer; check their websites for details.

By car, take the SS163 coastal road at Vietri sul Mare.

POSITANO
POP 4000

Approaching Positano by boat, you will be greeted by an unforgettable view of colourful, steeply stacked houses clinging to near-vertical green slopes. This is a destination where people come to see and be seen – the main activities are hanging out on the small beach, drinking and dining on flower-laden terraces, and browsing the expensive boutiques that are scattered around town. Be warned that all of this activity occurs only in summer – there's absolutely no good reason to come here in the low season.

The **tourist office** (☑089 87 50 67; Via del Saracino 4; ☺8am-2pm & 3.30-8pm Mon-Sat Apr-Oct, 9am-3pm Mon-Fri Nov-Mar) can provide information on walking in the densely wooded Lattari Mountains, including details of the spectacular 12km **Sentiero degli Dei** (Path of the Gods) between Positano and Praiano, and the **Via degli Incanti** (Trail of Charms) between Positano and Amalfi.

🛏 Sleeping

Pensione Maria Luisa   PENSION €
(☑089 87 50 23; www.pensionemarialuisa.com; Via Fornillo 42; r €70-85; ☺Apr-Oct; @🛜) The best budget choice in town is run by Carlo, a larger-than-life character who will go out of his way to assist and advise. Rooms are attractive and have modern bathrooms; those with private terraces are well worth the extra €10 to €15 for the view of the bay. Breakfast costs an additional €5.

Albergo Miramare   HOTEL €€€
(☑089 87 50 02; www.miramarepositano.it; Via Trara Genoino 29; s €150-175, d €195-480; ☺Apr-Oct; ❂@🛜) Every room at this gorgeous hotel has a terrace with sea view, just one of the features that makes it a dream holiday destination. Rooms are extremely comfortable, sporting all mod cons, and the common areas include a comfortable lounge and breakfast room with spectacular views.

Hostel Brikette   HOSTEL €
(☑089 87 58 57; www.brikette.com; Via Marconi 358; dm from €22, d from €75, without bathroom d from €65; ☺late Mar-Nov; ❂🛜) Close to the Bar Internazionale bus stop on the coastal road, this bright and cheerful hostel offers the cheapest accommodation in town. There are

ℹ UNICO COSTIERA

If you are travelling in Sorrento and along the Amalfi Coast on a SITA bus, you can save money and time by investing in a Unico Costiera travel card, available for durations of 45 minutes (€2.40), 90 minutes (€3.60), 24 hours (€7.20) and 72 hours (€18). The 24-hour and 72-hour tickets also cover one trip on the city sightseeing bus that travels between Amalfi and Ravello and Amalfi and Maiori. Buy the cards from bars, *tabacchi* and SITA or Circumvesuviana ticket offices.

various options: six- to eight-person dorms (single sex and mixed), double rooms, and apartments for two to five people.

🍴 Eating & Drinking

Next 2   NEAPOLITAN €€
(☑089 812 35 16; www.next2.it; Viale Pasitea 242; mains €18; ☺7-11pm) We're not sure which is the more enticing: Next 2's outside terrace with oversized white parasols and wicker seating, or its menu, which showcases organic ingredients as much as possible and includes interesting takes on classic Neapolitan dishes.

Da Vincenzo   TRATTORIA €€
(☑089 87 51 28; Viale Pasitea 172-178; mains €18; ☺Apr-Nov, closed lunch Tue Jul & Aug) The emphasis at this old-fashioned place is on fish dishes. Listen to the sound of Neapolitan guitarists during the summer months and be sure to try co-owner Marcella's legendary desserts, which are widely considered to be the best in town.

Da Costantino   TRATTORIA €
(☑089 87 57 38; Via Montepertuso; mains €12, pizzas from €4; ☺closed Wed) One of the few authentic trattorias in Positano, this place high up the hill serves honest, down-to-earth Italian grub. Expect amazing views, good pastas and pizzas and a selection of fail-safe grilled meats.

La Zagara   CAFE
(☑089 812 28 92; Via dei Mulini 4; panini €5, cakes €3) A terrace draped with foliage and flowers is but one of the attractions of this cafe, bar and *pasticceria*, alongside decadent cakes, live music and plenty of Positano poseur-watching potential.

AMALFI
POP 5400

Amalfi is a popular summer holiday destination for no good reason. The beach is unappealing, there's a surfeit of souvenir shops and crowds can be oppressive. Outside the high season, its tangle of narrow alleyways, whitewashed houses and sun-drenched piazzas make it worthy of a day trip but little more.

The **tourist office** (☑089 87 11 07; www.amalfitouristoffice.it; Corso delle Repubbliche Marinare 33; ☺8.30am-1.30pm & 3-7.15pm Mon-Fri, 8.30am-noon Sat) can provide information about sights, activities and transport.

◉ Sights & Activities

Cattedrale di Sant'Andrea　CHURCH
(☑089 87 10 59; Piazza del Duomo; ☺9am-7pm)
Looming over the central piazza is the town's landmark Duomo, one of the few relics of Amalfi's past as an 11th-century maritime superpower. In high season, entrance between 10am and 5pm is through the adjacent **Chiostro del Paradiso** (☑089 87 13 24; Piazza del Duomo; adult/reduced €2.50/1; ☺9am-7pm).

Grotta dello Smeraldo　CAVE
(admission €6; ☺9am-4pm; 🚤) The local version of Capri's famous sea cave can be visited on one-hour boat trips from Amalfi's harbour (€14 return, 9.20am to 3pm daily May to October).

🛏 Sleeping & Eating

Hotel Lidomare　HOTEL €€
(☑089 87 13 32; www.lidomare.it; Largo Duchi Piccolomini 9; s €55-65, d €103-145; ☺year-round; ✹@🛜) The spacious rooms at this old-fashioned, family-run favourite have an endearing air of gentility; the best have sea views.

A'Scalinatella Hostel　HOSTEL €
(☑089 87 14 92; www.hostelscalinatella.com; Piazza Umberto I; dm €30, d €70-140) This barebones operation, just around the headland in Atrani, has dorms, rooms and apartments scattered across the village. Breakfast is included in the price.

🌿 Marina Grande　SEAFOOD €€€
(☑089 87 11 29; www.ristorantemarinagrande.com; Viale Delle Regioni 4; mains €16-26, tasting menu lunch €22, dinner €48; ☺Tue-Sun Mar-Oct) Run by the third generation of the same family and patronised primarily by locals, this classy restaurant fronting the beach serves food made with seasonal ingredients. It's known for its fresh fish dishes.

Dolcería dell' Antíco Portico　PASTICCERIA €
(☑089 87 11 43; Via Supportico Rua 10; cakes from €3) Named for its location under the arches, this celebrated cake shop and small cafe gives a contemporary twist to traditional sweet treats such as *sfogliatella*.

Matera
POP 60,900

Set atop two rocky gorges, Matera is one of Italy's most remarkable towns and is the most compelling reason to visit the region of Basilicata. Dotting the ravines are the famous *sassi* (cave dwellings), where up to half the town's population lived until the late 1950s. These *sassi* now underpin Matera's economy, attracting visitors from all over the world.

The geographical centre of the town is handsome Piazza Vittorio Veneto, from where you can access the *sassi*.

◉ Sights & Activities

Sassi　CAVES
Within Matera there are two *sassi* areas: the largely restored **Barisano** and more impoverished and run-down **Caveoso**. Both feature serpentine alleyways and staircases, Byzantine-era cave churches and hidden piazzas. With a map you can explore them on your own, although you might find an audioguide (€8) from **Viaggi Lionetti** (☑0835 33 40 33; www.viaggilionetti.com; Via XX Settembre 9; ☺9am-1pm & 4-8pm Mon-Fri, 9am-1pm Sat) helpful. It and **Ferula Viaggi** (www.ferulaviaggi.it) also offer guided tours.

Inhabited since the Paleolithic Age, the *sassi* were brought to public attention with the publication of Carlo Levi's book *Cristo si é fermato a Eboli* (Christ Stopped at Eboli; 1945). His description of children begging for quinine to stave off endemic malaria shamed the authorities into action and about 15,000 people were forcibly relocated in the late 1950s. In 1993 the *sassi* were declared a Unesco World Heritage site.

Accessible from Via Ridola, Sasso Caveoso is older and more evocative than Sasso Barisano. Its highlights include the *chiese rupestre* (rock churches) of **Santa Maria d'Idris** (Piazza San Pietro Caveoso; adult/reduced €3/2; ☺10am-1pm & 2.30-7pm Tue-Sun Apr-Oct, 10.30am-1.30pm Tue-Sun Nov-Mar) and **Santa Lucia alle Malve** (Via la Vista; adult/reduced €3/2; ☺10am-1pm & 2.30-7pm Apr-Oct, 10.30am-1.30pm Tue-Sun Nov-Mar) with their well-preserved 13th-century frescos.

The countryside outside of Matera, the **Murgia Plateau**, is littered with dozens of Paleolithic caves and monastic developments. It's best explored with a guide.

🛏 Sleeping

TOP CHOICE Hotel in Pietra
BOUTIQUE HOTEL €€

(📞0835 34 40 40; www.hotelinpietra.it; Via San Giovanni Vecchio 22; s €55-100, d €95-150, ste €180-220; ✳@🛜) Housed in a 13th-century rock-hewn church in the Sasso Barisano, this boutique hotel features butter-yellow stone walls, a chic minimalist decor and stylish bathrooms set in rocky embrasures. A light gourmet breakfast provides the final touch of class.

La Dolce Vita B&B
B&B €

(📞0835 31 03 24; www.ladolcevitamatera.it; Rione Malve 51; s €40-60, d €60-80; 🛜) This delightful ecofriendly B&B in Sasso Caveoso offers cool, comfortable and homey rooms. Owner Vincenzo is passionate about Matera and is a mine of information on the *sassi*.

Le Monacelle
HOSTEL €

(📞0839 34 40 97; www.lemonacelle.it; Via Riscatto 9-10; dm €18, s/d €55/86; ✳🛜) Behind the Duomo and incorporating the delightful chapel of the Chiesa di San Franceso d'Assisi, this HI-run hostel is set in a 15th-century monastery (look for the 'Casa del Pellegrino Le Monacelle' signs). It offers large, mixed-sex dorms with bathrooms as well as plainly furnished private rooms. Its best feature is an atmospheric cobbled terrace, which has stunning *sassi* views. Breakfast costs an extra €4.

🍴 Eating

TOP CHOICE Il Cantuccio
RISTORANTE €€

(📞0835 33 20 90; Via delle Beccherie 33; antipasto €15, mains €10-15; ⊙Tue-Sun) Family-run Il Cantuccio is a Slow Food–recommended restaurant serving creative regional fare. The speciality of the house is a lavish, seven-dish antipasto, which includes delights such as a deliciously creamy ricotta with fig syrup and a tasty *caponata* (sweet-and-sour aubergine ratatouille).

Le Botteghe
TRATTORIA €€

(📞0835 34 40 72; Piazza San Pietro; mains €11.50-16; ⊙lunch & dinner daily Apr-Sep, closed lunch Tue-Thu Oct-Mar) This endearingly old-fashioned place offers a menu featuring local specialities that utilise products celebrated by the Presidio Slow Food. The freshly made pasta dishes and *salsiccia di maiale pezzente* (lo-cal 'beggar style' pork sausages) are particularly tasty.

ℹ️ Information

The **Agenzia di Promozione Territoriale Basilicata** (APT; 📞0835 33 19 83; www.aptbasilicata.it; 1st fl, Via De Viti De Marco 9; ⊙9am-1.30pm Mon-Fri, 4-6.30pm Mon & Tue) has a Matera office near the train station that can supply maps and brochures. In summer, tourist information booths operate next to the Convento Santa Lucia next to Sasso Barisano, and opposite the Palazzo della Provincia next to Sasso Caveoso. Online information is available at the APT's website and at www.sassiweb.it.

ℹ️ Getting There & Away

You can reach Matera by bus from Rome, Tuscany and Naples, or by train from Bari. The train station is close to the *sassi*, but the long-distance bus station is at Villa Longo on the edge of town, from where it's a 40-minute walk up Via Nazionale and Via Annunziatella to get to Piazza Vittorio Veneto.

Marozzi (📞06 225 21 47; www.marozzivt.it) runs two or three daily buses to/from Rome's Stazione Tiburtina (€34.50, 6½ hours) and one service per day to Siena (€46, 8¼ hours), Florence (€51, 9½ hours) and Pisa (€57.50, 12 hours). **Marino** (www.marinobus.it, 📞080 311 23 35) runs two daily services (one on Sunday) to/from Naples (€19, 4¼ hours).

By train, the **Ferrovie Appulo Lucano** (📞080 572 52 29; www.fal-srl.it) runs services to/from Bari (€4.50, 1¼ hour, 14 daily). Note that these do not run on Sundays.

Bari

TRANSPORT HUB

Most travellers visit Puglia's main town to take the Ferrovie Appulo Lucano to Matera or catch a ferry to Greece, Croatia or Montenegro. While it has no sights that in themselves demand a visit, the Old City (Bari Vecchia) has some architecturally notable Norman buildings that are worth exploring if you have a few hours to while away before your ferry leaves.

Bari Vecchia isn't particularly safe at night. Be aware of your personal safety and watch your bags and wallets.

🛏 Sleeping & Eating

B&B Casa Pimpolini
B&B €

(📞080 521 99 38; www.casapimpolini.com; Via Calefati 249; s €45-60, d €70-80; ✳@) This lovely B&B in the new town is within easy walking distance of shops, restaurants and Bari Vecchia. Its two guest rooms are warm and welcoming, and the homemade breakfast is a treat.

Hotel Adria HOTEL €€

(☑080 524 66 99; www.adriahotelbari.com; Via Zuppetta 10; s/d €70/110; ℙ❄@) This safe option near the train station offers comfortable, bright and modern rooms.

TOP CHOICE Alberosole MODERN ITALIAN €€

(☑080 523 54 46; www.alberosole.com; Corso Vittorio Emanuele II 13; mains €13-21; ⊙lunch & dinner Tue-Sun; ☎) Brioni-suited bankers and a loyal coterie of ladies-who-lunch are regulars at this elegant restaurant, drawn by its refined and perfectly executed modern Italian cuisine. Fantastic value considering the quality of the food on offer.

☕ Drinking

Bar Savoia CAFE

(cnr Via Sparano da Bari & Via Celefati; ⊙7am-midnight) The *passaggiata* crowds head towards this ever-fashionable cafe on the new town's main pedestrian mall for coffee and liberal doses of people-watching.

❶ Information

There's a helpful **tourist information point** (☑080 990 93 41; www.infopointbari.com; Piazza Aldo Moro; ⊙9am-7pm Mon-Sat, 9am-1pm Sun) in front of the train station, and another at the port which is only open May to October and whose hours are dependent on ferry arrivals.

❶ Getting There & Away

Air

Bari is served by **Karol Wojtyla airport** (BRI; ☑080 580 03 58; www.seap-puglia.it), 15km northwest of town in Palese. **Tempesta** (www.autoservizitempesta.it) runs an hourly shuttle bus (€4.15, 30 minutes) between the airport and the train station. Alternatively, take local bus 16 (€0.90, 40 minutes).

Boat

Ferries run from Bari to Greece (Igoumenitsa and Patra), Croatia (Dubrovnik) and Montenegro (Bar). Ferries to Corfu and Kefallonia (also Patra) in Greece leave from Brindisi, approximately 115km south of Bari and easily accessed by train.

Ferry companies have offices at Bari's port, accessible by bus 20/ (€0.90) from the train station. Note: only board a bus with / after the 20.

Train

Bari is on the main east-coast rail line and there are trains to/from Rome (Freccia Argento from €54, 4½ hours), Brindisi (Regionale €7.70, one hour 20 minutes) and Lecce (Regionale €9.70, 1½ to two hours).

Lecce

POP 95,600

Its profusion of opulent *barocco leccese* (Lecce baroque) architecture has earned this opulent city a reputation as the 'Florence of the South'. The presence of a highly regarded university means that there is a vibrant bar scene, and the elegant *centro storico* is easily explored on foot.

⊙ Sights

Basilica di Santa Croce CHURCH

(☑0832 24 19 57; www.basilicasantacroce.eu; Via Umberto I; ⊙9am-noon & 5-8pm) This basilica is the city's most celebrated example of *barocco leccese*. It took a team of 16th- and 17th-century craftsmen more than a century to create the carved facade that you see today, which features a magnificent allegorical feast of writhing sheep, dodos, cherubs and beasties.

Piazza del Duomo PIAZZA

During times of invasion the inhabitants of Lecce would barricade themselves in this bombastically baroque square, which has conveniently narrow entrances. The 12th-century **cathedral** (⊙8.30am-12.30pm & 4-6.30pm) is unusual in that it has two facades, one on the western end and the other, more ornate, facing the piazza. It's framed by the 15th-century **Palazzo Vescovile** (Episcopal Palace) and the 18th-century Seminario, which now houses the **Museo Diocesano** (Piazza del Duomo; admission museum €4, cloisters €1; ⊙9.30am-12.30pm & 4-7pm Mon-Sat).

🛏 Sleeping

There are no youth hostels in Lecce, and no budget options worth recommending. The following boutique hotels are well worth an extra slice of your daily budget, though.

TOP CHOICE Suite 68 BOUTIQUE HOTEL €

(☑0832 30 35 06; www.kalekora.it; Via Prato 7-9; s €70-80, d €80-120; ❄@☎) Vaulted ceilings, contemporary art and colourful rugs give the comfortable, well-sized rooms here loads of character. There's also a communal terrace on the roof, an attractive breakfast room downstairs and free use of bicycles. Prices are a steal for what's on offer.

Palazzo Rollo BOUTIQUE HOTEL, APARTMENT €

(☑0832 30 71 52; www.palazzorollo.it; Via Vittorio Emanuele II 14; s €50-60, d €70-90, ste €100-120, apt €70-90; P❄@) Stay in a 17th-century palace – the family seat for over 200 years. Six gorgeous upstairs suites are furnished with antiques and some have painted ceilings. Downstairs, small self-catering apartments sleeping two or three people open onto an ivy-hung courtyard. The rooftop garden has a wonderful view of the Duomo. Parking costs €7 per day.

✗ Eating

The main eating and drinking strip is on Via Umberto I, north of the Basilica di Santa Croce.

TOP CHOICE **Cucina Casareccia** TRATTORIA €€
(☑0832 24 51 78; Viale Costadura 19; mains €12; ☺lunch Tue-Sun, dinner Tue-Sat) Ring the bell to gain entry into a place that feels like a private home and is run with great warmth by Anna Carmela Perrone. In fact, it's known locally as *Trattoria le Zie* (The Aunts' Trattoria). Here you'll taste true Puglian cuisine, including an outstanding stuffed calamari. Booking is essential.

Alle due Corti TRATTORIA €€
(☑0832 24 22 23; www.alleduecorti.com; Via Prato 42; mains €12; ☺lunch & dinner daily, closed winter) For a taste of sunny Salento, check out this no-frills, fiercely traditional restaurant. The seasonal menu is classic Pugliese, written in a dialect that even some Italians struggle with. Celebrated chef Rosalba De Carla also runs cooking classes.

Trattoria di Nonna Tetti TRATTORIA €
(☑0832 24 60 36; Piazzetta Regina Maria 28; mains €8-12; ☺lunch & dinner daily) A warmly inviting restaurant that is popular with all ages and budgets, and serves a wide choice of tasty and traditional dishes.

❶ Information

Tourist Office (☑0832 24 80 92; Corso Vittorio Emanuele 24; ☺9am-1pm & 4-8.30pm Mon-Sat Apr-Sep, to 6pm Nov-Mar) The tourist information office is of little use, as staff speak no languages other than Italian. It's best to ask your hotel for advice instead.

Ufficio Informazioni Duomo (☑0832 52 18 77; www.infolecce.it; Piazza del Duomo 2; ☺9.30am-1.30pm & 3.30-7.30pm Mon-Fri Sep-Jul, from 10am Sat, 9.30am-7.30pm daily Aug) Rents out bikes (per hour/day €4/18) and runs guided tours (€40 for two hours). There's a second office at Via G Palmieri 47.

❶ Getting There & Away

Lecce is the end of one of the main southeastern rail line and there are frequent direct trains to/from Brindisi (Regionale €2.60, 30 minutes, hourly), Bari (Regionale €9.70, 1½ to two hours) and Rome (Freccia Argento; €66, 5½ hours, three daily). The train station is in the centre of town, an easy 15-minute walk from the Duomo.

Long-distance buses arrive at and leave from the **STP bus station** (☑800 43 03 46; Viale Porta D'Europa) opposite Grand Hotel Tiziano, past Porta Napoli. Miccolis has services to Naples (€32, six hours, three daily) and STP services travel to Brindisi airport (€6, 35 minutes, nine daily).

By car, take the SS16 to Bari via Monopoli and Brindisi. For Taranto take the SS7.

SICILY

Everything about the Mediterranean's largest island is extreme – the beauty of the rugged landscape, the robust flavours of the regional cuisine, the relentless summer sun and the all-powerful influence of its criminal underbelly.

Over the centuries, the strategic location and agricultural riches of Sicily have lured foreign invaders ranging from the Phoenicians and ancient Greeks to the Spanish Bourbons. All have contributed to the island's cultural landscape, leaving in turn Greek temples, Arab domes, Byzantine mosaics, Norman castles, Angevin churches and baroque facades.

This cultural complexity is complemented by Sicily's volcanic geography. Dominating the east coast, Mt Etna (3350m) is Sicily's most famous volcano, although not its most active; Stromboli usually claims that accolade. All round the island aquamarine seas lap at the craggy coastline, while inland, hilltop towns are strewn across the countryside.

❶ Getting There & Away
Air
Flights from Italy's mainland cities, Tunisia (Tunis) and some European destinations land at Sicily's two main air hubs: Palermo's **Falcone-Borsellino airport** (PMO; ☑091 702 01 11; www.gesap.it) and Catania's Fontanarossa airport (p532).

Boat
Regular car and passenger ferries cross to Sicily (Messina) from Villa San Giovanni in Calabria. The island is also accessible by ferry from Genoa, Livorno, Civitavecchia (near Rome),

Naples, Salerno (on the Amalfi Coast) and Cagliari, as well as Tunisia. The main ports are Palermo, Milazzo, Catania, Trapani, Termini Imerese (near Palermo) and the Aeolian Islands.

Timetables are seasonal, so get up-to-date information and book your tickets at www.traghettiweb.it. Note that you should book well in advance during summer, particularly if you have a car.

The major routes and the companies that operate them:

PORT	TO/FROM	COMPANY
Aeolian Islands	Naples	SNAV, Siremar
Catania	Naples	TTT Lines
Milazzo	Naples	Siremar
Palermo	Cagliari	Tirrenia
Palermo	Civitavecchia	Grandi Navi Veloci, SNAV
Palermo	Genoa	Grandi Navi Veloci
Palermo	Livorno	Grandi Navi Veloci
Palermo	Naples	SNAV, Tirrenia
Palermo	Tunis	Grandi Navi Veloci, Grimaldi
Termini Imerese	Livorno	Grandi Navi Veloci
Termini Imerese	Salerno	Caronte & Tourist
Trapani	Cagliari	Tirrenia
Trapani	Civitavecchia	Grimaldi Lines
Trapani	Naples	Ustica Lines
Trapani	Tunis	Grimaldi Lines

Bus

Bus services between Rome and Sicily are operated by **SAIS** (☑800 21 10 20; www.saisautolinee.it), **Interbus** (☑0935 2 24 60; www.interbus.it) and **Segesta** (☑091 616 79 19; www.segesta.it), departing from Rome's Piazza Tiburtina. There are daily buses to Messina, Catania, Palermo and Syracuse.

Train

Direct trains run from Milan, Florence, Rome, Naples and Reggio di Calabria to Palermo and Catania. For further information go to the **Trenitalia** (☑89 20 21; www.trenitalia.com) website.

❶ Getting Around

Generally the best way to get around Sicily is by bus. Trains tend to be cheaper on the major routes, but once you're off the coast, they can be painfully slow.

Roads are generally good and autostradas connect major cities.

Palermo

POP 655,875

Exploring this chaotic yet compelling city can be exhausting, but once you've acclimatised to the congested and noisy streets you'll be rewarded with some of southern Italy's most imposing architecture, impressive art galleries, vibrant street markets and an array of tempting restaurants and cafes.

Palermo's centre is large but it's relatively easy to explore on foot. The main street is Via Maqueda, which runs parallel to Via Roma, the busy road running north from the train station. Corso Vittorio Emanuele crosses Via Maqueda at a junction known as the Quattro Canti (Four Corners). You'll find that most sights and hotels are within easy walking distance of this intersection.

◉ Sights

At the time of research the city's famous Archeological Museum on Piazza Olivella was closed for restoration and the date of its reopening was unknown.

Churches   CHURCH

Around the corner from Piazza Pretoria, Piazza Bellini is home to three churches: the **Chiesa di Santa Caterina** (☑338 722 87 75; Piazza Bellini; admission €2; ⊗9.30am-1pm & 3-7pm Mon-Sat, to 1.30pm Sun Apr-Nov, to 1.30pm daily Dec-Mar & 25 Nov), one of the city's most impressive baroque churches; **La Martorana** (Chiesa di Santa Maria dell'Ammiraglio; Piazza Bellini 3; donation requested; ⊗8.30am-1pm & 3.30-5.30pm Mon-Sat, 8.30am-1pm Sun), Palermo's most famous medieval church; and the red-domed **Chiesa Capitolare di San Cataldo** (Piazza Bellini 3; admission €2; ⊗9.30am-1.30pm & 3.30-5.30pm Mon-Sat, 9.30am-1.30pm Sun), of interest more for its Arab-Norman exterior than its surprisingly bare interior.

A short walk west up Corso Vittorio Emanuele II brings you to the **Cattedrale di Palermo** (www.cattedrale.palermo.it; Corso Vittorio Emanuele; admission free; ⊗7am-7pm), a visual riot of arches, cupolas and crenellations. Modified many times over the centuries, it's a stunning example of Sicily's unique Arab-Norman architectural style. Its impressive **Museo Diocesano** (☑tel info 091 60 77 215; www.museodiocesanopa.it; Via Matteo Bonello 2; adult/6-17 & over 65/child under 6 €4.50/3/free; ⊗9.30am-1.30pm Tue-Fri & Sun, 10am-6pm Sat) is in a building on the opposite side of Via Matteo Bonello, on the western side of the cathedral.

Central Palermo

Central Palermo

◎ Top Sights

Cappella Palatina	A4
Cattedrale di Palermo	A3
Galleria Regionale della Sicilia	D3
Teatro Massimo	B2

◎ Sights

Chiesa Capitolare di San Cataldo	(see 1)
1 Chiesa di Santa Caterina	C3
2 Giardino Garibaldi	C3
La Martorana	(see 1)
3 Museo Diocesano	A3
4 Oratorio del Rosario di San Domenico	C2
5 Oratorio del Rosario di Santa Zita	C2
6 Oratorio di San Lorenzo	C3
7 Palazzo Reale	A4

⊜ Sleeping

8 A Casa di Amici	A2
9 Al Giardino dell'Alloro	C3
10 Ambasciatori Hotel	C3
11 B&B Panormus	C4
12 Butera 28	D3

⊗ Eating

13 Antico Caffè Spinnato	B1
14 Cappello Pasticceria	A1
15 Piccolo Napoli	B1
16 Pizzeria Biondo	A1
17 Trattoria Il Maestro del Brodo	C3

⊕ Drinking

18 Kursaal Kalhesa	D3
19 Pizzo & Pizzo	A1

Palazzo Reale PALACE

(Palazzo dei Normanni; Piazza Indipendenza 1; incl Cappella Palatina adult/concession €8.50/6.50; ⌚8.15am-5pm Mon-Sat, to 12.15pm Sun) Barely less dramatic than the cathedral is the theatrical seat of the Sicilian parliament. Guided tours lead you to the **Sala di Ruggero II**, the mosaic-decorated bedroom of King Roger II. Downstairs is Palermo's premier tourist attraction, the 12th-century **Cappella Palatina** (Palatine Chapel; ⌚8.15am-5pm Mon-Sat, 8.15-9.30am & 11.30am-12.15pm Sun), a jaw-dropping jewel of Arab-Norman architecture lavishly decorated with exquisite mosaics. If you visit the chapel on a day when the rest of the *palazzo* is closed, the entry price is reduced to adult/concession €7/5.

Oratories HISTORIC BUILDING

(Tesori della Loggia combined ticket adult/student/child under 6 €5/4/free; ⌚Tesori della Loggia 9am-1pm Mon-Sat) Hidden in the ancient streets of the Vucciria district are three ornate baroque oratories: **Oratorio di San Lorenzo** (Via dell'Immacolatella 5; adult/reduced €2.50/1.50; ⌚10am-6pm), **Oratorio del Rosario di Santa Zita** (Via Valverde) and **Oratorio del Rosario di San Domenico** (Via dei Bambinai 2). These places were the social clubs for the celebs of the time. The latter two are known collectively as the **Tesori della Loggia** and can be visited on a single ticket that will in turn give you a €1 discount at the Museo Diocesano and other church-run museums in the city.

Galleria Regionale della Sicilia MUSEUM

(Palazzo Abatellis; ☎091 623 00 11; www.regione.sicilia.it/beniculturali/palazzoabatellis/; Via Alloro 4; adult/EU 18-25/EU under 18 & over 65 €8/4/free; ⌚9am-6pm Tue-Fri, to 1pm Sat & Sun) Tucked down a side street in the stately 15th-century Palazzo Abatellis, this splendid museum has a wide-ranging collection featuring works by Sicilian artists from the Middle Ages to the 18th century.

Teatro Massimo CULTURAL BUILDING

(☎tour reservations 091 605 32 67; www.teatromassimo.it; Piazza Giuseppe Verdi; guided tours adult/reduced €8/5; ⌚10am-2.30pm Tue-Sun) A Palermo landmark, this grand neoclassical opera house took more than 20 years to complete and has become a symbol of the triumph and tragedy of the city. Appropriately, the closing scene of *The Godfather: Part III,* with its visually stunning juxtaposition of high culture, low crime, drama and death, was filmed here.

Catacombe dei Cappuccini ARCHAEOLOGICAL SITE

(☎091 21 21 17; Piazza Cappuccini; admission €3; ⌚9am-1pm & 3-5pm Mon-Sat, 9am-1pm Sun) These catacombs house the mummified bodies and skeletons of some 8000 Palermitans who died between the 17th and 19th centuries. Earthly power, gender, religion and professional status are still rigidly distinguished, with men and women occupying separate corridors, and a first-class section set aside for virgins. From Piazza Indipendenza, it's a 15-minute walk.

Sleeping

Butera 28 APARTMENT €€

(☎333 316 54 32; www.butera28.it; Via Butera 28; apt per day €50-170, per week €300-950; ❄📶) Delightful bilingual owner Nicoletta offers 11 well-equipped and comfortable apartments sleeping from two to eight persons in her elegant old *palazzo* near Piazza della Kalsa. Four apartments face the sea (No 9 is especially nice), and all have CD and DVD players, plus kitchens stocked with basic essentials.

A Casa di Amici HOSTEL €

(☎091 58 48 84; www.acasadiamici.com; Via Volturno 6; dm €17-23, d €56-72, without bathroom d €40-75, tr €60-84; ❄@📶) This hostel-style place behind Teatro Massimo is run by artist Claudia and her family. It offers two double and two triple rooms with shared bathrooms, as well as a communal lounge, guest kitchen and laundry. The annexe across the street has four additional rooms, including one with private bathroom and terrace. Internet costs €1 per 30 minutes; wi-fi is free – neither is available in the annexe.

B&B Panormus B&B €

(☎091 617 58 26; www.bbpanormus.com; Via Roma 72; s €43-65, d €55-85, tr €75-110; ❄📶) Keen prices, charming host Giovanni and five attractive and extremely comfortable rooms make this one of the city's most popular B&Bs. Each room has its own small private bathroom down the passageway (bathrobes are supplied).

Al Giardino dell'Alloro B&B €

(☎091 617 69 04; www.giardinodellalloro.it; Vicolo San Carlo 8; s €40-45, d €80-90, tr €120) This bijou B&B with flat-screen TVs, free wi-fi and walls hung with artwork from the nearby academy is a very pleasant retreat. The rooms are painted in vivid colours and there's a communal fridge for guests' use.

It's tucked down a slender alley opposite a wisteria-draped wall.

Ambasciatori Hotel HOTEL €€

(☑info 091 616 68 81; www.ambasciatorihotelpalermo.com; Via Roma 111, 5; s €50-75, d €60-95, tr €75-110; ❄@☎) A decent option occupying the 5th floor of an old *palazzo;* the Ambasciatori has clean, reasonably comfortable rooms and a marvellous rooftop terrace where you can eat your breakfast in the morning and sip cocktails in the evening. Request a quiet room with a view (there are eight of these).

✗ Eating

Like its architecture, Palermo's food is a unique mix of influences. Traditional yet spicy, it marries the island's superb produce – praised by Homer in *The Odyssey* – with recipes imported by the Arab Saracens in the 9th century. The street food is also superb. Three specialities to try are *arancini, panelle* (chickpea fritters) and cannoli (pastry tubes filled with sweetened ricotta and candied fruit).

For an adrenalin-charged food experience, head to one of Palermo's legendary markets: Capo on Via Sant'Agostino or Il Ballarò in the Albergheria quarter, off Via Maqueda. Both are open 7am to 8pm Monday to Saturday (to 1pm on Wednesday). The Capo is also open on Sunday mornings.

 Piccolo Napoli SEAFOOD €€

(☑091 32 04 31; Piazzetta Mulino a Vento 4; antipasti €4-8, mains from €8; ❤lunch Mon-Sat, dinner Thu-Sat) Known throughout the city for its spectacularly fresh seafood, delectable antipasti (try the *caponata* and the green olives) and fried morsels including *panelle,* this is a destination that serious foodies should not miss. The atmosphere is bustling and the genial owner greets most customers by name – a clear sign that once sampled, the food here exerts a true siren's call. Booking is advisable.

Pizzeria Biondo PIZZERIA €

(☑091 58 36 62; Via Nicolò Garzilli 27; pizzas €5-14; ❤dinner Thu-Tue) Made with super-fresh *mozzarella di bufala,* Biondo's pizzas are often described as the best in Palermo. An animated crowd fills the sidewalk tables and inside rooms every night.

Trattoria Il Maestro del Brodo TRATTORIA €€

(Via Pannieri 7; mains €8-16; ❤lunch Tue-Sun, dinner Fri & Sat) A Slow Food–recommended eatery, this no-frills place in the Vucciria offers a sensational antipasto buffet with loads of vegetarian choices (€8), delicious pastas and soups, and an array of ultra-fresh seafood.

Cappello Pasticceria PASTICCERIA €

(Via Niccolò Garzilli 10; ❤7am-9.30pm Thu-Tue) The chocolates and cakes here are true works of art, as beautiful to look at as they are delicious to eat. There's a boudoir-style salon at the back of the shop.

Antico Caffè Spinnato CAFE €

(☑091 32 92 20; Via Principe di Belmonte 107-15; snacks €4-8) Join Palermo's snappily dressed shoppers for a daytime coffee or an early evening drink at this sophisticated cafe, which dates to 1860.

☕ Drinking

Pizzo & Pizzo WINE BAR

(www.pizzoepizzo.com; Via XII Gennaio 5; ❤closed Sun) Patrons here are enticed by an extensive and excellent list of wines by the glass, a buzzing atmosphere and a tempting array of cheeses, cured meats and smoked fish.

Kursaal Kalhesa BAR

(www.kursaalkalhesa.it; Foro Umberto I 21; ❤noon-3pm & 6pm-1am Tue-Sun) A lively, unpretentious crowd is attracted by Kursaal Kalhesa's program of music and literary events. Meals (mains €16) are served upstairs on a leafy patio flanked by 15th-century walls.

❶ Information

Emergency
Police Station (Questura; ☑091 23 90 00; Piazza della Vittoria)

Medical Services
Presidio Ospedaliero Villa Sofia (☑091 780 40 33; www.ospedaliriunitipalermo.it/presidio_villa_sofia.html; Piazza Salerno; ❤24hr emergency) In the New City, near Parco della Favorita.

Tourist information
The **central tourist office** (☑091 58 38 47; www.palermotourism.com; Piazza Castelnuovo 34; ❤8.30am-2pm & 2.30-6pm Mon-Fri) is operated by the Provincia Regionale di Palermo, as is the **tourist information point** (☑091 59 16 98; in downstairs hall, Falcone-Borsellino airport; ❤8.30am-7.30pm Mon-Fri, to 2pm Sat) at Falcone-Borsellino airport. The Città di Palermo (City of Palermo) operates tourist information booths at Piazza Bellini, Piazza Castelnuovo (corner Via R Settimo), Piazza Marina, Piazza della Vittoria, the port and the train station. All of these are open from 9am to 1pm Monday to Friday; in

WORTH A TRIP

CATTEDRALE DI MONREALE

Just 8km southwest of Palermo, the 12th-century **Cattedrale di Monreale** (☑091 640 44 03; Piazza del Duomo; admission to cathedral free, north transept €2, terrace €2; ☺8am-6pm) is the finest example of Norman architecture in Sicily. The entire 6400-sq-metre ceiling is covered in mosaics depicting 42 Old Testament stories, including the Creation, Adam and Eve, and Noah and his Ark. Try to visit in the morning, when there is enough light in the building to see the mosaics properly. Afterwards, pop into the cathedral's tranquil **cloisters** (adult/EU 18-25/EU under 18 & over 65 €6/3/free; ☺9am-1.30pm & 2-7pm).

To get here from Palermo, take bus 389 (€1.30 from *tabacchi,* €1.70 on bus, every 25 minutes Monday to Saturday, hourly Sunday) from Piazza Indipendenza. A taxi costs €15 to €20.

high season those at Piazza Bellini and Piazza Castelnuovo are also open from 3pm to 7pm.

❶ Getting There & Away

National and international flights arrive at Falcone-Borsellino airport, 35km west of Palermo.

The ferry terminal is northeast of the *centro storico,* off Via Francesco Crispi. Ferries for Cagliari and Naples leave from Molo Vittorio Veneto; for Genoa they leave from Molo Santa Lucia.

The new intercity bus station is in Piazza Cairoli, behind the train station. Sicily's buses are privatised and different routes are serviced by various companies, most of which have ticket offices here. The main companies:

Cuffaro (☑091 616 15 10; www.cuffaro.info; Via Paolo Balsamo 13) Services to Agrigento (€8.70, two hours, three to nine daily).

Interbus (☑0935 56 51 11; www.interbus.it) To/from Syracuse (€12, 3¼ hours, three daily Monday to Saturday, two on Sunday).

SAIS Autolinee (☑091 616 60 28; www.saisautolinee.it) To/from Catania (€14.90, 2½ hours, every 30 minutes Monday to Saturday, eight services Sunday).

Regular trains leave from the Stazione Centrale for Messina (Regionale €11.80, 3¼ hours, hourly) via Milazzo (Regionale €10.40, 2½ hours), the jumping-off point for the Aeolian Islands. There are also slow services to Catania, Syracuse and Agrigento, as well as to nearby towns such as Cefalù. Long-distance trains go to Naples (Intercity €56.50, 9¼ hours, three daily) and Rome (Intercity €69, 11½ hours, four daily).

❶ Getting Around

To/From the Airport

A half-hourly bus service run by **Prestia e Comandé** (☑091 58 63 51; www.prestiaecomande.it) connects the airport with the train station via Piazza Politeama and operates between 5am and 10.30pm. Tickets for the 50-minute journey cost €6.10 and are available on the bus.

A taxi from the airport to the centre costs €45 (set fare).

Bus

Walking is the best way to get around Palermo's centre but if you want to take a bus, most stop outside or near the train station. Tickets cost €1.30 (€1.70 on bus) and are valid for 90 minutes. There are two small lines – Gialla and Rossa – that operate in the *centro storico.*

Aeolian Islands

Rising out of the cobalt-blue seas off Sicily's northeastern coast, the Unesco-protected Aeolian Islands (Isole Eolie) have been seducing visitors since Odysseus' time. Their wild, windswept mountains, hissing volcanoes and rich waters attract divers, sun seekers and adrenalin junkies.

Part of a huge volcanic ridge, the seven islands (Lipari, Salina, Vulcano, Stromboli, Alicudi, Filicudi and Panarea) represent the very pinnacle of a 3000m-high outcrop that was formed one million years ago. Lipari is the biggest and busiest of the seven, and the main transport hub. From there you can pick up connections to all the other islands, including Vulcano, famous for its therapeutic mud, and Stromboli, whose permanently active volcano supplies spectacular fire shows.

❂ Sights & Activities

Lipari   ISLAND

On Lipari you can explore the volcanic history of the islands and – even more interestingly – an impressive collection of classical-era artefacts at the **Museo Archeologico Regionale Eoliano** (☑090 988 01 74; www.regione.sicilia.it/beniculturali/museolipari; Castello di Lipari; adult/18-25/EU under 18 & over 65 €6/3/free; ☺9am-1pm & 3-6pm Mon-Sat, 9am-1pm Sun) located in the Spanish-built **citadel**. For sunbathing, head to Canneto and the Spiaggia Bianca or to Porticello for Spiaggia Papesca. Snorkelling and diving are popular – contact **Diving Center**

La Gorgonia (☏090 981 26 16; www.lagorgoniadiving.it; Salita San Giuseppe, Marina Corta; dive/night dive/beginner course €30/40/55) for equipment and guided dives. For tours of the islands, **Da Massimo Dolce Vita Group** (☏090 981 30 86; www.damassimo.it; Via Maurolico 2) offers various packages, ranging from a €15 tour of Lipari and Vulcano to a €80 summit climb of Stromboli.

Vulcano   ISLAND

From Lipari, it's a short boat ride to Vulcano, a malodorous and largely unspoilt island. Most people come here to make the hour-long trek up the **Fossa di Vulcano**, the island's active volcano (€3 for crater entrance in summer), or to wallow in the sulphurous **Fanghi di Vulcano** thermal mud baths (€2, plus €1 for shower). To get to the volcano, follow the signs from the port along Strada Provinciale and then turn left onto the gravel track.

Stromboli   ISLAND

Famous for its spectacular fireworks, Stromboli's **volcano** is the most active in the region, last exploding in April 2009. To make the tough six- to seven-hour ascent to the 920m summit you are legally required to hire a guide. At the top you're rewarded with incredible views of the Sciara del Fuoco (Trail of Fire) and constantly exploding crater. **Magmatrek** (☏090 986 57 68; www.magmatrek.it; Via Vittorio Emanuele) organises afternoon climbs for €28 per person (minimum 10 people).

🛏 Sleeping & Eating

Most accommodation is on Lipari. Always try to book ahead, as summer is busy and many places close over winter. Prices fall considerably outside of high season.

Villa Diana   HOTEL €€

(☏090 981 14 03; www.villadiana.com; Via Edwin Hunziker 1; s €43-80, d €67-145; ☺closed Nov-Mar; 🅿🕸🛜) Swiss artist Edwin Hunziker converted this Aeolian house into a bohemian-spirited hotel in the 1950s. It stands above Lipari town in a garden of citrus trees and olives and offers panoramic views from the terrace. Amenities include free wi-fi (in the reception area only) and use of the tennis court.

Diana Brown   B&B €

(☏090 981 25 84; www.dianabrown.it; Vico Himera 3; s €30-90, d €40-100, tr €50-130; 🕸🛜) South African–born Diana runs this excellent-value B&B, which is tucked down a narrow alley off the main drag. Rooms have abundant hot water, cheerful decor and welcome extras such as kettles, fridges, clothes-drying racks and satellite TV. Some downstairs rooms have kitchenettes, but these are a bit dark. Breakfast costs €5 extra.

E Pulera   SICILIAN €€

(☏090 981 11 58; Via Isabella Vainicher Conti; mains from €17; ☺dinner May-Oct) Its serene garden setting and exquisite food make this an upscale but relaxed choice for dinner. Choose from a vast array of Aeolian and Sicilian meat and fish dishes, then finish off with biscotti and sweet Malvasia wine.

Kasbah   SICILIAN €€

(☏090 981 10 75; Via Maurolico 25, Lipari; pizzas €6-9, mains from €15; ☺dinner, closed Wed Oct-Mar) Choose the environment that suits you best: the sleek, contemporary interior dining room or the vine-covered, candlelit garden out back. Menu choices include delicious pizzas and seafood delicacies.

Bar Pasticceria Subba   PASTICCERIA €

(☏090 981 13 52; Corso Vittorio Emanuele 92, Lipari; pastries from €1; ☺7am-10pm) Subba has been supplying indulgent cakes, pastries and gelato to locals since 1930.

🍷 Drinking

Bar Chicco Tosto   CAFE

(Corso Vittorio Emanuele II 281; ☺6am-7pm Mon-Sat) The name says it all – Chicco Tosto roasts its own beans and makes the best coffee on the islands. It's opposite the port and opens at 6am, which is convenient for those leaving or arriving early.

Eden Bar   BAR

(Corso Vittorio Emanuele II 133; ☺daily year-round) The bar of choice for locals of every age, plus almost every tourist in town. It hops on a Saturday evening when its tables and crowd spill onto the street, which is closed to traffic.

ℹ Information

The islands' only **tourist office** (☏090 988 00 95; www.aasteolie.191.it; Corso Vittorio Emanuele 202; ☺8.30am-1.30pm & 4.30-7.30pm Mon-Fri, 8.30am-1.30pm Sat & Sun Jul & Aug) is on Lipari.

ℹ Getting There & Away

The main departure point for the islands is Milazzo. If arriving in Milazzo by train, you'll need to catch a bus (€1) or taxi (€15) to the port, 4km from the station. At the port you'll find ticket offices lined up on Corso dei Mille.

Ustica Lines (www.usticalines.it) runs hydrofoils from the islands to/from Messina (€22.70, 1¾ hours) and Milazzo (€23.70, one hour). Siremar ferries travel to/from Milazzo (€16.20) but take longer than the hydrofoils. Frequency of service varies wildly according to the season.

Siremar also runs ferries from Naples to Lipari, the other islands and Milazzo (seat from €70.20).

❶ Getting Around

Lipari is the main transport hub. Ustica Lines runs regular services to Vulcano (€7, 10 minutes), Stromboli (€18.30, 1¾ hours) and the other islands. You can get full timetable information and buy tickets at Lipari's port.

Lipari's Guglielmo Urso Bus service travels around the island (€7 for six trips). Its terminus is at the port.

Taormina

POP 11,100

Crowning a clifftop terrace overlooking the Ionian Sea and Mt Etna, this sophisticated town has attracted socialites, artists and writers ever since Greek times. Its pristine medieval core, proximity to beaches, grandstand coastal views and chic social scene make it a hugely popular summer holiday destination, meaning that crowds can be oppressive in July and August.

◉ Sights & Activities

The principal pastime in Taormina is wandering the pretty hilltop streets, browsing the shops and eyeing up fellow holidaymakers.

For a swim you'll need to take the **funivia** (cable car; one-way/return €2/3.50; ⊙9am-8.15pm, to 1am Apr-Sep) down to Taormina's beach, **Lido Mazzarò**, and **Isola Bella**, a tiny island set in its own picturesque cove.

SAT (☑0942 2 46 53; www.satgroup.it; Corso Umberto I 73) is one of a number of agencies that organises day trips to Mt Etna (€40), as well as to Syracuse (€45), Palermo and Cefalù (€55), and Agrigento (€50).

Teatro Greco
AMPHITHEATRE

(☑0942 2 32 20; Via Teatro Greco; adult/reduced/EU under 18 & over 65 €8/4/free; ⊙9am-1hr before sunset) Suspended between sea and sky, and with Mt Etna looming on the southern horizon, this horseshoe-shaped theatre is Taormina's premier attraction. Built in the 3rd century BC, it's the most dramatically situated Greek theatre in the world and the second largest in Sicily (after Syracuse). In summer the theatre is used as a venue for international arts and film festivals. In peak season, explore early in the morning to avoid the crowds.

Corso Umberto
STREET

One of the chief delights of Taormina is wandering along its pedestrianised main street, which is lined with antique and jewellery shops, delis and designer boutiques. Midway down, pause to revel in the stunning panoramic views of Mt Etna and the sea coast from **Piazza IX Aprile**. A few blocks further along is **Piazza del Duomo**, where teenagers congregate around an ornate baroque fountain dating from 1635. On the eastern side of this piazza is the 13th-century **cathedral** (Piazza del Duomo; ⊙9am-8pm).

🛏 Sleeping & Eating

TOP CHOICE **Hotel Villa Belvedere** HOTEL €€€

(☑094 22 37 91; www.villabelvedere.it; Via Bagnoli Croce 79; s €70-190, d €80-280, ste €120-450; ⊙Mar–late-Nov; ❄@�︠🏊) Built in 1902, the jaw-droppingly pretty Villa Belvedere is in a quiet but central pocket and has fabulous views, luxuriant gardens and a swimming pool. Rooms are small but comfortable and most have terraces overlooking the sea – the best are on the 3rd floor. Suites have large dining/lounge areas, excellent kitchens and private terraces; they're perfect for families. Internet and wi-fi cost an extra €3 for the duration of your stay.

Hostel Taormina
HOSTEL €

(☑094 262 55 05, mobile 349 102 61 61; www.hosteltaormina.com; Via Circonvallazione 13; dm €18-25, d €58-80; ❄@�︠) The town's only hostel opened for business in 2011 and operates year-round. It's small (only 23 beds in three dorms and one private room) and the facilities are basic, but it has a roof terrace commanding panoramic sea views, comfortable beds and a communal kitchen. No breakfast.

Tiramisù
PIZZERIA, SICILIAN €€

(☑0942 2 48 03; Via Cappuccini 1; pizzas €7-14, mains €13-20; ⊙closed Tue) Known for its excellent pizzas and trademark *tiramisù*, this casual place close to Porta Messina offers indoor and outdoor eating areas and is a good choice for a casual meal.

Al Duomo
SICILIAN €€€

(☑0942 62 56 56; Vico Ebrei 11; mains €20-22; ⊙lunch & dinner, closed Mon Nov-Mar) A romantic terrace overlooking the cathedral and a menu of classic Sicilian dishes are the attractions here. The chef's six-course tasting menu (€60) is a great introduction to the best that the island has to offer.

ℹ Information

Tourist Office (☑0942 2 32 43; www.gate2 taormina.com; Piazza Santa Caterina, off Corso Umberto I; ⊙8.30am-2.30pm & 3.30-7pm Mon-Fri year-round, 9am-1pm & 4-6.30pm Sat Apr-Oct) Has helpful multilingual staff, plenty of practical information and tour bookings.

ℹ Getting There & Away

Taormina is best reached by bus. From the bus terminus on Via Pirandello, Interbus serves Messina (€3.90, 1½ hours, seven daily Monday to Saturday, one on Sunday) and **Etna Trasporti** (☑095 53 27 16; www.etnatrasporti.it) connects with Catania airport (€7, 1½ hours, five daily Monday to Saturday, three on Sunday).

Taormina's train station is some 2km downhill from the main town, making the train a last resort. If you do arrive by train, catch the Interbus service (€1.80) up to town. Buses run roughly every 30 to 90 minutes, less often on Sunday.

Mt Etna

The dark silhouette of Mt Etna (3350m) broods ominously over the east coast, more or less halfway between Taormina and Catania. One of Europe's highest and most volatile volcanoes, it erupts frequently, most recently in April 2012.

By public transport the best way to get to the mountain is to take the daily AST bus from Catania. This departs from in front of the main train station at 8.15am daily (returning at 4.30pm; €5.60 return) and drops you at the Rifugio Sapienza (1923m), where you can pick up the **Funivia dell'Etna** (☑095 91 41 41; www.funiviaetna.com; cable car one-way/return €14.50/27, incl bus & guide €51; ⊙9am-4.30pm) to 2500m. From June to September there is another departure at 11.20am. From Rifugio Sapienza buses courier you up to the official crater zone (2920m). If you want to walk, allow up to four hours for the round trip.

Gruppo Guide Alpine Etna Sud (☑095 791 47 55; www.etnaguide.com) is one of hundreds of outfits offering guided tours, typically involving 4WD transport and a guided trek. These cost from €45 per person for a half-day tour (usually morning or sunset) and about €60 for a full-day tour.

Armchair excursionists can enjoy Etna views by hopping on a **Ferrovia Circumetnea train** (www.circumetnea.it; single/re-turn €7.25/11.60). Catch the metro from Catania's main train station to the FCE station at Via Caronda (metro stop Borgo). Note that the service doesn't operate on Sundays from mid-September to March.

Further Etna information is available from the **municipal tourist office** (☑095 742 55 73; www.comune.catania.it; Via Vittorio Emanuele II 172; ⊙8.15am-7.15pm Mon-Fri, to 12.15pm Sat) in Catania.

Syracuse

POP 123,900

Syracuse (Siracusa) has a fascinating past. Founded in 734 BC by Corinthian settlers, it became the dominant Greek city state on the Mediterranean and was known as the most beautiful city in the ancient world. After falling to the Romans in 212 BC its power waned, and Palermo took over as the island's most important city. A devastating earthquake in 1693 destroyed most of the Syracuse's buildings; their replacements, built in the fashionable Sicilian baroque style, remain largely intact and visually resplendent in the streets of Ortigia, the *centro storico*.

◉ Sights

Ortygia HISTORIC AREA
Connected to the town centre by a bridge, the island of Ortygia is an atmospheric warren of baroque *palazzi*, lively piazzas and busy trattorias. Just off Via Roma, the 7th-century **Duomo** (Piazza del Duomo; ⊙8am-7pm) was built over a pre-existing 5th-century BC Greek temple, incorporating most of the original columns in its three-aisled structure. Its sumptuous baroque facade was added in the 18th century.

Parco Archaeologico della Neapolis ARCHAEOLOGICAL SITE
(☑0931 6 50 68; Viale Paradis; adult/18-25/under 18 & EU over 65 €10/5/free; ⊙9am-6pm Apr-Oct, to 4pm Nov-Mar) For the classicist, Syracuse's real attraction is this archaeological park with its 5th-century BC **Teatro Greco** hewn out of the rock above the city. This theatre staged the last tragedies of Aeschylus, which were first performed here in his presence. In summer it is brought to life again with an annual season of classical theatre.

Just beside the theatre is the mysterious **Latomia del Paradiso**. The stone for the ancient city was extracted from these deep, precipitous limestone quarries.

Back outside this area you'll find the entrance to the 2nd-century AD **Anfiteatro Romano**, which was used originally for gladiatorial combats and horse races. The Spaniards largely destroyed the site in the 16th century, and used it as a quarry to build Ortigia's city walls.

To reach the park, take bus 1, 3 or 12 (€1) from in front of the post office on Piazza Poste in Ortigia and get off at the corner of Corso Gelone and Viale Teocrito. Buy bus tickets from a *tabacchi*. Alternatively, the walk from Ortigia will take about 30 minutes. If driving, you can park along Viale Augusto (tickets available at the nearby souvenir kiosks).

Museo Archeologico Paolo Orsi　　MUSEUM
(Viale Teocrito; adult/reduced €8/4; ⊙9am-6pm Tue-Sat, 9am-1pm Sun) Head to the grounds of Villa Landolina, about 500m east of the archaeological park, to find this huge, well-organised and incredibly impressive archaeological museum. Allow plenty of time to get through the four distinct sectors; serious archaeology buffs may even want to consider splitting their visit into two days. A tip: don't miss the coin collection – it's quite extraordinary. A combined ticket is available for the museum and the archaeological park (adult/EU student 18-25/ EU under 18 & over 65 €13.50/7/free).

🛏 Sleeping

TOP CHOICE **Palazzo del Sale**　　B&B €
(☑0931 6 59 58; www.palazzodelsale.com; Via Santa Teresa 25, Ortigia; s €75-95, d €90-115, d with terrace €100-125; ❋@☎) This is as stylish as Syracuse gets: the six rooms at this designer B&B are well sized, with high ceilings and good beds. Extra touches include free coffee and tea in the comfortable communal lounge. The owners also operate a second property right on the beach near Porto Piccolo (www.giuggiulena.it).

B&B dei Viaggiatori, Viandanti e Sognatori　　B&B €
(☑0931 2 47 81; www.bedandbreakfastsicily.it; Via Roma 156, Ortigia; s €35-50, d €55-70, tr €75-80; ❋☎) On the 4th floor of an old *palazzo* at the end of Via Roma, this welcoming B&B is run by a young couple and their toddler, who live on site. It offers simple, colourfully decorated rooms and a sunny roof terrace with sweeping sea views. No lift.

Lol Hostel　　HOSTEL €
(☑0931 46 50 88; www.lolhostel.com; Via Francesco Crispi 94; dm €20-27, d €56-65; ❋@☎)

This modern, well-kept hostel is located in a scruffy street near the bus and train stations. It has six mixed dorms (sleeping eight, 10 and 20) and two doubles. The pleasant common spaces include an open, airy guest kitchen, an outdoor patio and a sprawling lounge with computers (€1 per 30 minutes) and bar (April to September only). It's 10 minutes on foot to Ortigia, or five minutes with one of the hostel's rental bikes.

🍴 Eating & Drinking

The two best bars in Ortigia are **Il Blu** (Via Nizza) and **Biblios Cafe** (Via del Consiglio Reginale 11; ⊙10am-1.30pm & 5-9pm, closed Wed).

Sicilia in Tavola　　SICILIAN €
(☑392 461 08 89; Via Cavour 28; pasta €7-12; ⊙closed Mon) There are only a dozen tables available at this popular local eatery specialising in seafood antipasti and homemade pasta dishes, so arrive early or be prepared to queue.

Ristorante Regina Lucia　　SICILIAN €€
(☑0931 2 25 09; www.reginalucia.it; Piazza Duomo 6, Ortigia; mains €13-18, degustation menus €45-65; ⊙lunch & dinner Wed-Mon) Romantics will adore this atmospheric place with its ancient-meets-arty decor featuring Kartell chairs, vaulted stone ceilings, candelabras and contemporary art. This complements a menu of modern Sicilian dishes dictated by the season.

Gelati Bianca　　GELATERIA €
(Via Pompeo Picherali 2; cone/cup from €1.80; ⊙daily) It's not just the location off Piazza Duomo that's the attraction here – the house-made gelati is pretty good, too.

ⓘ Information

The most useful **tourist information office** (☑0800 05 55 00; infoturismo@provsr.it; Via Roma 31; ⊙8am-8pm Mon-Sat, 9.15am-6.45pm Sun) is operated by the municipality.

ⓘ Getting There & Around

It's quickest and most convenient to get here by bus rather than train. Buses use the terminus close to the train station. Interbus runs services to/from Catania airport (€6, one hour, hourly Monday to Saturday, six Sunday) and Catania (€6, 1¼ hours). It also operates a service to Palermo (€12, 3¼ hours, three daily Monday to Saturday, two Sunday).

Regional trains service Taormina (€8.30, two hours, five daily), Catania (€6.35, 1¼ hours, seven daily) and Messina (€9.70, 2¾ hours, five daily).

A free shuttle bus (No 20) runs between the bus station and Ortigia every 30 minutes from 6.30am to 9.30pm, stopping at Parcheggio Talete, Piazza Archimede and Via Maestranza.

Note that there's a ZTL in Ortigia – the car park at Talete, just inside the bridge, charges €6 per day.

Agrigento

POP 59,200

Agrigento was founded around 581 BC by Greek settlers and became an important trading centre under the Romans and Byzantines. These days, the only trading that occurs is around the souvenir stands surrounding one of Italy's most wonderful ancient sights, the Valley of the Temples (Valle dei Templi).

Up in the main town, the tourist information desk in the office of the **Provincia Regionale di Agrigento** (☑0922 59 32 27; www.provincia.agrigento.it; Piazza Vittorio Emanuele; ◉8.30am-1pm & 2.30-7pm Mon-Fri, 8.30am-2pm Sat) can supply maps but little else.

◉ Sights

Valley of the Temples ARCHAEOLOGICAL SITE
(Valle dei Templi) One of the most magnificent archaeological sites in Southern Europe, this Unesco-listed complex of temples and old city walls from the ancient city of Akragas dates from 581 BC. The five Doric temples actually stand along a ridge, not a valley, and were designed to be visible from all around and a beacon for homecoming sailors.

Though in varying states of ruin, the temples give a tantalising glimpse of what must truly have been one of the most luxurious cities in Magna Graecia. You'll need a full day to do justice to the **Archaeological Park** (☑0922 49 72 26; adult/EU reduced/child €10/5/free; ◉8.30am-7pm, later in summer), which is divided into eastern and western zones. The most spectacular temples are in the eastern zone. First up is the oldest, the **Tempio di Ercole**, built at the end of the 6th century BC and equivalent in size to the Parthenon. Continuing east, the intact **Tempio della Concordia** was transformed into a Christian church in the 6th century, and the **Tempio di Giunone** boasts an impressive sacrificial altar.

Over the road in the western zone, the remains of the 5th-century BC **Tempio di Giove** suggest just how big the original must have been. In fact, it covered an area of 112m by 56m with 20m-high columns interspersed with *telamoni* (giant male statues), one of which now stands in the valley's

Museo Archeologico (☑0922 4 01 11; Contrada San Nicola; incl Archaeological Park adult/EU reduced €13.50/7; ◉9am-7pm Tue-Sat, 9am-1pm Sun & Mon), north of the temples.

If you are planning to visit both the park and the museum, purchase a combined ticket (adult/EU reduced €13.50/7).

The most scenic time to visit is in February and March when the valley is awash with almond blossoms.

🛏 Sleeping & Eating

TOP CHOICE Villa Athena LUXURY HOTEL €€€
(☑0922 59 62 88; www.hotelvillaathena.it; Via Passeggiata Archeologica 33; s €130-190, d €150-350, ste €240-890; P✳@🛜⛲) Close proximity to the Valley of the Temples (a five-minute walk), views of the Tempio della Concordia, a landscaped garden with swimming pool and a recently refurbished and extremely classy interior fitout make this five-star hotel an irresistibly indulgent choice.

Atenea 191 B&B €
(☑349 59 55 94; www.atenea191.com; Via Atenea 191; s €45-60, d €65-85) Though musty and worn, this B&B on Agrigento's main shopping thoroughfare is open all year and has a breakfast terrace with sweeping views over the valley.

Kalòs MODERN SICILIAN €€
(Piazzetta San Calogero; mains €15; ◉closed Mon) This stylish eatery compensates for bland decor by focusing full attention on its well-prepared fish, meat and pasta.

🍷 Drinking

Mojo Wine Bar WINE BAR
(☑0922 46 30 13; Piazza San Francesco 11-13; ◉Mon-Sat) A trendy *enoteca* in a pretty piazza. Enjoy a cool white Inzolia and munch on olives and spicy salami as you listen to some laid-back jazz.

ℹ Getting There & Away

Bus is generally the easiest way to get to Agrigento. Intercity buses arrive on Piazzale F Rosselli, from where it's a short walk downhill to the train station on Piazza Guglielmo Marconi, to catch local bus 1, 2 or 3 to the Valley of the Temples (€1.10). Buy tickets at the station *tabacchi*.

A taxi from the bus station to the Valley of the Temples costs €10.

Cuffaro runs buses to/from Palermo (€8.70, two hours, nine daily Monday to Saturday, three Sunday) and SAIS services go to Catania (€13, three hours, hourly).

SARDINIA

The Mediterranean's second-largest island, Sardinia, is a rugged and beautiful place. Tourist interest is largely focused on the coast, which is one of Italy's most impressive, with stunning sandy beaches, crystal-line waters and idyllic coves; but venture inland and you'll discover an altogether different island, of untamed nature and proud tradition, dark granite peaks, dizzying valleys and silent cork forests. Adding a sense of mystery are the 7000 *nuraghi* (circular stone towers) that pepper the landscape, all that's left of Sardinia's mysterious prehistoric past.

Sardinia's top coastal resorts, including the celeb-studded Costa Smeralda (Emerald Coast), are among the most expensive holiday destinations on the Med and get extremely busy in peak season. Visit out of high summer, though, and you'll find that space is not a problem and prices compare very favourably with the mainland (or 'continent' as Sardinians refer to it).

You can get around Sardinia on public transport but you'll discover much more with your own wheels.

❶ Getting There & Away

Air

Flights from Italian and European cities serve Sardinia's three airports: Elmas (p522) in Cagliari; Alghero's **Fertilia** (☑079 93 52 82; www.aeroportodialghero.it); and **Olbia Costa Smeralda** (OLB; ☑0789 56 34 44; www.geasar.it).

Boat

Car and passenger ferries sail year-round from various Italian ports, including Genoa, Livorno, Piombino, Civitavecchia, Naples and Palermo. Several companies ply these routes and services are at their most frequent between June and September. There are also summer-only routes from Fiumicino. The major routes and the companies that operate them are:

Civitavecchia To/from Olbia (Moby Lines, SNAV, Tirrenia); Cagliari (Tirrenia); Golfo Aranci (Sardinia Ferries); Arbatax (Tirrenia).

Genoa To/from Porto (Grandi Navi Veloci, Tirrenia); Torres (Grandi Navi Veloci, Tirrenia); Olbia (Grandi Navi Veloci, Moby Lines, Tirrenia).

Livorno To/from Olbia (Moby Lines); Golfo Aranci (Sardinia Ferries).

Naples To/from Cagliari (Tirrenia)

Palermo To/from Cagliari (Tirrenia)

Piombion To/from Olbia (moby Lines); Golfo Aranci (Sardinia Ferries).

Get up-to-date information and book tickets at www.traghettiweb.it.

❶ Getting Around

Getting round Sardinia by public transport is time-consuming but not impossible. In most cases buses are preferable to trains. The main transport provider, **ARST** (☑800 86 50 42; www.arst.sardegna.it), operates bus services across the island, as well as the **Trenino Verde** (☑070 58 02 46; www.treninoverde.com), a tiny tourist train that trundles through Sardinia's most inaccessible countryside.

Cagliari

POP 156,500

Sardinia's capital and most cosmopolitan city, Cagliari rises from the sea in a helter-skelter of golden-hued *palazzi*, domes and facades. Yet for all its splendour, it remains what it always has been – a busy working port with a gritty, down-to-earth atmosphere and a vibrant buzz. With its landmark citadel, great restaurants and popular, sandy beach, Cagliari is very much its own city.

◉ Sights & Activities

Cagliari's sights are concentrated in four central districts: Castello, the medieval citadel that towers over the city; Marina, the bustling seafront area; Stampace, which extends westwards of Largo Carlo Felice, modern Cagliari's showpiece street; and Villanova, east of Castello.

Museo Archeologico Nazionale MUSEUM
(☑070 68 40 00; Piazza dell'Arsenale; adult/reduced €3/1.50; ⊙9am-8pm Tue-Sun) Housed in what was once Cagliari's arsenal, the **Citadella dei Musei** is the city's main museum complex. Of its four museums, the most impressive is the Museo Archeologico Nazionale whose collection of archaeological artefacts includes a number of pint-sized bronze figurines. In the absence of any written records, these provide vital clues to the island's mysterious *nuraghic* culture.

Torre di San Pancrazio TOWER
(Piazza Indipendenza; adult/reduced €4/2.50; ⊙10.30am-7pm Tue-Sun summer, to 4.30pm winter) Guarding the entrance to the Citadella dei Musei, this 36m-high tower was completed in 1305 on the city's highest point.

Climb to the top for grandstand views of the Golfo di Cagliari.

Cattedrale di Santa Maria   CHURCH
(Piazza Palazzo 4; ⏱7.30am-8pm Mon-Sat, 8am-1pm & 4.30-8.30pm Sun) Cagliari's graceful, 13th-century cathedral sits aloft in the hilltop Castello district. Apart from its bell tower, little remains of the original Gothic structure, but it's still an impressive sight with an imitation Pisan-Romanesque facade and a baroque interior. Inside, note the imposing Romanesque pulpits.

Bastione San Remy   LOOKOUT
This monumental terrace, formerly a strong point in the defensive walls, affords sweeping views over Cagliari's higgledy-piggledy rooftops and distant lagoons.

Anfiteatro Romano   AMPHITHEATRE
(www.anfiteatroromano.it; Viale Sant'Ignazio) This 2nd-century amphitheatre is the most important Roman monument in Sardinia. Summer concerts are staged here; at the time of research the amphitheatre was closed for restoration.

Spiaggia di Poetto   BEACH
A short bus ride from the centre, Cagliari's vibrant beach boasts inviting blue waters and a happening summer bar scene. Take bus PQ or PF.

⭐ Festivals & Events
Cagliari's annual bonanza, the **Festa di Sant'Efisio**, involves four days of costumed processions from 1 May.

🛏 Sleeping

Il Cagliarese   B&B €
(☎339 654 40 83; www.ilcagliarese.it; Via Vittorio Porcile 19; s €45-70, d €60-90; ❄🛜) In the heart of the lively Marina district, this snug B&B gets everything right – the location is central, its three guest rooms are clean, comfortable and quiet, there's free wi-fi, and a great breakfast spread. Overseeing it all, the friendly owners are a mine of local information.

Hotel A&R Bundes Jack   HOTEL €
(☎070 65 79 70; www.hotelbjvittoria.it; Via Roma 75; s €52-72, d €80-92; ❄) An excellent seafront option is this old-fashioned family-run *pensione*. Run by a garrulous old gent, it has spacious, high-ceilinged rooms decorated with solid antique furniture and sparkling chandeliers. Breakfast is not included but is available for €7.

Hostel Marina   HOSTEL €
(☎070 67 08 18; www.hostelmarinacagliari.it; Scalette S Sepolcro; dm/s/d/q €22/40/60/100; ❄🛜) This central hostel, housed in a beautifully converted 800-year-old former monastery, has oodles of historic charm and a wide range of accommodation, from single-sex six-person dorms to private rooms with en suite bathrooms.

🍴 Eating & Drinking

Monica e Ahmed   SEAFOOD €€
(☎070 640 20 45; Corso Vittorio Emanuele 119; mains €20, fixed-price menus €15/25/30; ⏱closed dinner Sun) Search out this colourful, laid-back restaurant for fresh seafood served with a smile. Kick off with a lavish antipasto spread of swordfish, mussels, fried calamari, cuttlefish and tuna, before diving into spaghetti with *ricci* (sea urchins) and grilled catch of the day.

Il Fantasma   PIZZERIA €
(☎070 65 67 49; Via San Domenico 94; pizzas €6.50-10; ⏱Mon-Sat) A five-minute walk east of Piazza Martiri d'Italia, this unpretentious pizzeria prepares some of the best pizza in town. Grab a table in the barrel-vaulted interior and bite into classic pizzas served blisteringly hot from the wood-fired oven. Bookings recommended.

Sa Schironada   TRATTORIA €
(☎070 451 07 71; Via Baylle 39; set menus €13-38, pizza & drink €10) A big, barnlike trattoria that's good for a cheap, tasty fill-up. There are several menu options but take it easy when you order – the portions are huge and the antipasto is a minor meal in itself.

Antico Caffè   CAFE
(www.anticocaffe1855.it; Piazza Costituzione 10; ⏱7am-2am) Authors DH Lawrence and Grazia Deledda once frequented this grand old cafe, Cagliari's most famous. Join the locals to chat over leisurely coffees, cocktails and snacks.

❶ Information
Tourist Information Points (☎070 677 71 87; www.infopointcagliari.it; ⏱8am-8pm) The most useful information points are at Piazza Indipendenza, near the Torre di San Pancrazio, and at Piazza Costituzione, under Bastione San Remy.

WORTH A TRIP

CALA GONONE

Cala Gonone is a popular resort on the eastern **Gulf of Orosei**. It sits at the heart of one of Italy's most beautiful coastlines where the rocky mountains of the **Parco Nazionale del Golfo di Orosei e del Gennargentu** abruptly meet the sea, forming a curtain of plunging white cliffs riven by hidden coves and lapped by crystalline waters. The swimming is sublime and, inland, the rugged terrain is ideal for hiking and climbing.

In town, there's a small beach but the best swimming spots, including **Cala Fuili** and **Cala Luna**, lie to the south. Also to the south is the **Grotta del Bue Marino** (adult/reduced €8/4; ⊙guided tours hourly 9am-noon & 3-5pm Aug, 10am-noon & 3pm Jul, 10am, 11am & 3pm Sep, 11am & 3pm Oct-Nov & Mar-Jun), a complex of stalactite- and stalagmite-filled caves where monk seals used to pup. The easiest way to reach these places is to take a boat trip from Cala Gonone's small port. The **Nuovo Consorzio Trasporti Marittimi** (☑0784 9 33 05; www.calagononecrociere.it; Porto Cala Gonone) is one of several operators that sails to Cala Luna (€15 to €23) and the Grotta del Bue Marino (€19 to €22, including Cala Luna €26 to €35) between March and October.

For accommodation lists and information on tour operators offering excursions and guided hikes, contact the helpful **tourist office** (☑0784 9 36 96; www.dorgali.it; Viale Bue Marino 1a; ⊙9am-7pm Jul & Aug, 9am-1pm & 3-7pm Easter-Jun & Sep-Oct, to noon rest of year).

If travelling by public transport, Cala Gonone is accessible by ARST bus from Nuoro (€3.50, 70 minutes, up to six daily).

❶ Getting There & Away

Air

Flights from mainland Italy and European cities arrive at **Elmas airport** (☑070 21 12 11; www.cagliariairport.it), 6km northwest of the city. Half-hourly **ARST** (www.arst.sardegna.it) buses connect the airport with the bus station on Piazza Matteotti; the 10-minute journey costs €4.

Boat

Cagliari's ferry port is just off Via Roma. **Tirrenia** (☑892 123; www.tirrenia.it; Via dei Ponente 1) is the main ferry operator, with year-round services to Civitavecchia (from €58, 16½ hours), Naples (from €47, 16¼ hours) and Palermo (from €45, 14½ hours).

Bus

From the bus station on Piazza Matteotti, daily **ARST** (☑800 865 042; www.arst.sardegna.it) buses serve Oristano (€7, 1½ hours, two daily) and Nuoro (€15.50, 3½ hours, two daily), as well as destinations on the Costa del Sud and Costa Rei. Get tickets from the McDonald's on the square.

Turmo Travel (☑0789 2 14 87; www.gruppo turmotravel.com) runs a daily bus to Olbia (€19, 4¼ hours).

Car & Motorcycle

Down by the port, you can rent cars, bikes and scooters at **CIA Rent a Car** (☑070 65 65 03; www.rentcagliari.com; Via S Agostino 13). Bank on from €38 per day for a small car.

Train

From the station on Piazza Matteotti direct trains run to Oristano (€5.95, one to 1½ hours, hourly) and Sassari (€15.75, 3¾ hours, two daily).

Alghero

POP 40,700

Alghero, a picturesque medieval town, is the main resort on Sardinia's northwest coast. Interest is centred on the *centro storico*, a small tangle of tight-knit lanes and busy piazzas enclosed by robust honey-coloured sea walls.

The town was founded in the 11th century by the Genovese and later became an important outpost of the Aragonese Catalans. Still today the local dialect is a form of Catalan and the town retains something of a Spanish atmosphere.

◉ Sights & Activities

If you're in town for a few days, consider the **A-ticket** (1 adult & child €20, 2 adults & children

€40), a discount card that covers admission to the Grotta di Nettuno, Nuraghe di Palmavera and various museums. It's available at the tourist office and participating sites.

Centro Storico
NEIGHBOURHOOD

Alghero's medieval core is a charming mesh of narrow cobbled alleys hemmed in by Spanish Gothic *palazzi*. Of the various churches, the most interesting is the **Chiesa di San Francesco** (Via Carlo Alberto), with its mix of Romanesque and Gothic styles. A short walk away, the **campanile** (bell tower; 079 973 30 41; Via Principe Umberto; adult/child €2/free; 10.30am-12.30pm Mon-Fri & 7-9pm Mon & Fri Jun-Aug, 10.30am-12.30pm Mon, Tue, Thu, Fri & 4-6pm Mon & Fri Sep-Oct, on request Nov-May) of the **Cattedrale di Santa Maria** (Piazza Duomo; 7am-noon & 5-7.30pm) is a fine example of Gothic-Catalan architecture.

For lovely sea views, walk the town's honey-coloured **ramparts** from Piazza Sulis to the **Bastioni della Maddalena**, the only remnant of the town's former land battlements.

Grotta di Nettuno
CAVE

(079 94 65 40; adult/child €13/7; 9am-7pm May-Sep, to 6pm Apr-Oct, to 3pm Nov-Mar) From the port you can take a boat trip along the impressive northern coast to the grandiose Grotta di Nettuno cave complex. The cheapest boat is the Navisarda ferry (adult/child return €15/8), which departs hourly between 9.30am and 5.30pm from June to September, and twice daily between March and May and in October. Cheaper still, you can get a bus to the caves from Via Catalogna (€4.50 return, 50 minutes, three times daily summer, once winter).

Nuraghe di Palmavera
RUIN

(admission €3; 9am-7pm May-Sep, to 6pm Apr & Oct, 10am-2pm Nov-Mar) Ten kilometres west of Alghero, this 3500-year-old *nuraghe* village is well worth a visit.

🛏 Sleeping

There's plenty of accommodation in Alghero but you'll need to book between June and September.

TOP CHOICE Angedras Hotel
HOTEL €€

(079 973 50 34; www.angedras.it; Via Frank 2; s €60-130, d €65-150; ❄🐾) A model of white-washed Mediterranean style, the Angedras (Sardegna backwards) has cool white-tiled rooms with big French doors opening onto sunny patios. Note that it's a good 15-minute walk from the *centro storico*.

Hotel San Francesco
HOTEL €

(079 98 03 30; www.sanfrancescohotel.com; Via Ambrogio Machin 2; s €52-63, d €82-101, tr €110-135; ❄@🐾) This welcoming three-star is the only hotel in Alghero's *centro storico*. Housed in an ex-convent – monks still live on the 3rd floor – it has modest, comfortable rooms set around an attractive 14th-century cloister where summer concerts are sometimes staged.

🍴 Eating

Angedras Restaurant
SARDINIAN €€

(079 973 50 78; www.angedrasrestaurant.it; Bastioni Marco Polo 41; mains €14, lunch menu €16) Alghero's sea-facing ramparts set a memorable stage for alfresco dining. This is one of the better restaurants on the walls, serving a largely regional menu of pasta, meat and elegantly presented seafood.

Gelateria I Bastioni
GELATERIA €

(Bastioni Marco Polo 5; cones €1-3, milkshakes €3.50, granite €2.50; Apr-Oct) Homemade ice creams, creamy milkshakes, lush smoothies and cooling *granite* – this hole-in-the-wall gem does the lot. Particularly fab are the fresh fruit flavours, ideally topped by a generous squirt of whipped cream.

Il Ghiotto
FAST FOOD €

(079 97 48 20; Piazza Civica 23; mains €8) Part bar, part canteen, part shop, the Ghiotto is ideal for a cheap and cheerful fill-up. Grab a tray and stock up from the tantalising spread of panini, pastas, salads and main courses. There's seating in a dining area behind the main hall or outside on a busy wooden terrace.

ℹ Information

On the eastern fringe of the *centro storico*, the superhelpful **tourist office** (079 97 90 54; www.comune.alghero.ss.it; Piazza Porta Terra 9; 8am-8pm, closed Sun winter) can answer every imaginable question.

ℹ Getting There & Around

Alghero's **Fertilia airport** (079 93 52 82; www.aeroportodialghero.it) is used by a number of low-cost carriers, with connections to mainland Italy and destinations across Europe. To get into town take the hourly bus (€1, on board €1.50, 20 minutes) to the bus terminus on Via Cagliari.

In town you can walk most places, but for the beach, local bus AF runs along the seafront to/from Via Cagliari.

UNDERSTAND ITALY

History

Despite having an ancient history, Italy is actually a very young country. It only came into being with Italian unification in 1861; until then the Italian peninsula had been a complex patchwork of often warring empires, city states and maritime republics.

The Etruscans & Greeks

Of the many Italic tribes that emerged from the Stone Age, the Etruscans left the most enduring mark. By the 7th century BC their city states – places such as Caere (modern-day Cerveteri) and Tarquinii (Tarquinia) – were the dominant forces in central Italy, important Mediterranean powers rivalled only by the Greeks on the south coast. Greek traders had been settling in Italy since the 8th century BC and over the centuries had founded a number of independent city states, collectively known as Magna Graecia. Despite Etruscan attempts to conquer the Greeks, both groups thrived until the 3rd century BC, when legionnaires from the emerging city of Rome began to expand their territory and power.

Rise & Fall of Rome

Rome's origins are mired in myth. Romantics hold that the city was founded by Romulus in 753 BC on the site where he and his twin brother Remus had been suckled by a she-wolf. Few historians accept this as fact, although they acknowledge the existence of a settlement on Palatine Hill dating to the 8th century BC and it is generally accepted that Romulus was the first of Rome's seven kings. The last king, the Etruscan Tarquinius Superbus, was ousted in 509 BC, paving the way for the creation of the Roman Republic.

The fledgling republic got off to a shaky start but soon found its feet and by the 2nd century BC had seen off all its main rivals – the Etruscans, Greeks and Carthaginians – to become the undisputed master of the Western world. The republic's most famous leader was Julius Caesar, a gifted general and ambitious politician whose lust for power eventually proved his, and the republic's, undoing. His assassination on the Ides of March (15 March) in 44 BC sparked a power struggle between his chosen successor and great-nephew Octavian and Mark Antony, talented soldier and the lover of Egyptian queen,

Cleopatra. Octavian prevailed and in 27 BC became Augustus, Rome's first emperor.

Augustus ruled well and Rome flourished, reaching its zenith in the 2nd century AD. Unfortunately, the same can't be said for his crazy successors Caligula and Nero. By the 3rd century, economic decline and the spread of Christianity were fuelling discontent. Diocletian tried to stop the rot by splitting the empire into eastern and western halves, but when his successor, Constantine (the first Christian emperor), moved his court to Constantinople, Rome's days were numbered. Sacked by the Goths in 410 and plundered by the Vandals in 455, the Western Empire finally fell in 476.

From the Renaissance to the Risorgimento

The Middle Ages in Italy was a period of almost constant warfare. While the Papal States fought the Holy Roman Empire for control over Europe's Catholics, the French and Spanish battled over southern Italy, and Italy's prosperous northern city states struggled for territorial gain. Eventually Milan, Venice and Florence (the latter under the powerful Medici family) emerged as regional powers. Against this fractious background, art and culture thrived. In the latter half of the 15th century, the Renaissance emerged in Florence. A sweeping intellectual and artistic movement, it soon spread south to Rome before snowballing into a Europe-wide phenomenon.

By the end of the 16th century most of Italy was in foreign hands – the Spanish in the south and the Austrians in the north. Three centuries later, Napoleon's brief Italian interlude gave rise to the Risorgimento (unification movement). With Count Cavour providing the political vision and Garibaldi the military muscle, the movement culminated in the 1861 unification of Italy under King Vittorio Emanuele. In 1870 Rome was wrested from the papacy and became Italy's capital.

Fascism, WWII & the Italian Republic

Following a meteoric rise to power, Benito Mussolini became Italy's leader in 1925, six years after he had founded his Fascist Party. Invoking Rome's imperial past, Mussolini embarked on a disastrous invasion of Abyssinia (modern-day Ethiopia) and in 1940 entered WWII on Germany's side. Three years later, after the Allies invaded Sicily, his nation rebelled: King Vittorio Emanuele III had Mussolini arrested and Italy surrendered soon after. Mussolini was killed by Italian partisans in April 1945.

In the aftermath of the war Italy voted to abolish the monarchy, declaring itself a constitutional republic in 1946.

A founding member of the European Economic Community, Italy enjoyed a largely successful postwar period. Consistent economic growth survived domestic terrorism in the 1970s and continued well into the 1980s.

The Berlusconi Era

The 1990s heralded a period of crisis. In 1992 a minor bribery investigation ballooned into a nationwide corruption scandal known as Tangentopoli ('kickback city'). Top business figures were imprisoned and the main political parties were reduced to tatters, creating a power vacuum into which billionaire media mogul Silvio Berlusconi deftly stepped. A controversial and deeply divisive figure, Berlusconi dominated Italian public life from his first foray into government in 1994 until he was forced out of office in 2011 amid a severe national economic downturn. Economist Mario Monti took over as prime minister and committed to an agenda of economic reform, but his tenure was built on an unstable alliance with Berlusconi's People of Freedom party. Elections in February 2013 saw Berlusconi's bid to regain overall power fail, but the outcome was far from decisive, with the centre-left Democratic Party (PD) gaining a majority in the lower house, the PDL gaining a majority in the upper house, and the maverick Five Star Movement led by satirist Beppe Grillo gaining the highest overall vote (25.5%). After a two-month stalemate, the PD and PDL formed an uneasy parliamentary alliance, installing the PD's Enrico Letta as prime minister and Angelino Alfano from the PDL as deputy prime minister.

People

With a population of 60.62 million, Italy is Europe's fourth-most populous country after Germany, France and the UK. Almost half of all Italians live in the industrialised north and one in five is aged over 65 years. At the other end of the age scale, Italy is dragging its heels. The country has one of the world's lowest birth rates (0.38%, or an average of 1.4 children for every mother) and, were it not for immigration, the Italian population

would be in decline. Foreign residents now constitute 7.5% of Italy's population.

Traditionally, Italians are very conscious of their regional identity and very family oriented. Times are changing, but it is still common for Italian children to remain at home until they marry.

For a fascinating portrait of Italy's people and its national character, read Luigi Barzini's 1964 book *The Italians*.

Religion

Up to 80% of Italians consider themselves Catholic, although only about one in three regularly attends church. Similarly, the Vatican remains a powerful voice in national debate, but can't find enough priests for its parish churches. Still, first Communions, church weddings and regular feast days remain an integral part of Italian life.

There are no official figures but it's estimated that there are up to 1.5 million Muslims in Italy, making Islam Italy's second and fastest-growing religion. Italy also has small but well-established Orthodox, Protestant and Jewish communities.

Arts

Literature

Italian literature runs the gamut from Virgil's *Aeneid* to the chilling WWII stories of Primo Levi, the fantastical writings of Italo Calvino and the powerful contemporary writing of Niccolò Ammaniti, author of *Io non ho paura* (I'm Not Scared; 2001).

Dante, whose *Divina commedia* (Divine Comedy) dates to the early 1300s, was one of three 14th-century greats alongside Petrarch and Giovanni Boccaccio. The latter is considered the first Italian novelist.

Italy's southern regions provide rich literary pickings. Giuseppe Tomasi di Lampedusa depicts Sicily's melancholic resignation in *Il gattopardo* (The Leopard; 1958), a theme that Leonardo Sciascia later returns to in *Il giorno della civetta* (The Day of the Owl; 1961). Carlo Levi denounces southern poverty in *Cristo si é fermato a Eboli* (Christ Stopped at Eboli; 1945), an account of his internal exile under the Fascists, and more recently, Andrea Camilleri's Sicilian-based Montalbano detective stories have enjoyed great success. *The Shape of Water* (1994) is the first title in the series.

ITALY ON SCREEN

A few films that are sure to whet your appetite for an Italian vacation:

» *Il Postino* (1994) – spectacular Aeolian Island scenery sets the stage for this heartbreaking tale of thwarted dreams.

» *Room with a View* (1985) – dreamy shots of Florence and some great performances in a Merchant Ivory treatment of EM Forster's novel of the same name.

» *Cinema Paradiso* (1988) – bittersweet tale about a successful film director who returns to his home village in Sicily for a funeral, triggering memories of his early years.

» *Roman Holiday* (1953) – Gregory Peck and Audrey Hepburn give great performances, but director William Wyler hands the starring role to the Eternal City itself.

» *Pane e Tulipani* (2000) – an eccentric, feel-good romance set in Venice.

Cinema

The influence of Italian cinema goes well beyond its success at the box office. In creating the spaghetti western Sergio Leone inspired generations of film-makers, as did horror master Dario Argento and art-house genius Michelangelo Antonioni.

Italy has won more Academy Awards for Best Foreign-Language Film than any other country. Many of the winning films were made during the post-WWII period, when the neo-realists Vittorio de Sica and Roberto Rossellini created masterpieces such as *Ladri di biciclette* (Bicycle Thieves; 1948) and *Roma città aperta* (Rome Open City; 1945).

Taking a decidedly different turn, Federico Fellini created his own highly visual style and won an international audience with films such as *La dolce vita* (The Sweet Life; 1959). His contemporary Lucino Visconti made films melding extraordinary visual beauty and powerful narrative; these include *Morte a Venezia* (Death in Venice; 1961) and his masterpiece, *Il Gattopardo* (The Leopard; 1963).

Of Italy's notable contemporary directors, Roberto Benigni won an Oscar for *La vita è bella* (Life is Beautiful; 1997), Nanni Moretti won Cannes' Palme D'Or for *La stanza del figlio* (The Son's Room; 2001) and brothers Paolo and Vittorio Taviani won the Palme D'Or for *Padre padrone* (Father and Master; 1971) and the Golden Bear at Berlin for *Cesare deve morire* (Ceasar Must Die; 2012).

Music

Emotional and highly theatrical, opera has always appealed to Italians. Performances of Verdi and Puccini are regularly staged at legendary theatres such as Milan's Teatro alla Scala and Naples' Teatro San Carlo.

On the classical front, Antonio Vivaldi (1675–1741) created the concerto in its present form and wrote *Le quattro stagione* (The Four Seasons). In more recent times, pop singer Eros Ramazzotti and operatic tenor Andrea Bocelli have enjoyed considerable international success.

Architecture & Visual Arts

Italy is littered with architectural and artistic reminders of the country's convoluted history. Etruscan tombs at Tarquinia and Greek temples at Agrigento tell of glories long past, while Pompeii's skeletal ruins offer insights into the day-to-day life of ancient Romans, and Byzantine mosaics in Ravenna, Venice and Palermo reveal influences sweeping in from the East.

The Renaissance left an indelible mark, particularly in Florence and Rome. This was the period when Filippo Brunelleschi designed and oversaw construction of the Duomo's huge dome and Michelangelo swept aside all convention in his Sistine Chapel decoration. Contemporaries Leonardo da Vinci and Raphael further enriched the scene.

Controversial and highly influential, Michelangelo Merisi da Caravaggio dominated the late 16th century with his revolutionary use of light. He painted in Rome and in the south of the country; both destinations where the baroque style of art and architecture became prominent in the 17th-century.

Signalling a return to sober classical lines, neoclassicism majored in the late 18th and early 19th centuries. Its most famous Italian exponent was Canova, who carved a name for himself with his smooth, sensual style.

In sharp contrast to backward-looking neoclassicism, Italian futurism provided a rallying cry for modernism, with Giacomo Balla proving hugely influential.

Continuing in this modernist tradition are Italy's two superstar architects: Renzo

Piano, the visionary behind Rome's Auditorium, and Rome-born Massimiliano Fuksas.

Environment

Bound on three sides by four seas (the Adriatic, Ligurian, Tyrrhenian and Ionian), Italy has more than 8000km of coastline. Inland, about 75% of the peninsula is mountainous – the Alps curve around the northern border and the Apennines extend down the boot.

The peninsula and its surrounding seas harbour a rich fauna. You're unlikely to spot them but there are bears, wolves and wildcats in the national parks of central Italy, as well as over 150 types of bird. Swordfish, tuna and dolphins are common along the coastline, and although white sharks are known to exist, attacks are rare.

Italy has 24 national parks, covering about 5% of the country, and more than 400 nature reserves, natural parks and wetlands. It also boasts 47 Unesco World Heritage sites, more than any other country in the world.

Environmental Issues

The three most insidious environmental issues affecting Italy are air pollution, waste disposal and coastal development. Heavy industry and high levels of car ownership have combined to produce dense smog and poor air quality. This affects many Italian cities but is especially widespread in the industrialised north.

Inadequate waste disposal is another major cause of pollution, particularly in Naples, where the sight of rubbish rotting on the streets has become sadly familiar. At the heart of the problem lies a chronic lack of facilities – there are insufficient incinerators to burn the refuse and the landfill sites that do exist are generally full, often with waste dumped illegally by organised crime outfits.

Italy's coast has been subject to almost continuous development since the boom in beach tourism in the 1960s. While this has undoubtedly brought short-term advantages, it has also put a great strain on natural resources.

Food & Drink

Despite the ubiquity of pasta and pizza, Italian cuisine is highly regional. Local specialities abound and regional traditions are proudly maintained, so expect pesto in Genoa, pizza in Naples and *ragù* (bolog-

EARTHQUAKES & VOLCANOES

Italy is one of the world's most earthquake-prone countries. A fault line runs through the entire peninsula – from eastern Sicily, up the Apennines and into the northeastern Alps. The country is usually hit by minor quakes several times a year and devastating earthquakes are not uncommon in central and southern Italy. The most recent, measuring 6.3 on the Richter scale, struck the central region of Abruzzo on 6 April 2009, killing 295 people and leaving up to 55,000 homeless.

Italy also has six active volcanoes: Stromboli and Vulcano in the Aeolian Islands; Vesuvius and the Campi Flegrei and the island of Ischia near Naples; and Etna on Sicily. Stromboli and Etna are among the world's most active volcanoes, while Vesuvius has not erupted since 1944.

nese sauce) in Bologna. It's the same with wine – Piedmont produces Italy's great reds, Barolo, Barbaresco and Dolcetto, while Tuscany is famous for its Chianti, Vino Nobile di Montepulciano, Brunello di Montalcino and Vernaccia di San Gimignano.

Vegetarians will find delicious fruit and veg in the hundreds of daily markets, and although few restaurants cater specifically to vegetarians, most serve vegetable-based antipasti (starters), pastas, *contorni* (side dishes) and salads.

Where to Eat & Drink

The most basic sit-down eatery is a *tavola calda* (literally 'hot table'), which offers canteen-style food. Pizzerias, the best of which have a *forno a legna* (wood-fired oven), often serve a full menu as well as pizzas. For takeaway, a *rosticceria* sells cooked meats and a *pizza al taglio* joint sells pizza by the slice.

For wine, make for an *enoteca* (wine bar), many of which also serve light snacks and a few hot dishes. Alternatively, most bars and cafes serve *tramezzini* (sandwiches) and panini (bread rolls). A cheaper option is to go to an *alimentari* (delicatessen) and ask them to make a panino with the filling of your choice. At a *pasticceria* you can buy pastries, cakes and biscuits. *Forni* (bakeries) are another good choice for a cheap snack.

For a full meal you'll want a trattoria or a *ristorante*. Traditionally, trattorias were family-run places that served a basic menu of local dishes at affordable prices and thankfully, a few still are. *Ristoranti* offer more choice and smarter service.

Restaurants, all of which are nonsmoking, usually open for lunch from noon to 3pm and for dinner from 7.30pm (earlier in tourist areas).

On the bill expect to be charged for *pane e coperto* (bread and a cover charge). This is standard and is added even if you don't ask for or eat the bread. Typically it ranges from €1 to €4. *Servizio* (service charge) of 10% to 15% might or might not be included; if it's not, tourists are expected to leave around 10% tip.

Habits & Customs

A full Italian meal consists of an antipasto, a *primo* (first course; pasta or rice dish), *secondo* (second/main course; usually meat or fish), an *insalata* (salad) or *contorno* (vegetable side dish), *dolci* (dessert) and coffee, though most Italians will only eat a meal this large at Sunday lunch or for special occasions. When eating out it's perfectly acceptable to mix and match any combination and order, say, a *primo* followed by an *insalata* or *contorno*.

Italians don't tend to eat a sit-down *colazione* (breakfast), preferring instead a cappuccino and *cornetto* (pastry filled with custard, chocolate or jam) at a bar. *Pranzo* (lunch) was traditionally the main meal of the day, although many people now have a light lunch and bigger *cena* (dinner). Italians are late diners, often not eating until after 9pm.

SURVIVAL GUIDE

Directory A–Z
Accommodation

The bulk of Italy's accommodation is made up of *alberghi* (hotels) and *pensioni* – often housed in converted apartments. Other options are youth hostels, camping grounds, B&Bs, *agriturismi* (farm-stays), mountain *rifugi* (Alpine refuges), monasteries and villa/apartment rentals.

Prices fluctuate enormously between the high, shoulder and low seasons. High-season rates apply at Easter, in summer (mid-June to August), and over the Christmas to New Year period.

The north of Italy is generally more expensive than the south.

Many city-centre hotels offer discounts in August to lure clients from the crowded coast. Check hotel websites for last-minute offers.

Most hotels in coastal resorts shut for winter, typically from November to March. The same applies to *agriturismi* and villa rentals in rural areas.

PRICE RANGES

In this chapter prices quoted are the minimum-maximum for rooms with a private bathroom, and unless otherwise stated include breakfast. The following price indicators apply (for a high-season double room):

€€€ more than €200

€€ €110 to €200

€ less than €110

HOTEL TAX

Since early 2011 a number of Italian cities, including Rome, Florence and Venice, have introduced a hotel occupancy tax *(tassa di soggiorno)*. This is charged on top of your regular hotel bill and must sometimes be paid in cash. The exact amount, which varies from city to city, depends on your type of accommodation, but as a rough guide expect to pay €1 per night in a one-star hotel or hostel, €2 in a B&B, €2 to €3 in a three-star hotel etc.

Note that prices quoted in this book do not include the tax.

B&BS

There's a huge number of bed and breakfasts (B&Bs) across the country. Quality varies, but the best offer comfort greater than you'd get in a similarly priced hotel room.

Prices are typically €70 to €180 for a double room.

CAMPING

Campers are well catered for in Italy.

Lists of camping grounds are available from local tourist offices or online at www.campeggi.com, www.camping.it and www.italcamping.it.

In high season expect to pay up to €20 per person and a further €25 for a tent pitch.

Independent camping is not permitted in many places.

CONVENTS & MONASTERIES

Basic accommodation is often available in convents and monasteries. See www.monasterystays.com, a specialist online booking service.

FARM-STAYS

An *agriturismo* (farm-stay) is a good option for a country stay, although you will usually need your own transport to access these.

Accommodation varies from spartan billets on working farms to palatial suites at luxurious rural retreats.

For information and lists check out www. agriturist.it or www.agriturismo.com.

HOSTELS

Official HI-affiliated *ostelli per la gioventù* (youth hostels) are run by the Italian Youth Hostel Association (Associazione Italiana Alberghi per la Gioventù; Map p434; ☑06 487 11 52; www.aighostels.com; Via Cavour 44). A valid HI card is required for these; you can get one in your home country or directly at hostels.

There are many privately run hostels offering dorms and private rooms.

Dorm rates are typically between €15 and €30, with breakfast usually included.

REFUGES

Italy boasts an extensive network of mountain *rifugi*.

Open from July to September, refuges offer basic dorm-style accommodation, although some larger ones have double rooms.

Reckon on €20 to €30 per person per night with breakfast included.

Further information is available from the Club Alpino Italiano (CAI; www.cai.it), which owns and runs many of the refuges.

Activities

Cycling Tourist offices can provide details on trails and guided rides. The best time is spring. Lonely Planet's *Cycling in Italy* offers practical tips and several detailed itineraries.

Diving There are hundreds of schools offering courses and guided dives for all levels.

Hiking & Walking Thousands of kilometres of *sentieri* (marked trails) criss-cross Italy; the hiking season is June to September. Useful websites include www.cai.it and www.parks.it. Lonely Planet's *Hiking in Italy* includes descriptions of 59 hikes.

Skiing Italy's ski season runs from December to March. Prices are generally high, particularly in the top Alpine resorts; the Apennines are cheaper. The best way to save money is to buy a *settimana bianca* (literally 'white week') package deal, covering seven days' accommodation, food and ski passes.

Business Hours

In this chapter, opening hours are provided in Information, Eating, Drinking, Entertainment and Shopping sections when they differ from the following standard hours:

Banks 8.30am-1.30pm & 3-4.30pm Mon-Fri

Bars & Cafes 7.30am-8pm; many open earlier and some stay open until the small hours; pubs often open noon-2am

Discos & Clubs 10pm-4am

Pharmacies 9am-1pm & 4-7.30pm Mon-Fri, to 1pm Sat; outside of these hours, pharmacies open on a rotation basis – all are required to post a list of places open in the vicinity

Post offices Major offices 8am-7pm Mon-Fri, to 1.15pm Sat; branch offices 8.30am-2pm Mon-Fri, to 1pm Sat

Restaurants noon-3pm & 7.30-11pm or midnight; most restaurants close one day a week

Shops 9am-1pm & 3.30-7.30pm, or 4-8pm Mon-Sat; in larger cities many chain stores and supermarkets open from 9am to 7.30pm Mon-Sat; some also open Sun morning, typically 9am -1pm; food shops are generally closed Thu afternoon; some other shops are closed Mon morning

Many museums, galleries and archaeological sites operate summer and winter opening hours. Typically, winter hours will apply between November and late March or early April.

Embassies

The following embassies are based in Rome.

Australian Embassy (☑06 85 27 21; www. italy.embassy.gov.au; Via Antonio Bosio 5)

New Zealand Embassy (☑06 853 75 01; rome@nzembassy.it; Via Clitunno 44)

UK Embassy (☑06 422 00 001; http://ukinitaly.fco.gov.uk/en/; Via XX Settembre 80a)

US Embassy (☑06 4 67 41; italy.usembassy. gov; Via Vittorio Veneto 121)

Food

Throughout this chapter, the following price indicators have been used (prices refer to the cost of a main course):

€€€ more than €18

€€ €10 to €18

€ less than €10

Gay & Lesbian Travellers

Homosexuality is legal in Italy, but same-sex couples have no shared rights to property, social security and inheritance. There is a push to legalise gay marriage, but this seems unlikely in the near future.

Homosexuality is well tolerated in major cities but overt displays of affection could attract a negative response, particularly in small towns and in the more conservative south.

Italy's main gay and lesbian organisation is **Arcigay** (www.arcigay.it), based in Bologna.

Internet Access

Most hotels, hostels, B&Bs and *pensioni* offer wi-fi, either free or for a daily charge.

The 🛜 icon in accommodation reviews means wi-fi is available. An @ icon denotes availability of a computer for guest use.

Access is also available in internet cafes throughout the country, although many have closed in recent years. Charges are typically around €5 per hour.

To use internet points in Italy you must present photo ID.

Money

Italy's currency is the euro.

ATMs, known in Italy as *bancomat,* are widespread and will accept cards displaying the appropriate sign. Visa and MasterCard are widely recognised, as are Cirrus and Maestro; American Express is less common. If you don't have a PIN, some, but not all, banks will advance cash over the counter.

Credit cards are widely accepted, although many small trattorias, pizzerias and *pensioni* only take cash. Don't assume museums, galleries and the like accept credit cards.

If your credit/debit card is lost, stolen or swallowed by an ATM, telephone toll-free to block it: **Amex** (☑06 729 00 347); **MasterCard** (☑800 870866); and **Visa** (☑800 819014).

ADMISSION PRICES

EU citizens aged between 18 and 25 years and students from countries with reciprocal arrangements generally qualify for a discount (usually half-price) at galleries and museums. EU citizens who are under 18 and over 65 often get in free. In all cases you'll need proof of your age, ideally a passport or ID card.

Post

Italy's postal system, **Poste Italiane** (☑803 160; www.poste.it), is reasonably reliable.

The standard service is *posta prioritaria.* Registered mail is known as *posta raccomandata,* insured mail as *posta assicurato.*

Francobolli (stamps) are available at post offices and *tabacchi* (tobacconists) – look for a big white 'T' against a blue/black background. Tobacconists keep regular shop hours.

Public Holidays

Most Italians take their annual holiday in August. This means that many businesses and shops close down for at least a part of the month, usually around Ferragosto (15 August). Easter is another busy holiday.

Public holidays:

New Year's Day (Capodanno) 1 January

Epiphany (Epifania) 6 January

Anniversary of the Unification of Italy (Anniversario dell'Unità d'Italia) 17 March

Easter Monday (Pasquetta) March/April

Liberation Day (Giorno delle Liberazione) 25 April

Labour Day (Festa del Lavoro) 1 May

Republic Day (Festa della Repubblica) 2 June

Feast of the Assumption (Ferragosto) 15 August

All Saints' Day (Ognisanti) 1 November

Day of National Unity and the Armed Forces (Giornata dell'Unità Nazionale e delle Forze Armate) 4 November

Feast of the Immaculate Conception (Immacolata Concezione) 8 December

Christmas Day (Natale) 25 December

Boxing Day (Festa di Santo Stefano) 26 December

Individual towns also have holidays to celebrate their patron saints:

St Mark (Venice) 25 April

St John the Baptist (Florence, Genoa and Turin) 24 June

Sts Peter and Paul (Rome) 29 June

St Rosalia (Palermo) 15 July

St Janarius (Naples) First Sunday in May, 19 September and 16 December

St Ambrose (Milan) 7 December

Safe Travel

Petty theft is prevalent in Italy. Be on your guard against pickpockets and moped thieves in popular tourist centres such as Rome, Florence and Venice, and especially in Naples.

Don't take it for granted that cars will stop at red lights.

Telephone

Area codes are an integral part of all Italian phone numbers and must be dialled even when calling locally. The area codes have been listed in telephone numbers throughout this chapter.

To call Italy from abroad, dial ✆0039 and then the area code, including the first zero.

To call abroad from Italy, dial ✆00, then the relevant country code followed by the telephone number.

To make a reverse-charge (collect) international call, dial ✆170. All operators speak English.

You'll find cut-price call centres in all of the main cities. For international calls, their rates are often cheaper than at payphones.

Skype is available in many internet cafes and on hostel computers.

MOBILE PHONES

Italy uses the GSM 900/1800 network, which is compatible with the rest of Europe and Australia, but not with the North American GSM 1900 or the Japanese system (although some GSM 1900/900 phones do work here).

If you have a GSM dual- or tri-band cellular phone that you can unlock (check with your service provider), you can buy a *pre-pagato* (prepaid) SIM card in Italy.

Companies offering SIM cards include **TIM** (Telecom Italia Mobile; www.tim.it), **Wind** (www.wind.it) and **Vodafone** (www.vodafone.it). You'll need ID to open an account.

PHONE CODES

Italy's country code is ✆39.

Mobile phone numbers begin with a three-digit prefix starting with a 3.

Toll-free (free-phone) numbers are known as *numeri verdi* and start with 800. These are not always available if calling from a mobile phone.

PHONECARDS

To phone from a public payphone you'll need a *scheda telefonica* (telephone card; €3, €5). Buy these at post offices, *tabacchi* and newsstands.

Tourist Information

For pre-trip information, check out the website of the **Ministro del Turismo** (www.italia.it). The ministry also runs a multilingual telephone information service, **Easy Italy** (✆039 039 039; ⏰9am-10pm).

Tourist offices in Italy are listed throughout this chapter.

Travellers with Disabilities

Italy is not an easy country for travellers with disabilities. Cobbled streets, blocked pavements and tiny lifts all make life difficult. Rome-based **Consorzio Cooperative Integrate** (COIN; ✆06 712 90 11; www.coinsociale.it) is the best point of reference for travellers with disabilities.

If you're travelling by train, **Trenitalia** (www.trenitalia.com) runs a telephone info line (✆199 30 30 60) with details of assistance available at stations.

Visas

Schengen visa rules apply for entry to Italy.

Unless staying in a hotel/B&B/hostel etc, all foreign visitors are supposed to register with the police within eight days of arrival.

Non-EU citizens who want to study in Italy must obtain a study visa from their nearest Italian embassy or consulate.

A *permesso di soggiorno* (permit to stay) is required by all non-EU nationals who stay in Italy longer than three months. You must apply within eight days of arriving in Italy. Check the exact documentary requirements on www.poliziadistato.it.

EU citizens do not require a *permesso di soggiorno.*

Getting There & Away

Getting to Italy is straightforward. It is well served by Europe's low-cost carriers and there are plenty of bus, train and ferry routes into the country. Flights, tours and rail tickets can be booked online at lonelyplanet.com/bookings.

Air

There are direct intercontinental flights to/from Rome and Milan. European flights also serve regional airports.

Italy's main international airports:

Rome Leonardo da Vinci (✆06 6 59 51; www.adr.it/fiumicino) Italy's main airport, also known as Fiumicino.

Milan Malpensa (✆02 23 23 23; www.milano malpensa1.eu/it) Milan's principal airport.

Rome Ciampino (✆06 6 59 51; www.adr.it/ciampino) Rome's second airport. Hub for Ryanair flights.

Pisa International Airport Galileo Galilei (✆050 84 93 00; www.pisa-airport.com) Main gateway for Florence and Tuscany.

Venice Marco Polo (✆041 260 92 60; www.veniceairport.i

Cagliari Elmas (✆070 21 12 11; www.cagliari airport.it) Sardinia's main airport.

Naples Capodichino (✆081 789 61 11; www.gesac.it)

Catania Fontanarossa (✆095 723 91 11; www.aeroporto.catania.it) Sicily's busiest airport.

Italy's national carrier is **Alitalia** (✆89 20 10; www.alitalia.com).

Land

BORDER CROSSINGS

Italy borders France, Switzerland, Austria and Slovenia. The main points of entry:

From France The coast road from Nice; the Mont Blanc tunnel from Chamonix.

From Switzerland The Grand St Bernard tunnel; the Simplon tunnel; the Lötschberg Base tunnel.

From Austria The Brenner Pass.

BUS

Eurolines (www.eurolines.com) operates buses from European destinations to many Italian cities.

CAR & MOTORCYCLE

If traversing the Alps, note that border crossings from the Brenner Pass, Grand St Bernard tunnel, Simplon tunnel and Lötschberg Base tunnel are open year-round. Other mountain passes are often closed in winter and sometimes even in spring and autumn. Make sure you have snow chains in your car.

TRAIN

Direct international trains connect with various cities:

Milan To/from Paris, Basel, Lugano, Geneva and Zürich.

Rome To/from Munich

Venice To/from Paris, Munich, Geneva, Innsbruck.

There are also international trains from Verona, Padua, Bologna and Florence. Get details at www.trenitalia.com.

In the UK, the **Rail Europe Travel Centre** (✆0844 848 40 78; www.raileurope.co.uk) can provide fare information on journeys to/from Italy, most of which require a change at Paris. Another excellent resource is www.seat61.com.

Eurail and Inter-Rail passes are both valid in Italy.

Sea

Dozens of ferry companies connect Italy with other Mediterranean countries. Timetables are seasonal, so always check ahead – you'll find details of routes, companies and online booking at www.traghettiweb.it.

MAIN INTERNATIONAL FERRY ROUTES

FROM	TO	COMPANY	MIN-MAX FARE (€)	DURATION (HR)
Ancona	Igoumenitsa	Minoan, Superfast	75-111	16
Ancona	Patra	Minoan, Superfast	75-111	15½-22
Ancona	Split	Jadrolinija, SNAV	46-63	4½-11
Bari	Igoumenitsa	Superfast	78-93	8-12
Bari	Patra	Superfast	78-93	16
Bari	Dubrovnik	Jadrolinija	46-63	10-12
Bari	Bar	Montenegro	50-55	9
Brindisi	Igoumenitsa	Endeavor, Agoudimos	48-83	8
Brindisi	Patra	Endeavor	56-94	14
Brindisi	Corfu	Endeavor, Agoudimos	48-83	6½-11½
Brindisi	Kefallonia	Endeavor	56-94	12½
Genoa	Barcelona	GNV, SNAV	95	19½
Genoa	Tunis	GNV, SNAV	99	23½

Prices quoted here are for a one-way *poltrona* (reclinable seat). Holders of Eurail and InterRail passes should check with the ferry company if they are entitled to a discount or free passage.

Major ferry companies:

Agoudimos (www.agoudimos-lines.com)

Endeavor Lines (www.endeavor-lines.com)

Grandi Navi Veloci (www.gnv.it)

Jadrolinija (www.jadrolinija.hr)

Minoan Lines (www.minoanlines.it)

Montenegro (www.montenegrolines.com)

SNAV (www.snav.it)

Superfast (www.superfast.com)

Tirrenia (www.tirrenia.it)

Getting Around

Air

Domestic flights serve most major Italian cities and the main islands (Sardinia and Sicily), but are expensive. Airlines serving national routes include:

Alitalia (☑89 20 10; www.alitalia.com)

Air One (☑89 24 44; www.flyairone.it)

Blu-Express (☑06 989 56 666; www.blu-express.com)

Meridiana (☑89 29 28; www.meridiana.it)

easyJet (☑199 20 18 40; www.easyjet.com)

Ryanair (☑899 55 25 89; www.ryanair.com)

Bicycle

» Tourist offices can generally provide details of designated bike trails and bike hire (at least €10 per day).

» Bikes can be taken on regional and international trains carrying the bike logo, but you'll need to pay a supplement (€3.50 on regional trains, €12 on international trains). Bikes can be carried free if dismantled and stored in a bike bag.

» Bikes generally incur a small supplement on ferries, typically €10 to €15.

Boat

Navi (large ferries) service Sicily and Sardinia; *traghetti* (smaller ferries) and *aliscafi* (hydrofoils) cover the smaller islands.

The main embarkation points for Sardinia are Genoa, Piombino, Livorno, Civitavec-

chia and Naples; for Sicily, it's Naples and Villa San Giovanni in Calabria.

The major domestic ferry companies:

Grandi Navi Veloci (☑010 209 45 91; www.gnv.it) To/from Sardinia and Sicily.

Moby (☑199 30 30 40; www.mobylines.it) To/from Sardinia and Sicily.

Sardinia Ferries (☑199 40 05 00; www.corsica-ferries.it) To/from Golfo Aranci (Sardinia).

SNAV (☑Ancona 071 207 61, Naples 081 428 55 55; www.snav.it) To/from Sardinia, Sicily, Aeolian Islands, Capri.

Tirrenia (☑89 21 23; www.tirrenia.it) To/from Sardinia and Sicily.

Bus

» Italy boasts an extensive and largely reliable bus network.

» Buses are not necessarily cheaper than trains, but in mountainous areas they are often the only choice.

» In larger cities, companies have ticket offices or operate through agencies but in most villages and small towns tickets are sold in bars or on the bus.

» Reservations are only necessary for high-season long-haul trips.

Car & Motorcycle

» Roads are generally good and there's an excellent system of autostradas (motorways).

» There's a toll to use most autostradas, payable in cash or by credit card at exit barriers.

» Autostradas are indicated by an A with a number (eg A1) on a green background; *strade statali* (main roads) are shown by an S or SS and number (eg SS7) against a blue background.

» Italy's motoring organisation **Automobile Club d'Italia** (ACI; www.aci.it; Via Colombo 261) provides 24-hour roadside assistance – call ☑803 116 from a landline or Italian mobile, ☑800 116 800 from a foreign mobile.

» Cars use unleaded petrol *(benzina senza piombo)* and diesel *(gasolio);* both are expensive but diesel is slightly cheaper.

DRIVING LICENCES

All EU driving licences are recognised in Italy. Holders of non-EU licences must get an International Driving Permit (IDP) to accompany their national licence.

HIRE

To hire a car you must:

» have a valid driving licence (plus IDP if required)

» have had your licence for at least a year

» be 21 or over. Under-25s will often have to pay a young-driver's supplement on top of the usual rates

» have a credit card

Make sure you understand what is included in the price (unlimited kilometres, tax, insurance, collision damage waiver etc) and what your liabilities are. For the best rental rates, book your car before leaving home. Note also that most cars have manual gear transmission.

The most competitive agencies:

Avis (☑199 10 01 33; www.avis.com)

Budget (☑800 472 33 25; www.budget.com)

Europcar (☑199 30 70 30; www.europcar.com)

Hertz (☑199 11 22 11; www.hertz.com)

Italy by Car (☑091 639 31 20; www.italybycar.it)

Maggiore (☑199 15 11 20; www.maggiore.it)

You'll have no trouble hiring a scooter or motorcycle (provided you're over 18); there are agencies in all Italian cities. Rates start at about €30 a day for a 50cc scooter.

INSURANCE

If you're driving your own car, you'll need an international insurance certificate, known as a Carta Verde (Green Card), available from your insurance company.

ROAD RULES

» Drive on the right, overtake on the left and give way to cars coming from the right.

» It's obligatory to wear seatbelts, to drive with your headlights on when outside built-up areas, and to carry a warning triangle and fluorescent waistcoat in case of breakdown.

» Wearing a helmet is compulsory on all two-wheeled vehicles.

» The blood alcohol limit is 0.05% or zero for drivers who have had their licence for less than three years.

Unless otherwise indicated, speed limits are as follows:

» 130km/h (in rain 110km/h) on autostradas

» 110km/h (in rain 90km/h) on all main, non-urban roads

» 90km/h on secondary, non-urban roads

» 50km/h in built-up areas

Most major Italian cities operate a Limited Traffic Zone in their *centro storico*. You can enter a ZTL *(Zona a Traffico Limitato)* on a *motorino* (moped/scooter) but not in private or hire cars.

Train

Italy has an extensive rail network. Trains are relatively cheap, and many are fast and comfortable. Most services are run by **Trenitalia** (☑89 20 21; www.trenitalia.com) but as of April 2012 **Italo Treno** (☑06 07 08; www.italotreno.it) high-speed trains also connect Salerno, Naples, Rome, Florence, Bologna, Milan, Turin, Padua and Venice.

There are several types of train:

Frecciarossa Italy's fastest trains capable of 360km/h.

Frecciargento Slightly quicker than the Frecciabianca with a top speed of 250km/h.

Frecciabianca High-speed trains that run up to 200km/h.

Eurostar Italia (ES) Similar to InterCity but faster.

InterCity (IC) Trains between major cities.

Regionale or interregionale (R) Slow local services.

TICKETS

» Train prices quoted here are for the most common trains on any given route – that might be a slow Regionale train or a fast Frecciarossa.

» Regional trains are the cheapest.

» InterCity trains require a supplement, which is incorporated in the ticket price. If you have a standard ticket and board an InterCity you'll have to pay the difference on board.

» Eurostar and the Freccia trains require prior reservation.

» Generally, it's cheaper to buy all local train tickets in Italy.

» If your ticket doesn't include a reservation with an assigned seat, you must validate it before boarding by inserting it into one of the machines dotted around stations.

» Some services offer 'ticketless' travel – book and pay for your seat on www.trenitalia.com and then communicate your booking code to the controller on board.

» Children under four travel free; kids between four and 12 are entitled to discounts of between 30% and 50%.

Montenegro

Includes »

Herceg Novi 538
Kotor 540
Tivat 543
Budva 544
Ulcinj 547
Lake Skadar
National Park 549
Podgorica 551
Kolašin 554
Durmitor National
Park 555
Understand
Montenegro...................557
Survival Guide..............560

Best Places to Eat

» Konoba Ćatovića Mlini (p539)

» Konoba kod Rada Vlahovića (p555)

» Stari Most (p550)

» Blanche (p545)

» Miško (p548)

Best Places to Stay

» Old Town Hostel (p541)

» Palazzo Radomiri (p541)

» Vila Drago (p545)

» Eko-Oaza Suza Evrope (p556)

Why Go?

Imagine a place with sapphire beaches as spectacular as Croatia's, rugged peaks as dramatic as Switzerland's, canyons nearly as deep as Colorado's, *palazzi* as elegant as Venice's and towns as old as Greece's. Then wrap it up in a Mediterranean climate and squish it into an area two-thirds the size of Wales, and you start to get a picture of Montenegro (Црна Гора).

More adventurous travellers can easily sidestep the peak-season hordes on the coast by heading to the rugged mountains of the north. This is, after all, a country where wolves and bears still lurk in forgotten corners.

Montenegro, Crna Gora, Black Mountain: the name itself conjures up romance and drama. There are plenty of both on offer as you explore this perfumed land, bathed in the scent of wild herbs, conifers and Mediterranean blossoms. Yes, it really is as magical as it sounds.

When to Go
Podgorica

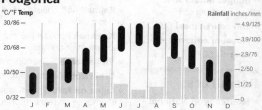

Jun Beat the peak-season rush and prices but enjoy the balmy weather.

Sep Warm water but fewer bods to share it with; not as scorching in Podgorica.

Oct The leaves turn golden, making a rich backdrop to walks in the national parks.

AT A GLANCE

» **Currency** Euro (€)

» **Language** Montenegrin

» **Money** ATMs in larger towns, banks open Monday to Friday and Saturday morning

» **Visas** None for citizens of EU, Canada, USA, Australia, New Zealand and many other countries

Fast Facts

» **Area** 13,812 sq km

» **Capital** Podgorica

» **Country code** ☑382

» **Emergency** Ambulance ☑124, fire ☑123, police ☑122

Exchange Rates

Australia	A$1	€0.82
Canada	C$1	€0.77
Japan	¥100	€0.83
New Zealand	NZ$1	€0.65
UK	UK£1	€1.18
USA	US$1	€0.78

Set Your Budget

» **Budget hotel room** €10–15 per person

» **Two-course meal** €10–30

» **Museum entrance** €1–5

» **Beer** €1.50

Resources

» **Montenegrin National Tourist Organisation** (www.montenegro.travel)

» **National Parks of Montenegro** (www.nparkovi.me)

» **Explore Montenegro** (www.exploremontenegro.com)

Connections

Many travellers make the most of the close proximity of Dubrovnik Airport to Herceg Novi to tie in a visit to Croatia with a Montenegrin sojourn. At the other end of the coast, Ulcinj is the perfect primer for exploring Albania and is connected by bus to Shkodra. Likewise, Rožaje captures elements of Kosovar culture and is well connected to Peja (Peć). A train line and frequent bus connections make a trip to Montenegro's closest cousins in Serbia a breeze. Montenegro shares a longer border with Bosnia and Hercegovina (BiH) than any of its neighbours. There are three main crossings for drivers, as well as regular bus services to Trebinje and Sarajevo. Ferries connect Bar to the Italian ports of Bari and Ancona.

ITINERARIES

One Week

Base yourself in the Bay of Kotor for two nights. Drive through Lovćen to Cetinje, then the next day continue to Šćepan Polje via Ostrog Monastery. Go rafting the following morning and spend the night in Podgorica. Head to Virpazar for a boat tour of Lake Skadar and then take the scenic lakeside road to Ulcinj. Finish in Sveti Stefan.

Two Weeks

Follow the itinerary above, but allow extra time in Kotor, Lake Skadar and Sveti Stefan. From Šćepan Polje, head instead to Žabljak and then to Biogradska Gora National Park before continuing to Podgorica.

Essential Food & Drink

» **Njeguški pršut i sir** Smoke-dried ham and cheese from the heartland village of Njeguši.

» **Ajvar** Spicy spread of fried red peppers and eggplant, seasoned with garlic, salt, vinegar and oil.

» **Kajmak** Soft cheese made from the salted cream from boiled milk.

» **Kačamak** Porridgelike mix of cream, cheese, potato and buckwheat or cornflour.

» **Riblja čorba** Fish soup, a staple of the coast.

» **Crni rižoto** Black risotto, coloured with squid ink.

» **Ligne na žaru** Grilled squid, sometimes stuffed (punjene) with cheese and smoke-dried ham.

» **Jagnjetina ispod sača** Lamb cooked (often with potatoes) under a metal lid covered with hot coals.

» **Rakija** Domestic brandy, made from nearly anything. The local favourite is grape-based loza.

» **Vranac** Local red wine varietal.

» **Krstač** Local white wine varietal.

BOSNIA & HERCEGOVINA

Foča

Priboj

Nova Varoš

SERBIA

Prijepolje

Sjenica

Šćepan Polje

Pljevlja Ranče

Dobrakovo

⑤ Tara Canyon

Durmitor National Park Žabljak

Plužine

Bobotov Kuk (2523m) Savin Kuk (2313m)

Bijelo Polje

Dobrilovina

Dračenovac

Donja Brezna

Mojkovac

Biogradska Gora National Park ⑥

Rožaje

Savnik

Crna Glava (2137m)

Berane

Kulina

Kapa Moračka (2227m)

Kolašin

Andrijevica

Peć

Morača Monastery

KOSOVO

Nikšić

Plav

④ Ostrog Monastery

Surdup (2182m)

Trebinje

Dolovi

Kolac (2534m)

CROATIA

Risan Perast

Debeli Brijeg

Morinj Ljuta

PODGORICA

Herceg Novi

① Kotor

Njeguši

② Cetinje

Bay of Kotor

Golubovci

Hani i Hotit

Luštica Peninsula Mt Lovćen (1749m)

Rijeka Crnojevića

ALBANIA

Lovćen National Park

Žabljak Crnojevića

Budva

③ Virpazar

Vranjina

Sveti Stefan

Lake Skadar ⑦

Petrovac

Murići

ADRIATIC SEA

Bar

Shkodra

Sukobin

0   40 km
0   20 miles

Ulcinj

Velika Plaža

Montenegro Highlights

① Marvel at the majesty of the **Bay of Kotor** (p538) and exploring the historic towns hemmed in by the limestone cliffs.

② Drive the vertiginous route from Kotor to the Njegoš Mausoleum at the top of **Lovćen National Park** (p548).

③ Enjoying the iconic island views while lazing on the sands of **Sveti Stefan** (p545).

④ Seeking the spiritual at peaceful **Ostrog Monastery** (p553).

⑤ Floating through paradise, rafting between the kilometre-plus walls of the **Tara Canyon** (p556).

⑥ Wandering through primeval forest mirrored in a tranquil alpine lake at **Biogradska Gora National Park** (p555).

⑦ Splashing through the floating meadows of water lilies garlanding vast **Lake Skadar** (p549).

BAY OF KOTOR

Coming from Croatia, the Bay of Kotor (Boka Kotorska) starts simply enough, but as you progress through fold upon fold of the bay and the surrounding mountains get steeper and steeper, the beauty meter gets close to bursting. It's often described as the Mediterranean's only fjord, and even though the geological label is not technically correct, the mental image that phrase conjures is spot on.

Herceg Novi   Херцег Нови

POP 12,700

It's easy to drive straight through Herceg Novi without noticing anything worth stopping for, especially if you've just come from Croatia with visions of Dubrovnik still dazzling your brain. However, just below the uninspiring roadside frontage hides an appealing Old Town with ancient walls, sunny squares and a lively atmosphere. The water's cleaner here, near the mouth of the bay, and while the town's pebbly coves and concrete swimming terraces aren't all that great, taxi boats do a brisk trade ferrying people to the secluded beaches on the Luštica Peninsula.

◉ Sights

Stari Grad   NEIGHBOURHOOD

Herceg Novi's Old Town is at its most impressive when approached from the pedestrian-only section of ul Njegoševa, which is paved in the same shiny marble as Dubrovnik and lined in elegant, mainly 19th-century buildings. The street terminates in cafe-ringed Trg Nikole Đurkovića, where steps lead up

---

ADVENTURE RACE MONTENEGRO

Started by a bunch of British expats operating outdoor-adventure businesses out of Herceg Novi, the **Adventure Race** (www.adventureracemontenegro. com) should be high on the agenda for anyone who fancies themselves an action man or wonder woman. Held in late September/early October, the Coastal Challenge is a day of kayaking, mountain biking, hiking and orienteering amid the exceptional scenery of the Bay of Kotor.

---

to an elegant crenulated **clock tower** (1667) which was once the main city gate.

Just inside the walls is Trg Herceg Stjepana (commonly called Belavista Sq), a gleaming white piazza that's perfect for relaxing, drinking and chatting in the shade. At its centre is the Orthodox **Archangel Michael's Church** (Crkva Sv Arhanđela Mihaila; ⊘7am-midnight Jun-Aug, to 9pm Sep-May). Built between 1883 and 1905, its lovely proportions are capped by a dome and flanked by palm trees. Its Catholic counterpart, **St Jerome's** (Crkva Sv Jeronima), is further down the hill, dominating Trg Mića Pavlovića.

Kanli-Kula   FORTRESS

(Bloody Tower; admission €1; ⊘8am-midnight) The big fort visible from the main road was a notorious prison during Turkish rule (roughly 1482–1687). You can walk around its sturdy walls and enjoy views over the town. In the dungeon below the lower set of flagpoles, former inmates have carved crosses and ships into the walls.

Savina Monastery   MONASTERY

(Braće Grakalić bb; ⊘6am-8pm) From its hillside location in the town's eastern fringes, this peaceful Orthodox monastery enjoys wonderful coastal views. It's dominated by the elegant 18th-century Church of the Dormition, carved from pinkish stone. Inside there's a beautiful gilded iconostasis, but you'll need to be demurely dressed to enter (no shorts, singlets or bikinis). The smaller church beside it has the same name but is considerably older (possibly 14th century) and has the remains of frescos.

The monastery is well signposted from the large roundabout on the highway at Meljine.

Regional Museum   MUSEUM

(Zavičajni muzej; www.rastko.rs/rastko-bo/muzej; Mirka Komnenovića 9; admission €1.50; ⊘9am-6pm Mon-Sat) Apart from the building itself (which is a fab bougainvillea-shrouded baroque palace with absolute sea views), the highlight of this little museum is its impressive icon gallery.

Španjola Fortress   FORTRESS

Situated high above the town, this fortress was started and finished by the Turks but named after the Spanish (yep, in 1538 they had a brief stint here as well). If the graffiti and empty bottles are anything to go by, it's now regularly invaded by local teenagers.

🏃 Activities

🪧 **Black Mountain** ADVENTURE TOURS
(☑067-640 869; www.montenegroholiday.com)
Can arrange pretty much anything, anywhere in the country, including mountain
biking, diving, rafting, hiking, paragliding,
canyoning, boat trips, wine tasting, accommodation, car hire and transfers.

🪧 **Kayak Montenegro** KAYAKING
(☑067-382 472; www.kayakmontenegro.com;
per 1/4/8hr from €5/15/25) Offers paddling
day tours across the bay to Rose and Dobreč
or Mamula and Mirišta (€45 including
equipment), as well as day trips to explore
Lake Skadar.

Yachting Club 32 OUTDOORS
(www.yachtingclub32.com; Šetalište Pet Danica 32)
Hires jet skis (€50 per 20 minutes), pedal
boats (€8 per hour) and mountain bikes
(€3/6/15 per one hour/three hours/day).

🛏 Sleeping

Private rooms start at about €15 per person.
Either look for signs saying 'sobe' or book
through a local agency such as **Trend Travel**
(☑031-321 639; www.trendtravelmontenegro.com;
Bus Station, Jadranski Put).

🪧 **Camp Full Monte** CAMPGROUND €
(☑067-899 208; www.full-monte.com; campsites
per person €10; ☻May-Sep) Hidden in the
mountains near the Croatian border, this
small British-run camping ground offers
solar-generated hot water, odourless com-
posting toilets and a whole lot of seclusion.
If you hadn't guessed already, clothing is optional. Tents (with full bedding) can be hired
and meals can be arranged.

Hotel Perla HOTEL €€€
(☑031-345 700; www.perla.me; Šetalište Pet Danica
98; s €84-112, d €104-140, apt €170-215; P❋☎)
It's a 15-minute stroll from the centre but if
it's beach you're after, Perla's position is perfect. The front rooms of this medium-sized
modern block have private terraces and sea
views.

Izvor HOSTEL €
(☑069-397 957; www.izvor.me; Jadranski Put bb,
Igalo; dm €12; P☎) On the slopes above Igalo, this simple place consists of four basic
shared rooms which open on to a terrace
overlooking the bay. There's a traditional
restaurant downstairs (mains €4 to €9).

WORTH A TRIP

KONOBA ĆATOVIĆA MLINI

A crystalline stream flows around and
under this rustic former mill which
masquerades as a humble konoba (a
simple, family-run establishment) but in
reality is one of Montenegro's best **restaurants** (☑032-373 030; www.catovi-
camlini.me; mains €8-24; ☻11am-11pm).
Watch the geese idle by as you sample
the magical bread and olive oil, which
appears unbidden at the table. Fish is
the focus but traditional specialities
from the heartland village of Njeguši are
also offered. You'll find it in the village
of Morinj, in the western corner of the
inner section of the Bay of Kotor.

Vila Aleksandar HOTEL €€
(☑031-345 806; www.hotelvilaaleksandar.com;
Save Kovačevića 64; s/d €51/82; ❋☎☻) The
decor's a little dated but almost all of the
rooms have balconies with sea views, and
the blue-tiled pool on the sunny terrace is
extremely enticing. The restaurant opens
onto the waterfront promenade.

🍴 Eating

If you want to take on the local women in a
tussle for the best fresh fruit and vegetables,
get to the **market** (Trg Nikole Đurkovića; ☻6am-
3pm Mon-Sat, to noon Sun) before 8am.

Konoba Feral SEAFOOD €€
(Vasa Ćukovića 4; mains €7-17) A feral is a ship's
lantern, so it's seafood that takes pride
of place on the menu – not wild cat. The
grilled squid is excellent and comes with a
massive serving of seasonal vegetables and
salads.

ℹ Information

Tourist Information Kiosk (Šetalište Pet
Danica bb; ☻9am-11pm May-Sep)
Tourist Office (☑031-350 820; www.herceg-
novi.travel; Jova Dabovića 12; ☻9am-10pm
daily Jul & Aug, 9am-4pm Mon-Fri, 9am-2pm
Sat Sep-Jun)

ℹ Getting There & Around

BOAT Taxi boats ply the coast during summer,
charging about €10 to €15 to the beaches on the
Luštica Peninsula.
BUS Buses stop at the station just above the Old
Town. There are frequent buses to Kotor (€4,

one hour), Budva (€6, 1¾ hours), Cetinje (€7, 2½ hours) and Podgorica (€9, three hours). At least two buses head to Dubrovnik daily (€10, two hours).

CAR A tortuous, often gridlocked, one-way system runs through the town, so you're best to park in the parking building opposite the bus station. If you're driving to Tivat or Budva, it's usually quicker to take the **ferry** (car/motorcycle/passenger €4/1.50/free; 24hr) from Kamenari (15km northeast of Herceg Novi) to Lepetane (north of Tivat). Queues can be long in summer.

Perast Пераст

Looking like a chunk of Venice that has floated down the Adriatic and anchored itself onto the Bay of Kotor, Perast hums with melancholy memories of the days when it was rich and powerful. This tiny town boasts 16 churches and 17 formerly grand *palazzi*, one of which has been converted into **Perast Museum** (Muzej grada Perasta; 032-373 519; adult/child €2.50/1.50; 9am-7pm) and showcases the town's proud seafaring history.

The 55m bell tower belongs to **St Nicholas' Church** (Crkva Sv Nikole; museum €1; museum 10am-6pm), which also has a museum containing relics and beautifully embroidered vestments.

Just offshore are two peculiarly picturesque islands. The smaller **St George's Island** (Sveti Đorđe) rises from a natural reef and houses a Benedictine monastery shaded by cypresses. Boats (€5 return) regularly head to its big sister, **Our-Lady-of-the-Rock Island** (Gospa od Škrpjela), which was artificially created in the 15th century. Every year on 22 July, the locals row over with stones to continue the task. Its magnificent church was erected in 1630.

Perast makes an atmospheric and peaceful base from which to explore the bay. Several houses rent rooms or you can try the **Hotel Conte** (032-373 687; www.hotel-conte.com; apt €100-160; P), where options range from deluxe studios to two-bedroom seaview apartments in historic buildings around St Nicholas' Church. Its wonderful restaurant (mains €9 to €20) serves fresh fish with lashings of romance on a waterside terrace.

Not far from Perast, **Risan** is the oldest town on the bay, dating to at least the 3rd century BC. Signposts point to some superb Roman **mosaics** (admission €2; 9am-7pm mid-May–mid-Oct), discovered in 1930.

Kotor Котор

POP 13,500

Wedged between brooding mountains and a moody corner of the bay, this dramatically beautiful town is perfectly at one with its setting. Its sturdy walls – started in the 9th century and tweaked until the 18th – arch steeply up the slopes behind it. From a distance they're barely discernible from the mountain's grey hide but at night they're spectacularly lit, reflecting in the water to give the town a golden halo. Within those walls lie labyrinthine marbled lanes where churches, shops, bars and restaurants surprise you on hidden piazzas.

Kotor's funnel-shaped **Stari Grad** (Old Town) sits between the bay and the lower slopes of Mt Lovćen. Newer suburbs surround the town, linking up to the old settlement of **Dobrota** to the north. Continuing around the bay towards Tivat, the coastal road narrows to a single lane and passes cute villages such as **Prčanj**, **Stoliv** and **Lastva**.

WORTH A TRIP

BACK ROAD TO MT LOVĆEN

The journey from Kotor to Mt Lovćen, the ancient core of the country, is one of Montenegro's great drives. Take the road heading towards the Tivat tunnel and turn right just past the graveyard. After 5km, follow the sign to Cetinje on your left opposite the fort. From here there's 17km of narrow road snaking up 25 hairpin turns, each one revealing a vista more spectacular than the last. Take your time and keep your wits about you; you'll need to pull over and be prepared to reverse if you meet oncoming traffic. From the top, the views stretch over the entire bay to the Adriatic. At the entrance to Lovćen National Park you can continue straight ahead through Njeguši for the shortest route to Cetinje or turn right and continue on the scenic route through the park.

WORTH A TRIP

LUŠTICA PENINSULA

Reaching out to form the southern headland of the Bay of Kotor, this gorgeous peninsula hides secluded beaches such as **Dobreč**, **Žanjic** and **Mirišta**, and the pretty fishing village **Rose**. They're all popular destinations for day trippers travelling from Herceg Novi by taxi boat

At **Bjelila**, a cluster of old stone houses, **Villa Kristina** (☑032-679 739; www.villakristina.me; Bjelila bb; apt €60-80; ❋ 🛜) has four apartments, each with its own little balcony gazing over the bay. It's terribly romantic, and there's a little private beach and a restaurant.

👁 Sights

The best thing to do in Kotor is to get lost and found again in the maze of streets. You'll soon know every corner, as the town is quite small, but there are plenty of churches to pop into and many coffees to be drunk in the shady squares.

Sea Gate   GATE
(Vrata od Mora) The main entrance to the town was constructed in 1555 when the town was under Venetian rule. Stepping through onto Trg od Oružja (Weapons Square), you'll see a strange stone pyramid in front of a **clock tower** (1602); it was once used as a pillory to shame wayward citizens.

St Tryphon's Cathedral   CHURCH
(Katedrala Sv Tripuna; Trg Sv Tripuna; admission €2; ⊙8am-7pm) Kotor's most impressive building is its Catholic Cathedral, which was originally built in the 12th century but reconstructed after several earthquakes. The gently hued interior is a masterpiece of Romanesque architecture, with slender Corinthian columns alternating with pillars of pink stone, thrusting upwards to support a series of vaulted roofs. Its gilded silver bas-relief altar screen is considered Kotor's most valuable treasure.

Town Walls   FORTRESS
(admission €2; ⊙24hr, fees apply 8am-8pm May-Sep) The energetic can make a 1200m-long ascent up the fortifications via 1350 steps to a height of 260m, for unforgettable views and a huge sense of achievement. There are entry points near the **River Gate** (North Gate) and Trg od Salate.

Maritime Museum of Montenegro   MUSEUM
(Pomorski muzej Crne Gore; www.museummaritimum.com; Trg Bokeljske Mornarice; adult/child €4/1; ⊙9am-6.30pm Mon-Sat, to 1pm Sun Apr-Oct, 9am-2pm daily Nov-Mar) Kotor's proud history as a naval power is celebrated in three storeys of displays housed in a wonderful early-18th-century palace.

🛏 Sleeping

Although the Stari Grad is a charming place to stay, you'd better pack earplugs. In summer the bars blast music onto the streets until 1am every night and rubbish collectors clank around at 6am. Some of the best options are just out of Kotor in quieter Dobrota. Enquire about private accommodation at the tourist information booth.

TOP CHOICE **Old Town Hostel**   HOSTEL **€**
(☑032-325 317; www.hostel-kotor.me; near Trg od Salata; dm €12-14, r without bathroom €30, apt €40) Sympathetic renovations have brought this 13th-century *palazzo* back to life, and the ancient stone walls now echo with the chatter of happy travellers. Comfortable, sociable, reasonable, historical... exceptional.

TOP CHOICE **Palazzo Radomiri**   HISTORIC HOTEL **€€€**
(☑032-333 172; www.palazzoradomiri.com; Dobrota; s €80-90, d €120-130, ste €150-220; ⊙Mar-Oct; P❋🛜🏊) Exquisitely beautiful, this honey-coloured early-18th-century *palazzo* in Dobrota has been transformed into a first-rate boutique hotel. Some rooms are bigger and grander than others, but all 10 have sea views and luxurious furnishings.

Forza Mare   BOUTIQUE HOTEL **€€€**
(☑032-333 500; www.forzamare.com; Kriva bb, Dobrota; r €180-252; ⊙Apr-Oct; P❋🛜🏊) A bridge arches over a small pool before you even reach the front door of this opulent Dobrota

Kotor

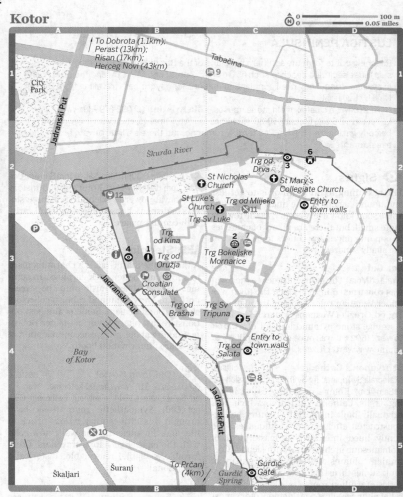

hotel. Downstairs there's a tiny private beach, restaurant and spa centre.

Hotel Monte Cristo
HOTEL €€
(☎032-322 458; www.montecristo.co.me; near Trg Bokeljske Mornarice; r €75-90, apt €115-150; P ✳ 🖭) It's not going to win any hip design awards but this old stone place offers a cheerful welcome and clean, brightly tiled rooms in a supremely central (but potentially noisy) location.

Tianis
APARTMENT €€
(☎032-302 178; www.tianis.net; Tabačina 569; apt €60-120; P ✳ 🖭) Well located without being

in the midst of the melee, this friendly establishment has a clutch of reasonably priced apartments, some of which have magical views of the Old Town.

✕ Eating & Drinking

There are dozens of cafe-bars, restaurants, bakeries and takeaway joints on Kotor's cobbled lanes.

⭐TOP CHOICE Galion
SEAFOOD €€€
(☎032-325 054; Šuranj bb; meals €10-21) With an achingly romantic setting, upmarket Galion gazes directly at the Old Town across the

Kotor

◎ Sights
1 Clock Tower B3
2 Maritime Museum of Montenegro C3
3 River Gate C2
4 Sea Gate B3
5 St Tryphon's Cathedral C4
6 Town Walls D2

🛏 Sleeping
7 Hotel Monte Cristo C3

8 Old Town Hostel C4
9 Tianis C1

✴ Eating
10 Galion A5
11 Stari Grad C2

⊙ Drinking
12 Maximus B2

yachts in the marina. Fresh fish is the focus, served as traditional grills. It usually closes in winter.

Restoran Stari Mlini　　SEAFOOD €€€
(☑032-333 555; www.starimlini.com; Jadranski Put; meals €12-20) It's well worth making the trip to Ljuta, just north of Dobrota, to this romantic restaurant set in an 18th-century mill by the edge of the bay. It's pricier than most and the service is variable, but the food is excellent.

Stari Grad　　SEAFOOD €€
(☑032-322 025; www.restoranstarigrad.com; Trg od Mlijeka; mains €8-18) Head straight through to the stone-walled courtyard, grab a seat under the vines and prepare to get absolutely stuffed full of fabulous food – the serves are huge.

☆ Entertainment

Maximus　　CLUB
(☑067-216 767; www.discomaximus.com; near Trg od Oružja; admission free-€5; ⊙11pm-5am Thu-Sat, nightly in summer) Montenegro's most pumping club comes into its own in summer, hosting big-name international DJs and local starlets.

⊙ Information

Tourist Information Booth (www.kotor.travel; ⊙8am-8pm)

⊙ Getting There & Away

The **bus station** (☑032-325 809; ⊙6am-9pm) is to the south of town, just off the road leading to the Tivat tunnel. Buses to Herceg Novi (€4, one hour), Budva (€3.50, 40 minutes), Tivat (€2.20, 20 minutes) and Podgorica (€7, two hours) are at least hourly. Further-flung destinations include Kolašin (€12, four daily).

A taxi to Tivat airport should cost around €10.

Tivat　　Тиват

POP 9,450

In the throes of a major makeover, courtesy of the multimillion-dollar redevelopment of its old naval base into the **Porto Montenegro** (www.portomontenegro.com; ⊙7am-1am) super-yacht marina, Tivat is becoming noticeably more schmick each year. While it will never rival Kotor for charm, it makes a pleasant stop on a trip around the bay, and a useful base for exploring the sweet villages of the Vrmac and Luštica Peninsulas.

🛏 Sleeping & Eating

Hotel Villa Royal　　HOTEL €€
(☑032-675 310; www.rotortivat.com; Kalimanjska 18; s/d €42/68; ❋@ই) It's not a villa and it's certainly not fit for a king, but this minihotel near the old marina has clean, bright rooms and friendly staff, making it our pick of Tivat's extremely limited accommodation options...at least until the Regent opens in 2014.

TOP CHOICE One　　ITALIAN €€€
(☑067-486 045; Porto Montenegro; mains €10-20; ⊙8am-1am) Murals and sail-like flourishes on the ceiling invoke the yachtie lifestyle in this smart but informal brasserie, while the menu sails clear across the Adriatic for an authentic take on Italian cuisine.

Prova　　MEDITERRANEAN €€
(www.prova.co.me; Šetalište Iva Vizina 1; mains €8-18; ⊙8am-1am) Shaped like a boat with chandeliers that look like mutant alien jellyfish, this upmarket eatery is the very epitome of the new, increasingly chic Tivat. The pasta is excellent.

⊙ Information

Tourist Office (☑032-671 324; www.tivat. travel; Palih Boraca 8; ⊙8am-8pm Mon-Fri,

8am-noon & 6-8pm Sat, 8am-noon Sun Jun-Aug, 8am-3pm Mon-Sat Sep-May)

❶ Getting There & Away

AIR Tivat airport is 3km south of town and 8km through the tunnel from Kotor. Major local and international rental-car companies have counters here. Taxis charge around €5 to €7 for Tivat, €10 for Kotor and €25 to Budva.

BUS Buses to Kotor (€2.20, 20 minutes) stop outside a silver kiosk on Palih Boraca. The main stop for longer trips is inconveniently located halfway between Tivat and the airport.

ADRIATIC COAST

Much of Montenegro's determination to re-invent itself as a tourist mecca has focused firmly on its gorgeous Adriatic coastline. In July and August it seems that the entire Serbian world and a fair chunk of its northern Orthodox brethren can be found crammed onto this scant 100km stretch. Avoid these months and you'll find a charismatic set of fortified towns and fishing villages to explore, set against clear Adriatic waters and Montenegro's mountainous backdrop.

Budva   Будва

POP 13,400

The poster child of Montenegrin tourism, Budva – with its atmospheric Old Town and numerous beaches – certainly has a lot to offer. Yet the child has moved into a difficult adolescence, fuelled by rampant development that has leeched much of the charm from the place. In the height of the season the sands are blanketed with package holidaymakers from Russia and the Ukraine, while the nouveau riche park their multimillion-dollar yachts in the town's guarded marina. By night you'll run a gauntlet of scantily clad women attempting to cajole you into the beachside bars. It's the buzziest place on the coast so if you're in the mood to party, this is the place to be.

◎ Sights & Activities

Stari Grad   HISTORIC AREA
Budva's best feature and star attraction is the Old Town – a mini-Dubrovnik with marbled streets and Venetian walls rising from the clear waters below. Much of it was ruined by two earthquakes in 1979 but it has since been completely rebuilt and now

houses more shops, bars and restaurants than residences. At its seaward end, the **Citadela** (admission €2; ⊙9am-midnight May-Oct, to 5pm Nov-Apr) offers striking views, a small museum and a library full of rare tomes and maps. In the square in front of the citadel is a cluster of interesting churches. Nearby is the entry to the **town walls** (admission €1).

Archaeological Museum   MUSEUM
(Arheološki muzej; ☑033-453 308; Petra I Petrovića 11; adult/child €2/1; ⊙9am-9pm Tue-Fri, 2-9pm Sat & Sun) This museum shows off the town's ancient and complicated history – dating back to at least 500 BC – over three floors of exhibits.

FREE **Modern Gallery**   GALLERY
(Moderna galerija; Cara Dušana 19; ⊙8am-2pm & 6-9pm Mon-Fri, 6-9pm Sat) An attractive gallery displaying temporary exhibitions.

Montenegro Adventure Centre   PARAGLIDING
(☑067-580 664; www.montenegrofly.com) Rafting, hiking, mountain biking, diving and accommodation can all be arranged, as well as paragliding from launch sites around the country. An unforgettable tandem flight landing 750m below at Bečići beach costs €65.

⬛ Sleeping

TOP CHOICE **Hotel Astoria**   HOTEL €€€
(☑033-451 110; www.astoriamontenegro.com; Njegoševa 4; s €90-105, d €110-130, ste €130-210; ❄@) Water shimmers down the corridor wall as you enter this chic boutique hotel hidden in the Old Town's fortifications. The rooms are on the small side but they're beautifully furnished.

Hotel Oliva   HOTEL €€
(☑033-459 429; olivai@t-com.me; Velji Vinogradi bb; s/d €30/58; ⓟ❄🛜) Don't expect anything flashy, just a warm welcome, clean and comfortable rooms with balconies, and a nice garden studded with the olive trees that give this small hotel its name.

Saki Hostel & Apartmani   HOSTEL, APARTMENTS €
(☑067-368 065; www.saki-apartmani.com; IV Proleterska bb; dm €10, apt per person €25; ⓟ❄🛜) Not quite a hostel and not quite an apartment hotel, this friendly family-run block on the outskirts of town offers elements of both. Individual beds are rented, hostel-style, in a rambling set of rooms.

Eating

Porto
SEAFOOD €€

(☑033-451 598; www.restoranporto.com; City Marina, Šetalište bb; mains €8-20; ☉10am-1am) From the waterfront promenade, a little bridge arches over a fish pond and into this romantic restaurant where jocular bow-tie-wearing waiters flit about with plates laden with fresh seafood.

Pizza 10 Maradona
PIZZERIA €

(Petra I Petrovića 10; pizza slice €2) A reader alerted us to this late-night hole-in-the-wall eatery selling pizza by the slice. We can confirm that after a hard night's hitting the city's night spots, Maradona's crispy-based pizza does indeed seem to come straight from the hand of God.

Drinking

Top Hill
CLUB

(www.tophill.me; Topliški Put; events €10-25; ☉11pm-5am Jul & Aug) The top cat of Montenegro's summer party scene attracts up to 5000 revellers to its open-air club atop Topliš hill, offering them top-notch sound and lighting, sea views, big-name touring DJs and performances by local pop stars.

Information

Tourist Office (☑033-452 750; www.budva.travel; Njegoševa 28; ☉9am-9pm Mon-Sat, 5-9pm Sun)

Getting There & Away

The **bus station** (☑033-456 000; Popa Jola Zeca bb) has frequent services to Herceg Novi (€6), Kotor (€3.50), Bar (€4.50) and Podgorica (€6).

Pržno & Sveti Stefan
Пржно И Свети Стефан

Gazing down on impossibly picturesque Sveti Stefan, 5km south of Budva, provides the biggest 'wow' moment on the entire coast. And gazing on it is all most people will get to do, as this tiny island – connected to the shore by a narrow isthmus and crammed full of terracotta-roofed dwellings dating from the 15th century – was nationalised in the 1950s and the whole thing is now a luxurious resort.

Sveti Stefan is also the name of the settlement that's sprung up onshore. From its steep slopes you get to look down at that iconic view all day – which some might suggest is even better than staying in the surreally glamorous enclave below.

The general public can access the main Sveti Stefan beach, which faces the island. From the beach there's a very pleasant walk north to the cute village of Pržno where there are some excellent restaurants and another attractive, often crowded beach.

Sleeping & Eating

Vila Drago
GUESTHOUSE €€

(☑030-468 477; www.viladrago.com; Slobode 32; r €45-60, apt €120-130; ❄🛜) The only problem with this family-run place is that you may never want to leave your terrace, as the views are so sublime. Watch the sunset over Sveti Stefan island from the grapevine-covered terrace restaurant (mains €5 to €17).

Aman Sveti Stefan
RESORT €€€

(☑033-420 000; www.amanresorts.com; ste €750-3000; P❄🛜☂) Truly unique, this island resort offers 50 luxurious suites that showcase the stone walls and wooden beams of the ancient houses. Back on the shore, **Villa Miločer** has a further eight suites by the beach. Nonguests can avail themselves of three eateries: the **Olive Tree** at Sveti Stefan Beach, the **Beach Cafe** at Miločer and **Queen's Chair**, perched on a wooded hill facing Budva.

Vila Levantin
APARTMENTS €

(☑033-468 206; www.villalevantin.com; Vukice Mitrović 3; r €30-50, apt €50-130; P❄🛜☂) Levantin has a variety of modern rooms and apartments at extremely reasonable prices. The block is modern and well finished, with red stone walls, blue-tiled bathrooms and an attractive plunge pool on the terrace.

Hotel Residence Miločer
HOTEL €€

(☑033-427 100; www.residencemontenegro.com; Jadranski Put; s €69-99, d €79-119; P❄🛜☂) The decor's fresh and modern, there's secure parking, the breakfast buffets are excellent, and the staff aren't afraid to smile. It's worth paying the additional €10 for a spacious junior suite.

Blanche
EUROPEAN €€

(☑062-504 272; www.blanche-restaurant.com; Obala 11; mains €8-24; ☉10am-midnight) Higher than usual prices and upmarket decor don't necessary signal quality but in the case of this Pržno waterfront restaurant, you can breathe easy. Sharing the menu with Dalmatian seafood classics are succulent steaks and a wide selection of Italian dishes.

❶ Getting There & Away

Olimpia Express buses head to and from Budva (€1.50, 20 minutes) every 30 minutes in summer and hourly in winter.

Petrovac   Петровац

POP 1400

The Romans had the right idea, building their summer villas on this lovely bay. The pretty beachside promenade is perfumed with the scent of lush Mediterranean plants, and a picturesque 16th-century **Venetian fortress** guards a tiny stone harbour. This is one of the best places on the coast for families: the accommodation is reasonably priced, the water's clear and kids roam the esplanade at night with impunity.

In July and August you'll be lucky to find an inch of space on the town beach, but wander south and there's cypress- and oleander-lined **Lučice Beach** and, beyond it, the 2.5km-long sweep of **Buljarica Beach**.

⌖ Sleeping & Eating

Hotel Danica   HOTEL €€
(☏033-462 304; www.hoteldanica.net; s/d €55/60; P✳︎🕸🛜🛝) With a quiet location under the pine-covered hill immediately west of the town beach, this four-storey hotel is small enough to maintain a relaxed family ambience. There's a little pool on the terrace.

Camping Maslina   CAMPGROUND €
(☏033-461 215; akmaslina@t-com.me; Buljarica bb; per adult/child/tent/car/caravan €3/1.50/3/3/5; P🛜) Just off the road to Buljarica Beach, this well-kept campground has a tidy ablutions block with proper sit-down toilets and solar-powered hot water. As Montenegrin campsites go, this is one of the best.

Hotel Đurić   HOTEL €€
(☏033-462 005; www.hoteldjuric.com; Brežine bb; s/d €72/96; ⊙May-Sep; ✳︎🛜🛝) There's a vaguely Spanish Mission feel to this smart boutique hotel. All rooms have kitchen facilities and there's a restaurant at the back under a canopy of kiwifruit and grapevines.

Konoba Bonaca   MONTENEGRIN, SEAFOOD €€
(☏069-084 735; mains €8-15) Set back slightly from the main beach drag, this traditional restaurant focuses mainly on seafood but

the local cheeses and olives are also excellent. Grab a table under the grapevines on the terrace.

❶ Getting There & Away

Petrovac's bus station is near the top of town. Regular services head to Budva and Bar (both €2.50, 30 minutes).

Bar   Бар

POP 13,500

Dominated by Montenegro's main port and a large industrial area, Bar is unlikely to be anyone's highlight, but it is a handy transport hub welcoming trains from Belgrade and ferries from Italy. More interesting are the ruins of Stari Bar (Old Bar) in the mountains behind.

◉ Sights

Stari Bar
TOP CHOICE   RUIN
(Old Bar; adult/child €2/1; ⊙8am-10pm) Bar's original settlements stands on a bluff 4km northeast, off the Ulcinj road. A steep cobbled hill takes you past a cluster of old houses and shops to the fortified entrance, where a short, dark passage pops you out into a large expanse of vine-clad ruins and abandoned streets overgrown with grass and wild flowers. A small museum just inside the entrance explains the site and its history.

The Illyrians founded the city in around 800 BC. It passed in and out of Slavic and Byzantine rule until Venice took it in 1443 and held it until the Ottoman conquest in 1571. Nearly all the 240 buildings now lie in ruins, a result of Montenegrin shelling when the town was captured in 1878.

Buses marked Stari Bar depart from the centre of new Bar every hour (€1).

King Nikola's Palace   MUSEUM
(Dvorac Kralja Nikole; ☏030-314 079; Šetalište Kralje Nikole; adult/child €1/.50; ⊙8am-2pm & 5-11pm) Presenting an elegant facade to the water, this former palace (1885) now houses a collection of antiquities, folk costumes and royal furniture. Its shady gardens contain plants cultivated from seeds and cuttings collected from around the world by Montenegro's sailors.

⌖ Sleeping & Eating

Hotel Princess   HOTEL €€€
(☏030-300 100; www.hotelprincess.me; Jovana Tomaševića 59; s €83-98, d €126-156, ste €205-275;

(P❄@🌐📶📺) The standards aren't what you'd expect for the price but this resort-style hotel is the best option in Bar by far. Get your money's worth at the private beach, swimming pool and spa centre.

🍴 Kaldrma
MONTENEGRIN €€

(☎030-341 744; kaldrmarestoran@t-com.me; mains €6-11; ☺lunch & dinner; 🍴) Located on the steep road leading to Stari Bar's main gate, this wonderful little eatery manages to be simultaneously very traditional and slightly hippy-dippy. The focus is on the cuisine of Stari Bar itself, including tender lamb and seasonal vegetarian options. Accommodation is offered in a room upstairs with mattresses laid on woven rugs (€25).

❶ Information

Tourist Information Centre (☎030-311 633; www.visitbar.org; Obala 13 Jula bb; ☺8am-8pm Mon-Sat, to 2pm Sun Jul-Sep, 8am-4pm Mon-Fri Oct-Jun)

❶ Getting There & Away

The bus station and adjacent train station are 1km southeast of the centre. Frequent buses head to Kotor (€6.50), Budva (€4.50), Ulcinj (€3) and Podgorica (€4.50). Trains head to Virpazar (€1.20, 23 minutes, seven daily), Podgorica (€2.40, one hour, nine daily) and Kolašin (€5.40, 2½ hours, four daily).

Montenegro Lines (☎030-311 164; www.montenegrolines.net) ferries to Italy (Bari and Ancona) leave from the ferry terminal near the centre of town.

Ulcinj
Улцињ

POP 10,700

If you want a feel for Albania without actually crossing the border, buzzy Ulcinj's the place to go. The population is 61% Albanian and in summer it swells with Kosovar holidaymakers for the simple reason that it's nicer than any of the Albanian seaside towns. The elegant minarets of numerous mosques give Ulcinj a distinctly Eastern feel, as does the music echoing out of the kebab stands.

For centuries Ulcinj had a reputation as a pirate's lair. By the end of the 16th century as many as 400 pirates, mainly from Malta, Tunisia and Algeria, made Ulcinj their main port of call – wreaking havoc on passing vessels and then returning to party up large on Mala Plaža. Ulcinj became the centre of a thriving slave trade, with people – mainly from North Africa – paraded for sale on the town's main square.

👁 Sights & Activities

Beaches
BEACHES

Mala Plaža may be a fine grin of a cove but it's a little hard to see the beach under all that suntanned flesh in July and August. You are better off strolling southeast where a succession of rocky bays offers clear water and a little more room to breathe. **Lady Beach 'Dada'** (admission €1.50) has a women-only policy, while a section of the **Hotel Albatros Beach** is clothing-optional.

The appropriately named **Velika Plaža** (Big Beach) starts 4km southeast of the town and stretches for 12 sandy kilometres. Sections of it sprout deckchairs but there's still plenty of relatively empty space. To be frank, this large flat expanse isn't as picturesque as it sounds and the water is painfully shallow – great for kids but you'll need to walk a fair way for a decent swim.

On your way to Velika Plaža you'll pass the murky Milena canal, where local fishermen use nets suspended from long willow rods attached to wooden stilt houses. The effect is remarkably redolent of Southeast Asia. There are more of these contraptions on the banks of the Bojana River at the other end of Veliki Plaža.

Stari Grad
NEIGHBOURHOOD

The ancient Old Town is still largely residential and somewhat dilapidated – a legacy of the 1979 earthquake. A steep slope leads to the Upper Gate, where there's a small **museum** (admission €1; ☺9am-8pm Tue-Sun) just inside the walls, containing Roman and Ottoman artefacts.

D'Olcinium Diving Club
DIVING

(☎067-319 100; www.uldiving.com; Detarёt e Ulqinit bb) Local dive sites include various wrecks (this is pirate territory, after all) and the remains of a submerged town. If you've got up-to-date qualifications you can rent gear (€20), take a guided shore dive (€15) or head out on a boat for a day's diving (€50).

🛏 Sleeping

TOP CHOICE Haus Freiburg
HOTEL €€

(☎030-403 008; www.hotelhausfreiburg.me; Kosovska bb; s/d/apt €50/65/85; P❄📶📺) High on the slopes above the town, this family-run hotel has well-kitted-out apartments and rooms, and a particularly attractive roof terrace with sea views, a swimming pool and small restaurant.

Dvori Balšića HOTEL €€€
(☎030-421 609; www.hotel-dvoribalsica-montenegro.com; Stari Grad bb; s/d €65/100; ❋☎) This stone *palazzo* and its equally grand sister, the **Palata Venecija**, are reached by the cobbled lanes and stairs of the Old Town. The sizeable rooms all have kitchenettes and sea views.

Real Estate Travel Agency ACCOMMODATION SERVICES €
(☎030-421 609; www.realestate-travel.com; Hazif Ali Ulqinaku bb; per person from €15) Obliging English-speaking staff can help you find private rooms, apartments or hotel rooms. They also rent bikes (€10) and cars, run tours and sell maps of Ulcinj.

 Eating

TOP CHOICE **Miško** SEAFOOD €€€
(Bojana River; mains €9-17) The most upmarket of the Bojana River restaurants (14km east of Ulcinj) is focused completely on seafood, including octopus, shrimps, shellfish, a big selection of fresh fish, and delicious *riblja čorba* (fish soup).

Restaurant Pizzeria Bazar PIZZERIA, SEAFOOD €
(Hazif Ali Ulqinaku bb; mains €4-10; ⊙10am-1pm) An upstairs restaurant that's a great idling place when the streets below are heaving with tourists. People-watch in comfort as you enjoy a plate of *lignje na žaru* (grilled squid).

ℹ **Getting There & Away**

The bus station is on the northeastern edge of town. Services head to Herceg Novi (€10, daily), Kotor (€9, daily), Budva (€7, eight daily), Podgorica (€6, 12 daily) and across the Albanian border to Shkodra (€6, two daily).

CENTRAL MONTENEGRO

The heart of Montenegro – physically, spiritually and politically – is easily accessed as a day trip from the coast but it's well deserving of a longer exploration. Two wonderful national parks separate it from the Adriatic and behind them lie the two capitals, the ancient current one and the newer former one.

Lovćen National Park Ловћен

Directly behind Kotor is Mt Lovćen (1749m), the black mountain that gave *Crna Gora* (Montenegro) its name (*crna/negro* means 'black' and *gora/monte* means 'mountain' in Montenegrin and Italian respectively). This locale occupies a special place in the hearts of all Montenegrins. For most of its history it represented the entire nation – a rocky island of Slavic resistance in an Ottoman sea. The old capital of Cetinje nestles in its foothills.

Lovćen's star attraction is the magnificent **Njegoš Mausoleum** (Njegošev Mauzolej; admission €3; ⊙8am-6pm) at the top of its second-highest peak, Jezerski Vrh (1657m). Take the 461 steps up to the entry, where two granite giantesses guard the tomb. Inside, under a golden mosaic canopy, a 28-tonne Petar II Petrović Njegoš rests in the wings of an eagle, carved from a single block of black granite. The actual tomb lies below and a path at the rear leads to a dramatic circular viewing platform.

The national park's 6220 hectares are criss-crossed with well-marked hiking paths. The **National Park Visitor Centre** (www.nparkovi.me; ⊙9am-5pm) at Ivanova Korita offers accommodation in four-bedded bungalows (€40). If you're driving, the park can be approached from either Kotor or Cetinje (entry fee €2). Tour buses provide the only services into the park.

Cetinje Цетиње

POP 14,000

Rising from a green vale surrounded by rough, grey mountains, Cetinje is an odd mix of former capital and overgrown village, where single-storey cottages and stately mansions share the same street. Pretty Njegoševa is a partly traffic-free thoroughfare lined with interesting buildings, including the **Blue Palace** (Plavi Dvorac), which houses the president, and various former embassies marked with plaques. Everything of significance is in the immediate vicinity.

◉ **Sights**

TOP CHOICE **National Museum of Montenegro** MUSEUM
(www.mnmuseum.org; Narodni muzej Crne Gore; all museums adult/child €10/5; ⊙9am-4pm) The

National Museum is actually a collection of four museums and two galleries housed in a clump of important buildings. A joint ticket will get you into all of them or you can buy individual tickets.

Two are housed in the former parliament (1910), Cetinje's most imposing building. The fascinating **History Museum** (Istorijski muzej; ☑041-230 310; Novice Cerovića 7; adult/child €3/1.50) is very well laid out, following a timeline from the Stone Age to 1955. There are few English signs but the enthusiastic staff will walk you around and give you an overview before leaving you to your own devices.

Upstairs you'll find the equally excellent **Montenegrin Art Gallery** (Crnogorska galerija umjetnosti; adult/child €4/2). In 2012 an offshoot of the national gallery opened in a striking building on Cetinje's main street. The edgy **Miodrag Dado Đurić Gallery** (Galerija; Balšića Pazar; ◷10am-2pm & 6-9pm Tue-Sun) is devoted to 20th-century and contemporary Montenegrin art. The same ticket covers both galleries.

Entry to the **King Nikola Museum** (Muzej kralja Nikole; Dvorski Trg; adult/child €5/2.50) is by guided tour, which the staff will only give to a group, even if you've prepaid a ticket. Still, this 1871 palace of Nikola I, last sovereign of Montenegro, is worth the delay.

The castle-like **Njegoš Museum** (Njegošev muzej; Dvorski Trg; adult/child €3/1.50) was the residence of Montenegro's favourite son, prince-bishop and poet Petar II Petrović Njegoš. The palace was built in 1838 and housed the nation's first billiard table, hence the museum's alternative name, Biljarda. When you leave, turn right and follow the walls to the glass pavilion housing a fascinating large-scale **Relief Map** (admission €1) of Montenegro created by the Austrians in 1917.

Occupying the former Serbian Embassy, the **Ethnographic Museum** (Etnografski Muzej; Dvorski Trg; adult/child €2/1) is the least interesting of the six but if you've bought a joint ticket you may as well check it out. The collection of costumes and tools is well presented and has English notations.

Cetinje Monastery   MONASTERY
(Cetinjski Manastir; ◷8am-6pm) It's a case of four times lucky for the Cetinje Monastery, having been repeatedly destroyed during Ottoman attacks and rebuilt. This sturdy incarnation dates from 1786, with its only exterior ornamentation being the capitals of columns recycled from the original building, founded in 1484.

The chapel to the right of the courtyard holds what is said to be the mummified right hand of St John the Baptist. The casket's only occasionally opened for veneration, so if you miss out you can console yourself with the knowledge that it's not a very pleasant sight.

The monastery **treasury** (admission €2) is only open to groups but if you are persuasive enough and prepared to wait around, you may be able to get in (mornings are best). It holds a wealth of fascinating objects that form a blur as you're shunted around the rooms by one of the monks.

If your legs, shoulders or cleavage are on display you'll either be denied entry or given an unflattering smock to wear.

🛏 Sleeping & Eating

Pansion 22   GUESTHOUSE €€
(☑069-055 473; pansion22@mtel-cg.net; Ivana Crnojevića 22; s/d €22/40; 🛜) They may not be great at speaking English or answering emails, but the family that runs this central guesthouse offers a warm welcome nonetheless. The rooms are simply decorated yet clean and comfortable.

Kole   MONTENEGRIN, EUROPEAN €
(☑041-231 620; www.restaurantkole.me; Bul Crnogorskih Junaka 12; mains €3-12; ◷7am-11pm) Omelettes and pasta are served at this snazzy modern eatery, but what are really great are the local specialities. Try the *Njeguški ražanj*, smoky spit-roasted meat stuffed with *pršut* and cheese.

❶ Information

Tourist Information (☑078-108 788; www.cetinje.travel; Novice Cerovića bb; ◷8am-6pm)

❶ Getting There & Away

Cetinje is on the main Budva–Podgorica highway and can also be reached by a glorious back road from Kotor via Lovćen National Park. Buses stop at Trg Golootočkih Žrtava, two blocks from the main street. There are regular services to Podgorica (€4) and Budva (€4).

Lake Skadar National Park   Скадарско Језеро

The Balkans' largest lake, dolphin-shaped Lake Skadar has its tail and two-thirds of its body in Montenegro and its nose in Albania.

Covering between 370 and 550 sq km (depending on the time of year), it's one of the most important reserves for wetland birds in the whole of Europe. The endangered Dalmatian pelican nests here, along with 256 other species, while 48 species of fish lurk beneath its smooth surface. On the Montenegrin side, an area of 400 sq km is protected by a national park. It's a blissfully pretty area, encompassing steep mountains, hidden villages, island monasteries, clear waters and floating meadows of waterlilies.

◉ Sights

Rijeka Crnojevića   VILLAGE
The northwestern end of the lake thins into the serpentine loops of the Crnojević River and terminates near the pretty village of the same name. It's a charming, tucked-away kind of place, accessed by side roads that lead off the Cetinje–Podgorica highway. Taxi boats dock at the marble riverside promenade, near the photogenic arched stone bridge (1854).

Žabljak Crnojevića   RUIN
For a brief time in the 15th century, this was the capital of Zetan ruler Ivan Crnojević. Now the enigmatic ruins stand forlornly on a hillside surrounded by green plains. The site's a little hard to find but well worth the effort. Heading towards Podgorica, turn left at the only set of traffic lights in Golubovci. After the railway bridge and the one-way bridge, turn left. Continue for about 4.5km until you see a bridge to your left. Cross the bridge and continue to the car park near the village. Take the stone stairs heading up from the path near the river and follow your nose along the overgrown path.

Virpazar   TOWN
This little town, gathered around a square and a river blanketed with water lilies, serves as the main gateway to the national park. Most of the boat tours of the lake depart from here.

Murići   BEACH
The southern edge of the lake is the most dramatic, with the Rumija Mountains rising precipitously from the water. From Virpazar there's a wonderful drive following the contours of the lake through the mountains towards the border before crossing the range and turning back towards Ulcinj. About halfway, a steep road descends to the village of Murići. This is one of the lake's best swimming spots. Local boatmen offer trips to the historic monasteries on the nearby islands for around €10 per hour.

Activities

Green Boats   BOAT TOUR
(Zeleni Brodovi; ☑069-998 737; greenboats.me@gmail.com; per hr from Virpazar/Vranjina €25/40) Lake cruises are offered every two hours by this association of small local operators. Two-hour cruises are the norm, although longer trips can be arranged. We've heard glowing reports about one particular lake, the **Golden Frog** (☑069-413 307; www.skadar-lakecruise.blogspot.co.uk).

Undiscovered Montenegro   ADVENTURE TOURS
(☑069-402 374; www.lake-skadar.com; ◉Apr-Nov) Specialises in weeklong, all-inclusive, lake-based itineraries (per person €530 including accommodation at Villa Miela), but also offers an accommodation booking service and day tours. Options include guided hikes, kayaking, caving, boat tours, fishing, car safaris, wine tours and expert-led birdwatching.

🛏 Sleeping & Eating

Villa Miela   GUESTHOUSE €€
(☑020-3287 0015; www.undiscoveredmontenegro.com; r €80; ◉Apr-Nov) Sitting pretty on the slopes near Virpazar, this lovingly renovated stone farmhouse has four rooms sharing a kitchen, BBQ area, orchard and lake views. In July and August it's reserved for Undiscovered Montenegro's seven-day activity holidays, but shorter stays are accepted at other times.

TOP CHOICE Stari Most   SEAFOOD €€
(☑041-239 505; mains €8-25) You wouldn't expect it, but sleepy Rijeka Crnojevića is home to one of Montenegro's best restaurants. Freshwater fish – particularly eel, trout and carp – is the speciality.

Konoba Badanj   MONTENEGRIN €€
(mains €6-12; ◉8am-midnight) Near the bridge in Virpazar, a cool stone-walled interior with solid wooden beams makes this an atmospheric eating option. The fish soup comes with big chunks of fish and delicious scone-like homemade bread.

ℹ Information

National Park Visitor Centre (☑020-879 103; www.nparkovi.me; admission €2, free with national park entry ticket; ◉8am-4pm, to 6pm summer) In Vranjina, this centre has excellent displays about all of Montenegro's national parks. A kiosk here and at Virpazar sells park entry tickets (per day €4) and fishing permits (per day summer/winter €10/5). In the busy months, tour operators have kiosks in the vicinity. Just across the busy highway and railway tracks are the remains of the 19th-century fortress Lesendro.

Virpazar Tourist Office (✆020-711 102; www.visitbar.org; ⊙8am-5pm May-Sep, to 4pm Mon-Fri Oct-Apr; ⛛) This big new office on the main square can assist you with arranging anything in the area, including boat trips, wine tastings and private accommodation. Upstairs there are displays about the national park, and the office operates as a storefront for the region's small wine producers.

❶ Getting There & Away

Buses on the Bar–Podgorica route stop on the highway. Virpazar's train station is off the main road, 800m south of town. There are seven trains to/from Bar (€1.20, 23 minutes) and Podgorica (€1.40, 30 minutes) every day.

Podgorica Подгорица

POP 151,000

Podgorica's never going to be Europe's most happening capital, but if you can get past the sweltering summer temperatures and concrete apartment blocks, you'll find a pleasant little city with lots of green space and some excellent galleries and bars.

The city sits at the confluence of two rivers. West of the broad Morača is what passes for the business district. The smaller Ribnica River divides the eastern side in two. To the south is Stara Varoš, the heart of the former Ottoman town. North of the Ribnica is Nova Varoš, an attractive, mainly low-rise precinct of late-19th-century and early-20th-century buildings housing a lively mixture of shops and bars. At its centre is the main square, Trg Republika.

◉ Sights & Activities

FREE **Museums & Galleries of Podgorica** MUSEUM
(Muzeji i Galerije Podgorice; ✆020-242 543; Marka Miljanova 4; ⊙9am-8pm) Despite Cetinje nabbing most of the national endowment, the new capital is well served by this collection of art and artefacts. There's an interesting section on Podgorica's history which includes antiquities exhumed from its Roman incarnation, Doclea.

FREE **Petrović Palace** PALACE, GALLERY
(Dvorac Petrovića; ✆020-243 513; www.csucg.co.me; Ljubljanska bb; ⊙9am-2pm & 5-10pm Mon-Fri, 10am-2pm Sat) The Contemporary Art Centre operates two galleries in Podgorica. The bottom two floors of this former palace are given over to high-profile exhibitions, while the top floor has an oddball collection from its days as Yugoslavia's gallery devoted to art from Non-Aligned Movement countries.

Temporary exhibitions are also staged in the small **Galerija Centar** (✆020-665 409; Njegoševa 2; ⊙10am-1pm & 6-pm Mon-Fri, 10am-1pm Sat).

Cathedral of Christ's Resurrection CHURCH
(Saborni Hram Hristovog Vaskrsenja; www.hramvaskrsenjapg.org; Bul Džordža Vašingtona) The large dome, white stone towers and gold crosses of this immense Serbian Orthodox cathedral are striking additions to Podgorica's skyline. Work commenced in 1993 and it's still a long way from completion, but you can usually enter and check out the glistening gold frescos inside.

Montenegro Adventures ADVENTURE TOURS
(✆020-208 000; www.montenegro-adventures.com; Jovana Tomaševića 35) This well-respected and long-standing agency creates tailor-made adventure tours, country-wide. It can organise mountain guides, cycling logistics, kitesurfing, hiking, cultural activities, accommodation, flights...you name it.

🛏 Sleeping

Most visitors to Podgorica are here for business, either commerce or government-related. Hotels set their prices accordingly and private accommodation isn't really an option.

Hotel Podgorica HOTEL €€€
(✆020-402 500; www.hotelpodgorica.co.me; Bul Sv Petra Cetinjskog 1; s €125-155, d €170-180, ste €190-200; P❋@⛛) A wonderful showcase of 1960s Yugoslav architecture, the Podgorica has been luxuriously modernised yet retains its riverstone cladding and period charm. The best rooms have terraces facing the river.

Aria HOTEL €€
(✆020-872 572; www.hotelaria.me; Mahala bb; s €56-76, d €93, apt €132-205; ❋⛛) An oasis of green lawns in the scorched field surrounding the airport, this new hotel offers better

Podgorica

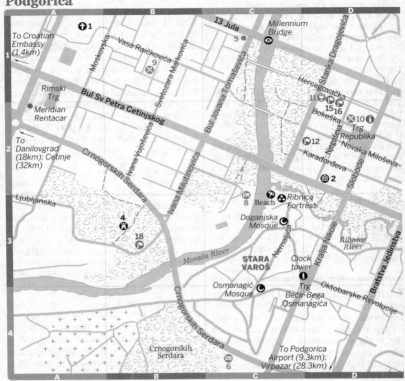

MONTENEGRO PODGORICA

value than its city equivalents and is a great option if you've got a badly timed flight.

City Hotel HOTEL **€€€**
(☑020-441 500; www.cityhotelmn.com; Crnogorskih serdara 5; s €75-95, d €100-120, apt €130-170; P❄@☎) A business-orientated makeover in 2008 has thankfully kept the 1970s exterior angularity of this city-fringe hotel, while the surrealist art of Dado Đurić has prevented a total beige-out inside.

Hotel Evropa HOTEL **€€**
(☑020-623 444; www.hotelevropa.co.me; Orahovačka 16; s €40-55, d €70-90; P❄@☎) It's hardly a salubrious location, but Evropa is handy to the train and bus stations, and offers good clean rooms with comfortable beds, writing desks and decent showers.

✗ Eating & Drinking

Podgorica's nightlife is centred on Nova Varoš, particularly in the blocks west of ulica Slobode. The hippest strip right now is ulica Bokeška.

TOP CHOICE Lupo di Mare SEAFOOD **€€**
(Trg Republika 22; mains €8-20; ☺8am-midnight) As you may have guessed from the name, there's a distinct Italian bent to this excellent seafood restaurant. Nautical knick-knacks hang from the pale stone walls and there's an interesting wine list.

Leonardo ITALIAN **€€**
(☑020-242 902; www.leonardo-restoran.com; Svetozara Markovića bb; mains €5-17; ☺8am-midnight; ☎✗) Leonardo's unlikely position at the centre of a residential block makes it a little tricky to find but the effort's well rewarded by accomplished Italian cuisine. The pasta dishes are delicious and reasonably priced.

Buda Bar BAR
(☑067-344 944; www.facebook.com/Budabarpg; Stanka Dragojevića 26; ☺8am-2am) A golden

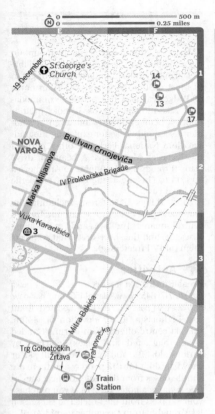

Podgorica

⊙ Sights
1 Cathedral of Christ's Resurrection A1
2 Galerija Centar.................................D2
3 Museums & Galleries of Podgorica....E3
4 Petrović Palace..............................B3

⊕ Activities, Courses & Tours
5 Montenegro Adventures...................C1

⊜ Sleeping
6 City Hotel.....................................C4
7 Hotel Evropa E4
8 Hotel Podgorica...........................C3

⊗ Eating
9 Leonardo B1
10 Lupo di Mare D2

⊙ Drinking
11 Buda Bar......................................D1

ⓘ Information
12 Albanian Embassy.........................D2
13 Bosnia & Hercegovinian Embassy F1
14 French Embassy.............................F1
15 German Embassy D1
16 Serbian Embassy...........................D2
17 UK Embassy F1
18 USA Embassy B3

Buddha smiles serenely as you search for the eternal truth at the bottom of a cocktail glass. The semi-enclosed terrace is the place to be on balmy summer nights.

ⓘ Information
Tourist Organisation Podgorica (☎020-667 535; www.podgorica.travel; Slobode 47; ☺8am-8pm Mon-Fri)

ⓘ Getting There & Around
AIR Podgorica airport is 9km south of the city. Airport taxis have a standard €15 fare to the centre.

BUS Podgorica's **bus station** (☎020-620 430; Trg Golootočkih Žrtava 1) has services to all major towns, including Herceg Novi (€9, three hours), Kotor (€7, 2¼ hours), Budva (€6, 1½ hours), Ulcinj (€6, one hour) and Cetinje (€3.50, 30 minutes)

TRAIN From Podgorica's **train station** (☎020-441 211; www.zpcg.me; Trg Golootočkih Žrtava

13) there are services to Bar (€2.40, one hour, nine daily), Virpazar (€1.40, 30 minutes, seven daily), Kolašin (€5.90, 1½ hours, five daily) and Belgrade (€20, 10 hours, three daily).

Ostrog Monastery
Манастир Острог

Resting in a cliff face 900m above the Zeta valley, the gleaming white Ostrog Monastery (Manastir Ostrog) is the most important site in Montenegro for Orthodox Christians. Even with its numerous pilgrims, tourists and trashy souvenir stands, it's a strangely affecting place.

The **Lower Monastery** (Donji manastir) is 2km below the main shrine. Stop here to admire the vivid frescos in the **Holy Trinity Church** (Crkva Sv Trojice; 1824). Behind it is a natural spring where you can fill your bottles with deliciously fresh water and potentially benefit from an internal blessing as you sup it. From here the faithful, some of them barefoot, plod up the steep road to the top. Nonpilgrims and the pure of heart may drive directly to the main car park and limit their penitance to just the final 200m.

The **Upper Monastery** (Gornji manastir; the really impressive one) is dubbed 'Sv Vasilije's miracle', because no one seems to understand how it was built. Constructed in 1665 within two large caves, it gives the impression that it has grown out of the very rock. Sv Vasilije (St Basil) brought his monks here after the Ottomans destroyed Tvrdoš Monastery near Trebinje. Pilgrims queue to enter the shrine where the saint's fabric-wrapped bones are kept. To enter you'll need to be wearing a long skirt or trousers (jeans are fine) and cover your shoulders. At the very top of the monastery is another cave-like chapel with faded frescos dating from 1667.

A **guesthouse** (☑020-811 133; dm €5) near the Lower Monastery offers tidy single-sex dorm rooms, while in summer sleeping mats are provided for free to pilgrims in front of the Upper Monastery.

NORTHERN MOUNTAINS

This really is the full Monte: soaring peaks, hidden monasteries, secluded villages, steep river canyons and a whole heap of 'wild beauty', to quote the tourist slogan. It's well worth hiring a car for a couple of days to get off the beaten track – some of the roads are truly spectacular.

Morača Canyon

Heading north from Podgorica, it doesn't take long before the scenery becomes breathtaking. The highway gets progressively more precarious as it follows the Morača River into a nearly perpendicular canyon, 300m to 400m deep. If you're driving, pull over into one of the viewing areas to enjoy it properly, as this is an extremely busy and unforgiving stretch of road.

Near the canyon's northern end is **Morača Monastery**. As you enter the walled compound it's like stepping back into the 13th century, when the monastery was founded. The larger of its two churches has faded external frescos by the celebrated master Đorđe Mitrofanović and a wealth of religious art inside.

Kolašin   Колашин
POP 2800

Kolašin is Montenegro's main mountain resort. Although the skiing's not as reliable as Durmitor, Kolašin's much easier to get to (it's just off the main highway, 71km north of Podgorica) and has better accommodation. Like most ski towns, it looks prettier under a blanket of snow but even in summer it's a handy base for exploring Biogradska Gora National Park and other parts of the Bjelasica Mountains. A beautiful drive leads through the mountains to Andrijevica and on to Gusinje at the base of Prokletije National Park.

Most things of interest, including the banks and post office, are set around the two central squares (Trg Borca and Trg Vukmana Kruščića) and the short street that connects them (ul IV Proleterske).

🏃 Activities

Kolašin 1450 Ski Resort   SKIING
(☑020-717 845; www.kolasin1450.com; half-day/ day/week ski pass €12/20/104) Located 10km east of Kolašin, at an elevation of 1450m, this ski centre offers 30km of runs (graded green, blue, red and black) reached by various ski lifts. You can hire a full ski or snowboard kit for €13 per day and there are shuttle buses from the Hotel Bianca; they're free if you're a hotel guest or if you purchase your ski pass from the hotel. The ski season lasts roughly from December to mid-April.

Hiking   HIKING
Three marked hiking paths start from Trg Borca and head into the Bjelasica mountains. From the ski centre there's a 16km, five-hour loop route through the forest to Mt Ključ (1973m) and back.

Explorer Tourist Agency   ADVENTURE TOURS
(☑020-864 200; www.montenegroexplorer.co.me; Mojkovačka bb) Located near the bus station, this agency specialises in action-packed holidays, including hiking, skiing, rafting, mountain biking, canyoning, caving, mountain climbing, jeep safaris, horse riding, paragliding and fishing expeditions. It also hires mountain bikes.

🛌 Sleeping & Eating

TOP CHOICE **Bianca Resort & Spa**   RESORT €€€
(☑020-863 000; www.biancaresort.com; Mirka Vešovića bb; s/d from €79/108; P ☎ 🅰) Take one

large angular hotel with quirky hexagonal windows, completely gut it and give it a designer rustic look, and you end up with an atmospheric, idiosyncratic and first-rate ski resort.

Brile HOTEL, RESTAURANT €€
(☑020-865 021; www.montenegrohotelsonline.com/eng/hotel/46/brile.html; Buda Tomovića 2; s/d €35/70; ☜) On the edge of the main square, this attractive family-run hotel has comfy rooms with polished wooden floors. There's a sauna for an après-ski defrost and a restaurant (mains €5 to €10) downstairs serving warming comfort food.

TOP **Konoba kod Rada**
CHOICE
Vlahovića MONTENEGRIN €€
(Trg Vukmana Kruščića; mains €6-8) Set on the square that was the heart of the old Turkish town, this rustic eatery is a standard-bearer for Montenegrin mountain cuisine, such as tender roast lamb which falls off the bone.

Vodenica MONTENEGRIN €€
(☑020-865 338; Dunje Dokić bb; mains €5-7) Set in a traditional watermill, Vodenica offers a taste of traditional stodgy mountain food designed to warm your belly on cold nights. Ease back and let your arteries clog.

Savardak MONTENEGRIN €€
(☑069-051 264; savardak@t-com.me; mains €8-9) Located 2.8km from Kolašin on the road to the ski centre, Savardak serves traditional food in what looks like a big haystack with a chimney attached. Four-person apartments (€40) are available in a thatch-roofed wooden chalet.

ⓘ Information

Bjelasica & Komovi Regional Tourism Organisation (☑020-865 110; www.bjelasica-komovi.com; Trg Borca 2; ☉9am-8pm Mon-Fri, 9am-noon & 4-8pm Sat & Sun)

Kolašin Tourist Office (☑020-864 254; www.kolasin.travel; Mirka Vešovića bb; ☉8am-8pm Mon-Fri, 9am-3pm Sat)

ⓘ Getting There & Away

BUS The **bus station** (☑020-864 033; Mojkovačka bb) is a shed set back from the road leading into town, about 200m from the centre. There are regular services to Podgorica (€5).

TRAIN Kolašin's train station is 1.5km from the centre. Trains head to Podgorica (€5, 90 minutes, five daily) and Bar (€5.48, 2½ hours, four daily). Buy your tickets onboard.

Biogradska Gora National Park Биоградска Гора

Nestled in the heart of the Bjelasica Mountain Range, this pretty national park has as its heart 16 sq km of virgin woodland – one of Europe's last primeval forests. The main entrance to the park is between Kolašin and Mojkovac on the Podgorica–Belgrade route. After paying a €2 entry fee you can drive the further 4km to the lake.

You can hire rowboats (per hour €8) and buy fishing permits (per day €20) from the **park office** (☑020-865 625; www.nparkovi.me; campsites per small tent/large tent/caravan €3/5/10, cabins €20; ☉7.30am-8.30pm) by the car park. Nearby there's a camping ground and a cluster of 12 windowless log cabins. The ablutions block for the cabins is much nicer than the campsite's basic squat toilets. **Restoran Biogradsko Jezero** (mains €5.70-9) has a terrace where you can steal glimpses of the lake through the trees as you tuck into a traditional lamb or veal dish.

The nearest bus stop is an hour's walk away, at Kraljevo Kolo, and the nearest train station is a 90-minute walk, at Štitarička Rijeka.

Durmitor National Park Дурмитор

Magnificent scenery ratchets up to the stupendous in this national park (€2 entry fee per day), where ice and water have carved a dramatic landscape from the limestone. Eighteen glacial lakes known as *gorske oči* (mountain eyes) dot the Durmitor range, with the largest, **Black Lake** (Crno jezero), a pleasant 3km walk from Žabljak. The rounded mass of **Međed** (The Bear; 2287m) rears up behind the lake flanked by others of the park's 48 peaks over 2000m, including the highest, **Bobotov Kuk** (2523m). From late December to March, Durmitor is Montenegro's main ski resort; in summer it's a popular place for hiking, rafting and other active pursuits.

Žabljak, at the eastern edge of the range, is the park's principal gateway and the only town within its boundaries. It's not very big and neither is it attractive, but it has a supermarket, post office, bank, hotels and restaurants, all gathered around the parking lot that masquerades as the main square.

🏃 Activities

Rafting

Slicing through the mountains at the northern edge of the national park like they were made from the local soft cheese, the Tara River forms a canyon that at its peak is 1300m deep. The best views are from the water, which explains why rafting along the river is one of the country's most popular tourist activities.

There are a few rapids but don't expect an adrenaline-fuelled white-water experience. You'll get the most excitement in April and May, when the last of the melting snow revs up the flow. Various operators run trips between April and October.

The 82km section that is raftable starts from Splavište, south of the Tara Bridge, and ends at Šćepan Polje on the Bosnian border. The classic two-day trip heads through the deepest part of the canyon on the first day, stopping overnight at Radovan Luka. **Summit Travel Agency** (☑052-360 082; www.summit.co.me; Njegoševa 12, Žabljak) offers trips, including transfers from Žabljak (half-/one-/two-day tour €50/110/200).

Most of the day tours from the coast traverse only the last 18km from Brstanovica – this is outside the national park and hence avoids hefty fees. You'll miss out on the canyon's depths but it's still a beautiful stretch, including most of the rapids. The buses follow a spectacular road along the Piva River, giving you a double dose of canyon action.

If you've got your own wheels you can save a few bucks and avoid a lengthy coach tour by heading directly to Šćepan Polje. It's important to use a reputable operator; in 2010, two people died in one day on a trip with inexperienced guides. At a minimum, make sure you're given a helmet and lifejacket – wear them and do them up.

One good operator is **Kamp Grab** (☑040-200 598; www.tara-grab.com; half-day incl lunch €44, 2-day all-inclusive €180), with lodgings blissfully located 8km upstream from Šćepan Polje. To get there, you'll need to cross the Montenegrin side of the border crossing and hang a right (tell the guards you're heading to Grab); the last 3.5km is unsealed. Accommodation is available, and Grab also offers guided riverboarding (hydrospeed), where you direct yourself down the river on what looks like a kick board (€35).

Tara Tour (☑069-086 106; www.tara-tour.com) offers an excellent half-day trip (€40, including two meals) and has a cute set of wooden chalets in Šćepan Polje; accommodation, three meals and a half-day's rafting costs €55.

Hiking

Durmitor has dozens of hiking trails, some of which traverse seriously high-altitude paths which are prone to fog and summer thunderstorms. Ask the staff at the visitors centre about tracks that suit your level of experience and fitness.

Skiing

On the slopes of Savin Kuk (2313m), you'll find Durmitor's main ski centre. Its 3.5km run starts from a height of 2010m and is best suited to advanced skiers. On the outskirts of Žabljak, near the bus station, **Javorovača Ski Centar** (☑067-800 971) has a gentle 300m slope that's good for kids and beginners. One of the big attractions for skiing in Durmitor is the cost: day passes are around €15, weekly passes €70, and ski lessons cost between €10 and €20.

🛏 Sleeping & Eating

TOP CHOICE Eko-Oaza Suza

Evrope CABINS, CAMPGROUND €
(☑069-444 590; ekooazatara@gmail.com; Dobrilovina; campsites per tent/person/campervan €5/1/10, cabins €50; ☺Apr-Oct) Consisting of four comfortable wooden cottages (each sleeping five people) and a fine stretch of lawn, this magical family-run 'eco oasis' offers a genuine experience of Montenegrin hospitality. Home-cooked meals are provided on request.

Hotel Soa HOTEL €€
(☑052-360 110; www.hotelsoa.com; Njegoševa bb, Žabljak; s €55-82, d €75-110, ste €130-160; 🛜) Rooms are kitted out with monsoon shower heads, Etro toiletries, robes and slippers, and downstairs there's an appealing terrace restaurant. Best of all, the staff are genuinely friendly and the prices reasonable.

Zlatni Papagaj PIZZERIA, CAFE €
(Vuka Karadžića 5, Žabljak; mains €4-13; 🛜) The 'Golden Parrot' has the feel of a pirate lair, with wine-barrel tables and a thick fug of cigarette smoke in the air. The menu offers a crowd-pleasing selection of pizza and steaks.

ℹ Information

Durmitor National Park Visitor Centre (www.nparkovi.co.me; Jovana Cvijića bb; ☺9am-5pm Mon-Fri)

PIVA CANYON

The highway to Šćepan Polje is a beautiful drive and quite a feat of engineering. It clings to the cliffs of the Piva Canyon and passes through 56 small tunnels carved out of the stone. The Piva River was blocked in 1975 by the building of a 220m-high hydroelectric dam at Plužine, flooding part of the canyon to create Lake Piva, which reaches depths of over 180m.

Great care was taken to move the **Piva Monastery** (Manastir Piva) to higher ground – a feat that took 12 years to complete. This Serbian Orthodox monastery has the distinction of being the only one to be built during the Turkish occupation.

Accommodation is available at the rafting camps around Šćepan Polje and in various *eko sela* (eco villages), scattered around Plužine and the back road to Žabljak. One excellent option is **Eko Selo Meadows** (069-718 078; www.meadows-eco.com; Donja Brezna bb; s/d/tr/q €20/30/42/50, mains €6-10; P), signposted from the highway, 17.5km south of Piva Monastery. Set on a flat plain edged by hills, the complex consists of a large restaurant serving local specialities and a collection of tidy wooden cabins.

ℹ Getting There & Away

All of the approaches to Durmitor are spectacular. If you're coming from the coast, the quickest route is through Nikšić and Šavnik. There's a wonderful back road through the mountains leaving the highway near Plužine, but it's impassable as soon as the snows fall.

The bus station is at the southern edge of Žabljak, on the Šavnik road. Three buses head to Podgorica daily (€9.50).

UNDERSTAND MONTENEGRO

Montenegro Today

Going it alone was a brave move for a nation of this size but toughing it out is something this gutsy people have had plenty of experience in. Their national identity is built around resisting the Ottoman Empire for hundreds of years in a mountainous enclave much smaller than the nation's current borders.

The Never-Changing Government

In the 2012 general election, the Democratic Party of Socialists (DPS) fell two seats short of ruling in their own right but quickly formed a coalition with ethnic Bosniak, Albanian and Croat parties to form a government (ethnicity still plays a large role in political affiliation here). What's extraordinary about this is that the DPS has won every single vote since multiparty elections were established, marking the end of Communism in Yugoslavia.

Part of the party's continued popularity is the role they played in gaining Montenegro its independence. Several of the main opposition parties, especially the Serb-aligned parties, were strongly opposed to the break with Serbia, although most have publicly dropped their anti-independence stance.

The Đukanović Factor

Another factor in the DPS's success is the charismatic figure of returning Prime Minister Milo Đukanović. As a tall (198cm), handsome 26-year-old he was part of the 'antibureaucratic revolution' that took control of the Communist Party in 1989. At the age of 29 he became the first prime minister of post-Communist Montenegro and apart from a few years of 'retirement' he has been prime minister or president ever since.

However, Đukanović remains a controversial figure. While still president he was investigated by an Italian antimafia unit and charged for his alleged role in a multibillion-dollar cigarette-smuggling operation; the charges were dropped in 2009.

NATO and the EU

Shortly after independence, Montenegro applied to join both NATO and EU, and in June 2012 it opened formal EU accession negotiations. While most Montenegrins strongly favour EU membership, joining NATO is much more contentious. Memories of the NATO bombing of Serbia during the Kosovo conflict are still fresh. However, the

Montenegrin goverment has stood firm in its resolve, publicly stating that it expects to be invited to join the alliance in 2014.

History

Like all the modern states of the Balkan peninsula, Montenegro has a long, convoluted and eventful history. History is worn on the sleeve here and people discuss 600-year-old events (or their not-always-accurate versions of them) as if they happened yesterday. Events such as the split of the Roman Empire, the subsequent split in Christianity between Catholic and Orthodox, and the battles with the Ottoman Turks still have a direct bearing on the politics of today.

Before the Slavs

The Illyrians were the first known people to inhabit the region. By 1000 BC they had established a loose federation of tribes across much of the Balkans. By around 400 BC the Greeks had established some coastal colonies and by AD 10 the Romans had absorbed the entire region into their empire. In 395 the Roman Empire was split into two halves: the western half centred on Rome and the eastern half, which eventually became the Byzantine Empire, centred on Constantinople. Modern Montenegro lay on the fault line between the two entities.

In the early 7th century, the Slavs arrived from north of the Danube. Two main Slavic groups settled in the Balkans: the Croats along the Adriatic coast and the Serbs in the interior. With time most Serbs accepted the Orthodox faith, while the Croats accepted Catholicism.

First Serbian States

In the 9th century the first Serb kingdom, Raška, arose near Novi Pazar (in modern Serbia) followed shortly by another Serb state, Duklja, which sprang up on the site of present-day Podgorica. Raška eventually became known as Serbia and Duklja as Zeta. From the 12th century, Raška/Serbia became dominant over Zeta, which nonetheless remained a distinct area. At its greatest extent Serbia reached from the Adriatic to the Aegean and north to the Danube.

Expansion was halted in 1389 at the battle of Kosovo Polje, where the Serbs were defeated by the Ottoman Turks. By 1441 the Turks had rolled through Serbia and in the late 1470s they took on Zeta. The remnants of the Zetan nobility fled first to Žabljak Crnojevića, near Lake Skadar, and eventually into the mountains. In 1480 they established a stronghold at Cetinje on Mt Lovćen.

Montenegro & the Ottomans

This mountainous area became the last redoubt of Serbian Orthodox culture when all else fell to the Ottomans. It was during this time that the Venetians, who ruled Kotor, Budva and much of the Adriatic Coast, began calling Mt Lovćen the Monte Negro (Black Mountain). The Montenegrins, as they became known, built a reputation as fearsome warriors. The Ottomans opted for pragmatism, and largely left them to their own devices.

With the struggle against the Ottomans, the highly independent Montenegrin clans began to work collaboratively and the *vladika*, previously a metropolitan position within the Orthodox Church, began mediating between tribal chiefs. As such, the *vladika* assumed a political role, and *vladika* became a hereditary title: the prince-bishop.

In the late 18th century the Montenegrins under *vladika* Petar I Petrović began to expand their territory, doubling it within the space of a little over 50 years. Serbia achieved independence in 1835 and a similar rebellion against Ottoman control broke out in Bosnia in 1875. Montenegrins joined the insurgency and made significant territorial gains as a result. At the Congress of Berlin in 1878, Montenegro and Bosnia officially achieved independence.

In the early years of the 20th century there were increasing calls for union with Serbia and rising political opposition to Montenegro's autocratic Petrović dynasty. The Serbian king Petar Karadjordjević was suspected of involvement in an attempt to overthrow King Nikola Petrović, and Montenegrin–Serbian relations reached their historic low point.

The Balkan Wars of 1912–13 saw the Montenegrins joining the Serbs, Greeks and Bulgarians, and succeeding in throwing the Ottomans out of southeastern Europe. Now that Serbia and Montenegro were both independent and finally shared a border, the idea of a Serbian–Montenegrin union gained more currency. King Nikola pragmatically supported the idea on the stipulation that both the Serbian and Montenegrin royal houses be retained.

The Two Yugoslavias

Before the union could be realised WWI intervened. Serbia quickly entered the war and Montenegro followed in its footsteps. Austria-Hungary invaded Serbia shortly afterwards and swiftly captured Cetinje, with King Nikola escaping to France. In 1918 the Serbian army reclaimed Montenegro, and the French, keen to implement the Serbian–Montenegrin union, refused to allow Nikola to leave France. The following year Montenegro was incorporated in the Kingdom of the Serbs, Croats and Slovenes, the first Yugoslavia.

During WWII the Italians occupied Montenegro. Tito's Partisans and the Serbian Chetniks engaged the Italians, sometimes lapsing into fighting each other. Ultimately, the Partisans put up the best fight and with the support of the Allies, the Partisans entered Belgrade in October 1944 and Tito was made prime minister. Once the communist federation of Yugoslavia was established, Tito decreed that Montenegro have full republic status and the border of the modern Montenegrin state was set. Of all the Yugoslav states, Montenegro had the highest per-capita membership of the Communist Party and it was highly represented in the armed forces.

Union then Independence

In the decades following Tito's death in 1980, Slobodan Milošević used the issue of Kosovo to whip up a nationalist storm in Serbia and rode to power on a wave of nationalism. The Montenegrins largely supported their Orthodox coreligionists. In 1991 Montenegrin paramilitary groups were responsible for the shelling of Dubrovnik. In 1992, by which point Slovenia, Croatia and Bosnia and Hercegovina (BiH) had opted for independence, the Montenegrins voted overwhelmingly in support of a plebiscite to remain in Yugoslavia with Serbia.

In 1997 Montenegrin leader Milo Djukanović broke with an increasingly isolated Milošević and immediately became the darling of the West. As the Serbian regime became an international pariah, the Montenegrins increasingly wanted to re-establish their distinct identity.

In 2003 Yugoslavia was consigned to the dustbin of history, and Montenegro entered into a state union with Serbia. In theory this union was based on equality between the two republics; however, in practice Serbia was such a dominant partner that the union

proved infeasible. In May 2006 the Montenegrins voted for independence.

People

In the last census (2011), 45% of the population identified as Montenegrin, 29% as Serb, 12% as Bosniak or Muslim, 5% as Albanian, 1% as Croat and 1% as Roma. Montenegrins are the majority along most of the coast and the centre of the country, while Albanians dominate in Ulcinj, Bosniaks in the far east (Rožaje and Plav), and Serbs in the north and Herceg Novi. Religion and ethnicity broadly go together in these parts. Over 72% of the population are Orthodox Christians (mainly Montenegrins and Serbs), 19% Muslim (mainly Bosniaks and Albanians) and 3% Roman Catholic (mainly Albanians and Croats).

Montenegrins traditionally considered themselves 'the best of the Serbs', and while most Montenegrins still feel a strong kinship to their closest siblings, this is coupled with a determination to maintain their distinct identity. After negotiating a reasonably amicable divorce from the unhappy state union in 2006, relations between the two countries took a turn for the worse. In 2008 Serbia expelled Montenegro's ambassador after Montenegro officially recognised the Serbian province of Kosovo as an independent country. Diplomatic relations have since resumed, but issues of ethnicity and identity remain thorny.

Food & Drink

Loosen your belt; you're in for a treat. Eating in Montenegro is generally an extremely pleasurable experience. By default, most of the food is local, fresh and organic, and hence very seasonal. The food on the coast is virtually indistinguishable from Dalmatian cuisine: lots of grilled seafood, garlic, olive oil and Italian dishes. Inland it's much more meaty and Serbian-influenced. The village of Njeguši in the Montenegrin heartland is famous for its *pršut* (dried ham) and cheese. Anything with Njeguški in its name is going to be a true Montenegrin dish and stuffed with these goodies.

Eating in Montenegro can be a trial for vegetarians and almost impossible for vegans. Pasta, pizza and salad are the best fallback options. Nonsmoking sections are a rumour from distant lands that have yet to trouble the citizens of Montenegro.

SURVIVAL GUIDE

Directory A–Z

Accommodation

Hotels and private accommodation (rooms and apartments for rent) form the bulk of the sleeping options, although hostels have been popping up in the more touristy areas in recent years. Camping grounds operate in summer and some of the mountainous areas have cabin accommodation in 'eco villages' or mountain huts.

In the peak summer season, some places require minimum stays (three days to a week). Many establishments on the coast, even some of the established hotels, close during winter.

An additional tourist tax (usually less than €1 per night) is added to the rate for all accommodation types. For private accommodation it's sometimes left up to the guest to pay it, but it can be nigh on impossible finding the right authority to pay it to (the procedure varies from area to area). Theoretically you could be asked to provide white accommodation receipt cards (or copies of invoices from hotels) when you leave the country, but in practice this is rarely required.

The following price categories for the cost of a room for a couple in the shoulder season (roughly June and September) are used in the listings in this chapter.

€ less than €20

€€ €30 to €90

€€€ more than €90

Business Hours

Business hours in Montenegro are a relative concept. Even if hours are posted on the doors of museums or shops, they may not be heeded.

Banks Usually 8am to 5pm Monday to Friday, 8am to noon Saturday

Cafes 10am to midnight (later in high season in busy areas)

Pubs 9pm to 2am

Restaurants 8am to midnight

Shops 8am to 7pm Monday to Friday, to 2pm Saturday; often closed in late afternoon

Supermarkets 8am to 8pm Monday to Friday, to 6pm Saturday, to 1pm Sunday

Embassies & Consulates

The following are all in Podgorica, unless otherwise stated. For a full list, see www.mip.gov.me.

Albanian Embassy (☏020-667 380; www.mfa.gov.al; Stanka Dragojevića 14)

Bosnia & Hercegovina Embassy (☏020-618 105; www.mvp.gov.ba; Atinska 58)

Croatian Embassy (☏020-269 760; Vladimira Ćetkovića 2)

Croatian Consulate (☏032-323 127; Trg od Oružja bb, Kotor)

French Embassy (☏020-655 348; Atinska 35)

German Embassy (☏020-441 000; www.auswaertiges-amt.de; Hercegovačka 10)

Serbian Embassy (☏020-667 305; www.podgorica.mfa.gov.rs; Hercegovačka 18)

Serbian Consulate (☏031-350 320; www.hercegnovi.mfa.gov.rs; Njegoševa 40, Herceg Novi)

UK Embassy (☏020-618 010; www.ukinmontenegro.fco.gov.uk; Ulcinjska 8)

US Embassy (☏020-410 500; http://podgorica.usembassy.gov; Ljubljanska bb)

Food

The following price categories for the cost of a main course are used in the listings in this chapter.

€ less than €5

€€ €5 to €10

€€€ more than €10

Gay & Lesbian Travellers

Although homosexuality was decriminalised in 1977 and discrimination outlawed in 2010, attitudes to homosexuality remain hostile and life for gay people is extremely difficult. Many gay men resort to online connections (try www.gayromeo.com) or take their chances at a handful of cruisy beaches. Lesbians will find it even harder to access the local community.

Money

» Montenegro uses the euro (€). You'll find banks with ATMs in all the main towns, most of which accept Visa, MasterCard, Maestro and Cirrus. Don't rely on restaurants, shops or smaller hotels accepting credit cards.

» Tipping isn't expected, although it's common to round up to the nearest euro.

Public Holidays

New Year's Day 1 and 2 January

Orthodox Christmas 6, 7 and 8 January

Orthodox Good Friday & Easter Monday Usually April/May

Labour Day 1 May

Independence Day 21 May

Statehood Day 13 July

Telephone

» The international access prefix is ⌒00 or ⌒+ from a mobile.

» Mobile numbers start with ⌒06.

» Local SIM cards are easy to find. The main providers are T-Mobile, Telenor and M:tel.

Women Travellers

Other than a cursory interest shown by men towards solo women travellers, travelling is hassle-free and easy. In Muslim areas some women wear a headscarf but most don't.

Getting There & Away

Air

Montenegro has two international airports – **Tivat** (TIV; ⌒032-670 930; www.montenegroairports.com) and **Podgorica** (TGD; ⌒020-444 244; www.montenegroairports.com) – although many visitors use Croatia's Dubrovnik Airport, which is very near the border. While various airlines run summer charter flights, the following airlines have regular scheduled flights to/from Montenegro.

Adria Airlines (www.adria.si) Ljubljana to Podgorica.

Austrian Airlines (www.austrian.com) Vienna to Podgorica.

Croatia Airlines (www.croatiaairlines.com) Zagreb to Podgorica.

Jat Airways (www.jat.com) Belgrade to Podgorica and Tivat.

Montenegro Airlines (www.montenegroairlines.com) Tivat to Belgrade and Moscow. Podgorica to Belgrade, Frankfurt, Ljubljana, Moscow, Niš, Paris, Rome, Vienna and Zurich.

Moskovia Airlines (www.ak3r.ru) Moscow to Tivat.

Rossiya Airlines (FV; www.rossiya-airlines.ru) St Petersburg to Tivat.

S7 Airlines (S7; www.s7.ru) Moscow to Tivat.

Turkish Airlines (www.turkishairlines.com) Istanbul to Podgorica.

Land
BORDER CROSSINGS

Albania The main crossings link Shkodra to Ulcinj (Sukobin) and to Podgorica (Hani i Hotit).

BiH The main checkpoints are at Dolovi and Šćepan Polje.

Croatia There's a busy checkpoint on the Adriatic highway between Herceg Novi and Dubrovnik; expect delays in summer.

Kosovo The only crossing is Kulina, between Rožaje and Peć.

Serbia The busiest crossing is Dobrakovo (north of Bijelo Polje), followed by Dračenovac (northeast of Rožaje) and Ranče (east of Pljevlja).

BUS

There's a well-developed bus network linking Montenegro with the major cities of the region.

Belgrade (Serbia) To Podgorica (€27, frequent), Budva (€26, 15 daily), Ulcinj (€33, four daily), Kotor (€32, seven daily) and Herceg Novi (€33, seven daily).

Dubrovnik (Croatia) To Herceg Novi (€10, two daily), Kotor (€14, two daily), Petrovac (€18, daily) and Podgorica (€19, daily).

Priština (Kosovo) To Podgorica (€17, daily) and Ulcinj (€18, six daily).

Sarajevo (BiH) To Podgorica (€19, six daily), Budva (€22, four daily), Herceg Novi (€24, two daily) and Ulcinj (€26, daily).

Shkodra (Albania) To Ulcinj (€6, two daily).

Trebinje (BiH) To Nikšić (€6.50, three daily).

CAR & MOTORCYCLE

Drivers are recommended to carry an International Driving Permit (IDP) as well as their home country's driving licence. Vehicles need Green Card insurance or insurance must be bought at the border.

TRAIN

At least two trains head between Bar and Belgrade daily (€21, 11 hours), with one continuing on to Novi Sad and Subotica.

Sea

Montenegro Lines (☑030-303 469; www.montenegrolines.net) has boats to Bar from the Italian ports of Bari and Ancona.

Getting Around

Bicycle

Cyclists are a rare species, even in the cities. Don't expect drivers to be considerate. Wherever possible, try to get off the main roads.

Bus

The local bus network is extensive and reliable. Buses are usually comfortable and air-conditioned, and are rarely full. It's slightly cheaper to buy your ticket on the bus rather than at the station, but a station-bought ticket theoretically guarantees you a seat. Luggage carried below the bus is charged at €1 per piece.

Car & Motorcycle

Independent travel by car or motorcycle is an ideal way to gad about and discover the country; some of the drives are breathtakingly beautiful. Traffic police are everywhere, so stick to speed limits and carry an IDP. Allow more time than you'd expect for the distances involved, as the terrain will slow you down.

The major international car-hire companies have a presence in various centres. **Meridian Rentacar** (☑020-234 944; www.meridian-rentacar.com), which has offices in Budva, Bar, Podgorica and the airports, is a reliable local option; one-day hire starts from €30.

Train

Montenegro Railways (Željeznica Crne Gore; www.zpcg.me) runs the passenger train service, heading north from Bar. The trains are old and can be hot in summer but they're priced accordingly and the route through the mountains is spectacular. Useful stops include Virpazar, Podgorica and Kolašin.

Portugal

Includes »

Lisbon	566
Sintra	581
Faro	585
Lagos	586
Sagres	588
Évora	588
Monsaraz	590
Estremoz	590
Peniche	591
Nazaré	592
Serra da Estrela	595
Porto	595
Braga	602

Best Places to Eat

» The Decadente (p576)
» Bistro 'oPorto' (p586)
» A Forja (p586)
» Botequim da Mouraria (p589)
» DOP (p599)

Best Places to Stay

» Lisbon Story Guesthouse (p571)
» Albergaria Calvario (p589)
» Casa das Marés (p591)
» Casa das Obras (p595)
» Guest House Douro (p598)

Why Go?

With medieval castles, frozen-in-time villages, captivating cities and golden-sand beaches, the Portuguese experience can mean many things. History, great food and wine, idyllic scenery and blazing nightlife are just the beginning...

Portugal's capital, Lisbon, and its northern rival, Porto, are gems among the urban streetscapes of Europe. Both are magical places for the wanderer, with picturesque views over the river, rattling trams and atmospheric lanes that hide boutiques and old-school record shops, stylish lounges and a vibrant mix of restaurants, fado clubs and open-air cafes.

Outside the cities, Portugal's landscape unfolds in all its variegated beauty. Here you can stay overnight in converted hilltop fortresses fronting age-old vineyards, hike amid granite peaks or explore historic villages of the little-visited hinterland. More than 800km of coast offers more outdoor enticements. You can gaze out over dramatic end-of-the-world cliffs, surf stellar breaks off dune-covered beaches or laze peacefully on sandy islands fronting calm blue seas.

When to Go

Lisbon

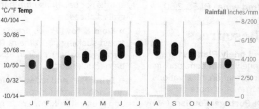

Apr & May Sunny days and wild-flowers set the stage for hiking and outdoor activities.

Jun–Aug Lovely and lively, with a packed festival calendar and steamy beach days.

Late Sep & Oct Crisp mornings and sunny days; prices dip, crowds disperse.

AT A GLANCE

» **Currency** euro (€)

» **Language** Portuguese

» **Money** ATMs widespread; banks open Mon-Fri

» **Visas** Schengen rules apply

Fast Facts

» **Area** 91,470 sq km

» **Capital** Lisbon

» **Country code** ☑351

» **Emergency** ☑112

Exchange Rates

Australia	A$1	€0.82
Canada	C$1	€0.77
Japan	¥100	€0.83
New Zealand	NZ$1	€0.65
UK	UK£1	€1.18
USA	US$1	€0.78

Set Your Budget

» **Budget hotel room** €40

» **Two-course meal** €10–18

» **Museum entrance** €4–6

» **Glass of vinho tinto (red wine)** €1.50-2.50

Resources

» **Lonely Planet** (www.lonelyplanet.com/portugal) Information, reservations, forum and more

» **Portugal Tourism** (www.visitportugal.com) Official tourism site

Connections

Travelling overland from Portugal entails a trip through Spain. Good places to cross the (invisible) border include ferry crossing from Vila Real de Santo António in The Algarve, with onward connections to Seville. There are also links from Elvas (going across to Badajoz) and rail links from Valença do Minho in the north (heading up to Santiago de Compostela in Galicia).

ITINERARIES

One Week

Devote three days to Lisbon, including a night of fado in the Alfama, bar-hopping in Bairro Alto and Unesco-gazing and pastry-eating in Belém. Spend a day taking in the wooded wonderland of Sintra, before continuing to Coimbra, Portugal's own Cambridge. End your week in Porto, gateway to the magical wine-growing region of the Douro Valley.

Two Weeks

On week two, stroll the historic lanes of Évora and visit the nearby megaliths. Take in the picturesque castle towns of Monsaraz and Estremoz before hitting the beaches of the Algarve. Travel along the coast, visiting the pretty riverfront town of Tavira and the dramatic cliffs of Sagres. End the grand tour back in sunny Lisbon.

Essential Food & Drink

» **Seafood** Char-grilled *lulas* (squid), *polvo* (octopus) or *sardinhas* (sardines). Other treats: *cataplana* (seafood and sausage cooked in a copper pot), *caldeirada* (hearty fish stew) and *açorda de mariscos* (bread stew with shrimp).

» **Cod for all seasons** Portuguese have dozens of ways to prepare *bacalhau* (salted cod). Try *bacalhau a brás* (grated cod fried with potatoes and eggs), *bacalhau espiritual* (cod soufflé) or *bacalhau com natas* (baked cod with cream and grated cheese).

» **Field & fowl** *Porco preto* (sweet 'black' pork), *leitão* (roast suckling pig), *alheira* (bread and meat sausage – formerly Kosher), *cabrito assado* (roast kid) and *arroz de pato* (duck risotto).

» **Drink** Port and red wines from the Douro valley, *alvarinho* and *vinho verde* (crisp, semi-sparkling wine) from the Minho and great, little-known reds from the Alentejo and the Beiras (particularly the Dão region).

» **Pastries** The *pastel de nata* (custard tart) is legendary, especially in Belém. Other delicacies: *travesseiros* (almond and egg pastries) and *queijadas* (mini-cheese pastries).

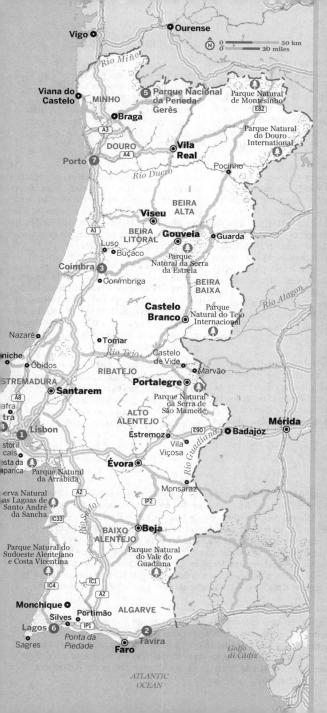

Portugal Highlights

1 Follow the sound of fado spilling from the lamplit lanes of the **Alfama** (p566), an enchanting old-world neighbourhood in the heart of Lisbon

2 Take in the laid-back charms of **Tavira** (p585), before hitting some of The Algarve's prettiest beaches

3 Catch live music in a backstreet bar in **Coimbra** (p593), a festive university town with a stunning medieval centre

4 Explore the wooded hills of **Sintra** (p581), studded with fairy-tale-like palaces, villas and gardens

5 Conquer the trails of the ruggedly scenic **Parque Nacional da Peneda-Gerês** (p603)

6 Enjoy heady beach days in **Lagos** (p586), a surf-loving town with a vibrant drinking and dining scene

7 Explore the Unesco World Heritage–listed centre of **Porto** (p595), sampling velvety ports at riverside wine lodges

LISBON

POP 550,000

Spread across steep hillsides overlooking the Rio Tejo, Lisbon has captivated visitors for centuries. Windswept vistas at breathtaking heights reveal the city in all its beauty: Roman and Moorish ruins, white-domed cathedrals and grand plazas lined with sun-drenched cafes. The real delight of discovery, though, is delving into the narrow cobblestone lanes.

As bright-yellow trams clatter through curvy tree-lined streets, Lisboetas (residents of Lisbon) stroll through lamplit old quarters, much as they've done for centuries. Village-life gossip is exchanged over fresh bread and wine at tiny patio restaurants as fado singers perform in the background. In other parts of town, Lisbon reveals her youthful alter ego at stylish dining rooms and lounges, late-night street parties, riverside nightspots and boutiques selling all things, classic and cutting-edge.

Just outside Lisbon, there's more to explore: enchanting woodlands, gorgeous beaches and seaside villages – all ripe for discovery.

⊙ Sights

At the riverfront is the grand Praça do Comércio. Behind it march the pedestrian-filled streets of Baixa (lower) district, up to Praça da Figueira and Praça Dom Pedro IV (aka Rossio). From Baixa, it's a steep climb west, through swanky shopping district Chiado, into the narrow streets of nightlife haven Bairro Alto. Eastward from Baixa it's another climb to Castelo de São Jorge and the labyrinthine Alfama below it. The Unesco World Heritage sites of Belém lie further west along the river, an easy tram-ride from Praça do Comércio.

BAIXA & ALFAMA

Alfama is Lisbon's Moorish time capsule: a medina-like district of tangled alleys, hidden palm-shaded squares and narrow terracotta-roofed houses that tumble down to the glittering Tejo. The terrace at **Largo das Portas do Sol** provides a splendid view over the neighbourhood.

Elevador de Santa Justa ELEVATOR
(Map p572; cnr Rua de Santa Justa & Largo do Carmo; admission €5; ⊙7am-10pm) Lisbon's only vertical street lift, this lanky neo-Gothic marvel provides sweeping views over the city's skyline. From the top, it's a short stroll to the fasci-

PORTUGAL LISBON

LISBOA CARD

If you're planning on doing a lot of sightseeing, you might consider this discount card. It offers free or discounted entry to key museums and attractions, plus unlimited use of public transport. The 24-/48-/72hr versions cost €19/32/39; it's available at tourist offices.

LISBON IN...

Two Days

Take a roller-coaster ride on tram 28, hopping off to scale the ramparts of **Castelo de São Jorge**. Sample Portugal's finest at **Wine Bar do Castelo**, then stroll the picturesque lanes of **Alfama**, pausing for a pick-me-up in arty **Pois Café**. Glimpse the fortress-like **Sé** cathedral en route to shopping in pedestrianised **Baixa**. By night, return to lantern-lit Alfama for first-rate fado at **Mesa de Frades**.

On day two, breakfast on cinnamon-dusted pastries in **Belém**, then explore the fantastical Manueline cloisters of **Mosteiro dos Jerónimos**. River-gaze from the **Torre de Belém** and see cutting-edge art at the **Museu Colecção Berardo**. Head back for sundowners and magical views at **Noobai Café**, dinner at **100 Maneiras** and bar crawling in **Bairro Alto**.

Four Days

Go window-shopping and cafe-hopping in well-heeled **Chiado**, then head to futuristic **Parque das Nações** for riverfront gardens and the head-spinning **Oceanário**. That night, dine at **Mezzaluna** or **The Decadente** then go dancing in clubbing temple **Lux**.

On day four, catch the train to **Sintra**, for walks through boulder-speckled woodlands to fairy-tale palaces. Back in **Rossio**, toast your trip with cherry liqueur at **A Ginjinha** and alfresco dining at **Chapitô**.

HEAVENLY VIEWS

Lisbon's *miradouros* (viewpoints) provide memorable settings to take in the panorama. Some have outdoor cafes attached.

Largo das Portas do Sol (Map p572) With a stylish bar and cafe.

Miradouro da Graça (Map p568; ⊙10:30am-3am) A pine-fringed square that's perfect for sundowners.

Miradouro da Senhora do Monte (Map p568) The highest lookout, with memorable castle views.

Miradouro de São Pedro de Alcântara (Map p572; Rua São Pedro de Alcântara; underground rail Restauradores) Drinks and sweeping views on the edge of Bairro Alto.

Miradouro de Santa Catarina (Map p568; Rua de Santa Catarina; ⊙24hr; 🚋Elevador da Bica) Youthful spot with guitar-playing rebels, artful graffiti and a first-rate eating/drinking spot (Noobai Café) attached.

nating ruins of **Convento do Carmo**, mostly destroyed in an earthquake in 1755 (and today housing an archaeological museum).

Castelo de São Jorge   CASTLE, RUINS
(Map p572; admission €7.50; ⊙9am-9pm) Dating from Visigothic times, St George's Castle sits high above town with stunning views of the city and river. Inside the Ulysses Tower, a **camera obscura** offers a unique 360-degree angle on Lisbon, with demos every half-hour. If you'd rather not walk, take scenic tram 28 from Largo Martim Moniz.

Museu do Fado   MUSEUM
(Map p568; www.museudofado.pt; Largo do Chafariz de Dentro; admission €5; ⊙10am-6pm Tue-Sun) This engaging museum provides vibrant audiovisual coverage of the history of fado from its working-class roots to international stardom.

BELÉM

This quarter, 6km west of Rossio, reflects Portugal's golden age and is home to several iconic sights. In addition to heritage architecture, Belém spreads some of the country's best *pastéis de nata* (custard tarts).

To reach Belém, hop aboard tram 15 from Praça da Figueira or Praça do Comércio.

Mosteiro dos Jerónimos   MONASTERY
(Praça do Império; admission €7; ⊙10am-6pm Tue-Sun) Dating from 1496, this Unesco World Heritage site is one of Lisbon's icons, and is a soaring extravaganza of Manueline architecture with stunning carvings and ceramic tiles.

FREE **Museu Colecção Berardo**   MUSEUM
(www.museuberardo.pt; Praça do Império; admission free; ⊙10am-7pm) Houses an impressive collec-

tion of abstract, surrealist and pop art, along with some of the city's best temporary exhibits. There's also a great indoor-outdoor cafe.

Torre de Belém   TOWER
(admission €5; ⊙10am-6pm Tue-Sun) Another of Belém's Unesco World Heritage–listed wonders, the Tower of Belém symbolises the voyages that made Portugal powerful. Brave the cramped winding staircase to the turret for fantastic river views.

SALDANHA

Museu Calouste Gulbenkian   MUSEUM
(Map p568; Avenida de Berna 45; admission €4; ⊙10am-6pm Tue-Sun) This celebrated museum showcases an epic collection of Eastern and Western art: Egyptian mummy masks, Mesopotamian urns, Qing porcelain and paintings by Rembrandt, Renoir and Monet.

Centro de Arte Moderna   MUSEUM
(Modern Art Centre; Map p568; Rua Dr Nicaulau de Bettencourt; admission €5; ⊙10am-6pm Tue-Sun) In a sculpture-dotted garden alongside Museu Calouste Gulbenkian, the modern art museum contains a stellar collection of 20th-century Portuguese art.

SANTA APOLÓNIA & LAPA

The museums listed here are west and east of the city centre, but are well worth visiting.

Museu Nacional do Azulejo   MUSEUM
(Map p568; Rua Madre de Deus 4; admission €5; ⊙10am-6pm Tue-Sun) Languishing in a sumptuous 17th-century convent, this museum showcases Portugal's artful *azulejos* (ceramic tiles), as well as a fascinating 36m-long panel depicting pre-earthquake Lisbon.

Greater Lisbon

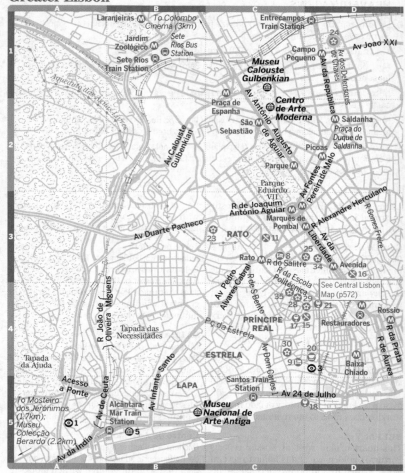

Museu Nacional de Arte Antiga MUSEUM
(Ancient Art Museum; Map p568; Rua das Janelas Verdes; admission €5; ⊙10am-6pm Tue-Sun) Set in a lemon-fronted, 17th-century palace, this museum presents a star-studded collection of European and Asian paintings and decorative arts.

PARQUE DAS NAÇÕES

The former Expo '98 site, a revitalised 2km-long waterfront area in the northeast, equals a family fun day out. There's weird

and wonderful public art on display, gardens and casual riverfront cafes. Other highlights include the epic **Oceanário** (www.oceanario.pt; Doca dos Olivais; adult/child €13/9; ⊙10am-8pm), Europe's second-largest oceanarium, and **Pavilhão do Conhecimento**, (Living Science Centre; adult/child €7/4; ⊙10am-6pm Tue-Fri, 11am-7pm Sat & Sun) with over 300 interactive exhibits for kids of all ages. Take the metro to Oriente station – a stunner designed by star Spanish architect Santiago Calatrava.

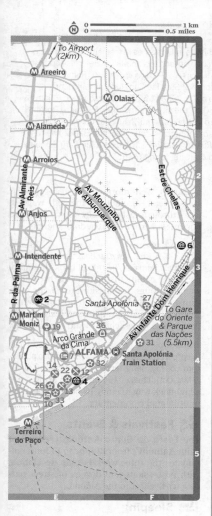

Greater Lisbon

◎ Top Sights
Centro de Arte Moderna	C2
Museu Calouste Gulbenkian	C1
Museu Nacional de Arte Antiga	B5

◎ Sights
1	LX Factory	A5
2	Miradouro da Senhora do Monte	E3
3	Miradouro de Santa Catarina	D4
4	Museu do Fado	E4
5	Museu do Oriente	B5
6	Museu Nacional do Azulejo	F3

⊜ Sleeping
7	Alfama Patio Hostel	E4
8	Lisbon Dreams	C3
9	Oasis Lisboa	C4
10	Pensão São João da Praça	E4

⊗ Eating
11	Mezzaluna	C3
12	Páteo 13	E4
13	Pois Café	E4
14	Santo António de Alfama	E4
15	Terra	D4
16	Zé Varunca	D3

◎ Drinking
17	Cinco Lounge	C4
18	Meninos do Rio	D5
19	Miradouro da Graça	E4
20	Noobai Café	D4
21	Pavilhão Chinês	D4

◎ Entertainment
22	A Baîuca	E4
23	Amoreiras Cinema	C3
24	Campo Pequeno	D1
25	Cinemateca Portuguesa	D3
26	Clube de Fado	E4
27	Clube Ferroviário	F3
28	Construction	C4
29	Finalmente	D4
30	Incógnito	C4
31	Lux	F4
32	Mesa de Frades	E4
33	Onda Jazz Bar	E4
34	São Jorge	D3
35	Trumps	C4

◎ Shopping
36	Feira da Ladra	E4

ALCÂNTARA

Today, these former wharves house a sleek and modern strip of bars and restaurants with tables spilling onto the long promenade. It's an intriguing place for a waterfront stroll, a bite or a drink, though the metallic drone of traffic across the bridge can be rather grating.

FREE **Museu do Oriente** MUSEUM
(Map p568; ☎213 585 200; www.museudooriente. pt; Doca de Alcântara; adult/child €5/2, 6-10pm Fri;

PORTUGAL LISBON

FREE LISBOA

Aside from the Castelo de São Jorge, many sights in Lisbon have free entrance on Sundays from 10am to 2pm. For a free cultural fix on other days, make for Belém's **Museu Colecção Berardo** for great art exhibits, **Museu do Teatro Romano** (Roman Theatre Museum; Map p572; Pátio do Aljube 5; ⊙10am-1pm & 2-6pm Tue-Sun) for Roman theatre ruins, and the fortresslike **Sé** (Cathedral; Map p572; ✆218 866 752; admission free; ⊙9am-7pm Tue-Sat, 9am-5pm Mon & Sun), built in 1150 on the site of a mosque. For more Roman ruins, take a free tour of the **Núcleo Arqueológico** (Map p572; Rua dos Correeiros 9; ⊙10am-5pm Mon-Sat), which contains a web of tunnels hidden under the Baixa. The new **Museu de Design e da Moda** (Map p572; Rua Augusta 24; ⊙10am-8pm Tue-Sun) exhibits eye-catching furniture, industrial design and couture dating to the 1930s.

⊙10am-6pm Tue-Thu, Sat & Sun, 10am-10pm Fri) Set in a revamped 1940s *bacalhau* (salted cod) warehouse, the Museu do Oriente explores Portugal's ties with Asia with a fascinating collection of art and relics from China, Japan and East Timor.

LX Factory   ART CENTRE
(Map p568; www.lxfactory.com; Rua Rodrigues de Faria 103, Alcântara) Lisbon's new hub of creativity hosts a dynamic menu of events from live concerts and film screenings to fashion shows and art exhibitions. You'll find restaurants, a bookshop and design-minded shops.

👉 Tours

We Hate Tourism Tours   DRIVING TOUR
(✆913 776 598; www.wehatetourismtours.com; tours from €25 per person) Offers unique perspectives of Lisbon. Popular outings include the three-hour 'King of the Hills' open-topped jeep tour, dinner outings and Sintra trips.

Lisbon Walker   WALKING
(Map p572; ✆218 861 840; www.lisbonwalker. com; Rua dos Remédios 84; 3hr walk €15; ⊙10am

CYCLING THE TEJO

A **cycling/jogging path** courses along the Tejo for 7km, between Cais do Sodré and Belém. Complete with artful touches – including the poetry of Pessoa printed along parts of it – the path takes in ageing warehouses, weathered docks and open-air restaurants and nightspots.

A handy place to rent bikes is a short stroll from Cais do Sodré: **Bike Iberia** (Map p572; www.bikeiberia.com; Largo Corpo Santo 5; bike hire per hr/day €4/14; ⊙9.30am-7.30pm).

& 2.30pm) Well-informed, English-speaking guides lead fascinating themed walking tours through Lisbon. They depart from the northwest corner of Praça do Comércio.

Lisbon Explorer   WALKING
(✆213 629 263; www.lisbonexplorer.com; tours adult/child from €34/free) Peel back the many layers of Lisbon's history during three-hour walking tours (admission to sights and transport included). It also hosts a nightly Taste of Portugal: sample (and learn about) Portuguese wines, cheeses and cured meats.

Transtejo   BOAT TOUR
(Map p572; ✆210 422 417; www.transtejo.pt; Terreiro do Paço ferry terminal; adult/child €20/10; ⊙May-Oct) These 2½-hour river cruises are a laid-back way to enjoy Lisbon's sights with multilingual commentary.

✨ Festivals & Events

The **Festa de Santo António** (Festival of Saint Anthony), from 12 June to 13 June, culminates the three-week **Festas de Lisboa**, with processions and dozens of street parties; it's liveliest in the Alfama.

🛏 Sleeping

Lisbon has a good mix of boutique hotels, stylish hostels and old-fashioned pensions that won't break the bank. Book well ahead during high season (July to mid-September).

BAIXA, ROSSIO & CAIS DO SODRÉ

Lavra Guest House   GUESTHOUSE €€
(Map p572; ✆218 820 000; www.lavra.pt; Calçada de Santano 198, Rossio; d from €59; ☎) Set in a former convent, the Lavra Guest House has a range of rooms, from basic quarters facing onto an inner courtyard, to brighter rooms with wood floors and tiny balconies.

Lisbon Story Guesthouse GUESTHOUSE €€
(Map p572; ☑211 529 313; www.lisbonstoryguest
house.com; Largo de São Domingos 18, Rossio; d
€90-110, without bathroom €40-80 ; @⚡) Overlooking the Praça São Domingos is a small,
welcoming guesthouse with small, well-
maintained rooms and a shoe-free lounge
with throw pillows and low tables.

Lisbon Destination Hostel HOSTEL €
(Map p572; ☑213 466 457; www.rossiopatio.com;
top floor, Rossio Train Station; dm/d/tr €22/60/75;
@⚡) Despite its location inside a train station, this hostel has loads of style, with a
glass ceiling flooding the spacious plant-
filled common area with light. Rooms are
crisp and and well-maintained, and there
are loads of activities (bar crawls, beach day
trips, etc), plus excellent multi-course meals
available (€8 per person including wine).

Beach Destination Hostel HOSTEL €
(Map p572; ☑210 997 735; Cais do Sodré Train
Station; dm/d €22/60; @⚡) New in 2012,
this beautifully designed hostel has comfy
rooms, a swanky dining room, a top-notch
kitchen and a roof terrace with impressive
river views.

Goodnight Hostel HOSTEL €
(Map p572; ☑213 430 139; www.goodnighthostel.
com; Rua dos Correiros 113, Baixa; dm/d €20/50;
@⚡) Set in a converted 18th-century townhouse, this glam hostel rocks with its fab location and retro design. The high-ceilinged
dorms offer vertigo-inducing views over Baixa.

Lounge Hostel HOSTEL €
(Map p572; ☑213 462 061; www.lisbonloungehostel.
com; Rua de São Nicolau 41, Baixa; dm/d incl breakfast €25/64; @⚡) These ultrahip Baixa digs
have a party vibe. Bed down in immaculate
dorms and meet like-minded travellers in
the funky lounge watched over by a wacky
moose head.

Travellers House HOSTEL €
(Map p572; ☑210 115 922; www.travellershouse.
com; Rua Augusta 89, Baixa; dm from €22; @⚡)
This superfriendly hostel is set in a converted 250-year-old house and offers cosy
dorms, a retro lounge with beanbags, an internet corner and a communal kitchen.

Residencial Florescente GUESTHOUSE €€
(Map p572; ☑213 426 609; www.residencial
florescente.com; Rua das Portas de Santo Antão 99,
Rossio; s/d from €45/65; ✻@⚡) On a vibrant
street lined with alfresco restaurants, lemon-
fronted Florescente has comfy rooms in

muted tones with shiny modern bathrooms.
It's a two-minute walk from Rossio.

Pensão Imperial GUESTHOUSE €
(Map p572; ☑213 420 166; Praça dos Restauradores
78, Rossio; s/d €25/40) Above Praça dos Restauradores, four flights up, this simple pension
has high-ceilinged rooms with basic wooden
furniture; it's nothing flash, but some rooms
have balconies overlooking the plaza.

ALFAMA
Alfama Patio Hostel HOSTEL €
(Map p568; ☑218 883 127; http://alfamapatio.
com; Rua das Escolas Gerais 3; dm/d from €20/60;
@⚡) Located in the heart of the Alfama, this
place attracts a cool, laid-back crowd. There
are loads of activities (pub crawls, day trips
to the beach), plus barbecues on the gardenlike patio.

Solar dos Mouros BOUTIQUE HOTEL €€€
(Map p572; ☑218 854 940; www.solardosmouros.
pt; Rua do Milagre de Santo António 4; d €87-187; ✻)
Affording river or castle views, the 12 rooms
at this boutique charmer bear the imprint of
artist Luís Lemos and offer high-end trappings, plus a tiny water garden.

Pensão Ninho das Águias GUESTHOUSE €
(Map p572; ☑218 854 070; Costa do Castelo 74; s/d/
tr without bathroom €30/40/60) It isn't called
'eagle's nest' for nothing: this guest-house has
a Rapunzel-esque turret affording magical
360-degree views over Lisbon. Book ahead.

Pensão São João da Praça GUESTHOUSE €
(Map p568; ☑218 862 591; 218 862 591@sapo.pt;
Rua de São João da Praça 97, 2nd fl; s/d without
bathroom €30/40, d €45-55; ⚡) So close to the
Sé you can almost touch the gargoyles, this
19th-century guesthouse has a pick-and-mix
of clean, sunny rooms; the best has a river-
facing veranda.

CHIADO, BAIRRO ALTO &
PRÍNCIPE REAL
Oasis Lisboa HOSTEL €
(Map p568; ☑213 478 044; www.oasislisboa.com;
Rua de Santa Catarina 24, Principe Real; dm incl
breakfast €17-21; @⚡) Behind yellow wonder

WANT MORE?

For in-depth information, reviews and
recommendations at your fingertips,
head to the Apple App Store to purchase Lonely Planet's *Lisbon City
Guide* iPhone app.

PORTUGAL LISBON

PORTUGAL LISBON

Central Lisbon

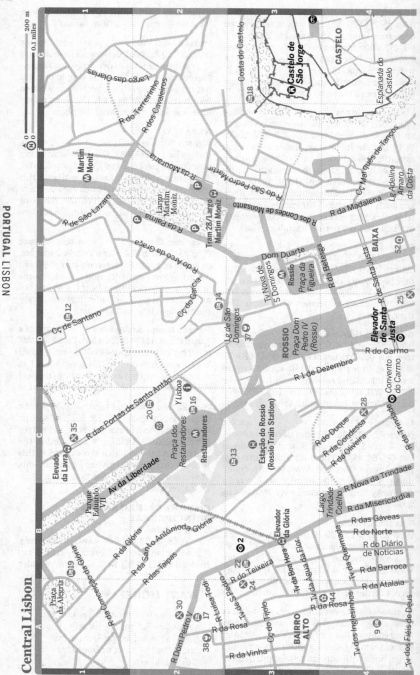

Castelo de São Jorge

CASTELO

Costa do Castelo

Esplanada do Castelo

Largo das Olarias

R do Terreirinho

R dos Cavaleiros

R da Mouraria

R de São Lazaro

Largo Martim Moniz

Tram 28/Largo Martim Moniz

R do São Pedro Mártir

R da Palma

R do Arco da Graça

Cç do Garcia

Martim Moniz

Lg Adelino Amaro da Costa

Cç Marquês de Tancos

R dos Condes de Monsanto

R da Madalena

BAIXA

Dom Duarte

Rossio Praça da Figueira

Tv.Nova de S Domingos

R da Betesga

R de Santa Justa

52

Cç de Santano

Cç de Santano

12

14

Lg de São Domingos

37

ROSSIO

Praça Dom Pedro IV (Rossio)

Elevador de Santa Justa

25

R do Carmo

R 1 de Dezembro

Convento do Carmo

Elevado da Lavra

35

R das Portas de Santo Antão

Y Lisboa

16

20

Praça dos Restauradores

Restauradores

13

Estação do Rossio (Rossio Train Station)

28

R do Duque

R da Condessa

R da Oliveira

R da Trindade

Av da Liberdade

Parque Eduardo VII

R Nova da Trindade

Largo Trindade Coelho

R da Misericórdia

R das Gáveas

R do Norte

R do Diário de Notícias

R da Barroca

R da Atalaia

R da Glória

R de Santo António da Glória

R das Taipas

Elevador da Glória

2

R da Boa Hora

Tv da Água da Flor

19

Praça da Alegria

R da Conceição da Glória

30

17

R Dom Pedro V

R Luísa Todi

Tv de S Pedro

22

R do Teixeira

24

Tv da Queimada

44

R da Rosa

38

Cç do Tijolo

R da Vinha

BAIRRO ALTO

R da Rosa

9

Tv dos Inglesinhos

Tv dos Fiéis de Deus

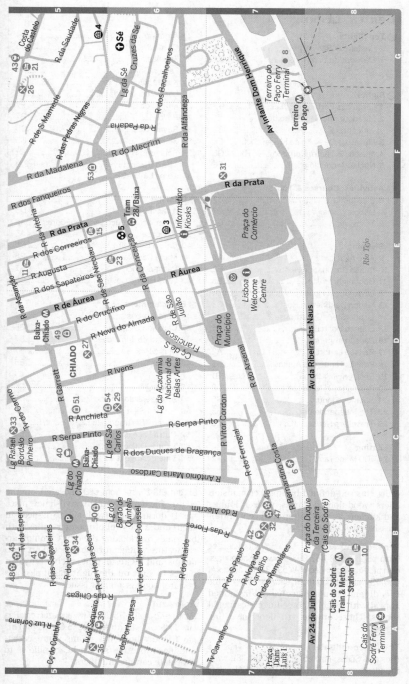

Central Lisbon

◉ Top Sights

Castelo de São Jorge	G3
Elevador de Santa Justa	D4
Sé	G6

◉ Sights

1	Largo das Portas do Sol	G3
2	Miradouro de São Pedro de Alcântara	B3
3	Museu de Design e da Moda	E6
4	Museu do Teatro Romano	G5
5	Núcleo Arqueológico	E6

✪ Activities, Courses & Tours

6	Bike Iberia	C7
7	Lisbon Walker	E7
8	Transtejo	G7

⊜ Sleeping

9	Anjo Azul	A4
10	Beach Destination Hostel	B8
11	Goodnight Hostel	E5
12	Lavra Guest House	D1
13	Lisbon Destination Hostel	C3
14	Lisbon Story Guesthouse	D2
15	Lounge Hostel	E5
16	Pensão Imperial	C2
17	Pensão Londres	A2
18	Pensão Ninho das Águias	G3
19	Residencial Alegria	B1
20	Residencial Florescente	C2
21	Solar dos Mouros	G5
22	The Independente	B3
23	Travellers House	E6

✸ Eating

24	100 Maneiras	A3
25	Amorino	D4
26	Chapitô	G5
27	Fábulas	D5
28	Faca & Garfo	C4
29	Kaffee Haus	C6
30	Lost in Esplanada	A2
31	Museu da Cerveja	F7
32	Povo	B7
33	Royale Café	C5
34	Sea Me	B5
35	Solar dos Presuntos	C1
	The Decadente	(see 22)
36	Toma Lá-Dá-Cá	A5

◉ Drinking

37	A Ginjinha	D3
38	Associação Loucos & Sonhadores	A2
39	Bicaense	A5
40	Café a Brasileira	C5
41	Maria Caxuxa	B5
42	Pensão Amor	B7
43	Wine Bar do Castelo	G5

◉ Entertainment

44	Catacumbas	A4
45	Clube da Esquina	B5
46	Discoteca Jamaica	B7
47	Music Box	B7
48	Zé dos Bois	B5

⊜ Shopping

49	Armazéns do Chiado	D5
50	Fábrica Sant'Ana	B5
51	Livraria Bertrand	C5
52	Outra Face da Lua	E4
53	Santos Oficios	F5
54	Vida Portuguesa	C6

walls, this self-defined backpacker mansion offers wood-floored dorms, a sleek lounge and kitchen, and a rooftop terrace with impressive river views.

Pensão Londres GUESTHOUSE €€
(Map p572; ☎213 462 203; www.pensaolondres.com.pt; Rua Dom Pedro V 53, Bairro Alto; s/d €50/75, without bathroom €35/45; @🛜) This friendly and popular place has old-fashioned appeal with large, high-ceilinged, carpeted rooms. Those on the 4th floor have fine views.

The Independente HOSTEL €
(Hostel & Suites; Map p572; ☎213 461 381; www.theindependente.pt; Rua de São Pedro de Alcântara

81; dm €18-20, ste from €80) Located on the edge of the Bairro Alto, this stylish new place has 11 dorm rooms (with six- to 12-beds in each) and a handful of roomier suites with balconies overlooking the city. Common areas feature vintage furnishings and art deco details, and the restaurant and bar are great places to start off the night. Light sleepers beware: noise is a major issue.

Anjo Azul GUESTHOUSE €€
(Map p572; ☎213 478 069; www.anjoazul.com; Rua Luz Soriano 75, Bairro Alto; r €45-65; @🛜) This gay-friendly hotel has rooms from scarlet-and-black love nests with heart pillows to chocolate-caramel numbers.

AVENIDA DE LIBERDADE, RATO & MARQUÊS DE POMBAL

Lisbon Dreams
GUESTHOUSE €€

(Map p568; ☎213 872 393; www.lisbondreamsguesthouse.com; Rua Rodrigo da Fonseca 29, Rato; s/d without bathroom incl breakfast €50/60; @🛜) On a quiet street lined with jacaranda trees, Lisbon Dreams offers excellent value with its bright modern rooms with tall ceilings and high-end mattresses. Bathrooms are shared, but spotlessly clean.

Residencial Alegria
GUESTHOUSE €€

(Map p572; ☎213 220 670; www.alegrianet.com; Praça da Alegria 12; d €60-83; ❄) Overlooking a palm-dotted plaza, this lemon-fronted belle époque gem has airy and peaceful rooms, with antique-filled corridors.

✗ Eating

New-generation chefs, first-rate ingredients and a generous pinch of old-world spice have helped put Lisbon on the gastronomic map. In addition to creative newcomers, you'll find inexpensive, traditional dining rooms home to classic Portuguese fare.

BAIXA, ROSSIO & CAIS DO SODRÉ

Solar dos Presuntos
PORTUGUESE €€€

(Map p572; ☎213 424 253; Rua das Portas de Santo Antão 150, Rossio; mains €15-26; ⊙lunch & dinner Mon-Sat) Renowned for its excellent seafood as well as its smoked and grilled meats, this buzzing restaurant serves up memorable lobster and prawn curry, salt-baked sea bass and delectable seafood paella, among other great picks.

Povo
PORTUGUESE €

(Map p572; Rua Nova do Carvalho 32; small plates €4-8; ⊙noon-2am Tue-Sat, 6pm-1am Sun & Mon) On bar-lined Rua Nova do Carvalho, Povo serves up tasty Portuguese comfort food in the form of *petiscos* (small plates). Try the *favinhas e chouriço* (fava beans with chorizo), *salada de polvo* (octopus salad) or *camarão ao alhinho* (garlic prawns). There's also outdoor seating and live fado nights (Thursdays are best).

Museu da Cerveja
PORTUGUESE €€

(Map p572; Praça do Comércio 62; mains €10-16; ⊙9am-2am) One of a number of new eating and drinking spaces lining the east and west sides of the Praça do Comércio, this sprawling restaurant serves up grilled meats and seafood as well as microbrews and beers from Angola. The outdoor tables are great for people watching.

Amorino
ICE CREAM €

(Map p572; Rua Augusta 209; small/large ice cream €3.50/5.50; ⊙11am-9pm) Amorino serves the city's best gelato – creamy, rich decadence made from organic, high-quality ingredients.

ALFAMA

Santo António de Alfama
PORTUGUESE €€€

(Map p568; ☎218 881 328; Beco de São Miguel 7; mains €14-20; ⊙lunch & dinner) With a lovely front courtyard and atmospheric interior, this bistro is one of the Alfama's stars, with tasty appetisers (try gorgonzola-stuffed mushrooms or roasted aubergines with yoghurt), as well as more filling traditional Portuguese dishes.

Páteo 13
PORTUGUESE €€

(Map p568; Calçadinha de Santo Estêvão 13; mains €8-12) Follow the scent of chargrilled fish to this local favourite, tucked away on a small, festively decorated plaza in the Alfama. Join buzzing crowds hunkered over picnic tables as they feast on barbecued seafood and meats, washed down with ever-flowing Alentejan reds.

Chapitô
CONTEMPORARY €€€

(Map p572; ☎218 867 334; Costa do Castelo 7; mains €17-20; ⊙lunch & dinner) This creative spot (which shares space with a circus school) has a gardenlike courtyard and a top-floor restaurant, affording mesmerising views over Lisbon. The small menu leans toward grilled meats and fish and the bar onsite often features live music, film screenings and other events.

Pois Café
CAFE €€

(Map p568; Rua de São João da Praça 93; mains €5-12; ⊙11am-10pm Tue-Sun) Boasting a laid-back vibe, Pois Café has creative salads, sandwiches and fresh juices, plus daily specials (soup and main for €9.50). Its sofas invite lazy afternoons reading novels and sipping coffee.

AVENIDA DE LIBERDADE, RATO & MARQUÊS DE POMBAL

Mezzaluna
ITALIAN €€€

(Map p568; ☎213 879 944; Rua Artilharia Um 16; mains €16-20; ⊙lunch Mon-Fri, dinner Mon-Sat) Run by a Neopolitan chef who grew up in New York, Mezzaluna prepares beautifully turned out dishes that blend classic Italian recipes with mouthwateringly fresh Portuguese ingredients. Start off with tender carpaccio or endive leaves wrapped in prosciutto, parmesan and *ginjinha* (cherry brandy) reduction, before moving on to linguine with octopus or pan-seared duck breast with prune sauce.

Zé Varunca
PORTUGUESE €€

(Map p568; Rua de São José 54; mains €10-14; ⏱lunch & dinner Mon-Sat) This charming, rustically decorated restaurant specialises in Alentejo cooking, with a changing menu of regional favourites such as oven-roasted duck and *migas de bacalhau* (a bread-based dish cooked with cod).

CHIADO, BAIRRO ALTO & PRÍNCIPE REAL

The Decadente
PORTUGUESE €€

(Map p572; ☎913 069 345; Rua de São Pedro de Alcântara 81, The Independente; mains €10-14) This beautifully designed restaurant, with touches of industrial chic, geometric artwork and an enticing back patio, attracts a mix of hip Lisboetas and foreign guests staying at the Independente. All come for inventive dishes showcasing high-end Portuguese ingredients at excellent prices. The changing three-course lunch menu (€10) is first-rate. Start off with creative cocktails in the front bar.

100 Maneiras
FUSION €€€

(Map p572; ☎210 990 475; Rua do Teixeira 35, Bairro Alta; tasting menus €45; ⏱dinner) One of Lisbon's best-rated restaurants, 100 Maneiras has no menu, just a 10-course tasting menu that changes daily and features creative, delicately prepared dishes. There's a lively buzz to the small space. Reservations essential.

Sea Me
SEAFOOD €€€

(Map p572; ☎213 461 564; Rua do Lareto 21; mains €17-28; ⏱lunch & dinner) One of Lisbon's best seafood restaurants serves up magnificent grilled fish by the kilo (check out the tempting fresh selection in back), as well as flavourful plates with international accents – risotto with shrimp, Thai green curry with grilled salmon, seared scallops with mango relish and fish ceviche among other standouts.

Lost in Esplanada
INTERNATIONAL €€

(Map p572; Rua Dom Pedro V 56; mains €11-15; ⏱4pm-midnight Mon, 12.30pm-midnight Tue-Sat) Hidden behind an Indian textile shop, this well-concealed terrace is set with painted whicker chairs, a gurgling fountain, and a Krishna mural, though the view over the city is the real star. Vegie burgers, prawn curry, Portuguese sharing plates and the like make up the menu. Live jazz on Thursdays (from 9 to 11pm).

Fábulas
CAFE €€

(Map p572; Calçada Nova de São Francisco 14, Chiado; mains €9-13; ⏱10am-midnight Mon-Sat, noon-10pm Sun; 🛜) Stone walls, low lighting and twisting corridors that open onto cosy nooks and crannies do indeed conjure a storybook *fábula* (fable). Sink into a comfy couch with coffee or wine, or have a bite to eat from the menu of creative salads, curries, burritos and daily specials.

Faca & Garfo
PORTUGUESE €€

(Map p572; Rua da Condessa 2, Chiado; mains €7-9; ⏱lunch & dinner Mon-Sat) The sweet *azulejo*-filled Faca & Garfo ('knife and fork') serves carefully prepared Portuguese recipes at reasonable prices. Try the authentic *alheira de Mirandela* (chicken sausage) or the *bife à casa* (steak with cream and port wine sauce).

🌱Terra
VEGETARIAN €€

(Map p568; ☎213 421 407; Rua da Palmeira 15, Príncipe Real; buffet €13-16; ⏱lunch & dinner Tue-Sun; 🌱) Terra is famed for its superb vegetarian buffet (including vegan options) of salads, kebabs and curries, plus organic wines and juices. A fountain gurgles in the tree-shaded courtyard, lit by twinkling lights after dark.

Toma Lá-Dá-Cá
PORTUGUESE €

(Map p572; ☎213 479 243; Travessa do Sequeiro 38; mains €7-12; ⏱lunch & dinner) Get your tongue in a twist pronouncing the name of this Santa Catarina gem, where there's often an anaconda of a queue. The inviting space rolls out perfectly grilled fish, along with superb desserts.

Kaffee Haus
CAFE €€

(Map p572; Rua Anchieta 3, Chiado; mains €9-13; ⏱11am-midnight Tue-Thu, 11am-2am Fri & Sat, 11am-8pm Sun) Overlooking a peaceful corner of Chiado, this cool but unpretentious cafe has daily chalkboard specials – big salads, tasty schnitzels, vegetarian risotto, strudels, cakes and more.

Royale Café
CAFE €

(Map p572; ☎213 469 125; Largo Rafael Bordalo Pinheiro 29, Chiado; mains around €10; ⏱10am-midnight Mon-Sat, to 8pm Sun) This chichi cafe has a pleasant vine-clad courtyard that's ideal for drinks, create-your-own sandwiches, salads and Portuguese fusion fare.

BELÉM

Antiga Confeitaria de Belém
BAKERY €

(☎213 637 423; Rua de Belém 86-88; ⏱8am-11pm) Since 1837, this patisserie has been transporting locals to sugar-coated nirvana with heavenly *pastéis de belém*: crispy crusted pastry nests filled with custard cream.

Nosolo Italia ITALIAN €€
(Av de Brasília 202; mains €10-14; ⏰noon-10pm) This bustling eatery with outdoor tables perched over the water has a big menu of tasty thin-crust pizzas, pastas, salads and crepes; there's also a popular ice cream counter.

🍷 Drinking

All-night street parties in Bairro Alto, sunset drinks from high-up terraces, and sumptuous art deco cafes scattered about Chiado – Lisbon has many enticing options for imbibers.

Pensão Amor BAR
(Map p572; Rua Nova do Carvalho 36; ⏰noon-2am Mon-Wed, to 4am Thu & Fri, 6pm-4am Sat) Set inside a former brothel, this cheeky bar pays homage to its passion-filled past with colourful wall murals, a library of erotic-tinged works and a boutique selling amorous accoutrements. Numerous other bars line the street (including O Bar da Velha Senhora where you can sometimes catch burlesque shows); expect huge crowds on weekends.

Pavilhão Chinês LOUNGE
(Map p568; Rua Dom Pedro V 89-91, Príncipe Real) An old curiosity shop of a bar with oil paintings and model spitfires dangling from the ceiling, and cabinets brimming with glittering Venetian masks and Action Men. Play pool or bag a comfy armchair with a port or beer in hand.

Bicaense BAR
(Map p572; Rua da Bica de Duarte Belo 42a, Bica) Indie kids have a soft spot for this chilled Santa Catarina haunt, kitted out with retro radios, projectors and squishy beanbags. DJs spin house to the pre-clubbing crowd and the back room stages occasional gigs.

Wine Bar do Castelo WINE BAR
(Map p572; Rua Bartolomeu de Gusmão 13, Castelo; ⏰noon-10pm) Near the entrance to the Castelo de São Jorge, this welcoming place serves more than 150 Portuguese wines by the glass, along with gourmet smoked meats, cheeses, olives and other tasty accompaniments.

Associação Loucos & Sonhadores BAR
(Map p572; Travessa do Conde de Soure 2) Though it's in Bairro Alto, this bohemian drinking den feels secreted away from the heaving masses on nearby streets. Kitschy decor, free (salty) popcorn and eclectic tunes – it's a great place for conversation rather than pounding shots.

Cinco Lounge LOUNGE
(Map p568; Rua Ruben António Leitão 17, Príncipe Real; ⏰9pm-2am) Take an award-winning London-born mixologist, add a candlelit, gold-kissed setting and give it a funky twist and you have Cinco Lounge. Come for the laid-back scene and legendary cocktails.

Meninos do Rio BAR
(Map p568; Rua da Cintura do Porto de Lisboa, Armação 255, Santos; ⏰12.30pm-1am Sun-Thu, to 4am Fri & Sat) Perched on the river's edge, Meninos do Rio has palm trees, wooden decks, DJs and tropical cocktails, giving it a vibe that's more Caribbean than Iberian.

Maria Caxuxa BAR
(Map p572; Rua Barroca 6, Bairro Alto; ⏰8am-2am) Maria Caxuxa has effortless style, its several rooms decked with giant mixers, *azulejo*-lined walls and 1950s armchairs and sofas, as funk-laden jazz plays overhead.

Café a Brasileira CAFE, BAR
(Map p572; ☎213 469 547; Rua Garrett 120, Chiado; ⏰8am-2am) An historic watering hole for Lisbon's 19th-century greats, with warm wooden innards and a busy counter serving daytime coffees and pints at night.

Noobai Café CAFE, BAR
(Map p568; Miradouro de Santa Catarina, Santa Catarina; ⏰noon-midnight) Lisbon's best-kept secret is next to Miradouro de Santa Catarina, with a laid-back vibe, jazzy beats and magnificent views from the terrace.

A Ginjinha BAR
(Map p572; Largo de São Domingos 8, Rossio; ⏰9am-10pm) Join a wide swath of society for a refreshingly potent quaff of *ginjinha* at this tiny bar/stand-up counter near Rossio.

☆ Entertainment

For the latest goings-on, pick up the weekly *Time Out Lisboa* (www.timeout.pt) from bookstores, or the free monthly *Follow me Lisboa* or *Agenda Cultural Lisboa* from the tourist office.

Live Music

Zé dos Bois LIVE MUSIC
(Map p572; ☎213 430 205; www.zedosbois.org; Rua da Barroca 59, Bairro Alto) Focusing on tomorrow's performing arts and music trends, Zé dos Bois is an experimental venue with a laid-back courtyard. Come for concerts, DJs and changing exhibitions.

PORTUGUESE SOUL

Infused by Moorish song and the ditties of homesick sailors, bluesy, bittersweet **fado** encapsulates the Lisbon psyche like nothing else. The uniquely Portuguese style was born in the Alfama, still the best place in Lisbon to hear it live. Minimum consumption charges range from €15 to €25 per person.

A Baîuca (Map p568; Rua de São Miguel 20; ☺dinner Thu-Mon) On a good night, walking into A Baîuca is like gatecrashing a family party. It's a special place with *fado vadio*, where locals take a turn and spectators hiss if anyone dares to chat during the singing.

Clube de Fado (Map p568; ☎218 852 704; www.clube-de-fado.com; Rua de São João da Praça; ☺9pm-2.30am Mon-Sat) Hosts the cream of the fado crop in vaulted, dimly lit surrounds. Big-name *fadistas* perform here alongside celebrated guitarists.

Mesa de Frades (Map p568; ☎917 029 436; www.mesadefrades.com; Rua dos Remédios 139a; admission from €15; ☺dinner Wed-Mon) A magical place to hear fado, tiny Mesa de Frades used to be a chapel. It's tiled with exquisite *azulejos* and has just a handful of tables. Reserve ahead.

Onda Jazz Bar JAZZ
(Map p568; www.ondajazz.com; Arco de Jesus 7, Alfama) This vaulted cellar features a menu of mainstream jazz, plus more-eclectic beats from bands hailing from Brazil and Africa.

Catacumbas JAZZ
(Map p572; Travessa da Água da Flor 43, Bairro Alto) Moodily lit and festooned with portraits of legends such as Miles Davis, this den is jam-packed when it hosts live jazz on Thursday nights.

Nightclubs

Cover charges for nightclubs typically run from €5 to €12.

Lux CLUB
(Map p568; www.luxfragil.com; Avenida Infante Dom Henrique, Santo Apolónia) Still Lisbon's best club, this beautifully conceived two-storey club attracts a mixed crowd who come for an eclectic lineup of concerts, along with big-name DJs. The rooftop terrace has fine views over the Tejo.

Music Box CLUB
(Map p572; www.musicboxlisboa.com; Rua Nova do Carvalho 24, Cais do Sodré) Under the brick arches on Rua Nova do Carvalho lies one of Lisbon's hottest clubs. Music Box hosts loud and bouncy club nights with music shifting from electro to rock, as well as ear-splitting gigs by rising bands.

Incógnito CLUB
(Map p568; Rua dos Poiais de São Bento 37, Santa Catarina) No-sign, pint-sized Incógnito offers an alternative vibe and DJs thrashing out indie rock and electro-pop. Sweat it out with a fun crowd on the tiny basement dance floor, or breathe more easily in the loft bar upstairs.

Discoteca Jamaica CLUB
(Map p572; Rua Nova do Carvalho, Cais do Sodré; ☺11pm-4am) Gay and straight, black and white, young and old – everyone has a soft spot for this long-running club. It gets going around 2am at weekends with DJs pumping out reggae, hip hop and retro.

Clube Ferroviário CLUB
(Map p568; Rua de Santa Apolónia 59) Above Santa Apolónia Train Station, this former social club of Lisbon's railworkers has been transformed into an intriguing nightspot with DJs and occasional concerts; the best feature is the roof terrace with Tejo views.

Gay & Lesbian Venues

Lisbon's small gay scene is headquarted in Príncipe Real, though you'll also find a few gay bars in Bairro Alto. Lux draws both a gay and straight crowd.

Construction GAY, CLUB
(Map p568; Rua Cecílio de Sousa 84; ☺midnight-6am Fri & Sat) New in 2012, Construction is the hot club of the moment, with pumping house music and a dark room. Popular with bears.

Finalmente GAY, CLUB
(Map p568; Rua da Palmeira 38) This popular club has a tiny dance floor, nightly drag shows and wall-to-wall crowds.

Trumps GAY, CLUB
(Map p568; www.trumps.pt; Rua da Imprensa Nacional 104b) Lisbon's hottest gay club, with

cruisy corners, a sizeable dance floor and events from live music to drag.

Clube da Esquina
GAY, BAR

(Map p572; Rua da Barroca 30; ⊙10pm-4am; underground rail Baixa-Chiado) DJs playing hip hop and house to an eye-candy crowd. Several other gay bars are nearby.

Cinemas

Lisbon's cinematic standouts are the grand **São Jorge** (Map p568; Avenida da Liberdade 175) and, just around the corner, **Cinemateca Portuguesa** (Map p568; www.cinemateca.pt; Rua Barata Salgueiro 39); both screen offbeat, arthouse, world and old films. For Hollywood fare, visit multiscreen **Amoreiras Cinema** (Map p568; Avenida Eng Duarte Pacheco, Amoreiras Shopping Centre) or **Colombo Cinema.** (Centro Colombo, Avenida Lusíada)

Sport

Lisbon's football teams are Benfica, Belenenses and Sporting. Euro 2004 led to the upgrading of the 65,000-seat **Estádio da Luz** and the construction of the 54,000-seat **Estádio Nacional**. Bullfights are staged on Thursday from May to October at **Campo Pequeno** (Map p568; Avenida da República; tickets €10-75). Tickets are available at **ABEP ticket kiosk** (Praça dos Restauradores). State-of-the-art stadium **Estádio José de Alvalade** (Rua Prof Fernando da Fonseca) seats 54,000 and is just north of the university. Take the metro to Campo Grande.

🛍 Shopping

Shops in Lisbon are a mix of the classic and the wild, with antiques, frozen-in-time button and tinned-fish shops, and edgy boutiques all sprinkled across the hilly landscape. Rua Garrett and nearby Largo do Chiado, across Rua da Misericórdia, are home to some of Lisbon's oldest and most upmarket boutiques. Meanwhile, Bairro Alto attracts vinyl lovers and vintage fans to its cluster of late-opening boutiques.

Feira da Ladra

MARKET

(Map p568; Campo de Santa Clara, Alfama; ⊙7am-5pm Sat) You'll find old records, coins, jewellery, vintage postcards, dog-eared poetry books and other attic treasure/trash at this lively Saturday market.

Vida Portuguesa
PORTUGUESE

(Map p572; Rua Anchieta 11, Chiado) With high ceilings and polished cabinets, this store lures nostalgics with all-Portuguese prod-

ucts, from retro-wrapped Tricona sardines to lime-oil soap and Bordallo Pinheiro porcelain swallows.

Santos Oficios
HANDICRAFTS

(Map p572; Rua da Madalena 87, Baixa) Touristy but fine selection of Portuguese folk art.

Armazéns do Chiado
MALL

(Map p572; Rua do Carmo 2, Chiado) A convenient, well-concealed shopping complex. The Fnac store here is good for books, music and booking concert tickets.

Outra Face da Lua
VINTAGE

(Map p572; Rua da Assunção 22, Baixa) A fun-to-explore vintage shop in Baixa, with a cafe inside.

Fábrica Sant'Ana
HANDICRAFTS

(Map p572; Rua do Alecrim 95, Chiado) Great spot for purchasing fabulous new and old *azulejos*.

Livraria Bertrand
BOOKS

(Map p572; ✆213 421 941; Rua Garrett 73, Chiado) Bertrand has both Portuguese and foreign-language books sold amid 18th-century charm.

ℹ Information

Emergency

Police, Fire & Ambulance (✆119)
Police Station (✆217 654 242; Rua Capelo 13)
Tourist Police (✆213 421 634; Palácio Foz, Praça dos Restauradores; ⊙24hr)

Internet Access

Most hostels and mid-range guesthouses offer wireless (usually free). Loads of cafes and restaurants also offer wi-fi – just ask for the *codigo* (access code).
Portugal Telecom (Praça Rossio 68; ⊙9am-10pm) Handy place to get online next to Praça Rossio. Also has rows of telephone booths.

Internet Resources

Time Out (www.timeout.pt) Details on upcoming gigs, cultural events and interesting commentary, in Portuguese.
Go Lisbon (www.golisbon.com) Up-to-date info on sightseeing, eating, nightlife and events.
Visit Lisboa (www.visitlisboa.com) Lisbon's comprehensive tourism website, with the low-down on sightseeing, transport and accommodation.

Medical Services

Farmácia Estácio (Rossio 62) A central pharmacy.
British Hospital (✆217 213 400; Rua Tomás da Fonseca) English-speaking staff and doctors.

Money

Cota Câmbios (Rossio 41) One of the best exchange rates in town.

Post

Main Post Office (Praça do Comércio)
Post Office (Praça dos Restauradores)

Tourist Information

Ask Me Lisboa (www.askmelisboa.com; Praça dos Restauradores; ⊙9am-8pm) The largest and most helpful tourist office. Can book accommodation or reserve rental cars.

Y Lisboa (www.askmelisboa.com; Rua Jardim do Regedor 50; ⊙9am-8pm)

Lisboa Welcome Centre (www.visitlisboa.com; Praça do Comércio; ⊙9am-6pm)

Information Kiosks (near Rua Conceição; ⊙10am-1pm & 2-6pm) Santa Apolónia (door 47, inside train station, Santa Apolónia; ⊙8am-1pm Tue-Sat) ;Belém (Largo dos Jernónimos, Belém; ⊙10am-1pm & 2-6pm Tue-Sat) ;Airport (Airport; ⊙7am-midnight).

Getting There & Away

Air

Around 6km north of the centre, **Aeroporto de Lisboa** (Lisbon Airport; www.ana.pt) operates direct flights to many European cities.

Bus

Lisbon's long-distance bus terminal is **Sete Rios** (Rua das Laranjeiras), conveniently linked to both Jardim Zoológico metro station and Sete Rios train station. The big carriers, **Rede Expressos** (☏213 581 460; www.rede-expressos.pt) and **Eva** (☏213 581 466; www.eva-bus.com), run frequent services to almost every major town.

The other major terminal is Gare do Oriente (at Oriente metro and train station), concentrating on services to the north and to Spain. The biggest companies operating from here are **Renex** (☏218 956 836; www.renex.pt)and the Spanish operator **Avanza** (☏218 940 250; www.avanzabus.com).

Train

Santa Apolónia station is the terminus for northern and central Portugal. You can catch trains from Santa Apolónia to Gare do Oriente train station, which has departures to The Algarve and international destinations. Cais do Sodré station is for Belém, Cascais and Estoril. Rossio station is the terminal for trains to Sintra via Queluz.

The overnight Lusitânia Comboio Hotel train (one-way seat/berth €61/84) departs Lisbon daily at 9.18pm, passing through Coimbra and Salamanca (Spain) before reaching Madrid the next morning at 8.20am.

For fares and schedules, visit www.cp.pt.

Getting Around

To/From the Airport

The **AeroBus** runs every 20 minutes from 7am to 11pm, taking 30 to 45 minutes between the airport and Cais do Sodré; buy your ticket (€3.50) on the bus.

The red line of the **metro** (€1.40) goes from the airport into town. Change at Alameda (green line) to reach Rossio and Baixa. A **taxi** into town is about €10 to €15.

Car & Motorcycle

On the outskirts of the city there are cheap **car parks** near Parque das Nações and Belém. The most central underground car park is at Praça dos Restauradores, costing around €2 per hour. On Saturday afternoons and Sunday, parking is normally free in the pay-and-display areas in the centre.

Public Transport

A 24-hour **Bilhete Carris/Metro** (€5) gives unlimited travel on all buses, trams, metros and funiculars. Pick it up from Carris kiosks and metro stations.

BUS, TRAM & FUNICULAR Buses and trams run from 6am to 1am, with a few all-night services. Pick up a transport map from tourist offices or Carris kiosks. A single ticket costs more if you buy it on board (€2.85/1.75/3.50 for tram/bus/funicular), and much less (€1.25 per ride) if you buy a refillable *Viva Viagem* card (€0.50), available at Carris offices and in metro stations.

There are three funiculars: Elevador da Bica; Elevador da Glória; Elevador do Lavra.

Don't leave the city without riding tram 28 from Largo Martim Moniz through the narrow streets of the Alfama; tram 12 goes from Praça da Figueira out to Belém.

FERRY Car, bicycle and passenger ferries leave frequently from the Cais do Sodré ferry terminal to Cacilhas (€1.15, 10 minutes). From Terreiro do Paço terminal catamarans zip across to Montijo (€2.70, every 30 minutes) and Seixal (€2.30, every 30 minutes).

METRO The **metro** (www.metrolisboa.pt; 1-/2-zone single €0.85/1.15; ⊙6.30am-1am) is useful for hops across town and to the Parque das Nações. Buy tickets from metro ticket machines, which have English-language menus.

Taxi

Lisbon's taxis are metered and best hired from taxi ranks. Beware of rip-offs from the airport. From Rossio to Belém is around €8 and to the castle about €6. To call one, try **Rádio Táxis** (☏214 942 527) or **Autocoope** (☏217 932 756).

COSTA DA CAPARICA

Located 10km southwest of Lisbon, Costa da Caparica's seemingly never-ending beach attracts sun-worshipping Lisboetas craving all-over tans, surfer dudes keen to ride Atlantic waves, and day-tripping families seeking clean sea and soft sand. It hasn't escaped development, but head south and the high-rises soon give way to pine forests and mellow beach-shack cafes.

During the summer, a **narrow-gauge railway** runs the length of the beach for 20 stops. The nearer beaches, including **Praia do Norte** and **Praia do São Sebastião**, are great for families, while the further ones are younger and trendier, including **Praia da Sereia** (stop 15), with its cool beachfront bar, Bar Waikiki. **Praia do Castelo** (stop 11) and **Praia da Bela Vista** (stop 17) are more-secluded gay and nudist havens.

The **main beach** (called Praia do CDS, or Centro Desportivo de Surf) is lined with cafes, bars and surfing clubs along its promenade.

The best way to get here is by ferry (€1.20, 12 minutes) to Cacilhas from Lisbon's Cais do Sodré, where buses 135 (express) and 124 (local) run to Costa da Caparica town (€3.50, 30 to 45 minutes, every 20 minutes).

Sport-minded folk can also get there by bike and ferry, by riding along the **Tejo bike path** 7km from Cais do Sodré to Belém, taking the ferry from there to Trafaria, then continuing on another new bike path (also separate from traffic) that runs for another 6km down to Costa da Caparica.

AROUND LISBON

Sintra

POP 26,200

Lord Byron called this hilltop town a 'glorious Eden' and, although best appreciated at dusk when the coach tours have left, it *is* a magnificent place. Less than an hour west of Lisbon, Sintra was the traditional summer retreat of Portugal's kings. Today it's a fairy-tale setting of stunning palaces and manors surrounded by rolling green countryside.

◉ Sights & Activities

Although the whole town resembles a historical theme park, there are several compulsory eye-catching sights. Multi-sight admission tickets, available at the tourist office, will save you a few euros.

TOP CHOICE **Quinta da Regaleira**   NOTABLE BUILDING, GARDENS

(www.regaleira.pt; Rua Barbosa du Bocage; adult/child €6/3; ⊙10am-8pm) Exploring this neo-Manueline manor and gardens is like delving into another world. The villa has ferociously carved fireplaces, frescos and Venetian glass mosaics with wild mythological and Knights Templar symbols. The playful gardens hide fountains, grottoes, lakes and underground caverns. All routes seem to lead to the 30m-deep initiation well, **Poço Iniciáto**, with mysterious hollowed-out underground galleries lit by fairy lights.

Palácio Nacional de Sintra   PALACE

(Largo Rainha Dona Amélia; admission €7; ⊙10am-5.30pm Thu-Tue) The whimsical interior of Sintra's iconic twin-chimney palace is a mix of Moorish and Manueline styles, with arabesque courtyards, barley-twist columns and stunning 15th- and 16th-century geometric *azulejos*.

Castelo dos Mouros   CASTLE

(adult/child €7/6; ⊙10am-8pm) An energetic, 3km greenery-flanked hike from the centre, the 8th-century ruined ramparts of this castle provide fine views.

Palácio Nacional da Pena   PALACE

(adult/child €13.50/11; ⊙10am-7pm) This exuberantly kitsch palace is 800m from the Castelo dos Mouros, and is an architectural extravaganza crammed with treasures.

Convento dos Capuchos   RELIGIOUS, SPIRITUAL

(Capuchin Monastery; ✆219 237 300; adult/child €6/5; ⊙9.30am-8pm) Hidden in the woods is this bewitchingly hobbit-hole-like convent, built in 1560 to house 12 monks who lived in incredibly cramped conditions, their tiny cells having low, narrow doors. The warren of cells, chapels, kitchen and cavern make for fascinating exploring.

WORTH A TRIP

PARQUE NATURAL DA ARRÁBIDA

Thickly green, hilly and edged by gleamingly clean, golden beaches and chiselled cliffs, the Arrábida Natural Park stretches along the southeastern coast of the Setúbal Peninsula, some 40km south of Lisbon. Highlights here are the long, golden beaches of windsurfer hot-spot **Figueirinha** and the sheltered bay of **Galapo**. Most stunning of all is **Portinho da Arrábida**, with fine sand, azure waters and a small 17th-century fort built to protect the monks from Barbary pirates.

Further west lies the former fishing village turned resort town of **Sesimbra**, with a fine beach, a hilltop castle and good seafood restaurants. Keep heading west to reach the haunting **Cabo Espichel**, home to a desolate church and striking ocean views over the cliffs.

Your best option for getting here and exploring the area is to rent a car. Be warned: parking is tricky near the beaches.

Monserrate Park GARDENS, PALACE
(www.parquesdesintra.pt; adult/child €7/6; ☉9.30am-8pm) This wild, rambling 30-hectare wooded garden 3.5km west of Sintra bristles with exotic foliage. A manicured lawn sweeps up to the whimsical, 19th-century Moorish-inspired **palácio** (palace).

🛏 Sleeping

Hotel Sintra Jardim GUESTHOUSE €€
(☎219 230 738; hotelsintrajardim@gmail.com; Travessa dos Avelares 12; d incl breakfast €65-80; @🄿🛜🏊) This stately 1850s manor overlooks rambling gardens and an inviting pool, and offers captivating views of the castle. The bright, high-ceilinged rooms are decorated in crisp hues with shiny wood floors.

Almaa HOSTEL €€
(☎219 240 008; www.almaasintrahostel.com; Caminho dos Frades; dm/d/tr €26/64/84) Sustainably-minded Almaa is an idyllic spot to recharge for a few days, with a quirky design scheme (featuring recycled furniture) and a beautiful setting – some rooms have views to the sea. The surrounding 3.5 hectares of lush grounds is set with walking paths and an old spring-fed reservoir for swimming. It's a 10-minute walk from the village centre.

Casa de Hóspedes
Dona Maria da Parreirinha GUESTHOUSE €
(☎219 232 490; Rua João de Deus 12-14; d €45-55) A short walk from the train station, this small, homely guesthouse has old-fashioned but spotless rooms, with dark-wood furnishings and floral fabrics.

🍴 Eating & Drinking

Sintra is famous for its pastries, including *queijadas* (crisp pastry shells filled with marzipan-like cheese, sugar, flour and cinnamon) and *travesseiros* (light rolled and folded puff pastries filled with almond-and-egg yolk cream). Sample the goods at **Fábrica das Verdadeiras Queijadas da Sapa** (Alameda Volta do Duche 12; ☉closed Mon) and **Casa Piriquita** (Rua das Padarias 1-5; ☉closed Wed).

Tulhas PORTUGUESE €€
(Rua Gil Vicente 4; mains €10-14; ☉closed Wed) This converted grain warehouse is dark, tiled and quaint, with twisted chandeliers and a relaxed, cosy atmosphere. It's renowned for its *bacalhau com natas* (baked cod with cream and grated cheese).

Saudade CAFE €
(Avenida Dr Miguel Bombardo 8; snacks €2-4; ☉8.30am-midnight Mon-Tue & Thu-Sat, 9am-8pm Sun; 🛜) This former bakery with changing art exhibitions has cherub-covered ceilings and a rambling interior. It's a charming spot for pastries or lighter fare, plus daily specials.

Dom Pipas PORTUGUESE €€
(Rua João de Deus 62; mains €7-12; ☉9am-midnight Tue-Sun) A local favourite, Dom Pipas serves up excellent Portuguese dishes, amid *azulejos* and rustic country decor. It's behind the train station (left out of the station, first left, then left again to the end).

❶ Information

Tourist Office (www.cm-sintra.pt; Praça da República 23; ☉9am-7pm) Has useful maps and can help with accommodation.

❶ Getting There & Away

The **Lisbon–Sintra railway** terminates in Sintra, a 1km scenic walk northeast of the town's historic centre. Sintra's **bus station**, and another train station, are a further 1km east in the new town Portela de Sintra. Frequent **shuttle buses** link the historic centre with the bus station.

Train services (€2.05, 40 minutes, every 15 minutes) run between Sintra and Lisbon's Rossio station. Buses run regularly from Sintra to Cascais (€4, 60 minutes), Estoril (€4, 40 minutes) and Mafra (45 minutes).

ℹ Getting Around

A handy bus for accessing the castle is the hop-on, hop-off Scotturb bus 434 (€5), which runs from the train station via Sintra-Vila to Castelo dos Mouros (10 minutes), Palácio da Pena (15 minutes) and back.

A **taxi** to Pena or Monserrate costs around €6 one-way.

Cascais

POP 34,000

Cascais is a handsome seaside resort with elegant buildings, an atmospheric old town and a happy abundance of restaurants and bars.

◉ Sights & Activities

Coast & Beaches BEACH

Cascais' three sandy bays – **Praia da Conceição**, **Praia da Rainha** and **Praia da Ribeira** – are great for a sunbake or a tingly Atlantic dip, but attract crowds in summer.

Estoril is a somewhat faded resort 2km east of Cascais with a popular sandy beach and Europe's largest **casino**.

The sea roars into the coast at **Boca do Inferno** (Hell's Mouth), 2km west of Cascais. Spectacular **Cabo da Roca**, Europe's westernmost point, is 16km from Cascais and Sintra and is served by buses from both towns.

FREE **Casa das Histórias Paula Rego** GALLERY

(www.casadashistoriaspaularego.com; Avenida da República 300; ☺10am-7pm) A boon to Sintra's cultural cache, this small museum showcases the disturbing, fairy-tale-like paintings of Paula Rego, one of Portugal's finest living artists.

Museu Condes de Castro Guimarães MUSEUM

(☺10am-5pm Tue-Sun) The picturesque gardens of **Parque Marechal Carmona** (Avenida Rei Humberto II) house this museum in a whimsical early-19th-century mansion, complete with castle turrets and Arabic cloister.

🛏 Sleeping & Eating

Residencial Solar Dom Carlos GUESTHOUSE €€

(☎214 828 115; www.solardomcarlos.pt; Rua Latino Coelho 104; s/d €50/70; 🅿@🛜) Hidden down a sleepy alley, this 16th-century former royal residence turned guest house retains lots of original features, from chandeliers to wood beams, *azulejos* and a frescoed breakfast room.

Confraria Sushi JAPANESE €€

(Rua Luís Xavier Palmeirim 16; mains €8-13; ☺noon-midnight Tue-Sun) This art-slung cafe, jazzed up with technicolour glass chandeliers, is a fun spot for sushi and tasty salads. Patio seating.

Viriato PORTUGUESE €€

(Av Vasco da Gama 34; mains €8-12; ☺lunch daily, dinner Wed-Mon) Amid rustic country decor, Viriato is a local favourite for its chargrilled fish and Portuguese classics.

ℹ Information

Tourist Office (www.visiteestoril.com; Rua Visconde de Luz 14) Can provide accommodation lists and bus timetables.

ℹ Getting There & Around

Trains run frequently to Cascais via Estoril (€2.05, 40 minutes) from Cais do Sodré station in Lisbon.

THE ALGARVE

Love it or loathe it, it's easy to see the allure of The Algarve: breathtaking cliffs, golden sands, scalloped bays and long sandy islands. Although overdevelopment has blighted parts of the coast, head inland and you'll land solidly in lovely Portuguese countryside once again. Algarve highlights include the forested slopes of Monchique, the pretty riverside town of Tavira and windswept, historic Sagres. Underrated Faro is the regional capital.

BIKE TO THE BEACH

Free bikes are available from 8am to 7pm from a kiosk on Largo da Estação near the train station (bring ID). There's a bicycle path that runs the entire 9km stretch from Cascais to wild **Guincho beach**, a popular surf spot.

PORTUGAL CASCAIS

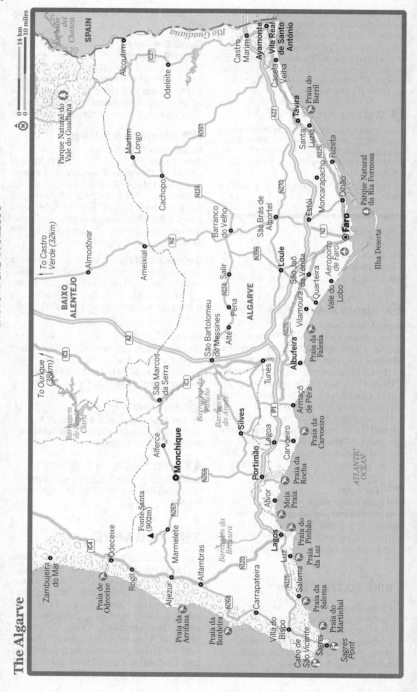

The Algarve

Faro

POP 65,000

Faro is an attractive town with a palm-clad waterfront, well-maintained plazas and a small pedestrianised centre sprinkled with outdoor cafes. There are no beaches in Faro itself, though it's an easy jaunt by ferry to picturesque beaches nearby. A boat trip through the Ria Formosa Natural Park is another highlight.

Sights & Activities

Ilha Deserta   ISLAND

Around six ferries per day make the 35-minute trip (€10 return) out to Ilha da Barreta (aka Ilha Deserta), a long narrow-strip of sand just off the mainland. There's a good seafood restaurant there, but little other development. Boats depart from the west side of Cidade Velha; exiting the tourist office, turn left and follow the edge of the old walls. Other depatures from here go to **Praia de Faro** (bus 14 and 16 also go here) and **Praia de Farol**.

Parque Natural da Ria Formosa   PARK

For visits to the Ria Formosa Natural Park, sign up for a boating or birdwatching tour with the environmentally friendly outfits of **Ria Formosa** (918 720 002; www.formosamar.pt) and **Lands** (289 817 466; www.lands.pt), both in the Clube Naval in Faro's marina.

Sleeping & Eating

Residencial Oceano   GUESTHOUSE €

(289 823 349; Rua Ivens 21; s/d €40/50; @) Up a tile-lined stairway, you'll find this simple and friendly option with tidy rooms (some of which lack windows).

Residencial Dandy   GUESTHOUSE €€

(289 824 791; Rua Filipe Alistão 62; d from €40; *) Plastic flowers, African masks and museum-style paraphernalia are features of this rambling place. The best rooms have antique furniture, high ceilings and wrought-iron balconies.

Pousada da Juventude   HOSTEL €

(289 826 521; www.pousadasjuventude.pt; Rua da Polícia de Segurança Pública 1; dm/d from €15/34;) Adjoining a small park, this hostel offers basic, clean rooms with no frills but is a good ultrabudget option.

Adega Nova   PORTUGUESE €€

(Rua Francisco Barreto 24; mains €7-13) This much-loved place serves tasty meat and fish dishes amid country charm. The daily specials are superb value.

Restaurante A Taska   PORTUGUESE €€

(289 824 739; Rua do Alportel 38; mains €7-14; ☉lunch & dinner Mon-Sat) Popular with locals, this cosy, busy trattoria-style restaurant serves delicious regional food such as *xarém* (corn meal), and has daily specials on a blackboard.

ℹ Information

Tourist Office (www.visitalgarve.pt; Rua da Misericórdia 8) A helpful, multilingual office.

ℹ Getting There & Away

Faro airport has both domestic and international flights.

From the **bus station**, just west of the centre, there are at least six daily express coaches to Lisbon (€20, four hours), plus several slower services, and frequent buses to other coastal towns.

The **train station** is a few minutes' walk west of the bus station. Five trains run daily to Lisbon (€22, four hours).

ℹ Getting Around

The **airport** is 6km from the centre. **Buses** 14 and 16 (€1.90) run into town until 9pm. A **taxi** from the airport to the town centre costs about €12.

Tavira

POP 25,400

Set on either side of the meandering Rio Gilão, Tavira is a charming town with a hilltop castle, an old Roman bridge and a smattering of Gothic churches. The pretty sands of Ilha da Tavira are a short boat ride away.

Sights & Activities

FREE Castle   CASTLE

(Rua da Liberdade; ☉10am-5pm) Tavira's ruined castle dominates the town. Nearby, the 16th-century **Palácio da Galeria** (281 320 540; Calçada da Galeria; admission €2; ☉10am-12.30pm & 3-6.30pm Tue-Sat) holds occasional exhibitions.

Igreja da Misericórdia   CHURCH

(Rua da Galeria) One of the town's 30-plus churches, the 16th-century Igreja da Misericórdia is among the most striking in The Algarve.

Ilha da Tavira   ISLAND, BEACH

You can reach this island beach by a ferry at Quatro Águas (€1.40 return) or Tavira (summer only, €1.90 return). It's a 2km walk to Quatro Águas (from the south bank of the river, follow the road south-southwest).

Casa Abilio   BICYCLE RENTAL

(Rua João Vaz Corte Real 23; per day around €7) Enjoy pedal power with a rented bike.

Sport Nautica   KAYAKING

(Rua Jacques Pessoa 26; per half-/full day €15/25) Rent kayaks for a paddle along the river.

🛏 Sleeping & Eating

Pensão Residencial Lagôas   GUESTHOUSE €

(☎281 328 243; Rua Almirante Cândido dos Reis 24; s/d from €20/30) A long-standing favourite, friendly Lagôas has small (some cramped), well-maintained rooms. There's a sunny terrace with views.

Residencial
Princesa do Gilão   GUESTHOUSE €€

(☎281 325 171; www.residencial-gilao.com; Rua Borda d'Água de Aguiar 10; s/d €52/58; ❄) This '80s-style place on the river has tight but neat rooms with identical decor. Go for a room with a river view.

Restaurante Bica   SEAFOOD €€

(Rua Almirante Cândido dos Reis 24; mains €8-14) Deservedly popular, Bica serves splendid food, such as fresh grilled fish and *cataplana* (seafood and sausage cooked in a copper pot), which diners enjoy with good-value Borba wine.

Bistro 'oPorto'   INTERNATIONAL €€

(Rua Dr José Pires Padinha 180; mains €10-15; ☻lunch & dinner Tue-Sun) Head to this artfully decorated French-owned restaurant with a relaxed riverside setting for octopus rice, codfish cakes, coconut curry and other flavourful bites.

❶ Information

Câmara Municipal (Praça da Republica; ☻9am-8pm Mon-Fri, 10am-1pm Sat) Free internet access.

Tourist Office (Praça da República) Can help with accommodation.

❶ Getting There & Away

Some 15 **trains** and six express **buses** run daily between Faro and Tavira (€3.50, one hour).

Lagos

POP 29,700

In summer, the pretty fishing port of Lagos has a party vibe; its picturesque cobbled streets and pretty nearby beaches are packed with revellers and sun-seekers.

◉ Sights & Activities

Museu Municipal   MUSEUM

(Rua General Alberto da Silveira; admission €3; ☻10am-5.30pm Tue-Sun) The municipal museum houses an eclectic mix of archaeological and ecclesiastical treasures (and oddities). Admission includes the adjacent **Igreja de Santo António**, one of the best baroque churches in Portugal.

Beaches   BEACH

The beach scene includes **Meia Praia**, a vast strip to the east; **Praia da Luz** to the west; and the smaller **Praia do Pinhão**.

Blue Ocean   OUTDOORS

(☎964 665 667; www.blue-ocean-divers.de) Organises diving trips. Along the promenade, fishermen can offer motorboat jaunts to nearby grottoes.

Kayak Adventures   KAYAKING

(☎913 262 200; www.kayakadventures-lagos.com) Offers kayaking trips from Batata Beach.

🛏 Sleeping

Pensão Marazul   GUESTHOUSE €€

(☎282 770 230; www.pensaomarazul.com; Rua 25 de Abril 13; s/d €45/55; @☎) Draws a good mix of foreign travellers to its small but cheerfully painted rooms – the best of which offer sea views.

Sol a Sol   HOTEL €€

(☎282 761 290; www.residencialsolasol.com; Rua Lançarote de Freitas 22; r €55-65) This central, small hotel has neat rooms with tiny balconies and views over the town.

Caza de São Gonçalo   GUESTHOUSE €€

(☎919 841 622; Rua Candido dos Reis 73; dm/d €25/60) New in 2012, this beautifully restored mansion has a handful of attractive dorm rooms and roomier doubles, all with en-suite bathrooms. There's also a jacuzzi and a lounge area.

🍴 Eating

oA Forja   PORTUGUESE €€

(Rua dos Ferreiros 17; mains €8-15; ☻lunch & dinner Sun-Fri) This buzzing place pulls in the crowds for its hearty, top-quality traditional food. Plates of the day are always reliable, as are the fish dishes.

Casinha do Petisco PORTUGUESE, SEAFOOD €€
(Rua da Oliveira 51; mains €7-13; ⊗Mon-Sat) This tiny traditional gem comes highly recommended by locals for its seafood grills and shellfish dishes. Come early to beat the lines.

❶ Information

Tourist Office (www.visitalgarve.pt; Praça Gil Eanes) In the centre of town.

❶ Getting There & Away

Bus and **train** services depart frequently for other Algarve towns, and around eight times daily to Lisbon (€21, 4¼ hours).

❶ Getting Around

A **bus service** (tickets €1-2; ⊗7am-8pm Mon-Sat) provides useful connections to the beaches of Meia Praia and Luz. Rent bicycles and motorbikes from **Motorent** (☏282 769 716; www.motorent.pt; Rua Victor Costa e Silva; bike/motorcycle per 3 days from €21/60).

Monchique

POP 5900

High above the coast, in cooler mountainous woodlands, the picturesque hamlet of Monchique makes a lovely base for exploring, with some excellent options for walking, cycling and canoeing.

◉ Sights & Activities

Caldas de Monchique, 6km south, is a peaceful hamlet with a **spa resort** (www.monchiquetermas.com). Some 8km west is The Algarve's 'rooftop', the 902m **Fóia** peak atop the Serra de Monchique, with breezy views through a tangle of radio masts.

Igreja Matriz CHURCH
(Rua da Igreja) This church features a stunning Manueline portal, with its stone seemingly tied in knots. Keep climbing to reach the ruins of the 17th-century Franciscan monastery, **Nossa Senhora do Desterro**, which overlooks the town from its wooded hilltop. From there, it's another 5km along a marked trail to the lookout at **Fóia**.

Outdoor Tours OUTDOORS
(☏282 969 520; www.outdoor-tours.com; Mexilhoeira Grande; trips from €20) Offers cycling, kayaking and walking trips.

🍴 Sleeping & Eating

Residencial Miradouro GUESTHOUSE €
(☏282 912 163; Rua dos Combatentes do Ultramar; s/d from €25/40) This 1970s hilltop place offers sweeping views and neat rooms, some with balcony.

A Charrete PORTUGUESE €€
(Rua Dr Samora Gil 30-34; mains €11-15; ⊗lunch & dinner Thu-Tue) Touted as the town's best eatery for its regional specialities, this place serves reliably good cuisine amid country rustic charm.

❶ Information

Tourist Office (Largo de São Sebastião; ⊗9.30am-1pm & 2-5.30pm Mon-Fri) Uphill from the bus stop.

❶ Getting There & Away

There are five to nine **buses** daily from Portimão (€4.20, 45 minutes) to Monchique.

Silves

POP 11,000

The one-time capital of Moorish Algarve, Silves is a pretty town of jumbling orange rooftops scattered above the banks of the Rio Arade. Clamber around the ramparts of its fairy-tale **castle** for superb views.

🍴 Sleeping & Eating

Residencial Ponte Romana GUESTHOUSE €
(☏282 443 275; Horta da Cruz; s/d €20/35) Floral-themed rooms beside the Roman bridge, with castle views and a cavernous bar-restaurant full of old-timers and Portuguese families.

Quinta da Figueirinha INN €€
(☏282 440 700; www.qdf.pt; 2-/4-/6-person apt from €54/94/135; ☀) Four kilometres outside of Silves, this 36-hectare organic farm offers simple apartments in idyllic, farmlike surroundings.

Café Ingles INTERNATIONAL €€
(☏282 442 585; mains €10-23; ☂) Situated at the castle entrance, this funky English-owned place with romantic rooftop terrace has wood-fired pizzas, prawn curry, lamb cutlets with rosemary and other global dishes. In summer, there's live music on weekends.

PORTUGAL MONCHIQUE

ⓘ Getting There & Away

Silves **train station** is 2km from town; trains from Lagos (€2.85, 35 minutes) stop eight times daily (from Faro, change at Tunes), to be met by local buses. Four to seven **buses** run daily connecting Silves and Albufeira (€4.20, 50 minutes).

Sagres

POP 2100

The small, elongated village of Sagres has an end-of-the-world feel with its sea-carved cliffs and empty, wind-whipped fortress high above the ocean.

◉ Sights & Activities

Coast & Beaches   BEACH
Visit Europe's southwestern-most point, the **Cabo de São Vicente** (Cape St Vincent), 6km to the west. A solitary lighthouse stands on this barren cape.

This coast is ideal for surfing; hire windsurfing gear at sand-dune fringed **Praia do Martinhal**. Rental shops on the main street hire out bikes, surfboards and wetsuits. You can sign up for surfing lessons with **Sagres Natura** (☑282 624 072; www.sagresnatura.com; Rua São Vicente). **DiversCape** (☑965 559 073; www.diverscape.com; Porto da Balereira) organises diving trips.

Fortaleza de Sagres   FORTRESS
(adult/child €3/1.50, free 10am-2pm Sun ; ☺10am-8.30pm) Sagres' fort offers breathtaking views over the seaside cliffs. According to legend, this is where Henry the Navigator established his navigation school and primed the early Portuguese explorers.

Mar Ilimitado   BOAT TOUR
(☑916 832 625; www.marilimitado.com; Porto da Balereira) **Mar Ilimitado** offers dolphin-spotting boat trips (€32) from the marina.

🛏 Sleeping & Eating

**Casa do Cabo de
Santa Maria**   GUESTHOUSE €€
(☑282 624 722; www.casadocabodesantamaria.
com; Rua Patrão António Faústino; r/apt from €50/80; ☏🅿) These squeaky-clean rooms and apartments might not have sweeping views, but they are handsomely furnished.

A Tasca   SEAFOOD €€
(Porto da Balereira; mains €12-17; ☺lunch & dinner Thu-Tue) Overlooking the marina, this cosy place whips up tasty *cataplana* and other seafood dishes, best enjoyed on the sunny terrace.

ⓘ Information

Tourist Office (Rua Comandante Matoso; ☺Tue-Sat) Central to town.

ⓘ Getting There & Away

Frequent **buses** run daily to Sagres from Lagos (€3.80, one hour), with fewer on Sunday. One continues to Cabo de São Vicente on weekdays.

CENTRAL PORTUGAL

The vast centre of Portugal is a rugged swath of rolling hillsides, whitewashed villages and olive groves and cork trees. Richly historic, it is scattered with prehistoric remains and medieval castles. It's also home to one of Portugal's most architecturally rich towns, Évora, as well as several spectacular walled villages. There are fine local wines and, for the more energetic, plenty of outdoor exploring in the dramatic Beiras region.

Évora

POP 54,300

Évora is an enchanting place to delve into the past. Inside the 14th-century walls, Évora's narrow, winding lanes lead to a striking medieval cathedral, a Roman temple and a picturesque town square. These old-fashioned good looks are the backdrop to a lively student town surrounded by wineries and dramatic countryside.

◉ Sights & Activities

Sé   CHURCH
(Largo do Marquês de Marialva; admission €2-5; ☺9am-noon & 2-5pm) Évora's cathedral has fabulous cloisters and a museum jam-packed with ecclesiastical treasures.

Templo Romano   RUINS
(Temple of Diana; Largo do Conde de Vila Flor) Once part of the Roman Forum; it's a heady slice of drama right in town.

Capela dos Ossos   CHAPEL
(Praça 1 de Maio; admission €2; ☺9am-1pm & 2.30-6pm) Built from the skeletons of several thousand people, the ghoulish Chapel of Bones in the Igreja de São Francisco provides a real *Addams Family* day out.

MEGALITHS

Ancient Greek for 'big stones', **megaliths** are found all over the ancient landscape that surrounds Évora. Such prehistoric structures, built around 5000 to 6000 years ago, dot the European Atlantic coast, but here in Alentejo, there is an astounding number of Neolithic remains.

The star attraction is the **Cromeleque dos Almendres**, the Iberian peninsula's most important megalithic group. The site consists of a huge oval of some 95 rounded granite monoliths – some of which are engraved with symbolic markings. They were erected over different periods it seems, with geometric and astral consideration, probably for social gatherings or sacred rituals. It lies 15km west of Évora.

Two and a half kilometres before Cromeleque dos Almendres stands **Menhir dos Almendres**, a single stone about 4m high, with some faint carvings near the top.

A bit further out (25km west of Évora) is the recently reopened **Gruta do Escoural** (☑266 857 000; admission €2; ⊙11am & 2.30pm Wed-Sat), a cave containing Neolithic rock art.

To get to this area, your best option is to rent a car or bike (note that about 5km of the route is rough and remote). Stop by the tourist office for exact driving directions.

Sleeping

TOP
CHOICE **Albergaria Calvario** BOUTIQUE HOTEL €€€
(☑266 745 930; www.albergariadocalvario.com; Travessa dos Lagares 3; d/studio incl breakfast €108/125) Elegant, friendly and comfortable, this place has an ambience that travellers adore. Pleasant lounge areas, a terrace, books and classical music, plus comfortable beds, ensure a homely stay.

Hostel Namaste HOSTEL €
(☑266 743 014; www.hostelnamasteevora.pt; Largo Doutor Manuel Alves Branco 12; dm/s/d €17/30/40; 🛜) New in 2012, this welcoming guesthouse has two attractively decorated four-bed dorm rooms and two private rooms (one with ensuite). The young, well-travelled owners create a familial ambience, and you can join them for dinner (€7 per person).

Casa dos Teles GUESTHOUSE €
(☑266 702 453; casadosteles.planetaclix.pt; Rua Romão Ramalho 27; s/d €30/35, with shared bathroom €20/25; 🌀🛜) These nine rooms – mostly light and airy – are good value; quieter rooms at the back overlook a pretty courtyard.

✕ Eating

TOP
CHOICE **Botequim da Mouraria** PORTUGUESE €€
(☑266 746 775; Rua da Mouraria 16a; mains €13-16.50; ⊙lunch & dinner Mon-Fri, lunch Sat) Poke around the old Moorish quarter to find this cosy spot serving some of Évora's finest food and wine. There are no reservations, just 12 stools at a counter.

Dom Joaquim PORTUGUESE €€
(☑266 731 105; Rua dos Penedos 6; mains €12-15; ⊙lunch Tue-Sun, dinner Tue-Sat) Amid stone walls and modern artwork, Dom Joaquim serves excellent traditional cuisine including meats (game and succulent, fall-off-the bone oven lamb) and seafood dishes.

Vinho e Noz PORTUGUESE €€
(Ramalho Orgigão 12; mains €11-12; ⊙lunch & dinner Mon-Sat) This family-run place has a warmly lit, brick-walled interior, a large wine list and good-quality cuisine.

Um Quarto Para as Nove PORTUGUESE €€
(Rua Pedro Simões 9; mains €12-19; ⊙lunch & dinner Thu-Tue) Serves up some of Évora's best seafood, including a tasty *açorda de mariscos* (a shrimp, clam and bread stew).

Pastelaria Conventual Pão de Rala BAKERY €
(Rua do Cicioso 47; pastries from €2; ⊙7.30am-8pm) Specialises in heavenly pastries, all made on the premises.

Drinking

Bar do Teatro BAR
(Praça Joaquim António de Aguiar; ⊙8pm-2am) This small, inviting bar with its high ceilings and old-world decor draws a friendly mixed crowd. Come early for an outdoor table overlooking the park.

Spettus CAFE, BAR
(Praça de Sertório 3; ⊙noon-2am) On a peaceful plaza near the town hall, laid-back Spettus

has outdoor tables that fill with a student crowd by night.

Terrazza BAR
(Jardim do Paço; Palácio das Cinco Quinas) A few steps from the Templo Romano, this plant-filled garden courtyard attracts a slightly more sophisticated crowd.

❶ Information

Câmara Municipal (◎9am-12.30pm & 2-5pm Mon-Fri) Free internet inside; free 24-hour wi-fi out front.

Tourist Office (www.cm-evora.pt; Praça do Giraldo 73) Has an excellent city map.

❶ Getting There & Away

Évora has six to 12 **buses** daily to Lisbon (€12, two hours) and three to Faro (€16.20, five hours), departing from the station off Avenida São Sebastião (700m southwest of the centre). Regular **trains** go direct to Lisbon (€12-16, 90 minutes) and indirectly, via Pinhal Novo, to Faro (€28, 4¼ hours) and Lagos (€31, five hours). The train station is 600m south of the Jardim Público.

Monsaraz

POP 970

In a dizzy setting high above the plain, this walled village has a moody medieval feel and magnificent views. The biennial **Monsaraz Museu Aberto** held in July on even-numbered years, features exhibitions and concerts.

The **Museu do Fresco** (Plaça Dom Nuno Álvares; admission €1.80; ◎10am-12.30pm & 2-6pm) has a superb 15th-century fresco. Situated 3km north of town is **Menhir of Outeiro**, one of the tallest megalithic monuments ever discovered.

There are several places to stay in town, including the friendly **Casa St Condestável** (✆266 557 181; www.condestavel-monsaraz. com; Rua Direita 4; r/ste €55/80) with wooden trimmings, whitewashed walls and heavy wooden furniture.

Casa do Forno (Travessa da Sanabrosa; ✆266 557 190; mains €8-10; ◎lunch & dinner Wed-Mon) is a small local favourite for its classic Alentejan cooking. There's a terrace with views.

The **tourist office** (✆266 557 136; Rua Direita 2) can offer advice on accommodation.

Up to four daily **buses** connect Monsaraz with Reguengos de Monsaraz (€3, 35 minutes, Monday to Friday), with connections to Évora.

Estremoz

POP 9000

One of three marble towns in these parts, Estremoz has an attractive centre set with peaceful plazas, orange-tree-lined lanes and a hilltop castle and convent. In its prime, the town was one of the most strongly fortified in Portugal, with its very own palace (now a luxurious *pousada;* upmarket inn).

◉ Sights

Museu Municipal MUSEUM
(✆268 339 219; Rua D Dinis; adult €1.55; ◎9am-12.30pm & 2-5.30pm Tue-Sun) In a beautiful 17th-century almshouse, the municipal museum specialises in fascinating pottery figurines, including an entire Easter parade.

⊨ Sleeping & Eating

Hotel O Gadanha HOTEL €
(✆268 339 110; www.hotelogadanha.com; Largo General Graça 56; s/d/tr €23/38/50 ; ❋🛜) This whitewashed house offers excellent value for its bright, fresh and clean rooms overlooking the square.

Adega do Isaías PORTUGUESE €€
(Rua do Almeida 21; mains €11-13; ◎lunch & dinner Mon-Sat; ✍) This award-winning, rustic *tasca* (tavern) serves tender fish, meat and Alentejan specialities inside a wine cellar crammed with tables and huge wine jars.

❶ Information

Tourist Office (www.cm-estremoz.pt; Rossio Marquês de Pombal) On the south side of Rossio, the huge main square.

❶ Getting There & Away

Estremoz is linked to Évora by three local **buses** (€4, 1¼ hours), Monday to Friday.

WORTH A TRIP

PALÁCIO DUCAL

Located in another marble town 17km from Estremoz, the **Palácio Ducal** (Terreiro do Paço, Vila Viçosa; admission €6, armoury/coach collection/Chinese Porcelain/treasury €3/2/2.50/2.50; ◎2.30-5.30pm Tue, 10am-1pm & 2.30-5.30pm Wed-Sun) is the magnificent ancestral home of the dukes of Bragança, and is rich with *azulejos*, frescoed ceilings and elaborate tapestries.

Peniche

POP 16,000

Popular for its nearby surfing beaches and also as a jumping-off point for the beautiful Ilhas Berlengas nature reserve, the coastal city of Peniche remains a working port, giving it a slightly grittier and more 'lived-in' feel than its beach-resort neighbours. It has a walled historic centre and lovely beaches east of town.

From the bus station, it's a 10-minute walk west to the historic centre.

◉ Sights

FREE Fortress   FORTRESS

(admission free, museum admission €1.50; ⊙9am-12.30pm & 2-5.30pm Tue-Fri, from 10am Sat & Sun) Peniche's imposing 16th-century fortress served as one of dictator Salazar's infamous jails for political prisoners and was later a temporary home for African refugees. The on-site **museum** houses the chilling interrogation chambers and cells on the top floor.

Islands   ISLAND

About 5km to the northeast of Peniche is the scenic island-village of **Baleal**, connected to the mainland village of Casais do Baleal by a causeway. The fantastic sweep of sandy beach here offers some fine surfing. Surf schools dot the sands, as do several bar-restaurants.

Sitting about 10km offshore from Peniche, **Berlenga Grande** is a spectacular, rocky and remote island, with twisting, shocked-rock formations and gaping caverns. It's the only island of the Berlenga archipelago you can visit; the group consists of three tiny islands surrounded by clear, calm, dark-blue waters full of shipwrecks – great for snorkelling and diving. Several outfits make the 40-minute trip to the island, including **Viamar** (✆262 785 646; www.viamar-berlenga.com; return adult/child €18/10).

⚡ Activities

Surfing

Surf camps offer week-long instruction (from €250 to 500 per week including lodging) as well as two-hour classes (€35 to 50), plus board and wetsuit hire. Well-established names include **Baleal Surfcamp** (www.baleal surfcamp.com), **Maximum Surfcamp** (www. maximumsurfcamp.com) and **Peniche Surfcamp** (www.penichesurfcamp.com).

Diving

There are good diving opportunities around Peniche, and especially around Berlenga Grande. Expect to pay about €65 to €75 for two dives (less around Peniche) with **Acuasuboeste** (www.acuasuboeste.com; Porto de Pesca) or **Haliotis** (www.haliotis.pt; Avenida Monsenhor Bastos).

⊨ Sleeping

TOP CHOICE **Casa das Marés**   B&B €€

(✆262 769 371, 262 769 200, 262 769 255; www. casadasmares2.com; Praia do Baleal; d €80; ☎) At the picturesque, windswept tip of Baleal, this unique place is loaded with character and all rooms have great sea views.

Peniche Hostel   HOSTEL €

(✆969 008 689; www.penichehostel.com; Rua Arquitecto Paulino Montês 6; dm/d €20/50; @☎) This cosy, welcoming hostel has a colourfully decorated lounge and very clean rooms. Surfboards and bikes are available for hire, and there's an attached surf school.

✗ Eating & Drinking

Restaurante A Sardinha   SEAFOOD €€

(Rua Vasco da Gama 81; mains €6-12; ⊙lunch & dinner) This simple place on a narrow street parallel to Largo da Ribeira does a roaring trade with locals and tourists alike.

Bar da Praia   BAR

(Praia do Baleal; ⊙noon-2am) One of several lively bars right on Baleal beach, with an outdoor terrace and DJs most nights.

❶ Getting There & Away

Peniche's **bus station** (✆968 903 861) is located 400m northeast of the tourist office (cross the Ponte Velha connecting the town to the isthmus). Buses go to Lisbon (€9, 1½ hours, every one to two hours), Coimbra (€14.50, 2¾ hours, three daily) and Óbidos (€3.15, 40 minutes, five to 13 daily).

Óbidos

POP 3100

This exquisite walled village was a wedding gift from Dom Dinis to his wife Dona Isabel (beats a fondue set), and its historic centre is a delightful place to wander. Highlights include the **Igreja de Santa Maria** (Rua Direita), with fine *azulejos,* and views from the town walls.

From mid-July to mid-August, Óbidos hosts the **Mercado Medieval** (www.mercadomedievalobidos.pt), featuring jousting matches, wandering minstrels and abundant medieval mayhem.

🛏 Sleeping & Eating

Hostel Argonauta   HOSTEL €
(☏262 958 088; http://hostel-argonauta.blogspot.com; Rua Adelaide Ribeirete 14; dm/d incl breakfast from €20/40; @🛜) The friendly and welcoming Señora Rozas runs this cosy place with spacious, handsomely furnished rooms, a short stroll (uphill) to the heart of the medieval centre.

Casal da Eira Branca   GUESTHOUSE €€
(☏966 629 868; www.casaldaeirabranca.com; Travessa do Facho 45; d/apt €65/105) Offers character-filled rooms with beamed ceilings and decorative balconies, one block from the main street (Rua Direita).

Petrarum Domus   PORTUGUESE €€
(Rua Direita; mains €9-18; ⊙lunch & dinner) Amid age-old stone walls, Petrarum serves up hearty dishes like pork with mushrooms, mixed seafood sautes and several *bacalhau* plates. The multilevel dining room is one of Óbidos' most atmsopheric settings.

ℹ Information

Espaço Internet (Rua Direita 107) Free internet access.

Tourist Office (Rua Direita) This helpful tourist office is just outside Porta da Vila, the town's main entrance gate.

ℹ Getting There & Away

Rodotejo (www.rodotejo.pt), runs frequent buses (every 45 minutes weekdays, eight daily weekends) between Obidos and Lisbon (€8, 70 minutes).

Nazaré

POP 16,000

Nazaré has a bustling coastal setting with narrow cobbled lanes running down to a wide, cliff-backed beach. The town centre is jammed with seafood restaurants and bars; expect huge crowds in July and August.

◉ Sights & Activities

The **beaches** here are superb, although swimmers should be aware of dangerous currents. Climb or take the funicular to the clifftop **Sítio**, with its cluster of fishermen's cottages and great view.

Historic Monasteries   ARCHITECTURE
Two of Portugal's big-time architectural masterpieces are close by. Follow the signs to Alcobaça where, right in the centre of town, is the immense **Mosteiro de Santa Maria de Alcobaça** (admission €6; ⊙9am-7pm) dating from 1178; don't miss the colossal former kitchen.

Batalha's massive **Mosteiro de Santa Maria de Vitória** (admission €6; ⊙9am-6.30pm), dating from 1388, is among the supreme achievements of Manueline architecture.

🛏 Sleeping & Eating

Many townspeople rent out rooms; doubles start at €35. Ask around near the seafront Av da República.

Vila Conde Fidalgo   GUESTHOUSE €
(☏262 552 361; http://condefidalgo.planetaclix.pt; Avenida da Independência Nacional 21a; d/apt from €40/80) This pretty little complex uphill a few blocks from the beach is built around a series of flower-filled courtyards. Rooms all have kitchenettes.

Adega Oceano   HOTEL €
(☏262 561 161; www.adegaoceano.com; Avenida da República 51; d €60; ❄🛜) This little oceanfront place offers pleasantly set rooms – renovated modern rooms in back, beach-view quarters in front.

A Tasquinha   SEAFOOD €€
(Rua Adrião Batalha 54; mains €7-11; ⊙lunch & dinner Tue-Sun) This enormously popular family-run tavern serves high-quality seafood at reasonable prices. Expect queues on summer nights.

ℹ Information

Tourist Office (www.cm-nazare.pt; Av Manuel Remígio) On the beachfront (south of the main centre).

ℹ Getting There & Away

Nazaré has numerous **bus** connections to Lisbon (€10.50, two hours).

Tomar

POP 16,000

A charming town straddling a river, Tomar has the notoriety of being home to the Knights Templar; check out their headquarters, the outstanding monastery **Convento** de Cristo (admission €6; ⊙9am-6.30pm), a steep climb above town. Other rarities include a medieval **synagogue** (Rua Dr Joaquim Jacinto 73; admission free; ⊙10am-7pm Tue-Sun). The town is backed by the dense greenery of the **Mata Nacional dos Sete Montes** (Seven Hills National Forest).

🛏 Sleeping & Eating

Residencial União   GUESTHOUSE €
(☎249 323 161; www.hotel-ami.com/hotel/uniao; Rua Serpa Pinto 94; s/d €30/40; 🖲) Tomar's most atmospheric budget choice, this once-grand townhouse features large and sprucely maintained rooms with antique furniture and fixtures.

Estalagem de Santa Iria   INN €€
(☎249 313 326; www.estalagemsantairia.com; Mouchão Parque; s/d/ste €65/85/125; 🖲) Centrally located on an island in Tomar's lovely riverside park, this '40s-style inn has large comfortable rooms, most with balconies overlooking the leafy grounds or the river.

Calça Perra   INTERNATIONAL €€
(Rua Pedro Dias 59; mains €12-15; ⊙lunch & dinner Tue-Sun) A charming restaurant specializing in delicious grilled fish; eat in the elegant dining room or in the bougainvillea-draped courtyard below.

Restaurante Tabuleiro   PORTUGUESE €
(☎249 312 771; Rua Serpa Pinto 140; mains €7.50; ⊙lunch & dinner Mon-Sat) This family-friendly local eatery with outdoor seating has attentive service and great food served up in ample portions. It's located just off Tomar's main square.

ℹ Information

Tourist Office (Rua Serpa Pinto) Can provide town and forest maps.

ℹ Getting There & Away

Frequent **trains** run to Lisbon (€9.50, two hours).

Coimbra

POP 107,000

Coimbra is a dynamic, fashionable, yet comfortably lived-in city, with a student life centred on the magnificent 13th-century university. Aesthetically eclectic, there are elegant shopping streets, ancient stone walls and backstreet alleys with hidden *tascas* and fado bars. Coimbra was the birth and burial place of Portugal's first king, and was

WORTH A TRIP

ROMAN RUINS

Conimbriga, 16km south of Coimbra, is the site of the well-preserved ruins of a **Roman town** (⊙10am-7pm), including mosaic floors, elaborate baths and trickling fountains. It's a fascinating place to explore, with a good **museum** (www.conimbriga.pt; admission €4, free Sun before 2pm; ⊙10am-7pm) that describes the once-flourishing and later abandoned town. There's a sunny cafe serving good lunch buffets. Frequent buses run to Condeixa, 2km from the site; there are also two direct buses (€2.50) from Coimbra.

the country's most important city when the Moors captured Lisbon.

⦿ Sights & Activities

Sé Velha   CATHEDRAL
(Old Cathedral; ☎239 825 273; Largo da Sé Velha; admission €2; ⊙10am-6pm Mon-Sat) Coimbra's stunning **old cathedral**, dating from the late 12th century, is one of the finest examples of Romanesque architecture in all of Portugal.

Velha Universidade   UNIVERSITY
(Old University; admission €7; ⊙10am-noon & 2-5pm) The old university is unmissable in its grandeur. You can visit various buildings, including the library with its gorgeous book-lined hallways and the Manueline chapel dating back to 1517.

O Pioneiro do Mondego   KAYAKING
(☎239 478 385; www.opioneirodomondego.com; per person €23) Offers daily kayak excursions along the Rio Mondego up to Penacova. The 18km trip departs at 10am from Torres de Mondego, 7km southwest of Coimbra's Largo da Portagem.

🎉 Festivals & Events

Coimbra's annual highlight is **Queima das Fitas**, a boozy week of fado and revelry that begins on the first Thursday in May when students celebrate the end of the academic year.

🛏 Sleeping

TOP CHOICE **Casa Pombal Guest House**   GUESTHOUSE €€
(☎239 835 175; www.casapombal.com; Rua das Flores 18; d €45-68, without bathroom €35-52;

(@🛜) This winning, Dutch-run guesthouse squeezes tons of charm into a small space. Also has an ample morning buffet.

**Pensão-Restaurante
Flôr de Coimbra**   GUESTHOUSE €€
(📞239 823 865; flordecoimbrahr.com.sapo.pt; Rua do Poço 5; s/d/tr €50/60/70, without bathroom €20/35/45; 🛜) This once-grand 19th-century home with its own (recommended) restaurant offers loads of character in a great location.

Grande Hostel de Coimbra   HOSTEL €
(📞239 108 212; www.grandehostelcoimbra.com; Rua Antero Quental 196; dm/d €18/40; @🛜) You won't find a hostel more laid-back than this and it's hard to beat the location in a grand, century-old townhouse near the nightlife of Coimbra's university campus.

✗ Eating & Drinking

Self-caterers should stop by the modern **Mercado Municipal Dom Pedro V** (Rua Olímpio Nicolau Rui Fernandes; ⏱Mon-Sat) for fruit, vegetables and more.

Restaurante Zé Manel   PORTUGUESE €€
(Beco do Forno 12; mains €8-10; ⏱lunch & dinner Mon-Fri, lunch Sat) Great food, huge servings and a zany atmosphere, with walls papered with diners' comments, cartoons and poems.

Restaurante Zé Neto   PORTUGUESE €€
(Rua das Azeiteiras 8; mains €6-10; ⏱lunch & dinner Mon-Sat) This marvellous family-run place specialises in homemade Portuguese standards, including *cabrito* (kid).

Italia   ITALIAN €€
(Parque Dr Manuel de Braga; mains €8-15; ⏱noon-midnight) Expand your midriff at this excellent Italian restaurant on the riverfront, with laden dishes of excellent pizza and pasta.

Cafetaria do Museu   CAFE
(Sé Nova; ⏱8am-7pm Sun-Thu to 4am Fri & Sat) This stylish cafe attracts a hip crowd who come for gourmet burgers, crepes, coffees and cocktails, with fine views from the breezy terrace. It's located near the Sé Nova (the 'New Cathedral', although it's facade dates to the 17th century).

Café Santa Cruz   CAFE
(Praça 8 de Maio; ⏱Mon-Sat) An atmospheric cafe inside a former chapel. Outdoor seating and occasional fado nights.

Café Tropical   BAR
(Praça da República 35; ⏱10am-2am Mon-Sat) One of several indoor-outdoor bars overlooking Praça da República, Café Tropical is a favourite place to start out the night.

☆ Entertainment

Coimbra-style fado is more cerebral than the Lisbon variety, and its adherents are staunchly protective.

oÁ Capella   LIVE MUSIC
(📞918 113 307; www.acapella.com.pt; Rua Corpo de Deus; admission incl 1 drink €10; ⏱9pm-2am) Housed in a fabulous 14th-century former chapel, Á Capella regularly hosts the city's most renowned fado musicians.

❶ Information

Ciberespaço (Loja 4, Av Sá da Bandeira; per hr €2.20; ⏱10am-11pm Mon-Sat, 1-9pm Sun) Paid access on the ground floor of the shopping centre.

Tourist Office (Praça da Porta Férrea) Located near the bridge (Ponte de Santa Clara).

❶ Getting There & Away

There are at least a dozen buses to Lisbon (€13.30, 2½ hours) and Porto (€12, 1½ hours), and regular service to Faro and Évora via Lisbon. There are also frequent trains to Lisbon (€19 to €25, 2 to 3 hours) and Porto (€9 to 17, 1¼ to 2 hours). The main train stations are **Coimbra B**, 2km northwest of the centre, and the central **Coimbra A**. Most long-distance trains call at Coimbra B. The **bus station** (Avenida Fernão Magalhães) is about 400m northeast of the centre.

Luso & the Buçaco Forest

POP 2000

This sylvan region harbours a lush forest of century-old trees surrounded by countryside that's dappled with heather, wildflowers and leafy ferns. There's even a fairy-tale **palace** (📞231 937 970; www.almeidahotels.com; Mata Nacional do Buçaco; 7–8-course meal €35/40; ⏱lunch & dinner; 🛜) here, a 1907 neo-Manueline extravagance, where deep-pocketed visitors can dine or stay overnight. The palace lies amid the Mata Nacional do Buçaco, a forest crisscrossed with trails, dotted with crumbling chapels and graced with ponds, fountains and exotic trees. Buçaco was chosen as a retreat by 16th-century monks, and it surrounds the lovely spa town of Luso. From the centre, it's a 2km walk through forest up to the palace.

The **Maloclinic Spa** (www.maloclinicspa.com; Rua Álvaro Castelões; ⊙10am-6pm Mon-Fri, 9am-6pm Sat & Sun, extended hours summer) offers a range of treatments.

🛏 Sleeping & Eating

Alegre Hotel　　　　　　BOUTIQUE HOTEL €€
(☑231 930 256; www.alegrehotels.com; Rua Emídio Navarro 2; s €45-55, d €60-86; P🅿🛜🏊) This grand, peach-coloured 19th-century townhouse has polished period furniture and other appealing touches. There's a formal parlour and a vine-draped garden with pool.

ℹ Information

Tourist Office (Avenida Emídio Navarro 136; ⊙Mon-Sat) Has maps and leaflets about the forest and trails.

ℹ Getting There & Away

Buses to/from Coimbra (€3.50, 45 minutes) run four times daily each weekday and twice daily on Saturdays. **Trains** to/from Coimbra B station (€2.55, 35 minutes) run several times daily; it's a 15-minute walk to town from the station.

Serra da Estrela

The forested Serra da Estrela has a raw natural beauty and offers some of the country's best hiking. This is Portugal's highest mainland mountain range (1993m), and the source of its two great rivers: Rio Mondego and Rio Zêzere. The town of **Manteigas** makes a great base for hiking and exploring the area (plus skiing in winter). The **main park office** (☑275 980 060; pnse@icn.pt; Rua 1 de Maio 2, Manteigas; ⊙Mon-Fri) provides details of popular walks in the Parque Natural da Serra da Estrela – some of which leave from town or just outside it; additional offices are at Seia, Gouveia and Guarda.

🛏 Sleeping

Casa das Obras　　　　　　B&B €€
(☑275 981 155; www.casadasobras.pt; Rua Teles de Vasconcelos, Manteigas; r summer/winter €68/80; P🅿🛜🏊) This lovely 18th-century townhouse has antique-filled rooms, and a pool in a grassy courtyard across the street.

Albergaria Berne　　　　　　HOTEL €€
(☑275 981 351; www.albergariaberne.com; Quinta de Santo António, Manteigas; s/d from €35/55; P✳@🛜🏊) At the base of town, Albergaria Berne has wood-accented rooms, some with balconies and views of Manteigas and the mountains above. Also has an excellent restaurant.

Pensão Serradalto　　　　　　GUESTHOUSE €
(☑tel/fax 275 981 151; Rua 1 de Maio 15; s/d/ste winter €35/45/60, summer €25/35/50) In the heart of town, the Serradalto has clean simple, wood-floored rooms, most with fine valley views.

ℹ Getting There & Around

Two regular weekday **buses** connect Manteigas with Guarda, from where there are onward services to Coimbra and Lisbon.

THE NORTH

Beneath the edge of Spanish Galicia, northern Portugal is a land of lush river valleys, sparkling coastline, granite peaks and virgin forests. This region is also gluttony for wine lovers: it's the home of the sprightly *vinho verde* wine and ancient vineyards along the dramatic Rio Douro. Gateway to the north is Porto, a beguiling riverside city blending both medieval and modern attractions. Smaller towns and villages also offer cultural allure, from majestic Braga, the country's religious heart, to the seaside beauty Viana do Castelo.

Porto

POP 208,000

At the mouth of the Rio Douro, the hilly city of Porto presents a jumble of styles, eras and attitudes: narrow medieval alleyways, extravagant baroque churches, prim little squares, and wide boulevards lined with beaux-arts edifices. A lively walkable city with chatter in the air and a tangible sense of history, Porto's old-world riverfront district is a Unesco World Heritage site. Across the water twinkle the neon signs of Vila Nova de Gaia, the headquarters of the major port manufacturers.

⊙ Sights & Activities

Head for the riverfront Ribeira district for an atmospheric stroll around, checking out the gritty local bars, sunny restaurants and river cruises.

A few kilometres west of the city centre, the seaside suburb of **Foz do Douro** is a prime destination on hot summer weekends. It has a long beach promenade and a smattering of oceanfront bars and restaurants.

Porto

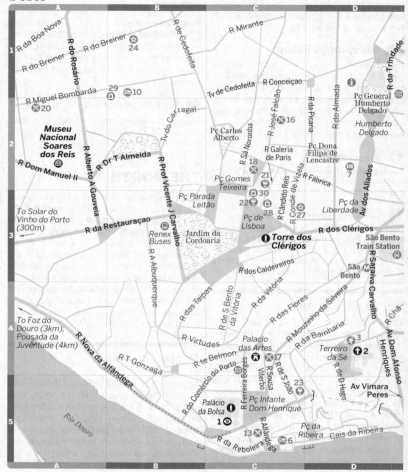

Museums
MUSEUM

Within the verdant gardens 4km west of the city, the arrestingly minimalist **Museu de Arte Contemporânea** (www.serralves.pt; Rua Dom João de Castro 210; admission €7; ⏰10am-5pm Tue-Fri, to 8pm Sat & Sun) features works by contemporary Portuguese artists. Take bus 201 from SaPraça Dom João I.

Porto's best art museum, the **Museu Nacional Soares dos Reis** (Rua Dom Manuel II 44; admission €5, free Sun 10am-2pm; ⏰10am-6pm Wed-Sun, 2-6pm Tue), exhibits Portuguese painting and sculpture masterpieces from the 19th and 20th centuries.

Torre dos Clérigos
TOWER

(Rua dos Clérigos; admission €2; ⏰9am-7pm) This tower rewards those who ascend the 225 steps to the top with an excellent view over the city.

Sé
CHURCH

(Terreiro da Sé; cloisters €3; ⏰9am-12.15pm & 2.30-6.30pm; ♿) Dominating Porto, the cathedral is worth a visit for its mixture of architectural styles and vast ornate interior.

Igreja de São Francisco
ARCHITECTURE

(☎222 062 100; Rua Infante Dom Henrique; admission €3.50; ⏰9am-6pm) Near the water-

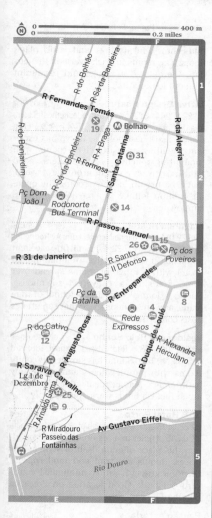

Porto

◎ Top Sights
Museu Nacional Soares dos Reis.......A2
Torre dos Clérigos............................C3

◎ Sights
1 Igreja de São Francisco.....................C5
2 Sé..D4

⊕ Activities, Courses & Tours
3 Porto Tours..D4

⊟ Sleeping
4 6 Only F3
5 B&B Hotel Porto E3
6 Guest House Douro..........................C5
7 Hotel Aliados....................................D2
8 Magnólia Hostel F3
9 Pensão Astória..................................E4
10 Pensão Favorita................................B1
11 Residencial Belo Sonho F3
12 Tattva Design Hostel........................E4

⊗ Eating
13 A Grade...C5
14 Café Majestic F2
15 Cafe Santiago F3
16 Café Vitória C2
17 DOP..C4
18 Leitaria Quinta Do Paço C2
19 Mercado do Bolhão E1
20 Rota do Chá A2

⊙ Drinking
21 Casa do Livro C2
22 Era Uma Vez no Porto C3
23 Vinologia...C5

✪ Entertainment
24 Breyner 85 .... B1
25 Hot Five Jazz & Blues Club E4
26 Maus Hábitos F3
27 Plano B C3

⊡ Shopping
28 A Vida Portuguesa............................C3
29 CC Bombarda B1
30 Livraria Lello....................................C3
31 Via Catarina Shopping Centre...........F2

PORTUGAL PORTO

front, this Gothic church – austere from the outside – hides one of Portugal's most dazzling displays of gilded baroque finery.

Port-Wine Lodges   TOUR
Many of the port-wine lodges in Vila Nova de Gaia offer daily tours and tastings, including **Taylor's** (www.taylor.pt; Rua do Choupelo 250; admission €3; ⊘10am-6pm Mon-Fri, to 5pm Sat & Sun), **Croft** (www.croftport.com; free; ⊘10am-6pm) and **Graham's** (www.grahamsportlodge.com; Rua Rei Ramiro 514; per person €3; ⊘9.30am-6pm Mon-Sat).

Teleférico de Gaia   CABLE CAR
(one-way/return €5/8; ⊘10am-8pm) In Vila Nova de Gaia, this new aerial gondola provides fine views over the Douro and Porto on its short, five-minute jaunt. It runs 562m between the south end of the Ponte Dom Luís I and the riverside.

PORT WINE PRIMER

With its intense flavours, silky textures and appealing sweetness, port wine is easy to love, especially when taken with its proper accompaniments: cheese, nuts and dried fruit.

It was probably Roman soldiers who first planted grapes in the Douro valley some 2000 years ago, but tradition credits the discovery of port itself to 17th-century British merchants. With their country at war with France, they turned to their old ally Portugal to meet their wine habit. According to legend, the British threw in some brandy with grape juice, both to take off the wine's bite and preserve it for shipment back to England – port wine was the result.

✪ Festivals & Events

Festa de São João   FESTIVAL
(St John's Festival) From 20 to 24 June; Porto's biggest festival, with processions, live music and merry-making all across town.

Noites Ritual Rock   MUSIC FESTIVAL
Late August; music festival.

Serralves Em Festa   CULTURAL FESTIVAL
(http://serralvesemfesta.com) Concerts, exhibitions, theatre and loads of events at this fest in early June.

🛏 Sleeping

TOP CHOICE Guest
House Douro   BOUTIQUE HOTEL €€€
(☎222 015 135; www.guesthousedouro.com; Rua de Fonte Taurina 99-101; r €140-180; ❋@☎) In a restored relic overlooking the Douro, this friendly guesthouse has excellent service and beautifully designed rooms; the best have river views. There's a 1am curfew.

6 Only   GUESTHOUSE €€
(☎222 013 971; www.6only.pt; Rua Duque de Loulé 97; d €70-80; @☎) True to name, 6 Only has just six rooms, all with simple but stylish details. There's a lounge, a Zen-like courtyard and friendly staff.

Pensão Favorita   GUESTHOUSE €€
(☎220 134 157; www.pensaofavorita.pt; Rua Miguel Bombarda 267; s/d from €60/80; ☎) An artful addition to Porto, Pensão Favorita has inviting rooms of ample size with big windows, mid-century furnishings and wide plank floors. The rooms in back overlook the garden; there's also a lounge and restaurant with outdoor seating.

Tattva Design Hostel   HOSTEL €
(☎220 944 622; www.tattvadesignhostel.com; Rua do Cativo 26; dm/d from €15/44; @☎) One of Portugal's best hostels, Tattva has excellent facilities and attractive rooms with thoughtful touches – big lockers, good lighting, privacy curtains around every bed, and a bathroom in every room. The open-air rooftop lounge is a great place for a sundowner.

Magnólia Hostel   HOSTEL €
(☎222 014 150; magnoliahostel.com; Av Rodrigues de Freitas 387; dm €17-22; ☎) You'll find excellent ambience at this attractive, well-maintained hostel with a range of rooms spread over three floors of a converted townhouse. There's a lounge with a spooky out-of-tune piano, and an outdoor space that sometimes hosts concerts.

Residencial Belo Sonho   GUESTHOUSE €
(☎222 003 389; Rua Passos Manuel 186; s/d €25/35; ☎) Belo Sonho has simple but comfy rooms with parquet floors and small, tidy bathrooms. Management doesn't speak much English but is warm and friendly.

B&B Hotel Porto   HOTEL €
(☎222 407 000; www.hotelbb.pt; Praça da Batalha 32; d €46; ☎) Set in a restored art deco building, this place offers a dash of style at low prices. Rooms are trim and modern, and there's a grassy if rather minimalist courtyard out back. Good location on Praça da Batalha.

Pensão Astória   GUESTHOUSE €
(☎222 008 175; Rua Arnaldo Gama 56; r €25-35) In an aging town house above the Rio Douro, Astória has old-world charm; several rooms have superb views.

Hotel Aliados   GUESTHOUSE €€
(☎222 004 853; www.hotelaliados.com; Rua Elísio de Melo 27; r €55-80; ❋☎) Set in one of Porto's marvellous beaux-arts buildings, offering comfortable rooms with wooden floors and dark-wood furnishings.

Eating

A Grade
PORTUGUESE €€€

(☎223 321 130; Rua da São Nicolau 9; mains €12-20; ⊙lunch & dinner Mon-Sat) Both a humble operation and a masterwork of traditional fare, with standouts such as baked octopus in butter and wine, roast goat, and lime tart for dessert. Reservations recommended.

DOP
PORTUGUESE €€€

(☎222 014 313; www.ruipaula.com; Largo S Domingos 18; mains €30-60; ⊙lunch & dinner) Sit at the 'long table' and watch the chef prepare tapas tableside, or find a romantic corner and linger over duck risotto and a bottle of Douro red. This is one of Porto's finest dining rooms.

Café Vitória
INTERNATIONAL €€

(Rua José Falcão 156; mains €6-14; ⊙noon-1am Mon, Wed, Thu, 2pm-2am Fri & Sat) This little-known gem serves lighter fare in the bar downstairs (noodles with shitake mushrooms, smoked salmon sandwiches, good-value daily specials) and heartier Portuguese fare in the elegant upstairs dining room. There's a pleasant garden in back, and a festive cocktail-sipping scene on weekends.

Café Majestic
CAFE €

(Rua Santa Catarina 112; snacks €2-3; ⊙9.30am-midnight Mon-Sat) An art-nouveau extravagance where old souls linger over afternoon tea.

Cafe Santiago
PORTUGUESE €€

(Rua Passos Manuel 226; mains €8-12; ⊙lunch & dinner) One of the best places to try Porto's classic belly-filling treat, the *francesinha*: a thick open-faced sandwich, piled with cheese, sausage, egg and/or assorted other meats, plus a tasty rich sauce.

Leitaria Quinta Do Paço
CAFE €

(Praça Guilherme Gomes Fernandes 47; sandwiches €4; ⊙9am-8pm Sun-Thu, to 1am Fri & Sat) The Leitaria is famed for its heavenly eclairs. You can dine al fresco at tables on the plaza.

Rota do Chá
CAFE €

(Rua Miguel Bombarda 457; 2-course lunch €7.50; ⊙noon-8pm Sun-Thu, noon-midnight Fri & Sat; ✐) This proudly bohemian cafe has a verdant but rustic back garden and a magnificent tea selection.

Mercado do Bolhão
MARKET €

(Rua Formosa; ⊙8am-5pm Mon-Fri, to 1pm Sat) Fruit, vegies, cheese and deli goodies in a 19th-century wrought-iron building.

Tattva
CAFE

(Rua do Cativo 26; 3-course lunch €7; ⊙lunch Mon-Fri, dinner Fri & Sat) This hostel serves excellent set lunches, and there's always a vegetarian option. Come on Friday nights for Portuguese cuisine and on Saturday nights for superb Indian cooking.

Drinking

The bar-lined Rua Galeira de Paris and nearby streets are packed with revellers most nights. Down by the water, the open-air bar scene on Praça da Ribeira is a pleasant but touristy option on warm nights.

Era Uma Vez no Porto
BAR

(Rua das Carmelitas 162) Artwork lines the walls of this cosy, lowlit Baixa bar, and there's a mellow buzz to the place, making it a fine retreat from the mayhem of nearby Rua Galeria de Paris. Step onto the tiny balcony for views of the Torre dos Clérigos across the way.

Casa do Livro
LOUNGE

(Rua Galeria de Paris 85; ⊙9pm-3am Mon-Sat) Vintage wallpaper, gilded mirrors and walls of books give a discreet charm to this perfectly lit bar. On weekends, DJs spin funk, soul and retro sounds in the back room for pretty people.

Vinologia
WINE BAR

(Rua de São João 46; ⊙4pm-midnight) This oaky French-owned wine bar is an excellent place to sample Porto's fine quaffs.

Solar do Vinho do Porto
WINE BAR,

(Rua Entre Quintas 220; ⊙4pm-midnight Mon-Sat) In a 19th-century house near the Palácio de Cristal, this upmarket spot has a manicured garden with picturesque views of the Douro and hundreds of ports by the glass.

☆ Entertainment

Plano B
GALLERY

(Rua Cândido dos Reis 30; ⊙closed Aug) This creative space has an art gallery and cafe, with a cosy downstairs space where DJs and live bands hold court.

Maus Hábitos
CLUB

(www.maushabitos.com; Rua Passos Manuel 178, 4th fl) This bohemian, multiroom space hosts art exhibits, while live bands and DJs work the back stage.

Breyner 85
LIVE MUSIC

(www.breyner85.com; Rua do Breyner 85; ⊙3-9pm Mon, to 2am Tue-Sun) This creative space with a grassy terrace features an eclectic line-up of bands covering rock, jazz and blues. Sunday night's jam sessions are particularly popular.

Hot Five Jazz & Blues Club
JAZZ

(www.hotfive.eu; Largo Actor Dias 51; ⊙10pm-3am Wed-Sun) Hosts live jazz and blues as well as acoustic, folk and all-out jam sessions.

🛍 Shopping

Major shopping areas are eastward around the Bolhão market and Rua Santa Catarina.

A Vida Portuguesa
SOUVENIRS

(Rua Galeria de Paris 20) This lovely shop showcases a medley of vintage Portuguese products – classic toys, old-fashioned soaps and retro journals, plus those emblematic ceramic *andorinhas* (swallows).

CC Bombarda
GALLERIA

(Rua Miguel Bombarda) For something a little edgier, visit this gallery of stores selling urban wear, stylish home knick-knacks, Portuguese indie rock and other hipster-pleasing delights.

Livraria Lello
BOOKS

(Rua das Carmelitas 144) Even if you're not after books, don't miss this beautiful 1906 neo-Gothic confection.

Via Catarina Shopping Centre
MALL

(Rua Santa Catarina) The best central shopping mall.

ℹ Information

Santo António Hospital (☑222 077 500; Largo Prof Abel Salazar) Has English-speaking staff.

Main Post Office (Praça General Humberto Delgado) Across from the main tourist office.

Main Tourist Office (www.portoturismo. pt; Rua Clube dos Fenianos 25) Opposite the *câmara municipal*.

ℹ Getting There & Away
Air

Porto is connected by daily flights from Lisbon and London, and direct links from other European cities, particularly with easyJet and Ryanair.

Bus

Porto has many private bus companies leaving from different terminals; the main tourist of-fice can help. In general, for Lisbon (€18) and The Algarve (€30), the choice is **Renex** (www. renex.pt; Campo Mártires de Pátria 37) or **Rede Expressos.** (www.rede-expressos.pt; Rua Alexandre Herculano 370).

Three companies operate from or near Praceto Régulo Magauanha, off Rua Dr Alfredo Magalhães: Transdev-Norte goes to Braga (€6); and AV Minho goes to Viana do Castelo (€8).

Train

Porto is a northern Portugal rail hub with three stations. Most international trains, and all intercity links, start at **Campanhã**, 2km east of the centre. Inter-regional and regional services depart from Campanhã or the central **São Bento station** (Praça Almeida Garrett). Frequent local trains connect these two.

At **São Bento station** you can book tickets to any other destination.

ℹ Getting Around
To/From the Airport

The **metro's 'violet' line** provides handy service to the airport. A one-way ride to the centre costs €1.80 and takes about 45 minutes. A daytime **taxi** costs €20 to €25 to/from the centre.

Public Transport

Save money on transport by purchasing a refillable **Andante Card** (€0.50), valid for transport on buses, metro, funicular and tram. You can buy them from STCP kiosks or newsagents.

Metro Porto's metro currently comprises four metropolitan lines that all converge at the Trinidade stop. Tickets cost €1.15 with an Andante Card. There are also various day passes (€4 to €7) available.

Tram Porto has three antique trams that trundle around town. The most useful line, 1E, travels along the Douro towards the Foz district.

Bus Central hubs of Porto's extensive bus system include Jardim da Cordoaria, Praça da Liberdade and São Bento station. Tickets purchased on the bus are €1.80 one-way, or €1.15 with the Andante Card.

Funicular A panoramic funicular shuttles up and down a steep incline from Avenida Gustavo Eiffel to Rua Augusto Rosa (€1.80, from 8am to 8pm).

Taxi

To cross town, expect to pay between €5 and €8. There's a 20% surcharge at night, and an additional charge to leave city limits, which includes Vila Nova de Gaia. There are taxi ranks throughout the centre or you can call a **radio taxi** (☑225 076 400).

Along the Douro

Portugal's best-known river flows through the country's rural heartland. In the upper reaches, port-wine grapes are grown on steep terraced hills, punctuated by remote stone villages and, in spring, splashes of dazzling white almond blossom.

The Rio Douro is navigable right across Portugal. Highly recommended is the train journey from Porto to Pinhão (€11, 2½ hours, five trains daily), the last 70km clinging to the river's edge; trains continue to Pocinho (from Porto €13, 3½ hours). **Porto Tours** (☑222 000 045; www.portotours. com; Calçada Pedro Pitões 15, Torre Medieval), situated next to Porto's cathedral, can arrange tours, including idyllic Douro cruises. Cyclists and drivers can choose river-hugging roads along either bank, and visit wineries along the way (check out www.rvp.pt for an extensive list of wineries open to visitors). You can also stay overnight in scenic wine lodges among the vineyards.

Viana do Castelo

POP 38,000

The jewel of the Costa Verde (Green Coast), Viana do Castelo has both an appealing medieval centre and lovely beaches just outside the city. In addition to its natural beauty, Viana do Castelo whips up some excellent seafood and hosts some magnificent traditional festivals, including the spectacular **Festa de Nossa Senhora da Agonia** in August.

◉ Sights

The stately heart of town is **Praça da República**, with its delicate fountain and grandiose buildings, including the 16th-century **Misericórdia**, a former almshouse.

FREE **Templo do Sagrado Coração de Jesus**   CHURCH
(Temple of the Sacred Heart of Jesus; ☺10am-5pm Sep-Jun, 9am-8pm Jul & Aug) Atop Santa Luzia Hill, the Temple of the Sacred Heart of Jesus offers a grand panorama across the river. It's a steep 2km climb; you can also catch a ride on a funicular railway (one-way/return €2/3).

Praia do Cabedelo   BEACH
Viana's enormous arcing beach is one of the Minho's best, with little development

to spoil its charm. It's across the river from town, best reached by **ferry** (adult/child €1.30/0.70; ☺hourly 9am to 8pm Mon-Fri, from 10am Sat & Sun) from the pier south of Largo 5 de Outubro.

Gil Eannes   SHIP
(☑258 809 710; www.fundacaogileannes.pt; Doca Comercial; admission €2; ☺9am-7pm) On the waterfront near Largo 5 de Outubro, this pioneering naval hospital ship once provided on-the-job care for those fishing off the coast of Newfoundland. You can clamber around the decks and cabins, or even overnight in a spooky youth hostel.

🛏 Sleeping

Margarida da Praça   BOUTIQUE HOTEL €€
(☑258 809 630; www.margaridadapraca.com; Largo 5 Outubro 58; r €50-75; @ 🞱) Fantastically whimsical, this friendly boutique inn offers colourful rooms accented by candelabra lanterns and lush duvets.

Hospedaria Senhora do Carmo   GUESTHOUSE €
(☑258 825 118; batistaesilva@sapo.pt; Rua Grande 72; r €35, without bathroom €20) Well-located in the historic centre, this friendly, family-run guesthouse is excellent value with its clean, freshly painted rooms with parquet floors. The best have views over the rooftops of Viana.

Pousada da Juventude Gil Eannes   HOSTEL €
(☑258 847 169; www.pousadasjuventude.pt; Gil Eannes; dm/d €12/26; 🞱) Sleep in the bowels of a huge, creaky hospital ship where men were stitched up and underwent emergency dentistry. This floating hostel scores well for novelty, but has few amenities.

🍴 Eating

Taberna do Valentim   SEAFOOD €€
(Campo do Castelo; mains €12-15; ☺lunch & dinner Mon-Sat) This popular seafood restaurant serves grilled fish by the kilogram, and rich seafood stews – *arroz de tamboril* (monkfish rice) and *caldeirada* (fish stew). It's on the main road facing Castelo de São Thiago, 400m west of the centre.

Os 3 Potes   PORTUGUESE €€€
(☑258 829 928; Rua Beco dos Fornos 7; mains €14-17; ☺lunch & dinner) Set in the former public kiln, this cosy restaurant serves traditional Minho delicacies.

Dolce Vianna   ITALIAN €
(☑258 824 860; Rua do Poço 44; pizzas €6-7)
In the centre, this pleasant local favourite
cooks up thin-crust, cheese-heavy pizzas in
a wood-burning oven.

Freguez   CAFE €
(Rua do Poço 42; snacks €2-3) A charming cafe
with a fado soundtrack and outdoor tables
on the pedestrian lane.

ℹ Information
Tourist Office (Rua Hospital Velho) Handily
located in the old centre.

ℹ Getting There & Away
Five to 10 **trains** go daily to Porto (€7 to €8, 1½
to 2¼ hours), as well as express **buses** (€8, 1 to
1½ hours).

Braga
POP 135,000

Portugal's third-largest city boasts a fine
array of churches, their splendid baroque
facades looming above the old plazas and
narrow lanes of the historic centre. Lively
cafes, trim little boutiques, and some good
restaurants add to the appeal.

◎ Sights

It's an easy day trip to **Guimarães** with its
medieval town centre and a palace of the
dukes of Bragança. It's also a short jaunt to
Barcelos, a town famed for its sprawling
Thursday market.

Sé   CHURCH
(Rua Dom Paio Mendes; admission free, treasury
€3, choir €2; ⊙8am-6.30pm) In the centre of
Braga, this is one of Portugal's most extraordinary cathedrals, with roots dating
back a thousand years. Within the cathedral you can also visit the **treasury** and
choir.

Escadaria do Bom Jesus   RELIGIOUS
At Bom Jesus do Monte, a hilltop pilgrimage
site 5km from Braga, there is an extraordinary stairway with allegorical fountains,
chapels and a superb view. City bus 2 runs
frequently from Braga to the site, where you
can climb the steps (pilgrims sometimes do
this on their knees) or ascend by funicular
railway (€1.50).

🛏 Sleeping

Pop Hostel   HOSTEL €
(☑253 058 806; dm/d from €16/45; @🛜) New in
2011, the small cosy Pop Hostel is a great addition to Braga, with a colourfully decorated
lounge and a friendly owner who knows all
the best eating and drinking spots in town.
Bike hire and tours available.

Casa Santa Zita   GUESTHOUSE €
(☑253 618 331; Rua São João 20; s/d from €22/35)
This impeccably kept pilgrims' lodge has
bright, spotless rooms (some with ensuite)
and an air of palpable serenity. Midnight
curfew.

Residencial Dos Terceiros   GUESTHOUSE €
(☑253 270 466; www.terceiros.com; Rua dos Cape-
listas 85; s/d €30/43) On a quiet pedestrianised
street near Praça da República, Terceiros offers simple rooms; some with small balconies.

🍴 Eating

Anjo Verde   VEGETARIAN €
(☑253 264 010; Largo da Praça Velha 21; mains
€8-9; ⊙lunch & dinner Mon-Sat; 🍴) Braga's best
vegetarian restaurant serves up elegantly
presented plates in a lovely, airy dining
room or on the peaceful lane in front. Several other attractive indoor-outdoor restaurants are on the same street.

Domus Vinum   TAPAS €
(www.domus-vinum.com; Largo da Nossa Senhora da
Boa Luz 12; tapas €4-6; ⊙6pm-2am Tue-Sun) With
Brazilian beats, a lantern-lit front patio and
excellent wines by the glass, Domus Vinum
draws a stylish crowd. The Portuguese and
Spanish tapas is excellent. It's just west of the
old town entrance portal, Arco da Porta Nova.

Manjar Bacalhau   PORTUGUESE €€
(Campo das Hortas; mains €8-12; ⊙closed Mon)
True to name, this place serves superb *ba-
calhau* dishes, as well as regional favourites.

Livraria Café   CAFE €
(Avenida Central 118; mains €4-5; ⊙9am-7.30pm
Mon-Sat) Tucked inside the bookshop Centési-
ma Página, this cafe with rustic garden
serves tasty sandwiches, salads and desserts.

ℹ Information
Tourist Office (www.cm-braga.pt; Praça da
República 1) Can help with accommodation and
maps.

❶ Getting There & Away

Trains arrive regularly from Lisbon (€33, 3½ to 4½ hours), Coimbra (€20, 2½ hours) and Porto (€3, 1¼ hours), and there are daily connections north to Viana do Castelo. Daily **bus** services link Braga to Porto (€6, one hour) and Lisbon (€19, 4½ hours). **Car hire** is available at **AVIC** (☎253 203 910; Rua Gabriel Pereira de Castro 28; ☺Mon-Fri), with prices starting at €35 per day.

Parque Nacional da Peneda-Gerês

Spread across four impressive granite massifs, this vast park encompasses boulder-strewn peaks, precipitous valleys, gorse-clad moorlands and forests of oak and pine. It also shelters more than 100 granite villages that, in many ways, have changed little since Portugal's founding in the 12th century. For nature lovers, the stunning scenery here is unmatched in Portugal for camping, hiking and other outdoor adventures. The park's main centre is at Vila do Gerês, a sleepy, hot-springs village.

🏃 Activities

Hiking

There are trails and footpaths through the park, some between villages with accommodation. Leaflets detailing these are available from the park offices.

Day hikes around Vila do Gerês are popular. An adventurous option is the **old Roman road** from Mata do Albergaria (10km up-valley from Vila do Gerês), past the **Vilarinho das Furnas** reservoir to Campo do Gerês. More distant destinations include **Ermida** and **Cabril**, both with simple accommodation.

Cycling & Horse Riding

Mountain bikes can be hired in Campo do Gerês (15km northeast of Vila do Gerês) from **Equi Campo** (☎253 161 405; www.equicampo.com; per hr/day €5/18; ☺10am-7pm). Guides here also lead horse-riding trips, hikes and combination hiking/climbing/abseiling excursions.

Water Sports

Rio Caldo, 8km south of Vila do Gerês, is the base for water sports on the Caniçada Reservoir. English-run **AML** (Água Montanha e Lazer; ☎253 391 779; www.aguamontanha.com;

Lugar de Paredes) rents kayaks, pedal boats, rowing boats and small motorboats. It also organises kayaking trips along the Albufeira de Salamonde.

🛏 Sleeping & Eating

Vila do Gerês has plenty of *pensões* (guesthouses), but you may find vacancies are limited; many are block-booked by spa patients in summer.

Hotel de Peneda   BOUTIQUE HOTEL €€
(☎251 460 040; www.hotelpeneda.com; Lugar da Peneda; r €50-75; P🖂) Set in the Serra da Peneda, in the northern reaches of the park, this mountain lodge has a waterfall backdrop and attractive rooms with picturesque views. Also has a good restaurant.

Beleza da Serra   GUESTHOUSE €€
(☎253 391 457; www.bserra.com; Lugar do Bairro 25, Vilar da Veiga; d/tr €59/79; 🖂) This friendly waterfront guesthouse overlooks the Caniçada Reservoir, 4.5km south of Vila do Gerês. It has simple, clean, comfortable rooms and a decent on-site restaurant.

Pousada da Juventude de Vilarinho das Furnas   HOSTEL €
(☎253 351 339; www.pousadasjuventude.pt; dm/bungalow €15/52; P@) Campo's woodland hostel offers spartan dormitories, simply furnished doubles (with bathrooms) and roomier bungalows with kitchen units.

Parque Campismo de Cerdeira   CAMPGROUND €
(☎253 351 005; www.parquecerdeira.com; camping per person/tent/car €5.50/5/5, bungalows €50-68; ☺year-round; P🖂) In Campo do Gerês, this place has oak-shaded sites, laundry, pool, minimarket and a particularly good restaurant. The ecofriendly bungalows open onto unrivalled mountain views.

❶ Information

The head park office is **Adere-PG** (☎258 452 250; www.adere-pg.pt; ☺Mon-Fri) in Ponte da Barca. Obtain park information and reserve cottages and other park accommodation through here. Other Adere-PG stations are at Mezio and Lamas de Mouro.

❶ Getting There & Away

Because of the lack of transport within the park, it's good to have your own wheels. You can rent cars in Braga.

UNDERSTAND PORTUGAL

History

Portugal has an early history of occupation, stretching back to 700 BC when the Celts arrived on the Iberian peninsula, followed by the Phoenicians, Greeks, Romans, Visigoths, Moors and Christians.

Life Under the Moors

The Moors ruled southern Portugal for more than 400 years, and some scholars describe that time as a golden age. The Arabs introduced irrigation, previously unknown in Europe. Two Egyptian agronomists came to Iberia in the 10th century and wrote manuals on land management, animal husbandry, plant and crop cultivation and irrigation designs. They also introduced bananas, rice, coconuts, maize and sugar cane, and also encouraged small-scale, cooperatively run communities, specialising in olive oil and wine production, and food markets – still embraced in many parts of Portugal.

The Moors opened schools and set about campaigns to achieve mass literacy (in Arabic of course), as well as the teaching of maths, geography and history. Medicine reached new levels of sophistication. There was also a degree of religious tolerance that evaporated when the Christian crusaders came to power. Much to the chagrin of Christian slave owners, slavery was not permitted in the Islamic kingdom – making it a refuge for runaway slaves. Muslims, Christians and Jews all peacefully coexisted, at times even collaborating together, creating the most scientifically and artistically advanced society the world had, until that time, ever known.

Age of Discovery

The 15th century marked a golden era in Portuguese history, when Portuguese explorers helped transform the small kingdom into a great imperial power.

The third son of King João I, Henrique 'O Navegador' (Henry the Navigator, 1394–1460) played a pivotal role in establishing Portugal's maritime dominance. As governor of The Algarve, he assembled the very best sailors, map-makers, shipbuilders, instrument-makers and astronomers.

By 1431, Portuguese explorers discovered the islands of Madeira and the Azores, fol-

lowed by Gil Eanes' 1534 voyage beyond Cape Bojador in West Africa, breaking a maritime superstition that this was the end of the world. More achievements followed over the next century. In 1488, Portuguese sailors, under navigator Bartolomeu Dias, were the first Europeans to sail around Africa's southern tip and into the Indian Ocean. This was followed by the epic voyage in 1497–98 when Vasco da Gama reached southern India, and in 1500 when Cabral discovered Brazil. With gold and slaves from Africa and spices from the East, Portugal was soon rolling in riches. As its explorers reached Timor, China and eventually Japan, Portugal cemented its power with garrison ports and trading posts. The monarchy, taking its 'royal fifth' of profits, became the wealthiest in Europe, and the lavish Manueline architectural style symbolised the exuberance of the age.

The Salazar Years

In 1908, King Carlos and his eldest son were assassinated in Lisbon. Two years later Portugal became a republic, which set the stage for an enormous power struggle. Over the next 16 years, chaos ruled, with an astounding 45 different governments coming to power, often the result of military intervention. Another coup in 1926 brought forth new names and faces, most significantly António de Oliveira Salazar, a finance minister who would rise up through the ranks to become prime minister – a post he would hold for 36 years.

Salazar hastily enforced his 'New State' – a republic that was nationalistic, Catholic, authoritarian and essentially repressive. All political parties were banned except for the loyalist National Union, which ran the show, and the National Assembly. Strikes were banned and propaganda, censorship and brute force kept society in order. The new secret police, Polícia Internacional e de Defesa do Estado (PIDE), inspired terror and suppressed opposition by imprisonment and torture. Various attempted coups during Salazar's rule came to nothing. The only good news was a dramatic economic turnaround, with surging industrial growth through the 1950s and 1960s.

Decolonisation finally brought the Salazarist era to a close. Independence movements in Portugal's African colonies led to costly and unpopular military interventions. In 1974, military officers reluctant to continue fighting bloody colonial wars staged a nearly bloodless coup – later nicknamed the Revolution of the Carnations (after victorious soldiers stuck carnations in their rifle barrels). Carnations are still a national symbol of freedom.

Portugal Today

After the revolution, Portugal faced enormous challenges as it modernized its economy and embraced a left-leaning democracy. Joining the EEC (European Economic Community) in 1986 and adopting the euro in 1999 gave the economy a boost, though the 2007 Global Financial Crisis hit the country hard. Portugal continues to struggle with a shrinking economy and EU-mandated austerity measures that have left many citizens disgruntled. The country has had more success in the realm of renewable energy (harvesting solar, wind and hydroelectric power). Today more than half of Portugal's energy comes from renewable sources, making it one of the world leaders in sustainability.

Arts
Music

The best-known form of Portuguese music is the melancholy, nostalgic songs called fado (literally 'fate'), said to have originated from troubadour and African slave songs. The late Amália Rodrigues was the Edith Piaf of Portuguese fado. Today it is Mariza who has captured the public's imagination with her extraordinary voice and fresh contemporary image. Lisbon's Alfama district has plenty of fado houses, ranging from the grandiose and tourist-conscious to small family affairs.

Architecture

Unique to Portugal is Manueline architecture, named after its patron, King Manuel I (1495–1521). It symbolises the zest for discovery of that era and is hugely flamboyant, characterised by fantastic spiralling columns and elaborate carving and ornamentation.

Visual Arts

Portugal's stunning painted *azulejo* tiles coat contemporary life, covering everything from houses to churches. The art form dates from Moorish times and reached a peak in the late 19th century when the art nouveau and art deco movements provided fantastic facades and interiors. Lisbon has its very own *azulejo* museum.

Environment

Portugal has made an astounding transformation from a nation powered largely by fossil fuels to one powered by solar, wind and hydropower. In 2005, only 17% of electricity in Portugal's grid came from green energy. By 2012, the figure had risen to over 50% – a gain unprecedented elsewhere in Europe. In 2008 one of the world's largest solar farms opened in the Alentejo, powering 30,000 homes. Portugal also has numerous wind farms as well as cutting-edge 'wave farms' to harness the ocean's power, located just north of Porto.

Food & Drink

Freshly baked bread, olives, cheese, red wine or crisp *vinho verde*, chargrilled fish, *cataplana* (seafood stew), smoked meats – the Portuguese have perfected the art of cooking (and eating) simple, delicious meals. Sitting down to table means experiencing the richness of Portugal's bountiful coastline and fertile countryside. Of course, you don't have to sit, you can take your piping-hot *pastel de nata* (custard tart) standing up, or wander through scenic vineyards, sipping the velvety ports of the Douro Valley – the oldest demarcated wine region on earth. For local specialties see p564.

SURVIVAL GUIDE

Directory A–Z
Accommodation

There's an excellent range of good-value accommodation in Portugal. Budget places offer some of Western Europe's cheapest rooms, while you'll find atmospheric accommodation in converted castles and farmhouses.

PRICE RANGES
We list high-season rates for a double room; breakfast is generally not included.

€€€ more than €100

€€ €50 to €100

€ less than €50

ECOTOURISM & FARMSTAYS
Turismo de Habitação (www.turihab.pt) is a private network of historic, heritage or rustic properties, ranging from 17th-century mansions

PORTUGAL DIRECTORY A–Z

SEASONS

High season mid-June to mid-September.

Mid-season May to mid-June and mid-September to October.

Low season November to April.

to quaint farmhouses or self-catering cottages. Doubles run from about €60 to €120.

POUSADAS

These are government-run former castles, monasteries or palaces, often in spectacular locations. For details, contact tourist offices or **Pousadas de Portugal** (www.pousadas.pt).

GUESTHOUSES

The most common types are the *residencial* and the *pensão:* usually simple, family-owned operations. Some have cheaper rooms with shared bathrooms. Double rooms with private bathroom typically run €40 to 60.

HOSTELS

Portugal has a growing number of hostels, particularly in Lisbon. Nationwide, Portugal has over 30 *pousadas da juventude* (youth hostels; www.pousadasjuventude.pt) within the Hostelling International (HI) system. The average price for a dorm room is about €20.

CAMPING

For detailed listings of campsites nationwide, pick up the **Roteiro Campista** (www.roteiro-campista.pt; €7), updated annually and sold at bookshops. The swishest places are run by **Orbitur** (www.orbitur.pt) and **Inatel** (www.inatel.pt).

Activities

The best **hiking** is found in Parque Nacional da Peneda-Gerês and Serra da Estrela. The ambitious can follow the 240km walking trail Via Algarviana across southern Portugal.

Popular **water sports** include surfing, windsurfing, canoeing, rafting and water skiing. For local specialists, see Lagos, Sagres, Tavira, Coimbra and Parque Nacional da Peneda-Gerês.

Good starting points for **cycling** trips are Tavira in The Algarve, Sintra in central Portugal and Parque Nacional da Peneda-Gerês in the north.

Modest alpine **skiing** is possible at Torre in the Serra da Estrela, usually from January through to March.

Business Hours

Standard hours are as follows:

Banks 8.30am to 3pm Monday to Friday

Bars 7pm to 2am

Cafes 9am to 7pm

Malls 10am to 10pm

Nightclubs 11pm to 4am Thursday to Saturday

Post offices 8.30am to 4pm Monday to Friday

Restaurants noon to 3pm & 7pm to 10pm

Shops 9.30am to noon & 2pm to 7pm Monday to Friday, 10am to 1pm Saturday

Sights 10am to 12.30pm & 2-5pm Tuesday to Sunday

Discount Cards

If you plan to do a lot of sightseeing in Portugal's main cities, the **Lisboa Card** and **Porto Card** are sensible investments. Sold at tourist offices, these cards offer discounts or free admission to many attractions, and free travel on public transport.

Embassies & Consulates

Australian Embassy (213 101 500; www.portugal.embassy.gov.au; 2nd fl, Av da Liberdade 200, Lisbon)

Canadian Embassy (213 164 600; Avenida da Liberdade 196, Edifício Victoria)

New Zealand Embassy (39 06 853 7501; www.nzembassy.com) The New Zealand embassy in Rome represents travellers.

UK Embassy (213 924 000; http://ukinportugal.fco.gov.uk; Rua de Saõ Bernardo 33) Also in Portimaõ.

US Embassy (217 273 300; http://portugal.usembassy.gov; Av das Forças Armadas, Lisbon)

Food

The following price indicators (per main course) are used here:

€€€ more than €15

€€ €8 to €15

€ less than €8

Money

There are numerous banks with ATMs located throughout Portugal. Credit cards are accepted in midrange and top-end hotels, restaurants and shops.

Public Holidays

New Year's Day 1 January

Carnaval Tuesday February/March – the day before Ash Wednesday

Good Friday March/April

Liberty Day 25 April – celebrating the 1974 revolution

Labour Day 1 May

Corpus Christi May/June – 9th Thursday after Easter

Portugal Day 10 June – also known as Camões and Communities Day

Feast of the Assumption 15 August

Republic Day 5 October – commemorating the 1910 declaration of the Portuguese Republic

All Saints' Day 1 November

Independence Day 1 December – commemorating the 1640 restoration of independence from Spain

Feast of the Immaculate Conception 8 December

Christmas Day 25 December

Telephone

Portugal's country code is ☎351. There are no regional area codes. Mobile phone numbers have nine digits and begin with 9.

All Portuguese phone numbers consist of nine digits. These include area codes, which always need to be dialled. For general information dial ☎118, and for reverse-charge (collect) calls dial ☎120.

Phonecards are the most reliable and cheapest way of making a phone call from a telephone booth. They are sold at post offices, newsagents and tobacconists in denominations of €5 and €10.

Visas

Schengen visa rules apply.

Getting There & Away

Air

TAP (www.tap.pt) is Portugal's international flag carrier as well as its main domestic airline. Portugal's main airports:

Lisbon (LIS; ☎218 413 500; www.ana-aeroportos.pt)

Porto Airport (OPO; ☎229 432 400; www.ana-aeroportos.pt)

Faro (☎289 800 800; www.ana-aeroportos.pt)

Land

BUS

UK–Portugal and France–Portugal Eurolines services cross to Portugal via northwest Spain. Buses from London (£169) take approximately 35 hours to reach Lisbon. Daily buses to Lisbon take 26 hours from Paris (€92-125) and 8 hours from Madrid (€40-50 euros). Operators include the following:

Alsa (www.alsa.es)

Avanza (www.avanzabus.com)

Damas (www.damas-sa.es)

Eurolines (www.eurolines.com)

Eva (www.eva-bus.com)

CAR & MOTORCYCLE

There is no border control in Portugal.

TRAIN

The most popular train link from Spain is on the Sud Express, operated by **Renfe** (www.renfe.com; one-way tickets from €59), which has a nightly sleeper service between Madrid and Lisbon (one-way from €61, 11 hours). Badajoz (Spain)–Elvas–Lisbon is slow and there is only one regional service daily, but the scenery is stunning. Coming from Galicia, in the northwest of Spain, travellers can go from Vigo to Valença do Minho (Portugal) (€9.25, 40 minutes) and continue on to Porto (€15, 2 hours).

SPAIN TO PORTUGAL BUS SERVICES

FROM	TO	VIA	COST (€)	DURATION (HRS)	COMPANY
Madrid	Porto	Guarda	47	8½	Eurolines
Madrid	Lisbon	Évora	39	8	Eurolines, Avanza, Alsa
Barcelona	Lisbon	Évora	70	19	Eurolines
Santiago de Compostela	Porto	Braga	31	4	Eurolines
Sevilla	Lisbon	Évora	38	7	Eurolines, Alsa
Sevilla	Faro	Huelva	21	3½	Eurolines, Eva, Damas

Getting Around

Air

TAP Portugal (TAP; www.flytap.com) has daily Lisbon–Faro flights (under an hour) year-round.

Bicycle

Mountain biking is a fine way to explore the country, although given the Portuguese penchant for overtaking on blind corners, it can be dangerous on lesser roads. Bicycle lanes are rare: veteran cyclists recommend the Parque Nacional da Peneda-Gerês. A handful of towns have bike-hire outfits (from €10 to €20 a day). If you're bringing your own, pack plenty of spare inner tubes. Bicycles can be taken free on all regional and inter-regional trains as accompanied baggage. They can also go on a few suburban services on weekends. Most domestic bus lines won't accept bikes.

Boat

Portugal is not big on water-borne transport as a rule; however, there are river cruises along the Rio Douro from Porto, Lisbon's river trips and commuter ferries.

Bus

A host of small bus operators, most amalgamated into regional companies, run a dense network of services across the country. Among the largest companies are **Rede Expressos** (www.rede-expressos.pt), **Rodonorte** (www.rodonorte.pt) and The Algarve line **Eva** (www.eva-bus.com).

Most bus-station ticket desks will give you a computer printout of fares, and services and schedules are usually posted at major stations.

CLASSES

Expressos Comfortable, fast buses between major cities

Rápidas Quick regional buses

Carreiras Marked CR, slow, stopping at every crossroad

COSTS

Travelling by bus in Portugal is fairly inexpensive. A Lisbon–Faro express bus costs €19; Lisbon–Porto costs about €18. Both take four hours. An under-26 card should get you a small discount on long-distance services.

Car & Motorcycle

AUTOMOBILE ASSOCIATIONS

Automóvel Clube de Portugal (ACP; ☎213 180 100; www.acp.pt) has a reciprocal arrangement with foreign automobile clubs, including AA and RAC. It provides medical, legal and breakdown assistance. The 24-hour emergency help number is ☎707 509 510.

HIRE

To hire a car in Portugal you must be at least 25 years old and have held your home licence for over a year (some companies allow younger drivers at higher rates). To hire a scooter of up to 50cc you must be over 18 years old and have a valid driving licence. For more powerful scooters and motorbikes you must have a valid driving licence covering these vehicles from your home country.

INSURANCE

Although most car-insurance companies within the EU will cover taking your car to Portugal, it is prudent to consider extra cover for assistance in case your car breaks down. The minimum insurance required is third party.

ROAD RULES

The various speed limits for cars and motorcycles are 50km/h within cities and public centres, 90km/h on normal roads and 120km/h on motorways (but 50km/h, 70km/h and 100km/h for motorcycles with sidecars).

Driving is on the right side of the road. Drivers and front passengers in cars must wear seatbelts. Motorcyclists and passengers must wear helmets, and motorcycles must have headlights on day and night. Using a mobile phone while driving could result in a fine.

Drink-driving laws are strict in Portugal, with a maximum legal blood-alcohol level of 0.05%.

Train

Caminhos de Ferro Portugueses (www.cp.pt) is the statewide train network and is generally efficient.

There are four main types of long-distance service. Note that international services are marked IN on timetables.

Regional (marked R on timetables) Slow trains that stop everywhere

Interregional (IR) Reasonably fast trains

Intercidade (IC) or **Rápido** Express trains

Alfa Pendular Deluxe, marginally faster and much pricier service.

Slovenia

Includes »

Ljubljana........................611
Lake Bled.......................624
Lake Bohinj....................628
Kranjska Gora................630
Soča Valley 631
Postojna........................633
Škocjan Caves..............634
Koper............................635
Piran 636
Portorož........................640
Maribor......................... 641
Ptuj.............................. 641
Understand Slovenia....642
Survival Guide..............644

Best Places to Eat

» Gostilna na Gradu (p618)
» Gostilna Ribič (p642)
» Gril Ranca (p641)
» Hiša Franko (p633)
» Gostilna Lectar (p625)

Best Places to Stay

» Antiq Palace Hotel & Spa (p617)
» Max Piran (p637)
» Hostel Pekarna (p641)
» Camping Bled (p625)
» Penzion Gasperin (p628)

Why Go?

It's a pint-sized place, with a surface area of just more than 20,000 sq km and two million people. But 'good things come in small packages', and never was that old chestnut more appropriate than in describing Slovenia. The country has everything from beaches, snowcapped mountains, hills awash in grape vines and wide plains blanketed in sunflowers to Gothic churches, baroque palaces and art nouveau buildings. Its incredible mixture of climates brings warm Mediterranean breezes up to the foothills of the Alps, where it can snow in summer.

The capital, Ljubljana, is a culturally rich city that values livability and sustainability over unfettered growth. This sensitivity towards the environment extends to rural and lesser-developed parts of the country as well. With more than half of its total area covered in forest, Slovenia really is one of the 'greenest' countries in the world.

When to Go
Ljubljana

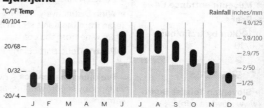

Apr–Jun Spring is a great time to be in the lowlands and the flower-carpeted valleys of the Julian Alps.

Sep This is the month made for everything – still warm enough to swim and tailor-made for hiking.

Dec–Mar Everyone (and their grandma) dons their skis in this winter-sport-mad country.

SLOVENIA

AT A GLANCE

» **Currency** Euro (€)

» **Language** Slovene

» **Money** ATMs are everywhere; banks open weekdays and Saturday morning

» **Visas** Not required for citizens of the EU, Australia, USA, Canada or New Zealand

Fast Facts

» **Area** 20,273 sq km

» **Capital** Ljubljana

» **Country code** ☏386

» **Emergency** Ambulance & fire ☏112, police ☏113

Exchange Rates

Australia	A$1	€0.82
Canada	C$1	€0.77
Japan	¥100	€0.83
New Zealand	NZ$1	€0.65
UK	UK£1	€1.18
USA	US$1	€0.78

Set Your Budget

» **Budget hotel room** €50

» **Two-course meal** €20

» **Museum entrance** €4

» **Beer** €3

» **100km by train/bus** €6/10

Resources

» **Slovenian Tourist Board** (www.slovenia.info)

» **E-uprava** (http://e-uprava.gov.si/e-unprava/en)

Connections

Border formalities with Slovenia's three European Union neighbours – Italy, Austria and Hungary – are nonexistent and all are accessible by train and bus. Venice can also be reached by boat from Piran. Expect a somewhat closer inspection of your documents when travelling to/from non-EU Croatia.

ITINERARIES

One Week

Spend a couple of days in Ljubljana, then head north to unwind in Bohinj or romantic Bled beside idyllic mountain lakes. Depending on the season, take a bus or drive over the hair-raising Vršič Pass into the valley of the vivid blue Soča River and take part in some adventure sports in Bovec or Kobarid before returning to Ljubljana.

Two Weeks

Another week will allow you to see just about everything: all of the above as well as the Karst caves at Škocjan and Postojna and the Venetian ports of Koper and Piran on the Adriatic. The country is small, so even the far eastern region, particularly the historically rich and picturesque city of Ptuj, is just a few hours away by car or train.

Essential Food & Drink

» **Pršut** Air-dried, thinly sliced ham from the Karst region not unlike Italian prosciutto.

» **Žlikrofi** Ravioli-like parcels filled with cheese, bacon and chives.

» **Žganci** The Slovenian stodge of choice – groats made from barley or corn but usually *ajda* (buckwheat).

» **Potica** A kind of nut roll eaten at teatime or as a dessert.

» **Wine** Distinctively Slovenian tipples include peppery red Teran from the Karst region and Malvazija, a straw-colour white wine from the coast.

» **Postrv** Trout, particularly the variety from the Soča River, is a real treat.

» **Prekmurska gibanica** A rich concoction of pastry filled with poppy seeds, walnuts, apples, and cheese and topped with cream.

» **Štruklji** Scrumptious dumplings made with curd cheese and served either savoury as a main course or sweet as a dessert.

» **Brinjevec** A very strong brandy made from fermented juniper berries (and a decidedly acquired taste).

LJUBLJANA

🔊 01 / POP 280,607

Slovenia's capital and largest city also happens to be one of Europe's greenest and most livable capitals. Car traffic is restricted in the centre, leaving the leafy banks of the emerald-green Ljubljanica River, which flows through the city's heart, free for pedestrians and cyclists. In summer, cafes set up terrace seating along the river, lending the feel of a perpetual street party. Slovenia's master of early-Modern, minimalist design,

Jože Plečnik, graced Ljubljana with beautiful alabaster bridges and baubles, pylons and pyramids that are both elegant and playful. The museums, hotels and restaurants are among the best in the country.

History

Legacies of the Roman city of Emona – remnants of walls, dwellings, early churches, even a gilded statuette – can be seen everywhere. Ljubljana took its present form in the mid-12th century as Laibach under the Habsburgs, but it gained regional prominence in 1809,

Slovenia Highlights

① Enjoy a flight up on the funicular to **Ljubljana Castle** (p612).

② Consider the genius of architect Jože Plečnik at Ljubljana's **National & University Library** (p613).

③ Gaze at the natural perfection that is **Lake Bled** (p624).

④ Gawk in awe at the 100m high walls of the incredible **Škocjan Caves** (p634).

⑤ Climb to the top of the country's tallest mountain, **Mt Triglav** (p629).

⑥ Get lost wandering the Venice-inspired, narrow alleyways of **Piran** (p636).

LJUBLJANA IN TWO DAYS

Take the funicular to **Ljubljana Castle**, then come down and explore the **Central Market** area. After a seafood lunch at **Ribca**, walk around the **Old Town** then cross the Ljubljanica River and walk north along Vegova ulica to **Kongresni Trg** and **Prešernov Trg**. Plan your evening over a fortifying libation at one of the many cafes along the Ljubljanica: low key at **Jazz Club Gajo** or alternative at **Metelkova Mesto**.

On your second day check out the city's museums and galleries, and then stroll or cycle on a **Ljubljana Bike**, stopping for an oh-so-local horse burger at **Hot Horse** along the way. In the evening, take in a performance at the **Križanke** or **Cankarjev Dom** and then visit one of the clubs you missed last night.

when it became the capital of Napoleon's short-lived 'Illyrian Provinces'. Some fine art nouveau buildings filled up the holes left by a devastating earthquake in 1895, and architect Jože Plečnik continued the remake of the city up until WWII. In recent years the city's dynamic mayor, Zoran Janković, has doubled the number of pedestrian streets, extended a great swathe of the river embankment and spanned the Ljubljanica River with two new footbridges.

◉ Sights

The easiest way to see Ljubljana is on foot. The oldest part of town, with the most important historical buildings and sights (including Ljubljana Castle) lies on the right (east) bank of the Ljubljanica River. Center, which has the lion's share of the city's museums and galleries, is on the left (west) side of the river.

CASTLE AREA

Begin an exploration of the city by making the trek up to **Castle Hill** (Grajska Planota) to poke around grand Ljubljana Castle. The castle area offers a couple of worthwhile exhibitions, and the castle watchtower affords amazing views out over the city. The prospect of lunch at one of the city's best restaurants, Gostilna na Gradu (p618), provides an added inducement.

There are several ways to access the castle, with the easiest (and for kids, the most fun) being a 70m-long **funicular** (vzpenjača; ☑reservations 306 42 00; www.ljubljanskigrad.si; Krekov trg 3-7; return adult/child €4/3; ☺9am-11pm Apr-Sep, 10am-9pm Oct-Mar) that leaves from Old Town not far from the market (p619) on Vodnikov trg. If you'd like to get some exercise, you can hike the hill in about 20 minutes. There are three main walking routes: Študentovska ulica, which runs south from Ciril Metodov trg; steep Reber ulica from Stari trg; and Ulica na Grad from Gornji trg.

TOP CHOICE ▸ **Ljubljana Castle** CASTLE
(Ljubljanski Grad; ☑306 42 93; www.ljubljanskigrad.si; Grajska Planota 1; adult/child incl funicular and castle attractions €8/5, castle attractions only €6/3; with guided tour €10/8; ☺9am-11pm May-Sep, 10am-9pm Oct-Apr) There's been a human settlement here since at least Celtic times, but the oldest structures these days date from around the 16th-century, following an earthquake in 1511. It's free to ramble around the castle grounds, but you'll have to pay to enter the **Watchtower**, the **Chapel of St George** (Kapela Sv Jurija) and to see the worthwhile **Exhibition on Slovenian History**.

There are several admission options available; some include the price of the funicular ride, while others include a **castle tour**. Consult the castle website for details. The **Ljubljana Castle Information Centre** (☺9am-9pm Apr-Sep, 9am-6pm Oct-Mar) can advise on tours and events that might be on during your visit.

PREŠERNOV TRG & OLD TOWN

Prešernov Trg SQUARE, PLAZA
This central and beautiful square forms the link between Center and the Old Town. Taking pride of place is the **Prešeren monument** (1905), designed by Maks Fabiani and Ivan Zajc and erected in honour of Slovenia's greatest poet, France Prešeren (1800–49). On the plinth are motifs from his poems.

Just south of the monument is the **Triple Bridge** (Tromostovje), called the Špital (Hospital) Bridge when it was built as a single span in 1842, which leads to the Old Town. The prolific architect Jože Plečnik added the two sides in 1931.

To the east of the monument at No 5 is the Italianate Central Pharmacy (Centralna Lekarna), an erstwhile cafe frequented by intellectuals in the 19th century. To the north, on the corner of Trubarjeva cesta and Miklošičeva cesta, is the delightful Secessionist **Palača Urbanc** (Urbanc Palace) building from 1903.

Mestni Trg
SQUARE

The first of the Old Town's three 'squares' (the other two – Stari trg and Gornji trg – are more like narrow cobbled streets), Mestni trg (Town Square) is dominated by the town hall, in front of which stands the **Robba Fountain** (the original is now in the National Gallery).

Town Hall
TOWN HALL

(Mestna Hiša; ☑306 30 00; Mestni trg; ☉7.30am-4pm Mon-Fri) The seat of the city government and sometimes referred to as the *Magistrat* or *Rotovž*. It was erected in the late 15th century and rebuilt in 1718. The Gothic courtyard inside, arcaded on three levels, is where theatrical performances once took place and contains some lovely sgraffiti.

If you look above the south portal leading to a second courtyard you'll see a relief map of Ljubljana as it appeared in the second half of the 17th century.

Stari Trg
SQUARE

The 'Old Square' is the true heart of the Old Town. It is lined with 19th-century wooden shopfronts, quiet courtyards and cobblestone passageways. From behind the medieval houses on the eastern side, paths once led to Castle Hill, which was a source of water. The buildings fronting the river had large passageways built to allow drainage in case of flooding.

Gornji Trg
SQUARE

Upper Square is the eastern extension of Stari trg. The five **medieval houses** at Nos 7 to 15 have narrow side passages (some with doors) where rubbish was once deposited so that it could be washed down into the river.

FREE Botanical Garden
PUBLIC GARDEN

(Botanični Vrt; ☑427 12 80; www.botanicni-vrt.si; Ižanska cesta 15; ☉7am-8pm Jul & Aug, 7am-7pm Apr-Jun, Sep & Oct, 7am-5pm Nov-Mar) About 800m southeast of the Old Town along Karlovška cesta and over the Ljubljanica River, this 2.5-hectare botanical garden was founded in 1810 as a sanctuary of native flora. It contains 4500 species of plants and trees, about a third of which are indigenous,

CENTER

This large district on the left bank of the Ljubljanica is the nerve centre of modern Ljubljana. It is filled with shops, commercial offices, government departments and embassies. The region is divided into several distinct neighbourhoods centred on town squares.

Trg Francoske Revolucije
SQUARE

'French Revolution Sq' was for centuries the headquarters of the Teutonic Knights of the Cross (Križniki). They built a commandery here in the early 13th century, which was transformed into the **Križanke** (☑241 60 00; Trg Francoske Revolucije 1-2) monastery complex in the early 18th century. Today it serves as the headquarters of the Ljubljana Festival (p617).

TOP CHOICE National & University Library
HISTORIC BUILDING

(☑200 11 09; Turjaška ulica 1; ☉9am-6pm Mon-Fri, 9am-2pm Sat) This library is Plečnik's masterpiece, completed in 1941. To appreciate this great man's philosophy, enter through the main door (note the horse-head doorknobs) on Turjaška ulica – you'll find yourself in near darkness, entombed in black marble. As you ascend the steps, you'll emerge into a colonnade suffused with light – the light of knowledge, according to the architect's plans.

The **Main Reading Room** (Velika Čitalnica), now open to nonstudents only by group tour in summer, has huge glass walls and some stunning lamps, also designed by Plečnik.

City Museum
MUSEUM

(Mestni Muzej; ☑241 25 00; www.mestnimuzej.si; Gosposka ulica 15; adult/child €4/2.50; ☉10am-6pm Tue & Wed, Fri-Sun, 10am-9pm Thu) The excellent city museum focuses on Ljubljana's history, culture and politics via imaginative multimedia and interactive displays. The reconstructed Roman street that linked the eastern gates of Emona to the Ljubljanica and the collection of well-preserved classical finds in the basement are worth a visit in themselves.

The permanent 'Faces of Ljubljana' exhibit of celebrated and lesser-known *žabarji* ('froggers', as natives of the capital are known) is memorable. They host some very good special exhibitions too.

National Museum of Slovenia
MUSEUM

(Narodni Muzej Slovenije; ☑241 44 00; www.nms.si; Prešernova cesta 20; adult/child €3/2.50, 1st Sun of month free; ☉10am-6pm Fri-Wed, 10am-8pm Thu) Highlights include a highly embossed *Vače situla*, a Celtic pail from the late 6th century BC unearthed in a town east of Ljubljana, and a Stone Age bone flute discovered near Cerkno in western Slovenia in 1995. There are also examples of Roman glass and jewellery found in 6th-century Slavic graves, along with many other historical finds.

Ljubljana

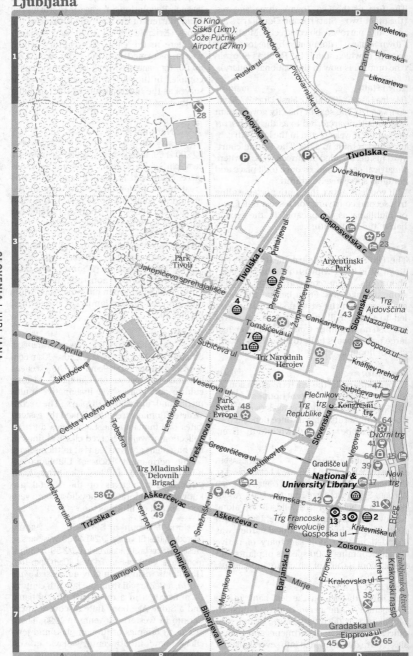

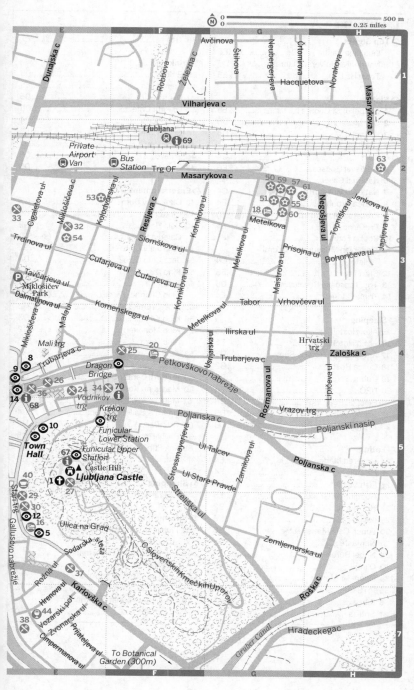

SLOVENIA LJUBLJANA

0 500 m
0 0.25 miles

Vilharjeva c

Ljubljana

69

Private
Airport
Van

Bus
Station

Trg OF

Masarykova c

33

Cigaletova ul
Miklošičeva c

53

32

54

Kolodvorska ul

Resljeva c

Slomškova ul

50 59 57 61
51 55 60
18
Metelkova

Kotnikova ul

Negošjeva ul

63

Topniška ul
Jenkova ul

Masarykova c

Trdinova ul

Tavčarjeva ul

Miklošičev
Park

Dalmatinova ul

Miklošičeva ul

Ma,clli

Mali trg

8

9

14

68

26

36

Cufarjeva ul

Čufarjeva ul

Komenskega ul

Metelkova ul

Prisojna ul
Bohoričeva ul

Maistrova ul

Tabor

Vrhovčeva ul

Ilirska ul

Hrvatski
trg

Zaloška c

Trubarjeva c

20

25

Dragon
Bridge

Petkovškovo nabrežje

Usnjarska ul

Rozmanova ul

Vrazov trg

Lipičeva ul

Trubarjeva c

24 34 70

Vodnikov
trg

Krekov
trg

Funicular
Lower Station

Funicular Upper
Station

Castle Hill

Ljubljana Castle

Poljanska c

Ul Talcev

Ul Stare Pravde

Strossmayerjeva c

Zarnikova ul

Poljanski nasip

Poljanska c

Vrazov trg

**Town
Hall**

40

67

1

10

29

30

12

16

5

Ulica na Grad

Strelliška ul

Zemljemerska ul

Sodarska steza

Ulica Slovenskih Kmečkih Uporov

Roška c

37

Rožna ul

Karlovška c

Gallusovo nabrežje

Hrenova ul

38

44

Vozarski pot

Zvonarska ul

Prijateljeva ul

Cimpermanova ul

To Botanical
Garden (300m)

Gruber Canal

Hradeckega c

Ljubljana

◎ Top Sights
Ljubljana Castle..E5
National & University Library...............D6
Town Hall...E5

◎ Sights
1 Chapel of St George E5
2 City Museum D6
3 Križanke D6
4 Ljubljana Museum of Modern
   Art..C4
5 Medieval Houses....................................E6
6 National Gallery......................................C3
7 National Museum of Slovenia C4
8 Palača Urbanc...E4
   Prešeren Monument ....(see 9)
9 Prešernov Trg..E4
10 Robba Fountain.......................................E5
11 Slovenian Museum of Natural
   History..C4
12 Stari Trg..E6
13 Trg Francoske Revolucije D6
14 Triple Bridge..E4

◎ Sleeping
15 Alibi Hostel...D5
16 Antiq Hotel...E6
17 Antiq Palace Hotel & Spa......................D6
18 Celica Hostel..G2
19 Cubo D5
20 H2O...F4
21 Penzion Pod Lipo C6
22 Slamič B&B...D3
23 Zeppelin Hostel D3

◎ Eating
24 Covered Market E4
25 Falafel F4
26 Fish Market..E4
27 Gostilna na Gradu...................................E5
28 Hot Horse..B2
29 Julija..E6
30 Lunch Café Marley & Me E6
31 Namasté..D6
32 Nobel Burek..E3
33 Olimpije...E2
34 Open-Air Market F4
35 Pri Škofu...D7
36 Ribca..E4
37 Špajza..E6

38 Trta...E7

◎ Drinking
39 BiKoFe..D5
40 Čajna Hiša E5
41 Dvorni Bar...D5
42 Le Petit Café..D6
43 Nebotičnik..D4
44 Open Cafe...E7
45 Šank Pub...D7
46 Žmavc..C6
47 Zvezda...D5

◎ Entertainment
48 Cankarjev Dom..C5
49 Cirkus..B6
50 Gala Hala...G2
   Galerija Mizzart...............................(see 50)
51 Jalla Jalla Club G2
52 Jazz Club Gajo...D4
53 Kino Dvor..E2
54 Kinoteka..E3
   Klub Channel Zero..........................(see 50)
55 Klub Gromka...G2
56 Klub K4..D3
57 Klub Monokel...G2
   Klub Roza..(see 56)
58 KMŠ..A6
   Križanke ....(see 3)
59 Kulturni Center Q G2
60 Menza pri Koritu......................................G2
61 Metelkova Mesto.....................................G2
62 Opera & Ballet Ljubljana C4
63 Orto Bar..H2
64 Philharmonic Hall...................................D5
65 Sax Pub...D7
   Tiffany...(see 59)

◎ Shopping
66 Knjigarna Behemot D5

◎ Information
67 Ljubljana Castle Information
   Centre...E5
68 Ljubljana Tourist Information
   Centre...E5
69 Ljubljana Tourist Information
   Centre Branch.......................................F2
70 Slovenian Tourist Information
   Centre..F4

SLOVENIA LJUBLJANA

Check out the ceiling fresco in the foyer, which features an allegorical Carniola surrounded by important Slovenes from the past and the statues of the Muses and Fates relaxing on the stairway banisters.

Slovenian Museum of Natural History
MUSEUM

(Prirodoslovni Muzej Slovenije; ☑241 09 40; www2. pms-lj.si; Prešernova cesta 20; adult/student €3/2.50, incl national museum €5/4; ☺10am-6pm Fri-Wed, 10am-8pm Thu; ℗) Housed in the same impressive building as the National Museum, the Natural History Museum contains the usual reassembled mammoth and whale skeletons, stuffed birds, reptiles and mammals. However, the mineral collections amassed by the philanthropic Baron Žiga Zois in the early 19th century and the display on Slovenia's unique salamander *Proteus anguinus* are worth a visit.

National Gallery
MUSEUM

(☑241 54 18; www.ng-slo.si; Prešernova cesta 24; adult/child €7/5, 1st Sun of month free; ☺10am-6pm Tue-Sun) Slovenia's foremost assembly of fine art is housed over two floors both in an old building dating to 1896 and an impressive modern wing.

Ljubljana Museum of Modern Art
MUSEUM

(☑241 68 00; www.mg-lj.si; Tomšičeva ulica 14; adult/student €5/2.50; ☺10am-6pm Tue-Sun) This museum houses the very best in Slovenian modern art. Keep an eye out for works by painters Tone Kralj *(Peasant Wedding)*, the expressionist France Mihelič *(The Quintet)* and the surrealist Štefan Planinc *(Primeval World series)* as well as sculptors such as Jakob Savinšek *(Protest)*.

The museum also owns works by the influential 1980s and 1990s multimedia group Neue Slowenische Kunst (NSK; *Suitcase for Spiritual Use: Baptism under Triglav)* and the artists' cooperative Irwin *(Kapital)*.

☞ Tours

Two-hour **walking tours** (adult/child €10/5; ☺10am, 2pm & 5pm Apr-Oct), combined with a ride on the funicular or the tourist train up to the castle or a cruise on the Ljubljanica, are organised by the TIC. They depart daily from the town hall on Mestni trg.

✸ Festivals & Events

Druga Godba
WORLD MUSIC

(http://festival.drugagodba.si; ☺May-Jun) This festival of alternative and world music, takes

place in the Križanke from late May to early June.

Ljubljana Festival
MUSIC & THEATRE

(www.ljubljanafestival.si; ☺Jul & Aug) The number-one event on Ljubljana's social calendar is the Ljubljana Festival, a celebration from early July to late August of music, opera, theatre and dance held at venues throughout the city, but principally in the open-air theatre at the Križanke.

International Ljubljana Marathon
MARATHON

(www.ljubljanskimaraton.si; ☺Oct) Takes off on the last Saturday in October.

🛏 Sleeping

The TIC has comprehensive details of private rooms (from single/double €30/50) and apartments (from double/quad €55/80) though only a handful are central.

TOP CHOICE Antiq Palace Hotel & Spa
BOUTIQUE HOTEL €€€

(☑051 364 124; www.antiqpalace.com; Gosposka ulica 10 & Vegova ul 5a; s/d €180/210; ℗☺✳@☎) Easily the city's most luxurious sleeping option, the Antiq Palace occupies a 16th-century townhouse, about a block from the river. Accommodation is in 13 individually designed suites, each with several rooms and some stretching to 250 sq m in size. The list of amenities is a mile long. The target market is upscale honeymooners and businessmen on expenses.

Cubo
BOUTIQUE HOTEL €€€

(☑425 60 00; www.hotelcubo.com; Slovenska cesta 15; s/d €120/140) This sleek boutique hotel in the centre of town boasts high-end, minimalist design that could have stepped out of the pages of *Wallpaper* magazine. The owners have placed great emphasis on using the best construction materials and high-quality bedding to ensure a good night's sleep. The in-house restaurant is very good.

Celica Hostel
HOSTEL €€

(☑230 97 00; www.hostelcelica.com; Metelkova ulica 8; dm €19-25, s/d/tr cell €53/60/70; ℗☺☎) This stylishly revamped former prison (1882) in Metelkova has 20 'cells', designed by different artists and architects and complete with original bars. There are nine rooms and apartments with three to seven beds and a packed, popular 12-bed dorm. The ground floor is home to a cafe and restaurant (set lunch €5 to €7, open 7.30am to midnight) and the hostel boasts its own gallery where everyone can show their work.

Slamič B&B
PENSION €€

(☏433 82 33; www.slamic.si; Kersnikova ulica 1; s €65-75, d €95-100, ste from €135; P☀@🛜) It's slightly away from the action but Slamič, a B&B above a famous cafe and teahouse, offers 11 bright rooms with antique(ish) furnishings and parquet floors. Choice rooms include the ones looking onto a back garden and the one just off an enormous terrace used by the cafe.

Penzion Pod Lipo
PENSION €€

(☏031 809 893; www.penzion-podlipo.com; Borštnikov trg 3; d/tr/q/ste €65/75/100/125; @) Sitting atop one of Ljubljana's oldest *gostilna* (inn-like restaurant) and a 400-year-old linden tree, this 10-room inn offers plain rooms, but excellent value in a part of the city that is filling up with bars and restaurants. We love the communal kitchen, the original hardwood floors and the east-facing terrace with deck chairs that catch the morning sun.

H2O
HOSTEL €

(☏041 662 266; www.h2ohostel.com; Petkovškovo nabrežje 47; dm €17-22, d €36-52, q €68-88; @🛜) One of our favourite hostels in Ljubljana, this six-room place wraps around a tiny courtyard bordering the Ljubljanica River and one room has views of the castle. Private doubles are available and guests have access to a common kitchen.

Antiq Hotel
BOUTIQUE HOTEL €€€

(☏421 35 60; www.antiqhotel.si; Gornji trg 3; s €75-120, d €85-150; ☀@🛜) This attractive boutique has been cobbled together from several townhouses in the Old Town. There are 16 spacious rooms and a multitiered back garden. The decor is kitsch with a smirk and there are fabulous touches everywhere. Among our favourite rooms are enormous No 8, with views of the Hercules Fountain, and No 13, with glimpses of Ljubljana Castle.

Zeppelin Hostel
HOSTEL €

(☏059 191 427; www.zeppelinhostel.com; 2 fl, Slovenska cesta 47; dm €18-24, d €49-60; @🛜) Located in the historic Evropa building on the corner of Gosposvetska cesta, this hostel offers clean and bright dorm rooms (four to eight beds) and doubles and is run by a young team of international travellers who keep their guests informed on parties and happenings around town.

Alibi Hostel
HOSTEL €

(☏251 12 44; www.alibi.si; Cankarjevo nabrežje 27; dm €15-18, d €40-50; ☀@) This very well-situated 106-bed hostel on the Ljubljanica has brightly painted, airy dorms with four to eight wooden bunks and a dozen doubles. There's a private suite at the top for six people.

 Eating

TOP CHOICE Gostilna na Gradu
SLOVENIAN €

(☏031 523 760; www.nagradu.si; Grajska planota 1; mains €8-14; ⏰10am-midnight Mon-Sat, noon-6pm Sun) Be sure to plan a meal here at this marvelous traditional Slovenian restaurant during your visit to the castle. The chefs pride themselves on using only Slovenian-sourced breads, cheeses and meats, and age-old recipes to prepare a meal to remember. The castle setting is ideal. Book a table in advance to avoid disappointment.

Julija
MEDITERRANEAN €€

(☏425 64 63; http://julijarestaurant.com; Stari trg 9; €10.90-18.90; ⏰noon-10pm) This is arguably the best of a trio of restaurants standing side by side on touristy Stari trg. We love the three-course set lunches served on the sidewalk terrace for €9. The cuisine here revolves around risottos and pastas, though the chicken breast special served in a spicy peanut sauce was one of the best meals on our trip.

Ribca
SEAFOOD €

(☏425 15 44; www.ribca.si; Adamič-Lundrovo nabrežje 1; dishes €5-8; ⏰8am-4pm Mon-Fri, to 2pm Sat) One of the culinary joys of a visit to Ljubljana is the chance to sample inexpensive and well-prepared fish dishes. This basement seafood bar below the Plečnik Colonnade in Pogačarjev trg is one of the best for tasty fried squid, sardines and herrings. The setting is informal, though the cuisine is top notch. Set lunch on weekdays is €7.50.

Špajza
SLOVENIAN €€

(☏425 30 94; www.spajza-restaurant.si; Gornji trg 28; mains €15-25; ⏰noon-11pm) This popular Old Town restaurant is the perfect spot for a splurge or romantic meal for two. The interior is decorated with rough-hewn tables and chairs, wooden floors, frescoed ceilings and nostalgic bits and pieces. The terrace in summer is a delight. The cooking is traditional Slovenian, with an emphasis on less-common mains like rabbit and veal.

Pri Škofu
SLOVENIAN **€€**

(☎426 45 08; Rečna ulica 8; mains €8-22; ☺7am-11pm; ☐) This wonderful little place in tranquil Krakovo, south of the centre, serves some of the best prepared local dishes and salads in Ljubljana, with an ever-changing menu. Weekday set lunches are good value at €8.

Lunch Café Marley & Me
INTERNATIONAL **€€**

(☎040 564 188; www.lunchcafe.si; Stari trg 9; mains from €7-20; ☺11am-11pm; ☐) The name couldn't be more misleading. It's more than a lunch cafe...and the 'Marley' bit? We just don't get it. Still, it's a very popular spot for lunch or dinner over salads, pastas and a variety of meats and seafood. There's sidewalk dining in nice weather.

Trta
ITALIAN **€**

(☎426 50 66; www.trta.si; Grudnovo nabrežje 21; pizza €8-10; ☺11am-10pm Mon-Fri, noon-10.30pm Sat; ☐) This award-winning pizzeria, with large pies cooked in a wood-fired oven, is slightly south of the centre, across the river opposite Trnovo.

Namasté
INDIAN **€€**

(☎425 01 59; www.restavracija-namaste.si; Breg 8; mains €10-20; ☺11am-midnight Mon-Sat, to 10pm Sun; ☐) Should you fancy a bit of Indian, head for this place on the left bank of the Ljubljanica. You won't get high-street-quality curry but the thalis and tandoori dishes are very good. The choice of vegetarian dishes is better than average and a set lunch costs between €6.50 €8.50. Eat along the river in nice weather.

Falafel
MIDDLE EASTERN **€**

(☎041 640 166; Trubarjeva cesta 40; sandwiches €4-6; ☺11am-midnight Mon-Fri, noon-midnight Sat, 1-10pm Sun) Authentic Middle Eastern food, like falafel and hummus, served up to go or eat in at a few tables and chairs scattered about. Perfect choice for a quick meal on the run or the late-night munchies.

Hot Horse
BURGERS **€**

(☎521 14 27; www.hot-horse.si; Park Tivoli, Celovška cesta 25; snacks & burgers €3-6; ☺9am-6pm Tue-Sun, 10am-6pm Mon) This little place in the city's biggest park supplies *Ljubljančani* (local people) with their favourite treat: horse burgers (€4). It's just down the hill from the Museum of Contemporary History.

Self-Catering

Self-caterers and those on a tight budget will want to head directly to Ljubljana's vast **open-air market** (Vodnikov trg; ☺6am-6pm Mon-Fri, 6am-4pm Sat summer, 6am-4pm Mon-Sat winter) on Vodnikov trg, just across the Triple Bridge to the southeast of Prešernov trg. Here you'll find stalls selling everything from wild mushrooms and forest berries to honey and homemade cheeses. The **covered market** (Pogačarjev trg 1; ☺7am-2pm Mon-Wed & Sat, 7am-4pm Thu & Fri) nearby sells meats and cheeses, and there's a **fish market** (Adamič-Lundrovo nabrežje 1; ☺7am-4pm Mon-Fri, 7am-2pm Sat) too. You'll also find open-air **fish stands** selling plates of fried calamari for as low as €6. Another budget option is *burek*, pastry stuffed with cheese, meat or even apple. Reputedly the best places in town are **Olimpije** (Pražakova ulica 2; burek €2; ☺24hr) southwest of the train and bus stations, and **Nobel Burek** (☎232 33 92; Miklošičeva cesta 30; burek €2, pizza slices €1.40; ☺24hr).

 Drinking

Few cities of this size have central Ljubljana's concentration of inviting cafes and bars, the vast majority with outdoor seating in the warmer months.

Bars & Pubs

TOP CHOICE Žmavc
BAR

(☎251 03 24; Rimska cesta 21; ☺7.30am-1am Mon-Fri, from 10am Sat, from 6pm Sun; ☐) A super-popular student hang-out west of Slovenska cesta, with *manga* comic-strip scenes and figures running halfway up the walls. There's a great garden terrace for summer-evening drinking, but try to arrive early to snag a table. Also excellent for morning coffee.

BiKoFe
BAR

(☎425 93 93; Židovska steza 2; ☺7am-1am Mon-Fri, 10am-1pm Sat & Sun; ☐) A favourite with the hipster crowd, this cupboard of a bar has mosaic tables, studenty art on the walls, soul and jazz on the stereo, and a giant water pipe on the menu for that long, lingering smoke outside. The shady outdoor patio is a great place to enjoy a recent purchase from the **Behemot** (☎251 13 92; www.behemot.si; Židovska steza 3; ☺10am-8pm Mon-Fri, 10am-3pm Sat) bookshop across the street.

Dvorni Bar
WINE BAR

(☎251 12 57; www.dvornibar.net; Dvorni trg 2; ☺8am-1am Mon-Sat, 9am-midnight Sun; ☐) This wine bar is an excellent place to taste Slovenian vintages; it stocks more than 100 varieties and has wine tastings every month (usually the second Wednesday).

Šank Pub
PUB

(Eipprova ulica 19; ⊙7am-1am; 🛜) Down in studenty Trnovo, this raggedy little place with brick ceiling and wooden floor is a relaxed alternative to the nearby Sax. The Šank is one of a number of inviting bars and cafes along this stretch of Eipprova ulica.

Cafes & Teahouses

TOP CHOICE Nebotičnik
CAFE

(📞040 601 787; www.neboticnik.si; 12th fl, Štefanova ulica 1; ⊙9am-1am Sun-Wed, 9am-3am Thu-Sat; 🛜) After a decade-long hibernation this elegant cafe with its breathtaking terrace atop Ljubljana's famed art deco Skyscraper (1933) has reopened, and the 360-degree views are spectacular.

Le Petit Café
CAFE

(📞251 25 75; www.lepetit.si; Trg Francoske Revolucije 4; ⊙7.30am-1am; 🛜) Just opposite the Križanke, this pleasant, boho place offers great coffee and a wide range of breakfast goodies, lunches and light meals, plus a good restaurant on the 1st floor.

Čajna Hiša
TEAHOUSE

(📞421 24 40; Stari trg 3; ⊙9am-10.30pm Mon-Fri, 9am-3pm & 6-10pm Sat; 🛜) This elegant and centrally located teahouse takes its teas very seriously. They also serve light meals and there's a tea shop next door.

Open Cafe
GAY & LESBIAN

(📞041 391 371; www.open.si; Hrenova ulica 19; ⊙4pm-midnight; 🛜) This very stylish gay-owned-and-run cafe south of the Old Town has become the meeting point for Ljubljana's burgeoning queer culture. In June 2009 it was attacked by fascist homophobes who attempted to torch the place and some patrons fought back.

Zvezda
CAFE

(📞421 90 90; Wolfova ulica 14; ⊙7am-11pm Mon-Sat, 10am-8pm Sun; 🛜) The 'Star' has all the usual varieties of coffee and tea but is celebrated for its shop-made cakes, especially *skutina pečena* (€3), an eggy cheesecake.

☆ Entertainment

Ljubljana in Your Pocket (www.inyourpocket. com), which comes out every two months, is a good English source for what's on in the capital. Buy tickets for shows and events at the venue box office, online through **Eventim** (📞430 24 05; www.eventim.si), or at Ljubljana Tourist Information Centre (p622). Expect to pay around €10 to €20 for tickets to live acts, and less for club entry and DJ nights.

Nightclubs

Cirkus
CLUB

(Kinoklub Vič; 📞051 631 631; www.cirkusklub.si; Trg Mladinskih Delovnih Brigad 7; €5; ⊙8pm-5am Tue-Sat) This popular dance club, with DJs at the weekends, occupies the former Kinoklub Vič.

Klub K4
CLUB

(📞040 212 292; www.klubk4.org; Kersnikova ulica 4; ⊙10pm-2am Tue, 11pm-4am Wed & Thu, 11pm-6am Fri & Sat, 10pm-4am Sun) This evergreen venue in the basement of the Student Organisation of Ljubljana University (ŠOU) headquarters features rave-electronic music Friday and Saturday, with other styles of music on weeknights, and a popular gay and lesbian night on Sunday.

KMŠ
CLUB

(📞425 74 80; www.klubkms.si; Tržaška cesta 2; ⊙8am-10pm Mon-Fri, 9pm-5am Sat) Located in the deep recesses of a former tobacco factory complex, the Maribor Student Club stays comatose till Saturday when it turns into a raucous place with music and dancers all over the shop.

Live Music

Kino Šiška
INDIE & ROCK

(📞box office 030 310 110; www.kinosiska.si; Trg Prekomorskih brigad 3; ⊙5-8pm Mon-Fri, 10am-1pm Sat) This renovated old movie theatre has been reopened as an urban cultural centre, hosting mainly indie, rock and alternative bands from around Slovenia and the rest of Europe.

Orto Bar
ROCK

(📞232 16 74; www.orto-bar.com; Graboličeva ulica 1; ⊙9pm-4am Tue & Wed, to 5am Thu-Sat) A popular bar-club for late-night drinking and dancing with occasional live music, Orto is just five minutes' walk from Metelkova. Note the program takes a two-month hiatus in summer during July and August.

Jazz Club Gajo
JAZZ

(📞425 32 06; www.jazzclubgajo.com; Beethovnova ulica 8; ⊙7pm-2am Mon-Sat) Now in its 18th year, Gajo is the city's premier venue for live jazz and attracts both local and international talent. Jam sessions are at 8.30pm Monday.

Sax Pub
ROCK

(📞283 90 09; Eipprova ulica 7; ⊙noon-1am Mon, 10am-1am Tue-Sat, 4-10pm Sun) Two decades in

SOMETHING COMPLETELY DIFFERENT: METELKOVO MESTO

For a scruffy antidote to trendy clubs in Ljubljana, try **Metelkova Mesto** (Metelkova Town; www.metelkova.org; Masarykova cesta 24), an ex-army garrison taken over by squatters in the 1990s and converted into a free-living commune – a miniature version of Copenhagen's Christiania. In this two-courtyard block, a dozen idiosyncratic venues hide behind brightly tagged doorways, coming to life generally after midnight daily in summer and on Friday and Saturday the rest of the year. While it's certainly not for the genteel and the quality of the acts and performances varies with the night, there's usually a little of something for everyone on hand.

Entering the main 'city gate' from Masarykova cesta, the building to the right houses **Gala Hala** (☑431 70 63; www.galahala.com), with live bands and club nights, and **Klub Channel Zero** (www.ch0.org), with punk and hardcore. Above it on the 1st floor is **Galerija Mizzart** (www.mizzart.net) with a great exhibition space (the name is no comment on the quality of the creations – promise!).

Easy to miss in the first building to the left is the **Kulturni Center Q** (Q Cultural Centre) including **Tiffany** (www.kulturnicenterq.org/tiffany/klub) for gay men and **Klub Monokel** (www.klubmonokel.com) for lesbians. Due south is the ever-popular **Jalla Jalla Club** (www.metelkovamesto.org), a congenial pub with concerts. Beyond the first courtyard to the southwest, **Klub Gromka** (www.klubgromka.org) has folk concerts, theatre and lectures. Next door is **Menza pri Koritu** (☑434 03 45; www.menzaprikoritu.org), under the creepy ET-like figures, with performance and concerts. If you're staying at the Hostel Celica (p617), all of the action is just around the corner.

Trnovo and decorated with colourful murals and graffiti inside and out, the tiny Sax has live jazz at 9pm or 9.30pm on Thursday from late August to December and February to June. Canned stuff rules at other times.

Performing Arts

Cankarjev Dom   OPERA, DANCE
(☑241 71 00, box office 241 72 99; www.cd-cc.si; Prešernova cesta 10; ⊙box office 11am-1pm & 3-8pm Mon-Fri, 11am-1pm Sat, 1hr before performance) Ljubljana's premier cultural and conference centre has two large auditoriums (the Gallus Hall is said to have perfect acoustics) and a dozen smaller performance spaces offering a remarkable smorgasbord of performance arts. Buy tickets at the box office.

Opera & Ballet Ljubljana   OPERA, DANCE
(☑box office 241 59 59; www.opera.si; Župančičeva ulica 1; ⊙box office 10am-5pm Mon-Fri, 1hr before performance) Home to the Slovenian National Opera and Ballet companies, this historic neo-Renaissance theatre was fully renovated in 2011 and restored to its former luster.

Philharmonic Hall   CLASSICAL
(Slovenska Filharmonija; ☑241 08 00; www.filharmonija.si; Kongresni trg 10; ⊙7am-10pm) Home to the Slovenian Philharmonic Orchestra, this smaller but more atmospheric venue

also stages concerts and hosts performances of the Slovenian Chamber Choir (Slovenski Komorni Zbor), which was founded in 1991.

Križanke   CLASSICAL, THEATRE
(☑241 60 00, box office 241 60 26; www.ljubljanafestival.si; Trg Francoske Revolucije 1-2; ⊙box office 10am-8pm Mon-Fri, 10am-1pm Sat Apr-Sep) The open-air theatre at this sprawling 18th-century monastery hosts the events of the Ljubljana Summer Festival. The smaller Knights Hall (Viteška Dvorana) is the venue for chamber concerts.

Cinema

Kinoteka   CINEMA
(☑547 15 80; www.kinoteka.si; Miklošičeva cesta 28) Shows archival art and classic films in their original language (not always English).

Kino Dvor   CINEMA
(Court Cinema; ☑239 22 13; www.kinodvor.org; Kolodvorska ulica 13) The sister cinema to Kinoteka nearby screens more contemporary films from around the world.

ℹ Information

Internet Access

Many cafes and restaurants offer free wi-fi for customers. Most hostels, and some hotels, maintain a public computer for guests to surf the internet. The Slovenia Tourist Information Centre has computers on-hand to check email (per 30 minutes €1).

Cyber Cafe Xplorer (☑430 19 91; Petkovškovo nabrežje 23; per 30min/1hr €2.50/4; ☺10am-10pm Mon-Fri, 2-10pm Sat & Sun; ☎) Ljubljana's best internet cafe; also has wi-fi and offers discount international calling.

Medical Services
Central Pharmacy (Centralna Lekarna; ☑230 61 00; Prešernov trg 5; ☺8am-7.30pm Mon-Fri, 8am-3pm Sat)

Health Centre Ljubljana (Zdravstveni Dom Ljubljana; ☑472 37 00; www.zd-lj.si; Metelkova ulica 9; ☺7.30am-7pm) For non-emergencies.

University Medical Centre Ljubljana (Univerzitetni Klinični Center Ljubljana; ☑522 50 50, emergencies 522 84 08; www4.kclj.si; Zaloška cesta 2; ☺24hr) University medical clinic with 24h accident and emergency service.

Money
There are ATMs at every turn, including a row of them outside the main Ljubljana Tourist Information (TIC) office. At the train station you'll find a **bureau de change** (train station; ☺7am-8pm) changing cash for no commission but not travellers cheques.

Abanka (☑300 15 00; www.abanka.si; Slovenska cesta 50; ☺9am-1pm & 3pm-5pm Mon-Fri)

Nova Ljubljanska Banka (☑476 39 00; www.nlb.si; Trg Republike 2; ☺8am-6pm Mon-Fri)

Post
Main Post Office (Slovenska cesta 32; ☺8am-7pm Mon-Fri, to 1pm Sat) Holds poste restante for 30 days and changes money.

Tourist Information
Ljubljana Tourist Information Centre (TIC; ☑306 12 15; www.visitljubljana.si; Adamič-Lundrovo nabrežje 2; ☺8am-9pm Jun-Sep, 8am-7pm Oct-May) Knowledgeable and enthusiastic staff dispense information, maps and useful literature and help with accommodation. Maintains an excellent website. Has a helpful **branch** (☑433 94 75; www.visitljubljana.si; Trg OF 6; ☺8am-10pm Jun-Sep, 10am-7pm Mon-Fri, 8am-3pm Sat Oct-May) at the train station.

Slovenian Tourist Information Centre (STIC; ☑306 45 76; www.slovenia.info; Krekov trg 10; ☺8am-9pm Jun-Sep, 8am-7pm Oct-May) Good source of information for the rest of Slovenia, with internet and bicycle rental also available.

Travel Agency
STA Ljubljana (☑439 16 90, 041 612 711; www.sta-lj.com; 1st fl, Trg Ajdovščina 1; ☺10am-5pm Mon-Fri) Discount air fares for students and its cafe has internet access.

Trek Trek (☑425 13 92; www.trektrek.si; Bičevje ulica 5; ☺10am-5pm Mon-Fri) Specialising in adventure travel in Slovenia, with emphasis on trekking and cycling holidays.

Websites
In addition to the websites of the Slovenian Tourist Information Centre and Ljubljana Tourist Information Centre the following sites might be useful:

City of Ljubljana (www.ljubljana.si) Comprehensive information portal on every aspect of life and tourism direct from city hall.

In Your Pocket (www.inyourpocket.com) Insider info on the capital updated regularly.

Lonely Planet (www.lonelyplanet.com/slovenia/ljubljana)

ⓘ Getting There & Away
Bus
Buses to destinations both within Slovenia and abroad leave from the **bus station** (Avtobusna Postaja Ljubljana; ☑234 46 00; www.ap-ljubljana.si; Trg Osvobodilne Fronte 4; ☺5.30am-10.30pm Sun-Fri, 5am-10pm Sat) just next to train station. Next to the ticket windows are multilingual information phones and a touchscreen computer. You do not usually have to buy a ticket in advance; just pay as you board the bus. But for long-distance trips on Friday, just before the school break and public holidays, book the day before to be safe. There's a **left luggage** (Trg OF 4; per day €2; ☺5.30am-10.30pm Sun-Fri, 5am-10pm Sat) area at window 3.

You can reach virtually anywhere in the country by bus.

Train
Domestic and international trains arrive at and depart from central Ljubljana's **train station** (Železniška Postaja; ☑291 33 32; www.slo-zeleznice.si; Trg Osvobodilne Fronte 6; ☺6am-10pm) where you'll find a separate Info Center next to the Ljubljana Tourist Information Centre branch. Buy domestic tickets from window nos 1 to 8 and international ones from either window no 9 or the Info Center. There are **coin lockers** (Trg OF 6; per day €2-3; ☺24hr) for left luggage on platform 1.

There's a surcharge of €1.55 on domestic InterCity (IC) and EuroCity (EC) train tickets.

ⓘ Getting Around
To/From the Airport
The cheapest way to Ljubljana's **Jože Pučnik Airport** (LJU/Aerodrom Ljubljana; ☑04-206 19 81; www.lju-airport.si/eng; Zgornji Brnik 130a, Brnik) is by public bus (€4.10, 45 minutes, 27km) from stop No 28 at the bus station. These run at 5.20am and hourly from 6.10am to 8.10pm

TRANSPORT FROM LJUBLJANA

Bus

DESTINATION	PRICE (€)	DURATION (HR)	DISTANCE (KM)	FREQUENCY
Bled	6.20	1½	57	hourly
Bohinj	9	2	91	hourly
Koper	12	2½	122	5 daily with more in season
Maribor	14	3	141	2-4 four daily
Piran	14	3	140	up to 7 daily
Postojna	7	1	53	up to 24 daily

Train

DESTINATION	PRICE (€)	DURATION	DISTANCE (KM)	FREQUENCY
Bled	6.20	55min	51	up to 21 daily
Koper	9	2½hr	153	up to 4 daily with more in summer
Maribor	15	1¾hr	156	up to 25 daily
Murska Sobota	14	3¼hr	216	up to 5 daily

Monday to Friday; at the weekend there's a bus at 6.10am and then one every two hours from 9.10am to 7.10pm. Buy tickets from the driver.

A **private airport van** (☑051 321 414; www. airport-shuttle.si) also links Trg OF, near the bus station, with the airport (€9) up to 11 times daily between 5.20am and 10.30pm, and is a 30-minute trip. It goes from the airport to Ljubljana 10 times a day between 5.45am and 11pm.

A taxi from the airport to Ljubljana will cost from €40 to €45.

Bicycle

Ljubljana is a pleasure for cyclists, and there are bike lanes and special traffic lights everywhere.

Ljubljana Bike (☑306 45 76; www.visitljubljana. si; Krekov trg 10; per 2hr/day €2/8; ☺8am-7pm or 9pm Apr-Oct) rents two-wheelers in two-hour or full-day increments from April through October from the Slovenia Tourist Information Centre.

For short rides, you can hire bikes as needed from **Bicike(lj)** (www.bicikelj.si; subscription weekly/yearly €1/€3 plus hourly rate; ☺24hr) bike stands located around the city. To rent a bike requires pre-registration and subscription over the company website plus a valid credit or debit card. After registration simply submit your card or an Urbana public-transport card plus a PIN number. The first hour of the rental is free, the second hour costs €1, the third hour €2, and each additional hour €4. Bikes must be returned within 24 hours.

Public Transport

Ljubljana's city buses operate every five to 15 minutes from 5am (6am on Sunday) to around 10.30pm. A flat fare of €1.20 (good for 90 minutes of unlimited travel, including transfers) is paid with a stored-value magnetic **Urbana** (☑430 51 74; www.jh-lj.si/urbana) card, which can be purchased at newsstands, tourist offices and the **LPP Information Centre** (☑430 51 75; www.jhl.si; Slovenska cesta 56; ☺7am-7pm Mon-Fri) for €2; credit can then be added (from €1 to €50).

JULIAN ALPS

Slovenia's Julian Alps, part of the wider European Alpine range, is the epicentre for all things outdoors. If you're into adventure sports, head to this area. Much of the region, including the country's highest mountain, Mt Triglav, is protected as part of the Triglav National Park. The park has hiking and biking trails galore. The beautiful alpine lakes at Bled and Bohinj offer boating and swimming amid shimmering mountain backdrops. The region is not just about nature pursuits; you'll also find some of the country's most attractive and important historical towns, like Radovljica. These are unexpected treasure troves of Gothic, Renaissance and baroque architecture.

Lake Bled

🗐 04 / POP 10900

With its emerald-green lake, picture-postcard church on an islet, a medieval castle clinging to a rocky cliff and some of the highest peaks of the Julian Alps and the Karavanke as backdrops, Bled is Slovenia's most popular resort, drawing everyone from honeymooners lured by the over-the-top romantic setting to backpackers, who come for the hiking, biking, boating and canyoning possibilities. Bled can be overpriced and swarming with tourists in mid-summer. But as is the case with many popular destinations around the world, people come in droves – and will continue to do so – because the place is special.

⊙ Sights

Lake Bled LAKE

(Blejsko jezero) Bled's greatest attraction is its crystal blue-green lake, measuring just 2km by 1380m. The lake is lovely to behold from almost any vantage point, and makes a beautiful backdrop for the 6km walk along the shore. Mild thermal springs warm the water to a swimmable 26°C from June through August. You can rent boats, go diving or simply snap countless photos.

Bled Castle CASTLE, MUSEUM

(Blejski Grad; www.blejski-grad.si; Grajska cesta 25; adult/child €8/3.50; ☉8am-8pm Apr-Oct, 8am-6pm Nov-Mar) Perched atop a steep cliff more than 100m above the lake, Bled Castle is how most people imagine a medieval fortress to be, with towers, ramparts, moats and a terrace offering magnificent views. The castle houses a museum collection that traces the lake's history from earliest times to the development of Bled as a resort in the 19th century.

The castle, built on two levels, dates back to the early 11th century, although most of what stands here now is from the 16th century. For 800 years, it was the seat of the Bishops of Brixen. Among the museum holdings, there's a large collection of armour and weapons (swords, halberds and firearms from the 16th to 18th centuries).

Bled Island ISLAND

(Blejski Otok; www.blejskiotok.si) Tiny, tear-shaped Bled Island beckons from the shore. There's a church and small museum, but the real thrill is the ride out by gondola (*pletna*). The boat sets you down on the south side at the monumental South Staircase (Južno Stopnišče), built in 1655.

Vintgar Gorge NATURE PARK

(Soteska Vintgar; adult/child/student €4/2/3; ☉8am-7pm late Apr-Oct) One of the easiest and most satisfying day trips from Bled is to Vintgar Gorge, some 4km to the north-west. The highlight is a 1600m wooden walkway, built in 1893 and continually rebuilt since. It criss-crosses the swirling Radovna River four times over rapids, waterfalls and pools before reaching 13m-high Šum Waterfall.

🏃 Activities

Several local outfits organise a wide range of outdoor activities in and around Bled, including trekking, mountaineering, rock climbing, ski touring, cross-country skiing, mountain biking, rafting, kayaking, canyoning, caving, horse riding and paragliding.

3glav Adventures ADVENTURE SPORTS

(🗐041 683 184; www.3glav-adventures.com; Ljubljanska cesta 1; ☉9am-7pm Apr-Oct) The number-one adventure-sport specialists in Bled for warm-weather activities from 15 April to 15 October. The most popular trip is the Emerald River Adventure (€65), an 11-hour hiking and swimming foray into Triglav National Park. Also rents bikes (half-day/full day €8/15), conducts hot-air balloon flights (€150) and leads diving expeditions of Lake Bled (€70).

Gondola BOATING

(Pletna; 🗐041 427 155; per person return €12) Riding a piloted gondola out to Bled Island is the archetypal tourist experience. There is a convenient jetty just below the TIC and another in Mlino on the south shore. You get about half an hour to explore the island. In all, the trip to the island and back takes about 1¼ hours.

Horse-drawn Carriages CARRIAGE

(Fijaker; 🗐041 710 970; www.fijaker-bled.si) A romantic way to experience Bled is to take a horse-drawn carriage from the stand near the **Festival Hall** (Festivalna Dvorana; Cesta Svobode 11). A spin around the lake costs €40, and it's the same price to the castle; an extra 30 minutes inside costs €50. You can even get a carriage for four to **Vintgar** (adult/child €4/2; ☉8am-7pm mid-May–Oct); the two-hour return trip costs €90.

🛏 Sleeping

Kompas has a list of private rooms and farmhouses, with singles/doubles starting at €24/38.

Hotel Triglav Bled `HOTEL €€€`

(☎575 26 10; www.hoteltriglavbled.si; Kolodvorska cesta 33; s €89-159, d €119-179, ste €139-209; P❅@🖵🌊) This 22-room boutique hotel in a painstakingly restored caravanserai that opened in 1906 raises the bar of accommodation standards in Bled. The rooms have hardwood floors and oriental carpets and are furnished with antiques. There's an enormous sloped garden that grows the vegetables served in the terrace restaurants. The location is opposite Bled Jezero train station.

TOP CHOICE Camping Bled `CAMPGROUND €`

(☎575 20 00; www.camping-bled.com; Kidričeva cesta 10c; adult €10.90-12.90, child €7.60-9, glamping huts €60-80; ☺Apr–mid-Oct; P@🖵) Bled's upscale campground is one of the nicest in the country and one of the few places around to try 'glamping' – aka glamorous camping – in this case, ecofriendly, all-natural A-frame huts, some equipped with hot-tubs. The campground setting is a well-tended rural valley at the western end of the lake, about 2.5km from the bus station.

Garni Hotel Berc `HOTEL €€`

(☎576 56 58; www.berc-sp.si; Pod Stražo 13; s €45-50, d €70-80; P@🖵) This purpose-built place, reminiscent of a Swiss chalet, has 15 rooms on two floors in a quiet location above the lake.

Penzion Mayer `PENSION €€`

(☎576 57 40; www.mayer-sp.si; Želeška cesta 7; s €57, d €77-82, apt €120-150; P@🖵) This flower-bedecked 12-room inn in a renovated 19th-century house is in a quiet location above the lake. The larger apartment is in a delightful wooden cabin and the in-house restaurant is excellent.

Traveller's Haven `HOSTEL €`

(☎041 396 545; www.travellers-haven.si; Riklijeva cesta 1; dm/d €19/48; P@🖵) This is arguably the nicest of several hostels clustered on a hillside on the eastern shore of the lake, about 500m north of the centre. The setting is a renovated villa, with six rooms (including one private double), a great kitchen and free laundry. Note the upstairs rooms get hot in mid-summer.

✗ Eating & Drinking

Vila Ajda `SLOVENIAN €€`

(☎576 83 20; www.vila-ajda.si; Cesta Svobode 27; mains €9-20; ☺11am-11pm; 🖵) Attractive destination restaurant with lovely views out over

SLOVENIA LAKE BLED

WORTH A TRIP

RADOVLJICA

The town of Radovljica, an easy day trip from Bled, just 7km away, is filled with charming, historic buildings and blessed with stunning views of the Alps, including Mt Triglav. It was settled by the early Slavs and by the 14th century had grown into an important market town centred on a large rectangular square, today's **Linhartov trg**, and fortified with high stone walls. Much of the original architecture is still standing and looks remarkably unchanged from those early days.

Besides simply strolling historic Linhartov trg, don't miss the town's **Beekeeping Museum** (Čebelarski Muzej; www.muzeji-radovljica.si; Linhartov trg 1; adult/child €3/2; ☺10am-6pm Tue-Sun May-Oct, 8am-3pm Tue, Thu & Fri, 10am-noon & 3-5pm Wed, Sat & Sun Mar, Apr, Nov & Dec, 8am-3pm Tue-Fri Jan & Feb), which is more interesting than it sounds. The museum's collection of illustrated beehive panels from the 18th and 19th centuries, a folk art unique to Slovenia, is the largest in the country. Ask to see a short, instructive video in English.

Radovljica's other claim to fame is food, and the town is blessed with several excellent restaurants. Our favourite is the traditional **Gostilna Lectar** (☎537 48 00; www.lectar. com; Linhartov trg 2; mains €9-15; ☺noon-11pm; 🖵), an inviting guesthouse on the main square. Everything from relatively common dishes like veal goulash to harder to find items like 'beef tongue served with kohlrabi' are given a gourmet touch.

Across the street, **Gostilna Augustin** (☎531 41 63; Linhartov trg 15; mains €10-17; ☺10am-10pm) serves excellent Slovenian dishes to order. Don't miss the cellar dining room, which was once part of a prison (and may have seen an execution or two), and the wonderful back terrace with stunning views of Mt Triglav. Why not have lunch at one and dinner at the other?

Bled

ŽELEČE

REČICA

PRISTAVA

Bled Castle

Grass Beach

◎2
Lake Bled

Bled Island

Boardwalk

MLINO

Mala Osojnica
(685m)

Straža Hill
(646m)

Bled Jezero

Kolodvorska c

Kidričeva c

C Svobode

Mlinska c

Pod Stražo

Zeleška c

Cankarjeva c

C Svobode

Kidričeva c

Grajska c

Rečiška c

Prešernova c

C Svobode

Mladinska c

Seliška c

Ljubljanska c

To Lesce-Bled
Train Station (4km);
Radovljica (8km)

Bled Shopping Centre

Spa Park

500 m
0.25 miles

Bled

◉ **Top Sights**
Bled Castle..E1
Bled Island C3

◉ **Sights**
1 Festival Hall F1
2 Lake Bled D3

◔ **Activities, Courses & Tours**
3 3glav Adventures G2
4 Gondolas Mlino E4
5 Gondolas TIC....................................F2
6 Horse-drawn Carriages......................F1

◔ **Sleeping**
7 Camping Bled.....................................A3
8 Garni Hotel Berc................................F3
9 Hotel Triglav Bled B2
10 Penzion Mayer F3
11 Traveller's Haven F1

◔ **Eating**
12 Ostarija Peglez'n F2
13 Penzion Mlino E4
14 Pizzeria Rustika................................F1
15 Vila Ajda F3

◔ **Drinking**
16 Pub Bled...F2
17 Slaščičarna Šmon...............................F1

the lake and a menu that features traditional Slovenian cooking made from locally sourced ingredients. Eat outdoors in the garden in nice weather, or in the upscale dining room. Book in advance on warm evenings in summer.

Ostarija Peglez'n SEAFOOD €€
(574 42 18; http://ostarija-peglezn.mestna-izlozba.com; Cesta Svobode 19a; mains €8-18; 11am-11pm) One of the better restaurants in Bled, the Iron Inn is just opposite the landmark Grand Hotel Toplice. It has fascinating retro decor with lots of old household antiques and curios (including the eponymous iron) and serves some of the best fish dishes in town.

Penzion Mlino SLOVENIAN €€
(www.mlino.si; Cesta Svobode 45; mains €8-15; noon-11pm) This is a wonderful choice for lunch along a quieter strip of the lake, about 3km outside the centre. The daily four-course set lunches (around €10) usually offer a fish choice, such as the unforgettable grilled trout we enjoyed on our stop.

Pizzeria Rustika PIZZA €
(576 89 00; www.pizzeria-rustika.com; Riklijeva cesta 13; pizza €6-10; noon-11pm) Conveniently located on the same hill as many of Bled's hostels, so the best pizza in town is just a couple of minutes' walk away.

Pub Bled PUB
(Cesta Svobode 19a; 9am-2am Sun-Thu, 9am-3am Fri & Sat) This friendly pub above the Oštarija Peglez'n restaurant has great cocktails and, on some nights, a DJ.

Slaščičarna Šmon CAFE
(http://slascicarna-smon.mestna-izlozba.com; Grajska cesta 3; 7.30am-10pm) Bled's culinary speciality is *kremna rezina* (€2.40), a layer of vanilla custard topped with whipped cream and sandwiched between two layers of flaky pastry, and while Šmon may not be its place of birth, it remains the best place in which to try it.

ℹ Information

A Propos Bar (574 40 44; Bled Shopping Centre, Ljubljanska cesta 4; per 15/30/60min €1.25/2.10/4.20; 8am-midnight Sun-Thu, to 1am Fri & Sat) In Bled Shopping Centre, wireless connection as well.

Gorenjska Banka (Cesta Svobode 15) Just north of the Park Hotel.

Kompas (572 75 01; www.kompas-bled.si; Bled Shopping Centre, Ljubljanska cesta 4; 8am-7pm Mon-Sat, 8am-noon & 4-7pm Sun) Full-service travel agency, organises excursions to Bohinj and Radovljica, airport transfers and transport, rents bikes and skis, sells fishing licenses and arranges accommodation in private homes and apartments.

Post Office (Ljubljanska cesta 10)

Tourist Information Centre Bled (574 11 22; www.bled.si; Cesta Svobode 10; 8am-7pm Mon-Sat, 11am-5pm Sun) Occupies a small office behind the Casino at Cesta Svobode 10; sells maps and souvenirs, rents bikes (half day/full day €8/11); has a computer for checking email.

ℹ Getting There & Around

BUS Bled is well connected by bus. There are buses every 30 minutes to Radovljica (€1.80, 15 minutes, 7km) and around 20 buses daily run from Bled to Lake Bohinj (€3.60, 45 minutes) via Bohinjska Bistrica, with the first bus leaving around 5am and the last about 9pm. Buses depart at least hourly for Ljubljana (€6.50, 1¼ hours, 57km).

TRAIN Bled has two train stations, though neither is close to the centre. Mainline trains for Ljubljana (€6.50, 55 minutes, 51km, up to 21 daily), via Škofja Loka and Radovljica, use

Lesce-Bled station, 4km to the east of town. Trains to Bohinjska Bistrica (€1.60, 20 minutes, 18km, eight daily), from where you can catch a bus to Lake Bohinj, use the smaller Bled Jezero station, which is 2km west of central Bled.

Lake Bohinj

📋04 / POP 5275

Many visitors to Slovenia say they've never seen a more beautiful lake than Bled...that is, until they've seen Lake Bohinj, just 26km to the southwest. We'll refrain from weighing in on the Bled vs Bohinj debate other than to say we see their point. Admittedly, Bohinj lacks Bled's glamour, but it's less crowded and in many ways more authentic. It's an ideal summer holiday destination. People come primarily to chill out or go for a swim in the crystal-clear, blue-green water. There are lots of outdoor pursuits like kayaking, cycling, climbing and horse riding if you've got the energy.

⊙ Sights

Church of St John the Baptist CHURCH
(Cerkev Sv Janeza Krstnika; Ribčev Laz; ⊙10am-noon & 4-7pm summer, by appointment other times) This church, on the northern side of the Sava Bohinjka river across the stone bridge, is what every medieval church should be: small, on a reflecting body of water and full of exquisite frescos. The nave is Romanesque, but the Gothic presbytery dates from about 1440.

Alpine Dairy Museum MUSEUM
(Planšarski Muzej; www.bohinj.si; Stara Fužina 181; adult/child €3/2; ⊙11am-7pm Tue-Sun Jul & Aug, 10am-noon & 4-6pm Tue-Sun early Jan-Jun, Sep-late Oct) This museum in Stara Fužina, 1.5km north of Ribčev Laz, has a small collection related to Alpine dairy farming. The four rooms of the museum – once a cheese dairy itself – contain a mock-up of a mid-19th-century herder's cottage.

Savica Waterfall WATERFALL
(Slap Savica; Ukanc; adult/child €2.50/1.25; ⊙9am-6pm Jul & Aug, 9am-5pm Apr-Jun, Sep & Oct; P) The magnificent Savica Waterfall, which cuts deep into a gorge 60m below, is 4km from the Hotel Zlatorog in Ukanc and can be reached by footpath from there.

🏃 Activities

While most people come to Bohinj to relax, there are more exhilarating pursuits available, including canyoning, caving, and paragliding from the top of Mt Vogel, among others. Two companies, Alpinsport and Perfect Adventure Choice (PAC) Sports, specialise in these activities.

Alpinsport ADVENTURE SPORTS
(📞572 34 86; www.alpinsport.si; Ribčev Laz 53; ⊙9am-8pm Jul-Sep, 9am-7pm Oct-Jun) Rents sporting equipment, canoes, kayaks and bikes; also operates guided rafting, canyoning and caving trips. Located in a kiosk at the stone bridge over the Sava Bohinjka river in Ribčev Laz.

Bohinj Cable Car HIKING, SKIING
(adult/child one way €9/7 return €13/9; ⊙every 30min 8am-6pm) The Bohinj cable car operates year-round, hauling skiers in winter and hikers in summer. There are several day hikes and longer treks that set out from Mt Vogel (1922m).

Mrcina Ranč HORSE RIDING
(📞041 790 297; www.ranc-mrcina.com; Studor; per hr €20) Mrcina Ranč in Studor, 5km from Ribčev Laz, offers a range of guided tours on horseback, lasting one hour to three days on sturdy Icelandic ponies.

PAC Sports ADVENTURE SPORTS
(Perfect Adventure Choice; 📞572 34 61; www.pac-sports.com; Hostel Pod Voglom, Ribčev Laz; ⊙7am-11pm Jul & Aug, 10am-6pm Sep-Jun) Popular youth-oriented sports and adventure company, located in the Hostel pod Voglom, 3km west of Ribcev Laz on the road to Ukanc. Rents bikes, canoes and kayaks, and operates guided canyoning, rafting, paragliding and caving trips. In winter, they rent sleds and offer winter rafting near Vogel (per person €15).

Tourist Boat BOATING
(Turistična Ladja; 📞574 75 90; one way adult/child €9/6.50, return €10.50/7.50; ⊙half-hourly 9.30am-5.30pm Jun–mid-Sep, 10am, 11.30am, 1pm, 2.30pm, 4pm & 5.30pm early Apr-May, 11.30am, 1pm, 2.30pm & 4pm mid-Sep–Oct) An easy family-friendly sail from Ribčev Laz to Ukanc and back.

🛏 Sleeping

The tourist office can help arrange accommodation in private rooms and apartments. Expect to pay anywhere from €38 to €50 for a two-person apartment.

TOP CHOICE **Penzion Gasperin** PENSION €€
(📞041 540 805; www.bohinj.si/gasperin; Ribčev Laz 36a; r €48-60; P⊝❄@🔊) This spotless

chalet-style guesthouse with 23 rooms is just 350m southeast of the TIC and run by a friendly British/Slovenian couple. Most rooms have balconies. The buffet breakfast is fresh and includes a sampling of local meats and cheeses.

Hotel Stare
PENSION €€

(☎040 558 669; www.bohinj-hotel.com; Ukanc 128; per person €42-50; P@🖧) This beautifully appointed 10-room pension is situated on the Sava Bohinjka river in Ukanc and is surrounded by 3.5 hectares of lovely garden. If you really want to get away from it all without having to climb mountains, this is your place. Rates are half-board, including breakfast and dinner.

Hotel Jezero
HOTEL €€€

(☎572 91 00; www.bohinj.si/alpinum/jezero; Ribčev Laz 51; s €65-75, d €120-140; P@🖧🏊) Further renovations have raised the standards at this 76-room place just across from the lake. It has a lovely indoor swimming pool, two saunas and a fitness centre.

Hostel Pod Voglom
HOSTEL €

(☎572 34 61; www.hostel-podvoglom.com; Ribčev Laz 60; dm €18, r per person €23-26, without bathroom €20-22; P@) Bohinj's youth hostel, some 3km west of the centre of Ribčev Laz on the road to Ukanc, has 119 beds in 46 rooms in two buildings.

Autokamp Zlatorog
CAMPGROUND €

(☎577 80 00; www.hoteli-bohinj.si; Ukanc 2; per person €6-9; ⊙May-Sep) This pleasant, pine-shaded 2.5-hectare camping ground accommodating 500 guests is at the lake's western end, 4.5km from Ribčev Laz. Prices vary according to site location, with the most expensive – and desirable – sites right on the lake.

✗ Eating

Gostilna Rupa
SLOVENIAN €€

(☎572 34 01; www.apartmajikatrnjek.com/rupa; Srednja Vas 87; mains €8-16; ⊙10am-midnight Jul & Aug, Tue-Sun Sep-Jun) If you're under your own steam, head for this country-style restaurant in the next village over from Studor and about 5km from Ribčev Laz. Among the excellent home-cooked dishes are *ajdova krapi*, crescent-shaped dumplings made from buckwheat and cheese, various types of local *klobasa* (sausage) and Bohinj trout.

Gostilna Mihovc
SLOVENIAN €

(☎572 33 90; www.gostilna-mihovc.si; Stara Fužina 118; mains €7-10; ⊙10am-midnight) This place in Stara Fužina is very popular – not least for its fiery homemade brandy. Try the *pasulj* (bean soup) with sausage (€6) or the beef *golač* (goulash; €5.20). Live music on Friday and Saturday evenings. In

SLOVENIA LAKE BOHINJ

SUMMITING MT TRIGLAV

The 2864m limestone peak called Mt Triglav (Mt Three Heads) has been a source of inspiration and an object of devotion for Slovenes for more than a millennium. Under the Habsburgs in the 19th century, the 'pilgrimage' to Triglav became, in effect, a confirmation of one's ethnic identity, and this tradition continues to this day: a Slovene is expected to climb Triglav at least once in his or her life.

You can climb Slovenia's highest peak too, but Triglav is not for the unfit or faint-hearted. We strongly recommend hiring a guide for the ascent, even if you have some mountain-climbing experience under your belt. A local guide will know the trails and conditions, and can prove invaluable in helping to arrange sleeping space in mountain huts and providing transport. Guides can be hired through 3glav (p624) in Bled or Alpinsport in Bohinj, or book in advance through the **Alpine Association of Slovenia** (PZS; www.pzs.si/).

Triglav is inaccessible from middle to late October to late May. June and the first half of July are the rainiest times in the summer months, so late July, August and particularly September and early October are the best times to make the climb.

There are many ways to reach the top, with the most popular approaches coming from the south, either starting from **Pokljuka**, near Bled, or from the Savica Waterfall, near Lake Bohinj. You can also climb Triglav from the north and the east (Mojstrana and the Vrata Valley). All of the approaches offer varying degrees of difficulty and have their pluses and minuses. Note that treks normally require one or two overnight stays in the mountains.

summer book in advance to secure a garden table.

Getting There & Away

Buses run regularly from Ljubljana (€9, two hours, 90km, hourly) to Bohinj Jezero and Ukanc – marked 'Bohinj Zlatorog' – via Bled and Bohinjska Bistrica. Around 20 buses daily run from Bled (€3.60, 45 minutes) to Bohinj Jezero (via Bohinjska Bistrica) and return, with the first bus leaving around 5am and the last about 9pm. From the end of June through August, **Alpetour** (☑532 04 45; www.alpetour.si) runs special tourist buses that leave from Ribčev Laz to Bohinjska Bistrica in one direction and to the Savica Waterfall (23 minutes) in the other.

Several trains daily make the run to Bohinjska Bistrica from Ljubljana (€6.70, two hours), though this route requires a change in Jesenice. There are also frequent trains between Bled's small Bled Jezero station (€1.60, 20 minutes, 18km, eight daily) and Bohinjska Bistrica.

Kranjska Gora

☑04 / POP 5510

Nestling in the Sava Dolinka Valley some 40km northwest of Bled, Kranjska Gora (Carniolan Mountain) is Slovenia's largest and best-equipped ski resort. It's at its most perfect under a blanket of snow, but its surroundings are wonderful to explore at other times as well. There are endless possibilities for hiking, cycling and mountaineering in Triglav National Park, which is right on the town's doorstep to the south, and few travellers will be unimpressed by a trip over Vršič Pass (1611m), the gateway to the Soča Valley.

⦿ Sights & Activities

Most of the sights are situated along the main street, Borovška cesta, 400m south of where the buses stop. The endearing **Liznjek House** (Liznjekova Domačija; www.gornjesavskimuzej.si; Borovška 63; adult/child €2.50/1.70; ⊙10am-6pm Tue-Sat, 10am-5pm Sun), an 18th-century museum house, has a good collection of household objects and furnishings peculiar to the alpine region.

Kranjska Gora is best known as a winter resort, and chairlifts up to the **ski slopes** on Vitranc (1631m) are at the western end of town off Smerinje ulica. There are more ski slopes and a **ski-jumping facility** 6km to the west, near the villages of Rateče and Planica, which is home to the annual **Ski-Jumping World Cup Championships** (☑1 200 6241; www.planica.info; Planica; adult/child €20/3) in

mid-March. There are lots of places offering ski tuition and hiring out equipment, including **ASK Kranjska Gora Ski School** (☑588 53 02; www.ask-kg.com; Borovška c 99a; ⊙9am-4pm Mon-Sat, 10am-6pm Sun mid-Dec–mid-Mar, 9am-3pm Mon-Fri mid-Mar–mid-Dec).

In summer, the town is quieter, but there are still plenty of things to do. Kranjska Gora makes an excellent base for **hiking** in the Triglav National Park, and Jasna Lake, the gateway to the park, is 2km to the south. The 1:30,000-scale *Kranjska Gora* hiking map is available at the **Tourist Information Centre** (TIC; ☑580 94 40; www.kranjska -gora.si; Tičarjeva cesta 2; ⊙8am-7pm Mon-Sat, 9am-6pm Sun Jun-Sep & mid-Dec–Mar, 8am-3pm Mon-Sat Apr, May & Oct–mid-Dec) for €9.

The hiking map also marks out 15 **cycling routes** of varying difficulty. Most ski-rental outfits hire out bikes in summer, including **Intersport** (www.intersport-bernik.com; Borovška cesta 88a; ⊙8am-8pm mid-Dec–mid-Mar, 8am-8pm Mon-Sat, 8am-1pm Sun mid-Mar–mid-Dec). Expect to pay €10 for a full-day rental and helmet.

⨴ Sleeping & Eating

Accommodation costs peak from December to March and in mid-summer. Private rooms and apartments can be arranged through the Tourist Information Centre.

Hotel Kotnik   HOTEL €€
(☑588 15 64; www.hotel-kotnik.si; Borovška cesta 75; s €50-60, d €72-80; P@☎) If you're not into big high-rise hotels with hundreds of rooms, choose this charming, bright-yellow, low-rise property. It has 15 cosy rooms, a great restaurant and pizzeria, and it couldn't be more central.

Natura Eco Camp Kranjska Gora   CAMPGROUND €
(☑064 121 966; www.naturacamp-kranjskagora. com; Borovška cesta 62; adult €8-10, child €5-7, cabin & tree tent €25-30) This wonderful site, some 300m from the main road on an isolated horse ranch in a forest clearing, is as close to paradise as we've been for awhile. Pitch a tent or stay in one of the little wooden cabins or the unique tree tents – great pouches with air mattresses suspended from the branches.

Hotel Miklič   HOTEL €€€
(☑588 16 35; www.hotelmiklic.com; Vitranška ulica 13; s €60-80, d €80-130; P@☎) This pristine 15-room small hotel south of the centre is

surrounded by luxurious lawns and flower beds and boasts an excellent restaurant and a small fitness room with sauna (€12 per hour). It's definitely a cut above most other accommodation in Kranjska Gora.

Hotel Kotnik　　　　　SLOVENIAN €€
(☑588 15 64; www.hotel-kotnik.si; Borovška c 75; mains €8-18; 🛜) One of Kranjska Gora's better eateries, the restaurant in this stylish inn, with bits of painted dowry chests on the walls, serves grilled meats – pepper steak is a speciality – that should keep you going for awhile. The adjoining pizzeria (pizza €6 to €9, open noon to 10.30pm) with the wood-burning stove is a great choice for something quicker.

Gostilna Pri Martinu　　　SLOVENIAN €
(☑582 03 00; Borovška c 61; mains €7-14; ⊘10am-11pm; 🛜) This atmospheric tavern-restaurant in an old house opposite the fire station is one of the best places in town to try local specialities, such as *ješprenj* (barley soup), *telečja obara* (veal stew) and *ričet* (barley stew with smoked pork ribs). One of the few places to offer a full three-course luncheon menu (€7).

ⓘ Getting There & Away

Buses run hourly to Ljubljana (€8.70, two hours, 91km) via Jesenice (€3.10, 30 minutes, 24km), where you should change for Bled (€2.70, 20 minutes, 19km). There's just one direct departure to Bled (€4.80, one hour, 40km) on weekdays at 9.15am and at 9.50am on weekends.

Alpetour (☑201 31 30; www.alpetour.si) runs regular buses to Trenta (€4.70, 70 minutes, 30km) and Bovec (€6.70, two hours, 46km) from June through September via the Vršič Pass. Check the website for a timetable. There are normally about four departures daily (more at the weekend). Buy tickets from the driver.

Soča Valley

The Soča Valley region (Posočje) stretches from Triglav National Park to Nova Gorica, including the outdoor activity centres of Bovec and Kobarid. Threading through it is the magically aquamarine Soča River. Most people come here for the rafting, hiking and skiing, though there are plenty of historical sights and locations, particularly relating to WWI, when millions of troops fought on the mountainous battle front here.

BOVEC
☑05 / POP 1810
Soča Valley's de facto capital, Bovec, offers plenty to adventure-sports enthusiasts. With

the Julian Alps above, the Soča River below and Triglav National Park all around, you could spend a week here hiking, kayaking, mountain biking and, in winter, skiing at Mt Kanin, Slovenia's highest ski station, without ever doing the same thing twice.

🏃 Activities

Rafting, **kayaking** and **canoeing** on the beautiful Soča River (10% to 40% gradient; Grades I to VI) are major draws. The season lasts from April to October.

Rafting trips of two to eight people over a distance of 8km to 10km (1½ hours) cost from €36 to €46 and for 21km (2½ hours) from €48 to €55, including neoprene long johns, windcheater, life jacket, helmet and paddle. Bring a swimsuit, T-shirt and towel. Canoes for two are €45 for the day; single kayaks €30. A number of beginners kayaking courses are also on offer (eg one-/two-days from €55/100). Longer guided kayak trips (up to 10km) are also available.

A 3km **canyoning** trip near the Soča, in which you descend through gorges and jump over falls attached to a rope, costs around €42.

Other popular activities include **cycling**, **hiking** and **fishing**. Visit the **Tourist Information Centre Bovec** (☑388 19 19; www.bovec.si; Trg Golobarskih Žrtev 8; ⊘8.30am-8.30pm summer, 9am-6pm winter) for specific information or check in with the following reputable agencies:

Soča Rafting　　　　ADVENTURE SPORTS
(☑041-724 472, 389 62 00; www.socarafting.si; Trg Golobarskih Žrtev 14; ⊘9am-7pm year-round)

Top Extreme　　　　ADVENTURE SPORTS
(☑041 620 636; www.top.si; Trg Golobarskih Žrtev 19; ⊘9am-7pm May-Sep)

Kanin Ski Centre　　　　　SKIING
(☑388 60 98; www.bovec.si; day pass adult/child/senior & student €22/16/18) The Kanin Ski Centre northwest of Bovec has skiing up to 2200m – the only real altitude alpine skiing in Slovenia. As a result, the season can be long, with good spring skiing in April and even May.

🛏 Sleeping & Eating

Private rooms are easy to come by in Bovec through the TIC.

TOP CHOICE ⟩ Dobra Vila　　BOUTIQUE HOTEL €€€
(☑389 64 00; www.dobra-vila-bovec.si; Mala Vas 112; d €120-145, tr €160-180; 🅿🌐🛜) This stunner

of a 10-room boutique hotel is housed in an erstwhile telephone-exchange building dating to 1932. Peppered with interesting artefacts and objets d'art, it has its own library and wine cellar and a fabulous restaurant with a winter garden and outdoor terrace.

Martinov Hram GUESTHOUSE €€
(☎388 62 14; www.martinov-hram.si; Trg Golobarskih Žrtev 27; s/d €33/54; P 📶) This lovely and very friendly guesthouse just 100m east of the centre has 14 beautifully furnished rooms and an excellent restaurant with an emphasis on specialities from the Bovec region.

Kamp Palovnik CAMPGROUND €
(☎388 60 07; www.kamp-polovnik.com; Ledina 8; adult €6.50-7.50, child €5-5.75; ⏲Apr–mid-Oct; P) About 500m southeast of the Hotel Kanin, this is the closest camping ground to Bovec. It is small (just over a hectare with 70 sites) but located in an attractive setting.

Gostišče Stari Kovač PIZZA €
(☎388 66 99; Rupa 3; starters €6.50-7, mains €8-11, pizza €5-7.50; ⏲noon-10pm Tue-Sun) The 'Old Blacksmith' is a good choice for pizza cooked in a wood-burning stove.

Getting There & Away

Buses to Kobarid (€3.10, 30 minutes) depart up to six times a day. There are also buses to Ljubljana (€13.60, 3½ hours) via Kobarid and Idrija. From late June to August a service to Kranjska Gora (€6.70, two hours) via the Vršič Pass departs four times daily, continuing to Ljubljana.

KOBARID

☎05 / POP 1250

The charming town of Kobarid is quainter than nearby Bovec, and despite being surrounded by mountain peaks, Kobarid feels more Mediterranean than Alpine. On the surface not a whole lot has changed since Ernest Hemingway described Kobarid (then Caporetto) in *A Farewell to Arms* (1929) as 'a little white town with a campanile in a valley' with 'a fine fountain in the square'. Kobarid was a military settlement during Roman times, was hotly contested in the Middle Ages and was hit by a devastating earthquake in 1976, but the world will remember Kobarid as the site of the decisive battle of 1917 in which the combined forces of the Central Powers defeated the Italian army.

Sights

Kobarid Museum MUSEUM
(☎389 00 00; www.kobariski-muzej.si; Gregorčičeva ul 10; adult/child €5/2.50; ⏲9am-6pm Mon-Fri, 9am-7pm Sat & Sun summer, 10am-5pm Mon-Fri, 9am-6pm Sat & Sun winter) This museum is devoted almost entirely to the Soča Front and WWI. There are many photographs documenting the horrors of the front, military charts, diaries and maps, and two large relief displays showing the front lines and offensives through the Krn Mountains and the positions in the Upper Soča Valley. Don't miss the 20-minute multimedia presentation.

Activities

A free pamphlet and map titled *The Kobarid Historical Trail* outlines a 5km-long route that will take you past remnants of WWI troop emplacements to the impressive **Kozjak Stream Waterfalls** (Slapovi Potoka Kozjak) and **Napoleon Bridge** (Napoleonov Most) built in 1750. More ambitious is the hike outlined in the free *Pot Miru/Walk of Peace* brochure.

Kobarid gives Bovec a run for its money in adventure sports, and you'll find several outfits on or off the town's main square that can organise rafting (from €34), canyoning (from €45), kayaking (€40) and paragliding (€110) between April and October. Two recommended agencies are listed below:

X Point ADVENTURE SPORTS
(☎041 692 290, 388 53 08; www.xpoint.si; Trg Svobode 6)

Positive Sport ADVENTURE SPORTS
(☎040 654 475; www.positive-sport.com; Markova ulica 2)

Sleeping

TOP CHOICE **Hiša Franko** GUESTHOUSE €€€
(☎389 41 20; www.hisafranko.com; Staro Selo 1; r €80-135; P 📶) This guesthouse in an old farmhouse 3km west of Kobarid in Staro Selo, halfway to the Italian border, has 10 themed rooms – we love the Moja Afrika (My Africa) and Soba Zelenega Čaja (Green Tea Room) ones – some of which have terraces and jacuzzis. Eat in their excellent restaurant.

Hotel Hvala HOTEL €€€
(☎389 93 00; wwww.hotelhvala.si; Trg Svobode 1; s €72-76, d €104-112; P ❄ 📶) The delightful 'Hotel Thanks' (actually it's the family's name), has 31 rooms. A snazzy lift takes you on a vertical tour of Kobarid (don't miss both the Soča trout and Papa Hemingway at work); there's a bar, a Mediterranean-style cafe in the garden and a superb restaurant.

Kamp Koren
CAMPGROUND €

(📞389 13 11; www.kamp-koren.si; Drežniške Ravne 33; per person pitch €11.50, chalets d/tr from €55/60; 🅿🛜) The oldest camping ground in the valley, this 2-hectare site with 70 pitches is about 500m northeast of Kobarid on the left bank of the Soča River and just before the turn to Drežniške Ravne. In full view is the Napoleon Bridge.

🍴 Eating

In the centre of Kobarid you'll find two of Slovenia's best restaurants.

TOP CHOICE Hiša Franko
SLOVENIAN €€

(📞389 41 20; www.hisafranko.com; Staro Selo 1; mains €22-24; ⏰noon-3pm & 6-11pm Tue-Sun) Foodies will love this superb gourmet restaurant in the guesthouse of the same name in Staro Selo, just west of town. Impeccable tasting menus, strong on locally sourced ingredients and which change according to the season, cost €50/75 for five/eight courses. It closes on Tuesday in winter.

Topli Val
SEAFOOD €€

(Trg Svobode 1; starters €8-10, mains €9.50-25; ⏰noon-10pm) Seafood is the speciality here, and it's excellent – from the carpaccio of sea bass to the Soča trout and signature lobster with pasta. Expect to pay about €30 to €60 per person with a decent bottle of wine. There's a lovely front terrace and back garden open in warmer months.

ℹ Information
Tourist Information Centre Kobarid (📞380 04 90; www.dolina-soce.com; Trg Svobode 16; ⏰9am-1pm & 2-7pm Mon-Fri, 10am-1pm & 4-7pm Sat & Sun) Free internet.

ℹ Getting There & Around
There are half a dozen buses a day to Bovec (€3.10, 30 minutes). Other destinations include Ljubljana (€11.40 three hours) via Most na Soči train station (good for Bled and Bohinj). Daily in July and August, buses cross the spectacular Vršič Pass to Kranjska Gora (€6.70, three hours).

KARST & COAST

Slovenia's short coast (47km) is an area for both history and recreation. The southernmost resort town of Portorož has some decent beaches, but towns like Koper and Piran, famed for their Venetian Gothic architecture, are the main drawcards here. En route from Ljubljana or the Soča Valley, you'll cross the Karst, a huge limestone plateau and a land of olives, ruby-red Teran wine, *pršut* (air-dried ham), old stone churches and deep subterranean caves, including Postojna and Škocjan.

Postojna
📞05 / POP 8910

The karst cave at Postojna is one of the largest in the world and its stalagmite and stalactite formations are unequalled anywhere. It's a busy destination (visited by as many as a third of all tourists coming to Slovenia). The amazing thing is how the large crowds at the entrance seem to get swallowed whole by the size of the caves.

The small town of Postojna lies in the Pivka Valley at the foot of Sovič Hill (677m) with Titov trg at its centre. Postojna's bus station is at Titova cesta 36, about 250m southwest of Titov trg. The train station is on Kolodvorska cesta about 600m southeast of the square.

◉ Sights
Postojna Cave
CAVE

(📞700 01 00; www.postojnska-jama.si; Jamska c 30; adult/child/student €22.90/13.70/18.30; ⏰tours hourly 9am-6pm summer, 3 or 4 times from 10am daily winter) Slovenia's single most-popular tourist attraction, Postojna Cave is about 1.5km northwest of Postojna. The 5.7km-long cavern is visited on a 1½-hour tour – 4km of it by electric train and the rest on foot. Inside, impressive stalagmites and stalactites in familiar shapes stretch almost endlessly in all directions.

Proteus Vivarium
MUSEUM

(www.turizem-kras.si; adult/child €8/4.80, with cave €27/16.20; ⏰9am-5.30pm May-Sep, 10.30am-3.30pm Oct-Apr) Just steps south of the Postojna Cave's entrance is Proteus Vivarium, a spelio-biological research station with a video introduction to underground zoology. A 45-minute tour then leads you into a small, darkened cave to peep at some of the endemic Proteus anguinus, a shy (and miniscule) salamander unique to Slovenia.

🛏 Sleeping & Eating
Hotel Kras
HOTEL €€

(📞700 23 00; www.hotel-kras.si; Tržaška cesta 1; s €68-74, d €84-96, apt €100-120; 🅿🛜) This rather flash, modern hotel has risen, phoenix-like, from the ashes of a decrepit old caravanserai in the heart of town, and now boasts 27 comfortable rooms with all the mod cons. If you've got the dosh, choose one

PREDJAMA CASTLE

The tiny village of Predjama (population 85), 10km northwest of Postojna, is home to remarkable **Predjama Castle** (☎700 01 03; www.postojnska-jama.eu; Predjama 1; adult/child/student €9/5.40/7.20; ☺9am-7pm summer, 10am-4pm winter). The castle's lesson is clear: if you want to build an impregnable redoubt, put it in the gaping mouth of a cavern halfway up a 123m cliff. Its four storeys were built piece-meal over the years since 1202, but most of what you see today is 16th century. It looks simply unconquerable.

The castle holds great features for kids of any age – a drawbridge over a raging river, holes in the ceiling of the entrance tower for pouring boiling oil on intruders, a very dank dungeon, a 16th-century chest full of treasure (unearthed in the cellar in 1991), and a hiding place at the top called Erazem's Nook.

In mid-July, the castle hosts the **Erasmus Tournament**, a day of medieval duelling, jousting and archery.

The cave below Predjama Castle is a 6km network of galleries spread over four levels. Casual visitors can see about 900m of it; longer tours are available by prior arrangement only. **Gostilna Požar** (☎751 52 52; Predjama 2; meals from €11; ☺10am-10pm Thu-Tue, daily Aug) is a simple restaurant next to the ticket kiosk and in heart-stopping view of the castle.

of the apartments on the top (5th) floor with enormous terraces.

Hotel Sport
HOTEL, HOSTEL €€

(☎720 22 44; www.sport-hotel.si; Kolodvorska c 1; dm €25, s/d from €55/70; P@☎) A hotel of some sort or another since 1880, the Sport offers reasonable value for money, with 37 spick-and-span and comfortable rooms, including five with nine dorm beds each. There's a kitchen with a small eating area. It's 300m north of the centre.

Jamski Dvorec
INTERNATIONAL €€

(☎700 01 81; starters €6.50-10, mains €13.50-22; ☺9am-6pm) Housed in a stunning 1920s-style building next to the entrance to the cave, the Cave Manor has fairly average international dishes but its set menus at €11 and €12 are a big attraction.

Čuk
PIZZA €

(☎720 13 00; Pot k Pivki 4; starters €5-7.50, pizza & pasta €6-9.50; ☺10am-11pm Mon-Fri, 11am-midnight Sat, noon-11pm Sun) Excellent restaurant southwest of Titov trg, just off Tržaška cesta, Čuk takes its pizza seriously but offers a wide range of Slovenian mains too.

❶ Getting There & Away

BUS Services from Ljubljana to the coast as well as Ajdovščina stop in Postojna (€6, one hour, 53km, hourly). Other destinations include Koper (€6.90, 1¼ hours, 68km, four to seven daily) and Piran (€8.30, 1½ hours, 86km, three or four a day).

TRAIN Postojna is on the main train line linking Ljubljana (€4.90, one hour, 67km) with Sežana and Trieste via Divača (€2.90 to €4.45, 40 minutes, 37km), and is an easy day trip from the capital. You can also reach here from Koper (€5.90 to €10.30, 1½ hours, 86km) on one of up to seven trains a day.

Škocjan Caves
☎05

The immense system of the **Škocjan Caves** (☎708 21 10; www.park-skocjanske-jame.si; Škocjan 2; adult/child €15/7; ☺10am-5pm), a Unesco World Heritage site, is more captivating than the larger one at Postojna, and for many travellers this will be the highlight of their trip to Slovenia.

Visitors walk in guided groups from the ticket office to the main entrance in the Globočak Valley. Through a tunnel built in 1933, you soon reach the head of the **Silent Cave**, a dry branch of the underground canyon that stretches for 500m. The first section, called **Paradise**, is filled with beautiful stalactites and stalagmites; the second part (called **Calvary**) was once the river bed. The Silent Cave ends at the **Great Hall**, a jungle of exotic dripstones and deposits; keep an eye out for the mighty stalagmites called the Giants and the Organ.

The sound of the Reka River heralds your entry into the **Murmuring Cave**, with walls 100m high. To get over the Reka and into Müller Hall, you must cross **Cerkvenik**

Bridge, some 45m high and surely the highlight of the trip.

Schmidl Hall, the final section, emerges into the Velika Dolina. From here you walk past **Tominč Cave**, where finds from a prehistoric settlement have been unearthed. A funicular takes you back to the entrance.

The temperature in the caves is constant at 12°C so bring along a light jacket or sweater. Good walking shoes, for the sometimes slippery paths, are recommended.

The nearest town with accommodation is **Divača**, 5km to the northwest. **Gostilna Malovec** (☎763 33 33; www.hotel-malovec.si; s/d €54/80; P@Wi-Fi) has a half-dozen basic but renovated rooms in a building beside its traditional restaurant.The nearby **Orient Express** (☎763 30 10; pizza €4.60-14; ⏰11am-11pm Sun-Fri, 11am-2am Sat) is a popular pizzeria.

Buses from Ljubljana to Koper and the coast stop at Divača (€7.90, 1½ hours, half-hourly). Divača is also on the rail line to Ljubljana (€7.30, 1½ hours, hourly), with up to five trains a day to Koper (€4.05, 50 minutes) via Hrpelje-Kozina. The Škocjan Caves are about 5km by road southeast of the Divača train station – the route is signed. A courtesy van sometimes meets incoming Ljubljana trains.

Koper

☎05 / POP 24,725

Coastal Slovenia's largest town, Koper (Capodistria in Italian) at first glance appears to be a workaday city that scarcely gives tourism a second thought. Yet its central core is delightfully medieval and far less overrun than its ritzy cousin Piran, 18km down the coast. Known as Aegida to the ancient Greeks, Koper grew rich as a key port trading salt and was the capital of Istria under the Venetian republic during the 15th and 16th centuries. It remains Slovenia's most important port.

Sights

The easiest way to see Koper's Old Town is to walk from the marina on Ukmarjev trg east along Kidričeva ulica to Titov trg and then south down Čevljarska ulica, taking various detours along the way.

Koper Regional Museum MUSEUM
(☎663 35 70; www.pmk-kp.si; Kidričeva ul 19; adult/child €2/1.50; ⏰9am-7pm Tue-Fri, to 1pm Sat & Sun) The **Belgramoni-Tacco Palace** houses this museum with displays of old maps and photos of the port and coast, Italianate sculpture, and paintings dating from the 16th to 18th centuries. Note the wonderful bronze knocker on the door of Venus arising from a seashell.

Cathedral of the Assumption CATHEDRAL
(Stolnica Marijinega Vnebovzetja; ⏰7am-9pm) Opposite the Armoury in Titov trg is the Cathedral of the Assumption and its 36m-tall belfry, now called the **City Tower**. The cathedral, partly Romanesque and Gothic but mostly dating from the 18th century, has a white classical interior with a feeling of space and light that belies the sombre exterior.

FREE **Beach** BEACH
(Kopališko nabrežje 1; ⏰8am-7pm May-Sep) Koper's tiny beach, on the northwest edge of the Old Town, has a small bathhouse with toilets and showers, grassy areas for lying in the sun and a bar and cafe.

Sleeping

Hotel Koper HOTEL €€€
(☎610 05 00; www.terme-catez.si; Pristaniška ul 3; s €76-92, d €120-150; ❄@≋) This pleasant, 65-room property on the edge of the historic Old Town is the only really central hotel in town. Rates include entry to an aquapark. Choose a harbour-facing room.

Hotel Vodišek HOTEL €€
(☎639 24 68; www.hotel-vodisek.com; Kolodvorska c 2; s €48-60, d €72-90; P❄@Wi-Fi) This small hotel with 35 reasonably priced rooms is in a shopping centre halfway between the Old Town and the train and bus stations. Guests get to use the hotel's bicycles for free.

Museum Hostel APARTMENTS €
(☎041 504 466, 626 18 70; bozic.doris@siol.net; Muzejski trg 6; per person €20-25; Wi-Fi) This place is more a series of apartments with kitchens and bathrooms than a hostel. Reception is at Museum Bife, a cafe-bar on Muzejski trg; the rooms are scattered nearby.

Eating

Istrska Klet Slavček ISTRIAN, SLOVENIAN €
(☎627 67 29; Župančičeva ul 39; dishes €3-12; ⏰7am-10pm Mon-Fri) The Istrian Cellar, situated below the 18th-century Carli Palace, is one of the most colourful places for a meal in Koper's Old Town. Filling set lunches go for less than €8, and there's local Malvazija and Teran wine from the barrel.

WORTH A TRIP

LIPICA'S LIPIZZANER HORSES

The impact of Lipica has been far greater than its tiny size would suggest. It's here where the famed snow-white 'Lipizzaner' horses, made famous at Vienna's Spanish Riding School, were first bred in the late 16th century.

The breed got its start by pairing Andalusian horses from Spain with the local Karst breed the Romans once used to pull chariots. The white colour came two centuries later, when white Arabian horses got into the act.

The breed has subsequently become scattered – moved to Hungary and Austria after WWI, to the Sudetenland in Bohemia by the Germans during WWII, and then shipped off to Italy by the American army in 1945. Only 11 horses returned when operations resumed at Lipica in 1947.

Today, some 400 Lipizzaners remain at the **Lipica Stud Farm** (☑739 15 80; www. lipica.org; Lipica 5; tour adult/child €11/5.50, training/classical performance €13/18; ⊙training & classical performance Tue, Fri & Sun Apr-Oct), while Lipizzaners are also bred in various locations around the world, including Piber in Austria, which breeds the horses for the Spanish Riding School. The stud farm offers equestrian fans a large variety of tours and riding presentations as well as lessons and carriage rides. Tour times are complicated; see the website for details.

Most people visit Lipica as a day trip from Sežana, 4km to the north, or Divača, 13km to the northeast, both of which are on the Ljubljana–Koper rail line. There is no public transport from either train station; a taxi will cost between €10 and €20.

For overnights, try the 59-room **Hotel Maestoso** (☑739 15 80; s/d €80/120; [P][⊛][≋]), managed by the stud farm. It has many upscale amenities, including a restaurant, swimming pool, sauna and tennis courts.

La Storia ITALIAN €€
(☑626 20 18; www.lastoria.si; Pristaniška ul 3; mains €8.50-25) This Italian-style trattoria with sky-view ceiling frescos focuses on salads, pasta and fish dishes and has outside seating in the warmer months.

ℹ Information

Banka Koper (Kidričeva ul 14)

Pina Internet Cafe (☑627 80 72; Kidričeva ul 43; per hr adult/student €4.20/1.20; ⊙noon-10pm Mon-Fri, from 4pm Sat & Sun)

Post Office (Muzejski trg 3)

Tourist Information Centre Koper (☑664 64 03; www.koper.si; Praetorian Palace, Titov trg 3; ⊙9am-8pm Jul & Aug, 9am-5pm Sep-Jun)

ℹ Getting There & Away

BUS Services run to Izola, Strunjan, Piran (€2.70, 30 minutes and Portorož every half-hour on weekdays. There's a handy bus stop at the corner of Piranška ulica. Some five daily buses make the run to Ljubljana (€11.10, 1¾ to 2½ hours). Buses to Trieste (€3, one hour) run along the coast via Ankaran and Muggia from Monday to Saturday. Destinations in Croatia include Rijeka (€11.20, two hours) and Rovinj (€12, three hours) via Poreč (€10, two hours).

TRAIN Half a dozen trains a day link Koper to Ljubljana (€10.70, 2½ hours, 153km) via Postojna and Divača.

Piran

☑05 / POP 4470

Picturesque Piran, sitting at the tip of a narrow peninsula, is everyone's favourite town on the coast. Its Old Town – one of the best preserved historical towns anywhere on the Adriatic – is a gem of Venetian architecture, but it can be a mob scene at the height of summer. In April or October, though, it's hard not to fall in love with the winding alleyways and tempting seafood restaurants.

⊙ Sights

Tartinijev Trg SQUARE
The **statue** of the nattily dressed gentleman in Tartinijev trg, an oval-shaped square that was the inner harbour until it was filled in 1894, is that of local boy-cum-composer Giuseppe Tartini (1692–1770). To the east is the **Church of St Peter** (Cerkev Sv Petra; Tartinijev trg), which contains the 14th-century **Piran Crucifix**. Across from the church is **Tartini House**, the composer's birthplace.

Sergej Mašera Maritime Museum
MUSEUM

(☑671 00 40; www.pommuz-pi.si; Cankarjevo nabrežje 3; adult/student & senior/child €3.50/2.50/2.10; ⊙9am-noon & 5-9pm Tue-Sun summer, 9am-5pm Tue-Sun winter) Located in the lovely 19th-century Gabrielli Palace on the waterfront, this museum focuses on the sea, sailing and salt-making. There are some old photographs showing salt workers going about their duties, as well as a wind-powered salt pump and little wooden weights in the form of circles and diamonds that were used to weigh salt during the Venetian republic.

Cathedral of St George
CATHEDRAL

(Stolna Cerkev Sv Jurija; Adamičeva ul 2) Piran's hilltop cathedral was founded in 1344 and rebuilt in baroque style in 1637. It's undergoing a massive renovation, and visitors are allowed only into the choir to view the magnificent marble altar and star-vaulted ceiling. If time allows, visit the attached **Parish Museum of St George** (☑673 34 40; admission €1; ⊙10am-1pm & 5-7pm Mon-Fri, 11am-7pm Sat & Sun), which contains paintings and a lapidary in the crypt.

Minorite Monastery
MONASTERY

(☑673 44 17; Bolniška ul 20) On your way up to Tartinijev trg are the Minorite Monastery with a wonderful cloister and the Church of St Francis Assisi, built originally in the early 14th century but enlarged and renovated over the centuries. Inside are ceiling frescos, a giant clam shell for donations and the Tartini family's burial plot.

🏃 Activities

The **Maona Tourist Agency** (☑673 45 20; www.maona.si; Cankarjevo nabrežje 7; ⊙9am-8pm Mon-Sat, 10am-1pm & 5-7pm Sun) and several other agencies in Piran and Portorož can book you on any number of **cruises** – from a loop that takes in the towns along the coast to day-long excursions to Brioni National Park and Rovinj in Croatia, or Venice and Trieste in Italy.

For **swimming**, Piran has several 'beaches' – rocky areas along Prešernovo nabrežje – where you might get your feet wet. They are a little better on the north side near Punta, but as long as you've come this far keep walking eastward on the paved path for just under 1km to Fiesa, which has a small but clean beach.

🛏 Sleeping

TOP CHOICE **Max Piran**
B&B €€

(☑041 692 928, 673 34 36; www.maxpiran.com; Ul IX Korpusa 26; d €60-70; ✳@🛜) Piran's most romantic accommodation has just six rooms, each bearing a woman's name rather than number, in a delightful coral-coloured 18th-century townhouse.

Miracolo di Mare
B&B €€

(☑051 445 511, 921 76 60; www.miracolodimare.si; Tomšičeva ul 23; s €50-55, d €60-70; @🛜) A lovely B&B on the coast, the Wonder of the Sea has a dozen charming (though smallish) rooms, some of which (like No 3 and the breakfast room) look on to the most charming raised back garden in Piran. Floors and stairs are wooden (and original).

Val Hostel
HOSTEL €

(☑673 25 55; www.hostel-val.com; Gregorčičeva ul 38a; per person €22-27; @🛜) This excellent central hostel on the corner of Vegova ulica has 22 rooms (including a few singles), with shared shower, kitchen and washing machine. It's a deserved favourite with backpackers, and prices include breakfast.

Kamp Fiesa
CAMPGROUND €

(☑674 62 30; autocamp.fiesa@siol.net; adult/child €12/4; ⊙May-Sep; 🅿) The closest camping ground to Piran is at Fiesa, 4km by road but less than 1km if you follow the coastal path (obalna pešpot) east from the Cathedral of St George. It's tiny and gets crowded in summer, but it's in a quiet valley by two small ponds and right by the beach.

🍴 Eating

There's an outdoor **fruit and vegetable market** (Zelenjavni trg; ⊙7am-2pm Mon-Sat) in the small square behind the town hall.

TOP CHOICE **Pri Mari**
MEDITERRANEAN, SLOVENIAN €€

(☑041 616 488, 673 47 35; Dantejeva ul 17; mains €8.50-16; ⊙noon-11pm Tue-Sun summer, noon-10pm Tue-Sat, noon-6pm Sun winter) This stylish and welcoming restaurant run by an Italian-Slovenian couple serves inventive Mediterranean and Slovenian dishes. Be sure to book ahead.

Riva Piran
SEAFOOD €€

(☑673 22 25; Gregorčičeva ul 46; mains €8-28; ⊙11.30am-midnight) The best waterfront seafood restaurant, and worth patronising, is

SLOVENIA PIRAN

Piran

Bathing Area

Prešernovo nabrežje

Pebble Beach

Pusterla

Vegova ul

🍴 11

📖 8

Bohinčeva ul

Gregorčičeva ul

Prešernovo nabrežje

Trg 1 Maja

Kosovelova ul

Židovski trg

Trubarjeva ul

Verdijeva ul

Levstikova ul

Obzidna ul

Zelenjavni trg

12

Piran Bay

Bathing Area

Tomažičev trg

Tomažičeva ul

Vidaljeva ul

Cankarjevo nabrežje

Župančičeva ul

Stjenkova ul

Marina

Piran Harbour

ADRIATIC SEA

Customs Wharf

To Hotel Riviera &
Hotel Slovenija (2.5km);
Stara Oljka (3km);
Staro Sidro (3km);
Portorož (5km)

Dantejeva ul

🍴 9

Piran

◉ Sights
1 Cathedral of St George	E2
2 Church of St Peter	E3
3 Minorite Monastery	F3
Parish Museum of St George	(see 1)
4 Sergej Mašera Maritime Museum	E4
5 Tartinijev Trg	E3

🛏 Sleeping
6 Max Piran	F2
7 Miracolo di Mare	E6
8 Val Hostel	B2

🍴 Eating
9 Pri Mari	D7
10 Restaurant Neptune	E5
11 Riva Piran	B2

🛍 Shopping
12 Fruit and Vegetable Market	D3

SLOVENIA PIRAN

this classy place with attractive decor and sea views.

Restaurant Neptune　　　　SEAFOOD €
(☑673 41 11; Župančičeva 7; mains €6-12; ☺noon-4pm, 6pm-midnight) It's no bad thing to be more popular with locals than tourists, and this family-run place hits all the buttons – a friendly welcome, big seafood platters (as well as meat dishes and salads), and a good-value, daily two-course set lunch.

ℹ Information

Banka Koper (Tartinijev trg 12)

Caffe Neptun (☑041 724 237; www.caffeneptun.com; Dantejeva ul 4; per 20min €1; ☺7am-1am; 🛜)

Post Office (Leninova ul 1)

Tourist Information Centre Piran (☑673 44 40, 673 02 20; www.portoroz.si; Tartinijev trg 2; ☺9am-8pm summer, 9am-5pm winter)

ℹ Getting There & Away

BUS Services run every 20 to 30 minutes to Koper (€2.70, 30 minutes). Other destinations include Ljubljana (€12, three hours) via Divača and Postojna, and Nova Gorica (€10.30, 2¾ hours).

Some five buses go daily to Trieste (€10, 1¾ hours) in Italy, except Sundays. One bus a day heads south for Croatian Istria from June to September, stopping at the coastal towns of Umag, Poreč and Rovinj (€10.30, 2¾ hours).

CATAMARAN There are catamarans from the harbour to Trieste (adult/child €8.30/4.75, 30 minutes) in Italy daily except Wednesday, departing around 7pm.

MINIBUS From Tartinijev trg, minibuses (€1 onboard, €0.40 in advance from newsagencies, €6 for 20 rides) shuttle to Portorož every half-hour from 5.40am to 11pm continuously year-round.

Portorož

⌖ 05 / POP 2900

Every country with a coast has got to have a honky-tonk beach resort and Portorož (Portorose in Italian) is Slovenia's. But the 'Port of Roses' is making a big effort to scrub itself up. Portorož's sandy beaches are relatively clean, and there are pleasant spas and wellness centres where you can take the waters or cover yourself in curative mud.

🏃 Activities

The **beaches** (⊘8am-8pm Apr-Sep) at Portorož, including the main one, which accommodates 6000 fried and bronzed bodies, have water slides and outside showers, and beach chairs (€4.10) and umbrellas (€4.10) are available for rent. Beaches are off-limits between 11pm and 6am and camping is forbidden.

A couple of boats make the run between the main pier in Portorož and Izola in summer on trips lasting four hours. They include the **Meja** (⌖041 664 132; adult/child €10/7; ⊘9.15am Tue & Fri) and the **Svetko** (⌖041 623 191; adult/child €15/10.50; ⊘2.30pm daily). The **Solinarka** (⌖031 653 682; www.solinarka.com; adult/child €12.50/6.25; ⊘varies) tour boat sails from Portorož to Piran and Strunjan and back.

Terme & Wellness Centre Portorož SPA
(⌖692 80 60; www.lifeclass.net; Obala 43; swimming pool 2/4hr pass Mon-Fri €8/12, Sat & Sun €10/15; ⊘8am-9pm Jun-Sep, 7am-7pm Oct-May, swimming pool 1-8pm Mon-Wed & Fri-Sun, 2-8pm Thu) This place is famous for treatments using sea water and by-products like mud, as well as a host of other therapies and beauty treatments. And there's a pool too.

🛌 Sleeping

Portorož counts upwards of two dozen hotels, and very few fit into the budget category. Many properties close for the winter in October and do not reopen until April or even May. The **Maona Tourist Agency** (⌖674 03 63; Obala 14/b; ⊘9am-8pm Mon-Sat, 10am-1pm & 5-8pm Sun Jul & Aug, 9am-7pm Mon-Fri, 10am-7pm Sat, 10am-1pm Sun Sep-Jun) has

private rooms (s €18-21, d €26-40, tr €36-52) and **apartments** (apt for 2 €40-50), with prices varying depending on both the category and the season.

TOP CHOICE **Kaki Plac** CAMPGROUND €
(⌖040 476 123; www.adrenaline-check/sea; Lucija; own tent €13, pitched tent €15, lean-to €20; ⊘Apr-Nov; P🐕) A small ecofriendly campsite tucked into the woods just outside Lucija on the outskirts of Portorož. Tents come with mattresses and linen, some sit snugly under thatched Istrian lean-tos, so you can sleep like a traditional shepherd (sort of).

Hotel Riviera & Hotel Slovenija HOTEL €€€
(⌖692 00 00; www.lifeclass.net; Obala 33; s €142-185, d €184-250; P🌸@🐕🏊) These four-star sister properties are joined at the hip and are good choices if you want to stay someplace central. The Riviera has 160 rooms, three fabulous swimming pools and an excellent wellness centre. The Slovenija is somewhat bigger with 183 rooms.

🍴 Eating

Staro Sidro SEAFOOD €
(⌖674 50 74; Obala 55; mains €8-19; ⊘noon-11pm Tue-Sun) A tried-and-true favourite, the Old Anchor is next to the lovely (and landmark) Vila San Marco. It specialises in seafood and has both a garden and a lovely terrace overlooking Obala and Portorož Bay.

Stara Oljka BALKAN €€
(⌖674 85 55; Obala 20; starters €5-9.60, mains €8.60-24; ⊘10am-midnight) The Old Olive Tree specialises in grills (Balkan, steaks etc), which you can watch being prepared in the open kitchen. There's a large and enticing sea-facing terrace.

❶ Getting There & Away

BUS Buses leave Portorož for Koper (€2.30, 25 minutes) and Izola (€1.80, 15 minutes) about every 30 minutes throughout the year. Other destinations from Portorož and their daily frequencies are the same as those for Piran.

MINIBUS Minibuses make the loop from the Lucija camping grounds through central Portorož to Piran throughout the year.

EASTERN SLOVENIA

The rolling vine-covered hills of eastern Slovenia are attractive but less dramatic than the Julian Alps or, indeed, the coast. Two cities worth a detour include lively Maribor, Slovenia's second-largest city, and postcard-perfect Ptuj, less than 30km down the road.

Maribor

📋 02 / POP 88,350

Despite being the nation's second-largest city, Maribor has only about a third the population of Ljubljana and often feels more like an overgrown provincial town. It has no unmissable sights but oozes charm thanks to its delightfully patchy Old Town along the Drava River. Pedestrianised central streets buzz with cafes and student life and the riverside Lent district hosts major cultural events – indeed, Maribor was European Capital of Culture in 2012.

◉ Sights

Grajksi Trg   SQUARE
The centre of the Old Town, this square is graced with the 17th-century **Column of St Florian**, dedicated to the patron saint of fire fighters.

Maribor Castle   MUSEUM
(Grajski trg 2) On Grajski Trg, the centre of Maribor's Old Town, is Maribor's 15th-century castle. It contains a **Knights' Hall** (Viteška Dvorana) with a remarkable painted ceiling, the baroque **Loretska Chapel** and a magnificent **rococo staircase**.

Inside the castle, the **Maribor Regional Museum** (📞228 35 51; www.pmuzej-mb.si; Grajski trg; adult/child €3/2; ⊘9am-1pm & 4pm-7pm Mon-Fri, 9am-1pm Sat) has one of the richest collections in Slovenia. The building is undergoing renovation, so parts may be off-limits. On the ground floor there are archaeological, clothing and ethnographic exhibits, including florid, 19th-century beehive panels. Upstairs are rooms devoted to Maribor's history and guilds.

🛏 Sleeping

TOP CHOICE **Hostel Pekarna**   HOSTEL €
(📞059 180 880; www.mkc-hostelpekarna.si; Ob železnici 16; dm/s/d €17/21/42; ☞🛈) This bright and welcoming hostel south of the river is a converted army bakery. Facilities, from the dorms to the cafe, are up to the minute, and there are several apartments with kitchens.

Hotel Lent   HOTEL €€
(📞250 67 69; www.hotel-lent.si; Dravska ulica 9; s/d €69/89; ❄☞) Shiny riverside hotel in Lent, with a café out front. Rooms are stylishly decorated and comfortable, though the suites are tricked out in unexpected gangster bling.

🍴 Eating

TOP CHOICE **Gril Ranca**   BALKAN €
(📞252 55 50; Dravska ul 10; dishes €4.80-7.50; ⊘8am-11pm Mon-Sat, noon-9pm Sun) This place serves simple but scrumptious Balkan grills such as *pljeskavica* (spicy meat patties) and *čevapčiči* (spicy meatballs of beef or pork) in full view of the Drava. It's cool on a hot night.

Pri Florjanu   MEDITERRANEAN €€
(📞059 084 850; Grajski trg 6; starters €5.50-7, mains €9-18; ⊘11am-10pm Mon-Thu, 11am-11pm Fri & Sat; 🖉🛈) A great spot in full view of the Column of St Florian, this stylish place has both an open front and an enclosed back terrace and a huge minimalist restaurant in between. It serves inspired Mediterranean food, with a good supply of vegetarian options.

ℹ Information

Tourist Information Centre Maribor (📞234 66 11; www.maribor-pohorje.si; Partinzanska c 6a; ⊘9am-7pm Mon-Fri, 9am-6pm Sat & Sun) Very helpful TIC in kiosk opposite the Franciscan church.

ℹ Getting There & Away

BUS Services are frequent to Celje (€6.7, 1½ hours), Murska Sobota (€6.30, 1¼ hours), Ptuj (€3.60, 45 minutes) and Ljubljana (€12.40, three hours).

TRAIN From Ljubljana there is the ICS express service (€15.20, 1¾ hours), or more frequent slower trains (€9, 2½ hours). Both stop at Celje.

Ptuj

📋 02 / POP 19,010

Rising gently above a wide valley, Ptuj forms a symphony of red-tile roofs best viewed from across the Drava River. One of the oldest towns in Slovenia, Ptuj equals Ljubljana in terms of historical importance but the compact medieval core, with its castle, museums, monasteries and churches, can easily be seen in a day.

◉ Sights

Ptuj's Gothic centre, with its Renaissance and baroque additions, can be viewed on a 'walking tour' taking in Minoritski trg and Mestni trg, Slovenski trg, Prešernova ulica, Muzejski trg and Ptuj Castle.

Ptuj Castle
CASTLE

(Grad Ptuj; ☑787 92 45, 748 03 60; Na Gradu 1) Ptuj castle is an agglomeration of styles from the 14th to the 18th centuries. It houses the **Ptuj Regional Museum** (☑787 92 30; www. pok-muzej-ptuj.si; adult/child €4/2.50; ☺9am-6pm Mon-Fri, 9am-8pm Sat & Sun summer, 9am-5pm daily winter) but is worth the trip for views of Ptuj and the Drava. The shortest way to the castle is to follow narrow Grajska ulica, which leads to a covered wooden stairway and the castle's Renaissance **Peruzzi Portal** (1570).

✷ Festivals

Kurentovanje
CARNIVAL

(www.kurentovanje.net) Kurentovanje is a rite of spring celebrated for 10 days in February leading up to Shrove Tuesday; it's the most popular and best-known folklore event in Slovenia.

🛌 Sleeping

TOP CHOICE **MuziKafe**
HOTEL €€

(☑787 88 60; www.muzikafe.si; Vrazov trg 1; 🅰) This quirky cracker of a place is tucked away off Jadranska ulica. Everything is bright, with each room idiosyncratically decorated by the hotel's artist owners. There's a terrace café, plus a vaulted brick cellar for musical and artistic events.

Hotel Mitra
HOTEL €€€

(☑051 603 069, 787 74 55; www.hotel-mitra.si; Prešernova ul 6; s €62-88, d €106; P🕸@🅰) This pleasant hotel has 25 generous-sized guest rooms and four humongous suites, each with its own name and story and specially commissioned paintings on the wall. There are lovely Oriental carpets on the original wooden floors and a wellness centre in an old courtyard cellar.

Hostel Eva
HOSTEL €

(☑040 226 522, 771 24 41; www.hostel-ptuj.si; Jadranska ul 22; per person €12-20) This welcoming, up-to-date hostel connected to a bike shop (per-day rental €10) has six rooms containing two to six beds and a large light-filled kitchen.

✕ Eating

TOP CHOICE **Gostilna Ribič**
GOSTILNA €€

(☑749 06 35; Dravska ul 9; mains €9.50-20; ☺10am-11pm Sun-Thu, 10am-midnight Fri & Sat) Arguably the best restaurant in Ptuj, the Angler Inn faces the river, with an enormous terrace, and the speciality here is – not surprisingly – fish, especially herbed and baked pike perch. The seafood soup served in a bread loaf bowl is exceptional.

Amadeus
GOSTILNA €€

(☑771 70 51; Prešernova ul 36; mains €6.50-20; ☺noon-10pm Mon-Thu, noon-11pm Fri & Sat, noon-4pm Sun) This pleasant *gostilna* (inn-like restaurant) above a pub and near the foot of the road to the castle serves *štruklji* (dumplings with herbs and cheese), steak, pork and fish.

ℹ Information

Tourist Information Centre Ptuj (☑779 60 11; www.ptuj.info; Slovenski trg 5; ☺8am-8pm summer, 9am-6pm winter)

ℹ Getting There & Away

BUS Services to Maribor (€3.60, 45 minutes) go every couple of hours, less frequently at weekends.

TRAIN Connections are better for trains than buses, with plentiful departures to Ljubljana (€8 to €13.60) direct or via Pragersko. Up to a dozen trains go to Maribor (€2.90 to €5.90, 50 minutes).

UNDERSTAND SLOVENIA

History
Early Years

Slovenes can make a credible claim to having invented democracy. By the early 7th century, their Slavic ancestors had founded the Duchy of Carantania (Karantanija), based at Krn Castle (now Karnburg in Austria). Ruling dukes were elected by enobled commoners and invested before ordinary citizens.

This unique model was noted by the 16th-century French political philosopher Jean Bodin, whose work was a reference for Thomas Jefferson when he wrote the American Declaration of Independence in 1776.

Carantania (later Carinthia) was fought over by the Franks and Magyars from the 8th to 10th centuries, and later divided up among Austro-Germanic nobles and bishops.

The Habsburgs & Napoleon

Between the late 13th and early 16th centuries, almost all the lands inhabited by Slovenes, with the exception of the Venetian-controlled coastal towns, came under the domination of the Habsburgs, ruled from Vienna.

Austrian rule continued until 1918, apart from a brief interlude between 1809 and 1813 when Napoleon created six so-called Illyrian Provinces from Slovenian and Croatian regions and made Ljubljana the capital.

Napoleon proved a popular conqueror as his relatively liberal regime de-Germanised the education system. Slovene was taught in schools for the first time, leading to an awakening of national consciousness. In tribute, Ljubljana still has a French Revolution Sq (Trg Francoske Revolucije) with a column bearing a likeness of the French emperor.

World Wars I & II

Fighting during WWI was particularly savage along the Soča Valley – the Isonzo Front– which was occupied by Italy then retaken by German-led Austro-Hungarian forces. The war ended with the collapse of Austria-Hungary, which handed western Slovenia to Italy as part of postwar reparations.

Northern Carinthia, including the towns of Beljak and Celovec (now Villach and Klagenfurt), voted to stay with Austria in a 1920 plebiscite. What remained of Slovenia joined fellow south (jug) Slavs in forming the Kingdom of Serbs, Croats and Slovenes, later Yugoslavia.

Nazi occupation in WWII was for the most part resisted by Slovenian partisans, though after Italy capitulated in 1943 the anti-partisan Slovenian Domobranci (Home Guards) were active in the west. To prevent their nemeses, the communists, from taking political control in liberated areas, the Domobranci threw their support behind the Germans.

The war ended with Slovenia regaining Italian-held areas from Piran to Bovec, but losing Trst (Trieste) and part of Gorica (Gorizia).

Tito's Yugoslavia

In Tito's Yugoslavia in the 1960s and '70s, Slovenia, with only 8% of the national population, was the economic powerhouse, creating up to 20% of the national GDP.

But by the 1980s the federation had become increasingly Serb-dominated, and Slovenes feared they would lose their political autonomy. In free elections, Slovenes voted overwhelmingly to break away from Yugoslavia and did so on 25 June 1991. A 10-day war that left 66 people dead followed; Yugoslavia swiftly signed a truce in order to concentrate on regaining control of coastal Croatia.

From Independence to Today

Shortly after the withdrawal of the federal army from Slovenian soil on 25 October 1991, Slovenia got a new constitution that provided for a bicameral parliamentary system of government.

The head of state, the president, is elected directly for a maximum of two five-year terms. Milan Kučan held that role from independence until 2002, when the late Janez Drnovšek (1950–2008), a former prime minister, was elected. Diplomat Danilo Türk has been president since 2007, having been re-elected in 2012.

Executive power is vested in the prime minister and his cabinet. The current premier is Janez Janša, who was returned to power in early 2012 after 3½ years in opposition.

Slovenia was admitted to the UN in 1992 as the 176th member-state. In May 2004, Slovenia entered the EU as a full member and less than three years later adopted the euro, replacing the tolar as the national currency.

People

The population of Slovenia is largely homogeneous. Just over 83% are ethnic Slovenes, with the remainder Serbs, Croats, Bosnians, Albanians and Roma; there are also small enclaves of Italians and Hungarians, who have special deputies looking after their interests in parliament.

Slovenes are ethnically Slavic, typically hardworking, multilingual and extrovert. Around 60% of Slovenes identify themselves as Catholics.

Arts

Slovenia's most cherished writer is the Romantic poet France Prešeren (1800–49). His patriotic yet humanistic verse was a driving force in raising Slovene national consciousness. Fittingly, a stanza of his poem 'Zdravljica' (A Toast) forms the lyrics of the national anthem.

Many of Ljubljana's most characteristic architectural features, including its recurring pyramid motif, were added by celebrated Slovenian architect Jože Plečnik (1872–1957), whose work fused classical building principles and folk-art traditions.

Postmodernist painting and sculpture were more or less dominated from the 1980s by the multimedia group NeueSlowenische Kunst (NSK) and the artists' cooperative Irwin. It also spawned the internationally known industrial-music group Laibach, whose leader, Tomaž Hostnik, died tragically in 1983 when he hanged himself from a *kozolec*, the traditional (and iconic) hayrack found only in Slovenia.

Slovenia's vibrant music scene embraces rave, techno, jazz, punk, thrash-metal and *chanson* (torch songs from the likes of Vita Mavrič); the most popular local rock group is Siddharta, formed in 1995 and still going strong. There's also been a folk-music revival: keep an ear out for the groups Katice and Katalena, who play traditional Slovenian music with a modern twist, and the vocalist Brina.

Films

Well-received Slovenian films in recent years include *Kruh in Mleko* (Bread & Milk, 2001), the tragic story by Jan Cvitkovič of a dysfunctional small-town family, and Damjan Kozole's *Rezerni Deli* (Spare Parts, 2003), about the trafficking of illegal immigrants through Slovenia from Croatia to Italy.

Much lighter fare is *Petelinji Zajtrk* (Rooster's Breakfast, 2007), a romance by Marko Naberšnik set on the Austrian border, and the bizarre US-made documentary *Big River Man* (John Maringouin, 2009) about an overweight marathon swimmer who takes on – wait for it – the Amazon and succeeds.

Environment

Slovenia is amazingly green; indeed, 58% of its total surface area is covered in forest and it's growing. Slovenia is home to almost 3200 plant species – some 70 of which are indigenous.

Triglav National Park is particularly rich in native flowering plants. Among the more peculiar endemic fauna in Slovenia is a blind salamander called *Proteus anguinus* that lives deep in Karst caves, can survive for years without eating and has been called a 'living fossil'.

Food & Drink

Slovenia boasts an incredibly diverse cuisine, but except for a few national favourites such as *žlikrofi* (pasta stuffed with cheese, bacon and chives) and *jota* (hearty bean soup) and incredibly rich desserts like *gibanica* (a layer cake stuffed with nuts, cheese and apple), you're not likely to encounter many of these regional specialities on menus.

Dishes like *brodet* (fish soup) from the coast, *ajdovi žganci z ocvirki* (buckwheat 'porridge' with savoury pork crackling) and salad greens doused in *bučno olje* (pumpkinseed oil) are generally eaten at home.

A *gostilna* or *gostišče* (inn) or *restavracija* (restaurant) more frequently serves *rižota* (risotto), *klobasa* (sausage), *zrezek* (cutlet/steak), *golaž* (goulash) and *paprikaš* (piquant chicken or beef 'stew'). *Riba* (fish) is excellent and usually priced by the *dag* (100g). Common in Slovenia are such Balkan favourites as *cevapčiči* (spicy meatballs of beef or pork) and *pljeskavica* (spicy meat patties), often served with *kajmak* (a type of clotted cream).

You can snack cheaply on takeaway pizza slices or pieces of *burek* (€2), flaky pastry stuffed with meat, cheese or apple. Alternatives include *štruklji* (cottage-cheese dumplings) and *palačinke* (thin sweet pancakes).

Wine, Beer & Brandy

Distinctively Slovenian wines include peppery red Teran (made from Refošk grapes in the Karst region), Cviček (a dry light red – almost rosé – wine from eastern Slovenia) and Malvazija (a straw-colour white from the coast that is light and dry). Slovenes are justly proud of their top vintages, but cheaper bar-standard *odprto vino* (open wine) sold by the decilitre (100mL) is just so-so.

Pivo (beer), whether *svetlo* (lager) or *temno* (porter), is best on *točeno* (draught) but always available in cans and bottles too.

There are dozens of kinds of *žganje* (fruit brandy) available, including *češnjevec* (made with cherries), *sadjevec* (mixed fruit), *brinjevec* (juniper), *hruška* (pears, also called *viljamovka*) and *slivovka* (plums).

SURVIVAL GUIDE

Directory A–Z
Accommodation

Accommodation runs the gamut from riverside camping grounds, hostels, mountain huts, cosy *gostišča* (inns) and farmhouses, to elegant castle hotels and five-star hotels in Ljubljana, so you'll usually have little trouble finding accommodation to fit your budget, except perhaps at the height of the season (July and August) on the coast, at Bled or Bohinj, or in Ljubljana.

The following price ranges refer to a double room, with en suite toilet and bath or shower and breakfast, unless otherwise indicated. Virtually every municipality in the land levies a tourist tax of between €0.50 and €1 per person per night.

€ less than €50

€€ €50 to €100

€€€ more than €100

FARMSTAYS

Hundreds of working farms in Slovenia offer accommodation to paying guests, either in private rooms in the farmhouse itself or in Alpine-style guesthouses. Many farms offer outdoor sport activities and allow you to help out with the farm chores if you feel so inclined.

Expect to pay about €15 per person in a room with shared bathroom and breakfast (from €20 for half-board) in the low season (September to mid-December and mid-January to June), rising in the high season (July and August) to a minimum €17 per person (from €25 for half-board).

For more information, contact the **Association of Tourist Farms of Slovenia** (Združenje Turističnih Kmetij Slovenije; ☑041 435 528, 03-425 55 11; www.farmtourism.si; Trnoveljska cesta 1) or check with the Slovenian Tourist Board.

Business Hours

The *delovni čas* (opening times) are usually posted on the door. *Odprto* is 'open', *zaprto* is 'closed'. The following hours are standard and reviews won't list business hours unless they differ from these.

Banks 9am to 5pm weekdays, and (rarely) from 8am until noon on Saturday.

Grocery stores 8am to 7pm weekdays and 8am until 1pm on Saturday.

Museums 10am to 6pm Tuesday to Sunday. Winter hours may be shorter.

Post offices 8am to 6pm or 7pm weekdays and until noon on Saturday.

Restaurant Hours vary but count on 11am to 10pm daily. Bars are usually open from 11am to midnight Sunday to Thursday and to 1am or 2am on Friday and Saturday.

Embassies & Consulates

All of the following are in Ljubljana:

Australian Consulate (☑01-234 86 75; Železna cesta 14; ☺9am-1pm Mon-Fri)

Canadian Consulate (☑01-252 44 44; 49a Linhartova cesta; ☺8am-noon Mon, Wed & Fri)

French Embassy (☑01-479 04 00; Barjanska cesta 1; ☺8.30am-12.30pm Mon-Fri)

German Embassy (☑01-479 03 00; Prešernova cesta 27; ☺9am-noon Mon-Thu, 9-11am Fri)

Irish Embassy (☑01-300 89 70; 1st fl, Palača Kapitelj, Poljanski nasip 6; ☺9.30am-12.30pm & 2.30-4pm Mon-Fri)

Netherlands Embassy (☑01-420 14 61; 1st fl, Palača Kapitelj, Poljanski nasip 6; ☺9am-noon Mon-Fri)

New Zealand Consulate (☑01-580 30 55; Verovškova ulica 57; ☺8am-3pm Mon-Fri)

UK Embassy (☑01-200 39 10; 4th fl, Trg Republike 3; ☺9am-noon Mon-Fri)

US Embassy (☑01-200 55 00; Prešernova cesta 31; ☺9-11.30am & 1-3pm Mon-Fri)

Festivals & Events

The official website of the **Slovenian Tourist Board** (www.slovenia.info), maintains a comprehensive list of major cultural events.

Food

The following price ranges are a rough approximation for a two-course sit-down meal for one person, with a drink. Many restaurants offer an excellent-value set menu of two or even three courses at lunch. These typically run from €5 to €9.

€ less than €15

€€ €16 to €30

€€€ over €30

Gay & Lesbian Travellers

National laws ban discrimination in employment and other areas on the basis of sexual preference. In recent years a highly visible campaign against homophobia has been put in place across the country. Outside Ljubljana, however, there is little evidence of a gay presence, much less a lifestyle.

Roza Klub (Klub K4 ; www.klubk4.org; Kersnikova ulica 4; ☺10pm-6am Sun Sep-Jun) in Ljubljana is made up of the gay and lesbian branches of **KUC** (www.skuc.org), which stands for Študentski Kulturni Center (Student Cultural

Centre) but is no longer student-orientated as such. It organises the gay and lesbian **Ljubljana Pride** (www.ljubljanapride.org) parade in late June and the **Gay & Lesbian Film Festival** (www.ljudmila.org/siqrd/fglf) in late November/early December. The gay male branch, **Magnus** (skucmagnus@hotmail.com), deals with AIDS prevention, networking and is behind the Kulturni Center Q (Q Cultural Centre) in Ljubljana's Metelkova Mesto, which includes Klub Tiffany for gay men and Klub Monokel for gay women.

A monthly publication called **Narobe** (Upside Down; www.narobe.si) is in Slovene only, though you might be able to at least glean some basic information from the listings.

Internet Access

Virtually every hotel and hostel now has internet access – a computer for guests' use (free or for a small fee), wi-fi – or both. Most of the country's tourist information centres offer free (or low-cost) access and many libraries in Slovenia have free terminals. Many cities and towns have at least one internet cafe (though they usually only have a handful of terminals), or even free wi-fi in town squares.

Money

The official currency is the euro. Exchanging cash is simple at banks, major post offices, travel agencies and *menjalnice* (bureaux de change), although many don't accept travellers cheques. Major credit and debit cards are accepted almost everywhere, and ATMs are ubiquitous.

Post

The Slovenian postal system (*Pošta Slovenije*), recognised by its bright yellow logo, offers a wide variety of services – from selling stamps and telephone cards to making photocopies and changing money. News stands also sell *znamke* (stamps). Post offices can sell you boxes.

Public Holidays

If a holiday falls on a Sunday, then the following Monday becomes the holiday.

New Year 1 and 2 January

Prešeren Day (Slovenian Culture Day) 8 February

Easter & Easter Monday March/April

Insurrection Day 27 April

Labour Day holidays 1 and 2 May

National Day 25 June

Assumption Day 15 August

Reformation Day 31 October

All Saints Day 1 November

Christmas Day 25 December

Independence Day 26 December

Telephone

Public telephones in Slovenia require a *telefonska kartica* or *telekartica* (telephone card) available at post offices and some newsstands. Phonecards cost €2.70/4/7.50/14.60 for 25/50/100/300 *impulzov* (impulses, or units).

To call Slovenia from abroad, dial the international access code, ☑386 (the country code for Slovenia), the area code (minus the initial zero) and the number. There are six area codes in Slovenia (☑01 to ☑05 and ☑07). To call abroad from Slovenia, dial ☑00 followed by the country and area codes and then the number. Numbers beginning with ☑80 in Slovenia are toll-free.

MOBILE PHONES

Network coverage amounts to more than 95% of the country. Mobile numbers carry the prefix ☑030 and ☑040 (SiMobil), ☑031, ☑041, ☑051 and ☑071 (Mobitel) and ☑070 (Tušmobil).

Slovenia uses GSM 900, which is compatible with the rest of Europe and Australia but not with the North American GSM 1900 or the totally different Japanese system. SIM cards with €5 credit are available for around €15 from **SiMobil** (www.simobil.si), **Mobitel** (www.mobitel.si) and **Tušmobil** (www.tusmobil.sil). Top-up scratch cards are available at post offices, news stands and petrol stations.

All three networks have outlets throughout Slovenia, including in Ljubljana.

Tourist Information

The **Slovenian Tourist Board** (Slovenska Turistična Organizacija, STO; ☑01-589 18 40; www.slovenia.info; Dunajska cesta 156), based in Ljubljana, is the umbrella organisation for tourist promotion in Slovenia, and produces a number of excellent brochures, pamphlets and booklets in English.

Walk-in visitors in Ljubljana can head to the **Slovenian Tourist Information Centre** (STIC; ☑306 45 76; www.slovenia.info; Krekov trg 10; ☺8am-9pm Jun-Sep, 8am-7pm Oct-May). In addition, the organisation oversees another five dozen or so local tourist offices and bureaus called 'tourist information centres' (TICs) across the country.

In the capital, the **Ljubljana Tourist Information Centre** (TIC; ☑306 12 15; www.visitljubljana.si; Adamič-Lundrovo nabrežje 2; ☺8am-9pm Jun-Sep, 8am-7pm Oct-May) knows just about everything there is to know about Ljubljana and almost as much about the rest of Slovenia. There's a branch at the train station.

Visas

Citizens of nearly all European countries, as well as Australia, Canada, Israel, Japan, New Zealand and the USA, do not require visas to visit Slovenia for stays of up to 90 days. Holders of EU and Swiss passports can enter using a national identity card.

Those who do require visas (including South Africans) can get them for up to 90 days at any Slovenian embassy or consulate – see the website of the **Ministry of Foreign Affairs** (www.mzz.gov.si) for a full listing. They cost €35 regardless of the type of visa or length of validity.

Getting There & Away

Border formalities with Slovenia's fellow European Union neighbours, Italy, Austria and Hungary, are virtually nonexistent. Croatia hopes to enter the EU in 2013 and plans to implement the Schengen border rules soon after. Until then expect a somewhat closer inspection of your documents – national ID (for EU citizens) or passport and, in some cases, visa when travelling to/from Croatia.

Air

Slovenia's only international airport is Ljubljana's **Jože Pučnik Airport** (LJU/Aerodrom Ljubljana; ☑04-206 19 81; www.lju-airport.si/eng; Zgornji Brnik 130a, Brnik) at Brnik, 27km north of Ljubljana. In the arrivals hall there's a **Slovenia Tourist Information Centre** (STIC; ☺11am-11pm Mon, Wed & Fri, 10am-10pm Tue & Thu, 10.30am-10.30pm Sat, 12.30pm-12.30am Sun) desk, a hotel-booking telephone and ATM. Car-rental agencies have outlets opposite the terminal.

From its base at Brnik, the Slovenian flag-carrier, **Adria Airways** (☑01-369 10 10, 080 13 00; www.adria-airways.com), serves some 20 European destinations on regularly scheduled flights.

Other airlines with regularly scheduled flights to and from Ljubljana include:

Air France (☑01-244 34 47; www.airfrance.com/si) Daily flights to Paris (CDG).

ČSA Czech Airlines (☑04-206 17 50; www.czechairlines.com) Flights to Prague.

EasyJet (☑04-206 16 77; www.easyjet.com) Low-cost daily flights to London Stansted.

JAT Airways (☑01-231 43 40; www.jat.com) Daily flights to Belgrade.

Lufthansa (☑01-434 72 46; www.lufthansa.com; Gosposvetska cesta 6) Code-shared flights with Adria.

Montenegro Airlines (☑04-259 42 52; www.montenegroairlines.com) Twice weekly flight to Podgorica.

Turkish Airlines (☑04-206 16 80; www.turkishairlines.com) Flights to Istanbul.

Land

BUS

International bus destinations from Ljubljana include Serbia, Germany, Croatia, Bosnia and Hercegovina, Macedonia, Italy and Scandinavia. You can also catch buses to Italy and Croatia from coastal towns, including Piran and Koper.

TRAIN

It is possible to travel to Italy, Austria, Germany, Croatia and Hungary by train; Ljubljana is the main hub, although you can, for example, hop on international trains in certain cities like Maribor and Ptuj). International train travel can be expensive. It is sometimes cheaper to travel as far as you can on domestic routes before crossing any borders.

Sea

Piran sends ferries to Trieste daily and catamarans to Venice at least once a week in season. There's also a catamaran between nearby Izola and Venice in summer months.

Getting Around

Bicycle

Cycling is a popular way of getting around. Bikes can be transported for €2.80 in the baggage compartments of some IC and regional trains. Larger buses can also carry bikes as luggage. Larger towns and cities have dedicated bicycle lanes and traffic lights.

ROAD RULES

» Drive on the right.

» Speed limits: 50km/h in town, 90km/h on secondary roads, 100km/h on highways; 130km/h on motorways.

» Seat belts are compulsory; motorcyclists must wear helmets.

» All motorists must illuminate their headlights throughout the day.

» Permitted blood-alcohol level for drivers is 0.05%.

Bus

Buy your ticket at the *avtobusna postaja* (bus station) or simply pay the driver as you board. In Ljubljana you should book your seat at least a day in advance if you're travelling on Friday, or to destinations in the mountains or on the coast on a public holiday. Bus services are restricted on Sunday and holidays.

A range of bus companies serve the country, but prices are uniform: €3.10/5.60/9.20/16.80 for 25/50/100/200km of travel.

Timetables in the bus station, or posted on a wall or column outside, list destinations and departure times. If you cannot find your bus listed or don't understand the schedule, get help from the *blagajna vozovnice* (information or ticket window), which are usually one and the same. *Odhodi* means 'departures' while *prihodi* is 'arrivals'.

Car & Motorcycle

Roads in Slovenia are generally good. There are two main motorway corridors – between Maribor and the coast (via the flyover at Črni Kal) and from the Karavanke Tunnel into Austria to Zagreb in Croatia – intersecting at the Ljubljana ring road, with a branch from Postojna to Nova Gorica. Motorways are numbered from A1 to A10 (for *avtocesta*).

Tolls are no longer paid separately on the motorways, instead all cars must display a *vinjeta* (road-toll sticker) on the windscreen. They cost €15/30/95 for a week/month/year for cars and €7.50/25/47.50 for motorbikes and are available at petrol stations, post offices and certain news stands and tourist information centres. These stickers will already be in place on a rental car; failure to display such a sticker risks a fine of up to €300.

Dial ☏1987 for roadside assistance.

HIRING A CAR

Renting a car in Slovenia allows access to cheaper out-of-centre hotels and farm or village homestays. Rentals from international firms such as Avis, Budget, Europcar and Hertz vary in price; expect to pay from €40/210 a day/week, including unlimited mileage, collision damage waiver (CDW), theft protection (TP), Personal Accident Insurance (PAI) and taxes. Some smaller agencies have somewhat more competitive rates; booking on the internet is always cheaper.

Train

Much of the country is accessible by rail, run by the national operator, **Slovenian Railways** (Slovenske Železnice, SŽ; ☏01-291 33 32; www.slo-zeleznice.si). The website has an easy-to-use timetable.

Figure on travelling at about 60km/h except on the fastest InterCity Slovenia (ICS) express trains that run between Ljubljana and Maribor (€13.60, 1¾ hours) at an average speed of 90km/h.

The provinces are served by *regionalni vlaki* (regional trains) and *primestni vlaki* (city trains), but the fastest are InterCity trains (IC).

An 'R' next to the train number on the timetable means seat reservations are available. If the 'R' is boxed, seat reservations are obligatory.

Purchase your ticket before travelling at the *železniška postaja* (train station); buying it from the conductor onboard costs an additional €2.50. Invalid tickets or fare dodging earn a €40 fine.

Spain

Includes »

Madrid 651
Toledo 681
Barcelona 683
Girona 700
Tarragona 702
Valencia 715
Ibiza 724
Seville 727
Córdoba........................ 733
Granada........................ 736
Costa de Almería.......... 739
Málaga 740
Gibraltar 746

Best Places to Eat

» La Cuchara de San Telmo (p707)

» Arzak (p707)

» Simply Fosh (p722)

» Tickets (p696)

» La Pepica (p717)

Best Places to Stay

» Hostal de San Marcos (p679)

» Hotel Meninas (p659)

» Hospedería Alma Andalusí (p735)

» Sabinas (p704)

» Casa Morisca Hotel (p737)

Why Go?

Passionate, sophisticated and devoted to living the good life, Spain is at once a stereotype come to life and a country more diverse than you ever imagined.

Spanish landscapes stir the soul, from the jagged Pyrenees and wildly beautiful cliffs of the Atlantic northwest to charming Mediterranean coves, while astonishing architecture spans the ages at seemingly every turn. Spain's cities march to a beguiling beat, rushing headlong into the 21st century even as timeless villages serve as beautiful signposts to Old Spain. And then there's one of Europe's most celebrated (and varied) gastronomic scenes.

But, above all, Spain lives very much in the present. Perhaps you'll sense it along a crowded after-midnight street when it seems all the world has come out to play. Or maybe that moment will come when a flamenco performer touches something deep in your soul. Whenever it happens, you'll find yourself nodding in recognition: *this* is Spain.

When to Go
Madrid

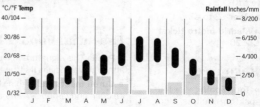

Mar–Apr Spring wildflowers, Semana Santa processions and mild southern temps.

May & Sep Mild and often balmy weather but without the crowds of high summer.

Jun–Aug Spaniards hit the coast in warm weather, but quiet corners still abound.

SPAIN

AT A GLANCE

- » **Currency** euro
- » **Language** Spanish (Castilian), Catalan, Basque, Galician (Gallego)
- » **Money** ATMs everywhere
- » **Visas** Schengen rules apply

Fast Facts

- » **Area** 505,370 sq km
- » **Capital** Madrid
- » **Country code** ☏34
- » **Emergency** ☏112

Exchange Rates

Australia	A$1	€0.82
Canada	C$1	€0.77
Japan	¥100	€0.83
New Zealand	NZ$1	€0.65
UK	UK£1	€1.18
USA	US$1	€0.78

Set Your Budget

- » **Budget hotel room** €60
- » **Two-course meal** €35 to €40
- » **Museum entrance** €8 to €10
- » **Beer** €2 to €3
- » **Madrid metro ticket** €12.20

Resources

- » **Tour Spain** (www.tourspain.org) Culture, food, hotels and transport links
- » **Turespaña** (www.spain.info) Official tourism site
- » **Lonely Planet** (www.lonelyplanet.com/spain)

Connections

Spanish airports are among Europe's best connected, while the typical overland route leads many travellers from France over the Pyrenees into Spain. Rather than taking the main road/rail route along the Mediterranean coast (or between Biarritz and San Sebastián), you could follow lesser known, pretty routes over the mountains. There's nothing to stop you carrying on to Portugal: numerous roads and the Madrid–Lisbon rail line connect the two countries.

The most obvious sea journeys lead across the Strait of Gibraltar to Morocco. The most common routes connect Algeciras or Tarifa with Tangier, from where there's plenty of transport deeper into Morocco. Car ferries also connect Barcelona with Italian ports.

There is a high-speed rail service between Paris and Barcelona (7½ hours), but at the time of writing it still required a change of trains in Figueres Vilafant. The Madrid–Paris line is also being upgraded to become a high-speed service.

ITINERARIES

One Week

Marvel at Barcelona's art nouveau–influenced Modernista architecture and seaside style before taking the train to San Sebastián, with a stop in Zaragoza on the way. Head on to Bilbao for the Guggenheim Museum and end the trip living it up in Madrid's legendary night scene.

One Month

Fly into Seville and embark on a route exploring the town and picture-perfect Ronda, Granada and Córdoba. Take the train to Madrid, from where you can check out Toledo, Salamanca and Segovia. Make east for the coast and Valencia, detour northwest into the postcard-perfect villages of Aragón and the Pyrenees, then travel east into Catalonia, spending time in Tarragona before reaching Barcelona. Take a plane or boat for the Balearic Islands, from where you can get a flight home.

Essential Food & Drink

- » **Paella** This signature rice dish comes in infinite varieties, although Valencia is its true home.
- » **Cured meats** Wafer-thin slices of *chorizo, lomo, salchichón* and *jamón serrano* appear on most Spanish tables.
- » **Tapas** These bite-sized morsels range from uncomplicated Spanish staples to pure gastronomic innovation.
- » **Olive oil** Spain is the world's largest producer of olive oil.
- » **Wine** Spain has the largest area of wine cultivation in the world. La Rioja and Ribera del Duero are the best-known wine-growing regions.

MADRID

POP 3.26 MILLION

No city on earth is more alive than Madrid, a beguiling place whose sheer energy carries a simple message: *madrileños* know how to live. Explore the old streets of the centre, relax in the plazas, soak up the culture in Madrid's excellent art museums, and spend at least one night exploring the city's legendary nightlife scene.

History

Established as a Moorish garrison in 854, Madrid was little more than a muddy provincial village when King Felipe II declared it Spain's capital in 1561. That began to change when it became the permanent home of the previously roaming Spanish court. Despite being home to generations of nobles, the city was a squalid grid of unpaved alleys and dirty buildings until the 18th century, when King Carlos III turned his attention to public works. With 175,000 inhabitants under Carlos' rule, Madrid had become Europe's fifth largest capital.

The postcivil war 1940s and '50s were trying times for the capital, with rampant poverty. When Spain's dictator, General Franco, died in 1975, the city exploded with creativity and life, giving *madrileños* the partyhard reputation they still cherish.

Terrorist bombs rocked Madrid in March 2004, just before national elections, and killed 191 commuters on four trains. In 2007 two people died in a Basque terrorist bomb attack at the city's airport. With remarkable aplomb, the city quickly returned to business as usual on both occasions.

Sights

Get under the city's skin by walking its streets, sipping coffee and beer in its plazas and relaxing in its parks. Madrid de los Austrias, the maze of mostly 15th- and 16th-century streets that surround Plaza Mayor, is the city's oldest district. Tapas-crazy La Latina, alternative Chueca, bar-riddled Huertas and Malasaña, and chic Salamanca are other districts that reward pedestrian exploration.

TOP CHOICE Museo del Prado MUSEUM
(Map p660; www.museodelprado.es; Paseo del Prado; adult/child €12/free, free 6-8pm Mon-Sat & 5-7pm Sun, audioguides €3.50; ⏱10am-8pm Mon-Sat, to 7pm Sun; Ⓜ Banco de España) Spain's premier art museum, the Prado is a seemingly endless parade of priceless works from Spain and beyond. The 1785 neoclassical Palacio de Villanueva opened as a museum in 1819.

The collection is roughly divided into eight major collections: Spanish paintings (1100–1850), Flemish paintings (1430–1700), Italian paintings (1300–1800), French paintings (1600–1800), German paintings (1450–1800), sculptures, decorative arts, and drawings and prints. There is generous coverage of Spanish greats including Goya, Velázquez and El Greco. In addition to these Spanish masterpieces, don't miss *El Jardín de las Delicias* (The Garden of Earthly Delights; Room 56A), a three-panelled painting by Hieronymus Bosch of the creation of man, the pleasures of the world, and hell, or the works by Peter Paul Rubens, Pieter Bruegel, Rembrandt, Anton Van Dyck, Albrecht Dürer, Raphael, Titian, Tintoretto, Joaquín Sorolla, Thomas Gainsborough, Fra Angelico and Tiepolo.

From the 1st floor of the Palacio de Villanueva, passageways lead to the Edificio Jerónimos, the Prado's modern extension. The main hall contains information counters, a bookshop and a cafe. Rooms A and B (and Room C on the 1st floor) host temporary exhibitions.

TOP CHOICE Museo Thyssen-Bornemisza MUSEUM
(Map p660; ☏902 760 511; www.museothyssen.org; Paseo del Prado 8; adult/child €9/free; ⏱10am-7pm Tue-Sun; Ⓜ Banco de España) Opposite Museo del Prado, the Museo Thyssen-Bornemisza is an outstanding collection of international masterpieces. Begin your visit on the 2nd floor, where you'll start with medieval art, and make your way down to modern works on the ground level, passing paintings by Titian, El Greco, Rubens, Rembrandt, Anton van Dyck, Canaletto, Cézanne, Monet, Sisley, Renoir, Pissarro, Degas, Constable, Van Gogh, Miró, Modigliani, Matisse, Picasso, Gris, Pollock, Dalí, Kandinsky, Toulouse-Lautrec, Lichtenstein and many others on the way.

TOP CHOICE Centro de Arte Reina Sofía MUSEUM
(Map p654; ☏91 774 10 00; www.museoreinasofia.es; Calle de Santa Isabel 52; adult/concession €6/free, free Sun, 7-9pm Mon-Fri & 2.30-9pm Sat; ⏱10am-9pm Mon-Sat, to 2.30pm Sun; Ⓜ Atocha) If modern art is your thing, the Reina Sofía is your museum. A stunning collection of mainly Spanish modern art, the Centro de Arte Reina Sofía is home to Picasso's *Guernica* – his protest against the German bombing of the Basque town of Guernica

Spain Highlights

1 Explore the **Alhambra** (p736), an exquisite Islamic palace complex in Granada

2 Visit Gaudí's singular work in progress, Barcelona's **La Sagrada Família** (p690), a cathedral that truly defies imagination

3 Wander amid the horseshoe arches of Córdoba's **Mezquita** (p733), close to perfection wrought in stone

4 Eat your way through **San Sebastián** (p706), a gourmand's paradise with an idyllic setting

5 Join the pilgrims making their way to magnificent **Santiago de Compostela** (p712)

6 Soak up the scent of orange blossom, admire the architecture and surrender to the party atmosphere in sunny **Seville** (p727)

7 Discover the impossibly beautiful Mediterranean beaches and coves of **Menorca** (p726)

8 Spend your days in some of Europe's best art galleries then revel amid the best nightlife in **Madrid** (p651)

9 Be carried away by the soulful strains of live **flamenco** (p753)

Madrid

A | B | C | D

1

Moncloa

Paseo de Moret

C de Guzmán el Bueno

Quevedo

Plaza del Conde del Valle de Suchil

Argüelles

ARGÜELLES

C de San Bernardo

C de Fuencarral

Paseo del Pintor Rosales

C del Marqués de Urquijo

C de Alberto Aguilera

San Bernardo

C de Carranza

2

C de la Princesa

C del Conde Duque

C del Acuerdo

C de San Bernardo

5 ⊗ 8

MALASAÑA

Plaza del Dos de Mayo

Glorieta de San Antonio de la Florida

C de Ferraz

⊛ 11

C de la Palma

⊙ 2

La Rosaleda

Ventura Rodríguez

⊙ 10

Noviciado

3

Paseo de la Florida

3

C de San Bernardino

Banco de España

Noviciado

C de la Madera

Jardines de Ferraz

Parque de la Montaña

Plaza de España

Gran Vía

Príncipe Pío

14

Santo Domingo

Príncipe Pío

See La Latina & Los Austrias Map (p664)

Callao

Casa de Campo

CAMPO

Campo del Moro

Ópera

4

Plaza de la Armería

Plaza de la Puerta del Sol

Puerta del Ángel

Sol

Paseo del Marqués de Monistrol

Paseo de la Virgen del Puerto

Parque de Atenas

Parque del Emir Mohamed I

Plaza Mayor

5

C de Bailén

LA LATINA

Tirso de Molina

6

Av de Manzanares

Río Manzanares

Ronda de Segovia

Paseo Imperial

Puerta de Toledo

Glorieta de Puerta de Toledo

Jardín del Rastro

Ronda de Toledo

7

Puente de San Isidro

Paseo de los Pontones

C de Toledo

Plaza de Ortega y Munilla

Paseo de las Acacias

Acacias

A | B | C | D

SPAIN MADRID

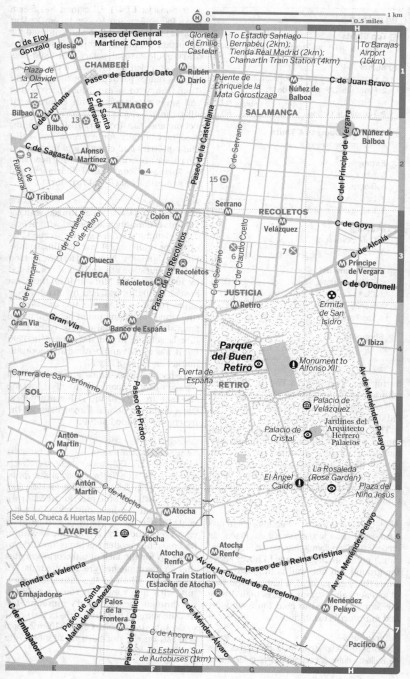

See Sol, Chueca & Huertas Map (p660)

SPAIN MADRID

Madrid

◉ **Top Sights**
Parque del Buen Retiro G4

◉ **Sights**
1 Centro de Arte Reina Sofía F6
2 Ermita de San Antonio de la
Florida A3
3 Templo de Debod B3

⊕ **Activities, Courses & Tours**
4 International House F2

⊗ **Eating**
5 Albur D2
6 Biotza G3
7 La Colonial de Goya G3
8 La Isla del Tesoro D2

⊖ **Drinking**
9 Café Comercial E2
10 El Jardín Secreto C2

⊕ **Entertainment**
11 Café La Palma D2
12 Clamores E1
13 Honky Tonk E2
14 Las Tablas C3

⊕ **Shopping**
15 Agatha Ruiz de la Prada G2

during the Spanish Civil War in 1937 – in addition to important works by surrealist Salvador Dalí and abstract paintings by the Catalan artist Joan Miró.

The main gallery's permanent display ranges over the 2nd and 4th floors. Key names in modern Spanish art on show include José Gutiérrez Solana, Juan Gris, Pablo Gargallo, Eusebio Sempere, Pablo Palazuelo, Eduardo Arroyo and Eduardo Chillida.

FREE Caixa Forum   MUSEUM, ARCHITECTURE
(Map p660; www.fundacio.lacaixa.es; Paseo del Prado 36; ☉10am-8pm; Ⓜ Atocha) The Caixa Forum, opened in 2008, seems to hover above the ground. On one wall is the *jardín colgante* (hanging garden), a lush vertical wall of greenery almost four storeys high. Inside are four floors used to hold top quality art and multimedia exhibitions.

Palacio Real   PALACE
(☎91 454 88 00; www.patrimonionacional.es; Calle de Bailén; adult/concession €10/5, guide/audio-guide/pamphlet €7/4/1, EU citizens free 5-8pm Wed & Thu; ☉10am-8pm Apr-Sep, to 6pm Oct-Mar; ⓂÓpera) Dating from 1755 and still used for important events of pomp and state, Madrid's opulent royal palace has 2800-plus rooms, of which 50 are open to the public.

Look out in particular for the **Salón de Gasparini**, with its exquisite stucco ceiling and walls resplendent with embroidered silks, the 215 clocks of the royal clock collection and the five Stradivarius violins, used occasionally for concerts and balls. The tapestries and chandeliers throughout the palace are original. Poke your head into the **Farmacia Real** (Royal Pharmacy) and the **Armería Real** (Royal Armoury).

Plaza Mayor   SQUARE
(Map p660; Plaza Mayor; ⓂSol) Ringed with cafes and restaurants and packed with people day and night, the 17th-century arcaded Plaza Mayor is an elegant and bustling square. First designed by Juan de Herrera in 1560 at the request of Phillip II, and completed by Juan Gómez de Mora in 1619, the plaza hosted bullfights watched by 50,000 spectators (until 1878), while the *autos-da-fé* (the ritual condemnation of heretics) of the Spanish Inquisition also took place here. Fire largely destroyed the square in 1790 but it was rebuilt and became an important market and hub of city life.

Today, the ochre-tinted apartments with wrought-iron balconies are offset by the exquisite frescoes of the 17th-century **Real Casa de la Panadería** (Royal Bakery); the frescoes were added in 1992.

**Catedral de Nuestra
Señora de la Almudena**   CATHEDRAL
(☎91 542 22 00; www.museocatedral.archi madrid.es; Calle de Bailén; cathedral & crypt by donation; ☉9am-8.30pm Mon-Sat, for Mass Sun; ⓂÓpera) Although the exterior of Madrid's cathedral sits in harmony with the adjacent Palacio Real, Madrid's cathedral is cavernous and largely charmless within; its colourful, modern ceilings do little to make up for the lack of old-world gravitas that so distinguishes great cathedrals. It's possible to climb to the cathedral's summit, with fine views. En route you climb up through the cathedral's museum; follow the signs to the **Museo de la Catedral y Cúpola** (adult/child €6/4; ☉10am-2.30pm Mon-Sat) on the northern facade, opposite the Palacio Real.

Basílica de San Francisco El Grande
CHURCH

(Plaza de San Francisco 1; adult/concession €3/2; ⏰Mass 8am-10.30am Mon-Sat, museum 10.30am-12.30pm & 4-6pm Tue-Sun; Ⓜ️La Latina, Puerta de Toledo) Lording it over the southwestern corner of La Latina, this imposing and recently restored baroque basilica is one of Madrid's grandest old churches. Its extravagantly frescoed dome is, by some estimates, the largest in Spain and the fourth largest in the world, with a height of 56m and diameter of 33m. The fresco in the neo-plateresque Capilla de San Bernardino was painted by Goya.

Iglesia de San Ginés
CHURCH

(Map p660; Calle del Arenal 13; ⏰8.45am-1pm & 6-9pm Mon-Sat, 9.45am-2pm & 6-9pm Sun; Ⓜ️Sol, Ópera) Due north of Plaza Mayor, San Ginés is one of Madrid's oldest churches: it has been here in one form or another since at least the 14th century. The church houses some fine paintings, including El Greco's *Expulsion of the Moneychangers from the Temple* (1614).

Convento de las Descalzas Reales
CONVENT

(Convent of the Barefoot Royals; Map p660; www.patrimonionacional.es; Plaza de las Descalzas 3; adult/child €7/4, incl Convento de la Encarnación €10/5, EU citizens free Wed & Thu afternoon; ⏰10.30am-2pm & 4-6.30pm Tue-Sat, 10am-3pm Sun; Ⓜ️Ópera, Sol) Opulent inside, though with a rather plain plateresque exterior, the Convento de las Descalzas Reales was founded in 1559 by Juana of Austria. Daughter of Spain's King Carlos I and Isabel of Portugal, Juana transformed one of her mother's palaces into the noblewomen's convent of choice. On the obligatory guided tour you'll see a gaudily frescoed Renaissance stairway and a number of extraordinary tapestries based on works by Rubens. Some 33 nuns still live here and there are 33 chapels dotted around the convent.

Parque del Buen Retiro
GARDENS

(Map p654; ⏰6am-midnight May-Sep, to 11pm Oct-Apr; Ⓜ️Retiro, Príncipe de Vergara, Ibiza, Atocha) The splendid gardens of El Retiro are littered with marble monuments, landscaped lawns, the occasional elegant building and abundant greenery. It's quiet and contemplative during the week, but comes to life on weekends.

The focal point for so much of El Retiro's life is the artificial *estanque* (lake), which is watched over by the massive ornamental structure of the **Monument to Alfonso XII** on the east side of the lake, complete with marble lions. Hidden among the trees south of the lake, the late-19th-century **Palacio de Cristal**, a magnificent metal and glass structure that is arguably El Retiro's most beautiful architectural monument, is now used for temporary exhibitions.

At the southern end of the park, near **La Rosaleda** (Rose Garden) with its more-than-4000 roses, is a statue of **El Ángel Caído** (the Fallen Angel, aka Lucifer), one of the few statues to the devil anywhere in the world. It sits 666m above sea level...

In the northeastern corner of the park is the ruined **Ermita de San Isidro**, a small country chapel noteworthy as one of the few, albeit modest, examples of Romanesque architecture in Madrid.

FREE Ermita de San Antonio de la Florida
CHURCH

(Map p654; Glorieta de San Antonio de la Florida 5; ⏰9.30am-8pm Tue-Fri, 10am-2pm Sat & Sun, hours vary Jul & Aug; Ⓜ️Príncipe Pío) The frescoed ceilings of the hermitage are one of Madrid's most surprising secrets. In the southern of the two small chapels you can see Goya's work in its original setting, rendered in 1798. The painter is buried in front of the altar.

FREE Templo de Debod
RUIN

(Map p654; www.munimadrid.es/templodebod; Paseo del Pintor Rosales; ⏰10am-2pm & 6-8pm Tue-Fri, 10am-2pm Sat & Sun Apr-Sep, 9.45am-1.45pm & 4.15-6.15pm Tue-Fri & 10am-2pm Sat & Sun Oct-Mar; Ⓜ️Ventura Rodríguez) This authentically ancient Egyptian Temple was transferred here stone by stone from Egypt in 1972 as a gesture of thanks to Spanish archaeologists who helped save Egyptian monuments from the rising waters of the Aswan Dam.

MADRID'S BEST PLAZAS

Madrid also has some lovely public squares, among the best are:

Plaza de Oriente (Ⓜ️Ópera)

Plaza de la Villa (Ⓜ️Ópera)

Plaza de la Paja

Plaza de Santa Ana (Map p660; Ⓜ️Sevilla, Sol, Antón Martín)

MUSEO DEL PRADO ITINERARY: ICONS OF SPANISH ART

The Museo del Prado's collection can be overwhelming in scope, but, if your time is limited, zero in on the museum's peerless collection of Spanish art.

Goya is displayed on all three floors of the Prado, but begin at the southern end of the ground or lower level. In rooms 64 and 65, Goya's *El Dos de Mayo* and *El Tres de Mayo* rank among Madrid's most emblematic paintings. In rooms 66 and 67, Goya's disturbing *Pinturas Negras* (Black Paintings) are so named for the distorted animalesque appearance of their characters. Of Goya's remarkable royal portraits, *La Família de Carlos V* (Room 32), on the 1st floor, is especially worth seeking out. Also on the 1st floor, in Room 36, are two more of Goya's best-known and most intriguing oils: *La Maja Vestida* and *La Maja Desnuda*. These portraits of an unknown woman, commonly believed to be the Duquesa de Alba (who some think may have been Goya's lover).

Having studied the works of Goya, turn your attention to Velázquez, beginning with *Las Meninas* (Room 12). Completed in 1656, it is more properly known as *La Família de Felipe IV* (The Family of Felipe IV). His mastery of light and colour is never more apparent than here. In the neighbouring rooms 14 and 15, watch also for his paintings of various members of royalty who seem to spring off the canvas – Felipe II, Felipe IV, Margarita de Austria (a younger version of whom features in *Las Meninas*), El Príncipe Baltasar Carlos and Isabel de Francia. In Room 9a, seek out his masterful *La Rendición de Breda* (The Surrender of Breda).

Further, Bartolomé Esteban Murillo (Room 17), José de Ribera (Room 9), the stark figures of Francisco de Zurbarán (Room 10a) and the vivid, almost surreal works of El Greco (Room 8b) should all be on your itinerary.

Real Academia de Bellas Artes de San Fernando   MUSEUM

(Map p660; ☑91 524 08 64; http://rabasf.insde.es; Calle de Alcalá 13; adult/child €5/free, free Wed; ⊙9am-3pm Tue-Sat, to 2.30pm Sun Sep-Jun, hours vary Jul & Aug; Ⓜ Sol, Sevilla) The somewhat fusty Real Academia de Bellas Artes de San Fernando offers a broad collection of old and modern masters, including works by Zurbarán, El Greco, Rubens, Tintoretto, Goya, Sorolla and Juan Gris.

🍴 Courses

International House   LANGUAGE SCHOOL
(Map p654; ☑902 141517; www.ihmadrid.es; Calle de Zurbano 8; Ⓜ Alonso Martínez) Some of the best and cheapest classes in town.

Academia Inhispania   LANGUAGE SCHOOL
(Map p660; ☑91 521 22 31; www.inhispania.com; Calle de la Montera 10-12; Ⓜ Sol) Language school.

Academia Madrid Plus   LANGUAGE SCHOOL
(☑91 548 11 16; www.madridplus.es, Calle del Arenal 21, 6th fl; Ⓜ Ópera) Language school.

Kitchen Club   COOKING SCHOOL
(Map p660; ☑91 522 62 63; www.kitchenclub.es; Calle de Ballesta 8; Ⓜ Gran Vía, Callao) Run by one of Madrid's most celebrated chefs, Andrés Madrigal, Kitchen Club spans the globe with a range of courses operating just off Gran Vía in the city centre. For further information about food and drink in Spain see p754.

☞ Tours

Visitas Guiadas Oficiales   GUIDED TOUR
(Official Guided Tours; ☑902 221424; www.esmadrid.com/guidedtours; Plaza Mayor 27; adult/child €3.90/free; Ⓜ Sol) Twenty highly recommended guided tours conducted in Spanish and English. Organised by the Centro de Turismo de Madrid (p672).

Madrid City Tour   BUS TOUR
(☑902 024758; http://www.esmadrid.com/en/tourist-bus; 1-day ticket adult €21, child free-€9; ⊙9am-10pm Mar-Oct, 10am-6pm Nov-Feb) Hop-on, hop-off, open-topped buses that run every 10 to 20 minutes along two routes: Historical Madrid and Modern Madrid. Information, including maps, is available at tourist offices, most travel agencies and some hotels, or you can get tickets on the bus.

🎉 Festivals & Events

Fiesta de San Isidro   CULTURAL
(www.esmadrid.com/sanisidro) Around 15 May, Madrid's patron saint is honoured with a week of nonstop processions, parties, bullfights and free concerts.

Suma Flamenca FLAMENCO

(www.madrid.org/sumaflamenca) A soul-filled flamenco festival that draws some of the biggest names in the genre in June.

Veranos de la Villa SUMMER FESTIVAL

(www.veranosdelavilla.esmadrid.com) Madrid's town hall stages a series of cultural events, shows and exhibitions throughout July and August, known as Summers in the City.

🛏 Sleeping

Madrid has a plethora of high-quality accommodation across all price ranges. Where you decide to stay will play an important role in your experience of Madrid. Los Austrias, Sol and Centro put you in the heart of the busy downtown area, while La Latina (the best *barrio* – neighbourhood – for tapas), Lavapiés and Huertas (good for nightlife) are ideal for those who love Madrid nights and don't want to stagger too far to get back to their hotel. You don't have to be gay to stay in Chueca, but you'll love it if you are, while Malasaña is another inner-city *barrio* with great restaurants and bars.

LOS AUSTRIAS, SOL & CENTRO

TOP CHOICE **Hotel Meninas** BOUTIQUE HOTEL €€

(☎91 541 28 05; www.hotelmeninas.com; Calle de Campomanes 7; s/d from €99/119; ✳☎; Mópera) Inside a refurbished 19th-century mansion, the Meninas combines old-world comfort with modern, minimalist style. The colour scheme is blacks, whites and greys, with dark-wood floors and splashes of fuchsia and lime-green.

Praktik Metropol BOUTIQUE HOTEL €€

(Map p660; ☎91 521 29 35; www.hotelpraktik-metropol.com; Calle de la Montera 47; s/d from €65/79; ✳☎; MGran Vía) The rooms here have a fresh, contemporary look with white wood furnishings and some (especially the corner rooms) have brilliant views down to Gran Vía and out over the city.

Posada del Dragón BOUTIQUE HOTEL €€

(Map p660; ☎91 119 14 24; www.posadadeldragon.com; Calle de la Cava Baja 14 ; r from €91; ✳☎; MLa Latina) This restored 19th-century inn sits on one of our favourite streets in Madrid and rooms either look out over the street or over the pretty internal patio. Bold, brassy colour schemes and designer everything dominates the rooms.

Cat's Hostel HOSTEL €

(Map p660; ☎91 369 28 07; www.catshostel.com; Calle de Cañizares 6; dm €15-20; ✳@☎; MAntón Martín) Forming part of a 17th-century palace, the internal courtyard here is one of Madrid's finest, with lavish Andalucian tilework, a fountain, a spectacular glass ceiling and stunning Islamic decoration. There's a supercool basement bar with free internet and fiestas.

Hostal Madrid HOSTAL, APARTMENT €

(Map p660; ☎91 522 00 60; www.hostal-madrid.info; Calle de Esparteros 6; s €35-55, d €45-75, d apt per night €55-150, per month €1200-2500; ✳☎; MSol) The 24 rooms at this well-run *hostal* have been wonderfully renovated with exposed brickwork, brand-new bathrooms and a look that puts many three-star hotels to shame. It also has terrific apartments (www.apartamentosmayorcentro.com).

Hotel Plaza Mayor HOTEL €€

(Map p660; ☎91 360 06 06; www.h-plazamayor.com; Calle de Atocha 2; s/d from €55/85; ✳☎; MSol, Tirso de Molina) Stylish decor, charming original elements of a 150-year-old building and helpful staff are selling points here. The rooms are attractive, some with a light colour scheme and wrought-iron furniture. The attic rooms have great views.

Hostal Acapulco HOSTAL €

(Map p660; ☎91 531 19 45; www.hostalacapulco.com; Calle de la Salud 13, 4th fl; s/d €55/65; ✳☎; MGran Vía, Callao) This immaculate little *hostal* has marble floors, renovated bathrooms, double-glazed windows and comfortable beds. Street-facing rooms have balconies overlooking sunny Plaza del Carmen.

Hotel de Las Letras HOTEL €€

(Map p660; ☎91 523 79 80; www.hoteldelasletras.com; Gran Vía 11; d from €100; ✳☎; MGran Vía) Hotel de las Letras started the rooftop hotel-bar trend in Madrid. The bar's wonderful, but the whole hotel is excellent with individually styled rooms, each with literary quotes scribbled on the walls.

HUERTAS & ATOCHA

Hotel Alicia BOUTIQUE HOTEL €€

(Map p660; ☎91 389 60 95; www.room-matehoteles.com; Calle del Prado 2; d €100-175, ste from €200; ✳☎; MSol, Sevilla, Antón Martín) With beautiful, spacious rooms, Alicia overlooks Plaza de Santa Ana. It has an ultra-modern look and the downstairs bar is oh-so-cool.

Sol, Chueca & Huertas

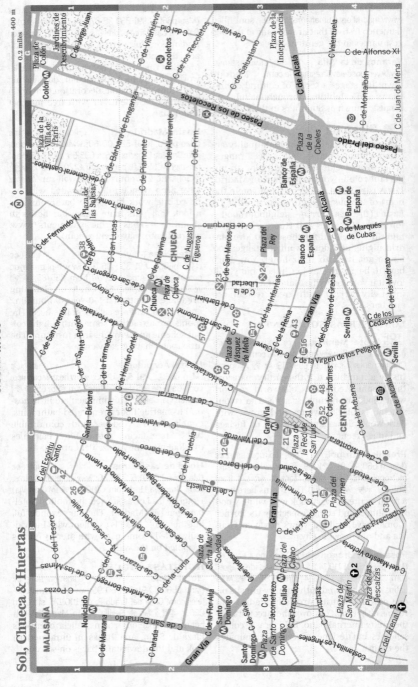

SPAIN MADRID

MALASAÑA

CHUECA

CENTRO

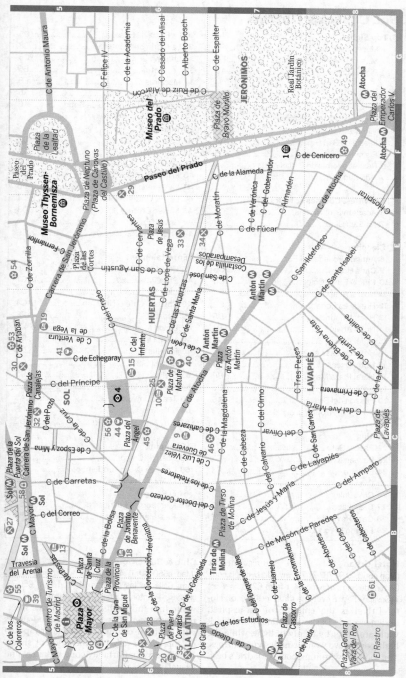

SPAIN MADRID

G
C de Antonio Maura
C Felipe IV
C de la Academia
C de Casado del Alisal
C de Alberto Bosch
C de Espalter
JERÓNIMOS
Real Jardín Botánico
Atocha
Plaza del Emperador Carlos V

Plaza de la Lealtad
C de Ruiz de Alarcón
Museo del Prado
Plaza de Bravo Murillo

F
Paseo del Prado
Plaza de Neptuno (Plaza de Cánovas del Castillo)
Museo Thyssen-Bornemisza
Paseo del Prado
29
C de la Alameda
C de la Verónica
C del Gobernador
C de Almadén
1
C de Cenicero
Atocha
49
C de Atocha
C de Hospital
Atocha

E
C de Zorrilla
C de Fernanflor
Carrera de San Jerónimo
Plaza de las Cortes
C de Cervantes
Plaza de Jesús
33
34
Costanilla de los Desamparados
C de Fúcar
C de Moratín
C de San Ildefonso
C de Santa Isabel
54

D
C de Alcalá
19
C de Ventura de la Vega
C del Prado
C del Infante
C de Lope de Vega
C de San José
C de las Huertas
C de Santa María
HUERTAS
Antón Martín
Plaza de Antón Martín
Antón Martín
C de Buena Vista
C de Zurita
C de Salitre
53
30
41
C de Echegaray
15
51
40
LAVAPIÉS
C de Tres Peces
C de la Fé
C de Primavera

C
SOL
C del Príncipe
C de la Cruz
C del Pozo
C de Espoz y Mina
4
25
56
44
45
Plaza del Ángel
10
Plaza de Matute
C de Atocha
C de Canizares
C de la Magdalena
C del Olmo
C de Cabeza
C del Calvario
C de San Carlos
Plaza de Lavapiés
C de Lavapiés
C del Amparo
C del Ave María
C del Olivar
46
6
C de Luiz Vélez de Guevara

B
Sol
Sol
27
C Mayor
C de Carretas
C del Correo
C de los Relatores
C del Doctor Cortezo
Tirso de Molina
Plaza de Tirso de Molina
C de Jesús y María
C de Mesón de Paredes
C de los Abades
C del Oso
C de Cabestreros
61

A
C de los Coloreros
Travesía del Arenal
55
39
Centro de Turismo de Madrid
Plaza de Santa Cruz
Plaza de la Provincia
13
18
Plaza de Jacinto Benavente
Plaza Mayor
60
28
C de la Cava de San Miguel
Plaza de Puerta Cerrada
36
20
35
LA LATINA
C de Grafal
C de la Concepción Jerónima
C de la Colegiata
C de los Estudios
C del Duque de Alba
Plaza de Cascorro
La Latina
C de Juanelo
C de la Encomienda
C de Ruda
El Rastro
Plaza General Vara del Rey

C de Toledo

Sol, Chueca & Huertas

◉ Top Sights

Museo del Prado......................................F6
Museo Thyssen-Bornemisza...............E5
Plaza Mayor A5

◉ Sights

1 Caixa Forum.......................................F7
2 Convento de las Descalzas
  Reales...B4
3 Iglesia de San Ginés A4
4 Plaza de Santa Ana..........................C6
5 Real Academia de Bellas Artes
  de San Fernando...............................C4

◎ Activities, Courses & Tours

6 Academia Inhispania.........................C4
7 Kitchen Club.......................................B2

⊜ Sleeping

8 Antigua Posada del Pez B2
9 Cat's Hostel.......................................C6
10 Chic & Basic Colors..........................C6
11 Hostal Acapulco.................................B4
12 Hostal La Zona C3
13 Hostal Madrid B5
14 Hotel Abalú...B1
15 Hotel Alicia D6
16 Hotel de Las Letras D3
17 Hotel Óscar D3
18 Hotel Plaza Mayor B6
19 Hotel Urban D5
20 Posada del Dragón A6
21 Praktik Metropol................................C3

✕ Eating

22 Baco y Beto D2
23 Bazaar E3
24 Bocaito E3
25 Casa Alberto D6
26 Casa Julio B1
27 Casa Labra B5
28 Casa Revuelta A6
29 Estado Puro F6

30 La Finca de Susana D5
31 La Gloria de Montera C3
32 Lhardy C5
33 Los Gatos E6
34 Maceiras E6
35 Posada de la Villa A6
36 Restaurante Sobrino de Botín............A6

◔ Drinking

37 Café Acuarela.....................................D2
38 Café Belén...E1
39 Chocolatería de San Ginés A5
40 El Imperfecto D6
41 La Venencia D5
42 Lolina Vintage Café C1
43 Museo Chicote D3
   Splash Óscar ....(see 17)
44 The Roof..C6

✪ Entertainment

45 Café Central.......................................C6
46 Casa Patas C7
47 Club 54 Studio D3
48 Costello Café & Niteclub....................C4
49 Kapital F8
   Liquid Madrid.............................(see 47)
50 Mamá Inés D3
51 Populart D6
52 Sala El Sol C4
53 Stella D5
54 Teatro de la Zarzuela E5
55 Teatro Joy Eslava A5
56 Villa Rosa C6
57 Why Not? D2

⊟ Shopping

58 Casa de Diego B5
59 Casa de Diego (workshop)..................B4
60 El Arco Artesanía...............................A5
61 El Rastro A8
62 Mercado de Fuencarral.......................C2
63 Real Madrid Store B4

Hotel Urban
LUXURY HOTEL €€€

(Map p660; ☑91 787 77 70; www.derbyhotels.com; Carrera de San Jerónimo 34; r from €225; ❋☞☎; Ⓜ Sevilla) The towering glass edifice of Hotel Urban is the epitome of art-inspired designer cool. Dark-wood floors and dark walls are offset by plenty of light, while the bathrooms have wonderful designer fittings. The rooftop swimming pool is Madrid's best.

Chic & Basic Colors
HOTEL €

(Map p660; ☑91 429 69 35; www.chicandbasic. com; Calle de las Huertas 14, 2nd fl; r €50-75; ❋☞☎; Ⓜ Antón Martín) The rooms here are white in a minimalist style with free internet, flat-screen TVs, dark hardwood floors with a bright colour scheme superimposed on top, with every room a different shade. It's all very comfortable, contemporary and casual.

MALASAÑA & CHUECA

TOP CHOICE Hotel Óscar BOUTIQUE HOTEL €€

(Map p660; ☑91 701 11 73; www.room-matehoteles.com; Plaza de Vázquez de Mella 12; d €90-200, ste €150-280; ✿🖳🔊; MGran Vía) Hotel Óscar's designer rooms ooze style and sophistication. Some have floor-to-ceiling murals, the lighting is always funky and the colour scheme is awash with pinks, lime-greens, oranges or a more minimalist black-and-white.

TOP CHOICE Hotel Abalú BOUTIQUE HOTEL €€

(Map p660; ☑91 531 47 44; www.hotelabalu.com; Calle del Pez 19; d/apt from €84/110; ✿🔊; MNoviciado) Malasaña's very own boutique hotel is an oasis of style amid the *barrio*'s timeworn feel. Suitably located on cool Calle del Pez, each room here has its own design, from retro chintz to Zen, baroque and pure white and most aesthetics in between. You're close to Gran Vía, but away from the tourist scrum.

Antigua Posada del Pez HOTEL €€

(Map p660; ☑91 531 42 96; www.antiguaposadadelpez.com; Calle de Pizarro 16; r €60-110; ✿🔊; MNoviciado) This place inhabits the shell of an historic Malasaña building, but the rooms are slick and contemporary with designer bathrooms. You're also just a few steps up the hill from Calle del Pez, one of Malasaña's most happening streets.

Hostal La Zona HOSTAL €

(Map p660; ☑91 521 99 04; www.hostallazona.com; Calle de Valverde 7, 1st fl; s/d incl breakfast €50/70; ✿🔊; MGran Vía) Catering primarily to a gay clientele, the stylish Hostal La Zona has exposed brickwork, wooden pillars and a subtle colour scheme. Other highlights include free internet, helpful staff and air-conditioning/heating in every room.

✗ Eating

It's possible to find just about any kind of cuisine and eatery in Madrid, from traditional to trendy fusion. Madrid is a magnet for cuisines from around the country and is particularly associated with seafood; despite not having a sea, Madrid has the world's second-largest fish market (after Tokyo).

From the chaotic tapas bars of La Latina to countless neighbourhood favourites, you'll have no trouble tracking down specialities like *cochinillo asado* (roast suckling pig) or *cocido madrileño* (a hearty stew made of chickpeas and various meats).

LOS AUSTRIAS, SOL & CENTRO

TOP CHOICE Mercado de San Miguel TAPAS, MARKET €

(www.mercadodesanmiguel.es; Plaza de San Miguel; tapas from €1; ☺10am-midnight Sun-Wed, to 2am Thu-Sat; MSol) One of Madrid's oldest and most beautiful markets, the Mercado de San Miguel has undergone a stunning major renovation and bills itself as a 'culinary cultural centre'. Within the early 20th-century glass walls, the market has become an inviting space strewn with tables (difficult to nab) where you can enjoy the freshest food or a drink. You can order tapas at most of the counter-bars.

TOP CHOICE Restaurante Sobrino de Botín CASTILIAN €€€

(Map p660; ☑91 366 42 17; www.botin.es; Calle de los Cuchilleros 17; mains €18.50-28; MLa Latina, Sol) It's not every day that you can eat in the oldest restaurant in the world (1725), which also appears in many novels about Madrid, most notably Hemingway's *The Sun Also Rises*. The secret of its staying power is fine *cochinillo* (suckling pig) and *cordero asado* (roast lamb) cooked in wood-fired ovens. Eating in the vaulted cellar is a treat.

Restaurante Sandó CONTEMPORARY SPANISH €€€

(☑91 547 99 11; www.restaurantesando.es; Calle de Isabel la Católica 2; mains €18-26, menú degustación €49; ☺lunch & dinner Tue-Sat, lunch Sun; MSanto Domingo) Juan Mari Arzak, one of Spain's most famous chefs, and his increasingly celebrated daughter Elena, have finally set up shop in Madrid. Bringing Basque innovation to bear upon local tradition, their cooking is assured with dishes such as bites of beef with fresh garlic and pineapple. If you can't decide, try the *menú degustación* (tasting menu).

La Gloria de Montera SPANISH €

(Map p660; www.lagloriademontera.com; Calle del Caballero de Gracia 10; mains €7-10; MGran Vía) Minimalist style, tasty Mediterranean dishes and great prices mean that you'll probably have to wait in line (no reservations taken) to eat here.

Taberna La Bola MADRILEÑO €€

(☑91 547 69 30; www.labola.es; Calle de la Bola 5; mains €16-24; ☺lunch & dinner Mon-Sat, lunch Sun, closed Aug; MSanto Domingo) Taberna La Bola (going strong since 1870 and run by the sixth generation of the Verdasco family) is known for its traditional local cuisine. If you're going to try *cocido madrileño* while in Madrid, this is a good place to do so.

La Latina & Los Austrias

N 0 _____ 200 m
0 _____ 0.1 miles

A · **B** · **C** · **D**

Cuesta de San Vicente

Jardines de Sabatini

Plaza de la Marina Española

C de Torija

C de Isabel la Católica 13

24

C de Bailén

C de la Encarnación

Guillermo Rolland

C de la Bola

14

C de San Quintín

Plaza de la Encarnación

C Pavia

C de Arrieta

Cuesta de Santo Domingo

Cuesta de Santo Domingo

6

C de Campomanes

Campo del Moro

Jardines Cabo Naval

Plaza de Oriente

C de Felipe V

Plaza de Isabel II

23

M Ópera

Farmacia Real

Plaza de la Armería

C de Carlos III

19

5

C de las Fuentes

Jardines de Lepanto

C Lepanto

C de Vergara

C de la Amnistia

C de Escalinata

Armería Real

Palacio Real

C de Requena

Plaza de Ramales

C de Noblejas

Plaza Santiago

C Lazo

Plaza Herradores

C de la Cruzada

25

Plaza del Comandante las Morenas

C del Factor

Plaza del Biombo

C de Biombo

C del Duque

2

Plaza de San Miguel

C Mayor

4

11

Parque de Atenas

C Mayor

C del Sacramento

C del Cordón

C del Codo

Plaza del Conde de Miranda

Plaza del Conde de Barajas

Cuesta de la Vega

C del Rollo

Plaza del Conde Cordón

C de San Justo

C de la Pasa

Parque del Emir Mohamed I

Plaza de la Cruz Verde

C de Segovia

Plaza de Puerta Cerrada

Plaza del Alamillo

Jardín del Príncipe Anglona

18

Viaduct

C de Alfonso VI

3

Costanilla de San Pedro

C del Nuncio

9

Jardines de las Vistillas

C de Beatriz Galindo

C de la Morería

C de Granado

Plaza de la Paja

12

C del Almendro

22

Plaza de Granada

C de Redondilla

C de Manebos

17

7

15

C de la Cava Baja

C de Yeseros

20

Plaza de San Andrés

8

C de la Cava Alta

Plaza de Gabriel Miró

Plaza de la Cebada

21

C de Don Pedro

Plaza de la Puerta de Moros

Plaza del Humilladero

C de San Buenaventura

C de la Morería

C de Bailén

Carrera de San Francisco

10

Plaza de San Francisco

16

C de Oriente

C de la Cebada

C de Toledo

1

SPAIN MADRID

La Latina & Los Austrias

◎ **Top Sights**
  Palacio Real...B3
  Plaza de Oriente C2

◎ **Sights**
  1 Basílica de San Francisco El
     Grande...B7
  2 Catedral de Nuestra Señora de la
     Almudena...B4
  3 Plaza de la Paja C6
  4 Plaza de la Villa D4

⊕ **Activities, Courses & Tours**
  5 Academia Madrid Plus D3

⊜ **Sleeping**
  6 Hotel Meninas..D2

⊗ **Eating**
  7 Almendro 13...D6
  8 Casa Lucio..D6
  9 Enotaberna del León de Oro.................D6

10 Juana La Loca..C7
11 Mercado de San Miguel D4
12 Naïa Restaurante C6
13 Restaurante Sandó D1
14 Taberna La Bola C1
15 Txacolina..D6
16 Txirimiri C7
17 Viva La Vida C6

◎ **Drinking**
18 Café del Nuncio D5
19 Café del Real...D3
20 Delic..C6
21 Taberna Tempranillo D6

◎ **Entertainment**
22 Corral de la Morería B6
23 Teatro Real D2

◎ **Shopping**
24 Antigua Casa Talavera...........................D1
25 El Flamenco Vive C3

LA LATINA & LAVAPIÉS

Naïa Restaurante   FUSION €€

(☏91 366 27 83; Plaza de la Paja 3; mains €12-19; ⊙lunch & dinner Tue-Sun; Ⓜ La Latina) On the lovely Plaza de la Paja, Naïa has a real buzz about it, with modern Spanish cuisine, a chill-out lounge downstairs and a cooking laboratory overseen by Carlos López Reyes.

Enotaberna del León de Oro   SPANISH €€

(☏91 119 14 94; www.posadadelleondeoro.com; Calle de la Cava Baja 12; mains €13-15; ⊙lunch & dinner; Ⓜ La Latina) At this fine, new bar–restaurant the emphasis is on matching carefully chosen wines with creative dishes in a casual atmosphere. It's a winning combination.

Viva La Vida   VEGETARIAN €

(www.vivalavida.com.es; Costanilla de San Andrés 16; buffet 500g plus drink €10; ⊙noon-midnight Mon-Wed, 11am-2am Thu-Sun; ☑; Ⓜ La Latina) This organic food shop has as its centrepiece an appealing vegetarian buffet with hot and cold food that's always filled with flavour. On the cusp of Plaza de la Paja, it's a great place at any time of the day, especially outside normal Spanish eating hours.

Casa Lucio   SPANISH €€

(☏91 365 32 52; www.casalucio.es; Calle de la Cava Baja 35; mains €12-25; ⊙lunch & dinner Sun-Fri, dinner Sat, closed Aug; Ⓜ La Latina) Lucio has been wowing *madrileños* with his light touch, quality ingredients and home-style local cooking for ages – think seafood, roasted meats and eggs (a Lucio speciality) in abundance.

Posada de la Villa   MADRILEÑO €€€

(Map p660; ☏91 366 18 80; www.posadadelavilla. com; Calle de la Cava Baja 9; mains €20-28; ⊙lunch & dinner Mon-Sat, lunch Sun, closed Aug; Ⓜ La Latina) This wonderfully restored 17th-century *posada* (inn) is something of a local landmark. The atmosphere is formal, the decoration sombre and traditional (heavy timber and brickwork), and the cuisine decidedly local.

HUERTAS & ATOCHA

Casa Alberto   SPANISH, TAPAS €€

(Map p660; ☏91 429 93 56; www.casaalberto.es; Calle de las Huertas 18; mains €16-20; ⊙lunch & dinner Tue-Sat, lunch Sun; Ⓜ Antón Martín) One of the most atmospheric old *tabernas* (taverns) of Madrid, Casa Alberto has been around since 1827. The secret to its staying power is vermouth on tap, excellent tapas at the bar and fine sit-down meals; Casa Alberto's *rabo de toro* (bull's tail) is famous among aficionados. The *raciones* have none of the frilly innovations that have come to characterise Spanish tapas. *Jamón,* Manchego cheese and *croquetas* are recurring themes.

A TAPAS TOUR OF MADRID

Madrid's home of tapas is La Latina, especially along Calle de la Cava Baja and the surrounding streets. **Almendro 13** (☑91 365 42 52; Calle del Almendro 13; mains €7-15; ☺12.30-4pm & 7.30pm-midnight Sun-Thu, 12.30-5pm & 8pm-1am Fri & Sat; Ⓜ La Latina) is famous for quality rather than frilly elaborations, with cured meats, cheeses, tortillas and *huevos rotos* (literally, 'broken eggs') the house specialities. Down on Calle de la Cava Baja, **Txacolina** (☑91 366 48 77; Calle de la Cava Baja 26; tapas from €3; ☺dinner Mon & Wed-Fri, lunch & dinner Sat, lunch Sun; Ⓜ La Latina) does some of the biggest *pintxos* (Basque tapas) you'll find. Not far away, **Juana La Loca** (☑91 364 05 25; Plaza de la Puerta de Moros 4; tapas from €4, mains €8-19; ☺lunch & dinner Tue-Sun, dinner Mon; Ⓜ La Latina) does a magnificent *tortilla de patatas* (potato and onion omelette). **Txirimiri** (☑91 364 11 96; www.txirimiri.es; Calle del Humilladero 6; tapas from €4; ☺lunch & dinner Mon-Sat, closed Aug; Ⓜ La Latina) is also outstanding.

In the centre, for *bacalao* (cod) the historic **Casa Labra** (Map p660; ☑91 532 14 05; www.casalabra.es; Calle de Tetuán 11; tapas from €1; ☺9.30am-3.30pm & 5.30-11pm; Ⓜ Sol) and **Casa Revuelta** (Map p660; ☑91 366 33 32; Calle de Latoneros 3; tapas from €2.60; ☺10.30am-4pm & 7-11pm Tue-Sat, 10.30am-4pm Sun, closed Aug; Ⓜ Sol, La Latina) have no peers.

Down the bottom of the Huertas hill, **Los Gatos** (Map p660; ☑91 429 30 67; Calle de Jesús 2; tapas from €3.50; ☺noon-1am Sun-Thu, to 2am Fri & Sat; Ⓜ Antón Martín) has eclectic decor and terrific canapés. Nearby, along the Paseo del Prado, there's supercool **Estado Puro** (Map p660; ☑91 330 24 00; www.tapasenestadopuro.com; Plaza de Cánovas del Castillo 4; tapas €5-12.50; ☺11am-1am Tue-Sat, to 4pm Sun; Ⓜ Banco de España, Atocha) with gourmet tapas inspired by Catalonia's world-famous (but now closed) El Bulli restaurant. In Salamanca, **Biotza** (Map p654; www.biotzarestaurante.com; Calle de Claudio Coello 27; tapas €2.50-3.50; ☺9am-midnight Mon-Thu, to 1am Fri & Sat; Ⓜ Serrano) offers creative Basque *pintxos* in stylish surrounds.

Chueca is another stellar tapas *barrio*. Don't miss **Bocaito** (Map p660; ☑91 532 12 19; www.bocaito.com; Calle de la Libertad 4-6; tapas from €3.50, mains €12-20; ☺lunch & dinner Mon-Fri, dinner Sat; Ⓜ Chueca, Sevilla), another purveyor of Andalucian *jamón* (ham) and seafood. **Casa Julio** (Map p660; ☑91 522 72 74; Calle de la Madera 37; 6/12 croquetas €5/10; ☺lunch & dinner Mon-Sat; Ⓜ Tribunal) is widely touted as the home of Madrid's best *croquetas* (croquettes). Another brilliant choice is **Baco y Beto** (Map p660; ☑91 522 84 81; Calle de Pelayo 24; tapas from €4; ☺dinner Mon-Fri, lunch & dinner Sat; Ⓜ Chueca).

Maceiras
GALICIAN €€

(Map p660; ☑91 429 15 84; Calle de las Huertas 66; mains €7-14; Ⓜ Antón Martín) Galician tapas (think octopus, green peppers etc) never tasted so good as in this agreeably rustic bar down the bottom of the Huertas hill, especially when washed down with a crisp white Ribeiro. The simple wooden tables, loyal customers and handy location make this a fine place to rest after (or en route to) the museums along the Paseo del Prado.

Lhardy
MADRILEÑO €€€

(Map p660; ☑91 521 33 85; www.lhardy.com; Carrera de San Jerónimo 8; mains €18.50-39; ☺lunch & dinner Mon-Sat, lunch Sun, closed Aug; Ⓜ Sol, Sevilla) This Madrid landmark (since 1839) is an elegant treasure-trove of takeaway gourmet tapas. Upstairs is the upscale preserve of house specialities. It's expensive, but the quality and service are unimpeachable.

La Finca de Susana
SPANISH €€

(Map p660; www.lafinca-restaurant.com; Calle de Arlabán 4; mains €7-12; Ⓜ Sevilla) It's difficult to find a better combination of price, quality cooking and classy atmosphere anywhere in the centre. The softly lit dining area is bathed in greenery and the sometimes innovative, sometimes traditional food draws a hip, young crowd. It doesn't take reservations.

MALASAÑA & CHUECA

Bazaar
CONTEMPORARY SPANISH €

(Map p660; www.restaurantbazaar.com; Calle de la Libertad 21; mains €6.50-10; ☺lunch & dinner; Ⓜ Chueca) Bazaar's popularity among the well-heeled and often-famous shows no sign of abating. Its pristine white interior design with theatre lighting may draw a crowd that looks like it stepped out of the pages of *Hola!* magazine, but the food is extremely well priced and innovative. It doesn't take reservations so be prepared to wait whether you're famous or not.

TOP CHOICE **Albur** TAPAS, SPANISH €€
(Map p654; ☎91 594 27 33; www.restaurantealbur.com; Calle de Manuela Malasaña 15; mains €13-18; ☺noon-1am Sun-Thu, to 2am Fri & Sat; MBilbao) One of Malasaña's best deals, this place has a wildly popular tapas bar and a classy but casual restaurant out the back. Albur is known for terrific rice dishes and tapas, and has a well-chosen wine list.

La Isla del Tesoro VEGETARIAN €€
(Map p654; ☎91 593 14 40; www.isladeltesoro.net; Calle de Manuela Malasaña 3; mains €12.50-14.50; ☺lunch & dinner; ☑; MBilbao) La Isla del Tesoro is loaded with quirky charm – the dining area is like someone's fantasy of a secret garden come to life. The cooking here is assured and wide-ranging in its influences and the menu is full of surprises.

SALAMANCA
La Colonial de Goya TAPAS €
(Map p654; www.restauranterincondegoya.es; Calle de Jorge Juan 34; tapas €3-4.50; ☺8am-midnight Mon-Fri, noon-1am Sat & Sun; MVelázquez) A mere 63 varieties of canapé should be sufficient for most, but La Colonial de Goya also serve a range of carpaccios, *croquetas* and main dishes at this engaging little tapas bar.

🍷 Drinking

The essence of Madrid lives in its streets and plazas, and bar-hopping is a pastime enjoyed by young and old alike. If you're after the more traditional, with tiled walls and flamenco tunes, head to Huertas. For gay-friendly drinking holes, Chueca is the place. Malasaña caters to a grungy, funky crowd, while La Latina has friendly bars that guarantee atmosphere most nights of the week. In summer, the terrace bars that pop up all over the city are unbeatable.

The bulk of Madrid bars open to 2am Sunday to Thursday, and to 3am or 3.30am Friday and Saturday.

LOS AUSTRIAS & CENTRO
TOP CHOICE **Museo Chicote** COCKTAIL BAR
(Map p660; www.museo-chicote.com; Gran Vía 12; ☺6pm-3am Mon-Thu, to 4am Fri & Sat; MGran Vía) The founder of this Madrid landmark is

---

ⓘ
MADRID'S FAVOURITE POST-CLUBBING MUNCHIES

Join the sugar-searching throngs who end the night at **Chocolatería de San Ginés** (Map p660; Pasadizo de San Ginés 5; ☺9.30am-7am; MSol), a legendary bar, famous for its freshly fried *churros* (fried sticks of dough) and syrupy hot chocolate.

---

said to have invented more than a hundred cocktails, which the likes of Hemingway, Ava Gardner, Grace Kelly, Sophia Loren and Frank Sinatra all enjoyed at one time or another. It's at its best after midnight when a lounge atmosphere takes over, couples cuddle on the curved benches and some of the city's best DJs do their stuff.

Café del Real BAR, CAFE
(Plaza de Isabel II 2; ☺9am-1am Mon-Thu, to 3am Fri & Sat; MÓpera) A cafe and cocktail bar in equal parts, this intimate little place serves up creative coffees and a few cocktails to the soundtrack of chill-out music. The best seats are upstairs, where the low ceilings, wooden beams and leather chairs are a great place to pass an afternoon with friends.

LA LATINA & LAVAPIÉS
Delic BAR, CAFE
(www.delic.es; Costanilla de San Andrés 14; ☺11am-2am Fri-Sun & Tue-Thu, 7pm-2am Mon; MLa Latina) We could go on for hours about this long-standing cafe-bar, but we'll reduce it to this most basic element: nursing an exceptionally good mojito (€8) or three on a warm summer's evening at Delic's outdoor tables on one of Madrid's prettiest plazas is one of life's great pleasures.

Taberna Tempranillo WINE BAR
(Calle de la Cava Baja 38; ☺1-3.30pm & 8pm-midnight Tue-Sun, 8pm-midnight Mon; MLa Latina) You could come here for the tapas, but we recommend Taberna Tempranillo primarily for its wines, of which it has a selection that puts many Spanish bars to shame, and many are sold by the glass.

Café del Nuncio BAR, CAFE
(Calle de Segovia 9; ☺noon-2am Sun-Thu, to 3am Fri & Sat; MLa Latina) Café del Nuncio straggles down a stairway passage to Calle de Segovia. You can drink on one of several cosy levels inside or, better still in summer, enjoy the

outdoor seating that one local reviewer likened to a slice of Rome.

HUERTAS & ATOCHA

The Roof
COCKTAIL BAR

(Map p660; www.memadrid.com/the-roof; Plaza de Santa Ana 14; admission €25; ⊗9pm-3am Wed & Thu, to 3.30am Fri & Sat; MAntón Martín, Sol) High above the Plaza de Santa Ana, this sybaritic open-air (7th floor) cocktail bar has terrific views over Madrid's rooftops. The high admission price announces straight away that riff-raff are not welcome and it's a place for sophisticates, with chill-out areas strewn with cushions, funky DJs and a dress policy designed to sort out the classy from the wannabes.

La Venencia
BAR

(Map p660; Calle de Echegaray 7; ⊗1-3.30pm & 7.30pm-1.30am; MSol, Sevilla) La Venencia is a *barrio* classic, with fine sherry from Sanlúcar and manzanilla from Jeréz poured straight from the dusty barrel, accompanied by a small selection of tapas with an Andalucian bent.

El Imperfecto
COCKTAIL BAR

(Map p660; Plaza de Matute 2; ⊗3pm-2am Mon-Thu, to 2.30am Fri & Sat; MAntón Martín) Its name notwithstanding, the 'Imperfect One' is our ideal Huertas bar, with live jazz most Tuesdays at 9pm and a drinks menu as long as a saxophone, ranging from cocktails (€7) and spirits to milkshakes, teas and creative coffees.

MALASAÑA & CHUECA

TOP CHOICE Café Comercial
CAFE

(Map p654; Glorieta de Bilbao 7; ⊗7.30am-midnight Mon-Thu, 7.30am-2am Fri, 8.30am-2am Sat, 9am-midnight Sun; MBilbao) This glorious old Madrid cafe proudly fights a rearguard action against progress with heavy leather seats, abundant marble and old-style waiters. As close as Madrid came to the intellectual cafes of Paris' Left Bank, Café Comercial now has a clientele that has broadened to include just about anyone.

Splash Óscar
LOUNGE BAR

(Map p660; Plaza de Vázquez de Mella 12; ⊗5pm-2am Mon-Thu, 4pm-3am Fri-Sun; MGran Vía) On of Madrid's stunning rooftop terraces (although this one has a small swimming pool), atop Hotel Óscar (p663), this chilled space with gorgeous skyline views has become a cause célèbre among A-list celebrities.

El Jardín Secreto
BAR, CAFE

(Map p654; Calle del Conde Duque 2; ⊗5.30pm-12.30am Sun-Thu, 6.30pm-2.30am Fri & Sat; MPlaza de España) 'The Secret Garden' is all about intimacy and romance in a *barrio* that's one of Madrid's best-kept secrets. Lit by Spanish designer candles, draped in organza from India and serving up chocolates from the Caribbean, it never misses a beat.

Café Belén
BAR

(Map p660; Calle de Belén 5; ⊗3.30pm-3am; MChueca) Café Belén is cool in all the right places – lounge and chill-out music, dim lighting, a great range of drinks (the mojitos are especially good) and a low-key crowd that's the height of casual sophistication.

Lolina Vintage Café
CAFE

(Map p660; www.lolinacafe.com; Calle del Espíritu Santo 9; ⊗9am-2.30am Mon-Fri, 10am-2.30am Sat, 11am-2.30am Sun; MTribunal) Lolina Vintage Café seems to have captured the essence of the *barrio* in one small space. With a studied retro look (comfy old-style chairs and sofas, gilded mirrors and 1970s-era wallpaper), it confirms that the new Malasaña is not unlike the old. It's low-key, full from the first breakfast to closing time and it caters to every taste with salads and cocktails.

☆ Entertainment

The **Guía del Ocio** (www.guiadelocio.com) is the city's classic weekly listings magazine. Also good are **Metropoli** (www.elmundo.es/metropoli) and **On Madrid** (www.elpais.com), respectively *ABC's* and *El País'* Friday listings supplements.

Nightclubs

No *barrio* is without a decent club or disco, but the most popular dance spots are in the centre. Don't expect dance clubs or *discotecas* (nightclubs) to get going until after 1am at the earliest. Standard entry fee is €12, which usually includes the first drink, although megaclubs and swankier places charge a few euros more.

Teatro Joy Eslava
CLUB

(Joy Madrid; Map p660; ☎91 366 37 33; www.joy-eslava.com; Calle del Arenal 11; ⊗11.30pm-6am; MSol) The only things guaranteed at this grand old Madrid dance club (housed in a 19th-century theatre) are a crowd and the fact that it will be open; the club claims to have opened every single day for the past 30 years. Every night's a little different. Loco Monday kicks off the week in spectacular

SPAIN MADRID

GAY & LESBIAN MADRID

The heartbeat of gay Madrid is the inner-city *barrio* of Chueca, where Madrid didn't just come out of the closet, but ripped the doors off in the process.

A good place to get the low-down is the laid-back **Mamá Inés** (Map p660; www.mamaines.com; Calle de Hortaleza 22; ⊙10am-2pm Sun-Thu, to 3am Fri & Sat; ⓂGran Vía, Chueca). **Café Acuarela** (Map p660; www.cafeacuarela.es; Calle de Gravina 10; ⊙11am-2am Sun-Thu, to 3am Fri & Sat; ⓂChueca) is another dimly lit centrepiece of gay Madrid.

Two of the most popular Chueca nightspots are **Club 54 Studio** (Map p660; www.studio54madrid.com; Calle de Barbieri 7; ⊙11.30am-3.30am Wed-Sat; ⓂChueca), modelled on the famous New York club Studio 54, and **Liquid Madrid** (Map p660; www.liquid.es; Calle de Barbieri 7; ⊙9pm-3am Mon-Thu, to 3.30am Fri & Sat; ⓂChueca). **Why Not?** (Map p660; www.whynotmadrid.com; Calle de San Bartolomé 7; admission €10; ⊙10.30pm-6am; ⓂChueca) is the sort of place where nothing's left to the imagination.

fashion, Thursday is student night and Friday's 'Fabulush' is all about glamour. Throw in occasional live acts and cabaret-style performances on stage and it's a point of reference for Madrid's professional party crowd.

Kapital   CLUB
(Map p660; ☎91 420 29 06; www.grupo-kapital.com; Calle de Atocha 125; ⊙5.30-10.30pm & midnight-6am Fri & Sat, midnight-6am Thu & Sun; ⓂAtocha) One of the most famous megaclubs in Madrid, this massive seven-storey nightclub has something for everyone: from cocktail bars and dance music to karaoke, salsa, hip hop and more chilled spaces for R&B and soul, as well as an area devoted to 'Made in Spain' music. It's such a big place that a cross-section of Madrid society (VIPs and the Real Madrid set love this place) all hang out here without ever getting in each other's way.

Stella   CLUB
(Map p660; ☎91 531 63 78; www.web-mondo.com; Calle de Arlabán 7; ⊙12.30am-6am Thu-Sat; ⓂSevilla) One of Madrid's enduring success stories, Stella is one of the city's best nightclubs. If you arrive here after 3am, there simply won't be room and those inside have no intention of leaving until dawn. The DJs here are some of Madrid's best and the great visuals will leave you cross-eyed – that's if you weren't already from the music in this heady place. Thursday and Saturday nights ('Mondo', for electronica) rely on resident and invited DJs, while Friday nights are more house-oriented.

Theatre

Teatro de la Zarzuela   THEATRE
(Map p660; ☎91 524 54 00; http://teatrodelazarzuela.mcu.es; Calle de Jovellanos 4; tickets €5-42; ⊙box office noon-6pm Mon-Fri, 3-6pm Sat & Sun; ⓂBanco de España, Sevilla) This theatre, built in 1856, is the premier place to see *zarzuela*, the uniquely Spanish combination of theatre and music. It also hosts a smattering of classical music and opera, as well as the cutting edge Compañía Nacional de Danza.

Teatro Real   OPERA
(☎902 24 48 48; www.teatro-real.com; Plaza de Oriente; ⓂÓpera) After spending €100 million-plus on a long rebuilding project, the Teatro Real is the city's grandest stage for elaborate operas, ballets and classical music. You'll pay as little as €6 for distant seats and as much as €125 for the best seats in the house.

Live Music
FLAMENCO

Corral de la Morería   FLAMENCO
(☎91 365 84 46; www.corraldelamoreria.com; Calle de la Morería 17; admission incl drink €42-45, meals from €43; ⊙8.30pm-2.30am, shows 9.30pm & 11.30pm Sun-Fri, 7pm, 10pm & midnight Sat; ⓂÓpera) This is one of the most prestigious flamenco stages in Madrid, with 50 years' experience as a leading flamenco venue and top performers most nights. The stage area has a rustic feel, and tables are pushed up close. We'd steer clear of the restaurant, which is overpriced, but the performances have a far better price-quality ratio.

Las Tablas   FLAMENCO
(Map p654; ☎91 542 05 20; www.lastablasmadrid.com; Plaza de España 9; admission €27; ⊙shows 10.30pm Sun-Thu, 8pm & 10pm Fri & Sat; ⓂPlaza de España) Las Tablas has a reputation for quality flamenco and reasonable prices; it could just be the best choice in town. Antonia

Moya and Marisol Navarro, leading lights in the flamenco world, are regular performers here.

Casa Patas FLAMENCO

(Map p660; ☑91 369 04 96; www.casapatas.com; Calle de Cañizares 10; admission €32; ☺shows 10.30pm Mon-Thu, 9pm & midnight Fri & Sat; ⓂAntón Martín, Tirso de Molina) One of the top flamenco stages in Madrid, this *tablao* (flamenco venue) always offers flawless quality that serves as a good introduction to the art. It's not the friendliest place in town, especially if you're only here for the show, and you're likely to be crammed in a little, but no one complains about the standard of the performances.

Villa Rosa FLAMENCO

(Map p660; ☑91 521 36 89; www.villa-rosa.es; Plaza de Santa Ana 15; admission €17; ☺shows 8.30pm & 10.45pm Sun-Thu, 8.30pm, 10.45pm & 12.15am Fri & Sat, 11pm-6am Mon-Sat; ⓂSol) The extraordinary tiled facade appeared in the Pedro Almodóvar film *Tacones Lejanos* (High Heels; 1991). It's been going strong since 1914 and has seen many manifestations – it has recently returned to its flamenco roots with well-priced shows and meals that won't break the bank.

JAZZ

TOP CHOICE Café Central JAZZ

(Map p660; ☑91 369 41 43; www.cafecentralmadrid .com; Plaza del Ángel 10; admission €10-15; ☺1.30pm-2.30am Sun-Thu, to 3.30am Fri & Sat; ⓂAntón Martín, Sol) In 2011, the respected jazz magazine *DownBeat* included this art-deco bar on the list of the world's best jazz clubs (said by some to be the jazz equivalent of earning a Michelin star) and with well over 9000 gigs under its belt, it rarely misses a beat. Performers usually play here for a week and then move on, so getting tickets shouldn't be a problem, except on weekends; shows start at 10pm and tickets go on sale an hour before the set starts.

FREE Populart JAZZ

(Map p660; ☑91 429 84 07; www.populart.es; Calle de las Huertas 22; ☺6pm-2.30am Sun-Thu, to 3.30am Fri & Sat; ⓂAntón Martín, Sol) One of Madrid's classic jazz clubs, this place offers a low-key atmosphere and top-quality music, which is mostly jazz with occasional blues, swing and even flamenco thrown into the mix. Shows start at 10.45pm but, if you want a seat, get here early.

OTHER LIVE MUSIC

TOP CHOICE Sala El Sol ROCK, SOUL

(Map p660; ☑91 532 64 90; www.elsolmad.com; Calle de los Jardines 3; admission €8-25; ☺11pm-5.30am Tue-Sat Jul-Sep; ⓂGran Vía) Sala El Sol opened in 1979, just in time for *la movida madrileña,* and quickly established itself as a leading stage for all the icons of the era. *La movida* may have faded into history, but it lives on at El Sol, where the music rocks and rolls and usually resurrects the '70s and '80s, while soul and funk also get a run. It's a terrific venue and although most concerts start at 11pm and despite the official opening hours, some acts take to the stage as early as 10pm. After the show, DJs spin rock, fusion and electronica from the awesome sound system.

Costello Café & Niteclub POP, ROCK

(Map p660; www.costelloclub.com; Calle del Caballero de Gracia 10; admission €5-10; ☺6pm-1am Sun-Wed, to 2.30am Thu-Sat; ⓂGran Vía) Costello Café & Niteclub is smooth-as-silk ambience wedded to an innovative mix of pop, rock and fusion in Warholesque surrounds. There's live music at 9.30pm every night of the week except Sundays, with resident and visiting DJs keeping you on your feet until closing time from Thursday to Saturday.

Café La Palma ROCK

(Map p654; ☑91 522 50 31; www.cafelapalma.com; Calle de la Palma 62; admission free-€12; ☺4.30pm-3am; ⓂNoviciado) It's amazing how much variety Café La Palma has packed into its labyrinth of rooms. Live shows featuring hot local bands are held at the back, while DJs mix it up at the front. You might find live music other nights as well, but there are always two shows at 10pm and midnight from Thursday to Saturday.

Clamores LIVE MUSIC

(Map p654; ☑91 445 79 38; www.clamores.es; Calle de Alburquerque 14; admission €5-15; ☺6pm-3am; ⓂBilbao) Clamores is one of the most diverse live music stages in Madrid. Jazz is a staple, but world music, flamenco, soul fusion, singer-songwriter, pop and rock all make regular appearances. Live shows can begin as early as 7pm on weekends but sometimes really only get going after 1am!

FREE Honky Tonk ROCK

(Map p654; ☑91 445 61 91; www.clubhonky.com; Calle de Covarrubias 24; ☺9pm-5am; ⓂAlonso Martínez) Despite the name, this is a great place to see blues or local rock 'n' roll, though many acts have a little country, jazz or R&B thrown into the mix too. It's a fun vibe in a smallish club that's been around since the heady 1980s and opens 365 days a year.

Sport

Estadio Santiago Bernabéu FOOTBALL
(☎902 301709, 91 398 43 00; www.realmadrid. com; Calle Concha Espina 1; ☺10am-7.30pm Mon-Sat, 10.30am-6.30pm Sun, except match days; ⓜSantiago Bernabéu) El Estadio Santiago Bernabéu is one of the world's great football arenas; watching a game here is akin to a pilgrimage for sports fans and doing so alongside 80,000 passionate *Madridistas* (Real Madrid supporters) in attendance will send chills down your spine. Those who can't come to a game can at least stop by for a **tour** (adult/child €19/13), a peek at the trophies or to buy some Real Madrid memorabilia in the **club shop** (Gate 57, Estadio Santiago Bernabéu, ☺10am-8.30pm). There is another **shop** (Tienda Real Madrid; Map p660; ☎91 521 79 50; Calle del Carmen 3; ☺10am-8.45pm Mon-Sat, 10am-6.45pm Sun; ⓜSol) in the centre of town.

The Spanish football season runs from September (or the last weekend in August) until May, with a two-week break just before Christmas until early in the New Year. Tickets for football matches in Madrid start at around €40 and run up to the rafters for major matches; you pay in inverse proportion to your distance from the pitch.

To buy tickets, turn up at the Estadio Santiago Bernabéu ticket office at Gate 42 on Calle de Conche de Espina early in the week before a scheduled game (eg Monday morning for a Sunday game). The all-important telephone number for booking tickets (which you later pick up at Gate 42) is ☎902 324 324, which only works if you're calling from within Spain. Tickets can also be bought on the website – click on 'Entradas'.

🔒 Shopping

The key to shopping Madrid-style is knowing where to look. Salamanca is the home of upmarket fashions, with chic boutiques lining up to showcase the best that Spanish and international designers have to offer. Some of it spills over into Chueca, but Malasaña is Salamanca's true alter ego, home to fashion that's as funky as it is offbeat and ideal for that studied underground look that will fit right in with Madrid's hedonistic after-dark crowd. Central Madrid – Sol, Huertas or La Latina – offers plenty of individual surprises.

During *las rebajas*, the annual winter and summer sales, prices are slashed on just about everything. The winter sales begin around 7 January and last well into February. Summer sales begin in early July and last into August.

Shops may (and many do) open on the first Sunday of every month and throughout December.

TOP CHOICE **El Rastro** MARKET
(Map p660; Calle de la Ribera de Curtidores; ☺8am-3pm Sun; ⓜLa Latina, Puerta de Toledo, Tirso de Molina) A Sunday morning at El Rastro, Europe's largest flea market, is a Madrid institution. You could easily spend an entire morning inching your way down the Calle de la Ribera de Curtidores and through the maze of streets that hosts El Rastro every Sunday morning. For every 10 pieces of junk, there's a real gem (a lost masterpiece, an Underwood typewriter) waiting to be found. A word of warning: pickpockets love El Rastro as much as everyone else.

Antigua Casa Talavera CERAMICS
(Calle de Isabel la Católica 2; ☺10am-1.30pm & 5-8pm Mon-Fri, 10am-1.30pm Sat; ⓜSanto Domingo) The extraordinary tiled facade of this wonderful old shop conceals an Aladdin's cave of ceramics from all over Spain. This is not the mass-produced stuff aimed at a tourist market, but comes from the small family potters of Andalucía and Toledo.

El Arco Artesanía HANDICRAFTS
(Map p660; www.artesaniaelarco.com; Plaza Mayor 9; ☺11am-9pm; ⓜSol, La Latina) This original shop in the southwestern corner of Plaza Mayor sells an outstanding array of homemade designer souvenirs, from stone and glass work to jewellery and home fittings. The papier mâché figures are gorgeous, but there's so much else here to turn your head.

El Flamenco Vive FLAMENCO
(www.elflamencovive.es; Calle Conde de Lemos 7; ☺10.30am-2pm & 5-9pm Mon-Sat; ⓜÓpera) This temple to flamenco has it all, from guitars and songbooks to well-priced CDs, polkadotted dancing costumes, shoes, colourful plastic jewellery and literature about flamenco. It's the sort of place that will appeal as much to curious first-timers as to serious students of the art.

Casa de Diego ACCESSORIES
(Map p660; www.casadediego.com; Plaza de la Puerta del Sol 12; ☺9.30am-8pm Mon-Sat; ⓜSol)

This classic shop has been around since 1858, making, selling and repairing Spanish fans, shawls, umbrellas and canes. Service is old style and occasionally grumpy, but the fans are works of antique art. It has another shop and workshop (Map p660; 91 531 02 23; www.casadediego.com; Calle del los Mesoneros Romanos 4; ⊗9.30am-1.30pm & 4.45-8pm Mon-Sat; MCallao, Sol) nearby.

Agatha Ruiz de la Prada   FASHION

(Map p654; www.agatharuizdelaprada.com; Calle de Serrano 27; ⊗10am-8.30pm Mon-Sat; MSerrano) This boutique has to be seen to be believed, with pinks, yellows and oranges everywhere you turn. It's fun and exuberant, but not just for kids. It also has serious and highly original fashion; Agatha Ruiz de la Prada is one of the enduring icons of Madrid's 1980s outpouring of creativity known as *la movida madrileña*.

Mercado de Fuencarral   CLOTHING

(Map p660; www.mdf.es; Calle de Fuencarral 45; ⊗11am-9pm Mon-Sat; MTribunal) Madrid's home of alternative club cool is still going strong, revelling in its reverse snobbery. With shops like Fuck, Ugly Shop and Black Kiss, it's funky, grungy and filled to the rafters with torn T-shirts and more black leather and silver studs than you'll ever need.

ⓘ Information

Dangers & Annoyances

Madrid is a generally safe city, although, as in most European cities, you should be wary of pickpockets in the city centre, on the metro and around major tourist sights.

Prostitution along Calle de la Montera means that you need to exercise extra caution along this street.

Discount Cards

The **Madrid Card** (⏹91 360 47 72; www.madridcard.com; 1-/2-/3-days adult €39/49/59, child age 6-12 €20/28/34) includes free entry to more than 40 museums in and around Madrid and discounts on public transport.

Emergency

Emergency (⏹112)

Policía Nacional (⏹091)

Servicio de Atención al Turista Extranjero (Foreign Tourist Assistance Service; ⏹902 102112, 91 548 85 37, 91 548 80 08; www.esmadrid.com/satemadrid; Calle de Leganitos 19; ⊗9am-10pm; MPlaza de España, Santo Domingo) To report thefts or other crime-related matters, cancel your credit cards, contact your embassy and other related matters, this is your best bet.

Internet Access

Café Comercial (Glorieta de Bilbao 7; per 50min €1; ⊗7.30am-midnight Mon-Thu, 7.30am-2am Fri, 8.30am-2am Sat, 9am-midnight Sun; MBilbao) One of Madrid's grandest old cafes, with internet upstairs.

Centro de Turismo de Madrid (www.esmadrid.com) Free 15-minute internet access, with more generous time limits (depending on demand) at the other tourist office underneath Plaza de Colón.

Left Luggage

At Madrid's Barajas airport, there are three *consignas* (left-luggage offices; ⊗24hr). In either, you pay €4.95 for the first 24-hour period (or fraction thereof). Thereafter, it costs €4.33/5.56 per day per small/large bag. Similar services operate for similar prices at Atocha and Chamartín train stations (⊗7am to 11pm).

Medical Services

Unidad Medica (Anglo American; ⏹91 435 18 23; www.unidadmedica.com; Calle del Conde de Aranda 1; ⊗9am-8pm Mon-Fri, 10am-1pm Sat; MRetiro) A private clinic with a wide range of specialisations and where all doctors speak Spanish and English, with some also speaking French and German. Each consultation costs around €125.

Farmacia Mayor (⏹91 366 46 16; Calle Mayor 13; ⊗24hr; MSol)

Post

Main Post Office (Map p660; www.correos.es; Plaza de la Cibeles; ⊗8.30am-9.30pm Mon-Fri, to 2pm Sat; MBanco de España)

Tourist Information

Centro de Turismo de Madrid (Map p660; ⏹91 588 16 36; www.esmadrid.com; Plaza Mayor 27; ⊗9.30am-8.30pm; MSol) Excellent city tourist office with a smaller office underneath Plaza de Colón and information points at Plaza de la Cibeles, Plaza de Callao, outside the Centro de Arte Reina Sofía and at the T4 terminal at Barajas airport.

Comunidad de Madrid (www.turismomadrid.es) The regional Madrid government maintains this useful site for the entire Madrid region.

ⓘ Getting There & Away

Air

Madrid's international Barajas airport (MAD), 15km northeast of the city, is Europe's fourth- or fifth-busiest airport (depending on the year), with flights coming in from all over Europe and beyond.

Bus

Estación Sur de Autobuses (⏹91 468 42 00; www.estaciondeautobuses.com; Calle de

Méndez Álvaro 83; Méndez Álvaro) just south of the M-30 ring road, is the city's principal bus station. It serves most destinations to the south and many in other parts of the country. Major bus companies:

ALSA (☎902 422242; www.alsa.es) One of the largest Spanish companies with many services throughout Spain. Most depart from Estación Sur but some buses headed north (including to Bilbao and Zaragoza, and some services to Barcelona) leave from the Intercambiador de Avenida de América with occasional services from T4 of Madrid's Barajas airport.

Avanzabus (☎902 020052; www.avanzabus. com) Services to Extremadura (eg Cáceres), Castilla y León (eg Salamanca and Zamora) and Valencia via Cuenca, as well as Lisbon, Portugal. All leave from the Estación Sur.

Car & Motorcycle

The city is surrounded by two main ring roads, the outermost M-40 and the inner M-30; there are also two additional partial ring roads, the M-45 and the more-distant M-50.

Train

Madrid is served by two main train stations. The bigger of the two is **Puerta de Atocha** (Atocha Renfe), at the southern end of the city centre. **Chamartín train station** (Chamartín) lies in the north of the city. The bulk of trains for Spanish destinations depart from Atocha, especially those going south. International services arrive at and leave from Chamartín. For bookings, contact **Renfe** (☎902 240202; www.renfe.es) at either station.

High-speed Tren de Alta Velocidad Española (AVE) services connect Madrid with Seville (via Córdoba), Valladolid (via Segovia), Toledo, Valencia, Málaga and Barcelona (via Zaragoza and Tarragona).

❶ Getting Around

To/From the Airport

BUS The **Exprés Aeropuerto** (Airport Express; www.emtmadrid.es; €5; ☺24hr; 📞) bus runs between Puerta de Atocha train station and the airport. Buses run every 13 to 23 minutes from 6am to 11.30pm, and every 35 minutes throughout the rest of the night. The trip takes 40 minutes. From 11.55pm until 5.35am, departures are from the Plaza de Cibeles, not the train station.

The excellent, privately run **AeroCITY** (☎91 747 75 70; www.aerocity.com; per person from €20, express service from €35 per minibus) operates a door-to-door service from the airport. **METRO** Line 8 of the metro (entrances in T2 and T4) runs to the Nuevos Ministerios transport interchange, which connects with lines 10 and 6. It operates from 6.05am to 2am. A one-way

WANT MORE?

For in-depth information, reviews and recommendations at your fingertips, head to the Apple App Store to purchase Lonely Planet's *Madrid City Guide* iPhone app.

Alternatively, head to **Lonely Planet** (www.lonelyplanet.com/madrid) for planning advice, author recommendations, traveller reviews and insider tips.

ticket to/from the airport costs €4.50. The journey from the airport to Nuevos Ministerios takes around 15 minutes, around 25 minutes from T4.

TAXI A taxi to the city centre will cost you around €25 in total (up to €35 from T4), depending on traffic and where you're going; in addition to what the meter reads, you pay a €5.50 airport supplement.

Public Transport

METRO Madrid's **metro** (www.metromadrid.es) is extensive and well maintained. A single ride costs €1.50 and a 10-ride ticket is €12.20. The metro is quick, clean, relatively safe and runs from 6.05am until 2am.

BUS The bus system is also good; contact **EMT** (www.emtmadrid.es) for more information. Twenty-six night-bus *búhos* (owls) operate from midnight to 6am, with all routes originating in Plaza de la Cibeles.

Taxi

You can pick up a taxi at ranks throughout town or simply flag one down. Flag fall is €2.15 from 6am to 10pm daily, €2.20 from 10pm to 6am Sunday to Friday and €3.10 from 10pm Saturday to 6am Sunday. Several supplementary charges, usually posted inside the taxi, apply; these include €5.50 to/from the airport and €2.95 from taxi ranks at train and bus stations.

Radio-Teléfono Taxi (☎91 547 82 00; www. radiotelefono-taxi.com)

Tele-Taxi (☎91 371 21 31; www.tele-taxi.es)

Around Madrid

The Comunidad de Madrid, the province surrounding the capital, has some of Spain's finest royal palaces and gardens that make for easy day trips from the city.

Places worth exploring include the royal palace complex at **San Lorenzo de El Escorial** (☎91 890 78 18; www.patrimonionacional.es; adult/concession €10/5, guide/audioguide €7/4, EU citizens free 5-8pm Wed & Thu; ☺10am-8pm Apr-

Sep, 10am-6pm Oct-Mar, closed Mon) Check also at www.sanlorenzoturismo.org.

Other worthwhile excursions include **Aranjuez** (www.aranjuez.es) and its **royal palace** (www.patrimonionacional.es; adult/child €5/2.50, EU citizens free Wed; ⊙palace 10am-6.15pm Tue-Sun, gardens 8am-8.30pm); the traditional village of **Chinchón** (www.ciudad-chinchon.com); and the university town (and birthplace of Miguel de Cervantes), **Alcalá de Henares** (www.turismoalcala.com). All of these places can be reached on the suburban rail network.

CASTILLA Y LEÓN

Spain's Castilian heartland, Castilla y León is scattered with hilltop towns sporting magnificent Gothic cathedrals, monumental city walls and mouth-watering restaurants.

Ávila

POP 59,010

Ávila's old city, surrounded by imposing city walls comprising eight monumental gates, 88 watchtowers and more than 2500 turrets, is one of the best-preserved medieval bastions in all of Spain. It's a perfect place to spend a day strolling narrow laneways and soaking up history. The city is known as the birthplace of Santa Teresa, a mystical writer and reformer of the Carmelite order.

◉ Sights

Murallas   WALLS
(adult/child €4/2.50; ⊙10am-8pm Tue-Sun) Ávila's splendid 12th-century walls rank among the world's best-preserved medieval defensive perimeters. Raised to a height of 12m between the 11th and 12th centuries, the walls stretch for 2.5km atop the remains of earlier Roman and Muslim battlements.

Two sections of the walls can be climbed – a 300m stretch that can be accessed from just inside the **Puerta del Alcázar**, and a longer 1300m stretch that runs the length of the old town's northern perimeter, in the process connecting the two access points at **Puerta de los Leales** and **Puerta del Puente Adaja**. The regional tourist office runs free guided tours.

Cathedral   CHURCH
(Plaza de la Catedral; admission €4; ⊙10am-7pm Mon-Fri, to 8pm Sat, noon-6pm Sun) Embedded into the eastern city walls, this splendid

12th-century cathedral was the first Gothic-style church built in Spain. It boasts rich walnut choir stalls and a long, narrow central nave that makes the soaring ceilings seem all the more majestic.

FREE **Convento de Santa Teresa**   MUSEUM
(Plaza de la Santa; ⊙8.45am-1.30pm & 3.30-9pm Tue-Sun) Built in 1636 over the saint's birthplace, this is the epicentre of the cult surrounding Teresa. In addition to the gilded main chapel, it's home to relics, including a piece of the saint's ring finger, as well as a small museum about her life.

🛌 Sleeping

TOP CHOICE **Hotel El Rastro**   HISTORIC HOTEL €
(☎920 35 22 25; www.elrastroavila.com; Calle Cepedas; s/d €35/55; ❀⊛) This superb choice occupies a former 16th-century palace with original natural stone, exposed brickwork and a warm colour scheme of earth tones exuding a calming understated elegance.

Hotel Las Leyendas   HISTORIC HOTEL €€
(☎920 35 20 42; www.lasleyendas.es; Calle de Francisco Gallego 3; s/d €56/79; ❀⊛) Occupying the house of 16th-century Ávila nobility, this intimate hotel overflows with period touches wedded to modern amenities. Some rooms have original wooden beams, exposed brick and stonework, others are more modern with muted tones.

Hostal Arco San Vicente   HOSTAL €€
(☎920 22 24 98; www.arcosanvicente.com; Calle de López Núñez 6; s/d €40/65; ❀⊛) This gleaming *hostal* has small, blue-carpeted rooms with pale paintwork and wrought-iron bed heads. Rooms on the 2nd floor have attic windows and air-con, some on the 1st floor look out at the Puerta de San Vicente.

✗ Eating & Drinking

Ávila is famous for its *chuleton de Ávila* (T-bone steak) and *judías del barco de Ávila* (white beans, often with chorizo, in a thick sauce).

TOP CHOICE **Hostería Las Cancelas**   CASTILIAN €€
(☎920 21 22 49; www.lascancelas.com; Calle de la Cruz Vieja 6; mains €16-25; ⊙Feb-Dec) This courtyard restaurant occupies a delightful interior patio dating back to the 15th century. Renowned for being a mainstay of Ávila cuisine, its traditional meals are prepared

with a salutary attention to detail. Reservations recommended.

Restaurante Reyes Católicos   CASTILIAN €€
(www.restaurante-reyescatolicos.com; Calle de los Reyes Católicos 6; mains €16-24, menú del día €16) Fronted by a popular tapas bar, this place has bright decor and an accomplished kitchen that churns out traditional dishes that benefit from a creative tweak. Its set menus include the *menú degustacion cocina tradicional de Ávila* (tasting menu of traditional Ávila cooking; €12).

TOP CHOICE La Bodeguita de San Segundo   WINE BAR
(www.vinoavila.com; Calle de San Segundo 19; ⊙11am-midnight Thu-Tue) Situated in the 16th-century Casa de la Misericordia, this superb wine bar is standing-room only most nights and more tranquil in the quieter afternoon hours. There's over 1000 wines to choose from, with tapas-sized servings of cheeses and cured meats the perfect accompaniment.

ⓘ Information

Centro de Recepción de Visitantes (☑920 35 40 00, ext 790; www.avilaturismo.com; Avenida de Madrid 39; ⊙9am-8pm) Municipal tourist office.

Regional Tourist Office (☑920 21 13 87; www.turismocastillayleon.com; Casa de las Carnicerías, Calle de San Segundo 17; ⊙9am-8pm)

ⓘ Getting There & Away

BUS From Ávila's bus station, there are frequent services to Segovia (€5, one hour) and Salamanca (€6.08, 1½ hours).

TRAIN More than 30 trains run daily to Madrid (from €6.80, 1¼ to two hours) and to Salamanca (€8.55, one to 1½ hours, nine daily).

Salamanca

POP 153,470

Whether floodlit by night or bathed in the midday sun, Salamanca is a dream destination. This is a city of rare architectural splendour, awash with golden sandstone overlaid with Latin inscriptions in ochre, and with an extraordinary virtuosity of plateresque and Renaissance styles. The monumental highlights are many but this is also Castilla's liveliest city, home to a massive Spanish and international student population who throng the streets at

DON'T MISS

CASTILLA Y LEÓN'S BEST CASTLES

While Segovia's Disneyesque Alcázar may get all the attention, lonely hilltop castles are something of a regional specialty. Our favourites include the following:

Pedraza de la Sierra (Pedraza de la Sierra; admission €5; ⊙11am-2pm & 5-8pm Wed-Sun) Has an unusually intact outer wall; northeast of Segovia.

Coca (guided tours €2.50; ⊙tours 10am-1.30pm & 4.30-7pm Mon-Fri, 11am-1pm & 4-7pm Sat & Sun) An all-brick, virtuouso piece of Gothic-Mudéjar architecture 50km northwest of Segovia.

Ponferrada (adult/concession €4/2; ⊙10am-2pm & 4.30-8.30pm Tue-Sun) A fortress-monastery built by the Knights Templar in the 13th century, west of León.

Peñafiel (Museo Provincial del Vino; Peñafiel; admission castle €3, incl museum €6, audioguides €2; ⊙11am-2.30pm & 4.30-8.30pm Tue-Sun) One of the longest castles in Spain and now a wine museum.

night and provide the city with youth and vitality.

⊙ Sights & Activities

Plaza Mayor   SQUARE
Built between 1729 and 1755, Salamanca's exceptional grand square is widely considered to be Spain's most beautiful central plaza. The square is particularly memorable at night when illuminated (until midnight) to magical effect.

Catedral Nueva & Catedral Vieja   CHURCHES
(www.catedralsalamanca.org) Curiously, Salamanca is home to two cathedrals: the newer and larger cathedral was built beside the old Romanesque one instead of on top of it, as was the norm. The **Catedral Nueva** (Plaza de Anaya; ⊙9am-8pm), completed in 1733, is a late-Gothic masterpiece that took 220 years to build. Its magnificent Renaissance doorways stand out. For fine views over Salamanca, head to the southwestern corner of the cathedral facade and the **Puerta de la**

FIND THE FROG

The Universidad Civil's facade is an ornate mass of sculptures and carvings, and hidden among this 16th-century plateresque creation is a tiny stone frog. Legend says that those who find the frog will have good luck in studies, life and love. If you don't want any help, look away now... It's sitting on a skull on the pillar that runs up the right-hand side of the facade.

Torre (Jeronimus; Plaza de Juan XXIII; admission €3.75; ⊙10am-7.15pm), from where stairs lead up through the tower.

The largely Romanesque **Catedral Vieja** (Plaza de Anaya; admission €4.75; ⊙10am-7.30pm) is a 12th-century temple with a stunning 15th-century altarpiece, which has 53 panels depicting scenes from the life of Christ and Mary, topped by a representation of the Final Judgement. The entrance is inside the Catedral Nueva.

Universidad Civil　　　HISTORIC BUILDING
(Calle de los Libreros; adult/child €4/2, Mon morning free; ⊙9.30am-1.30pm & 4-6.30pm Mon-Fri, 10am-1.30pm Sun) Founded initially as the Estudio Generál in 1218, Salamanca's university came into being in 1254 and reached the peak of its renown in the 15th and 16th centuries. Its facade is a tapestry in sandstone, bursting with images of mythical heroes, religious scenes and coats of arms. You can visit the old classrooms and the oldest university library in Europe. The latter is reached via the **Escalera de la Universidad** (University Staircase), which has symbols carved into the balustrade – to decode them was seen as symbolic of the quest for knowledge.

FREE Casa de
las Conchas　　　HISTORICAL BUILDING
(Calle de la Compañia 2; ⊙9am-9pm Mon-Fri, 10am-2pm & 4-7pm Sat & Sun) This glorious building has been a city symbol since it was built in the 15th century.

Convento de San Esteban　　　CONVENT
(Plaza del Concilio de Trento; adult/concession €3/2; ⊙10am-1.30pm & 4-7.30pm) The church here has an extraordinary altar-like facade,

with the stoning of San Esteban (St Stephen) as its central motif.

🛌 Sleeping

TOP CHOICE Microtel
Placentinos　　　BOUTIQUE HOTEL €€
(☎923 28 15 31; www.microtelplacentinos.com; Calle de Placentinos 9; s/d incl breakfast Sun-Thu €56/72, Fri & Sat €86/99; ❋🐾) One of Salamanca's most charming boutique hotels, Microtel Placentinos is tucked away on a quiet street and has rooms with exposed stone walls and wooden beams. The service is faultless, and the overall atmosphere is one of intimacy and discretion.

Aparthotel El Toboso　　　APARTMENT €
(☎923 21 14 62; www.hoteltoboso.com; Calle del Clavel 7; s/d €30/45, 3-/4-/5-person apt €75/85/95; ❋🐾) These rooms have a homey spare-room feel and are super value, especially the enormous apartments, which come with kitchens (including washing machines) and renovated bathrooms. It's ideal for families.

Hostal Concejo　　　HOSTAL €
(☎923 21 47 37; www.hconcejo.com; Plaza de la Libertad 1; s/d €45/60; 🅿❋🐾) A cut above the average *hostal,* the stylish Concejo has polished-wood floors, tasteful furnishings, light-filled rooms and a superb central location. Try and snag one of the corner rooms (like number 104) with its traditional glassed-in balcony.

Hostal Catedral　　　HOSTAL €
(☎923 27 06 14; www.hostalcatedralsalamanca.com; Rúa Mayor 46; s/d €30/48; ❋🐾) Just across from the cathedrals, this pleasing *hostal* with an attentive, motherly owner, has just six extremely pretty, impeccable, bright bedrooms with showers. All look out onto the street or cathedral, which is a real bonus.

🍴 Eating & Drinking

TOP CHOICE La Cocina de Toño　　　TAPAS €€
(www.lacocinadetoño.es; Calle Gran Via 20; menú del día €17, tapas €1.30-3.80, mains €6.90-23; ⊙lunch & dinner Tue-Sat, lunch Sun) We're yet to hear a bad word about this place and its loyal following owes everything to its creative *pinchos* (tapas) and half-servings of exotic dishes. The restaurant serves more traditional fare as befits the decor, but the bar is one of Salamanca's gastronomic stars.

Mesón Las Conchas
CASTILIAN €€

(Rúa Mayor 16; menú del día €12, mains €10-21; ⊙noon-midnight) Enjoy a choice of outdoor tables (in summer), an atmospheric bar or the upstairs, wood-beamed dining area. The bar caters mainly to locals who know their *embutidos* (cured meats). For sit-down meals, there's a good mix of roasts, *platos combinados* and *raciones*.

Mesón Cervantes
CASTILIAN €€

(www.mesoncervantes.com; Plaza Mayor 15; menú del día €13.50, mains €10-22; ⊙10am-midnight) Although there are outdoor tables on the plaza, the dark wooden beams and atmospheric buzz of the Spanish crowd on the 1st floor should be experienced at least once; if you snaffle a window table in the evening, you've hit the jackpot. The food's a mix of *platos combinados*, salads and *raciones*.

El Pecado
MODERN SPANISH €€

(☑923 26 65 58; www.elpecadorestaurante.es; Plaza de Poeta Iglesias 12; menú del día €15, mains €15-33) A trendy place that regularly attracts Spanish celebrities (eg Pedro Almodóvar and Ferran Adrià), El Pecado (The Sin) has an intimate dining room and a quirky, creative menu; it's a reasonably priced place to sample high-quality, innovative Spanish cooking.

[TOP CHOICE] Tío Vivo
MUSIC BAR

(www.tiovivosalamanca.com; Calle del Clavel 3-5; ⊙4pm-late) Sip drinks by flickering candlelight to a background of '80s music, enjoying the whimsical decor of carousel horses and oddball antiquities. There is live music Tuesdays to Thursdays from midnight, sometimes with a €5 cover charge.

ⓘ Information

Municipal Tourist Office (☑923 21 83 42; www.turismodesalamanca.com; Plaza Mayor 14; ⊙9am-2pm & 4.30-8pm Mon-Fri, 10am-8pm Sat, 10am-2pm Sun)

Regional Tourist Office (☑923 26 85 71; www.turismocastillayleon.com; Casa de las Conchas, Rúa Mayor; ⊙9am-8pm)

ⓘ Getting There & Away

BUS Services depart from the **bus station** (Avenida de Filiberto Villalobos 71-85) to Madrid (regular/express €12.88/20.30, three/2½ hours, hourly), Ávila (€6.08, 1½ hours, one to four daily) and Segovia (€11.08, 2¾ hours, two daily).

TRAIN Up to eight trains depart daily for Madrid's Chamartín station (€19.85, 2½ hours) via Ávila (€10.05, one hour). The train station is about 1km beyond Plaza de España.

Segovia

POP 55,220

Unesco World Heritage–listed Segovia has a stunning monument to Roman grandeur and a castle said to have inspired Walt Disney, and is otherwise a city of warm terracotta and sandstone hues set amid the rolling hills of Castilla.

⊙ Sights

Acueducto
ROMAN AQUEDUCT

El Acueducto, an 894m-long engineering wonder that looks like an enormous comb of stone blocks plunged into the lower end of old Segovia, is the obvious starting point of a tour of town. This Roman aqueduct is 28m high and was built without a drop of mortar – just good old Roman know-how.

Alcázar
CASTLE

(www.alcazardesegovia.com; Plaza de la Reina Victoria Eugenia; adult/child €4/3, tower €2, EU citizens free 3rd Tue of month; ⊙10am-7pm Apr-Sep) The fortified and fairy-tale Alcázar is perched dramatically on the edge of Segovia. Roman foundations are buried somewhere underneath the splendour, but what we see today is a 13th-century structure that burned down in 1862 and was subsequently rebuilt. Inside is a collection of armour and military gear, but even better are the ornate interiors of the reception rooms and the 360-degree views from the Torre de Juan II. Walt Disney reportedly used the Alcázar as inspiration for Sleeping Beauty's castle.

Catedral
CHURCH

(Plaza Mayor; adult/child €3/2, free 9.30am-1.15pm Sun; ⊙9.30am-6.30pm) In the heart of town, the resplendent late-Gothic Catedral was started in 1525 and completed a mere 200 years later. The Cristo del Consuelo chapel houses a magnificent Romanesque doorway preserved from the original church that burned down.

Iglesia de Vera Cruz
CHURCH

(Carretera de Zamarramala; admission €1.75; ⊙10.30am-1.30pm & 4-7pm Tue-Sun, closed Nov) The most interesting of Segovia's numerous churches, and one of the best preserved of its kind in Europe, is the 12-sided Iglesia de la Vera Cruz. Built in the 13th century by the

Knights Templar and based on the Church of the Holy Sepulchre in Jerusalem, it long housed what was said to be a piece of the Vera Cruz (True Cross).

🛏 Sleeping

TOP CHOICE Hospedería La Gran Casa Mudéjar
HISTORIC HOTEL €€

(📞921 46 62 50; www.lacasamudejar.com; Calle de Isabel la Católica 8; r €90; ❄@🖙) Spread over two buildings, this place has been magnificently renovated, blending genuine, 15th-century carved wooden ceilings in some rooms with modern amenities. In the newer wing, where the building dates from the 19th century, the rooms on the top floors have fine mountain views.

Hotel Alcázar
BOUTIQUE HOTEL €€€

(📞921 43 85 68; www.alcazar-hotel.com; Calle de San Marcos 5; s/d incl breakfast €135/163; ❄🖙) Sitting by the riverbank in the valley beneath the Alcázar, this charming, tranquil little hotel has lavish rooms beautifully styled to suit those who love old-world luxury. Breakfast on the back terrace is a lovely way to pass the morning, and there's an intimacy and graciousness about the whole experience.

Hostal Fornos
HOSTAL €

(📞921 46 01 98; www.hostalfornos.com; Calle de la Infanta Isabel 13; s/d €41/55; ❄) This tidy little *hostal* is a cut above most other places in this price category. It has a lovely, cheerful air and rooms with a fresh white-linen-and-wicker-chair look. Some rooms are larger than others, but the value is unbeatable.

Natura – La Hostería
HOTEL €

(📞921 46 67 10; www.naturadesegovia.com; Calle de Colón 5-7; r €60; ❄🖙) An eclectic choice a few streets back from Plaza Mayor. The owner obviously has a penchant for Dalí prints and the rooms have plenty of character, with chunky wooden furnishings and bright paintwork.

✗ Eating

Just about every restaurant proudly boasts its *horno de asar* (roasts) and the main speciality is *cochinillo asado* (roast suckling pig). Reservations are always recommended.

TOP CHOICE Restaurante El Fogón Sefardí
SEPHARDIC €€€

(📞921 46 62 50; www.lacasamudejar.com; Calle de Isabel la Católica 8; meals €30-40) Located within the Hospedería La Gran Casa Mudé-

jar, this is one of the most original places in town. Sephardic cuisine is served in either the intimate patio or splendid dining hall with original, 15th-century flourishes. The theme in the bar is equally diverse with dishes from all the continents.

TOP CHOICE Casa Duque
GRILL €€€

(📞921 46 24 87; www.restauranteduque.es; Calle de Cervantes 12; meals €25-35, menús del día €21-40) Casa Duque has been serving *cochinillo asado* here since the 1890s. For the uninitiated, try the *menú segoviano* (€30), which includes *cochinillo*, or the *menú gastronómico* (€43.50). Downstairs is the informal *cueva* (cave), where you can get tapas and full-bodied *cazuelas* (stews).

Mesón de Cándido
GRILL €€

(📞921 42 81 03; www.mesondecandido.es; Plaza del Azoguejo 5; meals €30-40) Set in a delightful 18th-century building in the shadow of the aqueduct, Mesón de Cándido is another place famous throughout Spain for its suckling pig and the more unusual roast boar with apple.

❶ Information

Centro de Recepción de Visitantes (Tourist Office; www.turismodesegovia.com; Plaza del Azoguejo 1; ⊙10am-7pm Sun-Fri, 10am-8pm Sat) Guided city tours are available, departing daily at 11.15 for a minimum of four people.

Regional Tourist Office (www.segoviaturismo. es; Plaza Mayor 10; ⊙9am-8pm Sun-Thu, 9am-9pm Fri & Sat)

❶ Getting There & Away

BUS Buses run half-hourly to Segovia from Madrid's Paseo de la Florida bus stop (€6.75, 1½ hours). Buses also run to/from Ávila (€5, 1¼ hours, five daily) and Salamanca (€11.08, 2¾ hours, two daily).

TRAIN Up to nine normal trains run daily from Madrid to Segovia (€6.75 one way, two hours), leaving you at the main train station, 2.5km from the aqueduct. The faster option is the high-speed Avant (€10.60, 35 minutes), which deposits you at the newer Segovia-Guiomar station, 5km from the aqueduct.

León

POP 132,740

León's stand-out attraction is the cathedral, one of the most beautiful in Spain. By day, this pretty city rewards long exploratory strolls. By night, the city's large student population floods into the narrow streets and plazas of the city's picturesque old quarter, the Barrio Húmedo.

Sights

Catedral CATHEDRAL
(www.catedraldeleon.org; adult/concession/child €5/4/free; ⏱8.30am-1.30pm & 4-8pm Mon-Sat, 8.30am-2.30pm & 5-8pm Sun) León's 13th-century cathedral, with its soaring towers, flying buttresses and truly breathtaking interior, is the city's spiritual heart. The extraordinary facade has a radiant rose window, three richly sculpted doorways and two muscular towers. After going through the main entrance, lorded over by the scene of *The Last Supper*, an extraordinary gallery of *vidrieras* (stained-glass windows) awaits. French in inspiration and mostly executed from the 13th to the 16th centuries, the windows evoke an atmosphere unlike that of any other cathedral in Spain; the kaleidoscope of coloured light is offset by the otherwise gloomy interior. There are 128 windows with a surface of 1800 sq metres in all, but mere numbers cannot convey the ethereal quality of light permeating this cathedral.

Real Basílica de San Isidoro CHURCH
Older even than León's cathedral, the Real Basílica de San Isidoro provides a stunning Romanesque counterpoint to the former's Gothic strains. The church remains open night and day by historical royal edict. The attached **Panteón Real** (admission €4, free Thu afternoon; ⏱10am-1.30pm & 4-6.30pm Mon-Sat, 10am-1.30pm Sun) houses sarcophagi beneath a canopy of some of the finest Romanesque frescoes in Spain.

FREE Museo de Arte Contemporáneo MUSEUM
(Musac; www.musac.org.es; Avenida de los Reyes Leóneses 24; ⏱11am-8pm Tue-Thu, to 9pm Fri, 10am-9pm Sat & Sun) León's showpiece Museo de Arte Contemporáneo belongs to the new wave of innovative Spanish architecture. A pleasing square-and-rhombus edifice of colourful glass and steel, it has been acclaimed for the 37 shades of coloured glass that adorn the facade; they were gleaned from the pixelisation of a fragment of one of the cathedral's stained-glass windows.

Although the museum has a growing permanent collection, it mostly houses temporary displays of cutting-edge Spanish and international photography, video installations and other similar forms.

Convento de San Marcos CONVENT
More than 100m long and blessed with a glorious facade, the plateresque exterior of this former pilgrims' hospital is sectioned off by slender columns and decorated with delicate medallions and friezes; most of it dates to 1513, by which time the edifice had become a monastery of the Knights of Santiago. Much of the former convent is now a supremely elegant *parador* (luxury hotel).

Barrio Gótico NEIGHBOURHOOD
On the fringes of León's Barrio Gótico (also known as the old town), Plaza de San Marcelo is home to the **ayuntamiento** (town hall), which occupies a charmingly compact Renaissance-era palace. The Renaissance theme continues in the form of the splendid **Palacio de los Guzmanes** (1560). Next door is Antoni Gaudí's sober contribution to León's skyline, the castle-like, neo-Gothic **Casa de Botines** (1893).

Down the hill, the delightful **Plaza de Santa María del Camino** (also known as Plaza del Grano) feels like a cobblestone Castilian village square. At the northeastern end of the old town is the beautiful and time-worn 17th-century **Plaza Mayor**.

🛏 Sleeping & Eating

TOP CHOICE La Posada Regia HISTORIC HOTEL €€
(☎987 21 31 73; www.regialeon.com; Calle de Regidores 9-11; s/d €65/120; ❄@🅿) You won't find many places better than this in northern Spain. The secret is a 14th-century building, magnificently restored (wooden beams, exposed brick and understated antique furniture), with individually styled rooms, character that overflows into the public areas and supremely comfortable beds and bathrooms.

Hostal de San Marcos HISTORIC HOTEL €€€
(☎987 23 73 00; www.parador.es; Plaza de San Marcos 7; d from €198; ❄@🅿) León's sumptuous *parador* is one of the finest hotels in Spain. With palatial rooms fit for royalty and filled with old-world luxury and decor, this is one of the Parador chain's flagship properties.

Hostal San Martín HOTEL €
(☎987 87 51 87; www.sanmartinhostales.com; Plaza de Torres de Omaña 1, 2nd fl; s/d/tr €31/43/55, s without bathroom €20) In a splendid central position, this recently overhauled 18th-century building has light, airy rooms painted in candy colours with small terraces.

BURGOS

The northern Castilian city of Burgos is home to a Unesco World Heritage–listed cathedral. A 13th-century French-Gothic creation, it has two extraordinary doors, the **Puerta del Sarmental**, the main entrance for visitors, and the **Puerta de la Coronería**.

Inside the main sanctuary, note the light and airy **Capilla de la Presentación** and the **Capilla de la Concepción** with its impossibly gilded, 15th-century **altar**. The main altar is a typically overwhelming piece of gold-encrusted extravagance, while directly beneath the star-vaulted central dome lies the **tomb of El Cid**. The **Capilla del Condestable**, behind the main altar, is a remarkable late-15th-century production.

If you're staying overnight, the **Hotel Norte y Londres** (☏947 26 41 25; www.hotelnorteylondres.com; Plaza de Alonso Martínez 10; s/d €66/100; ⓟⓐ⎷) **Hotel La Puebla** (☏947 20 00 11; www.hotellapuebla.com; Calle de la Puebla 20; s/d €50/65; ⎈ⓐ⎷) and **Hotel Mesón del Cid** (☏947 20 87 15; www.mesondelcid.es; Plaza de Santa María 8; s/d €70/100; ⓟ⎷⎈ⓐ⎷) are all excellent. For superb food, try **Cervecería Morito** (Calle de la Sombrerería 27; tapas €3, raciones €5-7).

The **tourist office** (www.aytoburgos.es; Plaza del Rey Fernando 2; ⊙10am-2pm & 4.30-7.30pm Mon-Fri, 10am-1.30pm & 4-7.30pm Sat & Sun) is in the town centre, and the city is well connected by train and bus to Madrid, León and Bilbao.

El Llar

TAPAS €€

(Plaza de San Martín 9; meals €25-30; ⏼) This old León *taberna* is a great place to *tapear* (eat tapas) with its innovative selection of *raciones*. The upstairs restaurant has a fine, classic look and the menu includes vegetarian options.

El Picoteo de la Jouja

TAPAS €

(Plaza de Torres de Omaña) This intimate little bar has earned a loyal following for its concentration on traditional local tapas (try the six tapas for €13.50) and local wines, including some from the nearby Bierzo region. The tapas include cured meats, snails and all manner of León specialties.

🍷 Drinking

The Barrio Húmedo's night-time epicentre is Plaza de San Martín – prise open the door of any bar here or in the surrounding streets (especially Calle de Juan de Arfe and Calle de la Misericordia), inch your way to the bar and you're unlikely to want to leave until closing time.

⟨TOP CHOICE⟩ Camarote Madrid

WINE BAR

(www.camarotemadrid.com; Calle Cervantes 8) We could equally recommend this fantastic and enduringly popular bar for its tapas (the little ceramic cup of *salmorejo* – a cold, tomato-based soup – is rightly famous), but the extensive wine list wins the day amid the buzz of a happy crowd swirling around the central bar. Recent renovations have thrust this sophisticated place into the 21st century.

Rebote

BAR

(Plaza de San Martín 9; ⊙8pm-1am Mon-Sat) A reliably popular bar at the lower end of Plaza de San Martín, Rebote is a good place for first drinks; the *croquetas* here are rightly famous.

ℹ Information

Tourist Office (www.turismocastillayleon.com; Calle el Cid 2; ⊙9am-8pm)

ℹ Getting There & Away

BUS From the **bus station** (Paseo del Ingeniero Sáez de Miera), there are numerous daily buses to Madrid (€22.60, 3½ hours) and Burgos (€14.50, two hours).

TRAIN Regular daily trains travel to Burgos (from €20.80, two hours), Oviedo (from €8.20, two hours), Madrid (from €34.75, 4½ hours) and Barcelona (from €70.70, nine hours).

CASTILLA-LA MANCHA

Known as the stomping ground of Don Quijote and Sancho Panza, Castilla-La Mancha conjures up images of lonely windmills, medieval castles and bleak, treeless plains. The characters of Miguel de Cevantes provide the literary context, but the richly historic cities of Toledo and Cuenca are the most compelling reasons to visit.

Toledo

POP 83,110

Toledo is Spain's equivalent of a downsized Rome. Commanding a hill rising above the Tajo River, it's crammed with monuments that attest to the waves of conquerors and communities – Roman, Visigoth, Jewish, Muslim and Christian – who have called the city home during its turbulent history. It's one of the country's major tourist attractions.

◉ Sights

TOP CHOICE Catedral   CATHEDRAL

(Plaza del Ayuntamiento; adult/child €7/free; ⊙10.30am-6.30pm Mon-Sat, 2-6.30pm Sun) Toledo's cathedral dominates the skyline, reflecting the city's historical significance as the heart of Catholic Spain. Within its hefty stone walls there are stained-glass windows, tombs of kings and art in the sacristy by the likes of El Greco, Zurbarán, Crespi, Titian, Rubens and Velázquez. Behind the main altar lies a mesmerising piece of 18th-century Churrigueresque baroque, the **Transparente**. Look out for the **Custodia de Arfe**, by the celebrated 16th-century goldsmith Enrique de Arfe. With 18kg of pure gold and 183kg of silver, this 16th-century conceit bristles with some 260 statuettes.

Alcázar   FORTRESS, MUSEUM

(Museo del Ejército; Calle Alféreces Provisionales; adult/child €5/free; ⊙10am-9pm Thu-Tue Jun-Sep, to 7pm Oct-May) At the highest point in the city looms the foreboding Alcázar. Abd ar-Rahman III raised an *al-qasr* (fortress) here in the 10th century, which was thereafter altered by the Christians. The Alcázar was heavily damaged during the siege of the garrison by loyalist militias at the start of the Spanish Civil War in 1936. The soldiers' dogged resistance, and the commander, Moscardó's, famous refusal to give it up in exchange for his son's life, made it a powerful nationalist symbol.

Rebuilt under Franco, the Alcázar has recently been reopened as an absolutely enormous military museum, with strict staff barking orders adding to the martial experience. The usual displays of uniforms and medals are here, but the best part is the exhaustive historical section, with an in-depth overview of the nation's history in Spanish and English.

Sinagoga del Tránsito   SYNAGOGUE

(http://museosefardi.mcu.es; Calle Samuel Leví; adult/child €3/1.50; ⊙9.30am-8pm Tue-Sat Apr-Sep, to 6.30pm Oct-Mar, 10am-3pm Sun) Toledo's former *judería* (Jewish quarter) was once home to 11 synagogues. The bulk of Toledo's Jews were expelled in 1492. This magnificent synagogue was built in 1355 by special permission of Pedro I (construction of synagogues was prohibited in Christian Spain). The synagogue now houses the **Museo Sefardi**.

Sinagoga de Santa María La Blanca   SYNAGOGUE

(Calle de los Reyes Católicos 4; admission €2.50; ⊙10am-6.45pm) This modest synagogue is characterised by the horseshoe arches that delineate the five naves – classic Almohad architecture.

Monasterio San Juan de los Reyes   MONASTERY

(Calle San Juan de los Reyes 2; admission €2.50; ⊙10am-6.45pm) This early 17th-century Franciscan monastery and church of San Juan de los Reyes is notable for its delightful cloisters. Provocatively built in the heart of the Jewish quarter, the monastery was founded by Isabel and Fernando to demonstrate the supremacy of the Catholic faith. The rulers had planned to be buried here but, when they took the greater prize of Granada in 1492, opted for the purpose-built Capilla Real. Throughout the church and cloister the coat of arms of Isabel and Fernando dominates, and the chains of Christian prisoners liberated in Granada dangle from the outside walls. The prevalent late-Flemish Gothic style is enhanced with lavish Isabelline ornament, counterbalanced by Mudéjar decoration.

FREE Museo de Santa Cruz   MUSEUM

(Calle Cervantes 3; ⊙10am-6.30pm Mon-Sat, to 2pm Sun) Just off the Plaza de Zocodover, the 16th-century Museo de Santa Cruz is a beguiling combination of Gothic and Spanish Renaissance styles. The cloisters and carved wooden ceilings are superb, as are the upstairs displays of Spanish ceramics. The ground-level gallery contains a number of El Grecos, a painting attributed to Goya (*Cristo Crucificado*), and the wonderful 15th-century *Tapestry of the Astrolabes*.

Iglesia de Santo Tomé CHURCH

(www.santotome.org; Plaza del Conde; admission €2.50; ⊙10am-6pm, to 7pm mid-Mar–mid-Oct) This otherwise modest church contains El Greco's masterpiece, *El Entierro del Conde de Orgaz* (The Burial of the Count of Orgaz). When the count was buried in 1322, Saints Augustine and Stephen supposedly descended from heaven to attend the funeral. El Greco's work depicts the event, complete with miracle guests including himself, his son and Cervantes.

Mezquita del Cristo de la Luz MOSQUE

(Calle Cristo de la Luz; admission €2.50; ⊙10am-2pm & 3.30-6.45pm Mon-Fri, 10am-6.45pm Sat & Sun) On the northern slopes of town you'll find this modest, yet beautiful mosque where architectural traces of Toledo's medieval Muslim conquerors are still in evidence. Built around AD 1000, it suffered the usual fate of being converted to a church (hence the religious frescoes), but the original vaulting and arches survived.

Sleeping

Accommodation is often full, especially from Easter to September. Many visitors choose to come on a day trip from Madrid.

TOP CHOICE Casa de Cisneros BOUTIQUE HOTEL €€

(⌨925 22 88 28; www.hostal-casa-de-cisneros.com; Calle Cardenal Cisneros; s/d incl breakfast €55/75; ❉⑨) Right by Toledo's cathedral, this lovely 16th-century house was once the home of the cardinal and Grand Inquisitor Cisneros (often known as Ximénes). It's a superb choice, with cosy, seductive rooms with original wooden beams and walls and voguish bathrooms.

Casa de los Mozárabes APARTMENT €€

(⌨925 21 17 01; www.casadelosmozarabes.com; Callejón de Menores 10; apt €96-170; ❉⑨) Occupying an historic Toledo house on a quiet central lane, these excellent apartments have modern furnishings that combine well with the exposed brick and historic features of the building. There's a common lounge area with a pool table and a few weights.

Hostal del Cardenal HISTORIC HOTEL €€

(⌨925 22 49 00; www.hostaldelcardenal.com; Paseo de Recaredo 24; s/d incl breakfast €90/120; ❉⑨) This wonderful 18th-century mansion has soft ochre-coloured walls, arches and columns. The rooms are grand, yet welcoming, with dark furniture, plush fabrics and parquet floors. Several rooms overlook the glorious terraced gardens.

La Posada de Manolo BOUTIQUE HOTEL €€

(⌨925 28 22 50; www.laposadademanolo.com; Calle de Sixto Ramón Parro 8; s/d incl breakfast €46/76; ❉⑨) This memorable hotel has themed each floor with furnishings and decor reflecting one of the three cultures of Toledo: Christian, Islamic and Jewish. There are stunning views of the old town and cathedral from the terrace.

✖ Eating

TOP CHOICE Alfileritos 24 MODERN SPANISH €€

(www.alfileritos24.com; Calle de los Alfileritos 24; mains €15-21, bar food €6-11; ⊙9.30am-midnight, to 1am Fri & Sat) The 14th-century surroundings of columns, beams and barrel-vault ceilings are snazzily coupled with modern artwork and bright dining rooms in an atrium space spread over four floors. The menu demonstrates an innovative flourish in the kitchen. The ground-floor bar offers good-value tapas and cheaper fare designed for sharing.

La Abadía TAPAS €

(www.abadiatoledo.com; Plaza de San Nicolás 3; raciones €4-15) In a former 16th-century palace, arches, niches and subtle lighting are spread over a warren of brick-and-stone-clad rooms. The menu includes lightweight dishes and tapas portions – perfect for small appetites.

Taberna El Embrujo TAPAS €

(www.tabernaembrujo.com; Calle Santa Leocadia 6; raciones €8-22) Near the top of the escalator up to the old town, this friendly bar has an appealing stone-clad dining area and an outdoor terrace across the street. It does a great line in high-quality deli-style tapas, with tasty tomato salads, delicious foie gras and seafood options, all served with a smile.

❶ Information

Main Tourist Office (⌨925 25 40 30; www.toledo-turismo.com; Plaza del Ayuntamiento; ⊙10am-6pm)

Provincial Tourist Office (www.diputoledo.es; Subida de la Granja; ⊙10am-5pm Mon-Sat, to 3pm Sun)

❶ Getting There & Away

For most major destinations, you'll need to backtrack to Madrid.

CUENCA

A World Heritage site, Cuenca is one of Spain's most memorable small cities, its old centre a stage set of evocative medieval buildings. Most emblematic are the 14th-century *casas colgadas*, the hanging houses that jut out precariously over the steep defile of Río Huécar. Inside one of the houses is the **Museo de Arte Abstracto Español** (Museum of Abstract Art; www.march.es/arte/cuenca; adult/child €3/free; ⊙11am-2pm & 4-6pm Tue-Fri, 11am-2pm & 4-8pm Sat, 11am-2.30pm Sun). Cuenca is also famous for its Semana Santa (Holy Week) processions; stop by the **Museo de la Semana Santa** (www.msscuenca. org; Calle Andrés de Cabrera 13; adult/child €3/free; ⊙11am-2pm & 4.30-7.30pm Thu-Sat, 11am-2pm Sun) to see why.

If you're staying overnight, the **Hostal Tabanqueta** (☑969 21 12 90; www.hostalta banqueta.com; Calle Trabuco 13; d €60; 🛜), **Posada de San José** (☑969 21 13 00; www. posadasanjose.com; Ronda de Julián Romero 4; d from €82, s/d without bathroom €30/43) and **Parador de Cuenca** (☑969 23 23 20; www.parador.es; Calle de Hoz de Huécar; s/d €138/173; 🅿❄🛜🏊) are all excellent. For a meal, try **La Bodeguilla de Basilio** (Calle Fray Luis de León 3; raciones €10-13; ⊙lunch & dinner Mon-Sat, lunch Sun).

There's a **tourist office** (http://turismo.cuenca.es; Calle Alfonso VIII 2; ⊙9am-9pm Mon-Sat, to 2.30pm Sun), and Cuenca is most easily reached along the Madrid–Valencia rail line.

BUS From Toledo's **bus station** (Avenida de Castilla La Mancha), buses depart for Madrid (from €5.25, one to 1½ hours) every half-hour from 6am to 10pm daily (less often on Sunday). There are also services on weekdays and Sunday to Cuenca (€12.80, 2¼ hours).

TRAIN The high-speed AVE service runs every hour or so to Madrid (€10.60, 30 minutes).

CATALONIA

Home to stylish Barcelona, ancient Tarragona, romantic Girona and countless alluring destinations along the coast, in the Pyrenees and in the rural interior, Catalonia (Catalunya in Catalan, Cataluña in Castilian) is a treasure box waiting to be opened.

Barcelona

POP 1.62 MILLION

Barcelona is one of Europe's coolest cities. Despite two millennia of history, it's a forward-thinking place, always on the cutting edge of art, design and cuisine. Whether you explore its medieval palaces and plazas, admire the Modernista masterpieces, shop for designer fashions along its bustling boulevards, sample its exciting nightlife or just soak up the sun on the beaches, you'll find it hard not to fall in love with this vibrant city.

As much as Barcelona is a visual feast, it will also lead you into culinary temptation. Anything from traditional Catalan cooking to the latest in avant-garde new Spanish cuisine will have your appetite in overdrive.

☉ Sights

LA RAMBLA

La Rambla is Spain's most talked-about boulevard. It certainly packs a lot of colour into a short walk, with flower stands, historic buildings, a sensory-rich produce market, overpriced beers and tourist tat, and a ceaselessly changing parade of people from all corners of the globe.

TOP CHOICE **Mercat de la Boqueria**   MARKET
(Map p688; ☑93 412 13 15; www.boqueria.info; La Rambla 91; ⊙8am-8.30pm Mon-Sat, closed Sun; Ⓜ Liceu) One of the greatest sound, smell and colour sensations in Europe is Barcelona's most central produce market, the Mercat de la Boqueria. It spills over with all the rich and varied colour of plentiful fruit and vegetable stands, seemingly limitless varieties of sea critters, sausages, cheeses, meat (including the finest Jabugo ham) and sweets. Note also its Modernista-influenced design.

Gran Teatre del Liceu   ARTS CENTRE
(Map p688; ☑93 485 99 14; www.liceubarcelona. com; La Rambla dels Caputxins 51-59; admission with/without guide €10/5; ⊙guided tour 10am, unguided visits 11.30am, noon, 12.30pm & 1pm; Ⓜ Liceu) If you can't catch a night at the opera, you can still have a look around one of Europe's greatest opera houses, known to locals as the Liceu. Smaller than Milan's La

Barcelona

SPAIN BARCELONA

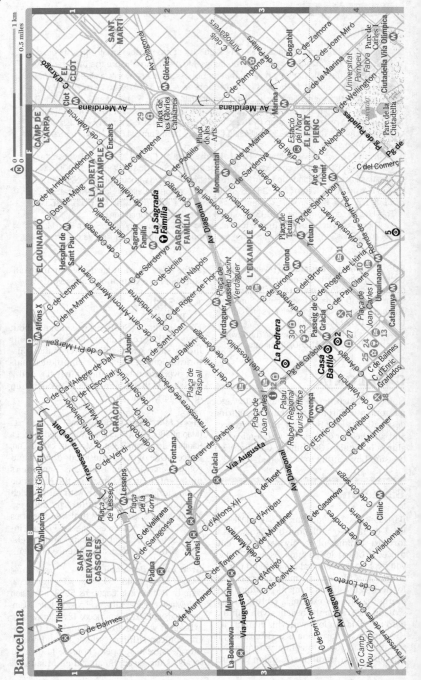

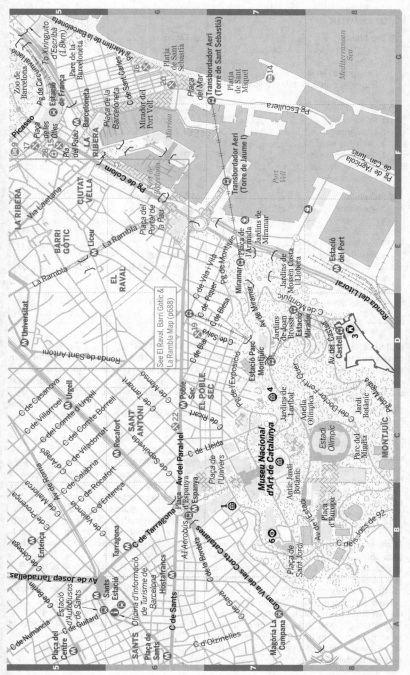

SPAIN BARCELONA

Mediterranean Sea

Platja de Sant Sebastià

Transbordador Aeri (Torre de Sant Sebastià)

Platja de Sant Miquel

Plaça del Mar

Pg Escullera

To Xiringuito d'Escribà (1.8km)

Pg Martinм alle de la Barceloneta

Zoo de Barcelona

Parc de la Barceloneta

Pg de Circu

Estació de França

C de Sant Carles

Plaça de la Barceloneta

LA BARCELONETA

Plaça del Palau

Pla del Palau

Mirador del Port Vell

Marina

Picasso

Plaça de les Olles

LA RIBERA

Pg de Colom

Pt de Cilunià

Transbordador Aeri (Torre de Jaume I)

Port Vell

Pg de l'Agricola de Can Tunis

CIUTAT VELLA

Via Laietana

Plaça del Portal de la Pau

Estació del Port

Jardins de Miramar

Jardins de Miramar

BARRI GÒTIC

Liceu

La Rambla

Plaça de l'Armada

Miramar

Pg de Montjuïc

Jardins de Mossèn Costa i Llobera

Universitat

EL RAVAL

La Rambla

Ronda de Sant Antoni

See El Raval, Barri Gòtic & La Rambla Map (p688)

C de Vila i Vilà

C de Piquer

C de Blesa

Avd Miramat

Ronda del Litoral

C de Casanova

C de Villarroel

C del Comte d'Urgell

C de Salvà

C de Bla

Estació Parc Montjuïc

Jardins de Joan Brossà

Estació Mirador

Av del Castell

MONTJUÏC

Pedralbes

3

SANT ANTONI

C del Comte Borrell

C de Viladomat

C de Calàbria

C de Rocafort

C d'Entença

Rocafort

C de Tamarit

C de Manso

Poble Sec

EL POBLE SEC

Pg de l'Exposició

Jardins de Laribal

Anella Olímpica

Jardí Botànic

22

Av del Paral·lel

C de Ricart

C de Lleida

4

C del Doctor Font

Quer

Jardins de Larbal

C de Provença

C de Mallorca

C de València

Av de Roma

Rocafort

SANT ANTONI

Tarragona

C de Tarragona

Plaça de l'Univers

Plaça d'Espanya

Espanya

Av Aerobús

Ai Aerobús

Gran Via de les Corts Catalanes

Estadi Olímpic

Antic Jardí Botànic

Parc del Migdia

Plaça d'Europa

C dels Jocs de 92

Av de l'Estadi

Plaça de Sant Jordi

Museu Nacional d'Art de Catalunya

1

6

C de Còrsega

Entença

C de Bellfort

Av de Josep Tarradellas

Estació d'Autobusos

Oficina d'Informació de Turisme de Barcelona

Plaça dels Països Catalans

C de Sants

SANTS

Sants

Estació Sants

C de Numància

C de Guilard

Plaça del Centre

Plaça de Sants

C d'Olzinelles

Magòria La Campana

C de la Bordeta

C de Gavà

Barcelona

⦿ Top Sights
Casa Batlló D4
La Pedrera D3
La Sagrada Família E2
Museu Nacional d'Art de Catalunya C7

⦿ Sights
1 CaixaForum B7
2 Casa Amatller D4
3 Castell de Montjuïc D8
4 Fundació Joan Miró C7
5 Palau de la Música Catalana E4
6 Poble Espanyol B7

🛏 Sleeping
7 Aparteasy D3
8 Barcelona On Line E3
9 Chic & Basic F5
10 Five Rooms E4
Hostal Goya .... (see 10)
11 Hotel Constanza E4
12 Hotel Omm D3
13 Hotel Praktik D4
14 W Barcelona G7

✴ Eating
15 Cal Pep F5
16 Can Majó G6
17 Casa Delfín F5
18 Cinc Sentits C4
19 Quimet i Quimet D6
20 Suquet De L'Almirall G6
21 Tapaç 24 .... D4
22 Tickets C6

🍷 Drinking
23 Les Gens Que J'Aime D3
24 Monvínic D4

✪ Entertainment
25 Arena Madre D4
Palau de la Música Catalana .... (see 5)
26 Razzmatazz G3

🛍 Shopping
27 Antonio Miró D4
28 Custo Barcelona F5
29 Els Encants Vells F2
30 Joan Murrià D3
31 Vinçon D3

Scala but bigger than Venice's La Fenice, it can seat up to 2300 people in its grand horseshoe auditorium. You can take a 20-minute quick turn around the main public areas of the theatre or join a one-hour guided tour.

Plaça Reial   SQUARE
(Map p688; Ⓜ Liceu) One of the most photogenic squares in Barcelona, the Plaça Reial is a delightful retreat from the traffic and pedestrian mobs on the nearby Rambla. Numerous eateries, bars and nightspots lie beneath the arcades of 19th-century neoclassical buildings, with a buzz of activity at all hours. The lamp posts by the central fountain are Antoni Gaudí's first known works in the city.

Mirador de Colom   VIEWPOINT
(Map p688; ☏ 93 302 52 24; Plaça del Portal de la Pau; lift adult/child €4/3; ⊙ 8.30am-8.30pm; Ⓜ Drassanes) High above the swirl of traffic on the roundabout below, Columbus keeps permanent watch, pointing vaguely out to the Mediterranean. Built for the Universal Exhibition in 1888, the monument allows you to zip up 60m in the lift for bird's-eye views back up La Rambla and across the ports of Barcelona.

BARRI GÒTIC
You could easily spend several days or even a week exploring the Barri Gòtic, Barcelona's oldest quarter, without leaving the medieval streets. In addition to major sights, its tangle of narrow lanes and tranquil plazas conceal some of the city's most atmospheric shops, restaurants, cafes and bars.

TOP CHOICE La Catedral   CHURCH
(Map p688; ☏ 933428260; www.website.es/catedral bcn; Plaça de la Seu; admission free, special visit €5, choir admission €2.20; ⊙ 8am-12.45pm & 5.15-8pm Mon-Sat, special visit 1-5pm Mon-Sat, 2-5pm Sun & holidays; Ⓜ Jaume I) Barcelona's Gothic Catedral was built atop the ruins of an 11th-century Romanesque church. Highlights include the cool cloister, the crypt tomb of martyr Santa Eulàlia (one of Barcelona's two patron saints), the choir stalls, the lift to the rooftop and the modest art collection in the **Sala Capitular** (Chapter House; admission €2; ⊙ 10am-12.15pm & 5.15-7pm Mon-Sat, 10am-12.45pm & 5.15-7pm Sun). You only pay the individual prices if you visit outside the special visiting hours.

Museu d'Història de Barcelona
TOP CHOICE   MUSEUM

(Map p688; ☑93 256 21 00; www.museuhistoria. bcn.cat; Plaça del Rei; adult/child €7/free, from 4pm 1st Sat of month and from 3pm Sun free; ☉10am-7pm Tue-Sat, 10am-8pm Sun; Ⓜ Jaume I) Not far from the Barcelona Catedral is pretty Plaça del Rei and the fascinating Museu d'Història de Barcelona, where you can visit a 4000-sq-metre excavated site of Roman Barcelona under the plaza. The museum encompasses historic buildings, including the **Palau Reial Major** (Main Royal Palace), once a residence of the kings of Catalonia and Aragón, and its **Saló del Tinell** (Great Hall).

Sinagoga Major
SYNAGOGUE

(Map p688; ☑93 317 07 90; www.calldebarcelona. org; Carrer de Marlet 5; admission by suggested donation €2.50; ☉10.30am-6.30pm Mon-Fri, to 2.30pm Sat & Sun; Ⓜ Liceu) When an Argentine investor bought a run-down electrician's store with an eye to converting it into central Barcelona's umpteenth bar, he could hardly have known he had stumbled onto the remains of what could be the city's main medieval synagogue. A guide will explain what is thought to be the significance of the site in various languages.

EL RAVAL

To the west of La Rambla is El Raval district, a once-seedy, now-funky area overflowing with cool bars and shops.

MACBA
MUSEUM

(Museu d'Art Contemporani de Barcelona; Map p688; ☑93 412 08 10; www.macba.cat; Plaça dels Àngels 1; adult/concession €7.50/6; ☉11am-8pm Mon & Wed, to midnight Thu-Fri, 10am-8pm Sat, 10am-3pm Sun & holidays; Ⓜ Universitat) Designed by Richard Meier and opened in 1995, MACBA has become the city's foremost contemporary art centre, with captivating exhibitions for the serious art lover. The permanent collection is on the ground floor and dedicates itself to Spanish and Catalan art from the second half of the 20th century, with works by Antoni Tàpies, Joan Brossa and Miquel Barceló, among others, though international artists, such as Paul Klee, Bruce Nauman and John Cage are also represented.

Església de Sant Pau
CHURCH

(Map p688; Carrer de Sant Pau 101; ☉cloister 10am-1pm & 4-7pm Mon-Sat; Ⓜ Paral·lel) The best example of Romanesque architecture in the city is the dainty little cloister of this church.

Set in a somewhat dusty garden, the 12th-century church also boasts some Visigothic sculptural detail on the main entrance.

LA RIBERA

In medieval days, La Ribera was a stone's throw from the Mediterranean and the heart of Barcelona's foreign trade, with homes belonging to numerous wealthy merchants. Now it's a trendy district full of boutiques, restaurants and bars.

Museu Picasso
TOP CHOICE   MUSEUM

(Map p688; ☑93 256 30 00; www.museupicasso. bcn.es; Carrer de Montcada 15-23; adult/senior & child under 16yr/student €11/free/6, temporary exhibitions adult/senior & child under 16yr/student €6/free/2.90, 3-8pm Sun & 1st Sun of month free; ☉10am-8pm Tue-Sun & holidays; Ⓜ Jaume I) The setting alone, in five contiguous medieval stone mansions, makes the Museu Picasso unique (and worth the probable queues). The pretty courtyards, galleries and staircases preserved in the first three of these buildings are as delightful as the collection inside.

While the collection concentrates on the artist's formative years – sometimes disappointing for those hoping for a feast of his better-known later works (they had better head for Paris) – there is enough material from subsequent periods to give you a thorough impression of the man's versatility and genius.

Església de Santa Maria del Mar
CHURCH

(Map p688; ☑93 319 05 16; Plaça de Santa Maria del Mar; ☉9am-1.30pm & 4.30-8pm; Ⓜ Jaume I) At the southwest end of Passeig del Born stands Barcelona's finest Catalan Gothic church, Santa Maria del Mar (Our Lady of the Sea). Built in the 14th century with record-breaking alacrity for the time (it took just 54 years), the church is remarkable for its architectural harmony and simplicity.

Palau de la Música Catalana
ARCHITECTURE

(Map p684; ☑902 475 485; www.palaumusica.org; Carrer de Sant Francesc de Paula 2; adult/child/student & EU senior €15/free/€7.50; ☉50min tours every 30 minutes 10am-6pm Easter week & Aug, 10am-3.30pm Sep-Jul; Ⓜ Urquinaona) The opulent Palau de la Música Catalana is one of the city's most delightful Modernista works. Designed by Lluís Domènech i Montaner in 1905, it hosts concerts regularly. It is well worth joining the guided tours to get a look inside if you don't make a concert.

El Raval, Barri Gòtic & La Rambla

SPAIN BARCELONA

Universitat de Barcelona

C d'Aribau

Gran Via de les Corts Catalanes

Ronda de la Universitat

C de Balmes

C de Bergara

Plaça de Catalunya

Oficina d'Informació de Turisme de Barcelona

11

M Universitat

C de Pelai

C de Jovellanos

C de Rivadeneyra

Catalunya

Catalunya

Rambla de Canaletes

C de Santa Anna

14

C dels Tallers

C dels Tallers

C de la Canuda

C d'en Bot

34

Plaça de Vicenç Martorell

C del Bonsuccés

C de Sepúlveda

Plaça de Joan Coromines

MACBA

Plaça dels Àngels

13

C del Notariat

C del Pintor Fortuny

24

C de

C de Casanova

C de Joaquín Costa

C de Valldonzella

C del Tigre

27

19

C del Lleó

C del Doctor Dou

C del Carme

Rambla de Sant Josep

21

4

C de Ferlandina

C de Sant Vicenç

C de la Lluna

C del Peu de la Creu

Jardins del Doctor Fleming

Plaça de la Gardunya

C de Jerusalem

Plaça del Pes de la Palla

C de les Egipcíaques

Plaça de Sant Agustí

18

C de la Riera Alta

C de la Riera Baixa

C de la Junta de Comerç

Ronda de Sant Antoni

C de la Cendra

Sant Antoni

Plaça del Padró

C de l'Hospital

Rambla del Raval

C de Sant Rafael

C d'en Robador

C de Manso

C de Sant Antoni Abat

C de la Cera

C de les Carretes

23

C de l'Aurora

C de Sant Pacià

C de la Riereta

Rambla del Raval

Plaça de Salvador Seguí

C de Sant Ramon

C del Parlament

C del Comte Borrell

C de la Reina Amàlia

C de les Tàpies

C de Sant Oleguer

C Nou de la Rambla

C de l'Om

C de les Flors

C d'Aldana

Ronda de Sant Pau

29

1

C de l'Abat Safont

C de Santa Madrona

Av del Paral·lel

M Paral·lel

Parc de les Tres Xemeneies

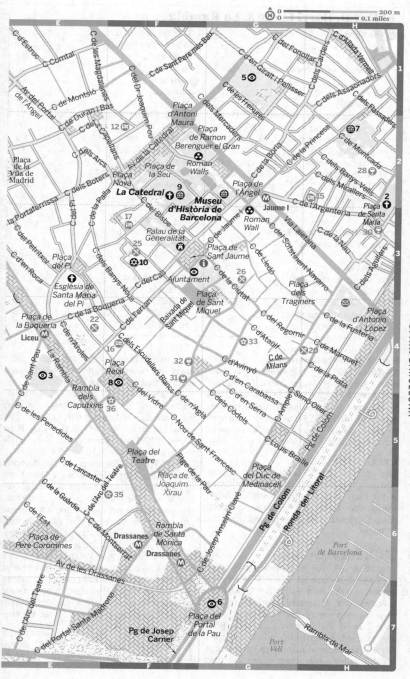

El Raval, Barri Gòtic & La Rambla

◎ Top Sights
La Catedral	F2
MACBA	B3
Museu d'Història de Barcelona	G2

◎ Sights
1	Església de Sant Pau	C7
2	Església de Santa Maria del Mar	H2
3	Gran Teatre del Liceu	E4
4	Mercat de la Boqueria	D4
5	Mercat de Santa Caterina	G1
6	Mirador de Colom	G7
7	Museu Picasso	H2
8	Plaça Reial	F4
9	Sala Capitular	F2
10	Sinagoga Major	F3

◎ Activities, Courses & Tours
11	Barcelona Walking Tours	D1

◎ Sleeping
12	Alberg Hostel Itaca	F2
13	Casa Camper	C3
14	Hostal Chic & Basic	A2
15	Hotel Banys Orientals	H2
16	Hotel California	F4
17	Hotel Neri	F3
18	Hotel San Agustín	D4
19	Whotells	B3

◎ Eating
20	Agut	H4
21	Bar Pinotxo	D3
22	Can Culleretes	E4
23	Can Lluís	B5
24	Granja Viader	D3
25	La Vinateria dell Call	F3
26	Pla	G3

◎ Drinking
27	33|45	B3
28	El Xampanyet	H2
29	La Confitería	C7
30	La Vinya del Senyor	H3
31	Marula Cafè	F4
32	Oviso	F4

◎ Entertainment
33	Harlem Jazz Club	G4
34	Metro	A2
35	Moog	F6
36	Sala Tarantos	F5

Mercat de Santa Caterina　MARKET
(Map p688; ☑93 319 17 40; www.mercatsantacaterina.net; Avinguda de Francesc Cambó 16; ⊘7.30am-2pm Mon, to 3.30pm Tue, Wed & Sat, to 8.30pm Thu & Fri; Ⓜ Jaume I) With its loopily pastel-coloured wavy roof, Mercat de Santa Caterina is a temple to fine foods designed by the adventurous Catalan architect Enric Miralles.

L'EIXAMPLE
Modernisme, the Catalan version of art nouveau, transformed Barcelona's cityscape in the early 20th century. Most Modernista works were built in L'Eixample, the grid-plan district that was developed from the 1870s on.

[TOP CHOICE] **La Sagrada Família**　CHURCH
(Map p684; ☑93 207 30 31; www.sagradafamilia.org; Carrer de Mallorca 401; adult/child under 10yr/senior & student €13/free/11; ⊘9am-8pm Apr-Sep, to 6pm Oct-Mar; Ⓜ Sagrada Família) If you have time for only one sightseeing outing, this should be it. La Sagrada Família inspires awe by its sheer verticality, and in the manner of the medieval cathedrals it emulates, it's still under construction after more than 100 years. When completed, the highest tower will be more than half as high again as those that stand today.

Unfinished though it may be, it still attracts around 2.8 million visitors a year and is the most visited monument in Spain. The most important recent tourist was Pope Benedict XVI, who consecrated the church in a huge ceremony in November 2010.

The Temple Expiatori de la Sagrada Família (Expiatory Temple of the Holy Family) was Antoni Gaudí's all-consuming obsession. Given the commission by a conservative society that wished to build a temple as atonement for the city's sins of modernity, Gaudí saw its completion as his holy mission.

Gaudí devised a temple 95m long and 60m wide, able to seat 13,000 people, with a central tower 170m high above the transept (representing Christ) and another 17 towers of 100m or more. Highlights among many include the apse, Nativity façade, Passion façade, Glory façade and the Museu Gaudí.

La Pedrera　ARCHITECTURE
(Casa Milà; Map p684; ☑902 400 973; www.lapedrera.com; Carrer de Provença 261-265; adult/

student/child €15/13.50/7.50; ⊙9am-8pm Mar-Oct, to 6.30pm Nov-Feb; MDiagonal) This undulating beast is another madcap Gaudí masterpiece, built in 1905–10 as a combined apartment and office block. Formally called Casa Milà, after the businessman who commissioned it, it is better known as La Pedrera (the Quarry) because of its uneven grey stone facade, which ripples around the corner of Carrer de Provença.

The Fundació Caixa Catalunya has opened the top-floor apartment, attic and roof, together called the Espai Gaudí (Gaudí Space), to visitors. The roof is the most extraordinary element, with its giant chimney pots looking like multicoloured medieval knights.

One floor below the roof, where you can appreciate Gaudí's taste for parabolic arches, is a modest museum dedicated to his work.

Casa Batlló   ARCHITECTURE
(Map p684; ☎93 216 03 06; www.casabatllo.es; Passeig de Gràcia 43; adult/child under 7yr/ €18.15/free; ⊙9am-8pm; MPasseig de Gràcia) One of the strangest residential buildings in Europe, this is Gaudí at his hallucinogenic best. The facade, sprinkled with bits of blue, mauve and green tiles and studded with wave-shaped window frames and balconies, rises to an uneven blue-tiled roof with a solitary tower.

FREE Casa Amatller   ARCHITECTURE
(Map p684; ☎93 487 72 17; www.amatller.org; Passeig de Gràcia 41; ⊙10am-8pm Mon-Sat, to 3pm Sun, guided tour in English noon Fri, in Catalan & Spanish noon Wed; MPasseig de Gràcia) One of Puig i Cadafalch's most striking bits of Mod-

ernista fantasy, Casa Amatller combines Gothic window frames with a stepped gable borrowed from Dutch urban architecture. But the busts and reliefs of dragons, knights and other characters dripping off the main facade are pure caprice.

MONTJUÏC
Southwest of the city centre and with views out to sea and over the city, Montjuïc serves as a Central Park of sorts and is a great place for a jog or stroll.

TOP CHOICE Museu Nacional d'Art de Catalunya   MUSEUM
(MNAC; Map p684; ☎93 622 03 76; www.mnac.es; Mirador del Palau Nacional; adult/senior & child under 15yr €10/free, 1st Sun of month free; ⊙10am-7pm Tue-Sat, to 2.30pm Sun & holidays, library 10am-6pm Mon-Fri, to 2.30pm Sat; MEspanya) From across the city, the bombastic neobaroque silhouette of the Palau Nacional can be seen on the slopes of Montjuïc. Built for the 1929 World Exhibition and restored in 2005, it houses a vast collection of mostly Catalan art spanning the early Middle Ages to the early 20th century. The high point is the collection of extraordinary Romanesque frescoes.

Fundació Joan Miró   MUSEUM
(Map p684; www.bcn.fjmiro.es; Plaça de Neptu; adult/senior & child €10/7; ⊙10am-8pm Tue, Wed, Fri & Sat, to 9.30pm Thu, to 2.30pm Sun & holidays; ☐50, 55, 193, funicular Paral·lel) Joan Miró, the city's best-known 20th-century artistic progeny, bequeathed this art foundation to his hometown in 1971. Its light-filled buildings

SPAIN BARCELONA

DON'T MISS

PARK GÜELL

North of Gràcia and about 4km from Plaça de Catalunya, **Park Güell** (☎93 413 24 00; Carrer d'Olot 7; ⊙10am-9pm Jun-Sep, to 8pm Apr, May & Oct, to 7pm Mar & Nov, to 6pm Dec-Feb; ☐24, MLesseps, Vallcarca) is where Gaudí turned his hand to landscape gardening. It's a strange, enchanting place where his passion for natural forms really took flight – to the point where the artificial almost seems more natural than the natural.

Park Güell originated in 1900, when Count Eusebi Güell bought a tree-covered hillside (then outside Barcelona) and hired Gaudí to create a miniature city of houses for the wealthy in landscaped grounds. The project was a commercial flop and was abandoned in 1914 – but not before Gaudí had created 3km of roads and walks, steps, a plaza and two gatehouses in his inimitable manner. In 1922 the city bought the estate for use as a public park. The park is extremely popular (it gets an estimated 4 million visitors a year, about 86% of them tourists) and there is talk of limiting access to keep a lid on damage done by the overkill. Its quaint nooks and crannies are irresistible to photographers – who on busy days have trouble keeping out of each other's pictures.

are crammed with seminal works, from Miró's earliest timid sketches to paintings from his last years.

FREE **Castell de Montjuïc**   FORTRESS, GARDENS
(Map p684; ⊙9am-9pm Tue-Sun Apr-Sep, to 7pm Tue-Sun Oct-Mar; ☐193, Telefèric de Montjuïc) The forbidding Castell (castle or fort) de Montjuïc dominates the southeastern heights of Montjuïc and enjoys commanding views over the Mediterranean. It dates, in its present form, from the late 17th and 18th centuries.

Poble Espanyol   CULTURAL CENTRE
(Map p684; www.poble-espanyol.com; Avinguda de Francesc Ferrer i Guàrdia; adult/child €9.50/5.60; ⊙9am-8pm Mon, to 2am Tue-Thu, to 4am Fri, to 5am Sat, to midnight Sun; ☐50, 61 or 193, Ⓜ Espanya) A showcase of typical Spanish architecture from around the country, Poble Espanyol has craft shops, restaurants and nightlife.

CaixaForum   GALLERY
(Map p684; www.fundacio.lacaixa.es; Avinguda de Francesc Ferrer i Guàrdia 6-8; adult/student & child €3/2, first Sun of the month free; ⊙10am-8pm Tue-Fri & Sun, to 10pm Sat; Ⓟ; Ⓜ Espanya) CaixaForum is housed in a remarkable former Modernista factory designed by Puig i Cadafalch and puts on major art exhibitions.

BARCELONA'S WATERFRONT
Barcelona has two major ports: **Port Vell** (Old Port), at the base of La Rambla, and **Port Olímpic** (Olympic Port), 1.5km up the coast. Shops, restaurants and nightlife options are plentiful around both marinas, particularly Port Olímpic. Barcelona boasts 4km of city *platjas* (beaches), beginning with the gritty **Platja de la Barceloneta** and continuing northeast, beyond Port Olímpic, with a series of cleaner, more attractive strands. All get packed in summer.

☞ Tours

Barcelona Walking Tours   WALKING TOUR
(Map p688; ☎93 285 38 34; www.barcelonaturisme.com; Plaça de Catalunya 17-S; Ⓜ Catalunya) The Oficina d'Informació de Turisme de Barcelona organises guided walking tours. One explores the **Barri Gòtic** (adult/child €14/5; ⊙in English 9.30am daily, in Spanish & Catalan 11.30am Sat); another follows in the footsteps of **Picasso** (adult/child €20/7; ⊙in English 3pm Tue, Thu & Sun) and winds up at the Museu Picasso, entry to which is included in the price; and a third takes in the main jewels of **Modernisme** (adult/child €14/5; ⊙in English

4pm Fri & Sat Oct-May, 6pm Fri & Sat Jun-Sep). Also offered is a **gourmet tour** (adult/child €20/7; ⊙in English 10am Fri & Sat, in Spanish & Catalan 10.30am Sat) of traditional purveyors of fine foodstuffs across the old city. All tours last two hours and start at the tourist office. All tours are also available in both English and Spanish at 6pm from June to September.

Bus Turístic   BUS TOUR
(☎93 285 38 32; www.barcelonaturisme.com; day ticket adult/child €24/14; ⊙9am-8pm) This hop-on, hop-off service covers three circuits (44 stops) linking virtually all the major tourist sights. Tourist offices, TMB transport authority offices and many hotels have leaflets explaining the system.

⚒ Festivals & Events

The **Festes de la Mercè** (www.bcn.cat/merce), held around 24 September, is the city's biggest party, with four days of concerts, dancing, *castellers* (human castle-builders), fireworks and *correfocs* – a spectacular parade of firework-spitting dragons and devils.

The evening before the **Dia de Sant Joan** (24 June) is a colourful midsummer celebration with bonfires and fireworks. The beaches are crowded with revellers to the wee hours.

🛏 Sleeping

There's no shortage of hotels in Barcelona. Those looking for cheaper accommodation close to the action should check out the Barri Gòtic and El Raval. Some good lower-end *pensiones* are scattered about L'Eixample, as well as a broad range of midrange and top-end places, most in easy striking distance of the old town. A growing range of options now makes it easier to stay in La Ribera and near the beaches at La Barceloneta.

Numerous private apartment-rental companies operate in Barcelona. These can often be a better deal than staying in a hotel. Start your search at **Aparteasy** (Map p684; ☎93 451 67 66; www.aparteasy.com; Carrer de Santa Tecla 3; Ⓜ Diagnoal), **Barcelona On Line** (Map p684; ☎902 887017, 93 343 79 93; www.barcelona-on-line.es; Carrer de València 352) and **Rent a Flat in Barcelona** (☎93 342 73 00; www.rentaflatinbarcelona.com; Ronda del Guinardó 2).

LA RAMBLA & BARRI GÒTIC

TOP CHOICE **Hotel Neri**   DESIGN HOTEL €€€
(Map p688; ☎93 304 06 55; www.hotelneri.com; Carrer de Sant Sever 5; d from €270; ✳@🛜;

Ⓜ Liceu) This tranquil hotel occupies a beautifully adapted, centuries-old building backing on Plaça de Sant Felip Neri. The sandstone walls and timber furnishings lend a sense of history, while the rooms feature cutting-edge technology, including plasma-screen TVs and infrared lights in the stone-clad designer bathrooms.

Alberg Hostel Itaca
HOSTEL €

(Map p688; ☑ 93 301 97 51; www.itacahostel.com; Carrer de Ripoll 21; dm €11-26, d €60; @ 🛜; Ⓜ Jaume I) A bright, quiet hostel near Barcelona's Catedral, Itaca has spacious dorms (sleeping six, eight or 12 people) with parquet floors and spring colours, and two doubles. It also features two nearby apartments for six people (€120 per night).

Hotel California
HOTEL €€

(Map p688; ☑ 93 317 77 66; www.hotelcaliforniabcn.com; Carrer d'en Rauric 14; s/d €70/120; ❋ @ 🛜; Ⓜ Liceu) This (gay) friendly and central hotel has 31 straightforward but fastidiously sparkling-clean rooms, with light, neutral colours, satellite plasma TV and good-sized beds. Double glazing helps ensure a good night's sleep.

EL RAVAL

TOP CHOICE Casa Camper
DESIGN HOTEL €€€

(Map p688; ☑ 93 342 62 80; www.casacamper.com; Carrer d'Elisabets 11; s/d €240/270; ⊝ ❋ @; Ⓜ Liceu) The massive foyer looks like a contemporary-art museum, but the rooms are the real surprise. Decorated in red, black and white, each room has a sleeping and bathroom area, where you can put on your Camper slippers, enjoy the Vinçon furniture and contemplate the hanging gardens outside your window. Across the corridor is a separate, private sitting room with balcony, TV and hammock.

Whotells
APARTMENT €€

(Map p688; ☑ 93 443 08 34; www.whotells.com; Carrer de Joaquín Costa 28; apt from €180; ❋ @ 🛜; Ⓜ Universitat) These comfortable home-away-from-home apartments, decked out with Muji furniture, can sleep four to six people. Cook up a storm in the kitchen with products bought in the nearby La Boqueria market, or flop in front of the LCD TV.

Hostal Chic & Basic
HOSTAL €€

(Map p688; ☑ 93 302 51 83; www.chicandbasic.com; Carrer de Tallers 82; s €80, d €103-124; ❋ @; Ⓜ Universitat) The colour scheme here is predominantly white, with exceptions like the screaming orange fridge in the communal kitchen and chill-out area. Rooms are also themed lily white, from the floors to the sheets. Finishing touches include the plasma-screen TVs and the option of plugging your iPod into your room's sound system. The street can get noisy.

Hotel San Agustín
HOTEL €€

(Map p688; ☑ 93 318 16 58; www.hotelsa.com; Plaça de Sant Agustí 3; r from €80-180; ❋ @ 🛜; Ⓜ Liceu) This former 18th-century monastery opened as a hotel in 1840, making it the city's oldest. The location is perfect – a quick stroll off La Rambla on a curious square. Rooms sparkle, and are mostly spacious and light-filled.

LA RIBERA & LA BARCELONETA

TOP CHOICE Hotel Banys Orientals
BOUTIQUE HOTEL €€

(Map p688; ☑ 93 268 84 60; www.hotelbanysorientals.com; Carrer de l'Argenteria 37; s/d €88/105, ste €130; ❋ @; Ⓜ Jaume I) Book well ahead to get into this magnetically popular designer haunt. Cool blues and aquamarines combine with dark-hued floors to lend this clean-lined, boutique hotel a quiet charm. All rooms, on the small side, look onto the street or back lanes.

Chic & Basic
DESIGN HOTEL €€

(Map p684; ☑ 93 295 46 52; www.chicandbasic.com; Carrer de la Princesa 50; s €96, d €132-192; ❋ @; Ⓜ Jaume I) This is a very cool hotel indeed, with its 31 spotlessly white rooms and fairy-lights curtains that change colour, adding an entirely new atmosphere to the space. The ceilings are high and the beds enormous.

W Barcelona
LUXURY HOTEL €€€

(Map p684; ☑ 93 295 28 00; www.w-barcelona.com; Plaça de la Rosa del Vents 1; r from €310; Ⓟ ❋ @ 🛜 ≋; ☐ 17, 39, 57 or 64, Ⓜ Barceloneta) This spinnaker-shaped, beach-adjacent tower of glass contains 473 rooms and suites that are the last word in contemporary hotel chic. Self-indulgence is a byword and guests can flit between gym, infinity pool (with bar) and spa.

L'EIXAMPLE

TOP CHOICE Hotel Praktik
BOUTIQUE HOTEL €€

(Map p684; ☑ 93 343 66 90; www.hotelpraktikrambla.com; Rambla de Catalunya 27; r from €80-170; ❋ @ 🛜; Ⓜ Passeig de Gràcia) This Modernista gem hides a gorgeous little boutique experience. While the high ceilings and the bulk of the original tile floors have been maintained, the 43 rooms have daring ceramic touches, spot lighting and contemporary art.

Five Rooms
BOUTIQUE HOTEL €€

(Map p684; ☑93 342 78 80; www.thefiverooms. com; Carrer de Pau Claris 72; s/d from €115/135, apt from €175; ✳@☎; ⓂUrquinaona) Like they say, there are five rooms (standard rooms and suites) in this 1st-floor flat virtually on the border between L'Eixample and the old centre of town. Each room is different; features include broad, firm beds, stretches of exposed brick wall, restored mosaic tiles and minimalist decor. There are also two apartments.

Hotel Omm
DESIGN HOTEL €€€

(Map p684; ☑93 445 40 00; www.hotelomm.es; Carrer de Rosselló 265; d from €360; P✳@☎; ⓂDiagonal) Design meets plain zany here, where the balconies look like strips of skin peeled back from the shiny hotel surface. The idea would no doubt have appealed to Dalí. In the foyer, a sprawling, minimalist and popular bar opens before you. Light, clear tones dominate in the ultramodern rooms, of which there are several categories.

Hotel Constanza
BOUTIQUE HOTEL €€

(Map p684; ☑93 270 19 10; www.hotelconstanza. com; Carrer del Bruc 33; s/d €130/150; ✳@; ⓂGirona, Urquinaona) This boutique beauty has stolen the hearts of many a visitor to Barcelona. Design touches abound, and little details like flowers in the bathroom add charm. Suites and studios are further options.

Hostal Goya
HOSTAL €€

(Map p684; ☑93 302 25 65; www.hostalgoya. com; Carrer de Pau Claris 74; s €70, d €96-113; ✳; ⓂPasseig de Gràcia, Urquinaona) The Goya is a modestly priced gem on the chichi side of L'Eixample. Rooms have a light colour scheme that varies from room to room. In the bathrooms, the original mosaic floors have largely been retained, combined with contemporary design features.

✗ Eating

Barcelona is foodie heaven. The city has firmly established itself as one of Europe's gourmet capitals, and innovative, cutting-edge restaurants abound. Some of the most creative chefs are one-time students of world-renowned chef Ferran Adrià, whose influence on the city's cuisine is strong.

Although Barcelona has a reputation as a hot spot of 'new Spanish cuisine', you'll still find local eateries serving up time-honoured local grub, from squid-ink *fideuà* (a satisfying paella-like noodle dish) to pigs' trotters, rabbit with snails, and *butifarra* (a tasty local sausage).

LA RAMBLA & BARRI GÒTIC

Skip the overpriced traps along La Rambla and get into the winding lanes of the Barri Gòtic.

Pla
TOP CHOICE
FUSION €€

(Map p688; ☑93 412 65 52; www.elpla.cat; Carrer de la Bellafila 5; mains €18-24; ☺dinner; ⚲; ⓂJaume I) One of Gòtic's long-standing favourites, Pla is a stylish, romantically lit medieval den (with a huge stone arch) where the cooks churn out such temptations as oxtail braised in red wine, seared tuna with roasted aubergine, and 'Thai-style' monkfish with prawns, lemongrass and apple foam. It has a tasting menu for €36 Sunday to Thursday.

La Vinateria dell Call
SPANISH €€

(Map p688; ☑93 302 60 92; www.lavinateriadelcall. com; Carrer de Sant Domènec del Call 9; small plates €7-11; ☺dinner; ⓂJaume I) In a magical setting in the former Jewish quarter, this tiny jewel-box of a restaurant serves up tasty Iberian dishes, including Galician octopus, cider-cooked chorizo and the Catalan *escalivada* (roasted peppers, aubergine and onions) with anchovies.

Can Culleretes
CATALAN €€

(Map p688; ☑93 317 30 22; www.culleretes.com; Carrer Quintana 5; mains €8-14; ☺lunch & dinner Tue-Sat, lunch Sun; ⓂLiceu) Founded in 1786, Barcelona's oldest restaurant is still going strong, with tourists and locals flocking to enjoy its rambling interior, old-fashioned tile-filled decor and enormous helpings of traditional Catalan food. The multicourse lunch specials are good value.

Agut
CATALAN €€

(Map p688; www.restaurantagut.com; Carrer d'en Gignàs 16; mains €16-25; ☺lunch & dinner Tue-Sat, lunch Sun; ⓂJaume I) Deep in the Gothic labyrinth lies this classic eatery. A series of cosy dining areas is connected by broad arches while, high up, the walls are tightly lined by artworks. There's art in what the kitchen serves up too, from the oak-grilled meat to a succulent variety of seafood offerings.

EL RAVAL

TOP CHOICE Bar Pinotxo TAPAS €€

(Map p688; www.pinotxobar.com; Mercat de la Boqueria; meals €20; ⊙6am-5pm Mon-Sat Sep-Jul; Ⓜ Liceu) Bar Pinotxo is arguably Barcelona's best tapas bar. It sits among the half-dozen or so informal eateries within Mercat de la Boqueria (p683), and the popular owner, Juanito, might serve up chickpeas with a sweet sauce of pine nuts and raisins, baby soft baby squid with cannellini beans, or a quivering cube of caramel sweet pork belly.

Can Lluís CATALAN €€€

(Map p688; Carrer de la Cera 49; meals €30-35; ⊙Mon-Sat, closed Aug; Ⓜ Sant Antoni) Three generations have kept this spick and span old-time classic in business since 1929. Beneath the olive-green beams in the back dining room you can see the spot where an anarchist's bomb went off in 1946, killing the then owner. Expect fresh fish and seafood.

Granja Viader CAFE €

(Map p688; ☎93 318 34 86; www.granjaviader.cat; Carrer d'en Xuclà 4; ⊙9am-1.45pm & 5-8.45pm Tue-Sat, 5-8.45pm Mon; Ⓜ Liceu) For more than a century, people have flocked down this alley to get to the cups of homemade hot chocolate and whipped cream (ask for a *suís*) ladled out in this classic Catalan-style milk bar cum deli.

LA RIBERA & WATERFRONT

La Barceloneta is the place to go for seafood; Passeig Joan de Borbó is lined with eateries but locals head for the back lanes.

TOP CHOICE Cal Pep TAPAS €€

(Map p684; ☎93 310 79 61; www.calpep.com; Plaça de les Olles 8; mains €8-18; ⊙lunch Tue-Sat, dinner Mon-Fri, closed Aug; Ⓜ Barceloneta) It's getting a foot in the door here that's the problem. Elbowing your way to the bar for some of the tastiest gourmet seafood tapas in town. Pep recommends *cloïsses amb pernil* (clams and ham) or the *trifàsic* (combo of calamari, whitebait and prawns). Its other pièce de résistance is a super smooth *tortilla de patatas* (Spanish omelette).

Casa Delfín SPANISH €

(Map p684; Passeig del Born 36; mains €4-12; ⊙noon-1am; Ⓜ Barceloneta) One of Barcelona's culinary delights, Casa Delfín is everything you dream of when you think of Catalan (and Mediterranean) cooking. Start with the tangy and sweet *calçots* (a cross between a leek and an onion; February and March only) or salt-strewn *padron* peppers, moving on to grilled sardines specked with parsley, then tackle the meaty monkfish roasted in white wine and garlic.

Can Majó SEAFOOD €€

(Map p684; ☎93 221 54 55; www.canmajo.es; Carrer del Almirall Aixada 23; mains €18-24; ⊙lunch & dinner Tue-Sat, lunch Sun; ▣45, 57, 59, 64, 157, Ⓜ Barceloneta) Virtually on the beach (with tables outside in summer), Can Majó has a long and steady reputation for fine seafood, particularly its rice dishes and bountiful *suquets* (fish stews). The *bollabessa de peix i marisc* (fish and seafood bouillabaisse) is succulent. Or try a big *graellada* (mixed seafood grill).

Suquet De L'Almirall SEAFOOD €€€

(Map p684; ☎93 221 62 33; www.suquetdelalmirall.com; Passeig de Joan de Borbó 65; meals €45-50; ⊙lunch & dinner Tue-Sat, lunch Sun; ▣17, 39, 57, 64, Ⓜ Barceloneta) A family business run by an alumnus of Ferran Adrià's El Bulli, the order of the day is top-class seafood with the occasional unexpected twist. The house specialty is *suquet*. A good option is the *pica pica marinera* (a seafood mix) or you could opt for the tasting menu (€44). Grab one of the few outdoor tables.

L'EIXAMPLE & GRÀCIA

Tapaç 24 TAPAS €€

(Map p684; www.carlesabellan.com; Carrer de la Diputació 269; mains €10-20; ⊙9am-midnight Mon-Sat; Ⓜ Passeig de Gràcia) Carles Abellán runs this basement tapas haven known for its gourmet versions of old faves. Specials include the *bikini* (toasted ham and cheese sandwich – here the ham is cured and the truffle makes all the difference) and a thick black *arròs negre de sípia* (squid-ink black rice).

Cinc Sentits INTERNATIONAL €€

(Map p684; ☎93 323 94 90; www.cincsentits.com; Carrer d'Aribau 58; mains €10-20; ⊙lunch & dinner Tue-Sat; Ⓜ Passeig de Gràcia) Enter this somewhat overlit realm of the 'Five Senses' to indulge in a tasting menu (from €49 to €69), consisting of a series of small, experimental dishes. A key is the use of fresh local produce, such as fish landed on the Costa Brava and top-quality suckling pig from Extremadura. Less ambitious, but cheaper, is the set lunch at €30.

SPAIN BARCELONA

Montjuïc, Sants & Poble Sec

TOP CHOICE Tickets
SPANISH €€

(Map p684; www.ticketsbar.es; Avinguda del Paral·lel 164; tapas €4-12; ⊗lunch & dinner; MParal·lel) This is, literally, one of the sizzling tickets in the restaurant world. It's the new tapas bar opened by Ferran Adrià, of the legendary (now closed) El Bulli, and his brother Albert. And unlike El Bulli, it's an affordable venture – if you can book a table, that is (you can only book online, and two months in advance).

Quimet i Quimet
TAPAS €€

(Map p684; Carrer del Poeta Cabanyes 25; tapas €3-11; ⊗lunch & dinner Mon-Fri, noon-6pm Sat; MParal·lel) Quimet i Quimet is a family-run business that has been passed down from generation to generation. There's barely space to swing a calamari in this bottle-lined, standing-room-only place, but it is a tapas treat for the palate.

🍷 Drinking

Barcelona abounds with day-time cafes, laid-back lounges and lively night-time bars. Closing time is generally 2am from Sunday to Thursday, and 3am Friday and Saturday.

BARRI GÒTIC

Oviso
BAR

(Map p688; Carrer d'Arai 5; ⊗10am-2am; MLiceu) Oviso is a popular, budget-friendly restaurant with outdoor tables on the plaza, but shows its true bohemian colours by night, with a wildly mixed crowd, a rock-and-roll vibe and a two-room fin-de-siècle interior plastered with curious murals.

Marula Cafè
BAR

(Map p688; www.marulacafe.com; Carrer dels Escudellers 49; ⊗11pm-5am; MLiceu) A fantastic funk find in the heart of the Barri Gòtic, Marula will transport you to the 1970s and the best in funk and soul. James Brown fans will think they've died and gone to heaven.

EL RAVAL

TOP CHOICE La Confitería
BAR

(Map p688; Carrer de Sant Pau 128; ⊗11am-2am; MParal·lel) This is a trip into the 19th century. Until the 1980s it was a confectioner's shop and, although the original cabinets are now lined with booze, the look of the place has barely changed in its conversion into a laid-back bar.

33|45
BAR

(Map p688; Carrer Joaquín Costa 4; ⊗10am-1:30am Mon-Thu, to 3am Fri & Sat, to midnight Sun; MUniversitat) A supertrendy cocktail bar on the nightlife-laden Joaquín Costa street, this place has excellent mojitos – even pink, strawberry ones! – and a fashionable crowd. The main area has DJ music and lots of excited noise making, while the back room is scattered with sofas and armchairs for a post-dancing slump.

LA RIBERA

TOP CHOICE El Xampanyet
WINE BAR

(Map p688; Carrer de Montcada 22; ⊗noon-4pm & 7-11pm Tue-Sat, noon-4pm Sun; MJaume I) Nothing has changed for decades at El Xampanyet, one of the city's best-known *cava* (Catalan version of champagne) bars. Plant yourself at the bar or seek out a table against the decoratively tiled walls for a glass or three of *cava* and an assortment of tapas.

La Vinya del Senyor
WINE BAR

(Map p688; www.lavinyadelsenyor.com; Plaça de Santa Maria del Mar 5; ⊗noon-1am Tue-Sun; MJaume I) Relax on the *terrassa*, which lies in the shadow of Església de Santa Maria del Mar, or crowd inside at the tiny bar. The wine list is as long as *War and Peace* and there's a table upstairs for those who opt to sample by the bottle rather than the glass.

L'EIXAMPLE & GRÀCIA

TOP CHOICE Monvínic
WINE BAR

(Map p684; ☎932 72 61 87; www.monvinic.com; Carrer de la Diputació 249 ; ⊗wine bar 1.30-11.30pm, restaurant 1.30-3.30pm & 8.30-10.30pm; MPasseig de Gracia) Proclaimed as 'possibly the best wine bar in the world' by the *Wall Street Journal,* and apparently considered unmissable by El Bulli's former sommelier, Monvínic is an ode, a rhapsody even, to wine loving. The interactive wine list sits on the bar for you to browse on a digital tablet and boasts more than 3000 varieties.

But that's not to say that it's for connoisseurs only; you can also come here to taste wine by the glass – there are 60 selections.

Les Gens Que J'Aime
BAR

(Map p684; www.lesgensquejaime.com; Carrer de València 286; ⊗6pm-2.30am Sun-Thu, to 3am Fri & Sat; MPasseig de Gràcia) This intimate basement relic of the 1960s follows a deceptively simple formula: chilled jazz music in the background, minimal lighting from an assortment of flea-market lamps and a cosy, cramped scattering of red velvet-backed lounges around tiny dark tables.

☆ Entertainment

To keep up with what's on, pick up a copy of the weekly listings magazine, *Guía del Ocio* (€1) from news-stands.

Nightclubs

Barcelona clubs are spread a little more thinly than bars across the city. They tend to open from around midnight until 6am. Entry can cost from nothing to €20 (one drink usually included).

Elephant   CLUB
(☏93 334 02 58; www.elephantbcn.com; Passeig dels Til·lers 1; ⊙11.30pm-4am Thu, to 5am Fri & Sat; ⓂPalau Reial) Getting in here is like being invited to a private fantasy party in Beverly Hills. Models and wannabes mix with immaculately groomed lads who most certainly didn't come by taxi. A big tentlike dance space is the main game here, but smooth customers slink their way around a series of garden bars in summer too.

Moog   CLUB
(Map p688; www.masimas.com/moog; Carrer de l'Arc del Teatre 3; admission €10; ⊙midnight-5am; ⓂDrassanes) This fun and minuscule club is a standing favourite with the downtown crowd. In the main dance area, DJs dish out house, techno and electro, while upstairs you can groove to a nice blend of indie and occasional classic-pop throwbacks.

Razzmatazz   CLUB
(Map p684; ☏93 320 82 00; www.salarazzmatazz. com; Carrer de Pamplona 88; admission €15-30; ⊙midnight-3.30am Thu, to 5.30am Fri & Sat; ⓂMarina, Bogatell) Bands from far and wide occasionally create scenes of near hysteria in this, one of the city's classic live-music and clubbing venues. Five different clubs in one huge postindustrial space attract people of all dance persuasions and ages.

Gay & Lesbian Venues

Barcelona's gay and lesbian scene is concentrated in the blocks around Carrers de Muntaner and Consell de Cent (dubbed Gayxample). Here you'll find ambience every night of the week in the bars, discos and drag clubs.

Party hard at classic gay discos such as **Arena Madre** (Map p684; ☏93 487 83 42; www.

arenadisco.com; Carrer de Balmes 32; admission €6-12; ⊙12.30am-5.30am; ⓂPasseig de Gràcia) and **Metro** (Map p688; ☏93 323 52 27; www.met-rodiscobcn.com; Carrer de Sepúlveda 185; ⊙1am-5am Mon, midnight-5am Sun & Tue-Thu, midnight-6am Fri & Sat; ⓂUniversitat).

Live Music

TOP CHOICE **Palau de la Música Catalana**   CLASSICAL MUSIC
(☏902 442882; www.palaumusica.org; Carrer de Sant Francesc de Paula 2; ⊙box office 10am-9pm Mon-Sat; ⓂUrquinaona) A feast for the eyes, this Modernista confection is also the city's traditional venue for classical and choral music. Just being here for a performance is an experience. Sip a preconcert tipple in the foyer, its tiled pillars all a-glitter. Head up the grand stairway to the main auditorium, a whirlpool of Modernista whimsy. The *palau* has a wide-ranging programme.

Harlem Jazz Club   JAZZ
(Map p688; ☏93 310 07 55; www.harlemjazzclub. es; Carrer de la Comtessa de Sobradiel 8; admission €6-15; ⊙8pm-4am Tue-Thu & Sun, to 5am Fri & Sat; ⓂDrassanes) This narrow, old-town dive is one of the best spots in town for jazz. Every now and then it mixes it up with a little Latin, blues or African rhythms. It attracts a mixed crowd who maintain a respectful silence during the acts. Usually there are two sessions with different musos each night.

Sala Tarantos   FLAMENCO
(Map p688; ☏93 319 17 89; www.masimas.net; Plaça Reial 17; admission from €7; ⊙shows 8.30pm, 9.30pm & 10.30pm; ⓂLiceu) Since 1963, this basement locale has been the stage for up-and-coming flamenco groups performing in Barcelona. These days Tarantos has become a mostly tourist-centric affair, with half-hour shows held three times a night. Still, it's a good introduction to flamenco, and not a bad setting for a drink.

Sport

FC Barcelona (Barça for aficionados) has one of the best stadiums in Europe – the 99,000-capacity **Camp Nou** (☏93 496 36 00; www.fcbarcelona.com; Carrer d'Aristides Maillol; adult/child €23/17; ⊙10am-8pm Mon-Sat, to 2.30pm Sun; ⓂPalau Reial) in the west of the city. Tickets for national-league games are available at the stadium, by phone or online. For the latter two options, non-members must book 15 days before the match.

🛍 Shopping

Most mainstream fashion stores are along a shopping 'axis' that runs from Plaça de Catalunya along Passeig de Gràcia, then left (west) along Avinguda Diagonal.

The El Born area in La Ribera is awash with tiny boutiques, especially those purveying young, fun fashion. There are plenty of shops scattered throughout the Barri Gòtic (stroll Carrer d'Avinyò and Carrer de Portaferrissa). For secondhand stuff, head for El Raval, especially Carrer de la Riera Baixa.

Joan Murrià
FOOD

(Map p684; ☑93 215 57 89; www.murria.cat; Carrer de Roger de Llúria 85; Ⓜ️Passeig de Gràcia) Note the century-old Modernista shop-front advertisements featured at this culinary temple. For a century the gluttonous have trembled here at this altar of speciality food goods from around Catalonia and beyond.

Els Encants Vells
MARKET

(Fira de Bellcaire; Map p684; ☑93 246 30 30; www.encantsbcn.com; Plaça de les Glòries Catalanes; ⊙7am-6pm Mon, Wed, Fri & Sat; Ⓜ️Glòries) The 'Old Charms' flea market is the biggest of its kind in Barcelona. It's all here, from antique furniture through to secondhand clothes. A lot of it is junk, but occasionally you'll stumble across a *ganga* (bargain). The most interesting time to be here is from 7am to 9am on Monday, Wednesday and Friday, when the public auctions take place.

Vinçon
HOMEWARES

(Map p684; ☑93 215 60 50; www.vincon.com; Passeig de Gràcia 96; ⊙10am-8.30pm Mon-Sat; Ⓜ️Diagonal) An icon of the Barcelona design scene, Vinçon has the slickest furniture and household goods (particularly lighting), both local and imported. Not surprising, really, since the building, raised in 1899, belonged to the Modernista artist Ramon Casas.

WANT MORE?

For in-depth information, reviews and recommendations at your fingertips, head to the Apple App Store to purchase Lonely Planet's *Barcelona City Guide* iPhone app.

Alternatively, head to **Lonely Planet** (www.lonelyplanet.com/Spain/Barcelona) for planning advice, author recommendations, traveller reviews and insider tips.

Antonio Miró
FASHION

(Map p684; ☑93 487 06 70; www.antoniomiro.es; Carrer del Consell de Cent 349; ⊙10am-8pm Mon-Sat; Ⓜ️Passeig de Gràcia) Antonio Miró is one of Barcelona's haute couture kings. The entrance to the airy store, with dark hardwood floor, seems more like a hip hotel reception. Miró concentrates on light, natural fibres to produce smart, unpretentious men's and women's fashion.

Custo Barcelona
FASHION

(Map p684; ☑93 268 78 93; www.custo-barcelona.com; Plaça de les Olles 7; Ⓜ️Jaume I) The psychedelic decor and casual atmosphere lend this avant-garde Barcelona fashion store a youthful edge. The dazzling colours and cut of anything from dinner jackets to hot pants are for the uninhibited. It has five other stores around town.

ℹ Information

Dangers & Annoyances

Purse snatching and pickpocketing are major problems, especially around Plaça de Catalunya, La Rambla and Plaça Reial.

Emergency

Tourists who want to report thefts need to go to the Catalan police, known as the **Mossos d'Esquadra** (☑088; Carrer Nou de la Rambla 80; Ⓜ️Paral.lel), or the **Guàrdia Urbana** (Local Police; ☑092; La Rambla 43; Ⓜ️Liceu)

In an emergency, call ☑112.

Internet Access

Bornet (Carrer de Barra Ferro 3; per hr/10hr €2.80/20; ⊙10am-11pm Mon-Fri, 2-11pm Sat, Sun & holidays; Ⓜ️Jaume I) A cool little internet centre and art gallery.

Medical Services

Call ☑010 to find the nearest late-opening duty pharmacy.

Farmàcia Clapés (La Rambla 98; Ⓜ️Liceu)

Hospital Clínic i Provincial (Carrer de Villarroel 170; Ⓜ️Hospital Clínic)

Tourist Information

Oficina d'Informació de Turisme de Barcelona (Map p688; ☑93 285 38 34; www.barcelonaturisme.com; underground at Plaça de Catalunya 17-S; ⊙8.30am-8.30pm; Ⓜ️Catalunya) also has branches at Aeroport del Prat (Aeroport del Prat, terminals 1, 2B & 2A; ⊙9am-9pm), Estació Sants (Estació Sants; ⊙8am-8pm; 🚉Estació Sants) and Town hall (Plaça Sant Jaume; ☑93 285 38 32; Carrer de la Ciutat 2; ⊙8.30am-8.30pm

ANDORRA

This mini-country wedged between France and Spain offers by far the best ski slopes and resort facilities in all the Pyrenees. Once the snow melts, there's an abundance of great walking, ranging from easy strolls to demanding day hikes in the principality's higher, more remote reaches. Strike out above the tight valleys and you can walk for hours, almost alone.

The only way to reach Andorra is by road from Spain or France. If driving, fill up in Andorra; fuel is substantially cheaper there. There are bus services to/from Lleida, Barcelona's Estació del Nord, Barcelona's airport El Prat de Llobregat, and Toulouse (France). All bus services arrive at and leave from Andorra la Vella. **Andorra Direct Bus** (www. andorradirectbus.es) is one of a number of companies offering direct services to/from Barcelona (three hours) and Barcelona's Prat Airport (3½ hours).

Mon-Fri, 9am-7pm Sat, 9am-2pm Sun & holidays; **M**Jaume I).

There is also a **Regional Tourist Office** (www.gencat.net/probert; Passeig de Gràcia 107; ⏰10am-7pm Mon-Sat, to 2.30pm Sun; **M**Diagonal).

 Getting There & Away

Air

Barcelona's airport, **El Prat de Llobregat** (☎902 404704; www.aena.es), is 12km southwest of the city centre. Barcelona is a big international and domestic destination, with direct flights from North America as well as many European cities.

Boat

Regular passenger and vehicular ferries to/from the Balearic Islands, operated by **Acciona Trasmediterránea** (☎902 454645; www.tras mediterranea.es), dock along both sides of the Moll de Barcelona wharf in Port Vell.

The Grimaldi group's **Grandi Navi Veloci** (www1.gnv.it) runs high-speed, thrice-weekly luxury ferries between Barcelona and Genoa, while **Grimaldi Ferries** (☎902 531333, www. grimaldi-lines.com) operates similar services to Civitavecchia (near Rome), Livorno (Tuscany) and Porto Torres (northwest Sardinia).

Bus

The main terminal for most domestic and international buses is the **Estació del Nord** (☎902 260606; www.barcelonanord.com; Carrer d'Ali Bei 80; **M**Arc de Triomf). ALSA goes to Madrid (€30, eight hours, up to 16 daily), Valencia (€27, 4½ hours to 6½ hours, up to 14 daily) and many other destinations.

Eurolines (www.eurolines.es) also offers international services from Estació del Nord and **Estació d'Autobusos de Sants** (Map p684; Carrer de Viriat; **M**Estació Sants).

Train

Virtually all trains travelling to and from destinations within Spain stop at **Estació Sants** (Plaça dels Països Catalans; **M**Estació Sants). High-speed trains to Madrid via Lleida and Zaragoza take as little as two hours and 40 minutes; prices vary wildly. Other trains run to Valencia (€36 to €45, three to 4½ hours, 15 daily) and Burgos (from €66, six to seven hours, four daily).

There are also international connections with French cities from the same station.

 Getting Around

To/From the Airport

The **A1 Aerobús** (☎93 415 60 20; one way €5.65) runs from Terminal 1 to Plaça de Catalunya from 6.05am to 1.05am, taking 30 to 40 minutes. A2 Aerobús does the same run from Terminal 2, from 6am to 12.30am. Buy tickets on the bus.

Renfe's R2 Nord train line runs between the airport and Passeig de Gràcia (via Estació Sants) in central Barcelona (about 35 minutes). Tickets cost €3.60, unless you have a T-10 multitrip public-transport ticket.

A taxi to/from the centre, about a half-hour ride depending on traffic, costs around €25 to €30.

Public Transport

Barcelona's metro system spreads its tentacles around the city in such a way that most places of interest are within a 10-minute walk of a station. Buses and suburban trains are needed only for a few destinations. A single metro, bus or suburban train ride costs €2, but a T-1 ticket, valid for 10 rides, costs €9.25.

Taxi

Barcelona's black-and-yellow taxis are plentiful and reasonably priced. The flag fall is €2.05. If you can't find a street taxi, call ☎93 303 30 33.

Monestir de Montserrat

The monks who built the Monestir de Montserrat (Monastery of the Serrated Mountain), 50km northwest of Barcelona, chose a spectacular spot. The Benedictine **monastery** (www.abadiamontserrat.net; ⊘9am-6pm) sits on the side of a 1236m-high mountain of weird, bulbous peaks. The monastery was founded in 1025 and pilgrims still come from all over Christendom to kiss the Black Virgin (La Moreneta), the 12th-century wooden sculpture of the Virgin Mary.

The **Museu de Montserrat** (www.museudemontserrat.com; Plaça de Santa Maria; adult/student €6.50/5.50; ⊘10am-6pm) has an excellent collection, ranging from an Egyptian mummy to art by El Greco, Monet, Degas and Picasso.

If you're around the basilica at the right time, you'll catch a brief performance by the **Montserrat Boys' Choir** (www.escolania.cat; ⊘performances 1pm & Mon-Thu, 1pm Fri, noon Sun late Aug–late Jun)

You can explore the mountain above the monastery on a web of paths leading to some of the peaks and to 13 empty and rather dilapidated hermitages. Running every 20 minutes, the **Funicular de Sant Joan** (one way/return €5.05/8; ⊘every 20min 10am-6.50pm, closed Jan & Feb) will carry you up the first 250m from the monastery.

❶ Getting There & Away

Montserrat is an easy day trip from Barcelona. The R5 line trains operated by FGC run from Plaça d'Espanya station in Barcelona to Monistrol de Montserrat up to 18 times daily starting at 5.16am. They connect with the rack-and-pinion train, or **cremallera** (☑902 312020; www.cremalleradmontserrat.com; one way/return €6/9), which takes 17 minutes to make the upwards journey.

Girona

POP 96,120

A tight huddle of ancient arcaded houses, grand churches, climbing cobbled streets and medieval baths, all enclosed by defensive walls and a lazy river, constitute a powerful reason for visiting north Catalonia's largest city, Girona (Castilian: Gerona).

◉ Sights

Catedral   CATHEDRAL
(www.catedraldegirona.org; Plaça de la Catedral; museum adult/child €5/1.20, Sun free; ⊘10am-8pm) The billowing baroque facade of the cathedral stands at the head of a majestic flight of steps rising from Plaça de la Catedral. Repeatedly rebuilt and altered down the centuries, it has Europe's widest Gothic nave (23m). The cathedral's **museum**, through the door marked 'Claustre Tresor', contains the masterly Romanesque *Tapís de la Creació* (Tapestry of the Creation) and a Mozarabic illuminated *Beatus* manuscript, dating from 975. The fee for the museum also admits you to the beautiful 12th-century Romanesque cloister.

[TOP CHOICE] **Passeig Arqueològic**   RUINS
Across the street from the Banys Àrabs, steps lead up into some heavenly gardens where town and plants merge into one organic masterpiece. The gardens follow the city walls up to the 18th-century Portal de Sant Cristòfol gate, from where you can walk back down to Girona's cathedral.

DALÍ'S CATALONIA

A short train ride north of Girona, Figueres is home to the zany **Teatre-Museu Dalí** (www.salvador-dali.org; Plaça de Gala i Salvador Dalí 5; admission incl Dalí Joies & Museu de l'Empordá adult/child €12/free; ⊘9am-8pm Jul-Sep, 9.30am-6pm Mar-Jun & Oct, shorter hr rest of yr), housed in a 19th-century theatre converted by Salvador Dalí (who was born here). 'Theatre-museum' is an apt label for this multidimensional trip through one of the most fertile (or disturbed) imaginations of the 20th century. It's full of surprises, tricks and illusions, and contains a substantial portion of Dalí's life's work.

Dalí fans will want to travel south to visit the equally kooky **Castell de Púbol** (www.salvador-dali.org; Plaça de Gala Dalí; adult/student & senior €8/5; ⊘10am-8pm daily mid-Jun–mid-Sep, shorter hr rest of yr) at La Pera, 22km northwest of Palafrugell, and the **Casa Museu Dalí** (☑972 25 10 15; www.salvador-dali.org; adult/child €11/free) at his summer getaway in Port Lligat (1.25km from Cadaqués), where entry is by advance reservation only.

The Call
HISTORIC DISTRICT

Until 1492 Girona was home to Catalonia's second-most important medieval Jewish community (after Barcelona), and its Jewish quarter, the Call, centred on Carrer de la Força. For an idea of medieval Jewish life and culture, visit the **Museu d'Història dels Jueus de Girona** (Carrer de la Força 8; adult/child €2/free; ⊙10am-8pm Mon-Sat, to 2pm Sun Jul & Aug, shorter hr rest of yr).

🛏️ Sleeping & Eating

Bed & Breakfast Bells Oficis
B&B €€

(📞972 22 81 70; www.bellsoficis.com; Carrer dels Germans Busquets 2; r incl breakfast €40-85; ❄️🛜) Up the wobbly-winding staircase of a 19th-century building right in the heart of Girona you'll discover six very desirable rooms, lovingly restored by knowledgeable Javi and his wife. Some have unusual pebble art in the bathrooms, while others have views over the street.

Casa Cúndaro
BOUTIQUE HOTEL €€

(📞972 22 35 83; www.casacundaro.com; Pujada de la Catedral 9; d €60-80; 🛜) The understated exterior of this medieval Jewish house, run by a friendly family, hides five sumptuous rooms and four self-catering apartments – all combining original exposed stone walls with modern luxuries, such as satellite TV.

Hotel Llegendes de Girona
HOTEL €€€

(📞972 22 09 05; www.llegendeshotel.com; Portal de la Barca 4; d from €123, 'Fountain of Lovers' room €288; P❄️🛜) The rooms at this restored 18th-century building are supremely comfortable, with all manner of high-tech gadgets, and the all-glass bathrooms have huge rain showers. This incongruous blend of modernity and antiquity includes a guide to tantric sex positions in each room; three of the rooms even have an 'Eros' sofa to try them out on.

🔝 TOP CHOICE Restaurant Txalaka
BASQUE €€

(📞972 22 59 75; www.restauranttxalaka.com; Carrer Bonastruc de Porta 4; mains €17-23, pintxos €2.50-4; ⊙closed Sun) For sensational Basque cooking and *pintxos* washed down with *txakoli* (the fizzy white wine from the Basque coast) poured from a great height, don't miss this popular local spot.

L'Alqueria
CATALAN €€

(📞972 22 18 82; www.restaurantalqueria.com; Carrer de la Ginesta 8; mains €18-22; ⊙lunch & dinner Wed-Sat, lunch only Tue & Sun) This smart minimalist *arrocería* serves the finest *arròs negre* (rice cooked in cuttlefish ink) and *arròs a la Catalan* in the city, as well as around 20 other superbly executed rice dishes, including paellas. Book ahead for dinner.

ℹ️ Information

Tourist Office (www.girona.cat; Joan Maragall 2; ⊙8am-8pm Mon-Fri, 8am-2pm & 4-8pm Sat, 9am-2pm Sun)

ℹ️ Getting There & Away

AIR Girona-Costa Brava airport, 11km south of the centre and just off the AP7 and A2, is Ryanair's Spanish hub.

TRAIN There are more than 20 trains per day to Figueres (€4.80 to €14.10, 30 to 40 minutes) and Barcelona (from €9.70, 1½ hours).

The Costa Brava

The Costa Brava (Rugged Coast) was Catalonia's first tourist centre, and after you visit its rocky coastline, romantic coves, turquoise waters and former fishing villages, you'll see why. Overdevelopment has ruined some stretches but much of the coast retains its spectacular beauty.

👁️ Sights & Activities

The Costa Brava is all about picturesque inlets and coves – and there are many. Although buses run along much of the coast, the best way to uncover some of these gems is with your own wheels.

The first truly pretty stop on the Costa Brava when heading northeast from Barcelona is **Tossa de Mar**, with its golden beach, ochre medieval village core and nearby coves. The coast road on to **Sant Feliu de Guíxols** is spectacular.

Further north are three gorgeous beach towns near Palafrugell: **Tamariu** (the smallest, least crowded and most exclusive), **Llafranc** (the biggest and busiest) and **Calella de Palafrugell**. There are further fine beaches and coves on the coast near Begur, a little further north.

North of the Costa Brava's main dive centre, **L'Estartit**, are the ruins of the Greek and Roman town of **Empúries** (📞972 77 02 08; www.mac.cat; adult/child €3/free; ⊙10am-8pm Jun-Sep, to 6pm Oct-May), 2km outside **L'Escala**.

Cadaqués, at the end of an agonising series of hairpin bends one hour from Figueres, is postcard perfect. Beaches are of the pebbly variety, so people spend a lot of time sitting at waterfront cafes or strolling. It's a pleasant 2km walk from central Cadaqués to Port Lligat, where you'll find Dalí's summer residence. Some 10km northeast of Cadaqués is **Cap de Creus**, an impressive cape that is Spain's easternmost point.

Of the many historic towns inland from the Costa Brava, the pretty walled town of **Pals**, 6km inland from Begur, and the nearby impeccably preserved medieval hamlet of **Peratallada** are the most charming.

🛏️ Sleeping & Eating

TOSSA DE MAR

TOP CHOICE **Hostal Cap d'Or**   HOSTAL €€
(☎972 34 00 81; www.hotelcapdor.com; Passeig de la Vila Vella 1; s/d incl breakfast €63/103; ❄️🖥️) Rub up against the town's history in this family-run spot right in front of the town walls. Rooms are lovingly decorated in sea-blues and whites, and the best of them look straight onto the beach.

Hotel Diana   HOTEL €€€
(☎972 34 18 86; www.hotelesdante.com; Plaça d'Espanya 6; d incl breakfast €145, with sea views €170-180; ☺Apr-Nov; 🅿❄️🖥️) Fronting Platja Gran, this artistic 1920s hotel has a Gaudí-built fireplace in the lounge and oozes Modernista decor and has stained glass in the central covered courtyard. Half of the spacious, tiled rooms have beach views.

TOP CHOICE **La Cuina de Can Simon**   CATALAN €€€
(☎972 34 12 69; www.lacuinadecansimon.com; Carrer del Portal 24; mains €30-50, taster menus €68-98; ☺lunch & dinner Wed-Sat & Mon, lunch Sun) Tossa's culinary star nestles by the old walls in a former fisherman's stone house and distinguishes itself by the most imaginative creations in town. Taking the *mar i muntanya* theme to its logical extreme, it presents you with pig trotters with sea cucumber as well as the more mainstream *fideuá* with rock fish.

CADAQUÉS

Hostal Vehí   PENSION €€
(☎972 25 84 70; www.hostalvehi.com; Carrer de l'Església 5; s/d without bathroom €30/55, d with bathroom €77; ❄️🖥️) Near the church in the heart of the old town, this simple *pensión* with clean-as-a-whistle rooms, run by a friendly family, tends to be booked up for July and August. It's a pain to get to if you have a lot of luggage, but it's easily the cheapest deal in town, and also about the best. Breakfast is €6 extra.

ℹ️ Information

There are tourist offices in **Palafrugell** (☎972 61 44 75; Carrer de les Voltes 6; ☺10am-8pm Jul-Aug, shorter hr rest of year) and other towns on the coast and inland.

ℹ️ Getting There & Away

Sarfa (☎902 30 20 25; www.sarfa.com) runs buses from Barcelona, Girona and Figueres to most towns along the Costa Brava.

Tarragona

POP 133.223

Barcelona's senior in Roman times (when the city was called Tarraco) and a lesser medieval city, Tarragona is a provincial sort of place with some outstanding attractions: Catalonia's finest Roman ruins, a magnificent medieval cathedral in a pretty old town and some decent beaches.

👁️ Sights

Museu d'Història de Tarragona   RUINS
(MHT; www.museutgn.com; adult/child per site €3/free, all MHT sites €10/free; ☺9am-9pm daily Easter-Sep, shorter hr rest of yr) The 'museum' title is somewhat misleading, as they are in fact four separate Roman sites (which, since 2000, together have constituted a Unesco World Heritage site).

Start exploring with the **Pretori i Circ Romans** (Plaça del Rei), which includes part of the vaults of the Roman circus, where chariot races were once held, ending at the Pretori tower on Plaça de Rei. Near the beach is the crown jewel of Tarragona's Roman sites, the well-preserved **Amfiteatre Romà** (Plaça d'Arce Ochotorena; ☺9am-9pm Tue-Sat, to 3pm Sun Easter-Sep, to 5pm Tue-Sat, 10am-3pm Sun & holidays Oct-Easter), where gladiators battled either each other or wild animals to the death. Much of the amphitheatre was picked to bits and the stone used to build the port, so what you see now is partial reconstruction. The northwest half of **Fórum Romà** (Carrer del Cardenal Cervantes) was occupied by a judicial basilica (where legal disputes were settled), from where the rest of the forum stretched downhill to the southwest. Linked to the site by a footbridge is another excavated area which includes a stretch of Roman street. The **Passeig Arqueològic** (admission €3; ☺9am-9pm Tue-Sat,

9am-3pm Sun Easter-Oct, shorter hr rest of yr) is a peaceful walk around part of the perimeter of the old town.

Museu Nacional Arqueològic de Tarragona
MUSEUM

(www.mnat.es; Plaça del Rei 5; adult/child €3.50/ free; ⊙10am-8pm Tue-Sat, to 2pm Sun & holidays Jun-Sep, shorter hr rest of yr) This carefully presented museum gives further insight into Roman Tarraco. Exhibits include part of the Roman city walls, mosaics, frescoes, sculpture and pottery.

Catedral
CATHEDRAL

(Pla de la Seu; adult/child €4/1.40; ⊙10am-7pm Mon-Sat Jun–mid-Oct, shorter hr rest of yr) Sitting grandly at the top of the old town, Tarragona's cathedral demands a solid chunk of your time. Built between 1171 and 1331 on the site of a Roman temple, it combines Romanesque and Gothic features, as typified by the main facade on Pla de la Seu. The entrance is by the cloister on the northwest flank of the building. The cloister and its perfectly presented gardens have Gothic vaulting and Romanesque carved capitals.

🛏 Sleeping & Eating

Look for tapas bars and inexpensive cafes on the Plaça de la Font. The Moll de Pescadors (Fishermen's Wharf) is the place to go for seafood restaurants.

Hotel Plaça de la Font
HOTEL €€

(☏977 24 61 34; www.hotelpdelafont.com; Plaça de la Font 26; s/d €55/70; ❄) Simple, spic-and-span rooms overlooking a bustling terrace in a you-can't-get-more-central-than-this location, right on the popular Plaça de la Font.

Hotel Lauria
HOTEL €€

(☏977 23 67 12; www.hotel-lauria.com; Rambla Nova 20; s/d from €49/69; P❄🐾🖥) In the newer part of town, a five-minute walk from the medieval part, this smart hotel offers modern rooms with welcome splashes of colour, large bathrooms and a small swimming pool.

Arcs Restaurant
MEDITERRANEAN €€

(☏977 21 80 40; www.restaurantarcs.com; Carrer Misser Sitges 13; menu €23; ⊙lunch & dinner Tue-Sat) Inside a medieval cavern with bright splashes of colour in the form of contemporary art, you are served some wonderful takes on Mediterranean dishes, including the most intense *salmorejo* (a cold, tomato-based soup) outside Andalucía.

Aq
CATALAN €€

(☏977 21 59 54; www.aq-restaurant.com; Carrer de les Coques 7; menus from €18; ⊙lunch & dinner Tue-Sat) This is a bubbly designer haunt with stark colour contrasts (black, lemon and cream linen), slick lines and intriguing plays on traditional cooking.

❶ Information

Regional Tourist Office (Carrer de Fortuny 4; ⊙9am-2pm & 4-6.30pm Mon-Fri, 9am-2pm Sat)

Tourist Office (www.tarragonaturisme.cat; Carrer Major 39; ⊙10am-8pm Mon-Sat, to 2pm Sun Jul-Oct, 10am-2pm & 4-7pm Mon-Sat)

❶ Getting There & Away

BUS Services run to Barcelona, Valencia, Zaragoza, Madrid, Alicante, Pamplona, the main Andalucian cities, Andorra and the north coast. The bus station is around 1.5km northwest of the old town.

TRAIN At least 16 regional trains per day run to/ from Barcelona's Passeig de Gràcia via Sants. Fares start at €15.90 and go up to €35.10; the journey takes one to 1½ hours.

ARAGÓN, BASQUE COUNTRY & NAVARRA

This northeastern area of Spain is brimming with fascinating destinations: the arid hills and proud history of Aragón; the lush coastline and gourmet delights of the Basque Country (País Vasco); and the wine country and famous festivals of Navarra.

Aragón

Zaragoza is the capital of the expansive Aragón region, though by no means is the city its only attraction. The national parks and pretty towns of the Pyrenees are well worth exploring too.

ZARAGOZA
POP 674,725

Sitting on the banks of the mighty Ebro River, Zaragoza (a contraction of Caesaraugusta, the name the Romans gave to this city when they founded it in 14 BC) is a busy regional capital with a seemingly voracious appetite for eating out and late-night revelry. The historic old centre, crowned by the majestic Basílica del Pilar, throws up echoes of its Roman and Muslim past. The old town is also home to El Tubo (The Tube), a maze of streets with countless tapas bars and cafes.

◉ Sights

FREE **Basílica de Nuestra Señora del Pilar** CHURCH
(Plaza del Pilar; lift admission €2; ☉7am-8.30pm, lift 10am-1.30pm & 4-6.30pm Tue-Sun) Brace yourself for the saintly and the solemn in this great baroque cavern of Catholicism. It was here on 2 January AD 40, that Santiago (St James the Apostle) is believed by the faithful to have seen the Virgin Mary descend atop a marble *pilar* (pillar). A chapel was built around the remaining pillar, followed by a series of ever-more-grandiose churches, culminating in the enormous basilica that you see today. Originally designed in 1681, it was greatly modified in the 18th century and the towers were not finished until the early 20th century. The exterior, with its splendid main dome lording over a flurry of 10 mini-domes, each encased in chunky blue, green, yellow and white tiles, creates a kind of rugged Byzantine effect. A lift whisks you most of the way up the north tower (Torre Pilar) for fine views.

Aljafería PALACE
(Calle de los Diputados; adult/under 12yr €3/free, free Sun; ☉10am-2pm Sat-Wed, 4.30-8pm Mon-Wed, Fri & Sat Jul & Aug, shorter hr rest of year) La Aljafería is Spain's finest Islamic-era edifice outside Andalucía. It's not in the league of Granada's Alhambra or Córdoba's Mezquita, but it's nonetheless a glorious monument. The Aljafería was built as a pleasure palace for Zaragoza's Islamic rulers, chiefly in the 11th century. After the city passed into Christian hands in 1118, Zaragoza's Christian rulers made alterations.

Inside the main gate, cross the rather dull introductory courtyard into a second, the Patio de Santa Isabel, once the central courtyard of the Islamic palace. Here you're confronted by the delicate interwoven arches typical of the geometric mastery of Islamic architecture.

La Seo CHURCH
(Catedral de San Salvador; Plaza de la Seo; admission €4; ☉10am-6pm Tue-Fri, 10am-2pm & 3-6pm Sat, 10-11.30am & 2.30-6pm Sun Jun-Sep) La Seo may lack the fame of the Basílica de Nuestra Señora del Pilar, but its interior is easily its architectural superior. Built between the 12th and 17th centuries, it displays a fabulous spread of architectural styles from Romanesque to baroque.

FREE **Museo Camón Aznar** MUSEUM
(Museo Ibercaja; Calle de Espoz y Mina 23; ☉10am-1.45pm & 5-8.45pm Tue-Sat, 10am-1.45pm Sun) This collection of Spanish art through the ages is dominated by an extraordinary series of etchings by Goya (on the 2nd floor), one of the premier such collections in existence. You'll also find paintings by other luminaries (including Ribera and Zurbarán), which spread over the three storeys of the Palacio de los Pardo, a Renaissance mansion.

Museo del Foro de Caesaraugusta MUSEUM
(Plaza de la Seo 2; admission €2.50; ☉9am-8.30pm Tue-Sat, 10am-2pm Sun Jun-Sep, shorter hr rest of year) The trapezoid building on Plaza de la Seo is the entrance to an excellent reconstruction of part of Roman Caesaraugusta's forum, now well below ground level.

Museo del Teatro de Caesaraugusta RUIN, MUSEUM
(Calle de San Jorge 12; admission €3.50; ☉9am-8.30pm Tue-Sat, to 1.30pm Sun) Discovered during the excavation of a building site in 1972, the ruins of Zaragoza's Roman theatre are the focus of this interesting museum; the theatre once seated 6000 spectators.

🛏 Sleeping

TOP
CHOICE **Sabinas** APARTMENT €
(☎976 20 47 10; www.sabinas.es; Calle de Alfonso I 43; d/apt €50/75; ❋⊛) Apartments with a kitchen and sitting room styled with a contemporary look and a location a few steps off Plaza del Pilar make this a terrific option. The bathrooms are lovely and the price is extraordinarily good considering the location and size of the rooms. Reception is at Hotel Sauce (☎976 20 50 50; www.hotelsauce.com; Calle de Espoz y Mina 33), around the corner.

Hotel Las Torres HOTEL €€
(☎976 39 42 50; www.hotellastorres.com; Plaza del Pilar 11; s/d incl breakfast from €75/85; ❋⊛) The rooms are designer cool with dazzling white furnishings and daring wallpaper in the public spaces. The bathrooms have hydromassage showers, and the views of the square and basilica from the balconies in most rooms are simply stunning. Our only complaint? Two years after it opened, the fittings are already showing considerable wear and tear.

Hostal el Descanso   HOSTAL €
(☑976 29 17 41; www.hostaleldescanso.es; Calle de San Lorenzo 2; s/d without bathroom €18/30; ☏) This welcoming family-run place combines a terrific location overlooking a pretty plaza near the Roman theatre with simple, bright rooms with comfortable mattresses. It adds up to one of the best budget choices in town.

✗ Eating & Drinking

Zaragoza has some terrific tapas bars, with dozens of places on or close to Plaza de Santa Marta. Otherwise the narrow streets of El Tubo, north of Plaza de España, are tapas central.

Calle del Temple, southwest of Plaza del Pilar, is the spiritual home of Zaragoza's roaring nightlife. This is where the city's students head out to drink. There are more bars lined up along this street than anywhere else in Aragón.

Casa Pascualillo   TAPAS €
(Calle de la Libertad 5; mains €5-14; ☉lunch & dinner Tue-Sat, lunch Sun) This celebrated bar groans under the weight of enticing tapas varieties; the house speciality is El Pascualillo, a 'small' *bocadillo* (filled roll) of *jamón*, mushrooms and onion. There's also a more formal restaurant attached.

Mery Limón Gastrobar   INTERNATIONAL €€
(www.merylimon.com; Calle de Santiago 30; mains €6-14; menú del día €15) This terrific little bar has an unusual menu divided into three parts – Italian, New York and Mediterranean. But what really stands out is the *menú del día* (daily set menu), which combines seven small dishes from the cutting-edge of Spanish gastronomy, and wines to go with them.

El Rincón de Aragón   ARAGONESE €€
(☑976 20 11 63; Calle de Santiago 3-5; mains €10-20) The decor here is basic and the food stripped down to its essence, but the eating is top-notch and ideal for finding out why people get excited about Aragonese cooking. If you're feeling hungry, numerous local dishes appear on the four-course *menú Aragonés*. The restaurant is in the covered lane between Calle de Santiago and Plaza del Pilar.

❶ Information

Main Tourist Office (☑976 39 35 37; www.zaragozaturismo.com; Plaza del Pilar; ☉9am-9pm Easter-Oct, 10am-8pm Nov-Easter) The city information office.

Oficina de Turismo de Aragón (www.turismodearagon.com; Avenida de César Augusto 25; ☉9am-2pm & 5-8pm Mon-Fri, from 10am Sat & Sun) Covers all of Aragón region.

❶ Getting There & Away

AIR **Zaragoza-Sanjurjo airport** (☑976 71 23 00) has domestic and international flights.

BUS Services from the bus station attached to the Estación Intermodal Delicias train station include Madrid (from €15.29, 3¾ hours) and Barcelona (€14.49, 3¾ hours).

TRAIN Zaragoza's **Estación Intermodal Delicias** (Calle Rioja 33) is connected by almost hourly high-speed AVE services to Madrid (€60.10, 1½ hours, 10 daily) and Barcelona (€65.80, from 1½ hours). There are also trains to Valencia (€29.80, 4½ hours, three daily) and Teruel (€16.55, 2¼ hours, four daily).

Around Aragón

In Aragón's south, little visited **Teruel** is home to some stunning Mudéjar architecture. Nearby, **Albarracín** is one of Spain's most beautiful villages.

In the north, the Pyrenees dominate and the **Parque Nacional de Ordesa y Monte Perdido** is excellent for hiking; the pretty village of **Torla** is the gateway. South of the hamlet of **La Besurta** is the great Maladeta massif, a superb challenge for experienced climbers. This forbidding line of icy peaks, with glaciers suspended from the higher crests, culminates in **Aneto** (3404m), the highest peak in the Pyrenees. There are plenty of hiking and climbing options for all levels in these mountain parks bordering France. Another enchanting base for exploration in the region is **Aínsa**, a hilltop village of stone houses.

In Aragón's northwest, **Sos del Rey Católico** is another gorgeous stone village draped along a ridge.

Basque Country

The Basques, whose language is believed to be among the world's oldest, claim two of Spain's most interesting cities – San Sebastián and Bilbao – as their own. Stately San Sebastián offers a slick seaside position and some of the best food Spain has to offer. Bilbao has the extraordinary Guggenheim Bilbao museum as its centrepiece.

SAN SEBASTIÁN
POP 185,500

Stylish San Sebastián (Donostia in Basque) has the air of an upscale resort, complete with an idyllic location on the shell-shaped Bahía de la Concha. The natural setting – crystalline waters, a flawless beach, green hills on all sides – is captivating. But this is one of Spain's true culinary capitals, with more Michelin stars (14) per capita here than anywhere else on earth.

◉ Sights & Activities

Beaches & Isla de Santa Clara   BEACH
Fulfilling almost every idea of how a perfect city beach should be formed, **Playa de la Concha** and its westerly extension, **Playa de Ondarreta**, are easily among the best city beaches in Europe. The **Isla de Santa Clara**, about 700m from the beach, is accessible by **glass-bottom boats** (to the island €3.80, tour the bay €6) that run every half-hour from June to September from the fishing port. Less popular, but just as showy, **Playa de Gros** (Playa de la Zurriola), east of Río Urumea, is the city's main surf beach.

Museo Chillida Leku   MUSEUM, PARK
(www.museochillidaleku.com; adult/child €8.50/free; ☺10.30am-8pm Mon-Sat, to 3pm Sun Jul & Aug, shorter hr rest of year) This open-air museum is the most engaging one in rural Basque Country. Amid the beech, oak and magnolia trees, you'll find 40 sculptures of granite and iron created by the renowned Basque sculptor Eduardo Chillida. Many more of Chillida's works appear inside the renovated 16th-century farmhouse.

To get here, take the G2 bus (€1.35) for Hernani from Calle de Okendo in San Sebastián and get off at Zabalaga.

Aquarium   AQUARIUM
(www.aquariumss.com; Paseo del Muelle 34; adult/4-12yr €12/6; ☺10am-8pm Mon-Fri, to 9pm Sat & Sun Apr-Jun & Sep, shorter hr rest of year) In San Sebastián's excellent aquarium, huge sharks bear down on you, and you'll be tripped out by fancy fluoro jellyfish. The highlights of a visit are the cinema-screen-sized deep-ocean and coral-reef exhibits and the long tunnel, around which swim monsters of the deep.

Monte Igueldo   VIEWPOINT
The views from the summit of Monte Igueldo, just west of town, will make you feel like a circling hawk staring over the vast panorama of the Bahía de la Concha and the surrounding coastline and mountains. The best way to get there is via the old-world **funicular railway** (return adult/child €2.80/2.10; ☺10am-10pm).

San Telmo Museoa   MUSEUM
(☎943 48 15 80; www.santelmomuseoa.com; Plaza Zuloaga 1; adult/child €5/free, free Tue; ☺10am-8pm Tue-Sun) This museum of Basque culture and society has displays that range from historical artefacts to the squiggly lines of modern art, and all the pieces are supposed to reflect Basque culture and society in some way or another.

Monte Urgull   CASTLE, MUSEUM
You can walk to the top of Monte Urgull, topped by low castle walls and a grand statue of Christ, by taking a path from Plaza de Zuloaga or from behind San Sebastián's aquarium. The views are breathtaking. The castle houses the well-presented **Mirando a San Sebastián** (admission free; ☺10am-2pm & 3-5.30pm), a small museum focusing on the city's history.

⌨ Sleeping

Pensión Bellas Artes   BOUTIQUE HOTEL €€
(☎943 47 49 05; www.pension-bellasartes.com; Calle de Urbieta 64; s €69-89, d €89-109; ☜) To call this magnificent place a mere *pensión* is to do it something of a disservice. Its rooms (some with glassed-in balconies), with their exposed stone walls and excellent bathrooms, should be the envy of many a more-expensive hotel. It also has to be the friendliest hotel in town.

Pensión Aida   BOUTIQUE HOTEL €€
(☎943 32 78 00; www.pensionesconencanto.com; Calle de Iztueta 9; s €60, d €82-88, studios €130-150; ✴@☜) The rooms here are bright and bold, full of exposed stone and everything smells fresh and clean. The communal area, stuffed with soft sofas and mountains of information, is a big plus. For our money, we'd say this one is very hard to beat.

Pensión Amaiur Ostatua   BOUTIQUE HOTEL €
(☎943 42 96 54; www.pensionamaiur.com; Calle de 31 de Agosto 44; s €45, d €54-65; @☜) This old town classic has always been one of the city's stand out accommodation options. At the time of research it was closed for major renovations that promise to make it even better than before. It will have re-opened by the time this book hits the shelves.

Pensión Altair
PENSION €€

(☎943 29 31 33; www.pension-altair.com; Calle Padre Larroca 3; s/d €60/86; ✳@⸂) This *pensión* is in a beautifully restored town house, with unusual church-worthy arched windows and modern, minimalist rooms that are a world away from the fusty decor of the old-town *pensiones*. Reception is closed between 1.30pm and 5pm.

✖ Eating

San Sebastián is paradise for food lovers. Considered the birthplace of *nueva cocina española* (Spanish nouvelle cuisine), this area is home to some of the country's top chefs. Yet not all the good food is pricey. Head to the Parte Vieja for San Sebastián's *pintxos,* Basque-style tapas.

Do what the locals do – go on crawls of the city centre's bars. *Pintxo* etiquette is simple. Ask for a plate and point out what *pintxos* (bar snacks – more like tasty mounds of food on little slices of baguette) you want. Keep the toothpicks and go back for as many as you'd like. Accompany with *txakoli,* a cloudy white wine poured like cider to create a little fizz. When you're ready to pay, hand over the plate with all the toothpicks and tell the bar staff how many drinks you've had. It's an honour system that has stood the test of time. Expect to pay €2.50 to €3.50 for a *pintxo* and *txakoli.*

TOP CHOICE La Cuchara de San Telmo
BASQUE €€

(www.lacucharadesantelmo.com; Calle de 31 de Agosto 28) This unfussy, hidden-away (and hard to find) bar offers miniature *nueva cocina vasca* from a supremely creative kitchen. Chefs Alex Montiel and Iñaki Gulin conjure up delights and a percentage of profits goes to the Fundación Vicente Ferrer charity.

Arzak
BASQUE €€€

(☎943 27 84 65; www.arzak.info; Avenida Alcalde Jose Elosegui 273; meals €175; ⸂closed Sun-Mon & Nov & late Jun) With three shining Michelin stars, acclaimed chef Juan Mari Arzak takes some beating when it comes to *nueva cocina vasca* and his restaurant is, not surprisingly, considered one of the best places to eat in Spain. Arzak is now assisted by his daughter Elena and they never cease to innovate. Reservations, well in advance, are obligatory. The restaurant is about 1.5km east of San Sebastián.

Astelena
BASQUE €€

(Calle de Iñigo 1) The *pintxos* draped across the counter in this bar, tucked into the corner of Plaza de la Constitución, stand out as some of the best in the city. Many of them are a fusion of Basque and Asian inspirations, but the best of all are perhaps the foie-gras-based treats.

Restaurante Alberto
SEAFOOD €

(☎943 42 88 84; Calle de 31 de Agosto 19; menus €15; ⸂closed Tue) A charming old seafood restaurant with a fishmonger-style window display of the day's catch. It's small and friendly and the pocket-sized dining room feels like it was once someone's living room. The food is earthy and good and the service swift.

La Mejillonera
BASQUE €€

(Calle del Puerto 15, mussels from €3) If you thought mussels only came with garlic sauce, come here to discover mussels by the thousand in all their glorious forms. Mussels not for you? Opt for the calamari and *patatas bravas* (fried potatoes with a spicy tomato and mayo sauce). We promise you won't regret it.

ℹ Information

Street signs are in Basque and Spanish.

Oficina de Turismo (☎943 48 11 66; www. sansebastianturismo.com; Alameda del Boulevard 8; ⸂9.30am-1.30pm & 3.30-7pm Mon-Thu, 10am-7pm Fri & Sat, 10am-2pm Sun)

ℹ Getting There & Away

AIR The city's **airport** (☎902 404704; www. aena.es) is 22km out of town, near Hondarribia. There are regular flights to Madrid and occasional charters to European cities.

BUS Daily bus services leave for Bilbao (€10.10 to €14, one hour), Bilbao Airport (€15.70, 1¼ hours), Biarritz (France; €6.60, 1¼ hours), Madrid (from €33.60, five hours) and Pamplona (€7.29, one hour).

TRAIN The main **Renfe train station** (Paseo de Francia) is just across Río Urumea. There are regular services to Madrid (from €54.20, five hours) and Barcelona (from €63.30, eight hours). There's only one direct train to Paris, but there are plenty more from the Spanish/ French border town of Irun (or sometimes Hendaye) (€2.20, 25 minutes), which is also served by **Eusko Tren/Ferrocarril Vasco** (www. euskotren.es). Trains depart every half-hour from Amara train station, about 1km south of the city centre.

BILBAO

POP 351.300

The commercial hub of the Basque Country, Bilbao (Bilbo in Basque) is best known for the magnificent Guggenheim Museum. An architectural masterpiece by Frank Gehry, the museum was the catalyst of a turnaround that saw Bilbao transformed from an industrial port city into a vibrant cultural centre. After visiting this must-see temple to modern art, spend time exploring Bilbao's Casco Viejo (Old Quarter), a grid of elegant streets dotted with shops, cafes, *pintxos* bars and several small but worthy museums.

◉ Sights

Museo Guggenheim   MUSEUM

(www.guggenheim-bilbao.es; Avenida Abandoibarra 2; adult/child €13/free; ⊙10am-8pm, closed Mon Sep-Jun) Opened in 1997, Bilbao's Museo Guggenheim lifted modern architecture and Bilbao into the 21st century – with sensation. Some might say, probably quite rightly, that structure overwhelms function here and that the Guggenheim is more famous for its architecture than its content. But Canadian architect Frank Gehry's inspired use of flowing canopies, cliffs, promontories, ship shapes, towers and flying fins is irresistible. The interior of the Guggenheim is purposefully vast. The cathedral-like atrium is more than 45m high. Light pours in through the glass cliffs. Permanent exhibits fill the ground floor and include such wonders as mazes of metal and phrases of light reaching for the skies. For most people, though, it is the temporary exhibitions that are the main attraction (check the Guggenheim's website for a full program of upcoming exhibitions).

Museo de Bellas Artes   MUSEUM

(Fine Arts Museum; www.museobilbao.com; Plaza del Museo 2; adult/child €6/free, free Wed; ⊙10am-8pm Tue-Sun) A mere five minutes from Museo Guggenheim is Bilbao's Museo de Bellas Artes. There are three main subcollections: Classical Art, with works by Murillo, Zurbarán, El Greco, Goya and van Dyck; Contemporary Art, featuring works by Gauguin, Francis Bacon and Anthony Caro; and Basque Art, with the works of the great sculptors Jorge de Oteiza and Eduardo Chillida, and also strong paintings by the likes of Ignacio Zuloaga and Juan de Echevarria.

Casco Viejo   OLD TOWN

The compact Casco Viejo, Bilbao's atmospheric old quarter, is full of charming streets, boisterous bars, and plenty of quirky and independent shops. At the heart of the Casco are Bilbao's original 'seven streets', Las Siete Calles, which date from the 1400s. The 14th-century Gothic **Catedral de Santiago** (Plaza de Santiago; ⊙10am-1pm & 4-7pm Tue-Sat, 10.30am-1.30pm Sun) has a splendid Renaissance portico and pretty little cloister. Further north, the 19th-century arcaded Plaza Nueva is a rewarding *pintxo* haunt.

Euskal Museoa   MUSEUM

(Museo Vasco; Plaza Miguel Unamuno 4; adult/child €3/free, free Thu; ⊙11am-5pm Tue-Sat, to 2pm Sun) This is probably the most complete museum of Basque culture and history in all the Basque regions. The story kicks off back in the days of prehistory and from this murky period the displays bound rapidly through to the modern age. The museum is housed in a fine old building, at the centre of which is a peaceful cloister that was part of an original 17th-century Jesuit College.

⌂ Sleeping

The Bilbao tourism authority has a useful **reservations department** (✆902 877298; www.bilbaoreservas.com) for accommodation.

Pensión Iturrienea
Ostatua   BOUTIQUE HOTEL €

(✆944 16 15 00; www.iturrieneaostatua.com; Calle de Santa María 14; r €50-70; ☏) Easily the most eccentric hotel in Bilbao, it's part farmyard, part old-fashioned toyshop, and a work of art in its own right. The nine rooms here are so full of character that there'll be barely enough room for your own! There's a lovely breakfast area and, with baby beds and chairs and lots of toys, it's family friendly.

Hostal Begoña   BOUTIQUE HOTEL €

(✆944 23 01 34; www.hostalbegona.com; Calle de la Amistad 2; s/d from €50/55; @☏) Begoña speaks for itself with colourful rooms decorated with modern artworks, all with funky tiled bathrooms and wrought-iron beds. It's probably the best hotel in the city in which to meet other travellers. There's a car park nearby.

Gran Hotel Domine   DESIGN HOTEL €€€

(✆944 25 33 00; www.granhoteldominebilbao.com; Alameda Mazarredo 61; r from €132; P ☀@☱) Designer chic all the way, from the Javier Mariscal interiors to the Phillipe Starck and Arne Jacobsen fittings – and that's just in the toilets. This stellar showpiece of the Silken chain has views of the Guggenheim from some of its pricier rooms, a giant column of rounded beach stones reaching for the heavens and a water feature filled with plates and glasses.

✕ Eating

Rio-Oja
BASQUE €

(☏944 15 08 71; Calle de Perro 4; mains €8-11) An institution that shouldn't be missed. It specialises in light Basque seafood and heavy inland fare, but to most foreigners the snails, sheep brains or squid floating in pools of its own ink are the makings of a culinary adventure story they'll be recounting for years.

Mina Restaurante
BASQUE €€€

(☏944 79 59 38; www.restaurantemina.es; Muelle Marzana; tasting menu from €61) Offering unexpected sophistication and fine dining in an otherwise fairly grimy neighbourhood, this riverside, and appropriately fish-based, restaurant has been making waves in the Bilbao culinary world, with some critics citing it as the new *número uno* of Basque cooking. Reservations are essential.

Nerua
BASQUE €€€

(☏944 00 04 30; www.nerua.com; tasting menu €80; ⊗closed Mon & Jan–mid-Feb) The Guggenheim's modernist, chic restaurant, Nerua, is under the direction of super chef Josean Martínez Alija. Needless to say, the *nueva cocina vasca* (Basque nouvelle cuisine) is breathtaking – even the olives come from 1000-year-old olive trees! Reservations are essential. If the gourmet restaurant is too extravagant for you try El Goog's bistro, which has set menus from €18.

❶ Information

Tourist Office (www.bilbao.net/bilbaoturismo; Plaza del Ensanche 11; ⊗9am-2pm & 4-7.30pm Mon-Fri) Other branches at the Teatro Arriaga, Museo Guggenheim and airport.

❶ Getting There & Away

AIR Bilbao's **airport** (BIO; ☏902 404704; www.aena.es), with domestic and a handful of international flights, is near Sondika, 12km northeast of the city. The airport bus Bizkaibus A3247 (€1.30, 30 minutes) runs to/from Termibus (bus station), where there is a tram stop and a metro station.

BUS Regular services operate to/from Madrid (€28.45, 4¾ hours), Barcelona (€43.81, seven hours), Pamplona (€13.75, two hours) and Santander (from €7.02, 1¼ hours).

TRAIN Two Renfe trains runs daily to Madrid (from €50.50, six hours) and Barcelona (€64.80, six hours) from the Abando train station. Slow **FEVE** (www.feve.es) trains run from Concordia station, heading west into Cantabria and Asturias.

Navarra

Navarra, historically and culturally linked to the Basque Country, is known for its fine wines and for the Sanfermines festival in Pamplona.

PAMPLONA

POP 195,800

Immortalised by Ernest Hemingway in *The Sun Also Rises,* the pre-Pyrenean city of Pamplona (Iruña in Basque) is home of the wild Sanfermines (aka Encierro or Running of the Bulls) festival, but is also an extremely walkable city that's managed to mix the charm of old plazas and buildings with modern shops and a lively nightlife.

◉ Sights

Catedral
CHURCH

(Calle Dormitalería; guided tours adult/child €4.40/2.60; ⊗10am-7pm Mon-Fri, to 2pm Sat mid-Jul–mid-Sep) Pamplona's main cathedral stands on a rise just inside the city ramparts amid a dark thicket of narrow streets. It's a late-medieval Gothic gem spoiled only by its rather dull neoclassical facade, an 18th-century appendage. The real joys are the vast interior and the Gothic cloister, where there is marvellous delicacy in the stonework.

Ciudadela & Parks
FORTRESS, PARK

(Avenida del Ejército) The walls and bulwarks of the grand fortified citadel, the star-shaped Ciudadela, lurk amid the verdant grass and trees in what is now a charming park, the portal to three more parks that unfold to the north and lend Pamplona a beautiful green escape.

Museo de Navarra
MUSEUM

(www.cfnavarra.es/cultura/museo; Calle Cuesta de Santo Domingo 47; adult €2, free Sat afternoon & Sun; ⊗9.30am-2pm & 5-7pm Tue-Sat, 11am-2pm Sun) Housed in a former medieval hospital, this superb museum has an eclectic collection of archaeological finds (including a number of fantastic Roman mosaics unearthed mainly in southern Navarra), as well as a selection of art including Goya's *Marqués de San Adrián.*

Museo Oteiza
MUSEUM

(www.museooteiza.org; Calle de la Cuesta 7, Alzuza; adult €4, free Fri; ⊗11am-7pm Tue-Sat, to 3pm

SANFERMINES

The Sanfermines festival is held from 6 to 14 July, when Pamplona is overrun with thrill-seekers, curious onlookers and, yes, bulls. The *encierro* (Running of the Bulls) begins at 8am daily, when bulls are let loose from the Coralillos Santo Domingo. The 825m race lasts just three minutes.

Since records began in 1924, 16 people have died during Pamplona's bull-run. Many of those who run are full of bravado (and/or drink) and have little idea of what they're doing. For dedicated *encierro* news, check out www.sanfermin.com.

Animal-rights groups oppose bull-running as a cruel tradition, and the participating bulls will almost certainly all be killed in the afternoon bullfight. The PETA-organised anti-bullfighting demonstration, the Running of the Nudes, takes place two days before the first bull-run.

Sun) Around 9km northeast of Pamplona in the town of Alzuza, this impressive museum contains almost 3000 pieces by the renowned Navarran sculptor Jorge Oteiza. Three buses a day run to Alzuza from Pamplona's bus station. If you're driving, Alzuza is signposted north off the NA150, just east of Huarte.

Sleeping

Accommodation is hard to come by during Sanfermines – book months in advance. Our prices don't reflect the huge (up to fivefold) mark-up you'll find in mid-July.

TOP CHOICE Palacio Guendulain HISTORIC HOTEL €€
(948 22 55 22; www.palacioguendulain.com; Calle Zapatería 53; d incl breakfast from €134; P✳🖳) To call this stunning hotel, inside the converted former home of the Viceroy of New Granada, sumptuous is an understatement. The rooms contain *Princess and the Pea*–soft beds, enormous showers and regal armchairs.

Hostel Hemingway HOSTEL €
(948 98 38 84; www.hostelhemingway.com; Calle Amaya 26; dm €19-22, s/d from €22/42; @) Bright, funky colours predominate at this well-run hostel a few minutes' walk from the old town. The dorms have four to six

beds and share three bathrooms. There's a TV lounge and a kitchen for guest use. It's just off Avenida de Carlos III.

Hotel Puerta del Camino BOUTIQUE HOTEL €€
(948 22 66 88; www.hotelpuertadelcamino.com; Calle Dos de Mayo 4; s/d from €89/95; P✳🖳) A very stylish hotel inside a converted convent beside the northern gates to the old city. The functional rooms have clean, modern lines and it's positioned in one of the prettier, and quieter, parts of town. Some rooms have Pyrenean views.

Eating & Drinking

Central streets such as Calle de San Nicolás and Calle de la Estafeta are lined with tapas bars, many of which morph into nightspots on weekends.

Baserri BASQUE €
(948 22 20 21; Calle de San Nicolás 32; menú del día €14) This place has won enough *pintxo* awards that we could fill this entire book listing them. In fact, it's staggering to know that so many food awards actually exist! As you'd expect from such a certificate-studded bar, the *pintxos* and full meals are superb.

Casa Otaño BASQUE €€
(948 22 50 95; Calle de San Nicolás 5; mains €15-18) A little pricier than many on this street but worth the extra. Its formal atmosphere is eased by the dazzling array of pink and red flowers spilling off the balcony. Great dishes range from the locally caught trout to heavenly duck dishes. The *menú del día* is good value.

Café Iruña CAFE
(www.cafeiruna.com; Plaza del Castillo 44) Opened on the eve of Sanfermines in 1888, Café Iruña's dominant position, powerful sense of history and frilly belle-époque decor make this by far the most famous and popular watering hole in the city.

ℹ Information
Tourist Office (www.turismo.navarra.es; Calle de Esclava 1; ⊙9am-8pm Mon-Sat, to 2pm Sun)

ℹ Getting There & Away
AIR Pamplona's **airport** (948 16 87 00), about 7km south of the city, has regular flights to Madrid and Barcelona. Bus 16 (€1.20) travels between the city (from the bus station) and the airport.

BUS From the **main bus station** (Calle Conde Oliveto 8), buses leave for Bilbao (€14.15, two hours) and San Sebastián (€7.29, one hour).

TRAIN Pamplona's train station is linked to the city centre by bus 9 from Paseo de Sarasate every 15 minutes. Trains run to/from Madrid (€57.90, three hours, four daily) and San Sebastián (from €21.20, two hours, two daily).

CANTABRIA, ASTURIAS & GALICIA

With a landscape reminiscent of parts of the British Isles, 'Green Spain' offers great walks in national parks, seafood feasts in sophisticated towns and oodles of opportunities to plunge into the ice-cold waters of the Bay of Biscay.

Cantabria

Cantabria may be small, but it is one of Spain's more varied regions. Here you'll find green hills and jagged peaks shadowing a coastline that's home to some of Spain's prettiest villages.

SANTILLANA DEL MAR
POP 4,200

Some 34km west of the regional capital, Santander, Santillana del Mar (www.santillanadelmar.com) is a bijou medieval village and the obvious overnight base for visiting the nearby Cueva de Altamira.

The country's finest prehistoric art, in the Cueva de Altamira, 2km southwest of Santillana del Mar, is off-limits to all but the scientific community. Since 2002, however, the **Museo Altamira** (www.museodealtamira.mcu.es; adult/child, EU senior or student €3/free, Sun & from 2.30pm Sat free; ⊙9.30am-8pm Tue-Sat, to 3pm Sun & holidays; P) has allowed all comers to view the inspired, 14,500-year-old depictions of bison, horses and other beasts (or rather, their replicas) in this full-size, dazzling re-creation of the cave's most interesting chamber, the Sala de Polícromos (Polychrome Hall).

Buses run three to four times a day from Santander to Santilla del Mar.

Asturias

If you ask Spaniards their favourite region of the country, many will nominate Asturias. With a gorgeous coast, the spectacular Picos de Europa and a food culture all its own, it's not difficult to see why.

WORTH A TRIP

PICOS DE EUROPA

These jagged mountains straddling Asturias, Cantabria and northeast Castilla y León amount to some of the finest walking country in Spain.

They comprise three limestone massifs (whose highest peak rises 2648m). The 647-sq-km **Parque Nacional de los Picos de Europa** (www.picosdeeuropa.com) covers all three massifs and is Spain's second-biggest national park.

There are numerous places to stay and eat all over the mountains. Getting here and around by bus can be slow going but the Picos are accessible from Santander and Oviedo (the latter is easier) by bus.

OVIEDO
POP 225,000

The elegant parks and modern shopping streets of Asturias' capital are agreeably offset by what remains of the *casco antiguo* (old town).

Just outside the city (within 3km) is a scattering of 9th-century, pre-Romanesque buildings, including the **Iglesia de San Julián de los Prados** (Iglesia de Santullano; adult/child €1.20/0.60, Mon free; ⊙10am-12.30pm Mon, 10am-12.30pm & 4-5.30pm Tue-Fri, 9.30am-noon & 3.30-5pm Sat, closed afternoons Oct-Apr), **Palacio de Santa María del Naranco** (adult/child incl Iglesia de San Miguel de Lillo €3/2, free Mon; ⊙9.30am-1pm & 3.30-7pm Tue-Sat, 9.30am-1pm Sun & Mon, shorter hours Oct-Mar) and the **Iglesia de San Miguel de Lillo** (⊙9.30am-1pm & 3.30-7pm Tue-Sat, 9.30am-1pm Sun & Mon, shorter hours Oct-Mar). Get information from the tourist offices in town.

⊙ Sights

Catedral de San Salvador   CATHEDRAL
(⊙10am-7pm Mon-Sat mid-May–Sep, 10am-1pm & 4-7pm Mon-Fri, 10am-1pm & 4-6pm Sat Sep–mid-May) In a sense, the mainly Gothic edifice you see today forms the outer casing of a many-layered history in stone of Spanish Christianity. Its origins lie in the **Cámara Santa**, a chapel built by Alfonso II to house holy relics. The chapel is now the inner sanctuary of the cathedral, which was chiefly built between the 14th and 16th centuries. The **cloister** is pure 14th-century Gothic, rare enough in Asturias, and just off it the

SPAIN CANTABRIA

sala capitular (chapter house) contains some well-restored Flemish Gothic choir stalls.

Old Town
HISTORIC AREA

The old town's nooks and crannies include **Plaza de la Constitución**, capped at one end by the Iglesia de San Isidoro and fronted by an eclectic collection of old shops, cafes and the 17th-century *ayuntamiento*. To the south, past the **Mercado El Fontán** food market, arcaded **Plaza Fontán** is equipped with a couple of *sidrerías* (cider houses). Other little squares include Plaza de Trascorrales, Plaza de Riego and Plaza del Paraguas.

🛏 Sleeping & Eating

Oviedo's *sidrería* rules include getting good food at reasonable prices. Calle de la Gascona is a particularly happy hunting ground.

Hotel de la Reconquista
HOTEL €€€

(☏985 24 11 00; www.hoteldelareconquista.com; Calle de Gil de Jaz 16; r €119-163; P❋@🕸) The city's fanciest lodgings, two blocks northwest of the central Campo de San Francisco, started life as an 18th-century hospice. Built around several patios, the somewhat formal rooms come in different shapes and sizes, with timber furniture, floor-to-ceiling windows and gentle ochre-and-white colour schemes.

Hotel Fruela
HOTEL €€

(☏985 20 81 20; www.hotelfruela.com; Calle de Fruela 3; r €72-79; P❋🕸) With a pleasing contemporary style and a touch of original art, plus professional yet friendly service, the 28-room Fruela achieves a cosy, almost intimate feel and is easily the top midrange option in central Oviedo.

Tierra Astur
SIDRERÍA €€

(☏985 20 25 02; www.tierra-astur.com; Calle de la Gascona 1; mains €9-21; ☉lunch & dinner) A particularly atmospheric *sidrería*/restaurant, Tierra Astur is famed for its grilled meats and prize-winning cider. People queue for tables, or give up and settle for tapas at the bar. Platters of Asturian sausage, cheese or ham are a good starter option.

La Corrada del Obispo
ASTURIAN €€

(☏985 22 00 48; www.lacorradadelobispo.com; Calle de la Canóniga 18; mains €16-24; ☉closed Sun dinner, Mon) Modern decor combines with the exposed stone walls of this 18th-century house to provide a welcoming setting for fine local cooking. It offers a tempting variety of fish and meat dishes, including game

such as wild boar and venison when they're in season. Woody Allen shot some scenes for *Vicky Cristina Barcelona* here.

ℹ Information

Oficina Municipal de Turismo (☏984 08 60 60; www.turismo.ayto-oviedo.es; Plaza de la Constitución 4 ; ☉9.30am-7.30pm)

Oficina de Turismo de Asturias (☏902 300202; www.infoasturias.com; Calle de Cimadevilla 4; ☉10am-7pm Mon-Sat year-round, to 5pm Sun Jul & Aug)

ℹ Getting There & Away

AIR The **Aeropuerto de Asturias** (☏902 404704) is at Santiago del Monte, 47km northwest of Oviedo and 40km west of Gijón. There are flights to European cities and around Spain. Buses run hourly to/from Oviedo's ALSA bus station (€7.50, 45 minutes).

BUS From the **ALSA bus station** (☏902 422242; www.alsa.es; Calle de Magnus Blikstad), 300m northeast of the train station, direct services head to Gijón (€2.25, 30 minutes) every 10 or 15 minutes. Other daily buses head to Asturian towns, Galicia, Cantabria and elsewhere.

TRAIN One **station** (Avenida de Santander; 🕸) serves both train companies, Renfe and FEVE (for buses to Santander and Bilbao), the latter located on the upper level. **Renfe** (www.renfe. com) runs trains to León, Madrid and Barcelona at least once daily. For Gijón, Renfe *cercanías* (local area trains; €2.85, 35 minutes) go once or twice an hour.

Galicia

Utterly unlike anywhere else in Spain, green Galicia has Spain's most beautiful coastline, fabulous food and Santiago de Compostela, one of Europe's most sacred pilgrimage destinations.

SANTIAGO DE COMPOSTELA
POP 95,400

The supposed burial place of St James (Santiago), Santiago de Compostela is a bewitching city. Christian pilgrims journeying along the Camino de Santiago often end up mute with wonder on entering its medieval centre. Fortunately, they usually regain their verbal capacities over a celebratory late-night foray into the city's lively bar scene.

◎ Sights

TOP CHOICE **Catedral de Santiago de Compostela**
CATHEDRAL

(www.catedraldesantiago.es; Praza do Obradoiro; ☉7am-9pm) The grand heart of Santiago, the cathedral soars above the city centre in a splendid jumble of moss-covered spires and statues. Though Galicia's grandest monument was built piecemeal through the centuries, its beauty is only enhanced by the mix of Romanesque, baroque and Gothic flourishes. What you see today is actually the fourth church to stand on this spot. The bulk of it was built between 1075 and 1211, in Romanesque style with a traditional Latin-cross layout and three naves.

The main entrance is via the lavish staircase and facade on the Praza do Obradoiro, or through the south door on Praza de Praterías. The baroque **Obradoiro facade** was erected in the 18th century partly to protect the cathedral's original entrance, which is now just inside it – the artistically unparalleled Pórtico de la Gloria (Galician: Porta da Gloria), with its 200 Romanesque sculptures by Maestro Mateo.

Towards the far (west) end of the cathedral's main nave, to the right of the Churrigueresque **Altar Mayor** (main altar), a small staircase leads up above the altar to a 13th-century statue of Santiago, which the faithful queue up to embrace.

A special pilgrims' Mass is usually celebrated at noon daily, with other Masses usually at 9.30am or 10am daily, 1.15pm Sunday, 6pm Saturday and Sunday, and 7.30pm daily. Touristic visits are not allowed during these services.

For an unforgettable bird's-eye view of the city, take the **cathedral rooftop tour** (981 55 29 85; per person €10; 10am-2pm & 4-8pm).

Museo da Catedral   MUSEUM
(www.catedraldesantiago.es; Praza do Obradoiro; adult/student & pilgrim/child €5/3/free; 10am-2pm & 4-8pm, closed Sun afternoon) The Cathedral Museum, entered to the right of the cathedral's Obradoiro facade, spreads over four floors and includes the cathedral's large, 16th-century, Gothic/plateresque cloister. You'll see a sizeable section of Maestro Mateo's original carved stone choir (destroyed in 1603 but recently pieced back together), an impressive collection of religious art (including the *botafumeiros*, in the 2nd-floor library), the lavishly decorated 18th-century *sala capitular* (chapter house) and, off the cloister, the Panteón de Reyes, which contains tombs of kings of medieval León.

FREE **Museo das Peregrinacións**   MUSEUM
(www.mdperegrinacions.com; Rúa de San Miguel 4; 10am-8pm Tue-Fri, 10.30am-1.30pm & 5-8pm Sat, 10.30am-1.30pm Sun) Explore the eight rooms investigating the Camino de Santiago phenomenon over the centuries.

Cidade da Cultura de Galicia   CULTURAL CENTRE
(City of Culture of Galicia; www.cidadedacultura.org; 8am-11pm, building interiors 10am-2pm & 4-8pm, museum closed Mon; P) This vast prestige project is taking shape atop Monte Gaiás, a hill about 1.5km southeast of the old town, to the designs of American Peter Eisenman. The first sections, the Library and Archive of Galicia, opened in 2011. The overall shape resembles a giant stone wave sliced into sections and is intended to be vaguely similar to a conch shell (symbol of the Camino de Santiago), while the passageways between the buildings are meant to recall the streets trodden by pilgrims arriving in Santiago.

A walk around the existing buildings and spaces is worth an hour or two of your time. Free guided visits in Spanish are given at 12.30pm and 6.30pm daily except Monday. You can reach the City of Culture on bus 9 (hourly Monday to Friday until 10.35pm and Saturday until 1.35pm) or bus C11 (5.35pm and 8.05pm Saturday and four times on Sunday), northbound from a stop opposite the market on Rúa da Virxe da Cerca.

AROUND THE CATHEDRAL
Catedral de Santiago de Compostela is surrounded by handsome plazas that invite you to wander through them. The grand **Praza do Obradoiro** (Workshop Plaza), to which most arriving Camino pilgrims instinctively find their way, earned its name from the stonemasons' workshops set up here while the cathedral was being built. At its northern end, the Renaissance **Hostal dos Reis Católicos** (admission €3; noon-2pm & 4-6pm Sun-Fri) was built in the early 16th century. Today it shelters well-off travellers instead, as a luxurious *parador*. Along the western side of the square is the elegant 18th-century **Pazo de Raxoi** (Praza do Obradoiro), now the city hall.

Around the corner, **Praza das Praterías** (Silversmiths' Square) is marked with the Fuente de los Caballos (1829) fountain, with the cathedral's south facade at the top of the steps. Curiously, the Casa do Cabildo, facing it on the lower side of the square, is no more than a 3m-deep facade, erected in 1758 to embellish the plaza.

Sleeping

Hotel Costa Vella   BOUTIQUE HOTEL €€
(981 56 95 30; www.costavella.com; Rúa da Porta da Pena 17; s €59, d €81-97;) The tranquil,

thoughtfully designed rooms (some with glassed-in galleries), friendly welcome and lovely garden cafe make this a wonderful option. Even if you don't stay, it's an ideal spot for breakfast or coffee.

Hotel Casas Reais
BOUTIQUE HOTEL €€

(☏981 55 57 09; www.casasreais.es; Rúa das Casas Reais 29; d incl breakfast €90; ❊❇) The 11 bright, contemporary rooms here are originally and discreetly themed after different real or pop-culture monarchs. White linen, mirrors and galleries all help to maximise light – this is undoubtedly one of the most attractive of Santiago's recent wave of new hotels in old buildings.

Casa-Hotel As Artes
BOUTIQUE HOTEL €€

(☏981 55 52 54; www.asartes.com; Travesía de Dos Puertas; r €95-105; @❇) On a quiet street close to the cathedral, As Artes' seven lovely stone-walled rooms exude a romantic rustic air. Breakfast (€10.80) is served in a homey dining room overlooking the street.

Parador Hostal dos Reis Católicos
HISTORIC HOTEL €€€

(☏981 58 22 00; www.parador.es; Praza do Obradoiro 1; s/d incl breakfast from €224/280; ❒❊❇) Opened in 1509 as a pilgrims' hostel, and with a claim to be the world's oldest hotel, this palatial *parador* is Santiago's top hotel, with regal (if rather staid) rooms. If you're not staying, stop in for a look round and coffee and cakes at the elegant cafe, or a meal in one of the restaurants (mains €20 to €35).

✖ Eating

O Curro da Parra
GALICIAN €€

(www.ocurrodaparra.com; Rúa do Curro da Parra 7; mains €14-20, tapas €5-8; ⊘closed Mon) With a neat little stone-walled dining room upstairs and a narrow tapas and wine bar below, this relative newcomer serves up a broad range of thoughtfully created, market-fresh fare. On weekday lunchtimes it serves a great-value *menú mercado* (market menu).

Bierzo de Enxebre
LEONESE €€

(www.bierzoenxebre.es; Rúa da Troia 10; raciones €8-14; ⊘closed Tue) The cuisine at this busy and atmospheric spot is that of El Bierzo, a rural area of northwest Castilla y León, meaning excellent grilled and cured meats, but also cheeses, pies and vegetables. There are two small, stone-walled, wood-beamed dining rooms and the outside tables are highly popular.

Mesón Ó 42
GALICIAN €€

(www.restauranteo42.com; Rúa do Franco 42; raciones €6-14, mains €16-19; ⊘closed Sun evening) With a solid list of favourite local *raciones* like *empanadas* (pies), shellfish, octopus and tortillas, as well as fish, meat and rice dishes, this popular place stands out from the crowd with well-prepared food and good service.

🍷 Drinking

If you're after tapas and wine, graze along Rúa do Franco and Rúa da Raíña. For people-watching, hit the cafes along Praza da Quinatana and Rúa do Vilar. The liveliest area lies east of Praza da Quintana, especially along Rúa de San Paio de Anteältares, known as a hot spot for live music.

ℹ Information

Turismo de Santiago (☏981 55 51 29; www.santiagoturismo.com; Rúa do Vilar 63; ⊘9am-9pm, to 7pm Nov-Mar) Efficient main municipal tourist office.

Oficina de Acogida de Peregrinos (Pilgrims' Reception Office; ☏981 56 88 46; www.peregrinossantiago.es; Rúa do Vilar 3; ⊘9am-9pm) People who have covered at least the last 100km of the Camino de Santiago on foot or horseback, or the last 200km by bicycle, with spiritual or religious motives, can obtain their 'Compostela' certificate to prove it here.

Oficina de Turismo de Galicia (www.turgalicia.es; Rúa do Vilar 30-32; ⊘10am-8pm Mon-Fri, 11am-2pm & 5-7pm Sat, 11am-2pm Sun) The scoop on all things Galicia as well as on the Camino de Santiago.

ℹ Getting There & Away

AIR Flights from various Spanish and European destinations land at **Lavacolla airport** (☏981 54 75 00; www.aena.es). Up to 36 Empresa Freire buses (€3) run daily between Lavacolla airport and Rúa do Doutor Teixeiro, in the new town southwest of Praza de Galicia.

BUS The **bus station** (☏981 54 24 16; www.tussa.org; Praza de Camilo Díaz Baliño; ❇) is about a 20-minute walk northeast of the centre. Castromil-Monbus runs to destinations throughout Galicia. ALSA has services to Oviedo (€28, 5¼ to 8¾ hours), León (€28, six hours) and Madrid (€44 to €63, 7¾ to 10 hours). ALSA also has direct daily services to Porto (€30, 4¼ hours) and Lisbon (€50, 9¾ hours).

TRAIN From the **train station** (☏981 59 18 59; Rúa do Hórreo), regional trains run up and down the coast, while a daytime Talgo and an overnight Trenhotel head to Madrid (from €50.60, 6¼ to 9½ hours).

Around Galicia

Galicia's dramatic Atlantic coastline is one of Spain's best-kept secrets, with wild and precipitous cliffs and isolated fishing villages. The lively port city of **A Coruña** has a lovely city beach and fabulous seafood (a recurring Galician theme). It's also the gateway to the stirring landscapes of the **Costa da Morte** and **Rías Altas**; the latter's highlight among many is probably **Cabo Ortegal**. Inland Galicia is also worth exploring, especially the old town of **Lugo**, surrounded by what many consider to be the world's best preserved Roman walls.

VALENCIA & MURCIA

A warm climate, an abundance of seaside resorts and interesting cities make this area of Spain a popular destination. The beaches of the Costa Blanca (White Coast) draw most of the visitors, but venture beyond the shore to get a real feel for the region.

Valencia

POP 815,000

Valencia, where paella first simmered over a wood fire, is a vibrant, friendly, slightly chaotic place. It has two outstanding fine-arts museums, an accessible old quarter, Europe's newest cultural and scientific complex, and one of Spain's most exciting nightlife scenes.

◉ Sights & Activities

TOP
CHOICE **Ciudad de las Artes y las Ciencias** SCIENCE CENTRE
(City of Arts & Sciences; ✆902 100031; www.cac. es; combined ticket adult/child €31.50/24) The aesthetically stunning City of Arts & Sciences occupies a massive 350,000-sq-metre swath of the old Turia riverbed. It's mostly the work of stellar local architect, the world-renowned Santiago Calatrava. The complex includes the **Oceanogràfic** (adult/child €24.90/18.80; ⊙10am-6pm or 8pm), a stunning aquarium; **Hemisfèric** (adult/child €7.85/6.10), a planetarium and IMAX cinema; **Museo de las Ciencias Príncipe Felipe** (adult/child €7.85/6.10; ⊙10am-7pm or 9pm), an interactive science museum; and the extraordinary **Palau de les Arts Reina Sofía** (www.lesarts. com) concert hall. Take bus 35 from Plaza del Ayuntamiento or bus 95 from Torres de Serranos or Plaza de América.

Barrio del Carmen HISTORIC AREA
You'll see Valencia's best face by simply wandering around the Barrio del Carmen. Valencia's Romanesque-Gothic-baroque-Renaissance **catedral** (Plaza de la Virgen; adult/child incl audioguide €4.50/3; ⊙10am-4.45pm or 5.45pm Mon-Sat, 2-4.45pm Sun) is a compendium of centuries of architectural history and home to the **Capilla del Santo Cáliz**, a chapel said to contain the Holy Grail (the chalice Christ supposedly used in the last supper). Climb the 207 stairs of the **Micalet bell tower** (adult/child €2/1; ⊙10am-7pm or 7.30pm) for sweeping city views.

Plaza del Mercado HISTORIC PLAZA
Over on Plaza del Mercado, two emblematic buildings, each a masterpiece of its era, face each other. Valencia's Modernista covered market, the **Mercado Central** (www.mercadocentralvalencia.es; ⊙7.30am-3pm Mon-Sat) recently scrubbed and glowing as new, was constructed in 1928. With over 900 stalls, it's a swirl of smells, movement and colour. **La Lonja** (adult/child €2/1; ⊙10am-7pm Tue-Sat, to 3pm Sun) is a splendid late-15th-century building, a Unesco World Heritage site and was originally Valencia's silk and commodity exchange.

FREE **Museo de Bellas Artes** MUSEUM
(www.museobellasartesvalencia.gva.es; Calle San Pío V 9; ⊙10am-7pm Tue-Sun, 11am-5pm Mon) Bright and spacious, the Museo de Bellas Artes ranks among Spain's best. Highlights include the grandiose Roman *Mosaic of the Nine Muses,* a collection of magnificent late-medieval altarpieces and works by El Greco, Goya, Velázquez, Murillo and Ribalta, plus artists such as Sorolla and Pinazo of the Valencian impressionist school.

Instituto Valenciano de Arte Moderno (IVAM) GALLERY
(www.ivam.es; Calle Guillem de Castro 118; adult/child €2/1; ⊙10am-8pm Tue-Sun) IVAM (pronounced 'ee-bam') hosts excellent temporary exhibitions and houses an impressive permanent collection of 20th-century Spanish art.

Beaches
Playa de la Malvarrosa runs into **Playa de las Arenas**. Each is bordered by the **Paseo Marítimo** promenade and a string of restaurants. **Playa El Salér**, 10km south, is backed

Valencia City

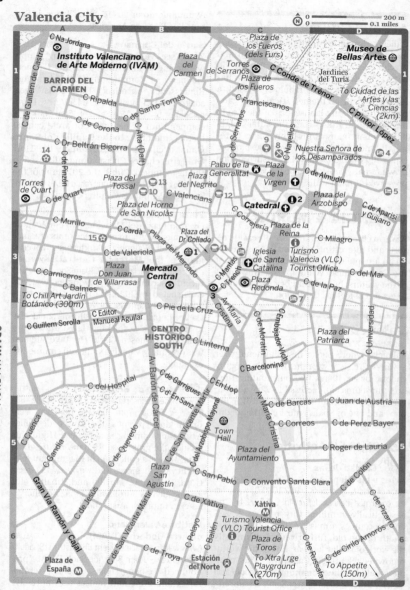

by shady pine woods. **Autocares Herca** (📞96 349 12 50; www.autocaresherca.com) buses run between Valencia and Perelló hourly (half-hourly in summer), calling by El Salér village. The beaches lie east and southeast of the city centre.

🛏 Sleeping

Caro Hotel
HOTEL €€€

(📞96 305 90 00; www.carohotel.com; Calle Almirante 14; r €140-200; ❄🐾) This spanking new hotel, housed in a sumptuous 19th-century mansion, sits atop some 2000 years of Va-

Valencia City

◎ Top Sights
Catedral.. C2
Instituto Valenciano de Arte
   Moderno (IVAM)................................. A1
Mercado Central..................................... B3
Museo de Bellas Artes...........................D1

◎ Sights
1 La Lonja.. B3
2 Miguelete Bell Tower............................C2
3 Plaza del Mercado C3

🛏 Sleeping
4 Ad Hoc Monumental D2
5 Caro Hotel...D2
6 Hostal Antigua Morellana C3

7 Petit Palace Bristol................................C3

✪ Eating
8 Delicat..C2
Seu-Xerea ....(see 8)

◎ Drinking
9 Café de las Horas C2
10 Café Infanta B2
11 Café Lisboa C3
12 Cafe-Bar Negrito C2
13 Sant Jaume B2

◎ Entertainment
14 Music Box A2
15 Radio City...A3

lencian history. Its recent restoration has revealed a hefty hunk of the Arab wall, Roman column bases and Gothic arches. Each room is furnished in soothing dark shades and is unique in design.

Chill Art Jardín Botánico
BOUTIQUE HOTEL €€
(☎96 315 40 12; www.hoteljardinbotanico.com; Calle Doctor Peset Cervera 6; s/d from €85/90; ❄️🛜) Welcoming and megacool, this intimate – only 16 rooms – hotel is furnished with great flair. Candles flicker in the lounge and each bedroom has original artwork.

Ad Hoc Monumental
HOTEL €€
(☎96 391 91 40; www.adhochoteles.com; Calle Boix 4; s €65-101, d €76-125; ❄️🛜) Friendly Ad Hoc offers comfort and charm deep within the old quarter and also runs a splendid small restaurant (☺dinner Monday to Saturday). The late-19th-century building has been restored to its former splendour with great sensitivity, revealing original ceilings, mellow brickwork and solid wooden beams.

Petit Palace Bristol
BOUTIQUE HOTEL €€
(☎96 394 51 00; www.hthoteles.com; Calle Abadía San Martín 3; r €60-130; ❄️@🛜) Hip and minimalist, this boutique hotel, a comprehensively made-over 19th-century mansion, retains the best of its past and does a particularly scrumptious buffet breakfast. Invest €15 extra for one of the superior top-floor doubles, with a broad wooden terrace giving panoramic views over the city. Free bikes for guests.

Hostal Antigua Morellana
HOSTAL €
(☎96 391 57 73; www.hostalam.com; Calle En Bou 2; s €45-55, d €55-65; ❄️) The friendly, family-run 18-room Hostal Antigua Morellana is tucked away near the central market. It occupies a renovated 18th-century *posada* (where wealthier merchants bringing their produce to the nearby food market would spend the night) and has cosy, good-sized rooms, most with balconies.

✖ Eating

At weekends, locals in their hundreds head for Las Arenas, just north of the port, where a long line of restaurants overlooking the beach all serve up authentic paella in a three-course meal costing around €15.

La Pepica
SEAFOOD €€€
(☎96 371 03 66; www.lapepica.com; Paseo de Neptuno 6-8; meals around €25; ☺lunch & dinner Mon-Sat, lunch Sun) More expensive than its many beachside competitors, La Pepica, run by the same family for more than a century, is renowned for its rice dishes and seafood. Here, Ernest Hemingway, among other luminaries, once strutted. Between courses, browse through the photos and tributes that plaster the walls.

Delicat
TAPAS, FUSION €
(☎96 392 33 57; seudelicat@hotmail.es; Calle Conde Almodóvar 4; mains €4-11; menus €12; ☺Tue-Sun) At this particularly friendly, intimate option (there are only nine tables, plus the terrace in summer), Catina, working up front, and her partner, Paco, on full view in the kitchen, offer an unbeatable

value five-course menu of samplers for lunch and a range of truly innovative tapas anytime.

TOP CHOICE **A Tu Gusto** MEDITERRANEAN €€
(☎96 322 70 26; www.atugusto.com; cnr Avenida Instituto Obrero & Calle Escritor Rafael Ferreres; mains €14-20, menus €10-36; ☺lunch & dinner Wed-Sat, lunch Sun & Tue) At this strictly contemporary place, the decor is sleek, all pistachio and pitch black but for the gleaming white bar. Salvador Furió, the powerhouse in the kitchen, has worked with some of Spain's finest chefs. His cuisine is modern, creative and attractively presented, and portions are generous.

Tridente FUSION €€
(☎96 356 77 77; Paseo de Neptuno 2; mains €16, menus €29-49; ☺lunch & dinner Mon-Sat, lunch Sun) Begin with an aperitif on the broad beachfront terrace of Tridente, restaurant of Neptuno hotel, then move inside, where filtered sunlight bathes its soothing cream decor. There's an ample à la carte selection but you won't find details of the day's *menús* in front of you – they're delivered verbally by the maître d', who speaks good English.

Appetite INTERNATIONAL, FUSION €€€
(☎96 110 56 60; www.appetite.es; Calle Salvador Abril 7; 6-/8-course menu €26/32; ☺dinner Thu-Mon, lunch Sat & Sun) 'Multicultural cuisine' is how Bonnie from Australia and her partner, Arantxa, as Valencian as they come, describe Appetite's fusion delights with an Asian slant, reflecting Bonnie's Singaporean origins. Sit back and let her compose your menu for you.

Seu-Xerea FUSION, MEDITERRANEAN €€€
(☎96 392 40 00; www.seuxerea.com; Calle Conde Almodóvar 4; mains around €20, menus €19-45; ☺Tue-Sat) Recently made over, this welcoming restaurant is favourably quoted in almost every English-language press article about Valencia city. The creative, regularly changing, rock-reliable à la carte menu features dishes both international and deep rooted in Spain. Wines, selected by the owner, a qualified sommelier, are uniformly excellent.

🍷 Drinking

The Barrio del Carmen, the university area (around Avenidas de Aragón and Blasco Ibáñez), the area around the Mercado de Abastos and, in summer, the new port area and Malvarrosa are all jumping with bars and clubs.

Sant Jaume CAFE, BAR
(Plaza del Tossal) At this converted pharmacy, you can still see the old potion bottles and jars ranged behind the counter. Its 1st floor is all quiet crannies and poky passageways.

Cafe-Bar Negrito CAFE, BAR
(www.cafenegrito.com; Plaza del Negrito) El Negrito's large terrace trumps the cramped interior. It occupies the whole of the square and traditionally attracts a more left-wing, intellectual clientele.

Café Lisboa CAFE, BAR
(Plaza del Doctor Collado 9) This lively, student-oriented bar has a large, street-side terrace. The bulletin board is a palimpsest of small ads for things like apartment shares and language tuition.

Café Infanta CAFE, BAR
(Plaza del Tossal) The interior is a clutter of cinema memorabilia, while its external terrace, beside the busy Plaza del Tossal, is great for people-watching.

Café de las Horas COCKTAIL BAR
(www.cafedelashoras.com; Calle Conde de Almodóvar 1) Offers high baroque, tapestries, music of all genres, candelabras, bouquets of fresh flowers and a long list of exotic cocktails.

☆ Entertainment

Terraza Umbracle LOUNGE BAR
(www.umbracleterraza.com; ☺midnight-8am Thu-Sat May–mid-Oct) At the southern end of the Umbracle walkway within the Ciudad de las Artes y las Ciencias, this is a cool, sophisticated spot to spend a hot summer night. Catch the evening breeze under the stars on the terrace, then drop below to **Mya** (Autopista del Saler; ☺1-7.30am Fri & Sat year round), a top-of-the-line club with an awesome sound system. Admission (around €20 including first drink) covers both venues.

Radio City CLUB
(www.radiocityvalencia.es; Calle de Santa Teresa 19; ☺11pm-3.30am) Almost as much mini-cultural centre as club, Radio City, always seething, pulls in the punters with activities including cinema, flamenco and dancing to an eclectic mix.

Music Box CLUB
(Calle del Pintor Zariñena 16; ☺midnight-7am Tue-Sat) The music here is eclectic with some-

LAS FALLAS

In mid-March, Valencia hosts one of Europe's wildest street parties: **Las Fallas de San José** (www.fallas.es). For one week (12 to 19 March), the city is engulfed by an anarchic swirl of fireworks, music, festive bonfires and all-night partying. On the final night, giant *ninots* (effigies), many of political and social personages, are torched in the main plaza.

If you're not in Valencia then, see the *ninots* saved from the flames by popular vote at the **Museo Fallero** (Plaza Monteolivete 4; adult/child €2/1; ⏲10am-7pm Tue-Sat, to 3pm Sun).

thing for everyone. Entry is free except after 3am on Friday and Saturday, when there's a €10 admission.

Xtra Lrge Playground BAR, CLUB
(cnr Gran Vía de las Germanias & Calle de Cádiz; ⏲midnight-4am Thu-Sat) Spread over 600 sq metres, this recently opened venue merits its outsize name. All soft pastel colours on brute metal and concrete, it offers live DJs, and is already popular with Valencia's movers and shakers. Sip something special at the Spanglishly named Gintonería-Coktelería, then dance away until late.

Black Note JAZZ
(www.blacknoteclub.com; Calle Polo y Peyrolón 15; ⏲from 11.30pm; Ⓜ Aragón) Valencia city's most active jazz venue, Black Note has live music daily except Sunday and good canned jazz. Admission, including first drink, ranges from free to €15, depending on who's grooving.

Information

Regional Tourist Office (☎96 398 64 22; www.comunitatvalenciana.com; Calle de la Paz 48; ⏲9am-8pm Mon-Sat, 10am-2pm Sun)

Turismo Valencia (VLC) Tourist Office (☎96 315 39 31; www.turisvalencia.es; Plaza de la Reina 19; ⏲9am-7pm Mon-Sat, 10am-2pm Sun) Has several other branches around town, including the train station and airport arrivals area.

Getting There & Away

AIR Valencia's **Aeropuerto de Manises** (☎96 159 85 00) is 10km west of the city centre. It's served by metro lines 3 and 5. Budget flights serve major European destinations.

BOAT **Acciona Trasmediterránea** (www.accionatrasmediterranea.es) operates car and passenger ferries to Ibiza, Mallorca and Menorca.

BUS Valencia's **bus station** (☎96 346 62 66) is beside the riverbed on Avenida Menéndez Pidal. **Avanza** (www.avanzabus.com) operates hourly bus services to/from Madrid (€27.50 to €34.50, four hours). **ALSA** (www.alsa.es) has numerous buses to/from Barcelona (€27 to €32, 4½ hours) and Alicante (€19, 2½ hours), most passing by Benidorm (€15.20, 1¾ hours).

TRAIN From Valencia's Estación del Norte, major destinations include Alicante (€17 to €29, 1¾ hours, eight daily) and Barcelona (€40 to €44, three to 3½ hours, at least 12 daily). The AVE, the high-speed train, now links Madrid and Valencia, with up to 15 high-speed services daily and a journey time of around 1¾ hours.

Getting Around

Metro line 5 connects the airport, city centre and port. The high-speed tram leaves from the FGV tram station, 500m north of the cathedral, at the Pont de Fusta. This is a pleasant way to get to the beach, the paella restaurants of Las Arenas and the port.

Alicante

TRANSPORT HUB

Although it's an attractive seaside city with palm-lined boulevards and lively nightlife, Alicante (Alacant in Valenciano) is primarily a gateway town for the Mediterranean – its airport is one of Spain's busiest in summer and the city is otherwise well-connected to the rest of Spain by train and bus.

Sleeping & Eating

The old quarter (known as El Barrio) around Catedral de San Nicolás is wall-to-wall bars of the tapas and drinking variety. Down by the harbour, the Paseo del Puerto, tranquil by day, is a double-decker line of bars, cafes and night-time discos.

Hostal Les Monges Palace HOSTAL €
(☎96 521 50 46; www.lesmonges.es; Calle San Agustín 4; s €37-45, d €53-60; ❄@📶) This agreeably quirky place is a treasure with its winding corridors, tiles, mosaics and antique furniture. Each room is individually decorated and reception couldn't be more welcoming.

Guest House Antonio BOUTIQUE HOTEL €
(☎650 718353; www.guesthousealicante.com; Calle Segura 20; s €35-40, d €45-50; ❄📶) Each of the eight large, tastefully decorated rooms

here has a safe, a full-sized fridge and free beverage-making facilities.

Piripi VALENCIAN €€
(☎96 522 79 40; Avenida Oscar Esplá 30; mains €12-26) This highly regarded restaurant is strong on rice, seafood and fish, and there's a huge variety of tapas.

❶ Getting There & Away

AIR Alicante's **El Altet airport**, gateway to the Costa Blanca, is around 12km southwest of the centre. It's served by budget airlines, charters and scheduled flights from all over Europe.
BUS Destinations include Murcia (€5.63, one hour, at least seven daily) and Valencia (€19, 2½ hours, 10 daily).
TRAIN Destinations from the main **Renfe Estación de Madrid** (Avenida de Salamanca) include Barcelona (€55, five hours, eight daily), Madrid (€60, 3¼ hours, seven daily), Murcia (from €8, 1¼ hours, hourly) and Valencia (€14 to €30, 1¾ to two hours, eight daily).

Costa Blanca

Clean white beaches, bright sunshine and a rockin' nightlife have made the **Costa Blanca** (www.costablanca.org) one of Europe's favourite summer playgrounds. Many resorts are shamefully overbuilt, but it is still possible to discover charming towns and unspoilt coastline. Some of the best towns to explore include **Benidorm**, a highrise nightlife hot spot in summer (but otherwise home to pensioners the rest of the year); **Altea**, famed for its church with a pretty blue-tiled dome; and **Calpe**, known for the Gibraltar-like **Peñón de Ifach** (332m). All are accessible by train from Alicante.

BALEARIC ISLANDS

POP 1.1 MILLION

The Balearic Islands (Illes Balears in Catalan) adorn the glittering Mediterranean waters off Spain's eastern coastline. Beach tourism destinations *par excellence,* each of the islands has a quite distinct identity and they have managed to retain much of their individual character and beauty. All boast beaches second to none in the Med but each offers reasons for exploring inland too.

Check out websites like www.illesbalears.es and www.platgesdebalears.com.

❶ Getting There & Away

AIR In summer, charter and regular flights converge on Palma de Mallorca and Ibiza from all over Europe. Major operators from the Spanish mainland include **Iberia** (www.iberia.es), **Air Europa** (www.aireuropa.com), **Spanair** (www.spanair.com), **Air Berlin** (www.airberlin.com) and **Vueling** (www.vueling.com).
BOAT Compare prices and look for deals at **Direct Ferries** (www.directferries.es). Ferry companies include:
Acciona Trasmediterránea (☎902 454 645; www.trasmediterranea.es)
Baleària (☎902 160 180; www.balearia.com)
Iscomar (☎902 119 128; www.iscomar.com)
The main ferry routes to the mainland are:
Ibiza (Ibiza City) To/from Barcelona (Acciona Trasmediterránea, Baleària), Valencia (Acciona Trasmediterránea)
Ibiza (Sant Antoni) To/from Denia, Barcelona and Valencia (Baleària)
Mallorca (Palma de Mallorca) To/from Barcelona and Valencia (Acciona Trasmediterránea, Baleària), Denia (Baleària)
Menorca (Maó) To/from Barcelona and Valencia (Acciona Trasmediterránea, Baleària)
The main interisland ferry routes:
Ibiza (Ibiza City) To/from Palma de Mallorca (Acciona Trasmediterránea and Baleària)
Mallorca (Palma de Mallorca) To/from Ibiza City (Acciona Trasmediterránea and Baleària) and Maó (Acciona Trasmediterránea and Baleària)
Mallorca (Port d'Alcúdia) To/from Ciutadella (Iscomar and Baleària)
Menorca (Ciutadella) To/from Port d'Alcúdia (Iscomar and Baleària)
Menorca (Maó) To/from Palma de Mallorca (Acciona Trasmediterránea and Baleària)

Mallorca

POP 402,000

The sunny, warm hues of the medieval heart of Palma de Mallorca, the archipelago's capital, make a great introduction to the islands. The northwest coast, dominated by the Serra de Tramuntana mountain range, is a beautiful region of olive groves, pine forests and ochre villages, with a spectacularly rugged coastline. Most of Mallorca's best beaches are on the north and east coasts, and although many have been swallowed up by tourist developments, you can still find the occasional exception. There is also a scattering of fine beaches along the south coast.

❶ Getting Around

BUS Most of the island is accessible by bus from Palma. All buses depart from or near the **bus station** (Carrer d'Eusebi Estada).

TRAIN Two train lines run from Plaça d'Espanya in Palma de Mallorca. The popular, old train runs to Sóller, a pretty ride. A standard train line runs inland to Inca, where the line splits with a branch to Sa Pobla and another to Manacor.

PALMA DE MALLORCA

◉ Sights

Catedral CATHEDRAL
(La Seu; ☎902 022445, 971 723 130; www.catedral demallorca.org; Carrer del Palau Reial 9; adult/child €6/free; ⏰10am-6.15pm Mon-Fri, to 2.15pm Sat) This awesome structure, completed in 1601, is predominantly Gothic, apart from the main facade (replaced after an earthquake in 1851) and parts of the interior. The cathedral's interior is stunning, with ranks of slender columns supporting the soaring ceiling and framing three levels of elaborate stained-glass windows. The front altar's centrepiece, a light, twisting wrought-iron sculpture suspended from the ceiling, is one of Gaudí's more eccentric creations. For once, Gaudí is upstaged by the island's top contemporary artist, Miquel Barceló, who reworked the Capella del Santíssim i Sant Pere, at the head of the south aisle, in a dream-fantasy, swirling ceramic rendition of the miracle of the loaves and fishes.

Palau de l'Almudaina PALACE
(Carrer del Palau Reial; adult/child €9/4, audio-guide €4, guided tour €6; ⏰10am-5.45pm Mon-Fri, to 1.15pm Sat) Originally an Islamic fort, this mighty construction was converted into a residence for the Mallorcan monarchs at the end of the 13th century. It is still occasionally used for official functions when King Juan Carlos is in town. At other times, you can wander through a series of cavernous and austere stone-walled rooms, a chapel with a rare Romanesque entrance, and upstairs royal apartments adorned with Flemish tapestries and period furniture.

Es Baluard MUSEUM
(Museu d'Art Modern i Contemporani; www.es baluard.org; Porta de Santa Catalina 10; adult/child €6/free, temporary exhibitions €4, free entry Tue; ⏰10am-8pm Tue-Sat, to 3pm Sun) This 21st-century concrete complex nests within Palma's grand Renaissance-era seaward fortifications. A playful game of light, surfaces and perspective, it makes the perfect frame-work for the creations within; these include works by Joan Miró, Miquel Barceló and Picasso.

Palau March MUSEUM
(Carrer de Palau Reial 18; adult/child €4.50/free; ⏰10am-6.30pm Mon-Fri, to 2pm Sat) This house, palatial by any definition, contains sculptures by such 20th-century greats as Henry Moore, Auguste Rodin, Barbara Hepworth and Eduardo Chillidan, which grace the outdoor terrace. Within is a set of Salvador Dalí prints.

FREE **Museu d'Art Espanyol Contemporani** MUSEUM
(Museu Fundació Juan March; www.march.es/arte/ palma; Carrer de Sant Miquel 11; ⏰10am-6.30pm Mon-Fri, 10.30am-2pm Sat) On permanent display within this 18th-century mansion are some 70 pieces held by the Fundación Juan March. Together they constitute a veritable who's who of mostly 20th-century artists, including Picasso, Miró, Juan Gris (of cubism fame), Dalí and the sculptor Julio González.

🛏 Sleeping

TOP CHOICE **Hotel Dalt Murada** HISTORIC HOTEL €€€
(☎971 425 300; www.daltmurada.com; Carrer de l'Almudaina 6A; s/d incl breakfast €177/210; ❄🔞 📶2) Gathered around a medieval courtyard, this carefully restored old townhouse, which dates from 1500, has 14 rooms and is a gorgeous option, with antique furnishings (including chandeliers and canopied beds) and art work, much of which belongs to the friendly family who still own and run the place.

Hotel Santa Clara BOUTIQUE HOTEL €€€
(☎971 72 92 31; www.santaclarahotel.es; Carrer de Sant Alonso 16; s/d from €122/168; ❄@🔞) Boutique meets antique in this historic mansion, converted with respect, where subdued greys, steely silvers and cream blend harmoniously with the warm stone walls, ample spaces and high ceilings of the original structure.

Misión de San Miguel BOUTIQUE HOTEL €€€
(☎971 214 848; www.urhotels.com; Carrer de Can Maçanet 1; r from €139; ❄❄@🔞) This 32-room boutique hotel is an astounding deal, with excellent prices and stylish designer rooms; it does the little things well with firm mattresses and rain showers, although some rooms open onto public areas and can be a little noisy.

Mallorca

✗ Eating

TOP CHOICE Simply Fosh　　INTERNATIONAL €€

(☏971 72 01 14; www.simplyfosh.com; Carrer de la Missió 7A; mains €18-26, dinner menús €48; ⊘Mon-Sat) Lovingly prepared Mediterranean grub with a special touch is the order of the day in the convent refectory, one of the home kitchens of Michelin-starred chef Marc Fosh. The range of set menus is a wonderful way to sample high-quality cooking at a reasonable price, but there are also à la carte choices.

Misa Braseria　　BRASSERIE, RESTAURANT €€

(☏971 595 301; www.misabraseria.com; Carrer de Can Maçanet 1; mains €16-20, menús from €17; ⊘1-3.30pm & 7.30-10.30pm Mon-Sat) The latest addition to Marc Fosh's ever-expanding restaurant empire, this attractive place consists of a basement restaurant adorned with famous restaurant menus on the walls, or offers lunchtime dining upstairs in its modern patio. The food is slickly presented and tastes are typically fresh with dishes that change weekly and with the seasons.

La Bodeguilla　　SPANISH €€

(☏971 71 82 74; www.la-bodeguilla.com; Carrer de Sant Jaume 3; mains €17.50-19.50; ⊘Mon-Sat) This gourmet restaurant does creative interpretations of dishes from across Spain; try the *cochinillo* (suckling pig) from Segovia or the *lechazo* (young lamb, baked Córdoba-style in rosemary). Also on offer is an enticing range of tapas.

13%　　TAPAS €€

(www.13porciento.com; Carrer Sant Feliu 13A; meals around €15; ⊘) At the quieter end of the old town, this L-shaped barn of a place is at once a wine and tapas bar, bistro and delicatessen. Most items are organic and there's plenty of choice for vegetarians. Wines are displayed on racks (both bar and takeaway prices are quoted, so you know the exact mark-up).

🍷 Drinking & Entertainment

The old quarter is the city's most vibrant nightlife zone. Particularly along the narrow streets between Plaça de la Reina and Plaça de la Drassana, you'll find an enormous selection of bars, pubs and bodegas. According to a much flouted law, bars should shut by 1am Sunday to Thursday (3am Friday and Saturday).

TOP CHOICE Puro Beach   BAR

(www.purobeach.com; ⊙11am-2am Apr-Oct) This uber-laid-back, sunset chill lounge has a tapering outdoor promontory with an all-white bar that's perfect for sunset cocktails, DJ sessions and fusion food escapes. It is just a two-minute walk east of Cala Estancia (itself just east of Ca'n Pastilla). It's southeast of Palma de Mallorca along the coast.

Ca'n Joan de S'Aigo   CAFE

(Carrer de Can Sanç 10; ⊙8am-9pm Wed-Mon) Dating from 1700, this is *the* place for a hot chocolate (€1.40) in what can only be described as an antique-filled milk bar. The house speciality is *quart,* a feather-soft sponge cake that children love, with almond-flavoured ice cream.

Abaco   BAR

(Carrer de Sant Joan 1; ⊙from 8pm) Inhabiting the restored patio of an old Mallorcan house, Abaco is filled with ornate candelabra, elaborate floral arrangements, cascading towers of fresh fruit and bizarre artworks. It hovers between extravagant and kitsch, but the effect is overwhelming, whatever your opinion. Paying this much for a cocktail is an outrage, but one might just be worth it here.

ℹ Information

Consell de Mallorca Tourist Office (✆971 17 39 90; www.infomallorca.net; Plaça de la Reina 2; ⊙8am-8pm Mon-Fri, 9am-2pm Sat) Covers the whole island. For cultural and sporting events, consult *On Anar,* its free quarterly 'what's happening' guide with a version in English.

Municipal Tourist Office (✆902 102365; ⊙9am-8pm Mon-Sat) In one of the railway buildings off Plaça d'Espanya.

AROUND MALLORCA

Mallorca's northwestern coast is a world away from the high-rise tourism on the other side of the island. Dominated by the Serra de Tramuntana, it's a beautiful region of olive groves, pine forests and small villages with shuttered stone buildings. There

are a couple of highlights for drivers: the hair-raising road down to the small port of **Sa Calobra**, and the amazing trip along the peninsula leading to the island's northern tip, **Cap de Formentor**.

Sóller is a good place to base yourself for hiking and the nearby village of **Fornalutx** is one of the prettiest on Mallorca.

From Sóller, it's a 10km walk to the beautiful hilltop village of **Deià** (www.deia.info), where Robert Graves, poet and author of *I Claudius,* lived for most of his life. From the village, you can scramble down to the small shingle beach of **Cala de Deià**. Boasting a fine monastery and pretty streets, **Valldemossa** (www.valldemossa.com) is further southwest down the coast.

Further east, **Pollença** and **Artà** are attractive inland towns. Nice beaches include those at **Cala Sant Vicenç**, **Cala Mondragó** and around **Cala Llombards**.

🛏 Sleeping & Eating

The **Consell de Mallorca tourist office** (✆971 71 22 16; www.infomallorca.net; Plaça de la Reina 2; ⊙8am-8pm Mon-Fri, 9am-2pm Sat) in Palma can supply information on rural and other types of accommodation around the island.

DEIÀ

TOP CHOICE S'Hotel des Puig   HISTORIC HOTEL €€€

(✆971 639 409; www.hoteldespuig.com; Carrer des Puig 4; s €95, d €150-160; ⊙Feb-Nov; ❄🌐) The eight rooms of this gem in the middle of the old town reflect a muted modern taste within ancient stone walls. Out the back are secrets impossible to divine from the street, such as the pool and lovely terrace.

Hostal Miramar   HOTEL €€

(✆971 63 90 84; www.pensionmiramar.com; Carrer de Ca'n Oliver; r incl breakfast €91, without bathroom €75; ⊙Mar–mid-Nov; 🅿) Hidden within the lush vegetation above the main road and with views across to Deià's hillside church and the sea beyond, this 19th-century stone house with gardens is a shady retreat with nine rooms. The rooms with shared bathrooms have the best views; others look onto the garden.

Restaurant Juame   MALLORCAN €€€

(✆971 63 90 29; www.restaurantejuame-deia.com; Avinguda del Arxiduc Lluís Salvador 22; mains €20-25; ⊙closed Mon) This is the kind of restuarant we like. Family-run and exceptionally friendly, with a relaxed, easy going vibe but simply superb gourmet Mallorcan dishes incorporating the very best local produce. It's a little more expensive than some of the other options in the village but it's worth every euro.

SÓLLER

The Sóller area has plenty of boutique hotels in historic buildings or country houses; many are listed on www.sollernet.com.

Ca'n Isabel
HOTEL €€

(☏971 638 097; www.canisabel.com; Carrer de d'Isabel ll 13; s €99.50-131.50, d €124.50-156.50; ☉mid-Feb–mid-Nov; ❋@☎) With just six rooms, this 19th-century house is a gracefully decorated hideaway, with a fine garden out the back. The decor won't be to everyone's taste, but the owners have retained the period style impeccably. The best (and dearest) of the rooms come with their own delightful terrace.

Ca's Carreter
MALLORCAN €€

(☏971 63 51 33; www.cascarreter.net; Carrer del Cetre 9; mains €13-17; ☉lunch & dinner Tue-Sat, lunch Sun) In an atmospheric former cart workshop, Ca's Carreter is a welcoming spot that serves unpretentious Mallorcan cooking, including fresh local fish and other mainly regional ingredients.

Ibiza

Ibiza (Eivissa in Catalan) is an island of extremes. Its formidable party reputation is completely justified, with some of the world's greatest clubs attracting hedonists from the world over. The interior and northeast of the island, however, are another world. Peaceful country drives, hilly green territory, a sprinkling of mostly laid-back beaches and coves, and some wonderful inland accommodation and eateries, are light years from the ecstasy-fuelled madness of the clubs that dominate the west.

IBIZA CITY

◉ Sights & Activities

Ibiza City's port area of **Sa Penya** is crammed with funky and trashy clothing boutiques and arty-crafty market stalls. From here, you can wander up into **D'Alt Vila**, the atmospheric old walled town.

Ramparts
HISTORIC SITE

A ramp leads from Plaça de Sa Font in Sa Penya up to the **Portal de ses Taules** gateway, the main entrance. Completed in 1585, the fortifications include seven artillery bastions joined by thick protective walls up to 22m in height. You can walk the entire perimeter of these impressive Renaissance-era walls, designed to withstand heavy artillery, and enjoy great views along the way.

Catedral
CATHEDRAL

(☉9.30am-1.30pm & 5-8pm) Ibiza's cathedral elegantly combines several styles: the original 14th-century structure is Catalan Gothic but the sacristy was added in 1592 and a major baroque renovation took place in the 18th century.

Centre d'Interpretació Madina Yasiba
MUSEUM

(Carrer Major 2; adult/child €2/1.50; ☉10am-2pm & 6-9pm Tue-Sat, 10am-2pm Sun) This small display replicates the medieval Muslim city of Madina Yabisa (Ibiza City) prior to the island's fall to Christian forces in 1235. Artefacts, audiovisuals and maps help transport you to those times.

⌂ Sleeping

Many of Ibiza City's hotels and *hostales* are closed in the low season and heavily booked between April and October. Make reservations well in advance.

Hotel La Ventana
HISTORIC HOTEL €€€

(☏971 30 35 37; www.laventanaibiza.com; Carrer de Sa Carossa 13; d from €165; ❋☎) This charming 15th-century mansion is set on a little tree-shaded square in the old town. Some rooms come with stylish four-poster beds and mosquito nets. The rooftop terrace, trim gardens and restaurant are welcome extras. Prices drop massively out of season.

Hostal Parque
HOTEL €€€

(☏971 30 13 58; www.hostalparque.com; Carrer de Vicent Cuervo 3; s €70-90, d €130-190; ❋☎) The rooms here are small, but otherwise what you get are the basics done very well indeed, and it manages to be modern and cool without being over the top. Rarely for central Ibiza City, there's decent double glazing so noise shouldn't be too much of an issue. The best doubles overlook pleasant Plaça des Parc and the downstairs cafe is a very popular place for a drink or a meal.

Hostal La Marina
HOTEL €€

(☏971 31 01 72; www.hostal-lamarina.com; Carrer de Barcelona 7; r €75-170; ❋) Looking onto both the waterfront and bar-lined Carrer de Barcelona, this mid-19th-century building has rooms that are as flamboyant and colourful as an Ibizan club night. A handful of singles and some doubles look onto the street (with the predictable noise problem), but you can opt for pricier doubles and attics with terraces and panoramic port and/or town views.

✕ Eating

TOP CHOICE Comidas

Bar San Juan   MEDITERRANEAN €

(Carrer de Guillem de Montgrí 8; mains from €6; ☺Mon-Sat) This family-run operation, with two small dining rooms, harks back to the days before Ibiza became a by-word for glam. It offers outstanding value, with fish dishes for around €10 and many small mains for €6 or less. It doesn't take reservations, so arrive early and expect to have other people sat at the same table as you.

Restaurant of Hotel Mirador de Dalt Vila   MEDITERRANEAN €€€

(☎971 30 30 45; Plaça d'Espanya 4; menú €45, mains €26-30; ☺Easter-Dec) At this intimate – do reserve – restaurant with its painted barrel ceiling and original canvases around the walls, you'll dine magnificently. Service is discreet yet friendly, and dishes are creative, colourful and delightfully presented.

♟ Drinking

Sa Penya is the nightlife centre. Dozens of bars keep the port area jumping. Alternatively, various bars at Platja d'en Bossa combine sounds, sand, sea and sangria.

Discobus   BUS

(www.discobus.es; per person €3; ☺midnight-6am Jun-Sep) Discobus runs around the major clubs, bars and hotels in Ibiza City, Platja d'en Bossa, Sant Rafel, Es Canar, Santa Eulària and Sant Antoni.

Teatro Pereira   MUSIC BAR

(www.teatropereyra.com; Carrer del Comte de Rosselló 3; ☺8am-4am) Away from the waterfront hubbub, this hugely atmospheric time warp of a place, which is all stained wood and iron girders, was once the foyer of the long-abandoned 1893 theatre at its rear. It's packed most nights with a more eclectic crowd than the standard preclubbing bunch, and offers nightly live music sessions.

Bora Bora Beach Club   BEACH BAR

(☺noon-4am May-Sep) At Platja d'en Bossa, about 2km from the old town, this is *the* place – a long beachside bar where sun and fun worshippers work off hangovers and prepare new ones. Entry's free and

---

CLUBBING IN IBIZA

In summer (late May to the end of September), the west of the island is a continuous party from sunset to sunrise and back again. In 2011 the International Dance Music Awards ranked four Ibiza clubs (see below) among their worldwide top eight.

The clubs operate nightly from around 1am to 6am and each has something different. Theme nights, fancy-dress parties and foam parties (where you are half-drowned in the stuff) are regular features. Admission can cost anything from €25 to €60.

Space (www.space-ibiza.es; admission €29-60; ☺Jun–mid-Oct) In Platja d'en Bossa, aptly named Space, which can pack in as many as 40 DJs and up to 12,000 clubbers, is considered one of the world's best nightclubs. Action here starts mid-afternoon and regular daytime boats make the trip between Platja d'en Bossa and Ibiza City (€6 return).

Pacha (www.pacha.com; admission €23-57; ☺nightly Jun-Sep, Fri & Sat Oct-May) In business on the northern side of Ibiza City's port since 1973, Pacha has 15 bars (!) and various dance spaces that can hold 3000 people. The main dance floor, a sea of colour, mirror balls and veils draped from the ceiling, heaves to deep techno. On the terrace, sounds are more gentle and relaxing.

Amnesia (www.amnesia.es; admission €40-65; ☺early Jun–Sep) Four kilometres out on the road to Sant Rafel, Amnesia has a sound system that seems to give your body a massage. A huge glasshouse-like internal terrace, filled with palms and bars, surrounds the central dance area with a seething mass of mostly tireless 20-something dancers.

Privilege (www.privilegeibiza.com; admission around €40) Five kilometres along the road to Sant Rafel, this club, with its 20 bars, interior pool and capacity for 10,000 clubbers, claims to be one of the world's largest. The main domed dance temple is an enormous, pulsating area, where the DJ's cabin is suspended above the pool.

the ambience is chilled, with low-key club sounds wafting over the sand. From midnight, everyone crowds inside. It's off Carrer del Fumarell.

ℹ Information

Tourist Office (☏971 39 92 32; www.eivissa. es; Plaça de la Catedral; ⊙10am-2pm & 6-9pm Mon-Sat, 10am-2pm Sun) Can provide audio-guides to the city; bring your passport or identity document. Other branches around the city.

AROUND IBIZA

Ibiza has numerous unspoiled and relatively undeveloped beaches. **Cala de Boix**, on the northeastern coast, is the only black-sand beach on the island, while further north are the lovely beaches of **S'Aigua Blanca**.

On the north coast near Portinatx, **Cala Xarraca** is in a picturesque, secluded bay, and near Port de Sant Miquel is the attractive **Cala Benirrás**.

In the southwest, **Cala d'Hort** has a spectacular setting overlooking two rugged rock islets, Es Verda and Es Verdranell.

The best thing about rowdy **Sant Antoni**, the island's second biggest town and north of Ibiza City, is heading to the small rock-and-sand strip on the north shore to join hundreds of others for sunset drinks at a string of chilled bars. The best known remains **Café del Mar** (⊙4pm-1am), our favourite, but it's further north along the pedestrian walkway.

Local **buses** (www.ibizabus.com) run to most destinations between May and October.

🛏 Sleeping & Eating

Check out rural accommodation at www. ibizaruralvillas.com. For more standard accommodation, start at www.ibizahotels guide.com.

Hostal Cala Boix　　　　　HOSTAL €€
(☏971 33 52 24; www.hostalcalaboix.com; Cala Boix; d €60-80; ⊙May-Oct; ❄) Set uphill and back from Cala Boix, this option couldn't be further from the Ibiza madness. All rooms have a balcony and many have sea views. At S'Arribiada, its hearty resturant, Thursday is barbeque day, while each Tuesday fresh sardines sizzle on the grill.

Hostal Restaurante Es Alocs　　HOTEL €€
(☏971 33 50 79; www.hostalalocs.com; Platja Es Figueral; s/d €40/65; ⊙May-Oct; ❄🖤) This very friendly choice sits right on the beach at Platja Es Figueral. Rooms occupy two floors and most have a small fridge and balcony.

The bar-restaurant has a wonderful terrace, deeply shaded with tangled juniper and chaste trees.

Bar Anita　　　　　　　　TAVERN €
(Sant Carles de Peralta; mains €8-16) A timeless tavern opposite the village church of Sant Carles de Peralta, this restaurant and bar has been attracting all sorts from around the island for decades. They come to enjoy pizza, pasta and a hearty meal – or simply to drink and chat.

Menorca

Renowned for its pristine beaches and archaeological sites, tranquil Menorca was declared a Biosphere Reserve by Unesco in 1993. The capital, Maó, is known as Mahón in Castilian.

ℹ Getting Around

TO/FROM THE AIRPORT Bus 10 (€1.80) runs between Menorca's airport, 7km southwest of Maó, and the city's bus station every half-hour. A taxi costs around €15.

◉ Sights & Activities

Maó absorbs most of the tourist traffic. North of Maó, a drive across a lunar landscape leads to the lighthouse at **Cap de Favàritx**. South of the cape stretch some fine sandy bays and beaches, including **Cala Presili** and **Platja d'en Tortuga**, reachable on foot.

Ciutadella, with its smaller harbour and historic buildings, has a more distinctly Spanish feel to it and is the more attractive of the two. A narrow country road leads south of Ciutadella (follow the 'Platges' sign from the *ronda,* or ring road) and then forks twice to reach some of the island's loveliest beaches: from west to east **Arenal de Son Saura**, **Cala en Turqueta**, **Es Talaier**, **Cala Macarelleta** and **Cala Macarella**. As with most beaches, you'll need your own transport.

In the centre of the island, the 357m-high **Monte Toro** has great views; on a clear day you can see Mallorca.

On the northern coast, the picturesque town of **Fornells** is on a large bay popular with windsurfers.

🛏 Sleeping

Many accommodation options on the island are closed between November and April.

MAÓ

TOP CHOICE **Casa Alberti** HISTORIC HOTEL €€€

(☎971 35 42 10; www.casalberti.com; Carrer d'Isabel II 9; s/d incl breakfast €130/160; ⏰Easter-Oct) Climb the central stairs with striking wrought-iron banisters to your vast room with white walls and whitest-of-white sheets. Each of the six bedrooms within this 18th-century mansion is furnished with traditional items, while bathrooms are designer cool and contemporary.

CIUTADELLA

Hotel Gèminis HOTEL €

(☎971 38 46 44; www.hotelgeminismenorca.com; Carrer de Josepa Rossinyol 4; s incl breakfast €31-56, d incl breakfast €45-92; ⏰April–mid-October; ❄📶🏊) A friendly, stylish two-star place, this graceful, three-storey, rose-and-white lodging offers comfortable if somewhat neutral rooms just a short walk away from the city centre. The best rooms have a sizeable balcony.

Hostal-Residencia Oasis PENSION €

(☎971 38 21 97; www.hostaloasismenorca.es; Carrer de Sant Isidre 33; r €34-64) Run by a delightful elderly couple, this quiet place is close to the heart of the old quarter. Rooms, mostly with bathroom, are set beside a spacious garden courtyard. Furnishings, though still trim, are from deep into the last century.

Eating & Drinking

The ports in both Maó and Ciutadella are lined with bars and restaurants.

MAÓ

El Varadero SPANISH €€

(☎971 35 20 74; Moll de Llevant 4; mains €13-17; ⏰Easter-Nov) With such a splendid vista from the harbourside terrace, El Varadero offers tempting rice dishes and a short, select choice of fish and meat mains. If a full meal is too much, drop by for a tapa or two with a glass of wine and savour the view.

CIUTADELLA

Cas Ferrer de sa Font MENORCAN €€

(☎971 48 07 84; www.casferrer.com; Carrer del Portal de sa Font 16; mains €15-20; ⏰Tue-Sun) Nowhere on the island will you find more authentic Menorcan cuisine – here you'll enjoy meats and vegetables from the owner's organic farm. Dine on the delightful interior patio of this charming 18th-century building or inside, below beams and soft curves, in what was once a blacksmith's forge.

Es Molí CAFE, BAR

(Plaça de ses Palmeres) Sit among the arches, pillars and mellow stonework of the interior, where the core of the old *molí* (windmill) still juts from its heart. Or, if you don't mind the traffic, plant yourself on the terrace for a fine prospect of the little square.

FORNELLS

Es Port SEAFOOD €€

(☎971 37 64 03; Passeig Marítim 5; menú €15.50, mains €10-21; ⏰Sat-Thu Easter-Oct) The fish and other seafood are of the freshest here – unsurprisingly since Es Port has its own boat and lobster pots. Like most of its neighbours, it does *caldereta de llagosta* (lobster stew; €65), but less financial outlay goes into a sizzling *paella de llomanto* (lobster paella; €35).

Information

Tourist Office (Plaça de la Catedral 5, Ciutadella; ⏰8.30am-3pm & 5-9pm)

ANDALUCÍA

Images of Andalucía are so potent, so quintessentially Spanish that it's sometimes difficult not to feel a sense of déjà vu. It's almost as if you've already been there in your dreams: a solemn Easter parade, an ebullient spring festival, exotic nights in the Alhambra. In the stark light of day the picture is no less compelling.

Seville

POP 703,000

A sexy, gutsy and gorgeous city, Seville is home to two of Spain's most colourful festivals, fascinating and distinctive *barrios*, and a local population that lives life to the fullest. A fiery place (as you'll soon see in its packed and noisy tapas bars), it is also hot climatewise – avoid July and August!

Sights

Cathedral & Giralda CHURCH

(www.catedraldesevilla.es; adult/child €8/free; ⏰11am-5.30pm Mon-Sat, 2.30-6.30pm Sun Sep-Jun, 9.30am-4.30pm Mon-Sat, 2.30-6.30pm Sun Jul & Aug) After Seville fell to the Christians in 1248 its main mosque was used as a church until 1401 when it was knocked down to make way for what would become one of the world's largest cathedrals and an icon of Gothic architecture. The building wasn't completed until 1507. Over 90m high, the perfectly proportioned and exquisitely decorated **La Giralda** was the minaret of the mosque that stood on the site before the cathedral. The views from the summit are exceptional.

Inside, the **Capilla de San Antonio** contains Murillo's large 1666 canvas depicting the vision of St Anthony of Padua. Inside the cathedral's southern door stands the elaborate **tomb of Christopher Columbus**, dating from 1902. Towards the east end of the main nave is the **Capilla Mayor**; its Gothic altarpiece is the jewel of the cathedral and reckoned to be the biggest altarpiece in the world with more than 1000 carved biblical figures. The **Sacristía de los Cálices** (Sacristy of the Chalices) contains Goya's 1817 painting of the Seville martyrs *Santas Justa y Rufina*. The room's centrepiece is the **Custodia de Juan de Arfe**, a huge 475kg silver monstrance made in the 1580s by Renaissance metalsmith Juan de Arfe. Displayed in a glass case are the city keys handed to the conquering Fernando III in 1248.

Alcázar
CASTLE
(adult/child €7.50/free; ☉9.30am-7pm Apr-Sep, to 6pm Oct-Mar) Seville's Alcázar, a royal residence for many centuries, was founded in 913 as a Muslim fortress. The Alcázar has been expanded and rebuilt many times in its 11 centuries of existence. The Catholic Monarchs, Fernando and Isabel, set up court here in the 1480s as they prepared for the conquest of Granada. Later rulers created the Alcázar's lovely gardens. The highlights include exquisitely adorned patios and the showpiece **Palacio de Don Pedro**.

FREE Archivo de Indias
MUSEUM
(Calle Santo Tomás; ☉10am-4pm Mon-Sat, to 2pm Sun & holidays) On the western side of Plaza del Triunfo, the Archivo de Indias is the main archive of Spain's American empire, with 80 million pages of documents dating from 1492 through to the end of the empire in the 19th century: a most effective statement of Spain's power and influence during its Golden Age.

Barrio de Santa Cruz
HISTORIC DISTRICT
Seville's medieval *judería* (Jewish quarter), east of the cathedral and Alcázar, is today a tangle of atmospheric, winding streets and lovely plant-decked plazas perfumed with orange blossom. Among its most characteristic plazas is **Plaza de Santa Cruz**, which gives the *barrio* its name. **Plaza de Doña Elvira** is another romantic perch, especially in the evening.

Metropol Parasol
LANDMARK
(www.metropolsevilla.com; Plaza de la Encarnación) The opinion-dividing Metropol Parasol which opened in March 2011 in the Plaza de la Encarnación claims to be the largest wooden building in the world. Its undulating honeycombed roof is held up by five giant mushroom-like pillars.

Six years in the making, the construction covers a former dead zone in Seville's central district. Roman ruins discovered during the building's conception have been cleverly incorporated into the foundations at the Museo Antiquarium, while upstairs on level 2 you can pay €1.20 to stroll along a surreal panoramic walkway with killer city views. The Metropol also houses the plaza's former market, a restaurant and a concert space.

Museo del Baile Flamenco
MUSEUM
(www.museoflamenco.com; Calle Manuel Rojas Marcos 3; adult/child €10/6; ☉9.30am-7pm) The brainchild of Sevillana flamenco dancer, Cristina Hoyos, this museum is spread over three floors of an 18th-century palace, although at €10 a pop it's a little overpriced. Exhibits include sketches, paintings, photos of erstwhile (and contemporary) flamenco greats, plus a collection of dresses and shawls.

Parque de María Luisa & Plaza de España
PARK
(☉8am-10pm) This is a large area transformed for Seville's 1929 international fair, the Exposición Iberoamericana. Architects adorned it with fantastical buildings, many of them harking back to Seville's past glory or imitating the native styles of Spain's former colonies. In its midst is the large Parque de María Luisa, a living expression of Seville's Moorish and Christian past.

✦ Festivals & Events
The first of Seville's two great festivals is **Semana Santa** (www.semana-santa.org), the week leading up to Easter Sunday. Throughout the week, thousands of members of religious brotherhoods parade in penitents'

garb with tall, pointed *capirotes* (hoods) accompanying sacred images through the city, while huge crowds look on.

The **Feria de Abril**, a week in late April, is a welcome release after this solemnity: the festivities involve six days of music, dancing, horse riding and traditional dress, plus daily bullfights.

The city also stages Spain's largest flamenco festival, the month-long **Bienal de Flamenco** (www.labienal.com). It's held in September in even-numbered years.

🛏 Sleeping

There's plenty of accommodation in the Barrio de Santa Cruz (close to the Alcázar), El Arenal and El Centro.

Prices over Semana Santa and the Feria de Abril can be up to double the high-season prices cited here. Accommodation is often full on weekends and is always booked solid during festivals, so make reservations well in advance.

TOP CHOICE **Hotel Casa 1800** LUXURY HOTEL €€€
(☎954 56 18 00; www.hotelcasa1800sevilla.com; Calle Rodrigo Caro 6; d €145-198; ❄@🌐) Straight in at number one as Seville's favourite hotel is this newly revived Santa Cruz jewel. This really is your home away from home (albeit a posh one!), with charming staff catering for your every need. Highlights include a sweet afternoon tea buffet, plus a quartet of penthouse garden suites with Giralda views.

Un Patio en Santa Cruz HOTEL €€
(☎954 53 94 13; www.patiosantacruz.com; Calle Doncellas 15; s €65-85; d €65-125; ❄🌐) Feeling more like an art gallery than a hotel, this place has starched white walls coated in loud works of art, and strange sculptures and preserved plants. The rooms are immensely comfortable, staff are friendly and there's a cool rooftop terrace with mosaic Moroccan tables.

Hotel Amadeus HOTEL €€
(☎954 50 14 43; www.hotelamadeussevilla.com; Calle Farnesio 6; s/d €85/95; P❄🌐) Just when you thought you could never find hotels with pianos in the rooms anymore, along came Hotel Amadeus. Run by an engaging musical family in the old Judería, several of the astutely decorated rooms come complete with soundproofed walls and upright pianos ensuring you don't miss out on your daily practice.

Hotel Puerta de Sevilla HOTEL €€
(☎954 98 72 70; www.hotelpuertadesevilla.com; Calle Puerta de la Carne 2; s/d €66/86; P❄@🌐) This superfriendly – and super-positioned – hotel is a great mix of the chintz and the stylish. The lobby, lined with superb Seville tile work, has an indoor water feature. The rooms are all flower-pattern textiles, wrought-iron beds and pastel wallpaper. It also features an unbeatable people-watching rooftop terrace.

Hotel Simón HOTEL €€
(☎954 22 66 60; www.hotelsimonsevilla.com; Calle García de Vinuesa 19; s €60-70, d €95-110; ❄@) A typically grand 18th-century Sevillan house, with an ornate patio and spotless and comfortable rooms, this place gleams way above its two-star rating. Some of the rooms are embellished with rich *azulejos* tile work.

Oasis Backpackers' Hostel HOSTEL €
(☎954 29 37 77; www.oasissevilla.com; Plaza de la Encarnación 29; dm/d incl breakfast €15/50; ❄@🌐💦) Seville's offbeat, buzzing backpacker central offers 24-hour free internet access. The new location is in Plaza Encarnación, a narrow street behind the Church of the Anunciación. Each dorm bed has a personal safe, and there is a small rooftop pool. There's no curfew: this is Spain!

Hotel Goya HOTEL €€
(☎954 21 11 70; www.hotelgoyasevilla.com; Calle Mateos Gago 31; s €39-60, d €65-95; ❄@🌐) The gleaming Goya is more popular than ever. Pets are welcome. Book ahead.

🍴 Eating

TOP CHOICE **Vinería San Telmo** TAPAS, FUSION €€
(☎954 41 06 00; www.vineriasantelmo.com; Paseo Catalina de Ribera 4; tapas €3.50, media raciones €10) San Telmo invented the *rascocielo* (skyscraper) tapa, an 'Empire State' of tomatoes, aubergine, goat's cheese and smoked salmon. If this and other creative nougats don't make you drool with expectation then there's something wrong.

Catalina TAPAS €€
(Paseo Catalina de Ribera 4; raciones €10) If your view of tapas is 'glorified bar snacks', then your ideas could be blown out of the water here with a creative mix of just about every ingredient known to Iberian cooking. Start with the cheese, aubergine and paprika special.

Seville

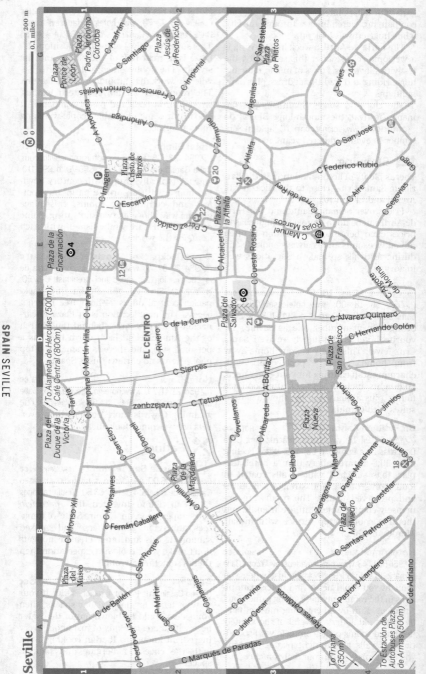

Seville

◎ Top Sights

Alcázar...E6
La Giralda..D5

◎ Sights

1 Archivo de Indias..............................D6
2 Barrio de Santa Cruz........................F5
3 Cathedral & Giralda..........................D5
4 Metropol Parasol..............................E1
5 Museo del Baile Flamenco.................E3
6 Plaza del Salvador............................D3

⌴ Sleeping

7 Hotel Amadeus...................................F4
8 Hotel Casa 1800................................E5
9 Hotel Goya..F5
10 Hotel Puerta de Sevilla....................G5
11 Hotel Simón.....................................C5
12 Oasis Backpackers' Hostel...............E1
13 Un Patio en Santa Cruz...................G5

✖ Eating

14 Bar Alfalfa..F3
15 Bodega Santa Cruz...........................E5
16 Catalina..G5
17 Extraverde.......................................E6
18 Mesón Cinco Jotas............................C4
19 Vinería San Telmo G5

⊖ Drinking

20 El Garlochi.......................................F2
21 La Antigua Bodeguita........................D3
22 La Rebótica......................................E2

✪ Entertainment

23 Casa de la Memoria de Al-
Andalus..F5
24 La Carbonería..................................G4

Bodega Santa Cruz   TAPAS €
(Calle Mateos Gago; tapas €2) Forever crowded
and with a mountain of paper on the floor,
this place is usually standing room only,
with tapas and drinks enjoyed alfresco as
you dodge the marching army of tourists
squeezing through Santa Cruz's narrow
streets.

⬗ **Extraverde**   TAPAS €
(www.extraverde.es; Plaza de Doña Elvira 8; tapas
€2.50-4; ⊙10.30am-11.30pm) Recent to the
Santa Cruz scene, Extraverde is a unique
bar-shop specialising in Andalucian products, such as olive oil, cheese and wine. You
can taste free samples standing up, or sit
down inside and order a full tapa.

Mesón Cinco Jotas
TAPAS €€

(www.mesoncincojotas.com; Calle Castelar 1; tapas €3.80, media raciones €10) In the world of *jamón*-making, if you are awarded 'Cinco Jotas' (Five Js) for your *jamón*, it's like getting an Oscar. The owner of this place, Sánchez Romero Carvajal, is the biggest producer of Jabugo ham, and has a great selection on offer.

Bar Alfalfa
TAPAS €

(cnr Calles Alfalfa & Candilejo; tapas €3) It's amazing how many people, hams, wine bottles and other knick-knacks you can stuff into such a small space. No matter, order through the window when the going gets crowded. You won't forget the tomato-tinged magnificence of the Italy-meets-Iberia *salmorejo* bruschetta.

Drinking

Bars usually open 6pm to 2am weekdays and 8pm till 3am at the weekend. Drinking and partying really get going around midnight on Friday and Saturday (daily when it's hot). In summer, dozens of open-air late-night bars *(terrazas de verano)* spring up along both banks of the river.

Plaza del Salvador is brimful of drinkers from mid-evening to 1am. Grab a drink from **La Antigua Bodeguita** next door and sit on the steps of the Parroquia del Salvador.

El Garlochi
BAR

(Calle Boteros 4) Dedicated entirely to the iconography, smells and sounds of Semana Santa, the ubercamp El Garlochi is a true marvel. A cloud of church incense hits you as you go up the stairs, and the faces of baby Jesus and the Virgin welcome you into the velvet-walled bar, decked out with more Virgins and Jesuses. Taste the rather revolting sounding cocktails Sangre de Cristo (Blood of Christ) or Agua de Sevilla, both heavily laced with vodka, whisky and grenadine, and pray they open more bars like this.

WANT MORE?

For in-depth information, reviews and recommendations at your fingertips, head to the Apple App Store to purchase Lonely Planet's *Seville City Guide* iPhone app.

La Rebótica
BAR

(Calle Pérez Galdós 11) Two's a crowd in the cramped, sinuous Rebótica, the place to come for cheap shots and 1980s flashbacks accompanied by an appropriately retro soundtrack.

Bulebar Café
BAR, CAFE

(Alameda de Hércules 83; ⏲4pm-late) This place gets pretty *caliente* (hot) at night but is pleasantly chilled in the early evening, with friendly staff. Don't write off its spirit-reviving alfresco breakfasts that pitch early-birds with up-all-nighters.

☆ Entertainment

Seville is arguably Spain's flamenco capital and you're most likely to catch a spontaneous atmosphere (of unpredictable quality) in one of the bars staging regular nights of flamenco with no admission fee. *Soleares,* Flamenco's truest *cante jondo* (deep song), was first concocted in Triana; head here to find some of the more authentic clubs.

TOP CHOICE Casa de la Memoria de Al-Andalus
FLAMENCO

(☏954 56 06 70; www.casadelamemoria.es; Calle Ximénez de Enciso 28; tickets €15; ⏲9pm) This flamenco *tablao* in Santa Cruz is without doubt the most intimate and authentic nightly flamenco show outside the Museo del Baile Flamenco (p728), offering a wide variety of *palos* (flamenco styles) in a courtyard of shifting shadows and overhanging plants. Reserve tickets a day or so in advance.

FREE La Carbonería
FLAMENCO

(Calle Levíes 18; ⏲8pm-4am) During the day there is no indication that this happening place is anything but a large garage. But, arrive after 8pm and this converted coal yard in the Barrio de Santa Cruz reveals two large bars, and nightly live flamenco (11pm and midnight) for no extra charge.

Casa Anselma
FLAMENCO

(Calle Pagés del Corro 49; ⏲midnight-late Mon-Sat) If you can squeeze in past the foreboding form of Anselma (a celebrated Triana flamenco dancer) at the door you'll quickly realise that anything can happen in here. Casa Anselma (beware: there's no sign, just a doorway embellished with *azulejos* tiles) is the antithesis of a tourist flamenco *tablao*, with cheek-to-jowl crowds, thick cigarette smoke, zero amplification and spontaneous outbreaks of dexterous dancing. Pure magic. To get here, cross the Puente de Isabel II, then turn right on Calle Pagés del Corro - Casa Anselma is around 100m along on your right.

ⓘ Information

There are branches of the regional tourist office at **Avenida de la Constitución** (☉9am-8pm Mon-Fri, 10am-2pm Sat & Sun, closed holidays) and **Estación de Santa Justa.** (☏954 53 76 26; Estación Santa Justa; ☉9am-8pm Mon-Fri, 10am-2pm Sat & Sun, closed holidays)

Discover Sevilla (www.discoversevilla.com) An excellent, comprehensive site.

Explore Seville (www.exploreseville.com) A good, informative site.

Seville Tourism (www.turismo.sevilla.org) The city's official tourism site; its 'Accessible Guide' is especially useful for travellers with a disability.

Turismo Sevilla (www.turismosevilla.org; Plaza del Triunfo 1; ☉10.30am-7pm Mon-Fri) Information on all Sevilla province.

ⓘ Getting There & Away

Air

A range of domestic and international flights land in Seville's **Aeropuerto San Pablo** (SVQ; www.sevilla-airport.com; ☉24hr), 7km from the city centre.

Bus

From the **Estación de Autobuses Prado de San Sebastián** (Plaza San Sebastián), there are 12 or more buses daily to/from Cádiz, Córdoba, Granada, Ronda and Málaga. From the **Estación de Autobuses Plaza de Armas** (www.autobusesplazadearmas.es; Avenida del Cristo de la Expiración), destinations include Madrid, Mérida, Cáceres and Portugal.

Train

The modern, efficient **Estación de Santa Justa** (☏902 43 23 43; Avenida Kansas City) is 1.5km northeast of the city centre. There's also a city-centre **Renfe ticket office** (Calle Zaragoza 29).

Twenty or more superfast AVE trains, reaching speeds of 280km/h, whiz daily to/from Madrid (€83.80, 2½ hours). Other services include Cádiz (€13.25, 1¾ hours, 13 daily), Córdoba (€17 to €33.20, 40 minutes to 1½ hours, 21 or more daily), Granada (€24.80, three hours, four daily) and Málaga (€38.70, two hours, 11 daily).

ⓘ Getting Around

Los Amarillos (www.losamarillos.es) runs buses between the airport and the Avenida del Cid near the bus station (€2.40, at 15 and 45 minutes past the hour). A taxi costs about €22.

Tussam's **Tranvia** (www.tussam.es), the city's sleek tram service, was launched in 2007. Individual rides cost €1.30, or you can buy a *Bono* (travel pass offering five rides for €5) from many newspaper stands and tobacconists.

Córdoba

POP 328,000

Córdoba was once one of the most enlightened Islamic cities on earth, and enough remains to place it in the contemporary top three Andalucian draws. The centrepiece is the gigantic and exquisitely rendered Mezquita. Surrounding it is an intricate web of winding streets, geranium-sprouting flower boxes and cool intimate patios that are at their most beguiling in late spring.

◉ Sights & Activities

| TOP CHOICE | **Mezquita** | MOSQUE |

(Mosque; ☏957 47 05 12; www.mezquitadecordoba.org; Calle Cardenal Herrero; adult/child €8/4, 8.30-10am Mon-Sat free; ☉10am-7pm Mon-Sat, 8.30-10am & 2-7pm Sun Mar-Oct, 8.30am-6pm Mon-Sat, 8.30-10am & 2-6pm Sun Nov-Feb) Founded in 785, Córdoba's gigantic mosque is a wonderful architectural hybrid with delicate horseshoe arches making this unlike anywhere else in Spain. The main entrance is the **Puerta del Perdón**, a 14th-century Mudéjar gateway, with the ticket office immediately inside. Within the gateway is the aptly named **Patio de los Naranjos** (Courtyard of the Orange Trees). Once inside, you can see straight ahead to the mihrab, the prayer niche in a mosque's qibla (the wall indicating the direction of Mecca) that was the focus of prayer. The first 12 transverse aisles inside the entrance, a forest of pillars and arches, comprise the original 8th-century mosque.

Judería NEIGHBOURHOOD

The medieval *judería*, extending northwest from the Mezquita almost to Avenida del Gran Capitán, is today a maze of narrow streets and whitewashed buildings with flowery window boxes. The beautiful little 14th-century **Sinagoga** (Calle de los Judíos 20; admission €0.30; ☉9.30am-2pm & 3.30-5.30pm Tue-Sat, 9.30am-1.30pm Sun & holidays) is one of

SPAIN CÓRDOBA

Córdoba

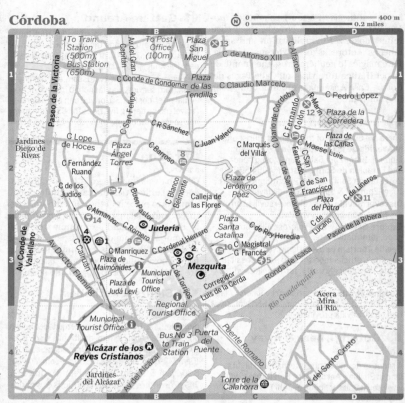

Córdoba

◎ Top Sights

Alcázar de los Reyes Cristianos	B4
Judería	B3
Mezquita	B3

◎ Sights

1	Casa de Sefarad	A3
2	Patio de los Naranjos & Minaret	B3
3	Puerta del Perdón	B3
4	Sinagoga	A3

✪ Activities, Courses & Tours

5	Hammam Baños Árabes	C3

🛏 Sleeping

6	Casa de los Azulejos	C2
7	Hospedería Alma Andalusí	B2
8	Hospedería Añil	B2
9	Hotel Lola	B3
10	Hotel Mezquita	C3

✖ Eating

11	Bodegas Campos	D2
12	Taberna Salinas	D1
13	Taberna San Miguel El Pisto	C1

🍷 Drinking

14	Bodega Guzmán	A3

only three surviving medieval synagogues in Spain and the only one in Andalucía. In the heart of the *judería*, and once connected by an underground tunnel to the Sinagoga, is the 14th-century **Casa de Sefarad** (www. casadesefarad.es; cnr Calle de los Judíos & Averroes; admission €4; ⊙10am-6pm Mon-Sat, 11am-2pm Sun). This small, beautiful museum is devoted to reviving interest in the Sephardic-Judaic-Spanish tradition.

SPAIN CÓRDOBA

Alcázar de los Reyes Cristianos CASTLE
(Castle of the Christian Monarchs; Campo Santo de Los Mártires; admission €4, Fri free; ⊙10am-2pm & 5.30-7.30pm Tue-Sat, 9.30am-2.30pm Sun & holidays) Just southwest of the Mezquita, the Alcázar began as a palace and fort for Alfonso X in the 13th century. From 1490 to 1821 the Inquisition operated from here. Today its gardens are among the most beautiful in Andalucía.

Medina Azahara RUINS
(Madinat al-Zahra; adult/EU citizen €1.50/free; ⊙10am-6.30pm Tue-Sat, to 8.30pm May–mid-Sep, to 2pm Sun) Even in the cicada-shrill heat and stillness of a summer afternoon, the Medina Azahara whispers of the power and vision of its founder, Abd ar-Rahman III. The self-proclaimed caliph began the construction of a magnificent new capital 8km west of Córdoba around 936, and took up full residence around 945. It was destroyed in the 11th century and just 10% of the site has been excavated. A taxi from Córdoba costs €37 for the return trip, with one hour to view the site, or you can book a three-hour coach tour for €6.50 to €10 through many Córdoba hotels.

Hammam Baños Árabes BATHHOUSE
(☑957 48 47 46; www.hammamspain.com/cordoba; Calle del Corregidor Luis de la Cerda 51; bath/bath & massage €26/33; ⊙2hr sessions 10am, noon, 2pm, 4pm, 6pm, 8pm & 10pm) Follow the lead of the medieval Cordobans and dip your toe in these beautifully renovated Arab baths, where you can enjoy an aromatherapy massage, with tea, hookah and Arabic sweets in the cafe afterwards.

🛏 Sleeping

Hospedería Alma Andalusí BOUTIQUE HOTEL €€
(☑957 76 08 88; www.almaandalusi.com; Calle Fernández Ruano 5; s/d €45/100; ❄🛜) The builders of this guesthouse in a quiet section of the *judería* have brilliantly converted an ancient structure into a stylish, modern establishment while keeping the rates down. Thoughtfully chosen furnishings, polished wood floors and solid colours make for a comfortable base.

Casa de los Azulejos HOTEL €€
(☑957 47 00 00; www.casadelosazulejos.com; Calle Fernando Colón 5; s/d incl breakfast from €85/107; ❄@🛜) Mexican and Andalucian styles converge in this chic hotel, where the patio is all banana trees, ferns and potted palms bathed in sunlight. Colonial-style rooms feature tall antique doors, massive beds, walls in lilac and sky blues, and floors adorned with the beautiful old *azulejos* tiles that give the place its name.

Hotel Mezquita HOTEL €€
(☑957 47 55 85; www.hotelmezquita.com; Plaza Santa Catalina 1; s/d €42/74; ❄) One of the best deals in town, Hotel Mezquita stands right opposite its namesake monument, amid the bric-a-brac of the tourism zone. The 16th-century mansion has large, elegant rooms with marble floors, tall doors and balconies, some affording views of the great mosque.

Hospedería Añil HOSTEL €
(☑957 49 15 44; www.sensesandcolours.com; Calle Barroso 4; dm/s/d from €12/30/42; 🛜) This vibrant, superfriendly establishment is aimed at the backpacker set, though it cuts no corners in the style and comfort departments. Primary colours and fanciful murals maintain an upbeat vibe. It's a skip and a jump to either the Mezquita or Plaza de las Tendillas.

Hotel Lola HOTEL €€
(☑957 20 03 05; www.hotellola.es; Calle Romero 3; r incl breakfast €129; ❄@🛜) Individualism and a quirky style are the prime ingredients here. Each room, named after an Arab princess, is decorated with large antique beds and covetable items that you will wish you could take home with you. What's more, you can eat your breakfast on the roof terrace overlooking the Mezquita's bell tower.

🍴 Eating & Drinking

Córdoba's liveliest bars are mostly scattered around the newer parts of town and start buzzing at about 11pm or midnight on weekends. Most bars in the medieval centre close around midnight.

ᴛᴏᴘ⁄ᴄʜᴏɪᴄᴇ Taberna San Miguel El Pisto TAPAS €
(www.casaelpisto.com/en; Plaza San Miguel 1; tapas €3, media raciones €5-10; ⊙closed Sun & Aug) Brimming with local character, El Pisto is one of Córdoba's best *tabernas*, both in terms of atmosphere and food. Traditional tapas and *media-raciones* are done perfectly, and inexpensive Moriles wine is ready in jugs on the bar.

Bodegas Campos ANDALUCIAN €€
(☑957 49 75 00; www.bodegascampos.com; Calle de Lineros 32; tapas €5, mains €13-21) One of Córdoba's most atmospheric and famous wine cellar/restaurants, this sprawling hall

features dozens of rooms and patios, with oak barrels signed by local and international celebrities stacked up alongside. The bodega produces its own house Montilla wine.

Taberna Salinas TAPAS €

(www.tabernasalinas.com; Calle Tundidores 3; tapas/raciones €2.50/8; ⊘closed Sun & Aug) A historic *taberna* that dates back to 1879, with a reputation that ensures the tables are always busy.

Bodega Guzmán BAR

(Calle de los Judíos 7; ⊘noon to 4pm & 8pm-midnight, closed Thu) Close to the Sinagoga, this atmospheric drinking spot bedecked with bullfighting memorabilia is frequented by both locals and tourists. Montilla wine is dispensed from three giant barrels behind the bar: don't leave without trying some *amargoso* (bitter).

ⓘ Information

Municipal Tourist Office (Plaza de Judá Levi; ⊘8.30am-2.30pm Mon-Fri)

Regional Tourist Office (Calle de Torrijos 10; ⊘9am-7.30pm Mon-Fri, 9.30am-3pm Sat, Sun & holidays) Inside the Palacio Episcopal.

ⓘ Getting There & Away

BUS The **bus station** (☑957 40 40 40; www.estacionautobusescordoba.es; Glorieta de las Tres Culturas) is 1km northwest of Plaza de las Tendillas. Destinations include Seville (€10.50, 1¾ hours, six daily), Granada (€12.50, 2½ hours, seven daily) and Málaga (€13, 2¾ hours, five daily).

TRAIN From Córdoba's **train station** (☑957 40 02 02; Glorieta de las Tres Culturas), destinations include Seville (€11 to €33, 40 to 90 minutes, hourly), Madrid (€53 to €68, 1¾ to 6¼ hours, hourly), Málaga (€22 to €45, one to

2½ hours, nine daily) and Barcelona (€138, 4½ hours, four daily).

Granada

POP 258,000 / ELEV 685M

Granada's eight centuries as a Muslim capital are symbolised in its keynote emblem, the remarkable Alhambra, one of the most graceful architectural achievements in the Muslim world. Islam was never completely expunged here, and today it seems more present than ever in the shops, restaurants, tearooms and the mosque of a growing North African community in and around the maze of the Albayzín. The tapas bars fill to bursting with hungry and thirsty revellers, while flamenco bars resound to the heart-wrenching tones of the south.

⊙ Sights & Activities

TOP CHOICE **Alhambra** PALACE

(☑902 44 12 21; www.alhambra-tickets.es; adult/under 8yr €13/free, Generalife only €6; ⊘8.30am-8pm 16 Mar-31 Oct, to 6pm 1 Nov-14 Mar, night visits 10-11.30pm Tue-Sat Mar-Oct, 8-9.30pm Fri & Sat Nov-Feb) The mighty Alhambra is breathtaking. Much has been written about its fortress, palace, patios and gardens, but nothing can really prepare you for seeing the real thing.

The **Alcazaba**, the Alhambra's fortress, dates from the 11th to the 13th centuries. There are spectacular views from the tops of its towers. The **Palacio Nazaríes** (Nasrid Palace), built for Granada's Muslim rulers in their 13th- to 15th-century heyday, is the centrepiece of the Alhambra. The beauty of

ALHAMBRA TICKETS

Up to 6600 tickets to the Alhambra are available for each day. About one-third of these are sold at the ticket office on the day, but they sell out early and you need to start queuing by 7am to be reasonably sure of getting one. It's highly advisable to book in advance (you pay €1 extra per ticket). You can book up to three months ahead in two ways:

Alhambra Advance Booking (☑international calls 0034 934 92 37 50, national calls 902 888001; www.alhambra-tickets.es; ⊘8am-9pm)

Servicaixa (www.servicaixa.com) Online booking in Spanish and English. You can also buy tickets in advance from Servicaixa cash machines (⊘8am to 7pm March to October, 8am to 5pm November to February), but only in the Alhambra grounds

For internet or phone bookings you need a Visa card, MasterCard or Eurocard. You receive a reference number, which you must show, along with your passport, national identity card or credit card, at the Alhambra ticket office when you pick up the ticket on the day of your visit.

its patios and intricacy of its stuccoes and woodwork, epitomised by the **Patio de los Leones** (Patio of the Lions) and **Sala de las Dos Hermanas** (Hall of the Two Sisters), are stunning. The **Generalife** (Palace Gardens) is a great spot to relax and contemplate the complex from a little distance.

Albayzín
NEIGHBOURHOOD

Exploring the narrow, hilly streets of the Albayzín, the old Moorish quarter across the river from the Alhambra, is the perfect complement to the Alhambra. The cobblestone streets are lined with gorgeous *cármenes* (large mansions with walled gardens, from the Arabic *karm* for garden). It survived as the Muslim quarter for several decades after the Christian conquest in 1492. Head uphill to reach the **Mirador de San Nicolás** – a viewpoint with breathtaking vistas and a relaxed scene.

Capilla Real
HISTORIC BUILDING

(www.capillarealgranada.com; Calle Oficios; admission €3.50; ☉10.30am-1.30pm & 4-7.30pm Mon-Sat, 11am-1.30pm & 4-7pm Sun Apr-Oct) The **Royal Chapel**, adjoins Granada's cathedral, and is an outstanding Christian building. Catholic monarchs Isabella and Ferdinand commissioned this elaborate Isabelline-Gothic-style mausoleum. It was not completed until 1521 and the monarchs lie in simple lead coffins in the crypt beneath their marble monuments in the chancel, enclosed by a stunning gilded wrought-iron screen.

🛏 Sleeping

Casa Morisca Hotel
HISTORIC HOTEL €€

(☎958 22 11 00; www.hotelcasamorisca.com; Cuesta de la Victoria 9; d €118-148; ✵@🛜) This late-15th-century mansion perfectly captures the spirit of the Albayzín. A heavy wooden door shuts out city noise, and rooms are soothing, with lofty ceilings, fluffy white beds and flat-weave rugs over brick floors.

Carmen de la Alcubilla
HISTORIC HOTEL €€

(☎958 21 55 51; www.alcubilladelcaracol.com; Calle del Aire Alta 12; s/d €100/120; ✵@🛜) This exquisitely decorated place is located on the slopes of the Alhambra. Rooms are washed in pale pastel colours contrasting with cool cream and antiques. There are fabulous views and a pretty terraced garden.

Parador de Granada
HISTORIC HOTEL €€€

(☎958 22 14 40; www.parador.es; Calle Real de la Alhambra; r €315; P✵@🛜) It would be remiss not to mention this hotel, the most luxurious of Spain's *paradors*. If you're looking for romance and history (it's in a converted 15th-century convent in the Alhambra grounds) and money is no object, then book well ahead.

Hotel Zaguán del Darro
HISTORIC HOTEL €€

(☎958 21 57 30; www.hotelzaguan.com; Carrera del Darro 23; s/d €55/70; ✵@) This place offers excellent value for the Albayzín. The 16th-century house has been tastefully restored, with sparing use of antiques. Its 13 rooms are all different; some look out over the Río Darro. There's a good bar-restaurant below.

Hostal Arteaga
HOSTAL €

(☎958 20 88 41; www.hostalarteaga.com; Calle Arteaga 3; s/d €40/49; ✵@🛜) A charming bargain option just off the Gran Vía de Colón, inching into the Albayzín. The rooms are spruced up with lavender walls, striped bedspreads and chequered blue bathroom tiles for a tidy, modern feel.

🍴 Eating

Granada is one of the last bastions of that fantastic practice of free tapas with every drink, and some have an international flavour. The labyrinthine Albayzín holds a wealth of eateries tucked away in the narrow streets. Calle Calderería Nueva is a fascinating muddle of *teterías* (tearooms) and Arabic-influenced takeaways.

Arrayanes
MOROCCAN €€

(☎958 22 84 01; www.rest-arrayanes.com; Cuesta Marañas 4; mains €8-15; ☉from 8pm; 🖉) The best Moroccan food in a city that is well known for its Moorish throwbacks? Recline on lavish patterned seating, try the rich, fruity tagine casseroles and make your decision. Note that Restaurante Arrayanes does not serve alcohol.

El Ají
SPANISH €€

(Plaza San Miguel Bajo 9; mains €12-20; 🖉) Up in the Albayzín, this chic but cosy neighbourhood restaurant is no bigger than a shoebox but serves from breakfast right through to the evening. Chatty staff at the tiny marble bar can point out some of the highlights of the creative menu.

Ruta del Azafrán
FUSION €€

(www.rutadelazafran.es; Paseo del Padre Manjón 1; mains €13-20) One of the few high-concept restaurants in Granada, this sleek spot with its steely-modern interior has an eclectic menu which ranges from Asian-inspired

Granada

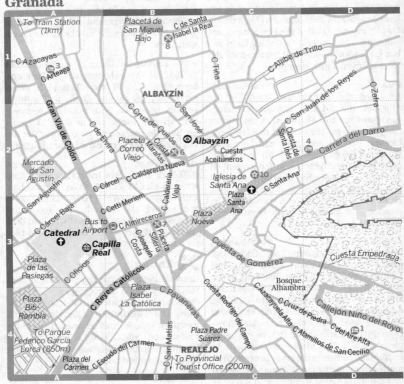

tempuras to broccoli-based pesto, lamb couscous and roasted pork. The terrace outside on the Río Darro is a great place for a snack, but you'll get better service inside.

Bodegas Castañeda   BAR €
(Calle Almireceros; tapas €2-3, raciones €6-8) An institution among locals and tourists alike, this buzzing bar doles out hearty portions of food (try a hot or cold *tabla,* or platter; a half order is ample for two) and dispenses drinks from big casks mounted in the walls.

☆ Entertainment
The excellent monthly *Guía de Granada* (€1), available from kiosks, lists entertainment venues and tapas bars.

Peña de la Platería   FLAMENCO
(www.laplateria.org.es; Placeta de Toqueros 7) Buried in the Albayzín warren, Peña La Platería claims to be the oldest flamenco aficionados'

club in Spain. It's a private affair, though, and not always open to nonmembers. Performances are usually Thursday and Saturday at 10.30pm – look presentable, and speak a little Spanish at the door, if you can.

Le Chien Andalou   FLAMENCO
(www.lechienandalou.com; Carrera del Darro 7; admission €8; ⊙shows 9pm) This is one of Granada's most atmospheric venues to enjoy some vigorous castanet-clicking flamenco, with a varied and professional line up of musicians and dancers throughout the week. The cave-like surroundings of a renovated *aljibe* (well) create a fittingly moody setting.

❶ Information
Provincial Tourist Office (www.turismode granada.org; Plaza de Mariana Pineda 10; ⊙9am-10pm Mon-Fri, 10am-7pm Sat) Information on the whole Granada region; a short walk east of Puerta Real.

Granada

◎ Top Sights
Albayzín..B2
Alhambra..E3
Capilla Real A3
Catedral...A3

🛏 Sleeping
1 Carmen de la Alcubilla D4
2 Casa Morisca Hotel E1
3 Hostal Arteaga A1
4 Hotel Zaguán del Darro....................D2
5 Parador de Granada.........................F3

✕ Eating
6 Arrayanes...B2
7 Bodegas Castañeda..........................B3
8 El Ají B1
9 Ruta del Azafrán E2

◉ Entertainment
10 Le Chien Andalou..............................C2
11 Peña de la Platería............................E1

four daily), Ronda (€15, three hours, three daily), Algeciras (€25, 4½ hours, three daily), Madrid (€68, four to five hours, one or two daily), Valencia (€52.50, 7½ to eight hours, one daily) and Barcelona (€58, 12 hours, one daily).

Municipal Tourist Office (www.granadatur. com; Calle Almona del Campillo, 2; ☺9am-7pm Mon-Fri, to 6pm Sat, 10am-2pm Sun) Opposite the city's Parque Federico García Lorca.

❶ Getting There & Away

AIR Destinations from Granada's airport include Madrid, Barcelona, Milan and Bologna. **Autocares J González** (www.autocaresjosegonzalez. com) runs buses between the airport and the city centre (€3, five daily) on Gran Vía de Colón.

BUS Granada's **bus station** (Carretera de Jaén) is 3km northwest of the city centre. Destinations include Córdoba (€13.50, 2¾ hours direct, nine daily), Seville (€20.50, three hours, ten daily), Málaga (€10.50, 1½ hours direct, 18 daily) and an overnight service to Madrid's Barajas Airport (€24.50, six hours).

TRAIN The **train station** (☎958 24 02 02; Avenida de Andaluces) is 1.5km west of the centre. Trains run to/from Seville (€24, three hours, four daily), Almería (€16.50, 2¼ hours,

Costa de Almería

The coast east of Almería in eastern Andalucía is perhaps the last section of Spain's Mediterranean coast where you can have a beach to yourself. This is Spain's sunniest region – even in late March it can be warm enough to strip off and take in the rays.

◉ Sights & Activities

The **Alcazaba** (Calle Almanzor; adult/EU citizen €1.50/free; ☺9am-8.30pm Tue-Sun Apr-Oct, to 6.30pm Tue-Sun Nov-Mar), an enormous 10th-century Muslim fortress, is the highlight of Almería City.

The best thing about the region is the wonderful coastline and semidesert scenery of the Cabo de Gata promontory. All along the 50km coast from El Cabo de Gata village to Agua Amarga, some of the most beautiful and empty beaches on the Mediterranean alternate with precipitous cliffs and scattered villages. The main village is laid-back San José, with excellent beaches nearby, such as **Playa de los Genoveses** and **Playa de Mónsul**.

SPAIN COSTA DE ALMERÍA

📖 Sleeping & Eating

ALMERÍA CITY

Hotel Catedral
HOTEL **€€**

(📞950 27 81 78; www.hotelcatedral.net; Plaza de la Catedral 8; r €70; @🖈) Cosied up to the Almería Cathedral and built with the same warm honey-coloured stone, the hotel building dates from 1850 and has been sensitively restored. Rooms are large, with luxury touches, and the sun terrace has heady cathedral views.

Plaza Vieja Alejandro
HOTEL **€€**

(📞950 28 20 96; www.plazaviejahl.com; Plaza de la Constitución 5; r €80-110; P🖈🖈) This is, arguably, the most stylish accommodation in the city. Part of the stunning Hammam Aire de Almería, the rooms are spacious and modern with high ceilings, lots of glass and shiny wood, soft natural colours and vast photo-friezes of local sights like the Cabo de Gato.

🏆 TOP CHOICE Tetería Almedina
TEAHOUSE **€€**

(www.restaurantetteriaalmedina.com; Calle Paz 2, off Calle de la Almedina; teas €3, mains €7-12; ⏰11am-11pm Tue-Sun; 🖈) This lovely little cafe in the old city serves a fascinating range of teas, delectable sweets and good couscous. It's run by a group dedicated to restoring and revitalising the old city, and functions as a sort of casual Islamic cultural centre. There's usually live music on Sundays, in addition to art shows and similar.

CABO DE GATA

Atalaya Hotel
HOTEL **€**

(📞950 38 00 85; www.atalayahotel.net; Avenida de San José, San José; r incl breakfast €75; 🖈🖈) This central hotel, situated over a bustling restaurant and bar, has rooms set around small terraces. At the time of research, the owners were in the throes of giving the rooms a Moroccan-style update with warm burgundy-painted walls, low beds and sparkling slate grey bathrooms.

Hostal Aloha
HOSTAL **€**

(📞950 38 04 61; www.hostalaloha.com; Calle Cala Higuera, San José; r €55; 🖈🖈) White walls, firm beds and gleaming bathrooms make this an appealing budget hotel to start with. Then throw in the enormous pool on the back terrace, and it's one of the best deals in San José. It's a few blocks back from the beach; to reach it, turn left off the main street at the tourist office.

Acá Charles
INTERNATIONAL **€€**

(Avenida de San José 51, San José; mains €14-19) Opened in 2012, this place has all the locals enthusing about the sophisticated menu where seafood doesn't necessarily take central stage. Dishes include truffles, crispy Serrano ham, fresh green asparagus with polenta, and similar.

ℹ️ Information

Regional Tourist Office (Parque de Nicolás Salmerón; ⏰9am-7pm Mon-Fri, 10am-2pm Sat & Sun)

ℹ️ Getting There & Away

AIR Almería **airport** (📞950 21 37 00), 10km east of the city centre, receives flights from several European countries, as well as Barcelona, Madrid and Melilla.

BOAT There are daily sailings to/from Melilla, Nador (Morocco) and Ghazaouet (Algeria). The tourist office has details.

BUS Destinations served from Almería's **bus station** (📞950 26 20 98) include Granada (€13, 2¼ hours, 10 daily), Málaga (€17, 3¼ hours, 8 daily), Madrid (€27, 10 hours, three daily) and Valencia (€37, 8½ hours, five daily).

TRAIN Daily trains run to Granada (€16.50, 2¼ hours), Seville (€40, 5½ hours) and Madrid (€45.50, 6¾ hours).

Málaga

POP 558,000

The exuberant port city of Málaga may be uncomfortably close to the overdeveloped Costa del Sol, but it's a wonderful amalgam of old Andalucian town and modern metropolis. The centre presents the visitor with narrow, old streets and wide, leafy boulevards, beautiful gardens and impressive monuments, fashionable shops and a burgeoning cultural life. The city's terrific bars and nightlife, the last word in Málaga *joie de vivre,* stay open very late.

⊙ Sights & Activities

🏆 TOP CHOICE Museo Picasso Málaga
MUSEUM

(📞902 44 33 77; www.museopicassomalaga.org; Calle San Agustín 8; permanent/temporary collection €6/4.50, combined ticket €8; ⏰10am-8pm Tue-Thu & Sun, to 9pm Fri & Sat) The hottest attraction on Málaga's tourist scene is tucked away on a pedestrian street in what was medieval Málaga's *judería.* The Museo Picasso Málaga has 204 Picasso works and also stages high-quality temporary exhibitions on Picasso themes. The Picasso paintings, drawings, engravings, sculptures and ceramics on show (many never previously on public display) span almost every phase and influence of the artist's colourful career. Picasso was born in Málaga in 1881 but moved to northern Spain with his family when he was nine.

Casa Natal de Picasso
MUSEUM

(Plaza de la Merced 15; admission €1; ☉9.30am-8pm) The house where Picasso was born in 1881 has a replica 19th-century artist's studio and small quarterly exhibitions of Picasso's work. Personal memorabilia of Picasso and his family make up part of the display.

Catedral
CATHEDRAL

(☎952 21 59 17; Calle Molina Lario; cathedral & museum €3.50; ☉10am-6pm Mon-Sat, closed holidays) Preserved rather magnificently, like an unfinished Beethoven symphony, Málaga's cathedral was begun in the 16th century on the former site of the main mosque and never properly completed. Consequently the building exhibits a mishmash of architectural styles absorbed during over two centuries of construction.

Alcazaba
CASTLE

(Calle Alcazabilla; admission €2.10, incl Castillo de Gibralfaro €3.40; ☉9.30am-8pm Tue-Sun Apr-Oct) At the lower, western end of the Gibralfaro hill, the wheelchair-accessible Alcazaba was the palace-fortress of Málaga's Muslim governors, dating from 1057. The brick path winds uphill, interspersed with arches and stone walls and refreshingly cool in summer. Roman artefacts and fleeting views of the harbour and city enliven the walk, while honeysuckle, roses and jasmine perfume the air.

Castillo de Gibralfaro
CASTLE

(admission €2.10; ☉9am-9pm Apr-Sep, to 6pm Oct-Mar) Above the Alcazaba rises the Castillo de Gibralfaro, built by Abd ar-Rahman I, the 8th-century Cordoban emir, and rebuilt in the 14th and 15th centuries. Nothing much remains of the castle's interior, but the walkway around the ramparts affords exhilarating views, and there's a tiny museum with a military focus.

There are plans to build a funicular railway up the hill to the Castillo but no completion date was available at research time.

Beaches
BEACHES

Sandy city beaches stretch several kilometres in each direction from the port. **Playa de la Malagueta**, handy to the city centre, has some excellent bars and restaurants close by. **Playa de Pedregalejo** and **Playa del Palo**, about 4km east of the centre, are popular and reachable by bus 11 from Paseo del Parque.

🛏 Sleeping

El Riad Andaluz
GUESTHOUSE €€

(☎952 21 36 40; www.elriadandaluz.com; Calle Hinestrosa 24; s/d €70/86; ❄@☎) This French-run guesthouse, near the **Teatro Cervantes** (www.teatrocervantes.com; Calle Ramos Marín; ☉closed mid-Jul–Aug), has eight rooms set around an atmospheric patio. The decoration is Moroccan but each room is different, including colourfully tiled bathrooms. Breakfast is available.

El Hotel del Pintor
HOTEL €€

(☎952 06 09 81; www.hoteldelpintor.com; Calle Álamos 27; r from €75; ❄@☎) The red, black and white colour scheme of this friendly small hotel echoes the abstract artwork of *malagueño* (person from Málaga) artist Pepe Bornov, whose paintings are on permanent display throughout the public areas and rooms. The rooms in the front can be noisy, especially on a Saturday night.

Room Mate Larios
HOTEL €€

(☎952 22 22 00; www.room-matehotels.com; Calle Marqués de Larios 2; s/d € 80/100; ❄@☎) Located on the central Plaza de la Constitución, this hotel is housed in a 19th-century building that has been elegantly restored. Rooms are luxuriously furnished with king-size beds and carpeting throughout; several rooms have balconies overlooking Calle Marqués de Larios.

Parador Málaga Gibralfaro
HISTORIC HOTEL €€€

(☎952 22 19 02; www.parador.es; Castillo de Gibralfaro; r €160-171; P❄☎☒) With an unbeatable location perched on the pine-forested Gibralfaro, Málaga's stone-built *parador* is a popular choice, although the rooms are fairly standard. Most have spectacular views from their terraces, however, and you can dine at the excellent terrace restaurant even if you are not a guest at the hotel.

✗ Eating

Most of the best eating places are sandwiched in the narrow streets between Calle Marqués de Larios and the cathedral.

⬛TOP CHOICE Vino Mio INTERNATIONAL €€

(www.restaurantevinomio.com/en; Plaza Jeronimo Cuervo 2; mains €10-15) This Dutch-owned restaurant has a diverse and interesting menu that includes dishes like kangaroo steaks, vegetable stir fries, duck breast with sweet chilli, pasta and several innovative salads.

La Moraga
Antonio Martín ANDALUCÍAN €€€

(✑952 22 41 53; www.lamoraga.com; Plaza Malagueta 4; tapas from €5, mains from €20) This is Michelin-star chef Dani Garcia's second Málaga-based La Moraga (the first is on Calle Fresca in the centre). The concept is based on traditional tapas given the nouvelle treatment.

Tapeo de Cervantes TAPAS €

(www.eltapeodecervantes.com; Calle Cárcer 8; tapas €4-6; ☺Tue-Sun) This place has caught on big time which, given its squeeze-in space, can mean a wait. Choose from traditional or more innovative tapas and *raciones* with delicious combinations and stylish presentation. Portions are generous.

♟ Drinking & Entertainment

On weekend nights, the web of narrow old streets north of Plaza de la Constitución comes alive. Look for bars around Plaza de la Merced, Plaza Mitjana and Plaza de Uncibay.

Málaga's substantial flamenco heritage has its nexus to the northwest of Plaza de la Merced. Venues here include **Kelipe** (✑692 82 98 85; www.kelipe.net; Calle Pena 11), a flamenco centre which puts on *muy puro* (authentic) performances Thursday to Saturday at 9.30pm; entry of €15 includes one drink and tapa; reserve ahead. Intensive weekend courses in guitar and dance are also held. **Amargo** (Calle R Franquillo 3) offers Friday and Saturday night gigs, while **Vino Mio** (www.restaurantevinomio.com; Calle Alamos) is a small restaurant with an international menu where musicians and dancers fill the wait for the food.

⬛TOP CHOICE Bodegas El Pimpi BAR

(www.bodegabarelpimpi.com; Calle Granada 62; ☺11am-2am) This rambling bar is an institution in this town. The cavernous interior encompasses a warren of rooms with a central courtyard and large open terrace overlooking the recently renovated Roman amphitheatre. Walls are decorated with historic *feria* (bullfighting) posters and photos of celeb-style visitors.

ⓘ Information

Municipal Tourist Office (Plaza de la Marina, www.malagaturismo.com) also has a branch at Casita del Jardinero (Avenida de Cervantes 1; ☺9am-8pm Mar-Sep, to 6pm Oct-Feb)

Regional Tourist Office (www.andalucia.org; Pasaje de Chinitas 4; ☺9am-7.30pm Mon-Fri, 10am-7pm Sat, 10am-2pm Sun) There is another branch at the airport; these offices cover the whole of Málaga and all of Andalucía.

ⓘ Getting There & Away

AIR Málaga's busy **airport** (✑952 04 88 38), the main international gateway to Andalucía, receives flights by dozens of airlines from around Europe. The Aeropuerto train station on the Málaga–Fuengirola line is a five-minute walk from the airport. Trains run about every half-hour to Málaga-Renfe station (€2.20, 11 minutes) and Málaga-Centro station.

BUS Málaga's **bus station** (✑952 35 00 61; www.estabus.emtsam.es; Paseo de los Tilos) is 1km southwest of the city centre. Frequent buses go to Seville (€30, 2½ hours), Granada (€10.50, 1½ to two hours), Córdoba (€13.50, 3½ hours) and Ronda (€9.50, 2½ hours).

TRAIN The main station, **Málaga-Renfe** (www.renfe.es; Explanada de la Estación), is around the corner from the bus station. The superfast AVE service runs to Madrid (€87, 2½ hours, 10 daily). Trains also go to Córdoba (from €26, 2½ hours, 10 daily) and Seville (from €18.50, 2¾ hours, 11 daily).

Ronda

POP 37,000 / ELEV 744M

Perched on an inland plateau riven by the 100m fissure of El Tajo gorge and surrounded by the beautiful Serranía de Ronda, Ronda is the most dramatically sited of Andalucía's *pueblos blancos* (white villages).

◉ Sights

The **Plaza de Toros** (built 1785), considered the national home of bullfighting, is a mecca for aficionados; inside is the small but fascinating **Museo Taurino** (Calle Virgen de la Paz; admission €6; ☺10am-8pm Apr-Sep, to 6pm Oct-Mar).

The amazing 18th-century **Puente Nuevo** (New Bridge) is an incredible engineering feat crossing the gorge to the originally Muslim La Ciudad (Old Town). At the **Casa del Rey Moro** (House of the Moorish King; Calle Santo Domingo 17), a romantically crumbling 18th-century house, supposedly built over the remains of an Islamic palace, you can visit the cliff-top gardens and climb down La Mina, a Muslim-era stairway cut inside the rock, right to the bottom of the gorge.

Also well worth a visit are the beautiful 13th-century **Baños Arabes** (Arab Baths; Hoyo San Miguel; admission €3, free on Sun; ⊙10am-7pm Mon-Fri, to 3pm Sat & Sun). Nearby, the amusing **Museo del Bandolero** (www.museobandolero.com; Calle de Armiñán 65; admission €3; ⊙10.30am-8pm Apr-Sep, to 6pm Oct-Mar) is dedicated to the banditry for which central Andalucía was renowned in the 19th century.

🛏 Sleeping & Eating

Hotel Alavera de los Baños HOTEL €€
(☑952 87 91 43; www.alaveradelosbanos.com; Hoyo San Miguel; s/d incl breakfast €70/95; ❄🐾) Taking its cue from the Arab baths next door, the Alavera de los Baños continues the Hispano–Islamic theme throughout, with oriental decor and tasty North African-inspired cuisine using predominantly organic foods.

Jardín de la Muralla HISTORIC HOTEL €€
(☑952 87 27 64; www.jardindelamuralla.com; Calle Espiritu Santo 13, Ronda; s/d incl breakfast €80/91; ❄@🐾) José María has ensured that his historic family home retains plenty of evocative atmosphere with antiques, chandeliers, ancestral portraits and wonderful claw-foot bath-tubs. The terraced gardens lead to the 15th-century city walls. Pets allowed.

Parador de Ronda HOTEL €€€
(☑952 87 75 00; www.parador.es; Plaza de España; r €160-171; P❄@🐾) Acres of shining marble and deep-cushioned furniture give this modern *parador* a certain appeal. The terrace is a wonderful place to drink in views of the gorge with your coffee or wine, especially at night.

TOP CHOICE **Bodega San Francisco** TAPAS €
(www.bodegasanfrancisco.com; Calle Ruedo Alameda; raciones €6-10) With three dining rooms and tables spilling out onto the narrow pedestrian street, this may well be Ronda's top tapas bar. The menu is vast and should suit the fussiest of families, even vegetarians, with nine-plus salad choices.

❶ Information

Municipal Tourist Office (www.turismoderonda.es; Paseo de Blas Infante; ⊙10am-7.30pm Mon-Fri, 10.15am-2pm & 3.30-6.30pm Sat, Sun & holidays)

Regional Tourist Office (www.andalucia.org; Plaza de España 1; ⊙9am-7.30pm Mon-Fri May-Sep, to 6pm Oct-Apr, 10am-2pm Sat year-round)

❶ Getting There & Away

Trains and buses run to/from Algeciras, Granada, Córdoba and Málaga.

Algeciras

TRANSPORT HUB

A gritty industrial and fishing town between Tarifa and Gibraltar, Algeciras is the major port linking Spain with Morocco and, as such, is an important way station en route between the two countries. Otherwise, we can't think of a single reason to come here. Keep your wits about you around the port area.

🛏 Sleeping & Eating

Hostal Marrakech HOTEL €
(☑956 57 34 74; Calle Juan de la Cierva 5; s/d €25/40) The Moroccan family who run this place have a handful of bold and tarty rooms with communal bathrooms only.

Hotel Reina Cristina HOTEL €€€
(☑956 60 26 22; www.hotelesglobales.com; Paseo de la Conferencia s/n; s/d €89/149) For old-world ambience head south to this colonial-style hotel with two swimming pools.

Restaurante Montes ANDALUCIAN €€
(☑956 65 42 07; Calle Juan Morrison 27; menú €9.50, mains €15) The Montes has a hugely fishy lunch *menú* consisting of three courses, bread and wine. There is also a long list of tempting à la carte seafood.

❶ Getting There & Away

BOAT The fastest ferry services, **FRS** (☑956 68 18 30; www.frs.es), run from Algeciras to Tangier (passenger/car €23/84, 70 minutes, eight daily).

BUS The bus station is on Calle San Bernardo. Buses arrive regularly from for La Línea (for Gibraltar; 30 minutes), Tarifa (30 minutes), Cádiz (2½ hours) and Seville (2½ hours).

TRAIN The **train station** (☑956 63 10 05) runs services to/from Madrid (€70.90, five hours 20 minutes, two daily) and Granada (€24.80, 4¼ hours, three daily).

Cádiz

POP 125,000

Cádiz, widely considered the oldest continuously inhabited settlement in Europe, is crammed onto the head of a promontory like an overcrowded ocean liner. Columbus sailed from here on his second and fourth voyages, and after his success in the Americas, the town grew into Spain's richest and most cosmopolitan city in the 18th century. The best time to visit is during the February *carnaval* (carnival).

Sights & Activities

Catedral
CHURCH

(Plaza de la Catedral; adult/student €5/3, free 7-8pm Tue-Fri, 11am-1pm Sun; ☉10am-6.30pm Mon-Sat, 1.30-6.30pm Sun) Cádiz' yellow-domed cathedral is an impressively proportioned baroque–neoclassical construction. It fronts a broad, traffic-free plaza where the cathedral's ground-plan is picked out in the paving stones. From a separate entrance on Plaza de la Catedral, climb to the top of the **Torre de Poniente** (Western Tower; adult/child €4/3; ☉10am-6pm, to 8pm mid-Jun–mid-Sep) for marvellous views.

Museo de Cádiz
MUSEUM

(Plaza de Mina; admission €1.50; ☉2.30-8.30pm Tue, 9am-8.30pm Wed-Sat, 9.30am-2.30pm Sun) The Museo de Cádiz, on one of Cádiz' leafiest squares, is outstanding with fine Phoenician and Roman artefacts on the ground floor and fine arts upstairs; in the latter look especially for the 18 superb canvases of saints, angels and monks by Francisco de Zurbarán.

Playa de la Victoria
BEACH

This lovely, wide strip of fine Atlantic sand stretches about 4km along the peninsula from its beginning at the Puertas de Tierra. At weekends in summer almost the whole city seems to be out here.

Sleeping & Eating

Hotel Argantonio
HOTEL €€

(☎956 21 16 40; www.hotelargantonio.com; Calle Argantonio 3; s/d incl breakfast €90/107; ❄@☎) At this small-is-beautiful hotel in Cádiz' old quarter, the stand-out features are the hand-painted doors, beautifully tiled floors that adorn both bedrooms and bathrooms, and the intricate Moorish arch in the lobby.

Hotel Patagonia Sur
HOTEL €€

(☎856 17 46 47; www.hotelpatagoniasur.es; Calle Cobos 11; d €80-130; ❄@☎) This sleek gem opened in Cádiz' old town in 2009 and offers clean-lined modernity just steps from the 18th-century cathedral. Bonuses include its sun-filled attic rooms on the 5th floor with cathedral views.

Casa Caracol
HOSTEL €

(☎956 26 11 66; www.caracolcasa.com; Calle Suárez de Salazar 4; dm/hammock incl breakfast €16/10; @☎) Casa Caracol is the only backpacker hostel in the old town. Friendly, as only Cádiz can be, it has bunk dorms for four and eight, a communal kitchen and a roof terrace with hammocks.

TOP CHOICE El Aljibe
TAPAS €€

(www.pablogrosso.com; Calle Plocia 25; tapas €2-3.50, mains €10-15) Refined restaurant upstairs and supercool tapas bar downstairs, El Aljibe on its own is almost reason enough to come to Cádiz. The cuisine developed by *gaditano* chef Pablo Grosso is a delicious combination of the traditional and the adventurous.

Arrocería La Pepa
SPANISH €€

(☎956 26 38 21; www.restaurantelapepa.es; Paseo Marítimo 14; paella per person €12-17) To get a decent paella you have to leave the old town behind and head for a few kilometres southeast along Playa de la Victoria – a pleasant, appetite-inducing ocean-side walk or a quick ride on the No 1 bus. Either method is worth it.

ℹ Information

Municipal Tourist Office (Paseo de Canalejas; ☉8.30am-6pm Mon-Fri, 9am-5pm Sat & Sun)

Regional Tourist Office (Avenida Ramón de Carranza; ☉9am-7.30pm Mon-Fri, 10am-2pm Sat, Sun & holidays)

ℹ Getting There & Away

BUS Destinations include Seville (€9, one hour), Tarifa (€7, 1½ hours), Málaga (€25, four hours) and Granada (€33, 5½ hours).

TRAIN From the **train station** (☎902 240202) trains run daily to Seville (€13.50, 1¾) and Madrid (€72.50, 4½ hours). High-speed AVE services to Madrid are due to commence in 2015.

Tarifa

POP 17,900

Windy, laid-back Tarifa is so close to Africa that you can almost hear the call to prayer issuing from Morocco's minarets. The town is a bohemian haven of cafes and crumbling Moorish ruins. There's also a lively windsurfing and kitesurfing scene.

Stretching west are the long, sandy (and largely deserted) beaches of the Costa de la Luz (Coast of Light), backed by cool pine forests and green hills.

◉ Sights

A wander round the old town's narrow streets, of mainly Islamic origin, is an appetiser for Morocco. The Mudéjar **Puerta de Jerez** was built after the Reconquista. Wind your way to the mainly 15th-century **Iglesia de San Mateo** (Calle Sancho IV El Bravo; ⊙9am-1pm & 5.30-8.30pm). South of the church, the **Mirador El Estrecho**, atop part of the castle walls, has spectacular views across to Africa, only 14km away. The 10th-century **Castillo de Guzmán** (Calle Guzmán El Bueno; admission €2; ⊙11am-4pm) is also worth a wander; tickets for the latter must be bought at the tourist office.

🏃 Activities

Beaches

On the isthmus leading out to Isla de las Palomas, tiny **Playa Chica** lives up to its name. Spectacular **Playa de los Lances** is a different matter, stretching northwest for 10km to the huge sand dune at **Ensenada de Valdevaqueros**.

Kitesurfing & Windsurfing

Tarifa now has around 30 kitesurf and windsurf schools, many of them with offices or shops along Calle Batalla del Salado or Calle Mar Adriático. Most rent equipment and run classes. Most of the action occurs along the coast between Tarifa and Punta Paloma.

Horse Riding

Located on Playa de los Lances, **Aventura Ecuestre** (☑956 23 66 32; www.aventura ecuestre.com; N340 Km79.5, Hotel Dos Mares) and **Hurricane Hípica** (☑646 964279; N340 Km78, Hurricane Hotel) both rent well-kept horses with excellent guides. An hour's beach ride costs €30. Three- or four-hour inland rides cost €70.

Whale-watching

The Strait of Gibraltar is a top site for viewing whales and dolphins. Killer whales visit in July and August, huge sperm and fin whales lurk here from spring to autumn, and pilot whales and three types of dolphin stay all year. Several organisations in Tarifa run daily two- to 2½-hour boat trips to observe these marine mammals, and most offer a free second trip if you don't at least see dolphins. **Firmm** (☑956 62 70 08; www.firmm. org; Calle Pedro Cortés 4; ⊙Mar-Oct) is the best and uses every trip to record data.

🛏 Sleeping & Eating

Posada La Sacristía   BOUTIQUE HOTEL €€
(☑956 68 17 59; www.lasacristia.net; Calle San Donato 8; r incl breakfast €115-135; 🕸@🛜) Tarifa's most elegant boutique accommodation is in a beautifully renovated 17th-century town house. Attention to detail is impeccable with 10 stylish rooms, tasteful colour schemes, large comfortable beds and rooms on several levels around a central courtyard.

Hostal Africa   HOSTAL €
(☑956 68 02 20; www.hostalafrica.com; Calle María Antonia Toledo 12, Tarifa; s/d €50/65, with shared bathroom €35/50; 🛜) This revamped 19th-century house close to the Puerta de Jerez is one of the best *hostales* along the coast. The owners are hospitable and the rooms sparkle with bright colours and plenty of space. There's a lovely, expansive roof terrace with an exotic cabana and views of Africa.

Mandrágora   MOROCCAN €€
(☑956 68 12 91; www.mandragoratarifa.com; Calle Independencia 3; mains €12-18; ⊙from 8pm Mon-Sat) Behind Iglesia de San Mateo, this intimate place serves Andalucían-Arabic food and does so terrifically well.

❶ Information

Tourist Office (☑956 68 09 93; www.ayto tarifa.com; Paseo de la Alameda; ⊙10am-2pm daily, 6-8pm Mon-Fri Jun-Sep) Near the top end of the palm-lined Paseo de la Alameda.

❶ Getting There & Away

BUS Daily services are offered by **Comes** (☑956 68 40 38; www.tgcomes.es; Calle Batalla del Salado 13) to Cádiz (€9, 1½ hours), Algeciras (€2.50, 30 minutes), La Línea de la Concepción (for Gibraltar; €4.50, 45 minutes), Seville (€18.50, three hours) and Málaga (€13.50, two hours).

BOAT Fast ferries are operated by **FRS** (☑956 68 18 30; www.frs.es; Avenida Andalucía 16) between Tarifa and Tangier (passenger/car/motorcycle €37/93/31, 35 minutes, eight daily).

WORTH A TRIP

MOROCCO

At once African and Arab, visible from numerous points along Spain's Andalucían coast, Morocco is an exciting detour from your Western European journey. The country's attractions are endless, from the fascinating souqs and medieval architecture of Marrakesh and Fes to the Atlantic charms of Asilah and Essaouira, from the High Atlas and Rif Mountains to the soulful sand dunes of Sahara. For further information, head to www.shop.lonelyplanet.com to purchase Lonely Planet's *Morocco* guide.

Casablanca and Marrakesh in particular are well-connected by air to numerous European cities, while car-and-passenger ferry services connect Tangier with Algeciras, Barcelona, Gibraltar and Tarifa, with an additional service between Nador and Almería.

GIBRALTAR

POP 30,000

The British colony of Gibraltar is like 1960s Britain on a sunny day, with Bobbies, double-decker buses and fried-egg-and-chip-style eateries. In British hands since 1713, the island was the starting point for the Muslim conquest of Iberia a thousand years earlier. Spain has never fully accepted UK control of the island but, for the moment at least, talk of joint sovereignty seems to have gone cold. Inhabitants speak English and Spanish, and signs are in English.

◉ Sights & Activities

In town, the **Gibraltar Museum** (www.gibmuseum.gi; Bomb House Lane; adult/child £2/1; ☺10am-6pm Mon-Fri, to 2pm Sat), with its interesting historical collection and Muslim-era bathhouse, is worth a peek.

The large **Upper Rock Nature Reserve** (adult/child incl attractions £10/5, vehicle £2, pedestrian excl attractions £0.50; ☺9am-6.15pm, last entry 5.45pm), covering most of the upper rock, has spectacular views. The rock's most famous inhabitants are its colony of Barbary macaques, the only wild primates in Europe. Some of these hang around the **Apes' Den** near the middle cable-car station; others can often be seen at the top station or Great Siege Tunnels. Other at-

tractions include **St Michael's Cave**, a large natural grotto renowned for its stalagmites and stalactites, and the **Great Siege Tunnels** (adult/child £8/4, price given is for admission by road - pedestrians pay less; ☺9.30am-7pm; walking downhill from top cable-car station), a series of galleries hewn from the rock by the British during the Great Siege by the Spaniards (1779–83) to provide new gun emplacements.

Dolphin-watching is an option from April to September. Most boats go from Watergardens Quay or adjacent Marina Bay. The trips last about 1½ hours and cost around £20 per adult. Tourist offices have full details.

🛏 Sleeping & Eating

Compared with Spain, expect to pay through the nose for accommodation and food.

Bristol Hotel HOTEL **££**
(☏20 07 68 00; www.bristolhotel.gi; 10 Cathedral Sq; s/d/tr £63/81/93; P❄❖🛜🏊) Veterans of bucket-and-spade British seaside holidays can wax nostalgic at the stuck-in-the-70s Bristol with its creaking floorboards, red patterned carpets and Hi-de-Hi reception staff.

Caleta Hotel HOTEL **£££**
(☏20 07 65 01; www.caletahotel.gi; Sir Herbert Miles Rd; d without/with sea view £110/150) This has a wonderful location overlooking Catalan Bay, on the east side of the Rock, five minutes from town. Its cascading terraces have panoramic sea views, and there's a host of gym and spa facilities. Bedrooms are large and luxurious.

TOP CHOICE **Bistro Madeleine** CAFE, BISTRO **£**
(256 Main St; cakes from £3; ☺9am-11pm; 🛜🖉) If you've just polished off a steak and ale pie in the local pub, have your dessert here, a refined, smoke-free bistro that serves Illy coffee with big chunks of English-inspired cake.

ℹ Information

Money

The currency is the Gibraltar pound. You can also use euros or pounds sterling.

Telephone

To dial Gibraltar from Spain, you precede the five-digit local number with the code ☏00350; from other countries, dial the international access code, then the Gibraltar country code

(☎350) and local number. To phone Spain from Gibraltar, just dial the nine-digit Spanish number.

Tourist Information

Gibraltar Tourist Board (www.gibraltar.gov. uk; Duke of Kent House, Cathedral Sq; ☉9am-5.30pm Mon-Thu, to 5.15pm Fri)

Tourist Office (Grand Casemates Sq; ☉9am-5.30pm Mon-Fri, 10am-3pm Sat, to 1pm Sun & holidays)

Visas

To enter Gibraltar, you need a passport or EU national identity card. EU, USA, Canadian, Australian, New Zealand and South African passport-holders are among those who do not need visas for Gibraltar.

❶ Getting There & Away

AIR Budget airline **easyJet** (www.easyjet.com) flies daily to/from London-Gatwick and three times a week from Liverpool, **British Airways** (www.ba.com) operate seven weekly flights from London Heathrow, and **Monarch Airlines** (www. flymonarch.com) flies daily to/from London Luton and Manchester.

BUS There are no regular buses to Gibraltar, but La Línea de la Concepción bus station is only a five-minute walk from the border.

CAR & MOTORCYCLE Snaking vehicle queues at the 24-hour border and congested traffic in Gibraltar often make it easier to park in La Línea and walk across the border. To take a car into Gibraltar (free) you need an insurance certificate, registration document, nationality plate and driving licence, which will be more trouble than it's worth for most.

FERRY One ferry (www.frs.es) a week sails between Gibraltar and Tangier in Morocco (€46/30 per adult/child one way, 70 minutes).

EXTREMADURA

A sparsely populated stretch of vast skies and open plains, Extremadura is far enough from most beaten tourist trails to give you a genuine sense of exploration.

Trujillo

POP 9690

With its medieval architecture, leafy courtyards, fruit gardens, churches and convents, Trujillo truly is one of the most captivating small towns in Spain. It can't be much bigger now than it was in 1529, when its most famous son, Francisco Pizarro, set off with his three brothers and a few buddies for an expedition that culminated in the bloody conquest of the Incan empire.

◉ Sights

Plaza Mayor   SQUARE
On the south side of the spectacular Plaza Mayor, carved images of Pizarro and his lover Inés Yupanqui (sister of the Inca emperor Atahualpa) decorate the corner of the 16th-century **Palacio de la Conquista**. Through a twisting alley above the Palacio de la Conquista is the **Palacio Juan Pizarro de Orellana** (admission free; ☉10am-1pm & 4.30-6.30pm Mon-Sat, 10am-12.30pm Sun), converted from miniature fortress to Renaissance mansion by one of the Pizarro cousin conquistadors. Overlooking the Plaza Mayor from the northeast corner is the 16th-century **Iglesia de San Martín** (adult/child €1.40/free; ☉10am-2pm & 4-7pm) with delicate Gothic ceiling tracing, stunning stained-glass windows and a grand organ (climb up to the choir loft for the best view).

Upper Town   HISTORIC AREA
The 900m of walls circling the upper town date from Muslim times and it was here that the newly settled noble families built their mansions and churches after the Reconquista.

The 13th-century **Iglesia de Santa María la Mayor** (adult/child €1.40/free; ☉10am-2pm & 4-7pm) has a mainly Gothic nave and a Romanesque tower that you can ascend (all 106 steps) for fabulous views.

At the top of the hill, Trujillo's impressive **castle** (adult/under 12yr €1.40/free; ☉10am-2pm & 4-7pm) has 10th-century Muslim origins (evident by the horseshoe-arch gateway just inside the main entrance) and was later strengthened by the Christians. Patrol the battlements for magnificent 360-degree sweeping views.

🛏 Sleeping & Eating

[TOP CHOICE] **Posada dos Orillas**   HISTORIC HOTEL €€
(☎927 65 90 79; www.dosorillas.com; Calle de Cambrones 6; d €70-90 Sun-Thu, €80-107 Fri & Sat; ❋❀) This tastefully renovated 16th-century mansion is in a great location in the walled town. Rooms replicate Spanish colonial taste, and are named for the countries in which towns called Trujillo are found. Personal service from the owners is excellent.

El Mirador de las Monjas
HOTEL €

(☑927 65 92 23; www.elmiradordelasmonjas.com; Plaza de Santiago 2; s/d incl breakfast €50/60 Mon-Thu, €60/70 Fri-Sun; ❊) High in the old town, this six-room *hostería* attached to a quality restaurant has spotless, light, modern rooms decorated in minimalist style. The upstairs ones with sloping ceilings and pleasant vistas are slightly better than the ones below.

Restaurante La Troya
SPANISH €€

(Plaza Mayor 10; menus €15) Famed for its copious servings of no-frills *comida casera* (home-style cooking), Troya enjoys a prime location on the main town square. On entering, you'll be directed to one of several dining areas, to be presented with plates of tortilla and chorizo, followed by a three-course *menú*. It's all about quantity, and queues stretch out the door on weekends.

Mesón Alberca
SPANISH €€

(Calle de Cambrones 8; mains €11-17; ⊘Thu-Sun) A pretty ivy-clad terrace or dark-timber tables laid with gingham tablecloths create a choice of warm atmospheres for sampling classic *extremeño* cooking. The specialities here are oven roasts and local cheeses. The regional set menu is excellent value at €24.50.

ℹ Information

Tourist Office (www.trujillo.es; Plaza Mayor; ⊘10am-2pm & 4-7pm Oct-May, 10am-2pm & 5-8pm Jun-Sep)

ℹ Getting There & Away

The **bus station** (☑927 32 12 02; Avenida de Miajadas) is 500m south of Plaza Mayor. There are services to/from Madrid (€18 to €30, three to 4¼ hours, five daily), Cáceres (€3.50, 40 minutes, eight daily) and Mérida (€8.25, 1½ hours, three daily).

Cáceres

POP 95,030

Cáceres' *ciudad monumental* (old town), built in the 15th and 16th centuries, is perfectly preserved. The town's action centres on Plaza Mayor, at the foot of the old town, and busy Avenida de España, a short distance south.

◉ Sights

Plaza de Santa María
SQUARE

Enter the old town from Plaza Mayor through the 18th-century **Arco de la Es-** trella, built with a wide span for the passage of carriages. The 15th-century Gothic cathedral, **Concatedral de Santa María** (Plaza de Santa María; admission €1; ⊘9.30am-2pm & 5.30-8.30pm Mon-Sat, 9.30-11.50am & 5.30-7.15pm Sun May-Sep), creates an impressive opening scene. Climb the **bell tower** (€1) for stunning views.

Also on the plaza are the **Palacio Episcopal** (Bishop's Palace), the **Palacio de Mayoralgo** and the **Palacio de Ovando**, all in 16th-century Renaissance style. Heading back through Arco de la Estrella, you can climb the 12th-century **Torre de Bujaco** (Plaza Mayor; adult/child €2/free; ⊘10am-2pm & 5.30-8.30pm Mon-Sat, 10am-2pm Sun Apr-Sep, 10am-2pm & 4.30-7.30pm Mon-Sat, 10am-2pm Sun Oct-Mar) for good stork's-eye views of the Plaza Mayor.

Plaza de San Mateo & Plaza de las Veletas
SQUARE

From Plaza de San Jorge, Cuesta de la Compañía climbs to Plaza de San Mateo and the **Iglesia de San Mateo**, traditionally the church of the land-owning nobility and built on the site of the town's mosque.

Below the square is the excellent **Museo de Cáceres** (Plaza de las Veletas 1; non-EU/EU citizens €1.20/free; ⊘9am-2.30pm & 5-8.15pm Tue-Sat, 10.15am-2.30pm Sun) in a 16th-century mansion built over an evocative 12th-century *aljibe* (cistern), the only surviving element of Cáceres' Muslim castle. It has an impressive archaeological section and an excellent fine-arts display (open only in the mornings), with works by Picasso, Miró, Tapiès and others.

🛏 Sleeping & Eating

TOP CHOICE / Hotel Casa Don Fernando
BOUTIQUE HOTEL €€

(☑927 21 42 79; www.casadonfernando.com; Plaza Mayor 30; d €60-140; ❊🖥) The classiest midrange choice in Cáceres, this boutique hotel sits on Plaza Mayor directly opposite the Arco de la Estrella. Spread over four floors, the designer rooms and bathrooms are tastefully chic; superior rooms have the best plaza views and come with free minibar (€30 more than the standards).

Parador de Cáceres
HOTEL €€€

(☑927 21 17 59; www.parador.es; Calle Ancha 6; s/d €139/173; 🅿❊@🖥) A substantial makeover has given this 14th-century Gothic palace in the old town a swish modern look to its interiors, with bedrooms and bathrooms exhibiting a distinctively nonmedieval level of style and comfort. If you're driving here, pay close attention to the directions you're given when booking.

TOP CHOICE Atrio SPANISH €€€
(☑927 24 29 28; www.restauranteatrio.com; Plaza de San Mateo 1; menus €99-119; ⏲lunch & dinner) With a stunning location in the heart of old Cáceres, the city's fine-dining highlight seems to be going from strength to strength. The focus is on local produce of highest quality; there's a tasting menu chosen by the chef or you can pick from a selection of daily specials to make up your own menu.

Restaurante Torre de Sande FUSION €€
(☑927 21 11 47; www.torredesande.com; Calle Condes 3; mains €12-20; ⏲lunch & dinner Tue-Sat, lunch Sun) Dine in the pretty courtyard at this elegant gourmet restaurant in the heart of the Ciudad Monumental. More modestly, stop for a drink and a tapa at the interconnecting *tapería* (tapas bar), which has appealing streetside tables.

❶ Information

Main Tourist Office (www.turismoextremadura.com; Plaza Mayor 3; ⏲8.30am-2.30pm & 4-6pm or 5-7pm Mon-Fri, 10am-2pm Sat & Sun) At the entrance to the Ciudad Monumental. Opens later in the afternoon in summer.

Municipal Tourist Office (Calle de los Olmos 3; ⏲10am-2pm & 4.30-7.30pm or 5.30-8.30pm)

❶ Getting There & Away

BUS The **bus station** (Carretera de Sevilla; ☑927 23 25 50) has services to Trujillo (€4.40, 40 minutes) and Mérida (€5.60, one hour).

TRAIN Up to five trains per day run to/from Madrid (€27, four hours) and Mérida (€6.10, one hour).

Mérida

POP 57,000

Once the biggest city in Roman Spain, Mérida is home to more ruins of that age than anywhere else in the country and is a wonderful spot to spend a few archaeologically inclined days.

◉ Sights

Roman Remains RUINS
The **Teatro Romano** (Calle Álvarez de Buruaga; ⏲9.30am-7.30pm Jun-Sep, 9.30am-1.45pm &

4-6.15pm Oct-May), built around 15 BC to seat 6000 spectators and set in lovely gardens, has a dramatic and well-preserved two-tier backdrop of Corinthian stone columns; the stage's *scaenae frons* (facade) was inaugurated in AD 105. The theatre hosts performances during the Festival del Teatro Clásico in summer. The adjoining **Anfiteatro**, opened in 8 BC for gladiatorial contests, had a capacity of 14,000.

Los Columbarios (Calle del Ensanche; ⏲9.30am-1.45pm & 5-7.15pm Jun-Sep, 9.30am-1.45pm & 4-6.15pm Oct-May) is a Roman funeral site. A footpath connects it with the **Casa del Mitreo** (Calle Oviedo; adult/child €4/free; ⏲9.30am-1.45pm & 5-7.15pm Jun-Sep, 9.30am-1.45pm & 4-6.15pm Oct-May), a 2nd-century Roman house with several intricate mosaics and a well-preserved fresco.

Don't miss the extraordinarily powerful spectacle of the **Puente Romano** over the Río Guadiana, which at 792m in length with 60 granite arches, is one of the longest bridges built by the Romans.

The **Templo de Diana** (Calle de Sagasta) stood in the municipal forum, where the city government was based. The restored **Pórtico del Foro**, the municipal forum's portico, is just along the road.

Museo Nacional de Arte Romano MUSEUM
(http://museoarteromano.mcu.es; Calle de José Ramón Mélida; adult/child €3/free, EU seniors & students free; ⏲9.30am-3.30pm & 5.30-8.30pm Tue-Sun Jul-Sep, shorter hr rest of year) On no account miss this fabulous museum, which has a superb collection of statues, mosaics, frescoes, coins and other Roman artefacts, all beautifully displayed. Designed by the architect Rafael Moneo, the soaring brick structure makes a remarkable home for the collection.

Alcazaba FORTRESS
(Calle Graciano; ⏲9.30am-1.45pm & 5-7.15pm Jun-Sep, 9.30am-1.45pm & 4-6.15pm Oct-May) This large Muslim fort was built in the 9th century on a site already occupied by the Romans and Visigoths. Down below, its pretty, goldfish-populated *aljibe* (cistern) reuses Visigothic marble and stone slabs, while the ramparts look out over the Guadiana.

🛏 Sleeping & Eating

TOP CHOICE La Flor de al-Andalus HOSTAL €
(☑924 31 33 56; www.laflordeal-andalus.es; Avenida de Extremadura 6; s/d €33/45; ❄⏲) If only all

hostales were this good. Describing itself as a 'boutique *hostal*', La Flor de al-Andalus has beautifully decorated rooms in an Andalucían style, with friendly service and a good location within walking distance of all of the main sights. This is hotel standard at a great price. Try to avoid the rooms on the ground floor by reception.

Hotel Adealba HOTEL €€
(☎924 38 83 08; www.hoteladealba.com; Calle Romero Leal 18; d incl breakfast from €96; P❋⊛) This chic but cordial hotel occupies a 19th-century town house close to the Templo de Diana and does so with a classy, contemporary look. The designer rooms have big windows, some with balcony, a minimalist feel, and there's a compact on-site spa complex. It's cheaper midweek. Valet parking available.

TOP CHOICE Casa Benito SPANISH €€
(Calle San Francisco 3; tapas €3.30, mains €14-22) Squeeze onto a tiny stool in the wood-panelled dining room, prop up the bar or relax on the sunny terrace for tapas at this bullfighting enthusiasts' hang-out; its walls plastered with photos, posters and memorabilia from the ring. The tapas are original and supertasty, while the upstairs restaurant specialises in roasts and is also a fine choice.

Tábula Calda SPANISH €€€
(www.tabulacalda.com; Calle Romero Leal 11; meals €20-25; ⊘lunch & dinner Mon-Sat, lunch Sun) This inviting space, with tilework and abundant greenery, serves up well-priced meals (including set menus from €12 to €24.50) that cover most Spanish staples. It effortlessly combines traditional home cooking, thoughtful presentation and subtle innovations.

ⓘ Information
Municipal Tourist Office (www.merida.es; Paseo de José Álvarez Sáenz de Buruaga; ⊘9.30am-2pm & 5-7.30pm)

ⓘ Getting There & Away
BUS From the **bus station** (☎924 37 14 04; Avenida de la Libertad), destinations include Seville (€13.50, 2½ hours), Cáceres (€5.50, 50 minutes), Trujillo (€8.50, 1¼ hours) and Madrid (from €26.50, four to five hours).

TRAIN Services to Madrid (from €33, 4½ to 6½ hours), Cáceres (from €5.50, 50 minutes) and Seville (€17, four hours).

UNDERSTAND SPAIN

History
Ancient Civilisations

Spain's story is one of European history's grand epics, and it's a story that begins further back than most – the oldest pieces of human bone in Europe (dating back a mere 780,000 years) have been found in Spain, in the Sierra de Atapuerca near Burgos.

The point at which Spanish history really gets interesting, however, is when the great civilisations of the Ancient Mediterranean began to colonise what we now know as the Iberian Peninsula, from around 1000 BC. The sea-going Phoenicians founded a great seafaring empire which depended on the establishment of ports around the Mediterranean rim. One of these ports, Cádiz, is widely believed to be Europe's oldest continuously inhabited settlement.

The Romans arrived in the 3rd century BC and while they took 200 years to subdue the peninsula, they would hold it for six centuries. Called Hispania, Roman Spain became an integral part of the Roman Empire, with its impact upon language, architecture and religion lasting to this day. Reminders of Roman times include Segovia's aqueduct, the ancient theatres and other monuments of Mérida, Tarragona and Zaragoza.

Muslim Spain & the Reconquista

In 711 Muslim armies invaded the peninsula, most of which they would end up occupying. Muslim dominion would last almost 800 years in parts of Spain. In Islamic Spain (known as al-Andalus), arts and sciences prospered, new crops and agricultural techniques were introduced, and palaces, mosques, schools, public baths and gardens were built. The spirit of these times lives on most powerfully in Andalucía.

In 1085 Alfonso VI, king of Castile, took Toledo, the first definitive victory of the Reconquista (the struggle to wrestle Spain into Christian hands). By the mid-13th century, the Christians had taken most of the peninsula, except for the emirate of Granada.

The kingdoms of Castile and Aragón emerged as Christian Spain's two main powers, and in 1469 they were united by the marriage of Isabel, princess of Castile, and Fernando, heir to Aragón's throne. Known as the Catholic Monarchs, they laid the foundations for the Spanish Golden Age, but were also responsible for one of the darkest hours in Spain's history – the Spanish Inquisition: a witch-hunt to expel or execute Jews and other non-Christians. In 1492 the last Muslim ruler of Granada surrendered to them, marking the end of the Reconquista. In the same year, Jews were expelled from Spain, with Muslims sent into exile eight years later.

The Golden Age

In the same year that marked the end of the Reconquista, Christopher Columbus (Colón in Castilian) landed in the Bahamas and later Cuba. His voyages sparked a period of exploration and exploitation that was to yield Spain enormous wealth, while destroying the ancient American empires. Over the centuries that followed, Spain's growing confidence was reflected in an extravagant cultural outpouring, producing towering figures such as Velázquez and Cervantes. For three centuries, gold and silver from the New World were used to finance the rapid expansion of the Spanish empire but were not enough to prevent its slow decline. By the 18th century, the mighty Spanish empire was on its way out, the life sucked out of it by a series of unwise kings, a self-seeking noble class and ceaseless warfare.

Struggle for the Soul of Spain

By the early 19th century, Spain's royal court had descended into internecine squabbles over succession to the Spanish throne. The consequences for the rest of the country were profound.

In 1807–08 Napoleon's forces occupied a weakened Spain, and King Carlos IV abdicated without a fight. In his place Napoleon installed his own brother, Joseph Bonaparte. The Spaniards retaliated with a five-year war of independence. The French were expelled in 1813 after defeat at Vitoria. A Bourbon, Fernando VII, was restored to the Spanish throne – despite periods of interruption to their rule, the Bourbon royal family rule Spain to this day.

Independence may have been restored, but Spain spent much of the next century embroiled in wars at home and abroad. The Spanish-American War of 1898 marked the end of the Spanish empire. The USA crushed Spanish forces and took over its last overseas possessions – Cuba, Puerto Rico, Guam and the Philippines. Spain was in a dire state.

Franco's Spain

Begun in the 19th century, the battle between conservatives and liberals, and between monarchists and republicans came to a head in July 1936 when Nationalist plotters in the army rose against the Republican government, launching a civil war (1936–39) that would create bitter wounds that are still healing today. The Nationalists, led by General Francisco Franco (who stood at the head of an alliance of the army, Church and the Fascist-style Falange Party), received military support from Nazi Germany and Fascist Italy, while the elected Republican government received support from the Soviet Union and other foreign leftists.

The war ended in 1939, with Franco the victor. Some 350,000 Spaniards died in the war, most of them on the battlefield but many others in executions, prison camps or simply from disease and starvation. After the war, thousands of Republicans were executed, jailed or forced into exile, and Franco's 36-year dictatorship began with Spain isolated internationally and crippled by recession. It wasn't until the 1950s and '60s, when the rise in tourism and a treaty with the USA combined to provide much-needed funds, that the country began to recover, although Franco retained an iron grip over the country.

The New Spain

Franco died in 1975, having named Juan Carlos, the grandson of Alfonso XIII, as his successor. Despite Franco's careful grooming, King Juan Carlos opted for the creation of a constitutional monarchy and a democratic government. The first elections were held in 1977 and a new constitution was drafted in 1978. It was a dramatic shift and although deep schisms remain to this day, the country's democratic transition has been an extraordinary success.

Post-Franco Spain bore little resemblance to what went before and the country revelled in its new-found freedoms. Seemingly everything – from political parties to drugs – was legalised and the 1980s, despite the spectre of killings by the Basque terrorist group ETA, was a period of great cultural innovation, and Spain's reputation as Europe's party capital was born. Spain joined the European Community (EC) in 1986 and celebrated its return to the world stage in style in 1992, with Expo '92 in Seville and the Olympic Games in Barcelona.

At a political level, Spain was ruled from 1982 until 1996 by the Partido Socialista Obrero Español (Spanish Socialist Party; PSOE) of Felipe González. By 1996 the PSOE government stood accused of corruption and was swept from power by the centre-right Partido Popular (Popular Party; PP), led by José María Aznar. The PP went on to establish programs of economic decentralisation and liberalisation.

Long accustomed to terrorist attacks by ETA (which has killed more than 800 people in the past four decades), Spain was nonetheless shaken to its core by the largest-ever terrorist attack on Spanish soil (later claimed by al-Qaeda), in Madrid on 11 March 2004. In national elections held three days later, the PP lost the presidential election to the PSOE. Among his first actions as president, José Luís Rodríguez Zapatero withdrew Spanish troops from Iraq.

The Socialists embarked on something of a social revolution, legalising gay marriage, regularising the status of hundreds of thousands of illegal immigrants, removing the Church's role in religious education in schools, making abortions easier to obtain, and pushing through a law aimed at investigating the crimes and executions of the Franco years; the latter broke the 'pact of silence' that had prevailed throughout the transition to democracy in the late 1970s.

Within months of the Socialists' re-election in 2008, years of economic boom came shuddering to an end amid the global financial crisis; unemployment jumped from around 7% in 2007 to above 20% in 2010. With the economy deep in recession, the Socialists' popularity plummeted.

Spain Today

Prime Minister Zapatero's delay in acknowledging the crisis sealed the government's fate, and it was defeated by the PP of Prime Minister Mariano Rajoy in a landslide on 20 November 2011. By late 2012, unemployment was stuck at around 25%, youth unemployment was close to 50% and the government was forced to seek billions of euros of assistance from the EU. The government's deeply unpopular austerity program slashed public services and ushered in regular protests in Madrid and across the country. Many of Spain's regions were also forced to seek bailouts from the central government in Madrid.

Against this backdrop of economic meltdown, Spain's restive regions of Catalonia and the Basque Country began demanding greater autonomy, with plans also underway in both regions for de facto referenda on independence.

Good news may be hard to come by, but the announcement of a ceasefire by a much-weakened ETA in September 2010, followed a year later by what ETA announced was a 'definitive cessation of its armed activity'.

Religion

Only about 20% of Spaniards are regular churchgoers, but Catholicism is deeply ingrained in the culture and an estimated 94% of Spaniards identify themselves as Catholics. As the writer Unamuno said, 'Here in Spain we are all Catholics, even the atheists'.

However, many Spaniards have a deep-seated scepticism about the Church. During the civil war and the four decades of Franco's rule, the Catholic Church was, for the most part, a strong supporter of his policies. The Church retains a powerful public voice in national debates.

Spain's most significant (and growing) religious community after the Catholics are Muslims.

Arts

Literature

Miguel de Cervantes' novel *Don Quijote* is the masterpiece of the literary flowering of the 16th and 17th centuries, not to mention one of the world's great works of fiction. Centuries later, the towering figure of the early 20th century was poet and playwright Federico García Lorca, who won international acclaim before he was murdered in the civil war for his Republican sympathies.

Popular contemporary authors include Arturo Pérez Reverte, Almudena Grandes and Javier Marías.

Cinema

Modern Spanish cinema's best-known director is Pedro Almodóvar, whose humorous, cutting-edge films are often set amid the great explosion of drugs and creativity that occurred in Madrid in the 1980s. His *Todo Sobre Mi Madre* (All About My Mother;

1999) and *Habla Con Ella* (Talk to Her; 2002) are both Oscar winners, while *Volver* (2006) is his most acclaimed recent work.

Alejandro Amenábar, the young Chilean-born director of *Abre los Ojos* (Open Your Eyes; 1997), *The Others* (2001) and the Oscar-winning *Mar Adentro* (The Sea Inside; 2004), is Almodóvar's main competition for Spain's 'best director' title. That latter film's star, Javier Bardem, won the Oscar for Best Supporting Actor in the Coen brothers' disturbing *No Country for Old Men* in 2008. The Madrid-born actress Penélope Cruz won an Oscar for Best Supporting Actress for her role in Woody Allen's *Vicky Cristina Barcelona* (2008).

Architecture

The Muslims left behind some of the most splendid buildings in the Islamic world, particularly in Andalucía. Examples include Granada's Alhambra, Córdoba's Mezquita and Seville's Alcázar – the latter is an example of Mudéjar architecture, the name given to Islamic artistry built in Christian-held territory. Outside of Andalucía, Zaragoza's Aljafería captures the same spirit, albeit on a smaller scale.

The first main Christian architectural movement was Romanesque, best seen in churches and monasteries across the north of the country. Later came the great Gothic cathedrals, such as those in Toledo, Burgos, León, Ávila, Salamanca and Seville of the 12th to 16th centuries. Spain then followed the usual path to baroque (17th and 18th centuries) and neoclassicism (19th century).

Around the turn of the 20th century, Catalonia produced its startling Modernista movement and many buildings in this style adorn Barcelona's streets; Antoni Gaudí's La Sagrada Família is the most stunning example.

Of the daring contemporary structures appearing all over Spain, Valencia's Ciudad de las Artes y las Ciencias and Bilbao's Guggenheim are the most eye-catching.

Painting

The giants of Spain's Golden Age (around 1550 to 1650) were Toledo-based El Greco (originally from Crete) and Diego Velázquez, considered Spain's best painter by greats including Picasso and Dalí. El Greco and Velázquez are well represented in Madrid's Museo del Prado, as is the genius of the 18th and 19th centuries, Francisco Goya. Goya's versatility ranged from unflattering royal portraits and anguished war scenes to bullfight etchings and tapestry designs.

Catalonia was the powerhouse of early-20th-century Spanish art, claiming the hugely prolific Pablo Picasso (although born in Málaga, Andalucía), the colourful symbolist Joan Miró and surrealist Salvador Dalí. To get inside the latter's world, head for Figueres or the Castell de Púbol. The two major museums dedicated to Picasso's work are the Museu Picasso in Barcelona and the Museo Picasso Málaga, while his signature *Guernica* and other works are found in Madrid's Centro de Arte Reina Sofía. The Reina Sofía also has works by Joan Miró, as does the Fundació Joan Miró.

Important artists of the late 20th century include the Basque sculptor Eduardo Chillida; his Museo Chillida Leku is south of San Sebastián.

Flamenco

Most musical historians speculate that flamenco probably dates back to a fusion of songs brought to Spain by the Roma people, with music and verses from North Africa crossing into medieval Muslim Andalucía.

FLAMENCO – THE ESSENTIAL ELEMENTS

A flamenco singer is known as a *cantaor* (male) or *cantaora* (female); a dancer is a *bailaora*. Most of the songs and dances are performed to a blood-rush of guitar from the *tocaora* (flamenco guitarist). Percussion is provided by tapping feet, clapping hands and sometimes castanets. Flamenco *coplas* (songs) come in many different types, from the anguished *soleá* or the intensely despairing *siguiriya* to the livelier *alegría* or the upbeat *bulería*. The first flamenco was *cante jondo* (deep song), an anguished instrument of expression for a group on the margins of society. *Jondura* (depth) is still the essence of pure flamenco.

The traditional flamenco costume – shawl, fan and long, frilly *bata de cola* (tail gown) for women, flat Cordoban hats and tight black trousers for men – dates from Andalucian fashions in the late 19th century.

Flamenco as we now know it first took recognisable form in the 18th and early 19th centuries among Roma people in western Andalucía. Suitably, for a place considered the cradle of the genre, the Seville–Jerez de la Frontera–Cádiz axis is still considered the flamenco heartland and it's here, purists believe, that you must go for the most authentic flamenco experience.

Environment

The Land

Spain is a geographically diverse country, with landscapes ranging from the near-deserts of Almería to the emerald green countryside of Asturias and deep coastal inlets of Galicia, from the rolling sunbaked plains of Castilla-La Mancha to the rugged Pyrenees. The country covers 84% of the Iberian Peninsula and spreads over 505,370 sq km, about 40% of which is high *meseta* (tableland).

Wildlife

The brown bear, wolf, Iberian lynx (the world's most endangered cat species, although it's making a hesitant and much-assisted comeback) and wild boar all survive in Spain, although only the boar exists in abundance. Spain's high mountains harbour the chamois and Spanish ibex, and big birds of prey such as eagles, vultures and lammergeier. The marshy Ebro Delta and Guadalquivir estuary are important for waterbirds, among them the spectacular greater flamingo.

Environmental Issues

Spain faces some of the most pressing environmental issues of our time. Drought, massive overdevelopment of its coastlines, overexploitation of scarce water resources by tourism projects and intensive agriculture, and spiralling emissions of greenhouse gases are all major concerns. It's a slightly more nuanced picture than first appears – Spain is a leading player in the wind-power industry, it has locked away around 40,000 sq km of protected areas, including 14 national parks, and its system of public transport is outstanding – but the apparent absence of any meaningful political will to tackle these issues is storing up problems for future generations.

Food & Drink

Reset your stomach's clock in Spain unless you want to eat alone, with other tourists or, in some cases, not at all.

Most Spaniards start the day with a light *desayuno* (breakfast), perhaps coffee with a *tostada* (piece of toast) or *pastel/bollo* (pastry), although they might stop in a bar later for a mid-morning *bocadillo* (baguette). *La comida* (lunch) is usually the main meal of the day, eaten between about 2pm and 4pm. The *cena* (evening meal) is usually lighter and most locals won't sit down for it before 9pm. The further south you go, the later start times tend to be – anything from 10pm to midnight!

At lunchtime from Monday to Friday, most places offer a *menú del día* – a fixed-price lunch menu and the traveller's best friend. For €10 to €14 you typically get three courses, bread and a drink. The *plato combinado* (combined plate) is a cousin of the *menú* and usually includes a meat dish with some vegetables.

JAMÓN – A PRIMER

Unlike Italian prosciutto, Spanish *jamón* is a bold, deep red and well marbled with buttery fat. Like wines and olive oil, Spanish *jamón* is subject to a strict series of classifications. *Jamón serrano* refers to *jamón* made from white-coated pigs introduced to Spain in the 1950s. Once salted and semidried by the cold, dry winds of the Spanish sierra, most now go through a similar process of curing and drying in a climate-controlled shed for around a year. *Jamón serrano* accounts for approximately 90% of cured ham in Spain.

Jamón ibérico – more expensive and generally regarded as the elite of Spanish hams – comes from a black-coated pig indigenous to the Iberian Peninsula and a descendant of the wild boar. If the pig gains at least 50% of its body weight during the acorn-eating season, it can be classified as *jamón ibérico de bellota*, the most sought-after designation for *jamón*.

Staples & Specialities

The variety in Spanish cuisines is quite extraordinary, and each region has its own styles and specialities. One of the most characteristic dishes, from the Valencia region, is paella – rice, seafood, the odd vegetable and often chicken or meat, all simmered together and traditionally coloured yellow with saffron. *Jamón serrano* (cured ham) is a delicacy available in many different qualities.

Many would argue that tapas are Spain's greatest culinary gift to the world, not least because the possibilities are endless. You can also order *raciones*, a large-sized serving of tapas. Anything can be a tapa, from a handful of olives or a piece of *tortilla de patatas* (potato and onion omelette) to more elaborate and often intensely surprising combinations of tastes. For tapas, the cities of Andalucía are usually (but not always) bastions of tradition, while the undoubted king of tapas destinations is San Sebastián, in Basque country, where they call tapas '*pintxos*'. It all comes together in Madrid.

Drinks

Start the day with a strong coffee, either as a *cafe con leche* (half-coffee, half-milk), *cafe solo* (short black, espresso-like) or *cafe cortado* (short black with a little milk).

The most common way to order a *cerveza* (beer) is to ask for a *caña* (small draught beer). In Basque Country this is a *zurrito*. A larger beer (about 300mL) is often called a *tubo*. All these words apply to *cerveza de barril* (draught beer) – if you just ask for a *cerveza* you're likely to get bottled beer, which is a little more expensive.

Vino (wine) comes *blanco* (white), *tinto* (red) or *rosado* (rosé). Exciting wine regions include Penedès, Priorat, Ribera del Duero and La Rioja. There are also many regional specialities, such as *jerez* (sherry) in Jerez de la Frontera and *cava* (a sparkling wine) in Catalonia. Sangria, a sweet punch made of red wine, fruit and spirits, is a summer drink and especially popular with tourists.

Agua del grifo (tap water) is usually safe to drink.

Vegetarians & Vegans

Vegetarians may have to be creative in Spain. You'll find dedicated vegetarian restaurants in larger cities. Otherwise, most traditional restaurants will offer salads and egg tortillas, but little else for non-carnivores. Even salads may come laden with sausages or tuna. Pasta and pizza are readily available, as is seafood for those who eat it. Vegans will have an especially hard time away from the big cities (and not an easy time in them).

SURVIVAL GUIDE

Directory A–Z
Accommodation

Budget options include everything from dorm-style youth hostels to family-style *pensiones* and slightly better-heeled *hostales*. At the upper end of this category you'll find rooms with air-conditioning and private bathrooms. Midrange *hostales* and hotels are more comfortable and most offer standard hotel services. Business hotels, trendy boutique hotels and luxury hotels are usually in the top-end category.

Virtually all accommodation prices are subject to IVA *(impuesto sobre el valor añadido)*, the Spanish version of value-added tax, which is 10%. This may or may not be included in the quoted price. To check, ask: *Está incluido el IVA?* (Is IVA included?)

PRICE RANGES

Our reviews refer to double rooms with a private bathroom, except in hostels or where otherwise specified. Quoted rates are for high season, which is generally May to September (though this varies greatly from region to region).

€ less than €65 (less than €75 for Madrid/Barcelona)

€€ €65 to €140 (€75 to €200 for Madrid/Barcelona)

€€€ more than €140 (more than €200 for Madrid/Barcelona)

CAMPING

Spain has around 1000 officially graded *campings* (camping grounds) and they vary greatly in service, cleanliness and style. They're officially rated as 1st class (1ªC), 2nd class (2ªC) or 3rd class (3ªC). Camping grounds usually charge per person, per tent and per vehicle – typically €5 to €10 for each. Many camping grounds close from around October to Easter.

The following are useful websites:

Campings Online (www.campingsonline.com/espana) Booking service.

Campinguía (www.campinguia.com) Contains comments (mostly in Spanish) and links.

Guía Camping (www.guiacampingfecc.com)
Online version of the annual *Guía Camping* (€13.60), which is available in bookshops around the country.

HOTELS, HOSTALES & PENSIONES
Most options fall into the categories of
hotels (one to five stars, full amenities),
hostales (high-end guesthouses with private bathroom; one to three stars) or *pensiones* (guesthouses, usually with shared
bathroom; one to three stars). A gem of
Spain's accommodation scene, **paradores**
(☎902 547979; www.parador.es) are luxury, but
well-priced state-run hotels, often inhabiting beautiful old castles, monasteries and
former palaces.

YOUTH HOSTELS
Albergues juveniles (youth hostels) are
cheap places to stay, especially for lone travellers. Expect to pay from €15 to €28 per
night, depending on location, age and season. Spain's Hostelling International (HI)
organisation, **Red Española de Albergues
Juveniles** (REAJ, Spanish Youth Hostel Network;
www.reaj.com), has around 250 youth hostels
throughout Spain. Official hostels require
HI membership (you can buy a membership
card at virtually all hostels) and some have
curfews.

Activities
HIKING
» Lonely Planet's *Walking in Spain* – read
more about some of the best treks in the
country.
» Maps by Editorial Alpina –useful for
hiking, especially in the Pyrenees. Buy at
bookshops, sports shops and sometimes
petrol stations near hiking areas.
» GR (*Grandes Recorridos,* or long
distance) trails – indicated with red-and-
white markers.

SKIING
» Cheaper, less varied than much of rest
of Europe.
» Season: December to mid-April.

SURFING, WINDSURFING &
KITESURFING
The Basque Country has good surf spots,
including San Sebastián, Zarautz and the
legendary left at Mundaka. Tarifa, with its
long beaches and ceaseless wind, is generally considered to be the windsurfing capital
of Europe. It's also a top spot for kitesurfing.

Business Hours
Reviews in this guidebook won't list business hours unless they differ from the following standards:

Banks 8.30am to 2pm Monday to Friday;
some also open 4pm to 7pm Thursday and
9am to 1pm Saturday

Central post offices 8.30am to 9.30pm
Monday to Friday, 8.30am to 2pm Saturday

Nightclubs midnight or 1am to 5am or
6am

Restaurants lunch 1pm to 4pm, dinner
8.30pm to midnight or later

Shops 10am to 2pm and 4.30pm to
7.30pm or 5pm to 8pm; big supermarkets
and department stores generally open
from 10am to 10pm Monday to Saturday

Embassies & Consulates
Australia Embassy (☎91 353 66 00; www.
spain.embassy.gov.au; Paseo de la Castellana 259D,
24th fl, Madrid)

Canada Embassy (☎91 382 84 00; www.
espana.gc.ca; Paseo de la Castellana 259D, Torre
Espacio, Madrid)

New Zealand Embassy (☎91 523 02 26;
www.nzembassy.com/spain; Calle de Pinar 7, 3rd
Fl, Madrid)

UK Embassy (☎91 714 62 00; www.ukinspain.
fco.gov.uk; Paseo de la Castellana 259D, Torre
Espacio, Madrid)

USA Embassy (☎91 587 22 00; http://span-
ish.madrid.usembassy.gov/; Calle de Serrano 75,
Madrid)

Food
The following price categories for the cost of
a main course are used in the listings in this
chapter.

€€€ more than €20

€€ €10 to €20

€ less than €10

Gay & Lesbian Travellers
Homosexuality is legal in Spain. In 2005 the
Socialists gave the country's conservative
Catholic foundations a shake with the legali-
sation of same-sex marriages in Spain.

Lesbians and gay men generally keep a
fairly low profile, but are quite open in the
cities. Madrid, Barcelona, Sitges, Torremo-
linos and Ibiza have particularly lively scenes.

Internet Access

» Wi-fi increasingly available at most hotels and some cafes, restaurants and airports; generally (but not always) free.

» Good cybercafes are increasingly hard to find; ask at the local tourist office. Prices per hour range from €1.50 to €3.

Language Courses

» Popular places to learn Spanish: Barcelona, Granada, Madrid, Salamanca and Seville.

» **Escuela Oficial de Idiomas** (EOI; www. eeooiinet.com) is a nationwide institution teaching Spanish and other local languages. On the website's opening page, hit 'Centros' under 'Comunidad' and then 'Centros en la Red' to get to a list of schools.

Legal Matters

Drugs Cannabis is legal but only for personal use and in very small quantities. Public consumption of any drug is illegal.

Smoking Not permitted in any enclosed public space, including bars, restaurants and nightclubs.

Money

ATMs Many credit and debit cards can be used for withdrawing money from *cajeros automáticos* (automatic teller machines) that display the relevant symbols such as Visa, MasterCard, Cirrus etc.

Cash Most banks will exchange major foreign currencies and offer the best rates. Ask about commissions and take your passport.

Credit & Debit Cards Can be used to pay for most purchases. You'll often be asked to show your passport or some other form of identification, or to type in your pin. The most widely accepted cards are Visa and MasterCard.

Moneychangers Exchange offices, indicated by the word *cambio* (exchange), offer longer opening hours than banks, but worse exchange rates and higher commissions.

Taxes & Refunds In Spain, value-added tax (VAT) is known as IVA (*ee*-ba; *impuesto sobre el valor añadido*). Visitors are entitled to a refund of the 18% IVA on purchases costing more than €90.16 from any shop if they are taking them out of the EU within three months.

Tipping Menu prices include a service charge. Most people leave some small change. Taxi drivers don't have to be tipped but a little rounding up won't go amiss.

Travellers Cheques Can be changed (for a commission) at most banks and exchange offices.

Public Holidays

The two main periods when Spaniards go on holiday are Semana Santa (the week leading up to Easter Sunday) and July or August. At these times accommodation can be scarce and transport heavily booked.

There are at least 14 official holidays a year – some observed nationwide, some locally. National holidays:

Año Nuevo (New Year's Day) 1 January

Viernes Santo (Good Friday) March/April

Fiesta del Trabajo (Labour Day) 1 May

La Asunción (Feast of the Assumption) 15 August

Fiesta Nacional de España (National Day) 12 October

La Inmaculada Concepción (Feast of the Immaculate Conception) 8 December

Navidad (Christmas) 25 December

Regional governments set five holidays and local councils two more. Common dates include the following:

Epifanía (Epiphany) or **Día de los Reyes Magos** (Three Kings' Day) 6 January

Día de San José (St Joseph's Day) 19 March

Jueves Santo (Good Thursday) March/April. Not observed in Catalonia and Valencia.

Corpus Christi June; the Thursday after the eighth Sunday after Easter Sunday.

Día de San Juan Bautista (Feast of St John the Baptist) 24 June

Día de Santiago Apóstol (Feast of St James the Apostle) 25 July

Día de Todos los Santos (All Saints Day) 1 November

Día de la Constitución (Constitution Day) 6 December

SPAIN DIRECTORY A–Z

Safe Travel

Most visitors to Spain never feel remotely threatened, but a sufficient number have unpleasant experiences to warrant an alert. The main thing to be wary of is petty theft (which may of course not seem so petty if your passport, cash, travellers cheques, credit card and camera go missing). Stay alert and you can avoid most thievery techniques. Algeciras, Barcelona, Madrid and Seville are the worst offenders, as are popular beaches in summer (never leave belongings unattended). Common scams include the following:

» Kids crowding around you asking for directions or help.

» A person pointing out bird droppings on your shoulder (some substance their friend has sprinkled on you) – as they help clean it off they are probably emptying your pockets.

» The guys who tell you that you have a flat tyre. While your new friend and you check the tyre, his pal is emptying the car.

» The classic snatch-and-run. Never leave your belongings unattended.

» An old classic: the ladies offering flowers for good luck. We don't know how they do it, but your pockets always wind up empty.

Telephone

Blue public payphones are common and fairly easy to use. They accept coins, phonecards and, in some cases, credit cards. Phonecards come in €6 and €12 denominations and, like postage stamps, are sold at post offices and tobacconists.

International reverse-charge (collect) calls are simple to make: dial ✆900 99 followed by the appropriate code. For example: ✆900 99 00 61 for Australia, ✆900 99 00 44 for the UK, ✆900 99 00 11 (AT&T) for the USA etc.

To speak to an English-speaking Spanish international operator, dial ✆1008 (for calls within Europe) or ✆1005 (rest of the world).

MOBILE PHONES

All Spanish mobile phone companies (Telefónica's MoviStar, Orange and Vodafone) offer *prepagado* (prepaid) accounts for mobiles. The SIM card costs from €50, which includes some prepaid phone time.

Mobile phone numbers in Spain start with the number 6.

PHONE CODES

Area codes in Spain are an integral part of the phone number. All numbers are nine digits and you just dial that nine-digit number.

Numbers starting with 900 are national toll-free numbers, while those starting 901 to 905 come with varying costs; most can only be dialled from within Spain. In a similar category are numbers starting with 800, 803, 806 and 807.

Tourist Information

All cities and many smaller towns have an *oficina de turismo*. In the country's provincial capitals you'll sometimes find more than one tourist office – one specialising in information on the city alone, the other carrying mostly provincial or regional information. National and natural parks also often have visitor centres offering useful information. Spain's official tourism site is *Turespaña* (www.spain.info).

Visas

Spain is one of 26 member countries of the Schengen Convention and Schengen visa rules apply.

Citizens/residents of EU & Schengen countries No visa required.

Citizens/ residents of Australia, Canada, Israel, Japan, NZ and the USA No visa required for tourist visits of up to 90 days.

Other countries Check with a Spanish embassy or consulate.

To work or study in Spain A special visa may be required – contact a Spanish embassy or consulate before travel.

Work

Norwegian, Swiss, Icelandic and EU nationals may work in Spain without a visa. Everyone else must obtain a work permit (from a Spanish consulate in their country of residence) and, if they plan to stay more than 90 days, a residence visa.

Teaching English is an obvious option; a TEFL (Teaching English as a Foreign Language) certificate will be a big help. Other possibilities include summer bar and restaurant work, as well as getting work on yachts in major ports.

Getting There & Away
Entering the Country

Immigration and customs checks usually involve a minimum of fuss, although there are exceptions. Your vehicle could be searched on arrival from Morocco; they're looking for controlled substances. Expect long delays at these borders, especially in summer.

The tiny principality of Andorra is not in the EU, so border controls (and rigorous customs checks for contraband) remain in place.

Air

Flights from all over Europe, including numerous budget airlines, serve main Spanish airports. All of Spain's airports share the user-friendly website and flight information telephone number of **Aena** (☎902 404 704; www.aena.es), the national airports authority. For more information on each airport on Aena's website, choose English and click on the drop-down menu of airports. Each airport's page has details on practical information (such as parking and public transport) and a full list of (and links to) airlines using that airport.

Madrid's Aeropuerto de Barajas is Spain's busiest (and Europe's fifth-busiest) airport.

Land

Spain shares land borders with France, Portugal and Andorra.

Apart from shorter cross-border services, **Eurolines** (www.eurolines.com) is the main operator of international bus services to Spain from most of Western Europe and Morocco.

In addition to the rail services connecting Spain with France and Portugal, there are direct trains between Zürich and Barcelona (via Bern, Geneva, Perpignan and Girona), and between Milan and Barcelona (via Turin, Perpignan and Girona). For these and other services, visit the website of **Renfe** (☎902 24 34 02; www.renfe.com), the Spanish national railway company.

Regular buses connect Andorra with Barcelona (including winter ski buses and direct services to the airport) and other destinations in Spain (including Madrid) and France.

TRANSPORT FROM FRANCE

Bus

DESTINATION	COMPANY	DURATION	FREQUENCY
Paris to Madrid	Eurolines	17¾ hr	daily
Paris to Barcelona	Eurolines	14¾ hr	daily

Car & Motorcycle

The main road crossing into Spain from France is the highway that links up with Spain's AP7 tollway, which runs down to Barcelona and follows the Spanish coast south (with a branch, the AP2, going to Madrid via Zaragoza). A series of links cut across the Pyrenees from France and Andorra into Spain, as does a coastal route that runs from Biarritz in France into the Spanish Basque Country.

Train

The main rail lines into Spain cross the Franco–Spanish frontier along the Mediterranean coast and via the Basque Country. Another minor route runs inland across the Pyrenees from Latour-de-Carol to Barcelona.

TGV (high-speed) trains connect Paris Montparnasse with Irún, where you change to a normal train for the Basque Country and on towards Madrid. Up to three TGVs also put you on track to Barcelona (leaving from Paris Gare de Lyon), with a change at Montpellier or Narbonne.

There are plans for direct high-speed rail links from Paris to Madrid and Barcelona.

DESTINATION	COMPANY	PRICE	DURATION	FREQUENCY
Paris Austerlitz to Madrid Chamartín	*Trenhotel Francisco de Goya*	chair/sleeper class €162.30/177.80	13½ hours	one daily
Paris Austerlitz to Barcelona Estacio de Franca	*Trenhotel Joan Miró*	chair/sleeper class €153.10/166.50	12 hours	one daily
Montpellier to Lorca	Talgo	€105	12½ hours	daily

FERRIES TO SPAIN

Ferries run to mainland Spain regularly from the Canary Islands, Italy, North Africa (Algeria, Morocco and the Spanish enclaves of Ceuta and Melilla) and the UK. Most services are run by the Spanish national ferry company, **Acciona Trasmediterránea** (☎902 454645; www.trasmediterranea.es). You can take vehicles on the following routes.

Algeria

DESTINATION	COMPANY	DURATION	FREQUENCY
Almería–Ghazaouet	Acciona Trasmediterránea	eight hours	four weekly (late June–mid Sep)
Almería–Oran	Acciona Trasmediterránea	eight hours	two weekly (May–Sep)

France

DESTINATION	COMPANY	DURATION	FREQUENCY
Gijón-Saint–Nazaire	LD Lines (www.ldlines.com)	14 hours	three weekly

Italy

DESTINATION	DURATION	FREQUENCY
Barcelona–Genoa	18 hours	three weekly
Barcelona–Civitavecchia (near Rome)	20½ hours	six to seven weekly
Barcelona–Livorno (Tuscany)	19½ hours	three weekly
Barcelona–Porto Torres (Sardinia)	12 hours	one daily

Morocco

In addition to the following services, there are also ferries to the Spanish enclaves of Melilla (from Almería and Málaga) and Ceuta (from Algeciras).

DESTINATION	DURATION	FREQUENCY
Tangier–Algeciras	90 minutes	up to eight daily
Tangier–Barcelona	24-35 hours	weekly
Tangier–Tarifa	35 minutes	up to eight daily
Nador–Almería	five to eight hours	up to three daily

UK

From mid-March to mid-November, **Brittany Ferries** (www.brittanyferries.com) runs the following services:

DESTINATION	DURATION	FREQUENCY
Plymouth–Santander	20 hours	weekly
Portsmouth–Santander	24 hours	weekly
Portsmouth-Bilbao	24 hours	twice weekly

Getting Around

Students and seniors are eligible for discounts of 30% to 50% on most types of transport within Spain.

Air

Domestic Spanish routes are operated by the following airlines:

Air Berlin (www.airberlin.com) Madrid to Valencia, Palma de Mallorca, Ibiza, Seville,

TRANSPORT FROM PORTUGAL

Bus

DESTINATION	COMPANY	PRICE	DURATION	FREQUENCY
Lisbon–Madrid	Avanza (www.avanzabus.com)	€37.50	7½ to 9hr	two daily

Other bus services run north via Porto to Tui, Santiago de Compostela and A Coruña. Local buses cross the border from towns such as Huelva, Badajoz and Ourense.

Car & Motorcycle

The A5 freeway linking Madrid with Badajoz crosses the Portuguese frontier and continues on to Lisbon, and there are many other road connections up and down the length of the Hispano–Portuguese frontier.

Train

From Portugal, the main line runs from Lisbon across Extremadura to Madrid.

DESTINATION	PRICE	DURATION	FREQUENCY
Lisbon–Madrid	chair/sleeper class €63.20/91.40	10½ hours	one daily
Lisbon–Irún	chair/sleeper class €73.80/103.50	14½ hours	one daily

Jerez de la Frontera, Alicante, Bilbao and Santiago de Compostela.

Air Europa (www.aireuropa.com) Madrid to Ibiza, Palma de Mallorca, Vigo and Santiago de Compostela.

easyJet (www.easyjet.com) Madrid to Ibiza, Menorca, Asturias (Gijón) and Santiago de Compostela.

Iberia (www.iberia.es) Spain's national airline and its subsidiary, Iberia Regional-Air Nostrum, have an extensive domestic network.

Ryanair (www.ryanair.com) Numerous domestic Spanish routes.

Volotea (www.volotea.com) New budget airline; domestic and international flights.

Vueling (www.vueling.com) Spanish low-cost company with loads of domestic flights.

Bicycle

Regional trains have space for carrying bikes, and they're also permitted on most *cercanías* (local trains in cities like Madrid and Barcelona); long-distance trains have more restrictions. As a rule, you have to be travelling overnight in a sleeper or couchette for (dismantled) bikes to be accepted as normal luggage.

Boat

Regular ferries connect the Spanish mainland with the Balearic Islands.

Bus

Spain's bus network is operated by countless independent companies, and reaches into the most remote towns and villages. Many towns and cities have one main station for arrivals and departures, which usually has an information desk. Tourist offices can also help with information on bus services.

Local services can get you nearly anywhere, but most buses connecting rural towns aren't geared to tourist needs. Frequent weekday services drop off to a trickle on weekends. It's not necessary, and often not possible, to make reservations for local bus journeys. It is, however, a good idea to turn up at least 30 minutes before the bus leaves to guarantee a seat.

Generally, bus fares are cheaper than on the faster, long-distance trains. For longer trips, you should buy your ticket in advance.

Among the hundreds of bus companies operating in Spain, the following have the largest networks:

ALSA (☎902 422242; www.alsa.es)

Avanza (☎902 020999; www.avanzabus.com)

Car & Motorcycle

Spain's roads vary enormously but are generally good. Fastest are the *autopistas;* on some, you have to pay hefty tolls.

Every vehicle should display a nationality plate of its country of registration and you must always carry proof of ownership of a private vehicle, as well as a warning triangle and a reflective jacket (to be used in case of breakdown). Third-party insurance is required throughout Europe.

AUTOMOBILE ASSOCIATIONS

The **Real Automóvil Club de España** (RACE; ☑902 404 545; www.race.es) is the national automobile club. They may well come to assist you in case of a breakdown, but you should obtain an emergency telephone number for Spain from your own insurer.

DRIVING LICENCES

All EU driving licences are recognised. Other foreign licences should be accompanied by an International Driving Permit (although in practice local licences are usually accepted).

HIRE

To rent a car in Spain you have to have a licence, be aged 21 or over and have a credit or debit card. Rates vary widely: the best deals tend to be in major tourist areas, including airports. Prices are especially competitive in the Balearic Islands. Expect a compact car to cost from €30 and up per day.

INSURANCE

Third-party motor insurance is a minimum requirement and it is compulsory to have an internationally recognised proof of insurance, which can be obtained from your insurer. Also ask your insurer for a European Accident Statement form, which can simplify matters in the event of an accident.

ROAD RULES

Blood-alcohol limit 0.05%.

Legal driving age for cars 18.

Legal driving age for motorcycles & scooters 16 (80cc and over) or 14 (50cc and under). A licence is required.

Motorcyclists Must use headlights at all times and wear a helmet if riding a bike of 125cc or more.

Side of the road Drive on the right.

Speed limits In built-up areas 50km/h (and in some cases, such as inner-city Barcelona, 30km/h), which increases to 100km/h on major roads and up to 120km/h on *autovías* and *autopistas* (toll-free and tolled dual-lane highways). Cars towing caravans are restricted to 80km/h.

Train

Renfe (☑902 240 202; www.renfe.es) is the national railway company. Trains are mostly modern and comfortable, and late arrivals are the exception rather than the rule. The high-speed network is in constant expansion.

Passes are valid for all long-distance Renfe trains; Inter-Rail users pay supplements on Talgo, InterCity and AVE trains. All passholders making reservations pay a small fee.

Among Spain's numerous types of trains:

Alaris, Altaria, Alvia, Arco and Avant Long-distance intermediate-speed services.

Cercanías For short hops and services to outlying suburbs and satellite towns in Madrid, Barcelona and 11 other cities.

Euromed Similar to the AVE trains, they connect Barcelona with Valencia and Alicante.

Regionales Trains operating within one region, usually stopping at all stations.

Talgo and Intercity Slower long-distance trains.

Tren de Alta Velocidad Española (AVE) High-speed trains that link Madrid with Barcelona, Burgos, Córdoba, Cuenca, Huesca, Lerida, Málaga, Seville, Valencia, Valladolid and Zaragoza. There are also Barcelona–Seville and Barcelona–Málaga services. In coming years Madrid–Cádiz and Madrid–Bilbao should come on line.

Trenhotel Overnight trains with sleeper berths.

CLASSES & COSTS

All long-distance trains have 2nd and 1st classes, known as *turista* and *preferente*. The latter is 20% to 40% more expensive.

Fares vary enormously depending on the service (faster trains cost considerably more) and, in the case of some high-speed services such as the AVE, on the time and day of travel.

Children aged between four and 12 years are entitled to a 40% discount; those aged under four travel for free (except on high-speed trains, for which they pay the same as those aged four to 12). Buying a return ticket often gives you a 10% to 20% discount on the return trip. Students and people up to 25 years of age with a Euro<26 Card (Carnet Joven in Spain) are entitled to 20% to 25% off most ticket prices.

RESERVATIONS

Reservations are recommended for long-distance trips; you can make them in train stations, Renfe offices, travel agencies and online. A growing number of stations let you pick up prebooked tickets from machines scattered about the station concourse.

Turkey

Includes »

İstanbul 765
Gallipoli Peninsula 784
İzmir 790
Selçuk 793
Ephesus 794
Bodrum 797
Fethiye 802
Kaş 806
Olympos & Çirali 809
Antalya 811
Ankara 818
Konya 820
Cappadocia 821
Göreme 823
Mt Nemrut
National Park 828
Mardin 829

Best Places to Eat

» Asmalı Cavit (p778)
» Köy Evi (p824)
» İkbal (p807)
» Reis (p804)

Best Places to Stay

» Hotel Ibrahim Pasha (p775)
» Esbelli Evi (p825)
» Hotel Villa Mahal (p805)
» Tuvana Hotel (p811)
» Assos Alarga (p788)

Why Go?

While many Turks see their country as European, Turkey packs in as many towering minarets and spice-trading bazaars as its Middle Eastern neighbours. This bridge between continents has absorbed the best of Europe and Asia. Travellers can enjoy historical hot spots, mountain outposts, expansive steppe and *caravanserai*-loads of the exotic, without forgoing comfy beds and buses.

Despite its reputation as a continental meeting point, Turkey can't be pigeonholed. Cappadocia, a dreamscape dotted with fairy chimneys (rock formations), is unlike anywhere else on the planet. Likewise, spots like Mt Nemrut (Nemrut Dağı), littered with giant stone heads, and Olympos, where Lycian ruins peek from the undergrowth, are quintessentially Turkish mixtures of natural splendour and ancient remains.

The beaches and mountains offer enough activities to impress the fussiest Ottoman sultan. Worldly pleasures include the many historic hotels, the meze to savour on panoramic terraces and, of course, Turkey's famous kebaps.

When to Go

Ankara

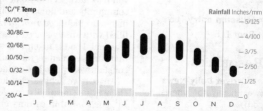

Apr–May Spring sunshine without summer crowds, apart from in İstanbul, where it is high season.

Jun–Aug İstanbul's shoulder season; music festivals and lazy summer days by the Bosphorus.

Sep–Oct Autumn walking and diving; outside of İstanbul crowds thin.

AT A GLANCE

» **Currency** Turkish lira (TL)

» **Languages** Turkish, Kurdish

» **Money** ATMs widespread; credit cards accepted in cities and tourist areas

» **Visas** On arrival

Fast Facts

» **Area** 783,562 sq km

» **Capital** Ankara

» **Country code** 📞90

» **Emergency** Police 📞155; Ambulance 📞112; Fire 📞110

Exchange Rates

Australia	A$1	TL1.88
Canada	C$1	TL1.77
Euro Zone	€1	TL2.32
Japan	¥100	TL1.94
New Zealand	NZ$1	TL1.51
UK	UK£1	TL2.75
USA	US$1	TL1.80

Set Your Budget

» **Budget hotel room** TL80

» **Midrange meal** TL9 to TL25

» **Museum entry** TL5

» **Beer** TL6

Resources

» **Hürriyet Daily News** (www.hurriyetdailynews. com)

» **Cornucopia** (www. cornucopia.net/blog)

» **tulumba.com** (www. tulumba.com)

Connections

İstanbul is well connected to Europe, with two international airports. Buses leave the *otogar* (bus station) for countries including Austria, Bulgaria, Germany, Greece, Italy, Macedonia, Romania and Slovenia.

Currently, the only daily train between İstanbul and Europe is the overnight Bosphorus/Balkan Express to Bucharest (Romania, 21 hours), Sofia (Bulgaria, 13 hours) and Belgrade (Serbia, 21½ hours). A suggested train route from London to İstanbul is the three-night journey via Paris, Munich, Vienna, Budapest and Bucharest; see www.seat61. com/turkey for more information and other routes.

Ferries connect Turkey's Aegean and Mediterranean coasts with Greek islands and Northern Cyprus; İstanbul with Ukraine; and Trabzon on the Black Sea coast with Russia.

ITINERARIES

One Week

Devote a few days to magical İstanbul, then cross the Sea of Marmara to Anatolia and head south to laid-back Selçuk or coastal Kuşadası, both convenient bases for visiting the marvellous ruins of Ephesus.

Two Weeks

From Ephesus, head inland to Pamukkale's shiny travertine formations, then return to the coast at the vibrant city of Antalya, with its Roman-Ottoman heritage quarter, and work your way around the glorious Teke Peninsula. Stop in Çıralı to see the eternal flame of the Chimaera, Kaş for activities and boat trips, and Patara for Turkey's longest beach. From Dalaman airport you can fly back to İstanbul and Europe.

Essential Food & Drink

Far from the uninspiring kebaps and stuffed vine leaves you may have seen at home, Turkish food is a celebration of community and life in its home country. Kebaps are swooningly succulent, *yaprak dolması* (stuffed vine leaves) are filled with subtly spiced rice and eating is social, slow and seasonal. Food is taken very seriously, with delicious results that vary between regions, meaning that travelling here will constantly surprise and seduce your taste buds.

Apart from kebaps, classic Turkish dishes and tipples include *köfte* (meatballs), meze, pide, *lahmacun* (Arabic pizza), *gözleme* (thin savoury crepes), *mantı* (Turkish ravioli), *börek* (filled pastries), baklava and *çay* (tea).

Rakı (a fiery, highly alcoholic aniseed drink) is best accompanied by meze, especially *beyaz peynir* (ewe's- or goat's-milk cheese) and melon, and *balık* (fish).

İSTANBUL

📞 0212 / POP 14 MILLION

Some ancient cities are the sum of their monuments. But others, such as İstanbul, factor a lot more into the equation. Here, you can visit Byzantine churches and Ottoman mosques in the morning, shop in chic boutiques during the afternoon and party at glamorous clubs through the night. In the space of a few minutes, you can hear the evocative strains of the call to prayer issuing from the Old City's minarets, the sonorous horn of a commuter ferry crossing between Europe and Asia, and the strident cries of a street hawker selling fresh seasonal produce. This marvellous metropolis is an exercise in sensory seduction like no other.

In terms of orientation, the Bosphorus strait, between the Black Sea and the Sea of Marmara, divides Europe from Asia. On its western shore, the European part of İstanbul is further divided by the Golden Horn (Haliç), an inlet of the Bosphorus, into the Old City in the southwest and Beyoğlu in the northeast.

Overlooked by the Galata Tower, the Galata Bridge (Galata Köprüsü) spans the Golden Horn between Eminönü, north of Sultanahmet in the Old City, and Karaköy. Ferries depart from Eminönü and Karaköy for the Asian shore.

Beyoğlu, uphill from Karaköy, was the city's 'European' quarter in the 19th century. The Tünel funicular railway links Karaköy up to the bottom of Beyoğlu's pedestrianised main street, İstiklal Caddesi. From here İstiklal Caddesi climbs to Taksim Sq, the heart of 'modern' İstanbul.

History

Late in the 2nd century AD, the Romans conquered the small city-state of Byzantium, which was renamed Constantinople in AD

MUSEUM PASS

The **Museum Pass İstanbul** (www.muze.gov.tr/museum_pass) offers a possible TL36 saving on entry to the Old City's major sights, and allows holders to skip admission queues.

330 after Emperor Constantine moved his capital there. Following the collapse of the Roman Empire, the city became the capital of the Christian, Greek-speaking Byzantine Empire.

In 1453, Mehmet the Conqueror (Mehmet Fatih) took Constantinople from the Byzantines and made it capital of the Ottoman Empire. During the glittering reign of Süleyman the Magnificent (1520–66), the great city was graced with many beautiful new buildings, and retained much of its charm even during the empire's long decline.

Occupied by Allied forces after WWI, the city came to be thought of as the decadent playpen of the sultans, notorious for its extravagant lifestyle, espionage and intrigue. As a result, when the Turkish Republic was proclaimed in 1923, Ankara became the new capital, in an attempt to wipe the slate clean. Nevertheless, İstanbul (Atatürk officially changed the city's name in the 1920s) remains a commercial, cultural and financial centre: Turkey's number-one city in all but title.

◉ Sights & Activities

SULTANAHMET & AROUND

The Sultanahmet area is the centre of the Old City, a World Heritage site packed with so many wonderful sights you could spend several weeks here.

Blue Mosque   MOSQUE
(Sultan Ahmet Camii; Map p770; Atmeydanı Caddesi; ⊘9am-12.15pm, 2-4.30pm & 5.30-6.30pm Sat-Thu, 9-11.15am, 2.30-4.30pm & 5.30-6.30pm Fri; 🚇Sultanahmet) In this 17th-century Ottoman mosque, Sultan Ahmet I attempted to rival the grandeur and beauty of the Byzantines' nearby Aya Sofya – with some success. Its exterior creates a visual wham-bam effect similar to the one achieved by Aya Sofya's interior, with voluptuous curves, six slender minarets and the biggest courtyard of all Ottoman mosques. Inside, the blue İznik tiles that give the building its unofficial name number in the tens of thousands, there are 260 windows and the central prayer space is huge.

TURKEY İSTANBUL

İSTANBUL IN TWO DAYS

On day one, visit the **Blue Mosque**, **Aya Sofya** and **Basilica Cistern** in the morning and the **Grand Bazaar** in the afternoon. Cross the Golden Horn from Sultanahmet for dinner in **Beyoğlu**.

Spend your second morning in **Topkapı Palace**, then board a private excursion boat for a **Bosphorus cruise**. Afterwards, walk up through Galata (or catch the funicular) to **İstiklal Caddesi** to enjoy Beyoğlu's nightlife again.

BLACK SEA
(KARADENIZ)

BULGARIA

Burgas

Sinop
İnebolu
Cide
Amasra
Zonguldak
Safranbolu
Kastamonu
Karabük
Tosya
Osmancı

Kapıkule
Edirne
Kırklareli
GREECE
İpsala Tekirdağ
Çorlu
İstanbul
Kocaeli
(İzmit)
Gerede
Kurşunlu
Ilgaz
Çankırı
Çorum
Keşan
The Bosphorus
Sea of Marmara
Darıca
Yalova
Adapazarı
Bolu
Sungurlu
Gelibolu
The Dardanelles
Gemlik
İznik
Ankara
Hattu
Gallipoli Peninsula
Lapseki
Bandırma
Bursa
Sakarya River
Eskişehir
Gordion
Kırıkkale
Yozg
Çanakkale
Uludağ (2543m)
Polatlı
Troy (Truva)
Ayvacık
Edremit
Balıkesir
Kütahya
Kırşehir
Lesvos
Assos
Ayvalık
Afyon
Cappadocia
Göre
Bergama
Pergamum
Uşak
Akşehir
Mustafapaşa
Nevşehir
Ü
Chios
Yeni Foça
Aliağa
Manisa
Egirdir Gölü
Beyşehir Gölü
Tuz Gölü (Salt Lake)
Aksaray
Derinkuyu
Yah
İzmir
Sardis
Çivril
Çeşme
Odemis
Hierapolis/Pamukkale
Konya
Niğ
Selçuk
Aydın
Nazilli
Denizli
Isparta
Beyşehir
Ereğli
Ikaria
Kuşadası
Priene
Ephesus
Afrodisias
Burdur
Suğla Gölü
Karaman
Samos
Didyma
Milas
Yatağan
Çavdır
Perge
Akseki
Taurus Mountains
Ada
Güllük
Gökova (Akyaka)
Muğla
Termessos
Antalya
Side
Kırobası
Tarsus
Mers (İçel)
Bodrum
Ortaca
Dalaman
Aspendos
Kemer
Uzuncaburç
Kos
Marmaris
Fethiye
Ölüdeniz
Çıralı
Olympos
Alanya
Silifke
Kızkalesi
Olukbaşı
Patara Beach
Kaş
Finike
Anamurium
Meis/Kastellorizo
Kekova
Lycian Way
Anamur

Köprülü Kanyon

Lefkoşa/Lefkosia (Nicosia)
CYPRUS

Crete

MEDITERRANEAN SEA
(AKDENIS)

Turkey Highlights

1 Uncover **İstanbul** (p765), the glorious one-time Ottoman and Byzantine capital and one of the world's truly great cities.

2 Sleep in a fairy chimney in jaw-droppingly bizarre and beautiful **Cappadocia** (p821).

3 Imagine the tourists streaming down the Curetes Way are wearing togas in **Ephesus** (p794), one of the greatest surviving Graeco-Roman cities.

4 Hike through the Mediterranean countryside on

a section of the 500km **Lycian Way** (p803).

5 Explore Turkey's exotic east at **Nemrut Dağı** (p828), where decapitated stone heads litter a king's burial mound.

6 Cruise over a sunken city at **Kekova** (p807), one of many blue voyages offered at Aegean and Mediterranean harbours.

7 Wander the Roman-Ottoman old quarter of **Antalya** (p811), a stylish Mediterranean hub and gateway to the Turquoise Coast.

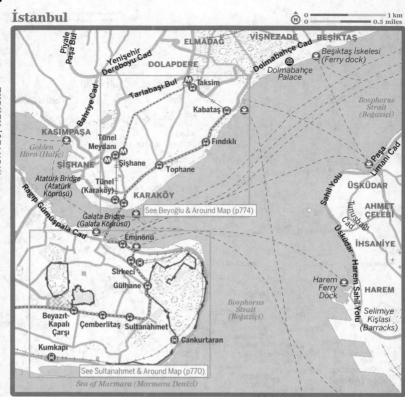

To the southeast, the **Arasta Bazaar** (Map p770; 🚇Sultanahmet), a great place for hassle-free shopping, specialises in carpets, jewellery, textiles and ceramics.

Topkapı Palace
PALACE

(Topkapı Sarayı; Map p770; www.topkapisarayi.gov.tr; Babıhümayun Caddesi; palace TL25, Harem TL15; ⏰9am-6pm Wed-Mon mid-Apr–Sep, to 4pm Oct–mid-Apr, Harem closes 4.30pm Apr-Oct, 3.30pm Nov-Mar; 🚇Sultanahmet) This great palace features in more colourful stories than most of the world's royal residences put together. Mehmet the Conqueror started work on the palace shortly after the Conquest in 1453, and Ottoman sultans lived in this rarefied environment until the 19th century. Visiting the palace's opulent **pavilions**, jewel-filled **Treasury** and sprawling **Harem**, once inhabited by libidinous sultans, ambitious courtiers, beautiful concubines and scheming eunuchs, gives a glimpse of life in the Ottoman court.

🔝 Grand Bazaar
MARKET

(Kapalı Çarşı, Covered Market; Map p770; www.kapalicarsi.org.tr; ⏰9am-7pm Mon-Sat; 🚻; 🚇Beyazıt-Kapalı Çarşı) This colourful and chaotic bazaar is the heart of the Old City and has been so for centuries. Starting as a small vaulted *bedesten* (warehouse) in 1461, it grew to cover a vast area as laneways between the *bedesten*, neighbouring shops and *hans* (*caravanserais* – trader's inns) were roofed and the market assumed the sprawling, labyrinthine form that it retains today.

Be sure to peep through doorways to discover hidden *hans*, veer down narrow laneways to watch artisans at work and wander the main thoroughfares to differentiate treasures from tourist tack.

Basilica Cistern
CISTERN

(Yerebatan Sarnıçı; Map p770; www.yerebatan.com; Yerebatan Caddesi 13; admission TL10; ⏰9am-6.30pm; 🚇Sultanahmet) Across the tram lines from the Aya Sofya is the entrance to this majestic underground chamber, built by Justinian in AD 532 and visited by James Bond in *From Russia with Love*. The vast, atmospheric, column-filled cistern stored up to 80,000 cubic metres of water for the Great Palace and surrounding buildings. Its cavernous depths stay wonderfully cool in the summer.

İstanbul Archaeology Museums   MUSEUM
(Map p770; www.istanbularkeologi.gov.tr; Osman Hamdi Bey Yokuşu, Gülhane; admission TL10; ⊘9am-6pm Tue-Sun mid-Apr–Sep, to 4pm Oct–mid-Apr; ⌂Gülhane) Downhill from the Topkapı Palace's First Court, this superb museum complex houses ancient artefacts, artistic treasures and objects showcasing Anatolian history. The **Archaeology Museum** houses an outstanding collection of classical statuary, including the magnificent sarcophagi from the Royal Necropolis at Side in Lebanon. The 'İstanbul Through the Ages' exhibition traces the city's history through its neighbourhoods during different periods.

In a separate building, the **Museum of the Ancient Orient** houses Hittite and other pre-Islamic archaeological finds. Also in the complex is the **Tiled Pavilion** (1472), with a display of Seljuk, Anatolian and Ottoman tiles and ceramics.

Hippodrome   PARK
(Atmeydanı; Map p770; ⌂Sultanahmet) The Byzantine emperors loved nothing more than an afternoon at the chariot races, and this rectangular arena was their venue of choice. In its heyday, it was decorated by **obelisks** and **statues**, some of which remain in place today. Recently relandscaped, it is one of the city's most popular meeting places and promenades, and was the scene of many popular uprisings during the Byzantine and Ottoman eras.

Museum of Turkish & Islamic Arts   MUSEUM
(Türk ve Islam Eserleri Müzesi; Map p770; www.tiem.gov.tr; Atmeydanı Caddesi 46; admission TL10; ⊘9am-6.30pm Tue-Sun Apr-Oct, to 4.30pm Nov-Mar; ⌂Sultanahmet) This 16th-century Ottoman palace on the western edge of the Hippodrome houses a magnificent collection of artefacts, including exquisite examples of calligraphy and a collection of antique carpets that is generally held to be the best in the world. Don't miss the extraordinary collection of carpets in the *divanhane* (ceremonial hall), and stop for a Turkish coffee at **Müzenin Kahvesi** (⊘9am-6.30pm Tue-Sun Apr-Oct, to 4.30pm Nov-Mar) in the courtyard.

Süleymaniye Mosque   MOSQUE
(Map p770; Prof Sıddık Sami Onar Caddesi; ⌂Beyazıt-Kapalı Çarşı) One of the grandest Ottoman mosque complexes dominates the Golden Horn from atop one of the city's seven hills, providing a prominent landmark. It was commissioned by the greatest Ottoman sultan, Süleyman the Magnificent (r 1520–66), and designed by Mimar Sinan, the most famous imperial architect.

Spice Bazaar   MARKET
(Mısır Çarşısı, Egyptian Market; Map p770; ⊘8am-6pm Mon-Sat, 9am-6pm Sun; ⌂Eminönü) This bustling marketplace, constructed in the 1660s, was called the Egyptian Market because it was famous for selling goods shipped in from Cairo. As well as *baharat* (spices),

---

DON'T MISS

AYA SOFYA

No doubt you will gasp at the overblown splendour of the **Aya Sofya** (Hagia Sophia; Map p770; www.ayasofyamuzesi.gov.tr; Aya Sofya Meydanı 1; adult/under 12yr TL25/free; ⊘9am-6pm Tue-Sun mid-Apr–Sep, to 4pm Oct–mid-Apr; ⌂Sultanahmet). Known as Sancta Sophia in Latin, Haghia Sofia in Greek and the Church of the Divine Wisdom in English, it is one of the world's most glorious buildings. Built as part of Emperor Justinian's effort to restore the greatness of the Roman Empire, it was completed in AD 537 and reigned as the grandest church in Christendom until the Ottomans took Constantinople in 1453. The victorious Mehmet the Conqueror converted the building to a mosque and it continued in that role until Atatürk declared it a museum in 1935.The basilica's interior, with its seemingly floating dome, frescos, and glittering mosaics of Byzantine emperors and empresses alongside Jesus and Mary, is truly a knockout.

Afterwards, visit the ornate **Aya Sofya Tombs** (Aya Sofya Müzesi Padişah Türbeleri; Map p770; Kabasakal Caddesi; ⊘9am-5pm; ⌂Sultanahmet), the final resting place of five Ottoman sultans.

Sultanahmet & Around

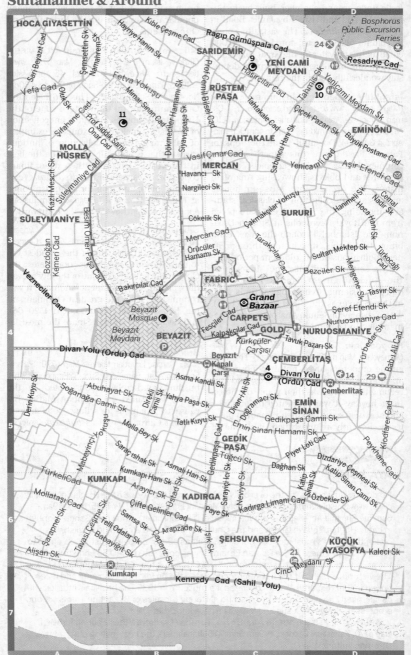

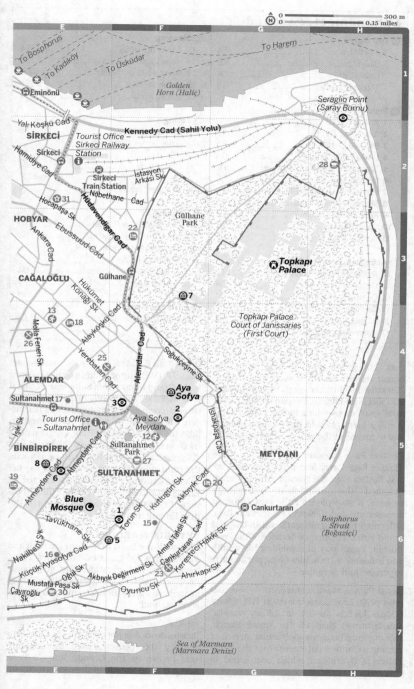

Sultanahmet & Around

◎ **Top Sights**
Aya Sofya F4
Blue Mosque E6
Grand Bazaar C4
Topkapı Palace G3

◎ **Sights**
1 Arasta Bazaar F6
2 Aya Sofya Tombs F5
3 Basilica Cistern F5
4 Divan Yolu Caddesi......................C4
5 Great Palace Mosaic Museum........F6
6 Hippodrome E5
7 İstanbul Archaeology Museums......F3
8 Museum of Turkish & Islamic Arts....E5
9 Rüstem Paşa Mosque C1
10 Spice Bazaar D1
11 Süleymaniye Mosque..................B2

◎ **Activities, Courses & Tours**
12 Ayasofya Hürrem Sultan Hamamı F5
13 Cağaloğlu Hamamı E4
14 Çemberlitaş Hamamı D4
15 Cooking Alaturka........................F6
16 İstanbul Walks...........................E6
17 Urban Adventures E5

◎ **Sleeping**
18 Agora Life Hotel.........................E4
19 Hotel Ibrahim Pasha E5
20 Marmara Guesthouse..................G5
21 Saruhan Hotel............................C6
22 Sirkeci Konak.............................F3

◎ **Eating**
23 Ahırkapı Balıkçısı.......................F6
24 Balık Ekmek (Fish Kebap)
  Boats D1
25 Cihannüma E4
  Cooking Alaturka.................(see 15)
26 Sefa Restaurant E4

◎ **Drinking**
27 Derviş Aile Çay Bahçesi F5
28 Set Üstü Çay Bahçesi H2
29 Türk Ocağı Kültür ve Sanat
  Merkezi İktisadi
  İşletmesi Çay Bahçesi.................D4
30 Yeni Marmara E7

◎ **Entertainment**
31 Hocapaşa Culture Centre.............E2

nuts, honeycomb and olive-oil soaps, the bazaar sells truckloads of *incir* (figs), *lokum* (Turkish delight) and *pestil* (fruit pressed into sheets and dried). Despite the increasing number of shops selling tourist trinkets, this is still a great place to buy edible souvenirs and to marvel at the well-preserved building.

Rüstem Paşa Mosque MOSQUE
(Rüstem Paşa Camii; Map p770; Hasırcılar Caddesi, Rüstem Paşa; ⓜEminönü) Mimar Sinan designed this diminutive 16th-century mosque, a showpiece of the best Ottoman architecture and tilework, for Rüstem Paşa, Süleyman the Magnificent's son-in-law and grand vizier. The preponderance of tiles was Rüstem Paşa's way of signalling his wealth and influence – İznik tiles being particularly expensive and desirable.

Great Palace Mosaic Museum MUSEUM
(Map p770; Torun Sokak; admission TL8; ⓣ9am-6.30pm Tue-Sun Apr-Oct, to 4.30pm Nov-Mar; ⓜSultanahmet) Next to the Arasta Bazaar, this museum houses a spectacular stretch of mosaic Byzantine pavement from the Great Palace of Byzantium, which once stood in this area.

Divan Yolu Caddesi HISTORIC AREA
(Map p770) Walking or taking a tram westward to the Grand Bazaar from Sultanahmet, you'll pass various monuments, including a shady Ottoman cemetery with an attached tea garden, **Türk Ocağı Kültür ve Sanat Merkezi İktisadi İşletmesi Çay Bahçesi** (Map p770; cnr Divan Yolu & Bab-ı Ali Caddesis; ⓣ8am-midnight; ⓜÇemberlitaş). Also on the right, overlooking the tram stop of the same name, is the tall column known as **Çemberlitaş**, erected by Emperor Constantine to celebrate the dedication of Constantinople as capital of the Roman Empire in AD 330.

BEYOĞLU & AROUND
Beyoğlu is the heart of modern İstanbul and *the* hot spot for galleries, boutiques, cafes, restaurants and nightlife. The neighbourhood is a showcase of cosmopolitan Turkey at its best – miss Beyoğlu and you haven't seen İstanbul.

İstiklal Caddesi STREET
(Independence Ave; Map p774) In the late 19th century, this pedestrianised thoroughfare was known as the Grande Rue de Pera, and it carried the life of the modern city up

and down its lively promenade. It's still the centre of İstanbullu life, and a stroll along its length is a must. You can also catch the antique tram (see p780). Come between 4pm and 8pm daily – especially on Friday and Saturday – and you'll see İstiklal at its busy best.

Galata Tower TOWER

(Galata Kulesi; Map p774; www.galatatower.net; Galata Meydanı, Galata; admission TL12; ⏰9am-8pm; ⛴Karaköy) Constructed in 1348, this cylindrical tower was the city's tallest structure for centuries, and it still dominates the skyline north of the Golden Horn. Its vertiginous upper balcony offers 360-degree views; the steep admission cost is just about worth it if you visit when it's quiet and don't have to queue.

Dolmabahçe Palace PALACE

(Dolmabahçe Sarayı; www.millisaraylar.gov.tr; Dolmabahçe Caddesi, Beşiktaş; Selâmlık TL30, Harem TL20, joint ticket TL40; ⏰9am-6pm Tue-Wed & Fri-Sun Mar-Sep, to 4pm Oct-Feb; ⛴Kabataş) On the Bosphorus shore, northeast of Kabataş tram and funicular stops, this grandiose 19th-century royal pad housed some of the last Ottoman sultans. Its neobaroque and neoclassical flourishes reflect the decadence of the decaying empire. The palace was guaranteed a place in the Turkish history books when Atatürk died here on 10 November 1938 and all the palace clocks stopped.

Visitors are taken on separate guided tours of two sections: the over-the-top **Selamlık** (ceremonial suites) and slightly more restrained **Harem**. Afterwards, make sure you visit the **Crystal Kiosk**, with its fairy tale-like conservatory featuring a crystal piano.

BOSPHORUS

Don't leave İstanbul without exploring the Bosphorus on a cruise on one of the boats departing from Eminönü. Private excursion boats (TL10, 90 minutes) travel to Anadolu Hisarı and back, without stopping. İDO's **Bosphorus Public Excursion Ferry** (www.ido.com.tr; Boğaz İskelesi; long tour 1 way/return TL15/25, short tour TL10; ⏰long tour 10.35am, plus 1.35pm Apr–Oct & noon summer, short tour 2.30pm Apr-Oct) travels all the way to Anadolu Kavağı at the Black Sea (90 minutes one way), stopping en route on the European and Asian sides. Its two-hour 'short tour' travels to Fatih Bridge and back.

The shores are sprinkled with monuments and sights, including the Dolmabahçe Palace, the majestic Bosphorus Bridge, numerous mosques, lavish *yalıs* (waterfront wooden summer residences) and affluent suburbs on the hills above the strait.

For the thrill of crossing from Europe to Asia (and back), you can catch a commuter ferry across the Bosphorus (TL2) from Eminönü, Karaköy or Beşiktaş (near Dolmabahçe Palace) to Kadıköy.

 Courses

Cooking Alaturka COOKING

(Map p770; ☎0536 338 0896; www.cookingalaturka.com; Akbıyık Caddesi 72a, Cankurtaran; cooking class per person €60; ⛴Sultanahmet) Dutch-born Eveline Zoutendijk's hands-on classes offer a great introduction to Turkish cuisine, suitable for both novices and experienced cooks, and include a five-course meal in the school's restaurant (p777).

Turkish Flavours COOKING

(☎0532 218 0653; www.turkishflavours.com; Apartment 3, Vali Konağı Caddesi 14; per person tours TL180-290, cooking classes TL180) As well as running excellent foodie tours of the Spice Bazaar and Kadıköy markets, which include a huge lunch (TL290 per person), Selin Rozanes conducts small-group cooking classes in her elegant Nişantaşı home (TL180 per person). The results are enjoyed over a four-course lunch with drinks.

☞ Tours

İstanbul Walks WALKING TOUR

(Map p770; ☎212-516 6300; www.istanbulwalks.net; 2nd fl, Şifa Hamamı Sokak 1; walking tours €25-75, child under 6yr free; ⛴Sultanahmet) This small company, run by a group of history buffs, offers a range of guided walking tours, concentrating on İstanbul's various neighbourhoods or taking in major monuments including Topkapı Palace. Student discounts are available.

Culinary Backstreets WALKING TOUR

(www.culinarybackstreets.com) Full-day walking tours of the Old City and Beyoğlu (with lunch), and a colourful evening tasting regional dishes from southeastern Anatolia in a progression of eateries. The guides produce the excellent foodie blog of the same name.

Urban Adventures WALKING, CULTURAL TOURS

(Map p770; ☎212-512 7144; www.urbanadventures.com; 1st fl, Ticarethane Sokak 11; all tours TL50; ⏰8.30am-5.30pm; ⛴Sultanahmet) International

Beyoğlu & Around

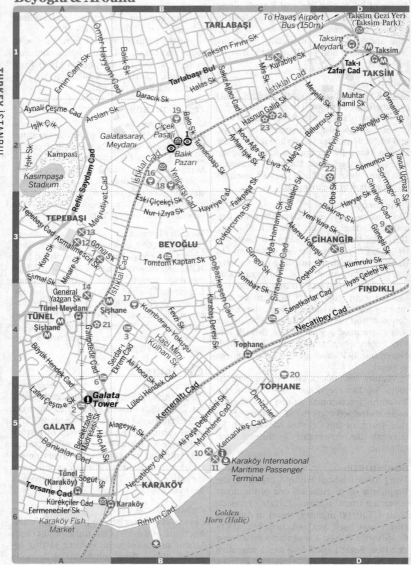

tour company Intrepid offers tours including a popular four-hour guided walk around Sultanahmet and the Bazaar District. The 'Home Cooked İstanbul' tour includes a no-frills dinner with a local family in their home.

🛏 Sleeping

During low season (October to April, but not around Christmas or Easter) you should be able to negotiate discounts of at least 20%. Before confirming bookings, ask if the hotel will give you a discount for cash payment

Beyoğlu & Around

◉ Top Sights
Galata Tower...................................A5

◉ Sights
1 İstiklal Caddesi.............................B2

🛏 Sleeping
2 Anemon Galata..............................A5
3 Beş Oda.......................................B4
4 TomTom Suites..............................B3
5 Witt Istanbul Hotel.........................C4
6 World House Hostel.........................A5

⊗ Eating
7 Asmalı Cavit..................................A3
8 Demeti...D3
9 Jash..D3
10 Karaköy Lokantası.........................B5
11 Lokanta Maya...............................C5
12 Meze by Lemon Tree......................A3
13 Mikla..A3
14 Sofyalı 9.....................................A4
Zencefil...................................(see 15)
15 Zübeyir Ocakbaşı...........................C1

☕ Drinking
16 360..B2
17 Leb-i Derya..................................B4
18 Litera...B2
Mikla.......................................(see 13)
19 Nevizade Sokak.............................B2
20 Tophane Nargile Cafes....................C4

✴ Entertainment
21 Galata Mevlevi Museum..................A4
22 MiniMüzikHol................................D2
23 Munzur Cafe & Bar.........................C2
24 Toprak..C2

SULTANAHMET & AROUND

The Sultanahmet area has the most budget and midrange options, as well as some more luxurious accommodation. Most have stunning views from their roof terraces, and are close to the Old City's sights.

TOP CHOICE **Hotel Ibrahim Pasha** BOUTIQUE HOTEL €€
(Map p770; ☎212-518 0394; www.ibrahimpasha.com; Terzihane Sokak 7; r standard €99-195, deluxe €139-265; ❄@⑤; 🚊Sultanahmet) Successfully combining Ottoman style with contemporary decor, the Ibrahim Pasha offers comfortable rooms, high levels of service, gorgeous ground-floor common areas and a terrace bar with Blue Mosque views.

(usually 5% or 10%) and whether there are discounts for extended stays. A pick-up from the airport is often included if you stay more than three nights. Book ahead from May to September and for the Christmas–New Year period.

HAMAMS

After a long day's sightseeing, few things could be better than relaxing in a *hamam* (Turkish bath). The ritual is invariably the same. First, you'll be shown to a cubicle where you can undress, store your clothes and wrap the provided *peştamal* (cloth) around you. Then an attendant will lead you through to the hot room, where you sit and sweat for a while.

It's cheapest to bring soap and a towel and wash yourself. The hot room is ringed with individual basins, which you can fill from the taps above, before sluicing the water over yourself with a plastic scoop. It's most enjoyable to let an attendant do it for you, dousing you with warm water and scrubbing you with a coarse cloth mitten. You'll be lathered with a sudsy swab, rinsed off and shampooed. When all this is complete, you'll likely be offered a massage.

Traditional *hamams* have separate sections for men and women or admit men and women at separate times. In tourist areas, many *hamams* are happy for foreign men and women to bathe together.

The Old City's pricey tourist *hamams*, including the following, are well worth a visit for the their gorgeous historic interiors, although their massages are generally short and not particularly good.

Ayasofya Hürrem Sultan Hamamı (Map p770; ☎212-517 3535; www.ayasofyahamami. com; Aya Sofya Meydanı; bath treatments €70-165, massages €40-75; ☺8am-11pm; ☒Sultanahmet) This restored 16th-century *hamam* offers the Old City's most luxurious traditional bath experience.

Cağaloğlu Hamamı (Map p770; ☎212-522 2424; www.cagalogluhamami.com.tr; Yerebatan Caddesi 34; bath, scrub & massage packages €50-110; ☺8am-10pm; ☒Sultanahmet) This 18th-century *hamam* is undoubtedly the city's most atmospheric. Bath services are overpriced; sign up for the self-service treatment (€30) only.

Çemberlitaş Hamamı (Map p770; ☎212-522 7974; Vezir Han Caddesi 8; bath, scrub & soap massage €29; ☺6am-midnight; ☒Çemberlitaş) Mimar Sinan designed this beautiful bathhouse dating back to 1584.

TOP CHOICE **Sirkeci Konak** HOTEL €€
(Map p770; ☎212-528 4344; www.sirkecikonak. com; Taya Hatun Sokak 5, Sirkeci; standard d €155-185, superior & deluxe r €170-270; ☒@☎☒; ☒Gülhane) Overlooking Gülhane Park, this terrific hotel's rooms are impeccably clean, well sized and loaded with amenities. It has a restaurant, a roof terrace, an indoor pool and a *hamam* (Turkish bath) and incredibly helpful staff. The complimentary entertainment program includes cooking classes, walking tours and afternoon teas.

Marmara Guesthouse PENSION €
(Map p770; ☎212-638 3638; www.marmaraguesthouse.com; Terbıyık Sokak 15, Cankurtaran; s €30-65, d €40-70, f €60-100; ☒@; ☒Sultanahmet) Manager Elif Aytekin and her family go out of their way to make guests feel welcome, offering plenty of advice and serving a delicious breakfast on the vine-covered, sea-facing roof terrace. Rooms have comfortable beds and double-glazed windows.

Saruhan Hotel HOTEL €
(Map p770; ☎212-458 7608; www.saruhanhotel. com; Cinci Meydanı Sokak 34, Kadırga; s €25-65, d €35-70, f €60-100; ☒@☎; ☒Çemberlitaş) In the quiet residential pocket of Kadırga, the impressive family-run Saruhan offers comfortable and well-equipped rooms plus a lovely terrace with a sea view. It's a 20-minute walk to Sultanahmet's sights and a shorter (but steep) walk to the Grand Bazaar.

Agora Life Hotel HOTEL €€
(Map p770; ☎212-526 1181; www.agoralifehotel.com; Cağoloğlu Hamamı Sokak 6, Cağoloğlu; s €69-129, d €79-209, ste €199-259; ☒@☎) This hotel in a quiet cul-de-sac focuses on service and quiet elegance as its signatures. There are plenty of amenities in the rooms, and the rooftop terrace has a simply extraordinary view. Opt for a deluxe or suite room if possible.

BEYOĞLU & AROUND

Stay here to avoid the Old City touts, and because buzzing, bohemian Beyoğlu has

İstanbul's best wining, dining and shopping. It's also where most of the suite hotels and apartment rentals are located.

TOP CHOICE Beş Oda
BOUTIQUE HOTEL €€

(Map p774; ☎212-252 7501; www.5oda.com; Şahkulu Bostan Sokak 16, Galata; ste €85-150; ✳@🌐; 🚇Karaköy, then funicular to Tünel) The name means 'Five Rooms', and that's exactly what this stylish and friendly suite hotel in bohemian Galata is offering. Suites have equipped kitchenette, lounge area, custom-designed furniture, large bed and black-out curtains.

Witt Istanbul Hotel
BOUTIQUE HOTEL €€€

(Map p774; ☎212-293 1500; www.wittistanbul. com; Defterdar Yokuşu 26, Cihangir; ste €160-390; ✳@🌐; 🚇Tophane) Showcasing countless designer features, this stylish apartment hotel in trendy Cihangir has 18 suites with fully equipped kitchenette, seating area, CD/DVD player, iPod dock, Nespresso machine, king-sized bed and huge bathroom.

TomTom Suites
BOUTIQUE HOTEL €€€

(Map p774; ☎212-292 4949; www.tomtomsuites. com; Tomtom Kaptan Sokak 18; ste €185-720; 🚇Karaköy, then funicular to Tünel) This suite hotel occupies a former Franciscan nunnery, with understated but elegant contemporary decor, impressive bathrooms and beautifully appointed suites. There's also a rooftop bar/restaurant with fantastic views

Anemon Galata
HOTEL €€

(Map p774; ☎212-293 2343; www.anemonhotels. com; cnr Galata Kulesi Sokak & Büyük Hendek Sokak, Galata; s US$140-210, d US$160-230, ste US$225-270; ✳@; 🚇Karaköy) Located on the attractive square surrounding Galata Tower, this 19th-century wooden building has been completely rebuilt inside. Rooms are elegantly decorated and well equipped; some have water views. There's a rooftop bar/restaurant with great views and an atmospheric basement wine bar.

World House Hostel
HOSTEL €

(Map p774; ☎212-293 5520; www.worldhouseistan-bul.com; Galipdede Caddesi 85, Galata; d €45-55; @🌐; 🚇Karaköy, then funicular to Tünel) Reasonably small and very friendly, World House is excellently located: close to Beyoğlu's entertainment strips but not too far from the sights in Sultanahmet. There are large and small dorms (one shower for every six beds), but none are female-only.

✖ Eating

İstanbul is a food-lover's paradise, but Sultanahmet has the least impressive range of eating options; we recommend crossing the Galata Bridge to join the locals.

If we've included a telephone number in the review, it means you should book ahead.

İstanbul Eats (www.culinarybackstreets.com /istanbul) is a good local foodie website.

SULTANAHMET & AROUND

İstanbul's favourite fast-food treat is the *balık ekmek* (fish kebap). On bobbing boats tied to the quay at the Eminönü end of Galata Bridge, fish fillets are grilled and crammed into fresh bread. You can buy the resulting snack at the adjoining stands (Map p770) on dry land for about TL5.

Avoid the rip-off eateries near the accommodation and bars on Akbıyık Caddesi.

TOP CHOICE Ahırkapı Balıkçısı
SEAFOOD €€

(Map p770; ☎212-518 4988; Keresteci Hakkı Sokak 46, Cankurtaran; meze TL5-25, fish TL15-70; ⊙4-11pm; 🚇Sultanahmet) Tiny and relatively cheap, this neighbourhood fish restaurant's food is so good (and the nearby eating alternatives are so bad) that we're sharing the locals' secret.

Cihannüma
TURKISH €€€

(Map p770; ☎212-520 7676; www.cihannuma istanbul.com; And Hotel, Yerebatan Caddesi 18; meze TL5-19, mains TL27-47; 🚇Sultanahmet) The view from the top-floor restaurant of this modest hotel is probably the best in the Old City. You can see as far as the Dolmabahçe Palace and Bosphorus Bridge, and it all provides a stunning backdrop for a menu showcasing good kebaps, Ottoman-influenced stews and a few vegetarian dishes.

Cooking Alaturka
TURKISH €€

(Map p770; ☎212-458 5919; www.cookingalaturka. com; Akbıyık Caddesi 72a, Cankurtaran; set lunch or dinner TL50; ⊙lunch Mon-Sat & dinner by reservation Mon-Sat; 🍴; 🚇Sultanahmet) This tranquil Dutch-Turkish restaurant serves a set four-course menu of simple Anatolian dishes. The menu can be tailored to suit vegetarians or those with food allergies (call ahead). No children under six at dinner and no credit cards.

Sefa Restaurant
TURKISH €

(Map p770; Nuruosmaniye Caddesi 17; portions TL7-12, kebaps TL12-18; ⊙7am-5pm; 🍴; 🚇Sultanahmet)

DON'T MISS

MEYHANES

A classic İstanbul night out involves carousing to live *fasıl*, a raucous local form of gypsy music, in Beyoğlu's *meyhanes* (Turkish taverns). A dizzying array of meze and fish dishes is on offer, washed down with *rakı*. On Friday and Saturday nights, the *meyhane* precinct **Nevizade Sokak** (Map p774) literally heaves with merrymakers.

Good, upmarket *meyhanes* include the following:

Asmalı Cavit (Asmalı Meyhane; Map p774; ☏212-292 4950; Asmalımescit Sokak 16, Asmalımescit; mezes TL6-20, mains TL18-24; ◨Karaköy, then funicular to Tünel)Quite possibly the city's best *meyhane*. Stand-out dishes include *yaprak ciğer* (liver fried with onions), *patlıcan salatası* (eggplant salad), *muska boreği* (filo stuffed with beef and onion) and *kalamar tava* (fried calamari).

Karaköy Lokantası (Map p774; ☏212-292 4455; Kemankeş Caddesi 37a, Karaköy; mezes TL6-10, portions TL7-12, grills TL11-16; ◷dinner daily, lunch Mon-Sat; ◪; ◨Karaköy) Known for its gorgeous tiled interior, genial owner and bustling vibe, the *lokanta* morphs into a *meyhane* at night.

Sofyalı 9 (Map p774; ☏212-245 0362; Sofyalı Sokak 9, Asmalımescit; mezes TL2.50-10, mains TL13-25; ◷closed Sun; ◨Karaköy, then funicular to Tünel) The food is fresh and tasty, and the atmosphere is convivial. Stick to meze rather than ordering mains.

Demeti (Map p774; ☏212-244 0628; www.demeti.com.tr; Şimşirci Sokak 6, Cihangir; mezes TL5-20, mains TL16-25; ◷4pm-2am Mon-Sat; ◨Kabataş, then funicular to Taksim) Bosphorus views from the terrace and occasional live music.

Jash (Map p774; ☏212-244 3042; www.jashistanbul.com; Cihangir Caddesi 9, Cihangir; mezes TL8-20, mains TL20-42; ◷lunch & dinner; ◨Kabataş, then funicular to Taksim) Armenian specialities and, at weekends, live accordion feature at Cihangir's bijou *meyhane*.

Locals rate this (unlicensed) place near the bazaar, which serves *hazır yemek* (ready-made) dishes and kebaps at reasonable prices. Order from an English menu or choose daily specials from the bain-marie, and arrive earlyish for lunch because many dishes run out by 1.30pm.

BEYOĞLU & AROUND

TOP CHOICE Lokanta Maya MODERN TURKISH €€€
(Map p774; ☏212-252 6884; www.lokantamaya. com; Kemankeş Caddesi 35a, Karaköy; meze TL11-28, mains TL26-35; ◷lunch Mon-Sat, dinner Tue-Sat, brunch Sun; ◪; ◨Karaköy) At her stylish restaurant near the Karaköy docks, chef Didem Şenol showcases her light, flavoursome, occasionally quirky and always assured food. Lunch is cheaper and more casual than dinner.

Zübeyir Ocakbaşı KEBAP €€
(Map p774; ☏212-293 3951; www.zubeyirocakbasi. com; Bekar Sokak 28; meze TL4-6, kebaps TL10-20; ◷noon-1am; ◨Kabataş, then funicular to Taksim) At this popular *ocakbaşı* (grill house), top-quality meats are grilled on handsome copper-hooded barbecues: spicy chicken wings and Adana kebaps, flavoursome ribs,

pungent liver kebaps and well-marinated lamb *şiş* kebaps (small pieces of lamb grilled on a skewer).

Meze by Lemon Tree MODERN TURKISH €€€
(Map p774; ☏212-252 8302; www.mezze.com.tr; Meşrutiyet Caddesi 83b, Tepebaşı; meze TL8-25, mains TL26-36; ◨Karaköy, then funicular to Tünel) Chef Gençay Üçok creates some of the most delicious, modern Turkish food in the city, including triumphs such as the monkfish casserole, and grilled lamb sirloin with baked potatoes and red beets.

Mikla MODERN TURKISH €€€
(Map p774; ☏212-293 5656; www.miklarestaurant. com; Marmara Pera Hotel, Meşrutiyet Caddesi 15, Tepebaşı; appetisers TL25-38, mains TL51-79; ◷dinner; ◨Karaköy, then funicular to Tünel) Local celebrity chef Mehmet Gürs is a master of Mod Med, and the Turkish accents on the menu here make his food memorable. Extraordinary views, luxe surrounds and professional service complete the experience.

Zencefil VEGETARIAN €
(Map p774; Kurabiye Sokak 8; soup TL7-9, mains TL9-17; ◷10am-11pm Mon-Sat, noon-10pm Sun; ◪; ◨Kabataş, then funicular to Taksim) Zencefil's

interior is comfortable and stylish, with a glassed courtyard and bright colour scheme, and its food is 100% homemade, fresh and varied. One chicken dish always features on the otherwise strictly vegetarian menu.

 Drinking & Entertainment

For an overview of what's on, pick up *Time Out İstanbul*, check out its *Istanbul Beat* (www.istanbulbeatblog.com) blog and visit the *Biletix* (www.biletix.com), where you can buy tickets for major events.

SULTANAHMET & AROUND

Sultanahmet isn't as happening as Beyoğlu, but it has a few watering holes. The area's alcohol-free, atmosphere-rich *çay bahçesi* (tea gardens) and *kahvehanes* (coffee houses) are great for relaxing and sampling that great Turkish institution, the *nargile* (water pipe), along with a *Türk kahvesi* (Turkish coffee) or *çay*.

Set Üstü Çay Bahçesi TEAHOUSE
(Map p770; Gülhane Park, Sultanahmet; ⊙9am-10.30pm; 🚇Gülhane) Come to this terraced tea garden to watch the ferries plying the route from Europe to Asia and enjoy an excellent pot of tea.

Yeni Marmara TEAHOUSE
(Map p770; Çayıroğlu Sokak, Küçük Ayasofya; ⊙10am-1am; 🚇Sultanahmet) This is the genuine article: a neighbourhood teahouse frequented by backgammon-playing regulars who slurp tea and puff on *nargiles*. In winter a wood stove keeps the place cosy; in summer patrons sit on the rear terrace, overlooking the Sea of Marmara.

Derviş Aile Çay Bahçesi TEAHOUSE
(Map p770; Mimar Mehmet Ağa Caddesi; ⊙9am-11pm Apr-Oct; 🚇Sultanahmet) Comfortable cane chairs, shady trees, efficient service, reasonable prices and peerless people-watching opportunities make this a great place for tea, *nargile* and backgammon.

Hocapaşa Culture Centre PERFORMING ARTS
(Hodjapasha Culture Centre; Map p770; ☎212-511 4626; www.hodjapasha.com; Hocapaşa Hamamı Sokak 3b, Sirkeci; 🚇Sirkeci) Occupying a 550-year-old *hamam*, Hocapaşa stages one-hour whirling-dervish performances for tourists (adult/child under 12 years TL50/30; 7.30pm Monday, Wednesday, Friday, Saturday and Sunday; children under seven not admitted) and 1½-hour Turkish dance shows (adult/child under 12 years

TL60/40; 8pm Tuesday and Thursday and 9pm Saturday and Sunday).

BEYOĞLU & AROUND

CAFES & BARS

There's a thriving bar scene in Beyoğlu, which is almost permanently crowded with locals who patronise the atmosphere-laden side-street bars and *meyhanes* (Turkish taverns).

The city's bohemian and student set tends to gravitate to the bars in Beyoğlu's Cihangir, Asmalımescit and Nevizade enclaves.

Tophane Nargile Cafes CAFE
(Map p774; off Necatibey Caddesi, Tophane; ⊙24hr; 🚇Tophane) This atmospheric row of *nargile* cafes is always packed with locals enjoying tea, *nargile* and snacks. Follow your nose to find it – the smell of apple tobacco is incredibly enticing.

Mikla BAR
(Map p774; www.miklarestaurant.com; Marmara Pera Hotel, Meşrutiyet Caddesi 15, Tepebaşı; ⊙from 6pm Mon-Sat summer only; 🚇Karaköy, then funicular to Tünel) It's worth overlooking the occasional uppity service at this stylish rooftop bar to enjoy one of the best views in İstanbul.

Leb-i Derya BAR
(Map p774; www.lebiderya.com; 6th fl, Kumbaracı Yokuşu 57, Galata; ⊙4pm-2am Mon-Thu, to 3am Fri, 10am-3am Sat, to 2am Sun; 🚇Karaköy, then funicular to Tünel) On the top floor of a dishevelled building off İstiklal, Leb-i Derya has wonderful views across to the Old City and down the Bosphorus.

Litera BAR
(Map p774; www.literarestaurant.com; 5th fl, Yeni Çarşı Caddesi 32, Galatasaray; ⊙11am-4am; 🚇Karaköy, then funicular to Tünel) Occupying the 5th floor of the handsome Goethe Institute building, Litera revels in its views and hosts plenty of cultural events.

360 BAR
(Map p774; www.360istanbul.com; 8th fl, İstiklal Caddesi 163; ⊙noon-2am Mon-Thu & Sun, 3pm-4am Fri & Sat; 🚇Karaköy, then funicular to Tünel) İstanbul's most famous bar, with an extraordinary view from the bar stools on the terrace. It morphs into a club after midnight on Friday and Saturday, when a cover charge of around TL40 applies.

NIGHTCLUBS, MUSIC & PERFORMANCE

MiniMüzikHol CLUB, LIVE MUSIC
(MMH; Map p774; www.minimuzikhol.com; Soğancı Sokak 7, Cihangir; ⊙Wed-Sat 10pm-late; 🚇Kabataş,

then funicular to Taksim) This small, slightly grungy venue hosts live sets by local and international musicians midweek and the best dance party in town on weekends. It's best after 1am.

Munzur Cafe & Bar LIVE MUSIC
(Map p774; www.munzurcafebar.com; Hasnun Galip Sokak, Galatasaray; ☺1pm-4am Tue-Sun, music from 9pm; 🚇Kabataş, then funicular to Taksim) The best of this street's *Türkü evleri*, Kurdish-owned bars where musicians perform live, emotion-charged *halk meziği* (folk music). Nearby **Toprak** (Map p774; ☑212-293 4037; www.toprakturkubar.tr.gg/ana-sayfa.htm; Hasnun Galip Sokak, Galatasaray; ☺4pm-4am, show from 10pm) offers more of the same.

Galata Mevlevi Museum PERFORMING ARTS
(Galata Mevlevihanesi Müzesi; Map p774; Galipdede Caddesi 15, Tünel; TL40; ☺performances 4pm Sun; 🚇Karaköy, then funicular to Tünel) The 15th-century *semahane* (whirling-dervish hall) at this *tekke* (dervish lodge) is the venue for a *sema* (ceremony) held most Sundays. Tickets are only available on the day of the performance; head to the museum as early as possible to purchase tickets (the ticket office opens at 9am).

ⓘ Information

Emergency

Tourist Police (☑212-527 4503; Yerebatan Caddesi 6) Across the street from the Basilica Cistern.

Medical Services

Private hospitals, such as the following, charge around TL200 for a standard consultation (credit card accepted).

Universal Taksim Alman Hastanesi (Universal German Hospital; ☑212-293 2150; www.uhg.com.tr; Sıraselviler Caddesi 119; ☺8.30am-6pm Mon-Fri, to 5pm Sat) Has a 24 hour emergency clinic and English-speaking staff.

Money

Banks, ATMs and exchange offices are widespread, including next to Sultanahmet's Aya Sofya Meydanı, in the Grand Bazaar and along İstiklal Caddesi (Beyoğlu). The exchange rates offered at Atatürk International Airport are usually as good as those offered in town.

Telephone

İstanbul has two area codes: ☑212 for the European side, ☑216 for the Asian zone.

Tourist Information

None of İstanbul's offices are particularly helpful.

Tourist office (☑212-465 3451; International Arrivals Hall, Atatürk International Airport; ☺9am-10pm)

ⓘ Getting There & Away

AIR Atatürk International Airport (IST, Atatürk Havalimanı; ☑212-463 3000; www.ataturkairport.com) Located 23km west of Sultanahmet.

Sabiha Gökçen International Airport (SAW, Sabiha Gökçen Havalimanı; ☑216-588 8888; www.sgairport.com) Located 50km east of Sultanahmet, and popular with low-cost European airlines.

BOAT Yenikapı is the main dock for **İDO** (İstanbul Deniz Otobüsleri; ☑212-444 4436; www.ido.com.tr) car and passenger ferries across the Sea of Marmara to Yalova, Bursa and Bandırma (from where you can catch a train to İzmir or a bus to Çanakkale).

BUS The aptly titled **Büyük İstanbul Otogarı** (Big İstanbul Bus Station; ☑212-658 0505; www.otogaristanbul.com), 10km west of Sultanahmet, is the city's main *otogar* for intercity and international routes. Regular services from here include Ankara (TL38 to TL43, six hours), Bursa (TL25 to TL30, four hours) and Çanakkale (TL45, six hours).

» Many bus companies offer a *servis* (free shuttle bus) to/from the *otogar*.

» The metro stops here en route between Atatürk International Airport and Aksaray, where you can pick up a tram to Sultanahmet.

» Bus 830/910 leaves for Taksim Sq/Eminönü (one hour) every 15 to 25 minutes from 6am and 8.45pm.

» A taxi to Sultanahmet/Taksim Sq costs around TL30/35 (30 minutes).

» If you're arriving from Anatolia, rather than travelling all the way to the Büyük İstanbul Otogarı, it's quicker to get out at the smaller **Harem Otogar** (☑216-333 3763) on the Asian shore, and take the ferry to Sirkeci/Eminönü.

TRAIN The daily Bosphorus/Balkan Express links İstanbul with Bucharest, Sofia and Belgrade (see p843).

Services to/from destinations in Anatolia have been severely curtailed by work on the line to/from Ankara. When this reopens in 2014 or 2015, it will feature high-speed trains that will depart from a new railway hub in Üsküdar, on the Asian shore.

ⓘ Getting Around

Tickets on public transport in İstanbul generally cost TL2.

DANGERS & ANNOYANCES

İstanbul is no more nor less safe than any large metropolis, but are there some dangers worth highlighting. (See also p841.)

» Some İstanbullus drive like rally drivers, and there is no such thing as a generally acknowledged right of way for pedestrians.

» Bag-snatchings and muggings occasionally occur on Beyoğlu's side streets.

» In Sultanahmet, if a shoe cleaner drops his brush, don't pick it up. He will insist on giving you a 'free' clean in return, before demanding an extortionate fee.

» There has been a recent police crackdown on gay venues in the city, especially *hamams* (Turkish baths) and saunas.

» Males travelling alone or in pairs should be wary of being adopted by a friendly local who is keen to take them to a club for a few drinks – many such encounters end up at *pavyons*, sleazy nightclubs run by the mafia where a drink or two with a female hostess will end up costing hundreds – sometimes thousands – of euros. If you don't pay up, the consequences can be violent.

» The PKK (Kurdistan Workers Party) and other terrorist groups sporadically target İstanbul with bombings, normally aimed at affluent, touristy neighbourhoods. In October 2010 a Kurdish suicide bomber injured 32 people on Taksim Sq.

TO/FROM THE AIRPORT

Havataş (Havaş) Airport Bus (www.havas.net) Travels between the airports and Cumhuriyet Caddesi, just off Taksim Sq. Buses leave Atatürk (TL10, one hour) every 30 minutes between 4am and 1am, and Sabiha Gökçen (TL12, 1½ hours) between 5am and midnight, thereafter 30 minutes after flight arrivals.

Metro From Atatürk to Zeytinburnu, where you can connect with the tram to Sultanahmet (total TL4, one hour).

Shuttle Many hotels will provide a free pick-up service from Atatürk airport if you stay with them for three nights or more.

Taxi From Atatürk/Sabiha Gökçen to Sultanahmet should cost around TL40/120.

BUS İstanbul's efficient bus system runs between 6.30am and 11.30pm. You must have a ticket before boarding; buy tickets from the white booths near major stops or, for a small mark-up, from some nearby shops (look for 'İETT *otobüs bileti satılır*' signs).

FUNICULAR RAILWAY The 19th-century Tünel climbs the hill from Karaköy (near the tram stop) to the bottom of İstiklal Caddesi (every 10 minutes from 7.30am to 9pm). A funicular railway also climbs from the Bosphorus shore at Kabataş (near the tram stop) to the metro station at Taksim Sq.

METRO Connects Aksaray with the airport, stopping at 15 stations, including the *otogar*, along the way. Services depart every 10 minutes or so between 5.40am and 1.40am.

TAXI İstanbul is full of yellow taxis, all of them with meters; do not let drivers insist on a fixed rate. From Sultanahmet to Taksim Sq costs around TL15.

TRAM A *tramvay* (tramway) service runs between Zeytinburnu (where it connects with the metro to/from the airport) and Kabataş via Aksaray, Sultanahmet, Eminönü and Karaköy. Trams run every five minutes or so from 6am to midnight.

A quaint antique tram rattles up and down İstiklal Caddesi in Beyoğlu, from the Tünel station to Taksim Sq via Galatasaray Lycée.

AROUND İSTANBUL

Since İstanbul is such a vast city, few places are within easy reach on a day trip. If you make an early start, however, it's just possible to see the sights of Edirne in Thrace (Trakya), the only bit of Turkey that is geographically within Europe. Ferries cross the Sea of Marmara to Bursa, although it's better to overnight there.

Edirne

☑ 0284 / POP 144,531

European Turkey's largest settlement outside İstanbul, Edirne was the Ottoman capital before Constantinople (İstanbul), and many of its key buildings are in excellent shape. You can enjoy mosques as fine as almost any in İstanbul – without the crowds. With Greece and Bulgaria a half-hour's drive away, Edirne is also a bustling border town.

◉ Sights

Selimiye Camii　　　　　　　　　MOSQUE
(Selimiye Mosque; Mimar Sinan Caddesi) Great Ottoman architect Mimar Sinan designed Edirne's grandest mosque (1569–75), and it is said that he considered it his finest work. Lit up at night, the complex is a spectacular sight, with four 71m-high minarets and a broad, lofty dome – marginally wider than that of İstanbul's Aya Sofya.

Eski Cami　　　　　　　　　　MOSQUE
The 15th-century Old Mosque exemplifies one of the two classic mosque styles used by the Ottomans in their earlier capital, Bursa. Like Bursa's Ulu Cami, the Eski Cami has rows of arches and pillars supporting a series of small domes.

Üç Şerefeli Cami　　　　　　　MOSQUE
With its four strikingly different minarets, the 15th-century Üç Şerefeli Cami dominates Hürriyet Meydanı (Freedom Sq). Its name refers to the three balconies on the tallest minaret, and its design is halfway between Konya and Bursa's Seljuk Turkish-style mosques and the truly Ottoman style.

Museum of Health　　　　　　MUSEUM
(Sağlık Müzesi; admission TL5; ⊙9am-5.30pm) Part of the Bayezid II mosque complex, north of the centre by the Tunca River, this museum illustrates the therapy and teaching that took place here. One of the most important Ottoman hospitals, it operated from 1488 to 1909, and music therapy was employed from 1652.

🛏 Sleeping & Eating

There's an assortment of eateries along Saraçlar and Maarif Caddesis. The riverside restaurants south of the centre are more atmospheric, but most open only in summer and are booked solid at weekends.

Efe Hotel　　　　　　　BOUTIQUE HOTEL €€
(☎213 6166; www.efehotel.com; Maarif Caddesi 13; s/d TL100/150; ❄@) The off-red Efe stands out for its atmospheric, archival lobby with tartan carpets and polished wood. There's an English pub open outside the summer months and a decent bar-restaurant called Patio.

Selimiye Taşodalar　　　BOUTIQUE HOTEL €€€
(☎212 3529; www.tasodalar.com.tr; Selimiye Arkası Hamam Sokak 3; s/d from TL160/210; ❄@) Next to Selimiye Camii and the 14th-century Sultan Selim Saray Hamam, the shared spaces

OIL WRESTLING

One of the world's oldest and most bizarre sporting events takes place annually in late June/early July at Sarayiçi in northern Edirne. At the 650-year-old **Tarihi Kırkpınar Yağlı Güreş Festivali** (Historic Kırpınar Oil Wrestling Festival), muscular men, naked bar a pair of heavy leather shorts, coat themselves with olive oil and throw each other around. For more information, visit **Kırpınar Evi** (Kırkpınar House; ☎212 8622; www.kirkpinar.com; ⊙10am-noon & 2-6pm) in Edirne or www.turkish-wrestling.com.

of this 15th-century Ottoman house have an air of elegance, although the dusty kitsch in the rooms disappoints. The tea garden is pleasant and shady.

Grand Altunhan Hotel　　　　HOTEL €€
(☎213 2200; www.altunhanhotel.com; Saraçlar Caddesi; s/d TL80/130) Located on a popular shopping strip, this friendly midrange hotel's rooms are modern, with flat-screen TVs, colourful furniture and brightly tiled bathrooms.

Melek Anne　　　　　　　　　CAFE €
('Angel' Anne's; ☎213 3263; Maarif Caddesi 18; mains TL7; ✍) Popular with students and foodies, 'Angel' Anne's occupies a 120-year-old house with a spacious courtyard. The rotating menu of homemade dishes includes unusual salads and hearty vegetarian choices.

❶ Getting There & Away

For the Bulgarian border crossing at Kapıkule, catch a *dolmuş* (minibus that follows a prescribed route; TL5, 25 minutes) from opposite the tourist office on Talat Paşa Caddesi. For the Greek border post at Pazarkule, catch a *dolmuş* (TL1, 20 minutes) from outside the tourist office on Maarif Caddesi.

Edirne's *otogar* is 9km southeast of the centre. There are regular buses to Çanakkale (TL30, four hours) and İstanbul (TL12, 2½ hours).

Bursa

☎0224 / POP 1.7 MILLION
The first capital of the Ottoman Empire, today Bursa mixes traditional Turkish flavour with modern vitality. Allow at least a day to take in the ancient mosques, tombs and

market. The thermal springs in the villagelike suburb of Çekirge, 3km west of central Bursa, are the perfect salve after exploring the city.

The city centre is along Atatürk Caddesi, between the Ulu Camii and, to the east, the main square, Cumhuriyet Alanı, commonly called Heykel.

◉ Sights & Activities

Yeşil Camii
MOSQUE

(Green Mosque; Yeşil Caddesi) Built for Mehmet I, this 15th-century mosque represents a departure from the previous, Persian-influenced Seljuk architecture. Exemplifying Ottoman stylings, the mosque was named for the interior wall's greenish-blue tiles – fragments of a few original frescos remain.

Ulu Camii
MOSQUE

(Atatürk Caddesi) This enormous Seljuk-style shrine (1396) is Bursa's most dominant and durable mosque. Having pledged to build 20 mosques after defeating the Crusaders in the Battle of Nicopolis, Sultan Beyazıt I settled for one mosque, with 20 small domes. Behind Ulu Camii is the sprawling **Kapalı Çarşı** (Covered Market; Kapalı Çarşı Caddesi).

Bursa Citadel
CASTLE

(Osman Gazi ve Orhan Gazi Türbeleri; admission by donation) Some ramparts and walls still survive on the steep cliff, the site of Bursa's citadel and oldest neighbourhood. From Ulu Cami, walk west and up Orhan Gazi (Yiğitler) Caddesi. On the summit, a park contains the **Tombs of Sultans Osman and Orhan** (Osman Gazi ve Orhan Gazi Türbeleri; Timurtaş Paşa Park; admission by donation), the Ottoman Empire's founders. The six-storey **clock tower** adjoins a **tea garden** overlooking the valley.

Uludağ
NATURE RESERVE

Whether it's winter or summer, it's worth taking a cable-car ride up the Great Mountain (2543m) to take advantage of the views and the cool, clean air of Uludağ National Park. As well as one of Turkey's most popular ski resorts (the season runs from December to early April), the park offers pine forests and snowy peaks. Hiking to the summit of Uludağ takes three hours. To get to the **teleferik** (cable car; return TL8) from Bursa, take a city bus from stop 1 or a *dolmuş* from behind the City Museum (Kent Müzesi).

🛌 Sleeping

There are a few decent options in Bursa, mostly business hotels. Consider Çekirge, which has tranquil hotels for some R&R; prices can be higher, but generally include the use of the mineral baths.

Kitap Evi
BOUTIQUE HOTEL €€

(Book House; ☑225 4160; www.kitapevi.com.tr; cnr Kavaklı Mahallesi & Burç Üstü 21; s/d/ste €100/140/230; ❄@) 'The Book House', a former Ottoman house and bookstore, draws an artistically inclined clientele with its eclectic decor. The 12 rooms each have their own style, while well-polished wood fixtures and touches like artwork and stained glass complement the bookshelves and empty leather suitcases. The restaurant is excellent.

Hotel Gönlüferah
LUXURY HOTEL €€

(☑233 9210; www.gonluferah.com; Murat Caddesi; s/d €90/120; ❄@🛜🏊) Dating from 1890 and a hotel since the early 20th century, Çekirge's hilltop Gönlüferah combines old-world charm with modern luxuries such as spa packages and an opulent bar. Day-use spa packages (TL30 per person) are available for nonguests too.

Safran Otel
PENSION €€

(☑224 7216; www.safranotel.com; Orta Pazar Caddesi; s/d TL90/150; ❄🛜) The Safran occupies an elegant restored Ottoman house near the Osman and Orhan tombs, in a historic district. Rooms are modern, spacious and well lit (with a hint of the Ottoman retained in the distinctive carpets).

Otel Güneş
HOSTEL €

(☑222 1404; İnebey Caddesi 75; s/d TL35/50) The Güneş has seen better days but remains the only true budget accommodation in Bursa's centre. Rooms are small but clean (choose between those with regular and 'Turkish traditional' toilets).

🍴 Eating & Drinking

Arap Şükrü
SEAFOOD €€

(Sakarya Caddesi; meze TL7-20; ⊙lunch & dinner) Situated in a cobblestoned lane in the former Jewish quarter, a 10-minute walk from Ulu Cami, this historic restaurant serves fresh seafood meze and mains. Similar restaurants line the same street, regaled by accordion-wielding Roma bands. After eating, have a drink at nearby 'photography cafe' **Gren** (☑223 6064; www.grencafe.com; Sakarya Caddesi 46), with exhibitions and antique-camera decor.

Kebapçı İskender
KEBAP €€

(Ünlü Caddesi 7; iskender kebap TL18; ⊙lunch & dinner) This famous refuge for serious carnivores is where the legendary *İskender* kebap – *döner* lamb on crumbled pide and yoghurt, topped with tomato and burnt butter sauces – was created in 1867. This is the main branch of the local chain.

Cafe My Kitchen INTERNATIONAL **€€**

(☑234 6200; Çekirge Caddesi 114; pizzas TL11-18, mains TL17-24; ☺lunch & dinner; ☎) This 'international' restaurant, fashionable among up-and-coming young Bursans, is somewhat upscale, serving excellent pastas and salads. The wine bar's also good for a drink.

Mahfel Mado RESTAURANT, BAR **€**

(Namazgah Caddesi 2; mains TL5-10; ☺breakfast, lunch & dinner) Bursa's oldest cafe is known for its *dondurma* (ice cream), and has a nice, shady ravine setting.

❶ Information

Post office, payphones and ATMs are on Atatürk Caddesi; for exchange offices visit the Covered Market.

Tourist Office (☺9am-5pm Mon-Fri, to 6pm Sat) Beneath Atatürk Caddesi, in the shop row at the pedestrian subway Orhan Gazi Alt Geçidi's northern entrance.

❶ Getting There & Around

Bursa's *otogar* is 10km north of the centre; take bus 38 (TL3, 45 minutes) from stop 4 on Atatürk Caddesi or a taxi (TL25 to TL30).

For İstanbul (TL24), *karayolu ile* (by road) buses drag you around the Bay of İzmit (four to five hours); better *feribot ile* (by ferry) buses go to Topçular, east of Yalova, and then by ferry to Eskihisar near İstanbul (three hours).

The fastest route to İstanbul is the metro-bus combo to Mudanya (take Bursa's metro to the final stop, then continue by public bus), then an İDO ferry (www.ido.com.tr) across the Sea of Marmara to Yenikapı. Alternatively, take a bus to Yalova (TL9, 1¼ hours, half hourly), then a ferry to Yenikapı (TL24). Catch a bus leaving Bursa's otogar at least 90 minutes before the scheduled boat departure. On both routes, to travel on a weekend or public holiday, purchase your ferry ticket in advance.

A *dolmuş* (in Bursa, these are cars as well as minibuses) to Çekirge from the terminal immediately south of Heykel costs TL2; a taxi is TL10.

THE AEGEAN COAST

Turkey's Aegean coast can convincingly claim more ancient ruins per square kilometre than any other region in the world.

Since time immemorial, conquerors, traders and travellers have beaten a path to the mighty monuments, and few leave disappointed.

Gallipoli (Gelibolu) Peninsula

☑0286

Antipodeans and many Brits won't need an introduction to Gallipoli; it's the backbone of the 'Anzac legend', in which an Allied campaign in 1915 to knock Turkey out of WWI and open a relief route to Russia turned into one of the war's greatest fiascos. Some 130,000 men died, roughly a third from Allied forces and the rest Turkish.

Today the Gallipoli battlefields are peaceful places, covered in brush and pine forests. But the battles fought here nearly a century ago are still alive in many memories, both Turkish and foreign, especially Australians and New Zealanders, who view the peninsula as a place of pilgrimage. The Turkish officer responsible for the defence of Gallipoli was Mustafa Kemal (the future Atatürk); his victory is commemorated in Turkey on 18 March. On **Anzac Day** (25 April), a dawn service marks the anniversary of the Allied landings.

The easiest way to see the battlefields is with your own transport or an afternoon minibus tour from nearby Eceabat/ Çanakkale (typically TL60/90) with **Crowded House Tours** (☑814 1565; www.crowded housegallipoli.com; Eceabat) or **Hassle Free Travel Agency** (☑213 5969; www.anzachouse. com; Çanakkale). With a tour you get the benefit of a guide who can explain the battles as you go along.

Most people use Çanakkale or, on the Thracian (European) side of the strait, Eceabat as a base. From Eceabat, take a *dolmuş* (TL2.50) or taxi to the **Kabatepe Information Centre & Museum**, 750m from the bottom of the road up to the main battlefields.

Crowded House offers one- and two-day packages starting in İstanbul.

Eceabat (Maydos)

☑0286 / POP 5300

Eceabat is a small waterfront town with the best access to the main Gallipoli battlefields. Ferries dock by the main square, Cumhuriyet Meydanı, which has hotels, restaurants, ATMs, a post office,

Aegean Coast

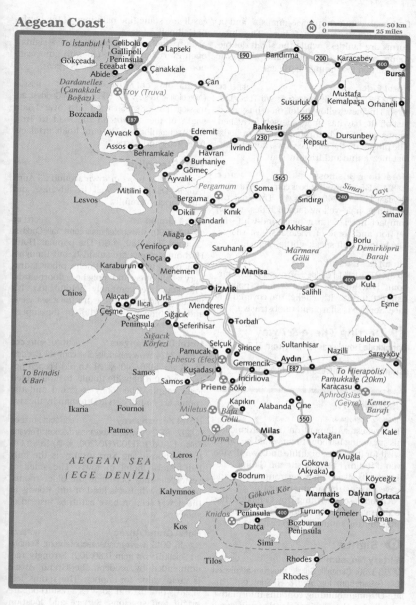

bus-company offices, *dolmuş* stands and taxis. Like most of the peninsula, Eceabat is swamped with students and tour groups at weekends from 18 March to mid-June and in late September.

🛏 Sleeping & Eating

TOP CHOICE **Hotel Crowded House** HOSTEL €
(☏814 1565; www.crowdedhousegallipoli.com; Hüseyin Avni Sokak 4; dm/s/d TL20/50/65; ✱@) Guests of all budgets and persuasions will

find real comfort, professionalism and a truly accommodating staff here. The three dorms are faultless, while the small double rooms represent excellent value. There's a beer garden for summer barbecues.

Hotel Ejder   HOTEL €€
(☑8023 8757; Ataturk Caddesi 5; s/d TL60/120; 🅿🛜) This new yellow hotel, on a busy road just off the bay, has small, sparsely furnished rooms with tiled bathrooms and firm beds. The pluses are the terrace views, huge breakfast mezzanine and friendly staff.

Hotel Boss Business   HOTEL €
(☑814 1464; www.heyboss.com; Cumhuriyet Meydanı 14; s/d TL40/70; ❄@) This narrow building's pale yellow facade hides a cool, compact hotel, with a black-and-white reception and some of Eceabat's best rooms. The helpful staff speak a little English.

Liman Restaurant   SEAFOOD €€
(☑814 2755; İstiklal Caddesi 67; mains TL12) 'Harbour' is a humble and extremely popular fish restaurant with a delightful covered terrace. Service is sharp and unobstrusive.

🛈 Getting There & Away

Çanakkale Hourly car ferries (from TL2, 25 minutes).

İstanbul Hourly buses (TL40, five hours).

Çanakkale
☑0286 / POP 104,400

The liveliest settlement on the Dardanelles, this sprawling harbour town would be worth a visit for its sights, nightlife and overall vibe even if it didn't lie opposite the Gallipoli Peninsula. Its sweeping waterfront promenade heaves during the summer months.

A good base for visiting Troy, Çanakkale has become a popular destination for weekending Turks; during summer, try to visit midweek.

👁 Sights

Military Museum   MUSEUM
(☑213 1730; Çimenlik Sokak; museum admission TL4; ☺9am-5pm Tue, Wed & Fri-Sun; 🅿) This late-Ottoman building contains informative exhibits on the Gallipoli battles and some war relics, including fused bullets that hit each other in mid-air. Also here is a replica of the **Nusrat minelayer** (Nusrat Mayın Gemisi), which sank or crippled three Allied ships, and the impressive 15th-century **Çimenlik Kalesi** (Meadow Castle). Inside the

castle are some fine paintings of the battles of Gallipoli.

Entry to the park containing these sights – open every day and dotted with guns, cannons and military artefacts – is free.

Archaeological Museum   MUSEUM
(Arkeoloji Müzesi; ☑217 6565; 100 Yil Caddesi; admission TL5; ☺8am-5pm; 🅿) Just over 1.5km south of the *otogar,* on the road to Troy, the Archaeological Museum holds artefacts from Troy and Assos.

🛏 Sleeping

If you intend to be in town around 25 April (Anzac Day), book well in advance and check prices carefully.

Hotel Limani   HOTEL €€
(☑217 4090; www.hotellimani.com; Yalı Caddesi 12; rooms TL130-180; ❄@) The popular Hotel Harbour's rooms are smallish, but thoughtfully fitted with quality linens, pillows, drapery, wallpaper and polished floorboards. The staff are genuinely helpful too. It's worth spending a little extra for a sea view, and stopping for a cocktail in the superb lobby restaurant.

Hotel Des Etrangers   BOUTIQUE HOTEL €€€
(☑214 2424; www.yabancilaroteli.com; Yali Caddesi 25-27; s/d TL180/240; ❄🛜) An old French hotel has found new life thanks to a dedicated local couple. The lobby is grand and the rooms are country-style Ottoman by the sea.

Hotel Kervansaray   BOUTIQUE HOTEL €€
(☑217 8192; www.otelkervansaray.com; Fetvane Sokak 13; s/d/tr TL100/170/200; ❄@) In an Ottoman house, the Kervansaray is the only half-historic hotel in town. The smell of yesteryear may permeate the older rooms, but the dowdiness is kind of fun. Rooms in the newer section have bathtubs instead of showers.

Hotel Grand Anzac   HOTEL €€
(☑216 0016; www.grandanzachotel.com; Kemalyeri Sokak 11; s/d from TL80/100) Strongly recommended by readers, the Grand Anzac is great value for money. The rooms feel slightly prefab (and noisy as a result) but are bright and spacious. Service and location are both excellent.

Anzac House Hostel   HOSTEL €
(☑213 5969; www.anzachouse.com; Cumhuriyet Meydanı 59; dm/s/d without bathroom & excl breakfast TL20/30/45; @) The base of **Hassle Free Travel Agency** (☑213 5969; Cumhuriyet Meydanı

61) is Çanakkale's only genuine backpackers. The bright colours and friendly staff go some way to alleviate the cramped confines.

Eating & Drinking

Licensed restaurants line the waterfront, where stalls also offer corn on the cob, mussels and other simple items. Head to Fetvane and buzzing, pedestrianised Matbaa Sokaks for bars.

Yalova   SEAFOOD €€
(☎217 1045; www.yalovarestaurant.com; Gümrük Sokak 7; mains TL15-20) Yalova is a pure seafood restaurant that combines impeccable service with the best produce and preparation in Çanakkale. Ask for a tour of the 2nd floor, where you can select your own fish. Wine is matched to order.

Cafe du Port   RESTAURANT €€
(☎217 2908; Yalı Caddesi 12; ☺8am-11pm) Stylish and inviting, Hotel Limani's popular restaurant occupies a glass-fronted building on the *kordon* (seafront), with Çanakkale's most versatile chefs and good service. Specialities include steaks, salads, pastas and superb cocktails.

Benzin   BAR, CAFE
(Eski Balıkhane Sokak 11; ☎) This grungy waterfront bar-cafe, done out in 1960s decor, is a relaxing spot for a drink and a bite (pizzas TL8 to TL12.50). Heaves at weekends.

Time Out   LIVE MUSIC
(Kayserili Ahmet Paşa Caddesi; beer TL6) A rock club of the stylish (rather than dingy) variety, with pictures of Elvis et al, and outside tables.

🛈 Information

The **tourist office** (☎217 1187; Cumhuriyet Meydanı; ☺8.30am-5.30pm) is 150m from the ferry pier, and you can access the internet at **Araz Internet** (Fetvane Sokak 21; per hr TL1.50; ☺9am-midnight).

🛈 Getting There & Away

BUS Ayvalık TL25, 3½ hours, hourly
Bandırma TL20, 2½ hours, hourly
İstanbul TL35, six hours, frequent
İzmir TL35, 5½ hours, hourly
FERRY Eceabat Car ferries (from TL3, 15 minutes, several daily).

Behramkale & Assos

☎0286

Behramkale is an old hilltop Greek village spread out around the ruins of the 6th-century-BC Ionic **Temple of Athena** (☎217 6740; admission TL8; ☺8am-7.30pm), which has spectacular views of Lesvos and the dazzling Aegean. Next to the temple ticket booth, the 14th-century **Hüdavendigar Camii** is a simple, early-Ottoman mosque.

Just before the entrance to the village, a road winds down the steep hill to Assos, the ideal place to unwind over a glass of *çay*. Overlooking the picture-perfect harbour, the old stone buildings have been transformed into hotels and fish restaurants.

Try to avoid visiting on weekends and public holidays from the beginning of April to the end of August, when tourists pour in by the coachload.

WORTH A TRIP

TROY (TRUVA)

Of all the ancient centres in Turkey, the remains of the great city of Troy are in fact among the least impressive; you'll have to use your imagination. Still, for history buffs and fans of Homer's *Iliad*, it's an important site to tick off the list, and a new national archaeological and history museum is set to open here by 2015.

Approaching the ruins of Troy from the ticket booth, the first thing you see is a reconstruction of the Trojan Horse. The site is rather confusing for nonexpert eyes (guides are available), but the most conspicuous features include the **walls** from various periods; **megarons** (houses inhabited by the elite); and the Roman **Odeon**, where concerts were held.

The travel agencies offering Gallipoli tours also offer morning trips to Troy (around TL60 per person).

From Çanakkale, *dolmuşes* to Troy (TL4, 35 minutes, 9.30am to 4.30/7pm winter/summer) leave on the half hour (less frequently at weekends) from a station at the northern end of the bridge over the Sarı River. Returning, *dolmuşes* leave on the hour (7am to 3pm/5pm winter/summer).

🛏 Sleeping

BEHRAMKALE

TOP CHOICE Assos Alarga BOUTIQUE HOTEL €€€
(📞721 7260; www.assosalarga.com; Berhamkale 88; r from TL200; P❄@🛜🏊) Located in the quiet end of the village, just behind the temple ruins, Alarga may only have three rooms, but this ensures stellar service. All rooms have amazing views over the mountains and very cool bathrooms. There's a deluxe outdoor pool, garden, sauna and pool table.

Eris Pansiyon PENSION €€
(📞721 7080; www.erispansiyon.com; s/d incl afternoon tea TL70/120) This guesthouse has three pleasant, peaceful rooms; those facing the sea are less impressive inside. Afternoon tea is served on a terrace with spectacular views over the hills. Call ahead out of season.

Dolunay Pansiyon PENSION €€
(📞721 7172; s/d TL50/100; ❄) In the centre of the village on the main square, this basic, family-run place has six spotless rooms. You can have breakfast on the pretty terrace with sea views.

ASSOS

In high season most hotels here insist on *yarım pansiyon* (half board), though you could try negotiating.

Hotel Kervansaray HOTEL €€€
(📞721 7093; www.assoskervansaray.com; s/d with sea view TL140/180; ❄🏊) A 19th-century acorn store, the Kervansaray is pretty good value in its newer 'Butik' section, although the restaurant's popularity can detract from the guest experience. The outdoor pool almost laps into the sea.

Yıldız Saray Hotel PENSION €€
(📞721 7025; www.yildizsaray-hotels.com; s/d/f TL100/140/220; ❄) The Star Palace is drifting into postretro territory in its tired decor, but it's friendly, the upstairs terrace is sublime and the family apartment is good value. Breakfast is served on a floating platform.

Dr. No Antik Pansiyon PENSION €
(📞721 7397; www.assosdrnoantikpansiyon.com; s/d TL40/80; ❄) This simple, friendly pension, with cramped rooms and a pleasant outdoor area, is the best budget option near the sea.

🍴 Eating

Proximity to the sea accounts for higher prices at the harbour. Be sure to check the cost of fish and bottles of wine before ordering.

Ehl-i Keyf TURKISH €
(📞721 7106; www.assosehlikeyf.com.tr; gozleme TL5; 🛜) This multilevel restaurant in Behramkale combines fresh food with attentive service and a pleasant outlook. Choose from a long menu of *izgara* (grills), *gozleme* (thin savoury crepes), cocktails, coffee and ice cream amid flowering plants.

Uzunev SEAFOOD €€
(📞721 7007; mains TL15-20; ⊙lunch & dinner) The pick of the nonhotel restaurants in Assos, Uzunev garners a lively crowd, especially on high-season weekends. Try the speciality, sea bass à l'Aristotle (steamed in a special stock), or the delicious seafood meze (TL10).

ℹ Getting There & Away

Behramkale Regular buses run from Çanakkale to Ayvacık (TL12, 1½ hours), where you can pick up a *dolmuş* to Behramkale (TL3, 20 minutes). In low season the *dolmuşes* run less frequently; a taxi from Ayvacık costs around TL30.

Assos Some *dolmuşes* continue to Assos. In summer there's a half-hourly shuttle service between the villages (TL1). In winter *dolmuşes* occasionally link the two (TL8).

Ayvalık

📞0266 / POP 37,200

Back from the palm trees and fish restaurants on Ayvalık's waterfront, the tumble-down old Greek village is a kind of outdoor museum. Horses and carts clatter down narrow streets, past headscarf-wearing women holding court outside picturesque shuttered houses.

Olive-oil production is the traditional business here, and the town is a gateway to local islands and the Greek isle of Lesvos.

Offshore is **Alibey Island** (known locally as Cunda), which is lined with open-air fish restaurants and linked to the mainland by ferries (June to early September) and a causeway. Summer **cruises** (TL50 per person including lunch) include it in their day tours of the bay's islands, leaving Ayvalık around 11am and stopping here and there for sunbathing and swimming.

🛏 Sleeping & Eating

Istanbul Pansiyon PENSION €
(📞312 4001; www.istanbulpansiyonayvalik.com; Neşe Sokak Aralığı 4; s/d TL35/70; P❄🛜) This lovely pension's blue and pink exterior gives way to six spacious rooms. Breakfast is a delight in the lush garden.

Kelebek Pension
PENSION €€

(☑312 3908; www.kelebek-pension.com; Mareşal Çakmak Caddesi 108; s/d/tr TL60/100/135; 圖) In this colourful seven-room pension, you can see the sea from your bedroom. The white-and-blue building has a terrace for having breakfast in the fresh air.

Balıkçı
SEAFOOD €€

(☑312 9099; Balıkhane Sokak 7; mains TL17; ⊙dinner) Run by a local fishing association, this is a fine place to sample seafood and settle into the tiled terrace, or sit inside for a better view of the Turkish troubadours.

Tarlakusu Gurmeko
CAFE €€

(☑312 3312; Cumhuriyet Caddesi 53; ⊙8.30am-8.30pm; 🔊) This artsy coffee house serves top-notch brews. Nibbles include cookies, brownies, soup, salads, cheese plates and *börek* (TL4.50).

ℹ Information

In high season, an information **kiosk** (⊙Jun-Sep) opens on the waterfront south of the main square.

ℹ Getting There & Away

BUS & DOLMUŞ The *otogar* is 1.7km northeast of the centre.

Alibey Island *Dolmuş* taxis (white with red stripes) run from the south side of Ayvalık main square (TL2, 20 minutes).

Bergama (TL7, 1¾ hours, hourly) Jump on a Bergama-bound bus at the main square.

Çanakkale (TL15, 3¼ hours, five a day) Smaller companies may drop you on the main highway outside Ayvalık. Larger companies, such as Ulusoy, provide a *servis* to the centre.

İzmir (TL16, three hours, hourly)

BOAT Alibey Island (TL4; 15 minutes; every 15 minutes) From a quay behind the tourist kiosk just off Ayvalık main square.

Lesvos (one way/return €60/70, 1½ hours) Daily except Sunday between May and September, with three boats a week from October to May. Advance reservations are essential; contact **Jale Tour** (☑331 3170; www.jaletour. com; Yeni Liman Karsisi).

Bergama (Pergamum)
☑0232 / POP 60,600

As Selçuk is to Ephesus, so Bergama is to Pergamum: the workaday market town has become a stop on the tourist trail because of its proximity to the remarkable ruins of Pergamum, site of ancient Rome's pre-eminent

medical centre. During Pergamum's heyday (between Alexander the Great and the Roman domination of Asia Minor) it was one of the Middle East's richest and most powerful small kingdoms.

◉ Sights

A **cable car** (one way TL4) ascends to the Acropolis. A taxi from the centre to the Asclepion/Acropolis is TL8/15. A taxi tour, including waiting time at the Asclepion, Red Basilica and Acropolis, costs around TL50.

Asclepion
RUIN

(Temple of Asclepios; admission/parking TL15/3) Treatments at this anvient medical centre included mud baths, the use of herbs and ointments, enemas and sunbathing. Diagnosis was often by dream analysis. The centre came to the fore under the great early physician Galen (AD 131–210), whose work was the basis for Western medicine well into the 16th century.

The Asclepion is 2km uphill from the town centre as the crow flies (but it's a winding road), signposted from Cumhuriyet Caddesi just north of the tourist office. Walk down the Roman **bazaar street**, to ruins including the circular **Temple of Asclepios**, **library**, **Roman theatre**, **sacred well** and, accessed along a vaulted underground corridor, the **Temple of Telesphorus**.

Acropolis
RUIN

(Akropol; admission TL20) The road to the acropolis winds 5km uphill from the Red Basilica. At the top, the magnificent ruins include the **library**, the marble-columned **Temple of Trajan**, and the vertigo-inducing, 10,000-seat **theatre**. Impressive and unusual, the theatre is built into the hillside.

To escape the crowds and get a good view of the theatre and Temple of Trajan, walk downhill behind the **Altar of Zeus**, or turn left at the bottom of the theatre steps, and follow the sign to the *antik yol* (antique street). Ruins sprawl down the hill and you can follow this route to walk back to the Red Basilica.

Red Basilica
RUIN

(Kınık Caddesi; admission TL5) The cathedral-sized Red Basilica was originally a giant temple to the Egyptian gods Serapis, Isis and Harpocrates, built in the 2nd century AD. The building is so big that the Christians didn't convert it into a church but built a basilica inside it.

🛏 Sleeping

Hera Boutique Hotel
BOUTIQUE HOTEL €€€

(☏631 0634; www.hotelhera.com; Tabrak Körpü Caddesi 21; d from TL200; P❋☀) These two 200-year-old Greek houses have 10 rooms with timber ceilings, parquetry floors and curios handpicked by the erudite couple in charge. The breakfast spread is highly recommended.

Odyssey Guesthouse
PENSION €

(☏631 3501; www.odysseyguesthouse.com; Abacıhan Sokak 13; s/d from TL45/50, without bathroom from TL35/45) This grand old house has superb views of the Red Basilica from the upstairs terrace. The main building has some basic doubles, with excellent showers, and self-caterers can enjoy the small kitchenette.

Citi Hostel
HOSTEL €

(☏830 0668; Bankalar Caddesi 10; s/d/t TL35/60/80; ❋☀) Beside the *hamam*, this great new hostel run by the friendly Imdat, a Turkish-Australian chap. Basic, spotless rooms on two levels encircle a spacious courtyard.

🍴 Eating

Kervan
FAMILY RESTAURANT €€

(☏633 2632; İzmir Caddesi; mains TL12; ❋) Popular locally for its large outdoor terrace and excellent food, Kervan's menu features a good range of kebaps, pide and *çorba* (soup). It's cheap but prices are not listed.

Bergama Ticaret Odası Sosyal Tesisleri
RESTAURANT €€

(☏632 9641; Ulucamii Mahallesi; mains TL15; ☉9am-midnight) This licensed restaurant's outdoor terrace and cafeteria-style interior offer panoramic views and reasonable food. It's in a park 300m up the hill behind the main street. Avoid walking in the area at night.

ℹ Information

The elongated main street (İzmir/Cumhuriyet/Bankalar Caddesi) is where you'll find banks, ATMs and the post office. The **tourist office** (☏631 2851; İzmir Caddesi 54; ☉8.30am-noon & 1-5.30pm) is north of the museum.

ℹ Getting There & Away

Between 6am and 7pm, a *servis* shuttles between Bergama's new *otogar* (7km from the centre, at the junction of the highway and the main road into town) and the central old *otogar*. A taxi costs about TL25.

Ayvalık TL8, 1¼ hours, hourly

İzmir TL10, two hours, every 45 minutes

İzmir

☏0232 / POP 2.8 MILLION

The grand port of İzmir, Turkey's third-largest city, is a proudly liberal, long-time centre of commerce that has emerged as a smart alternative base for travel in the west of the country. Formerly the famed Greek city of Smyrna, İzmir lives by its *kordon* and, especially around leafy Alsancak, is as fetching and lively as any large seaside city in the world.

👁 Sights

Kordon & Alsancak
SEAFRONT, NEIGHBOURHOOD

A triumph of urban renewal, the pedestrianised *kordon* is home to a great selection of bars and restaurants for watching the picture-perfect sunsets.

Konak Meydanı
SQUARE

On a pedestrianised stretch of Cumhuriyet Bulvarı, this wide plaza, named after the Ottoman government mansion (*hükümet konağı*), pretty much marks the heart of the city. The ornate Oriental style of the late Ottoman clock tower (*saat kulesi*) may have been meant to atone for Smyrna's European ambience. Beside it is the lovely, tile-covered **Konak Camii** (1755).

Agora
RUIN

(Agora Caddesi; admission TL8; ☉8.30am-7pm, to 5.30pm Sat; P) The ancient Agora, built for Alexander the Great, was ruined in an earthquake in AD 178, but rebuilt soon after by the Romans. Colonnades of reconstructed Corinthian columns, vaulted chambers and arches give a good idea of what a Roman bazaar must have looked like.

Kemeraltı Bazaar
BAZAAR

(☉8am-5pm) A great place to get lost for a few hours, with bargains galore, especially leather goods, clothing and jewellery. Within the main bazaar, the glorious **Kızlarağası Han** is touristy, with many items from the far end of the Silk Road (China), but good for a wander.

🛏 Sleeping

İzmir's waterfront is dominated by large, high-end business hotels, while inland are more budget and midrange options, particularly around Kemeraltı Bazaar and Basmane train station. West of the station, 1368 Sokak is good for budget hotels.

TOP CHOICE Key Hotel BOUTIQUE HOTEL €€€
(☑482 1111; www.keyhotel.com; Mimar Kemalettin Caddesi 1; d TL270; P❋☙) This black, gold and brown masterpiece, located in a former bank building down by Konak Pier, has a glass-topped atrium, glass elevators, a superb ground-floor restaurant and concierge service. Rooms have hi-tech touches, rain showers and king-size beds.

İzmir Palas Oteli HOTEL €€
(☑465 0030; www.izmirpalas.com.tr; Atatürk Caddesi; s/d from TL120/165; P❋) Established in 1927 and rebuilt in 1972, the 138-room Palas is a storied beast, but it's popular, quite comfortable and overlooks the bay, with fine fish restaurants nearby.

Hotel Baylan Basmane HOTEL €€
(☑483 1426; www.hotelbaylan.com; 1299 Sokak 8; s/d TL80/140) Basmane's best option, the Baylan is a spacious and attractive hotel with a welcoming rear terrace. The rooms have polished floorboards and large bathrooms.

Güzel İzmir Oteli HOTEL €
(☑483 5069; www.guzelizmirhotel.com; 1368 Sokak 8; s/d TL40/70) One of Basmane's better choices, the Good İzmir is friendly, safe and convenient for bus and train access. Rooms are nothing special (avoid the small and damp few) but it's good value at the low end.

✖ Eating & Drinking

For fresh fruit and veg, freshly baked bread and delicious savoury pastries, head for the **canopied market** just off Anafartalar Caddesi. The *kordon* restaurants have outside tables with views of the bay – some serve excellent food. On and around Kıbrıs Şehitleri Caddesi in Alsancak, you'll lose the sunset views but gain on atmosphere; in particular try 1453 Sokak.

Sakız MODERN TURKISH €€
(☑484 1103; Şehit Nevresbey Bulvarı 9a; mains TL12-25; ☙noon-2pm & 7.30-10pm Mon-Sat) With a wooden terrace and red-and-white tablecloths, Sakız is informal and fabulous. Its fresh meze and unusual mains include sardines, octopus, sea bass with asparagus, and stir-fried fish with artichoke.

Veli Usta Balık Pişiricisi SEAFOOD €€
(☑464 2705; Atatürk Caddesi 212; mains TL20; ☙noon-10.30pm) This relaxed, quality seafood

restaurant outstrips the strip thanks to dishes such as fresh, good-value *dil şiş* (grilled sole).

Aksak Lounge BAR
(1452 Sokak 10) In a typical İzmir mansion with high ceilings, balconies and a courtyard garden, Aksak attracts a cultured crowd to its jazz nights on Tuesday and Sunday.

❶ Information

Banks, ATMs, internet cafes and wi-fi networks are found throughout the centre.
Tourist Office (☑483 5117; 1344 Sokak 2) Just off Atatürk Caddesi. Has English-, German- and French-speaking staff.

❶ Getting There & Away

AIR There are many flights to İzmir's **Adnan Menderes Airport** (☑455 0000; www.adnanmenderesairport.com) from European destinations. Turkish Airlines flies to/from İstanbul (both airports), Ankara and 11 other Turkish locations. Onur Air, Atlasjet, Pegasus Airlines, Sun Express and Izair also serve İzmir.
BUS From the mammoth *otogar*, 6.5km northeast of the centre, frequent buses leave for nationwide destinations including the following:
Bergama TL10, two hours
Çeşme TL15, 1¾ hours. Buses also leave from a local bus terminal in Üçkuyular, 6.5km southwest of Konak.
Kuşadası TL15, 1¼ hours
Selçuk TL9, one hour
TRAIN Most intercity services arrive at Basmane station, although Alsancak is being vamped up.
Ankara TL27, 15 hours. Two a day in both directions; via Eskişehir (TL21, 11 hours).
Bandırma TL18, six hours. Every afternoon in both directions. Apart from on Tuesday, morning trains coordinate with the ferry to/from İstanbul.
Selçuk TL4.75, 1½ hours, six daily

❶ Getting Around

TO/FROM THE AIRPORT Havaş buses (TL10, 30 minutes) leave from Gazi Osman Paşa Bulvarı near the Swissôtel on the half hour; and from domestic arrivals 25 minutes after flights arrive.
BUS Intercity bus companies operate *servises* to/from the *otogar*. *Dolmuşes* run to the centre; to the *otogar*, take the metro to Bornova and catch bus 505.
FERRY Roughly half-hourly services (TL3), with more at the beginning and end of the working day, link piers including Alsancak, Pasaport and Konak.

Çeşme Peninsula

📞0232

The Çeşme Peninsula is İzmir's summer playground, which means it fills with Turkish tourists over weekends and during school holidays, when prices rise accordingly. Çeşme itself is a transit point for the Greek island of Chios, and a pleasant base with a dramatic Genoese fortress. Alternatively, nearby Alaçatı is a boutique bolt-hole with old Greek stone houses and a windsurfing beach.

🛌 Sleeping

ÇEŞME

Levant Apart Otel   APARTMENT €€
(📞712 6553; www.cesmelevantaparts.com; 105 Sokak 23; 1/2-bedroom apt TL135/250; P❄️🛜) Levant's slick designer apartments, one street back from the sea, are well ahead of Çeşme's otherwise humble digs. The 35-sq-metre studios are bright and cool, with plasmas, hairdryers, cute bathrooms and self-catering facilities.

Nese Hotel   HOTEL €
(📞712 6543; www.neseotel.net; Inkılap Caddesi, 3025 Sokak; s/d TL40/80; P❄️🛜) A hit with readers, this charming white-and-blue hotel is a few streets from the sea. Rooms are tiled and pastel, cool and clean. The canopied restaurant is lovely in summer.

ALAÇATI

Prices plummet out of season, although most hotels open only from mid-May to mid-October and for Christmas and New Year. For more boutique hotels, visit www.charmingalacati.com.

Vintage Boutique Hotel   BOUTIQUE HOTEL €€€
(📞716 0716; www.vintagealacati.com; 3046 Sokak 2; TL250-400; P❄️🛜) The Vintage's hip interior is aesthetically more modern than some may want in a historic neighbourhood, but its confidence and popularity are indicative of Alaçatı's maturing hotel scene. The all-white rooms feature high-end beauty products and linen.

Alaçatı Taş Otel   BOUTIQUE HOTEL €€€
(Stone Hotel; 📞716 7772; www.tasotel.com; s/d incl afternoon tea from TL150/200; ❄️🛜) The Stone Hotel, Alaçatı oldest, continues to lead the boutique scene, with seven understated rooms overlooking a walled garden. The poolside afternoon teas are lavish, featuring freshly baked cakes. Open year-round.

🍴 Eating & Drinking

ÇEŞME

The most touristy restaurants are along the waterfront. For cheaper, more locally oriented places, head to İnkılap Caddesi.

Some of the restaurants along the marina morph into live-music venues during the summer.

Tiko's Cafe   TURKISH €
(2008 Sokak 8A; mains TL8-12; ⏰6am-3am winter, 24hr summer) This new, Ottoman-feeling establishment gets crammed with locals at lunchtime and with sailors and partygoers through summer. The regular menu includes seafood and grilled meat and a revolving display of fresh meze.

Pasifik Otel Restaurant   SEAFOOD €€
(📞712 1767; Tekke Plajı Mevkii 16; mains TL10-20; ⏰noon-midnight) If you fancy a walk and some fish, head to this hotel restaurant at the far northern end of the seafront, overlooking a small beach.

ALAÇATI

Restaurants here are mostly smart, gourmet affairs, with mains typically starting at around TL20. Many close for lunch, and open only at weekends (if at all) in low season. The cafes by the mosque serve cheaper fare.

Asma Yapraği   AEGEAN €€
(📞716 0178; 1005 Sokak 50; meze TL10-15) Communal meals in this one-room restaurant are an Alaçatı experience for gastronomes and lucky stragglers. Expect plenty of fresh herbs, lashings of olive oil, Aegean vegetables and vine leaves.

ℹ️ Information

Çeşme's **tourist office** (📞712 6653; fax 712 6653; İskele Meydanı 4; ⏰8.30am-noon & 1-5.30pm Mon-Fri), ferry and bus ticket offices, banks with ATMs, restaurants and hotels are all within two blocks of Cumhuriyet Meydanı, the main square near the waterfront.

ℹ️ Getting There & Around

BOAT Between mid-May and mid-September, **Ertürk** (📞712 6768; www.erturk.com.tr; Beyazıt Caddesi 6; ⏰9am-7.30pm) sails once or twice daily to Chios (one way/return TL65/100, 1½ hours); outside that period, twice a week.

BUS Buses from Çeşme *otogar* run every 15 minutes to İzmir *otogar* (TL12, 1¾ hours) and the smaller, western Üçkuyular terminal (TL10, 1½ hours). *Dolmuşes* link Çeşme and Alaçatı (TL3.50).

Selçuk

☎0232 / POP 28,200

The normal gateway to Ephesus, this provincial town has an impressive number of sights, including graceful Byzantine aqueduct ruins and one of the Seven Wonders of the Ancient World. The down-to-earth town acts more as a weigh station for the throngs of passers-through than a vibrant tourist hub.

◉ Sights

Temple of Artemis   RUIN

(Artemis Tapınağı; ◷8.30am-5.30pm) Just beyond Selçuk's western extremities, in an empty field, stands a solitary reconstructed pillar: all that remains of the massive Temple of Artemis, one of the Seven Wonders of the Ancient World. At its height, the structure had 127 columns; Didyma's better-preserved Temple of Apollo (p797), which had 122 columns, gives a sense of this vanished grandeur.

Ephesus Museum   MUSEUM

(☎892 6010; Uğur Mumcu Sevgi Yolu Caddesi; admission TL5; ◷8.30am-6.30pm summer, to 4.30pm winter) This museum holds artefacts from Ephesus' Terrace Houses, including scales, jewellery and cosmetic boxes, plus coins, funerary goods and ancient statuary. Look out for the famous effigy of phallic god Priapus, visible by pressing a button, and the multi-breasted, egg-holding marble Artemis statue. After midday, the museum gets crowded with cruise crowds being rushed through.

Basilica of St John   RUIN

(St Jean Caddesi; admission TL5; ◷8.30am-6.30pm summer, to 4.30pm winter) This once-great basilica is a skeleton of its former self, but makes a pleasant stroll and warm-up to Ayasuluk Fortress, with excellent hilltop views. St John reportedly visited Ephesus twice and wrote his gospel on this hill. These legends, and the existence of a 4th-century tomb, supposedly housing John's relics, inspired the Byzantine Emperor Justinian to build the basilica.

Ayasuluk Fortress   CASTLE

(St Jean Caddesi; admission €8; ◷8.30am-6.30pm summer, to 4.30pm winter) Selçuk's crowning achievement is accessed via the Basilica of St John – and on the same ticket. The partially restored fortress' remains date from Byzantine and Ottoman times.

🛏 Sleeping

Selçuk specialises in good-value, family-run pensions, though upscale hotels do exist. With all of the attentive service, free extras and bus-station pick-ups, there can be pressure to buy (carpets, tours etc). You should be OK at the following.

TOP CHOICE Atilla's Getaway   HOSTEL €

(☎892 3847; www.atillasgetaway.com; Acarlar Köyü; s/d incl breakfast & dinner €24/40; ❄🖥☞🏊) This friendly 'backpacker's resort' is 2.5km south of town (linked to the *otogar* by regular free shuttles). Basic rooms and spacious dorms (no bunk beds) are spread around an outdoor pool, itself flanked by a billiards table, 'chill-out area', outdoor bar and dining area. Campers can use the lawn beside the sand volleyball court. Delicious home-cooked dinners are included (if eating out instead, deduct €5 from the given prices).

Akay Hotel   HOTEL €€

(☎892 3172; www.hotelakay.com; 1054 Sokak 7; s/d/tr from €30/50/80; ❄@☞🏊) This smart, Swiss-run hotel near İsa Bey Camii offers impeccable service, attention to detail, and the quiet elegance of its stone foundations, white walls and green doors. The well-appointed rooms overlook a turquoise pool and patio. Dinners (mains TL12 to TL15) are on the roof terrace.

Homeros Pension   PENSION €€

(☎892 3995; www.homerospension.com; 1048 Sokak 3; s/d/tr TL50/80/110; ❄☞) This long-time favourite has a dozen rooms with colourful hanging textiles and handcrafted furniture made by the friendly owner. Enjoy good views, coffee and dinners (TL15) from the roof terraces.

Wallabies Aquaduct Hotel   HOTEL €

(☎892 3204; www.wallabiesaquaducthotel.com; Cengiz Topel Caddesi 2; s/d/tr from TL50/70/105; ❄☞) Right beside the aqueducts in Selçuk centre, Wallabies has clean, modern rooms, some overlooking the storks' nests atop the ruins. There's a great buffet breakfast, and the ground-floor restaurant is among the town's best.

Barım Pension   PENSION €

(☎892 6923; barim_pansiyon@hotmail.com; 1045 Sokak 34; s/d TL40/80; ❄☞) Barım stands out for its unusual wire art, crafted by the owners, two friendly metalworking brothers. The pension occupies a 140-year-old stone house, with a leafy back garden for breakfasts and coffees.

Hotel Bella
HOTEL €€€

(📞892 3944; www.hotelbella.com; St Jean Caddesi 7; s/d from €80/120; ❄@🛜) Well-situated near St John's Hill, this upmarket little hotel comes complete with a pricey carpet and jewellery shop. The well-designed rooms have Ottoman flourishes in the decor, and the roof terrace offers refined dinners (TL25).

✕ Eating

Most pensions offer good meals at reasonable prices. The Saturday **market** (Şahabettin Dede Caddesi; ⊙9am-5pm Sat winter, 8am-7pm Sat summer) and **Wednesday market** (respectively behind the bus and train stations) are great places to stock up for a picnic.

Ejder Restaurant
ANATOLIAN €€

(Cengiz Topel Caddesi 9e; mains TL7-17) Roughly opposite the aqueduct, this tiny but time-tested local favourite serves delicious Turkish dishes – if you can't decide, take the whole sizzling Anatolian meat platter.

Wallabies Aquaduct Restaurant
TURKISH €€

(📞892 3204; Cengiz Topel Caddesi 2; mains TL10-16) Beneath the hotel of the same name, Wallabies spills out onto the square beneath the aqueduct, guaranteeing atmospheric summer dining. The traditional Anatolian fare is complemented by more international offerings, including veggie dishes and fish. Try the house chicken dish, *krep tavuk sarması*.

Selçuk Köftecisi
KÖFTE €

(Şahabettin Dede Caddesi; mains TL6-9) This classic *köfte* joint, family-run since 1959, offers great but small meat portions and tasty side salads.

Sişçı Yaşarın Yeri
KÖFTE €

(Atatürk Caddesi; mains from TL6) A popular spot for *köfte* and kebaps, this stall has tables.

St John's Café
MEDITERRANEAN €

(www.stjohn-cafe-ephesus.com; Uğur Mumcu Sevgi Yolu Caddesi 4c; mains TL8-13; 🛜) Selçuk's most touristy cafe-shop has the town's widest coffee selection, various toasts and other international snacks. There's a play area for restless youngsters, too.

❶ Information

Tourist Office (www.selcuk.gov.tr; Agora Caddesi 35; ⊙8am-noon & 1-5pm daily summer, Mon-Fri winter)

❶ Getting There & Away

Frequent *dolmuşes* run to Kuşadası (TL5, 30 minutes) and the beach at Pamucak (TL2.50, 10 minutes). There's a train to İzmir Adnan Menderes Airport (TL4.50, 55 minutes), which drops you a 20-minute stroll from the departures terminal. Buses include:

Bodrum TL25, 3¼ hours, three daily in summer

Denizli For Pamukkale and the Mediterranean, TL25, 4½ hours, two daily

İzmir TL9, one hour, every 40 minutes in summer

Ephesus (Efes)

Even if you're not an architecture buff, you can't help but be dazzled by the sheer beauty of the ruins of Ephesus (📞892 6010; admission/parking TL25/7.50; ⊙8am-6.30pm May-Oct, to 4.30pm Nov-Apr), the most complete classical metropolis in Europe. Once the capital of the Roman province of Asia Minor, with 250,000-plus inhabitants, today it's *the* place to get a feel for life in Greco-Roman times.

There's a couple of hours' worth of sights to explore, including the **Great Theatre**, reconstructed by the Romans between AD 41 and 117, and capable of holding 25,000 people; the 110-sq-metre **Lower Agora**, a textile and food market; and the **Library of Celsus**, adorned with niches holding statues of the classical Virtues. Going up Ephesus' Champs Élysées, the **Curetes Way**, you can't miss the impressive Corinthian-style **Temple of Hadrian** on the left, its arches decorated with deities; the magnificent **Terraced Houses** (Yamaç Evleri; admission TL15), which are well worth the extra outlay; and

Ephesus (Efes)

◉ Sights

1	Great Theatre	B4
2	Library of Celsus	B4
3	Lower Agora	B4
4	Lower Gate	B3
5	Magnesia Gate (Upper Gate)	C6
6	Memius Monument	B5
7	Odeon	C5
8	Pollio Fountain	B5
9	Prytaneum	C5
10	Temple of Hadrian	B5
	Temple of Hestia Boulaea	(see 9)
11	Terraced Houses	B5
12	Trajan Fountain	B5

the **Trajan Fountain**. At the top of the Curetes Way, the **Pollio Fountain** and **Memius Monument** also hint at the lavish nature of the fountains that covered the ancient capital. Up the hill on the left are the ruined remains of the **Prytaneum** (Town Hall) and the **Temple of Hestia Boulaea**, where vestal virgins tended to a perpetually burning flame. Beyond, the **Odeon**, a 5000-seat theatre with marble seats and carved ornamentation, was used for municipal meetings.

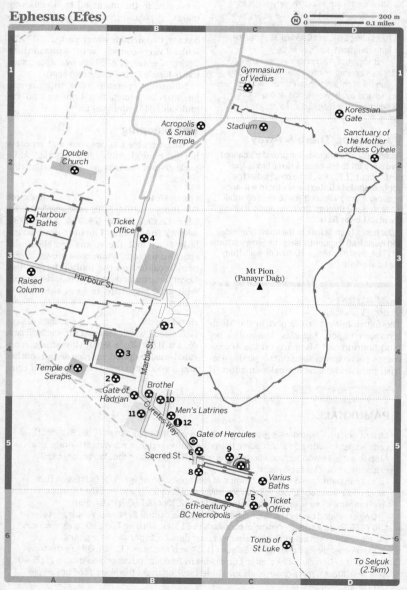

Ephesus (Efes)

N ⬆
0 —————————— 200 m
0 —————————— 0.1 miles

Gymnasium of Vedius

Koressian Gate

Acropolis & Small Temple

Stadium

Sanctuary of the Mother Goddess Cybele

Double Church

Harbour Baths

Ticket Office ✪ 4

Raised Column

Harbour St

Mt Pion (Panayır Dağı) ▲

Temple of Serapis ✪

✪ 3

Marble St

✪ 1

2 ✪

Gate of Hadrian

Brothel ✪ 10

11 ✪

Men's Latrines

✪ ❶ 12

Curetes Way

Gate of Hercules

6 ✪

9 ✪ 7 ✪

Sacred St

8 ✪

Varius Baths ✪

6th-century-BC Necropolis

✪ 5 Ticket Office

Tomb of St Luke ✪

To Selçuk (2.5km)

VISITING EPHESUS

The mediocre audioguide is not recommended, nor are the 'guides' loitering at the entrances. Organise a guide in advance through a company such as the Selçuk-based **No-Frills Ephesus Tours** (☑892 8838; www.nofrillsephesustours.com; Sen Jean Caddesi 3a ; ⊙8am-8pm summer, 9am-5pm winter).

Bring your own snacks and water, as prices are high here. Heat and crowds can be problematic so come early or late and avoid weekends and public holidays. The site lacks restrooms.

❶ Getting There & Away

Technically, accommodation providers cannot give you a lift to Ephesus. A taxi from Selçuk costs about TL20. Ask to be dropped at the upper **Magnesia Gate** (the southern entrance or *güney kapısı*), allowing you to walk downhill (roughly 3km) through the ruins and out through the main **Lower Gate**.

Dolmuşes from Selçuk to the coast (Pamucak and Kuşadası) frequently pass the Ephesus turn-off (TL4, five minutes), a 20-minute walk from the Lower Gate.

Kuşadası

☑0256 / POP 68,300

The fourth-busiest cruise port in the Mediterranean region, Kuşadası languishes behind Bodrum and Marmaris on the Aegean coast's party scene, though the plethora of Irish pubs and discos do make an effort. If you want nightlife, or simply like being near the sea, this is a good base.

◎ Sights & Activities

Kuşadası is short on specific sights, although the minor **stone fortress** on an island connected to the mainland by a causeway makes a pleasant stroll. There are also **beaches** south of town, a tourist-orientated **bazaar**, two sizeable **water parks**, and PADI scuba-diving courses with **Aquaventure Diving Center** (☑612 7845; www.aquaventure.com.tr; Miracle Beach Club; ⊙8am-6pm).

Numerous operators offer trips to major attractions including Ephesus and Pamukkale (€45), and boat tours.

🛏 Sleeping

Kuşadası centre has pensions and business hotels, none terribly atmospheric, while package-tour resorts cover the outlying coasts.

Liman Hotel PENSION €€
(Mr Happy's; ☑614 7770; www.limanhotel.com; Kıbrıs Caddesi, Buyral Sokak 4; s/d €25/38; ❈@ᗅ) The friendly Liman is not particularly fancy, but the rooms are clean and spacious enough, while great views accompany breakfast on the rooftop terrace/bar. Local information is on hand, as is help with arranging trips to local sites and to Samos.

Hotel Ilayda BUSINESS HOTEL €€
(☑614 3807; www.hotelilayda.com; Atatürk Bulvarı 46; s/d TL80/140; ❈@ᗅ) This shiny, renovated seaside option has nice design touches and a good restaurant. It has all mod cons,

WORTH A TRIP

PAMUKKALE

East of Selçuk, Pamukkale's gleaming white **travertines** (admission TL30; ⊙daylight), calcite shelves with pools cascading down the plateau edge, are a World Heritage site. Atop this fragile wonder, you can tour the magnificent ruins of the Roman city of **Hierapolis**, an ancient spa resort.

You can bathe amid sunken columns at Hierapolis' **Antique Pool** (admission TL25, public pool admission TL7.50; ⊙9am-7pm, public pool 9am-8pm) and visit the **Hierapolis Archaeology Museum** (admission TL3; ⊙9am-12.30pm & 1.30-7pm Tue-Sun).

One of several budget pensions in the village, the central **Artemis Yoruk Hotel** (☑272 2073; www.artemisyorukhotel.com; Atatürk Caddesi; s/d from TL40/50; ❈@ᗅ❈) has simple rooms with balconies set around a palm-lined outdoor swimming pool.

In summer direct buses serve Selçuk (TL27) and Kuşadası (TL30). Otherwise, travel via local hub Denizli, connected to Pamukkale by frequent buses and *dolmuşes* (TL5, 40 minutes). Most people choose advance hotel booking to get the free lift to Pamukkale (and often back again).

and great views from the rooftop terrace and some rooms.

Club Caravanserail   HISTORIC HOTEL €€
(☑614 4115; www.kusadasihotelcaravanserail.com; Atatürk Bulvarı 2; s/d/ste €80/100/150; ❋⌨) A grand 17th-century stone *caravanserai*, this photogenic structure is spotlit at night. The rooms' Ottoman decor is authentic, the kitschy 'Turkish nights' less so.

✖ Eating & Drinking

Waterfront dining is atmospheric but can be expensive; verify seafood prices before ordering. Head inland for cheaper but tasty kebap shops. Kaleiçi, Kuşadası's old quarter, offers characterful backstreet eats and some fun, more Turkish, cafes.

Raucous Barlar Sokak (Bar St) is chock-a-block with Irish-theme pubs. Locals prefer Kaleiçi's laid-back old cafes, while Cape Yılancı on the southern coast has giant bar-club-concert complexes.

Ferah   SEAFOOD €€
(☑614 1281; İskele Yanı Güvercin Parkı İçi; mains TL15-25; ⊙lunch & dinner) This waterfront restaurant pairs great sunset sea views with good-quality meze and seafood.

Bebop   INTERNATIONAL €€
(☑618 0727; www.bebopjazzclub.com; mains from TL9; ⊙lunch & dinner) Located within the marina, Bebop offers breakfasts, a pool to laze by over drinks, generous portions of Turkish and international fare, and late-night live jazz.

Köfteci Ali   KÖFTE €
(Arslanlar Caddesi 14; mains TL5; ⊙24hr summer, 9am-midnight winter) This Bar St kebap booth caters to both well-mannered Turks and drunken foreign louts. The spicy wrapped pide kebap is nourishing.

ⓘ Information

There's a post office and several banks with ATMs on Barbaros Hayrettin Bulvarı. The **tourist office** (Liman Caddesi, İskele Meydanı; ⊙8am-noon & 1-5pm Mon-Fri) is near the cruise-ship dock, and under the walls.

ⓘ Getting There & Around

BOAT All Kuşadası travel agents sell tickets to the Greek island of **Samos**. Boats (one way/same-day return €35/40) depart daily between April and October.

BUS *Dolmuşes* run to/from the *otogar*, out on the bypass road, and along the coast. Heading

---

DON'T MISS

PRIENE, MILETUS & DIDYMA

Kuşadası makes a good base for visiting a trio of ancients sites to the south. Perched high on the craggy slopes of Mt Mykale, **Priene** has a beautiful, windswept setting; **Miletus**, another ruined Graeco-Roman port city, boasts a spectacular theatre and a **museum** (admission TL3; ⊙8.30am-4.30pm); and in Didyma is the stupendous **Temple of Apollo** (☑811 0035; admission TL3; ⊙9am-7.30pm mid-May–mid-Sep, to 5.30pm mid-Sep–mid-May), the ancient world's second-largest. *Dolmuşes* don't serve Miletus; the easiest way to visit the sites is on a 'PMD' tour from Kuşadası or Selçuk (€50).

---

out of Kuşadası, *dolmuşes* leave from the central Adnan Menderes Bulvarı and the *otogar*.

Bodrum In summer three daily buses (TL25, 2½ hours); in winter take a *dolmuş* to Söke (TL5).

Selçuk *Dolmuşes* (TL5, 30 minutes, every 30 minutes) via Pamucak and the Ephesus turn-off.

Bodrum

☑0252 / POP 34,900

The beating heart of a holiday-happy peninsula, Bodrum is a famously posh paradise where sun-kissed travellers dance the breezy summer nights away. With laws restricting the height of its buildings, the town has a nice architectural uniformity; the idyllic whitewashed houses with their bright-blue trim call out to tourists' cameras. Even when the clubs are bumpin' there's something rather refined about the town.

⊙ Sights & Activities

Castle of St Peter   MUSEUM
(☑316 2516; www.bodrum-museum.com; admission TL10; ⊙9am-noon & 1-7pm Tue-Sun summer, 8am-noon & 1-5pm winter) Tamerlane's Mongol invasion of Anatolia (1402) not only gave Byzantine Constantinople a reprieve from Turkish besiegers, it also allowed the Knights Hospitaller, based in Rhodes, to build a castle at ancient Halicarnassus, using marble and stones from the famed mausoleum. By 1437 they had finished the construction, adding defensive features right up until

Bodrum

Cevat Şakir Cad

Castle of St Peter

Kumbahçe Bay

Kambahçe Bay

Pamili Sk

Yaka Sk

Derviş Görgün Cad

Yılmaz Sk

Uslu Sk

Sevenceler Sk

Mandalin Sk

Atatürk Cad

Tarla Sk

Zeki Müren Cad

Çıkrık Sk

İğinli Sk

Cumhuriyet Cad

Omurga Dere Sk

2430 Sk

Kraft Sk

Artemis Cad

Fabrika Sk

Bahçe Sk

Heykelciler Sk

Adliye Sk

Uslu Sk

Taşlık Sk

Hüseyin Nafiz Özsoy Cad

Cemil Uyar Cad

Küleü Sk

Marsmabedi Cad

Atatürk Cad

Türkkuyusu Cad

Bazaar

Belediye

Adliye Camii

Kale Cad

Dr Alim Bey Cad

Bodrum Ferryboat Association

Göktepe Sk

Gerence Sk

Davut Sk

Turgutreis Cad

1201 Sk

Ancient Harbour

Marsmabedi Cad

Araplar Sk

TEPECİK

İmbat Çık

Hamam Sk

Tepecik Camii

Salmakis Bay

1205 Sk

Saray Sk

Adnan Toker Sk

Fırkateyn Sk

Neyzen Tevfik Cad

Marina

Kıbrıs Şehitler Cad

ESKİÇEŞME

Şafak Sk

Shipyard

400 m
0.2 miles

Bodrum

◉ **Top Sights**

    Castle of St Peter D4

◉ **Sights**

    1 Ancient Theatre...................................B1
    2 Mausoleum C2
    3 Museum of Underwater
        Archaeology......................................D4

🛏 **Sleeping**

    4 Anfora F3
    5 Bahçeli Ağar Aile Pansiyonu..............B2
    6 Kaya Pension D2
    7 Otel Atrium...F2
    8 Su Otel D2

✖ **Eating**

    9 Döner Tepecik.....................................C2
   10 Fish Market E2
   11 Fruit & Vegetable Market....................E2
   12 La Pasión...E3
       Marina Köftecisi...........................(see 5)
   13 Meyhane Deniz Feneri.........................E2

🍷 **Drinking**

   14 Marina Yacht Club B3

🎭 **Entertainment**

   15 Helva..D2
   16 Marine Club Catamaran......................D3
   17 Mavi Bar F4

1522, when Süleyman the Magnificent captured Rhodes and this castle.

Renovations started in the 1960s, and the underwater archaeology treasures amassed therein became Bodrum's **Museum of Underwater Archaeology** (📞316 2516; Castle of St Peter; admission €5.55; ☺9am-7pm Tue-Sun summer). The battalions offer splendid views and the castle contains numerous historic sights.

Mausoleum   RUIN
(Turgutreis Caddesi; admission TL8; ☺8.30am-5.30pm Tue-Sun) One of the Seven Wonders of the Ancient World, the Mausoleum was the greatest achievement of Carian King Mausolus (r 376–353 BC). The king planned his own tomb and, following his death, his wife (and sister), Artemisia, oversaw the completion of an enormous, white-marble tomb topped by stepped pyramids.

The site includes relaxing gardens, a scale model of the Mausoleum and a few ancient fragments, among them the entry to Mausolus' tomb chamber.

Blue Cruises   BOAT TOUR
Countless excursion boats are moored along Neyzen Tevfik Caddesi; a 'blue cruise' on board one of these is a fun day trip. Like the ferry companies, some even access peninsula bays, saving you a sweaty minibus ride (check locally). **Karaada** (Black Island), with hot-spring waters gushing from a cave, is a popular destination where you can swim and loll in orange mud.

Book cruises at your hotel, or on the moored excursion boats, ideally a day ahead. Group tours start from €12.

🛏 Sleeping

With an efficient *dolmuş* shuttle system linking Bodrum to the rest of the peninsula, it's worth checking out hotels, apartments and villas on the other bays. Plan in advance: many hotels offer discounted rates for advance bookings, and places fill up fast in high summer. The marina-area hotels get the most noise from the clubs and bars.

TOP CHOICE Su Otel   BOUTIQUE HOTEL €€€
(📞316 6906; www.bodrumsuhotel.com; Turgutreis Caddesi, 1201 Sokak; s/d/ste from €70/95/115; ❄🛜🏊) Epitomising Bodrum's traditional white-and-bright-blue decor, the Su has sun-filled bedrooms, some with balconies overlooking the terraced gardens and inviting pool. The friendly management helps with all local activities; out of high season, it even runs a cooking class.

Kaya Pension   PENSION €€
(📞316 5745; www.kayapansiyon.com.tr; Eski Hükümet Sokak 14; s/d/tr TL100/120/140; ❄🛜) Kaya has clean, simple rooms in town and a beautiful flowering courtyard for breakfast and drinks. Reception has a safe for valuables, and the helpful staff can arrange activities.

Otel Atrium   HOTEL €€
(📞316 2181; www.atriumbodrum.com; Fabrika Sokak 21; s/d incl half board from TL100/120; 🅿❄🛜🏊) This midsize hotel amid tangerine trees has bright and fairly spacious rooms. It's good value for families and independent travellers. There's a pool (with separate kid's section), a poolside bar, two restaurants and free parking. It's a five- to 10-minute walk to both centre and beach.

Marmara Bodrum LUXURY HOTEL €€€
(☑999 1010; www.themarmarahotels.com; Suluhasan Caddesi 18; r/ste from €180/600; ❈@☒)
High on a bluff, the Marmara has great views, elegant rooms, and facilities including tennis, spa, gym and two pools. A free shuttle accesses a private beach in Torba.

Bahçeli Ağar Aile Pansiyonu PENSION €€
(☑316 1648; 1402 Sokak 4; s/d €50/65) This friendly little pension has small but spotless rooms with balconies, some overlooking a vine-draped courtyard, and a kitchen.

Anfora PENSION €
(☑316 5530; www.anforapansiyon.com; Omurça Dere Sokak 23; s/d from TL45/70; ❈🛜) Rooms are well kept and clean (though can be cramped) at this friendly pension. Although Bar St's a few blocks away, it's not too loud at night.

✕ Eating & Drinking

Bodrum's waterfront has pricey, big-menu restaurants (not all bad), while nearby are discreet backstreet contenders, fast-food stalls and a **fruit and veg market** (Cevat Şakir Caddesi).

Generally, Bodrum's western-bay eateries are more upscale, while the eastern bay has more informal, soak-up-the-Efes fare.

For drinking, follow the same rule of thumb: for cheap and cheerful head to the eastern bay; for expensive and classy, think western bay. Dr Alim Bey Caddesi and Cumhuriyet Caddesi function as Bodrum's waterfront 'Bar St'.

TOP CHOICE Fish Market SEAFOOD €€
(Cevat Şakir Caddesi; meze from TL4, fish TL20; ⏱dinner Mon-Sat) Bodrum's fish market offers a unique sort of direct dining: you choose between myriad fresh fish and seafood on ice at fishmongers' tables, and have them cooked (about TL6 extra) at any adjoining restaurant. The plain restaurants spill across the small streets; **Meyhane Deniz Feneri** (☑316 3534; Belediye Gıda Çarşısı 12; fish TL18-35) is the area's oldest, and many residents still consider it the best. Dinner for two with a few meze, drinks and fish will run at least TL100 here. In any fish-market restaurant, book ahead for evening dining.

TOP CHOICE La Pasión SPANISH €€
(Restaurante Español; www.lapasion-bodrum.com; cnr Atatürk Caddesi & Uslu Sokak; set menus TL18-35; ⏱lunch & dinner) To see just how far Bodrum has come in its quest to join the ranks of international seaside sophistication, try this refined Spanish restaurant down a side street off Cumhuriyet Caddesi. The good-value lunch menus (appetiser, mains, dessert and first drink are TL18 per person) change weekly.

Marina Köftecisi KÖFTE €€
(☑313 5593; Neyzen Tevfik Caddesi 158; mains TL10-17) With a waterfront view, this is an excellent spot for various traditional *köfte* recipes. Try *kaşarlı köfte* (meatballs with cheese from sheep's milk), served with pita bread drizzled with tomato sauce and yoghurt.

Döner Tepecik KEBAP €
(Neyzen Tevfik Caddesi; kebaps from TL6; ⏱breakfast, lunch & dinner) Across from the eponymous mosque, this local favourite does tasty kebabs on homemade bread.

Marina Yacht Club BAR
(☑316 1228; Neyzen Tevfik Caddesi 5; ⏱8am-late) Marina serves meals (Italian and Turkish flavours, average TL22 per person), but its primary identity is as a big, breezy waterfront nightspot. Merrymakers congregrate around the extended, wrap-around bar or at the scattered tiny tables dotting the way to the water-facing deck, where cover bands liven things up.

☆ Entertainment

Nightclubs such as the floating **Marine Club Catamaran** (www.clubcatamaran.com; Dr Alim Bey Caddesi; admission weekday/weekend TL35/40; ⏱10pm-4am mid-May–Sep) are famous party spots, and the likes of **Helva** (www.helvabodrum.com; Neyzen Tevfik Caddesi 54; ⏱2pm-3am) are slicker clubs aimed at Turkish trendsetters. **Mavi Bar** (Cumhuriyet Caddesi 175; ⏱6pm-6am) hosts live music, as do the **castle** and **ancient theatre** (Kıbrıs Şehitler Caddesi); for upcoming events, visit www.biletix.com.

ℹ Information

Head to Cevat Şakir Caddesi for ATMs.
Post office (Cevat Şakir Caddesi; ⏱8.30am-5pm, telephone exchange 8am-midnight)
Tourist Office (Kale Meydanı; ⏱8am-6pm Mon-Fri, daily in summer)

ℹ Getting There & Away

AIR Almost 50 airlines, including charter and budget operators, Turkish Airlines, AtlasJet and Pegasus Airlines, fly from Europe, İstanbul and elsewhere to Bodrum International Airport, 36km away. Havaş shuttle buses (TL19) tie in with Turkish Airlines, AnadoluJet, Onur Air, Sun Express and Pegasus Airlines flights; otherwise an expensive taxi (TL90 from the city centre; TL100 from the airport) is your only option.

BOAT For tickets and the latest times, contact the **Bodrum Ferryboat Association** (☑316 0882; www.bodrumferryboat.com; Kale Caddesi Cümrük Alanı 22; ⊗8am-8pm).

Kos (one way or same-day return €32, one hour) Daily ferries to/from the Greek island.

Rhodes (one way or same-day return €60, 2¼ hours) From June to September there are two weekly hydrofoils to/from the Greek island.

Datça (single/return TL25/40, two hours) Daily ferries from mid-June to September; four weekly from April to mid-June and in October.

BUS There are services to more or less anywhere you could wish to go.

İstanbul TL68, 12 hours, 10 nightly

Kuşadası TL20, 2½ hours, four each afternoon

Marmaris TL15, three hours, hourly

Marmaris

☑0252 / POP 31,400

A popular resort town with a nonstop party atmosphere and good nearby beaches, in-your-face Marmaris is Mediterranean Turkey's version of Spain's Costa del Sol. Bar St offers unparalleled decadence, and charter boats will happily whisk you to Fethiye and beyond.

⊙ Sights & Activities

Marmaris Castle & Museum   FORTRESS, MUSEUM
(Marmaris Kalesi ve Müzesi; ☑412 1459; admission TL3; ⊗8am-noon & 1-5pm Tue-Sun) Marmaris' hilltop castle (1522) hosts **Marmaris Museum**, which exhibits amphorae, glassware, coins and other local finds. Saunter the castle's **walls** and gaze down on the bustling marina.

Boat Trips   BOAT TOUR
Marmaris Bay *dolmuş*-boat **day trips** (TL30 to TL35) offer eye-opening views and inviting swimming holes, and you can even hire a yacht, which offers the pleasure of a blue voyage down the coast (see p803). Cruises offered by the long-established **Yeşil Marmaris Travel & Yachting** (☑412 2290; www.yesilmarmaris.com; Barbaros Caddesi 13; 4 people from €300, incl all meals & soft drinks; ⊗7am-11.30pm Mon-Sat high season, 8.30am-6.30pm low season) are recommended. As for the rest of the old salts advertising tours, compare prices, ask around, negotiate and, before signing up,

DON'T MISS

DATÇA & BOZBURUN PENINSULAS

Not far south, these deeply indented peninsulas hide azure bays backed by pine-covered mountains and gorgeous fishing villages. Reach them from Marmaris by *dolmuş*, boat or scooter (rentals average TL45 per day in high season).

confirm all details (exact boat, itinerary, lunch etc). Yachts sail from May to October.

From May to October, hourly water taxis, docked around the Atatürk statue, serve the beaches at **İçmeler** and **Turunç** (TL13, 45 minutes), respectively 10km and 20km southwest of Marmaris.

Diving   DIVING
Several harbourside companies along Yeni Kordon Caddesi offer scuba-diving excursions and courses (April through October), including **Marmaris Diving Center** (aytac.ozan@hotmail.com) and **Deep Blue Dive Center** (☑0541 374 5881, 0506 614 6408; www.sealung.com).

🛏 Sleeping

Marmaris is geared towards all-in package tour groups, so good independent sleeping options are rare.

Halıcı Hotel   HOTEL €€
(☑412 3626; www.halicihotel.com; Sokak 1; s/d TL80/130; ᴾ❄@⚛⚛) Despite being a big and somewhat dated package-tour hotel, this place is good value, with a big outdoor pool in a leafy tropical garden. It's a 10-minute walk west of the central waterfront.

Maltepe Pansiyon   PENSION €
(☑412 1629; www.maltepepansiyon.com; 66 Sokak 9; s/d/tr/q TL35/75/90/120; ❄@) A small pension in a shady garden, the Maltepe offers small but spotless rooms (most ensuite). You can use the kitchen.

Bariş Motel & Pansiyon   PENSION €
(☑413 0652; www.barismotel.com; 66 Sokak 10; s/d TL50/70; ❄) Opposite the canal, this friendly little pension has spartan but clean rooms. Breakfast costs TL6. If coming by taxi, specify that you mean this Bariş (and not the similarly named apartment complex).

🍴 Eating & Drinking

Marmaris by night offers more neon than Vegas. Hedonistic crowds descend on the aptly named Bar St (39 Sokak) for foam parties, laser beams, dance music and tequilas by the half-dozen.

Ney
TURKISH €€

(☑412 0217; 26 Sokak 24; meze TL5-6, mains TL15-20) Up from the western marina, atmospheric little Ney occupies a 250-year-old Greek house. The home-cooked specialties include *tavuklu mantı böreği* (Turkish ravioli with chicken; TL14).

Liman Restaurant
SEAFOOD €€

(☑412 6336; 40 Sokak 38; mains TL10-20; ⊗8am-1am) This old favourite in the bazaar serves excellent meze and fish dishes (check prices in advance), including grilled sea bass, fish soup and calamari. Landlubbers will enjoy the *kavurma* (stir-fried lamb).

Panorama Restaurant & Bar
INTERNATIONAL €€

(☑413 4835; Hacı İmam Sokağı 40; mains TL10-15; ⊗9am-1am) Panorama's marina-view terrace is more famous than the food, though it's still pleasant for pizza or pasta and sunset drinks.

Aquarium Restaurant
INTERNATIONAL €€

(☑413 1522; Barbaros Caddesi; mains TL15-30; ⊗9am-midnight) A portside restaurant with sublime views, this is a good spot for large grills and steaks.

Meryemana
TURKISH €

(☑412 7855; 35 Sokak 5b; mains TL5-6; 📶) Meryemana's nourishing traditional tastes, including *mantı* (TL6), meze, spicy dips and homemade bread, attract Turks and foreigners alike.

ℹ Information

Tourist Office (☑412 1035; İskele Meydanı 2; ⊗8am-noon & 1-5pm Mon-Fri, daily Jun–mid-Sep) Below the castle; unhelpful.

ℹ Getting There & Away

AIR The nearest airports are at Dalaman, reached on the Havaş shuttle bus (TL25), and Bodrum.

BOAT Rhodes (Greece; one way/same-day return from €45/55, 50 minutes) Catamarans sail twice daily from April to October. In low season, cargo boats go two to three times weekly. Buy tickets from Marmaris agencies at least one day in advance.

BUS The *otogar* is 3km north of the centre, served by *dolmuşes*. Buses include:

Bodrum TL15, three hours, at least every two hours

Fethiye TL20, three hours, half-hourly

İzmir TL32, 4¼ hours, hourly

THE MEDITERRANEAN COAST

The western Mediterranean, known as the 'Turquoise Coast', is a region of endless azure sea lined with kilometres of sandy beaches and backed by mountains rising up to almost 3000m. It also has an embarrassment of ancient ruins strewn through the aromatic scrub and pine forests, and a broad menu of sports and activities.

The Med's seamless mix of history and holiday inspires and excites. The most dramatic way to see this stretch of coastline is aboard a *gület* (traditional wooden yacht) or by walking sections of the 500km-long Lycian Way, high above the crystal waters known locally as the Akdeniz (White Sea).

The eastern Mediterranean, meanwhile, has long lived in its more fashionable western neighbour's shadow. But the area facing Syria has Christian sites, Hittite settlements and Crusader castles between its timeless hillside villages, mountains and stunning coastline.

Fethiye

☑0252 / POP 81,500

In 1958 an earthquake levelled the harbour city of Fethiye, sparing only the ancient remains of Telmessos. Half a century on, Fethiye is once again a prosperous, growing hub of the western Mediterranean. Its natural harbour, tucked away in the southern reaches of a broad bay scattered with pretty islands, is perhaps the region's finest.

⊙ Sights

Dolmuşes run southeast to the **Lycian ruins** dotting the countryside, including Tlos, Pınara, Letoön and Xanthos.

Telmessos
RUIN

The mammoth **Tomb of Amyntas** (admission TL8; ⊗8am-7pm May-Oct, to 5pm Nov-Apr), an Ionic temple facade, was carved into the sheer rock face in 350 BC. Located south of the centre, it is best visited at sunset.

BLUE CRUISE

Fethiye is the hub of Turkey's cruising scene, and the most popular route is the 'Blue Voyage' (Mavi Yolculuk) to Olympos: a four-day, three-night journey on a *gület* (traditional wooden sailing boat) that attracts young party animals. Boats usually call in at Ölüdeniz and Butterfly Valley and stop at Kaş, Kalkan and/or Kekova, with the final night at Gökkaya Bay opposite the eastern end of Kekova. A less-common (but some say prettier) route is between Marmaris and Fethiye.

Depending on the season, the price is typically €165 to €195 per person (food should be included, but you sometimes have to pay for water and soft drinks and always for alcohol). Make sure you shop around; many shoddy operators work the waters and wallets. Recommended operators include **Before Lunch Cruises** (☑0535 636 0076, 0532 623 4359; www.beforelunch.com), **Ocean Yachting Travel Agency** (☑612 4807; www.oceantravelagency.com; İskele Meydanı 1; ☺9am-9pm Apr-Oct), **Olympos Yachting** (☑892 1145; www.olymposyachting.com) and **V-Go Yachting & Travel Agency** (☑612 2113; www.bluecruisesturkey.com).

Other, smaller rock tombs lie about 500m to the east.

Behind the harbour in the centre of town are the partly excavated remains of a 2nd-century BC Roman **theatre**. In town you'll also see curious **Lycian stone sarcophagi** dating from around 450 BC.

On the hillside south of town, and along the Kayaköy road, is the ruined tower of a 15th-century **Crusader fortress**.

Kayaköy   HISTORIC AREA
(admission TL5; ☺8.30am-5pm) *Dolmuşes* (TL4) run to this nearby open-air museum, an evocative Ottoman Greek 'ghost town' that was abandoned during the population exchange of 1923.

🏃 Activities

Lycian Way   WALK
Acclaimed as one of the top 10 long-distance walks in the world, the Lycian Way follows signposted paths around the Teke peninsula to Antalya. The route leads through pine and cedar forests in the shadow of mountains rising almost 3000m, past villages, stunning coastal views and an embarrassment of ruins at ancient Lycian cities. Walk it in sections (unless you have plenty of time and stamina).

Fethiye is at the western end of this 500km walking trail, which leads south from here to Faralya and Butterfly Valley.

Fethiye offers numerous water-based activities and boat trips, including the **12-Island Tour** (per person TL30-50) and the **Butterfly Valley tour** (TL25) via Ölüdeniz. On dry land, the **Dalyan tour** (TL50)

includes Lake Köyceğiz, the Sultaniye mud baths, Kaunos ruins and İztuzu Beach, and the **Saklıkent Gorge tour** (TL45) includes Tlos and a trout lunch.

Seven Capes (☑0537 403 3779; www.seven-capes.com) offers sea kayaking, **European Diving Centre** (☑614 9771; www.europeandivingcentre.com; Fevzi Çakmak Caddesi 133) runs diving trips and courses, and **Ocean Yachting Travel Agency** (☑612 4807; www.oceantravelagency.com; İskele Meydanı 1) organises activities from rafting to horse riding.

🛏 Sleeping

Most accommodation is up the hill behind the marina in Karagözler or further west. Many pensions organise transport from the *otogar*.

Yıldırım Guest House   PENSION, HOSTEL €
(☑614 4627, 0543 779 4732; www.yildirimguesthouse.com; Fevzi Çakmak Caddesi 21;, dm/d/tr TL25/80/120; ❄@🛜) Shipshape Yıldırım, opposite the marina, features four- to six-bed dorms (two by gender and one mixed) and spotless rooms. The well-travelled host Ömer offers excursions, pick-ups, laundry, evening meals (TL15), Saturday hikes on the Lycian Way (TL10) and free bikes.

Villa Daffodil   HOTEL €€
(☑614 9595; www.villadaffodil.com; Fevzi Çakmak Caddesi 115; s/d TL85/120; ❄🛜🏊) This large Ottoman-styled and flower-bedecked guesthouse, one of the few older buildings to survive the earthquake and development, has 41 rooms with stylish furnishings, a homely feel and, in some cases, balconies and sea views. The terrace and pool are centres of activity.

V-Go's Hotel & Guesthouse
PENSION, HOSTEL €€

(☏614 4004, 612 5409; www.v-gohotel.com; Fevzi Çakmak Caddesi 109; r per person €20, f €60; ✳@🤶🛰) This modern hostel/guesthouse at the western end of Karagözler has 28 rooms (four are four- to eight-bed dorms) across two buildings, most overlooking the sea or pool. There's a terrace with chill-out chairs and a bar with self-service music and DVDs.

✖ Eating & Drinking

Fethiye's enormous canalside Tuesday **market** takes place between Atatürk Caddesi and Pürşabey Caddesi next to the stadium. Bars and nightclubs are mostly on Hamam Sokak in the Old Town, and along Dispanser Caddesi south of the Martyrs' Monument.

TOP CHOICE Reis
SEAFOOD €€

(☏612 5368, 0532 472 5989; www.reisrestaurant.com; Hal ve Pazar Yeri 62; mains TL12-20; ⊘10am-midnight) To taste Fethiye's fabulous fish, buy your own (per kilo TL18 to TL25) from the fishmongers in the central covered market, then take it to one of the restaurants opposite. Reis charges TL5 per head for cooking the fish, plus a sauce, green salad, garlic bread and fruit. It also does meze and meat dishes. You should book.

İskele Ocakbaşı
BARBECUE €€

(☏614 9423; Şehit Feti Bey Parkı; meze TL6-19, grills TL12-26; ⊘9am-1am) This grill restaurant overlooks the water and a small park (outside seating), and serves excellent meat dishes from its central barbecue.

Meğri Lokantası
TURKISH €€

(☏614 4047; www.megrirestaurant.com; Çarşı Caddesi 26; mains TL7-13, mixed plates TL17-25; ⊘8am-11.30pm low season, to 1am high season) Packed with locals who spill onto the streets, the Meğri offers hearty home-style cooking at palatable prices. Choose from the huge display of meze and savoury mains or try the güveç (casserole; TL20 to TL25).

Deniz Restaurant
SEAFOOD €€

(☏612 0212; Uğur Mumcu Parkı Yanı 10/1; mains TL15-30) The 'Sea' exhibits everything alive and swimming in tanks (the grouper is best) and excels in unusual meze. Try the semizotu (purslane) in yoghurt and the ceviche (fish preserved in lemon juice).

Kismet
BAR, CABARET

(☏0545 922 2301; Uğur Mumcu Parkı Yanı) This welcoming bar and cabaret venue (shows most Friday nights in season; phone for an update) off Dispanser Caddesi is open all day until the wee hours. Good for a sundowner or something cold much later.

❶ Information

Tourist Office (☏614 1527; İskele Meydanı; ⊘8am-7pm Mon-Fri, 10am-5pm Sat & Sun May-Sep, 8am-noon & 1-5pm Mon-Fri Oct-Apr) Helpful centre opposite the marina.

❶ Getting There & Away

BOAT Catamarans sail to Rhodes (Greece; one way/same-day return €50/60, 1½ hours) between late April and October.

BUS Fethiye's otogar is 2.5km east of the centre, connected to the centre and Karagözler by dolmuş (TL1.50).

Buses to Antalya either go via the quicker, inland (yayla) route (TL20, 3½ hours), or the the less-direct coastal (sahil) route (TL28, 6½ hours, hourly in summer), via Kalkan (TL11, 1½ hours), Kaş (TL13, two hours) and Olympos (TL35, 4¾ hours).

DOLMUŞ From the stops near the mosque, minibuses run to local destinations including Ölüdeniz (TL5) and Faralya (TL5.50).

Ölüdeniz
☏0252 / POP 4600

Ölüdeniz's many charms – a sheltered lagoon beside a lush national park, a long spit of sandy beach, and Baba Dağ (Mt Baba) casting its shadow across the sea – have been a curse as much as a blessing. Many people think package tourism has turned 'Dead Sea' into a Paradise Lost. But Ölüdeniz remains a good place to party between trips along the serene coastline.

The **lagoon** remains a lovely place to while away a few hours on the beach with mountains soaring above you. Ölüdeniz is also a hot spot for **paragliding** (and parasailing). Companies here offer tandem paragliding flights off Baba Dağ (1960m) for TL120 to TL150.

Day cruises (TL15 to TL25) explore the coast, and shuttle boats head south to the beautiful **Butterfly Valley** (TL20 return).

⛺ Sleeping & Eating

Ölüdeniz's camping grounds are almost like budget resorts, with comfortable and stylish bungalows. There are also laid-back accommodation options in the valley and nearby Faralya and Kabak.

Sugar Beach Club CAMPGROUND, RESORT €
(📞617 0048; www.thesugarbeachclub.com; Ölüdeniz Caddesi 20; camp site per person/car/caravan TL15/15/15, bungalows per person TL50-140; ❄️@🛜) About 500m north of the entrance to the park, this ultrachilled spot is the pick of the crop for backpackers. The strip of beach is shaded by palms and lounging areas, with a waterfront bar-restaurant. There's free entry to the beach, and canoes and pedalos to hire, and regular events such as barbecues. Nonguests can use the sun lounges, parasols and showers for TL7.

Oba Motel Restaurant INTERNATIONAL €€
(📞617 0158; www.obamotel.com.tr/Erestaurant. asp; Mimar Sinan Caddesi; mains TL15-25; ⊗8am-midnight) Partly housed in a wooden cabin, the Oba has a reputation for home-style food at good prices. It does great Turkish/European breakfasts (from TL12), snacks and full-on mains, including a half-dozen veggie options.

ⓘ Getting There & Away

There are frequent minibuses to Fethiye (TL5, 25 minutes).

Patara

📞0242 / POP 950

With Turkey's longest uninterrupted **beach**, laid-back little Patara (Gelemiş) is the perfect spot to mix your ruin-rambling with some dedicated sand-shuffling. The extensive **ruins** (admission TL5; ⊗9am-7pm May-Oct, 8am-5pm Nov-Apr) include a 5000-seat theatre and the *bouleterion* (council chamber), ancient Patara's 'parliament' where it is believed the Lycian League met. All in all, the former hippy-trail stop offers a good combination of nature, culture and traditional village life.

🛏️ Sleeping & Eating

TOP CHOICE Patara View Point Hotel HOTEL €€
(📞843 5184, 0533 350 0347; www.pataraviewpoint.com; s/d TL70/100; ❄️@🛜🏊) Up the hill from the main road, the *très* stylish Patara View has a pleasant pool, an Ottoman-style cushioned terrace, 27 rooms with balconies, and killer views over the valley. You'll find old farm implements inside and out,

including a 2000-year-old olive press. There's a tractor-shuttle to and from the beach at 10am and 3pm.

Akay Pension PENSION €
(📞843 5055, 0532 410 2195; www.pataraakaypension.com; s/d/tr TL45/60/80; ❄️@) Kazım and wife Ayşe's pension has 13 well-maintained rooms with comfortable beds and balconies overlooking citrus groves, and an Ottoman-style lounge. Sample at least one set meal (from TL18).

Flower Pension PENSION €
(📞843 5164, 0530 511 0206; www.pataraflowerpension.com; s/d TL45/60, 4-/6-person apt TL100/150; ❄️@🛜) On the road before the turn-off to the centre, the Flower has simple and airy rooms with balconies overlooking the garden, plus kitchen-equipped studios and apartments. There's a free shuttle to the beach.

Tlos Restaurant TURKISH €€
(📞843 5135; meze TL3-6, pide TL6-15, mains TL12-20; ⊗8am-midnight) The BYO Tlos has an open kitchen by the centre under a large plane tree. Its *guveç* (TL15) is recommended.

ⓘ Getting There & Away

Buses on the Fethiye–Kaş route drop you on the highway 4km from the village. From here *dolmuşes* run to the village every 30 to 40 minutes.

In high season minibuses run from the beach through the village to Fethiye (TL12, 1½ hours), Kalkan (TL7.50, 20 minutes) and Kaş (TL10, 45 minutes).

Kalkan

📞0242 / POP 3250

Kalkan is a stylish hillside harbour town overlooking a sparkling blue bay. It's as rightly famous for its restaurants as its small but central beach, and makes an upmarket alternative to neighbouring Kaş. Development continues on the hills, driven by the many tourists and expats, and the former Ottoman-Greek fishing village's charms are found in its compact Old Town.

🛏️ Sleeping

TOP CHOICE Hotel Villa Mahal LUXURY HOTEL €€€
(📞844 3268, 0532 685 2136; www.villamahal.com; d €200-300, ste €550; ❄️🛜🏊) One of Turkey's most elegant and stylish hotels lies atop a cliff on the western side of Kalkan Bay, about

2km by road from town. The 13 rooms, individually designed in whiter-than-white minimalist fashion, have private terraces and sea views. The sail-shaped infinity pool is spectacularly suspended on the edge of the void and steps descend to the sea and a bathing platform. There's a free water taxi into the centre and sailboats can be hired.

Caretta Boutique Hotel HOTEL €€
(844 3435, 0505 269 0753; www.carettaboutiquehotel.com; İskele Sokak 6; s €45-58, d €69-85; ❄@) A perennial favourite with isolated swimming platforms, excellent home-style cooking, a warm welcome, and 13 bright and sunny rooms. For an away-from-it-all experience, nab one of the two terrace rooms reached down steps along the cliff. There's a free boat service from below the lighthouse in the marina.

White House Pension PENSION €€
(844 3738, 0532 443 0012; www.kalkanwhitehouse.co.uk; Süleyman Yilmaz Caddesi 24-26; s/d/f TL100/150/175; ❄@) Situated on a quiet corner at the top of the hill, this attentively run pension has 10 compact, breezy rooms (four with balconies) in a spotless family home. The real winner here, though, is the view from the terrace. Sharing the garden is sister property the **Courtyard Hotel Kalkan** (844 3738, 0532 443 0012; www.courtyardkalkan.com; s & d TL350), cobbled out of a couple of 19th-century village houses.

Kelebek Hotel & Apartments HOTEL, APARTMENT €
(844 3770, 0543 375 7947; www.butterflyholidays.co.uk; Mantese Mah 4; s TL45-50, d TL70-85, 1-/2-bedroom apt TL75/125; ❄@❄) Though slightly away from the action to the north of the centre, and a couple of hundred metres off the D400, the family-run 'Butterfly' offers remarkably good value for Kalkan. Choose between rooms in the main building, with a pool table in the tiled lobby, and apartments with kitchens in a separate block.

✕ Eating & Drinking

Kalkan's main market day is Thursday, though there is a smaller one in the Akbel district to the northwest on Sunday. In high season, always book ahead.

Korsan Fish Terrace SEAFOOD €€€
(844 3076; www.korsankalkan.com; Atatürk Caddesi; mains TL26-40; ⊙10am-midnight) On the roof of the 19th-century Patara Stone House, Korsan offers a fine seafood experience.

There's live jazz on Tuesday and Saturday from 8.30pm, and an alternative, fishless menu of modern Turkish and international dishes.

Guru's Place ANATOLIAN €€
(844 3848, 0536 331 1016; www.kalkanguru.com; Kaş Yolu; meze plate TL20, mains TL9-28; ⊙8am-11pm) Affable Hüseyin and family have been running this seaside restaurant for 20 years. Food is authentic and fresh, coming from their own garden. The menu is often limited to daily specials such as the lamb shanks. It's a bit out of town on the road to Kaş, so a free transfer service is provided.

Hünkar Ocakbaşı TURKISH €€
(844 2077; Şehitler Caddesi 38e; mains TL9-17) This authentic grill house serves all the traditional favourites, as well as pide (TL6 to TL9), pizzas (TL8 to TL11) and *guveç*, including a vegetarian option.

The Lighthouse TEA GARDEN, CAFE
(844 3752; Yat Limanı; beer TL6; ⊙8.30am-2.30am) The erstwhile Fener ('lighthouse' in Turkish – and no prizes for guessing its location) is popular with locals, expats and visitors.

❶ Getting There & Away

Minibuses go to Fethiye (TL11, 1½ hours), Kaş (TL5, 35 minutes) and Patara (TL5, 25 minutes).

Kaş

🗷 0242 / POP 7200

A more genuine destination than Kalkan, Kaş (pronounced 'cash') may not sport the region's finest beaches, but this yachties' haven has a wonderfully mellow atmosphere. The surrounding areas are ideal for day trips by sea or scooter, and a plethora of adventure sports are on offer, in particular some excellent wreck diving.

◉ Sights & Activities

Apart from enjoying the small pebble **beaches**, you can walk 500m west of the main square to the well-preserved **Hellenistic theatre**. Other ancient remnants from the Lycian port of Antiphellos include the **rock tombs** in the cliffs above town, which you can walk to. It's well worth climbing the hilly street to the east of the main square to reach the **King's Tomb**, a Lycian sarcophagus mounted on a high base. Overland excursions and *dolmuşes* go to **Saklıkent Gorge**.

Boat Trips
CRUISE

(TL40-TL50) The most popular trip is to Üçağız and Kekova, a three-hour bus-and-boat excursion that includes time to see several interesting ruins as well as swim. Off Kekova Island is the Batık Şehir (Sunken City), the submerged remains of Lycian Simena. Other standard tours go to the Mavi Mağara (Blue Cave), Patara and Kalkan, or to Longos and several small nearby islands.

Bougainville Travel
OUTDOOR

(836 3737; www.bougainville-turkey.com; İbrahim Serin Sokak 10, Kaş) This long-established English-Turkish tour operator organises a plethora of activities, including canyoning, mountain biking, paragliding, scuba diving and sea kayaking. They are also experts on Lycian Way trekking.

Sleeping

Hideaway Hotel
HOTEL €€

(836 1887, 0532 261 0170; www.hotelhideaway.com; Eski Kilise Arkası Sokak 7; s TL40-60, d TL60-120; ❋@☞☀) The aptly named Hideaway, located at the far end of town on a quiet street, has comfortable rooms with balcony, some facing the sea. There's also a roof terrace with terminals, DVD player, honour-system bar, and views over the water and amphitheatre. Full meals are available.

Hotel Hadrian
RESORT €€€

(836 2856; www.hotel-hadrian.de; Doğan Kaşaroğlu Sokak 10; s €80-100, d €125-140, ste from €160; ❋☀) About halfway out on the peninsula, the German-owned Hadrian is a tropical, Teutonic oasis. The large seawater pool, private swimming platform and terrace bar with wow-factor views are all excellent.

White House Pension
PENSION €€

(836 1513, 0532 550 2663; www.orcholiday.com; Yeni Cami Caddesi 10; s TL60-85, d TL100-140; ❋☞) Decked out in wood, wrought iron, marble and terracotta paint, this stylish little gem has attractive rooms and a pretty terrace. Very warm welcome.

Anı Pension & Guesthouse
PENSION €

(836 1791, 0533 326 4201; www.motelani.com; Süleyman Çavuş Caddesi 12; s TL30-50, d TL50-60; ❋@☞) Host Ömer offers smallish but spotless rooms with balconies, a relaxing roof terrace with DVD player, lounge with cushions and water pipes, and a bar. Guests can use the kitchen (occasional barbecues for TL15) and borrow a chaise longue and umbrella for the beach.

Eating

There are some excellent restaurants southeast of the main square, especially around Sandıkçı Sokak. A big outdoor Friday market takes place along the old road to Kalkan.

TOP CHOICE İkbal
MODERN TURKISH €€€

(836 3193; Sandıkçı Sokak 6; mains TL20-34; ☺9am-midnight) This Turkish-German restaurant serves excellent prepared fish dishes and the house speciality – slow-cooked leg of lamb – from a small but well-chosen menu. There's also a good selection of Turkish wines from Mediterranean vineyards.

TOP CHOICE Şaraphane
TURKISH €€

(836 2715, 0532 520 3262; Yeni Cami Caddesi 3; mains TL12-25) In the old part of Kaş, the 'Wine House' emphasises the fruit of the vine amid cosy surrounds with an open kitchen, bleached wooden floors and a roaring fire in the cooler months. Nice touches include complimentary homemade meze.

Köşk
MEZE €€

(836 3857; Gürsoy Sokak 13; mains TL14-25) In a lovely little square off a cobbled street just up from the water, Köşk occupies a rustic, 150-year-old house with two terraces. It serves good grills and gorgeous meze (TL6 to TKL7).

Blue House
MEZE €€

(836 1320; Sandıkçı Sokak 8; mains TL20-34) This family-run restaurant, with its blue doorway and balcony, has a great ambience and lovely views. The ladies work from the kitchen of their home, which you have to pass through to reach the terrace.

Bi Lokma
MEZE €€

(836 3942; www.bilokma.com.tr; Hükümet Caddesi 2; mains TL13-21; ☺9am-midnight) Also known as 'Mama's Kitchen', this place has tables meandering around a terraced garden overlooking the harbour. The great traditional dishes include *mantı* (TL13) and *börek* (TL13).

Drinking

Giorgio's Bar
BAR

(0544 608 8687; Cumhuriyet Meydanı) Facing the main square, Georgio's has great music

Kaş

(played live several times a week). Cocktails from TL18.

Hideaway Bar & Cafe
BAR, CAFE

(☐836 3369; Cumhuriyet Meydanı 16/A; beer TL6-8; ☺4pm-3am) The enchanting Hideaway is tucked away in a garden accessed via a secret doorway. Turkish breakfast, Sunday brunch, snacks and cakes are offered.

Moon River
BAR

(☐836 4423; İbrahim Serin Caddesi 1d; beer TL5; ☺8am-3am; ☎) This lounge offers live music throughout the week, good coffee, and reasonably priced drinks.

Echo Cafe & Bar
BAR, CLUB

(☐836 2047; www.echocafebar.com; Limanı Sokak; ☺8am-4am) Hip and stylish, this lounge near an ancient cistern on the harbour has Kaş high society sipping fruit daiquiris to both live and canned jazz.

ℹ Information

The **tourist office** (☐836 1238; Cumhuriyet Meydanı; ☺8am-5pm daily May-Oct, 8am-noon & 1-5pm Mon-Fri Nov-Apr) is on the main square.

ℹ Getting There & Away

BOAT The **Meis Express** (www.meisexpress. com; one way or same-day return TL40; 20 minutes) fast ferry sails daily throughout the year to the tiny Greek island of Meis (Kastellorizo). It's possible to spend the night there, or continue to Rhodes. Tickets can be bought from travel agencies or directly from Meis Express in the harbour.

BUS İstanbul TL65, 15 hours, 6.30am daily
İzmir TL40, 8½ hours, daily

DOLMUŞ There are regular *dolmuşes* to:
Antalya TL23, 3½ hours
Fethiye TL15; 2½ hours
Kalkan TL5, 35 minutes
Olympos TL18, 2½ hours
Patara TL7.50, 45 minutes.

Kaş

◎ Top Sights
Hellenistic Theatre	A2
King's Tomb	E3

Activities, Courses & Tours
1	Boat Trips	D3
2	Bougainville Travel	E2

Sleeping
3	Anı Pension & Guesthouse	B2
4	Hideaway Hotel	B2
5	White House Pension	C3

Eating
6	Bi Lokma	E3
7	Blue House	E3
8	İkbal	E3
9	Köşk	E3
10	Şaraphane	B3

Drinking
11	Giorgio's Bar	E3
12	Hideaway Bar & Cafe	D2

Entertainment
13	Echo Cafe & Bar	D3
14	Moon River	E2

Olympos & Çirali

📞 0242

Olympos has long had ethereal appeal to travellers. It was an important Lycian city in the 2nd century BC, when the Olympians devoutly worshipped Hephaestus (Vulcan), the god of fire. No doubt this veneration sprang from reverence for the mysterious Chimaera, an eternal flame that still burns in the ground nearby. Along with the other Lycian coastal cities, Olympos went into decline in the 1st century BC, before its fortunes twisted and turned through Roman rule, 3rd-century AD pirate attacks, and fortress building during the Middle Ages by the Venetians and Genoese.

Neighbouring Çiralı, over the mountain and the narrow Ulupınar Stream, is another gem of a place. While Olympos has a well-established party reputation (though it has gentrified considerably), Çiralı is a family-friendly place to experience the fine art of *keyif* (quiet relaxation).

◉ Sights & Activities

You can swim at the beach fronting the ruins of Olympos. Agencies and camps in Olympos offer activities including boat cruises, canyoning, mountain biking, rock climbing, diving, sea kayaking and hiking.

Ruins RUIN
(admission TL3, 10 entry pass to ruins & beach TL7.50; ◷9am-7.30pm May-Oct, 8am-6pm Nov-Apr) Set in a deep shaded valley running to the beach, the ruins of ancient Olympos appear undiscovered among the vines and flowered trees. Rambling along the trickling stream that runs through this rocky gorge is a treat.

Chimaera HISTORIC SITE
(admission TL4, torch/flashlight rental TL3) This cluster of flames blazes from the crevices on the rocky slopes of Mt Olympos, near Çıralı and 7km from Olympos. Pensions and agencies offer lifts/evening tours (TL5/15).

🛏 Sleeping & Eating

OLYMPOS

Staying in an Olympos 'tree house' has long been the stuff of travel legend. The camps lining the valley have become overcrowded and institutionalised compared with their hippy-trail incarnations, and few huts are actually up in the trees. Still, they offer good value and an up-for-it party atmosphere in a lovely setting.

Unless specified otherwise, any prices listed here are for half board per person. Bathrooms are generally shared, but some bungalows have private facilities and even air-conditioning. Not all tree houses have reliable locks, so store valuables at reception.

Be extra attentive to personal hygiene while staying here; every year some travellers get ill. Especially in summer, the huge influx of visitors can overwhelm the camps' capacity for proper waste disposal. Be vigilant about where and what you eat.

Şaban Pansion   CAMPGROUND, PENSION €
(☑892 1265, 0532 457 3439; www.sabanpansion. com; tree house TL35-40, bungalow with bathroom TL45-50; ✳@) The place to come if you want to snooze in a hammock or on cushions in the shade of orange trees, Şaban sells itself on tranquillity, space and great home cooking. Room 7 really is a tree house.

Kadır's Tree Houses   CAMPGROUND, PENSION €
(☑892 1250, 0532 347 7242; www.kadirstree-houses.com; bungalow with bathroom TL40-65; ✳@) The place that put Olympos on the map looks like a Wild West boom town that just kept a-growin'. Kadır's has pillows in wooden bungalows, cabins and dorm rooms for 350 heads, the Bull and Hangar bars and travel agency **Adventure Centre** (☑892 1316; ⏱8.30am-10pm).

Bayrams   CAMPGROUND, PENSION €
(☑892 1243, 0532 494 7454; www.bayrams. com; dm TL30-35, tree house TL35-40, bungalow with air-con TL45-60, without air-con TL40-55; ✳@) Guests relax on cushioned platforms, play backgammon in the garden, puff on *nargiles* at the bar and socialise without necessarily partying.

Varuna Pansiyon   RESTAURANT €€
(☑892 1347, 0532 602 7839; www.olymposvaruna. com; mains TL10-15; ⏱8am-11pm) This popular restaurant serves snacks and mains including pide (TL7 to TL9), trout and *şiş* kebaps in an attractive open dining room. There's also accommodation in bungalows (room TL30 to TL60).

ÇIRALI

Çıralı may initially look like two dirt roads lined with pensions, but it's a delightful beach community for nature lovers and post-backpackers. There are about 60 pensions here, some near the path up to the Chimaera and others close to the beach and the Olympos ruins. A dozen restaurants line the beach.

📗 Myland Nature   PENSION €€€
(☑825 7044, 0532 407 9656; www.mylandnature. com; s TL113-167, d TL168-225, tr TL205-279; ✳🗺) This artsy, holistic and very green place is sure to rub you up the right way (massage, free yoga and meditation workshops offered). Spotless and spacious wooden bungalows are set around a pretty garden. Food (vegetarian set meal TL20) and bikes are available.

TOP CHOICE Hotel Canada   HOTEL €€
(☑0532 431 3414, 825 7233; www.canadahotel.net; d €55-60, 4-person bungalow €85-90; ✳@🗺🏊) This beautiful Canadian-Turkish operation offers the quintessential Çıralı experience: warmth, friendliness and house-made honey. The garden is filled with hammocks, citrus trees, a pool and bungalows (some ideal for families), and the comfortable main building also has rooms. Excellent set meals (€10) are served.

Sima Peace Pension   PENSION €€
(☑825 7245, 0532 238 1177; www.simapeace.com; s/d/tr TL80/120/140; ✳@) A comfortable '60s throwback and Çıralı stalwart just down from the beach, Sima has five rooms and two bungalows hidden in an orange grove. Host Aynur cooks like a dream (evening buffet TL15–20).

❶ Getting There & Away

Buses and minibuses plying the Fethiye–Antalya coast road will halt at the stops near the Olympos and Çıralı junctions. From there, minibuses leave for both destinations (TL5). To Olympos (9km), they depart roughly hourly/half-hourly in winter/summer; to Çıralı (7km), roughly every two hours. Many accommodation options will pick you up from the highway (TL20 to TL25) if you book in advance.

The most pleasant way to travel between Olympos and Fethiye is on a cruise.

Antalya

☎ 0242 / POP 964,000

Once seen simply as the gateway to the 'Turkish Riviera', Antalya is is today very much a destination in its own right. Situated on the Gulf of Antalya (Antalya Körfezi), the largest city on Turkey's Mediterranean coast is both stylishly modern and classically beautiful. It boasts the wonderfully preserved Roman-Ottoman quarter of Kaleiçi, a splendid Roman harbour, plus superb ruins in the surrounding Beydağları (Bey Mountains). Kaleiçi's good-value boutique hotels are of an international standard, the museum is one of Turkey's finest, and there are excellent bars and clubs. The opera and ballet season at the Aspendos amphitheatre continues to draw attention.

◉ Sights & Activities

Antalya Museum   MUSEUM
(☎ 236 5688; www.antalya-ws.com/english/museum; Konyaaltı Caddesi 1; admission TL15; ⊙9am-7pm Tue-Sun mid-Apr–Oct, 8am-5pm Tue-Sun Nov–mid-Apr) This comprehensive museum is about 2km west of the centre and accessible on the old-fashioned *tramvay* (tram, TL1.25, Müze stop). Exhibitions in 14 big halls cover everything from the Stone and Bronze Ages to Byzantium, including finds from ancient Lycian cities (eg Patara and Xanthos) and sublime statues of Olympian gods.

KALEIÇI

Around the harbour is the lovely historic district Kaleiçi (literally 'within the castle'). It's a charming area full of twisting alleys, huge stone walls, atmosphere-laden courtyards, souvenir shops and lavishly restored mansions. Cliffside vantage points, including **Karaalioğlu Parkı** (Atatürk Caddesi), provide stunning views over the beautiful marina and soaring Beydağları. Kaleiçi is downhill from the main square, **Kale Kapısı** (Fortress Gate), with its old stone **clock tower** *(saat kalesi)*.

Yivli Minare   LANDMARK
(Fluted Minaret) Antalya's symbol, this handsome and distinctive 'fluted' minaret was erected by the Seljuks in the early 13th century. The adjacent mosque (1373) is still in use. Within the complex is a restored **Mevlevi Tekke** (whirling-dervish monastery), and nearby to the west are two 14th- and 16th-century **türbe** (tombs). Cumhuriyet Meydanı to the west has an equestrian **statue of Atatürk**.

Hadriyanüs Kapısı   LANDMARK
(Hadrian's Gate) The monumental Hadrian's Gate was erected for the Roman emperor's visit to Antalya (130 BC).

Suna & İnan Kıraç
Kaleiçi Museum   MUSEUM
(☎ 243 4274; www.kaleicimuzesi.org; Kocatepe Sokak 25; admission TL2; ⊙9am-noon & 1-6pm Thu-Tue) This small but well-formed ethnography museum is housed in a lovingly restored Antalya mansion. Most impressive is the collection of ceramics in the exhibition hall behind the former Greek Orthodox church of Aya Yorgi (St George).

Balık Pazarı Hamamı   HAMAM
(Fish Market Bath; ☎ 243 6175; Balık Pazarı Sokak; bath TL15, package TL40; ⊙8am-11pm) Kaleiçi is a great place to experience a traditional Turkish *hamam*. At the 700-year-old Fish Market Bath, a bath, peeling, and soap and oil massage costs TL40 (TL15 for bath and scrub only). There are separate sections for men and women.

Boat Trips   CRUISE
(TL20 to TL80) Excursion yachts tie up in the marina, offering trips to the Gulf of Antalya islands and local beaches or further afield.

🛏 Sleeping

The best place to stay is Kaleiçi, where signs point the way to some excellent pensions.

TOP CHOICE Tuvana Hotel   BOUTIQUE HOTEL €€€
(☎ 247 6015; www.tuvanahotel.com; Karanlık Sokak 18; s & d €140-300; ❄ 🎧 🌐) Among the most beautiful and intimate hotels on the Mediterranean coast, this discreet compound of six Ottoman houses has been converted into a refined city hotel. Rooms are suitably plush, with kilims, linen and brass light fittings as well as modcons. The main restaurant Seraser is world-class.

TOP CHOICE White Garden Pansiyon   PENSION €
(☎ 241 9115; www.whitegardenpansion.com; Hesapçı Geçidi 9; s/d TL40/60, 4-person apt TL120; @🌐) The 15-room White Garden offers tidiness, class beyond its price level and impeccable service. The building itself is a fine restoration with a charming courtyard. Guests can use the pool at the **Secret Palace** (☎ 244 1060; www.secretpalacepansion.

Kaleiçi (Antalya)

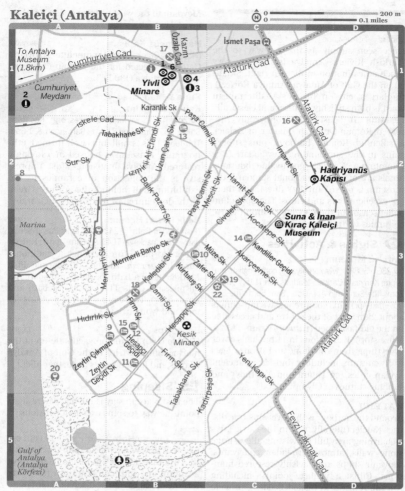

TURKEY ANTALYA

com; Fırın Sokak 10; s/d TL50/70; ❇@❄), an Ottoman conversion in the same stable behind the White Garden.

Hotel Hadrianus
HOTEL €€
(☎244 0030; www.hadrianushotel.com; Zeytin Çıkmazı 4; s TL65-80, d TL80-120; ❇❞) This 10-room hotel is set in a 750-sq-metre garden, a veritable oasis in Kaleiçi. Rooms at the top are larger and contain faux-antique and Ottoman-style furnishings.

Mediterra Art Hotel
BOUTIQUE HOTEL €€
(☎244 8624; www.mediterraart.com; Zafer Sokak 5; s €50-80, d €70-120; ❇@❄) This up-

scale masterpiece of wood and stone once housed a Greek tavern (see the 19th-century frescos and graffiti on the restaurant wall). The Mediterra offers sanctuary by a cutting-edge pool, a marvellous winter dining room, small, modestly luxurious rooms spread over four buildings, and an art gallery.

Sabah Pansiyon
PENSION €
(☎247 5345, 0555 365 8376; www.sabahpansiyon. com; Hesapçı Sokak 60; dm TL25, s/d with shower TL40/55, s/d without shower TL35/45, 2-bedroom apt TL200; ❇❞❄) The Sabah brothers run their place with aplomb while Mama takes

Kaleiçi (Antalya)

◎ Top Sights
Hadriyanüs Kapısı	D2
Suna & İnan Kıraç Kaleiçi Museum	C3
Yivli Minare	B1

◎ Sights
1	14th-Century Tombs	B1
2	Atatürk Statue	A1
3	Clock Tower	B1
4	Kale Kapısı	B1
5	Karaalioğlu Parkı	B5
6	Mevlevi Tekke	B1

◎ Activities, Courses & Tours
7	Balık Pazarı Hamamı	B3
8	Boat Trips	A2

◎ Sleeping
9	Hotel Hadrianus	B4
10	Mediterra Art Hotel	B3
11	Sabah Pansiyon	B4
12	Secret Palace	B4
13	Tuvana Hotel	B2
14	Villa Perla	C3
15	White Garden Pansiyon	B4

◎ Eating
16	Dönerciler Çarşısı	C2
17	Parlak Restaurant	B1
	Seraser	(see 13)
18	Sim Restaurant	B3
19	Vanilla	C3

◎ Drinking
20	Castle Café	A4
21	Kale Bar	A3
	The Lounge	(see 19)

◎ Entertainment
22	Dem-Lik	C3

care of the kitchen. Attractions include the shaded courtyard and five new villas that can accommodate six people. Great for families. The 22 rooms vary greatly, so ask to see a couple.

Villa Perla PENSION €€
(☎248 4341; www.villaperla.com; Hesapçı Sokak 26; s/d €50/70; ❄️🛜🏊) At this authentic Ottoman place hidden in a courtyard (with pool and tortoises), the wooden ceilings are the real deal, and some rooms have four-poster beds and folk-painted cupboards. Mama Perla's in-house restaurant offers meze (plate TL19) and nine rabbit dishes (from TL19).

✕ Eating

A nearly endless assortment of cafes and eateries is tucked in and around the harbour area. For cheap eating, walk east to the **Dönerciler Çarşısı** (Market of Döner Makers; Atatürk Caddesi), or north to the rooftop kebap places around Kale Kapısı.

Vanilla INTERNATIONAL €€€
(☎247 6013; www.vanillaantalya.com; Zafer Sokak 13; mains TL22-40) At this outstanding, ultramodern restaurant led by a British chef and his Turkish wife, banquettes, glass surfaces and cheery orange bucket chairs provide a streamlined and unfussy setting for the Mediterranean-inspired international dishes. For dessert, retire next door to slick cafe-bar **The Lounge** (ice creams TL3.50, cakes TL10; ⊙9am-1am; 🛜) for Mövenpick ice cream and Lavazza coffee.

Seraser MEDITERRANEAN €€€
(☎247 6015; www.seraserrestaurant.com; Karanlık Sokak 18, Tuvana Hotel; mains TL29-50; ⊙1pm-midnight) The Tuvana Hotel's signature restaurant offers international dishes with a Mediterranean twist in fine Ottoman surrounds. The Turkish coffee *crème brûlée* is legendary.

Sim Restaurant MEZE €€
(☎248 0107; Kaledibi Sokak 7; mains TL12.50-20) This simple but charming restaurant offers a choice of seated areas: underneath the canopy in the narrow passageway at the front, wedged against ancient Byzantine walls; or inside, with global graffiti on the ground floor and, upstairs, eclectic antiques to complement *köfte* and glorious *çorbalar* (soups).

Parlak Restaurant ANATOLIAN €€
(☎241 6553; www.parlakrestaurant.com; Kazım Özlap Caddesi 7; mains TL10-24) Opposite the jewellery bazaar and just off pedestrian Kazım Özlap Caddesi, this sprawling open-air patio restaurant in an old *caravanserai* is famous for its charcoal-grilled chicken and meze, and favoured by locals.

🍺 Drinking

Kaleiçi offers buzzy beer gardens with million-dollar views, live-music venues, as well as raunchy clubs with outrageously expensive drinks.

It's worth seeking out the **Kale Bar** (☎248 6591; Mermerli Sokak 2; beer TL9, cocktails from TL21; ⊙11am-midnight), attached to the

WORTH A TRIP

AROUND ANTALYA

There are several magnificent Graeco-Roman ruins in the Mediterranean hinterland around Antalya. The ruins of **Perge** (admission TL15; ☉9am-7pm Apr-Oct, 8am-5.30pm Nov-Mar), one of the most important towns of ancient Pamphylia, are located 17km east of Antalya and 2km north of Aksu. On the access road you will see the stadium and theatre, which each sat 12,000 spectators.

At stunning **Aspendos** (admission TL15, parking TL5; ☉9am-7pm Apr-Oct, 8am-5pm Nov-Mar), 47km east of Antalya, you'll see the world's best-preserved Roman theatre, dating from the 2nd century AD and still used for performances during the **Aspendos Opera & Ballet Festival** (Aspendos Opera ve Bale Festivalı; www.aspendosfestival.gov.tr) every June and September.

The fierce Pisidians inhabited the ruined but still massive city of **Termessos** (admission TL5; ☉9am-7pm Apr-Oct, 8am-5pm Nov-Mar) for centuries, and repelled Alexander the Great from this rugged mountain valley. The ruins, 34km northwest of Antalya, have a spectacular setting, but demand some vigorous walking and climbing.

The Roman ruins continue at **Köprülü Kanyon**, about 100km northeast of Antalya and deservedly popular for hiking and white-water rafting. More than two-dozen companies offer rafting trips in the canyon, including **Medraft** (☎312 6296, in UK +44 20 8150 0687; www.medraft.com). An excursion on the intermediate rapids is about TL30, including a lesson, a two- to three-hour trip and lunch.

The easiest way to see these sights is with your own transport (Antalya has plenty of car-rental agencies) or on a tour with one of the many agencies based in Kaleiçi. A tour to Perge and Aspendos, with a side trip to Manavgat waterfall, should cost around TL115; an excursion/taxi tour to Termessos costs about TL100/150; and a tour to Köprülü Kanyon costs about TL100.

CH Hotels Türkevi and commanding some of Antalya's best harbour and sea views; the lively **Castle Café** (☎248 6594; Hıdırlık Sokak 48/1; beer TL7.50; ☉8am-11pm), filled with students; and **Dem-Lik** (☎247 1930; Zafer Sokak 6; beer TL5, coffee TL4; ☉noon-midnight), for jazz, reggae and blues (live at the weekend).

ℹ Information

Tourist Office (☎241 1747; Cumhuriyet Meydanı; ☉8am-6pm May-Oct, 8.30am-5.30pm Nov-Mar) Tiny but helpful office.

ℹ Getting There & Away

AIR Antalya's airport is 10km east of the city centre on the D400 highway. Turkish Airlines and budget AnadoluJet have several daily flights to/from İstanbul and Ankara year-round.

To reach the airport, catch bus 600 (TL2), which can be boarded along 100 Yıl. A taxi costs about TL35.

BUS From Kaleiçi, board the AntRay tram at the İsmet Paşa stop and travel for 20 minutes (TL1.50) to reach the *otogar*, 4km north of the centre on the D650 highway. A taxi costs TL25. Regular buses serve destinations including:

Göreme/Ürgüp TL40, nine hours
Kaş TL20, 3½ hours
Konya TL38, five hours
Olympos/Çıralı TL13, 1½ hours
Side/Manavgat TL13, 1½ hours

Side

☎0242 / POP 11,400

To some, the once-docile fishing town of Side (pronounced *see*-day) is mass tourism at its worst: endless rows of souvenirs, and matching restaurant menus in various European languages.

But move a couple of streets over and you'll find a different side to Side. Entering the town through the monumental Vespasian Gate is like walking onto a film set: Roman and Hellenistic ruins mark out the road, and a rebuilt agora could just as easily contain togas as T-shirts. The town is also blessed with sandy beaches.

◉ Sights

Side's impressive structures include the 2nd-century AD **theatre** (admission TL10; ☉9am-7.30pm mid-Apr–mid-Oct, 8am-5.30pm mid-Oct–mid-Apr) with 20,000 seats - one of the region's most dramatic; seaside **temples** to

Apollo and Athena (2nd century BC); and a 5th-century bathhouse, now **Side Museum** (admission TL10; ⊘9am-7.30pm Tue-Sun), with an excellent small collection of statues and sarcophagi.

🛏 Sleeping & Eating

Some accommodation has parking; otherwise you have to use the car park just beyond the theatre (TL3/15 per hour/day).

Beach House Hotel   HOTEL €€
(☑753 1607; www.beachhouse-hotel.com; Barbaros Caddesi; s/d TL50/100; ✳@🛜) Once the Pamphylia Hotel, a celebrity magnet in the 1960s, the Beach House's prime seafront location and welcoming staff lure a loyal band of regulars. Rooms have balconies and mostly face the sea. The roof terrace has a jacuzzi, and the garden boasts both a ruined Byzantine villa and rabbits.

Özden Pansiyon   PENSION €
(☑753 1337, 0534 552 3328; www.yoga-holidays-turkey.com; Gül Sokak 50; s/d TL30/60; 🛜) Simple but stylish wood-lined rooms frame a leafy courtyard that's a tranquil retreat from the souvenir-shop buzz outside. One-week yoga holidays here cost £395 per person.

Emir   TURKISH €€
(☑753 2224; Menekşe Caddesi; meze TL8-10, mains TL16-25; 🍴) The Emir almost leans on the ruins of the Roman baths where Cleopatra is said to have dallied. The open kitchen produces excellent meze, grills and an array of vegetarian dishes.

❶ Getting There & Away

In summer Side has daily buses to Ankara, İzmir and İstanbul. Otherwise, frequent minibuses connect Side with Manavgat *otogar* (TL2), 4km away, from where buses go to Antalya (TL10, 1½ hours), Alanya (TL10, 1½ hours) and Konya (TL25, four hours).

Alanya

📞0242 / POP 103,700

Alanya has mushroomed from a sparsely populated highway town with a sandy beach to a densely populated tourist town. Aside from a quick boat cruise or waterfront stroll, many visitors to Alanya shuffle between their hotel's pool and all-inclusive buffet, venturing to the throbbing, laser-shooting nightclubs after dark. But Alanya has something special up its ancient sleeve. Looming high above the promontory south of the modern centre is an impressive fortress complex, with the remains of a Seljuk castle, some atmospheric ruins and a small traditional village.

◎ Sights

Alanya Castle   FORTRESS
(Alanya Kalesı; admission TL10; ⊘9am-7pm Apr-Oct, 8am-5pm Nov-Mar) Alanya's awesome Seljuk-era castle overlooks the city, Pamphylian plain and Cilician mountains. Before reaching the entrance, the road passes a turn-off for the village of **Ehmedek**, which was the Turkish quarter during Ottoman and Seljuk times. Old wooden houses cluster around the 16th-century **Süleymaniye Camii**, Alanya's oldest; also here are an Ottoman **bedesten** and the **Akşebe Türbesi**, a 13th-century mausoleum.

In the castle's **İç Kale** (Inner Fortress), you'll mostly find poorly preserved ruins.

Catch a bus from opposite the tourist office (TL1.25). Taxis are around TL15 each way.

Kızılkule   HISTORIC BUILDING
(Red Tower; admission TL4; ⊘9am-7pm Apr-Oct, 8am-5pm Nov-Mar) Seljuk Sultan Alaeddin Keykubad I, who also built the fortress, constructed this five-storey octagonal tower by the harbour in 1226.

🏃 Activities

Every day at around 10.30am **boats** (per person incl lunch TL35) leave from near Rıhtım Caddesi for a six-hour voyage around the promontory, visiting several caves and Cleopatra's Beach.

Many local operators organise tours for landlubbers. A typical tour to Aspendos, Side and Manavgat waterfall costs around TL75 per person, while a **4WD safari** in the Taurus Mountains costs about TL60.

🛏 Sleeping

Alanya has hundreds of hotels and pensions, almost all designed for groups and those in search of *apart oteller* (self-catering flats). The best alternatives are found along İskele Caddesi and in Tophane, the heritage district beneath the castle.

Centauera   BOUTIQUE HOTEL €€€
(☑519 0016; www.centauera.com; Andızlı Camii Sokak 4, Tophane; r €110-140; 🅿✳🛜) A

10-minute stroll from the harbour, the romantic Centauera fills a restored Ottoman house. Views take in the elegant sweep of Alanya bay, and birdsong emanates from the surrounding Tophane neighbourhood. Dinner is available on request and for outside guests.

Seaport Hotel BUSINESS HOTEL €€
(☑513 6487; www.hotelseaport.com; İskele Caddesi 82; s/d TL120/200; 🕸) The last hotel on the İskele strip, the Seaport offers efficient service and sea views from half of its rooms, which are not huge but are well appointed. Rates include a dinner buffet, but the food can be disappointing.

✖ Eating & Drinking

Many restaurants will pick you up from and bring you back to your accommodation.

İskele Sofrası SEAFOOD €€
(Tophane Caddesi 2b; meze TL6-8, mains TL15-30) This intimate, family-run place just off İskele Caddesi serves more than 70 meze. The terrace with harbour views is perfect for a cold beer and the shrimp *güveç*.

Ottoman House TURKISH €€€
(☑511 1421; www.ottomanhousealanya.com; Damlataş Caddesi 31; mains TL20-32) Alanya's most atmospheric eatery occupies a 100-year-old stone villa surrounded by lush gardens. Thursday and Sunday nights see an all-you-can-eat barbecue (€15); on Tuesdays there's a meze buffet (€15) and Turkish dancing.

Sofra ANATOLIAN €€
(İskele Caddesi 8a; mains TL8-16) Sofra delivers a modern spin on the traditional Turkish eatery with tasty kebaps, *mantı*, eastern Anatolian *içli köfte* (ground lamb and onion in a bulgur wheat shell) and a complimentary self-serve salad bar.

Cello BAR, LIVE MUSIC
(İskele Caddesi 36) This rustic wooden bar, showcasing 'protest and folk music', is a top spot for an acoustic-fuelled night. Friendly locals crowd in, and gigs kick off at 9.30pm most nights.

❶ Information

Tourist Office (☑513 1240; Damlataş Caddesi 1; ⊙8am-5pm Mon-Fri) Opposite Alanya Museum, with a smaller branch (Damlataş Caddesi; ⊙9am-6pm Mon-Fri) near the *belediye* (town hall).

❶ Getting There & Away

BOAT Fergün Denizcilik (☑511 5565, 511 5358; www.fergun.net; İskele Caddesi 84) runs ferries twice a week to **Girne/Kyrenia** (Northern Cyprus; one way/return TL77/127 plus harbour tax).
BUS The *otogar* is on the coastal highway (Atatürk Caddesi), 3km west of the centre (TL1.50/12 by *dolmuş*/taxi).

There are regular buses to Antalya (TL15, two hours), and to Adana (TL40, 10 hours) via Anamur.

Anamur

☑0324 / POP 35,100
Anamur has a pretty beach and waterfront at İskele, but the main reason to stop here is the ruined Byzantine city of **Anemurium** (Anemurium Ancient City; admission TL3; ⊙8am-7pm Apr-Oct, to 5pm Nov-Mar), 8.5km west of the town. The sprawling site is eerily quiet, with ruins stretching 500m to the pebble beach, and city walls scaling the mountainside. About 7km east of town, the 13th-century **Mamure Castle** (Mamure Kalesi; admission TL3; ⊙8am-7.30pm Apr-Oct, to 5pm Nov-Mar) is the biggest and best-preserved fortification on the Turkish Mediterranean coast, with 39 towers.

Good sleeping options are **Hotel Esya** (☑816 6595, 0532 491 0211; www.mersintatil.com/esyahotel.htm; İnönü Caddesi 55; s/d TL50/80; 🕸🛜) and **Hotel Luna Piena** (☑814 9045; www.hotellunapiena.com; Süleyman Bal Sokak; s TL60-80, d TL90-110; 🕸🛜).

Buses run to Alanya (TL25, three hours), Taşucu/Silifke (TL25, three hours) and Adana (TL35, six hours).

Kızkalesi

☑0324 / POP 1750
Wonderful 'Maiden's Castle', an easygoing and welcoming village with one of the region's loveliest beaches, is named after the astounding **Byzantine castle** (Maiden's Castle; admission TL3; ⊙8am-5pm May-Oct) offshore, which looks from a distance as if it's suspended on top of the water. Unless you're up to swimming 300m, take a boat (TL5) or pedalo (TL10) to get there. The ruins of **Corycus Castle** (Korykos Kalesi; admission TL3; ⊙8am-8pm Apr-Oct, to 5pm Nov-Mar) are on the beach; the two were once linked by a causeway.

Friendly **Rain Hotel** (☑523 2782; www.rain-hotel.com; per person €40-70; 🕸@) has spotless rooms and a long list of activities.

There are frequent buses to/from Silifke (TL4, 30 minutes).

From Taşucu, 11km southwest of Silifke, **Akgünler Denizcilik** (☑741 2303; www.akgunler.com.tr; İsmet İnönü Caddesi) *feribotlar* (car ferries; one way/return from TL59/99 plus harbour tax, four to 10 hours, Sunday to Thursday) and faster *ekspresler* (hydrofoils; one way/return TL69/114 plus harbour tax, two hours, daily) depart for Girne (Kyrenia) in Northern Cyprus.

Adana

TRANSPORT HUB

Turkey's fourth-largest city is a thoroughly modern affair, and its main use for travellers is as a transport hub. You may pass through en route along the Mediterranean coast or inland.

If you get stuck overnight, the boutique **Hotel Bosnalı** (☑359 8000; www.hotelbosnali.com; Seyhan Caddesi 29; s/d €75/85, ste €130-160; ❄️🛜) occupies a 19th-century mansion, and the **Ibis Hotel** (☑355 9500; www.ibishotel.com; Turhan Cemal Beriker Bulvari 49; r TL100; ♨️❄️🛜) is a dependable chain choice.

Ova Ev Yemekleri (off Ataturk Caddesi; soups & rice TL3, mains TL6-11; ⊙Lunch) serves *yöresel yemekler* (hearty renditions of traditional homestyle recipes), and **Öz Asmaaltı** (☑351 4028; Pazarlar Caddesi 9; mains TL15-20) is another local favourite for its kebaps and meze.

❶ Getting There & Away

AIR Şakirpaşa airport is 4km west of the centre; a taxi costs about TL15.

BUS Adana's *otogar*, 2km beyond the airport, serves destinations throughout Turkey, including Antakya (TL20, 3½ hours), Konya (TL40, six hours), Ankara (TL40, seven hours) and İstanbul (TL60, 12 hours).

TRAIN Sleeper trains run nightly to/from Ankara (TL55, 12 hours).

Antakya (Hatay)

☑0326 / POP 213,300

Part of Syria until 1938, you might recognise Antakya by its biblical name, Antioch. Under the Romans, the city's important Christian community developed out of the already large Jewish population that was at one time led by St Paul. In today's prosperous, modern city, Arab influences permeate local life, food and language, and the ba-

zaars, back lanes and Orontes (Asi) River are well worth a wander.

At the time of writing, regions close to the Syrian border were offlimits due to the unrest in Syria and fighting between the Turkish army and PKK (Kurdistan Workers Party). Antakya is usually accessible and safe, but visitors should check on the current security situation before travel.

👁 Sights

Hatay Archaeology Museum   MUSEUM
(Hatay Arkeoloji Müzesi; Gündüz Caddesi 1; admission TL8; ⊙9am-6.30pm Tue-Sun Apr-Oct, 8.30am-noon & 12.30-4.30pm Nov-Mar) This museum contains one of the world's finest collections of Roman and Byzantine mosaics, covering a period from the 1st century AD to the 5th century.

Church of St Peter   CHURCH
(St Pierre Kilisesi; admission TL8; ⊙9am-noon & 1-6pm Apr-Oct, 8am-noon & 1-5pm Nov-Mar) Both Peter and Paul almost certainly preached at this early Christian church, cut into the slopes of Mt Staurin (Mountain of the Cross) 2.5km northeast of town.

🛏 Sleeping

Belkis Konuk Evi ve Pansiyon   PENSION €€
(☑212 1511; www.belkisev.com; Gazipasa Caddesi, Güllübahçe Sokak; s/d TL60/120; ❄️) Rooms in this cute family pension frame a white-washed inner courtyard dotted with leafy trees. Expect decor merging rustic with chintzy, and a warm welcome.

Mozaik Otel   HOTEL €€
(☑215 5020; www.mozaikotel.com; İstiklal Caddesi 18; s/d TL85/130; ❄️🛜) Near the bazaar, rooms are decorated with folksy bedspreads and mosaic reproductions.

🍴 Eating

For restaurants head south of Ulus Alanı on (or just off) Hürriyet Caddesi. Tea gardens are found in the park on the left bank of the Orontes, southwest of the museum.

Syrian influences permeate Antakya's cuisine. Handfuls of mint and wedges of lemon accompany many kebaps. Hummus is readily available and local specialities abound, including *künefe*, a cake of fine shredded wheat laid over a dollop of fresh, mild cheese, on a layer of sugar syrup, topped with chopped walnuts. You can try it at several places near the Ulu Camii, including **Kral Künefe** (Çarşı Caddesi 7).

Antakya Evi
TURKISH €€

(Silahlı Kuvvetler Caddesi 3; mains TL7-12) In this old villa decorated with photos and antique furniture, there are numerous spicy Hatay specialities, local meze (TL6 to TL8) and robust grills. Turkish folk music is played on Friday and Saturday night.

Hatay Sultan Sofrası
TURKISH €€

(www.sultansofrasi.com; İstiklal Caddesi 20a; mains TL10-16) A top spot for a diverse array of meze, spicy local kebaps, and (just maybe) Hatay's best *künefe*.

ℹ Getting There & Away

Turkish Airlines and Pegasus Airlines serve İstanbul, İzmir and Ankara from Hatay aiport, 20km north of Antakya (TL10/30 by Havaş bus/taxi).

The *otogar* is 7km northwest of the centre. Destinations include Adana (TL20, 3½ hours).

CENTRAL ANATOLIA

On central Turkey's hazy plains, the sense of history is so pervasive that the average kebap chef can remind you that the Romans preceded the Seljuks. This is, after all, the region where the whirling dervishes first swirled, Atatürk began his revolution, Alexander the Great cut the Gordion knot and King Midas turned everything to gold. Julius Caesar came here to utter his famous line, *'Veni, vidi, vici'* ('I came, I saw, I conquered').

Ankara
📞 0312 / POP 4.5 MILLION

İstanbullus may quip that the best view in Ankara is the train home, but the Turkish capital has more substance than its reputation as a staid administrative centre suggests. The capital established by Atatürk offers a mellower, more manageable vignette of urban Turkey than İstanbul, and claims two of the country's most important sights: the Museum of Anatolian Civilisations and the Anıt Kabir. Ankara's flat, modest surroundings are hardly the stuff of national poetry, but a few neighbourhoods have some charm, notably the historic streets in the hilltop citadel and Kızılay, one of Turkey's hippest urban quarters.

◉ Sights

TOP CHOICE Museum of Anatolian Civilisations
MUSEUM

(Anadolu Medeniyetleri Müzesi; 📞 324 3160; Gözcü Sokak 2, Ulus; admission TL15; ⊙ Apr-Oct 8.30am-7pm, Nov-Mar to 5pm; Ⓜ Ulus) Displaying artefacts cherry-picked from just about every significant archaeological site in Anatolia, all housed in a beautifully restored 15th-century *bedesten*, the museum is the perfect introduction to the complex weave of Turkey's ancient past.

Citadel
NEIGHBOURHOOD

(Ankara Kalesi; Ⓜ Ulus) Just up the hill from the museum, the imposing *hisar* (citadel) is the most interesting part of Ankara to poke about in. This well-preserved quarter of thick walls and intriguing winding streets took its present shape in the 9th century AD, and locals still live here as if in a traditional Turkish village.

FREE Anıt Kabir
MONUMENT

(Atatürk Mausoleum and Museum; Gençlik Caddesi; audio guide TL5; ⊙ 9am-5pm May-Oct, to 4pm Nov-Apr; Ⓜ Tandoğan) The monumental mausoleum of Mustafa Kemal Atatürk (1881–1938), the beloved founder of modern Turkey, sits high above the city (2km west of Kızılay) with its abundance of marble and air of veneration.

FREE Vakıf Eserleri Müzesi
MUSEUM

(Ankara Museum of Religious Foundation Works; Atatürk Bulvarı, Ulus; ⊙ 9am-5pm Tue-Sun; Ⓜ Ulus) The tradition of carpets being gifted to mosques has helped preserve many of Turkey's finest specimens. This extensive collection once graced the floors of mosques throughout the country.

⌖ Sleeping

The Ulus area is most convenient for the Museum of Anatolian Civilisations and the citadel, but most of the restaurants and nightlife are in Kızılay and Kavaklıdere.

Angora House Hotel
HISTORIC HOTEL €€

(📞 309 8380; www.angorahouse.com.tr; Kalekapısı Sokak 16; s/d/tr €50/69/75; 📶; Ⓜ Ulus) This restored Ottoman house oozes subtle elegance at every turn. The six spacious rooms are infused with old-world atmosphere, while the walled courtyard garden is the perfect retreat from the citadel streets. Delightfully helpful staff add to the appeal.

Deeps Hostel HOSTEL €
(☑213 6338; www.deepshostelankara.com; Ataç Sokak 46; dm/s/d without bathroom €10/18/32; ☎; MKızılay) Ankara's best budget choice, friendly Deeps has colourful, light-filled rooms, a spacious dorm, and squeaky-clean, modern shared bathrooms. It's all topped off by a fully equipped kitchen (breakfast isn't included) and a cute communal area downstairs.

Divan Çukurhan HISTORIC HOTEL €€€
(☑306 6400; www.divan.com.tr; Depo Sokak 3, Ankara Kalesi; s/d €130/150, ste €180-400; ✴☎; MUlus) This distinctive hotel offers a chance to stay in the 16th-century Çukurhan *caravanserai*. Set around a dramatic glass-ceilinged interior courtyard, each individually themed room blends ornate decadence with sassy contemporary style.

Hotel Eyüboğlu HOTEL €€
(☑417 6400; www.eyubogluhotel.com; Karanfil Sokak 73; s/d €69/89; ✴☎; MKızılay) Although lacking in character, this great-value option is wonderfully efficient. Staff go out of their way to help (despite a shortage of English), and the no-nonsense rooms boast supremely comfy beds.

🍴 Eating & Drinking

Most Ulus options are basic. **Ulus Hali food market** sells provisions from oversized chilli peppers to jars of honey. In and around the citadel, inviting, atmospheric licensed restaurants occupy old wood-and-stone houses.

It's all about street stalls, hip bistros and cafe culture in Kızılay, where terraces line virtually every inch of space south of Ziya Gökalp Caddesi. Kızılay's tall, thin buildings also pack in up to five floors of studenty bars, cafes and *gazinos* (nightclubs).

Zenger Paşa Konağı ANATOLIAN €€
(☑311 7070; www.zengerpasa.com; Doyran Sokak 13; mains TL12-17; MUlus) Crammed with Ottoman ephemera, the Zenger Paşa at first looks like a deserted ethnographic museum, but climb up the rickety stairs and you'll find views of the city that are worth a visit alone. Wealthy Ankaralıs love the pide, meze and grills.

And Evi Cafe MODERN TURKISH €€
(☑312 7978; İçkale Kapısı; mains TL12-24; MUlus) This cafe, set into the citadel walls, is a winner for its cosy Ottoman-style interior and panoramic city views from the terrace. Tuck into a lunchtime crepe (TL11), sample the divine carrot cake (TL6) with a latte for afternoon tea, or choose a pasta dish for dinner.

Le Man Kültür INTERNATIONAL €
(☑310 8617; Konur Sokak 8; mains TL6-16; MKızılay) Named after a Turkish comic strip (and decorated accordingly), this is the pre-party pick for a substantial feed among Ankara's beautiful young educated things. Drinks are reasonably priced and the speakers crank everything from indie-electro to Türk pop.

Aylak Madam CAFE
(☑419 7412; Karanfıl Sokak 2, Kızılay; ⊙10am-late) A supercool French bistro/cafe with a mean weekend brunch (from 10am to 2.30pm), plus sandwiches, head-kicking cappuccinos, and a kick-backed jazz-fusion soundtrack.

ℹ Information

There are lots of banks with ATMs in Ulus, Kızılay and Kavaklıdere.

Main Post Office (Atatürk Bulvarı) In Ulus, with branches in Kızılay.

Tourist Office (☑310 8789; Gazi Mustafa Kemal Bulvarı; ⊙9am-5pm Mon-Fri, 10am-5pm Sat) Also branches (usually unmanned) at the *otogar* and train station.

ℹ Getting There & Away

AIR Domestic and international carriers serve Esenboğa airport, 33km north of the city, but İstanbul's airports offer more choice and better deals. Lufthansa, Pegasus Airlines and Qatar Airways offer international connections, while AnadoluJet has direct flights to/from destinations nationwide.

BUS Ankara's huge AŞTİ (Ankara Şehirlerarası Terminali İşletmesi) *otogar*, 4.5km west of Kızılay, is the vehicular heart of the nation, with buses to/from every Turkish city or town of any size. Apart from over public holidays, you can often turn up, buy a ticket and be on your way in less than an hour. Services include İstanbul (TL40, six hours).

TRAIN A high-speed train serves Konya (economy/business class TL25/35, two hours, eight daily) and long-distance trains run overnight to eastern Anatolia. Services to/from İstanbul have been cancelled until at least 2014.

ℹ Getting Around

To/From the Airport

Havaş shuttle buses depart from Gate B at 19 May Stadium (Kazım Karabekir Caddesi, Ulus) every half hour between 2am and 10pm daily

SAFRANBOLU & AMASYA

Safranbolu and Amasya, respectively 145km north and 270km northeast of Ankara, are slightly off the beaten Anatolian track, but beckon savvy travellers with their ethereal settings and historic atmosphere.

Safranbolu is such an enchanting town that Unesco declared it a World Heritage site. It boasts a wonderful old Ottoman quarter bristling with 19th-century half-timbered houses; as part of the ongoing restoration, many have been turned into hotels or museums.

Blissfully located on riverbanks beneath cliffs carved with Pontic tombs, **Amasya** is one of Turkey's best-kept secrets, harbouring historic sites including a lofty castle, Seljuk mosques and enough picturesque Ottoman piles to satisfy the fussiest sultan.

Both towns boast excellent accommodation, with a profusion of delightful pensions set in skilfully restored Ottoman mansions. In Safranbolu, **Kahveciler Konağı** (☑725 5453; www.kahvecilerkonagi.com; Mescit Sokak 7; s/d TL60/TL120; 🐾) was once the host's grandfather's house; Amasya's family-run **Gönül Sefası** (☑212 9461; Yalıboyu Sokak 24; s/d/tr TL60/100/120) has lots of local character.

There are buses from Ankara to Safranbolu (TL25, three hours) and Amasya (TL30, five hours), as well as from İstanbul.

(TL10, 35 minutes). After 10pm buses leave according to flight departure times. Havaş also links the airport and *otogar*. From the airport, buses leave 25 minutes after each flight arrival.

Don't pay more than TL60 for a taxi.

Public Transport

BUS Buses marked 'Ulus' and 'Çankaya' run the length of Atatürk Bulvarı. Those marked 'Gar' go to the train station, those marked 'AŞTİ' to the *otogar*. You can buy transport cards (TL3.50), valid for two journeys (bus or metro), from metro stations and major bus stops or anywhere displaying an EGO Bilet sign.

TAXI It costs about TL10 to cross the centre; charges rise at night.

METRO The network has two lines: the Ankaray line, running between AŞTİ *otogar* and Dikimevi via Kızılay; and the Metro line, runing from Kızılay northwest via Sıhhiye and Ulus to Batıkent. Trains run from 6.15am to 11.45pm daily. Tickets cost TL3.50/8.75 for two/five journeys.

Konya

☑0332 / POP 1.07 MILLION

Turkey's equivalent of the 'Bible Belt', conservative Konya treads a delicate path between its historical significance as the home town of the whirling-dervish orders and a bastion of Seljuk culture, and its modern importance as an economic boom town. The city derives considerable charm from this juxtaposition of old and new, and boasts one of Turkey's finest and most characteristic sights, the Mevlâna Museum.

The centre stretches from Alaaddin Tepesi, the hill topped by the Seljuk **Alaaddin Camii**, along Mevlâna Caddesi to the Mevlâna Museum.

The two-week **Mevlâna Festival** culminates on 17 December, the anniversary of Mevlâna's 'wedding night' with Allah. **Semas** (dervish ceremonies) also take place on Saturday evenings throughout the year; contact the tourist office about both.

👁 Sights

TOP CHOICE **Mevlâna Museum** MUSEUM

(☑351 1215; admission TL3, audio guide TL5; ☺9am-5pm Tue-Sun, 10am-5pm Mon) Join the pilgrims at this wonderful museum-cum-shrine, where embroidered velvet shrouds cover the turban-topped tombs of Mevlâna (Celaleddin Rumi) and other eminent dervishes. The former lodge of the whirling dervishes, it is topped by a brilliant turquoise-tiled dome. Although it's virtually under siege from devout crowds, there's a palpable mystique here.

Tile Museum MUSEUM

(Karatay Medresesi Çini Müzesi; ☑351 1914; Alaaddin Meydanı; admission TL3; ☺9am-5pm) The interior central dome and walls of this former Seljuk theological school (1251) showcase some finely preserved blue-and-white Seljuk tilework. There is also an outstanding collection of ceramics on display.

Museum of Wooden Artefacts & Stone Carving MUSEUM

(Tas ve Ahsap Eserler Müzesi; ☑351 3204; Adliye Bulvarı; admission TL3; ☉Tue-Sun 9am-5pm) The İnce Minare Medresesi (Seminary of the Slender Minaret), housing this museum, was built in 1264 for a Seljuk vizier. Inside, many of the carvings feature motifs similar to those used in tiles and ceramics.

🛏 Sleeping

Derviş Otel BOUTIQUE HOTEL €€

(☑350 0842; www.dervishotel.com; Güngör Sokak 7; s/d/tr TL100/160/210; ❄️🛜) This airy, light-filled 200-year-old house has been converted into a rather wonderful boutique hotel, which has a taste of local character without scrimping on modern luxuries.

Ulusan Otel HOTEL €

(☑351 5004; Çarşi PTT Arkasi 4; s/d without bathroom TL30/60; 🛜) The pick of the Konya cheapies, with basic but bright and spotlessly clean rooms, both private and (immaculately kept) shared bathrooms, a communal area full of homely knick-knacks, and an enthusiastic and graceful host.

Hotel Rumi HOTEL €€€

(☑353 1121; www.rumihotel.com; Durakfakih Sokak 5; s/d/tr/ste €60/90/110/130; ❄️🛜) Rooms are a tad on the small side, but are elegantly styled in soft mauves and sage green. Staff seem to delight in offering genuine service and the top-level breakfast room has killer views of the nearby Mevlâna Museum.

Mevlâna Sema Otel HOTEL €€

(☑350 4623; www.semaotel.com; Mevlâna Caddesi 67; s/d TL60/90; ❄️🛜) Despite the strange plaster mouldings all over the room walls, this is a safe, solid choice with a great location and friendly staff. Ask for a rear-facing room to avoid the din of the main road.

🍴 Eating & Drinking

Restaurants around the Mevlâna Museum and tourist office have great views, but their food is not recommended – with the exception of Gülbahçesi Konya Mutfağı (☑351 0768; Gülbahçe Sokak 3; mains TL8-18; ☉8am-10pm). The fast-food restaurants on Adilye Bulvarı are lively places for a snack, but check the swift grub is thoroughly cooked. Head to Alaaddin Tepesi for tea gardens.

Konak Konya Mutfağı ANATOLIAN €

(☑352 8547; Piriesat Caddesi 5; mains TL8-16; ☉11am-10pm) This excellent traditional restaurant is run by food writer Nevin Halıcı, who puts her personal twist on Turkish classics. Grab an outside table to rub shoulders with vine-draped pillars and a fragrant rose garden.

Osmanlı Çarşısı CAFE

(☑353 3257; İnce Minare Sokak) An atmospheric, early-20th-century house with terraces, pavement seating and cushions galore where students talk politics while sucking on *nargiles*.

ℹ Information

Tourist Office (☑353 4020; Aslanı Kışla Caddesi; ☉8.30am-5.30pm Mon-Sat) Gives out a city map and a leaflet covering the nearby Mevlâna Museum; can also organise guides.

ℹ Getting There & Away

AIR Turkish Airlines and Pegasus Airlines both operate daily flights to/from İstanbul. The airport is 13km northeast of the centre; TL40 by taxi. Havaş runs shuttle buses (TL9).

BUS From the *otogar*, 7km north of the centre and accessible by tram from Alaaddin Tepesi, regular buses serve all major destinations.

Ankara TL18, 3½ hours

İstanbul TL45, 11½ hours

Kayseri TL30, four hours

TRAIN Eight high-speed trains run to/from Ankara daily (adult/child TL25/12.50, 1¾ hours). A taxi from the station to the centre should cost about TL15.

CAPPADOCIA (KAPADOKYA)

Cappadocia's surreal fairy chimneys – rock columns, pyramids, mushrooms and even a few shaped like camels – were formed, alongside the area's valleys of cascading white cliffs, when Erciyes Daği (Mt Erciyes) erupted. The intervening millennia added to the remarkable Cappadocian canvas, with Byzantines carving out cave churches and subterranean complexes large enough to house thousands. You could spend days hiking through the canyons and admiring the rock-cut churches and their frescos.

When the day's done, spots such as Göreme and Ürgüp have some of Anatolia's best restaurants and guesthouses, allowing guests to experience troglodyte living first hand.

☞ Tours

Most itineraries finish at a carpet shop, onyx factory or pottery workshop. It is interesting to see traditional Cappadocian craftsmen at work, but make it clear before the trip begins if you are not interested. Most tour companies offer full-day tours and guided day hikes.

Full-day tours To destinations such as the Ihlara Valley, the underground cities (which are best visited with a guide) and Soğanlı's valleys of rock-cut churches. The Ihlara Valley trip usually includes a short guided hike in the gorge, lunch and a trip to an underground city; most operators charge about TL90.

Guided day-hikes Usually in the Güllüdere (Rose), Kızılçuker (Red) or Meskendir Valleys. Costs vary according to the destination, degree of difficulty and length.

The following Göreme-based agencies offer good daily tours. There are also agencies in Avanos and Ürgüp. Do not book tours in Nevşehır, which has a reputation for unscrupulous operators; or in İstanbul, which will be more expensive than booking in Cappadocia.

Middle Earth Travel　　ADVENTURE TOUR
(🖉271 2559; www.middleearthtravel.com; Cevizler Sokak 20) The adventure-travel specialist offers climbing and treks ranging from local, one-day expeditions to one-week missions, including the rugged Ala Dağlar National Park.

Heritage Travel　　GUIDED TOUR
(🖉271 2687; www.turkishheritagetravel.com; Uzundere Caddesi) The knowledgeable Mustafa is recommended (group/private tours €45/100 per person).

Mehmet Güngör　　WALKING TOUR
(🖉0532 382 2069; www.walkingmehmet.com; Noriyon Cafe, Müze Caddesi; four hours/full day €60/80) Recommended walking guide.

Yama Tours　　GUIDED TOUR
(🖉271 2508; www.yamatours.com; Müze Caddesi 2) Also offers three-day trips to Nemrut Dağı (Mt Nemrut).

Neşe Tour　　GUIDED TOUR
(🖉271 2525; www.nesetour.com; Avanos Yolu 54) Also organises two- to four-day trips to Nemrut Dağı.

Nomad Travel　　GUIDED TOUR
(🖉271 2767; www.nomadtravel.com.tr; Belediye Caddesi) Offers an excellent Soğanlı tour.

New Göreme Tours　　GUIDED TOUR
(🖉271 2166; www.newgoreme.com) Fun and friendly private tours.

❶ Getting There & Away

AIR To travel between central Cappadocia and the two nearby airports, the easiest solution is to organise a transfer through your accommodation or **Cappadocia Express** (🖉0384-271 3070; www.cappadociatransport.com; Iceridere Sokak 3, Göreme; per passenger TL20).

Kayseri airport Turkish Airlines and Pegasus Airlines have several daily flights to/from İstanbul.

Nevşehır airport Turkish Airlines has two daily flights to/from İstanbul.

BUS It's easy to get to Cappadocia by bus, although from İstanbul it will likely be an overnight journey. When you purchase your ticket, make sure it clearly states your final destination (Göreme, Ürgüp etc), not just 'Cappadocia'. There should be a *servis* from Nevşehır to the surrounding villages. If you get stuck, phone your accommodation for a pick-up and do *not*

ABOVE THE FAIRY CHIMNEYS

Cappadocia is one of the best places in the world to try hot-air ballooning, with favourable flight conditions and a wonderful network of valleys to explore. Flights take place at dawn (later-morning flights are also offered, but not recommended) and balloons operate most mornings throughout the year. The major drawback is that, with the activity's burgeoning popularity, dozens of balloons now fill the sky on typical mornings, and the numerous operators vary in expertise and safety standards. The following have good credentials:

Butterfly Balloons (🖉271 3010; www.butterflyballoons.com; Uzundere Caddesi 29, Göreme) Standard flights (one hour, up to 16 passengers) cost €175.

Royal Balloon (🖉271 3300; www.royalballoon.com; Dutlu Sokak 9) Standard flights (one hour, up to 20 passengers) cost €175.

Voyager Balloons (🖉271 3030; www.voyagerballoons.com; Müze Caddesi 36/1, Göreme) Standard flights (one hour) cost €160.

book a tour in Nevşehir. A taxi to Göreme should cost around TL35.

Departing Cappadocia, Göreme and Ürgüp have *otogars*, as do Kayseri and Nevşehir. From Göreme buses go to:

Ankara TL30, 4½ hours

Antalya TL45, nine hours

İstanbul TL50, 12 hours

Konya TL20, three hours

ℹ Getting Around

Travelling the quieter roads is a great way to cover the central sights and appreciate the landscape. Prices (in Göreme) for a day's rental:

Mountain bikes TL25

Mopeds and scooters TL45 to TL55

Small car TL90 to TL130

DOLMUŞ Belediye Bus Corp *dolmuşes* (TL2.50 to TL3) travel between Ürgüp and Avanos via Ortahisar, Göreme Open-Air Museum, Göreme village, Çavuşin and (on request) Paşabaği and Zelve. The services leave Ürgüp at 10am, noon, 4pm and 6pm; and Avanos at 9am, 11am, 1pm, 3pm and 5pm.

There's also an hourly *belediye* (municipal) bus between Avanos and Nevşehir (TL4) via Çavuşin (10 minutes), Göreme (15 minutes) and Uçhisar (30 minutes), leaving Avanos from 7am to 7pm.

Göreme

✓0384 / POP 6350

Göreme is the archetypal travellers' utopia: a beatific village where the surreal surroundings spread a fat smile on everyone's face. Beneath the honeycomb cliffs, the locals live in fairy chimneys – or increasingly, run hotels in them. The encroaching maze of wavy white and pink valleys is dotted with hiking trails, panoramic viewpoints and rock-cut churches.

Tourism has inevitably changed this village, where you can start the day in a hot-air balloon before touring a valley of rock-cut Byzantine churches. Nonetheless, you can still see rural life continuing in a place where, once upon a time, if a man couldn't lay claim to one of the rock-hewn pigeon houses, he would struggle to woo a wife.

🏃 Activities

Hiking   HIKING

There are many hiking options around Göreme village. It's surrounded by a handful of gorgeous interconnected valleys that are easily explored on foot, allowing about one to

DON'T MISS

GÖREME OPEN-AIR MUSEUM

Cappadocia's top attraction and a World Heritage site, the **Göreme Open-Air Museum** (Göreme Açık Hava Müzesi; **✓**271 2167; admission TL15, Karanlık Kilise admission TL8; ⊙8am-5pm) preserves a rock-hewn Byzantine monastic settlement, where some 20 monks lived. Frescos cover the 10th- to 13th-century cave churches – notably the stunning **Karanlık Kilise** (Dark Church), which is well worth the extra TL8. Across the road from the main entrance, the **Tokalı Kilise** (Buckle Church), with an underground chapel and fabulous frescos, is included in the museum entrance fee.

three hours for each. The valleys are remote in places and it's easy to get lost in them, so stick to the trails and walk with a companion if possible.

Recommended guides include Mehmet Güngör.

Horse Riding   HORSE RIDING

Cappadocia is excellent for horse riding, which allows you to access untrodden parts of the valleys. **Dalton Brothers** (**✓**0532 275 6869; Müze Caddesi; 1 hr TL45, 2 hr TL90), run by the Göreme-born 'horse whisperer' Ekrem Ilhan, uses sure-footed Anatolian horses from Erciyes Dağı.

🛏 Sleeping

If you're visiting between October and May, pack warm clothes as pension owners may delay putting the heating on, and ring ahead to check your choice is open. This is only a small sample of the huge number of rock-cut retreats.

TOP CHOICE **Kelebek Hotel & Cave Pension**   HOTEL **€€**

(**✓**271 2531; www.kelebekhotel.com; Yavuz Sokak 31; fairy chimney s/d €40/50, deluxe s/d €52/65, ste s €64-144, ste d 80-180; 🗟🗷) Spread over two gorgeous stone houses, each with fairy chimney protruding skyward, rooms here exude Anatolian inspiration. One of Göreme's original boutique hotels, Kelebek (Butterfly) continues to innovate, offering complimentary village garden breakfast visits.

TURKEY GÖREME

`TOP CHOICE` Koza Cave Hotel
HOTEL €€

(☑271 2466; www.kozacavehotel.com; Cakmaklı Sokak 49; s/d €75/90, ste €115-140; ☏) Bringing eco-inspired chic to Göreme, Koza Cave is a masterclass in stylish sustainable tourism. Owner Derviş lived in Holland, and has incorporated Dutch ecosensibility into every cave crevice. Recycled materials and local handcrafted furniture are utilised to create sophisticated, elegant spaces.

Aydınlı Cave House
HOTEL €€

(☑271 2263; www.thecavehotel.com; Aydınlı Sokak 12; r €70-140; ☏) Proprietor Mustafa has converted his family home into a haven for honeymooners and those requiring a little rock-cut style with their solitude. Guests rave about the warm service and immaculate, spacious cave rooms, which include a family suite.

Dorm Cave
HOSTEL €

(☑271 2770; www.travellerscave.com; Hafız Abdullah Efendi Sokak 4; dm €10, d/tr €30/45; ☏) In this superb hostel, three spacious cave rooms are home to the dorm beds, and share small, modern bathrooms across a pretty courtyard. Upstairs a couple of snug private rooms also offer brilliant value.

Kismet Cave House
HOTEL €€

(☑271 2416; www.kismetcavehouse.com; Kağnı Yolu 9; d €75; ☏) Guests consistently hail the intimate experience created by the unobtrusive Faruk and his family at this cave house. The rooms host local antiques, colourful rugs and quirky artwork, while communal areas have cosy, cushion-scattered nooks.

Fairy Chimney Inn
HOTEL €€

(☑271 2655; www.fairychimney.com; Güvercinlik Sokak 5-7; r from €55-111; ☏) This highbrow retreat is run by Dr Andus Emge and his wife, who offer academic asides to their wonderful hospitality. The views from the garden and various peepholes are magnificent, while the rooms have simple furniture and traditional textiles.

Cappadocia Cave Suites
LUXURY HOTEL €€€

(☑271 2800; www.cappadociacavesuites.com; Ünlü Sokak 19; r €135-275; ❋☏) Uncomplicated service, spacious, modern-meets-megalithic suite rooms and cool, converted stables. Fairy Chimney 1 is our pick for its cosy living room, ideal for balloon-viewing.

Eating

`TOP CHOICE` Köy Evi
ANATOLIAN €€€

(☑271 2008; Aydınkıragı Sokak 40; set menu TL25; ☏) The simple, wholesome, tasty flavours of village food are the main act at this brilliant set-menu restaurant, which offers a taste-bud tour of Göreme. The warren of cave rooms has been kept authentically basic, adding to the homespun appeal.

Seten Restaurant
MODERN TURKISH €€

(☑271 3025; www.setenrestaurant.com; Aydınlı Sokak; mains TL16-40) Brimming with an artful Anatolian aesthetic, Seten offers an education for newcomers to Turkish cuisine and a treat for well-travelled tongues. The classic dishes done right, and dazzling array of meze done differently, keep you coming back.

Topdeck Cave Restaurant
ANATOLIAN €€

(☑271 2474; Hafız Abdullah Efendi Sokak 15; mains TL15-20; ⊘dinner only; ☏) Talented chef Mustafa and his gracious family have transformed an atmospheric cave room in their house into this cosy restaurant. Kids pitch in with the serving and diners dig into hearty helpings of Anatolian favourites with a spicy twist. Mustafa also offers reservation-only, morning **cooking classes** (€40; ⊘classes 9-11am).

Nazar Börek
TURKISH €

(☑271 2441; Müze Caddesi; gözleme & börek TL6-9; ☏) Head here for supremely tasty traditional Turkish staples, including hearty plates of *gözleme* and *sosyete böregi* (stuffed spiral pastries served with yoghurt and tomato sauce).

Dibek
ANATOLIAN €€

(☑271 2209; Hakkı Paşa Meydanı 1; mains TL10-22; ☏) Diners sprawl on cushions and feast on traditional dishes and homemade wine at this family restaurant, set inside a 475-year-old building. Book ahead (at least three hours) for the slow-cooked *testi* kebap meal ('pottery kebap', with meat or mushrooms and vegetables cooked in a sealed terracotta pot, which is broken at the table; TL28).

Local Restaurant
MODERN TURKISH €€

(☑271 2629; Müze Caddesi 38; mains TL11-32) Local's steak dishes are scrumptious enough, but do order the *patlican* (aubergine) salad for gloriously smoky perfection on a plate.

Information

Services useful to travellers are mostly around the central *otogar*, including ATMs and a **tourist information booth** (☏271 2558; www.goreme. org). The **post office** (PTT; Posta Sokak), a good option for changing money, is nearby.

Uçhisar

☏0384 / POP 3800

Between Göreme and Nevşehir is picturesque, laid-back yet stylish Uçhisar, built around a **rock castle** (Uçhisar Kalesi; admission TL3; ☺8am-8.15pm) that offers panoramic views from its summit. The local 'kilometre zero' for French holidaymakers, Uçhisar is nonetheless quieter than Göreme and worth considering as an alternative base.

There are some excellent places to stay, mostly with views across the rocky valleys.

Underground passageways, reading corners and shady terraces add magic to **Kale Konak** (☏219 2828; www.kalekonak.com; Kale Sokak 9; s/d/ste €90/110/140; ☎), with a marble *hamam* and minimalist retreat-chic rooms in the shadow of Uçhisar castle.

Hospitable and spacious, **Kilim Pension** (☏219 2774; www.sisik.com; Tekelli Mahallesi; s/d/tr TL70/130/170; ☎) has smartly simple, light-filled rooms and a vine-draped terrace.

At cosy **Uçhisar Pension** (☏219 2662; www.uchisarpension.com; Göreme Caddesi; s/d/tr €25/40/55; ☎), Mustafa and Gül dispense lashings of old fashioned Turkish hospitality.

Eating options in the village range from **Elai** (☏219 3181; www.elairestaurant.com; Eski Göreme Yolu; mains TL24-45; ☺10.30am-2.30pm & 6.30-11pm), which serves modern Anatolian dishes with international influences in sharp surrounds, to the humble **Center Café & Restaurant** (☏219 3117; Belediye Meydanı; mains TL10-25), offering crispy salads and *dondurma* (ice cream) in the town square.

Zelve Valley

Three valleys of abandoned rock-cut churches and homes converge at the excellent **Zelve Open-Air Museum** (admission TL8, parking TL2; ☺8am-7pm Apr-Oct, to 5pm Nov-Mar), off the Göreme–Avanos road. Inhabited until 1952, its sinewy valley walls with rock antennae could have been made for poking around. In the same area, a three-headed formation and fine examples of mushroom-shaped fairy chimneys can be seen at **Paşabağı**. You can climb inside one chimney to a monk's quarters. Near Zelve on the Ürgüp–Avanos road, **Devrent Valley** is also known as 'Imagination Valley' for its chimneys' anthropomorphic forms.

Ürgüp

☏0384 / POP 18,700

Ninety years after Ürgüp's Greek residents were evicted in the population exchange, international visitors are pained to leave their temporary boutique residences here. Like your favourite Turkish aunt, Ürgüp is elegant without even trying. With a few restaurants, the fabulous **Tarihi Şehir Hamamı** (☏341 2241; İstiklal Caddesi; soak, scrub & massage TL25; ☺7am-11pm), the up-and-coming **Turasan Winery** (☏341 4961; Tevfik Fikret Caddesi; vineyard tour & wine tasting €5; ☺8.30am-7pm) and valley views, the town is the connoisseurs' base for exploring the heart of Cappadocia.

🛏 Sleeping

Most of Ürgüp's boutique hotels are on Esbelli hill.

TOP CHOICE **Esbelli Evi**　　　BOUTIQUE HOTEL €€€
(☏341 3395; www.esbelli.com; Esbelli Sokak 8; d €120, ste €150-235; ❉☎) Jazz in the bathroom, whiskey by the tub, secret tunnels to secluded walled gardens covered in vines: Esbelli is the pick of Cappadocia's accommodation. Occupying 12 properties, the cultured yet unpretentious hotel has 14 rooms, which feel like first-class apartments for visiting dignitaries.

Serinn House　　　BOUTIQUE HOTEL €€€
(☏341 6076; www.serinnhouse.com; Esbelli Sokak 36; d €120-140; ☎) Jetsetter hostess Eren Serpen has set a new standard for hotel design in Cappadocia with this contemporary effort, seamlessly merging İstanbul's European aesthetic with Turkish provincial life. The six minimally furnished rooms feature Archimedes lamps, signature chairs, hip floor rugs and tables too cool for coffee.

Melekler Evi　　　BOUTIQUE HOTEL €€
(☏341 7131; www.meleklerevi.com.tr; Dere Sokak 59; d €90-115, ste 145; ☎) Architectural duo Muammer and Arzu have created a sweet little hideaway that brims with inspired artistic flourishes. Each room is an individual piece of interior-design heaven, where hi-fi

music and hi-tech shower systems merge with smatterings of winged sculpture, grand old stone fireplaces and homespun whimsy.

Cappadocia Palace HOTEL €€
(☑341 2510; www.hotel-cappadocia.com; Mektep Sokak 2; s/d €30/44, cave €60/88; ☜) An Ürgüp old-timer with helpful management and a choice of either enormous cave rooms hosting bathrooms big enough to boogie in, or plainer (and smaller) motel-style rooms.

✕ Eating & Drinking

The main square is the best place to grab an alcoholic or caffeinated beverage at an outside table and watch Cappadocia cruise by. The pedestrian walkway running northeast from Ehlikeyf restaurant is full of cafes, bars and old men playing backgammon. The most convivial and relaxed place for a drink is at the bar in Han Çirağan.

TOP CHOICE Ziggy's MODERN TURKISH €€€
(☑341 7107; Yunak Mahallesi, Teyfik Fikret Caddesi 24; meze TL6-12, set menus TL45, mains TL25; ☻) With the finest meze menu in Cappadocia, and a terrace that fills day and night with humming tunes, strong cocktails and a hip clientele, Ziggy's backs up its glowing reputation with professional service and an innovative menu.

Han Çirağan Restaurant RESTAURANT, BAR €€
(☑341 2566; Cumhuriyet Meydanı; mains TL15-25; ☻) Offering atmospheric yet casual dining, the Han's service is superfriendly and the menu meanders through Turkish favourites with a modern twist. After dinner, retire to the cool bar downstairs, under the vine trellis, for an excellent wine list and mean Martinis.

Cafe In INTERNATIONAL €€
(Cumhuriyet Meydanı; mains TL13-17; ☻) For a pasta-orientated break from Turkish cuisine, this wee cafe should be your first port of call. Servings are on the generous side, service is swift and it does some excellent salads.

Develili Deringöller Pide ve Kebap Salonu PIDE €
(Dumlupınar Caddesi; pide TL6-8; ☻) Shush. We're going to tell you a secret the locals have been trying to hide for years. This is, hands down, the best pide in Cappadocia.

Ailanpa Wine House WINE BAR
(☑341 6927; İstiklal Caddesi; wine TL10) This trendy wine house mixes chatty staff, comfy red velvet seating and a decent soundtrack.

ℹ Information

Around Cumhuriyet Meydanı, the main square, you'll find banks with ATMs. The **tourist office** (☑341 4059; Kayseri Caddesi 37; ☺8am-5.30pm Mon-Fri) gives out a map and has a list of hotels.

Travel agencies **Argeus Tours** (☑341 4688; www.argeus.com.tr; İstiklal Caddesi 47) and **Peerless Travel Services** (☑341 6970; www.peerlessexcursions.com; İstiklal Caddesi 41) can arrange tours and transfers.

Mustafapaşa

☑0384 / POP 1600

Mustafapaşa is the sleeping beauty of Cappadocia – a peaceful village with pretty, old stone-carved houses, some minor rock-cut churches and a scattering of hotels. If you want to get away from it all, this is the place to base yourself. Until WWI it was called Sinasos and was a predominantly Ottoman-Greek settlement.

Ukabeyn Pansiyon (☑353 5533; www.ukabeyn.com; Gazi Sokak 62; s/d TL85/120; ☜☻) is a well-presented, friendly cave hotel with light-filled, stone-vaulted rooms and, backing onto the downstairs terrace, more characterful cave rooms.

Old Greek House (☑353 5306; www.oldgreekhouse.com; Şahin Caddesi; s TL100, d TL150-200; ☜) is well known for its Ottoman-flavoured set menus (TL35 to TL45), starring good versions of the usual suspects: *mantı*, *köfte*, lima beans, crispy salads and baklava. If the Turkish coffee hasn't kicked in, the large bedrooms have polished floorboards and an antique feel.

Dolmuşes to Mustafapaşa leave roughly every 30 minutes from Ürgüp's Mustafapaşa *otogar* (TL2, 10 minutes), next to the main bus station.

Kayseri

TRANSPORT HUB

Mixing Seljuk tombs, mosques and modern developments, Kayseri is both central Turkey's most devoutly Islamic city after Konya and one of the economic powerhouses nicknamed the 'Anatolian tigers'. You may well pass through en route to/from central Cappadocia.

⌂ Sleeping & Eating

If you get caught here overnight, the reasonable midrange options **Hotel Almer** (☑320 7970; www.almer.com.tr; Osman Kavuncu

WORTH A TRIP

IHLARA VALLEY

A beautiful canyon full of greenery and rock-cut churches dating back to Byzantine times, **Ihlara Valley** (TL8, parking TL2; ☺8am-6.30pm) is an excellent, if popular, spot for a walk. Footpaths follow the course of the river, Melendiz Suyu, which flows between the narrow gorge at Ihlara village and the wide valley around **Selime Monastery** (admission TL8; ☺dawn-dusk).

The easiest way to see the valley is on a day tour, which allows a few hours for a one-way walk through the stretch of the gorge with most churches. To get there by bus from Göreme, you must change in Nevşehir and Aksaray, making it a tricky day trip on public transport.

Midway along the gorge, below Belisırma village, four low-key riverside restaurants feed the hungry hikers. If you want to walk the whole valley, it takes about five to six hours, and there are modest pensions at both ends: **Akar Pansion & Restaurant** (☑453 7018; www.ihlara-akarmotel.com; Ihlara Village; s/d/tr TL40/70/90; ☎) in Ihlara village and **Çatlak Hotel** (☑454 5006; www.catlakturizm.com.tr; Selime; s/d TL45/90; ☎) in Selime. Note that most accommodation is closed out of season (December to March).

On weekdays six *dolmuşes* travel to/from Aksaray (TL4, 45 minutes), stopping in Selime, Belisırma and Ihlara village. In Belisırma, *dolmuşes* stop up on the plateau, and you have to hike a few hundred metres down into the valley. On the weekend there are fewer services.

Caddesi 1; s/d TL70/110; ✳☎), **Bent Hotel** (☑221 2400; www.benthotel.com; Atatürk Bulvarı 40; s/d/tr TL70/110/120; ✳☎) and **Hotel Çapari** (☑222 5278; Donanma Caddesi 12; s/d/tr/ste TL60/90/110/120; ✳☎) are all a few hundred metres east of main square Cumhuriyet Meydanı. **Novotel** (☑207 3000; www.novotel. com; Kocasinan Bulvarı; r from €60; ✳☎), 3km from the centre en route to the airport, is a very good version of the dependable international chain. Book accommodation in advance.

The western end of Sivas Caddesi has a strip of fast-food joints that still seem to be pumping when everything else in town is quiet, including the fish-loving **İstanbul Balık Pazarı** (☑231 8973; Sivas Caddesi; mains TL5-10; ☺8am-11pm). For an alcoholic tipple with your tucker, try Hotel Almer or, 500m northeast, **Kale Rooftop Restaurant** (☑207 5000; Hilton Hotel, Cumhuriyet Meydanı, İstasyon Caddesi 1; mains TL20-40; ☺noon-2am) at the Hilton.

❶ Getting There & Away

AIR Turkish Airlines and Pegasus Airlines have several daily flights to/from İstanbul.

A taxi between Kayseri city centre and the *havaalanı* (airport) costs TL15 and a *dolmuş* is TL1.25.

BUS The *otogar* is 9km west of the centre, reached by *servis*, taxi (TL15), local bus (TL1.25)

or a tram to Selimiye (TL1), a 10-minute walk away. On an important north–south and east–west crossroads, Kayseri has many services:

Göreme TL10, one hour

Malatya TL25, five hours

Van TL80, 13 hours

TRAIN There are daily long-distance trains to/from destinations including Adana, Ankara and Tatvan (Lake Van). The station is about 1.5km northwest of Cumhuriyet Meydanı.

EASTERN TURKEY

Like a challenge? Eastern Anatolia – vast, remote and culturally very Middle Eastern – is the toughest part of Turkey to travel in but definitely the most exotic, and certainly the least affected by mass tourism. Winter here can be bitterly cold and snowy.

Rugged southeastern Anatolia, bordering Syria, Iran and Iraq, makes a fascinating addition to an eastern Mediterranean or Cappadocian itinerary. A good selection of eastern Turkey's major sights are found among its expansive steppe and soaring mountains. Particularly near Iraq, a few places and roads are sometimes offlimits due to fighting between the military and the PKK. The same is also true of roads and regions close to the Syrian border owing to the unrest in Syria.

However, the southeast is mostly safe and accessible to independent travellers. What will linger longest in your memory is the incredibly warm-hearted welcome from the (predominantly Kurdish) locals. Expect a military presence, keep your passport handy for army checkpoints, and check the current security situation before you visit the area.

Mt Nemrut National Park

Nemrut Dağı Milli Parkı (admission TL8; ☉dawn-dusk) contains one of the country's most awe-inspiring sights. Two thousand years ago, right on top of **Nemrut Dağı** (Mt Nemrut; 2150m) and pretty much in the middle of nowhere, a meglomaniac Commagene king erected fabulous temples and a funerary mound. The fallen heads of the gigantic decorative statues of gods and kings, toppled by earthquakes, form one of the country's most enduring images.

Tours

There are a few possible bases for visiting Mt Nemrut:

MALATYA

The **Nemrut Dağı Information Booth** (☑0535 760 5080; kemalmalatya@hotmail.com; Atatürk Caddesi; ☉8am-7pm May-Sep) organises all-inclusive daily **minibus tours** (TL100, early May–mid-Oct, min 2 people), with a night at the Güneş Hotel below the summit and visits to the heads at sunset and sunrise.

KAHTA

Hotels and guesthouses offer eight-hour sunrise and sunset 'long tours', as well as the less-interesting three-hour 'short tour'. This route is more scenic, and Kahta is slowly losing its reputation as a rip-off town. The **Kommagene Hotel** (www.nemrutguide.com; 'long tour' incl accommodation TL125 per person, daily Apr-Nov) and **Zeus Hotel** offer tours. Alternatively, hire a taxi at the *otogar* (short/long tour TL100/130); Kahta's 'tours' are usually just glorified taxi services anyway.

KARADUT

Near the park's southern entrance, hotels offer return trips to the summit for about TL50 per vehicle (Karadut Pension) or TL100 (Hotel Euphrat).

ŞANLIURFA

Several agencies run tours, including **Harran-Nemrut Tours** (☑215 1575, 0542 761 3065; www.aslankonukevi.com; Demokrasi Caddesi 12; per person €50, min two people), **Mustafa Çaycı** (☑0532 685 2942, 313 1340; musma63@yahoo.com; Hotel Uğur, Köprübaşı Caddesi 3; per person TL130, min 2 people) and **Nomad Tours Turkey** (☑0533 747 1850; www.nomadtoursturkey.com; per person €100).

CAPPADOCIA

Some people take a two-day tour (about TL350, mid-April to mid-November), but it's a tedious drive. If you have enough time, it's better to opt for a three-day tour, which usually also includes Harran and Şanlıurfa.

🛏 Sleeping

MALATYA

Grand W Aksaç Hotel　　　　HOTEL €€
(☑0422-324 6565; www.aksachotel.com; Saray Mahallesi, Ömer Efendi Sokak 19; s/d TL100/140; ❋🛜) In a quiet central location, with flash services including a *hamam*, spacious bathrooms, flat-screen TVs, huge beds, and chocolate-covered apricots for sale in reception.

KAHTA

Kommagene Hotel　　　　HOTEL €
(☑0416-725 9726, 0532 200 3856; ; Mustafa Kemal Caddesi 1; s/d TL45/70; ❋@🛜) The wood-lined rooms are cosy and colourful, and breakfast is served in a spacious top-floor salon with good views of Kahta's dusty main drag. A kitchen, laundry and free pickups from the Adıyaman and Kahta *otogars* are also offered.

Zeus Hotel　　　　HOTEL €€
(☑0416-725 5694; www.zeushotel.com.tr; Mustafa Kemal Caddesi; camp sites per person TL20, s/d/ste €60/80/110; ❋🛜🏊) At this solid three-star option, with its pool and manicured garden, angle for the renovated rooms, which feature top-notch bathrooms and flat-screen TVs. Campers can pitch tents on the parking lot, and have access to their own ablutions block. Opposite, the recommended **Papatya Restaurant** (Mustafa Kemal Caddesi; mains TL8-10) whips up all the usual Turkish suspects.

KARADUT

Karadut Pension　　　　PENSION €
(☑0416-737 2169, 0532 566 2857; www.karadutpansiyon.net; Karadut; d per person TL35; ❋@) This pension has neat, compact rooms (some with air-con), cleanish bathrooms and a shared kitchen. Meals are available with alcoholic drinks on the alfresco terrace bar. Campers can pitch their tent and they'll pick you up from Kahta for TL18.

Hotel Euphrat   HOTEL €€
(☑0416-737 2175; www.hoteleuphratnemrut.com; s/d/tr with half board €45/58/68; ❄✿🏊) Popular with tour groups in peak season. Renovations have made the rooms larger and more comfortable, and the views from the restaurant terrace and pool are spectacular.

ŞANLIURFA
Aslan Konuk Evi   PENSION €€
(☑0414-215 1575, 0542 761 3065; www.aslankonukevi.com; Demokrasi Caddesi 12; r TL90-120; ❄@🛜) Efficiently run by English teacher Özcan, with good food and cold beer available in this heritage building's rooftop terrace restaurant. Accommodation options range from shared dorm rooms to newer double rooms with private bathrooms. A good-value deal is TL120 for two people including breakfast and dinner.

Hotel Uğur   HOTEL €
(☑0414-313 1340, 0532 685 2942; musma63@yahoo.com; Köprübaşı Caddesi 3; per person with shared bathroom TL20; ❄🛜) Rooms are sparsely decorated and relatively compact, but clean and spotless. There's a great travellers' vibe, enhanced by a few cold beers on the hotel's terrace. Rates exclude breakfast, but there's a good *kahvaltı salonu* (breakfast restaurant) downstairs.

🛈 Getting There & Away

AIR Malatya and Şanlıurfa's airports both have daily Turkish Airlines and Pegasus Airlines flights to/from Ankara and İstanbul. Pegasus also links Urfa with İzmir, and Onur Air flies İstanbul–Malatya.

BUS Malatya, Kahta and Şanlıurfa are well connected, with regular buses to/from locations including Ankara, İstanbul and Kayseri.

DOLMUŞ During the summer season, there are minibuses (TL10) around every two hours between Kahta and the Çeşme Pansion, about 6km from the summit, via Karadut. Pension owners can pick you up at Kahta's *otogar* (set the price beforehand).

Mardin
☑0482 / POP 88,000
Pretty-as-a-picture Mardin is an addictive, unmissable spot. With its minarets poking out of a labyrinth of brown lanes, its castle dominating the Old City, and honey-coloured stone houses cascading down the hillside, Mardin emerges like a phoenix from the sun-roasted Mesopotamian plains. A mosaic of Kurdish, Yezidi, Christian and Syrian cultures, it also has a fascinating cultural mix.

The city has started to become popular with Turkish travellers – get here before it becomes too touristy.

Mardin is only 25km north of Turkey's border with Syria, and areas near this border are sometimes off limits due to the unrest in Syria and fighting between the Turkish army and the PKK. See p841 for advice on safe travel in the region.

👁 Sights & Activities

Sakıp Sabancı
Mardin City Museum   MUSEUM
(Sakıp Sabancı Mardin Kent Müzesi; www.sabancimuzesimardin.gov.tr; Eski Hükümet Caddesi; admission TL3; ⏰8am-5pm Tue-Sun) Housed in a carefully restored former army barracks, this superb museum showcases Mardin's cosmopolitan and multicultural past. Downstairs is used as an art gallery.

Bazaar   MARKET
Mardin's rambling commercial hub parallels Cumhuriyet Caddesi one block down the hill. Donkeys are still a main form of transport, and saddle repairers ply their trade. Look for the secluded **Ulu Camii**, a 12th-century Iraqi Seljuk structure with delicate reliefs adorning its minaret.

Forty Martyrs Church   CHURCH
(Kırklar Kilisesi; Sağlık Sokak) This 4th-century church was renamed in the 15th century to commemorate Cappadocian martyrs, now remembered in the fine carvings above the entrance.

Cumhuriyet Caddesi
Mardin Museum   STREET
(Mardin Müzesi; admission TL5; ⏰8am-5pm Tue-Sun) is housed in a restored late-19th-century mansion; east of there, the ornately carved **old Mardin house**, featuring a three-arched facade, is a fabulous example of the city's domestic architecture. **Sultan İsa (Zinciriye) Medresesi** (admission TL2) has an imposing recessed doorway, pretty courtyards and city views from the roof. Opposite the former **post office**, housed in a 17th-century *caravanserai*, rises the elegant, slender minaret of the 14th-century **Şehidiye Camii**. It's superbly carved, with colonnades all around and three small bulbs superimposed at the summit. **Emir Hamamı** (treatments from T20; ⏰men 6.30am-noon & 6-10pm, women noon-5.30pm) dates back to Roman times and has views of the plains from its terrace.

🍽 Sleeping & Eating

Mardin's popularity means that accommodation is expensive, and summer weekends are particularly busy. Rooms are often small and lack natural light; ask the right questions when you book.

Şahmeran Otanik Pansiyon   PENSION €
(☏213 2300; www.sahmeranpansiyon.com; Cumhuriyet Caddesi, 246 Sokak 10; per person with/without bathroom TL35/40 ; ☎) In Old Mardin, this good-value historic option is arrayed around a honey-coloured stone courtyard just a short uphill meander from Mardin's main thoroughfare. Breakfast is an additional TL5.

Reyhani Kasrı   BOUTIQUE HOTEL €€€
(☏212 1333; www.reyhanikasri.com.tr; Cumhuriyet Caddesi; s/d TL150/190; ❄☎) Sleek and modern rooms are concealed within a lovingly restored historic mansion, providing a contemporary spin on the boutique-hotel experience. Multiple floors cascade down the hillside, making it one of Mardin's more spectacular buildings, and the 'Sky Terrace' bar has unbeatable Mesopotamian views.

Antik Tatlıede Butik Hotel   BOUTIQUE HOTEL €€
(☏213 2720; www.tatlidede.com.tr; Medrese Mahallesi; s/d/tr TL100/150/200; ❄☎) In a quiet location near Mardin's bazaar, a labyrinthine heritage mansion is filled with rooms of varying sizes (mostly fairly spacious). Huge terraces have views across the plains.

Kamer Cafe Mutfak   ANATOLIAN €€
(Cumhuriyet Caddesi; mains TL10-15) Operated by the Kamer Vakif (Moon Foundation), a support organisation for women who are victims of domestic violence, this terrific

---

DON'T MISS

AKDAMAR KILISESI

This carefully restored island **church** (Church of the Holy Cross; admission TL3; ☻8am-6pm) is one of the marvels of Armenian architecture. The wonderful relief carvings on its well-preserved walls are masterworks of Armenian art, and inside are frescos. Akdamar Island is 3km out in Lake Van, reached on boats from the south shore (TL8) and most easily on a day trip from Van.

---

restaurant serves some of Mardin's best local cuisine. There's occasional live music amid the rustic and arty ambience.

❶ Getting There & Away

AIR Any minibus to Kızıltepe can drop you at Mardin airport (TL3), 20km south of town. Turkish Airlines has daily flights to/from İstanbul and Ankara.

DOLMUŞ There are frequent minibuses to Diyarbakır (TL10, 1¼ hours), Midyat (TL9, 1¼ hours) and Şanlıurfa (TL25, three hours).

Van

☏0432 / POP 353,500

With young couples walking hand in hand on the main drag and live bands knocking out Kurdish tunes in pubs, Van is more urban, more casual and less rigorous than the rest of southeastern Anatolia. Its resilient population is rebuilding after the devastating earthquakes of 2011, and its satisfying urban buzz complements its brilliant location, near the eponymous lake.

◉ Sights & Activities

Van Castle (Van Kalesi)   RUIN
(Rock of Van; admission TL3; ☻9am-dusk) Try to visit Van's imposing castle, about 4km west of the centre, at sunset for great views of the lake. On the southern side of the rock are the foundations of **Eski Van** (the old city).

Van Museum   MUSEUM
(Van Müzesi; Kişla Caddesi; admission TL3; ☻8am-noon & 1-5pm Tue-Sun) This compact museum was closed at the time of writing, and a potential move to near Van Castle was rumoured. It boasts an outstanding collection of Urartian exhibits, with gold jewellery, bronze belts, helmets, horse armour and terracotta figures.

Alkan Tours   GUIDED TOURS
(☏215 2092, 0530 349 2793; www.easternturkeytour.org; Ordu Caddesi) Guided day trips (per person €20) taking in **Akdamar Island**, the photogenic 17th-century **Hoşap Castle** and the Urartian site at **Çavuştepe** are a time-efficient way to see the region's main sights.

🛏 Sleeping

Accommodation is often in high demand, and rates can be higher than elsewhere in eastern Turkey.

Büyük Asur Oteli HOTEL **€€**
(☑216 8792; www.buyukasur.com; Cumhuriyet Caddesi, Turizm Sokak; s/d TL100/150; ❀⊚) This reliable midrange venture's colourful rooms come complete with fresh linen, TV and well-scrubbed bathrooms. English is spoken and the hotel can organise tours to Akdamar Island, Hoşap Castle and other attractions.

Akdamar Otel HOTEL **€€**
(☑214 9923; www.otelakdamar.com; Kazım Karabekir Caddesi; s/d TL120/160; ❀⊚) The Akdamar is centrally located, close to good restaurants and pastry shops, and has flat-screen TVs, and newly decorated, spacious bathrooms. The young, English-speaking staff have lots of recommendations.

✕ Eating & Drinking

Tamara Ocakbaşı STEAKHOUSE **€€**
(Yüzbaşıoğlu Sokak; mains TL15-20; ⏲5pm-late) Dining at the Hotel Tamara's restaurant is dizzying, especially for carnivores: each table has its own grill. High-quality meat and fish dishes feature prominently, but the list of meze is equally impressive. Downstairs, you can get a cold beer at the **North Shield** pub.

Kervansaray ANATOLIAN **€€**
(Cumhuriyet Caddesi; mains TL12-18) Van's go-to spot for an elegant and refined dining experience. Share plates of meze as you peruse a menu containing more than a few local specialities. Fans of incredibly tender lamb should definitely consider the *kağıt* kebap (paper kebab).

Halay Türkü Bar LIVE MUSIC, BAR
(Kazım Karabekir Caddesi) At the multilevel Halay Türkü, enjoy tasty meze and grilled meat before graduating to draught beer, local spirits and regular live music.

ℹ Information

Hotels, restaurants, ATMs, internet cafes, bus-company offices, the post office and the **tourist office** (☑216 2530; ⏲8.30am-noon & 1-5.30pm Mon-Fri) lie on and around Cumhuriyet Caddesi.

ℹ Getting There & Away

AIR Turkish Airlines, AnadoluJet and Pegasus Airlines fly daily to/from İstanbul and Ankara. A taxi to the airport costs about TL30. Buses leave frequently from near the Akdamar Hotel (TL1.25).

BOAT A twice-daily ferry crosses Lake Van between Tatvan and Van (TL10, four hours), but there's no fixed schedule.

> ### BREAKFAST OF CHAMPIONS
>
> Van is famed for its tasty *kahvaltı* (breakfast), best tried on pedestrianised Eski Sümerbank Sokak, also called 'Kahvaltı Sokak' (Breakfast St). Here, a row of eateries offers complete Turkish breakfasts (around TL12 to TL15). Sample honey, olives, tomatoes, cucumbers, *sucuklu yumurta* (omelette with sausage) and dairy goodness including *otlu peynir* (cheese mixed with a tangy herb, Van's speciality) and *kaymak* (clotted cream).

BUS Daily buses connect Van with Ankara (TL90, 17 hours), Malatya (TL60, 12 hours) and Şanlıurfa (TL60, 11 hours).

TRAIN The twice-weekly *Vangölü Ekspresi* train from Ankara meets the ferry in Tatvan. The weekly *Trans Asya Ekspresi* connects Ankara to Tehran (Iran) via Van; a train also runs to Tabriz (Iran) on Tuesday.

UNDERSTAND TURKEY

History

The sheer weight and depth of history in Turkey is overwhelming. The Anatolian plateau features in various guises in both Homer's *Iliad* and the Bible; it has produced some of the world's longest-lasting dynasties, been the centre of ancient empires covering much of Europe and the Middle East, and still holds a strategic position at the meeting of two continents.

By about 6500 BC a Neolithic city, one of the oldest ever recorded, was established at Çatalhöyük, near Konya. The greatest of the early civilisations of Anatolia (Asian Turkey) was that of the Hittites, a force to be reckoned with from 2000 to 1200 BC, with their capital at Hattuşa, east of Ankara. Traces of their existence remain throughout central Turkey.

After the collapse of the Hittite empire, Anatolia splintered into several small states until the Graeco-Roman period, when parts of the country were reunited. Later, Christianity spread through Anatolia, carried by the apostle Paul, a native of Tarsus (near Adana).

Byzantine Empire & the Crusades

In AD 330 the Roman emperor Constantine founded a new imperial city at Byzantium (modern İstanbul). Renamed Constantinople, this strategic city became the capital of the Eastern Roman Empire and was the centre of the Byzantine Empire for 1000 years. During the European Dark Ages, the Byzantine Empire kept alive the flame of Western culture, despite threats from the empires of the East (Persians, Arabs and Turks) and the West (the Christian powers of Europe).

The Byzantine Empire's decline came with their defeat at the hands of the Seljuk Turks in 1071. Seljuks overran most of Anatolia, establishing a provincial capital at Konya, ruling domains that included today's Turkey, Iran and Iraq. The Byzantines endeavoured to protect their capital and reclaim Anatolia, but, during the Fourth Crusade (1202–04), a combined Venetian and crusader force took and plundered Constantinople. The Byzantines eventually regained the ravaged city in 1261.

Ottoman Empire

A Mongol invasion in the late 13th century ended Seljuk power, but new small Turkish states soon arose in western Anatolia. One, headed by Gazi Osman (1258–1326), grew into the Ottoman Empire. In 1453 Constantinople finally fell to the Ottoman sultan Mehmet II (the Conqueror), replacing Edirne as the capital of the dynasty.

A century later, under Süleyman the Magnificent, the Ottoman Empire reached its peak, spreading deep into Europe, Asia and North Africa. Ottoman success was based on military expansion; when their march westwards stalled at Vienna in 1683, the rot set in. İstanbul's Topkapı Palace became a centre of indolence and decadence for increasingly out-of-touch sultans.

Nationalist ideas swept through Europe after the French Revolution. In 1830 the Greeks won their independence, followed by Romania, Montenegro, Serbia and Bosnia in 1878. By the early 20th century, European diplomats were plotting how to cherry-pick the choicest parts of 'the sick man of Europe'.

Having sided with the Axis powers in 1914, the Turks emerged from WWI in disarray, with the French, Italians, Greeks, Armenians and Russians contolling much of Anatolia. The Treaty of Sèvres (1920) divvied out Anatolia among the European powers, leaving the Turks with a slither of steppe.

Mustafa Kemal Atatürk

At this low point, Mustafa Kemal, the father of modern Turkey, took over. Atatürk, as he was later called, had made his name by repelling the Anzacs in their heroic but futile attempt to capture the strategic Dardanelles strait at Gallipoli during WWI.

Rallying the remnants of the Turkish army during the Turkish War of Independence that followed WWI, Kemal pushed the last of the Ottoman rulers aside and out-manoeuvred the Allied forces. The Turks finally won in 1922 by repelling the invading Greeks at Smyrna (present-day İzmir). In the ensuing population exchange, whole communities were uprooted as Greek-speaking people from Anatolia were shipped to Greece, while Muslim residents of Greece were transferred to Turkey. One result of this upheaval was the 'ghost villages' that were vacated but never reoccupied.

After the Treaty of Lausanne (1923) undid the humiliations of Sèvres, a new Turkish republic, reduced to Anatolia and part of Thrace, was born. Atatürk embarked on a rapid modernisation program, establishing a secular democracy, introducing the Latin script and European dress, and adopting equal rights for women (at least in theory). The capital was moved from İstanbul to Ankara.

Relations with Greece improved in the 1930s (the Greek president even nominated Atatürk for the Nobel Peace Prize), but soured again after WWII due to the conflict over Cyprus, particularly after the Greek-led anti-Makarios coup and the subsequent Turkish invasion in 1974.

Modern Turkey

Atatürk died in 1938 and his successor, İsmet İnönü, stepped carefully to avoid involvement in WWII. The war over, Turkey found itself allied to the US, later becoming a NATO member. However, the second half of the 20th century was a tumultuous era. The political and economic turmoil included military coups in 1960, 1971 and 1980, and 1997's military memorandum (or 'postmodern coup'). The military considered themselves the guardians of Atatürk's vision – pro-Western and secular – and stepped in when they considered it necessary.

During the 1980s and '90s the country was wracked by the ongoing conflict with the PKK, led by Abdullah Öcalan, who wanted the creation of a Kurdish state in southeastern Anatolia. The conflict led to an estimated 35,000 deaths and huge population shifts. In 1999 Öcalan was captured, but Kurdish discontent and terrorist activities continue.

The current millennium has been a more positive era for Turkey, led by the Justice and Development (AKP) party, which began its third term in 2011. The next general election is due in 2015.

Turkey Today

The very heart of the world during the Ottoman and Byzantine empires, Turkey remains pivotal on the global stage. Its position at the meeting of Europe and Asia informs its political bent: the secular country has a moderate Islamic government and good relations with the West, for which Turkey is a key ally in the Middle East.

With eight neighbouring countries, cross-border tensions are a fact of life for the Turkish government. In 2012 its biggest concern was the unrest in Syria. Refugee camps sprung up along the border in southeastern Anatolia, and Turkey returned fire after stray Syrian shells hit the Turkish border town of Akçakale and killed five civilians.

Meanwhile, efforts to normalise Turkish–Armenian diplomatic relations, long strained over the alleged massacre of Ottoman Armenians during WWI, have faltered. The countries' border remains closed, but there are glimmers of hope in their increasing cultural and trade ties.

Turkey's bid to join the EU continues. Obstacles include Turkey's refusal to recognise EU member Cyprus, the marginalisation of its Kurdish minority, and freedom of speech. Turks resent the slow pace of the talks, especially given Turkey's economic boom and Eurozone woes. Turkey's economy was Europe's fastest growing in 2011.

Domestically, Turkey's most pressing problem is the Kurdish issue, which sparked a near civil war between the military and the PKK, classed as a terrorist group by organisations including the EU and the US government in the 1980s and '90s. Having simmered down, the situation worsened during the Syrian unrest, which made it easier for the PKK to move around and launch attacks. Clashes in the remote mountains of southeastern Anatolia claimed hundreds of lives during 2012, and 600 Kurdish prisoners went on hunger strike. Nonetheless, with relations seemingly thawing between Prime Minister Erdoğan and the Kurdish figurehead Abdullah Öcalan, there are hopes that peace talks may finally bring end the insurgency.

Despite the misgivings of groups from Kurds to secularist Kemalists, Erdoğan's AKP government has overseen a broadly positive era for Turkey. Decades of military coups have given way to stability, and the 2010 referendum on constitutional reform, in which Turkey voted for change, will lead to greater democracy.

People

Turkey's population (79.8 million) is predominantly made up of Turks, with a big Kurdish minority (about 15 million) and much smaller groups of Laz, Hemşin, Arabs, Jews, Greeks and Armenians. The Laz and Hemşin people are natives of the northeastern corner of Turkey, around the Black Sea coast and Kaçkar Mountains, while Arab influence is strongest in the Antakya (Hatay) area abutting Syria. Southeastern Turkey is pretty solidly Kurdish, although the problems of the last 30 years have led many to head west in search of a better life.

As a result of Atatürk's reforms, republican Turkey has largely adapted to a modern Westernised lifestyle, at least on the surface. In the big cities and coastal resorts, you will not feel much need to adapt to fit in. In smaller towns and villages, however, particularly in the east, you may find people warier and more conservative.

The gregarious, nationalistic Turks have an acute sense of pride and honour. They are fiercely proud of their history and heros, especially Atatürk, whose portrait and statues are ubiquitous. The extended family still plays a key role, and formality and politeness are important; if asked 'how is Turkey?', answer 'çok güzel' (very beautiful).

Religion

Turkey is 99% Muslim – about 80% Sunni, with Shiites and Alevis mainly in the east. The religious practices of Sunnis and Alevis differ markedly, with the latter incorporating aspects of Anatolian folklore and less-strict segregation of the sexes.

The country espouses a more relaxed version of Islam than many Middle Eastern nations. Many men drink alcohol (although almost no one touches pork) and many women uncover their heads.

Today most of Turkey's Jews live in İstanbul, and some still speak Ladino, a Judaeo-Spanish language. The Christian minority includes some 70,000 Armenians, also mostly in İstanbul, Greeks and ancient southeastern Anatolian communities, such as Chaldean Catholics and Aramaic-speaking adherents of the Syriac Orthodox Church.

Arts

Turkey's artistic traditions are rich and diverse, displaying influences of the many cultures and civilisations that have waxed and waned in Anatolia over the centuries.

Carpets

Turkey is famous for its beautiful carpets and *kilims* (flat-weave rugs). It's thought that the Seljuk Turks introduced handwoven carpet-making techniques to Anatolia in the 12th century. During the Ottoman era, textile production and trade contributed significantly to the economy.

Traditionally, village women wove carpets for their family's use, or for their dowry. Today, the dictates of the market rule, but carpets still incorporate traditional symbols and patterns. The Ministry of Culture has sponsored projects to revive aged weaving and dyeing methods in western Turkey; some shops stock these 'project carpets'.

Architecture

Turkey's architectural history encompasses everything from Hittite stonework and Graeco-Roman temples to modern tower blocks, but perhaps the most distinctively Turkish styles are Seljuk and Ottoman. The Seljuks left magnificent mosques, *madrasas* (Islamic schools) and *hans (caravanserais)*, distinguished by their elaborate entrances. The Ottomans also built grand religious structures, and fine wood-and-stone houses in towns such as Safranbolu and Amasya.

Literature

The most famous Turkish novelists are Yaşar Kemal, nominated for the Nobel Prize for Literature on numerous occasions, and Orhan Pamuk, the Nobel Prize laureate in 2006. Kemal's novels, which include *Memed, My Hawk, The Wind from the Plain* and *Salman the Solitary,* chronicle the desperate lives of villagers battling land-grabbing lords.

An inventive prose stylist, Pamuk's books include the Kars-set *Snow,* and the existential İstanbul whodunit *Black Book,* told through a series of newspaper columns. Other well-regarded contemporary writers include Elif Şafak *(The Flea Palace),* Latife

---

LOCAL KNOWLEDGE

CELAL COŞKUN: CARPET SELLER

Celal Coşkun learned to make carpets and weave *kilims* at his grandmother's knee in southeastern Anatolia, before apprenticing as a carpet repairer in İstanbul and opening **Old Orient Carpet & Kilim Bazaar** (☑0532 510 6108; c.c_since.1993@hotmail.com; Çarşı Caddesi 5) in Fethiye. We asked this veteran of the trade for his top carpet tips.

» Know the basics: a carpet is wool or silk pile with single (Persian) or double (Turkish) knots; a *kilim* is a flat weave and reversible; a *cicim* is a *kilim* with one side embroidered.

» Establish in advance your price range and what you want in terms of size, pattern and colour.

» Deal only with a seller who you feel you can trust, be it through reputation, recommendation or instinct.

» Counting knots is only important on silk-on-silk carpets, though a double-knotted wool carpet will wear better than a single-knotted one.

» Most reputable carpet shops can negotiate discounts of between 5% and 10%, depending on how you may pay; anything higher than that and the price has been inflated in the first place.

» To extend a carpet's life, always remove your shoes when walking on it and never beat it, as this breaks the knots and warp (vertical) and weft (horizontal) threads.

» If professional cleaning is too expensive and the traditional method – washing it with mild soap and water and drying it on wood blocks to allow air to circulate beneath it – is too much like hard work, lay the carpet face (pattern) side down for a few minutes in fresh snow (if available!).

» Anything made by hand – including a carpet – can be repaired by hand.

Tekin *(Dear Shameless Death)* and Ayşe Kulin *(Farewell)*.

Cinema

Several Turkish directors have won worldwide recognition, including the late Yılmaz Güney, whose *Yol* (The Road) explores the dilemmas of convicts on weekend-release. Cannes favourite Nuri Bilge Ceylan's films include *Uzak* (Distant), which probes the lives of village migrants in the big city, and *Once Upon a Time in Anatolia*, an intriguing all-night search for a corpse in the Turkish back woods.

Ferzan Özpetek's *Hamam* addresses the hitherto hidden issue of homosexuality in Turkish society. Golden Bear–winning Fatih Akın ponders the Turkish experience in Germany in *Duvara Karsi* (Head On) and *Edge of Heaven*. Yılmaz Erdoğan's *Vizontele* is a black comedy about the first family to get a TV in a southeastern Anatolian town.

Music

The big pop stars include pretty-boy Tarkan, and chanteuse Sezen Aksu. Burhan Öçal is one of Turkey's finest percussionists; his seminal *New Dream* is a funky take on classical Turkish music.

With an Arabic spin, Arabesk is also popular. The genre's stars are Orhan Gencebay and the Kurdish former construction worker İbrahim Tatlıses.

Two folk singers to listen out for are Kurdish chanteuses Aynur Doğan and the ululating Rojin.

For an excellent overview of Turkish music, watch Fatih Akın's documentary *Crossing the Bridge: the Sound of İstanbul,* which explores styles from rock and hip hop to *fasıl* (gypsy music), or listen to Baba Zulu's classic *Duble Oryantal*. Featuring *saz* (Turkish lute), electronic and pop, it's mixed by British dub master Mad Professor.

Sport

Turkish men are fanatical lovers of soccer, and will happily opine about English teams as well as domestic sides. Major teams include Bursaspor, Trabzonspor and İstanbul's Galatasaray, Fenerbahçe and Beşiktaş.

A major home-grown spectator sport is *yağlı güreş* (oil wrestling, p782), where burly men in leather shorts grease themselves up with olive oil and grapple – most famously in Edirne.

Environment

The Land

The Dardanelles, the Sea of Marmara and the Bosphorus divide Turkey into Asian and European parts. Eastern Thrace (European Turkey) comprises only 3% of the country's 769,632-sq-km land area; the remaining 97% is Anatolia, a vast plateau rising eastward towards the Caucasus mountains. With 7200km of coastline, snowcapped mountains, rolling steppe, vast lakes and broad rivers, Turkey is geographically diverse. Turkey's 33 national parks include Uludağ National Park near Bursa, Cappadocia's Ala Dağlar National Park and southeastern Anatolia's Mt Nemrut National Park.

Wildlife

Turkey's location at the junction between Asia and Europe and its varied geography has made it one of the most biodiverse temperate-zone countries, blessed with an exceptionally rich flora of more than 9000 species, 1200 of them endemic. In addition, some 400 bird species are found here, with about 250 of these passing through on migration from Africa to Europe.

In theory, you could see bears, deer, jackals, caracal, wild boars and wolves in Turkey, although you're unlikely to spot any wild animals unless you're hiking. Instead look out for Kangal dogs, originally bred to protect sheep from wolves and bears on mountain pastures. People wandering off the beaten track, especially in eastern Turkey, are often alarmed at the sight of these huge, yellow-coated, black-headed animals, especially as they often wear spiked collars to protect them against wolves.

Environmental Issues

Turkey's embryonic environmental movement is making slow progress; discarded litter and ugly concrete buildings (some half-finished) disfigure the west in particular.

Short of water and electricity, Turkey is one of the world's main builders of dams. The 22-dam Southeast Anatolia Project, known as GAP, is changing eastern Turkey's landscape as it generates hydroelectricity for industry. Parched valleys have become fish-filled lakes, causing an explosion of diseases such as malaria; communities have been uprooted; and archaeological sites are disappearing under dam water. Hasankeyf, which was a Silk Road commercial centre on the border of Anatolia and Mesopotamia, is slated to be submerged in 2015. There are also controversial plans to build three nuclear power plants, despite the risks posed by the country's seismic vulnerabilities.

Another major environmental challenge is the threat from maritime traffic along the Bosphorus. On the Mediterranean coast, the beach nesting grounds of the loggerhead turtle *(Caretta caretta)* – such as at İztuzu Beach at Dalyan, the Göksu Delta and Patara Beach – have long been endangered by tourism and development. Various schemes are underway to protect these areas during the breeding season – look out for signs telling you when to avoid certain stretches.

On the plus side, Turkey is slowly reclaiming its architectural heritage: central Anatolia's Ottoman towns Safranbolu and Amasya are masterpieces of restoration. The country is doing well when it comes to beach cleanliness, with 352 beaches qualifying for Blue Flag status (which recognises success in areas such as water quality and environmental management); go to www.blueflag. org for the complete list. Turkey's intended accession to the EU is also forcing it to lift its environmental standards.

İstanbul has a branch of **Greenpeace Mediterranean** (☏0212-292 7619; www.greenpeace.org/mediterranean).

Food & Drink

Afiyet olsun (bon appétit)! Not without reason is Turkish food regarded as one of the world's greatest cuisines. Kebaps are, of course, the mainstay of many restaurant meals; omnipresent *kebapçıs* (kebap restaurants) and *ocakbaşıs* (grill houses) sell a range of meat feasts. The ubiquitous *dürüm döner* kebap contains compressed meat (usually lamb) cooked on a revolving upright skewer over coals, then thinly sliced. When laid on crumbled pide bread and yoghurt, and topped with tomato sauce and browned butter, *döner* kebap becomes *İskender* kebap. Equally ubiquitous are *şiş* kebap (small pieces of lamb grilled on a skewer) and *köfte* (meatballs).

For a quick, cheap fill you could hardly do better than a freshly cooked pide, Turkey's version of pizza, topped with *peynir* (cheese), *yumurta* (egg) or *kıymalı* (minced meat). Alternatively, *lahmacun* is a paperthin Arabic pizza topped with chopped onion, lamb and tomato. Other favourites are *gözleme* (thin savoury crepes) and *börek* (filled pastries – go for the white-cheese-and-parsley *su böreği*). *Mantı* (Turkish ravioli) is perfect in winter but can be overly rich and heavy in hot weather.

Balık (fish) dishes, although excellent, are often expensive; always check the price before ordering.

For vegetarians, a meal made up of meze can be an excellent way to ensure a varied diet. Most restaurants will be able to rustle up at least *beyaz peynir* (ewe's- or goat's-milk cheese), *sebze çorbası* (vegetable soup), *dolma* (stuffed vegetables), a *salata* (salad) such as the basic *çoban salatası* (shepherd's salad), *fasulye pilaki* (beans) and *patlıcan kızartması* (fried aubergine with tomato).

For dessert, try *fırın sütlaç* (rice pudding), baklava (honey-soaked flaky pastry stuffed with walnuts or pistachios), *kadayıf* (dough soaked in syrup and topped with clotted cream), *künefe* (*kadayıf* with sweet cheese, doused in syrup and served hot with a sprinkling of pistachio) and *dondurma* (ice cream). *Lokum* (Turkish delight) has been made here since the Ottoman sultans enjoyed it with their harems.

The national hot drink, *çay* (tea), is served in tiny tulip-shaped glasses with copious quantities of sugar. The wholly chemical *elma çay* (apple tea) is caffeine-free and only for tourists – locals wouldn't be seen dead drinking the stuff. If you're offered a tiny cup of traditional, industrial-strength Turkish *kahve* (coffee), you will be asked how sweet you like it: *çok şekerli* (very sweet), *orta şekerli* (middling), *az şekerli* (slightly sweet) or *sade* (not at all). Unfortunately, Nescafé is much more readily available than filter coffee or cappuccino. Don't miss the love-it-or-hate-it savoury dairy drink *ayran*, made by whipping up yoghurt with water and salt.

The Turks' meze accompaniment of choice is *rakı*, a fiery aniseed spirit like the Greek ouzo, Arab arrack or French pastis. Do as the Turks do and turn it milky white by adding water if you don't want to suffer ill effects. Turkish *şarap* (wine), both *kırmızı* (red) and *beyaz* (white), is improving in quality, particularly in Cappadocia and the Aegean island of Bozcaada. You can buy Tuborg or Efes Pilsen beers everywhere, although less Westernised towns may have only one licensed restaurant and/or liquor store. It's also worth remembering that licensed restaurants are generally more expensive than local eateries just serving *ayran* and *çay*.

SURVIVAL GUIDE

Directory A–Z

Accommodation

Rates quoted here are for high season (June to August; in İstanbul: April, May, September and October) and, unless otherwise mentioned, include tax (KDV), private bathroom and breakfast. Listings are ordered by preference.

In tourist-dependent areas, many accommodation options close from mid-October to late April. In those that remain open, rooms are discounted by about 20%, apart from around Christmas, Easter and major Islamic holidays.

Hotels quote tariffs in Turkish lira or euros, sometimes both, so we've used the currency quoted by the business being reviewed. Particularly in more-touristy locations, many places accept euros.

Virtually nowhere in Turkey is far from a mosque; light sleepers might want to bring earplugs for the early-morning call to prayer. In small tourist towns, touts or taxi drivers may try to persuade you to stay at a certain pension. Decide where you want to stay and stick to your guns; if you do view the pension in question, make it clear that you're only looking.

PRICE RANGES

The below prices indicators are based on the cost of a double room with private bathroom, and breakfast included.

İstanbul

€ less than €70

€€ €70 to €180

€€€ more than €180

Rest of Turkey

€ less than TL80

€€ TL80 to TL170

€€€ more than TL170

CAMPING

» Camping facilities dotted about Turkey, mostly along the coasts and in Cappadocia and Mt Nemrut National Park.

» Pensions and hostels often let you camp in their grounds and use their facilities for a fee.

HOSTELS

» Plenty of hostels with dormitories in popular destinations.

» Dorm beds usually cost about TL20 to TL45 per night.

» Hostelling International members in İstanbul, Cappadocia and the Aegean and western Mediterranean areas.

HOTELS

Budget In most cities and resort towns, good, inexpensive beds are readily available. Difficult places to find good, cheap rooms include İstanbul, Ankara, İzmir and package-holiday resort towns such as Alanya and Çeşme. The cheapest hotels, which charge around TL40/35 for a single with/without bathroom, are mostly used by working-class Turkish men, and are not suitable for solo women.

Midrange One- and two-star hotels vary from TL80 to TL125 for an ensuite double. They are generally less oppressively masculine in atmosphere, and three-star establishments are normally used to catering for female travellers.

Top End Turkey offers top-notch boutique accommodation in Ottoman mansions and other historic buildings, refurbished or completely rebuilt as hotels with all mod cons and bags of character.

PENSIONS

» Most tourist areas offer simple, family-run pensions where you can get a good, clean single/double from around TL40/70.

» Often cosy and represent good value, distinguished from cheap hotels by extras such as a choice of simple meals, laundry service and staff who speak a foreign language.

Activities

HIKING

The Lycian Way, which runs around the coast and mountains of Lycia from Fethiye to Antalya, and the St Paul Trail (Perge to Lake Eğirdir) are waymarked trails, each about 500km long. For more info on these and new trails in development, visit http://cultureroutesinturkey.com.

Popular hiking destinations include southern Cappadocia's Ala Dağlar National Park and northeastern Anatolia's Kaçkar Mountains. The spectacular valleys of central Cappadocia are excellent for day walks.

If you're a serious hiker, you could consider conquering Turkey's highest mountain, Mt Ararat (5137m), near Doğubayazıt, but you need a permit. **Tamzara Turizm**

(☑0544 555 3582; www.mtararattour.com; off Dr İsmail Beşikçi Caddesi) and **Mount Ararat Trek** (☑0537 502 6683; www.mountararattrek.com) in Doğubayazıt are good contacts.

WATER & WIND SPORTS

All sorts of activities, including windsurfing, rafting and kayaking, are available on the Aegean and Mediterranean coasts. The best diving spots are Ayvalık, Kuşadasi, Bodrum, Marmaris and Kaş. You can also try tandem paragliding in Ölüdeniz.

WINTER SPORTS

Most Turkish ski resorts are cheaper than their Western European counterparts and offer good facilities. The season lasts from December to April.

Palandöken, near Erzurum, has the best facilities, and pine-studded Sarıkamış, near Kars, has the most scenic runs. You can also ski on Uludağ, near Bursa, and Erciyes Dağı, above Kayseri.

RELAXING & REJUVENATING

Those of a lazier disposition may want to take a *gület* cruise along the coast, stopping off to swim in bays along the way.

Visiting one of the many *hamams*, some in historic Seljuk or Ottoman buildings, for a scrub and massage is a traditional Turkish activity.

Business Hours

Most museums close on Monday and, from April to October, close 1½ to two hours later. A bar is likely to open later in summer, when tourist offices in popular locations also open longer hours and at weekends.

The working day shortens during the holy month of Ramazan, which currently falls during summer. More-Islamic cities such as Konya and Kayseri virtually shut down during noon prayers on Friday (the Muslim sabbath); apart from that, Friday is a normal working day.

Bars 4pm to late

Government departments, offices and banks 8.30am to noon and 1.30pm to 5pm Monday to Friday

Nightclubs 11pm to late

Restaurants, cafes Breakfast 7.30am to 10am, lunch noon to 2.30pm, dinner 7.30pm to 10pm

Shops 9am to 6pm Monday to Friday (longer in tourist areas and big cities – including weekend opening)

Tourist information 8.30am to noon and 1.30pm to 5pm Monday to Friday

Children

Çocuklar (children) are the beloved centrepiece of family life and your children will be welcomed wherever they go.

However, Turkish safety consciousness rarely meets Western standards and children are not well catered for, although hotels and restaurants will often prepare special dishes for children.

Dangerous Turkish drivers and uneven surfaces can make using strollers, or just walking the streets with little ones, challenging. Other hazards include open power points and carelessly secured building sites.

Shops such as Migros supermarket sell baby food, although fresh milk is uncommon and formula is expensive.

Customs Regulations

IMPORT

Goods including the following can be imported duty-free:

» 600 cigarettes
» 200g of tobacco
» 1L of spirits (over 22%)
» 2L of wine and beer (under 22%)

EXPORT

» Buying and exporting antiquities is illegal.
» Carpet shops should be able to provide a form certifying that your purchase is not antique.
» Ask for advice from vendors and keep receipts and paperwork.

Discount Cards

The following offer discounts on accommodation, eating, entertainment, shopping and transport.

International Student Identity Card (ISIC; www.isic.org)

International Youth Travel Card (IYTC; http://tinyurl.com/25tlbv7)

International Teacher Identity Card (ITIC; http://tinyurl.com/25tlbv7)

Embassies & Consulates

Embassies are generally in Ankara. Many countries also have consulates in İstanbul and elsewhere. In general they open from 8am or 9am to noon Monday to Friday, then after lunch until 5pm or 6pm. For more information, visit http://tinyurl.com/6ywt8a.

Armenia (www.mfa.am/en) Contact Russian embassy.

Australian Embassy (☎0312-459 9500; www.embaustralia.org.tr; Uğur Mumcu Caddesi 88, MNG Bldg, Gaziosmanpaşa)

Azerbaijan Embassy (☎0312-491 1681; www.mfa.gov.az/eng; Baku Sokak 1, Diplomatik Site, Oran)

Bulgarian Embassy (☎0312-467 2071; www.bulgaria.bg/en/; Atatürk Bulvarı 124, Kavaklıdere)

Canadian Embassy (☎0312-409 2700; www.canadainternational.gc.ca; Cinnah Caddesi 58, Çankaya)

Georgian Embassy (☎0312-491 8030; www.turkey.mfa.gov.ge; Kılıç Ali Sokak 12, Diplomatik Site, Oran)

Greek Embassy (☎0312-448 0647; www.mfa.gr; Zia Ur Rahman Caddesi 9-11, Gaziosmanpaşa)

Iranian Embassy (☎0312-468 2820; www.mfa.gov.ir; Tahran Caddesi 10, Kavaklıdere)

Iraqi Embassy (☎0312-468 7421; http://iraqmissions.hostinguk.com; Turan Emeksiz Sokak 11, Gaziosmanpaşa)

New Zealand Embassy (☎0312-467 9054; www.nzembassy.com/turkey; İran Caddesi 13, Kavaklıdere)

Russian Embassy (☎0312-439 2122; www.turkey.mid.ru; Karyağdı Sokak 5, Çankaya)

Syrian Embassy (☎0312-440 9657; Sedat Simavi Sokak 40, Çankaya)

UK Embassy (☎0312-455 3344; http://ukinturkey.fco.gov.uk; Şehit Ersan Caddesi 46/A, Çankaya)

US Embassy (☎0312-455 5555; http://turkey.usembassy.gov; Atatürk Bulvarı 110, Kavaklıdere)

Food

Listings in this book are ordered by preference, and the following price indicators are used, based on the cost of a main course.

İstanbul

€ less than TL15

€€ TL15 to TL25

€€€ more than TL25

Rest of Turkey

€ less than TL9

€€ TL9 to TL17.50

€€€ more than TL17.50

Gay & Lesbian Travellers

Homosexuality is legal in Turkey and attitudes are changing, but prejudice remains strong – the message is discretion. İstanbul has a flourishing gay scene, as does Ankara.

Kaos GL (www.kaosgl.com) The lesbian, gay, bisexual, transgender (LGBT) rights organisation's website has content in English.

Lambda (www.lambdaistanbul.org) LGBT support group.

Pride Travel Agency (www.turkey-gay-travel.com) Gay-friendly travel agent.

Health

In addition to the routine vaccinations that all travellers should have, typhoid and hepatitis A and B are recommended for Turkey.

Rabies is endemic here, so if you will be travelling off the beaten track you might want to consider a vaccination.

Malaria is found in a few areas near the Syrian border.

Internet Access

» Most accommodation offers free wi-fi, as do many other businesses.

» Internet cafes are widespread.

» Fees typically about TL1.50 per hour (İstanbul TL3).

Language Courses

The most popular Turkish-language courses are offered by **Dilmer** (www.dilmer.com), near Taksim Sq in İstanbul, and the Ankara University–affiliated **Tömer** (www.tomer.com.tr), with branches throughout the country.

Legal Matters

» Technically, you should carry your passport at all times, but you may prefer to carry a photocopy.

» There are laws against treason, buying and smuggling antiques, and illegal drugs.

Money

» Turkey's currency, the Türk Lirası (Turkish Lira; TL), replaced the Yeni Türk Lirası (New Turkish Lira; YTL) in 2009.

» Lira come in notes of 5, 10, 20, 50, 100 and 200, and 1 lira coins.

» One lira is worth 100 kuruş, which are available in 1, 5, 10, 25 and 50 coins.

» Watch out for people dumping their old-currency coins on you.

» Prices in this book are quoted in lira or euros, depending on which currency is used by the business.

ATMS

ATMs dispense Turkish lira, and occasionally euros and US dollars, to Visa, MasterCard, Cirrus and Maestro card holders. Machines are found in most towns.

It's possible to get around Turkey using only ATMs, if you keep some cash in reserve to tide you through the villages, and for the inevitable day when the ATM throws a wobbly.

Some banks levy high charges for the conversion and/or withdrawal, so check your bank's fees before you leave home.

CASH

» Euros and US dollars the most readily accepted foreign currencies, and the easiest to change.
» Many exchange offices and banks change other major currencies such as UK pounds and Japanese yen.
» Foreign currencies accepted in shops, hotels and restaurants in many tourist areas, and by taxi drivers for big journeys.

CREDIT CARDS

» Visa and MasterCard widely accepted by hotels, shops and restaurants.
» Often not accepted by pensions and local restaurants outside main tourist areas.
» You can also get cash advances on these cards.
» Amex less commonly accepted outside top-end establishments.
» Inform your credit-card provider of your travel plans.

MONEY CHANGERS

» Turkish lira is weak against Western currencies; you will likely get a better exchange rate in Turkey than elsewhere.
» Exchange offices offer better rates than banks, and often don't charge commission. They offer the best rates in market areas.
» Offices also found at some post offices, shops and hotels.
» Banks more likely to change minor currencies, although will often make heavy weather of it.

TIPPING & BARGAINING

Turkey is fairly European in its approach to tipping and you won't be pestered with demands for baksheesh. Tipping is customary in restaurants, hotels and taxis; optional elsewhere.

» Round up metered taxi fares and leave waiters and masseurs around 10% to 15% of the bill. In more-expensive restaurants, check a *servis ücreti* (service charge) hasn't been automatically added to the bill.
» Hotel prices are sometimes negotiable, and you should always bargain for souvenirs.

TRAVELLERS CHEQUES

Banks, shops and hotels usually see it as a burden to change travellers cheques, and will either try to persuade you to go elsewhere or charge you a premium. If you do have to change them, try one of the major banks.

Photography

» People in Turkey are generally receptive to having their photo taken, apart from when they are praying or performing other religious activities.
» As in most countries, do not take photos of military sites, airfields, police stations and so on.

Post

Postanes (post offices) are indicated by blue-on-yellow 'PTT' signs.
» Postcards sent abroad cost about TL2.
» If you are shipping something from Turkey, don't close your parcel before it has been inspected by a customs official.
» Airmail tariffs are typically around TL40 for the first kilo, with an additional charge for every extra kilo (typically TL5 to Europe).

Public Holidays

New Year's Day 1 January

National Sovereignty & Children's Day 23 April

International Workers' Day 1 May

Youth & Sports Day 19 May

Victory Day 30 August

Republic Day 28–29 October

Turkey also celebrates the main Islamic holidays, the most important of which are Şeker Bayramı (Sweets Holiday; roughly 28 July 2014 and 17 July 2015), which marks the end of the holy month of Ramazan; and about two months later, Kurban Bayramı (Festival of the Sacrifice; roughly 4 October 2014 and 23 September 2015). Due to the fact that these holidays are celebrated according to the Muslim lunar calendar, they take place around 11 days earlier every year.

Safe Travel

Although Turkey is in no way a dangerous country to visit, it's always wise to be a little cautious, especially if you're travelling alone.

» As a pedestrian, note that there is no such thing as a generally acknowledged right of way, despite the little green man. İstanbullus in particular drive like rally drivers; give way to cars and trucks in all situations.

» Drugging is a risk, especially for lone men, and most commonly in İstanbul. It may involve so-called friends, a bar and perhaps a willowy temptress. Another İstanbul scam with these elements ends with the traveller buying a couple of drinks and receiving a bill for hundreds of euros. Be cautious about who you befriend, especially when you're new to the country.

» Sexual assaults have occurred against travellers of both sexes in hotels in central and eastern Anatolia. Make enquiries and do a little research if you are travelling alone or heading off the beaten track.

» Receiving the hard sell from carpet salesmen in places such as İstanbul's Grand Bazaar can drive you to distraction. Remember you're under no obligation to look or buy. 'Free' lifts and other suspiciously cheap services often lead to near-compulsory visits to carpet showrooms or hotel commission for touts.

» Do not buy coins or other artefacts offered to you by touts at ancient sites such as Ephesus and Perge.

» Fighting between the Turkish military and PKK continues in remote southeastern Anatolia. More of a risk are the bomb attacks, also linked to Kurdish separatist groups, that target affluent areas frequented by tourists, including attacks in İstanbul in 2008 and 2010. Check for travel warnings before visiting southeastern Anatolia, particularly areas near the Syrian and Iraqi borders.

» Nationalistic laws against insulting, defaming or making light of Atatürk, the Turkish flag and so on are taken seriously. Turks have been known to claim derogatory remarks were made in the heat of a quarrel, which is enough to get a foreigner carted off to jail.

Telephone

Türk Telekom (www.turktelekom.com.tr) has a monopoly on phone services, which are efficient if costly.

» Payphones are found in many major public buildings and facilities, public squares and transport terminals. International calls can be made from payphones, which require phonecards. Some accept credit cards.

» If you're only going to make one quick call, it's easier to look for a booth with a sign saying '*kontörlü telefon*', where the cost of your call is metered.

» Numbers starting with ☑444 don't require area codes and, wherever you call from, are charged at the local rate.

MOBILE PHONES

» Reception is generally excellent.

» Mobile phone numbers start with a four-figure number beginning with ☑05.

» If you set up a roaming facility with your home network, most mobiles can connect to Turkcell (the most comprehensive network), Vodafone and Avea.

» To buy a Turkcell SIM card (TL30 to TL40), you need to show your passport and ensure the seller phones through or inputs your details. If you plan to use a local SIM card in your phone for longer than two weeks, try to register the phone, or it will later be barred.

* *Kontör* (credit) is readily available at streetside booths, shops and mobile-phone outlets. You can pick up a basic mobile phone for about TL50.

PHONECARDS

» Phonecards can be bought at telephone centres or, for a small mark-up, from some shops.

» The cheapest option for international calls is phonecards such as IPC.

Toilets

» Most hotels have sit-down toilets, but hole-in-the-ground models are common.

» Toilet paper is often unavailable; keep some on you.

» In an emergency it's worth remembering that mosques have basic men and women's toilets.

Tourist Information

Local tourist offices, run by the **Ministry of Culture and Tourism** (www.goturkey.com), can often do little more than hand out glossy brochures. Tour operators, pension owners and so on are often better sources of information.

Travellers with Disabilities

Turkey is challenging for disabled (engelli or özürlü) travellers, and not just because of the scarce facilities. Obstacles abound and crossing the dangerous roads is tough, although Selçuk, Bodrum and Fethiye are relatively user friendly.

Airlines, some trains and the top hotels and resorts have some provision for wheelchair access, with discounts offered by Turkish Airlines.

Hotel Rolli (www.hotel-rolli.de) Specially designed for wheelchair users.

Mephisto Voyage (📞 532 7070; www.mephistovoyage.com) Tours of Cappadocia for mobility-impaired people, utilising the Joëlette system.

Visas

» Nationals of countries including Denmark, Finland, France, Germany, Israel, Italy, Japan, New Zealand, Sweden and Switzerland don't need a visa to visit Turkey for up to 90 days.

» Nationals of countries including Australia, Austria, Belgium, Canada, Ireland, the Netherlands, Norway, Portugal, Spain, the UK and the USA need a visa, but it is just a sticker bought on arrival at the airport or border post.

» The above nationals are given a 90-day multiple-entry visa. In many cases it stipulates 'per period 180 days'. This means you can spend three months in Turkey within a six-month period; when you leave after three months, you can't re-enter for three months.

» The cost of the visa varies. At the time of writing, Americans paid US$20 (or €15), Australians and Canadians US$60 (or €45) and British citizens UK£10 (or €15 or US$20).

» Some major entry points accept Visa and MasterCard, but it is generally worth having the fee ready in cash in one of the above currencies.

» Your passport must be valid for at least six months from the date you enter the country.

» See the **Ministry of Foreign Affairs** (www.mfa.gov.tr) for the latest information.

Volunteering

Alternative Camp (www.ayder.org.tr) Runs camps for people with disabilities.

Culture Routes in Turkey (tinyurl.com/d6fld8l) Help waymark and repair hiking trails.

Gençlik Servisleri Merkezi (Youth Services Centre; www.gsm-youth.org) Voluntary work camps.

Gençtur (genctur.com.tr) Voluntourism, including farmstays.

Women Travellers

Turkish society is still basically sexually segregated, especially once you get away from the big cities and tourist resorts. Although younger Turks are questioning the old ways and women hold positions of authority (there's even been a female prime minister), foreign women can find themselves being harassed. It's mostly just catcalls and dubious remarks, but assaults do occasionally occur.

» Travelling with companions usually helps. Dressing modestly will also reduce unwanted attention, and encourage most men to treat you with kindness and generosity.

» Tailor your behaviour and your clothing to your surrounds. Look at what local women are wearing. On the streets of Beyoğlu (İstanbul) you'll see skimpy tops and tight jeans, but cleavage and short skirts without leggings are a no-no everywhere except nightclubs in İstanbul and heavily touristed destinations along the coast.

» Bring a shawl to cover your head when visiting mosques.

» On the street, you don't need to don a headscarf, but keeping your legs, upper arms and neckline covered is often a good idea, particularly in eastern Anatolia. Here, long sleeves and baggy long pants should attract the least attention, and you should keep your dealings with men formal and polite, not friendly.

» When travelling by taxi and dolmuş, avoid getting into the seat beside the driver. Men and unrelated women are not supposed to sit together on long-distance buses, although the bus companies rarely enforce this in the case of foreigners. Lone women are often assigned seats at the front of the bus near the driver.

» Restaurants and tea gardens that aim to attract women often set aside a family room or section. Look for the term aile salonu (family dining room), or just aile.

» Stick to official camping grounds and camp where there are plenty of people around, especially out east.

Work

Travellers sometimes work illegally for room and board in pensions, bars and other businesses in tourist areas. These jobs are generally badly paid and only last a few months maximum, but they are a fun way to stay in a place and get to know the locals.

Job hunters may have luck with:
» http://istanbul.craigslist.org
» www.sahibinden.com/en/
» www.mymerhaba.com
» www.expatinturkey.com
» istanbul.angloinfo.com

NANNYING

One of the most lucrative nonspecialist jobs available to foreigners is nannying for the wealthy urban elite, with opportunities for English, French and German speakers.

TEACHING ENGLISH

There is lots of work available for qualified English teachers, although many employers are reluctant to deal with the bureaucratic headache of helping you get a work permit.

The best option is working for a university or a *dershane* (private school). Jobs are mostly advertised in May and June, then run from September until the following June.

Getting There & Away

Air

The cheapest flights are usually to İstanbul's **Atatürk International Airport** (Atatürk Havalimanı; ☏212-463 3000; www.ataturkairport. com), 23km west of Sultanahmet, and **Sabiha Gökçen International Airport** (Sabiha Gökçen Havalimanı; ☏216-588 8888; www.sgairport.com), 50km east of Sultanahmet on the Asian side of the city. To reach other Turkish airports you often have to transit in İstanbul.

Other international airports include Ankara, Antalya, Bodrum, Dalaman and İzmir.

It's a good idea to book at least two months in advance if you plan to arrive between April and August. If you plan to visit a resort, check with your local travel agents for flight and accommodation deals.

Turkey's national carrier, **Turkish Airlines** (☏0850-333 0849; www.thy.com), flies worldwide.

Asia and Middle East One of the cheapest ways to fly further afield is from İstanbul via Dubai.

Australia and New Zealand You can fly to İstanbul, normally via Dubai, Kuala Lumpur or Singapore. You can often get cheaper flights with European airlines, which involves a second flight change in Europe.

Europe İstanbul is connected to most major European cities by Turkish Airlines, with flights also available with its budget subsidiaries **Sun Express** (☏444 0797; www. sunexpress.com) and **AnadoluJet** (☏444 2538; www.anadolujet.com), its Turkish competitors including **Pegasus Airlines** (www.flypgs.com), and European carriers including **easyJet** (www.easyjet.com). Charter flights are a good option, particularly at the beginning and end of the peak summer holiday season.

North America Most flights connect with İstanbul-bound flights in the UK or Continental Europe, so it's worth looking at European airlines in addition to North American carriers. Another option is to cross the Atlantic to Europe and continue on a separate ticket with a budget carrier.

Land

Turkey shares borders with Armenia (closed), Azerbaijan, Bulgaria, Georgia, Greece, Iran, Iraq and Syria. There are many routes into and out of the country.

BUS

Austria, Bulgaria, Germany, Greece, Macedonia and Romania have the most direct buses to İstanbul.

The Turkish companies **Varan Turizm** (☏444 8999; www.varan.com.tr), **Metro Turizm** (☏444 3455; www.metroturizm.com.tr) and **Ulusoy** (☏444 1888; www.ulusoy.com.tr) operate on these routes. Ulusoy has weekly departures to/from Germany (about €200), with one line running through Slovenia and eastern Europe, and the other through Italy and Greece with a sea crossing.

If you're travelling from other European countries, you'll likely have to catch a connecting bus.

TRAIN

The daily Bosphorus/Balkan Express links İstanbul with Bucharest (Romania), Sofia (Bulgaria) and Belgrade (Serbia). Visit www.seat61.com/turkey2 and tinyurl.com/b3cx85s for more information.

Sea

Departure times and routes change between seasons, with less ferries running in winter. **Ferrylines** (www.ferrylines.com) is a good starting point for information.

FERRIES TO/FROM TURKEY

ROUTE	FREQUENCY	DURATION	FARE (ONE WAY/RETURN)	COMPANY
Ayvalık–Lesvos, Greece	Mon-Sat May-Sep; 3 weekly Oct-Apr	1½hr	TL60/70, car TL120/130	Jale Tour (www.jaletour.com)
Alanya–Girne (Kyrenia), Northern Cyprus	2 weekly in summer	3½hr	TL77/127	Fergün Denizcilik (www.fergun.net)
Bodrum–Kos, Greece	daily	1hr	single or same-day return €32; open return €60	Bodrum Ferryboat Association (www.bodrumferryboat.com); Bodrum Express Lines (www.bodrumexpresslines.com)
Bodrum–Rhodes, Greece	2 weekly Jun-Sep	2¼hr	single or same-day return €60; open return €120	Bodrum Ferryboat Association (www.bodrumferryboat.com)
Çeşme–Chios, Greece	daily mid-May–mid-Sep; 2 weekly mid-Sep–mid-May	1½hr	TL65/100, car TL150/260	Ertürk (www.erturk.com.tr)
Datça–Rhodes, Greece	Sat May-Sep	45min	TL90/180	Knidos Yachting (www.knidosyachting.com)
Datça–Simi, Greece	hydrofoil Sat May-Sep, gület 2 weekly	hydrofoil 15min, gület 70min	hydrofoil TL60/120, gület TL140	Knidos Yachting (www.knidosyachting.com)
İstanbul–Illyichevsk (Odessa), Ukraine	2 weekly	28½hr	one way US$150, car US$325	Sea Lines (www.sea-lines.net)
Kaş–Meis (Kastellorizo), Greece	daily	20min	single or same-day return €20	Meis Express (www.meisexpress.com)
Kuşadası– Samos, Greece	daily Apr-Oct	1¼hr	€35/55	Meander Travel (www.meandertravel.com)
Marmaris–Rhodes, Greece	daily Apr-Oct	50min	from €45/65, car from €110/190	Yeşil Marmaris Travel & Yachting (www.yesil-marmaris.com)
Taşucu–Girne (Kyrenia), Northern Cyprus	daily	from 2hr	TL69/114	Akgünler Denizcilik (www.akgunler.com.tr)
Trabzon–Sochi, Russia	weekly	5-12hr	one way US$100 to US$200	Olympia Line (www.olympia-line.ru), Öz Star Denizcilik (Princess Victoria), Sarı Denizcilik (www.saridenizcilik.com/en); see also www.seaport-sochi.ru and www.al-port.com
Turgutreis–Kos, Greece	daily 25 May–31 Oct	30min	€12/20	Bodrum Ferryboat Association (www.bodrumferryboat.com)

Getting Around

Air

Turkey is well connected by air throughout the country, although many flights go via hubs İstanbul or Ankara. Internal flights are a good option in such a large country, and competition between the following Turkish airlines keeps tickets affordable.

AnadoluJet (☑444 2538; www.anadolujet.com)

Atlasjet (☑0850-222 0000; www.atlasjet.com)

Onur Air (☑0850-210 6687; www.onurair.com.tr)

Pegasus Airlines (☑0850-250 0737; www.pegasusairlines.com)

Sun Express (☑444 0797; www.sunexpress.com)

Turkish Airlines (☑0850-333 0849; www.thy.com)

Bicycle

Riding a bike is a great way of exploring the countryside, especially in touristy areas, where you can hire bikes from pensions and rental outfits. Road surfaces are generally acceptable, if a bit rough, though Turkey's notorious drivers are a hazard.

Bus

The Turkish bus network is excellent: coaches go just about everywhere, they're cheap and comfortable, smoking isn't permitted, drinks and snacks are often provided, and regular toilet stops are built into longer routes.

» The premium companies have nationwide networks offering greater speed and comfort for slightly higher fares. They also have the best safety records. Departures on popular routes can be as frequent as every 15 minutes, with hourly services the norm from major cities.

Fares vary according to distance and the popularity of the route; typically, from İstanbul to Çanakkale costs TL45, İstanbul to Ankara TL38 to TL43, and İstanbul to Göreme (Cappadocia) TL65.

» Although you can usually walk into an *otogar* (bus station) and buy a ticket for the next bus, it's wise to plan ahead for public holidays, at weekends and during the school holidays from mid-June to early September. You can reserve seats online with the better companies.

» A town's *otogar* is often on the outskirts, but most bus companies provide a *servis* (free shuttle bus) to/from the centre.

Besides intercity buses, *otogars* often handle *dolmuşes* (minibuses) to outlying districts or villages. Larger bus stations have an *emanetçi* (left luggage) room, which you can use for a fee.

The best bus companies, with extensive route networks:

Kamil Koç (☑444 0562; www.kamilkoc.com.tr)

Metro Turizm (☑444 3455; www.metroturizm.com.tr)

Ulusoy (☑444 1888; www.ulusoy.com.tr)

Varan Turizm (☑444 8999; www.varan.com.tr)

Car & Motorcycle

Public transport is a much easier and less stressful way of getting around the traffic-clogged cities. Turkey's main motoring organisation is the **Türkiye Turing ve Otomobil Kurumu** (TTOK, Turkish Touring & Automobile Club; ☑212-513 3660; www.turing.org.tr; Soğukçeşme Sokağı, Sultanahmet, İstanbul).

BRINGING YOUR OWN VEHICLE

You can bring your vehicle into Turkey for six months without charge, but details of your car are marked in your passport to ensure it leaves the country with you.

DRIVING LICENCES

An international driving permit (IDP) is not obligatory, but may be handy if your driving licence is from a country likely to seem obscure to a Turkish police officer.

FUEL & SPARE PARTS

Turkey has the world's second most expensive petrol prices. Petrol/diesel costs about TL4/4.70 per litre.

» There are plenty of modern petrol stations in the west. In the east they are slightly less abundant and it's a good idea to have a full tank when you start out in the morning.

* *Yedek parçaları* (spare parts) are readily available in the big cities and *sanayi bölgesi* (industrial zones) on the outskirts, especially for European models such as Renaults, Fiats and Mercedes-Benz. Repairs are usually quick and cheap.

CAR HIRE

» Rental charges are similar to those in Continental Europe.

» You need to be at least 21 years old, with a year's driving experience, to hire a car.

» Most companies require a credit card.

» The big international companies (including Avis, Budget, Europcar, Hertz,

ⓘ **TOLLS**

You must pay a toll to use the major motorways. You can buy green-and-orange toll cards and place *kontör* (credit) on them at the offices near motorway toll gates. The offices are not open 24 hours; most close on Sunday. There is a TL100 fine for nonpayment, which takes about two weeks to come through.

National and Sixt) are represented in the main cities, towns and airports. Particularly in eastern Anatolia, stick with these companies, as they have insurance and better emergency backup.

Economy Car Rentals (www.economycar-rentals.com) gets excellent rates with other companies, including Budget and National.

INSURANCE

You *must* have third-party insurance to drive in Turkey. Buying it at the border is a straightforward process (one month €80).

ROAD RULES & SAFETY

Turkey has one of the world's highest motor-vehicle accident rates.

Driving is hair-raising during the day because of fast, inappropriate driving and overladen trucks, and dangerous at night, when some drivers speed along with their headlights off. Always drive cautiously.

Unless otherwise posted, maximum speed limits are 50km/h in towns, 90km/h on highways and 120km/h on *otoyols* (motorways). Clamping is a fact of life in Turkey.

Hitching

Although we don't recommend hitching *(otostop)*, short hitches are not uncommon in Turkey, for example to get from the highway to an archaeological site.

Offer to pay something towards the petrol, although most drivers pick up foreign hitchers for their curiosity value.

Instead of sticking out your thumb for a lift, you should face the traffic and wave your arm up and down as if bouncing a basketball.

Local Transport

Short-distance and local routes are usually served by medium-sized 'midibuses' or smaller *dolmuşes* (minibuses that follow prescribed routes).

A few cities, including Bursa, have old-fashioned *taksi dolmuşes* (shared taxis).

Most towns have a municipal bus network; this may be supplemented by underground, tram, train and ferries in the largest cities.

Taxis are plentiful; they have meters – just make sure they're switched on.

Tours

Areas where an organised tour makes sense, particularly with limited time, include the Gallipoli Peninsula, Troy and Cappadocia. There are unscrupulous operators, particularly in Sultanahmet (İstanbul) and Nevesehir (Cappadocia), but also plenty of good outfits.

Train

Although most people still opt for buses as train journey times are notoriously long, the system is being overhauled and a few fast lines (Ankara–Konya and Ankara–Eskişehir) are appearing. A growing number of fans appreciate the no-rush experience of a train journey, such as the stunning scenery rolling by and immersion with fellow passengers.

The occasional unannounced hold-up and public toilets gone feral by the end of the long journey are all part of the adventure. If you're on a budget, overnight train journeys are a great way to save accommodation costs. Don't try to attempt a trans-Turkey trip in one go, as the country is large and the trains slow.

InterRail, Balkan Flexipass and Eurodomino passes are valid on the Turkish railway network, but Eurail passes are not.

Turkish State Railways (☎444 8233; www.tcdd.gov.tr)

Man in Seat Sixty-One (www.seat61.com/turkey2) Information and inspiration on Turkish train travel.

ROUTES

The train network covers the country fairly well, with the notable exception of the coast-lines. For the Aegean and Mediterranean coasts you can travel by train to either İzmir or Konya, and take the bus from there.

Trains are not currently running between İstanbul and destinations in Anatolia. From Ankara, long-distance destinations include Adana, Diyarbakır, İzmir, Kayseri, Kurtalan, Malatya and Tatvan (Lake Van).

Useful routes include the following:
» Ankara–Konya
» İstanbul–İzmir (including ferry to/from Bandırma)
» İzmir–Selçuk

Survival Guide

DIRECTORY A–Z ... 848

Accommodation........ 848
Activities 851
Business Hours 852
Children............... 852
Customs Regulations ... 853
Discount Cards......... 853
Electricity 854
Embassies & Consulates... 854
Food 854
Gay & Lesbian Travellers...854
Health................. 855
Holidays............... 856
Insurance.............. 856
Internet Access......... 856
Language Courses...... 856
Legal Matters 857
Maps.................. 857
Money................. 857
Photography 859
Post................... 859
Safe Travel............. 859
Telephone 861
Time 861
Toilets................. 862
Tourist Information 862
Travellers with
Disabilities............. 862
Visas.................. 862
Volunteering 863
Women Travellers....... 863

TRANSPORT 865

GETTING THERE & AWAY.. 865
Entering the Region..... 865
Air.................... 865
Land 866
Sea 868
GETTING AROUND...... 869
Air.................... 869
Bicycle 869
Boat 870
Bus 870
Car & Motorcycle....... 871
Hitching............... 873
Local Transport......... 873
Tours.................. 874
Train 874

LANGUAGE 877

Directory A–Z

Accommodation

There's a vast choice of accommodation in Mediterranean Europe, ranging from world-famous five-star hotels to modest family rooms.

The cheapest places to stay are camping grounds, followed by hostels and student dormitories. Guesthouses, pensions and private rooms often offer good value, as do rooms in religious institutes. Self-catering flats and cottages are also worth considering for group stays, especially for longer sojourns. You can also bunk down in a B&B, stay on a farm or crash on a couch.

Unless otherwise stated, prices in this book are high-season rates for rooms with a private bathroom. All listings are ordered according to preference, with the author's favourite place listed first.

Rates High-season rates apply at Easter, from June to August, and over Christmas and New Year. Prices are also high in April and May in many of the region's big cities. Conversely, many city hoteliers drop rates in August to lure punters away from the coast.

Reservations Book ahead for peak holiday periods, and year-round in big cities such as Paris, Rome, Venice, Madrid and Barcelona – at least for the first night or two. Most places can be booked online, and many require credit-card details in lieu of a deposit.

Reservation Services Most airports and many large train stations have accommodation-booking desks, although they rarely cover budget hotels. Tourist offices can generally supply accommodation lists and some will even help you find a hotel. There's usually a small fee for this service, but if accommodation is tight it can save you hassle. Agencies offering private rooms are also worth considering.

Bargaining It's often worth bargaining in the low season as, although they may not advertise the fact, many places reduce their rates.

Seasonal Closures Many coastal hotels close over winter, typically between November and March.

Touts In some destinations locals wait at train stations or ferry terminals, touting rented rooms. Don't necessarily reject these out of hand, as in some places they're genuine offers. Before accepting, though, make sure the accommodation isn't in a far-flung suburb or an outlying village that requires a difficult journey, and don't forget to confirm the price.

Website Deals It's always worth checking hotel websites for last-minute deals and discounts.

B&Bs

B&B accommodation is widely available across the region and usually provides excellent value. There's a huge selection of places, ranging from traditional B&B set-ups (private homes with a guest room or two) to smart boutique-style outfits offering quality accommodation at midrange and top-end prices. As a general rule, a B&B room will be cheaper than a hotel room of corresponding comfort.

» Most B&Bs will give you a key, allowing you to come and go as you like, although some places might insist that you're back by a certain time.

» Most smarter B&Bs will have private bathrooms; in some you might have to share with other guests or the host family.

» When booking, make sure you're happy with the location. City B&Bs are often not central, so check local transport connections. If it's in a remote rural spot, work

BOOK YOUR STAY ONLINE

For more accommodation reviews by Lonely Planet authors, check out www.lonelyplanet.com/hotels. You'll find independent reviews, as well as recommendations on the best places to stay. Best of all, you can book online.

PRACTICALITIES

» The metric system is in use throughout Mediterranean Europe, so expect litres not gallons and kilometres rather than miles. In some countries, decimal points are represented by commas (eg 0,5), and to separate thousands a full point is used (eg 1.000.000 for one million).

» Smoking bans exist in all of the countries listed in this book. The exact rules vary from place to place, so always check before lighting up.

» English-language newspapers and magazines are available in many of the region's big cities and popular resorts.

» Keep up to date with world news on BBC World Service, which is broadcast on a range of platforms: online, via satellite or cable, on digital and internet radio, on shortwave radio, and on FM or AM frequencies.

» Satellite TV is common across the area and in many hotels you'll be able to pick up BBC World and CNN International.

out in advance how it fits in with your plans.

» Contact tourist offices for lists of local B&Bs.

Useful resources include **Bed and Breakfast Europe** (www.bed-and-breakfast-europe.com), **Bed and Breakfast in Europe** (www.bedandbreakfastineurope.com) and **Europe and Relax** (www.europeandrelax.com).

Camping

Camping is very popular in Mediterranean Europe, and there are thousands of camping grounds dotted around the region. These range from large, resort-style operations with swimming pools and supermarkets to more simple affairs in isolated countryside locations. National tourist offices and local camping organisations can provide lists.

» If you're intent on camping around the region, consider the **Camping Card International** (CCI; www.campingcardinternational.com), an ID-style card that provides third-party insurance and entitles you to discounts of up to 25% at more than 1600 camping grounds across Europe. Note that in some cases discounts are

not available if you pay by credit card. CCIs are issued by automobile associations, camping federations and, sometimes, on the spot at camping grounds.

» At designated grounds, there are often charges per tent or site, per person and per vehicle.

» Many places have bungalows or cottages accommodating two to eight people.

» Free camping is often illegal without permission from the local authorities (the police or local council) or from the owner of the land. In some countries (eg France and Spain) it is illegal on all but private land, and in Greece, Croatia and Slovenia it's illegal altogether. This doesn't prevent hikers from occasionally pitching their tent for the night, and you'll usually get away with it if you have a small tent, stay only one or two nights, take the tent down during the day and don't light a campfire or leave rubbish. At worst, you'll be woken up by the police and asked to move on.

» Many camping grounds close over winter, typically between October and April.

» Carting your kit around with you is fine if you've got a car, but a real pain if you haven't.

» Most city camping grounds are some distance from the city centre, so the money you save on accommodation can quickly be eaten up in bus and train fares.

» For upmarket and quirky camping grounds check out listings on **Go Glamping** (www.goglamping.net).

Couchsurfing & House Swapping

The cheapest way of staying in the region is sleeping on a local's couch – a practice known as couchsurfing.

Through online agencies such as **Couch Surfing** (www.couchsurfing.org), **GlobalFreeloaders** (www.globalfreeloaders.com) or **Hospitality Club** (www.hospitalityclub.org), you can contact members across the world who'll let you sleep on their sofa or in their spare room for next to nothing.

Another cheap alternative is house swapping, whereby you sign up to an online agency such as **Home Exchange** (www.ihen.com) or **Global Home Exchange** (www.4homex.com) and arrange to swap houses with a fellow member for an agreed period of time.

Farmstays

Farmstays are an excellent way of escaping the crowds and experiencing the local countryside.

They are particularly popular in Italy, where an *agriturismo* can be anything from a working farm to a luxurious rural resort in a converted castle. Italian tourist offices can provide lists for specific areas. Online information is available at **Agriturist** (www.agriturist.it).

Farmstays are also popular in Slovenia – the **Slovenia Tourist Board** (www.slovenia.info) lists tourist farms – and in Portugal, where many farmhouses and country homes are affiliated with the **Turismo de Habitação** (www.turihab.pt) network.

In general, note the following:

» Room rates are usually much less than in hotels of comparable comfort.

» Many farmstays offer activities such as horse riding, hiking and cycling, and serve delicious food.

» Country locations mean that most have plenty of space for kids to run around in, making them a good choice for families.

» You'll almost certainly need a car to get to them.

» Always book ahead, as in high season places fill quickly, while in low season many open only on request.

Guesthouses & Pensions

» The distinction between a guesthouse and a hotel is fairly blurred. Most guesthouses are simple family affairs offering basic rooms and shared bathrooms, but more expensive guesthouses can have rooms of hotel standard.

» Pensions, which are widespread throughout the region, are basically small, modest hotels. In cities, they are often housed in converted flats that occupy one or two floors of a large apartment block. Rooms tend to be simple, often with just a basin and bidet.

Homestays & Private Rooms

» Renting a room in a local home is generally a good, cheap option, especially for longer stays.

» It's not so good for solo travellers (most rooms are set up as doubles or triples) or for quick stopovers (many places levy hefty surcharges, typically 30% to 40%, for stays of under three or four days).

» Room quality and price vary considerably – some rooms come with private bathrooms, some have cooking facilities, some might even have both.

» When you book, make sure you check if the price is per room or per person, and whether or not breakfast is included. Also make sure you're happy with the location.

» You can book rooms either privately or through an agency (to whom you'll have to pay a fee). Once you've booked a room, it's always worth phoning ahead to say when you're arriving as, in many cases, the owners will pick you up at the station or port.

» Room rentals are particularly widespread in Albania, Bosnia and Hercegovina (BiH), Croatia, Greece and Montenegro.

Hostels

Hostels are widespread across the region and provide a cheap roof over your head. Hostels referred to as 'official' are affiliated with **Hostelling International** (HI; www.hihostels.com), while private hostels are just that, operating independently of HI.

Membership Requirements To stay at an official hostel you'll need to be a HI member, although in practice you can usually stay by buying a 'welcome stamp' (generally about €3; buy six and you qualify for full HI membership) directly at the hostel. HI membership is available at affiliated hostels or through your national hostelling association – there's a full list on the HI website. Private hostels don't require membership.

Beds & Facilities Alongside dorms of varying sizes – small ones typically for four or five people, larger ones for up to 12 people – many hostels offer hotel-standard private rooms with en suite bathrooms. Dorms may or may not be single sex. Typical facilities include a communal kitchen, a TV room, a laundry, wi-fi and internet access.

Rules Generally speaking, independent hostels are a lot less rule-bound than HI hostels, some of which impose a maximum length of stay, a daytime lockout and a curfew. But with the rules come standards, and affiliated hostels have to comply with HI safety and cleanliness standards.

Age Limits These days few hostels impose age limits, with many now catering to families as well as backpackers

---

ALTERNATIVE ACCOMMODATION

In addition to typical accommodation in the region, there are various other options available.

Convents & Monasteries Particularly widespread in Italy, these are a good bet for cheap, modest lodging, often in historic buildings. You'll need your own transport to get to convents and monasteries in country locations outside of towns and cities.

Mountain Refuges A favourite with hikers, refuges offer high-altitude mountain accommodation between July and September. Don't expect frills, but breakfast is generally included in the price and dinner is sometimes available. Bookings are usually required.

Pousadas These are former castles, monasteries or palaces providing simple accommodation in Portugal.

Tree Houses Olympos on Turkey's Mediterranean coast is the place to go to stay in a tree house. Accommodation is pretty basic but the forest setting and nearby beaches are a major plus.

and young travellers. Some hostels may give priority to younger, student-age travellers in peak periods.

Meals Many hostels offer a complimentary breakfast and some serve an evening meal (typically about €10).

Reservations It's a good idea to book ahead whenever possible, especially in summer, when popular hostels are packed to the gills. The easiest way to book is online, either through individual hostel websites or the HI website. Many hostels also accept reservations over the phone or by fax (but during peak periods you will probably have to call to bag a bed). If you are heading on to another hostel, most places will book the next place for you for a small fee.

Resources Useful websites include **Hostel World** (www. hostelworld.com), **Hostel Bookers** (www.hostelbookers. com), **Hostels.com** (www. hostels.com) and **Hostelz** (www.hostelz.com).

Hotels

Hotels in the region range from dodgy fleapits with rooms to rent by the hour to some of the world's grandest five-star palaces.

Classification Each country operates its own hotel-classification system, so a three-star hotel in İstanbul might not correspond to a three-star hotel in Barcelona. Stars are awarded according to facilities only and give no indication of value, comfort, atmosphere or friendliness. As a rule, the hotels we recommend range from one to three stars.

Location Inexpensive hotels are often clustered around bus and train stations. These can be useful for late-night/early-morning arrivals or departures, but are rarely the best options around. Generally, you'll do better looking elsewhere in town.

Rates Rates fluctuate enormously from high to low season, sometimes by up to 40% or 50%. Always make sure you know exactly what your room rate covers (eg air-con, breakfast, internet access). If breakfast is extra, bear in mind that you'll often be able to get a better, and cheaper, breakfast in a regular cafe.

Discounts Particularly in the slower winter months, discounts are often available for groups or longer stays. In slack periods, hoteliers may even be open to a little bargaining – it's worth trying. It's also worth checking hotel websites for last-minute deals and weekend discounts, as many business hotels (usually three stars and upwards) slash their rates by up to 40% on Friday and Saturday nights.

Reservations Well-known hotels in major destinations fill quickly in high season, so always book ahead. If you're not booking online, many hotels will insist on an email or faxed confirmation. Most will also require credit card details in place of a deposit. If you don't have a credit card you might be asked to send a money order to cover the first night's stay.

Payment To avoid embarrassing scenes at reception, always check that your hotel accepts credit cards. Most do, but it's dangerous to assume that a request for a credit card number with your booking means that the hotel accepts payment by plastic.

Resources Check out **Booking.com** (www.booking.com), **Venere** (www.venere.com), **DHR** (www.dhr.com) and **i-escape** (www.i-escape.com).

Rental Accommodation

Ranging from luxurious country villas to small studio flats, rental accommodation is good for families or groups travelling together, and for longer stays. All should come with kitchens – or at the very least cooking facilities – which will help save on the food bill.

For leads, try **Air BnB** (www.airbnb.com) and **Vacations-Abroad** (www. vacations-abroad.com).

University Accommodation

» Student accommodation is sometimes opened to travellers in the holidays and provides an alternative to sleeping in a hostel.

» Beds are available in single rooms but more commonly in doubles or triples. There might also be cooking facilities available.

» Enquire at the university, at student information services or at local tourist offices.

Activities

Beautiful beaches, tempting seas, mountains, lakes and rivers – Mediterranean Europe is a magnificent outdoor playground. Activities run the gamut from gentle strolls to tough mountain hikes, and from windsurfing and scuba diving to mountain biking, paragliding and white-water rafting.

Cycling

Cycling opportunities abound across the region – tourist offices can usually provide maps and local information.

» The best time for cycling is generally spring, when the weather is sunny but not too hot and the countryside is at its most colourful. In summer, resorts in the Alps, Dolomites and Pyrenees offer excellent mountain biking.

» Never underestimate the effects of the heat. Always cover your head (helmets are mandatory in some countries) and make sure you drink plenty of fluids. Sunburn can be highly unpleasant and heatstroke very serious.

Diving

The Med's warm waters, with their abundant marine life, underwater caves and sunken shipwrecks, are ideal for diving. Throughout the region there are hundreds of diving centres offering everything from beginners courses to trips exploring wrecks. Most dive schools hire out equipment.

Extreme Sports

Hang-gliding, paragliding, caving, canyoning and hydrospeed (boogie boarding down a river) are among the adventure sports available across the region.

» Adventure sports are popular in Slovenia and the Balkan countries, with a growing number of ecotourism groups offering tailor-made activity packages.

» Climbing is also popular, particularly in the Alps, where the icy slopes attract mountaineers, rock climbers and ice climbers.

Hiking

Keen hikers could spend a lifetime exploring Mediterranean Europe's many trails.

» As a rule, spring and autumn are the best periods.

» Between June and September, the region's mountain chains offer stunning hiking, with mountain refuges providing accommodation on many of the longer, high-altitude routes.

» While most high-level mountain paths are only open in the summer, there are possibilities for hiking in the winter snow.

» Contact tourist offices for information on routes and local guides.

Kayaking & Rafting

The region's lakes, rivers and reservoirs offer ample opportunities for water-sport lovers. In mountainous areas, kayaking and white-water rafting provide thrills (and possibly the odd spill). Bosnia and Hercegovina, Montenegro and Slovenia are popular destinations.

Skiing & Snowboarding

Winter sports are big business in southern Europe, and

each year thousands take to the pistes to ski (downhill or cross-country), snowboard and snowshoe.

» For a ski holiday you'll need to budget for ski lifts, accommodation and the inevitable après-ski entertainment. You'll save a bit by bringing your own equipment, but often not enough to compensate for the hassle of lugging it around with you. As a general rule, cross-country skiing costs less than downhill.

» The ski season traditionally lasts from early December to late March, though at higher altitudes in the French and Italian Alps it may extend an extra month either way. Snow conditions vary greatly from one year to the next and from region to region, but January and February tend to be the best, busiest and most expensive months.

Surfing, Windsurfing & Kitesurfing

» Windsurfing is one of the most popular of the region's water sports. It's easy to rent sailboards in many tourist centres, and courses are usually available for beginners.

» Surfers can strut their stuff, too, with excellent waves on the western seaboard off the coast of France, Spain and Portugal.

» Kitesurfing is also readily available across the region.

Business Hours

Although there are no hard and fast rules respected by all countries (or even by all of the businesses in any one country), most Mediter-

ranean nations share some habits.

Banks Generally open early and either close for the day at around 1.30pm or reopen for a brief two-hour window in the early afternoon, say from 2.30pm to 4.30pm.

Museums Many are closed on Mondays.

Offices Usually operate from Monday to Friday and possibly Saturday morning. Sunday opening is not unheard of, but it's not widespread.

Shops It's common, especially outside the main cities, for small shops to close for a long lunch. Typically a shop might open from 8am or 9am until 1.30pm, and then from about 4pm to 8pm. Larger department stores tend to stay open all day.

Children

Despite a dearth of child-friendly sights and activities, the Mediterranean is a great place to travel with children. Kids are universally adored and are welcome just about everywhere.

» You should have no problems finding baby food, formulas or disposable nappies.

» Remember that shop opening hours might be different from those at home, so if you run out of nappies on Saturday afternoon you could be in for a messy weekend.

» Most car-rental firms have safety seats for hire at a nominal cost, but it's essential you book them in advance. The same goes for high chairs and cots – they're

WINTER & SUMMER HOURS

Opening hours sometimes change between summer and winter. In general, summer hours are longer, with later closing times. In coastal areas, many seasonal businesses (hotels, souvenir shops, bars etc) close over winter, generally from November to March.

available in most restaurants and hotels, but numbers will be limited.

» Don't overdo it on the beach – the Mediterranean sun is strong and sunburn is a risk, particularly in the first couple of days of your trip.

» For more information, see Lonely Planet's *Travel with Children,* or check out **TravelWithYourKids** (www.travelwithyourkids.com) or **Family Travel Network** (www.familytravelnetwork.com).

Customs Regulations

Travelling within the EU

Travelling from one EU country to another you're allowed to carry:

» 800 cigarettes

» 200 cigars or 1kg of loose tobacco

» 10L of spirits (anything more than 22% alcohol by volume)

» 20L of fortified wine or aperitif

» 90L of wine

Entering or Leaving the EU

On leaving the EU, non-EU residents can reclaim value-added tax (VAT) on expensive purchases. You can carry the following duty-free:

» 200 cigarettes or 50 cigars or 250g of tobacco

» 1L of spirits or 2L of fortified wine, sparkling wine or any alcoholic drink under 22% volume

» 4L of still wine

» 16L of beer

» Goods, including perfume and electronic devices, up to a value of €430 for air and sea travellers, and €300 for land travellers

Non-EU Countries

Non-EU countries each have their own regulations, although most forbid the exportation of antiquities and cultural treasures.

TAX-FREE SHOPPING

Tax-free shopping is available across the region – look for signs in shop windows – and while it won't save you a fortune, it won't cost you anything extra.

Value-added tax (VAT) is a sales tax imposed on most goods and services sold in Europe; it varies from country to country but is typically between 6% and 23%. In most countries, non-EU residents who spend more than a certain amount – ranging from €50 to €175 depending on the country – can claim VAT back on their purchases when they leave the EU. EU residents, however, are not entitled to a refund on goods bought in another EU country.

The procedure is straightforward. When you make your purchase ask the shop assistant for a tax-refund voucher (sometimes called a tax-free shopping cheque), which is filled in with the date of your purchase and its value. When you leave the EU, get this voucher stamped at customs – the customs agent might want to check the item so try to ensure you have it at hand – and take it to the nearest tax-refund counter. Here you can get an immediate refund, either in cash or onto your credit card. If there's no refund counter at the airport or you're travelling by sea or overland, you'll need to get the voucher stamped at the port or border crossing and mail it back for your refund.

Discount Cards

Many major cities now offer cards that provide discounts on public transport and entry to selected sights. Alternatively, **European Cities Marketing** (www.european-citycards.com) sells cards for cities in Croatia, France, Italy, Portugal, Slovenia and Spain.

Senior Cards

EU citizens over 65 are often entitled to free or discounted entry to museums and tourist attractions, provided proof of age can be shown. A passport or ID card is usually sufficient.

There are a growing number of tour operators who specialise in senior travel and can provide information about special packages and discounts.

Student & Youth Cards

There are a range of discount cards available to young travellers, students and teachers.

Note also that membership of **Hostelling International** (HI; www.hihostels.com) guarantees discounts and benefits, as does possession of the **Camping Card International** (CCI; www.campingcardinternational.com).

The **International Student Identity Card** (ISIC; www.isic.org) offers worldwide discounts on transport, museum entry, youth hostels and even some restaurants, as well as access to a 24-hour emergency telephone help line. It's available to full-time students and gappers who have a confirmed place at uni or college. The price varies from country to country but in the UK it costs UK£9, in Australia A$25 and in the USA US$25.

If not eligible for the ISIC, teachers and professors can apply for the International Teacher Identity Card (ITIC), and nonstudents aged under

26 for the International Youth Travel Card (IYTC). Both offer the same benefits as the ISIC.

See the ISIC website for details of worldwide issuing offices.

The **European Youth Card** (www.euro26.org), sometimes still known as the Euro<26 card, is available to people aged under 30 (26 in some countries), and offers a wide selection of benefits and discounts. It costs €5 to €19 depending on the country of purchase.

The **International Student Exchange Card** (www.isecards.com) is available to full-time students, teachers and under-26s, and costs US$25. Benefits include discounts, US medical insurance, 24-hour emergency assistance and a global phone card.

Electricity
Voltages & Cycles

Most of Europe runs on 230V/50Hz AC (as opposed to, say, North America, where the electricity is 120V/60Hz AC). Chargers for phones, iPads, laptops and tablets can usually handle any type

of electricity. If in doubt, read the fine print.

Plugs & Sockets

Countries in Mediterranean Europe use the 'europlug' (two round pins).

Embassies & Consulates

As a traveller, it's important to realise what your embassy can and can't do for you. Remember, you're bound by the laws of the country you're in. If you end up in jail after committing a crime locally (even if such actions are legal in your own country), your embassy will not be sympathetic. Also remember if the trouble you're in is even remotely your own fault, they generally won't be much help.

In genuine emergencies you might get some assistance, but only if other channels have been exhausted. Most importantly, your consulate can issue an emergency passport, help get a message to friends or family, and offer advice on money transfers.

Nations such as Australia, Canada, New Zealand, the UK and the US have embassies and consulates across the region in capitals and major cities. To locate them consult the following websites:
Australia (www.dfat.gov.au)
Canada (www.international.gc.ca)
New Zealand (www.mfat.govt.nz)
UK (www.fco.gov.uk)
US (www.travel.state.gov)

Food

Eating out is a way of life on the Med, and with everything from Michelin-starred restaurants, beachside tavernas, designer bistros, cafes and bars, there's no shortage of choices. If you're on a budget, look out for self-service canteens or roadside kiosks serving local snacks (think

takeaway pizza in Italy or souvlaki in Greece) and shop at local markets.

» Lunch is the main meal of the day in most Mediterranean countries.

» Meals are eaten later in southern Europe than in more northerly climes – dinner is typically served from about 8pm.

» Children are usually welcome in all but the very smartest establishments. Kids menus are uncommon but you can often ask for half portions.

» Vegetarianism is not widespread in the region and vegetarians might have a hard time in Portugal and some of the Eastern European countries.

» Eat better and save money by choosing seasonal dishes and local wines/beers/spirits.

Gay & Lesbian Travellers

Discretion is the key. Although homosexuality is acknowledged and in the large part tacitly accepted in Mediterranean Europe, attitudes remain conservative and overt displays of affection could elicit hostility, especially outside of main cities and in some eastern countries.

» Antidiscrimination legislation is in place everywhere except Turkey.

» Same-sex relationships are recognised in Croatia, Slovenia, France, Spain and Portugal and same-sex marriages are legal in Spain and Portugal.

» Paris, Madrid, Barcelona, Lisbon and Athens all have thriving gay scenes and the Greek islands of Mykonos and Lesvos are popular beach destinations for gay travellers.

» Further information is listed in individual country directories.

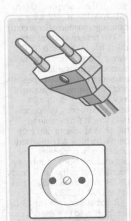

230V/50Hz

Useful resources:

Damron (www.damron.com) Publishes various guides and apps for gay travellers.

Gay Journey (www.gay-journey.com) Travel services (package deals, accommodation, insurance etc), gay-friendly listings and loads of links.

Spartacus World.com (www.spartacusworld.com) Extensive listings and sells the *Spartacus International Gay Guide* (€25.95, US$32.99, UK£19.99), a male-only directory of worldwide gay venues, as well as a guide to gay-friendly hotels, restaurants and saunas. Apps are also available.

Health

Required Vaccinations

No vaccinations are mandatory for any of the countries in this book.

» The World Health Organization (WHO) recommends that all travellers, regardless of their destination, should be covered for diphtheria, tetanus, measles, mumps, rubella and polio.

» Vaccinations against typhoid and hepatitis A and B are recommended for Turkey.

» Since most vaccines don't produce immunity until at least two weeks after they're given, visit a physician at least six weeks before departure.

Health Insurance

» With a European Health Insurance Card, EU nationals are entitled to free or reduced-cost public health care in EU countries. The card, which is available from your national health provider, does not cover private treatment, nonemergency treatment or emergency repatriation.

» Non-EU citizens should find out if there is a reciprocal arrangement for free or reduced-cost medical care between their country and the country visited. For example, Australian residents are entitled to subsidised medical treatment in Italy and Slovenia.

» US citizens should check if their health-insurance plan covers medical care abroad – many don't.

» As a rule, non-EU nationals should take out health insurance.

» If you do need health insurance, consider a policy that covers you for the worst possible scenario, such as an accident requiring an emergency flight home.

» Find out in advance if your insurance plan will make payments directly to providers, or will reimburse you later for overseas health expenditures. The former option is generally preferable, as it doesn't require you to be out of pocket in a foreign country.

Availability of Health Care

» Good health care is readily available throughout the region.

» For minor illnesses, pharmacists can give valuable advice and sell over-the-counter medication. They can also advise when more specialised help is required and point you in the right direction.

» The standard of dental care is usually good; however, it is sensible to have a dental check-up before a long trip.

Common Problems
HEAT EXHAUSTION & HEATSTROKE

Heat exhaustion occurs when excessive fluid loss is combined with inadequate replacement of fluids and salt. Symptoms include headache, dizziness and tiredness. Dehydration is already happening by the time you feel thirsty – aim to drink sufficient water to produce pale, diluted urine. Replace lost fluids by drinking water and/or fruit juice, and cool the body with cold water and

TRAVEL HEALTH WEBSITES

Before travelling to the region, you can get up-to-date health advice from your government's website:

Australia (www.smartraveller.gov.au/tips/health.html)

Canada (www.phac-aspc.gc.ca/tmp-pmv/index-eng.php)

New Zealand (www.safetravel.govt.nz/beforeugo/health.shtml)

UK (www.fco.gov.uk/en/travel-and-living-abroad/staying-safe/health/)

USA (www.cdc.gov/travel)

Another useful resource is www.mdtravelhealth.com, a US website with detailed destination advice.

CAN YOU DRINK THE TAP WATER?

Tap water is safe to drink in most of the countries listed in this book. However, in Albania, Bosnia and Hercegovina, Montenegro and Turkey, it's best to stick to bottled or purified water.

Don't drink water from rivers or lakes, as it may contain bacteria or viruses that can cause diarrhoea or vomiting.

fans. Treat salt loss with salty fluids such as soup, or add a little more table salt to foods than usual.

Heatstroke is much more serious, resulting in irrational and hyperactive behaviour, and eventually loss of consciousness and death. Rapid cooling by spraying the body with water and fanning is ideal. Emergency fluid and electrolyte replacement by intravenous drip is recommended.

INSECT BITES & STINGS

Mosquitoes are found in most parts of Mediterranean Europe. They may not carry malaria, but they can cause irritation and infected bites. Use a DEET-based insect repellent.

Sandflies are found around Mediterranean beaches. They usually cause only a nasty, itchy bite, but can carry a rare skin disorder called cutaneous leishmaniasis.

TRAVELLER'S DIARRHOEA

If you develop diarrhoea, be sure to drink plenty of fluids, preferably an oral rehydration solution such as Dioralyte. You should seek medical attention if diarrhoea is bloody, persists for more than 72 hours, or is accompanied by a fever, shaking, chills or severe abdominal pain.

Holidays

» Most holidays in the southern European countries are based on the Christian calendar.

» In Turkey, the month-long holiday of Ramazan (Ramadan) is celebrated. Its exact timing depends on lunar events.

» August is the peak holiday period for Mediterranean dwellers.

» The major school holidays run from July to September, and many businesses simply shut up shop for much of August. Schools also pause for breaks over Easter and Christmas.

» For details of the school calendar, check out http://eacea.ec.europa.eu/education/eurydice, which lists holiday dates for many European countries.

Insurance

Travel insurance to cover theft, loss and medical problems is highly recommended. It may also cover you for cancellation of and delays in your travel arrangements.

Also see p872 for info on car and motorcycle insurance.

» There is a whole range of policies available so make sure you get one that's tailored to your needs – while one policy may be suitable if you're going skiing, you'll need another if you're planning a beach holiday. And always check the small print.

» Don't forget to keep all paperwork. If you have to claim for medical expenses you'll need all the relevant documentation. Similarly, to claim for a theft, you'll require a statement from the local police.

» The policies handled by **STA Travel** (www.statravel.com) and other student travel agencies are usually good value.

» Price comparison website **Money Supermarket** (www.moneysupermarket.com) compares 450 policies and comes up with the best for your needs. It also has a useful FAQ section and some good general information.

» Worldwide travel insurance is available at www.lonelyplanet.com/travel-insurance. You can buy, extend and claim online anytime – even if you're already on the road.

Things to consider when choosing a policy:

» Are 'dangerous activities' (scuba diving, motorcycling and, for some policies, trekking) covered? Some policies might not cover you if you're riding a motorbike with a locally acquired motorcycle licence.

» Does the policy cover every country you're planning to visit? Some policies don't cover certain countries, such as Montenegro or BiH.

» Does the policy cover ambulance service or an emergency flight home?

Internet Access

» Wi-fi is widely available across the region. Hostels, B&Bs and midrange hotels often offer free wi-fi, while top-end places generally charge a fee.

» Wi-fi is often available in public parks, at cafes and restaurants, in railway stations and at airports.

» Many hotels and hostels provide computer terminals for guests' use, either free or for a small fee.

» The diffusion of wi-fi means that there aren't as many internet cafes as there once were. They still exist, though, and you'll find them across the region. You might also be able to log on at department stores, post offices, libraries, tourist offices, phone centres and universities. Costs range from about €1.50 to €5 per hour.

» If you're using your own kit, note that you might need a power transformer (to convert from 110V to 230V if your computer isn't set up for dual voltage) and a plug adaptor.

Language Courses

A language course is a great way of tapping into the local culture. Courses are available to foreigners at universities and in private language schools across the region.

France Details of language schools and courses are available at www.qualitefle.fr and www.europa-pages.com/france. See also p316.

Greece Try the **Athens Centre** (www.athenscentre.gr).

Italy The **Università per Stranieri** (www.unistrapg.it)

in Perugia is a popular place to study, with hundreds of courses available to non-Italians.

Spain Check out the **Escuela Oficial de Idiomas** (www.eeooiinet.com) or look for schools at www.europa-pages.com/spain.

Turkey Popular schools include **Dilmer** (www.dilmer.com) in İstanbul and the nationwide **Tömer** (www.tomer.com.tr).

Information about courses is also available from the cultural institutes maintained by many European countries around the world, such as the Spanish **Istituto Cervantes** (www.cervantes.es) or French **Alliance Française** (www.alliancefr.org). National tourist authorities, student-exchange organisations and student travel agencies should also be able to help. Ask about special holiday packages that include a course.

If you don't fancy a language course there are many other subjects to choose from – cooking, art, literature, architecture, drama, music, fashion and photography.

Legal Matters

Driving Drink-driving laws apply and road checks are common in some areas. When driving make sure you have the correct documents at hand.

Drugs Drugs are widespread. Legislation and local attitudes vary, but if you're caught with a small quantity of cannabis you might get away with a warning and/or a fine. Possession of hard drugs or quantities of cannabis deemed 'dealable' could lead to imprisonment. Note that prescription drugs that are legal in your home country might not be legal abroad – check before travelling.

Proof of Identity You are required by law to prove your identity if asked by police, so always carry your passport, or ID card if you're an EU citizen.

Theft If you have something stolen and you want to claim it on insurance, you must make a statement to the police, as insurance companies won't pay up without official proof of a crime.

Maps

Proper road maps are essential if you're driving or cycling. Quality European map publishers include **Michelin** (www.michelin.com), **Freytag & Berndt** (www.freytagberndt.com) and **Kümmerly+Frey** (www.kuemmerly-frey.ch).

» As a rule, maps published by automobile associations (for example ACI in Italy or ELPA in Greece) are excellent, and are sometimes free if membership of your local association gives you reciprocal rights.

» Tourist offices are a good source of free, basic maps.

» Good maps are easy to find in bookshops throughout the region.

Money

France, Greece, Italy, Montenegro, Portugal, Slovenia and Spain use the euro. The euro is also widely accepted in Albania, BiH and Croatia.

There are seven euro notes (€5, €10, €20, €50, €100, €200 and €500) and eight euro coins (€1 and €2, then 1, 2, 5, 10, 20 and 50 cents); one euro is equivalent to 100 cents.

While travelling in the region, the best way to carry your money is to bring an ATM card, credit card and cash. Internet-banking accounts are useful for tracking your spending – if you don't have one, set one up before you leave home.

ATMs

ATMs are widely available in the region and easy to use (many have instructions in English). It's always prudent, though, to have a backup option in case something goes wrong with your card or you can't find a working ATM – in remote villages and islands they can be scarce.

There are four types of card you can use in an ATM:

ATM Cards Use to withdraw money from your home bank account. They can be used in ATMs linked to international networks such as Cirrus and Maestro.

Debit Cards Like ATM cards but can also be used to make purchases over the counter.

Credit Cards Can be used in ATMs displaying the appropriate logos.

Prepaid Cards Like credit/debit cards, they can be used in ATMs displaying the appropriate logos.

» Note that you'll need a four-digit PIN (in numbers rather than letters) for most European ATMs.

» As a security measure, be wary of people who offer to help you use an ATM or, at ports or stations, people who claim that there are no ATMs at your destination.

» Note that ATMs impose a limit on daily withdrawals, typically around €250.

TELL THE BANK

Before leaving home, always let your bank or credit-card company know of your travel plans. If you don't, you risk having your card blocked, as banks often block cards as a standard security measure when they notice out-of-the-ordinary transactions.

ATM CHARGES

When you withdraw money from an ATM, the amounts are converted and dispensed in local currency. However, there are hidden costs. Typically, you'll be charged a transaction fee (usually 1% to 3% with a minimum of €3 or more), as well as a 1% to 3% conversion charge. You might also be charged by the owner of the ATM, and, if you're using a credit card, you'll be hit by interest on the cash withdrawn.

Fees vary from company to company so it's worth doing some research before you travel – check out the British website **Money Supermarket** (www.money-supermarket.com) or the US site **Card Ratings** (www.cardratings.com). Two companies that apply reduced fees are the British Halifax, whose Clarity Card charges no fees for cash withdrawals and foreign exchanges, and the US bank Capital One, which charges no fees for foreign-currency transactions.

Despite all the hidden charges, having the right card is still generally cheaper than exchanging money directly. To minimise costs, try making fewer but larger withdrawals. It's also worth checking whether your bank has reciprocal arrangements with foreign banks allowing you to use their ATMs free of charge.

Black Market

Black-market money exchange is relatively rare in Mediterranean Europe, although it's not totally absent. If you do encounter it, stay well clear. The rates rarely outweigh the risk of being caught, and by dealing with unofficial moneychangers you greatly increase your chances of being conned – many people offering illegal exchanges are professional thieves.

Cash

Nothing beats cash for convenience, or risk. If you lose it, it's gone forever and very few travel insurers will come to your rescue. Those that will insure you limit the amount to somewhere around US$300. As a general rule of thumb, carry no more than 10% to 15% of your total trip money in cash.

It's still a good idea, though, to bring some local currency in cash, if only to tide you over until you find an ATM.

Credit Cards

Credit cards are good for major purchases such as airline tickets or car hire, as well as for providing emergency cover. They also make life a lot easier if you need to book hotels while on the road – many places request a credit-card number when you reserve a room.

» Credit cards are widely accepted in most countries, although don't rely on them in small restaurants, shops or private accommodation in Albania, Croatia and Montenegro. As a general rule, Visa and MasterCard are more widely accepted in the region than American Express and Diners Club.

» Many European countries use a 'chip and PIN' system for credit and debit cards. If your card isn't enabled for this, as many US cards are not, or you don't know your card's PIN, you can often still sign a printed receipt in the usual way. However, you might find your card is refused in automatic payment machines at railway stations, petrol stations etc.

» Using your credit card in ATMs is costly. On every transaction there's a fee as well as interest per withdrawal. Check the charges with your issuer before leaving home. As a rule, debit cards cost less for withdrawing money from an ATM.

» Make sure you can always see your card when making transactions – it'll lessen the risk of fraud.

International Transfers

If you need money sent to you, international bank transfers are good for secure, one-off movements of large amounts of money, but they might take three to five days and there will be a fee. Be sure to specify the name of the bank, plus the IBAN (International Bank Account Number) and the address of the branch where you'd like to pick up your money.

It's quicker and easier (although more expensive) to have money wired via **Western Union** (www.western union.com) or **MoneyGram** (www.moneygram.com).

A cheaper option is **Skrill** (www.skrill.com), a British money-transfer website that allows you to send and receive money via email.

Moneychangers

» US dollars, British pounds and the euro are the easiest currencies to exchange in Europe. You might have trouble exchanging Canadian, Australian and New Zealand dollars.

» Most airports, central train stations, big hotels and many border posts have exchange facilities. Post offices are another option, although while they'll always exchange cash, they might not change travellers cheques unless they're in the local currency.

» The best exchange rates are generally offered by banks. *Bureaux de changes* usually, but not always, offer worse rates or charge higher commissions. Hotels are almost always the worst places to change money.

Prepaid Cards

In recent years prepaid cards (also called travel money cards, prepaid currency cards or cash passport cards) have become a popular way of carrying money.

These enable you to load a card with as much foreign currency as you want to spend. You then use it to withdraw cash at ATMs – the money comes off the card and not out of your account – or to make direct purchases. You can reload it via telephone or online.

Many prepaid cards are linked to Visa or MasterCard.

Advantages of a prepaid card:

» you avoid foreign-exchange fees as the money you put on your card is converted into foreign currency at the moment you load it

» you can control your outlay by only loading as much as you want to spend

» security: if your card is stolen your losses are limited to the balance on the card – it's not directly linked to your bank account

» lower ATM withdrawal fees

» many cards have a chip enabling you to use them in automatic payment machines – especially good for US travellers whose regular cards probably won't have a chip

Against this you'll need to weigh up the costs:

» fees are charged for buying the card and then every time you load it

» ATM withdrawal fees apply

» you might be charged a fee if you don't use the card for a certain period of time or if you need to redeem any unused currency

» if the card has an expiry date, you'll forfeit any money loaded onto the card after that date

Tipping

There are no hard-and-fast rules about tipping.

» Many restaurants add service charges, making a tip discretionary. In such cases, it's common practice, and often expected of visitors, to round bills up. If the service was particularly good and you want to leave a tip, 5% to 10% is fine.

» At bars or cafes it's not necessary but you might leave your change or a few small coins.

» In some places, such as Croatia, tour guides expect to be tipped.

Travellers Cheques

Although outmoded by cards and ATMs, travellers cheques are safer than cash and are a useful emergency backup, especially as you can claim a refund if they're stolen. Keep a separate record of their numbers and all original purchase receipts.

» American Express, Visa and Travelex cheques are the most widely accepted, par-

ticularly in US dollars, British pounds or euros.

» It's becoming increasingly hard to find places to cash travellers cheques, especially outside of the main centres.

» When changing, ask about fees and commissions, as well as the exchange rate. There may be a service fee charged per cheque, a flat transaction fee, or a fee that's a percentage of the total amount.

Photography

As a rule, there are very few photographic restrictions in Mediterranean Europe. However, remember the following:

» Many museums, art galleries and churches ban flash photography.

» Avoid taking pictures of military sites, airfields, police stations etc.

» Always ask permission before photographing people.

» For further tips, check out Lonely Planet's *Travel Photography*, a comprehensive guide to all aspects of the art.

Post

» From major European centres, airmail typically takes about five days to reach North America and a week to Australasian destinations. It might be slower from countries such as Albania and BiH, which has three parallel postal services.

» Postage costs vary from country to country, as does post-office efficiency.

» Courier services such as DHL (www.dhl.com) are best for essential deliveries.

Safe Travel

Travelling in Mediterranean Europe is pretty safe. The ongoing financial crisis has hit the region hard and austerity measures have been introduced in many countries, provoking strikes and

---

GET THE BILL IN LOCAL CURRENCY

Something to look out for when making payments with a credit card is what's known as **dynamic currency conversion**. This is used when a vendor offers to convert your bill into your home currency rather than charging you in the local currency. The catch here is that the exchange rate used to convert your bill will usually be highly disadvantageous to you, and the vendor might well add his or her own commission fee. Always ask to be billed in the local currency.

rioting in Greece, Spain, Italy and Portugal. That said, the region is relatively stable and violent crime is rare.

Travellers to remote areas in southeastern Anatolia in Turkey should check on the latest security situation, and visitors to BiH should note the presence of unexploded landmines in certain areas of the country.

Petty crime is widespread in the region, so watch out for bag snatchers, pickpockets and scam artists. In cities, take note of any local crime hot spots (a particular neighbourhood, bus route, metro station etc) and areas to avoid after dark.

As always, common sense and a little healthy scepticism are the best defence.

Scams

Mediterranean con artists are good at what they do and you should be on your guard against scams. Typical scenarios:

Bar Scam Typically worked on solo male travellers. You're approached by a guy who claims to be a lone out-of-towner like you but who's heard of a great bar. You go to the bar and enjoy a boozy evening with a crowd of new friends. At the end of the evening you're presented with an outrageous bill.

Druggings These are unlikely but do happen, especially on trains. A new 'friend' slips something into your drink or food and then fleeces you of your valuables as you sleep off the effects.

Flat-Tyre Ruse While driving you stop to help someone with a flat tyre (or someone stops to help you change your tyre, which they've just punctured). As you change the tyre, an accomplice takes valuables from the interior of your car.

Phoney Cops These often appear as the end-play in cons involving money-changers or arguments about money. If approached by someone claiming to be a police officer, offer to go with them to the nearest police station.

Swapping Banknotes You pay for a taxi fare or a train ticket with a €20 note. The taxi driver or ticket seller deftly palms the note and produces a €5 note, claiming that you paid with this. In your confusion you're not sure what you did and accept their word.

Touts & Unofficial Guides Be wary of people directing you to hotels or shops (they'll usually be collecting a commission) and people offering to show you around tourist sites (they'll demand hefty payment afterwards).

Theft

Theft is the biggest problem facing travellers in Mediterranean Europe. There's no need for paranoia but be aware that pickpockets and bag snatchers are out there.

» Don't store valuables in train-station lockers or at luggage-storage counters, and be careful if people offer to help you operate a locker.

» Be vigilant if someone offers to carry your luggage: they just might carry it away.

» Carry your own padlock for hostel lockers. Be careful even in hotels; don't leave any valuables lying around in your room.

» When going out, spread your valuables, cash and cards around your body or in different bags. A money belt with your essentials (passport, cash, credit cards, airline tickets) is usually a good idea. However, to avoid delving into it in public, carry a wallet with a day's cash.

» Don't flaunt watches, cameras and other expensive goods.

» Cameras and shoulder bags are an open invitation for snatch thieves, many of whom work from motorcycles or scooters. A small day pack is better, but watch your rear. Also be very careful at cafes and bars – always loop your bag's strap around your leg while seated.

» Pickpockets are particularly active in dense crowds, especially in busy train stations and on public transport. A common ploy is for one person to distract you while another whips through your pockets. Beware of gangs of dishevelled-looking kids waving newspapers and demanding attention. In the blink of an eye, a wallet or camera can go missing. Remember also that some of the best pickpockets are well dressed.

» Parked cars, especially those with foreign number plates or rental-agency stickers, are prime targets for petty criminals. While driving through cities, beware of thieves at traffic lights; keep your doors locked and the windows rolled up.

» A favourite tactic of scooter snatchers is for a

GOVERNMENT TRAVEL ADVICE

The following government websites offer travel advisories and information on current hot spots.

Australian Department of Foreign Affairs (www.smartraveller.gov.au)

British Foreign & Commonwealth Office (www.fco.gov.uk/en/travel-and-living-abroad)

Canadian Department of Foreign Affairs (www.voyage.gc.ca)

US State Department (http://travel.state.gov)

first rider to brush past your car, knocking the side mirror out of position; then, as you reach out to readjust the mirror, an accomplice on a second scooter will race past, snatching the watch off your wrist as he goes.

» In case of theft or loss, always report the incident to the police and ask for a statement. Without one, your travel insurance company won't pay up.

Telephone

Domestic and international calls can be made from public payphones using prepaid phonecards, and from hotels, post offices, internet cafes (via Skype) and private call centres.

Phoning from a post office or a public payphone is almost always cheaper than calling from a hotel. Private call centres often have good long-distance rates but always check before calling.

To call abroad simply dial the international access code (IAC) of the country you're calling *from* (most commonly 00), the country code (CC) of the country you're calling *to*, the local area code (usually, but not always, dropping the leading zero if there is one) and then the number.

To have someone else pay for your call, you can often dial directly to your home-country operator and make a reverse-charge (collect) call. Alternatively, you can use the Country Direct system (such as AT&T's USADirect), which lets you phone home by billing the long-distance carrier you use at home. Home Direct numbers, which can often be dialled from public phones without even inserting a phonecard, vary from country to country.

Emergency Numbers

The EU-wide general emergency number is ☎112. This can be dialled, toll-free, for emergencies in BiH, Croatia, France, Greece, Italy (for the

SMARTPHONES

For making calls and sending text messages, smartphones are just like any other mobile phone, so if you can unlock yours, the best bet is to get a local SIM card. But be careful when accessing the internet: high data-roaming charges quickly add up and even checking your email can become a costly business. A way around this is to turn off data roaming and only use the internet when you have access to free wi-fi. Once online, you can then use Skype or Google Voice to make cheap (sometimes free) calls.

carabinieri, who can forward you to the other emergency services), Montenegro, Portugal, Slovenia, Spain and Turkey (for ambulances only).

See the individual country directories for country-specific emergency numbers.

Mobile Phones

» Most European mobile phones operate on the GSM 900/1800 system, which also covers Australia and New Zealand, but is not compatible with the North American GSM 1900 system. Some American GSM 1900/900 phones do work in Europe, although high roaming charges make it an expensive option.

» If you have a GSM tri- or quad-band phone that you can unlock (check with your service provider), the easiest way of using it is to buy a prepaid SIM card in each country you visit.

» You can often buy European SIM cards in your home country but you'll generally pay less in Europe.

» Note that most SIMs expire if not used within a certain time and that most country-specific SIMs can only be used in the country of origin.

Phone Codes

Toll-free numbers in Mediterranean Europe often have an 0800 or 800 prefix (also 900 in Spain).

Phonecards

» Phonecards for public payphones are available from post offices, telephone centres, news stands and retail outlets.

» There's a wide range of local and international phonecards. Most international cards come with a toll-free number and a PIN code, which gives access to your prepaid credit. However, for local calls you're usually better off with a local phonecard.

» Cards sold at airports and train stations are rarely good value for money.

» Note that many cards have an expiry date.

» Both the International Student Identity Card and Hostelling International offer a range of phonecards and SIM cards – see www.isiconnect.ekit.com or www.hi.ekit.com for details.

» If you don't have a phonecard, you can often telephone from a booth inside a post office or telephone centre and settle your bill at the counter.

Time

Most Mediterranean Europe countries are on Central European Time (GMT/UTC plus one hour), except for Portugal, which runs on Western European Time (GMT/UTC), and Greece and Turkey, which are on Eastern European Time (GMT/UTC plus two hours).

In most European countries, clocks are put forward one hour for daylight-saving time on the last Sunday in March and turned back again on the last Sunday in October. Thus, during daylight-saving time, Western European Time is GMT/UTC plus one hour, Central European Time is GMT/UTC plus two hours and Eastern European Time is GMT/UTC plus three hours.

Toilets

» Public toilets are pretty thin on the ground in much of the region. The best advice if you're caught short is to nip into a train station, fast-food outlet, bar or cafe and use their facilities.

» A small fee (typically €0.20 to €1) is often charged in public toilets, so try to keep some small change handy.

» Most toilets in the region are of the sit-down Western variety, but don't be surprised to find the occasional squat toilet. And don't ever assume that public toilets will have paper – they almost certainly won't.

Tourist Information

» Tourist information is widely available throughout the region. Most towns, big or small, have a tourist office of some description, which at the very least will be able to provide a rudimentary map and give information on accommodation. Some even provide a hotel-reservation service, which might or might not be free.

» In the absence of a tourist office, useful sources of information include travel agencies and hotel receptionists.

» Tourist-office staff will often speak some English in the main centres, but don't bank on it away from the tourist hot spots.

Travellers with Disabilities

With the notable exception of Croatia – and to a lesser extent BiH – which has improved wheelchair access due to the large number of wounded war veterans, the region does not cater well to travellers with disabilities. Steep cobbled streets, ancient lifts and anarchic traffic all make life difficult for wheelchair-using visitors. Wheelchair access is often limited to the more expensive hotels and major airports, public transport is usually woefully ill-equipped, and tourist sites rarely cater well to those with disabilities.

However, it's not impossible to travel the region, even independently. If you're going it alone, pre-trip research and planning is essential:

» find out about facilities on public transport

» work out how to get to your hotel or hostel

» check if there are care agencies available and how much they cost

» give your wheelchair a thorough service before departing and prepare a basic tool kit, as punctures can be a problem

» national support organisations can help; they often have libraries devoted to travel, and can put you in touch with travel agents who specialise in tours for those with disabilites

Other useful resources:
Flying with Disability (www.flying-with-disability.org) Comprehensive and easy-to-use site covering all aspects of air travel – pre-trip planning, navigating the airport, boarding the flight, on the plane etc.

Global Access (www.global accessnews.com) A worldwide network for wheelchair users with a monthly e-zine and tonnes of reader-generated articles.

Lonely Planet (www.lonely planet.com) Check out the Travellers with Disabilities branch on the Thorn Tree travel forum.
Society for Accessible Travel and Hospitality (www.sath.org) Has loads of useful information, including a need-to-know section and travel tips.

Visas

Citizens of Australia, New Zealand, Canada, the UK and the US do not need a visa to enter most Mediterranean Europe countries and stay for up to three months (90 days).

France, Greece, Italy, Portugal, Slovenia and Spain have all signed the Schengen Agreement, which abolishes customs checks between signatory states.

For the purposes of visa requirements, the Schengen area should be considered a single unit, as all member states have the same entry requirements. These include the following:

» Legal residents of one Schengen country do not need a visa for another Schengen country.

» Nationals of Australia, Canada, Israel, Japan, New Zealand and the USA do not need a visa for tourist or business visits of up to 90 days.

» The UK and Ireland are not part of the Schengen area but their citizens can stay indefinitely in other EU countries, and only need to fill in paperwork if they want to work long term or take up residency.

Of the non-Schengen countries, only Turkey requires visas from Australian, Canadian, British and US nationals. These can be bought at any point of entry into the country.

Visa requirements change, and you should always check with the embassy of your destination country or a reputable travel agent before travelling.

Schengen Visa

If you do require a Schengen visa for a tourist visit, you'll need the category C short-stay visa. There are two versions of this: a single-entry visa allows for an uninterrupted stay of up to 90 days within a six-month period (180 days). A multiple-entry visa allows you to enter and leave the Schengen area as long as your combined stay in the area does not exceed 90 days in any 180-day period.

In both cases, the clock starts ticking from the moment you enter the Schengen area. You cannot exit the Schengen area for a short period and start the clock on your return.

Other rules:

» It's obligatory to apply for a Schengen visa in your country of residence at the embassy of your main destination country or, if you have no principal destination, of the first Schengen country you'll be entering.

» A visa issued by one Schengen country is generally valid for travel in other Schengen countries, but individual countries may impose restrictions on certain nationalities.

» You can only apply for two Schengen visas in any 12-month period.

» You cannot work in a Schengen country without a specific work permit.

» Always check which documents you'll need. You'll almost certainly require a passport valid for three months beyond the end of your proposed visit; a return air or train ticket; proof of a hotel reservation or similar accommodation arrangement; proof of your ability to support yourself financially; and medical insurance.

Work Visas

» Most EU citizens can work in any other EU country without a visa or specific permit. Paperwork, which can be complicated, only really becomes necessary for long-term employment or if you want to apply for residency.

» Non-EU nationals require work permits. There is no universal Schengen work visa or permit – each individual member state issues its own. These can be difficult to arrange and usually require you to have a job lined up and an employer ready to do the paperwork for you.

» If one of your parents or a grandparent was born in an EU country, you may have certain rights you never knew about. Get in touch with that country's embassy and ask about dual citizenship and work permits – if you go for citizenship, ask about any obligations, such as military service and residency. Also be aware that your home country may not recognise dual citizenship.

» For details of individual country regulations check with the embassy of the country you want to work in.

» For temporary vacation work in France and Italy, the Working Holiday Visa Program is open to Australian, Canadian and New Zealand citizens aged between 18 and 35. To apply for the visa, which is valid for a year and allows work with certain restrictions, contact the Italian or French embassy in your country of residence.

» Students enrolled in a recognised study program should apply to their destination country's embassy for a student visa. Proof of enrolment as well as health insurance and documents attesting to your financial means will generally be required.

Volunteering

If you can afford it, a volunteer work placement is a great way to gain an insight into local culture. Typical volunteer jobs include working on conservation projects, participating in research programs, or helping out at animal-welfare centres. In some cases volunteers are paid a living allowance; sometimes they work for their keep; and sometimes volunteers are required to pay for the experience, typically from about US$300 per week.

Lonely Planet's *The Big Trip* provides advice and practical information on volunteering and working abroad.

Other resources:

World Wide Opportunities on Organic Farms (WWOOF; www.wwoof.org) International organisation that puts volunteers in contact with organic farms across the world. In exchange for your labour, you'll receive free lodging and food.

Go Abroad (www.goabroad. com) Huge site with information on hundreds of jobs and volunteer opportunities.

Women Travellers

It's sad to report, but machismo is alive and well in Mediterranean Europe, a region in which gender roles are still largely based on age-old social norms. But even if attitudes are not always very enlightened, a deep sense of hospitality runs through many Mediterranean societies, and travellers (of both sexes) are usually welcomed with warmth and genuine kindness. That said, women travellers continue to face more challenging situations than men do, most often in the form of unwanted harassment. Other things to bear in mind:

» Staring is much more overt in Mediterranean countries than in the more reticent northern parts of Europe, and although it is almost always harmless, it can become annoying.

» If you find yourself being pestered by local men and

ignoring them isn't working, tell them you're waiting for your husband (marriage is highly respected in the area) and walk away. If they continue, call the police.

» Gropers, particularly on crowded public transport, can also be a problem. If you do feel someone start to touch you inappropriately, make a fuss – molesters are no more accepted in Mediterranean Europe than they are anywhere else.

» In Muslim countries, where women's roles are clearly defined and unmarried men have little contact with women outside of their family unit, women travelling alone or with other women will attract attention. This is rarely dangerous, but you'll need to exercise common sense. Dress conservatively, avoid eye contact and, if possible, don't walk alone at night.

» Security for solo travellers is mainly a matter of common sense – watch your possessions, don't go wandering down dark alleys at night and be wary of overly friendly people you've just met.

Sources of information and inspiration include the following:

Wanderlust & Lipstick (www.wanderlustandlipstick.com) Comprehensive site with loads of useful info.

Also sells *The Essential Guide for Women Travelling Solo*, a good guide for nervous first-timers.

Journeywoman (www.journeywoman.com) An online women's travel magazine full of tips, anecdotes and recommendations.

Lonely Planet (www.lonelyplanet.com) Exchange thoughts and ideas on the Women Travellers branch of the Thorn Tree travel forum.

Women Travel Tips (www.womentraveltips.com) US travel expert Marybeth Bond shares her experiences and provides plenty of on-the-road tips.

Transport

GETTING THERE & AWAY

Getting to Mediterranean Europe is easy. Most of the world's major airlines serve the region and there are plenty of budget airlines operating within Europe. Road and rail networks connect with countries in northern and eastern Europe, while ferries sail into the region from the UK and North Africa.

Flights, cars and tours can be booked online at lonelyplanet.com.

Entering the Region

There are no special entry requirements for EU citizens and nationals of Australia, Canada, New Zealand and the USA. For most places a valid passport is all you need for a stay of up to 90 days. Some nationalities, including South Africans, require visas for Schengen countries. For more on visas, see p862.

Passport

Exact passport requirements vary from country to country, even within the EU, but as a rule non-EU nationals require a passport valid for three to six months after their period of stay. EU citizens travelling to Albania, Bosnia and Hercegovina (BiH) and Turkey are also subject to minimum passport validity requirements.

As of June 2012, all children are required to have their own passport.

Air

It's not difficult to find a flight to the Med. Most major airlines fly into the region, and there are currently more than 30 low-cost carriers operating between hundreds of European airports. In summer, charter flights add to the congestion.

» Expect to pay high-season prices between June and August – the two months either side of this period are the shoulder seasons. Low season is November to March.

» Many no-frills airlines use secondary provincial airports.

Airports & Airlines

The region's main international airports serve flights to/from destinations in Europe, Africa, North and South America, the Middle East and Asia.

» Athens **Eleftherios Venizelos International** (www.aia.gr)

» Barcelona **El Prat** (☑902 404704; www.aena.es)

» İstanbul **Atatürk International** (www.ataturkairport.com)

» Lisbon **Lisboa** (www.ana.pt)

» Madrid **Barajas** (www.aena.es)

» Milan **Malpensa** (www.milanomalpensa1.eu)

» Paris **Orly** (www.aeroportsdeparis.fr)

» Paris **Roissy Charles de Gaulle** (www.aeroportsdeparis.fr)

» Rome **Leonardo da Vinci** (Fiumicino; www.adr.it)

CLIMATE CHANGE & TRAVEL

Every form of transport that relies on carbon-based fuel generates CO_2, the main cause of human-induced climate change. Modern travel is dependent on aeroplanes, which might use less fuel per kilometre per person than most cars but travel much greater distances. The altitude at which aircraft emit gases (including CO_2) and particles also contributes to their climate change impact. Many websites offer 'carbon calculators' that allow people to estimate the carbon emissions generated by their journey and, for those who wish to do so, to offset the impact of the greenhouse gases emitted with contributions to portfolios of climate-friendly initiatives throughout the world. Lonely Planet offsets the carbon footprint of all staff and author travel.

TICKET TIPS

For advice on booking tickets, check out the article *How to Buy Cheap Flights Online* (www.stanfords.co.uk/blog/post/How-to-Buy-Cheap-Flights-Online.aspx), which has some excellent tips.

Some considerations:

» Buy early. If booking for high season (June to August) try to sort out your ticket by about March.

» Travelling midweek generally costs less. Friday and Sunday are the most expensive days to travel.

» Get an early flight – you'll lose sleep but save bucks.

» Flights to major hubs tend to be cheaper. If you're heading to Eastern Europe consider taking a long-haul flight to a major Western European airport and then picking up an onward flight with a European low-cost carrier.

» When working out the cost of your ticket, factor in all price extras, such as fuel surcharges, seat selection, luggage fees etc.

» Consider an open-jaw return when you fly into one city and exit from another. They are usually more expensive than simple returns but might save you in the long run, particularly if travelling across the region. If, for example, you plan to fly into Rome and head across to Madrid, it might cost less to fly out of Madrid on an open-jaw ticket than to retrace your footsteps to Rome and fly out on a standard return ticket.

The following national airports operate mainly European flights:

» Ljubljana **Jože Pučnik** (www.lju-airport.si)

» Podgorica **Podgorica** (www.montenegroairports.com)

» Sarajevo **Sarajevo International** (www.sarajevo-airport.ba)

» Tirana **Nënë Tereza International** (www.tirana-airport.com.al)

» Zagreb **Zagreb** (www.zagreb-airport.hr)

The flag carriers for the countries covered in this book:

» Bosnia and Hercegovina **BH Airlines** (www.bhairlines.ba)

» Croatia **Croatia Airlines** (www.croatiaairlines.hr)

» France **Air France** (www.airfrance.com)

» Italy **Alitalia** (www.alitalia.com)

» Montenegro **Montenegro Airlines** (www.montenegroairlines.com)

» Portugal **TAP Portugal** (www.flytap.com)

» Slovenia **Adria Airways** (www.adria.si)

» Spain **Iberia** (www.iberia.com)

» Turkey **Turkish Airlines** (www.thy.com)

Tickets

Finding tickets to Mediterranean Europe isn't difficult, but to get the best deal you'll need to shop around.

» Check airline websites and flight-comparison sites. Lonely Planet has a flight search engine at www.lonelyplanet.com/bookings/flights.do.

» Note that some low-cost airlines, including Ryanair, only accept bookings made on their own website.

» If you're planning a complex itinerary talk to a travel agent, who can find you the best fares, advise on connections and sell travel insurance.

» Full-time students and people aged under 26 (under 30 in some countries) have access to discounted fares. You'll have to show a document proving your date of birth, such as a valid International Student Identity Card (ISIC) or an International Youth Travel Card (IYTC) when buying your ticket.

Land

There are plenty of options for getting to Mediterranean Europe by car, bus or train. In most Western European countries, buses are generally cheaper than trains, which tend to be more comfortable and more frequent. However, in the Balkan countries, buses are the main form of long-distance travel, serving more destinations than the limited train networks.

Bicycle

Transporting your bike to the region poses no great problems.

» Different airlines have different rules – some insist that you pack your bike in a bike bag; others require you to remove the pedals and deflate the tyres. Some sell specially designed bike boxes. Remember that the bike's weight will be included in your luggage allowance.

» Bikes can generally be carried on slower trains, subject to a small supplementary fee. On fast trains they might need to be sent as registered luggage and will probably end up on a different train from the one you take.

» In the UK, **European Bike Express** (☏ 01430 422 111; www.bike-express.co.uk) is a coach service on which cyclists can travel with their bikes. It runs in the summer from Stokesley in northeast England to France and northern Spain, with pick-up and drop-off points en route.

Standard return fares range from UK£239 to UK£249 (less if you pay online); single fares cost UK£144. Members of the **Cyclists' Touring Club** (CTC; 🖉0844 736 8450; www.ctc.org.uk; membership adult/senior/junior UK£41/25/16) qualify for a discount of UK£10 on return fares. The CTC can also offer advice and organise tours.

» If travelling from Britain to France by Eurostar (🖉in France 08 92 35 35 39, in the UK 08432 186 186; www.eurostar. com) you can take a bike on as part of your luggage only if it's in a bike bag. Otherwise it must go as registered baggage, for which there's a UK£30 fee.

» **Eurotunnel** (🖉in France 08 10 63 03 04, in the UK 08443 35 35 35; www.eurotunnel.com) runs two daily cycle services to the continent. These must be booked 24 hours in advance. The standard fare is UK£16 one way per bike.

Border Crossings

Border crossings into the region are pretty stress-free.

» If entering France, Greece, Italy, Portugal, Slovenia or Spain from another Schengen country, there are officially no border controls. However, spot checks are not unusual, particularly on trains, and individual countries are within their rights to reinstate controls. As a precaution, always have your passport or ID card ready to show when crossing a national border.

» Land crossings into the eastern Mediterranean countries are fairly straightforward, although delays are not uncommon between Albania and Greece, particularly in summer.

» Border crossings into Turkey often involve a one- to three-hour delay. Passengers are usually required to get off the bus or train for checks of paperwork and baggage. Note that if you require a visa, you will need to buy it at the border crossing. Some

crossings don't have ATMs or exchange facilities so ensure you have the money on hand.

Bus

Bus links between Mediterranean Europe and the rest of Continental Europe are comprehensive.

Eurolines (www.eurolines. com) is a consortium of coach companies that operates across Europe. You can book tickets through the website, which also has timetable information and details of ticket offices in each country.

At some border crossings you might be required to get off the bus to have your documents and bags checked.

Car & Motorcycle

Driving to the region from northern Europe is a definite possibility – the road network is good, border controls are simple and there are no special hazards. If you have to traverse the Alps, note that while the main mountain passes remain open year-round, some minor ones close over winter.

When driving make sure you have the following:

» a valid driving licence, and, if necessary, an International Driving Permit (IDP)

» vehicle-registration documents

» insurance certificate

» passport or ID card

» any compulsory equipment (such as snow chains, a warning triangle etc)

THE CHANNEL TUNNEL
To take your car through the Channel Tunnel, **Eurotunnel Le Shuttle** (🖉in France 08 10 63 03 04, in the UK 08443 35 35 35; www.eurotunnel.com) operates between Folkestone and Calais. Trains run 24 hours, every day, with up to three departures an hour at peak times.

» To save money, book in advance, although it is possible to drive into the terminal, buy a ticket and get on the next train.

» Fares for a car and passengers start at UK£30. As a rule, the more expensive tickets allow for a longer duration and increased flexibility. Check the website for details.

» Both terminals are directly linked to motorways (the M20 in the UK and the A16 in France) and both have petrol stations.

Train

Train is a viable option for getting to Mediterranean Europe, particularly if travelling from the UK. The high-speed **Eurostar** (🖉in France 08 92 35 35 39, in the UK 08432 186 186; www.eurostar.com) passenger service runs from London to Paris, where you can pick up trains to destinations across Europe.

Routes Direct trains from London's St Pancras International Station, Ebbsfleet and Ashford in the UK to Paris' Gare du Nord station, Lille, Calais and Avignon. There are also services to Paris Disneyland, several

EUROPEAN RAIL RESOURCES

German Deutsch Bahn (www.bahn.de) German Railway's excellent website with schedules for European trains.

The Man in Seat 61 (www.seat61.com) Encyclopedic site with information on how to get to Europe by train.

Thomas Cook European Timetable (www.european-railtimetable.co.uk) Order timetables of train, bus and ferry services; updated monthly.

French Alpine ski resorts, and Brussels.

Journey Times Approximately one hour to Calais, 1½ hours to Lille, 2¼ hours to Paris, and 6¼ hours to Avignon.

Fares There are 10 ticket types (adult/child/youth/senior, fully-/semi-/nonflexible etc), with a corresponding range of fares and restrictions. The cheapest are generally nonrefundable returns with restrictions on departure times and length of stay. As a rough guide, return fares to Paris start at UK£69. Always check the website for special deals.

Tickets Tickets are available direct from Eurostar, from travel agencies, at St Pancras, Ebbsfleet and Ashford, from other UK mainline stations, and from **Rail Europe** (⏴in the UK 0844 848 4064, in the USA 1-800-622-8600; www.raileurope.co.uk), which also sells other European rail tickets.

You can also get trains to the region from central and eastern Asia. Allow at least eight days.

Sea

The Mediterranean has an extensive ferry network. For timetables, routes, ports and prices, check out **AFerry** (www.aferry.com).

From North Africa

There are regular ferries from Morocco and Algeria to Spain and France, and from Tunisia to Italy and France.

The main ports are Tangier (Morocco), Algiers (Algeria) and Tunis (Tunisia). Note that ferries on popular routes are often filled to capacity in summer, so book well in advance if you're taking a vehicle across.

Main ferry companies operating to/from North Africa:

Acciona Trasmediterránea (⏴in Spain 902 45 46 45; www.trasmediterranea.es)

Tangier and Ceuta to Algeciras; Melilla and Nador to Almería; Melilla to Málaga. There are also services from Ghazaouet and Oran (both in Algeria) to Almería.

SNCM (⏴in France 3260; www.sncm.fr) Services from Tunisia (Tunis) and Algeria (Algiers, Oran, Béjaia and Annaba) to France (Marseille). Also from Tunis to Italy (Genoa).

From the UK

There are several UK–France ferry routes, including the following:

» Dover–Calais (1¼ to 1½ hours)
» Newhaven–Dieppe (four hours)
» Poole–Cherbourg (4½ to 6½ hours)
» Portsmouth–Cherbourg (5½ hours)

Fares depend on the usual mix of factors – the time of day/year, the flexibility of the ticket and, if you're driving, the length of your vehicle. Vehicle tickets include the driver and often up to five passengers free. There are also plenty of reductions on off-peak crossings and advance-purchase tickets. On most routes there is generally little price advantage in buying a return ticket rather than two singles. To compare fares check out **Ferry Savers** (www.ferrysavers.com).

Rail pass-holders are entitled to discounts or free travel on some lines, and most ferry companies give discounts to drivers with disabilities.

Major ferry companies include the following:

Brittany Ferries (⏴0871 244 0744; www.brittany-ferries.com) From Portsmouth to Caen, Cherbourg and St Malo (all France), Bilbao and Santander (Spain); from Poole to Cherbourg; and from Plymouth to Roscoff (France) and Santander.

Condor Ferries (⏴0845 609 1024; www.condorferries.

co.uk) From Portsmouth to Cherbourg; from Poole to St Malo; and from Weymouth to St Malo.

LD Lines (⏴0844 576 8836; www.ldlines.co.uk) From Dover to Calais (France); from Newhaven to Dieppe (France); and from Portsmouth to Le Havre (France).

My Ferry Link (⏴in France 08 11 65 47 65, in the UK 0844 248 2100; www.myferrylink.com) From Dover to Calais.

Norfolk Line (⏴0871 574 7235; www.norfolkline.com) From Dover to Calais and Dunkirk (France).

P&O Ferries (⏴0871 664 5645; www.poferries.com) From Dover to Calais.

From the USA

Sailing the Atlantic is slow (typically between seven and 13 days) and not cheap. You can either sign up for passage on a cruise ship or hop on a freighter as a paying passenger. Freighters are cheaper, more frequent and offer more routes.

» Freighters usually carry up to 12 passengers (more than 12 would require a doctor to be on board).
» Bank on between €80 and €125 per day plus port fees and insurance.
» Vehicles can often be included for an additional fee.
» If you're not travelling with a car, you'll need to organise transport from the port to the centre of town – ask the port agent (who'll be on board when the vessel docks) to arrange a taxi for you.
» You'll need to be flexible as shipping schedules can change at short notice due to weather conditions, delays in cargo loading, port congestion etc.
» Take seasick pills, as many cargo ships are not fitted with stabilisers.
» Useful resources include **Strand Travel** (⏴in the UK 020 7802 2136; www.strandtravel.co.uk), **A la Carte Freighter Travel** (www.freighter-travel.com) and **Sea**

Travel Ltd (☐in the UK 0203 371 9484; www.seatravelltd.co.uk).

GETTING AROUND

Getting around Mediterranean Europe poses no great difficulties. There's a comprehensive transport network, and relations between countries are generally good. Ensure that you have a valid passport and check any visa requirements before travelling.

Air

Flying around Mediterranean Europe is a good option. Alongside the main established carriers, there are more than 30 budget airlines serving hundreds of cities across Europe. You can usually pick up a reasonably priced flight, especially if you're prepared to fly very early in the morning or late at night.

Some considerations:

» Low-cost carriers rarely provide much in the way of comfort or service. Inflight food, checked-in baggage, airport check-in and priority boarding all incur extra charges.

» When booking online, always ensure that you untick any add-on options you don't want. The default page settings of many airline websites have them automatically ticked.

» Check baggage-weight allowances – they are often less than on the established airlines and they are enforced.

» Many budget carriers use provincial airports that might be some way from your destination city. For example, Ryanair's Venice flights actually land at Treviso, which is some 30km from the lagoon city. If you're arriving late at night, make sure you've checked transport options into town, otherwise you could end up

forking out for an expensive taxi ride.

Airlines

Europe's no-frills carriers are the obvious first port of call when looking for bargain flights, but don't write off the bigger established airlines. If travelling with a lot of luggage at peak holiday periods, there's often very little difference between the price of a 'low-cost' ticket, complete with extra charges for checked-in luggage, online booking etc, and a ticket from an established airline.

Listed here are the main budget airlines operating in the region:

Air Berlin (www.airberlin.com)
Air One (www.flyairone.com)
bmibaby (www.bmibaby.com)
easyJet (www.easyjet.com)
germanwings (www.germanwings.com)
Jet2.com (www.jet2.com)
Pegasus Airlines (www.flypgs.com)
Ryanair (www.ryanair.com)
Tuifly (www.tuifly.com)
Vueling (www.vueling.com)
Wizz Air (http://wizzair.com)

Air Passes

If you're planning to fly around the region and prefer to sort out flights before you leave, consider a European air pass. These are generally only available to non-Europeans, who must purchase them in conjunction with a long-haul international return ticket. Typically, they involve the purchase of flight coupons (usually around US$60 to US$205 each) for travel between a number of European destinations.

Oneworld Visit Europe Pass (www.oneworld.com) Available to non-Europeans who buy an intercontinental ticket with a Oneworld member airline. There's a minimum of two coupons, although you must only confirm the first flight when you buy. Valid on routes between 219 destinations in 52 countries.

SkyTeam Go Europe (www.skyteam.com) The pass is available with the purchase of an intercontinental flight with any of SkyTeam's 18 member carriers. Flight coupons are valid for flights in 44 countries. You must buy a minimum of three flight coupons and a maximum of 16. Advance booking is only required for the first European flight.

Star Alliance European Airpass (www.staralliance.com) Non-European residents who buy a round-trip international ticket with a Star Alliance operator can buy a minimum of three and a maximum of 10 coupons for one-way flights between 40 European countries. Coupons, the first of which you must reserve when you buy the pass, are valid for three months.

Bicycle

Although cycling is a popular sport in France, Spain and Italy, as a means of everyday transport it is not common in Mediterranean Europe. Outside certain areas there are few dedicated cycle lanes, and drivers tend to regard cyclists as an oddity. Poor road conditions, particularly in the Eastern European countries, and mountainous terrain provide further obstacles.

» There are no special road rules for cyclists, although it's advisable to carry a helmet, lights and a basic repair kit (containing spare brake and gear cables, spanners, Allen keys, spare spokes and some strong adhesive tape).

» Take a good lock and make sure you use it when you leave your bike unattended.

» Bike hire is available throughout the region – tourist offices can usually direct you to rental outlets.

» There are plenty of shops selling new and second-hand bikes, although you'll need a specialist outlet for a touring bike. European prices are quite high; expect to pay from €100 for a new bike.

Boat

The Mediterranean's modern ferry network is comprehensive, covering all corners of the region. There are routes between Spain and France; between Italy, Spain, Greece, Croatia and Turkey; and between the hundreds of Mediterranean islands. See the relevant country sections for further details. Popular routes get very busy in summer, so try to book ahead.

The main ferry operators in the region:

Acciona Trasmediter-ránea (☑in Spain 902 45 46 45; www.trasmediterranea.es) Spanish company with domestic services from Barcelona to Ibiza, Maó and Palma de Mallorca; from Valencia to Palma de Mallorca, Maó and Ibiza.

Agoudimos (☑in Greece 210 414 1300, in Italy 0831 56 03 81; www.agoudimos-lines.com) Services from Brindisi (Italy) to Igoumenitsa and Corfu (both Greece); from Brindisi to Vlora (Albania).

Corsica Ferries (☑in Italy 199 400 500; www.corsica-ferries.it) Services from Bastia (Corsica) to Toulon and Nice (both France), and to Savona and Livorno (both Italy); from Île Rousse (Corsica) to Toulon, Nice and Savona; from Ajaccio (Corsica) to Toulon and Nice; from Golfo Aranci (Sardinia) to Livorno.

Grandi Navi Veloci (☑in Italy 010 209 45 91; www.gnv.it) Services from Genoa (Italy) to Barcelona and Palermo (Sicily); from Civitavecchia (Italy) to Palermo; from Naples (Italy) to Palermo.

Grimaldi Lines (☑in Italy 081 496 444, in Spain 902 53 13 33; www.grimaldi-lines.com) Services from Barcelona to Porto Torres (Sardinia), Civitavecchia and Livorno; from Civitavecchia to Trapani

(Sicily); from Salerno (Italy) to Palermo; from Brindisi (Italy) to Corfu, Igoumenitsa and Patra (Greece).

Endeavor Lines (☑in Greece 210 940 5222, in Italy 0831 57 16 04; www.endeavor-lines.com) Services from Brindisi to Igoumenitsa, Patra, Corfu and Kefallonia (Greece).

Jadrolinija (☑in Croatia 051-666 111; www.jadrolinija.hr) Services from Ancona (Italy) to Split (Croatia); from Bari (Italy) to Dubrovnik (Croatia).

Minoan Lines (☑in Greece 210 414 5700; www.minoan.gr) Ferries from Ancona to Igoumenitsa and Patra.

SNAV (☑in Italy 081 428 55 55; www.snav.it) Italian company with services from Ancona to Split; from Naples to Palermo and the Aeolian Islands (Sicily); from Civitavecchia to Palermo; from Genoa to Palermo, Olbia and Porto Torres.

Superfast Ferries (www.superfast.com) Services from Ancona to Igoumenitsa and Patra; from Bari to Igoumenitsa, Patra and Corfu.

Tirrenia (☑in Italy 892 123; www.tirrenia.it) Italian company with domestic services from Genoa to Arbatax, Porto Torres and Olbia (all Sardinia); from Civitavecchia to Olbia, Arbatax and Cagliari (Sardinia); from Naples to Palermo and Cagliari; from Cagliari to Palermo.

Bus

Travelling by bus is generally the cheapest way of getting around the region, although it's neither comfortable nor particularly quick. In some of the eastern countries, including BiH, Croatia and Montenegro, the rail networks are limited and buses tend to be quicker (and more expensive) than trains. Buses also cover more routes, especially away from the main coastal areas. In mountainous countries (eg Albania and Greece)

they are sometimes the only option.

» **Eurolines** (www.eurolines.com) is a network of 32 European coach operators serving hundreds of destinations throughout Europe.

» London-based **Busabout** (☑in the UK 08450 267 514; www.busabout.com) runs bus tours around Europe, stopping off at major cities in Italy, France, Spain and other countries. Note, however, that you don't simply buy a ticket from A to B; rather, you pay for travel on a specified route, allowing you to hop off at any scheduled stop, then resume with a later bus. Busabout buses are often oversubscribed, so book each sector to avoid being stranded. Departures are every two days from May to October.

Bus Passes

Bus passes make sense if you want to cover a lot of ground as cheaply as possible. However, they're not always as extensive or as flexible as rail passes, and to get your money's worth you will need to spend a lot of time crammed into a bus seat.

Eurolines Pass (www.eurolines-pass.com) covers 51 European cities. Most of the trips must be international, although a few internal journeys are possible between major cities. There are two passes:

» 15 days (low/high season adult €210/310, under 26 €180/295)

» 30 days (low/high season adult €315/460, under 26 €245/380)

Busabout (☑in the UK 08450 267 514; www.busabout.com) runs hop-on hop-off circuits (loops) around Europe. Discounts are available for early booking. Passes come in many forms:

» A single loop costs per adult/student €515/495

» A double loop costs per adult/student €879/849

» A flexitrip pass allows you to choose where you want to go and buy tickets (flexistops) for those destinations. It's valid for the entire operating season (May to October) and costs from €449/435 per adult/student for six flexistops

» One-way route tickets start at €619/599 per adult/student

Costs & Reservations

Booking a seat in advance is not usually obligatory, but if you already know when you want to travel it makes sense to do so. In summer it is always advisable to book if you want to travel popular routes.

As a rough guide, a one-way bus ticket from Paris to Rome costs €86, and from Madrid to Lisbon €38.

Car & Motorcycle

Travelling around the region by car or motorbike gives you increased flexibility and allows you to venture off the beaten path. On the downside you'll often have to deal with congestion, urban one-way systems, traffic-free zones and nonexistent city parking. In winter, ice and fog can prove hazardous, particularly in mountainous areas such as Albania and BiH, where roads are badly signposted and often in poor condition.

Mediterranean Europe is well suited to motorcycle touring, as it has an active motorcycling scene and plenty of panoramic roads. On ferries, motorcyclists can sometimes be squeezed in without a reservation, although booking ahead is advisable in peak travelling periods. Take note of local customs about parking on pavements.

Some useful motoring resources include the following:

AA (www.theaa.com) The British Automobile Association's site has a comprehensive travel section covering all aspects of driving in Europe.

British Motorcyclists Federation (www.bmf.co.uk) Click on the 'Touring' link for information on all aspects of European touring, including specialist tour operators, recommended maps and updated European fuel prices.

Idea Merge (www.ideamerge.com/motoeuropa) An extensive US guide to motoring in Europe, with information on renting, leasing and purchasing, and tonnes of useful practical advice.

RAC (www.rac.co.uk) Has up-to-date country-by-country information, a route planner and a useful pretrip checklist.

Bringing Your Own Vehicle

Bringing your own vehicle into the region is fairly straightforward if you're coming from elsewhere in mainland Europe. In addition to your vehicle registration document you'll need a valid driving licence and proof of third-party (liability) insurance.

Shipping a vehicle from the US or Canada is time-consuming and costs approximately US$750 to US$2000 one-way, depending on the size of the car. For further information consult **Idea Merge** (www.ideamerge.com/motoeuropa).

» Some countries require you to carry certain pieces of equipment. For example, you'll need a first-aid kit in Croatia, Greece and Slovenia; a warning triangle in Greece, Italy, Portugal and Slovenia; a fire extinguisher in Greece and Turkey; and a set of spare headlight bulbs in Croatia and Spain.

» Note that there's sometimes a maximum time limit (typically six or 12 months) you can keep your car in a foreign country.

» For more information contact the RAC or AA in the UK,

or the **AAA** (www.aaa.com) in the USA.

Driving Licence

» An EU driving licence is valid for driving throughout Europe.

» If you've got an old-style, green UK licence or a licence issued by a non-EU country you'll need an International Driving Permit (IDP).

» To get an IDP, apply to your national automobile association – you'll need a passport photo and your home driving licence. They cost about US$15 or UK£10 and are valid for 12 months.

» When driving in Europe, always carry your home licence with the IDP, as the IDP is not valid on its own.

Fuel & Spare Parts

» Fuel prices vary from country to country, but are almost always more expensive than in the US or Australia.

» Fuel is sold by the litre (one US gallon is 3.8L). It comes as either unleaded petrol or diesel. Diesel is cheaper than unleaded petrol.

» As a rough guide, reckon on anything from €2/1.80 for unleaded petrol/diesel in Turkey and €1.40/1.30 in Croatia. Get updated prices at www.fuel-prices-europe.info.

» Prices tend to be higher at motorway service stations and lowest at supermarket petrol stations.

» You should have no great problems getting spare parts if needed.

Hire

AGENCIES

Car-hire agencies are widespread across the region. **Avis** (www.avis.com), **Budget** (www.budget.com), **Europcar** (www.europcar.com) and **Hertz** (www.hertz.com) have offices throughout the Med, and there are any number of local firms.

Regulations vary but there's often a minimum hire age (typically 21 or 23) and sometimes a maximum age (usually about 65 or 70).

The hire company might also insist that you've held your licence for at least a year. You'll almost certainly need a credit card.

Motorcycle and moped hire is common in Italy, Spain, Greece and the south of France. See the Getting Around section in individual countries for further details.

COSTS

» International agencies are generally more expensive, but they guarantee reliable service and a good standard of vehicle. You'll also usually have the option of returning the car to a different outlet at the end of the rental period.

» If you know in advance that you want a car, you'll get a better deal if you arrange it at home. Fly-drive packages and other programs are also worth considering.

» Note that very few cars in Mediterranean Europe have automatic transmission. To hire one order it in advance and expect to pay more.

» As an approximate guide, reckon on about €30 (from €40 in some places) per day for a small car, and between €200 and €280 per week. Check individual sections for country-specific prices.

» A useful online resource is www.traveljungle.co.uk, which finds the best rates available for your destination.

Brokers, such as those listed below, can also cut costs.

Autos Abroad (☑in the UK 0844 826 6536; www.autos abroad.com)

Holiday Autos (☑in Australia 1300 55 45 07, in the UK 0800 392 9288, in the USA 1-866-392-9288; www.holidayautos.com)

Kemwel Holiday Autos (☑in the USA 1-877-820-0668; www.kemwel.com)

LEASING

For longer stays, leasing can work out cheaper.

Renault Eurodrive (www. renault-eurodrive.com) This scheme provides new cars

for non-EU residents for a period of between 17 and 170 days. Under this arrangement, a Renault Clio Campus for four weeks in France costs about US$1375, including comprehensive insurance and roadside assistance.

Kemwel Holiday Autos (☑in the USA 1-877-820-0668; www.kemwel.com) In the US; arranges similar deals to Renault Eurodrive.

Check out www.ideamerge. com for further information on leasing in Europe.

RENTAL AGREEMENTS

» Make sure that you understand what's included in your rental agreement (collision waiver, unlimited mileage etc).

» Most agreements provide basic insurance that you can supplement by purchasing additional coverage. This supplemental insurance is often expensive if bought directly from the hire agency. As an alternative, check if your home car insurance covers foreign hire or if your credit-card company offers insurance.

» If you're going to be crossing national borders, make sure your insurance policy is valid in all the countries you plan to visit.

RAIL-&-DRIVE PASSES

You can combine train and car travel with a rail-and-drive pass.

Rail Europe (☑in the UK 0844 848 4064, in the USA 1-800-622-8600; www. raileurope.co.uk) sells several passes, including the Eurail Select Pass 'n' Drive, which covers 1st-class train travel and Hertz car hire. Available to non-European residents, it allows for five, six or eight days of rail travel in three bordering countries plus two days of car hire. Prices for a five-day package start at US$473 for two adults.

Insurance

» To drive in Mediterranean Europe you'll need third-party

(liability) insurance – most UK motor-insurance policies automatically provide this for EU countries.

» In Albania, BiH and Turkey you'll also need an International Insurance Certificate, commonly called a Green Card. This is a certificate attesting that your insurance policy meets the minimum legal requirements of the country you're visiting. When you get this, check with your insurance company that it covers all of the countries you intend to visit, and if you're driving in Turkey, make sure that it covers the European and Asian parts of the country.

» Consider taking out a European motoring assistance policy to cover roadside assistance and emergency repair. In the UK, both the AA and the RAC offer such services.

» Non-Europeans might find it cheaper to arrange international coverage with their national motoring organisation. Also ask about the services (eg free breakdown assistance) offered by European motoring organisations affiliated with your home organisation.

» In the event of an accident a useful document to have is a European Accident Statement form, which allows each party to record identical information for insurance purposes. Get it from your insurance company or download a copy from www. cartraveldocs.com.

Purchase

Buying a car in Mediterranean Europe is generally not worth the hassle. In EU countries you can only buy a car if you are a legal resident of the country or have a local tax registration number. For further information see www. ideamerge.com/motoeuropa/index.html.

Paperwork can be tricky wherever you buy, and many countries have compulsory roadworthy checks on older vehicles.

Road Conditions

» Road conditions vary enormously across the region. At best, you'll find well-maintained four- or six-lane dual carriageways or highways. At worst, you'll be driving on rough, badly sign-posted single-lane tracks.

» You'll encounter some pretty terrible roads in Albania and BiH, although conditions are improving all the time.

» Tolls are charged on motorways (autoroutes, autostrade etc) in many Mediterranean countries, including Croatia, France, Greece, Italy, Portugal, Slovenia, Spain and Turkey. You can generally pay by cash or credit card, and in some cases you can avoid the queues altogether by buying a prepaid card. See individual sections for details.

Road Rules

The AA and RAC can supply members with country-by-country information on road rules and conditions.

Some universal rules and considerations:

» Drive on the right.

» In European cars the steering wheel is on the left. If you're bringing over a UK or Irish right-hand-drive vehicle you should adjust its headlights (which are angled differently to those in Mediterranean Europe) to avoid blinding oncoming traffic at night.

» Some countries require you to have your headlights on even when driving during the day.

» Unless otherwise indicated, always give way to cars entering a junction from the left.

» Speed limits vary from country to country. You may be surprised at the apparent disregard for speed limits (and traffic regulations in general) in some places, but as a visitor it's always best to be cautious.

» Random police checks are common in some countries

and many driving infringements are subject to on-the-spot fines. If you're clobbered with a fine, always ask for a receipt.

» Drink-driving laws are strict, with the blood-alcohol concentration (BAC) limit generally between 0.05% and 0.08%.

» It's obligatory to wear a helmet on motorcycles, scooters and mopeds everywhere in Mediterranean Europe. It's also recommended that motorcyclists use their headlights during the day.

Hitching

Hitching is more common in northern Europe than in Mediterranean countries, and although it is possible, you'll need to be patient. It's never entirely safe, however, and we don't recommend it. If you do decide to go for it, there are a few simple steps you can take to minimise the risks:

» Travel in pairs – ideally with a man if you're a woman. A woman hitching on her own is taking a big risk.

» Let someone know where you're going and when you'll be on the road. If possible, carry a mobile phone.

» When a driver stops, ask where they're going before getting in. This gives you time to size up the driver and, if you don't like the look of them, to politely decline the ride.

» Don't let the driver put your backpack in the boot; if possible, keep it with you in the car.

» Don't try to hitch from city centres – take public transport to suburban exit routes.

» Hitching is often illegal on motorways, so stand on the slip roads or approach drivers at petrol stations and truck stops.

» Look presentable and cheerful, and make a cardboard sign indicating the road you want to take or your

destination. A sign will also mean you're less likely to use the wrong gesture – the thumbs-up sign, for example, means 'up yours' in Sardinia.

» Never hitch where traffic passes too quickly or where drivers can't stop without causing an obstruction.

» Drivers will want to check you out before stopping, so don't wear sunglasses.

» If your itinerary includes a ferry crossing, try to score a ride before the ferry rather than after, as vehicle tickets sometimes include all passengers free of charge.

» It is sometimes possible to arrange a lift in advance: scan student noticeboards in colleges, or check out the French-language car-sharing website **Allostop Provoya** (www.allostop.net).

Other online resources:
BUG (www.bugeurope.com) Has a page dedicated to hitching in Europe.
Digihitch (www.digihitch.com) A comprehensive site with hitchers' forums, links and country-specific information.

Local Transport

The region's local transport network is comprehensive and mostly pretty efficient. Services may be irregular in remote rural regions, but wait long enough and a bus will pass.

In many places you have to buy your ticket before you get on the bus/boat/train and then validate it once on board (if the driver hasn't already checked it). It's often tempting not to do this – many locals don't appear to – but if you're caught with an unvalidated ticket you risk a fine.

If you're going to use public transport frequently, check out the daily, weekly and monthly passes available.

Boat

In some parts of the region, jumping on a ferry is as common as taking a bus. In

Venice, *vaporetti* (small passenger ferries) ply the city's canals, ferrying tourists and locals alike. In Istanbul ferries are the cheapest way of getting around the city.

Bus

City buses usually require you to buy your ticket in advance from a kiosk or machine, and then validate it upon boarding. See the country sections and individual cities for more details on local bus routes.

Metro

All of the region's major capitals (Athens, Paris, Madrid and Rome) have metro systems, as do several other large cities (Milan, Barcelona and İstanbul). While it can often be quicker to travel underground, it can get unpleasantly hot and crowded, especially in summer rush hours.

Taxi

» Taxis are generally metered and rates are uniformly high. There can also be additional charges depending on the pick-up location or time of day, or for luggage or extra passengers.

» As a rule, always insist on a metered fare rather than an agreed price. Set fares to airports are an exception to this general rule of thumb.

» To catch a cab you'll usually have to phone for one or queue at a taxi rank, which are often found outside train stations and big hotels.

Tours

Tours exist for all ages, interests and budgets. Specialist operators offer everything from tours of the region's gardens to island-hopping cruises, walking holidays and adventure-sports packages.

Many national tourist offices organise trips ranging from one-hour city tours to excursions taking several days. While they often work out more expensive than a self-organised tour, they are sometimes worth it if you're pressed for time. A short city tour will give you a quick overview of the place and can be a good way to begin your visit.

Established tour operators include the following:

Austin-Lehman Adventures (☑in the USA 1-800-577-1540; www.austinlehman.com) A US tour operator specialising in adventure sports, walking and cycling holidays. Has packages in Croatia, France, Greece, Italy, Slovenia, Spain and Turkey.

Busabout (☑in the UK 08450 267 514; www.busabout.com) Best known for its pan-European bus tours, London-based Busabout also offers tours to Italy, Turkey, Spain and Portugal, the Balkans, island-hopping trips to Greece and Croatia, and packages to big European festivals such as Las Fallas in Valencia, Spain, and Sanfermines in Pamplona, Spain.

Contiki (www.contiki.com) Contiki runs a range of European tours for 18- to 35-year-olds, including city breaks, camping trips, foodie itineraries and island-hopping journeys.

Ramblers Holidays (☑in the UK 017 0733 11 33; www.ramblersholidays.co.uk) A British-based outfit that offers hiking holidays, ski packages, cooking trips and much more.

Saga Holidays (☑in the UK 0800 096 0074; www.saga.co.uk) Serving people aged over 50, Saga sells everything from travel insurance to bus tours, river cruises and special-interest holidays.

Top Deck (☑in the UK 0208 987 3300; www.topdecktravel.co.uk) This London-based outfit offers young travellers everything from Croatian coastal cruises to festival weekends and ski breaks.

Train

Trains are a popular way of getting around Mediterranean Europe. The region's rail network is comprehensive, and trains are comfortable, frequent and generally punctual. You'll have no trouble travelling between the region's main cities, although if you want to get off the beaten track, particularly in the eastern Balkan countries, you'll find buses a better option. Note also that as of February 2011 all international train services to Greece have been suspended indefinitely.

Other factors to bear in mind:

» The speed and cost of your journey depends on the type of train you take. Fast trains include the TGV in France, the Tren de Alta Velocidad Española (AVE) in Spain and the Frecciarossa in Italy. Extra charges apply for fast trains, and it's often obligatory to make seat reservations. See individual country sections for details.

» Most long-distance trains have a dining car or an attendant with a snack trolley. If possible, buy your food before travelling, as on-board prices tend to be high.

» You should be quite safe travelling on trains in Mediterranean Europe, but it pays to be security-conscious nonetheless. Keep an eye on your luggage at all times (especially when stopping at stations) and lock the compartment doors at night.

» Note that European trains sometimes split en route in order to service two destinations, so even if you're on the right train, make sure you're in the correct carriage.

» To check train schedules in any European country, get hold of the **Thomas Cook European Timetable** (www.europeanrailtimetable.co.uk), which lists train, bus and ferry times. Updated monthly, the timetable (UK£14.99) can be ordered online or bought from Thomas Cook outlets in the UK.

» Other resources include **The Man in Seat 61** (www.seat61.com), an exhaustive website touching on every aspect of European rail travel, and **German Deutsch Bahn** (www.bahn.de), where you can get up-to-the-minute train times for services across Europe.

Classes

On most trains there are 1st- and 2nd-class carriages. As a rough guide, a 1st-class ticket generally costs about double the price of a 2nd-class ticket. In 1st-class carriages there are fewer seats and more luggage space. On overnight trains, your comfort depends less on which class you're travelling than on whether you've booked a regular seat, couchette or sleeper.

Costs

Rail travel throughout the region is generally pretty economical. How much you pay depends on the type of train you take (high-speed trains are more expensive), whether you travel 1st or 2nd class, the time of year (or even the time of day), and whether or not you have a seat, a couchette or a sleeper. As a rough guide, the following are approximate ticket prices for high-speed trains:

» Barcelona–Madrid from €120

» Paris–Marseille from €57

» Rome–Florence from €43

Discounts are often available online or if you book well in advance. Check country sections for details.

Reservations

On many local services it's not possible to reserve a seat – just jump on and sit where you like. On faster, long-distance trains it's sometimes obligatory to make a reservation, although this will often be included in the ticket price. Regardless of whether it's necessary, it's a good idea to book on popular routes in peak periods.

Most international trains require a seat reservation, and you'll also need to book sleeping accommodation on overnight trains. Bookings can be made for a small, non-refundable fee (usually about €3) when you buy your ticket.

Supplements (applicable on some fast trains) and reservation costs are not covered by most rail passes.

Train Passes

There are a lot of rail passes for travel in the region, but before you buy work out whether you really need one. Unless you're planning to cover a lot of ground in a short time, you'd probably do as well buying regular train tickets. Advance-purchase deals, one-off promotions and special circular-route tickets are all available. Also, normal international tickets are valid for two months and allow you to stop as often as you like en route. However, rail passes provide a degree of flexibility that many discount tickets do not.

When choosing a pass, consider the following:

» how many countries you want to see

» how flexible your travel dates are

» if you want to travel 1st or 2nd class

» whether you need a Eurail pass (for residents of non-European countries) or an InterRail pass (for European residents)

Passes are available online or at travel agents. Prices vary, so it pays to shop around before committing yourself. Once you've purchased a pass, take care of it, as it cannot be replaced or refunded if it's lost or stolen.

Before travelling, always check that the train you're taking doesn't require a supplement or seat reservation – these additional costs are not covered by most rail passes. Note also that pass holders must always carry their passport for identification purposes.

Comprehensive information and online bookings are available at **Rail Europe** (☑ in the UK 0844 848 4064, in the USA 1-800-622-8600; www.raileurope.co.uk) and **Rail Pass** (www.railpass.com).

PASSES FOR NON-EUROPEAN RESIDENTS

If you are a resident in a non-European country you'll need a **Eurail** (www.eurail.com) pass. These are best bought before you leave home. You can buy them in Europe – provided you can prove you've been on the continent for less than six months – but sales outlets are limited and you'll pay up to 20% more than you would at home.

» There are four types of passes (the Global Pass, Select Pass, Regional Pass and One Country Pass) and four fare types – adult (over 26), youth (12 to 25 years of age), family and saver.

» Prices quoted here are for the adult and youth versions; savers, available for two to five people travelling together, cost about 15% less than adult

---

OVERNIGHT TRAINS

Overnight trains are often a good bet as they save you time and the price of a night's accommodation. They usually offer a choice of couchettes or sleepers.

» Couchettes are mixed sex, and are fitted with four or six bunks, for which pillows, sheets and blankets are supplied.

» Sleepers are for between one and four passengers, and are more expensive. They are generally single sex, come with towels and toiletries, and have a washbasin in the compartment.

» On some routes, you can get a private room with an en-suite shower and toilet.

passes. With adult passes, children under four travel free, and kids aged between four and 11 travel for half-price.

» Adult and saver passes are valid for 1st-class travel only; youths who want to upgrade to 1st class have to pay for an adult pass.

EURAIL GLOBAL PASS

This provides unlimited rail travel in 24 countries – including Croatia, France, Greece, Italy, Portugal, Slovenia, Spain and Turkey.

» Pass holders are entitled to free or discounted passage on some ferries between Italy and Greece.

» Before using the pass for the first time, you'll need to have it validated at a ticket counter (you'll need your passport to do this).

The pass comes in two forms:

Continuous (15 days/3 months adult US$589/1628, youth US$384/1059) Provides travel each day for a period ranging from 15 days to three months.

Flexi (10/15 days adult US$695/912, youth US$452/594) Opt for 10 or 15 travel days within a two-month period.

EURAIL SELECT PASS

The **Select Pass** (3 countries 5/10 days adult US$373/564, youth US$245/368, 4 countries 5/10 days adult US$418/607, youth US$273/396, 5 countries 5/15 days adult US$459/821, youth US$300/536) allows travel between three, four or five bordering countries for five, six, eight or 10 days within a two-month period (the five-country pass also has a 15-day option). Countries covered include Croatia, France, Greece, Italy, Montenegro, Portugal, Slovenia, Spain and Turkey.

EURAIL REGIONAL PASS

If you're planning to concentrate on a particular area

it makes sense to go for a Regional Pass, rather than a more expensive Global Pass.

Eurail has an extensive range of regional passes covering neighbouring countries, including for Austria, Croatia and Slovenia; France and Italy; France and Spain; Greece and Italy; and Spain and Portugal. These provide for between four and 10 days of unlimited travel within a two-month period.

Most of these passes can only be purchased prior to arrival in the country concerned.

Prices vary, but as a rough guide:

Austria, Croatia & Slovenia (4/10 days adult US$274/513, youth US$199/371)

France & Spain (4/10 days adult US$393/667, youth US$255/435)

France & Italy (4/10 days adult US$412/697, youth US$269/455)

EURAIL ONE COUNTRY PASS

One Country Passes are available for 19 countries, including Croatia, Greece, Italy, Portugal, Slovenia and Spain. These provide for between three and 10 days of travel within a two-month period.

Note that these passes do not cover charges for seat reservations, which are obligatory on many high-speed services.

Popular passes:

Italy Pass (3/10 days adult US$281/515, youth US$187/343)

Spain Pass (3/10 days adult US$229/466)

PASSES FOR EUROPEAN RESIDENTS

European residents of at least six months' standing (passport identification is required) will need an **InterRail** (www.interrailnet.com) pass. There are two types of pass: the Global Pass and the One Country Pass.

Adult passes are available in 1st and 2nd class, while the youth (12 to 25 years of age) passes are for 2nd class only. With adult passes, children under four travel free, and kids aged between four and 11 travel for half-price. Seniors (over 60) qualify for a 10% discount on the Global Pass.

INTERRAIL GLOBAL PASS

The Global Pass is valid for travel in 30 countries, including BiH, Croatia, France, Greece, Italy, Montenegro, Portugal, Slovenia, Spain and Turkey. There are various options:

» Five days of travel within 10 days (adult/youth €267/175)

» 10 days of travel within 22 days (adult/youth €381/257)

» every day for 15 days (adult/youth €422/298)

» every day for 22 days (adult/youth €494/329)

» every day for one month (adult/youth €638/422)

Before you start each trip, fill in the journey details on the provided form.

INTERRAIL ONE COUNTRY PASS

There are InterRail One Country Passes for 27 European countries. These provide three, four, six or eight days of travel within a one-month period. Among the most popular options are passes to Italy and Spain.

Italy Pass (3/4/6/8 days adult €181/205/267/311, youth €123/144/175/205)

Spain Pass (3/4/6/8 days adult €277/314/409/476, youth €123/144/175/205)

Greece Plus Pass (3/4/6/8 days adult €119/150/201/243, youth €78/98/129/160) The Greece Plus Pass also covers Superfast and Blue Star ferries between Ancona or Bari in Italy and Patra and Igoumenitsa in Greece.

For in-depth language information and handy phrases, check out Lonely Planet's *Mediterranean Europe Phrasebook*. You'll find it at **shop.lonelyplanet.com**, or you can buy Lonely Planet's iPhone phrasebooks at the Apple App Store.

Language

This chapter offers basic vocabulary to help you get around Mediterranean Europe. If you read our coloured pronunciation guides as if they were English, you'll be understood. The stressed syllables are indicated with italics.

Some of the phrases in this chapter have both polite and informal forms (indicated by the abbreviations 'pol' and 'inf' respectively). Use the polite form when addressing older people, officials or service staff. The abbreviations 'm' and 'f' indicate masculine and feminine gender respectively.

ALBANIAN

Note that ew is pronounced as 'ee' with rounded lips, uh as the 'a' in 'ago', dh as the 'th' in 'that', dz as the 'ds' in 'adds', and zh as the 's' in 'pleasure'.

Basics

Hello.	Tungjatjeta.	toon·dya·*tye*·ta
Goodbye.	Mirupafshim.	mee·roo·*paf*·sheem
Excuse me.	Më falni.	muh *fal*·nee
Sorry.	Më vjen keq.	muh vyen kech
Please.	Ju lutem.	yoo *loo*·tem
Thank you.	Faleminderit.	fa·le·meen·*de*·reet
Yes.	Po.	po
No.	Jo.	jo

Do you speak English?
A flisni anglisht? — a *flees*·nee ang·*leesht*

I don't understand.
Unë nuk kuptoj. — oo·nuh nook koop·*toy*

Accommodation

campsite	vend kampimi	vend kam·*pee*·mee
guesthouse	bujtinë	booy·*tee*·nuh
hotel	hotel	ho·*tel*

Do you have a singe/double room?
A keni një dhomë teke/dopjo? — a *ke*·nee nyuh *dho*·muh *te*·ke *dop*·yo

How much is it per night/person?
Sa kushton për një natë/njeri? — sa koosh·*ton* puhr nyuh *na*·tuh/*nye*·ree

Eating & Drinking

Is there a vegetarian restaurant near here?
A ka ndonjë restorant vegjetarian këtu afër? — a ka *ndo*·nyuh res·to·*rant* ve·dye·ta·ree·*an* kuh·*too* a·fuhr

I'd like the bill/menu, please.
Më sillni faturën/menunë, ju lutem. — muh *seell*·nee fa·*too*·ruhn/me·*noo*·nuh yoo *loo*·tem

| I'll have ... | Dua ... | *doo*·a ... |
| Cheers! | Gëzuar! | guh·*zoo*·ar |

Emergencies

Help!
Ndihmë! — *ndeeh*·muh

Call a doctor/the police!
Thirrni doktorin/policinë! — *theerr*·nee dok·*to*·reen/po·lee·*tsee*·nuh

I'm lost.
Kam humbur rrugën.   kam *hoom*·boor rroo·guhn

I'm ill.
Jam i/e sëmurë. (m/f)   yam ee/e suh·*moo*·ruh

Where are the toilets?
Ku janë banjat?   koo ya·nuh *ba*·nyat

Shopping & Services

I'm looking for ...
Po kërkoj për ...   po kuhr·*koy* puhr ...

How much is it?
Sa kushton?   sa koosh·*ton*

That's too expensive.
Është shumë   uhsh·tuh *shoo*·muh
shtrenjtë.   *shtreny*·tuh

bank	bankë	ban·kuh
post office	posta	pos·ta
tourist office	zyrë	zew·ra
	turistike	too·rees·*tee*·ke

Transport & Directions

Where's the ...?
Ku është ...?   koo uhsh·tuh ...

What's the address?
Cila është adresa?   tsee·la uhsh·tuh a·*dre*·sa

a ... ticket	Një biletë ...	nyuh bee·*le*·tuh ...
one-way	për vajtje	puhr *vai*·tye
return	kthimi	*kthee*·mee

boat	anija	a·*nee*·ya
bus	autobusi	a·oo·to·*boo*·see
plane	aeroplani	a·e·ro·*pla*·nee
train	treni	*tre*·nee

Numbers – Albanian		
1	një	nyuh
2	dy	dew
3	tre	tre
4	katër	*ka*·tuhr
5	pesë	pe·suh
6	gjashtë	*dyash*·tuh
7	shtatë	*shta*·tuh
8	tetë	te·tuh
9	nëntë	*nuhn*·tuh
10	dhjetë	*dhye*·tuh

Signs – Albanian	
Hyrje	Entrance
Dalje	Exit
Hapur	Open
Mbyllur	Closed
E Ndaluar	Prohibited
Nevojtorja	Toilets

CROATIAN

The national language of Croatia also has official status in Bosnia & Hercegovina and in Montenegro.

Note that r is a rolled sound, zh is pronounced as the 's' in 'pleasure', and the apostrophe (') indicates a slight y sound after a consonant.

Basics

Hello.	Dobar dan.	do·bar dan
Goodbye.	Zbogom.	zbo·gom
Excuse me.	Oprostite.	o·*pro*·sti·te
Sorry.	Žao mi je.	zha·o mi ye
Please.	Molim.	*mo*·lim
Thank you.	Hvala.	*hva*·la
Yes.	Da.	da
No.	Ne.	ne

Do you speak English?
Govorite/Govoriš li   go·vo·ri·te/go·vo·rish
engleski? (pol/inf)   li en·gle·ski

I don't understand.
Ja ne razumijem.   ya ne ra·zu·mi·yem

Accommodation

campsite	kamp	kamp
guesthouse	privatni	pri·vat·ni
	smještaj	smyesh·tai
hotel	hotel	ho·tel

Do you have a single/double room?
Imate li jednokrevetnu/   i·ma·te li yed·no·kre·vet·nu/
dvokrevetnu sobu?   dvo·kre·vet·nu so·bu

How much is it per night/person?
Koliko stoji po ...   ko·li·ko sto·yi po ...
noći/osobi?   no·chi/o·so·bi

Eating & Drinking

Do you have vegetarian food?
Da li imate   da li i·ma·te
vegetarijanski obrok?   ve·ge·ta·ri·yan·ski o·brok

I'd like the bill/menu, please.
Mogu li dobiti račun/   mo·gu li do·bi·ti ra·chun
jelovnik molim?   ye·lov·nik mo·lim

I'll have ...
Želim naručiti ...   zhe·lim na·ru·chi·ti ...

Cheers!
Živjeli!   zhi·vye·li

Emergencies

Help!
Upomoć!   u·po·moch

Call a doctor/the police!
Zovite liječnika/   zo·vi·te li·yech·ni·ka/
policiju.   po·li·tsi·yu

I'm lost.
Izgubio/Izgubila   iz·gu·bi·o/iz·gu·bi·la
sam se. (m/f)   sam se

I'm ill.
Ja sam bolestan/   ya sam bo·le·stan/
bolesna. (m/f)   bo·le·sna

Where are the toilets?
Gdje se nalaze zahodi?   gdye se na·la·ze za·ho·di

Shopping & Services

I'm looking for ...
Tražim ...   tra·zhim

How much is it?
Koliko stoji?   ko·li·ko sto·yi

That's too expensive.
To je preskupo.   to ye pre·skoo·po

ATM	bankovni automat	ban·kov·nee a·oo·to·mat
post office	poštanski ured	posh·tan·skee oo·red
tourist office	turistička agencija	too·ree·steech·ka a·gen·tsee·ya

Numbers – Croatian		
1	jedan	ye·dan
2	dva	dva
3	tri	tri
4	četiri	che·ti·ri
5	pet	pet
6	šest	shest
7	sedam	se·dam
8	osam	o·sam
9	devet	de·vet
10	deset	de·set

Signs – Croatian	
Ulaz	Entrance
Izlaz	Exit
Otvoreno	Open
Zatvoreno	Closed
Zabranjeno	Prohibited
Zahodi	Toilets

Transport & Directions

Where's the ...?
Gdje je ...?   gdye ye ...

What's the address?
Koja je adresa?   ko·ya ye a·dre·sa

One one-way/return ticket (to Sarajevo), please.
Jednu jednosmjernu/   yed·nu yed·no·smyer·nu/
povratnu kartu   po·vrat·nu kar·tu
(do Sarajeva),   (do sa·ra·ye·va)
molim.   mo·lim

boat	brod	brod
bus	autobus	a·u·to·bus
plane	avion	a·vi·on
train	vlak	vlak

FRENCH
French has nasal vowels (pronounced as if you're trying to force the sound through the nose), indicated in our pronunciation guides with o or u followed by an almost inaudible nasal consonant sound m, n or ng. Note also that air is pronounced as in 'fair', eu as the 'u' in 'nurse', ew as ee with rounded lips, r is a throaty sound, and zh is pronounced as the 's' in 'pleasure'. Syllables in French words are, for the most part, equally stressed.

Basics

Hello.	Bonjour.	bon·zhoor
Goodbye.	Au revoir.	o·rer·vwa
Excuse me.	Excusez-moi.	ek·skew·zay·mwa
Sorry.	Pardon.	par·don
Please.	S'il vous plaît.	seel voo play
Thank you.	Merci.	mair·see
Yes.	Oui.	wee
No.	Non.	non

Do you speak English?
Parlez-vous anglais?   par·lay·voo ong·glay

I don't understand.
Je ne comprends pas.   zher ner kom·pron pa

Accommodation

campsite	camping	kom·peeng
guesthouse	pension	pon·syon
hotel	hôtel	o·tel

Do you have a ... room?	Avez-vous une chambre ...?	a·vey·voo ewn shom·bre ...
single	à un lit	a un lee
double	avec un grand lit	a·vek ung gron lee

How much is it per night/person?
Quel est le prix par nuit/personne? — kel ey le pree par nwee/pair·son

Eating & Drinking

Do you have vegetarian food?
Vous faites les repas végétariens? — voo fet ley re·pa vey·zhey·ta·ryun

I'd like the bill/menu, please.
Je voudrais l'addition/ la carte s'il vous plaît. — zhe voo·drey la·dee·syon/ la kart seel voo pley

I'll have ...
Je prends ... — zhe pron ...

Cheers!
Santé! — son·tay

Emergencies

Help!
Au secours! — o skoor

Call a doctor!
Appelez un médecin! — a·play un mayd·sun

Call the police!
Appelez la police! — a·play la po·lees

I'm lost.
Je suis perdu(e). (m/f) — zhe swee·pair·dew

Numbers – French		
1	un	un
2	deux	der
3	trois	trwa
4	quatre	ka·trer
5	cinq	sungk
6	six	sees
7	sept	set
8	huit	weet
9	neuf	nerf
10	dix	dees

Signs – French	
Entrée	Entrance
Sortie	Exit
Ouvert	Open
Fermé	Closed
Interdit	Prohibited
Toilettes	Toilets

I'm ill.
Je suis malade. — zher swee ma·lad

Where are the toilets?
Où sont les toilettes? — oo son ley twa·let

Shopping & Services

I'd like to buy ...
Je voudrais acheter ... — zher voo·dray ash·tay ...

How much is it?
C'est combien? — say kom·byun

It's too expensive.
C'est trop cher. — say tro shair

ATM	guichet automatique de banque	gee·shay o·to·ma·teek der bonk
post office	bureau de poste	bew·ro der post
tourist office	office de tourisme	o·fees der too·rees·mer

Transport & Directions

Where's ...?
Où est ...? — oo ay ...

What's the address?
Quelle est l'adresse? — kel ay la·dres

one-way ticket
billet simple — bee·yey sum·ple

return ticket
billet aller et retour — bee·yey a·ley ey re·toor

boat	bateau	ba·to
bus	bus	bews
plane	avion	a·vyon
train	train	trun

GREEK

Greek has official status in Greece and Cyprus.

Note that dh is pronounced as the 'th' in 'that', dz as the 'ds' in 'lads', and that gh and kh are both throaty sounds, similar to the 'ch' in the Scottish *loch*.

Basics

Hello.	Γεια σου.	yia su
Goodbye.	Αντίο.	a·di·o
Excuse me.	Με συγχωρείτε.	me sing·kho·ri·te
Sorry.	Συγνώμη.	si·ghno·mi
Please.	Παρακαλώ.	pa·ra·ka·lo
Thank you.	Ευχαριστώ.	ef·kha·ri·sto
Yes.	Ναι.	ne
No.	Οχι.	o·hi

Do you speak English?
Μιλάς Αγγλικά;   mi·las ang·gli·ka

I don't understand.
Δεν καταλαβαίνω.   dhen ka·ta·la·ve·no

Accommodation

campsite	χώρος για κάμπινγκ	kho·ros yia kam·ping
guesthouse	ξενώνας	kse·no·nas
hotel	ξενοδοχείο	kse·no·dho·hi·o

Do you have a single/double room?
Εχετε ένα μονό/
διπλό δωμάτιο;   e·he·te e·na mo·no/
dhi·plo dho·ma·ti·o

How much is it per night/person?
Πόσο είναι για κάθε
νύχτα/άτομο;   po·so i·ne yia ka·the
nikh·ta/a·to·mo

Eating & Drinking

Do you have vegetarian food?
Εχετε φαγητό για
χορτοφάγους;   e·he·te fa·yi·to yia
khor·to·fa·ghus

I'd like the bill/menu, please.
Θα ήθελα το μενού/
λογαριασμό, παρακαλώ.   tha i·the·la to me·nu/
lo·gha·riaz·mo pa·ra·ka·lo

Numbers – Greek		
1	ένας	e·nas
2	δύο	dhi·o
3	τρεις	tris
4	τέσσερις	te·se·ris
5	πέντε	pe·de
6	έξι	ek·si
7	εφτά	ef·ta
8	οχτώ	okh·to
9	εννέα	e·ne·a
10	δέκα	dhe·ka

Signs – Greek	
Είσοδος	Entrance
Εξοδος	Exit
Ανοικτός	Open
Κλειστός	Closed
Απαγορεύεται	Prohibited
Τουαλέτες	Toilets

I'll have ...	Θα πάρω ...	tha pa·ro ...
Cheers!	Εις υγείαν!	is i·yi·an

Emergencies

Help!
Βοήθεια!   vo·i·thia

Call a doctor!
Κάλεσε ένα γιατρό!   ka·le·se e·na yia·tro

Call the police!
Κάλεσε την αστυνομία!   ka·le·se tin a·sti·no·mi·a

I'm ill.
Είμαι άρρωστος/
άρρωστη. (m/f)   i·me a·ro·stos/
a·ro·sti

Where are the toilets?
Που είναι η τουαλέτα;   pu i·ne i tu·a·le·ta

Shopping & Services

I'd like to buy ...
Θα ήθελα να αγοράσω ...   tha i·the·la na a·gho·ra·so ...

How much is it?
Πόσο κάνει;   po·so ka·ni

It's too expensive.
Είναι πολύ ακριβό.   i·ne po·li a·kri·vo

bank	τράπεζα	tra·pe·za
post office	ταχυδρομείο	ta·hi·dhro·mi·o
tourist office	τουριστικό γραφείο	tu·ri·sti·ko ghra·fi·o

Transport & Directions

Where's ...?
Που είναι ...?   pu i·ne ...

What's the address?
Ποια είναι η διεύθυνση;   pia i·ne i dhi·ef·thin·si

a ... ticket	ενα εισιτήριο ...	e·na i·si·ti·ri·o ...
one-way	απλό	a·plo
return	με επιστροφή	me e·pi·stro·fi

boat	πλοίο	pli·o
bus	λεωφορείο	le·o·fo·ri·o
plane	αεροπλάνο	a·e·ro·pla·no
train	τρένο	tre·no

ITALIAN

Italian vowels are generally shorter than those in English. The consonants sometimes have a stronger, more emphatic pronunciation – if the word is written with a double consonant, pronounce them stronger. Note that ow is pronounced as in 'how', dz as the 'ds' in 'lads', and r is a strong, rolled sound.

Basics

Hello.	Buongiorno.	bwon·jor·no
Goodbye.	Arrivederci.	a·ree·ve·der·chee
Excuse me.	Mi scusi. (pol)	mee skoo·zee
	Scusami. (inf)	skoo·za·mee
Sorry.	Mi dispiace.	mee dees·pya·che
Please.	Per favore.	per fa·vo·re
Thank you.	Grazie.	gra·tsye
Yes.	Sì.	see
No.	No.	no

Do you speak English?
Parla inglese?   par·la een·gle·ze

I don't understand.
Non capisco.   non ka·pee·sko

Accommodation

campsite	campeggio	kam·pe·jo
guesthouse	pensione	pen·syo·ne
hotel	albergo	al·ber·go

How much is it per night/person?
Quanto costa per   kwan·to kos·ta per
una notte/persona?   oo·na no·te/per·so·na

Do you have a single room?
Avete una   a·ve·te oo·na
camera singola?   ka·me·ra seen·go·la

Numbers – Italian

1	uno	oo·no
2	due	doo·e
3	tre	tre
4	quattro	kwa·tro
5	cinque	cheen·kwe
6	sei	say
7	sette	se·te
8	otto	o·to
9	nove	no·ve
10	dieci	dye·chee

Signs – Italian

Entrata	Entrance
Uscita	Exit
Aperto	Open
Chiuso	Closed
Proibito	Prohibited
Gabinetti	Toilets

Do you have a double room?
Avete una camera   a·ve·te oo·na ka·me·ra
doppia con letto   do·pya kon le·to
matrimoniale?   ma·tree·mo·nya·le

Eating & Drinking

Do you have vegetarian food?
Avete piatti   a·ve·te pya·tee
vegetariani?   ve·je·ta·rya·nee

I'd like the ..., please.
Vorrei il conto/menù,   vo·ray eel kon·to/me·noo
per favore.   per fa·vo·re

I'll have ...	Prendo ...	pren·do ...
Cheers!	Salute!	sa·loo·te

Emergencies

Help!
Aiuto!   ai·yoo·to

Call a doctor!
Chiami un medico!   kya·mee oon me·dee·ko

Call the police!
Chiami la polizia!   kya·mee la po·lee·tsee·a

I'm lost.
Mi sono perso/a. (m/f)   mee so·no per·so/a

I'm ill.
Mi sento male.   mee sen·to ma·le

Where are the toilets?
Dove sono i gabinetti?   do·ve so·no ee ga·bee·ne·tee

Shopping & Services

I'm looking for ...
Sto cercando ...   sto cher·kan·do ...

How much is it?
Quant'è?   kwan·te

It's too expensive.
È troppo caro/a. (m/f)   e tro·po ka·ro/a

ATM	Bancomat	ban·ko·mat
post office	ufficio postale	oo·fee·cho pos·ta·le
tourist office	ufficio del turismo	oo·fee·cho del too·reez·mo

Transport & Directions

Where's ... ?
Dov'è ... ? — do·ve ...

What's the address?
Qual'è l'indirizzo? — kwa·le leen·dee·ree·tso

One ... ticket	Un biglietto ...	oon bee·lye·to...
one-way	di sola andata	dee so·la an·da·ta
return	di andata e ritorno	dee an·da·ta e ree·tor·no
boat	nave	na·ve
bus	autobus	ow·to·boos
plane	aereo	a·e·re·o
train	treno	tre·no

PORTUGUESE

Most Portuguese vowel sounds have a nasal version (ie pronounced as if you're trying to force the sound through the nose), which is indicated in our pronunciation guides with ng after the vowel. Note also that oh is pronounced as the 'o' in 'note', ow as in 'how', rr is a throaty sound in Portuguese (similar to the French 'r'), and zh is pronounced as the 's' in 'pleasure'.

Basics

Hello.	Olá.	o·laa
Goodbye.	Adeus.	a·de·oosh
Excuse me.	Faz favor.	faash fa·vor
Sorry.	Desculpe.	desh·kool·pe
Please.	Por favor.	poor fa·vor
Thank you.	Obrigado. (m) Obrigada. (f)	o·bree·gaa·doo o·bree·gaa·da
Yes.	Sim.	seeng
No.	Não.	nowng

Do you speak English?
Fala inglês? — faa·la eeng·glesh

I don't understand.
Não entendo. — nowng eng·teng·doo

Accommodation

campsite	parque de campismo	paar·ke de kang·peezh·moo
guesthouse	casa de hóspedes	kaa·za de osh·pe·desh
hotel	hotel	o·tel

Do you have a single/double room?
Tem um quarto de solteiro/casal? — teng oong kwaar·too de sol·tay·roo/ka·zaal

How much is it per night/person?
Quanto custa por noite/pessoa? — kwang·too koosh·ta poor noy·te/pe·so·a

Eating & Drinking

Do you have vegetarian food?
Tem comida vegetariana? — teng koo·mee·da ve·zhe·ta·ree·aa·na

I'll have ...	Eu queria ...	e·oo ke·ree·a ...
Cheers!	Saúde!	sa·oo·de
I'd like the ..., please.	Queria ..., por favor.	ke·ree·a ... poor fa·vor
bill	a conta	a kong·ta
menu	um menu	oong me·noo

Emergencies

Help!
Socorro! — soo·ko·rroo

Call a doctor!
Chame um médico! — shaa·me oong me·dee·koo

Call the police!
Chame a polícia! — shaa·me a poo·lee·sya

I'm ill.
Estou doente. — shtoh doo·eng·te

Where are the toilets?
Onde é a casa de banho? — ong·de e a kaa·za de ba·nyoo

Shopping & Services

I'd like to buy ...
Queria comprar ... — ke·ree·a kong·praar ...

How much is it?
Quanto custa? — kwang·too koosh·ta

Numbers – Portuguese		
1	um	oong
2	dois	doysh
3	três	tresh
4	quatro	kwaa·troo
5	cinco	seeng·koo
6	seis	saysh
7	sete	se·te
8	oito	oy·too
9	nove	no·ve
10	dez	desh

Signs – Portuguese

Entrada	Entrance
Saída	Exit
Aberto	Open
Encerrado/Fechado	Closed
Proibido	Prohibited
Lavabos	Toilets

It's too expensive.
Está muito caro.   shtaa *mweeng*·too *kaa*·roo

ATM	*caixa automático*	kai·sha ow·too·maa·tee·koo
post office	*correio*	koo·*rray*·oo
tourist office	*escritório de turismo*	shkree·*to*·ryoo de too·*reezh*·moo

Transport & Directions

Where's ...?
Onde é ...?   ong·de e ...

What's the address?
Qual é o endereço?   kwaal e oo eng·de·*re*·soo

one-way ticket
bilhete de ida   bee·*lye*·te de *ee*·da

return ticket
bilhete de ida e volta   bee·*lye*·te de *ee*·da ee *vol*·ta

boat	*barco*	*baar*·koo
bus	*autocarro*	ow·to·*kaa*·roo
plane	*avião*	a·vee·*owng*
train	*comboio*	kong·*boy*·oo

SLOVENE

Note that uh is pronounced as the 'a' in 'ago', zh as the 's' in 'pleasure', r is rolled, and the apostrophe (') indicates a slight y sound.

Basics

Hello.	*Zdravo.*	*zdra*·vo
Goodbye.	*Na svidenje.*	na svee·den·ye
Excuse me.	*Dovolite.*	do·vo·*lee*·te
Sorry.	*Oprostite.*	op·ros·*tee*·te
Please.	*Prosim.*	*pro*·seem
Thank you.	*Hvala.*	*hva*·la
Yes.	*Da.*	da
No.	*Ne.*	ne

Do you speak English?
Ali govorite angleško?   a·lee go·vo·*ree*·te ang·*lesh*·ko

I don't understand.
Ne razumem.   ne ra·*zoo*·mem

Accommodation

campsite	*kamp*	kamp
guesthouse	*gostišče*	gos·*teesh*·che
hotel	*hotel*	ho·*tel*

Do you have a single/double room?
Ali imate enoposteljno/ dvoposteljno sobo?   a·lee ee·*ma*·te e·no·*pos*·tel'·no/ dvo·*pos*·tel'·no *so*·bo

How much is it per night/person?
Koliko stane na noč/osebo?   ko·lee·ko *sta*·ne na noch/o·*se*·bo

Eating & Drinking

Do you have vegetarian food?
Ali imate vegetarijansko hrano?   a·lee ee·*ma*·te ve·ge·ta·ree·*yan*·sko *hra*·no

I'd like the bill/menu, please.
Želim račun/ jedilni list, prosim.   zhe·*leem* ra·*choon*/ ye·*deel*·nee leest *pro*·seem

I'll have ...	*Jaz bom ...*	yaz bom ...
Cheers!	*Na zdravje!*	na *zdrav*·ye

Emergencies

Help!
Na pomoč!   na po·*moch*

Call a doctor/the police!
Pokličite zdravnika/ policijo!   pok·lee·chee·te zdrav·*nee*·ka/ po·lee·*tsee*·yo

I'm ill.
Bolan/Bolna sem. (m/f)   bo·*lan*/*boh*·na sem

Where are the toilets?
Kje je stranišče?   kye ye stra·*neesh*·che

Numbers – Slovene

1	*en*	en
2	*dva*	dva
3	*trije*	*tree*·ye
4	*štirje*	*shtee*·rye
5	*pet*	pet
6	*šest*	shest
7	*sedem*	*se*·dem
8	*osem*	*o*·sem
9	*devet*	de·*vet*
10	*deset*	de·*set*

Signs – Slovene

Vhod	Entrance
Izhod	Exit
Odprto	Open
Zaprto	Closed
Prepovedano	Prohibited
Stranišče	Toilets

Shopping & Services

I'm looking for ...
Iščem ...   eesh·chem ...

How much is this?
Koliko stane?   ko·lee·ko sta·ne

It's too expensive.
Predrago je.   pre·dra·go ye

bank	banka	ban·ka
post office	pošta	posh·ta
tourist office	turistični urad	too·rees·teech·nee oo·rad

Transport & Directions

Where's the ...?
Kje je ...?   kye ye ...

What's the address?
Na katerem naslovu je?   na ka·te·rem nas·lo·voo ye

one-way ticket
enosmerno vozovnico   e·no·smer·no o·zov·nee·tso

return ticket
povratno vozovnico   pov·rat·no o·zov·nee·tso

boat	ladja	ad·ya
bus	avtobus	av·to·boos
plane	letalo	le·ta·lo
train	vlak	vlak

Basics

Sorry.	Lo siento.	lo see·en·to
Please.	Por favor.	por fa·vor
Thank you.	Gracias.	gra·thyas
Yes.	Sí.	see
No.	No.	no

Do you speak English?
¿Habla/Hablas inglés? (pol/inf)   a·bla/a·blas een·gles

I don't understand.
Yo no entiendo.   yo no en·tyen·do

Accommodation

campsite	terreno de cámping	te·re·no de kam·peeng
guesthouse	pensión	pen·syon
hotel	hotel	o·tel

Do you have a single/double room?
¿Tiene una habitación individual/doble?   tye·ne oo·na a·bee·ta·thyon een·dee·vee·dwal/do·ble

How much is it per night/person?
¿Cuánto cuesta por noche/persona?   kwan·to kwes·ta por no·che/persona

Eating & Drinking

Do you have vegetarian food?
¿Tienen comida vegetariana?   tye·nen ko·mee·da ve·khe·ta·rya·na

I'd like the ... please.	Quisiera ... por favor.	kee·sye·ra ... por fa·vor
bill	la cuenta	la kwen·ta
menu	el menú	el me·noo

I'll have ...	Para mí ...	pa·ra mee ...
Cheers!	¡Salud!	sa·loo

SPANISH

Spanish vowels are generally pronounced short. Note that ow is pronounced as in 'how', kh as the 'ch' in the Scottish loch (a throaty sound), rr is rolled and stronger than in English, and v is a soft 'b' (pronounced between the English 'v' and 'b' sounds).

Basics

Hello.	Hola.	o·la
Goodbye.	Adiós.	a·dyos
Excuse me.	Perdón.	per·don

Numbers – Spanish

1	uno	oo·no
2	dos	dos
3	tres	tres
4	cuatro	kwa·tro
5	cinco	theen·ko
6	seis	seys
7	siete	sye·te
8	ocho	o·cho
9	nueve	nwe·ve
10	diez	dyeth

LANGUAGE TURKISH

Signs – Spanish	
Entrada	Entrance
Salida	Exit
Abierto	Open
Cerrado	Closed
Prohibido	Prohibited
Servicios/Aseos	Toilets

Emergencies

Help!
¡Socorro! so·ko·ro

Call a doctor!
¡Llame a un médico! lya·me a oon me·dee·ko

Call the police!
¡Llame a la policía! lya·me a la po·lee·thee·a

I'm ill.
Estoy enfermo/a. (m/f) es·toy en·fer·mo/a

Where are the toilets?
¿Dónde están los don·de es·tan los
servicios? ser·vee·thyos

Shopping & Services

I'd like to buy ...
Quisiera comprar ... kee·sye·ra kom·prar ...

How much is it?
¿Cuánto cuesta? kwan·to kwes·ta

That's too expensive.
Es muy caro. es mooy ka·ro

ATM	cajero automático	ka·khe·ro ow·to·ma·tee·ko
post office	correos	ko·re·os
tourist office	oficina de turismo	o·fee·thee·na de too·rees·mo

Transport & Directions

Where's ...?
¿Dónde está ...? don·de es·ta ...

What's the address?
¿Cuál es la dirección? kwal es la dee·rek·thyon

one-way ticket
billete sencillo bee·lye·te sen·thee·lyo

return ticket
billete de bee·lye·te de
ida y vuelta ee·da ee vwel·ta

boat	barco	bar·ko
bus	autobús	ow·to·boos
plane	avión	a·vyon
train	tren	tren

TURKISH

Turkish is the official language in Turkey and the northern part of Cyprus.

Double vowels are pronounced twice. Note that eu is pronounced as the 'u' in 'nurse', ew as 'ee' with rounded lips, uh as the 'a' in 'ago', zh as the 's' in 'pleasure', r is always rolled and v is a little softer than in English.

Basics

Hello.	Merhaba.	mer·ha·ba
Goodbye.	Hoşçakal. (when leaving)	hosh·cha·kal
	Güle güle. (when staying)	gew·le gew·le
Excuse me.	Bakar mısınız.	ba·kar muh·suh·nuhz
Sorry.	Özür dilerim.	eu·zewr dee·le·reem
Please.	Lütfen.	lewt·fen
Thank you.	Teşekkür ederim.	te·shek·kewr e·de·reem
Yes.	Evet.	e·vet
No.	Hayır.	ha·yuhr

Do you speak English?
İngilizce een·gee·leez·je
konuşuyor ko·noo·shoo·yor
musunuz? moo·soo·nooz

I don't understand.
Anlamıyorum. an·la·muh·yo·room

Accommodation

campsite	kamp yeri	kamp ye·ree
guesthouse	misafirhane	mee·sa·feer·ha·ne
hotel	otel	o·tel

Do you have a single/double room?
Tek/İki kişilik tek/ee·kee kee·shee·leek
odanız var mı? o·da·nuz var muh

Numbers – Turkish		
1	bir	beer
2	iki	ee·kee
3	üç	ewch
4	dört	dert
5	beş	besh
6	altı	al·tuh
7	yedi	ye·dee
8	sekiz	se·keez
9	dokuz	do·kooz
10	on	on

88

How much is it per night/person?
Geceliği/Kişi | ge·je·lee·ee/kee·shee
başına ne kadar? | ba·shuh·na ne ka·dar

Eating & Drinking

Do you have vegetarian food?
Vejeteryan | ve·zhe·ter·yan
yiyecekleriniz | yee·ye·jek·le·ree·neez
var mı? | var muh

I'd like the bill/menu, please.
Hesabı/Menüyü | he·sa·buh/me·new·yew
istiyorum. | ees·tee·yo·room

| I'll have ... | ... alayım. | ... a·la·yuhm |
| Cheers! | Şerefe! | she·re·fe |

Emergencies

Help!
İmdat! | eem·dat

Call a doctor!
Doktor çağırın! | dok·tor cha·uh·ruhn

Call the police!
Polis çağırın! | po·lees cha·uh·ruhn

I'm lost.
Kayboldum. | kai·bol·doom

I'm ill.
Hastayım. | has·ta·yuhm

Where are the toilets?
Tuvaletler nerede? | too·va·let·ler ne·re·de

Shopping & Services

I'd like to buy ...
... almak istiyorum. | ... al·mak ees·tee·yo·room
How much is it?
Ne kadar? | ne ka·dar

Signs – Turkish

Giriş	Entrance
Çıkışı	Exit
Açık	Open
Kapalı	Closed
Yasak	Prohibited
Tuvaletler	Toilets

It's too expensive.
Bu çok pahalı. | boo chok pa·ha·luh

ATM	bankamatik	ban·ka·ma·teek
post office	postane	pos·ta·ne
tourist office	turizm	too·reezm
	bürosu	bew·ro·soo

Transport & Directions

Where is ...?
... nerede? | ... ne·re·de

What's the address?
Adresi nedir? | ad·re·see ne·deer

I'd like a	... bir bilet	... beer bee·let
... ticket.	lütfen.	lewt·fen
one-way	Gidiş	gee·deesh
return	Gidiş-	gee·deesh-
	dönüş	deu·newsh

boat	vapur	va·poor
bus	otobüs	o·to·bews
plane	uçak	oo·chak
train	tren	tren

Behind the Scenes

SEND US YOUR FEEDBACK

We love to hear from travellers – your comments keep us on our toes and help make our books better. Our well-travelled team reads every word on what you loved or loathed about this book. Although we cannot reply individually to postal submissions, we always guarantee that your feedback goes straight to the appropriate authors, in time for the next edition. Each person who sends us information is thanked in the next edition – the most useful submissions are rewarded with a selection of digital PDF chapters.

Visit **lonelyplanet.com/contact** to submit your updates and suggestions or to ask for help. Our award-winning website also features inspirational travel stories, news and discussions.

Note: We may edit, reproduce and incorporate your comments in Lonely Planet products such as guidebooks, websites and digital products, so let us know if you don't want your comments reproduced or your name acknowledged. For a copy of our privacy policy visit lonelyplanet.com/privacy.

OUR READERS

Many thanks to the travellers who used the last edition and wrote to us with helpful hints, useful advice and interesting anecdotes:
Johanna Linder, Ian Roitt, Colleen Threadkell

AUTHOR THANKS

Duncan Garwood

A big thank you to fellow author James Bainbridge and all the other Lonely Planet writers who contributed to this big project. Thanks also to Dora Whitaker, Katie O'Connell and the hard-working mapping and SPP teams. On the home front, *grazie* to Lidia and the boys, Ben and Nick, who provided a welcome distraction from briefs, word counts and looming deadlines.

Alexis Averbuck

Hail Alexandra Stamopoulou for her spot-on recommendations. Marina Flenga was a superlative fairy godmother, connecting me to those in the know. Marilee Anargyrou Kyri-azakou and Cali Doxiadis (in Kerkyra), Eleni Doxiadi (in Lefkada) and Manita Scocimara-Ponghis (in Kefallonia) shared their love and knowledge of their islands. In Athens, Lena Lambrinou decoded the Acropolis, and Elina Lychoudi the nightlife. Anthy and Costas, as well as Margarita Kontzia and Kostas Karakat-sanis, made it home.

James Bainbridge

A heartfelt *çok teşekkürler*, once again, to everyone who helped me find my way around the steppe on my recent visit to northeastern Turkey. Celil in Kars and Necmettin in Akçaa-bat deserve special mention for their help on a few projects this year. Thanks, as ever, to everyone at Lonely Planet – Duncan, Dora, Angela, Cliff et al – and to my wife Leigh-Robin.

Mark Baker

I met many helpful people all along the way in researching this guide and their names are too numerous to mention here. In Slovenia, the staff of the Slovenia Tourist Board deserve special mention.

Peter Dragicevich

Many thanks to all of the wonderful people who helped me in Montenegro, especially Ivica Erdelja, Hayley Wright and Jack Delf, Emma and Ben Heywood, Krstinja Petranović, Danica Ćeranić and Matthew Lane. Also, I owe a debt of gratitude to James and Lorraine Hedder-man, Tim Benzie and Kerri Tyler for their con-tributions before and after the journey.

Mark Elliott

Many thanks to Snezhan, Vlaren, Semir, Ner-men, Žika, Sanila, Narmina and Branislav, the helpful folks at Travellers Home and New Age Hostel, and Jan Beran and Mišo Marić for such a wonderfully random *slivovice* (plum brandy) evening in Mostar. As ever my greatest thanks go to my endlessly inspiring family, notably my unbeatable parents who, nearly four decades ago, had the crazy idea of driving me to Bosnia in the first place.

Anthony Ham

Heartfelt thanks to all those *madrileños* who I have been proud to call friends during my decade in the city. A huge thank you to Dora Whitaker and to all of the authors of Lonely Planet's *Spain* guide. It was my great fortune a week after arriving in Madrid to meet my wife and soulmate, Marina, who has made this city a true place of the heart. And to Carlota and Valentina: you are Madrid's greatest gifts of all.

Tom Masters

An enormous debt of thanks to all of my hard-working fellow authors on this book, and the teams in London and Melbourne who commissioned, edited and oversaw the project. Special thanks in Albania to Ardi Pulaj, Catherine Bohne, Tedi Sina and Bledi Strakosha.

Virginia Maxwell

As always, many thanks to the staff of tourist offices throughout Italy. Thanks also to my ever-helpful Italy-based coauthor Duncan Garwood. In London, thanks to commissioning editors Helena Smith and Joe Bindloss. In Melbourne, love and thanks to Peter and Max Handsaker, who held the fort.

Craig McLachlan

A hearty thanks to all those who helped me out on the road, but most of all, to my exceptionally beautiful wife, Yuriko, who let me know when I'd had my daily quota of Mythos and gyros pitta.

Anja Mutić

Hvala mama, for your home cooking and contagious laughter. *Obrigada*, Hoji, for being there before, during and after. A huge *hvala* to my friends in Croatia who gave me endless recommendations – this book wouldn't be the same without you. Special thanks go to Lidija in Zagreb and Mila in Split, as well as the team at HTZ. Finally, to the inspiring memory of my father, who travels with me still.

Regis St Louis

In Lisbon, I'd like to thank Guida Moura for her friendship and hospitality, chef Michael Guerrieri for his kindness and insight into the dining scene, and João Teixeira for his mine of local knowledge. Thanks go out to Italian travellers Silvia Luraschi and Cesare Figini for tips on Braga, and to all of the helpful tourism officials across the country. As always, *beijos* to my family Cassandra, Magdalena and Genevieve for their support.

Nicola Williams

Kudos to my *France* coauthors who resolutely persevered with an ambitious project that, at times, felt akin to scaling the Eiffel Tower on tiptoes in stilettos. On the road *merci mille fois* to Corsica aficionado Vincent Lehoux (unsurpassable Ajaccio recommendations); Kasia Dietz and Lindsay Tramuta (Corsica tips by way of Paris); Charlie Johnson (best hidden beach camping); travel-mad husband Matthias and our trilingual tribe (only car sick once during 2000km of coastal hairpins covered at an average speed of 38km/h).

ACKNOWLEDGMENTS

Climate map data adapted from Peel MC, Finlayson BL & McMahon TA (2007) 'Updated World Map of the Köppen-Geiger Climate Classification', *Hydrology and Earth System Sciences*, 11, 163344.

Cover photograph: Burano, Venice, Italy, Jean-Pierre Lescourret/Getty Images

THIS BOOK

This 11th edition of Lonely Planet's *Mediterranean Europe* guidebook is part of Lonely Planet's Europe series. Other titles in this series include *Eastern Europe*, *Western Europe*, *Central Europe*, *Southeastern Europe*, *Scandinavia* and *Europe on a Shoestring*. Lonely Planet also publishes phrasebooks for these regions. This guidebook was commissioned in Lonely Planet's London office, and produced by the following:

Commissioning Editor
Dora Whitaker

Coordinating Editors
Carolyn Boicos, Samantha Forge

Coordinating Cartographer
Valentina Kremenchutskaya

Coordinating Layout Designer Adrian Blackburn

Managing Editors Annelies Mertens, Angela Tinson

Managing Cartographers Adrian Persoglia, Anthony Phelan, Amanda Sierp

Managing Layout Designer Jane Hart

Senior Editor Catherine Naghten

Assisting Editors Anne Mason, Fionnuala Twomey

Assisting Cartographer Gabriel Lindquist

Cover Research Kylie McLaughlin

Internal Image Research Aude Vauconsant

Language Content Branislava Vladisavljevic

Thanks to Elin Berglund, Joe Bindloss, Ryan Evans, Larissa Frost, Genesys India, Jouve India, Lucy Monie, Trent Paton, Helena Smith, Kerrianne Southway, Gerard Walker

index

A

A Coruña 715
Abd al Malik 311
accommodation 848-51, *see also individual cities & countries*
    language 877-87
Acropolis 329
activities 24, 25-9, 851-2, *see also individual activities & countries*
Adana 817
Aegean Coast 784-802, **785**
Aegina 358
Aeolian Islands 514-16
Agia Roumeli 377, 378
Agiasos 391
Agios Georgios 379
Agios Gordios 396
Agios Nikitas 396
Agios Nikolaos 379
Agrigento 519
Ahmet I of Turkey 765
Aínsa 705
air travel
    to/from Mediterranean Europe 865-6
    within Mediterranean Europe 869
Aix-en-Provence 285-7
Ajaccio 306-7
Alaçatı 792
Alanya 815-16
Albania 35, 42-74, **44**
    accommodation 42, 70-1
    activities 71
    business hours 71
    climate 42
    costs & money 43, 71
    drinking 70
    embassies 71
    environment 70
    exchange rates 43
    food 42, 43, 70, 71
    highlights 44
    history 66-9
    internet access 71

000 Map pages
000 Photo pages

internet resources 43
itineraries 43
language 877-8
planning 42-3
postal services 71-2
public holidays 72
telephone services 72
tourist offices 72
travel to/from 43, 72-3
travel within 73-4
visas 72
Albarracín 705
Albert I of Monaco 302
Albert II of Monaco 302
Alcaeus 402
Alcalá de Henares 674
Alcântara 569-70
alcohol, *see* drinks
Alexandroupolis 355
Alfama 14, 566-7, 571, 575, **14**
Alfonso VI of Spain 750
Algarve 583-8, **584**
Algeciras 743
Alghero 522-3
Alhambra 14, 736-7, **14**
Alicante 719-20
Almodóvar, Pedro 752
Alonnisos 393
Alpe di Siusi 474
Alps (French) 258-65
Alsace 237-42
Altea 720
Amalfi 506
Amalfi Coast 504-6
Amasya 820
Amboise 247-8
Amenábar, Alejandro 753
Amiens 223-4
Anamur 816
Anatolia 818-21
Anavatos 388
Andorra 699
Andrić, Ivo 105
Aneto 705
Anglet 274
Ankara 818-20
Annecy 261-3
Antakya 817-18
Antalya 811-14, **812**
Antiparos 364, **363**
Apollinaire 200
Apollonia 57
Appian Way, the 437
aquariums
    France 231, 302
    Italy 447
    Portugal 568
    Spain 706, 715

Aragón 703-5
Aranjuez 674
Arc de Triomphe 197
Arçais 270
archaeological sites 22
    Acrocorinth 345
    Acropolis 329
    Acropolis of Lindos 382
    Agora 330
    Akrotiri 369
    Amphitheatre of Durrës 56
    Asklipieion 384
    Butrint 64
    Conimbriga 593
    Corinth 345
    Delos 362
    Delphi 350-1, **16**
    Empúries 701
    Ephesus 15, 794-6, **795**, **15**
    Fortress of Justinian 46-7
    Herculaneum 502
    Ireon 387
    Kamiros 382
    Knossos 374
    Mérida 749
    Mycenae 347
    Nea Moni 388
    Olympia 350
    Ostia Antica 445
    Palatino 10, 417
    Parco Archaeologico della Neapolis 517
    Pergamum 789
    Phaestos 374-5
    Pompeii 502
    Roman Forum 417, 420, **10**
    Skarkos 367
    Stari Bar 546
    Teatro Greco 516
    Temple of Aphaia 358
    Temple of Apollo 365
    Temple of Artemis 793
    Temple of Olympian Zeus 330
    Temple of Zeus 350
    Terme di Caracalla 432
    Triumphal Arch of Sergius 137
    Vaison-la-Romaine 291
    Valley of the Temples 519
    Vézère Valley 268
    Žabljak Crnojevića 550
architecture 23
Areopoli 349
Argostoli 397
Arkadia 347
Arles 290
Arp, Hans Jean 238
Arroyo, Eduardo 656
Arsac-en-Médoc 272

89

Artà 723
art museums,
see museums & galleries
arts
Albania 69-70
Bosnia & Hercegovina 114-15
Croatia 174-5
France 310-12
Greece 402-3
Italy 525-7
Portugal 605
Slovenia 643-4
Spain 752-4
Turkey 834-5
Aspendos 814
Assisi 493-4
Assos 787-8
Asturias 711-12
Atatürk 832
Athani 396
Athens 325-41, **326-7, 334**
accommodation 332-5
drinking 337
entertainment 337-9
festivals & events 332
food 335-7
history 328-9
itineraries 329
safety 339
shopping 339
sights 329-31, 332
tourist offices 340
tours 331
travel to/from 340
travel within 340-1
ATMs 857, 858
Avignon 287-90, **288-9**
Ávila 674-5
Aya Sofya 769
Ayvalık 788-9

B
Badron Gorge 347
Baixa 566-7, 570-1, 575
Baleal 591
Balearic Islands 720-7
Balzac 200
Banja Luka 107-9
Bar 546-7
Barceló, Miquel 687, 721
Barcelona 683-99, **684-5, 688-9**
accommodation 692-4
drinking 696-7
entertainment 697
festivals & events 692
food 694-6
shopping 698
sights 683-92

tourist offices 698-9
tours 692
travel to/from 699
travel within 699
Barcelos 602
Bari 507-8
Basque Country 705-9
Bastia 303-5
bathrooms 862
Bay of Kotor 13, 538-44, **13**
Bayeux 226-7
beaches 23, 24
Beaune 250-2
beer
Albania 70
Croatia 176
France 221, 314
Slovenia 644
Spain 755
Behramkale 787-8
Belém 567, 576-7
Bellini, Giovanni 306, 460
Benidorm 720
Berat 14, 57-9, **14**
Bergama 789-90
Berlenga Grande 591
Berlusconi, Silvio 525
Bernini, Gian Lorenzo 426, 427
Besançon 265-6
Beuvron-en-Auge 224
Beyoğlu 772-3
Biarritz 274-5
bicycle travel, see cycling
BiH, see Bosnia & Hercegovina
Bihać 109-10
Bilbao 708-9
Bizet, Georges 311
Bjelašnica 91
Bjelila 541
Black Lake 555
black market 858
Blagaj 100
Bled 624-8, **626**
Blois 243-4
Blue Mosque 765, **13**
boat travel
to/from Mediterranean Europe
868-9
within Mediterranean Europe 870,
873-4
Bobotov Kuk 555
Boca do Inferno 583
Bodrum 797-801, **798**
Bohinj 628-30
Bologna 470-2
Bolzano 474
Bonaparte, Napoléon 192, 197, 303,
306, 309, 751

Bonifacio 307-8
books, see literature
Bordeaux 271-3
border crossings 867
Bosnia & Hercegovina 36, 75-118,
77, 112
accommodation 75, 115
activities 115-16
business hours 116
climate 75
costs & money 76, 116
drinking 76
exchange rates 76
food 75, 76, 116
highlights 77
history 111-14
internet access 116
internet resources 76
itineraries 76
language 115
planning 75-6
postal services 116
public holidays 116
safety 116
telephone services 116
travel to/from 76, 117
travel within 117-18
visas 117
Bosphorus 773
Botticelli, Sandro 197, 306, 427,
475, 479
Bouzianis, George 403
Bovec 631-2
Bozburun Peninsula 801
Braga 602-3
Braque, Georges 212, 312, 460
Brittany 229-34
Brunelleschi, Filippo 475
Buçaco Forest 594-5
budgeting 20, see also costs
Budva 544-5
Buoninsegna, Duccio di 488
Burano 461
Buren, Daniel 269
Burgos 680
Burgundy 248-58
Bursa 782-4
bus travel
to/from Mediterranean Europe 867
within Mediterranean Europe
870-1, 874
business hours 852, see also
individual countries
Butrint 64
Butterfly Valley 803, 804

C
Cabo da Roca 583
Cabo de São Vicente 588

Cabo Espichel 582
Cabo Ortegal 715
Cabril 603
Cáceres 748-9
Cadaqués 701-2
Cádiz 744
Caesar, Julius 524
Cagliari 520-2
Cala Gonone 522
Calais 222-3
Caldas de Monchique 587
Calella de Palafrugell 701
Calpe 720
Calvi 305
Cambremer 224
Çanakkale 786-7
Canal St-Martin 200, 207
Canaletto 263, 450, 651
Canazei 474
Cancale 231
Cannes 296-8
canoeing, see kayaking, rafting
Cantabria 711
Cap de Creus 702
Cap de Formentor 723
Cape Keri 399
Cappadocia 821-7
Capri 501-3
car travel
    to/from Mediterranean Europe 867
    within Mediterranean Europe 871-3
Caravaggio 224, 240, 426, 427, 479
Carcassonne 278
Carlos III of Spain 651
Carlos IV of Spain 751
Carnac 229
Carnival 25, 462, **7**
carpets 834
Carracci, Annibale 426
Casais do Baleal 591
Cascais 583
Casino de Monte Carlo 300
Cassis 280
Castilla y León 674-80
Castilla-La Mancha 680-3
castles, fortresses & palaces
    Alcázar 677
    Alhambra 14, 736-7, **14**
    Aljafería 704
    Bled Castle 624
    Castelo de São Jorge 567
    Castelo dos Mouros 581
    Castle of Lëkurësit 62
    Castle of St Peter 797

Château d'Azay-le-Rideau 246
Château de Chambord 244
Château de Chaumont 245
Château de Chenonceau 246, **19**
Château de Cheverny 244
Château de Versailles 217-18
Château de Villandry 246
Château Royal de Blois 243
Coca Castle 675
Diocletian's Palace 152-5
Doboj 109
Fortica 160
Fortress of Justinian 46-7
Gjirokastra Castle 65
Gradačac 109
Kalasa 58, **14**
Kamerlengo Fortress 160
Kanli-Kula 538
Kastel Banja Luka 108
Kruja 55
Ljubljana Castle 612
Maribor Castle 641
Ostrožac Fortress 110
Palácio da Galeria 585
Palácio Ducal 590
Palácio Nacional da Pena 581
Palácio Nacional de Sintra 581
Palacio Real 656
Palaio Frourio 395
Palais des Papes 287
Palais du Tau 234
Palazzo Reale di Capodimonte 498
Pedraza de la Sierra 675
Peñafiel 675
Peniche 591
Petrović Palace 551
Ponferrada 675
Predjama Castle 634
Ptuj Castle 642
Quinta da Regaleira 581
Rector's Palace 167
Rozafa Fortress 52-3
Španjola Fortress 538
Sponza Palace 167
Srebrenik 109
Stari Grad 105
Tešanj 109
Topkapı Palace 768
Trsat Castle 144
Vranduk 109
Catalonia 683-703
cathedrals, see churches & cathedrals
cell phones 861
cemeteries 48, 128, 191, 200, 228
Çeşme Peninsula 792
Cetinje 548-9
Cézanne, Paul 191, 212, 285, 286, 288, 312, 430

Chagall, Marc 198, 263, 269, 293, 390
Chamonix 258-61
Champagne 234-7
Champs-Élysées 209
Channel Tunnel 867
Charlemagne 308
Charles VII 227, 234, 308
Charles VIII 247
Chartres 218-19
Châteauneuf-du-Pape 294
chateaux, see castles, fortresses & palaces
cheese 228, 237
children, travel with 838, 852-3
Chillida, Eduardo 656, 706, 708, 753
Chinchón 674
Chios 387-9
Chirac, Jacques 310
churches & cathedrals
    Akdamar Kilisesi 830
    Baptistère St-Jean 271
    Basílica de Nuestra Señora del Pilar 704
    Basilica di San Lorenzo 479
    Basilica di San Marco 459
    Basilica di San Pietro in Vincoli 431
    Basilica di Santa Croce 508
    Basilique St-Rémi 234
    Berat 58
    Capela dos Ossos 588
    Cappella degli Scrovegni 457
    Catedral (Burgos) 680
    Catedral (León) 679
    Catedral (Palma de Mallorca) 721
    Catedral (Toledo) 681
    Catedral de Santiago de Compostela 712
    Cathedral & Giralda 727
    Cathedral of Christ's Resurrection 551
    Cathedral of St Domnius 153
    Cathedral of St George 637
    Cathedral of St Lovro 159-60
    Cathedral of the Assumption (Koper) 635
    Cathedral of the Assumption (Krk Island) 148
    Cathedral of the Assumption of the Blessed Virgin Mary 121
    Cathedral of the Assumption of the Virgin 167
    Cathédrale de Notre Dame de Paris 193
    Cathédrale Notre Dame (Amiens) 223
    Cathédrale Notre Dame (Chartres) 219-20
    Cathédrale Notre Dame (Reims) 234
    Cathédrale Notre-Dame (Strasbourg) 238

Cathédrale St-André 271
Cathédrale St-Bénigne 249
Cattedrale di Monreale 514
Cattedrale di Santa Maria del Fiore 475
Chiesa di Santa Maria del Popolo 427
Chiesa di Santa Maria della Salute 461
Church of the Dormition of St Mary 58
Duomo (Florence) 475, **18**
Duomo (Milan) 452
Duomo (Pisa) 485
Duomo (Siena) 487
Église St-Sulpice 193
Ermita de San Antonio de la Florida 657
Igreja da Misericórdia 585
Igreja de Santa Maria 591
Igreja de Santo António 586
Igreja de São Francisco 596
Igreja Matriz 587
La Catedral 686
La Sagrada Família 10, 690, **11**
Orthodox Cathedral of Christ Saviour 108
Pantheon 425
Sé (Braga) 602
Sé (Évora) 588
Sé (Porto) 596
Sé Velha 593
Sistine Chapel 425
St Mark's Cathedral 163
St Peter's Basilica 424
St Tryphon's Cathedral 541
Ste-Chapelle 193
Templo do Sagrado Coração de Jesus 601
cider 224
cinema 69, 115, 311, 403, 526, 644, 752-3, 835
cinemas 339, 391, 484, 579
Cinque Terre 448-9
Çirali 809-10
Ciutadella 726
climate 20, 25, 26, 27, 28, 29, see also individual countries
Clovis 234
Coimbra 593-4
Colette 200
Colosseum 416, **4**
concert halls, see opera houses, theatres & concert halls
Conimbriga 593
Constantinople, see İstanbul
consulates 854, see also individual countries
convents & monasteries
Agias Triados 351
Agias Varvaras Rousanou 351, **18**
Agiou Nikolaou Anapafsa 351
Agiou Stefanou 351
Cetinje Monastery 549
Convento de Cristo 592
Convento de las Descalzas Reales 657
Convento dos Capuchos 581
Dobrun Monastery 103
Dominican Monastery 167
Franciscan Monastery (Dubrovnik) 166-7
Franciscan Monastery (Hvar Town) 160
Megalou Meteorou 351
Minorite Monastery 637
Monasterio San Juan de los Reyes 681
Monastery of St John the Theologian 385
Monestir de Montserrat 700
Morača Monastery 554
Mosteiro de Santa Maria de Alcobaça 592
Mosteiro de Santa Maria de Vitória 592
Mosteiro dos Jerónimos 567
Nossa Senhora do Desterro 587
Ostrog Monastery 553-4
Piva Monastery 557
Savina Monastery 538
Varlaam 351
Córdoba 733-6, **734**
Corfu 393-6, **394**
Corinth 344-5
Corsica 303-8
Cortina d'Ampezzo 474
Coşkun, Celal 834
Costa Blanca 720
Costa Brava 701-2
Costa da Caparica 581
Costa da Morte 715
Costa de Almería 739-40
costs 858, see also individual countries
Côte d'Azur 291-303
Côte d'Opale 222
Coulon 270
courses 856-7
credit cards 858, 859
Cres 149
Crete 371-9, **372-3**
Croatia 15, 36, 119-82, **122-3**, **15**
    accommodation 119, 177
    activities 177-8
    business hours 178
    climate 119
    costs & money 120, 178-9
    drinking 176-7
    embassies 178
    exchange rates 120
    food 119, 120, 176-7, 178
    highlights 122
    history 173-4
    internet resources 120
    itineraries 120
    language 878-9
    planning 119-20
    public holidays 179
    telephone services 179
    tourist offices 179
    travel to/from 120, 180
    travel within 180-2
    visas 179-80
Cuenca 683
currency 21, 857, 859
customs regulations 838, 853
Cyclades 359-71
cycling 851, 866-7, 869-70
    Croatia 137, 140, 143, 165, 177
    France 200, 222, 242, 262, 320
    Greece 410
    Italy 533
    Montenegro 551, 554
    Portugal 570, 581, 583, 603, 608
    Slovenia 628, 630, 631
    Spain 761

D

da Vinci, Leonardo 197, 244, 247, 452, 475
Dalí, Salvador 651, 656, 700, 753
Dalmatia 149-72
dangers 873, see also safety
Dante Alighieri 473, 525
Datça Peninsula 801
D-Day beaches 227-8
de Gaulle, Charles 310
Degas, Edgar 191, 198, 201, 288, 312
Deià 723
Delacroix 193, 197, 200, 225, 265
Delanoë, Bertrand 185
Delos 362
Delphi 350-1, **16**
Devrent Valley 825
Dhërmi 61
Diakofto 344
Didyma 797
Digne-les-Bains 296
Dijon 248-50
Dilofo 357
Dimitsana 347
disabilities, travellers with 862
    Albania 72
    Bosnia & Hercegovina 116
    Croatia 179
    Greece 408
    Italy 531
    Turkey 842

Disneyland Resort Paris 217
diving 851-2
 Croatia 137, 140, 143, 165, 168, 177
 Italy 514, 529
 Montenegro 547
 Portugal 588, 591
 Spain 701
 Turkey 796, 801, 838
Dobrota 540
Dodecanese 379-86
Dolomites 474
Donatello 479, 487
Dordogne 266-8
drinks 22, see also beer, cider, ouzo, port wine, wine
driving, see car travel
Drymades 61
Dubrovnik 16, 166-72, **168-9**, **16**
Dumas, Alexandre 201, 281
Duncan, Isadora 200
Dune du Pilat 274
Dürer, Albrecht 265, 651
Durrës 56-7

E
Eceabat 784-6
economy
 Albania 66
 Bosnia & Hercegovina 111
 Croatia 173
 France 310
 Greece 402
 Montenegro 557-8
 Portugal 605
 Spain 752
 Turkey 833
Edirne 781-2
Efes, see Ephesus
Eiffel Tower 12, 185, 190, **12**
El Greco 403, 651, 657, 658, 681, 753
electricity 854
Elies 350
embassies 854, see also individual countries
emergencies 861
 language 877-87
Entrevaux 296
environment
 Albania 70
 Bosnia & Hercegovina 115
 Croatia 175-6
 France 312-13
 Greece 403-4
 Italy 527

000 Map pages
000 Photo pages

Portugal 605
Slovenia 644
Spain 754
Turkey 835-6
Épernay 236-7
Ephesus 15, 794-6, **795**, **15**
Epidavros 347
Ermida 603
Esquiline 431, 436-7, 440, **434-5**
Estoril 583
Estremoz 590
Eurail passes 875-6
Eurostar 867-8
events, see festivals & events
Évora 588-90
exchange rates, see individual countries
Extremadura 747-50

F
fado 578
Faro 585
Favret, Eric 259
ferries, see boat travel
festivals & events 25-9, see also music festivals
 Adventure Race 538
 Art-Athina 332
 Athens Biennial 332
 Bienal de Flamenco 729
 Carnaval de Nice 294
 Carnival 25, 462, **7**
 Dia de Sant Joan 692
 Estate Romana 432
 Fashion Week 200
 Feria de Abril 729
 Féria de Pentecôte 276
 Féria des Vendanges 276
 Festa de Nossa Senhora da Agonia 601
 Festa de Santo António 570
 Festa de São João 598
 Festa dei Santi Pietro e Paolo 433
 Festa del Redentore 462
 Festa de'Noantri 433
 Festa di San Gennaro 498
 Festa di San Giovanni 480
 Festa di Sant'Efisio 521
 Festas de Lisboa 570
 Festes de la Mercè 692
 Festival d'Avignon 27, 289
 Festival de Cannes 26, 297
 Festival Internazionale del Film di Roma 433
 Festival Off 289
 Fête des Lumières 253
 Fête des Vendanges de Montmartre 201

Fiesta de San Isidro 658
Formula One Grand Prix 302
Hartera 145
Hellenic Festival 332
Las Fallas de San José 25, 719
Maggio dei Monumenti 500
Maggio Musicale Fiorentino 26, 480
Mercado Medieval 592
Mondial de la Bière 238
Monsaraz Museu Aberto 590
Natale di Roma 432
Nuit Blanche 201
Palio 27, 488
Palio delle Quattro Antiche Repubbliche Marinare 462
Paris Plages 201
Patras Carnival 343
Procession Eucharistique 273
Queima das Fitas 593
Ravenna Festival 472
Regata Storica 462
ReMap 332
Riesling du Monde 238
RomaEuropa 433
Sanfermines 27, 710
Sarajevo Film Festival 84
Scoppio del Carro 480
Semana Santa 728
Serralves Em Festa 598
Settimana della Cultura 432
Suma Flamenca 659
Tirana International Film Festival 48
Venice Architecture Biennale 462
Venice Biennale 462
Venice Film Festival 28, 462
Veranos de la Villa 659
Fethiye 802-4
Figueirinha 582
films, see cinema
Filoti 365
Fira 368
Firenze, see Florence
Fiskardo 397
flamenco 659, 669-70, 728, 732, 738, 753-4
Flanders 219-24
Florence 18, 474-85, **476-7**, **18**
 accommodation 480-2
 drinking 483
 entertainment 484
 festivals & events 480
 food 482-3
 history 474
 sights 474-9
 tourist offices 484
 tours 480
 travel to/from 484
 travel within 484-5

Fóia 587
food 22, 854, *see also individual cities & countries*
  language 877-87
football 455
Fornalutx 723
Fornells 726
fortresses, *see* castles, fortresses & palaces
Fra Angelico 479, 651
Fra Bartolomeo 306
France 36, 183-322, **186-7**
  accommodation 183, 314-15
  activities 315
  business hours 315-16
  climate 183
  costs & money 184, 317
  drinking 313-14
  embassies & consulates 316
  food 183, 184, 313-14, 316
  highlights 186
  history 308-10
  holidays 317
  internet resources 184
  itineraries 184
  language 316-17, 879-80
  planning 183-4
  telephones services 317-18
  travel to/from 318-19
  travel within 320-2
  visas 318
Franco, General Francisco 751
François I 309
French Riviera 291-303
Frikes 398

G
Galapo 582
Galicia 712-14
galleries, *see* museums & galleries
Gallipoli Peninsula 784
gardens, *see* parks & gardens
Garnier, Charles 198
Gaudí, Antoni 679, 690, 691, 721
gay travellers 854-5
  Albania 71
  Bosnia & Hercegovina 116
  Croatia 132, 178
  France 213, 316
  Greece 389, 406
  Italy 530
  Montenegro 560
  Slovenia 645-6
  Spain 669, 756
  Turkey 839
Gefyra 348
gelato 439, 483
Gelibolu 784

Genoa 446-8
George II of Greece 401
Géricault 197
Gerolimenas 349
Giambologna 478
Gibraltar 746-7
Giorgione 460
Giotto 457
Girona 700-1
Giverny 226
Gjirokastra 65-6
glaciers 259
González, Julio 721
Göreme 823-5
Gouveia 595
Goya, Francisco 265, 651, 657, 658, 681, 704, 753
Granada 736-9, **738-9**
Grand Bazaar 768
Grand Canal 459
Grasse 297
Graves, Robert 723
Greece 16, 37, 323-412, **325**
  accommodation 323, 405-6
  business hours 406
  climate 323
  costs & money 324, 407
  drinking 404-5
  embassies & consulates 406
  food 323, 324, 404-5
  highlights 325
  history 400-2
  internet resources 324
  itineraries 324
  language 880-1
  public holidays 407
  telephone services 407
  tourist offices 408
  travel to/from 324, 408-9
  travel within 361, 410-12
  visas 408
Grenoble 263-5
Guarda 595
Guène, Faïza 311
Guimarães 602
Gythio 348-9

H
Habsburgs 642-3
Hadrian 445
Hagia Sophia 769
Halki 366
Halkidiki 355
hamams 776
Hania 375-6
Hatay 817-18
health 839, 855-6
heat exhaustion & heatstroke 855-6

Héloïse d'Argenteuil 200
Hemingway, Ernest 709
Henri IV 191
Henry VI 308
Herceg Novi 538-40
Hercegovina 91-102
Herculaneum 502
Hergé 244
hiking 852
  Albania 54, 59, 71
  Bosnia & Hercegovina 116
  Croatia 143, 178
  France 222, 264, 306
  Greece 350, 357
  Montenegro 554, 550, 551, 556
  Portugal 603
  Slovenia 624, 628, 630, 631
  Spain 756
  Turkey 803, 823, 837
Himara 61-2
Hippocrates 383
historical buildings, monuments & squares, *see also* archaeological sites
  Acropolis 329
  Arc de Triomphe 197
  Aya Sofya 769
  Bocca della Verità 421
  Casa Amatller 691
  Casa Batlló 691
  Casa di Giulietta 456
  Colosseum 416, **4**
  Conciergerie 193
  Dante's Tomb 473
  Eiffel Tower 12, 185, 190, **12**
  Galleria Vittorio Emanuele II 452
  Hôtel des Invalides 192
  La Pedrera 690
  Leaning Tower of Pisa 485
  Les Catacombes 191
  Metropol Parasol 728
  Morbihan Megaliths 229
  Panthéon 192
  Parthenon 329
  Piazza dei Miracoli 485
  Piazza San Marco 460
  Plaça Reial 686
  Place de la Bastille 199
  Plaza Mayor (Madrid) 656
  Plaza Mayor (Salamanca) 675
  Pont Neuf 193
  Pont St-Bénézet 287
  Pont St-Louis 193
  Ponte dei Sospiri 460
  Spanish Steps 427
  St Peter's Square 424
  Temple of Athena Nike 329
  Theatre of Dionysos 329
  Trevi Fountain 426

history, *see also individual cities & countries*, WWI, WWII
battle of Hastings 226
Byzantine Empire 400, 831-2
Crimean War 309
Franco-Prussian War 309
French Revolution 185, 309
Hundred Years War 308
Moors 604
Olympics 400
Ottoman Empire 400, 832
Reconquista 750
Roman Empire 524, 750
hitching 873
holidays 856
Hollande, François 310
Homer 368, 400, 402, 787
Hora Sfakion 378
horse riding
France 222
Portugal 603
Spain 745
Turkey 823
hot-air ballooning 822
Hugo, Victor 199, 310
Hvar Island 160-3, **24**
Hydra 358-9

I
Ibiza 724-6
Igoumenitsa 357
Ihlara Valley 827
Île de la Cité 193
Île Rousse 304
Île Ste-Marguerite 297
Île St-Honorat 297
Île St-Louis 193
Îles Lavezzi 308
Ilha da Tavira 586
Ilha Deserta 585
Iliad 400, 787
Il Postino 526
immigration 865
insurance 855, 856, 872
internet access 856, *see also individual countries*
internet resources 21, 855, *see also individual countries*
InterRail passes 876
Ioannina 356-7
Ionian Islands 393-400
Ios 367-8, **367**
Iraklio 372-4
Isola Bella 516

İstanbul 12, 765-81, **774-5, 768, 770-1, 2**
accommodation 774-7
drinking 779-80
entertainment 779-80
food 777-9
history 765
itineraries 765
safety 781
sights 765-73
tourist offices 780
tours 773-4
travel to/from 780
travel within 780-1
Istria 136-44
Italy 37, 413-534, **415**
accommodation 413, 528-9
activities 529
business hours 529
climate 413
costs & money 414, 530
drinking 527-8
embassies 529
food 413, 414, 527-8, 529
highlights 415
history 524-5
internet resources 414
itineraries 414
language 882-3
planning 413-14
public holidays 530
telephone services 531
tourist offices 531
travel to/from 414, 531-3
travel within 533-4
visas 531
Ithaki 398
itineraries 30-4, *see also individual countries*
İzmir 790-1

J
Jahorina 90-1
Jajce 106-7
Jal 62
jamón 754
Joan of Arc 224, 234, 308
Juan Carlos of Spain 751
Julian Alps 623-33
Jura, The 265-6

K
Kahta 828
Kalavryta 344
Kaleiçi, *see* Antalya
Kalkan 805-6
Kandinsky, Wassily 238, 269, 430, 460

Kapadokya, *see* Cappadocia
Karadut 828
Kardamyli 350
Karpathos 382-3
Kaş 806-8, **808-9**
Kassandra Peninsula 355
Kassiopi 395
Kastraki 351
Katzenthal 239
kayaking 852, *see also* rafting
Bosnia & Hercegovina 111
Croatia 168-9, 178
Montenegro 539, 550
Portugal 586, 593, 603
Slovenia 628, 631, 632
Turkey 838
Kayseri 826-7
Kazantzakis, Nikos 402
Kefallonia 397-8
Kelly, Grace 302
Kemal, Yaşar 834
Khadra, Yasmina 311
Kioni 398
kitesurfing 745, 756, 852
Kızkalesi 816-17
Klee, Paul 286, 460, 687
Klimt, Gustav 430
Knights of St John 381, 384
Knossos 374
Kobarid 632-3
Kolašin 554-5
Koliba 91
Konya 820-1
Koper 635-6
Köprülü Kanyon 814
Korčula Island 163
Kos 383-5
Kotor 540-3, **542**
Kozjak Stream Waterfalls 632
Kranjska Gora 630-1
Kravice Waterfalls 101
Krk Island 148-9
Kruja 55-6
Krupa na Vrbasu 109
Ksamil 64
Kuşadası 796-7
Kythira 399

L
La Besurta 705
La Sagrada Família 10, 690, **11**
Lac d'Annecy 261
Lacroix, Christian 202
Laganas Bay 399
Lagos 586-7
Lake Bled 624-8, **626**
Lake Bohinj 628-30

Lake Koman 55
Lake Pamvotida 356
Lakones 396
Lakonian Mani 349
language 877-87
    courses 856-7
Languedoc-Roussillon 275-9
Lapa 567-8
Lasithi Plateau 378-9
Last Supper, the 452
Lastva 540
Le Brun, Charles 218
Le Clézio, JMG 311
Le Corbusier 390
Le Nôtre, André 218
Lecce 508-9
Leaning Tower of Pisa 485
Lefkada 396
legal matters 857
Léger, Fernand 286
Lens 225
León 678-80
Leonidio 347
Leroux, Gaston 198
Les Baux de Provence 290-1
Les Calanques 280
Les Calanques de Piana 306
Les Eyzies-de-Tayac-Sireuil 268
lesbian travellers 854-5
    Albania 71
    Bosnia & Hercegovina 116
    Croatia 132, 178
    France 213, 316
    Greece 389, 406
    Italy 530
    Montenegro 560
    Slovenia 645-6
    Spain 669, 756
    Turkey 839
L'Escala 701
L'Estartit 701
Lesvos 389-91
Letta, Enrico 525
Levy, Marc 311
Lichtenstein, Roy 293
Lido, the 461
Lille 219-22
Limnionas 399
Lindos 382
Lipari 514
Lipica 636
Lippi, Filippo 427, 479
Lisbon 14, 566-80, **568-9**, **572-3**, **14**
    accommodation 570-5
    drinking 577
    entertainment 577-9
    festivals & events 570
    food 575-7

itineraries 566
    shopping 579
    sights 566-70
    tourist offices 580
    tours 570
    travel to/from 580
    travel within 580
Listrac-Médoc 272
literature
    Albania 69
    Bosnia & Hercegovina 114-15
    Croatia 174-5
    France 310-11
    Greece 402
    Italy 525
    Slovenia 643
    Spain 752
    Turkey 834-5
Litohoro 356
Ljubljana 611-23, **614-15**
    accommodation 617-18
    drinking 619-20
    entertainment 620-1
    festivals & events 617
    food 618-19
    history 611-12
    internet access 621-2
    itineraries 612
    sights 612-13, 617
    tourist offices 622
    tours 617
    travel to/from 622, 623
    travel within 622-3
Llafranc 701
Locmariaquer 229
Loire Valley 18, 242, 243-8
Lorca, Federico García 752
Lorenzetti, Ambrogio 487
Lorrain, Claude 240
Lorraine 237-42
Lošinj 149
Louha 399
Louis IX 193
Louis XIII 192
Louis XIV 192, 217, 218-19, 265, 309
Louis XV 192, 309
Louis XVI 185
Lourdes 273-4
Lousios Gorge 347
Loutro 378
Louvre 196-7
Lucca 489-91
Lugo 715
Lukomir 91
Luso 594-5
Lycian Way 803
Lyon 252-8, **254-5**

M
macarons 205
Madrid 651-73, **654-5**, **660-1**, **664**
    accommodation 659-63
    courses 658
    drinking 667-8
    entertainment 668-71
    festivals & events 658-9
    food 663-7
    history 651
    shopping 671-2
    sights 651-8
    tourist offices 672
    tours 658
    travel to/from 672-3
    travel within 673
magazines 849
Magritte 238
Málaga 740-2
Malatya 828
Malia 375
Mallarmé, Stéphane 311
Mallorca 720-4, **722**
Mamma Mia 392
Manet, Edouard 191, 288, 312, 450
Mani, the 349-50
Manolates 387
Mantegna, Andrea 456
Manteigas 595
Manuel I of Portugal 605
Maó 726
maps 857
Marathonisi islet 348
Mardin 829-30
Maribor 641
Marie Antoinette 185, 193, 217
markets
    Dolac Market 121
    El Rastro 671
    Feira da Ladra 579
    Gjirokastra 65
    Grand Bazaar 768
    Kruja 56
    Les Halles de Lyon 256
    Marché aux Enfants Rouges 206
    Marché aux Puces de la Porte de
        Vanves 215
    Marché aux Puces de Montreuil 215
    Marché aux Puces de St-Ouen 215
    Marché Bastille 206
    Marché Belleville 206
    Marché Couvert 241
    Marché Couvert St-Quentin 206
    Marché de Noël 238
    Marché Raspail 206
    Mercat de la Boqueria 683
    Mercat de Santa Caterina 690
    Monastiraki Flea Market 339

markets *continued*
  Odos 1866 373
  Porta Portese 442
  Tirana 50
  Zagreb 133
Marmaris 801-2
Marseille 280-5, **282-3**
Martin Brod 110
Matera 506-7
Matisse, Henri 263, 265, 286, 293, 312, 390, 450
Maydos 784-6
measures 849
Međed 555
medical services 855
Međugorje 100-1
Megalo Papingo 357
Mehmet the Conqueror 765, 768
Menalon Mountains 347
Menorca 726-7
Mérida 749-50
Messinian Mani 349-50
Mesta 388
Metaxas 401
Meteora 18, 351-2, **18**
metro travel 874
Metz 241-2
meyhanes 778
Mezquita 733
Michelangelo 197, 424, 425, 426, 431, 471, 475, 478, 479
Mikro Papingo 357
Milan 452-5, **453**
Miletus 797
Milišići 91
Miró, Joan 390, 651, 656, 691, 753
Mithymna 390-1
Mitterrand, François 185, 310
Mljet Island 164-6
mobile phones 861
Modigliani, Amedeo 200, 225, 430, 651
Molyvos 390-1
Monaco 300-3, **301**
monasteries, *see* convents & monasteries
Monchique 587
Monemvasia 348
Monet, Claude 191, 224, 225, 226, 238, 240, 263, 269, 286, 312, 567
money 20, 21, 853-4, 857-9
moneychangers 858-9
Monodendri 357
Monsaraz 590
Mont Blanc 260

Mont St-Michel 229, 313
Montaner, Lluís Domènech i 687
Montenegro 37, 535-62, **537**
  accommodation 535, 560
  business hours 560
  climate 535
  costs & money 536, 560
  drinking 536
  embassies 560
  exchange rates 536
  food 535, 536, 559, 560
  highlights 537
  history 558-9
  internet resources 536
  itineraries 536
  planning 535-6
  public holidays 561
  telephone services 561
  travel to/from 536, 561-2
  travel within 562
Monti, Mario 525
Montignac 268
Montmartre 201, 204, 212, **198**
Moore, Henry 430
Morača Canyon 554
Morandi, Giorgio 470
Morocco 746
mosques
  Blue Mosque 765, **13**
  Čaršija Mosque 101
  Et'hem Bey Mosque 45-6
  Fethija Mosque 110
  Gazi-Husrevbey Mosque 79
  Haji Alibey Mosque 105
  Karađozbeg Mosque 93
  Koski Mehmed Paša Mosque 93
  Many Coloured Mosque 105
  Mezquita (Córdoba) 733
  Mezquita del Cristo de la Luz 682
  Mosque of Süleyman 381
  Muradi Mosque 60
  Red Mosque 58
  Roznamedži Ibrahimefendi Mosque 93
  Selimiye Camii 782
  Süleymaniye Mosque 769
mosquitoes 856
Mostar 17, 92-100, **94-5**, **17**
motorcycle travel, *see* car travel
Moulin, Jean 192, 253
Moulin Rouge 212
movies, *see* cinema
Mt Athos 355
Mt Erciyes 821
Mt Etna 517, 527
Mt Ida 374
Mt Kynthos 362
Mt Lovćen 540

Mt Nemrut National Park 828
Mt Olympus 355-6
Mt Psiloritis 374
Mt Triglav 17, 629, **17**
Munster 237
Murano 461
Murcia 715
Murillo, Bartolomé Esteban 658
museums & galleries 22
  Acropolis Museum 329
  Archaeological Museum (Pula) 137
  Art Pavilion 127
  Batana House 140
  Beekeeping Museum 625
  Benaki Museum 330
  Byzantine & Christian Museum 331
  Capitoline Museums 421
  Casa Museu Dalí 700
  Centre Pompidou 197
  Centre Pompidou-Metz 241
  Centro de Arte Reina Sofía 651
  Cité de l'Espace 279
  City Museum (Zagreb) 127
  Ciudad de las Artes y las Ciencias 715
  Collezione Peggy Guggenheim 460
  Croatian Museum of Naïve Art 126
  Dražen Petrović Memorial Museum 128
  Ethnographic Museum 153
  Galerija Klovićevi Dvori 127
  Galleria degli Uffizi 475
  Galleria dell'Accademia 479
  Gallery of Fine Arts (Split) 155
  Gallery of Modern Art (Zagreb) 127-8
  Göreme Open-Air Museum 823
  Homeland War Museum 167
  İstanbul Archaeology Museums 769
  Louvre-Lens 225
  MACBA 687
  Marco Polo Museum 163
  Maritime & History Museum 145
  Meštrović Gallery 155
  Mevlâna Museum 820
  Musée Calvet 287
  Musée d'Art Contemporain 253
  Musée de Grenoble 263
  Musée de l'Annonciade 298
  Musée de l'Œuvre Notre Dame 238
  Musée des Beaux-Arts (Lyon) 253
  Musée des Beaux-Arts (Nancy) 240
  Musée des Beaux-Arts (Nantes) 269
  Musée des Beaux-Arts et d'Archéologie (Besançon) 265
  Musée d'Orsay 191
  Musée du Louvre 196-7

Musée National d'Art Moderne 197
Musée Picasso (Paris) 199
Musée Rodin 191
Museo Archeologico Nazionale
   (Naples) 495
Museo Civico (Siena) 487
Museo del Prado 651, 658
Museo dell'Ara Pacis 427
Museo di San Marco 479
Museo e Galleria Borghese 427
Museo Guggenheim 708
Museo Nazionale Romano 431
Museo Picasso Málaga 740
Museu d'Història de Barcelona 687
Museu d'Història de Tarragona 702
Museu Nacional d'Art de Catalunya
   691
Museu Picasso (Barcelona) 687
Museum Mimara 127
Museum of Anatolian
   Civilisations 818
Museum of Ancient Glass 150
Museum of Broken Relationships 121
Museum of Contemporary Art
   (Zagreb) 128
National Archaeological Museum
   (Athens) 330
Onufri Museum 58
Palazzo Ducale 460
Palazzo Pitti 479
Strossmayer Gallery of Old Masters
   127
Svrzo House 79
Teatre-Museu Dalí 700
Town Museum (Korčula Island) 163
Town Museum (Split) 153
Town Museum (Trogir) 160
Tusculum Museum 153
Vatican Museums 425
War Photo Limited 166
music
   Albania 69
   Bosnia & Hercegovina 115
   Croatia 175
   France 230, 311-12
   Greece 403
   Italy 526
   Portugal 605
   Slovenia 644
   Spain 753-4
   Turkey 835
music festivals
   Astropolis 230
   Eurochocolate 491
   Les Transmusicales de Rennes 230
   Les Vieilles Charrues de Carhaix
      230
   Music Biennale Zagreb 25-6, 128
   Nice Jazz Festival 294

Noites Ritual Rock 598
Primo Maggio 432
Puccini Festival 489
Sani Jazz Festival 355
Torino Milano Festival Internazionale
   della Musica 454
Umbria Jazz Festival 491
Mustafa Kemal Atatürk 832
Mustafapaşa 826
mustard 250
Mycenae 347
Mykonos 359-63, **360**
Mystras 348
Mytikas 356
Mytilini 389-90

N
Nafplio 345-7
Nancy 240-1
Nantes 268-70
Naples 494-501, **496-7**
Napoléon Bonaparte 192, 197, 303,
   306, 309, 751
Napoléon III 185, 309
national parks & reserves
   Biogradska Gora National Park 555
   Durmitor National Park 555-7
   Lake Skadar National Park 549-51
   Llogaraja Pass National Park 60
   Lovćen National Park 548
   Mljet National Park 165
   Mt Dajti National Park 52
   Mt Nemrut National Park 828
   National Marine Park of
      Alonnisos 392
   National Marine Park of
      Zakynthos 399
   Parc Naturel Interrégional du
      Marais Poitevin 270
   Parco Nazionale delle Cinque
      Terre 448
   Parque Nacional da Peneda-Gerês
      603
   Parque Nacional de los Picos de
      Europa 711
   Parque Natural da Arrábida 582
   Parque Natural da Serra da Estrela
      595
   Plitvice Lakes National Park 136
   Sutjeska National Park 103
   Una National Park 110
Navarra 709-11
Naxos 364-6, **365**
Nazaré 592
Nemrut Dağı 828-9
newspapers 849
Nice 291-6, **292-3**
Nijinsky, Vaslav 201
Nîmes 275-7

Normandy 224-9
Northeastern Aegean Islands 386-91
Nydri 396

O
Óbidos 591-2
Odyssey 398, 400
Oia 369
oil wrestling 782
Ölüdeniz 804-5
Olymbos 383
Olympia 350
Olympos 809-10
Omaha Beach 228
Omalos 377
Opal Coast 222
Opatija 147-8
opening hours 852, *see also
   individual countries*
opera houses, theatres & concert
   halls
   Arena di Verona 456
   Auditorium Parco della Musica 441
   Gran Teatre del Liceu 683
   La Cigale 213
   Le Lido de Paris 213
   Moulin Rouge 212
   National Theatre (Athens) 338
   Olympia Theatre 338
   Opéra de Lyon 257
   Palais Garnier 198
   Palau de la Música Catalana 697
   Teatro alla Scala 452, 454
   Teatro Carlo Felice 446, 448
   Teatro Comunale 484
   Teatro dell'Opera di Roma 441
   Teatro La Fenice 467
   Teatro Massimo 512
   Teatro Olimpico 441
   Teatro San Carlo 500
Orebić 164
Ortisei 474
Orvieto 493
Ostia Antica 445
Our-Lady-of-the-Rock Island 540
ouzo 404
Oviedo 711-12
oysters 231, 273

P
Padua 457-8
Paganini, Niccolò 446
Pakleni Islands 161
palaces, *see* castles, fortresses &
   palaces
Palatine Hill 10, 417
Palazuelo, Pablo 656
Pale di San Martino 474

Paleohora 377
Paleokastritsa 396
Palermo 510-14, **511**
Palma de Mallorca 721-3
Pals 702
Pamplona 709-11
Pamuk, Orhan 834
Pamukkale 796
Pane e Tulipani 526
Papandreou, George 401
paragliding 544, 804
parasailing 554
Parikia 363
Paris 185-217, **188-9**, **194-5**, **198**
    accommodation 201-4
    activities 200
    drinking 210-12
    entertainment 212-14
    festivals & events 200-1
    food 204-10
    history 185
    itineraries 185
    medical services 215
    shopping 214-15
    sights 185-200
    tourist offices 215
    tours 200
    travel to/from 215-16
    travel within 216-17
parks & gardens
    Canal St-Martin 200, 207
    Jardin du Luxembourg 191
    National Gardens (Athens) 331
    Park Güell 691
    Parque del Buen Retiro 657
    Villa Borghese 427, 430
Paros 363-4, **363**
Parthenon 329
Paşabağı 825
passports 865
Patara 805
patisseries 205
Patitiri 393
Patmos 385-6
Patra 343-4
Pauillac 272
Paxi 396
Pays d'Auge 224
Pelekas Beach 396
Pelion Peninsula 351
Peloponnese, the 343-50
Peniche 591
Perast 540
Peratallada 702

perfume 297
Pergamum 789-90
Perge 814
Pericles 328, 400
Perugia 491-3
Petrovac 546
Phaestos 374-5
Philip II of Macedon 329
Philippe-Auguste 196
phonecards 861
photography 859
Piana 306
Piano, Renzo 447
Picasso, Pablo 312, 460, 651, 753
    museums 199, 687, 740-1
Picos de Europa 711
Pigadia 383
Pindar 402
Pindos Mountains 356
Pinhão 601
Piraeus 341-3, **342**
Piran 636-40, **638-9**
Pisa 485-7
Pisano, Bonanno 485
Piva Canyon 557
planning, see also individual
        countries
    budgeting 20
    calendar of events 25-9
    internet resources 21
    itineraries 30-4
    Mediterranean Europe basics 20-1
    Mediterranean Europe's regions
        35-9
    travel seasons 20, 25, 26, 27, 28, 29
Plitvice Lakes 110
Pocinho 601
Počitelj 101
Podgorica 551-3, **552-3**
Poitiers 270-1
politics
    Albania 66
    Bosnia & Hercegovina 111
    Croatia 172-3, 174
    France 310
    Greece 401
    Italy 525
    Montenegro 557-8
    Portugal 605
    Spain 751-2
    Turkey 832-3
Pollença 723
Pollock, Jackson 430, 460
Pompeii 502
Pompidou, Georges 310
Poreč 142-4
Poros 358
port wine 597, 598
Portinho da Arrábida 582

Porto 595-600, **596-7**
Portorož 640
Portugal 38, 563-608, **565**
    accommodation 563, 605-6
    activities 606
    business hours 606
    climate 563
    costs & money 564, 606
    drinking 605
    embassies 606
    exchange rates 564
    food 563, 564, 605, 606
    highlights 565
    internet resources 564
    itineraries 564
    language 883-4
    public holidays 607
    telephone services 607
    travel to/from 564, 607
    travel within 608
    visas 607
Positano 505
postal services 859
Postojna 633-4
Prčanj 540
Predjama 634
Priene 797
Proust, Marcel 199
Prouvé, Jean 240
Provence 16, 280-91, **16**
Pržno 545-6
Psyhro 379
Ptuj 641-2
Puccini, Giacomo 490
Pula 136-9
Punta Corrente Forest Park 140
Pyla-sur-Mer 274
Pyrgi 388
Pythagoras 387
Pythagorio 387

Q
Quimper 230-1

R
radio 849
Radovljica 625
rafting 852, see also kayaking
    Albania 59, 71
    Bosnia & Hercegovina 111, 115
    Croatia 168-9, 178
    Montenegro 554, 556
    Slovenia 628, 631, 632
    Turkey 838
Rainier III of Monaco 302
Raphael 197, 225, 425, 426, 427, 479,
    498, 651

Ravel, Maurice 312
Ravenna 472-3
Rego, Paula 583
Reims 234-5
Rembrandt 567, 651
Reni, Guido 427
Renoir, Pierre-Auguste 191, 225, 227, 312, 450, 567
Rethymno 375
Rhodes 380-2, **380**
Rhône Valley 248-58
Rías Altas 715
Rijeka 144-7
Rijeka Crnojevića 550
Rimbaud, Arthur 311
Rio Douro 601-2
Risan 540
rock climbing 178, 629
Rodin, Auguste 191, 222, 265
Rodrigues, Amália 605
Roman Forum 417, 420, **10**
Roman Holiday 526
Rome 10, 416-45, **418-19**, **422-3**, **428-9**, **432**, **434-5**
accommodation 433-7
drinking 440-1
entertainment 441-2
festivals & events 432-3
food 437-40
history 416
internet access 442
itineraries 417
medical services 442
shopping 442
sights 416-32
tourist offices 443
travel to/from 443-4
travel within 444-5
Romeo & Juliet 456
Ronda 742-3
Room with a View 526
Rose 541
Rouen 224-6
Rousseau, Jean-Jacques 192, 310
Route des Vins d'Alsace 237
Route des Vins de Jura 266
Route du Chocolat et des Douceurs d'Alsace 237
Route du Cidre 224
Rovinj 139-42
Rt Kamenjak 137
Rubens, Peter Paul 224, 240, 265, 479, 651

S
Sa Calobra 723
safety 859-61, 873, *see also individual cities & countries*

Safranbolu 820
Sagres 588
Salamanca 675-7
Samaria Gorge 376-7
Samaris, Antonis 402
Samos 386-7, **386**
San Gimignano 491
San Martino di Castrozza 474
San Sebastián 19, 706-7
sand dunes 274
sandflies 856
Sanfermines 27, 710
Şanlıurfa 828, 829
Sant Antoni 726
Sant Feliu de Guíxols 701
Santa Cristina 474
Santiago de Compostela 712-14
Santillana del Mar 711
Santorini 368-71, **369**
Sappho 389, 402
Sarajevo 78-90, **80**, **82**
accommodation 84-5
activities 78-83
drinking 86-7
entertainment 87-8
festivals & events 84
food 85-6
history 78
itineraries 78
shopping 88
sights 78-83
tours 83-4
travel to/from 88, 89
travel within 88, 90
Saranda 62-4
Sardinia 520-3
Sarkozy, Nicolas 310, 313
Sarlat-La-Canéda 266-8
Saronic Gulf Islands 357-9
Saving Private Ryan 228
scams 860
Schengen visas 863
Seferis, George 402
Segovia 677-8
Seia 595
Selçuk 793-4
Selva Gardena 474
senior travellers 853
Serra da Estrela 595
Sesimbra 582
Seville 727-33, **730-1**
Sgombou 395
Shkodra 52-4
shopping 853, *see also individual cities*
Sicily 509-19
Side 814-15
Siena 487-9

Signac, Paul 299
Silves 587-8
Sintra 581-3
Sisley, Alfred 225, 288
Sistine Chapel 425
Sithonian Peninsula 355
Sitia 379
Sítio 592
Skala Eresou 389, 391
Skanderbeg 56
Skiathos 391-2
skiing 852
Bosnia & Hercegovina 90, 91, 115
France 260, 263, 264
Italy 474
Montenegro 554, 556
Slovenia 628, 630, 631
Spain 756
Turkey 783, 838
Škocjan Caves 634-5
Skopelos 392-3
Slovenia 38, 609-48, **611**
accommodation 609, 644-5
business hours 645
climate 609
costs & money 610, 646
drinking 644
embassies 645
exchange rates 610
festivals & events 645
food 609, 610, 644, 645
highlights 611
history 642-3
internet access 646
internet resources 610
itineraries 610
language 884-5
planning 609-10
postal services 646
public holidays 646
telephone services 646
tourist offices 646-7
travel to/from 610, 647
travel within 647-8
visas 647
smoking 849
snowboarding 852
Soča Valley 631-3
Solana, José Gutiérrez 656
Solin 153
Sóller 723
Somme, the 219-24
Sorrento 503-4
Sos del Rey Católico 705
Sougia 378
Spain 38, 649-762, **652-3**
accommodation 649, 755-6
activities 756

Spain continued
business hours 756
climate 649
costs & money 650, 757
drinking 754-5
embassies 756
food 649, 650, 754-5, 756
highlights 652-3
history 750-2
internet resources 650
itineraries 650
language 757, 885-6
planning 649-50
public holidays 757
telephone services 758
tourist offices 758
travel to/from 650, 758-60, 761
travel within 760-2
visas 758
Spanish Steps 427
Sparta 347-8
Spetses 359
Spinalonga Island 379
Split 152-9, **154-5**
Sporades 391-3
sporting grounds
Camp Nou 697
Estádio da Luz 579
Estádio Nacional (Lisbon) 579
Estadio Santiago Bernabéu 671
Stadio Giuseppe Meazza 455
St Francis de Assisi 493
St George's Island 540
St John the Baptist 223
St Peter's Square 424
St-Émilion 272
Stemnitsa 347
Stendhal 201
St-Malo 231-4, **232**
Stolac 101-2
Stoliv 540
Strasbourg 237-9
Štrbački Buk 110
Stromboli 515, 527
St-Tropez 298-300
Süleyman the Magnificent 765
surfing 852
France 274
Portugal 588, 591
Spain 756
Sveti Stefan 545-6, **6-7**
Symi 383
synagogues
Dubrovnik 167

Sinagoga (Córdoba) 733
Sinagoga del Tránsito 681
Sinagoga de Santa María La
Blanca 681
Sinagoga Major 687
Syracuse 517-19

T
Tamariu 701
Taormina 516-17
tapas 19, 666, **2**, **19**, **23**
Tarifa 745
Tarragona 702-3
Tavira 585-6
taxes 853
taxis 874
Taÿgetos Mountains 348, 349
telephone services 861, see also
individual countries
Termessos 814
Teruel 705
theatres, see opera houses, theatres
& concert halls
theft 860-1
Thessaloniki 352-5, **353**
Theth 54
Thira, see Santorini
Tiepolo, Giovanni 651
time 861-2
Tintin 244
Tintoretto 426, 460, 461, 651
tipping 859
Tirana 45-52, **46**
Titian 197, 265, 306, 426, 460, 461,
479, 498
Tivat 543-4
Tivoli 445-6
toilets 862
Toledo 681-3
Tomar 592-3
Torcello 461
Torla 705
Tossa de Mar 701, 702
Toulouse 277-9
Toulouse-Lautrec, Henri de 191
tourist offices 862
tours 874, see also individual cities
Tours 245-7
Tragaea 365
train travel
to/from Mediterranean Europe
867-8
within Mediterranean Europe 874-6
Trastevere 430-1, 435-6, 438-9, **432**
travel to/from Mediterranean Europe
865-9
travel within Mediterranean Europe
869-76
travellers cheques 859

Travnik 105-6
Trebinje 102-3
Trento 474
Trevi Fountain 426
Trogir 159-60
Troy 787
truffles 267
Trujillo 747-8
Truva 787
Turin 450-2
Turkey 39, 763-846, **766-7**
accommodation 763, 837
activities 837-8
business hours 838
climate 763
costs & money 764, 839-40
drinking 836
embassies 838
food 763, 764, 836, 839
highlights 766-7
history 831-3
internet access 839
internet resources 764
itineraries 764
language 886-7
public holidays 840
safety 841
telephone services 841
tourist offices 841
tours 801, 803
travel to/from 764, 843-4
travel within 845-6
visas 842
Tuscany 18, 473-91
TV 849
Tzermiado 379

U
Uçhisar 825
Ulcinj 547-8
Umbria 491-4
Umoljani 91
Ürgüp 825-6

V
vacations 856
Vaison-la-Romaine 291
Val di Fassa 474
Val Gardena 474
Valbonë 54
Valencia 715-19, **716**
Valldemossa 723
Van 830-1
Van Gogh, Vincent 191, 286, 288, 290
Vasiliki 396
Vasilikos Peninsula 399
Vathy 386-7, 398

000 Map pages
000 Photo pages

Vatican City 421-5, 426, 433, 437
vegetarian travellers
  Albania 70
  Bosnia & Hercegovina 177
  Croatia 177
  Greece 404
  Italy 527
  Montenegro 559
  Spain 755
  Turkey 836
Velázquez, Diego 426, 651, 658, 753
Venice 12, 458-70, **459**, **464-5**,
  468-9, **7**, **12**
  accommodation 462-3
  activities 461
  drinking 467
  entertainment 467
  festivals & events 462
  food 465-7
  history 458-9
  sights 459-61
  tourist offices 467-9
  tours 461
  travel to/from 469-70
  travel within 470
Venizelos, Eleftherios 401
Ventabren 286
Verlaine, Paul 311
Verne, Jules 269
Verona 456-7
Veronese, Paolo 306, 460
Versailles 217-18
Verudela Peninsula 137
Vesuvius 527
Vézère Valley 268
Via Appia Antica 437
Viana do Castelo 601-2
Vikos Gorge 357
Vila do Gerês 603
Vintgar Gorge 624
Virpazar 550
visas 862-3, see also individual
  countries

Višegrad 103-4
Visoko 104-5
Vivaldi, Antonio 526
Vlora 60-1
Volosko 148
Voltaire 192, 310
volunteering 842, 863
Voulismeni Lake 379
Vourliotes 387
Vrbas Canyons 109
Vršič Pass 17, 630, **17**
Vulcano 515
Vuno 62
Vyros Gorge 350

W
Warhol, Andy 293
water 855
weather, see climate
weights 849
Wells, Patricia 208
whale-watching 745
William the Conqueror 226, 227,
  308
windsurfing 852
  Croatia 178
  Greece 396
  Spain 745, 756
  Turkey 838
wine
  Bosnia & Hercegovina 101
  Croatia 176
  France 234, 314
  Italy 527
  Slovenia 644
wineries
  Albania 59
  France 234-6, 237, 239, 251, 266,
    272, 294
  Greece 345, 370
women travellers 863-4
  Albania 72
  Montenegro 561

Turkey 842
WWI
  Bosnia & Hercegovina 112
  France 309, 223
  Slovenia 643
  Turkey 784
WWII
  Bosnia & Hercegovina 112
  France 185, 222, 227-8, 253,
    263, 310
  Greece 371
  Italy 524
  Slovenia 643

Y
Yugoslavia 173, 559

Z
Žabljak 555
Zadar 150-2
Zagorohoria 357
Zagreb 121, 124-36, **124-5**
  accommodation 129-30
  drinking 131-2
  entertainment 132-3
  festivals & events 128-9
  food 130-1
  history 121
  itineraries 127
  shopping 133
  sights 121, 126-8
  tourist offices 134
  tours 128
  travel to/from 134, 135
  travel within 134, 136
Zakros 375
Zakynthos 398-400
Zapatero, José Luís Rodríguez 752
Zaragoza 703-5
Želenkovac 110
Zelve Valley 825
Zlatni Rt 140
Zola, Émile 192, 201, 285, 311

NOTES

how to use this book

These symbols will help you find the listings you want:

👁 Sights   ☞ Tours   🍸 Drinking

🏖 Beaches   🎊 Festivals & Events   ★ Entertainment

🏃 Activities   🛏 Sleeping   🔒 Shopping

🎓 Courses   🍴 Eating   ℹ Information/Transport

Look out for these icons:

TOP CHOICE — Our author's recommendation

FREE — No payment required

🍃 — A green or sustainable option

Our authors have nominated these places as demonstrating a strong commitment to sustainability – for example by supporting local communities and producers, operating in an environmentally friendly way, or supporting conservation projects.

These symbols give you the vital information for each listing:

📞 Telephone Numbers   🕐 Opening Hours   🅿 Parking   🚭 Nonsmoking   ❄ Air-Conditioning   @ Internet Access   🛜 Wi-Fi Access   🏊 Swimming Pool   🥗 Vegetarian Selection   📖 English-Language Menu   👪 Family-Friendly   🐾 Pet-Friendly   🚌 Bus   ⛴ Ferry   Ⓜ Metro   Ⓢ Subway   🚊 Tram   🚆 Train

Reviews are organised by author preference.

Map Legend

Sights: Beach, Buddhist, Castle, Christian, Hindu, Islamic, Jewish, Monument, Museum/Gallery, Ruin, Winery/Vineyard, Zoo, Other Sight

Activities, Courses & Tours: Diving/Snorkelling, Canoeing/Kayaking, Skiing, Surfing, Swimming/Pool, Walking, Windsurfing, Other Activity/Course/Tour

Sleeping: Sleeping, Camping

Eating: Eating

Drinking: Drinking, Cafe

Entertainment: Entertainment

Shopping: Shopping

Information: Post Office, Tourist Information

Transport: Airport, Border Crossing, Bus, Cable Car/Funicular, Cycling, Ferry, Monorail, Parking, S-Bahn, Taxi, Train/Railway, Tram, Tube Station, U-Bahn, Underground Train Station, Other Transport

Routes: Tollway, Freeway, Primary, Secondary, Tertiary, Lane, Unsealed Road, Plaza/Mall, Steps, Tunnel, Pedestrian Overpass, Walking Tour, Walking Tour Detour, Path

Boundaries: International, State/Province, Disputed, Regional/Suburb, Marine Park, Cliff, Wall

Population: Capital (National), Capital (State/Province), City/Large Town, Town/Village

Geographic: Hut/Shelter, Lighthouse, Lookout, Mountain/Volcano, Oasis, Park, Pass, Picnic Area, Waterfall

Hydrography: River/Creek, Intermittent River, Swamp/Mangrove, Reef, Canal, Water, Dry/Salt/Intermittent Lake, Glacier

Areas: Beach/Desert, Cemetery (Christian), Cemetery (Other), Park/Forest, Sportsground, Sight (Building), Top Sight (Building)

Anja Mutić

Croatia It's been more than two decades since Anja left her native Croatia. The journey took her to several countries before she made New York City her base 13 years ago. But the roots are calling and she's been returning to Croatia frequently for work and play. She's happy that Croatia's beauties are appreciated worldwide but secretly longs for the time when you could head to Hvar and hear the sound of crickets instead of blasting music. Anja is online at www.everthenomad.com.

Regis St Louis

Portugal Regis' long-time admiration for wine, rugged coastlines and soulful music made him easy prey for Portugal – a country he has travelled extensively over the past decade. Fine memories from his most recent trip include chatting with shepherds in the mountains near Manteigas, hearing avant-garde fado in Lisbon and feasting on delectable *percebes* (goose barnacles) in The Algarve. Regis is the coordinating author of the last three editions of Lonely Planet's *Portugal*, and he has written numerous articles about the Iberian Peninsula.

Nicola Williams

France British writer and editorial consultant Nicola Williams has lived in France and written about it for more than a decade. From her hillside home on Lake Geneva's southern shore, it is an easy hop to the French Alps (call her a ski fiend), Paris (art buff) and southern France (foodie). She has worked on numerous Lonely Planet titles, including *France, Discover France, Paris, Provence & the Côte d'Azur* and *The Loire*. She blogs at tripalong.wordpress.com and tweets @*Tripalong*.

Read more about Nicola at:
lonelyplanet.com/members/nicolawilliams

Peter Dragicevich

Montenegro After a dozen years working for newspapers and magazines in both his native New Zealand and Australia, Peter ditched the desk and hit the road. While it was family ties that first drew him to the Balkans, it's the history, natural beauty and the intriguing people that keep bringing him back. He wrote Lonely Planet's first guide to the newly independent Montenegro and has contributed to literally dozens of other Lonely Planet titles, including four successive editions of this book.

Mark Elliott

Bosnia & Hercegovina British-born travel writer Mark Elliott was only 11 when his family first dragged him to Sarajevo and stood him in the now-defunct concrete footsteps of Gavrilo Princip. Fortunately no Austro-Hungarian emperors were passing at the time. He has since visited virtually every corner of Bosnia and Hercegovina, supping fine Hercegovinian wines with master vintners, talking philosophy with Serb monks and Sufi mystics, and drinking more Bosnian coffee than any healthy stomach should be subjected to.

Anthony Ham

Spain In 2001, Anthony fell in love with Madrid on his first visit to the city. Less than a year later, he arrived on a one-way ticket, with not a word of Spanish and not knowing a single person. Having recently passed the 10-year mark in Madrid, he still adores his adopted city. Anthony also writes about and photographs Spain, Scandinavia, Africa and the Middle East for newspapers and magazines around the world.

Tom Masters

Albania Tom is a British writer and photographer whose work has taken him to some of the strangest and most challenging countries on earth. Having lived in Russia, travelled to all corners of eastern Europe in the decade that he's been working on the *Eastern Europe* guide and currently residing in East Berlin, he has a good understanding of what makes the former communist world tick. You can find more of Tom's work at www.tommasters.net.

Virginia Maxwell

Italy Though based in far-off Australia, Virginia is a regular visitor to Italy, lured by the country's history, art, architecture, food and wine. She is the coordinating author of Lonely Planet's *Florence & Tuscany*, has covered almost every corner of the country for multiple editions of *Western Europe*, and has also worked as coordinating author of *Sicily*. When pressed, she nominates Rome and Florence as her favourite Italian destinations.

Craig McLachlan

Greece Craig has covered the Greek Islands for the last five editions of Lonely Planet's Europe guidebooks. He runs an outdoor activity company in Queenstown, New Zealand in the southern-hemisphere summer, then heads north for another summer, writing for Lonely Planet and leading tours all over the world, including Greece. A 'freelance anything', he has an MBA from the University of Hawaii and leads other lives as a pilot, karate instructor and Japanese interpreter. Check out www.craigmclachlan.com.

OUR STORY

A beat-up old car, a few dollars in the pocket and a sense of adventure. In 1972 that's all Tony and Maureen Wheeler needed for the trip of a lifetime – across Europe and Asia overland to Australia. It took several months, and at the end – broke but inspired – they sat at their kitchen table writing and stapling together their first travel guide, *Across Asia on the Cheap*. Within a week they'd sold 1500 copies. Lonely Planet was born.

Today, Lonely Planet has offices in Melbourne, London and Oakland, with more than 600 staff and writers. We share Tony's belief that 'a great guidebook should do three things: inform, educate and amuse'.

OUR WRITERS

Duncan Garwood

Coordinating author; Italy British-born Duncan moved to Italy in 1997 and now lives near Rome with his Italian wife and two bilingual kids. He has travelled extensively in his adopted homeland and worked on about 30 Lonely Planet books, including *Italy, Rome, Sardinia* and *Italy's Best Trips*, as well as the past six editions of this guide. His first experience of the Mediterranean came on a kayaking holiday to France, but it was while island-hopping around the Aegean that he really fell for the region and its passionate way of life.

Read more about Duncan at:
lonelyplanet.com/members/duncangarwood

Alexis Averbuck

Greece Alexis Averbuck lives on Hydra, takes regular reverse R&R in Athens (she wrote *Pocket Athens*), and makes any excuse she can to travel the isolated back roads of her adopted land. She is committed to dispelling the stereotype that Greece is simply a string of sandy beaches. A travel writer for two decades, Alexis has lived in Antarctica for a year, crossed the Pacific by sailboat and written books on her journeys through Asia and the Americas. She's also a painter – visit www.alexisaverbuck.com.

James Bainbridge

Turkey Media assignments and extra-curricular wanderings have taken James to most of Turkey's far-flung regions, from Aegean islands to the eastern steppe via Cappadocia's surreal rock formations. He has coordinated three editions of Lonely Planet's *Turkey* guide, and deepened his local knowledge by living in İstanbul and grappling with suffixes during a Turkish-language course. For articles on Turkey, and a link to a blog with advice about travel writing, visit James's website at www.jamesbainbridge.net.

Read more about James at:
lonelyplanet.com/members/james_bains

Mark Baker

Slovenia Based permanently in Prague, Mark has lived, worked and enjoyed the splendours of central Europe for more than 20 years, first as a journalist for The Economist Group and then for Bloomberg News and Radio Free Europe/Radio Liberty. In addition to this book, Mark is coauthor of Lonely Planet's *Prague & the Czech Republic, Poland, Slovenia* and *Romania & Bulgaria*.

OVER MORE
PAGE WRITERS

Published by Lonely Planet Publications Pty Ltd

ABN 36 005 607 983
11th edition – Oct 2013
ISBN 978 1 74220 418 5
© Lonely Planet 2013   Photographs © as indicated 2013
10 9 8 7 6 5 4 3 2 1
Printed in Singapore

Although the authors and Lonely Planet have taken all reasonable care in preparing this book, we make no warranty about the accuracy or completeness of its content and, to the maximum extent permitted, disclaim all liability arising from its use.

All rights reserved. No part of this publication may be copied, stored in a retrieval system, or transmitted in any form by any means, electronic, mechanical, recording or otherwise, except brief extracts for the purpose of review, and no part of this publication may be sold or hired, without the written permission of the publisher. Lonely Planet and the Lonely Planet logo are trademarks of Lonely Planet and are registered in the US Patent and Trademark Office and in other countries. Lonely Planet does not allow its name or logo to be appropriated by commercial establishments, such as retailers, restaurants or hotels. Please let us know of any misuses: lonelyplanet.com/ip.